P9-DUN-300

West's Law School Advisory Board

R

MODERN ENVIRONMENTAL LAW

POLICY AND PRACTICE

By

Elizabeth Glass Geltman
Professor of Law
George Washington University Law School

AMERICAN CASEBOOK SERIES®

WEST PUBLISHING CO.
ST. PAUL, MINN., 1997

American Casebook Series, the key symbol appearing on the front
cover and the WP symbol are registered trademarks of West Publishing
Co. Registered in the U.S. Patent and Trademark Office.

COPYRIGHT © 1997 By WEST PUBLISHING CO.
    610 Opperman Drive
    P.O. Box 64526
    St. Paul, MN 55164–0526
    1–800–328–9352

Library of Congress Cataloging-in-Publication Data

Geltman, Elizabeth Glass.
  Modern environmental law policy and practice / by Elizabeth Glass
Geltman.
    p. cm. — (American casebook series)
   ISBN 0–314–20347–8 (hard cover)
   1. Environmental law—United States—Cases. I. Title.
  II. Series.
  KF3775.A7G45 1997
  344.73'046—dc20
  [347.30446]   96–46480
                      CIP

ISBN 0–314–20347–8

TEXT IS PRINTED ON 10% POST
CONSUMER RECYCLED PAPER

For my teachers, with special gratitude to the following:

James R. Howard, III
Kenneth Greif
Brooks Lakin
The Park School, Brooklandville, Maryland

Prof. William Lambert
Prof. Walter Lafeber
Cornell University, College of Arts & Sciences, Ithaca, New York

Prof. Edith Brown Weiss
Georgetown University Law Center, Washington, D.C.

Prof. Nancy Norris
Johns Hopkins University School of Continuing Studies,
Baltimore, Maryland

and

The Honorable Paul Alpert
The Honorable Kenneth Starr

*

Author's Note

The Author has provided the reader with her comments concerning the current laws and regulations affecting environmental activities as of June 1996. The reader is advised that environmental law is a fast changing area of law and others may reach different conclusions and recommendations due to either change in law or regulation or due to their differing views of those laws and regulations. The author does not warrant that her conclusions and recommendations will be adhered to by any or all courts and regulatory agencies that investigate or rule upon environmental matters. The reader should update his or her research (with particular emphasis on the state in question) or seek independent legal advice from his or her attorney before undertaking any activity that may be within the scope of any environmental law or regulation.

*

About the Author

Elizabeth Glass Geltman is an Associate Professor of Environmental Law at the George Washington University School of Law and is Counsel to Squire, Sanders & Dempsey, Washington, D.C. Prof. Geltman is the author of ten books on issues concerning environmental law, business and natural resources, including two multi-volume treatises entitled ENVIRONMENTAL ISSUES IN BUSINESS TRANSACTIONS AND SECURITIES DISCLOSURE OF CONTINGENT ENVIRONMENTAL LIABILITIES. She has spoken at various legal seminars and conferences and is widely published in newspapers, magazines and law reviews on issues of environmental law and natural resources. She has assumed numerous leadership positions in the Natural Resources and Environmental law sections of the District of Columbia, Maryland and American Bar Associations. Prof. Geltman is a member of the Maryland and District of Columbia bars.

*

Acknowledgments

The author would like to thank Mike Briggs, Beverly Calvert, Glynis Hammond, Winifred Hercules, John Jolley, Cynthia Webb-Manly, Carey Ann Mathews, Patrick Ryan, and Stacy Wahlberg for their research, editing, typing and computer assistance in writing this book. In addition, the author thanks Prof. Arnold Reitze and Prof. Larry Hourclé and her many students and colleagues of George Washington University's National Law School, all of whom gave countless hours and insight, making this project possible. The author also thanks Van Carson and Geoffrey K. Barnes and the environmental group of Squire, Sanders & Dempsey for their support and encouragement while writing this book.

The author also thanks West Publishing for their tireless efforts in bringing this book to press.

Finally, the author gives her greatest thanks to her children, Andy and Jeffrey, for giving her the inspiration to write this book; her husband, Edward Alan Geltman, and parents, Dr. & Mrs. Sheldon Glass, for their advice, wisdom and support through this and so may other projects; and her teachers, to whom this book is dedicated.

*

I regard it as the foremost task of education to insure the survival of these qualities:

> an enterprising curiosity, an undefeatable spirit, tenacity in pursuit, readiness for sensible self denial, and above all, compassion.

—Kurt Hahn
Founder of Outward Bound

*

Summary of Contents

*

Table of Contents

*

Table of Cases

The principal cases are in bold type. Cases cited or discussed in the text are roman type. References are to pages. Cases cited in principal cases and within other quoted materials are not included.

*

Table of Statutes

MODERN ENVIRONMENTAL LAW

POLICY AND PRACTICE

*

Chapter 1

INTRODUCTION

§ 1.1 OVERVIEW

Environmental law has been developing rapidly in the United States since the early 1970's and now constitutes an imposing body of statutes, rules, and case and common law that creates significant compliance and liability risks for all companies and private investors involved in commercial transactions. Environmental laws create two main categories of risk for investments in the United States—regulatory risks and liability

1

risks. The regulatory risks arise from a myriad of complicated environmental laws that regulate such matters as impact assessment, standard-setting, licensing, and enforcement. Compliance with these laws can be quite expensive, can constrain management's decision-making capacity, and can, in some cases, altogether preclude operation of a business. Failure to comply with these regulatory laws can result in exposure to fines and penalties that can reach more than $25,000 per day and can result in imprisonment.

Even more significant than the regulatory risks, however, are the civil liability risks associated with past or present ownership or operation of hazardous waste sites or of a company that created such wastes and shipped them offsite. Association with property contaminated by hazardous waste, or with a company that owns or operates such property, can result in millions of dollars of liability for cleanup costs, personal injury, or property damage. These potentially devastating liability risks have resulted primarily from enactment of the federal Superfund law and state Superfund-like laws enacted in virtually every state. The Superfund law is a harsh, retroactive civil liability scheme under which all past and present owners and operators associated with a hazardous waste site, even those that did not create or contribute to the hazardous condition, may be held liable for cleanup costs unless they qualify for certain extremely limited defenses. Persons associated with contaminated property must also contend with potential toxic tort liability under the common law.

In addition to these regulatory and liability risks, investors contemplating business transactions in America also have to contend with state and federal liens that may be placed on contaminated property for state or federal cleanup expenditures and damages; legislation that regulates the transfer or abandonment of contaminated property, including transfer of control in corporate mergers and acquisitions; state provisions requiring notice and disclosure prior to the transfer of an interest in land that has been used as a hazardous waste site; Security and Exchange Commission environmental disclosure requirements; the interrelationship of United States bankruptcy law and environmental law; and the fact that the huge Superfund and toxic tort risks have become essentially uninsurable.

Given the extent and magnitude of these environmental risks, it is critical that investors contemplating business transactions in the United States be familiar with environmental laws, and the impact they may have on a business deal, so that these risks are adequately identified and managed.

§ 1.2 THE STRUCTURE OF THE ENVIRONMENTAL LEGAL SYSTEM

To understand environmental regulation in the United States, it is necessary to understand the basic governmental structure of the United States and the role that environmental regulation plays within it. The

United States is a federal system comprised of fifty states. Under the United States Constitution, the individual states are the governmental entities with plenary governmental power. In theory, the "federal" or "national" government has only those powers delegated to it by the states through the Constitution. Historically, control over water, air, and other pollution has been a state governmental function arising under the general "police" power to protect public health and safety—the federal government has no general police power.

In the past few decades, however, the federal government has greatly expanded its role in environmental regulation through exercise of its constitutional power to regulate interstate and foreign commerce. To the extent that federal statutes or regulations conflict with state statutes or regulations, the former usually prevails through the constitutional doctrine of "preemption"—federal preemption generally exists, however, in the environmental law field, only with regard to state requirements that are *less stringent* than corresponding federal requirements.

The federal government, the structure of which is based on the separation of powers principle, is divided into executive, legislative, and judicial branches. Reduced to the simplest terms, the legislature enacts laws; the executive, through a system of administrative agencies, implements the laws by promulgating regulations and ensuring enforcement; and the courts interpret the statutes and regulations. The individual states have similar governmental frameworks consisting of state executive, legislative, and judicial branches.

As a result, there are several sources of environmental regulation in the United States, including (1) the United States Constitution, (2) state constitutions, (3) federal, state, and local statutes and ordinances, (4) regulations promulgated by federal, state, and local administrative agencies, (5) judicial decisions interpreting environmental laws and regulations, and (6) the common law.

§ 1.3 ENVIRONMENTAL LEGISLATION IN THE UNITED STATES

Although the right to a healthful environment is not a fundamental right under the United States Constitution, environmental protection has increasingly become a matter of national interest and has been the subject of much statutory regulation. Since the early 1970s, the United States Congress has had the primary role in environmental policy-making at the federal level. Comprehensive federal statutes have been enacted dealing with, among other things, environmental impact assessment, air pollution, water pollution, and solid and hazardous waste. The goals that Congress has set in these statutes are often extremely ambitious, with the executive frequently a somewhat reluctant partner in these initiatives. Similar statutes have been enacted at the state level in virtually every state.

§ 1.4 ADMINISTRATIVE ENFORCEMENT OF ENVIRONMEN- TAL LAWS IN THE UNITED STATES—ADMINISTRA- TIVE AGENCIES

The federal executive and administrative agencies are responsible for implementing Congress' ambitious environmental statutes. The primary federal administrative agency responsible for protection of the environment is the United States Environmental Protection Agency (EPA), which was created by an executive order in 1970 to consolidate most of the government's environmental regulatory activities into a single agency. EPA is headed by an administrator, currently William Reilly, who serves at the President's pleasure. EPA historically has been a highly decentralized agency that operates through ten regional offices.

Despite long-standing opposition from previous presidential administrations, the Bush administration has proposed elevating EPA to a cabinet level agency and creating a Department of the Environment. The impetus for elevation of EPA to cabinet level reflects the current administration's increasing willingness to consider the environmental point of view.

EPA is responsible for regulating air pollution under the Clean Air Act; water pollution and sewage treatment under the Clean Water Act; drinking water under the Safe Drinking Water Act; solid and hazardous waste under the Resource Conservation and Recovery Act; hazardous waste sites and community response to chemical releases under the Comprehensive Environmental Response, Compensation, and Liability Act; toxic substances under the Toxic Substances Control Act; pesticides under the Federal Insecticide, Fungicide, and Rodenticide Act; and ocean dumping under the Marine Protection, Research and Sanctuaries Act. EPA's primary responsibilities include establishing and enforcing environmental standards, monitoring and analyzing the environment, conducting environmental research, and assisting state and local governments in pollution control programs.

EPA establishes and enforces environmental standards primarily through administrative rulemakings that are preceded by a notice and a period during which written comment is allowed. Other vehicles for standard-setting and enforcement include licensing requirements and authority to review and approve state environmental programs under various federal statutes if they meet certain standards.

The Council on Environmental Quality (CEQ), which was created by the National Environmental Policy Act and is part of the Executive Office of the President, is responsible for advising the president on national policies for improving environmental quality, analyzing conditions and trends in environmental quality, and evaluating the effect of federal programs and authorities on the environment. CEQ is required under the National Environmental Policy Act to supervise the preparation of environmental impact statements by federal agencies. The role of CEQ was greatly diminished under the Clinton administration. The advisory functions formerly at CEQ were moved to the newly created

White House Office of Environmental Policy and the staff at CEQ was dramatically reduced.

Other United States agencies that have environmental responsibilities include: the Department of Agriculture (soil conservation); the National Oceanic and Atmospheric Administration (coastal zone management, air pollution, and marine mammals); the Army Corps of Engineers (navigable waters and ocean dumping); the Department of Energy (energy-related issues); the Department of Interior (endangered species, federal lands, and the outer continental shelf); the Federal Aviation Administration (aircraft noise); and the Department of Housing and Urban Development (certain community water supply and sewerage grants). EPA shares responsibility for control of radiation with the Nuclear Regulatory Commission. EPA, the United States Coast Guard, and the Federal Maritime Commission share responsibility for control of water pollution from oil and other hazardous substances.

§ 1.5 THE ROLE OF COURTS IN ENVIRONMENTAL PROTECTION

Courts have had a significant role in the development of environmental law. Environmental regulation in the United States is characterized by strong judicial review of agency implementation of federal regulation and extensive industry, citizen, and environmental group involvement in the formal administrative and judicial processes. In addition, there is much civil litigation over personal injury and property damage due to toxic torts in the United States. The net result of this process is a system of central planning through litigation that is costly, inefficient, and a barrier to new investments. New projects and new products must often undergo a gauntlet of legal review that is time consuming, difficult, and uncertain.

Compounding the matter is the fact that there are two sets of judicial systems in the United States—a federal system of courts established under the United States Constitution and state and local courts established under the authority of each state government. There are several levels of authority in each court system. The state courts generally have unlimited power to decide almost every type of case, whereas the federal courts have authority to entertain only certain types of cases that are specifically set forth in the United States Constitution. Cases involving federal environmental statutes may be heard by federal courts.

The net result of all of this is that court decisions on environmental matters often vary from jurisdiction to jurisdiction—especially from one state court system to another. Moreover, the weight of authority given to a decision will depend to a large extent on the level of the court that issues it. If the United States Supreme Court, the highest American court, decides a case, for example, it establishes law for the entire country, whereas, a decision by a lower state court generally is of major interest only to that local jurisdiction. Federal court decisions generally carry more weight than state court decisions, though this may not be true if there is a state court precedent in the state where an environmental problem arises, and the only federal court decisions addressing the problem are from jurisdictions that do not include that particular state. Thus, in evaluating the impact of court decisions on environmental matters, one must evaluate both federal and state court decisions and consider the weight of authority that each decision will carry.

§ 1.6 REGULATORY STYLE IN THE UNITED STATES

Some distinguishing characteristics of American regulation are as follows. First, American regulation is normally much more extensive and specific than is the case in many foreign countries, and is based much more explicitly on stated and reasoned conclusions drawn from technical, scientific, and economic data. Second, American regulation relies heavily on generic administrative rulemaking to achieve specificity and uniformity simultaneously and to gather the technical scientific and economic data that form the premises for public decisionmaking. No other legal system makes nearly the same use as does the United States of structured, legislative-style, public rulemaking (called "informal" rulemaking, as opposed to "formal" rulemaking, conducted on the judicial rather than the legislative model) as a vehicle for "fact" generation and decisionmaking. Further, the American administrative process is essentially political in nature. Nowhere is this more apparent than in informal rulemaking, which is in essence an extension of the American legislative process.

Third, American environmental regulation is born of political hyperbole and overreaction and develops rapidly, but once in place tends to be strict and rigid. The rules typically are overbroad and arbitrary, and frequently have to be tortured when applied, in order to conform them to reality and to render them at least minimally fair. Further, there are seldom, if ever, "safe harbors" under American environmental law. Fourth, American environmental regulation is characterized by a wide range of flexible enforcement tools that are vigorously used. Despite a great deal of complaining by Congressional staffs and environmental groups, environmental enforcement and resulting deterrence are alive and well in the United States, at least in the case of substantial compliance with the major statutes by most large companies. Fifth, American environmental regulation is characterized by strong judicial review and extensive industry, citizen, and environmental group involvement in the formal administrative and judicial processes, including citizen enforcement rights. There is, in short, a great deal of government accountability. Finally, there is much more civil litigation over personal injury and property damage due to toxic torts in the United States than in most foreign legal systems, for a number of structural and contextual reasons (which include: the American discovery system, contingent fees, and jury systems).

§ 1.7 STATE AND FEDERAL ROLES IN ENVIRONMENTAL REGULATION

The United States environmental regulatory system is a product of both federal and state standards, goals, requirements, limitations, and enforcement authorities. Federal environmental programs are a fairly recent development—states have been enacting environmental laws and regulations for a much longer time. The federal government has been expanding its role in environmental regulation through its constitutional power to regulate interstate and foreign commerce. Although the federal government often has taken the lead in developing and enforcing environmental requirements since the 1970s, states have continued to develop their own laws—sometimes in direct response to new federal programs that required the submission of state "plans" and federal approval of state programs, and sometimes to address environmental problems of particular concern to the state. In any case, many states have enacted environmental laws and regulations that go beyond and/or are more stringent than federal requirements. Thus, investors and businesses contemplating commercial transactions in the United States must consider both federal environmental laws and any state environmental laws in the state where any business or transaction is anticipated.

Federal legislation regulating environmental hazards and activities falls into three broad areas. The first area involves products that are marketed nationally, such as automobiles, chemicals, and pesticides. In this area, federal national standards and direct enforcement of those standards by federal authorities are used. The second broad category is regulation of industrial processes that cause air, water, and toxic waste pollution. Here the dominant approach is federal standard-setting, with primary reliance on states to implement and enforce the standards, and with some backup enforcement role by the federal government. Under the Clean Water Act, the Resource Conservation and Recovery Act, and the Safe Drinking Water Act, for example, EPA administers the regulatory program unless the state has a comprehensive alternative program that would be at least as protective as the federal program. The third area of regulation addresses problems that involve a large degree of state and local resource management and infrastructure, such as solid waste disposal or water supply planning. Here there is primary reliance on state and local governments, with inducements in federal law, often in the form of financial contributions or grants, accompanied by federal standards to steer the use of those grants to promote environmental goals.

In each of these three areas of regulation there is characteristically uniformity in the federal standards imposed in order to ensure, among other things, that one state does not obtain a competitive economic advantage over another state by enacting less stringent environmental standards. Thus, federal legislation generally imposes the same standards on industries in different states.

§ 1.8   REGULATORY RISKS POSED BY ENVIRONMENTAL LAWS

A company or investor doing business in the United States must comply with a host of detailed United States environmental regulatory laws. Comprehensive federal statutes have been enacted dealing with environmental impact assessment, air pollution, water pollution, and solid and hazardous waste. There is a host of related federal and state statutes that regulate the manufacture, distribution, and use of new and existing toxic chemicals and pesticides, chemicals and hazardous substances in consumer products, and toxic chemicals in food. There are also other federal and state environmental statutes that protect specific types of resources such as drinking water, rare or endangered species, or wild and scenic rivers. In addition to the federal regulatory regime, there are also detailed state environmental regulatory programs addressing air pollution, water pollution, waste disposal, resource management, and other environmental issues. While many of these laws are virtually identical to their federal counterparts, some are significantly different and may impose even more stringent environmental requirements.

Under these Acts, the chief environmental risks facing business flow from regulatory functions such as impact assessment, standard-setting, licensing, and enforcement. Compliance with detailed regulatory requirements is the key.

The most immediate business risk imposed by these statutes is that they govern whether permission can be obtained from the government to conduct the business at all, and on what terms. A second risk is that compliance costs money, largely through costs of (1) technology, (2) the business practices necessary to achieve compliance, and (3) fines or civil penalties for noncompliance. Civil and criminal penalties for noncompliance are set by statute and can reach $25,000 or more per day.

Environmental agencies, particularly those at the federal level, are frequently given little enforcement discretion, and citizens are empowered by federal statute in many cases to enforce the environmental laws against private companies when agencies do not.

Finally, federal and state regulatory statutes impose two important, but little noticed constraints on a management's future options. First, they inhibit the flexibility of plant and product changes that can be made if pollutant discharges will increase or differ materially. Second, they inhibit or, in some cases, altogether preclude future plant expansion at a site by placing overall limits on the amount of pollutants, from any source, that the air, water, land, or groundwater at or near the site may receive.

Discussion Problem

You are the EPA Administrator and you direct seventy-five of your most senior scientists and regulatory officials to scrutinize the available evidence concerning the health and ecological risks arising from the thirty most significant problems your agency must address. Following a nine-month review, they report to you that, while some abandoned hazardous waste disposal sites pose significant risks to people living nearby, from an overall national perspective these sites are of "medium to low" risk in terms of cancer and non-cancer health risks, ecological effects, and welfare effects. At the same time, your experts report that hazardous waste sites are at the very top of the list when the public is asked to rank those same thirty environmental problems according to its level of concern. In addition, as revealed by the fact that Congress appropriates more than a third of EPA's budget to hazardous waste programs. Congress clearly intends for you to concentrate on site cleanups.

What do you do? What, if anything, can you do? What are your legal restrictions in framing proposed solutions?

§ 1.9 ENVIRONMENTAL IMPACT ASSESSMENT REQUIREMENTS: THE NATIONAL ENVIRONMENTAL POLICY ACT (NEPA)

Perhaps the single most pervasive environmental law in the United States is the National Environmental Policy Act of 1969 (NEPA), 42 U.S.C.A. §§ 4331 *et seq.* (1988), which declared a national environmental policy and set forth a requirement that federal agencies prepare a "detailed statement" (known as an "Environmental Impact Statement" or "EIS") analyzing the environmental effects and potential alternatives of all "major Federal actions significantly affecting the quality of the human environment." 42 U.S.C.A. § 4332(2)(C). An action is "federal" under NEPA if it is (1) undertaken directly by a federal entity *or* (2) undertaken by a private party that is effectively "in partnership" with the federal government. Such a partnership can result when the government provides significant funding for the project or issues a lease, permit, license, insurance, contract extension or modification, conveyance, assistance authorization, or other entitlement that is a legal precondition to the activity. Thus, any activity or commercial transaction that involves government licensing, approval, or participation can trigger environmental assessment responsibilities.

EISs have been required, for example, for construction of highways; pipelines; housing developments; electric transmission lines; dams; drainage, irrigation and navigation improvements; hospital, airport, industrial, commercial, and recreational complexes; and many other activities such as timber sales and mineral leasing.

When environmental assessment responsibilities are triggered and a federal agency is required to prepare an EIS, the agency normally requires any private party involved to prepare a broad-ranging and expensive back-up study that will serve as a basis for the agency's preparation of its independent EIS. Agency rules generally provide for public notice, review, and comment on an agency's written statement of environmental impacts and alternatives.

An EIS must include an adequate discussion of:

    (1) the environmental impact of the proposed action;

    (2) any adverse environmental effects that cannot be avoided should the proposal be implemented;

    (3) alternatives to the proposed action;

(4) the relationship between local short-term uses of man's environment and the maintenance and enhancement of long-term productivity; and

(5) any irreversible and irretrievable commitments of resources that would be involved in the proposed action should it be implemented.

42 U.S.C.A. § 4332(2)(c)(i–v). Any failure by the agency to comply with these requirements can lead to court challenges and to delay or derailment of the private transaction in question. Counsel for a private participant must therefore be concerned that the environmental studies of both the client and the federal agency conform to NEPA requirements.

ALABAMA EX REL. SIEGELMAN v. UNITED STATES EPA
911 F.2d 499 (11th Cir.1990).

OPINION: EDMONDSON, CIRCUIT JUDGE.

Pursuant to the Resource Conservation and Recovery Act of 1976, 42 U.S.C. §§ 6901–6992k (1982 & Supp. V 1987)("RCRA"), the Environmental Protection Agency ("EPA") issued a final operating permit for the nation's largest hazardous waste management facility, located at Emelle, Alabama. We are asked to decide whether EPA's procedures in issuing the permit were sufficient to exempt EPA from performing an environmental impact study in compliance with the National Environmental Policy Act, 42 U.S.C. §§ 4321–4370b (1982 & Supp. V 1987)("NEPA"). The answer is "Yes." We are also asked to decide whether EPA violated its own procedural requirements governing public participation and whether EPA's waiver of a ground water monitoring requirement was arbitrary and capricious. The answer is "No." We affirm the EPA Administrator's decision to uphold EPA's issuance of the permit for the Emelle facility.

I. BACKGROUND

The Emelle facility, owned and operated by Chemical Waste Management, Inc. ("ChemWaste"), receives hazardous wastes from forty-eight states. The facility covers 2730 acres of land and includes twenty inactive landfill trenches, one active trench, an aqueous waste storage pond, a waste drum storage area, a liquid waste tank storage area, a liquid waste solidification unit, and a solvent and fuel recovery area. Emelle receives almost every type of hazardous waste identified in the RCRA regulations at 40 C.F.R. Part 261, including waste that is toxic, corrosive, flammable, and reactive, but does not accept municipal refuse or garbage, radioactive wastes, or explosive wastes.

RCRA, which establishes a "cradle-to-grave" system for regulating the treatment, storage, and disposal of hazardous wastes, requires hazardous waste management facilities like Emelle to receive an operating permit from EPA.... *See* 42 U.S.C. § 6925. Alabama requires that hazardous waste management facilities also obtain an operating permit from the state, see Ala. Code § 22–30–12 (1989); such permits are issued by the Alabama Department of Environmental Management ("ADEM").

Under RCRA, facilities that were already in operation in November 1980 are allowed to continue operating on an interim basis until a final permit can be issued.... *See* 42 U.S.C. § 6925(e). ChemWaste, operating the Emelle facility under an interim permit, filed its application for a final permit in 1983. ChemWaste's application requested authority to operate the facility permanently and to expand the facility. ChemWaste proposed adding four landfill trenches and a large amount of container storage facilities and asked for a waiver of ground water monitoring relative to the landfill disposal....

EPA's Regional Office, after determining that ChemWaste's application for a final RCRA permit was complete, issued a "draft" permit in 1986, commencing a period for public hearing and comments. Jointly with ADEM, EPA held a public hearing in Alabama and accepted and responded to comments from interested parties.... In 1987, EPA issued the final permit for the Emelle facility, approving ChemWaste's proposed expansions and waiving certain ground water monitoring requirements.... To our knowledge, ADEM has not issued a final state permit; ADEM's actions are not challenged in this appeal.

When EPA issued Emelle's permit, EPA did not prepare an environmental impact study ("EIS") under NEPA. EPA followed one of its own regulations, promulgated in 1980 shortly after RCRA took effect, which states EPA's position that the RCRA permit process supplants the requirements of NEPA and that EPA need not comply with NEPA when granting RCRA permits. *See* 40 C.F.R. § 124.9(b)(6)....

The petitioners in this case are the State of Alabama and four citizen organizations: Alabamians for a Clean Environment; the Alabama Chapter of the Sierra Club; the Alabama Conservancy; and Greenpeace, U.S.A. Petitioners appealed the EPA Regional Office's issuance of ChemWaste's permit to the EPA Administrator, who refused to rescind Emelle's permit, ruling that EPA had not violated NEPA because the RCRA permit process was functionally equivalent to the requirements of NEPA. The Administrator also said that EPA had satisfied all procedural requirements for issuing the permit and had not acted arbitrarily in allowing a waiver of ground water monitoring. The Administrator's decision is the basis of this appeal.... Under the Administrative Procedure Act, 5 U.S.C. §§ 701–706 (1982), our role is to determine: (1) whether EPA acted within the scope of its authority; (2) whether EPA's decision to issue the permit was "arbitrary, capricious, an abuse of discretion, or otherwise not in accordance with law"; and (3) whether EPA followed procedural requirements in issuing the permit. *See* 5 U.S.C. § 706(2)(A); *Citizens to Preserve Overton Park v. Volpe*, 401 U.S. 402, 413–17, 91 S.Ct. 814, 822–24, 28 L.Ed.2d 136 (1971).

II. DISCUSSION

* * *

B. COMPLIANCE WITH NEPA

By enacting NEPA, Congress declared a broad national commitment to protecting and promoting environmental quality. *See Robertson v. Methow Valley Citizens Council*, 490 U.S. 332, 109 S.Ct. 1835, 1844, 104 L.Ed.2d 351 (1989). To ensure that this commitment is implemented throughout the federal government, NEPA forces federal agencies to prepare detailed studies of the environmental effects of their actions. These studies serve two important purposes: (1) the agency is forced to consider carefully detailed information about significant environmental impacts; and (2) relevant environmental information is made available to the members of the public, who can then play a role in the agency's decisionmaking process and implementation of that decision. *See* Robertson, U.S. at , 109 S.Ct. at 1845.

NEPA requires that "to the fullest extent possible . . . all agencies of the Federal government shall . . . include in every recommendation or report on proposals for legislation and other major Federal actions significantly affecting the quality of the human environment, a detailed statement by the responsible official on—(i) the environmental impact of the proposed action. . . ." 42 U.S.C. § 4332. So, a federal agency must ordinarily prepare an EIS whenever the agency's action will have a significant effect on the environment. *See Environmental Defense Fund, Inc. v. EPA*, 160 U.S.App.D.C. 123, 489 F.2d 1247, 1255 (D.C.Cir.1973).

No one disputes that EPA's action in granting a final operating permit to the nation's largest commercial hazardous waste management facility—a facility that handles almost every type of hazardous waste identified by RCRA regulations—is a "major Federal action" that will significantly affect the human environment. The parties in this case, however, disagree about whether EPA had to comply with NEPA's EIS requirements. EPA contends that RCRA's permit issuance process takes the place of NEPA. In other words, EPA contends that, in the context of approving operating permits for hazardous waste management facilities, RCRA functions as the equivalent and more specific legislative safeguard of the environment. But petitioners contend that NEPA applies to EPA's action under RCRA and that RCRA is not functionally equivalent to NEPA.

We are not the first judges called upon to decide whether NEPA applies to actions taken by EPA. Although NEPA says that "all agencies" must comply with its terms, most circuits have already recognized—in some instances, as many as seventeen years ago—that an agency need not comply with NEPA where the agency is engaged primarily in an examination of environmental questions and where "the agency's organic legislation mandate[s] specific procedures for considering the environment that [are] functional equivalents of the impact statement process." *Texas Committee on Natural Resources v. Bergland*, 573 F.2d 201, 207 (5th Cir.1978). . . . *See also, e.g., State of Wyoming v. Hathaway*, 525 F.2d 66, 70 (10th Cir.1975); *Indiana & Michigan Elec. Co. v. EPA*, 509 F.2d 839, 843 (7th Cir.1975); *South Terminal Corp. v.*

EPA, 504 F.2d 646, 676 (1st Cir.1974); *Portland Cement Ass'n v. Ruckelshaus*, 158 U.S.App.D.C. 308, 486 F.2d 375, 380 (D.C.Cir.1973); *Buckeye Power, Inc. v. EPA*, 481 F.2d 162, 174 (6th Cir.1973); *Appalachian Power Co. v. EPA*, 477 F.2d 495, 508 (4th Cir.1973).

This idea of limiting the sweep of NEPA stems, in part, from the traditional view that specific statutes prevail over general statutes dealing with the same basic subjects. *See Merrell v. Thomas*, 807 F.2d 776, 778, 779 (9th Cir.1986)(NEPA inapplicable where Federal Insecticide, Fungicide, and Rodenticide Act, 7 U.S.C. §§ 136–136y (1982 & Supp. V 1987), provided more specific registration requirements). *See generally Busic v. United States*, 446 U.S. 398, 406, 100 S.Ct. 1747, 1753, 64 L.Ed.2d 381 (1980)(more specific statute is given precedence over more general one, regardless of temporal sequence). NEPA is the general statute forcing agencies to consider the environmental consequences of their actions and to allow the public a meaningful opportunity to learn about and to comment on the proposed actions. If there were no RCRA, NEPA would seem to apply here. But RCRA is the later and more specific statute directly governing EPA's process for issuing permits to hazardous waste management facilities. As such, RCRA is an exception to NEPA and controls here.

Petitioners complain, and EPA agrees, that RCRA does not require EPA to consider every point the agency would have to consider in preparing a formal EIS under NEPA; thus, NEPA and RCRA conflict. Still, RCRA is the functional (though not the structural or literal) equivalent and more specific counterpart of NEPA. . . . RCRA is comprehensive in its field of application. RCRA's substantive and procedural standards are intended to ensure that EPA considers fully, with the assistance of meaningful public comment, environmental issues involved in the permitting of hazardous waste management facilities. The RCRA permitting procedures "strike a workable balance between some of the advantages and disadvantages of full application of NEPA." Portland Cement, 486 F.2d at 386 (finding section 111 of Clean Air Act functionally equivalent to NEPA); *see Amoco Oil Co.*, 501 F.2d at 750; *Warren County v. State of North Carolina*, 528 F.Supp. 276, 287 (E.D.N.C. 1981). . . .

NEPA's environmental impact statement is merely an implement devised by Congress to require government agencies to think about and weigh environmental factors before acting. Considered in this light, an organization like EPA whose regulatory activities are necessarily concerned with environmental consequences need not stop in the middle of its proceedings in order to issue a separate and distinct impact statement just to be issuing it. To so require would decrease environmental protection activity rather than increase it.

Hathaway, 525 F.2d at 71–72 (footnote omitted). We believe that Congress did not intend for EPA to comply with NEPA when RCRA applies to the particular EPA activity. We hold that, in considering Chem-

Waste's application for a final permit for the Emelle facility, EPA did not have to comply with NEPA.

* * *

AFFIRMED.

NEPA at a Glance

Section	NEPA
§ 101	Sets Goals
§ 102	Requires All Federal Agencies to Conduct an Environmental Impact Statement (EIS) on Major Federal Action
§ 103	Requires All Federal Agencies to Promulgate Regulations to Ensure NEPA Compliance
§ 201	Requires an Annual Environmental Quality Report to Be Submitted (by CEQ) to Congress
§ 202	Establishes CEQ
§ 204	Outlines Duties and Functions of CEQ

A non-federal entity may be reached pursuant to NEPA when the non-federal entity is in a "partnership" or "joint venture" with a federal agency subject to NEPA. *See, e.g., Macht v. Skinner,* 916 F.2d 13, 20 (D.C.Cir.1990)(holding NEPA inapplicable where there was no " 'partnership' or 'joint venture' with the federal government"); *Silva,* 473 F.2d at 290 n. 5 ("once the partnership stage has been reached between the federal and non-federal entities, all parties in a project are subject to injunctive process"). The NEPA requirement of 42 U.S.C.A. § 4332 that federal agencies file environmental impact statements before undertaking major federal actions with significant environmental effects is a single aspect of NEPA. Nevertheless, the EIS requirement has proven a thorn in the side of many developers since it went into effect on January 1, 1970. The extensive impact of this law, however, is less due to its breadth, rather the requirement comes into play so much because federal agencies are so often involved in actions affecting the environment.

Although the cases often speak often of NEPA "partnerships" or "joint ventures," the courts typically use these terms with great imprecision, never referring to the common business association law definitions for these terms. Indeed, non-federal entities have sometimes been enjoined even when it was clear that a partnership with the federal entity no longer existed. *See, e.g., San Francisco Tomorrow v. Romney,* 472 F.2d 1021, 1025 (9th Cir.1973)(court held that "for purposes of NEPA, major federal action had terminated when" contract for HUD to provide loans was signed but non-federal entity could be enjoined where the federal financial assistance was not complete).....

A review of the cases indicates that, consciously or not, most courts are engaging in a two-part jurisdictional inquiry to determine if projects significantly affecting the environment, and which involve non-federal entities, may be enjoined pending the completion of an EIS. The first inquiry is simply to ask whether at any time the project involved a major federal action. Sometimes cases are disposed of at this point because there simply has not been enough federal involvement in the project to implicate NEPA. *See, e.g., City of Highland Park v. Train*, 519 F.2d 681, 695 (7th Cir.1975)("NEPA's requirement of an environmental impact statement [did] not apply to [a state] project" which involved only "[p]ossible future federal funding"), *cert. denied*, 424 U.S. 927, 96 S.Ct. 1141, 47 L.Ed.2d 337 (1976).

Second, if the answer to the first question is yes—there has been major federal action—then the project and any non-federal entities involved in it may be enjoined pending completion of an EIS if there is continued agency involvement in the project such that termination or modification of the agency involvement would terminate or significantly impact the project. The second inquiry then is to ask—whether termination or modification of federal agency involvement would end, cripple or at least significantly affect the project.

In making this inquiry the concept of "control" is key—not, however, in the limited sense that the federal agency must be actively exercising discretionary control over some aspect of the project in order for non-federal actors to be enjoined. Rather, the term "control" describes the minimum federal agency involvement that would permit federal court jurisdiction under NEPA if that term is viewed as also encompassing situations in which the cessation of federal involvement would control the destiny of some aspect of the project. *See Macht v. Skinner*, 916 F.2d 13 (D.C.Cir.1990).

MACHT v. SKINNER
916 F.2d 13 (D.C.Cir.1990).

WALD, CHIEF JUDGE.

* * *

NEPA requires that federal agencies consider the environmental consequences of "major Federal actions significantly affecting the quality of the human environment." 42 U.S.C. § 4332(2)(C). Thus the threshold issue in this case is whether, at this point, there is sufficient federal involvement in the Light Rail Project to constitute major federal action affecting the environment under NEPA.... Appellants base their claim that the Project involves major federal action on two facts: (1) UMTA has given Maryland $2.5 million for preliminary engineering studies and environmental impact statements for the proposed extensions to the Light Rail Project; and (2) Maryland must obtain from the Army Corps of Engineers a wetlands permit pursuant to § 404 of the Clean Water Act and § 10 of the Rivers and Harbors Act in order to build the state segment. We hold that neither is sufficient to transform the entirely state-funded Light Rail Project into "major federal action" affecting the environment within the meaning of NEPA. . . .

A. UMTA Funding for Preliminary Studies

On September 29, 1989, UMTA granted MTA a maximum of $2,587,500 to perform an Alternative Analysis and Draft Environmental Impact Statement for the possible extensions to the Light Rail Project. *Macht,* Mem. op. at 6, J.A. at 51. Appellants argue that this federal expenditure makes the entire Light Rail Project—the 22.5–mile state segment under construction as well as the proposed extensions—"major federal action" affecting the environment within the meaning of NEPA. This argument is based on a misconception about NEPA's requirements.

NEPA requires federal agencies to prepare or evaluate an EIS for any proposed "major federal action" that will "significantly affect[ ]the quality of the human environment." 42 U.S.C. § 4332(2)(C). NEPA does not require UMTA to prepare an EIS until it proposes or decides to participate in a project that will affect the environment. In this case, UMTA has not yet decided to assist Maryland in the final design or construction of the proposed extensions to the Light Rail Project. As the district court aptly recognized, "[t]o argue that the federal funding . . . for the preliminary analysis studies constitutes major federal action in the proposed extensions would be putting the proverbial cart before the horse because until these studies are done a decision cannot be reached on what projects—if any—are to be developed." *Macht,* Mem. op. at 6, J.A. at 51.

Our holding that UMTA funding of preliminary studies is not major federal action within the meaning of NEPA is consistent with other circuit court precedent. In *Rapid Transit Advocates, Inc. v. Southern California Rapid Transit District,* 752 F.2d 373 (9th Cir.1985)(per curiam), a group of homeowners sought to enjoin an UMTA grant to assist the local transit district in performing preliminary design and engineering studies for a proposed subway line, alleging that UMTA failed to comply with various provisions of the UMT Act and NEPA. The Ninth Circuit rejected their claim, saying: Neither [UMTA's] decision nor the design and engineering work that will follow will have any impact upon appellants in and of themselves. The UMT Administration has explicitly disavowed any advance commitment to approve construction. The process may never be completed; the Wilshire Subway may never be funded. If it is, appellants' present objections can be raised and fully considered in a suit to review the agency's final action in light of then existing circumstances. 752 F.2d at 378–79; *see also Atlanta Coalition on the Transportation Crisis, Inc. v. Atlanta Regional Commission,* 599 F.2d 1333, 1347 (5th Cir.1979)(development of regional transportation plan is not major federal action where the "federal financial assistance to the planning process in no way implies a commitment by any federal agency to fund any transportation project or projects or to undertake, fund or approve any action that directly affects the human environment").

Similarly in this case, UMTA's decision to fund preliminary studies, in and of itself, will have no impact on appellants or the environment. UMTA has expressly stated that its decision to provide funding for alternative analyses "is not a commitment to fund the construction of any project that may result." Letter from Alfred A. DelliBovi, Administrator of UMTA, to Ronald J. Hartman, Administrator of MTA (March 30, 1989), J.A. at 371. In fact, Maryland has not even decided to build the proposed extensions—with or without federal financial assistance. *See Macht,* Mem. op. at 8, J.A. at 53. At this point, the federal involvement is not the firm commitment that could transform the so far entirely state-funded Light Rail Project into major federal action affecting the environment within the meaning of NEPA. *Cf. Defenders of Wildlife v. Andrus,* 627 F.2d 1238, 1243 (D.C.Cir.1980)("only when an agency reaches the point ... where it is ready to propose a course of action need it be ready to produce an impact statement" pursuant to NEPA).

Nor are we persuaded that the Project involves major federal action because Maryland hopes to obtain a $40 million UMTA grant to build the extensions. The district court perceptively recognized that "in this era of federal fiscal shortcomings there is a wide gulf between what a state may want and what the federal government is willing to provide. The [appellants] have provided no evidence that the federal government is irretrievably committed to providing the funds for the proposed extensions." *Macht,* Mem. op. at 7–8, J.A. at 52–53. Absent such evidence, we cannot find major federal action in the Light Rail Project. *See Boston v. Volpe,* 464 F.2d 254, 258 (1st Cir.1972)(state's "present intention eventually to seek federal funds for yet another stretch of [airport] taxiway" does not convert present state construction of taxiway into a federal project).

Because we hold that the Light Rail Project does not yet involve major federal action, we do not decide whether NEPA may require an environmental analysis if UMTA ultimately decides to fund construction of the extensions, or whether such a decision may constitute major federal action within the meaning of NEPA. *Cf. Indian Lookout Alliance v. Volpe,* 484 F.2d 11, 16 (8th Cir.1973)("any project for which federal funds have been approved or committed constitutes a major federal action bringing into play the requirements of NEPA"). If such an eventuality occurs, appellants may renew their claim that an EIS is required prior to the disbursement of federal funds or question the scope of the EIS, i.e., whether it must encompass the baseline segment as well as the extensions. *See Kleppe v. Sierra Club,* 427 U.S. 390, 406 n. 15, 96 S.Ct. 2718, 2728 n. 15, 49 L.Ed.2d 576 (1976)("the time at which a court enters the [NEPA] process is when the report or recommendation on the proposal [for major federal action] is made, and someone protests either the absence or the adequacy of the final impact statement"). An adequate EIS would, of course, be a necessary prerequisite for the expenditure of federal funds on the project.

B. THE ARMY CORPS OF ENGINEERS' PERMIT

Appellants also claim that even though the state segment is financed entirely with state funds, it is major federal action under NEPA because the Army Corps of Engineers must issue a wetlands permit pursuant to § 404 of the Clean Water Act, 33 U.S.C. § 1344, and § 10 of the Rivers and Harbors Act, 33 U.S.C. § 403.... Appellants argue that because the Project has been "federalized," Maryland must comply with NEPA before it may construct the state segment. We disagree and take this opportunity to clarify what it means to "federalize" state or private action for purposes of NEPA.

NEPA requires federal agencies—not states or private parties—to consider the environmental impacts of their proposed actions. "[F]or any major Federal action funded under a program of grants to States," however, NEPA allows a state agency to prepare an EIS for a federal agency if certain conditions are met. 42 U.S.C. § 4332(2)(D); *see also* 23 C.F.R. § 771.109(c)(UMTA regulations). Regardless of whether the EIS is prepared by a federal or state agency, the twofold purpose of NEPA is "to inject environmental considerations into the federal agency's decisionmaking process" and "to inform the public that the [federal] agency has considered environmental concerns in its decisionmaking process." *Weinberger v. Catholic Action of Hawaii/Peace Education Project*, 454 U.S. 139, 143, 102 S.Ct. 197, 201, 70 L.Ed.2d 298 (1981)....

Appellants correctly assert that federal involvement in a nonfederal project may be sufficient to "federalize" the project for purposes of NEPA. *See, e.g., Maryland Conservation Council, Inc. v. Gilchrist*, 808 F.2d 1039 (4th Cir.1986); *Winnebago Tribe of Nebraska v. Ray*, 621 F.2d 269 (8th Cir.), *cert. denied*, 449 U.S. 836, 101 S.Ct. 110, 66 L.Ed.2d 43 (1980); *Sierra Club v. Hodel*, 544 F.2d 1036 (9th Cir.1976). But contrary to appellants' argument, none of these cases stand for the proposition that a state must comply with NEPA if one of its projects is found to involve major federal action.

The cases instead fall into two categories. Cases in the first category involve allegations that a federal agency failed to comply with NEPA when it issued a permit allowing a nonfederal project to go forward. In these cases the question is usually whether the federal agency had to prepare an EIS before issuing the permit or whether the EIS prepared by the federal agency was sufficiently broad in scope. *See, e.g., Winnebago Tribe of Nebraska*, 621 F.2d at 272–73 (challenge to Army Corps' decision that issuance of wetlands permit would have no significant impact and thus EIS was not required); *Save the Bay, Inc. v. United States Corps of Engineers*, 610 F.2d 322 (5th Cir.)(challenge to Army Corps' decision that issuance of pipeline construction permit was not major federal action requiring compliance with NEPA), *cert. denied*, 449 U.S. 900, 101 S.Ct. 269, 66 L.Ed.2d 130 (1980). Because the Army Corps is not a party to this case and there is no allegation that the Army Corps has failed to comply with NEPA, these cases are not controlling on the issue before us....

The issue in the second category of cases is whether state or private action on an entire project should be enjoined until the federal agencies that must approve particular portions of the project have complied with NEPA. The question in these cases is whether the federal participation in the project is so substantial that the state should not be allowed to go forward until all the federal approvals have been granted in accordance with NEPA. *See, e.g., Sierra Club v. Hodel*, 544 F.2d 1036 (9th Cir. 1976)(court enjoined construction of an ALCOA plant until the Bonneville Power Administration—a federal agency subject to NEPA—completed an EIS; by contracting to construct a transmission line and supply power to the ALCOA plant, the BPA federalized the entire project); *Dalsis v. Hills*, 424 F.Supp. 784, 787 (W.D.N.Y.1976)(court enjoined construction of shopping mall until HUD prepared an EIS because HUD financed demolition of "substandard structures" on the site, and the developer "could not lawfully have started the redevelopment project without HUD's approval").

Maryland Conservation Council, Inc. v. Gilchrist, 808 F.2d 1039 (4th Cir.1986), on which appellants primarily rely, falls in this latter category. Gilchrist involved an attempt to enjoin construction of a county highway designed to pass through a state park. The court found that the county highway project involved major federal action because: (1) the highway crossed a state park that had been purchased with a substantial federal grant; therefore, the county needed the approval of the Secretary of Interior, pursuant to § 6(f) of the Conservation Act, to convert the park land to other than recreational use; (2) the county needed a § 404 permit from the Army Corps to dredge a wetlands; and (3) the county might need the approval of the Secretary of Transportation to use park land for a transportation project under § 4(f) of the Transportation Act. 808 F.2d at 1042. On these facts, the court of appeals held that the district court should have considered the motion to enjoin the county's construction until the federal officials complied with NEPA. *Id.* at 1403.

Gilchrist did not hold that the state had to comply with NEPA because the approval of several federal agencies was a necessary precondition to the state project. Instead, *Gilchrist* held that because the state needed permits and discretionary approval from several federal agencies in order to build a substantial part of the highway, the state could not construct any portion of the highway until the federal agencies had approved the project in compliance with NEPA. The reasoning of the Fourth Circuit in *Gilchrist* is sound: the state may not begin construction of any part of a project if the effect of such construction would be to limit significantly the options of the federal officials who have discretion over substantial portions of the project. Nevertheless, we decline to extend *Gilchrist* to this case where the only federal involvement is the issuance of a wetlands permit covering a maximum of 3.58 acres of the 22.5–mile Project.

First, and most significantly, the district court found that the Army Corps has discretion over only "a negligible portion of the entire project." *Macht,* Mem. op. at 10, J.A. at 55. This case is thus distinguishable from *Gilchrist* where several federal agencies had discretion over a substantial part of the highway project. *See also Sierra Club v. Alexander*, 484 F.Supp. 455, 472 (N.D.N.Y.), aff'd mem., 633 F.2d 206 (2d Cir.1980)(court empowered to enjoin private construction of shopping mall until Army Corps complies with NEPA where completion of the project will require Army Corps approval to rechannel 2,000 linear feet of creek and fill 38 acres of wetlands).

Second, "the degree of federal involvement in the 22.5 mile Project is limited solely to the issuance of wetlands permits and no other federal activity is required for the Project's construction." *Macht,* Mem. op. at 11, J.A. at 56. Maryland has not, therefore, entered a "joint venture" with the federal government by contracting to obtain goods or services from a federal agency. *See Sierra Club v. Hodel*, 544 F.2d 1036 (9th Cir.1976)(construction of ALCOA plant may be enjoined until federal agency prepares EIS because ALCOA federalized the project by contracting to have a federal agency construct a transmission line and supply power to the plant).

Finally, Maryland has not entered a financial "partnership" with the federal government because the district court found that "the federal government has given no direct—or indirect, for that matter—financial aid to the state for the Project." *Macht,* Mem. op. at 11, J.A. at 56; *cf. Gilchrist*, 808 F.2d at 1042 (federal government provided indirect financial assistance because state highway would cross a park established with a "grant of substantial federal funds"); *Biderman v. Morton*, 497 F.2d 1141 (2d Cir.1974)("it is well settled that non-federal parties may be enjoined, pending completion of an EIS, where those non-federal entities have entered into a partnership or joint venture with the Federal Government, and are thus recipients of federal funding"); *Foundation on Economic Trends v. Heckler*, 756 F.2d 143 (D.C.Cir.1985)(enjoining University of California experiment that NIH approved and funded without complying with NEPA).

This is clearly not a case in which the state has entered a "partnership" or "joint venture" with the federal government by contracting with a federal agency to obtain goods, services, or financing. Nor is this a case where the federal government has discretion over substantial portions of the project. NEPA therefore provides no basis for enjoining Maryland's construction of the Light Rail Project.

* * *

§ 1.10 REGULATIONS IMPLEMENTING NEPA

The Council on Environmental Quality (CEQ) is responsible for supervising the preparation of EIS's by agencies and has promulgated regulations governing federal agency compliance with NEPA. The regulations establish uniform standards applicable throughout the federal government for conducting environmental reviews. *See* 40 C.F.R. Parts 1500–1508. In addition, most federal agencies have regulations governing their own NEPA procedures, which should be consulted in appropriate cases. EPA's NEPA regulations, for example, are set forth at 40 C.F.R. Part 6, and those of the Corps of Engineers are at 33 C.F.R. Part 230.

Discussion Problem

Prior to 1990, the United States Forest Service used herbicides when necessary to control vegetation in the Lake States National Forests. On those occasions when herbicides were used, the Forest Service prepared an Environmental Impact Statement ("EIS") as required by the National Environmental Policy Act, 42 U.S.C.A. §§ 4331–4334 (1988)("NEPA"). In 1990, the Forest Service decided it would not use herbicides in the forests and, accordingly, decided not to prepare an EIS examining the environmental impacts of their use. State Pesticide Information and Education, Inc. ("SPIE") filed suit alleging that NEPA required the Forest Service to prepare an EIS before it decided not to use herbicides in the forests.

You are the attorney for the Forest Service. What arguments do you make to oppose SPIE? What arguments is SPIE likely to raise?

§ 1.11 PERMIT OR OTHER "ADVANCE APPROVAL" REQUIREMENTS

Most federal and state environmental laws contain "permit" or other "prior approval" requirements. Permit or approval requirements can be triggered by certain facilities or land uses involving, among other things:

(1) Pollutant discharges

    (a) Water pollution discharges

    (b) Air pollution discharges

    (c) Solid or hazardous waste disposal

(2) Certain locations

    (a) Use of wetlands

    (b) Work in navigable (or state) waters

    (c) Use of state-owned bottom lands of state waters (subaqueous beds)

    (d) Use of flood plains

    (e) Withdrawal of water in "surface or groundwater management areas"

    (f) Construction or activities in aquifer recharge areas

    (g) Use of "critical environmental areas"

    (h) Building within a "historic district"

    (i) Activity within the State's coastal zone management area

    (j) Activities on federal lands

    (k) Activities in marine sanctuaries

    (l) Construction on a "wild and scenic" river

(3) Certain activities

(a) Construction or operation of water supply systems of a certain size

(b) Construction or operation of sewerage systems and treatment works

(c) Construction of dams or other impounding structures

(d) Open burning

(e) Land disturbing activity likely to lead to land erosion or stream sedimentation

(f) Strip mining of certain materials

(g) Discharge of dredged or fill material

(h) Construction of wells

(i) Construction or operation of nuclear power plants

(j) Construction or operation of hydroelectric power plants

(k) Construction or operation of tall buildings or towers

(4) Certain materials

(a) Manufacture or use of toxic or hazardous substances

(b) Manufacture or use of pesticides

(c) Manufacture or use of radioactive substances

(5) Certain protected items

(a) Destruction of rare or endangered species

(b) Destruction of historical buildings

(c) Alteration of terrain involving significant, historical, or archeological data

Permits normally must be obtained before construction or operation of facilities requiring them can be commenced. The definition of "commencing" construction or operation is not uniform among environmental laws, and this determination is frequently one of the key determinations that must be made.

Any one project may require a multitude of permits from separate agencies, and failure to obtain any one of these permits may kill the deal. Permit requirements are usually multitudinous and uncoordinated. Bureaucratic delays can be significant, so plan ahead.

§ 1.12 SUBSTANTIVE REQUIREMENTS UNDER ENVIRON-MENTAL LAWS AND REGULATIONS

In addition to the permit requirements, there are a whole host of substantive requirements to be complied with under environmental laws and regulations. Most, but not all, of these are applied through permit systems.

Compliance can be very costly in both time and money. In some cases, compliance will be impossible, and a new facility (or the expansion of an old one) will be "zoned out" of an area on environmental grounds. Economic and technical feasibility is frequently only a secondary consideration. Failure to comply with permit or substantive requirements subjects an owner or operator to injunctive relief and to severe civil and criminal penalties.

§ 1.13　ENVIRONMENTAL REGULATORY RISKS

1.　*The Rise of Federal and State Administrative Regulation of the Environment*

In 1970, environmental law took a sharp turn away from its common law tort liability roots toward administrative regulation. Comprehensive federal statutes were enacted dealing with:

- Environmental impact assessment (the National Environmental Policy Act, or NEPA, in 1969),
- Air pollution (the Clean Air Act in 1970),
- Water pollution (the Clean Water Act in 1972), and
- Solid and hazardous waste (the Resource Conservation and Recovery Act, or RCRA, in 1976).

Similar statutes were enacted at the state level in virtually every state.

2.　*The Resulting Business Risks*

Federal and state regulatory statutes impose three basic business risks:

　　a.　They govern whether permission can be obtained from the government to conduct the business at all, and on what terms.

　　b.　They impose compliance costs of essentially two types:

　　　　(1) The costs of technology or business practices necessary to achieve compliance, and

　　　　(2) The costs of fines or civil penalties for noncompliance.

　　c.　They also impose constraints on management's future options:

　　　　(1) They inhibit flexibility of plant and product changes through requirements for new or modified permits or licenses before changes can be made, and

　　　　(2) They may inhibit or altogether preclude future plant expansion at a site by placing overall limits on the amount of pollutants, from any source, that the air, water, land, or groundwater at or near the site may receive.

3.　*The Effect of Regulatory Risks on Real Estate Transactions*

The types of business transactions traditionally affected by administrative regulatory risks have included:

- land sales,

- leases, and

- business acquisitions and mergers.

These risks have been accommodated by:

- obtaining or transferring the necessary permits and licenses,

- using representations or warranties to identify the normally modest liabilities involved,

- using insurance to shift the risks, and

- using covenants or indemnities to allocate the risks.

4. The Characteristics of the Risks Posed by Administrative Regulation

The state and federal environmental regulatory statutes create a complex and pervasive web of administrative regulation to which the conduct of business must conform. Until that web is in place and relatively stable, they also create massive uncertainty for business planning. Once a regulatory program is established, however, uncertainty is reduced and costs become relatively determinable. The risk of noncompliance penalties falls on a relatively determinable class, since liability normally runs only to the "owner or operator" of a facility. Further, the maximum amount of such penalties is set by regulation and noncompliance liability is not normally so large as to provoke bankruptcy. In any case, regulatory risk is largely controllable in the last resort by shutting down.

In short, regulatory compliance risks typically (a) involve chiefly the right to do business, (b) cost relatively predictable and controllable amounts, related directly to the nature of the business being done, (c) fall on a few actors obviously identified with the risk, and (d) involve little risk of substantial, unanticipated liability.

§ 1.14 ENVIRONMENTAL PERMITTING ISSUES

Environmental permitting programs do not, in general, operate directly on a business transaction (*i.e.*, permit requirements do not prohibit a particular transaction). Rather, a permit program may govern the risk or legality of doing business after the transaction. Therefore, relevant environmental permit programs must be considered carefully when the transaction is structured and implemented. Issues that must be considered include:

- Who must be permitted?

- May an existing permit be transferred to a new permittee and must the regulatory agency be notified (and when) of the business transaction?

- Are other forms of notification required?

- How do permit transfer and notification requirements affect the structure of a transaction, especially the representations and warranties?

Both federal and state transfer and notice requirements for existing permits should be carefully reviewed. Although many facilities merely send the appropriate regulatory agencies a letter containing notification of the change and requesting permit modification as necessary, this procedure frequently does not technically comply with the formal permit modification requirements. While regulatory agencies may be quite flexible and make the requested permit transfer, in the interim the facility may be operating without complying with permit regulations. This possibility must be carefully considered if any warranties or representations regarding compliance with environmental laws are contained in the transaction.

§ 1.15 CIVIL LIABILITY RISKS POSED BY ENVIRONMENTAL LAWS

Though the regulatory system in the United States—consisting of environmental impact assessment requirements and comprehensive media-specific regulation of discharge sources or other forms of regulation—addresses current and future sources of pollution, it does little to address the already existing contamination of land and groundwater. Common law tort actions for personal injury and property damage historically were the only means of imposing liability for environmental harm, and outside of the asbestos industry, liability had been more theoretical than real since proof was difficult under most state laws, and plaintiffs seldom sued.

Around 1980, however, a major shift occurred in environmental policy from administrative regulation to heavy reliance on traditional civil liability, but in a new statutory form. By that time the United States Congress had already enacted comprehensive administrative regulatory requirements to control air pollution, water pollution, and solid waste disposal from currently operating sources. Congress then turned its attention to the clean up of toxic chemical dump sites. To accomplish cleanup, Congress abandoned the prospective regulatory approach of the 1970's in favor of a harsh retroactive civil liability scheme. Congress enacted the Comprehensive Environmental Response, Compensation and Liability Act of 1980 (CERCLA), commonly known as Superfund, which overnight created billions of dollars of potential new "clean-up" liability for business. The scope and magnitude of the Superfund liability are startling.

A company or investor may subject itself to millions of dollars in civil liability under Superfund if it buys or sells commercial real estate in the United States, builds or operates commercial or manufacturing facilities there, buys, sells, or merges with a United States company or a company with assets or operations in the United States, or lends money to a United States company or to a company with assets or operations in the United States.

A company or investor doing business in the United States or acquiring assets in the United States also must contend with liability under state common and statutory law for personal injury or property damages due to toxic or hazardous substances, especially when those substances are released to groundwater. In two such cases, for example, plaintiffs recovered $13.7 million and $12.7 million. There is also much study and talk in the United States today of creating a new federal statutory tort or administrative compensation system for personal injury and property damage due to toxics.

As a result of the types of liabilities just outlined, contaminated real estate in the United States may now have a large negative value, as may businesses that own such property. Insurance policies covering past conduct may not cover these liabilities and current insurance generally cannot be obtained. Businessmen who do not educate themselves about these realities, and who do not carefully identify and manage these risks in transactions involving businesses or assets, are playing a new form of "Russian Roulette."

§ 1.16 ENVIRONMENTAL RACISM AND OTHER ENVIRONMENTAL JUSTICE ISSUES

In 1992 EPA issued a report entitled "Environmental Equity: Reducing Risk for All Communities." In that report, EPA found that people of color and low-income communities experience higher than average exposure to toxic pollutants than the general population. *See* 58 Fed. Reg. 63955 (December 3, 1993). EPA defines environmental justice as "the fair treatment of people of all races, cultures and income with respect to the development, implementation and enforcement of environmental laws, regulations and policies." EPA explains:

> Fair treatment means that no racial, ethnic or socioeconomic group should bear a disproportionate share of the negative environmental consequences resulting from the operation of industrial, municipal, and commercial enterprises and from the execution of federal, state and local, and tribal programs and policies. Environmental justice seeks to ensure that the communities, private industry, local governments, states, tribes, federal government, grass-roots organizations, and individuals act responsibly and ensure environmental protection to all communities.

58 Fed. Reg. at 63957.

In June of 1993, the Office of Environmental Equity of the Environmental Protection Agency (EPA) was delegated granting authority to solicit projects, select suitable projects from among those proposed, supervise such projects, evaluate the results of projects, and disseminate information on the effectiveness of the projects, and feasibility of the practices, methods, techniques and processes in environmental justice areas. Each instrument approved under the environmental equity delegation must be consistent with the Federal Grant and Cooperative Agreements Act of 1977, Public Law 95–24, as amended, 31 U.S.C. 6301; Title 40 of the Code of Federal Regulations, parts 30, 31, 33, 40, 45 and 47, as appropriate; and existing media-specific regulations pertinent to the statement of work. The Office of Environmental Equity is interested in helping these communities to identify and assess these pollution sources, to implement environmental awareness and training programs for affected residents and work with local stakeholders (community-based organizations, academia, industry, local governments) to devise strategies for environmental improvements. According to EPA:

> Environmental justice projects or activities should enhance critical thinking, problem solving, and effective decision-making skills. Environmental justice efforts may include, but are not necessarily limited to enhancing the gathering, observing, measuring, classifying, experimenting and other data gathering techniques that assist individuals in discussing, inferring, predicting, and interpreting information about environmental justice issues and concerns. Environmental justice projects should engage and motivate individuals to weigh various issues to make informed and responsible decisions as they work to address environmental inequities.

Fiscal Year 1994 was the first year of the grants program with the amount of awards up to $10,000 per grant. Each of EPA's 10 regions had approximately $50,000 for grants with a Federal share of $10,000 or less. *See* 58 Fed. Reg. 63955 (December 3, 1993).

1. *Overview*

IN THE MATTER OF: GENESEE POWER STATION LIMITED PARTNERSHIP PERMITTEE

PSD Appeal Nos. 93–1 through 93–7.
United States Environmental Protection Agency.

OPINION OF THE BOARD BY JUDGE MCCALLUM:

The Environmental Appeals Board has received nine petitions seeking review of a Prevention of Significant Deterioration (PSD) permit issued to Genesee Power Station Limited Partnership (Genesee) for construction of a 35–megawatt steam/electric power plant designed to burn several types of wood waste. The PSD permit was prepared under an EPA delegation by the staff of the Air Quality Division of the Michigan Department of Natural Resources (MDNR) and issued by the Michigan Air Pollution Control Commission (Commission). *See* 40 CFR § 52.21(u)(authorizing Administrator to delegate responsibility for conducting source review under Section 52.21). As requested by the Board, the Commission through MDNR filed a response to six of the petitions (as discussed below, three other petitions were not filed in a timely fashion). Although not requested to do so by the Board, Genesee also filed a brief containing its responses to the petitions. For the reasons set forth below, with respect to one issue raised by the American Lung

Association of Michigan, we are remanding the permit to the Commission so that it may reconsider its determination of the best available control technology for lead emissions. With respect to all other issues raised in the petitions, we are denying review.

I. BACKGROUND

Genesee proposes to install and operate a 35–megawatt steam/electric power plant designed to burn several types of wood waste including demolition debris, pallets, dunnage, construction waste, tree trimmings, landclearing/inforest and sawmill residue. The plant, which will use a spreader stoker system to burn the fuel, will be located northeast of Flint, Michigan in an industrial park.

New major stationary sources of air pollution, such as the proposed Genesee facility, are required under the Clean Air Act to obtain an air pollution permit before commencing construction. If the facility is in an area where one or more national ambient air quality standards (NAAQS) are not being violated (attainment and unclassified areas), the permit is referred to as a prevention of significant deterioration of air quality (PSD) permit. CAA § 165, 42 U.S.C. § 7475. If the facility is in an area where the NAAQS are being violated (nonattainment area), the permit is referred to as a nonattainment area permit. CAA § 173, 42 U.S.C. § 7503. The PSD and nonattainment area permit requirements are pollutant-specific. For example, although a facility may emit many air pollutants, a PSD or nonattainment area permit will regulate only those pollutants that will be emitted in sufficient quantities to trigger the PSD or nonattainment area requirements. Also because a source may be located in an area that is attainment or unclassified for some pollutants and simultaneously nonattainment for others, the source may be required to obtain both PSD and nonattainment area permits.

Of the six pollutants for which NAAQS have been established (criteria pollutants), the area in which the proposed Genesee facility would be built is attainment for five PM–10 (particulate matter with particle diameter < 10 microns, carbon monoxide, lead, nitrogen oxides, and sulfur dioxide) and nonattainment for the sixth (ozone). The PSD permit under consideration here imposes emissions limitations for the following four criteria pollutants:

PM–10, carbon monoxide, nitrogen oxides, and lead. The permit does not impose an emissions limitation for sulfur dioxide, because that pollutant is not expected to be emitted in sufficient quantities to trigger the PSD requirements. The PSD permit also does not impose an emissions limitation for ozone, because the proposed site is in an area that is nonattainment for that pollutant.

In addition to the four criteria pollutants addressed in the permit, the permit also contains an emissions limitation for beryllium, for which a NAAQS has not been set.... The permit also contains State requirements relating to emissions of toxic pollutants that are not subject to PSD review....

The emissions limitations imposed under the federal PSD regulations for control of PM–10, carbon monoxide, nitrogen oxides, and lead emissions are required to meet the definition of Best Available Control Technology or BACT, which is, in relevant part, as follows:

[BACT] means an emissions limitation (including a visible emission standard) based on the maximum degree of reduction for each pollutant subject to regulation under [the] Act which would be emitted from any proposed major stationary source or major modification which the Administrator, on a case-by-case basis, taking into account energy, environmental, and economic impacts and other costs, determines is achievable for such source or modification through application of production processes or available methods, systems, and techniques, including fuel cleaning or treatment or innovative fuel combustion techniques for control of such pollutant.

40 CFR § 52.21(b)(12). Under the rules governing the PSD permitting process, the permit applicant is responsible for proposing an emissions limitation that constitutes BACT for each regulated pollutant and for providing information on the control alternatives that can be used to achieve it. 40 CFR 52.21(n)(1)(iii). Nevertheless, regardless of the control level proposed by the applicant as BACT, the ultimate BACT decision is made by the permit-issuing authority.

To meet the emissions limitations that represent BACT for particulate matter and lead, Genesee will install a multiclone collector and an electrostatic precipitator (ESP).... To meet the emissions limitation that is BACT for emissions of nitrogen oxides, Genesee will install a selective non-catalytic reduction (SNCR) system.... To meet the emissions limitation that is BACT for carbon monoxide, Genesee will employ proper combustion design and operation.

Genesee submitted an initial PSD permit application on June 8, 1992, and the application was deemed complete on October 1, 1992. The public comment period for the draft permit lasted 42 days, and two public hearings were held, one on October 27, 1992, and the other on December 1, 1992. The service of the notice of the issuance of the final permit decision was dated December 7, 1992. The Board has received petitions for review from the following groups and individuals: American Lung Association of Michigan (ALAM); Flint Branch of the NAACP; Society of Afro–American People; Flint/Genesee Neighborhood Association; Linda Elston and Betty Strong; Genesee County Medical Society; Violet Worthington; Cherie N. Misner; and Sister Marjorie Polys.

II. DISCUSSION

Under the rules that govern this proceeding, a PSD permit ordinarily will not be reviewed unless it is based on a clearly erroneous finding of fact or conclusion of law, or involves an important matter of policy or exercise of discretion that warrants review. *See* 40 CFR § 124.19; 45 Fed. Reg. 33,412 (May 19, 1980). The preamble to the promulgation of these rules states that "this power of review should be only sparingly exercised," and that "most permit conditions should be finally determined at the Regional [or State] level." *Id.* The burden of demonstrating that review is warranted is on the petitioner. In re Ogden Martin Systems of Onondaga, Inc., et al., PSD Appeal No. 92–7, at 2 (EAB, December 1, 1992); In re Hawaiian Commercial & Sugar Company, PSD Appeal No. 92–1, at 2 (EAB, July 20, 1992). For the reasons set forth below, we conclude that, with the exception of the BACT determination for lead emissions, none of the petitioners have met this burden. With respect to the BACT determination for lead emissions, we agree with ALAM that the Commission did not give adequate consideration to fuel cleaning as a control technology for such emissions. Accordingly, we are remanding the permit for further consideration by the Commission on this issue.

In the discussion below, we first address the environmental racism argument raised by the Society of Afro–American People. We then consider whether the opportunities for public participation in the decisionmaking process leading up to the issuance of the subject permit were adequate. We next focus on the arguments raised in the petition for review filed by the American Lung Association of Michigan, which challenges among other things MDNR's BACT determinations for PM–10, nitrogen oxides, lead and carbon monoxide. Finally, we consider whether the other petitions for review challenging the subject permit meet the procedural requirements that govern the filing of petitions for review.

A. ENVIRONMENTAL RACISM

Richard Dicks, Executive Director of the Society of Afro–American People in Michigan, argues that the Commission's issuance of the PSD permit represents an instance of "governmental environmental racism," because the facility will be located near the predominantly African American Flint/Genesee neighborhood.... According to Mr. Dicks, this environmental racism is evidenced by the manner in which the public hearings were held. Specifically, Mr. Dicks charges that:

> This conclusion [of environmental racism] is supported by the obvious promotion by the DNR for this project. And the inability for people of color and other resident's of the economically deprived area to attend, or be involved in the hearings properly, is a civil rights concern....

Mr. Dicks also notes that, as the residents of the Flint/Genesee neighborhood waited for their chance to speak at the December 1, 1992 public hearing, the Commission was considering a permit application for a different facility to be located in Marquette County, Michigan. According to Mr. Dicks, the Commission denied that permit because the white residents of the surrounding community did not want the incinerator to be built:

> Five or six white residents from Marquette, Michigan who addressed the commission just before us. Live in a rural farm area that was not populated. They told the Commission that they did not want an

incinerator built near their property because it might affect their farm animals.

At this time one of the commissioners immediately stated that "if the people don't want this in their community we shouldn't put it there, because I sure wouldn't want it in my community." The commission then voted not to issue the permit to build the incinerator and the five or six people from Marquette left.

Mr. Dicks contrasts this treatment with the treatment received by the residents of the Flint/Genesee neighborhood, who expressed strong opposition to the location of the proposed Genesee power plant at the hearing, but failed to persuade the Commission to deny the permit. Mr. Dicks also notes that: "The commissioner that took such a strong stance for the people from Marquette, who said that they just didn't want a[n] incinerator in their community—well he said nothing in support of our plea."

In its response to comments, MDNR declined to respond to comments raising the environmental racism issue on the ground that "they are beyond the scope of Air Quality's rules and regulations." Staff Activity Report Addendum, at 8. In its Response to the Petitions, MDNR only mentions the environmental racism issue in passing. It lists the issue along with several other issues and states that it is denying review of such issues because they are "vague and/or unsubstantiated" or "not subject to federal or state air quality rules and regulations," or because petitioners have failed to provide supporting evidence. MDNR's Response to Petitions, at 19. MDNR does not specify which reason or reasons apply to the environmental racism argument.

We read Mr. Dicks' petition as arguing that the Commission acted with a racially discriminatory intent when it granted the Genesee permit. As evidence of this intent, Mr. Dicks cites the disparate treatment received by the African American opponents of the Genesee facility at the December 1, 1992 meeting: While the Commission was swayed to deny the Marquette permit by the opposition of white Marquette residents, the Commission was not swayed to deny the Genesee permit by the opposition of the African American Flint/Genesee residents. For the following reasons, however, we conclude that there is no basis for concluding that the Commission acted with a racially discriminatory intent. . . .

First, it is clear from the petition that Mr. Dicks' environmental racism argument is a challenge to the proposed location of the Genesee facility near the Flint/Genesee neighborhood. Mr. Dicks does not challenge any of the emissions limitations set for the Genesee facility. Accordingly, we must first consider whether the Commission in administering the Clean Air Act or PSD regulations under a federal delegation may consider community opposition to the location of the proposed Genesee facility. The decision to locate the Genesee facility at its proposed site is a local land use or zoning decision. Our review of the Clean Air Act and the PSD regulations leads us to conclude that local land use or zoning decisions are not to be disturbed under the Clean Air Act. The Clean Air Act specifically provides that:

> Nothing in [the Clean Air Act] constitutes an infringement on the existing authority of counties and cities to plan or control land use, and nothing in [the Clean Air Act] provides or transfers authority over such land use.

CAA § 131, 42 U.S.C. § 7431. The legislative history of the above-quoted provision reveals that its "purpose is to preclude any inference that the Clean Air Act by its terms, as amended by this bill, authorizes air pollution control agencies to override individual project-specific land use decisions made by a city or county." H. Rep. No. 101–90 Part 1, 101st Cong., 2d Sess. 401 (1990). Under the Clean Air Act, therefore, the inquiry of a state agency acting in its capacity as a PSD permit-issuing authority under a federal delegation is limited to determining whether the facility at the proposed site would meet federal air quality requirements. As long as the air quality impacts of the proposed facility would meet such requirements, the permit-issuing authority may not deny a PSD permit for the facility because the proposed location of the facility is objectionable from a local land use perspective.

We are mindful that the permit-issuing authority is required under the PSD rules to consider non-air quality "environmental" impacts and "other costs" when it determines the best available control technology (BACT) for each covered pollutant.... The ultimate purpose of the BACT determination, however, is to determine the best way of controlling emissions from the facility. Moreover, it has been held that consideration of non-air quality collateral impacts "operates primarily as a safety valve whenever unusual circumstances specific to the facility make it appropriate to use less than the most effective technology." In re Columbia Gulf Transmission Company, PSD Appeal No. 88–11, at 6 (Adm'r, June 21, 1989). Hence, although non-air quality impacts must be considered when BACT for a covered pollutant is determined, this consideration does not extend to generalized community opposition to the proposed site of the facility. The BACT determination has nothing to do with the decision to locate the facility at a particular site.

Thus, in its capacity as a PSD permit-issuing authority under a federal delegation, the Commission does not have authority under the Clean Air Act to consider community opposition to the proposed location of the Genesee facility so long as the air quality impacts of the facility meet federal air quality requirements. Any failure on its part to consider such opposition in the exercise of its PSD authority, therefore, was appropriate and does not in and of itself indicate a racially discriminatory intent.

Of course, if the Commission, in granting the Genesee permit, was also exercising some non-PSD authority under State law that allowed it to consider community opposition to the location of the facility, then its decision to grant the permit in spite of the intense opposition of the Flint/Genesee residents conceivably could have been motivated by a racially discriminatory intent. It is not clear from the record, however, whether the Commission was exercising such authority. Nor is it clear that the Board would have authority to review the Commission's exercise of such authority. We need not decide these issues now, however, because even assuming that the Commission was exercising some non-PSD power and assuming that the Board does have authority to review the Commission's exercise of that power, our review of the record leads us to conclude that Mr. Dicks' petition should be rejected. Mr. Dicks argues that the Commission treated Marquette's white residents and Flint's African American residents differently when it denied the Marquette permit but granted the Flint permit. This argument is based on the assumption that the Commission denied the Marquette County permit because the white Marquette County residents had come to oppose it. Mr. Dicks supports his contention with a remark allegedly made by one of the Commissioners, i.e. "[I]f the people don't want this in their community we shouldn't put it there, because I sure wouldn't want it in my community." Mr. Dicks' contention, however, is not borne out by the minutes of the December 1, 1992 hearing. Those minutes indicate that the Commission denied the Marquette permit not because of the opposition of the white Marquette County residents, but because (i) local zoning approval for the facility had been denied, (ii) the facility's proximity to a wetland would violate the federal Wild and Scenic Rivers Act, and (iii) the facility would not comply with state law. Exhibit 1, Genesee's Response to Petitions. These are legitimate, nondiscriminatory reasons for denying a permit. They suggest that the opposition of local white residents was not the basis for the Commission's decision. The minutes, therefore, negate Mr. Dicks' assumption to the contrary. Accordingly, we can find no support for Mr. Dicks' claim of disparate treatment, and a thorough search of the record has revealed no other evidence that the Commission was acting with a racially discriminatory intent.

In these circumstances, we see no basis for concluding that the Commission acted with a racially discriminatory intent when it granted the Genesee permit, either in its capacity as a PSD permit-issuing authority or in some other, non-PSD capacity. Accordingly, we are denying review of Mr. Dicks' petition.

The residents of the Flint/Genesee neighborhood, however, should not feel that the Genesee facility permit gives Genesee a license to threaten their health and safety. The record demonstrates that emissions allowed under the permit will meet all applicable air quality regulations, which are specifically established to protect human health. For example, emissions allowed under the permit will not cause a violation of the federal primary National Ambient Air Quality Standards (NAAQS), which for covered pollutants specify the level of air quality that EPA has determined will protect the public health, "allowing an adequate margin of safety." CAA § 109(b)(1), 42 U.S.C. § 7409(b)(1). The permit also requires that emissions meet State health-based restrictions on toxic emissions. *See* Michigan Administrative Code R 336.1230

(Exhibit 11, MDNR's Response to Petitions). In fact, with respect to some of the pollutants that have been the subject of most concern, the predicted ambient impact of emissions will be far below levels that have been determined to protect human health. For example, the predicted ambient level for mercury is 250 times lower than the Initial Threshold Screening Level (ITSL) for mercury, which is based on a "conservative estimate of the daily exposure to the human population, including sensitive subgroups, that is likely to be without appreciable risk of deleterious effect during a lifetime." Michigan Administrative Code R 336.1115(d), R 336.1109(c), R 336.1232 (Exhibit 11, MDNR's Response to Petitions). In addition, the predicted ambient lead level is 375 times lower than the primary NAAQS for lead. MDNR's Staff Activity Report Addendum, at 7 (Response 12). Also, as discussed infra, the permit is being remanded so that the Commission may consider whether fuel cleaning should be required to reduce lead emissions even further. Thus, emissions allowed under the PSD permit will not be permitted to exceed, and in certain instances will be far below, applicable air quality standards adopted to protect human health and welfare.

B. Public Participation

* * *

... we conclude that the permit should be remanded so that the Commission may consider fuel cleaning (i.e., removal of wood waste that is painted or treated with lead-bearing substances) in its BACT determination for lead. In view of this remand, we need not reach the issue of whether the comment period should have been reopened to allow the public to comment on the removal of the prohibition on painted wood waste from the permit.

* * *

III. Conclusion

Except for the issue relating to fuel cleaning as BACT for lead, review of the petition of the American Lung Association of Michigan (ALAM) is denied. With respect to the fuel cleaning issue, the permit is remanded so that the Commission may consider fuel cleaning in its BACT determination for lead. The petition of the Society of Afro–American People is denied because there is no support in the record for Mr. Dicks' claim of environmental racism. The petition of the Flint Branch of the NAACP is denied because it was not filed within the appeal period and because it does not itself raise any issues but merely incorporates testimony presented at a public hearing. The petition of the Flint/Genesee Neighborhood Association is denied because it merely incorporates other documents and does not itself raise any issues for review. The petition of the Genesee County Medical Society is denied because the issues it raises are not stated with sufficient specificity to allow for meaningful review. The petitions of Violet Worthington, Cherie N. Misner, and Sister Marjorie Polys are denied because the petitions were not filed in a timely manner. With respect to all but one issue, the petition of Linda Elston and Betty Strong is denied because the issues raised in their petition are not stated with sufficient specificity to permit meaningful review. With respect to the remaining issue, review is denied because the petition does not demonstrate a clear error or an important policy consideration.

* * *

AIELLO v. BROWNING–FERRIS, INC.
1993 WL 463701, 24 ELR 20771 (N.D.Cal.1993).

Marilyn Hall Patel.

This is a class action brought by and on behalf of residents and property owners of a section of the city of Pittsburg, California, located in east Contra Costa County. Plaintiffs live and own property adjacent to the Keller Canyon Landfill and have filed claims against the County of Contra Costa and the County's Board of Supervisors (collectively, "the County"), under 42 U.S.C. §§ 1983 and 42 U.S.C. §§ 1985, alleging that the County violated their constitutional rights in making a racially discriminatory decision to locate and approve the landfill in a part of the county where a high proportion of the county's minorities reside.

In addition, the plaintiffs have sued Browning–Ferris, Inc., Browning–Ferris Industries of California, and Keller Canyon, Inc. (collectively, "BFI"), the operators of the landfill, for the alleged taking of their property without just compensation in violation of their rights under the Fifth and Fourteenth Amendments to the United States Constitution and under 42 U.S.C. §§ 1983 and 42 U.S.C. § 1985. . . .

The case is before the court on BFI's motion to dismiss plaintiffs' takings claim, and on the County's motion to dismiss plaintiffs' civil rights claims. Having carefully considered the papers submitted by the parties, the court enters the following Memorandum and Order.

BACKGROUND

Plaintiffs allege that in January 1987, the Contra Costa County Board of Supervisors appointed a Landfill Siting Task Force to recommend future landfill sites for the County. Plaintiffs further allege that in June 1987, the task force ranked the present site last among 13 potential landfill sites, in part because of its proximity to residential and commercial areas. One location that ranked higher than Keller Canyon was in the Tassajara section of the county. That potential site, contend plaintiffs, would have been farther away from residential areas; however the closest residential population to that site is primarily white.

On November 10, 1988, the Board of Supervisors voted to endorse the siting of the landfill at Keller Canyon. Construction of the landfill began in November 1991, and operations began in May of the following year. According to plaintiffs, the construction and operation of the landfill caused and continues to cause dust, unnamed toxic substances, odors and trash to blow over into the residential area where plaintiffs live. In addition, plaintiffs complain of the noise of heavy machinery and the steady stream of trucks to and from the landfill. Plaintiffs allege that the wind-borne substances cause respiratory problems for the nearby residents and may cause other medical problems in the future. Plaintiffs also allege that the proximity to the landfill has reduced the value of their property.

Plaintiffs filed suit in federal court on February 8, 1993. Plaintiffs originally stated their civil rights claim and their takings claim against all defendants, but subsequently dismissed the County from the takings claim and dismissed BFI from the civil rights claim.

* * *

II. *Civil Rights Claim*

Plaintiffs' civil rights claims are brought under 42 U.S.C. § 1983 and 42 U.S.C. § 1985. Where Congress has not established a time limitation for a federal cause of action, federal courts rely on state law to determine the length of the statute of limitations. *Hoesterey v. City of Cathedral City,* 945 F.2d 317, 318 (9th Cir.1991)(citing *Wilson v. Garcia,* 471 U.S. 261, 105 S.Ct. 1938, 85 L.Ed.2d 254 (1985)). The parties agree that, applying relevant California law, the statute of limitations for plaintiffs' federal civil rights claims is one year. *See McDougal v. County of Imperial,* 942 F.2d 668, 672–74 (9th Cir.1991). Plaintiffs filed their complaint on February 8, 1993.

Defendant County has moved to dismiss plaintiffs' action as time-barred. The County maintains that plaintiffs' complaint alleges only that the decision as to where to locate the landfill was discriminatory. This decision, claims the County, took place in July 1990. Alternatively, the County argues, the decision must have been made by November 1991, when construction on the landfill began. Either date precedes February 8, 1992, the date which is one year before this action commenced.

Plaintiffs counter in two ways. First, they argue that under the "continuing wrong doctrine," a cause of action does not accrue until the time of the final wrongful act. Second, they argue that the statute of limitations should not begin running until after an aggrieved party has had time to assess the full extent of its losses.

A. *The Continuing Wrong Exception*

The "continuing wrong" exception to statutes of limitations provides that where a challenged practice is a continuing one, the plaintiff need only allege one occurrence of the practice that falls within the statute of limitations. *See Havens Realty Corp. v. Coleman,* 455 U.S. 363, 380–81, 102 S.Ct. 1114, 1125, 71 L.Ed.2d 214 (1982). In *Havens,* the plaintiffs brought suit under the Fair Housing Act of 1968, 42 U.S.C. § 3604, alleging "racial steering" in the rental of apartment units. *Id.* Four of the five specific instances complained of fell outside the applicable limitations period. The Court concluded, however, that "where a plaintiff, pursuant to the Fair Housing Act, challenges not just one incident of conduct violative of the Act, but an unlawful practice [] that continues into the limitations period, the complaint is timely" as long as the last asserted occurrence of the practice falls within the limitations period. *Id.* at 1125 (footnote omitted). *See also Rapf v. Suffolk County,* 755 F.2d 282, 289 (2d Cir.1985)(allegation that county is not performing a continuing duty to maintain jetties not barred).

A somewhat different situation arises, however, where the sole wrong complained of falls outside the limitations period, and where it is only the effects of that wrong continue into the limitations period. In such a case, there is no "continuing wrong" and the plaintiff is time-barred. *Delaware State College v. Ricks,* 449 U.S. 250, 101 S.Ct. 498, 66 L.Ed.2d 431 (1980). In *Ricks,* the plaintiff brought suit under Title VII of the Civil Rights Act of 1964 and under 42 U.S.C. section 1981, alleging that the college where he was employed had denied him tenure on the basis of his national origin. The adverse tenure decision was initially made in February 1973 and approved in March 1974; the plaintiff was not actually terminated, however, until June 1975. The question before the Court was whether the applicable date for purposes of the statute of limitations was the date on which the decision was made, or the date on which plaintiff was actually terminated.

The Court held that "termination of employment ... [was] a delayed, but inevitable consequence of the denial of tenure." *Id.* at 257–58. The only alleged discriminatory act was the denial of tenure, which fell outside the applicable limitations period. The Court held that " 'the proper focus is upon the time of the discriminatory acts, not upon the time at which the consequences of the acts became most painful.' " *Id.* at 258 (citing *Abramson v. University of Hawaii,* 594 F.2d 202, 209 (9th Cir.1979))(emphasis added by *Ricks* Court).

The instant case falls more squarely within the *Ricks* line of cases than the *Havens* line of cases. The gravamen of plaintiffs' complaint is that the decision to site the landfill was discriminatory. That decision was made in 1988. At most, plaintiffs' complaint of discriminatory conduct continues up until approval of the landfill plan in 1989. This is not a case, however, where there is an allegedly continuing pattern of intentional wrongdoing, or where repeated acts each constitute an illegal act. Rather, this is a case where there was one allegedly unlawful act, from which other consequences flowed.

It is critical to remember that it is plaintiffs' civil rights causes of action that they claim fall under the "continuing wrong" exception. The Supreme Court has made clear that the wrong addressed by sections 1983 and 1985 is intentional discrimination, and that disparate impact alone is insufficient to state a claim under those provisions. *United Brotherhood of Carpenters v. Scott,* 463 U.S. 825, 829, 103 S.Ct. 3352, 3356, 77 L.Ed.2d 1049 (1983)(42 U.S.C. § 1985); *Village of Arlington Heights v. Metropolitan Hous. Dev.,* 429 U.S. 252, 50 L.Ed.2d 450, 97 S.Ct. 555 (1977)(42 U.S.C. § 1983). Plaintiffs have alleged such intentional discrimination, at least in regard to the siting decision. The "wrongs", if any, that "continue," however are plaintiffs' tort claims, not their civil rights claims. Plaintiffs' claims that they continue to be exposed to noise and harmful wind-borne substances may constitute continuing torts, and may be the effect of a section 1983 or a section 1985 violation, but such injury does not constitute a continuing civil rights violation.

It is clear from plaintiffs' complaint that any allegedly discriminatory intent by defendants occurred well before construction on the landfill began in late 1989. In their class action allegations, plaintiffs state that members of the class have all "suffered injuries, losses or deprivation of civil rights as a result of the County Defendants' discriminatory siting decision." Second Amended Complaint P 12(a).... In their claim for relief on their civil rights claim, plaintiffs allege that "the County Defendants' conduct in the planning, siting, permitting and approval of the [landfill]" deprived plaintiffs of their civil rights. *Id.* P 49....

Moreover, the only evidence of intent that plaintiffs cite is evidence of discriminatory intent in the siting decision. *See id.* P 51. Plaintiffs list the following evidence to demonstrate that their civil rights have been violated: 1) a comment by a county supervisor that discrimination may have played a part in the siting decision; 2) the disparate impact on minority residents of the siting and operation of the landfill; 3) the historical background of the siting decision; and 4) the fact that the County knew that locating the landfill where they did would result in substances being carried by wind over to the residential areas. *See id.* Only the second piece of evidence even refers to the operation of the landfill, to allege that the operation has a disparate impact on plaintiffs. Not only is such an allegation wholly dependent on the siting decision, ... it is also insufficient to state a claim under section 1983 or section 1985, which require more than disparate impact alone. *See Arlington Heights,* 429 U.S. at 264–65.

Plaintiffs now contend in their opposition papers that the County continues to violate their civil rights by permitting the landfill to continue to operate. They have not alleged in their complaint, however, that once the siting decision had been made, there was anything further in the County's conduct was intentionally discriminatory. As the Supreme Court stated in *Ricks,* it is necessary to allege that some later discrimination occurred in order to delay the commencement of the limitations period. *See Ricks,* 449 U.S. at 257–58, 101 S.Ct. at 504 ("in order for the limitations period to commence with the date of discharge, Ricks would have had to allege and prove that the manner in which his employment was terminated differed discriminatorily from the manner in which the College terminated other professors who also had been denied tenure."); *United Air Lines, Inc. v. Evans*, 431 U.S. 553, 558, 97 S.Ct. 1885, 1889, 52 L.Ed.2d 571 (1977)(no continuing violation based on "mere continuity" without any "present violation")....

Plaintiffs' reliance on takings cases is unhelpful, since in such cases it is often the effects or duration of the initial act by the government that determines whether a taking has occurred at all. For instance, in *Lockary v. Kayfetz*, 587 F.Supp. 631 (N.D.Cal.1984), cited by plaintiffs, the property owners alleged that an "emergency" water moratorium lasting twelve years was a taking. In holding that the claim was not time-barred, the court noted that "it is the unlawful duration of the moratorium which constitutes the continuing wrong." *Id.* at 636. Thus it was the very continuation of the conduct that turned the conduct into an illegal act. *See also United States v. Dickinson*, 331 U.S. 745, 748–49, 67 S.Ct. 1382, 1385, 91 L.Ed. 1789 (1947)(takings claims do not necessarily accrue at the time of the initial action by the government).

The court finds that plaintiffs have alleged only that the siting decision and approval of the landfill was discriminatory. Those events fell outside of the limitations period. The operation of the landfill is not a continuing wrong, but rather is an effect of the allegedly discriminatory decision.

B. *Speculative Damages*

Plaintiffs' second argument is that a cause of action does not accrue on the date of injury if the damages are speculative. *See Airweld, Inc. v. Airco, Inc.*, 742 F.2d 1184, 1190 (9th Cir.1984), *cert. denied*, 469 U.S. 1213, 84 L.Ed.2d 331, 105 S.Ct. 1184 (1985). This rule is an exception to the well-established rule that a civil rights cause of action accrues when the plaintiff "knows or has reason to know of the injury which is the basis of the action." *Norco Construction, Inc. v. King County*, 801 F.2d 1143, 1145 (9th Cir.1986)(citation omitted).

Although plaintiffs attempt to characterize this exception as providing that a cause of action does not accrue until the plaintiffs are able to assess the full extent of their losses, this overstates the exception. As the cases to which plaintiffs cite indicate, this exception derives from antitrust cases in which it would be too speculative, at the time of the wrongful act, to determine the nature and extent of the injury. *See Airweld*, 742 F.2d at 1189–91 (citing *In Re Multidistrict Vehicle Air Pollution*, 591 F.2d 68, 71 (9th Cir.), cert. denied, 444 U.S. 900 (1979)). In such a case, courts have held that it would be unfair to hold that a party is barred from bringing an action at the time that it is injured because damages would be too speculative, and then is barred from bringing an action when damages are accrued based on a statute of limitations. *See Multidistrict Vehicle*, 591 F.2d at 73.

In general, the speculative nature of damages that delays the accrual of a cause of action in antitrust cases is uncertainty as to whether there will be damages at all, rather than uncertainty as to the extent of such damages. *See Bigelow v. RKO Radio Pictures, Inc.*, 327 U.S. 251, 264, 90 L.Ed. 652, 66 S.Ct. 574 (1946); *Story Parchment Co. v. Paterson Parchment Paper Co.*, 282 U.S. 555, 565–66, 75 L.Ed. 544, 51 S.Ct. 248 (1931). Even in antitrust cases, it is possible to bring suit based on uncertain damages, as long as a jury will not be forced to resort to "speculation or guesswork" to determine the extent of damages. *Bigelow*, 327 U.S. at 263, 66 S.Ct. at 579–80.

The appropriate question before the court is therefore whether in February 1992, plaintiffs knew or should have known that they would be damaged by the siting of the landfill, and what the nature of that damage would be. By that point, not only had the siting decision been made, but construction on the landfill had already begun. Moreover, according to plaintiffs' original complaint, "soon after construction began" in 1991, the public began making a steady stream of complaints about the landfill. Although the nature and extent of plaintiffs' damages might not have been known with precision by February 1992, there was certainly sufficient injury by that time to begin the running of the statute of limitations. *See Compton v. Ide,* 732 F.2d 1429, 1433 (9th Cir.1984)(plaintiff need not have knowledge of all the details of the wrongful conduct at issue for his or her cause of action to accrue).

* * *

IT IS FURTHER ORDERED that plaintiffs' first claim for relief, alleging violations of civil rights under 42 U.S.C. §§ 1983 and 1985, is DISMISSED WITH PREJUDICE, as barred by the statute of limitations.

* * *

2. *Executive Order*

Executive Order 12898, "Federal Actions to Address Environmental Justice in Minority Populations and Low-income Populations" (February 11, 1994) requires each Federal agency, to the greatest extent practicable and permitted by law, and consistent with the principles set forth in the report on the National Performance Review, to achieve environmental justice as part of its mission by identifying and addressing, as appropriate, disproportionately high and adverse human health or environmental effects, including social and economic effects, of its programs, policies, and activities on minority populations and low-income populations in the United States. As such, Executive Order 12898 required Federal agencies to develop Environmental Justice strategies for carrying out the requirements of the Executive Order.

EXECUTIVE ORDER 12898 OF FEBRUARY 11, 1994
59 Fed. Reg. 7629 (Feb. 16, 1994).

By the authority vested in me as President by the Constitution and the laws of the United States of America, it is hereby ordered as follows:

Section 1–1.   Implementation.

1–101.   Agency Responsibilities. To the greatest extent practicable and permitted by law, and consistent with the principles set forth in the report on the National Performance Review, each Federal agency shall make achieving environmental justice part of its mission by identifying and addressing, as appropriate, disproportionately high and adverse human health or environmental effects of its programs, policies, and activities on minority populations and low-income populations in the United States and its territories and possessions, the District of Columbia, the Commonwealth of Puerto Rico, and the Commonwealth of the Mariana Islands.

1–102. Creation of an Interagency Working Group on Environmental Justice. (a) Within 3 months of the date of this order, the Administrator of the Environmental Protection Agency ("Administrator") or the Administrator's designee shall convene an interagency Federal Working Group on Environmental Justice ("Working Group"). The Working Group shall comprise the heads of the following executive agencies and offices, or their designees: (a) Department of Defense; (b) Department of Health and Human Services; (c) Department of Housing and Urban Development; (d) Department of Labor; (e) Department of Agriculture; (f) Department of Transportation; (g) Department of Justice; (h) Department of the Interior; (i) Department of Commerce; (j) Department of Energy; (k) Environmental Protection Agency; (*l*) Office of Management and Budget; (m) Office of Science and Technology Policy; (n) Office of the Deputy Assistant to the President for Environmental Policy; (*o*) Office of the Assistant to the President for Domestic Policy; (p) National Economic Council; (q) Council of Economic Advisers; and (r) such other Government officials as the President may designate. The Working Group shall report to the President through the Deputy Assistant to the President for Environmental Policy and the Assistant to the President for Domestic Policy.

(b) The Working Group shall: (1) provide guidance to Federal agencies on criteria for identifying disproportionately high and adverse human health or environmental effects on minority populations and low-income populations;

(2) coordinate with, provide guidance to, and serve as a clearinghouse for, each Federal agency as it develops an environmental justice strategy as required by section 1–103 of this order, in order to ensure that the administration, interpretation and enforcement of programs, activities and policies are undertaken in a consistent manner;

(3) assist in coordinating research by, and stimulating cooperation among, the Environmental Protection Agency, the Department of Health and Human Services, the Department of Housing and Urban Development, and other agencies conducting research or other activities in accordance with section 3–3 of this order;

(4) assist in coordinating data collection, required by this order;

(5) examine existing data and studies on environmental justice;

(6) hold public meetings as required in section 5–502(d) of this order; and

(7) develop interagency model projects on environmental justice that evidence cooperation among Federal agencies.

1–103. Development of Agency Strategies. (a) Except as provided in section 6–605 of this order, each Federal agency shall develop an agency-wide environmental justice strategy, as set forth in subsections (b)-(e) of this section that identifies and addresses disproportionately high and adverse human health or environmental effects of its programs, policies, and activities on minority populations and low-income populations. The environmental justice strategy shall list programs, policies, planning and public participation processes, enforcement, and/or rulemaking related to human health or the environment that should be revised to, at a minimum: (1) promote enforcement of all health and environmental statutes in areas with minority populations and low-income populations; (2) ensure greater public participation; (3) improve research and data collection relating to the health of and environment of minority populations and low-income populations; and (4) identify differential patterns of consumption of natural resources among minority populations and low-income populations. In addition, the environmental justice strategy shall include, where appropriate, a timetable for undertaking identified revisions and consideration of economic and social implications of the revisions.

(b) Within 4 months of the date of this order, each Federal agency shall identify an internal administrative process for developing its environmental justice strategy, and shall inform the Working Group of the process.

(c) Within 6 months of the date of this order, each Federal agency shall provide the Working Group with an outline of its proposed environmental justice strategy.

(d) Within 10 months of the date of this order, each Federal agency shall provide the Working Group with its proposed environmental justice strategy.

(e) Within 12 months of the date of this order, each Federal agency shall finalize its environmental justice strategy and provide a copy and written description of its strategy to the Working Group. During the 12 month period from the date of this order, each Federal agency, as part of its environmental justice strategy, shall identify several specific projects that can be promptly undertaken to address particular concerns identified during the development of the proposed environmental justice strategy, and a schedule for implementing those projects.

(f) Within 24 months of the date of this order, each Federal agency shall report to the Working Group on its progress in implementing its agency-wide environmental justice strategy.

(g) Federal agencies shall provide additional periodic reports to the Working Group as requested by the Working Group.

1–104. Reports to the President. Within 14 months of the date of this order, the Working Group shall submit to the President, through the Office of the Deputy Assistant to the President for Environmental Policy and the Office of the Assistant to the President for Domestic Policy, a report that describes the implementation of this order, and includes the final environmental justice strategies described in section 1–103(e) of this order.

Section 2–2. Federal Agency Responsibilities for Federal Programs. Each Federal agency shall conduct its programs, policies, and activities that substantially affect human health or the environment, in a manner that ensures that such programs, policies, and activities do not have the effect of excluding persons (including populations) from participation in, denying persons (including populations) the benefits of, or subjecting persons (including populations)

to discrimination under, such programs, policies, and activities, because of their race, color, or national origin.

Section 3–3. Research, Data Collection, and Analysis.

3–301. Human Health and Environmental Research and Analysis. (a) Environmental human health research, whenever practicable and appropriate, shall include diverse segments of the population in epidemiological and clinical studies, including segments at high risk from environmental hazards, such as minority populations, low-income populations and workers who may be exposed to substantial environmental hazards.

(b) Environmental human health analyses, whenever practicable and appropriate, shall identify multiple and cumulative exposures.

(c) Federal agencies shall provide minority populations and low-income populations the opportunity to comment on the development and design of research strategies undertaken pursuant to this order.

3–302. Human Health and Environmental Data Collection and Analysis. To the extent permitted by existing law, including the Privacy Act, as amended (5 U.S.C.A. section 552a): (a) each Federal agency, whenever practicable and appropriate, shall collect, maintain, and analyze information assessing and comparing environmental and human health risks borne by populations identified by race, national origin, or income. To the extent practical and appropriate, Federal agencies shall use this information to determine whether their programs, policies, and activities have disproportionately high and adverse human health or environmental effects on minority populations and low-income populations;

(b) In connection with the development and implementation of agency strategies in section 1–103 of this order, each Federal agency, whenever practicable and appropriate, shall collect, maintain and analyze information on the race, national origin, income level, and other readily accessible and appropriate information for areas surrounding facilities or sites expected to have a substantial environmental, human health, or economic effect on the surrounding populations, when such facilities or sites become the subject of a substantial Federal environmental administrative or judicial action. Such information shall be made available to the public, unless prohibited by law; and

(c) Each Federal agency, whenever practicable and appropriate, shall collect, maintain, and analyze information on the race, national origin, income level, and other readily accessible and appropriate information for areas surrounding Federal facilities that are: (1) subject to the reporting requirements under the Emergency Planning and Community Right-to-Know Act, 42 U.S.C.A. section 11001–11050 as mandated in Executive Order No. 12856; and (2) expected to have a substantial environmental, human health, or economic effect on surrounding populations. Such information shall be made available to the public, unless prohibited by law.

(d) In carrying out the responsibilities in this section, each Federal agency, whenever practicable and appropriate, shall share information and eliminate unnecessary duplication of efforts through the use of existing data systems and cooperative agreements among Federal agencies and with State, local, and tribal governments.

Section 4–4. Subsistence Consumption of Fish and Wildlife.

4–401. Consumption Patterns. In order to assist in identifying the need for ensuring protection of populations with differential patterns of subsistence consumption of fish and wildlife, Federal agencies, whenever practicable and appropriate, shall collect, maintain, and analyze information on the consumption patterns of populations who principally rely on fish and/or wildlife for subsistence. Federal agencies shall communicate to the public the risks of those consumption patterns.

4–402. Guidance. Federal agencies, whenever practicable and appropriate, shall work in a coordinated manner to publish guidance reflecting the latest scientific information available concerning methods for evaluating the human health risks associated with the consumption of pollutant-bearing fish or wildlife. Agencies shall consider such guidance in developing their policies and rules.

Section 5–5. Public Participation and Access to Information. (a) The public may submit recommendations to Federal agencies relating to the incorporation of environmental justice principles into Federal agency programs or policies. Each Federal agency shall convey such recommendations to the Working Group.

(b) Each Federal agency may, whenever practicable and appropriate, translate crucial public documents, notices, and hearings relating to human health or the environment for limited English speaking populations.

(c) Each Federal agency shall work to ensure that public documents, notices, and hearings relating to human health or the environment are concise, understandable, and readily accessible to the public.

(d) The Working Group shall hold public meetings, as appropriate, for the purpose of fact-finding, receiving public comments, and conducting inquiries concerning environmental justice. The Working Group shall prepare for public review a summary of the comments and recommendations discussed at the public meetings.

Section 6–6.   General Provisions.

6–601.   Responsibility for Agency Implementation. The head of each Federal agency shall be responsible for ensuring compliance with this order. Each Federal agency shall conduct internal reviews and take such other steps as may be necessary to monitor compliance with this order.

6–602.   Executive Order No. 12250. This Executive order is intended to supplement but not supersede Executive Order No. 12250, which requires consistent and effective implementation of various laws prohibiting discriminatory practices in programs receiving Federal financial assistance. Nothing herein shall limit the effect or mandate of Executive Order No. 12250.

6–603.   Executive Order No. 12875. This Executive order is not intended to limit the effect or mandate of Executive Order No. 12875.

6–604.   Scope. For purposes of this order, Federal agency means any agency on the Working Group, and such other agencies as may be designated by the President, that conducts any Federal program or activity that substantially affects human health or the environment. Independent agencies are requested to comply with the provisions of this order.

6–605.   Petitions for Exemptions. The head of a Federal agency may petition the President for an exemption from the requirements of this order on the grounds that all or some of the petitioning agency's programs or activities should not be subject to the requirements of this order.

6–606.   Native American Programs. Each Federal agency responsibility set forth under this order shall apply equally to Native American programs. In addition, the Department of the Interior, in coordination with the Working Group, and, after consultation with tribal leaders, shall coordinate steps to be taken pursuant to this order that address Federally-recognized Indian Tribes.

6–607.   Costs. Unless otherwise provided by law, Federal agencies shall assume the financial costs of complying with this order.

6–608.   General. Federal agencies shall implement this order consistent with, and to the extent permitted by, existing law.

6–609.   Judicial Review. This order is intended only to improve the internal management of the executive branch and is not intended to, nor does it create any right, benefit, or trust responsibility, substantive or procedural, enforceable at law or equity by a party against the United States, its agencies, its officers, or any person. This order shall not be construed to create any right to judicial review involving the compliance or noncompliance of the United States, its agencies, its officers, or any other person with this order.

/s/ WILLIAM J. CLINTON
THE WHITE HOUSE,
February 11, 1994.

Note

Environmental Justice strategies have been issued by many federal agencies in response to Executive Order 12898, signed by President Clinton on February 11, 1994. This Order directed each Federal agency to develop a strategy to address environmental justice concerns in its programs, policies and regulations. The thrust of the Executive Order is to avoid disproportionately high and adverse impacts on minority and low-income populations with respect to human health and the environment.

Discussion Problem

Big Corp plans to build and operate a recycling plant which will omit small quantities of lead. Lead has been linked to brain damage and learning disabilities in small children and adolescents.

After numerous studies, Big Corp determined that the most cost efficient area in which to build the plant is a low income area where most of the residents are non-English speaking. A large number of these residents speak Spanish, Korean, Portuguese and Chinese. Within 500 yards of the proposed plant is a community of garden apartments. As part of the community relations program, Big Corp offers to buy a vacant lot 700 yards from the proposed plant and build a company sponsored day care on the lot. Employees of the plant will be able to send their children to the day care at a dramatic discount over other comparable day care facilities. In addition, residents of the community will be able to send their kids to the day care at the same rate as employees on a space available basis. Big Corp also promises to make earnest efforts to hire from the neighboring community. Finally, Big Corp will take advantage of a federally funded grant to set up community based health care facilities and drug and alcohol rehabilitation clinics which will be available to community members for free.

Big Corp applies with the Regional Air Quality Board, the permitting authority, for the necessary permit to operate facility. The permit is granted with very few safety requirements in the permit. For example, there are no required recapture or re-use systems required to minimize the amount of lead going into the air, minimal monitoring is required and no limitations are placed on the permit as to when and under what conditions recycling should or should not occur.

The permit was issued after Executive Order 12898 was signed by President Clinton on Feb. 11, 1994.

Questions

As attorney for a community group, what do you do, advise or want to know?

As attorney for an environmental group?

As attorney for Big Corp?

As attorney for the State permitting agency?

As attorney for EPA?

As attorney in the White House Office of Environmental Policy?

As attorney for the municipality in which the plant will be located?

As attorney for the municipality in which Big Corp rejected an alternate site (Site B)?

* * *

3. State Constitutional Basis

In addition to relying on federal theories of protection, environmental justice issues have been raised using state constitution as the basis for claims.

IN RE AMERICAN WASTE & POLLUTION CONTROL CO.
642 So.2d 1258 (La.1994).

WATSON, JUSTICE.

The issue is whether an action taken by the Louisiana Department of Environmental Quality (DEQ) on a solid waste disposal permit application without an adjudicatory hearing is a "final decision or order" under LSA–R.S. 30:2024(C) which affords judicial review to persons aggrieved by the action.

In the early 1980's, solid waste disposal posed a serious problem for the governmental entities of St. Martin, Iberia, and Lafayette Parishes. American Waste and Pollution Control Company (*American Waste*) proposed a site outside St. Martinville near Cade, Louisiana, for construction of a solid waste disposal facility (*Cade I*). On February 26, 1987, DEQ Secretary Martha Madden denied a construction permit based on the site's geologic conditions and the proposed facility's proximity to the Chicot Aquifer. DEQ's Environmental Regulatory Code (1992) defines aquifer as "a formation, group of formations, or part of a formation that contains sufficient saturated permeable materials to yield significant quantities of water to wells and springs." Title 33: VII.501. The Chicot Aquifer is a major source of drinking water for southwest Louisiana.

In November of 1987, American Waste submitted a site selection study for a second facility in the Cade area (*Cade II*), approximately 1.5 miles from the *Cade I* proposed site, on the east side of La. Hwy. 182, almost one mile north of the highway's intersection with Duchamp Road.

Under DEQ rules, an application is first reviewed by DEQ staff to determine whether the format, technical engineering, geochemical, and environmental aspects of the application are consistent with DEQ regulations. If deficiencies are noted, the applicant is allowed an opportunity to correct them. When the application is deemed complete, the law requires a public hearing, followed by a thirty-day delay for public comment. After the thirty day period, DEQ staff again reviews the matter to determine whether additional information should be considered. DEQ department heads then make recommendations and the completed application is sent to the DEQ Secretary for a decision.

A public hearing was held December 15, 1987. No transcript or recording of this hearing exists. Despite local opposition to the site selection, DEQ informed American Waste that its permit application was deemed acceptable for public review. American Waste submitted its permit application to DEQ in February of 1988.

By letter dated December 2, 1988, attorney Robert L. Boese wrote to DEQ on behalf of the Episcopal School of Acadiana "and other concerned citizens of St. Martin and Lafayette Parishes" requesting both a fact-finding hearing and an adjudicatory hearing based on issues of technical merit and legal sufficiency.

In March of 1989, DEQ wrote the Headmaster of the Episcopal School of Acadiana, stating a final decision had not been made and would not be made "until the appropriate time, which is afte.‧ public hearings and any additional hearings that may follow, such as adjudicatory and court hearings."

A public hearing on American Waste's permit application was held April 3, 1989. Public interest was intense with approximately 1500 people in attendance and over 120 people commenting on the permit application.

On motion of American Waste, then-DEQ Secretary Paul Templet was recused July 5, 1990, from acting on American Waste's permit application. *See Matter of American Waste and Pollution Control Company,* 581 So.2d 738 (La.App. 1 Cir.1991). Retired Judge William V. Redmann was appointed Secretary pro tempore of DEQ to render a decision on American Waste's Cade II application.

On July 12, 1991, the president of War on Waste (WOW), a non-profit unincorporated association, wrote DEQ and requested an updated public hearing because American Waste's permit application was four years old. The environmental group pointed out that DEQ policy requirements had changed, that new solid waste regulations were about to be issued, that current DEQ staff had not studied this application and that citizens advisory committees had not had the opportunity to comment on the application. The letter included the following notation: "At one time, early in the process, a request was made for an adjudicatory hearing. Please determine and advise us on the status of that request." DEQ failed to respond to this request; no adjudicatory hearing was held.

On January 9, 1992, Judge Redmann, acting as DEQ Secretary pro tempore, granted American Waste a standard permit for the construction, installation, and operation of a solid waste facility at *Cade II.*

WOW, joined with the Acadiana Chapter of the National Audubon Society, a non-profit corporation (collectively referred to as WOW herein), filed an appeal with the First Circuit Court of Appeal. A copy of the appeal was filed with DEQ. The First Circuit considered the simultaneous filing and ordered that the appeal be transferred to DEQ for treatment as a motion and order for appeal. A DEQ hearing officer ordered that an appeal to the court of appeal be granted.

American Waste filed a motion to dismiss the appeal, arguing that the appellants were untimely, had incorrectly taken an appeal to the court of appeal rather than to DEQ and lacked standing under LSA–R.S. 30:2024(C) in that they were not "aggrieved parties." The motion to dismiss was denied; the appeal was deemed timely and in the proper forum. The appellate court found WOW had standing as an "aggrieved party" due to its claim that constitutionally protected rights of liberty and property would be violated by the facility.

On the merits, the court of appeal found DEQ erroneously issued the permit without proper evaluation of alternative sites, without a balancing of benefits versus the risk to the environment, without listing basic findings or ultimate findings, without articulating a rational connection between factual findings and the resulting order, and by misstating the test to be used. The court of appeal vacated the Secretary pro tempore's order and remanded to DEQ for further proceedings. 633 So.2d 188 (La.App. 1 Cir.1993). A writ was granted to review the matter. 93–3163 (La. 3/11/94), 634 So.2d 837. . . .

LAW AND ANALYSIS

Article IX, Section 1 of the Louisiana Constitution provides:

The natural resources of the state, including air and water, and the healthful, scenic, historic, and esthetic quality of the environment shall be protected, conserved, and replenished insofar as possible and consistent with the health, safety, and welfare of the people. The legislature shall enact laws to implement this policy.

This article continues the Public Trust Doctrine in environmental matters first recognized in the 1921 Constitution's Article VI, § 1 and "imposes a duty of environmental protection on all state agencies and officials, establishes a standard of environmental protection, and mandates the legislature to enact laws to implement fully this policy." *Save Ourselves v. Louisiana Environ. Cont. Com'n,* 452 So.2d 1152, 1156 (La.1984); McCowan, Charles S. *The Evolution of Environmental Law in Louisiana,* 52 La. L. Rev. 907 (1992). This constitutional standard has been interpreted as a "rule of reasonableness" which "requires a balancing process in which environmental costs and benefits must be given full and careful consideration along with economic, social and other factors." *Save Ourselves,* 452 So.2d at 1157.

The Constitution also ensures basic due process protections. *See* La. Const. art. I, § 2 (no deprivation of life, liberty or property without due process), La. Const. art. I, § 19 (no forfeiture of rights or property without the right of judicial review of the record), and La. Const. art. I, § 22 (right of access to courts).

Sweeping legislation implements the constitutional environmental mandate. LSA–R.S. 30:2002 provides "the maintenance of a healthful and safe environment for the people of Louisiana is a matter of critical state concern." In order to protect the state's resources, the Legislature created the DEQ and designated it the primary state agency concerned with environmental protection and regulation. DEQ has specific jurisdiction over solid waste disposal regulation. LSA–R.S. 30:2011(A)(1).

The Legislature has reposed the power to issue environmental permits in DEQ and has authorized the agency to exercise quasi-judicial authority. *Matter of American Waste & Poll. Control*, 588 So.2d 367 (La.1991). The Secretary of DEQ is empowered, inter alia, to grant or deny permits and "to hold meetings or hearings ... for purposes of factfinding, receiving public comments, conducting inquiries and investigations, or other purposes...." LSA–R.S. 30:2011(D)(2) and (5). In making a determination relative to the granting or denying of permits, the Secretary "shall act as the primary public trustee of the environment, and shall consider and follow the will and intent of the Louisiana Constitution and Louisiana statutory law." LSA–R.S.30:2014(A). DEQ's actions must be diligent, fair, and faithful to protecting the public interest in the state's resources. *Save Ourselves*, 452 So.2d at 1157. "The [DEQ's] role as the representative of the public interest does not permit it to act as an umpire passively calling balls and strikes for adversaries appearing before [the Secretary]; the rights of the public must receive active and affirmative protection at the hands of [DEQ]." Save Ourselves, 452 So.2d at 1157. The statutory framework places on the DEQ Secretary the burden of exercising responsible discretion to determine each permit application's substantive result.

Although the Legislature gave DEQ the primary responsibility for protecting the environment, the Legislature also provided statutory due process mechanisms to allow the participation of interested individual citizens and groups of citizens. In some instances, the statutes provide for mandatory public hearings to allow for public comment and reaction to proposed environmental actions or agency rule changes. *See* e.g. LSA–R.S. 30:2011(D)(1), 30:2011(D)(5), 30:2011(24)(c)(ii), 30:2158(A)(4). An interested citizen may file a civil action in district court on his own behalf against any person whom he alleges to be in violation of environmental statutes or regulations, subject to certain limitations. LSA–R.S. 30:2026. The remedies available include damages, civil penalties, injunctive relief, costs and attorney fees.

This legislatively authorized participation of the public achieves two goals, public input in substantive environmental matters and "a safeguard against abuses in the administrative process." *Concerned Citizens v. Lake Charles Refining*, 387 So.2d 1330, 1333 (La.App. 1 Cir.), writ refused, 392 So.2d 693 (La.1980).

WOW relies on LSA–R.S. 30:2024 as statutory authority for its appeal to the First Circuit. The statute sets forth the effective date of any enforcement or permit action and provides the procedure for appeals. At the time the permit was granted, the statute provided in pertinent part:

§ 2024. Finality of action; trial de novo; appeals

A. Any enforcement or permit action shall be effective upon issuance unless a later date is specified therein. Such action shall be final and shall not be subject to further review unless, no later than twenty days after the notice of the action is served by certified mail or by hand upon the respondent, he files with the secretary a request for hearing. Upon timely filing of the request, the secretary shall either grant or deny the request within twenty days. If the request for hearing is granted, the issues raised in the request shall be resolved by an adjudicatory hearing before a hearing officer. Any appeal from a final decision of the secretary shall be in accordance with the provisions of R.S. 30:2024(C). If the request for hearing is denied, or the secretary does not act on the request within twenty days after the timely filing, the respondent shall, within twenty days from the denial or the lapse of the period for the secretary to act, be entitled to file an application for de novo review of the secretary's action in the Nineteenth Judicial District Court for the parish of East Baton Rouge.

* * *

C. Any person aggrieved by a final decision or order of the secretary may appeal therefrom to the Court of Appeal, First Circuit, if a motion for an appeal is filed with the secretary within thirty days after the final decision or order is served upon the respondent. Any preliminary, procedural, or intermediate ruling or decision by the secretary is subject to the supervisory jurisdiction of the appellate court as provided by Article V, Section 10 of the Constitution of Louisiana. The Court of Appeal, First Circuit, shall promulgate rules of procedure to be followed in taking and lodging such appeals. The provisions of R.S. 49:962 and 964 shall not apply to decisions and orders of the secretary....

WOW and American Waste argue for conflicting interpretations of the phrase "final decision or order" in R.S. 30:2024(C), both of which find support in prior First Circuit decisions. WOW argues the term "final decision or order" means any action taken by the DEQ Secretary which considers the merits of an issue. *See Matter of Marine Shale Processors, Inc.*, 563 So.2d 278 (La.App. 1 Cir.1990); *Matter of Recovery I, Inc.*, 622 So.2d 272 (La.App. 1 Cir.), writ denied, 629 So.2d 383 (La.1993).

American Waste argues the phrase should be understood as defined in the Administrative Procedures Act (APA), LSA–R.S. 49:951(3), and as that phrase was interpreted in *Delta Bank & Trust Co. v. Lassiter*, 383 So.2d 330 (La.1980). *See Matter of Carline Tank Services, Inc.*, 626 So.2d 358 (La.App. 1 Cir.), rehearing denied, 627 So.2d 669 (La.App. 1 Cir. 1993); *Matter of Industrial Pipe, Inc.*, 626 So.2d 364 (La.App. 1 Cir. 1993). Under this interpretation, in order to be a "decision or order," the disposition must be required by constitution or statute to be preceded by notice and an opportunity for a hearing; and, if required, the hearing held must be an adjudication. An adjudicatory hearing is similar to a trial in that evidence is presented on the facts and law at issue. LSA–R.S. 49:955. Since only two public hearings were held in this case, and no adjudicatory hearing, American Waste argues no decision or order was reached which WOW could appeal.

It is unnecessary to look to the APA, or this Court's interpretations of the APA's requirements, however, to decide whether the acting-Secretary's grant of the permit was a final decision or order. Subsection A of R.S. 30:2024 provided at the time the permit was granted that, as between the permittee (American Waste) and DEQ, a permit action shall be final when issued (unless a later date is specified) unless American Waste files a request for a hearing with the DEQ Secretary within twenty days. Since no hearing was requested by American Waste, the agency action is final. There is no reason why the DEQ Secretary's final action should not be appealable for a person aggrieved by that action.

The rules of statutory interpretation support this conclusion. The language of the statute, the starting point of analysis, is not free from ambiguity. American Waste argues the phrase "final decision or order" may only be understood after reference to the APA. WOW argues the phrase should be understood in its ordinary and common sense meaning.

Because the statute is susceptible of different meanings, it is necessary to ascertain the legislative intent. *Touchard v. Williams*, 617 So.2d 885 (La.1993). The title or preamble of an act may be used to determine legislative intent. *Louisiana Associated Gen. Contr. v. Calcasieu*, 586 So.2d 1354 (La.1991); *Green v. Louisiana Underwriters Ins. Co.*, 571 So.2d 610 (La.1990). In addition, the act as a whole must be considered in order to ascertain the meaning of any phrase. *Green*, 571 So.2d at 613.

R.S. 30:2024 has undergone several amendments since its enactment as R.S. 30:1072 by 1979 Acts No. 449. The title of the statute was then "Commission Hearing" and the preamble stated, in pertinent part, that the act's purpose was "to create and provide with respect to the Environmental Control Commission [the precursor of the DEQ] and the office of environmental affairs of the Department of Natural Resources and their powers, duties, functions, and responsibilities."

Preambles to subsequent amendments have stated, in pertinent part, the purpose of the acts was "to provide for the effective time of orders" (1980 Acts No. 194), "to provide for appeals of any enforcement or permit action taken by the assistant secretary of the office of environmental affairs or the commission" (1982 Acts No. 322; title of the statute changed to "Finality of actions; appeals"), "to provide for appeals from decisions of the secretary of the Department of Environmental Quality" (1984 Acts No. 795), "to provide that any enforcement or permit action shall be effective upon issuance unless a later date is specified; to provide appeals of any enforcement or permit action to the commission, to provide that any person aggrieved by a final decision or order of the commission may appeal to the Court of Appeal, First Circuit" (1984 Acts No. 825), "to provide for hearings on enforcement and permit actions, to provide for appeals, to provide for time limitations" (1990 Acts No. 197), and "to provide for finality of action, and appeals" (1991 Acts No. 846).

When the preambles and all the provisions of R.S. 30:2024 are considered together, *see Green*, 571 So.2d at 613, it is evident the overall intent of the Legislature was to provide for finality of certain DEQ actions for respondents and parties affected by those actions, and to set forth appeal procedures.

The APA enunciates general procedural rules for administrative agencies. R.S. 30:2024 sets forth special procedural rules for appeal of DEQ actions. The APA "was not intended to supersede the specific provisions of other administrative acts, or to supersede the rights and remedies created under those acts. Instead, it was intended to create procedures in those instances where none existed." *Corbello v. Sutton,* 446 So.2d 301, 303 (La.1984). "When two statutes are in conflict, the statute that is more specifically directed to the matter at issue must prevail as an exception to the statute that is more general." *Smith v. Cajun Insulation, Inc.,* 392 So.2d 398, 402 (La.1980). Thus, the specific statutory definition of a final and appealable DEQ action in R.S. 30:2024 should prevail over the general appeal procedures in the APA.

In construing the meaning of statutes, "courts must endeavor to give an interpretation that will give them effectiveness and purpose, rather than one which makes them meaningless." *State v. Union Tank Car Co.,* 439 So.2d 377, 382 (La.1983); *Smith,* 392 So.2d at 400. Under the interpretation urged by American Waste, the appeal provisions of Section 2024(C) would be meaningless.

There is no statutory or constitutional requirement for DEQ to hold an adjudicatory hearing on a permit action for a solid waste facility. *Blackett v. Dept. of Environ. Quality,* 506 So.2d 749 (La.App. 1 Cir.1987). Although persons with a substantial interest may intervene in the agency determination under DEQ Rules of Procedure, see Rules of Procedure, Louisiana Environmental Control Commission [precursor to DEQ], Rule 5.1(B), even parties to the agency action are not assured of a requested adjudicatory hearing. *See Matter of Carline Tank Services, Inc.,* 626 So.2d at 361. The decision to hold an adjudicatory hearing after a party requests one is within the DEQ's discretion. *See* R.S. 30:2024(A).

The only way for a party aggrieved or a respondent, permittee, or intervenor to invoke an adjudicatory hearing at the agency level, when there is no constitutional or statutory requirement for an adjudicatory hearing, is solely within the discretion of DEQ. Thus, under American Waste's interpretation, DEQ would have sole discretion as to which actions were entitled to judicial review. In this case, agency action was taken despite repeated public requests for an adjudication.

This interpretation frustrates the legislative goal of authorizing aggrieved parties judicial review of agency abuses in Section 2024(C) and would deny citizens judicial review of environmental decisions which may have an immediate and sustained impact on their health and property. This Court has previously recognized that the legislature enacted laws to respect the right of private citizens to litigate environmental matters. Regarding R.S. 30:2024(C), the Court stated "this right of 'aggrieved' persons ... no doubt includes the opponents and parties who have been permitted to intervene in the DEQ permit action." *Matter of American Waste*, 588 So.2d at 372.

We find, therefore, that a final decision of the DEQ Secretary in this permit action was rendered on January 9, 1992, when Judge Redmann, acting as DEQ Secretary pro tempore, granted American Waste a standard permit for the construction, installation and operation of a solid waste facility at Cade II. This action was final and appealable under the provisions of R.S. 30:2024(C) when American Waste failed to request a hearing within the time constraints of R.S. 30:2024(A).

The court of appeal's action vacating the DEQ permit grant utilized the proper analysis and correctly remanded the matter to DEQ. In Save Ourselves, the standard of judicial review provided by LSA–R.S. 49:964 was applied by analogy to the quasi-judicial decisions of the DEQ Secretary. Pursuant to § 964, a reviewing court may affirm the decision of the agency or remand the case for further proceedings; or it may reverse or modify the decision if substantial rights of the appellant have been prejudiced because the administrative findings, inferences, conclusions, or decisions are: (1) in violation of constitutional or statutory provisions; (2) in excess of the statutory authority of the agency; (3) made upon unlawful procedure; (4) affected by other error of law; (5) arbitrary or capricious or characterized by abuse of discretion or clearly unwarranted exercise of discretion; or (6) manifestly erroneous in view of the reliable, probative, and substantial evidence on the whole record. *Save Ourselves*, 452 So.2d at 1158.

On review, a court should not reverse a substantive decision of DEQ on its merits unless it can be shown that the Secretary was arbitrary or clearly gave insufficient weight to environmental protection in balancing the costs and benefits of the proposed action. The court must reverse, however, if the decision was reached "without individualized consideration and balancing of environmental factors conducted fairly and in good faith." *Id.*, at 1159.

In making a decision, DEQ "is required to make basic findings supported by evidence and ultimate findings which flow rationally from the basic findings; and it must also articulate a rational connection between the facts found and the order issued." *Id.* Although the court will uphold a decision of less than ideal clarity if the agency's reasoning may be easily discernible on the record, it will not supply a finding from the evidence or a basis for the action which was not found by the Secretary. *Id.*, at 1160. Only by detailing its reasoning does the DEQ uphold its position as public trustee and justify the discretion with which it is entrusted by constitutional and statutory authority in a contested environmental matter. *Id.*, at 1159–60.

We find, as did the court of appeal, that the Secretary pro tempore did not list his basic findings or his ultimate findings, nor did he articulate a rational connection between his factual findings and his order, as required in *Save Ourselves*. Instead, his written decision contains only conclusions without stated bases. It cannot be determined from this order whether the Secretary pro tempore balanced the benefits of the *Cade II* proposed project against the site's inherent environmental risks, particularly the danger of Chicot Aquifer contamination. Nor can these important considerations be determined from the record. While the Secretary pro tempore found the proposed site would pose no "unreasonable danger" to clean air and water resources, and rejected an absolute such as "maximum protection" of the environment, he failed to utilize the constitutional standard enunciated in *Save Ourselves* which requires the agency "to determine that adverse environmental impacts have been minimized or avoided as much as possible consistently with the public welfare." *Id.*, 452 So.2d at 1157. We, therefore, affirm the court of appeal's decision to vacate the order granting American Waste's permit application for a solid waste disposal facility at the Cade II site.

* * *

A reviewing court may remand the case for further proceedings. *Save Ourselves*, 452 So.2d at 1159. A remand will allow such additional hearings and agency reports as are necessary for the Secretary to reach a decision on American Waste's permit application consistent with the constitutional, statutory, and jurisprudential standards detailed above.

For the foregoing reasons, the matter is remanded to DEQ for further proceedings.

* * *

MARCUS, J. (dissenting).

I disagree with the majority's conclusion that WOW is an aggrieved party entitled to appeal under La. R.S. 30:2024(C).

* * *

Chapter 2

COMMON LAW ORIGINS OF ENVIRONMENTAL LAW

Table of Sections

§ 2.1 INTRODUCTION

Courts have had and continue to have a significant role in the development of American environmental law. Environmental jurisprudence is characterized by strong judicial review of agency implementation of federal regulation and extensive industry, citizen, and environmental group involvement in the formal administrative and judicial processes. In addition, there is much civil litigation over personal injury and property damage due to toxic torts in the United States. The net

56

result of this process is a system of central planning through litigation that is costly, inefficient, and a barrier to new investments. New projects and new products often must undergo a gauntlet of legal review that is time consuming, difficult, and uncertain.

Compounding the matter is the fact that there are two sets of judicial systems in the United States—a federal system of courts established under the United States Constitution and state and local courts established under the authority of each state government. There are several levels of authority in each court system. The state courts generally have unlimited power to decide almost every type of case, whereas the federal courts have authority to entertain only certain types of cases that are specifically set forth in the United States Constitution. Cases involving federal environmental statutes may be heard by federal courts. The net result of separate court systems is that court decisions on environmental matters often vary from jurisdiction to jurisdiction—especially from one state court system to another.

§ 2.2   COMMON LAW TORT THEORIES OF LIABILITY

There are a variety of tort theories applied in the environmental law context. Overall the tort system has not been very effective at providing environmental protection.

The tort system has problems of proof, namely showing that the defendants' action caused plaintiff's injury. This has been relaxed somewhat in toxic torts, where courts will find the defendant liable if the conduct of the defendant was a substantial factor in causing the harm alleged.

The tort system has potentials for abuse because of monetary damages as an incentive to sue. A jury may impose liability whether or not the defendant's actions are actually responsible for plaintiff's injury. Much of the money recovered in tort cases goes to insurance companies and attorneys. The tort system is, thus, largely reduced to little more than a crap shoot that has little ability to protect the environment or the victims of pollution.

Tort remedies exist in parallel with the new regulatory and statutory programs. These programs have placed limits on the use of tort remedies by causing courts to remand cases to agencies on such grounds as the doctrines of primary jurisdiction or exhaustion of administrative remedies. Federal common law has been virtually eliminated, which further limits environmental tort actions.

Despite these limitations, the tort system remains the primary way a private person can receive compensation for personal injury or property caused by pollution emissions released to the environment. The federally funded research and reporting requirements imposed on polluters provide information that can be used by tort lawyers. The studies required by the Agency for Toxic Substances and Disease Registry (ATSDR), information required by the Employee Planing & Community Right to Know Act, and various state laws such as California's well publicized Proposition 65, provide information on pollutants which can be used by tort lawyers. In particular, the Employee Planing & Community Right to Know Act information may be used as ammunition in the battle to control toxics.

§ 2.3 TOXIC TORTS

Toxic tort liability has increased dramatically since 1980 under state common law, and there is much study and talk of creating a new federal tort or administrative compensation system for personal injury and property damage due to toxics. *See, e.g.,* National Science Foundation, Compensation for Victims of Toxic Pollution—Assessing the Scientific Knowledge Base (Mar. 1983); Superfund Section 301(e) Study Group, Injuries and Damages from Hazardous Wastes—Analysis and Improvement of Legal Remedies: Report to Congress in Compliance with Section 301(e) of the Comprehensive Environmental Response, Compensation, and Liability Act of 1980 (Pub. L. No. 96–510), 97th Cong., 2d Sess. (Comm. Print. 1982). For a general discussion of toxic tort litigation, *see* M. Dore, Law of Toxic Torts (1988).

Superfund does not create a federal cause of action for recovery of personal injury damages; it only allows recovery of cleanup costs and natural resource damages. But many Superfund sites are surrounded by potential plaintiffs lawyers, many of whom are already suing. Residents of Columbia, Mississippi, for example, filed a $10 billion suit ($1 billion in actual damages and $9 billion in punitive damages) against Reichold Chemical Co. in early 1988, alleging that the company had converted a site into a latent toxic chemical waste dump that caused actual physical injuries, psychological and emotional trauma, and a fear of cancer and other diseases caused by chemicals. *See Breeden v. Reichold Chemicals Inc.,* No. J–88–00–34(B)(S.D. Miss. Feb. 3, 1988); 2 Tox.L.Rep. (BNA) 969 (Feb. 10, 1988). The case ultimately was settled for an undisclosed sum. *See* 3 Tox.L.Rep. (BNA) 519 (Sept. 21, 1988).

Litigation over exposure to toxic substances in groundwater is now frequent. In the *Jackson Township* case, New Jersey landowners initially recovered a $15.6 million judgment against the municipal dump site owner, a judgment that was later reduced to $13.6 million on appeal. *Ayers v. Jackson Township,* No. L–5808 (N.J. Law Div. Nov. 22, 1983), *rev'd in part,* No. A–2103–83T3, *reprinted in* 1985 Haz. Was. Lit. Rep. (Andrews) 7569 (N.J. App. Div. June 4, 1985), *rev'd in part,* 25 Env't Rep. Cas. (BNA) 1953, (N.J. Sup. Ct. May 7, 1987). A federal district court judge in Tennessee also awarded over $12.7 million in compensatory and punitive damages to class action plaintiffs in a groundwater contamination case. *See Sterling v. Velsicol Chemical Corp.,* 647 F.Supp. 303 (W.D.Tenn.1986), *aff'd in part, rev'd in part,* 855 F.2d 1188 (6th Cir.1988)(remanding the case for recomputation of both compensatory and punitive damages). Such suits are spurred by developments in the law of class actions and product liability, by efforts to develop new theories of liability (*e.g.,* recovery for "cancer *risk*" and immune system injury or suppression), and by the willingness of some courts and juries to award large punitive damages.

§ 2.4   STRICT LIABILITY IN TORT

1. *Products Liability*

The term "products liability" refers to the liability of a manufacturer, processor, or non-manufacturing seller who supplies goods or products for injuries to purchasers, users, bystanders and property caused by defects in those products. Prosser & Keaton on The Law of Torts (5th Ed. 1984); 63 Am. Jur. 2d 33. The basis of products liability law is the responsibility put upon those who send goods out into the channels of trade for use by others. *Liberty Mutual Ins. Co. v. Hercules Powder Co.*, 224 F.2d 293 (3d Cir.1955). Traditional common law theories upon which liability for harm caused by a defective product include negligence, breach of warranty, fraud, misrepresentation, nuisance, and strict liability in tort.

There are three issues common to all product liability cases, regardless of the theory of liability: (1) the plaintiff cannot recover unless the product is defective (i.e. had an element capable of causing injury), (2) the defendant's act or omission is causally related to the injury; (3) the defendant is identified with the product, for example as its manufacturer or seller. 63 Am. Jur. 2d 47. Thus, the plaintiff always bears the initial burden of establishing that he has been injured by the product, the injury occurred because the product was defective and unreasonably unsafe, and the defect existed when the product left the defendant's hands. Prosser, at 671; 63 Am. Jur. 2d 47, n.21; *Franks v. National Dairy Products Corp.*, 414 F.2d 682 (5th Cir.1969).

Under the doctrine of strict liability in tort, the manufacturer or seller of a product is liable, notwithstanding exercise of due care, for harm or damage caused by a defective condition present in the product when it left the hands of the seller or manufacturer, if the defective condition rendered the product unreasonably dangerous or unsafe to the user. 54 A.L.R.3d 352. Many states have adopted Restatement of Torts 2d sec. 402A as the statement of this doctrine:

(1) One who sells any product in a defective condition unreasonably dangerous to the user or consumer or to his property is subject to liability for physical harm thereby caused to the ultimate user or consumer, or to his property, if

> (a) the seller is engaged in the business of selling such a product, and

> (b) it is expected to and does reach the user or consumer without substantial change in the condition in which it is sold.

(2) The rule stated in Subsection (1) applies although

> (a) the seller has exercised all possible care in the preparation and sale of his product, and

(b) the user or consumer has not bought the product from or entered into any contractual relation with the seller.

The justification for holding manufacturers liable without evidence of fault is to ensure that the costs of injuries resulting from defective products are borne by manufacturers who put products on the market, rather than by the injured person who is powerless to protect himself. *Roseleaf Corp. v. Chierighino*, 59 Cal.2d 35, 27 Cal.Rptr. 873, 378 P.2d 97 (1963).

To support a strict liability cause of action, the plaintiff must show the defendant's relationship to the product, the defective and unreasonably dangerous condition; proximate causal connection between the condition and damages, and that the defendant put the product into the stream of commerce. It is not necessary to prove negligence. 94 Misc.2d 336, 404 N.Y.S.2d 778, 63 Am. Jur. 2d 44. A product may be defective within the meaning of section 402A because of a flaw in the product at the time the manufacturer sold it, or the manufacturer's failure to warn of a risk inherent in the product's design, or the product's defective design. Prosser, at 695.

Merely causing harm does not render a product defective. *Moomey v. Massey Ferguson, Inc.*, 429 F.2d 1184 (10th Cir.1970). A product is defective under the Restatement only if it is unreasonably dangerous; that is, dangerous to an extent beyond that contemplated by the ordinary consumer. Restatement of Torts 2d sec. 402A, comment i.

Where the product is defective because of the manufacturer's failure to warn of the product's inherent danger, the manufacturer or seller has a duty to warn of only those dangers that are reasonably foreseeable.

The application of the strict liability in tort doctrine to environmental damage cases began with the asbestos cases, in which courts held asbestos manufacturers strictly liable in tort for health hazards caused by insulation materials. The asbestos was considered an unreasonably dangerous product because the manufacturers failed to test their product and failed to warn of the product's dangers despite the scientific knowledge regarding such dangers which had been available for many years.

BOREL v. FIBREBOARD PAPER PRODUCTS CORP.

493 F.2d 1076 (5th Cir.1973).

WISDOM, CIRCUIT JUDGE:

This product liability case involves the scope of an asbestos manufacturer's way to warn industrial insulation workers of dangers associated with the use of asbestos.

Clarence Borel, an industrial insulation worker, sued certain manufacturers of insulation materials containing asbestos to recover damages for injuries caused by the defendants' alleged breach of duty in failing to warn of the dangers involved in handling asbestos. Borel alleged that he had contracted the diseases of asbestosis and mesothelioma as a result of his exposure to the defendants' products over a thirty-three year period beginning in 1936 and ending in 1969. The jury returned a verdict in favor of Borel on the basis of strict liability. We affirm.

I.

Clarence Borel began working as an industrial insulation worker in 1936. During his career, he was employed at numerous places, mostly in Texas, until disabled by the disease of asbestosis in 1969. Borel's employment necessarily exposed him to heavy concentrations of asbestos dust generated by insulation materials. In his pre-trial deposition, Borel testified that at the end of a day working with insulation material containing asbestos his clothes were usually so dusty he could "just barely pick them up without shaking them." Borel stated: "You just move them a little bit and there is going to be dust, and I blowed this dust out of my nostrils by handfuls at the end of the day, trying to use water too, I even used Mentholatum in my nostrils to keep some of the dust from going down in my throat, but it is impossible to get rid of all of it. Even your clothes just stay dusty continually unless you blow it off with an air hose."

Borel said that he had known for years that inhaling asbestos dust "was bad for me" and that it was vexatious and bothersome, but that he never realized that it could cause any serious or terminal illness. Borel emphasized that he and his fellow insulation workers thought that the dust "dissolves as it hits your lungs". He said:

A.　Yes, I knew the dust was bad but we used to talk [about] it among the insulators, [about] how bad was this dust, could it give you TB, could it give you this, and everyone was saying no, that dust don't hurt you, it dissolves as it hits your lungs. That was the question you get all the time.

Q.　Where would you have this discussion, in your Union Hall?

A.　On the jobs, just among the men.

Q.　In other words, there was some question in your mind as to whether this was dangerous and whether it was bad for your health?

A.　There was always a question, you just never know how dangerous it was. I never did know really. If I had known I would have gotten out of it.

Q.　All right, then you did know it had some degree of danger but you didn't know how dangerous it was?

A.　I knew I was working with insulation.

Q.　Did you know that it contained asbestos?

A.　Yes, sir, but I didn't know what asbestos was.

When asked about the use of respirators, Borel replied that they were not furnished during his early work years. Although respirators were later made available on some jobs, insulation workers usually were not required to wear them and had to make a special request if they wanted one. Borel stated that he and other insulation workers found that the respirators furnished them were uncomfortable, could not be work in hot weather, and—"you can't breathe with the respirator." Borel further noted that no respirator in use during his lifetime could prevent the inhalation of asbestos dust. As an alternative precaution, therefore, he would sometimes wear a wet handkerchief over his nostrils or apply mentholatum, but these methods were also unsatisfactory and did not exclude all the dust.

Borel stated that throughout his early working life and until the mid–1960's he was in good health, except for pains caused by lung congestion that his doctor attributed to pleurisy. In 1964, a doctor examined Borel in connection with an insurance policy and informed him that x-rays of his lung were cloudy. The doctor told Borel that the cause could be his occupation as an insulation worker and therefore advised him to avoid asbestos dust as much as he possibly could.

On January 19, 1969, Borel was hospitalized and a lung biopsy performed. Borel's condition was diagnosed as pulmonary asbestosis. Since the disease was considered irreversible, Borel was sent home. Borel testified in his deposition that this was the first time he knew that he had asbestosis.

Borel's condition gradually worsened during the remainder of 1969. On February 11, 1970, Borel underwent surgery for the removal of his right lung. The examining doctors determined that Borel had a form of lung cancer known as mesothelioma, which had been caused by asbestosis. As a result of these diseases, Borel later died before the district case reached the trial stage.

The medical testimony adduced at trial indicates that inhaling asbestos dust in industrial conditions, even with relatively light exposure, can produce the disease of asbestosis. . . . The disease is difficult to diagnose in its early stages because there is a long latent period between initial exposure and apparent effect. This latent period may vary according to individual idiosyncrasy, duration and intensity of exposure, and the type of asbestos used. In some cases, the disease may manifest itself in less than ten years after initial exposure. In general, however, it does not manifest itself until ten to twenty-five or more years after initial exposure. This latent period is explained by the fact that asbestos fibers, once inhaled, remain in place in the lung, causing a tissue reaction that is slowly progressive and apparently irreversible. Even if no additional asbestos fibers are inhaled, tissue changes may continue undetected for decades. By the time the disease is diagnosable, a considerable period of time has elapsed since the date of the injurious exposure. Furthermore, the effect of the disease may be cumulative since each exposure to asbestos dust can result in additional tissue changes. A worker's present condition is the biological product of many years of exposure to asbestos dust, with both past and recent exposures contributing to the overall effect. All of these factors combine to make it impossible, as a practical matter, to determine which exposure or exposures to asbestos dust caused the disease.

A second disease, mesothelioma, is a form of lung cancer caused by exposure to asbestos. It affects the pleural and peritoneal cavities, and there is a similarly long period between initial contact and apparent effect. As with asbestosis, it is difficult to determine which exposure to asbestos dust is responsible for the disease. . . .

At issue in this case is the extent of the defendants' knowledge of the dangers associated with insulation products containing asbestos. We pause, therefore, to summarize the evidence relevant to this question.

Asbestosis has been recognized as a disease for well over fifty years. . . . The first reported cases of asbestosis were among asbestos textile workers. In 1924, Cooke in England discovered a case of asbestosis in a person who had spent twenty years weaving asbestos textile products. . . . In the next decade, numerous similar cases were observed and discussed in medical journals. An investigation of the problem among textile factory workers was undertaken in Great Britain in 1928 and 1929. . . . In the United States, the first official claim for compensation associated with asbestos was in 1927. . . . By the mid–1930s, the hazard of asbestosis as a pneumoconiotic dust was universally accepted. . . . Cases of asbestosis in insulation workers were reported in this country as early as 1934. . . . The U.S. Public Health Service fully documented the significant risk involved in asbestos textile factories in a report by Dreessen, et al., in 1938. . . . The authors urged precautionary measures and urged elimination of hazardous exposures.

The first large-scale survey of asbestos insulation workers was undertaken in the United States by Fleischer–Drinker, et al., in 1945. . . . The authors examined insulation workers in eastern Navy shipyards and had only three cases of asbestosis. They concluded that "asbestos covering of naval vessels is a relatively safe operation." Significantly, ninety-five percent of those examined had worked at the trade for less than ten years. Since asbestosis is usually not diagnosable until ten to twenty years after initial exposure, the authors' conclusion has been criticized as misleading. . . . Perhaps recognizing this possibility, the authors cautioned that the study did not "give a composite picture of the asbestos dust that a worker may breathe over a period of years", and that "if pipe coverers had worked steadily under conditions where the amount of asbestos dust in the air was consistently high, the incidence of asbestosis among these workers would have been considerably greater." The authors stated that "the suggestions relative to exhaust ventilation and respiratory protection are therefore of value in maintaining this low incidence of asbestosis". . . .

In 1947, the American Conference of Governmental Industrial Hygienists, a quasi-official body responsible for making recommendations concerning industrial hygiene, issued guidelines suggesting threshold limit values for exposure to asbestos dust. In its first report, the ACGIH recommended that there should be no more than five million parts per cubic foot of air. It later determined in 1968 that the threshold limit value should be reduced to two million. . . .

Throughout the 1950s and 1960s, further studies and medical reports on asbestosis were published. In 1965, J. Selikoff and his colleagues published a study entitled, "The Occurrence of Asbestosis Among Insulation Workers in the United States." . . . The authors examined 1,522 members of an insulation workers union in the New York–New Jersey metropolitan area. Evidence of pulmonary asbestosis was found in almost half the men examined. Among those with more than forty years experience, abnormalities were found in over ninety percent. The authors concluded that "asbestosis and its complications are significant hazards among insulation workers". . . . Other studies have since confirmed these findings. . . .

The plaintiff introduced evidence tending to establish that the defendant manufacturers either were, or should have been, fully aware of the many articles and studies on asbestosis. The evidence also indicated, however, that during Borel's working career no manufacturer ever warned contractors or insulation workers, including Borel, of the dangers associated with inhaling asbestos dust or informed them of the ACGIH's threshold limit values for exposure to asbestos dust. Furthermore, no manufacturer ever tested the effect of their products on the workers using them or attempted to discover whether the exposure of insulation workers to asbestos dust exceeded the suggested threshold limits.

On October 20, 1969, Borel initiated the present diversity action in the United States District Court for the Eastern District of Texas. Borel named as defendants eleven manufacturers of asbestos insulation materials used by him during his working career. He settled with four defendants before trial. The trial court instructed a verdict as to a fifth. The remaining defendants were: Fibreboard Paper Products Corporation, Johns–Manville Products Corporation, Pittsburgh Corning Corporation, Philip Carey Corporation, Armstrong Cork Corporation, and Ruberoid Corporation, a Division of GAF Corporation. . . . Borel died before trial and his widow was substituted as plaintiff under the Texas wrongful death statutes. Tex. Rev. Civ. Stat. arts. 4671, 5525.

The plaintiff sought to hold the defendants liable for negligence, gross negligence, and breach of warranty or strict liability. The negligent acts alleged in the complaint were: (1) failure to take reasonable precautions or to exercise reasonable care to warn Borel of the danger to which he was exposed as a worker when using the defendants' asbestos insulation products; (2) failure to inform Borel as to what would be safe and sufficient wearing apparel and proper protective equipment and appliances or method of handling and using the various products; (3) failure to test the asbestos products in order to ascertain the dangers involved in their use; and (4) failure to remove the products from the market upon ascertaining that such products would cause asbestosis. The plaintiff also alleged that the defendants should be strictly liable in warranty and tort. The plaintiff contended that the defendants' products were unreasonably dangerous because of the failure to provide adequate warnings of the foreseeable dangers associated with them.

The defendants denied the allegations in the plaintiff's complaint and interposed the defenses of contributory negligence and assumption of risk.

The trial court submitted the case to the jury on general verdicts accompanied by a special interrogatory as to Borel's contributory negligence. As to the negligence count, the jury found that all the defendants, except Pittsburgh and Armstrong, were negligent but that none of the defendants had been grossly negligent. It found also, however, that Borel had been contributory negligent.

As to the strict liability count, the jury found that all the defendants were liable and determined that the total damages were $79,436.24. Since four defendants originally named in the complaint had previously settled, paying a total of $20,902.20, the trial court gave full credit for the sums paid in settlement and held the remaining six defendants jointly and severally liable for the balance of $58,534.04. The defendants appealed.

II.

At the outset, we meet the question whether the trial court properly instructed the jury on strict liability. Since federal jurisdiction is based on diversity of citizenship, the substantive law of the forum state, Texas, controls. *Erie R.R. Co. v. Thompkins*, 1938, 304 U.S. 64, 58 S.Ct. 817, 82 L.Ed. 1188.

Under Texas law, a manufacturer of a defective product may be liable to a user or consumer in either warranty or tort.... With respect to personal injuries caused by a defective product, the Texas Supreme Court has adopted the theory of strict liability in tort as expressed in section 402A of the Restatement (Second) of Torts (1964).... *McKisson v. Sales Affiliates, Inc.*, 1967, 416 S.W.2d 787; *Shamrock Fuel & Oil Sales Co. v. Tunks*, 1967, 416 S.W.2d 779; *Texsun Feed Yards, Inc. v. Ralston Purina Co.*, 5 Cir.1971, 447 F.2d 660. Section 402A provides, in relevant part: "One who sells any product in a defective condition unreasonably dangerous to the user or consumer ... is subject to liability for physical harm thereby caused to the ultimate consumer or user".

Under the *Restatement*, liability may not be imposed merely because a product involves some risk of harm or is not entirely safe for all uses. Products liability does not mean that a seller is an insurer for all harm resulting from the use of his product. Rather, a product is "defective" under the *Restatement* only if it is "unreasonably dangerous" to the ultimate user or consumer.... The requirement that the defect render the product "unreasonably dangerous" reflects a realization that many products have both utility and danger. The determination that a product is unreasonably dangerous, or not reasonably safe, means that, on balance, the utility of the product does not outweigh the magnitude of the danger. *See Helene Curtis Industries, Inc. v. Pruitt*, 5 Cir.1967, 385 F.2d 841; James, Products Liability, 33 Tex. L. Rev. 114 (1955); Wade, Strict Tort Liability of Manufacturers, 19 S.W.L.J. 5, 15 (1965); Keeton, Products Liability–Inadequacy of Information, 48 Tex.L.Rev. 398, 403 (1970). The fulcrum for this balancing process is the reasonable man as consumer or as seller. Thus, a product is unreasonably dangerous only when it is "dangerous to an extent beyond that contemplated by the ordinary consumer who purchases it". Restatement (Second) of Torts, § 402A, comment i. In other words, for a product to be unreasonably dangerous, "it must be so dangerous that a reasonable man would not sell the product if he knew the risk involved".... *Helene Curtis Industries, Inc. v. Pruitt*, 385 F.2d at 850. *See Wade, supra* at 15; Keeton, Products Liability–Liability Without Fault and the Requirement of a Defect, 41 Tex. L. Rev. 855, 859 (1963).

Here, the plaintiff alleged that the defendants' product was unreasonably dangerous because of the failure to give adequate warnings of the known or knowable dangers involved. As explained in comment j to section 402A, a seller has a responsibility to inform users and consumers of dangers which the seller either knows or should know at the time the product is sold. The requirement that the danger be reasonably foreseeable, or scientifically discoverable, is an important limitation of the seller's liability.... In general, "[t]he rule of strict liability subjects the seller to liability to the user or consumer even though he has exercised all possible care in the preparation and sale of the product". Section 402A, Comment a. This is not the case where the product is alleged to be unreasonably dangerous because of a failure to give adequate warnings. Rather, a seller is under a duty to warn of only those dangers that are reasonably foreseeable. The requirement of foreseeability coincides with the standard of due care in negligence cases in that a seller must exercise reasonable care and foresight to discover a danger in his product and to warn users and consumers of that danger. *Davis v. Wyeth Laboratories, Inc.*, 9 Cir.1968, 399 F.2d 121. *See Basko v. Sterling Drug, Inc.*, 2 Cir.1969, 416 F.2d 417, 427.

As the plaintiff has argued, insulation materials containing asbestos may be viewed as "unavoidably unsafe products". As explained in comment k to section 402A of the *Restatement*, "unavoidably unsafe products" are those which, in the present state of human knowledge, are incapable of being made safe for their ordinary and intended use. Strict liability may not always be appropriate in such cases because of the important benefits derived from the use of the product. This is especially so with respect to new drugs that are essential in treating disease but involve a high degree of risk.... It may also be so with respect to other commercial products possessing both unparalleled utility and unquestioned danger. As a practical matter, the decision to market such a product requires a balancing of the product's utility against its known or foreseeable danger. But, as comment k makes clear, even when such balancing leads to the conclusion that marketing is justified, the seller still has a responsibility to inform the user or consumer of the risk of harm. The failure to give adequate warnings in these circumstances renders the product unreasonably dangerous. *See Alman Bros. Farm & Feed Mill, Inc. v. Diamond Lab. Inc.*, 5 Cir.1971, 437 F.2d 1295; *Davis v. Wyeth Laboratories, Inc.*, 9 Cir.1968, 399 F.2d 121; *Basko v. Sterling Drug. Inc.*, 2 Cir.1969, 416 F.2d 417; *Sterling Drug, Inc. v. Yarrow*, 8 Cir.1969, 408 F.2d 978; *Sterling Drug v. Cornish*, 8 Cir.1966, 370 F.2d 82. The rationale for this rule is that the user or consumer is entitled to make his own choice as to whether the product's utility or benefits justify exposing himself to the risk of harm. thus, a true choice situation arises, and a duty to warn attaches, whenever a reasonable man would want to be informed of the risk in order to decide whether to expose himself to it.

In *Davis v. Wyeth Laboratories, Inc.*, for example, the defendant manufacturer sold polio vaccine without warning of the statistical risk that one person in a million would contract polio by taking the vaccine. The court held that the manufacturer had a duty to warn the consumer of the risks involved and that the failure to meet this duty rendered the drug "unfit" and "unreasonably dangerous" within the meaning of section 402A. The court stated:

In such cases, then, the drug is fit and its danger is reasonable only if the balance is struck in favor of its use. Where the risk is otherwise known to the consumer, no problem is presented, since choice is available. Where not known, however, the drug can properly be marketed only in such fashion as to permit the striking of the balance; that is, by full disclosure of the existence and extent of the risk involved.

* * *

There will, of course, be cases where the personal risk, although existent and known, is so trifling in comparison with the advantage to be gained as to be de minimis. Appellee so characterizes this case. It would approach the problem from a purely statistical point of view; less than one out of a million is just not unreasonable. This approach we reject. When, in a particular case, the risk qualitatively (e.g., of death or major disability) as well as quantitatively, on balance with the end sought to be achieved, is such as to call for a true choice judgment, medical or professional, the warning must be given.

399 F.2d at 129–130.

So it is with the case at bar. The utility of an insulation product containing asbestos may outweigh the known or foreseeable risk to the insulation workers and thus justify its marketing. The product could still be unreasonably dangerous, however, if unaccompanied by adequate warnings. An insulation worker, no less than any other product user, has a right to decide whether to expose himself to the risk.

Furthermore, in cases such as the instant case, the manufacturer is held to the knowledge and skill of an expert. This is relevant in determining (1) whether the manufacturer knew or should have known the danger, and (2) whether the manufacturer was negligent in failing to communicate this superior knowledge to the user or consumer of its product. *Wright v. Carter Products, Inc.*, 2 Cir.1957, 244 F.2d 53. The manufacturer's status as expert means that at a minimum he must keep abreast of scientific knowledge, discoveries, and advances and is presumed to know what is imparted thereby.... But even more importantly, a manufacturer has a duty to test and inspect his product.... The extent of research and experiment must be commensurate with the dangers involved. A product must not be made available to the public without disclosure of those dangers that the application of reasonable foresight would reveal. Nor may a manufacturer rely unquestioningly on others to sound the hue and cry concerning a danger in its product. Rather, each manufacturer must bear the burden of showing that its own conduct was proportionate to the scope of its duty.

We now turn to the charge in the present case and the defendants objections to it. The trial judge instructed the jury in terms of both breach of warranty and strict liability in tort. He stated that strict liability could be imposed only if the product was unreasonably dangerous to the user or consumer at the time it was sold. He defined "unreasonably dangerous" as dangerous to an extent "beyond that contemplated by [an] insulation contractor or insulator [i.e. asbestos insulation worker] with knowledge available to them as to the characteristics of the product". Furthermore, the court stated that the danger "must have been reasonably foreseen by the manufacturer" and that the product's unreasonably dangerous condition must have been the proximate cause of Borel's injury....

The defendants first object to the court's use of breach of warranty language in some parts of the charge. It is argued that such terms as "unmerchantable", and "unfit for ordinary purposes" may have led the jury to believe that liability could be imposed simply because the product caused harm in its ordinary and intended use.

Although we agree that a reference to "breach of warranty" in a products liability charge may be unnecessarily confusing in some cases, since that is the language of contracts not torts, we are persuaded that no prejudice resulted to the defendants from its use in this case. Consistent with *Shamrock Fuel & Oil Sales v. Tunks*, the trial court accurately instructed the jury on strict liability in tort as defined in section 402A of the *Restatement*. With respect to breach of implied warranty, the court specifically equated "unfitness" or "unmerchantability" with the "unreasonably dangerous" standard of strict liability in tort.... Viewing the charge as a whole, we think that the jury fully understood that liability could be imposed only if the product was unreasonably dangerous.

The defendants also contend that the trial court erred in refusing to instruct the jury that liability could not be imposed if the utility of the product outweighed the danger involved. The trial court, however, did tell the jury that liability could not be imposed unless the product was "unreasonably dangerous," a concept that necessarily implies a balancing of a product;' s utility against the danger. Furthermore, as we noted earlier, even when such a balancing leads to the conclusion that marketing is justified, the seller still has a responsibility to inform the user or consumer of the risk. The failure to give adequate warnings in such circumstances can render the product unreasonably dangerous. *See* Restatement (Second) of Torts, § 402A, comment k; *Davis v. Wyeth Laboratories, Inc.* That was precisely the contention of the plaintiff in this case. We therefore find no error.

The defendants next contend that it was error for the trial court to imply that the defendants had an independent duty to test their product. As we have made clear, however, the manufacturer's duty to test his product is well-established. . . .

Finally, the defendants contend that the district court erred in refusing to instruct the jury that a product cannot be unreasonably dangerous if it conforms to the reasonable expectations of the industrial purchasers, here, the insulation contractors. The defendants assert, in effect, that it is the responsibility of the insulation contractors, not the manufacturers, to warn insulation workers of the risk of harm. We reject this argument. We agree with the *Restatement*; a seller may be liable to the ultimate consumer or user for failure to give adequate warnings. The seller's warning must be reasonably calculated to reach such persons and the presence of an intermediate party will not by itself relieve the seller of this duty. *Sterling Drug Co. v. Cornish*, 8 Cir.1969, 408 F.2d 978; Noel, Products Defective Because of Inadequate Directions or Warnings, 23 S.W.L.J. 256 (1969). In general, of course, a manufacturer is not liable for miscarriages in the communication process that are not attributable to his failure to warn or the adequacy of the warning. This may occur, for example, where some intermediate party is notified of the danger, or discovers it for himself, and proceeds deliberately to ignore it and to pass on the product without a warning. . . . But there is nothing in the trial court's charge in the present case to imply that the seller or manufacturer would be liable in such a situation. To the contrary, the trial court fully instructed the jury that the defect rendering the product unreasonably dangerous must be the proximate cause of the plaintiff's injury.

We conclude, therefore, that the trial court did not err in instructing the jury on strict liability.

* * *

Having concluded that each defendant was the cause in fact of some injury to Borel, we now come to the question of apportionment of damages. In general, a defendant is liable only for that portion of the harm which he in fact caused. A problem arises, however, where, as here, several causes combine to product an injury that is not reasonably capable of being divided. In the instant case, the trial court resolved this issue by holding the defendants jointly and severally liable for the entire harm. Asserting error, the defendants argue that if the injury cannot be reasonably apportioned, the plaintiff must bear the entire loss unless it can be shown that the tortfeasors acted in concert or with unity of design.

* * *

... we conclude that the defendants may be held jointly and severally liable for the total damages.

V.

We now turn to a consideration of the defensive issues raised in the trial court's charge. The principal issue on appeal is whether the trial court properly instructed the jury as to which forms of contributory negligence or assumption of risk are defenses to a strict liability action. The defendants contend that the plaintiff's recovery should have been barred by both the doctrine of volenti non fit injuria and contributory negligence. In brief, it is argued that Borel assumed the risk when he continued in his employment as an insulator after he knew and appreciated the danger from the defendants' product....

Volenti non fit injuria, an ancient maxim meaning that no wrong is done to one who consents, is essentially a form of assumption of risk. Under Texas law, the *volenti* doctrine has four elements: (1) the plaintiff knows the facts constituting a dangerous condition; (2) he knows the condition or activity to be dangerous; (3) he appreciates the nature or extent of the danger; and (4) he voluntarily exposes himself to the danger. *Halepeska v. Callihan Interests, Inc.*, Tex. Sup.1963, 371 S.W.2d 368. Texas courts have held that *volenti* is a subjective standard: the plaintiff must know, understand, and appreciate the danger, and consent to expose himself to it. *J. & W. Corp. Inc. v. Ball*, Tex. Sup. Ct. 1967, 414 S.W.2d 143.

In its most traditional form, contributory negligence consists of the plaintiff's failure to exercise the case of a reasonable person for his own protection. It may overlap with *volenti* in situations where the plaintiff has been contributory negligent in proceeding to encounter an unreasonable risk. This form of contributory negligence differs from *volenti* in two respects. First, contributory negligence is an objective rather than a subjective standard. The plaintiff is required to have the knowledge, understanding, and judgment of an ordinary reasonable man and must exercise due care to discover and understand the defect or danger. Second, justification, in terms of the reasonableness of the plaintiff's conduct, is an important element. The plaintiff is not contributory negligent unless his conduct in encountering the danger was unreasonable. Thus, unlike *volenti*, the contributory negligence doctrine requires a balancing of the utility of the plaintiff's conduct against the magnitude of the danger. *See generally*, (Second) Restatement of Torts S 463, 466 (1964); Restatement (Second) of Torts, §§ 496A–G (Tent. Draft No. 9, 1963).

Another form of contributory negligence consists of voluntary and unreasonable conduct in encountering a known risk. As found in comment n to section 402A office *Restatement*, ... it represents a hybridization of *volenti* and traditional contributory negligence. Applying a subjective standard, the jury must find the first three elements of *volenti*; the plaintiff must have had actual knowledge, understanding and appreciation of the danger. With respect to voluntariness, however, the jury must find that the plaintiff's action was both voluntary from a subjective standpoint and unreasonable from an objective standpoint.

The applicability of a *volenti* or contributory negligence defense to a strict liability action is unclear under Texas law. the leading Texas decision concerning the strict liability action is *Shamrock Fuel & Oil Sales v. Tunks*, Tex. Sup. Ct. 1967, 416 S.W.2d 779. In that case, the plaintiff sought damages for injuries sustained while using adulterated kerosene. The defendants asserted that recovery should be denied because of the plaintiff's contributory negligence in failing to discover the dangerous nature of the adulterated kerosene or to guard against the possibility of its existence. Following in part the position taken in comment n to section 402A of the Restatement, ... the Texas Supreme Court held that such negligence was not a defense to a strict liability action.

Later Texas decisions have re-affirmed the holding in *Shamrock* but have left unanswered what other forms of contributory negligence, assumption of risk, or *volenti* are a defense to a strict liability action. *See McKisson v. Sales Affiliates, Inc.* Our *Erie* ruminations in *Messick v. General Motors Corp.*, 5 Cir.1972, 460 F.2d 485, however, have led us to predict that Texas will adopt the position taken in comment n to section 402A of the *Restatement* that contributory negligence or assumption of risk is a defense to a strict liability action only when it consists of a voluntary and unreasonable conduct in encountering a known risk. In *Messick*, the plaintiff continued to drive his new car even after a private mechanic told him that its defective steering and suspension systems would cause his death. When the car later ran off the road, the plaintiff sued the manufacturer to recover damages for personal injuries sustained in the accident. The plaintiff alleged that the defendant was strictly liable because the car's defects rendered it unreasonably dangerous. After the jury returned a verdict in the plaintiff's favor, the defendant appealed, arguing that *volenti* was established as a matter of law by the plaintiff's voluntary decision to continue using the car. In affirming, this Court held that continued use of a product known to be defective is a defense to a strict liability action only when the continued use is unreasonable. The court stated: "The limits of a manufacturer's liability for releasing a defective and unreasonably dangerous product in *volenti* area are that the plaintiff's consent to incur the risk has been voluntarily given and is objectively unreasonable. The plaintiff at bar was entitled to go to the jury with the question of whether his consent was voluntary or was the product of duress of circumstances and unreasonable." 460 F.2d at 494.

We now turn to the trial court's instructions in the present case. The trial court, in informing the jury that assumption of risk was a defense to a strict liability action, stated as follows:

[T]he defendants contend that the deceased, Mr. Borel, knew of the dangerous nature of the asbestos product manufactured by the defendants in connection with his insulation work and appreciated the danger and with such knowledge voluntarily assumed the risk by continuing his employment. Further, that this knowledge of the danger of the insulation was known to Mr. Borel's contractor or employer. Therefore, the Court would instruct you that if you find from a preponderance of the evidence that the deceased knew of the dangerous nature of the asbestos products with which he was working and appreciated the danger of working with such products or that he had knowledge through his contractor of the dangerous nature of the product and that he assumed the risk by continuing his work, then you would find against the plaintiff and in favor of the defendants.

In effect, the trial court instructed the jury that *volenti*, consisting of voluntary conduct in encountering a known and appreciated danger, is a defense to a strict liability action. This was error since, as we have held, contributory negligence or assumption of risk is a defense to a strict liability action only if the plaintiff's conduct is both voluntary and unreasonable. *Messick v. General Motors Corp., supra*; Restatement Second of Torts, § 402A, comment (n); Prosser, Law of Torts, § 102. The trial court's charge was overly favorable to the defendants. Despite this error, the jury still found that Borel had not assumed the risk even under the harsh *volenti* doctrine. Reversal of the jury's verdict, therefore, is not required.

The defendants contend, however, that they are entitled to judgment as a matter of law even if the *Restatement* standard had been correctly applied. We disagree. There is strong evidence in the record that Borel never actually knew or appreciated the extent of the danger involved. Borel testified that he never realized that inhaling asbestos dust could cause serious illness until his doctors first diagnosed his condition as asbestosis in 1969. Nor can we say that the danger was so obvious that Borel should be charged with knowledge as a matter of law. *Halepeska v. Callihan Interests, Inc., supra*; *Schiller v. Rice*, Tex.Sup. 1952, 246 S.W.2d 607. Furthermore, there was evidence that Borel's decision to continue in his employment was neither voluntary nor unreasonable. *Messick v. General Motors Corp., supra*. In these circumstances, we find no cause to invade the province of the jury.

We next consider whether the trial court erred in instructing the jury that none of the alleged acts of contributory negligence was a defense to a strict liability action. The court described the acts of contributory negligence as follows:

In this connection, the defendants contend that the deceased was negligent in failing to use a mask and respirator for protection from dust containing some asbestos; in failing to request his employer to furnish blowers to remove dust laden air; in working in asbestos dust laden air with full knowledge that he was inhaling such dust laden air; in continuing to work with insulation material containing some asbestos after he knew or in the exercise of ordinary care should have known that it was affecting his health.

The defendants assert that Borel's allegedly negligent failure to wear a respirator constituted a misuse of the product that bars recovery.

"Misuse" involves a use of the product in a manner not reasonably foreseeable by the seller or manufacturer. . . . The most common form of misuse is a failure to follow adequate directions or warnings accompanying the product. In *Proctor & Gamble Manufacturing Co. v. Langley,* Tex.Civ.App.1967, 422 S.W.2d 773, for example, the plaintiff read and understood the instructions accompanying a home permanent hair wave product but nevertheless failed to follow them in several important respects. When injury resulted, the plaintiff sued the manufacturer, the wholesale distributor, and the retail seller for breach of implied warranty. The court held that the plaintiff's violation of the plain instructions and warnings was a misuse of the product and constituted a defense to her cause of action. On rehearing, the court stated:

> We do not believe that the strict liability doctrine means [that] . . . a consumer may knowingly violate the plain, unambiguous instructions and ignore the warnings, then hold the makers, distributors and sellers of a product liable in the face of the obvious misuse of the product. Appellees brought their suit on the theory of implied warranty. We agree that the product carried an implied warranty of fitness, but such warranty existed only if the product was used in accordance with directions. The implied warranty did not apply when the product was misused, as it undisputedly was in this case. 42 S.W.2d at 780.

Similarly, in *McDevitt v. Standard Oil Co. of Texas,* 1968, 391 F.2d 364, the plaintiff sued an automobile tire retailer to recover damages for injuries sustained when his automobile tires failed and the car left the road. There was evidence that the plaintiff was provided with manufacturer's instructions regarding proper tire size but that he purchased an improper size. In addition, the record indicated that the vehicle was driven with air pressure in the tires at time well above, and at times well below the recommended pressure as set out in the published manuals. There was also evidence that the vehicle was driven at excessive speeds and over rough terrain. The court, construing Texas law, held that the plaintiff's actions constituted a misuse of the product and was a defense to a strict liability action.

In the case at bar, we are not confronted with a failure to follow adequate instructions or warnings. Indeed, the evidence tended to establish that the defendants gave no instructions or warnings at all. They never suggested that respirators should be worn by insulation workers or provided any other directions as to the product's use. Nor are we confronted with any other type of conduct that was not reasonably foreseeable by the defendant manufacturers. From all that appears, Borel used the defendants' product exactly for its intended purpose. Rather, the defendants allege merely that Borel was contributory negligent in failing to use a respirator. This form of contributory negligence amounts to a failure to discover a defect in the product or to guard against the possibility of its existence and is not a defense to a strict liability action. *Smahrock Fuel & Oil Sales v. Tunks, McKisson v. Sales Affiliates, Inc.* We therefore find no error in the trial court's charge.

The defendants also assert that the trial court's instructions to the jury were confusing and ambiguous in some parts. The trial court's charge must be read as a whole and not as if each sentence were a solitary verbal phenomenon existing in an otherwise empty vacuum. The test is not whether the charge was faultless in every particular but whether the jury was misled in any way and whether it had understanding of the issues and its duty to determine those issues. *Gearhart v. SWAZ, Inc.*, 1957 E.D.Ky., 150 F.Supp. 98, aff'd 154; *Miller v. Pacific Mut. Life Ins. Co.*, D.C. Mich.1955, 17 F.R.D. 121, aff'd 228 F.2d 889. On reading the trial court's charge in this case, we find that it meets that standard.

The defendants further complain because the trial court refused to submit special interrogatories to the jury on several issues, including assumption of risk, but instead submitted the case on a general verdict. Rule 49 of the Federal Rules of Civil Procedure, however, gives the trial court wide discretion in determining the wording and form of verdicts. In the present case, we cannot say that the trial court abused its discretion. *See Car v. General Ins. Corp.*, 5 Cir. 1947, 159 F.2d 985; *De Eugenio v. Allis–Chalmers Mfg. Co.*, 3 Cir.1954, 210 F.2d 409; *Texas & P. Ry. Co. v. Friffen*, 5 Cir.1959, 265 F.2d 489.

* * *

Notes

1. In another case involving a strict liability action for failure to warn of the health hazards of asbestos exposure, the court refused the manufacturer's attempt to use a "state of the art" defense. This defense asserts that the distributor of a product cannot be held liable for injuries resulting from health hazards that were not scientifically discoverable at the time the products were made. *Beshada v. Johns–Manville Products Corp.*, 90 N.J. 191, 447 A.2d 539 (1982). This is a negligence defense which explains why the defendant is not culpable for failing to warn. However, in strict liability cases, culpability is irrelevant. The knowledge of hazards will be imputed to the manufacturer regardless of the state of scientific knowledge.

2. Where it is difficult for the plaintiff to prove the identity of the manufacturer of the injury-causing product, the plaintiff may be able to rely on the market share theory of liability. This theory was created by the California Supreme Court in *Sindell v. Abbott Laboratories*, 26 Cal.3d 588, 163 Cal.Rptr. 132, 607 P.2d 924 (1980), *cert. denied*, 449 U.S. 912, 101 S.Ct.

285, 66 L.Ed.2d 140 a personal injury action arising from the plaintiff's prenatal exposure to the drug DES. Since the plaintiff was suing years later as an adult, it was impossible for her to prove which defendant manufactured the drug her mother had taken. Accordingly, the court shifted the burden of proof to the defendants to prove that each could not have manufactured the product which caused plaintiff's injuries. Each defendant which could not make that exculpatory showing would be held liable for the proportion of the judgment corresponding to its share of the DES market.

The market share theory is not available in asbestos-related product liability cases. The asbestos actions are distinguishable from *Sindell*-type cases, in that it is difficult to identify an accurate division of liability concerning asbestos; asbestos fibers are of several types and are found in varying quantities in asbestos products; numerous uses of asbestos make relevant product and geographic markets difficult to identify; unlike the plaintiffs in the DES cases, the plaintiffs in the asbestos cases have information as to the identity of the defendants who caused the alleged injuries. *In re Related Asbestos Cases*, 543 F.Supp. 1152 (N.D.Cal.1982).

3. In addition, the manufacturer, processor, supplier, or seller of a product which causes environmental damage may also be liable under various federal and state environmental statutes, such as CERCLA and RCRA, which impose strict liability upon those who "own or operate" a hazardous waste facility or "arrange for the disposal or treatment of hazardous waste." Application of common law theories of liability to the supplier of products which cause environmental damage involves traditional analyses of the common law elements of each cause of action. Liability under CERCLA and RCRA, however, depends upon interpretation of statutory language and the case law which has developed recently in this area.

2. *Abnormally Dangerous Activities*

There are several other common law doctrines which provide remedies for environmental harm. These doctrines antedated the current environmental statutes and may be relied upon in addition to statutory causes of action. These theories are as follows:

One whose actions are "ultrahazardous" will be strictly liable for the resulting harm. In assessing whether a particular activity is ultrahazardous, the courts will view the magnitude of the risk presented, the probability of harm and the resulting severity.... The theory behind strict liability is that the actor is in a "better position than the victim 'to insure against the risk, allocate the cost, and reduce or warn against the dangers'"

The most obvious example of what may constitute an ultrahazardous activity is the operation of a hazardous waste disposal site. The risk of contaminated groundwater, increased risk of certain diseases to any nearby residents and severity of the harm, may deem such activities "ultrahazardous." Indeed, in *Sterling v. Velsicol Chemical Corp.,* 647 F.Supp. 303 (W.D.Tenn.1986) *aff'd in part, rev'd in part,* 855 F.2d 1188 (6th Cir. 1988), the plaintiff's successfully imposed strict liability on several defendants whose hazardous waste dump had contaminated drinking wells. The court stated that :

> Velsicol's actions in creating, maintaining and operating its chemical waste burial site, with superior knowledge of the highly toxic and harmful nature of the chemical contaminants it disposed therein, and specifically its failure to immediately cease dumping said toxic chemicals after being warned by several state and federal agencies several years prior to the final cessation of such abnormally hazardous and harmful activity, constituted gross, wilful and wanton disregard for the health and well-being of the plaintiffs. *Id.* at 323–24. Thus, one engaged in activities that have the potential for severe harm to the public would be well-advised to take precautions to mitigate the risk of harm. Otherwise, one faces the possibility of strict liability and the resulting damages which must be paid to injured parties.

* * *

T & E INDUSTRIES, INC. v. SAFETY LIGHT CORP.
123 N.J. 371, 587 A.2d 1249 (N.J.1991).

CLIFFORD, S.

* * *

B.

We focus now on the elements of the abnormally-dangerous-activity doctrine. That doctrine is premised on the principle that "one who carries on an abnormally dangerous activity is subject to liability for harm to the person, land or chattels of another resulting from the activity, although he has exercised the utmost care to prevent the harm." Restatement (Second) of Torts, *supra* § 519. The Restatement sets forth six factors that a court should consider in determining whether an activity is "abnormally dangerous." They are:

(a) existence of a high degree of risk of some harm to the person, land or chattels of others;

(b) likelihood that harm that results from it will be great;

(c) inability to eliminate the risk by the exercise of reasonable care;

(d) extent to which the activity is not a matter of common usage;

(e) inappropriateness of the activity to the place where it is carried on; and

(f) extent to which its value to the community is outweighed by its dangerous attributes.

[Restatement (Second) of Torts, supra § 520.]

In *Ventron*, this court concluded, after applying factors, that "mercury and other toxic wastes 'abnormally dangerous,' and the disposal of them past or present, is an abnormally dangerous activity." 94 N.J. at 493, 468 A.2d 150. As *Ventron* makes clear, "[u]nder Restatement analysis, whether an activity is abnormally dangerous is to be determined on a case-by-case basis, taking all relevant circumstances into consideration." *Id.* at 491, 468 A.2d 150. That proposition is consistent with the Restatement, which cautions against per se rulings. *See* Restatement (Second) of Torts, *supra*, § comment f ("In determining whether the danger is abnormal, the factors listed in Clauses (a) to (f) are all to be considered, and are all of importance. Because of the interplay of [those] factors, it is not possible to reduce abnormally dangers activity to any definition."). Thus, a court must make the determination about the abnormally-dangerous character of an activity one case at a time. The Appellate Division failed to observe that mandate in this case and consequently gave *Ventron* too broad a reading in concluding that "the processing of radium and the disposal of its waste product is an abnormally dangerous activity as a matter of law." 227 N.J.Super. at 240, 546 A.2d 570....

Defendant does not dispute that liability can be imposed on enterprisers who engage in abnormally-dangerous activities that harm others; but it contends that such liability is contingent on proof that the enterpriser knew or should have known of the "abnormally dangerous character of the activity." According to defendant, absent such knowledge the enterpriser "is in no position to make the cost-benefit calculations that will enable him to spread the risk and engage in the optimal level of activity." Defendant argues that absent such an opportunity, the policy basis for imposing strict liability on those who engage in abnormally-dangerous activities, namely, cost spreading, cannot be realized.

Defendant adds that knowledge, or the ability to acquire such knowledge, must be assessed as of the time the enterpriser engaged in the activity, not at a later time—that is, if the risk of harm from the activity was scientifically unknowable at that time, an enterpriser should not be held liable. Defendant also insists that the inquiry must focus on the enterpriser's ability to learn of the risks inherent in the precise activity that causes harm, not merely of the hazards inherent in the business in general. Thus, defendant stresses that strict liability should be imposed in this case only if USRC knew in 1926 of the specific dangers inherent in the discarded tailings, not simply of those associated with the processing and handling of radium.

Defendant's argument poses an interesting question concerning the availability of a state-of-the-art defense—that is, the risk of the activity was scientifically unknowable at the time—to a strict-liability claim for abnormally-dangerous activities. It is a question that we need not resolve here, however, because state-of-the-art becomes an issue only if we agree that knowledge is a prerequisite for strict-liability claims and if we accept defendant's narrow view of the "knowledge" inquiry.

Few cases discuss specifically the requisite state of mind for those who engage in abnormally-dangerous activities. *See, e.g., Garcia v. Estate of Norton*, 183 Cal.App.3d 413, 420, 228 Cal.Rptr. 108, 112 (1986) (defendant need not have "actual knowledge of the true extent of the danger involved in proceeding with an ultrahazardous activity"). Some commentators propose that the Restatement standards for abnormally-dangerous activities imply that the risk be foreseeable. *See, e.g.*, Zazzali & Grad, "Hazardous Wastes: New Rights and Remedies? The Report and Recommendations of the Superfund Study Group," 13 Seton Hall L. Rev. 446, 462 (1983)("The Restatement (Second) formula of strict liability, adopting an abnormally dangerous activity test, requires a balancing of numerous factors such as the utility of the activity, foreseeability of harm, and the appropriateness of the locale of the activity."); Ginsberg & Weiss, "Common Law Liability for Toxic Torts: A Phantom Remedy," 9 Hofstra L. Rev. 859, 918 (1981)(both versions of Restatement include foreseeability requirement); Comment, "Absolute Liability for Ultrahazardous Activities: An Appraisal of the Restatement Doctrine," 37 Calif. L. Rev. 269, 272 (1969)(hereinafter Comment, "Absolute Liability")(Restatement impliedly requires foreseeability of risk). One author suggests that foreseeability of the risk is "a necessary element in any adequate absolute liability doctrine." Comment, "Absolute Liability," *supra*, 37 Calif. L. Rev. at 275.

But requirements such as "knowledge" and "foreseeability" smack of negligence and may be inappropriate in the realm of strict liability. *See* Special Report to Congress, "Injuries and Damages From Hazardous Wastes—Analysis And Improvement of Legal Remedies, In Compliance With Section 301(c) Of The Comprehensive Environmental Response Compensation And Liability Act of 1980 By The 'Superfund Section 301(e) Study Group'" Vols. I & II, ___ to ___ (reprinted as Comm. Print for the Senate Comm. on Envtl. & Pub. Works, Serial No. 97–12, 97th Cong., 2d Sess., 1982)("Whenever a balancing of factors is required under a strict liability theory, a notion of duty of care, responsibility or fault is easily implied as to choice of location or means and strict liability begins to sound more like negligence").

We need not, however, determine whether knowledge is a requirement in the context of a strict-liability claim predicated on an abnormally-dangerous activity. Even if the law imposes such a requirement, we are convinced, for the reasons set forth more fully below, that defendant should have known about the risks of its activity, and that its constructive knowledge would fully satisfy any such requirement.

C

That brings us to the question of whether defendant's activity was such as to fall within the meaning of "abnormally-dangerous activity." As indicated above, our opinion in *Ventron, supra*, 94 N.J. at 491, 468 A.2d 150, instructs that in making such a determination a court must consider the factors set forth in the Restatement of Torts. *See supra* at

1259. As in *Ventron,* we apply those factors to the circumstances in this case.

Radium has always been and continues to able an extraordinarily-dangerous substance. Although radium processing has never been a common activity, the injudicious handling, processing, and disposal of radium has for decades caused concern; it has long been suspected of posing a serious threat to the health of those who are exposed to it. *See* articles of handbook referred to *supra* at 1252–1253. The harm that can result from excess radium exposure, namely, cancer is undoubtedly great. In light of those suspicions and the magnitude of the harm, it is not surprising that in the 1930s and 1940s experts concluded that radon exposure should be limited. Wisely, the government now regulates such exposure.

Furthermore, although the risks involved in the processing and disposal of radium might be curtailed, one cannot safely dispose of radium by dumping it onto the vacant portions of an urban lot. Because of the extraordinarily-hazardous nature of radium, the processing and disposal of that substance is particularly inappropriate in an urban setting. We conclude that despite the usefulness of radium, defendant's processing, handling, and disposal of that substance under the facts of this case constituted an abnormally-dangerous activity. Plaintiff's property is befouled with radium because of defendant's abnormally-dangerous activity. Radiation levels at the site exceed those permitted under governmental health regulations. Moreover, the property has been earmarked as a Superfund site. *See supra* at 1253. Because plaintiff vacated the premises in response to the health concerns posed by the radium-contaminated site and because the danger to the health is "the kind of harm, the possibility of which [made defendant's] activity abnormally dangerous," defendant is strictly liable for the resulting harm. Restatement of Torts, *supra* § 519. Defendant's asserted lack of knowledge cannot relieve it of that liability.

Recall that defendant argues that the knowledge required is of the precise dangers associated with the disposal of the tailings, not merely those inherent in the processing and handling of radium. Defendant has not, however, cited any authority that supports such a narrow inquiry, nor do we believe that the focus should be that narrow.

Here defendant knew that it was processing radium, a substance concededly fraught with hazardous potential. It knew that its employees who handled radium should wear protective clothing; it knew that some employees who had ingested radium had developed cancer; and prior to the sale of the property, it knew that the inhalation of radon could cause lung cancer. Despite the wealth of knowledge concerning the harmful effects of radium exposure, defendant contends that it could not have known that disposal of the radium-saturated by-products behind the plant would produce a hazard. That content appears to rest on the idea that somehow the radium's potential for harm miraculously disappeared once the material had been deposited in a vacant corner of any urban lot, or at the least that one might reasonably reach that conclusion—a proposition that we do not accept.

Surely someone engaged in a business as riddled with hazards as defendant's demonstrably was should realize the potential for harm in every aspect of that dangerous business. If knowledge be a requirement, defendant knew enough about the abnormally-dangerous character of radium processing to be charged with knowledge of the dangers of disposal.

* * *

Out of abundance of caution born of the occasional experience of having our opinions overread, we add a final note about the breadth of our opinion.

By no means do we signal an end to or undermining of that vast body of doctrine by which people regulate their everyday affairs in respect of the conveyancing of land. Today's decision is the proper judicial accommodation of those familiar principles of law to a highly unusual and highly dangerous form of human activity. The law has characterized that activity as "abnormally dangerous."

STATE DEP'T OF ENVTL. PROTECTION v. VENTRON CORP.
94 N.J. 473, 468 A.2d 150 (N.J.1983).

Pollock, J.

This appeal concerns the responsibility of various corporations for the cost of the cleanup and removal of mercury pollution seeping from a forth-acre tract of land into Berry's Creek, a tidal estuary of the Hackensack River that flows through the Meadowlands. The plaintiff is the State of New Jersey, Department of Environmental Protection (DEP); the primary defendants are Velsicol Chemical Corporation (Velsicol), its former subsidiary, Wood Ridge Chemical Corporation (Wood Ridge), and Ventron Corporation (Ventron), into which Wood Ridge was merged. Other defendants are F.W. Berk and Company, Inc. (Berk), which no longer exists, United States Life Insurance Company, which was dismissed by the lower courts in an unappealed judgment, and Robert M. and Rita W. Wolf (the Wolfs), who purchased part of the polluted property from Ventron.

Beneath its surface, the tract is saturated by an estimated 268 tons of toxic waste, primarily mercury. For a stretch of several thousand feet, the concentration of mercury in Berry's Creek is the highest found in fresh water sediments in the world. The waters of the creek are contaminated by the compound methyl mercury, which continues to be released as mercury, which continues to be released as the mercury interacts with other elements. Due to depleted oxygen levels, fish no longer inhabit Berry's Creek, but are present only when swept in by the tide and, thus, irreversibly toxified.

* * *

I.

From 1929 to 1960, first as lessee and then as owner of the entire forty-acre tract, Berk operated a mercury processing plant, dumping untreated waste material and allowing mercury-laden effluent to drain on the tract. Berk continued uninterrupted operations until 1960, at which time it sold its assets to Wood Ridge and ceased its corporate existence.

In 1960, Velsicol formed Wood Ridge as a wholly-owned subsidiary for the sole purpose of purchasing Berk's assets and operating the mercury processing plant. In 1967, Wood Ridge subdivided the tract and declared a thirty-three-acre land dividend to Velsicol, which continued to permit Wood Ridge to dump material on the thirty-three acres. As a Velsicol subsidiary, Wood Ridge continued to operate the processing plant on the 7.1–acre tract from 1960 to 1968, when Velsicol sold Wood Ridge to Ventron.

Although Velsicol created Wood Ridge as a separate corporate entity, the trial court found that Velsicol treated it not as an independent subsidiary, but as a division. From the time of Wood Ridge's incorporation until the sale of its capital stock to Ventron, Velsicol owned 100% of the Wood Ridge stock. All directors met monthly in the Velsicol offices in Chicago. At the meetings, the board not only reviewed financial statements, products development, and public relations, but also the details of the daily operations of Wood Ridge. For example, the Wood Ridge board considered in detail personnel practices, sales efforts, and production. Velsicol arranged for insurance coverage, accounting, and credit approvals for Wood Ridge. Without spelling out all the details, we find that the record amply supports the conclusion of the trial court that "Velsicol personnel, directors, and officers were constantly involved in the day-to-day operations of the business of [Wood Ridge]."

In 1968, Velsicol sold 100% of the Wood Ridge stock to Ventron, which began to consider a course of treatment for plant wastes. Until this time, the waste had been allowed to course over the land through open drainage ditches. In March 1968, Ventron engaged the firm of Metcalf & Eddy to study the effects of mercury on the land, and three months later, Ventron constructed a wire to aid in monitoring the effluent.

Ventron's action was consistent with a heightened sensitivity in the 1960's to pollution problems. Starting in the mid–1960's, DEP began testing effluent on the tract, but did not take any action against Wood Ridge. The trial court found, in fact, that the defendants were not liable under intentional tort or negligence theories.

Nonetheless, in 1970, the contamination at Berry's Creek came to the attention of the United States Environmental Protection Agency (EPA), which conducted a test of Wood Ridge's waste water. The tests indicated that the effluent carried two to four pounds of mercury into Berry's Creek each day. Later that year, Wood Ridge installed a waste treatment system that abated, but did not altogether hold, the flow of mercury into the creek. The operations of the plant continued until 1974, at which time Wood Ridge merged into Ventron. Consistent with N.J.S.A. 14A:10–6(e), the certificate of ownership and merger provided that Ventron would assume the liabilities and obligations of Wood Ridge. Ventron terminated the plant operations and sold the movable operating assets to Troy Chemical Company, not a party to these proceedings.

On February 5, 1974, Wood Ridge granted to Robert Wolf, a commercial real estate developer, an option to purchase the 7.1–acre tract on which the plant was located, and on May 20, 1974, Ventron conveyed the tract to the Wolfs. The Wolfs planned to demolish the plant and construct a warehousing facility. In the course of the demolition, mercury-contaminated water was used to wet down the structures and allowed to run into the creek. The problem came to the attention of DEP, which ordered a halt to the demolition, pending adequate removal or containment of the contamination. DEP proposed a containment plan, but the Wolfs implemented another plan and proceeded with their project. DEP then instituted this action.

Although Wolf knew he was buying from a chemical company land that had been the site of a mercury processing plant, Ventron knew other material facts that it did not disclose to the Wolfs. Ventron knew that the site was a man-made mercury mine. From a study conducted by Metcalf & Eddy at Ventron's request in 1972, Ventron knew the mercury content of the soil. Although the soil and water adjacent to the plant were still contaminated in 1974, that fact was not readily observable to the Wolfs, and Ventron intentionally failed to advise the Wolfs of the condition of the site and to provide them with the relevant part of the Metcalf & Eddy report. Based on these factual findings, the lower courts concluded that Ventron fraudulently concealed material facts from the Wolfs to their detriment. The trial court limited damages, however, to the recovery of the actual costs of the containment system on the 7.1–acre tract and other costs of abating the pollution. In affirming, the Appellate Division extended damages to include diminution in the fair market value of the premises below the purchase price because of the undisclosed mercury contamination. Both courts awarded to the Wolfs those counsel fees and costs incurred in defending the DEP action.

The trial court concluded that the entire tract and Berry's Creek are polluted and that additional mercury from the tract has reached, and may continue to reach, the creek via ground and surface waters. Every operator of the mercury processing plant contributed to the pollution; while the plant was in operation, the discharge of effluent resulted in a dangerous and hazardous mercurial content in Berry's Creek. The trial court found that from 1960–74 the dangers of mercury were becoming better known and that Berk, Wood Ridge, Velsicol, and Ventron knew of those dangers. Furthermore, the lower courts concluded that Velsicol so dominated Wood Ridge as to justify disregarding the separate entity of that corporation and imposing liability on Velsicol for the acts of Wood Ridge, Velsicol, and Ventron were liable for damages caused by the creation of a public nuisance and the conduct of an abnormally dangerous activity. 182 *N.J.Super.* at 219, 440 A.2d 455.

The trial court also determined that the 1977 Spill Act did not impose retroactive liability for discharges of mercury into a waterway of the State. After the entry of the judgment, however, the Legislature amended the act to impose retroactive strict liability on "[a]ny person who has discharged a hazardous substance or is in any way responsible for any hazardous substance" being removed by DEP. *See N.J.S.A.* 58:10–23.11g(c).

Exercising its original jurisdiction under *R.* 2:10–5, the Appellate Division found "overwhelming evidence of mercury pollution in the sediments and waters of Berry's Creek and its substantial and imminent threat to the environment, to marine life and to human health and safety." 182 *N.J.Super.* at 221, 440 A.2d 455. Consequently, the Appellate Division held Wood Ridge jointly and severally liable under the 1979 amendment to the Spill Act.

II.

The lower courts imposed strict liability on Wood Ridge under common-law principles for causing a public nuisance and for "unleashing a dangerous substance during non-natural use of the land." 182 *N.J.Super.* at 219, 440 A.2d 455. In imposing strict liability, those courts relied substantially on the early English decision of *Rylands v. Fletcher, L.R. 1 Ex.* 265 (1866), *aff'd, L.R. 3 H.L.* 330 (1868). An early decision of the former Supreme Court, *Marshall v. Welwood*, 38 *N.J.L* 339 (Sup.Ct. 1876), however, rejected *Rylands v. Fletcher.* But *see City of Bridgeton v. B.P. Oil, Inc.*, 146 N.J.Super. 169, 179, 369 A.2d 49 (Law Div.1976)(landowner is liable under *Rylands* for an oil spill).

Twenty-one years ago, without referring to either *Marshall v. Welwood* or *Rylands v. Fletcher*, this Court adopted the proposition that "an ultrahazardous activity which introduces an unusual danger into the community ... should pay its own way in the event it actually causes damage to others." *Berg v. Reaction Motors Div., Thiokol Chem. Corp.*, 37 N.J. 396, 410, 181 A.2d 487 (1962). Dean Prosser views *Berg* as accepting a statement of principle derived from *Rylands.* W. Prosser, *Law of Torts* § 78 at 509 & n.7 (4th ed. 1971).

In imposing liability on a landowner for an ultrahazardous activity, *Berg* adopted the test of the *Restatement of the Law of Torts* (1938). See *id.*, §§ 519–20. Since *Berg*, the *Restatement (Second) of the Law of Torts* (1977) has replaced the "ultrahazardous" standard with one predicated on whether the activity is "abnormally dangerous." Imposition of liability on a landowner for "abnormally dangerous" activities incorporates, in effect, the *Rylands* test. *Restatement (Second)* § 520, comments (d) & (e).

We believe it is time to recognize expressly that the law of liability has evolved so that a landowner is strictly liable to others for harm caused by toxic wastes that are stored on his property and flow onto the property of others. Therefore, we overrule *Marshall v. Welwood* and adopt the principle of liability originally declared in *Rylands v. Fletcher*. The net result is that those who use, or permit others to use, land for the conduct of abnormally dangerous activities are strictly liable for resultant damages. Comprehension of the relevant legal principles, however, requires a more complete explanation of their development.

Even in its nascent stages, the English common law recognized the need to provide a system for redressing unlawful interference with a landowner's right to the possession and quiet enjoyment of his land. *See* 2 W. Blackstone, Commentaries 218; 1 F. Harper & F. James, *The Law of Torts*, § 1.23 (1956); 2 F. Pollock and F. Maitland, *The History of English Law* 53 (1895). Trespass and nuisance developed as the causes of action available to a landowner complaining of an unauthorized intrusion on his lands. *See* Prosser, *supra*, §§ 13, 86; P. Keeton, "Trespass, Nuisance, and Strict Liability," 59 COLUM.L.REV. 457 (1959); Note, "The *Rylands v. Fletcher* Doctrine in America: Abnormally Dangerous, Ultrahazardous, or Absolute Nuisance," 1978 ARIZ.ST.L.J. 99, 123. In their early forms, predating the development of negligence as a basis for liability, neither trespass nor nuisance required a showing of fault as a prerequisite to liability. *See* Keeton, *supra*, at 462–65; Prosser, *supra*, § 13, at pp. 63–64. Historically, any actual invasion that was the direct result of the defendant's act and that interfered with the plaintiff's exclusive possession of his land constituted an actionable trespass, even in the absence of fault. Keeton, *supra*, at 464–65; *see* 1 Harper & James, *supra*, §§ 1.2–1.3. In contrast, nuisance required only an interference with the enjoyment and possession of land caused "by things erected, made, or done, not on the soil possessed by the complainant but on neighboring soil." 2 Pollack & Maitland, *supra*, at 53; *see* W. Seavey, "Nuisance; Contributory Negligence and Other Mysteries," 65 Harv. L.Rev. 984 (1952); Prosser, *supra*, § 86, at 571–74. The continuing nature of the interference was the essence of the harm, and was with trespass, fault was largely irrelevant. *See* Prosser, *supra*, at 576.

Such was the state of the common law in England when, in 1868, the English courts decided *Rylands v. Fletcher*. In that case, defendants, mill owners in a coal-mining region, constructed a reservoir on their property. Unknown to them, the land below the reservoir was riddled with the passages and filled shafts of an abandoned coal mine. The waters of the reservoir broke through the old mine shafts and surged through the passages into the working mine of the plaintiff. *Id.* As Dean Prosser explains, the courts were presented with an unusual situation: "[n]o trespass could be found, since the flooding was not direct or immediate; nor any nuisance, as the term was then understood, since there was nothing offensive to the senses and the damage was not continuing or recurring." Prosser, *supra*, § 78, at p. 505.

The Exchequer Chamber, however, held the mill owners liable, relying on the existing rule of strict liability for damage done by trespassing cattle. The rationale was stated:

We think that the true rule of law is that the person who for his own purposes brings on his land and collects and keeps there anything likely to do mischief if its escapes, must keep it at his peril, and if he does not do so, is *prima facie* answerable for all damage which is the natural consequence of its escape. [*Rylands v. Fletcher*, *L.R. 1 Ex.* 265, 279–80 (1866), *aff'd*, *L.R. 3 H.L.* 330 (1868)].

On appeal, the House of Lords limited the applicability of this strict liability rule to "nonnatural" uses of land. Consequently, if an accumulation of water had occurred naturally, or had been created incident to a use of the land for "any purpose for which it might in the ordinary course of enjoyment of land be used," strict liability would not be imposed. *Rylands v. Fletcher, L.R. 3 H.L.* 330, 338–39.

Early decisions of the State recognized the doctrine of nuisance as a basis for imposing liability for damages. *See, e.g., Cuff v. Newark & N.Y.R. Co.*, 35 N.J.L. 17, 22 (1870)(when the owner of land undertakes to do work that is, in the ordinary mode of doing it, a nuisance, he is liable for any injuries to third persons, even when an independent contractor is employed to do the work). The former New Jersey Supreme Court, however, became one of the first courts to reject the doctrine of *Rylands v. Fletcher. See Marshall v. Welwood*, 38 N.J.L. 339 (1876)(when the owner of land undertakes to do work that is, in the ordinary mode of doing it, a nuisance, he is liable for any injuries to third persons, even when an independent contractor is employed to do the work). That Court reached this result by referring to the Exchequer Chamber's broad formulation of the rule, which extended liability to anything on the land "likely to cause mischief," rather than the narrowed version affirmed by the House of Lords, which limited liability to "nonnatural" use of the land. Writing for the Court, Chief Justice Beasley refused to adopt *Rylands* because it did not require the challenged activity to be a nuisance *per se*. Using the example of an alkali works, however, he distinguished those situations in which the causes of injury partake "largely of the character of nuisances," even when they "had been erected upon the best scientific principles." *Marshall v. Welwood*, 38 N.J.L. at 342–43; *see also Ackerman v. Ellis*, 81 N.J.L. 1, 79 A. 883 (Sup.Ct. 1911)(trees whose branches overhand the premises of another are an actionable nuisance).

The confusion occasioned by the rejection of the *Rylands* principle of liability and the continuing adherence to the imposition of liability for a "nuisance" led to divergent results. *See Majestic Realty Assocs., Inc. v. Toti Contracting Co.*, 30 N.J. 425, 433–35, 153 A.2d 321 (1959); *see also McAndrews v. Collerd*, 42 N.J.L. 189 (1880)(storing explosives in Jersey City is a nuisance *per se*, and one who stores them is liable for all actual "injuries caused thereby)". In *Majestic Realty*, this Court abandoned the term "nuisance *per se*," 30 N.J. at 434–35, 153 A.2d 321, and adopted a rule of liability that distinguished between an "ultrahazardous" activity, for which liability is absolute, and an "inherently dangerous" activity, for which liability depends upon proof of negligence. *Id.* at 436, 153 A.2d

321. In making that distinction, the Court implicitly advocated by section 519 of the original *Restatement of Torts, supra.*

This rule, while somewhat reducing the confusion that permeated the law of nuisance, presented the further difficulty of determining whether an activity is "ultrahazardous" or "inherently dangerous." *See, e.g., Adler's Quality Bakery, Inc. v. Gaseteria, Inc.,* 32 N.J. 55, 159 A.2d 97 (1960)(discussing in *dicta* whether aviation should be considered an ultrahazardous activity). Subsequently, in *Berg,* this Court confirmed strict liability of landowners by noting that it was "primarily concerned with the underlying considerations of reasonableness, fairness and morality rather than with the formulary labels to be attached to the plaintiffs' causes of action or the legalistic classifications in which they are to be placed." 37 N.J. at 405, 181 A.2d 487.

More recently, the *Restatement (Second) of Torts* reformulated the standard of landowner liability, substituting "abnormally dangerous" for "ultrahazardous" and providing a list of elements to consider in applying the new standard. *Id.,* §§ 519–20. As noted, this standard incorporates the theory developed in *Rylands v. Fletcher.* Under the *Restatement* analysis, whether an activity is abnormally dangerous is to be determined on a case-by-case basis, taking all relevant circumstances into consideration. As set forth in the *Restatement:*

> In determining whether an activity is abnormally dangerous, the following factors are to be considered:
>
> (a) existence of a high degree of risk of some harm to the person, land or chattels of others;
>
> (b) likelihood that the harm that results from it will be great;
>
> (c) inability to eliminate the risk by the exercise of reasonable care;
>
> (d) extent to which the activity is not a matter of common usage;
>
> (e) inappropriateness of the activity to the place where it is carried on; and
>
> (f) extent to which its value to the community is outweighed by its dangerous attributes.

[*Restatement (Second) of Torts* § 520 (1977)].

Pollution from toxic wastes that seeps onto the land of others and into streams necessarily harms the environment. *See* Special Report to Congress, *Injuries and Damages from Hazardous Wastes—Analysis and Improvement of Legal Remedies in Compliance with section 301(e) of the Comprehensive Environmental Response Compensation and Liability Act of 1980 By the "Superfund Section 301(c) Study Group"* (reprinted as Comm. Print for the Senate Comm. on Envtl. & Pub. Works, Serial No. 97–12, 97th Cong., 2d Sess., 1982) [hereinafter cited as *Special Report*]. Determination of the magnitude of the damage includes recognition that the disposal of toxic waste may cause a variety of harms, including ground water contamination via leachate, surface water contamination via runoff or overflow, and poison via the food chain. *Special Report, supra,* at 27. The lower courts found that each of those hazards was present as a result of the contamination of the entire tract. 182 *N.J.Super.* at 217–18. Further, as was the case here, the waste dumped may react synergistically with elements in the environment, or other waste elements, to form an even more toxic compound. *See* W. Stopford & L.J. Goldwater, "Methylmercury in the Environment, A Review of Current Understanding," 12 *Envtl. Health Persp.* 115–18 (1975). With respect to the ability to eliminate the risks involved in disposing of hazardous wastes by the exercise of reasonable care, no safe was exists to dispose of mercury by simply dumping it onto land or into water.

The disposal of mercury is particularly inappropriate in the Hackensack Meadowlands, an environmentally sensitive area where the arterial waterways will disperse the pollution through the entire ecosystem. Finally, the dumping of untreated hazardous waste is a critical societal problem in New Jersey, which the Environmental Protection Agency estimates is the source of more hazardous waste than any other state. J. Zazzali and F. Grad, "Hazardous Wastes, New Rights and Remedies?," 13 *Seton Hall L.Rev.* 446, 449 n. 12 (1983). From the foregoing, we conclude that mercury and other toxic wastes are "abnormally dangerous," and the disposal of them, past or present, is an abnormally dangerous activity. We recognize that one engaged in the disposing of toxic waste may be performing an activity that is of some use to society. Nonetheless, "the unavoidable risk of harm that is inherent in it requires that it be carried on at his peril, rather than at the expense of the innocent person who suffers harm as a result of it." *Restatement (Second), supra,* comment h at 39.

The Spill Act expressly provides that its remedies are in addition to existing common-law or statutory remedies. N.J.S.A. 58:10–23.11v....

* * *

§ 2.5   TRADITIONAL TORT REMEDIES PERTAINING TO LAND

1. *Negligence*

A common law suit for negligence may be maintained where pollution or environmental harm results from the defendant's negligent actions. A prima facie case of negligence per se may be established by showing the violation of a statute or regulation. Otherwise, the plaintiff will be required to prove the traditional tort elements for negligence— breach of a duty by the defendant by failing to exercise the requisite degree of care.

Where recovery for environmental damage is sought based on a negligence theory, the plaintiff must establish the elements of actual negligence: (1) breach of duty on the part of the manufacturer to plaintiff; (2) injury to a party to whom a duty is owed; (3) the injury proximately resulted from the manufacturer's breach of duty. *Driekosen v. Black, Sivalls & Bryson, Inc.*, 64 N.W.2d 88 (Neb.1954). The manufacturer has a duty to exercise reasonable care to ensure that there is no risk of injury from negligent manufacture, where the product is used in the ordinary manner for which it is intended or in some other reasonably foreseeable manner. 63 Am. Jur. 2d 332. *See* Restatement of Torts 2d sec. 395. The three basic breaches of duty are failure to inspect and test the product, failure to warn of product-connected danger, and negligent product design. 63 Am. Jur. 2d 332, 357–460.

In cases involving claims of environmental or occupational hazards, perhaps the most frequently used theory of liability is negligent failure to warn of a product's inherent dangers. Duty to warn runs only to those dangers the manufacturer knew of.

For example, in *Jersey City Redevelopment Authority v. PPG Industries*, 655 F.Supp. 1257 (D.N.J.1987), the defendant's chromium processing operation produced tons of residue mud which contained chromium. This contaminated mud routinely was removed by a construction company and used as fill material in construction projects. The defendant's property was later sold to the construction company. In an action for damages, the court found that the defendant acted negligently in selling its land to the construction company without properly advising the buyer of the potential risks of chromium contamination. In light of the fact that the defendant knew at the time of the sale that there were major health risks associated with inhalation of chromium and minor risks from direct exposure to chromium even in residue, and it knew that the purchasing company would continue to use the contaminated fill and sell it to others, the court held the defendant was under a duty to advise the purchaser of such risks. The court also held that the purchaser construction company was negligent in distributing the chromium-contaminated fill without warning customers.

The courts have held that a manufacturer or seller is not liable for injuries caused by a defective product if the defect was created by an alteration which amounts to a superseding cause. Accordingly, manufacturers have been exonerated from liability where damage was proximately caused by a substantial alteration of the product subsequent to its sale and not contemplated by the manufacturer. 63 Am. Jur. 2d 249; Prosser, at 711. Likewise, the unforeseeable misuse of a product is a superseding cause; one that the manufacturer could not be expected to guard against in designing the product. Prosser, at 711. In this regard, the courts have found that the destruction and recycling of a product is not a reasonably foreseeable use. Thus the manufacturer has no liability for failure to warn of risks of injuries sustained during such activities.

2. Nuisance

The common law theory which has been the most widely utilized in environmental law is nuisance. Nuisance can be defined as the "wrongful invasion of a legal right or interest, comprehending . . . the wrongful invasion of the *use and enjoyment of property* . . . [and] as conduct that is either unreasonable or unlawful and causes annoyance, inconvenience, discomfort, or damage to others." Nuisance theory can be applied to all three environmental media—air, land and water.

The doctrine of nuisance appears to be centered around the "reasonable use and enjoyment" of one's property. Activities which annoy or disturb one's use of the property or substantially makes its ordinary use uncomfortable, may be nuisances. The determination of whether a nuisance exists if fact specific and will depend upon the extent of the injury suffered by the plaintiff. Thus, the plaintiff must demonstrate that he has suffered a cognizable injury and is not complaining for mere "inconvenience, discomfort, or annoyance."

In analyzing a nuisance claim, the courts have traditionally utilized a balancing approach. This involves determining whether the interference is unreasonable "in the sense that the harm to plaintiffs is greater than . . . the utility of the defendant's conduct." The harm suffered by the plaintiff must be greater than the social usefulness of the activity engaged in by the defendant. Thus, the relief in each case will be fact-specific and involve a balancing approach common to courts of equity.

The law of nuisance can be divided into interferences which invade both public and private interests. These are two distinct tort causes of action. Generally, the distinction does not depend on the nature of the interference with property rights, but rather on the number of individuals affected by the offensive conduct. A public nuisance involves a "right common to the public." The nuisance must affect the public, rather than a specific individual.

NEW YORK v. SHORE REALTY CORP.

759 F.2d 1032 (2d Cir.1985).

OAKES, CIRCUIT JUDGE:

* * *

Under New York law, Shore, as a landowner, is subject to liability for either a public or private nuisance on its property upon learning of the nuisance and having a reasonable opportunity to abate it. . . . *See Pharm v. Lituchy*, 283 N.Y. 130, 132, 27 N.E.2d 811, 812 (1940); *Conhocton Stone Road v. Buffalo, New York & Erie Railroad Co.*, 51 N.Y. 573 (1873); *New York Telephone Co. v. Mobil Oil Corp.*, 99 A.D.2d 185, 188–89, 473 N.Y.S.2d 172, 174 (1984). As noted in the Restatement (Second) of Torts § 839 comment d (1979) [hereinafter cited as Restatement]:

> [L]iability [of a possessor of land] is not based upon responsibility for the creation of the harmful condition, but upon the fact that he has exclusive control over the land and the things done upon it and should have the responsibility of taking reasonable measures to remedy conditions on it that are a source of harm to others. Thus a

> vendee ... of land upon which a harmful physical condition exists maybe liable under the rule here stated for failing to abate it after he takes possession, even though it was created by his vendor, lessor or other person and even though he had no part in its creation.

It is immaterial therefore that other parties placed the chemical on this site; Shore purchased it with knowledge of its condition—indeed of the approximate cost of cleaning it up—and with an opportunity to cleanup the site. LeoGrande knew that the hazardous waste was present without the consent of the State or its DEC, but failed to take reasonable steps to abate the condition. Moreover, Shore is liable for maintenance of a public nuisance irrespective of negligence or fault. *See McFarlane v. City of Niagara Falls*, 247 N.Y. 340, 343, 160 N.E. 391, 391–92 (1928); *Schenectady Chemicals*, 117 Misc.2d at 965, 970, 459 N.Y.S.2d at 976, 979. Nor is there any requirement that the State prove actual as opposed to threatened, harm from the nuisance in order to obtain abatement. *See Southern Leasing Co. v. Ludwig*, 217 N.Y. 100, 104, 111 N.E. 470, 472 (1916); *City of Rochester v. Gutberlett*, 211 N.Y. 309, 316, 105 N.E. 548, 550 (1914); *Wall Street Transcript Corp. v. 343 East 43rd Street Holding Corp.*, 81 A.D.2d 783, 439 N.Y.S.2d 23 (1981); *Buchanan v. Cardozo*, 24 A.D.2d 620, 621, 262 N.Y.S.2d 247, 249 (1965); W. Prosser, Handbook of the Law of Torts § 90, at 603 (1971). Finally, the State has standing to bring suit to abate such a nuisance "in its role as guardian of the environment." *Schenectady Chemicals*, 117 Misc.2d at 968, 459 N.Y.S.2d at 978; *accord State v. Monarch Chemicals, Inc.*, 90 A.D.2d 907, 907, 456 N.Y.S.2d 867, 869 (1982).

We also reject Shore's argument that its maintenance of the Shore Road site does not constitute a public nuisance. We have no doubt that the release or threat of release of hazardous waste into the environment unreasonably infringes upon a public right and thus is a public nuisance as a matter of New York law, *see Schenectady Chemicals*, 103 A.D.2d at 37, 479 N.Y.S.2d at 1013; *Monarch Chemicals*, 90 A.D.2d at 907, 456 N.Y.S.2d at 868–69, particularly in light of Title 13 of Article 27 of the New York Environmental Conservation Law, *see* Restatement § 821B comment c (statutes can indicate that conduct is an "unreasonable interference with a public right"). Shore challenges the existence of the releases or threatened releases claimed by the State. We have found, however, that several crucial facts are undisputed: the tanks have leaked and are corroding; and Shore is unwilling and unable to transform the site into a stable, licensed storage facility. It makes no difference that Shore has begun a cleanup. We simply hold that under New York law it is required to finish that cleanup.

The district court could have also found that Shore is maintaining an public nuisance under two alternative theories. Shore's continuing violations of N.Y. Envt'l. Conserv. Law § 27–0913 (1)(not having a permit to store or dispose of hazardous waste), and of *id.* § 27–0914(1) (possessing hazardous waste without authorization), constitute a nuisance per se. *See Delaney v. Philhern Realty Holding Corp.*, 280 N.Y. 461, 465, 21 N.E.2d 507, 509 (1939); *Driscoll v. New York City Transit*

Authority, 53 A.D.2d 391, 395, 385 N.Y.S.2d 540, 543 (1976). And while we recognize that determining whether an activity is abnormally dangerous depends on the circumstances. A review of the undisputed facts under the guidelines stated in *Doundoulakis v. Town of Hempstead*, 42 N.Y.2d 440, 448, 368 N.E.2d 24, 27, 398 N.Y.S.2d 401, 404 (1977), convinces us that a New York court would find as a matter of law that Shore's maintenance at the site—for example, allowing corroding tanks to hold hundreds of thousands of gallons of hazardous waste—constitutes abnormally dangerous activity and thus constitutes a public nuisance. *See Schenectady Chemicals*, 103 A.D.2d at 37, 479 N.Y.S.2d at 1013; *see also State v. Ventron Corp.*, 94 N.J. 473, 492, 468 A.2d 150, 160 (1983)(holding that "simply dumping [a hazardous substance] onto land or into water" is an abnormally dangerous activity). . . .

* * *

Note

The manufacturer of a defective product may also be held liable on a common law theory of nuisance. The essence of the tort of nuisance is one party using his property to the detriment of the use and enjoyment of others. *City of Bloomington v. Westinghouse Electric Corp.* (7th Cir.1989). Liability for damage caused by a nuisance turns on whether the defendant was in control over the instrumentality alleged to have caused the nuisance, either through ownership or otherwise. If the defendant no longer retains such control, then he has no power to abate the nuisance, and a remedy directed against him is of no use. *City of Manchester v. National Gypsum Co.*, 637 F.Supp. 646 (D.R.I.1986).

Accordingly, a manufacturer of a product may be liable where his product or manufacturing process creates a nuisance on his property, or where he retains control or ownership over the product and it creates a nuisance on another's property. However, it is established that a manufacturer is not liable for nuisance claims arising from the use of his product subsequent to its sale. In *City of Bloomington*, for example, Monsanto manufactured PCBs and sold them in sealed containers for electrical uses. The defendant used the PCBs to manufacture capacitors. PCB-contaminated waste was hauled to landfills and some got into the sewer effluent. The court held that the plaintiff had no viable claims against Monsanto for nuisance for discharging PCBs into the sewer system. The manufacturer did not retain the right to control the PCBs beyond the point of sale. The essence of the tort of nuisance is one party using his property to the detriment of the use and enjoyment of others. Here, the defendant was in control of the product and solely responsible for the nuisance created by not safely disposing of it. *See also City of Manchester v. National Gypsum Co.*, 637 F.Supp. 646, in which the court dismissed nuisance claims asserted against manufacturers of asbestos products for damages associated with the removal and replacement of the products from schools and other public buildings. The instrumentality which created the nuisance was in the possession and control of the plaintiff since the time it purchased the products containing asbestos. The defendants no longer had the power to abate the nuisance and therefore could not be liable for it.

WESTWOOD PHARMACEUTICALS, INC. v. NATIONAL FUEL GAS DISTRIBUTION CORP.

737 F.Supp. 1272 (W.D.N.Y.1990).

CURTIN, DISTRICT JUDGE.

BACKGROUND

Plaintiff Westwood Pharmaceuticals, Inc. ("Westwood"), claims that defendant National Fuel Gas Distribution Corporation ("National Fuel") is liable for Westwood's past and future response costs associated with the release of hazardous substances on a parcel of land in Buffalo, New York, purchased by Westwood from National Fuel's predecessor in interest, Iroquois Gas Corporation ("Iroquois"). Westwood has asserted four causes of action alleging that National Fuel is liable under either the Comprehensive Environmental Response, Compensation and Liability Act ("CERCLA"), 42 U.S.C. § 9601, et seq., as amended by the Superfund Amendments and Reauthorization Act of 1986 ("SARA"), Pub. L. No. 99–499, 100 Stat. 1613 (1986), or the New York State common law of nuisance and unjust enrichment. National Fuel has moved for summary judgment dismissing Westwood's complaint and holding Westwood liable on National Fuel's counter-claims for its past response costs and for any future response costs it may incur. Westwood has moved for partial summary judgment under Section 107(a) of CERCLA, 42 U.S.C. § 9607(a), for Westwood's past response costs; for declaratory judgment pursuant to CERCLA Sections 107(a) and 113(g)(2), 42 U.S.C. §§ 9607(a), 9613(g)(2), and the Declaratory Judgment Act, 28 U.S.C. § 2201(a), on National Fuel's liability for any future response costs that Westwood may incur; and for summary judgment as to most of the affirmative defenses asserted by National Fuel. . . .

FACTS

The site at issue encompasses approximate 8.8 acres bounded on the west by DeWitt Street, on the south by Bradley Street, on the east by Dart Street, and on the north by land owned by the Buffalo Structural Steel Corporation. The northwest corner of the site is bounded by Scajaquada Creek. It appears that the site has been put to industrial use since 1866. Before the land was purchased by People's Gas Company ("People's"), it was used for operations such as a sawmill, an iron-products manufacturing plant, a carriage and sleigh works, and a carriage-top manufacturing company. When People's bought the land in 1897, it constructed a gas-manufacturing plant. In 1925, Iroquois purchased the site for $375,000, gaining title by a referee's deed, and People's was subsequently dissolved in 1932.

Iroquois conducted gas-manufacturing and storage operations on the site through 1951. According to National Fuel,

> [t]ars and waste oils produced by the Iroquois operations were extracted in concrete tar separator pits and stored in tanks pending sale or off-site disposal. . . . Spent oxides generated in the gas purification process were taken off-site for disposal. . . . Ash and

cinders were stored on site temporarily and then removed for use or disposal elsewhere.

. . . Iroquois halted gas-manufacturing operations at the site in 1951, but continued to use the location for gas compression and storage for several years thereafter. In 1968, it had certain structures on the premises demolished, primarily, it appears, on the northern portion of the site. The structures that were demolished included a 1.75–million-cubic-foot gas holder, a one-million-gallon oil tank, a relief holder, a gas-purifying house, and at lease two tar-separator pits. Other structures on the southern portion of the premises were left standing. National Fuel states that

> [i]n connection with the demolition, oils, tars, coal, coke, spent oxides, and various wastes from the gas manufacturing process were removed from the site for sale or disposal. . . . Underground pipelines were purged with an inert gas and plugged. . . . The tar separator pits were pumped out, the above-ground portions were collapsed into the sub-surface sections . . . and were covered with a clay cap.

. . .

In 1972, Westwood, which since at least 1942 had occupied what appears to be an adjacent parcel, purchased the property from Iroquois in order to accommodate its planned expansion; the purchase price was $60,100. The sales contract, which provided that it was to be "governed by and construed in accordance with the laws of the State of New York," . . . provided Westwood the right to pre-closing access to the property to

> (a) inspect the Premises upon reasonable notice to the Seller; (b) enter the Premises for purposes of inspection and planning for Purchaser's occupancy and for the demolition of buildings and improvements; and (c) commence the demolition of buildings and improvements situated upon the Premises. . . .

Id., Exhibit L at ¶ 5. Westwood subsequent demolished the remaining structures at the site. According to Westwood, although it was told that "all buildings, tanks, pipelines and other improvements situate [sic] on the premises had been purged of natural gas and other chemicals" used in the business operations on the site, it was never told "of the existence of the partially demolished remains of buildings, process equipment, and waste residues left buried at the premises." . . . For its part, National Fuel claims that Iroquois was never told of Westwood's development plans prior to the sale, . . . although it seems unlikely that Iroquois was not aware that construction of some type would be undertaken at the site.

Westwood subsequently constructed a warehouse on the southern portion of the property. Soil borings associated with the construction were taken in 1973, and, according to National Fuel, those boring indicated "widespread petroleum-product contamination of the site." . . . Soil borings were also taken in 1984 and 1985 in connection with the construction of a warehouse on the northern portion of the site, . . . and they revealed petroleum-related contaminants and other wastes. During excavation for the second warehouse, Westwood encountered subsurface pipeline and the remains of three separator pits and a filtered bed. According to Westwood, the separator pits were filled with "demolition debris, and a mixture of water, tar, and waste oil"; the filter bed contained "oily contaminated water"; and the pipes contained "various process residues and waste materials." . . . In February, 1985, Westwood had a consultant dig a series of test pits on the location of the planned warehouse, and soil samplings from the pits apparently also displayed signs of petroleum-related contamination. . . .

National Fuel alleges that Westwood continued with construction far too prematurely. It claims that "[n]otwithstanding these repeated and detailed reports of widespread petroleum produce contamination of the project area, Westwood did not initiate an investigation into the origin or scope of the contamination." . . . National Fuel also claims that Westwood likewise failed to confer with "its environmental consultants, its architects, its general construction contractor, or anyone else, to determine whether the conditions encountered required action to protect against a release of these substances into the environment." *Id.* at 10–11. National Fuel asserts that "[o]n numerous occasions" in late 1985 and early 1986 it expressed concern to Westwood about the manner and pace of the construction activities, and that its concern over containing the migration of suspected wastes on or from the site led it to ask Westwood at least to modify those activities. National Fuel states that it reiterated these concerns by letter in February, 1986, . . . but that Westwood nonetheless proceeded with construction on an "expedited basis." . . .

In any event, it appears that the clay cap was removed from the site in October, 1985, during the early phases of construction of the second warehouse, and that Westwood subsequently continued with construction activities. The initial phase of construction apparently involved stripping topsoil to a depth of eighteen inches, and, according to National Fuel, it was during this process that the clay cap was removed. . . . It appears that the separator pits were initially discovered by Westwood in approximately November, 1985.

Westwood states that, after submitting the materials it discovered at the site for chemical analysis, it contracted for the removal of the contaminated soil and the water matter "in a manner which was consistent with the applicable waste management regulations of the New York Environmental Conservation Law." . . . Westwood also states that, subject to review and comment by the New York State Department of Environmental Conservation ("DEC"), it initiated procedures designed to investigate the extent of soil and groundwater contamination at the site that included "the installation, sampling and analysis of groundwater monitoring wells, in a manner which is consistent with the provisions of the National Contingency Plan." *Id.* It is not clear, however, precisely when these actions were taken.

Westwood asserts that "[t]he investigations conducted to date have established the existence of a release of hazardous substances at the Premises and have confirmed that the hazardous substances found at the site are constituents of the wastes and by-products from the gas manufacturing operations conducted there by [Iroquois]." ... Westwood states that it has thus far incurred over $650,000 in costs associated with the investigation and cleanup of the site, and that it expects to incur additional costs. National Fuel asserts that it has spent over $75,000 in costs associated with its own investigation of the site that was required by Westwood's construction activities.

* * *

DISCUSSION

* * *

c) Caveat Emptor
WESTWOOD'S CERCLA CLAIM

National Fuel ... argues that Westwood's CERCLA claim is barred by the New York State common-law doctrine of caveat emptor. National Fuel argues that the extremely low contract price "presumably" reflected the parties' understanding that, under New York law, National Fuel would not be liable to Westwood for any condition of the property.... The United States Court of Appeals for the Third Circuit, however, rejected such an argument in *Smith Land & Improvement Corp. v. Celotex Corp.*, 851 F.2d 86 (3d Cir.1988), cert. denied, 488 U.S. 1029, 109 S.Ct. 837, 102 L.Ed.2d 969 (1989), and the court finds the analysis done by the Third Circuit to be persuasive.... Accepting National Fuel's position clearly would be inconsistent with Congress's intent, in enacting CERCLA, to provide for swift clean-up of hazardous substances by all responsible parties under a uniform national scheme. *See also In Re Acushnet River & New Bedford Harbor*, 712 F.Supp. 1010, 1013–14 (D.Mass.1989); *United States v. Hooker Chemicals & Plastics Corp.*, 680 F.Supp. 546, 556–57 (W.D.N.Y.1988). Consequently, the court holds that Westwood's CERCLA claim is not barred by the doctrine of caveat emptor.

The court also notes the fundamental unfairness of National Fuel's argument. While National Fuel properly argues that, under New York law, the doctrine of caveat emptor bars Westwood's private-nuisance claim, see infra at subsection "iii," it is difficult to understand how National Fuel can argue that Westwood also bargained-away National Fuel's CERCLA liability in light of fact that that statutory scheme was passed approximately eight years after the site at issue was conveyed to Westwood. Rather, logic and fairness dictate that, barring appropriate contractual language amply indicating otherwise, Westwood bargained away National Fuel's future liability only insofar as National Fuel's liability was shaped by the legal principles operative at the time of the conveyance. In other words, while Westwood may have bargained-away its ability to bring an action based on private nuisance against National

Fuel in light of then-established New York common-law principles, it did not relinquish its right to bring an action based on statutes such as CERCLA and SARA that were not in existence at the time of the conveyance. The soundness of this result is buttressed by the fact that it furthers the compelling congressional goal underlying the enactment of these statutes—"respon[ding] to the severe environmental and public health effects posed by the disposal of hazardous wastes." *United States v. Hooker Chemicals & Plastics Corp.*, 680 F.Supp. at 548.

The case upon which National Fuel primarily relies, *Mardan Corp. v. C.G.C. Music, Ltd.*, 804 F.2d 1454 (9th Cir.1986), does not hold otherwise. In finding that a successor landowner had contracted away any claim it might have had under CERCLA, the district court in that case noted that the purchaser had at least constructive knowledge of any such potential claim because CERCLA had been in existence for nearly a year at the time the settlement agreement and release at issue were executed. *Mardan Corp. v. C.G.C. Music, Ltd.*, 600 F.Supp. 1049, 1057 (D.Ariz.1984). That factor was specifically cited by the Ninth Circuit in affirming the district court's decision. 804 F.2d at 1463.

WESTWOOD'S PUBLIC-NUISANCE CLAIM

National Fuel also contends that the doctrine of caveat emptor deprives Westwood of standing to maintain a public-nuisance action.... In support of its argument, National Fuel cite *Philadelphia Electric Co. v. Hercules, Inc.*, 762 F.2d 303, 315–16 (3d Cir.), *cert. denied*, 474 U.S. 980, 106 S.Ct. 384, 88 L.Ed.2d 337 (1985), a case in which the Third Circuit determined that Pennsylvania law did not provide a landowner with a cause of action based on public nuisance against the corporate successor of the vendor from whom the landowner had originally purchased the property.

New York law, however, supports Westwood's claim of standing. In *Copart Industries, Inc. v. Consolidated Edison Co.*, 41 N.Y.2d 564, 394 N.Y.S.2d 169, 362 N.E.2d 968 (1977), the New York Court of Appeals defined public nuisance as "conduct or omissions which offend, interfere with or cause damage to the public in the exercise of rights common to all ... in a manner such as to offend public morals, interfere with use by the public of a public place or endanger or injure the property, health, safety or comfort of a considerable number of persons." *Id.* at 172, 362 N.E.2d at 791 (citations omitted). In order for a private party to maintain an action for public nuisance, "the harm suffered must be 'of a different kind from that suffered by other persons exercising the same public right.' " *Burns Jackson Miller Summit & Spitzer v. Lindner*, 59 N.Y.2d 314, 464 N.Y.S.2d 712, 721, 451 N.E.2d 459, 468 (1983)(quoting Restatement (Second) of Torts § 821C comment b (1977)).

With regard to the issue of what constitutes a public nuisance under state law, the Second Circuit has held that "the release or threat of release of hazardous waste into the environment unreasonably infringes upon a public right and thus is a public nuisance as a matter of New York law." *State of New York v. Shore Realty Corp.*, 759 F.2d at 1051 (citations omitted).... *See also United States v. Hooker Chemicals & Plastics Corp.*, 722 F.Supp. 960, 965 (W.D.N.Y.1989); *United States v. Hooker Chemicals & Plastics Corp.*, 118 F.R.D. 321, 324 (W.D.N.Y.1987). Westwood has provided evidence that at least some of the materials found on the premises were hazardous substances associated with Iroquois's gas-manufacturing and storage operations. Consequently, resolving all ambiguities and drawing all reasonable inferences in its favor, Westwood has provided sufficient evidence for a reasonably jury to conclude that National Fuel is responsible for the release or threatened release of hazardous waste into the environment.

With regard to the issue of whether Westwood has suffered harm "of a different kind from that suffered by other persons exercising the same public right," the court finds that if Westwood can establish, as it claims, that it has incurred response costs consistent with the National Contingency Plan ("NCP"), see 42 U.S.C. §§ 9601(31), 9607(a), those costs will be sufficient to meet this criterion for bringing a public-nuisance action. *See* Restatement (Second) of Torts § 821C comment h (1977); *Philadelphia Electric Co. v. Hercules, Inc.*, 762 F.2d at 316.

The court thus rejects National Fuel's argument that Westwood's public-nuisance claim is barred because, according to National Fuel, Westwood had an adequate opportunity between 1972 and 1985 to investigate the site and to remove any alleged nuisance.... This conclusion is bolstered by the nature of the alleged public nuisance involved here—contamination of the environment by hazardous substances. Knowledge about the hazardous to public health and to the environment posed by hazardous wastes is increasing constantly, and this court is not willing to assume that the New York law of public nuisance is too inflexible to meet the growing public need for avenues to address these hazardous, including lawsuits where public interests are being protected through a cause of action brought by a private party.

WESTWOOD'S PRIVATE-NUISANCE CLAIM

National Fuel also contends that the doctrine of caveat emptor bars Westwood's common-law private-nuisance claim.... Westwood replies that under New York law there is no such bar to its claim, arguing that the New York doctrine against alienation of nuisance should be applied to "override" this defense....

The general rule under New York law is that the sale of real property is governed by the doctrine of caveat emptor. *See, e.g., Lindlots Realty Corp. v. Suffolk County*, 278 N.Y. 45, 54, 15 N.E.2d 393 (1938); *London v. Courduff*, 141 A.D.2d 803, 529 N.Y.S.2d 874, 875 (2d Dep't), lv. to appeal denied, 73 N.Y.2d 809, 537 N.Y. S.2d 494, 534, N.E.2d 332 (1988); *De Roche v. Dame*, 75 A.D.2d 384, 430 N.Y.S.2d 390, 392 (3d Dep't); appeal denied, 51 N.Y.2d 821, 433 N.Y.S.2d 427, 413 N.E.2d 366 (1980). While the New York Court of Appeals has abolished the defense of caveat emptor in cases involving contracts for the constructions and sale of homes, *see Caceci v. Di Canio Construction Corp.*, 72 N.Y.2d 52, 530 N.Y.S.2d 771, 526 N.E.2d 266 (1988), Westwood has provided no convincing reason for this court to assume that the Court of Appeals would likewise refuse to apply the doctrine where, as in the present case, the vendor and the vendee of the property at issue are both sophisticated commercial enterprises who agreed to a purchase price based, apparently in large part, on the condition of the property at the time of conveyance. (footnote omitted).

Westwood has cited three cases in support of its argument that New York courts would apply the doctrine against alienation of nuisances under these facts, but each is readily distinguishable from the case at bar.

Westwood correctly points out that in *Pharm v. Lituchy* the New York Court of Appeals recognized the principle that a landowner who creates a nuisance cannot escape liability to third persons for injuries caused by the nuisance simply by having sold the property before the injuries were sustained. The court, however, qualified its holding by stating that a vendor's liability "persists beyond conveyance *at least until the new owner has had reasonable opportunity to discover the condition on prompt inspection and to make necessary repairs*.... We need not determine its limits more precisely." 283 N.Y. at 132, 27 N.E.2d 811....

Subsequent case law has reaffirmed that there are limits to a vendor's liability in such cases. For example, in *New York Telephone Co. v. Mobil Oil Corp.*, 99 A.D.2d 185, 473 N.Y.S.2d 172 (1st Dep't 1984), one of New York's intermediate appellate courts held:

> The owner of land ceases to be liable in negligence for its dangerous condition when the ownership of the premises or possession and control pass to another before the injury is sustained. *Even where a continuing trespass or nuisance exists,* liability of the owner terminates after the conveyance at such time at the new owner has had a reasonable opportunity to discover the condition by making prompt inspection and necessary repairs.

Id., 473 N.Y.S.2d at 174 (emphasis added)(citing *Pharm v. Lituchy*). The court held that a former gasoline-station owner and its gasoline supplier were not liable in nuisance to an adjoining property owner for damage allegedly caused by leakage from subsurface gasoline tanks that had been installed by the owner and the supplier. In reaching its decision, the court found that the subsequent owner and its lessee.... had had ample opportunity to discover the nuisance and to make appropriate repairs during the more than nine years that, collectively, they had owned, possessed, and controlled the premises and had conducted opinions thereon. 473 N.Y.S.2d at 175.... *See also Zeledon v. Bowery Savings Bank*, 195 Misc. 933, 85 N.Y.S.2d 414 (1948), *appeal dismissed*, 276 A.D. 898, 95 N.Y.S.2d 345 (1st Dep't 1950)(six months "more than enough" time to give successor property owner reasonable opportunity to discover and to repair nuisance (defective fire escape), thereby terminating any potential liability of two prior owners to injured party); *Tri-Boro Bowling Center, Inc. v. Roosevelt Eighty–Fifth Estates, Inc.*, 77

N.Y.S.2d 74 (N.Y.Sup.Ct.1947)(former property owner not liable for damages caused by nuisance (collapsed ceiling) over four years after property was conveyed). *Cf. Rufo v. South Brooklyn Savings Bank*, 268 A.D. 1057, 52 N.Y.S.2d 469 (2d Dep't 1945), *appeal dismissed*, 295 N.Y. 981, 68 N.E.2d 60 (1946)(after verdict indicating that jury had found approximately one month to be sufficient time for successor property owner to discover and to repair nuisance (defective stair tread) that had existed at time property was conveyed, verdict against codefendant prior owner reversed). The court concludes that, whatever the precise limits they might otherwise place on the applicability of the doctrine against alienation of nuisances, New York courts would find on the present record that Westwood had a reasonable opportunity to discover and to take steps to abate the alleged nuisance between 1972 and 1985.

Westwood also cites the New York Court of Appeals' affirmance in *State v. Ole Olsen, Ltd.*, 65 Misc.2d 366, 317 N.Y.S.2d 538 (1971), aff'd, 38 A.D.2d 967, 331 N.Y.S.2d 761 (2d Dep't 1972), after trial, 76 Misc.2d 796, 352 N.Y.S.2d 97 (1973), *aff'd mem.*, 45 A.D.2d 821, 357 N.Y.S.2d 1016 (2d Dep't 1974), aff'd as modified, 35 N.Y.2d 979, 365 N.Y.S.2d 528, 324 N.E.2d 886 (1975), as a recent reaffirmation by the court of the doctrine against alienation of nuisances. Westwood relies on the court's statement that "these defendants had conveyed all their interest in the properties in question to the present homeowners or their predecessors in title several years ago." 35 N.Y.2d 979, 365 N.Y.S.2d at 529, 324 N.E.2d 886. . . .

Ole Olsen does not advance Westwood's position for three reasons. First, that case involved a public-nuisance action brought by the State of New York against the developers of a residential tract comprised of individual vacation homes. Second, National Fuel is not challenging the continuing viability of the doctrine against alienation of nuisances; rather, it is arguing that the doctrine does not apply in the present case. Third, while the doctrine against alienation of nuisances was discussed in *Ole Olsen*, see 317 N.Y.S.2d at 541; 331 N.Y.S.2d at 763; 352 N.Y.S.2d at 99–100, . . . Westwood is simply reading too much into the portion of the Court of Appeals' opinion that it cites. That statement was not made in the context of rejecting a defense of caveat emptor. Rather, when read in light of the history of that litigation, it is clear that the statement was made in response to the defendants' claim, maintained from the outset of the lawsuit, that the trial court did not have the power to order remedial relief that required the defendants to enter upon the land of another where the defendants had not reserved any right to reenter at the time of conveyance. *See* 317 N.Y.S.2d at 541–42; 331 N.Y.S.2d at 763. As the Court of Appeals went on to state in its opinion:

Problems of fashioning remedial relief other than by way of damage against these defendants who no longer hold any interest in the properties, have been obviated in this case. All presently affected homeowners have been made parties to this action. None has taken exception to that portion of the judgement by which each is directed to permit reasonable entrance on his property for [abatement of the nuisance].

365 N.Y.S.2d at 529, 324 N.E.2d at 886. The opinion simply does not vindicate Westwood's claim that the defense of caveat emptor is inapplicable to a private-nuisance claim brought by a commercial purchaser of land who had many years to discovery and to take steps to abate an alleged nuisance.

Finally, in *Tahini Investments, Ltd. v. Bobrowsky*, 99 A.D.2d 489, 470 N.Y.S.2d 431 (2d Dep't 1984), cited by Westwood as an example of how New York courts have recognized exceptions to the defense of caveat emptor, ... the court did not even discuss the defense.

Without a more definitive indication from New York's courts that the state's common-law doctrine of caveat emptor does not apply to cases such as the one at bar, well-established principles of federalism dictate that this court refrain from extending the scope of private-nuisance liability beyond its traditional bounds. National Fuel's motion for summary judgment with regard to Westwood's private-nuisance claim is, therefore, granted.

* * *

Notes

1. The *Westwood Pharmaceuticals, Inc. v. National Fuel Gas Distribution Corp.* court ruled "that a CERCLA claim is not barred by the doctrine of caveat emptor." Do you agree with the court's reasoning?

2. Compare this case with *Smith Land & Improvement Corp. v. Celotex Corp.*, 851 F.2d 86, in which the court held that the doctrine of although caveat emptor is not a defense to liability for contribution under CERCLA, the doctrine may be considered in mitigation of the amount due. Which ruling do you find more persuasive?

3. Trespass

An action for trespass may also be utilized in environmental cases. A trespass is defined as "any intentional invasion of the plaintiff's interest in the exclusive possession of property." This doctrine is closely related to nuisance; the basic distinction is that nuisance causes a "substantial and unreasonable interference" whereas trespass causes an actual "encroachment by 'something' upon the plaintiff's exclusive rights of possession."

Distinguishing between what conduct constitutes a trespass rather than a nuisance can be difficult. If any doubt exists, a practitioner may choose to assert both theories because of the doctrinal overlap of the two theories. For example, in the case where gases and odors enter the property, an action for trespass has been held not to exist. However, if airborne particulates fall onto another's land an action for trespass exists. Therefore, one should determine if there has been an actual invasion of a pollutants on the plaintiff's property to determine if a trespass action can be asserted.

§ 2.6   PUBLIC OBLIGATIONS

1. *Inverse Condemnation*

Inverse condemnation is a theory which may be asserted against a governmental entity when private property is taken because of environmental pollution. The plaintiff in an inverse condemnation action must establish that the property was "taken" in violation of the Fifth Amendment. Thus, pollution which invades an individual's property by air, land or water, done by federal, state or municipal authorities may constitute an inverse condemnation.

2. *Public Trust Doctrine*

The public trust doctrine provides that "when a state holds a resource which is available for the free use of the general public, a court will look with considerable skepticism upon any governmental conduct which is calculated either to reallocate that resource to more restricted uses or to subject public uses to the self-interest of private parties." The public trust doctrine typically applies to submerged lands and navigable waters. Thus, the government has the duty to act as trustee to protect the public resources; if it fails to do so, citizen's may attempt to bring their own cause of action to enforce this right.

3. *Aiding & Abetting Liability*

O'NEIL v. Q.L.C.R.I., INC.

750 F.Supp. 551 (D.R.I.1990).

PETTINE, SENIOR DISTRICT JUDGE.

I.   MOTIONS TO DISMISS AND AMEND

Davisville is involved in this case because it granted two mortgages on the land that is the subject of this case and because it currently holds a mortgage on the land. Plaintiff, the Attorney General, alleges three types of claims against Davisville. In the original complaint, plaintiff alleges that "[i]f the Davisville Credit Union forecloses upon the land under the Ryan mortgage and fails to halt the discharge, Davisville Credit Union, or its successors, will violate" federal and state statutory and common law and that Davisville's present mortgage interest is subject to a 1979 Department of Environmental (DEM) Management order. In its amended complaint, plaintiff alleges that Davisville aided and abetted violations of federal and state statutory and common law.

* * *

B.   *Aiding and Abetting Claims*

The futility of an amended claim is a proper basis for its denial. *Foman v. Davis*, 371 U.S. at 182, 83 S.Ct. at 230; *Vargas v. McNamara,*

608 F.2d 15, 18 (1st Cir.1979). This Court will begin, therefore, by analyzing the aiding and abetting claims under the same standards used in a motion to dismiss.

Plaintiff seeks to use the common law concept of aiding and abetting to find Davisville in violation of federal and state statutory and common law. The Restatement (Second) of Torts § 876 sets out the standard for aiding and abetting liability: "For harm resulting to a third person from the tortious conduct of another, one is subject to liability if he . . . (b) knows that the other's conduct constitutes a breach of duty and gives substantial assistance or encouragement to the other so to conduct himself. . . ." Plaintiff alleges that Davisville's close relationship with the principals is shown by the two "straw conveyances," namely the Davisville mortgages. They allege that Davisville "collaborated in a scheme to lend money to a borrower in the name of another." Most importantly, plaintiff alleges that Davisville had "influence and control" over the principal polluters because Davisville knew of the sewage problem and could have conditioned the loans on the fixing of the sewage problem.

Davisville argues that there is no aiding and abetting liability under the "citizen suit" provision of the Federal Water Pollution Control Act (FWPCA), 33 U.S.C. § 1365. Section 1365(a) allows for suit:

> (1) against any person . . . who is alleged to be in violation of (A) an effluent standard or limitation under this chapter or (B) an order issued by the Administrator or a State with respect to such a standard or limitation, or

> (2) against the Administrator where there is alleged a failure of the Administrator to perform any act or duty under this chapter which is not discretionary with the Administrator.

Davisville relies on a series of cases, primarily *Ringbolt Farms Homeowners Ass'n v. Town of Hull*, 714 F.Supp. 1246 (D.Mass.1989) and *Love v. New York State Dep't of Environmental Conservation*, 529 F.Supp. 832 (S.D.N.Y.1981), in support of its argument that § 1365 allows suit against only the principal polluter.

Plaintiff, in his reply brief, persuasively argues that Davisville's cases are not controlling. The cases cited by Davisville are suits against state regulators. The states have a special role under the FWPCA through the National Pollutant Discharge Elimination System (NPDES) program, see 33 U.S.C. § 1342(b). A number of cases have held that states' decisions regarding permits under NPDES are not reviewable in federal court. *See American Paper Institute, Inc. v. EPA*, 890 F.2d 869 (7th Cir.1989); *District of Columbia v. Schramm*, 631 F.2d 854 (D.C.Cir. 1980); *Mianus River Preservation Comm. v. Administrator, EPA*, 541 F.2d 899 (2d Cir.1976). *Love* and *Ringbolt Farms* were attempts to circumvent this series of cases and to find state agencies indirectly liable for being "in violation" under § 1365. As plaintiff's reply brief explains in great detail, the courts distinguished state agencies from direct polluters and held that plaintiffs could not reach state regulators in this fashion. *See Ringbolt Farms*, 714 F.Supp. at 1253; *Love*, 529 F.Supp. at

839. Because so much of the reasoning involved in these cases deals with the special role of the states, their holdings do not control a suit against a private party.

In the absence of controlling cases, this Court must determine whether the common law concept of aiding and abetting can be used to determine liability under the FWPCA. "[T]he applicability of common law doctrines in litigation under federal statutes depends on whether these principles advance the goals of the particular federal statute which plaintiffs allege has been violated." *Petro-Tech Inc. v. Western Co. of North America*, 824 F.2d 1349 (3d Cir.1987)(citations omitted). The doctrine of aiding and abetting has been found to further the goals of other federal statutes. *See, e.g., FDIC v. First Interstate Bank of Des Moines*, 885 F.2d 423 (8th Cir.1989)(banking laws); *Petro-Tech*, 824 F.2d 1349 (RICO); *Metge v. Baehler*, 762 F.2d 621 (8th Cir.1985), *cert. denied*, 474 U.S. 1057, 106 S.Ct. 798, 88 L.Ed.2d 774 (1986) (Securities Act of 1934).

The Supreme Court has ruled that the FWPCA preempts the federal common law of public nuisance. *Milwaukee v. Illinois and Michigan*, 451 U.S. 304, 319, 101 S.Ct. 1784, 1793, 68 L.Ed.2d 114 (1981). This does not mean that the FWPCA preempts consideration of an aiding and abetting theory. *Milwaukee* dealt with a separate cause of action, whereas aiding and abetting is a concept that can be used to interpret "in violation" under § 1365. *See Petro–Tech*, 824 F.2d at 1357 ("The doctrine of aiding and abetting is simply one way that an individual can violate the substantive ... law."). In *Milwaukee*, the Supreme Court reached its decision by noting that the vague federal common law nuisance standards had been replaced when Congress thoroughly addressed the issue of effluent standards in the FWPCA. *Milwaukee*, 451 U.S. at 320, 101 S.Ct. at 1794. As the Court stated, the "question was whether the legislative scheme 'spoke directly to a question.'" *Id.* at 315, 101 S.Ct. at 1791 (citations omitted). Nothing in the FWPCA rules out the use of the aiding and abetting doctrine. Because the concept could be useful in interpreting who is "in violation," claims based on aiding and abetting a violation of the FWPCA will not be ruled out.

Plaintiff has alleged sufficient involvement and possible control on the part of Davisville to present a viable claim of aiding and abetting. This Court, therefore, rejects Davisville's arguments that the FWPCA bars aiding and abetting claims. Davisville has presented no arguments for disallowing aiding and abetting claims in relation to the state statutory and common law claims. Thus, all the aiding and abetting claims can withstand a motion to dismiss and are not futile.

This Court further holds that it would not prejudice Davisville to allow plaintiff to amend the complaint to add the aiding and abetting claims because they are based on the same factual allegations as those in the original claims against Davisville. The motion to amend Counts I, II, III, and IV to add aiding and abetting claims is therefore granted.

C. Claim relating to 1979 DEM order.

Plaintiff seeks to have this Court find that Davisville's present mortgage is subject to the 1979 order of the DEM. Defendant argues that there is no basis for equitable subordination in this case and that the claim should be dismissed. This Court has already allowed the plaintiff to add a claim of aiding and abetting a violation of the DEM order. If plaintiff prevails on this claim, this Court may reach Davisville's security interest in fashioning relief. Plaintiff has thus alleged a basis for the requested relief to be granted. The motion to dismiss Count III, ¶ 115 is denied.

CONCLUSION

Davisville has demonstrated that the claims relating to the possibility it will foreclose in the future do not present a case or controversy and must be dismissed. The aiding and abetting claims are viable, however, and because adding them will not prejudice Davisville, plaintiff is given leave to amend the complaint. Plaintiff has also alleged facts sufficient to support the claim under the 1979 DEM order.

* * *

§ 2.7 CAUSES OF ACTION ARISING FROM THE LAND-LORD/TENANT RELATIONSHIP

1. Constructive Eviction

Constructive eviction due to the presence of hazardous substances will be recognized in two situations. If essential building services are materially disrupted in the course of removal or abatement, an action for constructive eviction may lie. Also, if the potential hazard of exposure or harm so significantly deprives the tenant of the use of the property, constructive eviction may be recognized. Glazerman, Asbestos in Commercial Buildings: Obligations and Responsibilities of Landlords and Tenants., 22 Real Prop., Prob. & Tr. J. 661, 680 (1987). *See also* 49 Am. Jur. 2d Landlord and Tenant § 310 (1970).

In *Versatile Metals, Inc. v. Union Corp.*, 693 F.Supp. 1563 (E.D.Pa. 1988), a tenant claimed that they were constructively evicted by the contamination on the leased property. However, the court refused to grant their claims because the tenant had contributed significantly to the contamination after taking possession. Citing *No. 14 Coal Co. v. Pennsylvania Co.*, 416 Pa. 218, 206 A.2d 57, 58 (1965), the court held that the covenant of quiet possession related only to the acts of the lessor and those acting under him and do not extend to the "conduct of other persons by which the value or the comfort of the lease hold may be diminished."

2. Waste

One court has held that the failure of a lessee to use reasonable care upon discovery of contamination may constitute waste. *See Versatile Metals, Inc. v. Union Corp.*, 693 F.Supp. 1563 (E.D.Pa.1988). In this case, the court upheld a jury verdict that the lessee/buyer was liable for reasonable cleanup costs incurred by the seller/lessor in restoring the property to its former condition before the tenancy. The court cited the basic tenet of landlord tenant law, that is, that under state law (here, Pennsylvania) there exists an implied covenant to return a leasehold premises in substantially the same condition in which it existed when received, except for unusual wear and tear, and uninjured by any willful or negligent act of the lessee. *United States Gypsum Co. v. Schiavo Bros. Inc.*, 450 F.Supp. 1291 (1978) *aff'd in part, rev'd in part*, 668 F.2d 172 (3d Cir.1981), *cert. denied*, 456 U.S. 961, 102 S.Ct. 2038, 72 L.Ed.2d 485 (1982) (*quoting Earle v. Arbogast*, 180 Pa. 409 36 A. 923 (1897)).

3. *Frustration of Purpose*

Another possible claim by a tenant upon discovery of contamination would be frustration of purpose. To prevail on this claim, a tenant would need to show that the intended use of the land was totally or absolutely frustrated. Glazerman, Asbestos in Commercial Buildings: Obligations and Responsibilities of Landlords and Tenants, 22 Real Prop., Prob. & Tr. J., 661, 681 (1987). The court in *Wooldridge v. Exxon Corp.*, 39 Conn. Supp. 190, 473 A.2d 1254 (1984), held that mere economic hardship due to circumstances beyond the control of the lessor and the lessee was insufficient to rescind a lease agreement for frustration of purpose.

§ 2.8 FRAUD, MISREPRESENTATION & THE LIKE

1. *Misrepresentation*

A manufacturer or seller of a product may also incur strict liability for misrepresentation. This liability arises for injury caused by a defective product where by advertising or labels or otherwise the seller makes to the public a misrepresentation of material fact concerning the character or quality of the product, and the injured party justifiably relies upon the misrepresentation, even though it is not made fraudulently or negligently. Restatement of Torts 2d sec. 402B; 63 Am Jur. 2d 836.

Liability may also arise for negligent misrepresentation of a product. A seller is liable if not knowing or caring whether representations are true or false, represents that the article is safe for a certain use, when in fact it is dangerous. In other words, an ordinarily careful person would not have made the representation under the circumstances. Failure to warn of a product's inherent danger may amount to negligent misrepresentation. 63 Am. Jur. 2d 840.

2. *Fraud*

A manufacturer or retailer who sells a product and represents it to be safe for the purposes for which it is designed to serve, when he knows it is dangerous because of concealed defects, has acted fraudulently and may be liable for injuries to a buyer who has no knowledge of its defective character. 63 Am. Jur. 2d 825. The fraud may arise in deceitful advertising, or purposeful concealment of the defect, or deliberate failure to disclose the defect. To sustain a cause of action for fraud, the plaintiff must prove the manufacturer made a misrepresentation or concealed a defect, knew it to be false or was reckless in disregarding the truth, and the fraud caused injury. *Id.*

Even though the Federal Rules of Civil Procedure require pleading fraud with particularity (FRCP 9(b)), in cases involving toxic substances, it is not necessary to plead fraud with a great deal of specificity. All that is required is a short and plain statement of the basis for the suit. *Johns-Manville Asbestosis Cases*, 511 F.Supp. 1229 (1981). Thus, in *United States v. Southeastern Pennsylvania Transportation Authority*, 1986 WL 7565 (E.D.Pa.1986), the court sustained as sufficient a complaint which alleged that the defendant fraudulently concealed the dangers and risk involved in its activities at the railroad yard, and they knew or should have known that plaintiffs were exposed to serious risk of PCBs, knew that runoff with PCBs was entering residences and adjacent properties, the environment and the community, and intentionally failed to issue warnings regarding the PCB contamination. Similarly, in *Town of Hooksett School District v. W.R. Grace & Co.*, 617 F.Supp. 126 (D.N.H.1984), the plaintiff adequately presented a claim for fraudulent concealment, where it was alleged that the asbestos manufacturer concealed the fact that it had reason to know that asbestos posed a serious health risk to all those who might come into contact with it.

WEYERHAEUSER CO. v. EDWARD HINES LUMBER CO.

1991 WL 169385 (N.D. Ill.1991).

KOCORAS, DISTRICT JUDGE.

* * *

Through this litigation the plaintiff seeks to recoup its contractual losses pursuant to noncontractual theories of liability. The focus of the suit is the sale of the "Wolcott property," a piece of land previously owned by Defendant Edward Hines Lumber Company ("Hines"). Plaintiff Weyerhaeuser Company ("Weyerhaeuser") alleges that it signed a contract for the purchase of this land from Hines on April 18, 1986.

According to the complaint, Hines used the Wolcott property for 75 years in the operation of its lumber business and, in the course of that business, stored and disposed of chemical wastes on the property. Hines also allegedly installed and maintained underground storage tanks from which chemical waste has been discharged into the structures, soil, subsoil, and underground water. Weyerhaeuser claims that Hines knew of the discharge or threat of discharge long before the parties entered into negotiations for the sale of the Wolcott property, but never notified the plaintiff of such problems.

On May 2, 1986, two weeks after the alleged execution of the sale contract Weyerhaeuser allegedly wrote to Hines, indicating

> Weyerhaeuser ... requires written disclosure that no hazardous substances are on, in, under, or otherwise associated with this property, or if any exist their location, content, age and extent.

Complaint Exhibit B. Hines allegedly never answered the letter. Weyerhaeuser asserts that it relied on the defendant's (silent) representation that there were no known environmental problems in determining whether to enter into the sales contract.

The complaint also states that the defendant's non-disclosure occurred prior to the consummation of the contract and during negotiations. However, there is no indication of the circumstances in which such non-disclosure took place. The plaintiff concludes that as a result of Hines' fraudulent concealment, the plaintiff has and will continue to incur the costs of investigating and cleaning up the environmental hazards present on the Wolcott property.

The plaintiff has framed its claims for relief in three counts. Count I, a fraud count, asserts that by failing to respond to the letter of May 2, 1986 Hines fraudulently concealed the existence of environmental problems on the Wolcott property, that Hines' silence led Weyerhaeuser to believe that such problems were not present, and that the plaintiff relied on that belief in determining whether to purchase the property. In Count II the plaintiff seeks to hold Hines liable for negligence in failing to use, dispose, or discharge waste in such a way as to avoid harm to Weyerhaeuser. Finally, Count III claims restitution for the money expended by the plaintiff in performance of the defendant's alleged duty to clean up the property. The relief sought under each count is the cost already incurred and, in the case of Counts I and II, to be incurred by Weyerhaeuser in remedying the property.

Through the instance motion, the defendant moves for dismissal of all three counts on the grounds that the facts alleged do not state a cause of action under the asserted theories. In addition the defendant argues that Edward Hines Lumber Company is no longer amenable to suit and therefore ought to be dismissed.

* * *

DISCUSSION

* * *

... Fraud

To state a claim for fraud under Illinois law, the plaintiff must allege: (1) a misrepresentation of material fact, (2) known or believed by the speaker to be false, (3) made with the intent to induce action, (4) action in reliance on the misrepresentations, (5) justifiable reliance or the right to rely, and (6) resultant harm to the claimant. *Dixie-Portland Flour Mills v. Nation Enterprises*, 613 F.Supp. 985, 990 (N.D.Ill.1985); *Coca-Cola Co. Foods Div. v. Olmarc Packaging Co.*, 620 F.Supp. 966, 973 (N.D.Ill.1985). Moreover, pursuant to the Federal Rules of Civil Procedure, the circumstances constituting fraud must be stated with particularity. Fed. R. Civ. P. 9(b). To satisfy this requirement the complaint must aver the "time and place of the fraud, the contents of the omissions or misrepresentations and the identity of the party or parties perpetrating the fraud." *Coronet Insurance Co. v. Seyfarth*, 665 F.Supp. 661, 666 (N.D.Ill.1987). The complaint in this case fails to allege facts indicating the existence of either an actionable misrepresentation or reasonable reliance on such representation.

A misrepresentation for purposes of this standard is not limited to the affirmative statement of a falsehood. It may also include the concealment or failure to disclose a material fact "under circumstances creating an opportunity and duty to speak." *Lagen v. Lagen*, 302 N.E.2d 201, 205, 14 Ill.App.3d 74 (Ill.App. 1 Dist.1973); *Perlman v. Time, Inc.*, 20 Ill.Dec. 831, 380 N.E.2d 1040, 1044, 64 Ill.App.3d 190 (Ill.App. 1 Dist.1978). Excluded from the definition of actionable concealment is the passive omission of facts in the course of a business transaction. *id.* at 1044. In addition, where property has been sold "as is," courts have found it appropriate to require very convincing proof of fraud before relief will be granted.... *CNC Service Center v. CNC Service Center*, 731 F.Supp. 293, 301 (N.D.Ill.1990).

The concealment alleged in Weyerhaeuser's complaint is passive in nature. It consists merely of failure to respond to a letter sent several weeks after the execution of a contract for the "as is" sale of property. There is no allegation that Hines engaged in deceptive conduct or disguised material facts. Therefore, as alleged in the complaint, the defendant's silence cannot be viewed as anything more than the passive omission of facts in the course of a business transaction.

The allegations of the complaint also fail to support Weyerhaeuser's contention that reliance was reasonable in this case. First, the plaintiff's conclusory statements to the effect that it relied on Hines to disclose the alleged contamination prior to execution of the April 18, 1986 contract are too lacking in specificity to survive a motion to dismiss. In particular, they fail to indicate who said what to whom and under what circumstances.

The only act of concealment specifically alleged in the complaint arose out of the opportunity to speak purportedly created by the May 2, 1986 letter. However, according to the complaint, the execution of the sales contract preceded this demand for information by two weeks. Under such circumstances the plaintiff could not possibly have relied on the defendant's non-disclosure when it signed the contract.

Weyerhaeuser improperly tries to correct this incongruity by alleging additional facts in its response to the instant motion. According to the new allegations, the plaintiff relied on Hines' silence in accepting title to the property approximately ten months after the mailing of the May 2, 1986 letter. However, even if such allegation were properly incorporated in the complaint, they would not aid the plaintiff in this case.

Illinois law does not allow a plaintiff to ignore a known risk or to recover "for walking into an obvious risk even if such risk was not perceived." *AMPAT/Midwest, Inc. v. Ill. Tool Works, Inc.*, 896 F.2d 1035, 1042 (7th Cir.1990). Thus, if the plaintiff has had time or opportunity to ascertain the truth of the allegedly misrepresented facts, it may not assert a cause of action for fraud. Moreover, if property has been sold "as is," reliance on an alleged misrepresentation "will be deemed reasonable only in circumstances indicating manifest inequality between the respective parties." *CNC Service Center*, 731 F.Supp. at 301.

The May 2, 1986 letter clearly calls for a response which was apparently never received. Nevertheless, no further inquiry is alleged to have been made in the ten months period preceding closing on the property. The complaint further does not aver that Weyerhaeuser inspected the property or would not have discovered the alleged defects had such inspection been made. At the same time, the May 2, 1986 letter suggests an awareness of the possibility that environment hazards obtained on the property. Finally, no manifest inequality in the knowledge or bargaining power of the parties is apparent from the allegations in the complaint. Therefore, under the alleged circumstances, it appears that Weyerhaeuser had ample opportunity to ascertain whether environmental problems were in fact present on the property. In this context, the plaintiff's alleged reliance on Hines' misrepresentation cannot be deemed reasonable.

Because the complaint does not properly allege facts necessary to state a claim for fraud, Count I of the complaint is dismissed.

... Negligence

As alleged in the complaint, Count II seeks to hold Hines liable for the negligent failure to dispose, use and maintain waste in such a way as to avoid harm to its prospective buyer. However, it is well settled under Illinois law that a vendor of real property may not be held liable to a future buyer for negligence. *Chapman v. Lily Cache Builders, Inc.*, 6 Ill.Dec. 176, 362 N.E.2d 811, 814, 48 Ill.App.3d 919 (Ill.App. 3 Dist.1977); *Century Display Mfg. Corp. v. D.R. Wager Construction Corp.*, 17 Ill.Dec. 664, 376 N.E.2d 993, 997 71 Ill.2d 428 (Ill.1978). Thus, as plead in the complaint, Count II must be dismissed for failure to state a claim for relief.

In its response to this motion Weyerhaeuser seeks to escape this conclusion by shifting to a new legal theory. The plaintiff argues that the defendant should be held liable for failing to disclose the presence of chemical waste on the Wolcott property prior to sale. In support of this claim the plaintiff cites Section 353 of the Restatement (Second) of Torts which has been cited with approval by the Illinois Supreme Court. *See Century Display*, 376 N.E.2d at 997.

Section 353 provides a limited exception to the general rule that a vendee of real property may not hold the vendor liable in tort. *Id.* Pursuant to its exception,

(1) A vendor of land who conceals or fails to disclose to his vendee any condition ... which involves unreasonable risk to persons on the land, is subject to liability to the vendee ... for physical harm caused by the condition after the vendee has taken possession, if

> (a) the vendee does not know or have reason to know of the condition of risk involved, and

> (b) the vendor knows or has reason to know of the condition, and realizes or should realize the risk involved, and has reason to believe that the vendee will not discover the condition or realize the risk.

Restatement (Second) of Torts § 353. Liability pursuant to this section extends only until the vendee has had reasonable opportunity to discover the condition and to take effective precautions against it. Restatement (Second) of Torts § 353(2).

A plaintiff may recover under Section 353 for personal injury or harm to property other than the subject of the sale caused by the dangerous condition. *See People ex rel. Skinner v. Graham*, 120 Ill.Dec. 612, 524 N.E.2d 642, 652, 170 Ill.App.3d 417 (Ill.App. 4 Dist.1988). Under Illinois law, however, recovery is not available for purely economic loss—i.e., disappointed expectations, costs of repair, or decrease in property value. See *Board of Education v. A. C. & S.*, 137 Ill.Dec. 635, 546 N.E.2d 580, 586, 131 Ill.2d 428 (Ill.1989) and cases cited therein. For relief for such injury, the plaintiff must look to the contract.

The allegations of the complaint do not allege damages for which Section 353 provides relief. The harm allegedly suffered by Weyerhaeuser is the unanticipated costs of putting the property into the condition Weyerhaeuser believed it to be when the contract was made. In other words, the alleged losses are purely contractual. Thus, the plaintiff's ability to hold the defendant liable depends on Hines' obligations under the contract. . . .

A similar result was reached in *Western v. Kerr McGee Chemical Corporation*, No. 82 C 2034, Memorandum Opinion (N.D.Ill.1983). As in this case, the plaintiff-vendee in *Western* attempted to sue the defendant-vendor for negligence in the maintenance, inspection, and removal of hazardous material which had collected on property previously owned and used by the defendant in the operation of its business. The plaintiff sought to recover the decrease in property value caused by the radiation. The district court held that the losses alleged by the plaintiff were economic losses consisting of their disappointed expectations as to the value of the building they purchased. As a result, the court held that the plaintiff could not recover in tort or under Section 353 of the Restatement.

The plaintiff argues in its response brief that because there is a risk that the chemical contamination may spread to the environment generally, it has sufficiently alleged damage to "other property" to proceed under Section 353. In support of this contention, the plaintiff cites the Illinois Supreme Court's opinion in *Board of Education v. A.C. and S*, 546 N.E.2d 580 (Ill.1989). In that case, the plaintiff landowners sought to recover the cost of removing asbestos materials from their property. The court found "that it would be incongruous to argue there is no damage to other property when a harmful element exists throughout a building or an area of a building which by law must be corrected and proven to exist at unacceptably dangerous levels." 546 N.E.2d at 588. The plaintiff suggests that a similar finding is warranted here.

There is however, a key factual distinction between *A, C and S* and his case. *A, C and S* was a products liability action brought not against the former owner and vendor of land but against the manufacturers of asbestos material contaminating the premises. Thus the Illinois Supreme Court did not have to contend with the tradition rule of non-tort liability of real estate vendors. In addition, the plaintiffs in the state case were seeking relief for damage to the premises as a whole and not for disappointment in the quality or effectiveness of the asbestos materials purchased from the defendants. As a result, allegations of damage to "other property" were clearly present. In this case, by contrast, the allegedly contaminated property is the very property that was the subject of the parties' transaction. In light of these factual distinctions the reasoning underlying *A, C and S* is inapplicable in this case.

As Weyerhaeuser's negligence claim fails to state a basis for relief, Count II of the complaint is accordingly dismissed.

... Restitution

The plaintiff bases its restitution claim on Section 115 of the Restatement of Restitution. Pursuant to that section, a person who performs another's duty to the public is entitled to restitution if

> (a) he acted unofficiously and with intent to charge therefor, and

> (b) the things or services supplied were immediately necessary to satisfy the requirements of public decency, health or safety.

Restatement of Restitution § 115. What the plaintiff fails to note, however, is that this remedy is not available where the relationship of the parties is governed by a contract. *Stanley Gudyka Sales v. Lacy Forest Products Co.*, 686 F.Supp. 1301, 1306 (N.D.Ill.1988), quoting *First Commodity Traders, Inc. v. Heinold Commodities, Inc.*, 766 F.2d 1007, 1011 (7th Cir.1985); *Industrial Lift Truck v. Mitsubishi International*, 60 Ill.Dec. 100, 432 N.E.2d 999, 1002, 104 Ill.App.3d 357(Ill.App. 1 Dist.1982). Such limitation operates regardless of the fact that the contract does not expressly address the matter sued upon. *First Commodity Traders*, 766 F.2d at 1011. This rule is based on the notion that, in the give and take of the bargaining process, parties to a contract agree to the allocation of certain risks in the hope of obtaining a beneficial return, and that allocation is reflected in the consideration paid by each party in reaching the agreement. If the remedy of restitution were available in this setting, one party would essentially be allowed to unilaterally shift the risks associated with the contract whenever its contractual expectations are not realized. *Batler, Capitel, & Schwartz v. Tapanes*, 115 Ill.Dec. 530, 517 N.E.2d 1216, 1219, 164 Ill.App.3d 427 (Ill.App. 2 Dist.1987)(citation omitted). The law does not allow such unilateral modification of private agreements. *Industrial Lift Truck*, 432 N.E.2d at 1002.

In this case there is a contract governing the relationship of the parties with respect to the Wolcott property. Illinois law therefore bars the plaintiff from recovery pursuant to a quasi-contractual theory of relief. Accordingly, Count III is also dismissed.

* * *

3. *Liability for Fraudulent Nondisclosure*

Vendors of land contaminated by hazardous wastes also may be liable to purchasers for fraudulent nondisclosure in the sale of realty where (1) the vendor knows of a latent defect, such as hazardous waste in the soil, but intentionally fails to disclose that fact to purchasers, (2) contamination is not readily observable by purchasers, and (3) purchasers relied upon the nondisclosure to their detriment. *See NJDEP v. Ventron Corp., supra* (purchaser recovered all costs incurred for abatement of the pollution and construction of a containment system, as well as for diminution of the fair market value of the property below the purchase price because of undisclosed mercury contamination.)

Practice Problems
#1

XYZ owns land in the South Valley area of County. ABC owns a wood treatment and preservation facility adjacent to XYZ's property. From 1908 to 1972, ABC used this facility to treat and preserve wooden railroad ties. XYZ would like to file a complaint alleging ABC improperly stored and disposed chemical waste which contaminated the groundwater and rendered XYZ's adjacent property unmarketable. What common law claims would XYZ have against ABC? How would your answer differ if ABC was the former owner of the adjacent site?

#2

Medical Center ("Center") would like to sue Contractor for damage to its building allegedly resulting from the installation of asbestos-containing fireproofing manufactured and supplied by Contractor. What common law theories of liability might Center allege in seeking recovery from Contractor?

#3

Mr. X was diagnosed with lung cancer. Mr. X believes his condition was caused by exposure to insecticides which were applied in his home from 1989 through 1991 to rid his home of termites. Only one extermination company treated his house with the insecticides claimed to have caused his injury.

Two companies, however, manufactured the insecticides alleged to have been used by the ExtermCo in treating Mr. X's home for termites.

For a number of years, Mr. X was covered under a Termite Protection Plan with the ExtermCo for the inspection and treatment of his home for termites. In October 1989, after Mr. X discovered termites and termite damage in his home, ExtermCo began treating his home for termites. Later, in 1991, when Mr. X again discovered termites in his home, ExtermCo returned and again treated the home for the termite infestation. Mr. X alleges that the pesticides applied by ExtermCo in the treatments for termites caused his injury and avers, more specifically, that as the result of his exposure to Pryfon, an organophosphorus insecticide manufactured by ABCCo, and to Permethrin, which is marketed by XYZCo under the trademark Dragnet FT, he sustained permanent injury to his lungs.

What common law causes of action might Mr. X allege? Against whom?

#4

PaperCo is a New York corporation engaged in the business of making paper. In 1928, PaperCo commenced operation of a "bleach kraft" paper pulp mill at X site, on the X River upstream from its confluence with the Y River. Treated effluent from the mill's papermaking process is discharged into the X River.

The owners of a Fishing Camp approach you. The Fishing Camp sells bait and tackle, rents and stores boats and other "marine appliances," serves as a launching point for boats, and provides other goods and services for persons using the X and Y Rivers. The owners of the Fishing Camp have also raised concern in a town meeting of some other persons that own real property which abuts the X and lies within its flood plain, concerned recreational users of the rivers and other persons that consume fish from the rivers as well as other

The Camp believes that PaperCo should have known, no later than 1985, that a by-product of the bleach kraft pulp making process is 2.3.7.8–tetrachlorodibenzo-p-dioxin (TCDD) and its mill was discharging at levels which resulted in contamination of the river system and aquatic life downstream from the mill discharge site. Despite possessing such knowledge, PaperCo continued its operations and at no time issued any warnings to the public that fish in the two Rivers might or would be contaminated with TCDD, or that there was any hazard to persons or property.

The PaperCo mill also discharges into the waters of the X River dark and foul smelling effluent in sufficient quantities that the color of the rivers is often altered. The operation of the mill has been conducted in a manner that has resulted in the aquatic life of the X and Y Rivers being so contaminated with TCDD and a closely related chemical known as TCDF that the State has considered banning commercial fishing and consumption of fish from the X River below the PaperCo mill. The Camp claims they have been damaged through injury to their business, loss of income, damage to real property, and resulting emotional anxiety and worry.

What common law causes of action might they bring? The other landowners? The fish eaters? The boaters and swimmers? Against whom?

#5

The Owners own real property and live near the County landfill. They raise livestock on their property. Between 1984 and 1989 more than 25 of the Bakers' cattle died from a suspected but unidentified poisoning. In the spring of 1990 some of Owner's cattle died, and approximately 31 trees have died on their property. Over time, the Owners' pond, they say, has become "nearly black," and a black run-off washes onto neighboring property. Owner observed chunks of "raw rubber" on her property and has seen pockets of carbon black in a creek on her land. Dust from the landfill blows over his property, making everything black. Owners claim that this has resulted in damages based on a devaluation of their property, physical impairment, and emotional and mental distress, all related to toxic or harmful materials dumped at the landfill.

Manufacturer makes rubber tires for motor vehicles at a plant that is served by the County landfill. The SWA oversees operations at the County landfill.

Both the Owners and the SWA contend that Manufacturer has improperly disposed of hazardous waste at the landfill or has improperly packaged harmful waste for disposal, resulting, they say, in migration of the waste and contamination of the landfill and nearby property. As to the Owners' claims against the SWA, Manufacturer states that the Owners "produced ample evidence that various kinds of trash and rainwater run-off had escaped from the County Landfill and gotten onto [the Owners'] property."

Identified at both the landfill and the Owners' property are substances that can be classified as hazardous waste or as potentially harmful waste.

What common law causes of action could be raised to remedy this environmental problem? by whom?

Chapter 3

THE ENVIRONMENTAL REGULATORY PROCESS

Table of Sections

The Company and its operations are subject to a number of federal, state and local laws and regulations governing the discharge of materials into the environment or otherwise relating to the protection of the environment. These environmental provisions may, among other things, impose liabilities for the cost of pollution clean-up....

The Company has conducted a review of its operations with particular attention to environmental compliance. The Company believes it has acted as a prudent operator and is in substantial compliance with environmental laws and regulations. The Company has and will continue to incur costs in its efforts to comply with these environmental standards. Although the costs incurred by Company to date solely to comply with environmental laws and regulations have not had a material adverse effect upon capital expenditures, earnings or the competitive position of the Company, the trend toward stricter environmental laws and regulations is expected to have an increasingly significant impact on the conduct of Company's business. The cost of expenditures to comply with evolving regulations and the related future impact on Company's business cannot be predicted at this time because of the uncertainties regarding future environmental standards, advances in technology, the timing for expending funds and the availability of insurance and third-party indemnification. However, Company believes that the evolving environmental stan-

*dards do not affect the Company in a materially different manner
from other similarly situated companies in the ... industry.*

§ 3.1 INTRODUCTION

As the above statement indicates, companies in the United States
are subject to a complex, ever changing fabric of environmental laws
which causes uncertainty in their financial planning. The Clinton administration announced efforts to "reinvent EPA" to make environmental
regulation more "flexible", "cost-effective" and in tune with "common-
sense." Below is a description of EPA's effort to undertake a "smarter
approach" to regulation.

60 FED. REG. 23928
(May 8, 1995).

REINVENTING ENVIRONMENTAL REGULATION

The Environmental Protection Agency is committed to reinventing
environmental regulation so as to offer greater protection for less cost.
To further this goal, the President has directed EPA to take immediate
steps to improve the current regulatory system through a comprehensive
review of all existing regulations. To meet this goal, the Agency is
performing a comprehensive reexamination of the Code of Federal Regulations (CFR) to identify rules that are obsolete or no longer applicable
or which could be modified or simplified to reduce compliance costs while
still protecting human health and the environment. By June 1, the
Agency expects to identify those regulations that can be removed from
the CFR in whole or in part, as well as those that are scheduled for
modification or for further study. At the same time, EPA is subjecting its
paperwork requirements to rigorous reexamination. The Agency has set
a target of reducing paperwork burden on the public by 25 percent.
Toward this end, the Agency is responding to the President's instruction
to reduce reporting requirements by half wherever legal and appropriate.

Additionally, EPA is building and enhancing partnerships with the
regulated community through increased stakeholder outreach and involvement. The Agency is seeking to increase participation by the private
sector and other governmental entities in its efforts to improve its
regulatory programs. In this respect, the President recently announced a
program of 25 substantial actions EPA will take to carry out its mission
of environmental protection in more flexible and publicly responsive
ways. These initiatives include such varied steps as expanding the use of
market incentives to promote environmentally responsible behavior,
addressing the most stringent regulation and enforcement to problems
posing the highest public risks, and experimenting with novel solutions
to the real environmental problems posed by an industry or locality
when generally applicable mandates may prove ineffective or inefficient
in a specific application.

* * *

The Regulatory Flexibility Act (RFA) requires the identification of those regulations which are likely to have a "significant economic impact on a substantial number of small entities" (i.e., small governments, small businesses, and small nonprofit organizations). Under the requirements of the Act, such regulations are subject to a "regulatory flexibility analysis." This analysis must consider the likely economic impacts on small entities, as well as any significant alternatives to the rule which accomplish the objectives of applicable statutes and which minimize significant economic impacts of the rulemaking on small entities.

In April 1992, EPA adopted a policy which exceeds the requirements of the RFA (this policy applies to rulemakings that were initiated on or after April 9, 1992). For rulemakings subject to this policy, EPA will perform a regulatory flexibility analysis if the rule is likely to have any economic impact on any small entity. For rulemakings not subject to this policy (i.e., initiated prior to April 9, 1992), a regulatory flexibility analysis will be conducted only if the rulemaking will meet the RFA's standard of having a "significant impact on a substantial number of small entities."

Each rulemaking listed in this agenda indicates in the "Analysis" section whether EPA expects to conduct a regulatory flexibility analysis. If EPA believes small entities will be affected by a rulemaking, this is indicated under the "Small Entities Affected" and/or the "Government Levels Affected" section of the summary for each listed rule. EPA invites public comment regarding EPA's assessment of which of the listed rulemakings are appropriate for regulatory flexibility analysis. (See "Small Entities Index to the Environmental Protection Agency Agenda" at the end of this document. It lists the regulatory actions EPA believes may have effects on small businesses, small governmental jurisdictions, or small organizations.)

The RFA requires that existing regulations with significant economic impact on a substantial number of small entities are to be reviewed within 10 years of promulgation of the regulations. While, as described above, EPA is currently reexamining all of its existing regulations, the Agency recognizes that many rules will require detailed study before they may be appropriately modified or retained. As part of that process, as well as under the requirements of the Regulatory Flexibility Act, EPA invites public comment identifying any existing EPA rules believed to have a significant economic impact on a substantial number of small entities.

Comments should be provided in the following format:

- Title
- Authorizing statute and CFR citation
- Description of economic effects on small entities, especially on the commenting person or organization
- Recommendations for changes

Any additional detailed comments or data are welcome.

When EPA completes its review of an existing rule, it will indicate in the agenda whether that rulemaking will be continued without change or will be amended or rescinded consistent with the stated objectives of applicable statutes to minimize any significant economic impact of the regulations upon a substantial number of small entities.

The agenda is organized by statute and ordered numerically within each statutory area. Entries within each statute are divided into four categories: (1) Prerule, (2) proposed rule, (3) final rule, and (4) completed or long-term actions (i.e., regulations that EPA is deleting from the agenda because the Agency has completed, withdrawn, or postponed them indefinitely, as well as actions under preparation that will not be published until after the 1–year horizon for this agenda). Detailed information on each of these categories is presented below. A bullet (●) preceding an entry indicates that this is the first time this entry appears in an agenda.

I. *Prerulemakings*

Prerulemaking actions are activities intended to determine whether to initiate rulemaking. These activities include anything that influences or leads to rulemaking, such as advance notices of proposed rulemaking, significant studies or analyses of the possible need for regulatory action, requests for public comment on the need for regulatory action, or important preregulatory policy proposals.

II. *Proposed and Final Rules*

This section includes all substantial EPA regulations. To focus the public's attention on the most timely actions, EPA lists regulations in this category of the agenda that are within a year of proposal or promulgation. The listings, however, generally exclude (a) specialized categories of actions (e.g., EPA approvals of State plans and other actions that do not apply nationally) and (b) routine actions (e.g., pesticide tolerances and minor amendments to existing rules).

The Agency has attempted to list all regulations and regulatory reviews except those considered as minor, routine, or repetitive actions. There is no legal significance to the inadvertent omission of an item from the listing. The agenda reflects dates for actions on each item; these dates are estimates that should not be construed as an Agency commitment to act on or by the date shown. The Administrator of EPA will review the items contained in this agenda over the next 6 months. Items in this agenda may be deleted, or new items may be added, as a result of that review.

III. *Completed or Long–Term Actions*

This section contains actions that appeared in the previous agenda but which EPA is deleting because they are completed or no longer under consideration for rulemaking. This section also includes previously listed actions with publication dates beyond the next 12 months. Please note that the Agency will continue to work with the public to develop partnerships and information necessary to support these rulemakings with long-term publication dates.

§ 3.2   REGULATORY NEGOTIATION

"Reg/neg" is the term popularly used to describe the complex manner in which federal agencies, in consultation with industry, environmental groups and other interested parties, writes environmental regulations designed to implement the federal statutes it administers. Below is a description of the process used by one federal agency.

60 FED. REG. 30506
(June 9, 1995).

Due to the increasing complexity and formalization of the written rulemaking process, it can be difficult for an agency to craft effective regulatory solutions to certain problems. During the rulemaking process, the participants may develop adversarial relationships that prevent effective communication and creative solutions. The exchange of ideas that can lead to solutions acceptable to all interested groups sometimes do not occur in the traditional notice and comment context. As the Administrative Conference of the United States (ACUS) noted in its Recommendation 82–4:

> Experience indicates that if the parties in interest work together to negotiate the text of a proposed rule, they might be able in some circumstances to identify the major issues, gauge their importance to the respective parties, identify the information and data necessary to resolve the issues, and develop a rule that is acceptable to the respective interests, all within the contours of the substantive statute.

ACUS adopted this recommendation in "Procedures for Negotiating Proposed Regulations," 47 FR 30708. The thrust of the recommendation is that representatives of all interests should be assembled to discuss the issue and all potential solutions, reach consensus, and prepare a proposed rule for consideration by the agency. After public comment on any proposal issued by the agency, the group would reconvene to review the comments and make recommendations for a final rule. This inclusive process is intended to make the rule more acceptable to all affected interests and prevent the need for petitions for reconsideration (and litigation) that often follow issuance of a final rule.

The movement toward negotiated rulemaking gained impetus with enactment of the Negotiated Rulemaking Act of 1990 (RegNeg), 5 U.S.C. Sec. 561 et seq. In 1993, Executive Order 12866 (58 FR 51735) added to this impetus:

> In particular, before issuing a notice of proposed rulemaking, each agency should, where appropriate, seek the involvement of those who are intended to benefit from and those expected to be burdened

by any regulation * * * Each agency is also directed to explore and, where appropriate, use consensual mechanisms for developing regulations, including negotiated rulemaking.

(Sec. 6(a), p. 51740)

Although relatively new, negotiated rulemakings have been used successfully by agencies within DOT: the Federal Aviation Administration, Federal Highway Administration, Federal Railroad Administration, and the United States Coast Guard. NHTSA now intends to begin this process in a formal manner for the first time in promulgating a Federal motor vehicle safety standard. It welcomes the opportunity to work with those who will be affected directly by such a rule, and is confident that the agency, industry, and the public will benefit with the creation of an effective and reasonable regulation.

Pursuant to section 563(a) of RegNeg, an agency considering rulemaking by negotiation should consider whether:

(1) There is need for the rule;

(2) There is a limited number of identifiable interests;

(3) These interests can be adequately represented by persons willing to negotiate in good faith to reach a consensus;

(4) There is a reasonable likelihood that the committee will reach consensus within a fixed period of time;

(5) The negotiated rulemaking procedure will not unreasonably delay the notice of proposed rulemaking;

(6) The agency has adequate resources and is willing to commit such resources to the process; and

(7) The agency is committed to use the result of the negotiation in formulating a proposed rule if at all possible.

For the reasons stated in this Notice, NHTSA believes that these criteria have been met with regard to headlamp amiability and beam pattern issues.

The regulatory negotiation NHTSA proposes would be carried out by an advisory committee (Committee) created under the Federal Advisory Committee Act (FACA), as amended, 5 U.S.C. App., and in a manner that reflects appropriate rulemaking directives, including pertinent executive Orders. NHTSA will be represented on the Committee and will take an active part in the negotiations as a Committee member. However, pursuant to section 566(c) of RegNeg, those representing NHTSA would not facilitate or otherwise chair the proceedings.

III. PROCEDURES AND GUIDELINES

The following proposed procedures and guidelines would apply to NHTSA's negotiated rulemaking process, subject to appropriate changes made as a result of comments received on this Notice or as are determined to be necessary during the negotiating process.

(A) Facilitator: The Facilitator will not be involved with substantive development of this regulation. This individual will chair the negotiations, may offer alternative suggestions toward the desired consensus, and will determine the feasibility of negotiating particular issues. The Facilitator may ask members to submit additional information or to reconsider their position. NHTSA has contracted with the Federal Mediation and Conciliation Service for a Facilitator.

(B) Feasibility: NHTSA has examined the issues and interests involved and has made a preliminary inquiry among representatives of those interests to determine whether it is possible to reach agreement on: (a) individuals to represent those interests; (b) the preliminary scope of the issues to be addressed; and (c) a schedule for developing a notice of proposed rulemaking. The results are sufficiently encouraging to believe that a workable proposal could be developed, and that there are potential participants who could adequately represent the affected interests.

(C) Participants and Interests: The number of Committee participants generally should not exceed 25. However, it is not necessary that each individual or organization affected by a final rule have its own representative on the Committee. Rather, each interest must be adequately represented, and the Committee should be fairly balanced. However, individuals who are not part of the Committee may attend sessions and confer with or provide their views to Committee members.

The following interests have been tentatively identified as those that are likely to be significantly affected by the rule:

HTSA proposes that persons selected by the various interests be named to the Committee.

In addition to NHTSA, the following interests have been tentatively identified as those that would supply Committee members:

As indicated previously in this Notice, NHTSA invites applications for representation from any interests that will be affected by a final rule on the subject but are not named in this list or who may not be represented or be able to be represented by the interests on the list. Such applications must be filed within thirty days from the date of publication of this Notice, and must meet the requirements set forth herein. Also, such interests should provide the name(s) of the individual(s) they propose to represent their interest. As noted, the Committee should not exceed 25 members.

(D) Good Faith: Participants must be committed to negotiate in good faith. It is therefore important that senior individuals within each interest group be designated to represent that interest. No individual will be required to "bind" the interest represented, but the individual should be at a high enough level to represent the interest with confidence. For this process to be successful, the interests represented should be willing to accept the final Committee product.

(E) Notice of Intent to Establish Advisory Committee and Request for Comment: In accordance with the requirements of FACA, an agency of the Federal government cannot establish or utilize a group of people in the interest of obtaining consensus advice or recommendations unless that group is chartered as a Federal advisory committee. It is the purpose of this Notice to indicate NHTSA's intent to create a Federal advisory committee, to identify the issues involved in the rulemaking, to identify the interests affected by the rulemaking, to identify potential participants who will adequately represent those interests, and to ask for comment on the use of regulatory negotiation and on the identification of the issues, interests, procedures, and participants.

(F) Requests for Representation: One purpose of this notice is to determine whether interests exist that may be substantially affected by a rule, but have not been represented in the list of prospective Committee members. Commenters should identify such interests if they exist. Each application or nomination to the Committee should include (i) the name of the applicant or nominee and the interests such person would represent; (ii) evidence that the applicant or nominee is authorized to represent parties related to the interest the person proposes to represent; and (iii) a written commitment that the applicant or nominee would participate in good faith. If any additional person or interest requests membership or representation on the Committee, NHTSA shall determine (i) whether that interest will be substantially affected by the rule, (ii) if such interest would be adequately represented by an individual on the Committee, and (iii) whether the requested organization should be added to the group or whether interests can be consolidated to provide adequate representation.

(G) Final Notice: After evaluating the comments received in response to this Notice, NHTSA will issue a further notice announcing the establishment of the Federal advisory committee, unless it determines that such action is inappropriate in light of comments received, and the composition of the Committee. After the Committee is chartered, the negotiations should begin.

(H) Administrative Support and Meetings: Staff support would be provided by NHTSA and meetings would take place in Washington, D.C. unless agreed otherwise by the Committee.

(I) Tentative Schedule: If the Committee is established and selected, NHTSA will publish a schedule for the first meeting in the Federal Register. The first meeting will focus on procedural matters, including dates, times, and locations of further meetings. Notice of subsequent meetings would also be published in the Federal Register before being held.

NHTSA expects that the Committee would reach consensus and prepare a report recommending a proposed rule within ten months of the first meeting. However, if unforeseen delays occur, the Administrator may agree to an extension of that time if it is the consensus of the Committee that additional time will result in agreement. The process may end earlier if the Facilitator so recommends.

(J) Committee Procedures: Under the general guidance of the Facilitator, and subject to legal requirements, the Committee would establish the detailed procedures for meetings which it considers appropriate.

(K) Records of Meetings: In accordance with FACA's requirements, NHTSA would keep a summary record of all Committee meetings. This record would be placed in Docket No. 95–28. Meetings of the Committee would be open to the public to observe, but not to participate.

(L) Consensus: The goal of the negotiating process is consensus. NHTSA proposes that the Committee would develop its own definition of consensus, which may include unanimity, a simple majority, or substantial agreement such that no member will disapprove the final recommendation of the Committee. However, if the Committee does not develop its own definition, consensus shall mean unanimous concurrence.

(M) Regulatory Approach: The Committee's first objective is to prepare a report recommending a regulatory approach for resolving the issues discussed in the BACKGROUND section of this notice. If consensus is not obtained on some issues, the report should identify the areas of agreement and disagreement, and explanations for any disagreement. It is expected that participants will be mindful of cost/benefit considerations.

NHTSA will issue a notice of proposed rulemaking based upon the approach recommended by the Committee.

(N) Key Issues for Negotiation: NHTSA has reviewed correspondence, reports, petitions, relevant data, and other information. Based on this information and rulemaking requirements, NHTSA has tentatively identified major issues that should be considered in this negotiated rulemaking. Other issues related to headlamp amiability and beam pattern not specifically listed in this Notice may be addressed as they arise in the course of the negotiation. Comments are invited concerning the appropriateness of these issues for consideration and whether other issues should be added. These issues are:

* * *

IV.   PUBLIC PARTICIPATION

NHTSA invites comments on all issues, procedures, guidelines, interests, and suggested participants embodied in this Notice. All comments and requests for participation should be submitted to the . . . .

The Regulatory/Negotiation Process as a Glance

```
Initiate Preruling Action
I
Formulate Regulatory Program
I
OMB Approval
I
Prepare proposed rule and Regulatory Impact Analysis (RIA)
(Must be sent to OMB at least 60 Days
prior to publication in the Federal Register)
I
Revise/Withdraw through Reg/Neg Process—OMB Review for
Consistency with Administrative Policies
I
Publish NPRM in Federal Register
I
Prepare final rule and RIA
(Send to OMB 30 days prior to publication in Federal Register)
I
Revise/Withdraw through Reg/Neg Process—OMB Review for
Consistency with Administrative Policies
I
Publish Final Rule in Federal Register
I
Final Rule Goes into Effect
(After 30 Days)
I
Judicial Challenges, If Any
I
Judicial Review
```

§ 3.3   CHEVRON DEFERENCE

A critical principal of administrative law is that the interpretations of the agency charged with administering a statute will be given deference. This has been termed *"Chevron"* deference, after the seminole supreme court case, *Chevron USA, Inc. v. NRDC*, 467 U.S. 837, 104 S.Ct. 2778, 81 L.Ed.2d 694 (1984).

ARCO OIL & GAS CO. v. EPA
14 F.3d 1431 (10th Cir.1993).

HOLLOWAY, CIRCUIT JUDGE.

ARCO Oil and Gas Company ("ARCO") petitions for review of a June 14, 1990 finding by the Administrator of the Environmental

Protection Agency ("EPA") that EPA Region VIII properly required ARCO to obtain a Class I EPA permit pursuant to the Safe Drinking Water Act ("SDWA"), 42 U.S.C. 300f to 300f–26 (1988), for operation of ARCO's Garcia #1 injection well in Colorado. Prior to the EPA's reclassification of the well, the Garcia #1 had been regulated as a Class II well by the Colorado Oil and Gas Conservation Commission ("COGCC"). We affirm the EPA Administrator's decision and deny ARCO's petition.

I

Since 1982, ARCO has been operating a gas extraction and processing project in Huerfano County, Colorado. The gas extracted by ARCO consists primarily of carbon dioxide (96%) and is used for enhanced oil recovery in Texas. In connection with ARCO's extraction activity, certain waste fluids are brought to the surface and subsequently disposed of in ARCO's Garcia #1 well, an underground injection well. . . .

On April 12, 1985, the EPA Region VIII directed ARCO to apply for a Class I permit for the Garcia # 1 well. I R., Doc. 4. In so doing, the agency relied on its characterization of the waste fluids disposed of in the Garcia #1 as "hazardous," "industrial" or "municipal" waste within the meaning of 40 C.F.R. 144.6(a)(1)–(2)(defining Class I wells). Designation of the Garcia #1 as a Class I well would result in direct—and more burdensome—regulation of the well by the EPA rather than continued regulation by the COGCC. . . .

ARCO objected, contending that the Garcia #1's waste fluids should instead be characterized as fluids "brought to the surface in connection with . . . conventional oil or natural gas production" within the meaning of 40 C.F.R. 144.6(b)(1), resulting in continued Class II designation of the Garcia #1 and regulation by the COGCC. I R., Doc. 6. ARCO's position was, and is, premised on its interpretation of the phrase "natural gas production" in 144.6(b)(1) as broadly encompassing carbon dioxide production of the kind undertaken by ARCO in connection with its Huerfano project.

Despite its objection to the EPA's reclassification, ARCO hedged its bets and applied for a Class I permit. Four years later, EPA Region VIII issued the requested Class I permit, indicating that the designation of Garcia #1 as a Class I well was appropriate because "the definition of 'natural gas' for the purpose of the underground injection control regulations was intended to include only 'energy-related' hydrocarbon series gases such as methane and butane," not carbon dioxide. I R., Doc. 2, Addendum at 2. This reading of the regulations was consistent with the EPA's advice to the COGCC in early 1984 that "the meaning of 'natural gas' in our regulations includes low molecular weight flammable gases and not just any naturally occurring gas." I R., Doc. 15 at 2.

In accordance with applicable administrative procedures (40 C.F.R. 124.19), ARCO petitioned for review to the EPA Administrator. I R., Doc. 1. The Administrator denied ARCO's petition, concluding ARCO did not demonstrate "that the Region's permit determination [was] either clearly erroneous (legally or factually) or that it involved an important question of policy or exercise of discretion warranting review." Petitioner's Opening Brief, Attach. A.

In its petition to this court, ARCO requests that we set aside the EPA's construction of the SDWA and its regulations. In the alternative, if the EPA's construction is upheld and the reclassification of the Garcia #1 as a Class I well is affirmed, ARCO urges us to invalidate the reclassification pursuant to the Administrative Procedures Act as "arbitrary, capricious, an abuse of discretion, or otherwise not in accordance with law. . . . " 5 U.S.C. 706. According to ARCO, "there is no rational basis for regulating the disposal of produced water from carbon dioxide operations more stringently than the disposal of produced water from hydrocarbon operations." Petitioner's Opening Brief at 20–21.

Our jurisdiction is reviewed based on 42 U.S.C. 300j–7(a)(2).

II

Here, as in *Exxon Corp. v. Lujan*, 970 F.2d 757, 759 (10th Cir.1992), and *Aulston v. United States*, 915 F.2d 584, 588–89 (10th Cir.1990), *cert. denied*, 114 L.Ed.2d 98, 111 S.Ct. 2011 (1991), we review the EPA's administrative findings under the deferential test established in *Chevron, U.S.A., Inc. v. NRDC*, 467 U.S. 837, 81 L.Ed.2d 694, 104 S.Ct. 2778 (1984):

> When a court reviews an agency's construction of the statute which it administers, it is confronted with two questions. First, always, is whether Congress has directly spoken to the precise question at issue. If the intent of Congress is clear, that is the end of the matter; for the court, as well as the agency, must give effect to the unambiguously expressed intent of Congress. If, however, the court determines Congress has not directly addressed the precise question at issue, the court does not simply impose its own construction on the statute, as would be necessary in the absence of an administrative interpretation. Rather, if the statute is silent or ambiguous with respect to the specific issue, the question for the court is whether the agency's answer is based on a permissible construction of the statute.

Id. at 842–43 (emphasis added; footnotes omitted). *Accord Sullivan v. Everhart*, 494 U.S. 83, 89, 108 L.Ed.2d 72, 110 S.Ct. 960 (1990); *Rives v. ICC*, 934 F.2d 1171, 1174 (10th Cir.1991), *cert. denied*, 118 L.Ed.2d 207, 112 S.Ct. 1559 (1992). The standard of review is the same whether the agency interpretation is performed through rulemaking or, as here, informal adjudication. *See Midtec Paper Corp. v. United States*, 857 F.2d 1487, 1496 (D.C.Cir.1988).

III

A

We first address whether the EPA properly characterized waste fluids disposed of in ARCO's Garcia #1 injection well as "hazardous," "industrial" or "municipal" waste within the meaning of 40 C.F.R.

144.6(a)(1)-(2), or whether the waste fluids should have been characterized as fluids "brought to the surface in connection with . . . conventional oil or natural gas production" under 144.6(b)(1).

The initial step in our analysis is to determine "whether Congress
has directly spoken to the precise question at issue," i.e., whether
Congress itself has defined the term "natural gas" in the context of the
SDWA and its regulations. *Chevron*, 467 U.S. at 842; *accord Good
Samaritan Hospital v. Shalala*, 124 L.Ed.2d 368, 113 S.Ct. 2151, 2157
(1993)("the starting point in interpreting a statute is its language"). In
so doing, we must consider the language of the relevant statutory
scheme as illuminated by "the provisions of the whole law, and . . . its
object and policy." *Aulston*, 915 F.2d at 589. *See also Sullivan v.
Everhart*, 494 U.S. 83, 89, 108 L.Ed.2d 72, 110 S.Ct. 960 (1990)(" 'in
ascertaining the plain meaning of the statute, the court must look to the
particular statutory language at issue, as well as the language and design
of the statute as a whole' ")(quoting *Kmart Corp. v. Cartier, Inc.*, 486
U.S. 281, 291, 108 S.Ct. 1811, 100 L.Ed.2d 313 (1988)).

1

The SDWA makes reference to "natural gas" in two sections, neither of
which provides any clear insight into the intended meaning of that term.
First, concerning underground injection of fluids brought to the surface
in connection with oil and natural gas production, 300h(b)(2) of the
statute provides:

> Regulations of the Administrator under this section for State under-
> ground injection control programs may not prescribe requirements
> which interfere with or impede—
>
> (A) the underground injection of brine or other fluids which are
> brought to the surface in connection with oil or natural gas produc-
> tion or natural gas storage operations, or
>
> (B) any underground injection for the secondary or tertiary
> recovery of oil or natural gas, unless such requirements are essential
> to assure that underground sources of drinking water will not be
> endangered by such injection.

. . . Second, with respect to the kinds of underground injection covered
by the SDWA, 300h(d)(1) of the statute (a 1980 amendment) excludes
injection of "natural gas for purposes of storage." . . .

Apart from simply employing the term "natural gas," the SDWA
does not elaborate on the term's intended meaning or scope. As we
recognized in *Exxon*, "in the absence of more specific linguistic evidence
of Congress's intention than the [mere] use of the term 'natural gas,' we
cannot say on the basis of the statute's plain language that Congress has
spoken directly to the question at issue." 970 F.2d at 761. Accordingly,
in order to discern the intended meaning of the term used, we consult
relevant secondary authorities, a task we previously undertook in both
Exxon, 970 F.2d at 760–61, and *Austin*, 915 F.2d at 589–90. However,
because our definitional inquiry in this case is the same as in *Exxon* and

Austin, we need not repeat the analysis here. Suffice it to say, we are not aware of any post-*Exxon* authorities that in any way alter or affect our previous conclusions....

1

... Because Congress' concern about undue interference with oil and gas production is secondary and expressly subject to the primary goal of ensuring clean water, the legislative history cited by ARCO in no way mandates that we override the EPA and adopt the broad construction or the term "natural gas" urged by ARCO.... Instead, we conclude that neither the language of the SDWA, nor the relevant legislative history reveals a clear congressional intent to treat carbon dioxide as "natural gas" within the meaning of the Act.

2

We next consider whether the EPA's narrow interpretation of the term "natural gas" is "a permissible construction of the [SDWA]" (*Chevron,* 467 U.S. at 842–43), i.e., whether the construction is " 'rational and consistent with the statute.' " *Sullivan,* 110 S.Ct. at 964 (quoting *NLRB v. United Food & Commercial Workers,* 484 U.S. 112, 123, 98 L.Ed.2d 429, 108 S.Ct. 413 (1987)). *Accord Salt Lake City v. Western Area Power Admin.,* 926 F.2d 974, 981 (10th Cir.1991)("when an administering agency's interpretation of a statute is challenged, and traditional tools of statutory construction yield no relevant congressional intent, the reviewing court must determine if the agency's construction is a permissible one"); *Aulston,* 915 F.2d at 597 ("we will defer to the [EPA's] interpretation unless it is inconsistent with the purpose and policy of the [statute]"). As recently reiterated by the Supreme Court:

> Confronted with an ambiguous statutory provision, we generally will defer to a permissible interpretation espoused by the agency entrusted with its implementation.... Of particular relevance is the agency's contemporaneous construction which "we have allowed ... to carry the day against doubts that might exist from a reading of the bare words of a statute." *FHA v. The Darlington, Inc.,* 358 U.S. 84, 90, 79 S.Ct. 141, 145, 3 L.Ed.2d 132 (1958).

Good Samaritan Hospital, 113 S.Ct. at 2159.

This is not the first time we have been asked to consider the propriety of EPA interpretations of the SDWA. In *Phillips Petroleum Co.,* we considered whether the EPA properly invoked the SDWA to make regulations applicable to Indian lands. We defined the relevant standard of review as follows:

> Because Congress has conferred ... sweeping authority on the [EPA] Administrator, courts afford considerable deference to the EPA's construction of the statutory scheme that it is entrusted to administer.... We need not find that the EPA's interpretation is the only permissible construction but only that the EPA's understanding of the statute is a sufficiently rational one to preclude a court from substituting its judgment for that of the EPA.... "The

need for judicial restraint is further heightened by the realization that courts do not share the [Administrator's] expertise in this highly technical area." [*American Mining Congress v. Marshall*, 671 F.2d 1251, 1255 (10th Cir.1982).]

Phillips Petroleum Co., 803 F.2d at 558 (citations omitted).

Affording the appropriate measure of deference to the EPA and recognizing the Administrator's technical expertise in this area, we find the agency's interpretation of "natural gas" as excluding carbon dioxide to be permissible and consistent with the purpose and policy of the SDWA. The overriding purpose of the Act is "to insure the quality of publicly supplied water" by "regulating the endangerment of under-ground drinking water sources." *Id.* at 547. Here, the EPA's narrow interpretation of the term "natural gas" has the effect of subjecting carbon dioxide injection wells to stricter regulatory scrutiny and placing a greater number of wells under direct EPA oversight. This result is consistent with the statutory goal of treating water pollution as "a national concern," the causes and effects of which are "national in scope" and which therefore require "national standards for protection of public health." *Id.* at 555 (quoting H.R. Rep. No. 1185, 93d Cong., 2d Sess. 1 (1974), U.S. Code Cong. & Admin. News 1974, p. 6454). Because "Congress emphasizes a national policy of clean water[] so, therefore, must we in interpreting the statute." *Id.* Accordingly, we are compelled to conclude that the EPA's interpretation of "natural gas" in the context of the SDWA "gives effect to the central purposes of [the] statute[] and is consequently permissible." *Exxon,* 970 F.2d at 763. "We should be especially reluctant to reject the agency's current view which, as we see it, so closely fits 'the design of the statute as a whole and . . . its object and policy.'" *Good Samaritan Hospital,* 113 S.Ct. at 2161 (quoting *Crandon v. United States,* 494 U.S. 152, 158, 108 L.Ed.2d 132, 110 S.Ct. 997 (1990)). . . .

B

Lastly, we address ARCO's alternative contention that regulation of the Garcia #1 as a Class I well is arbitrary and capricious and therefore in violation of the Administrative Procedures Act, 5 U.S.C. 706. ARCO says the produced waters from its Sheep Mountain wells are "virtually identical" to waters from wells producing mainly hydrocarbon gases; equipment and production methods for those Sheep Mountain wells are "virtually identical" to equipment and production methods for wells producing mainly hydrocarbon gases; ARCO injects the largely carbon dioxide gas stream from the field into old oil wells to enhance oil recovery; and Congress intended to limit as much as possible regulatory constraints on the oil and gas industry. Thus, ARCO concludes it is arbitrary and capricious to impose Class I regulation on the Garcia #1 well.

We are not persuaded. A very similar argument was discussed in *Exxon,* 970 F.2d at 763, where Exxon argued that the common carrier requirement emanating from the Secretary's ruling would "unduly burden the carbon dioxide industry and create perverse incentives to produce artificial carbon dioxide." We disagreed, holding that Exxon's argument struck us as a matter more appropriately addressed to the agency, and that the challenge really centered on the wisdom of the agency's policy, rather than on whether it was a reasonable choice within a gap left by Congress. *Id.* Here we have already upheld the administrative interpretation that carbon dioxide is not "natural gas" within the meaning of 40 C.F.R. 144.6(b)(1) as proper. This essentially disposes of ARCO's contention on arbitrariness.

It is true that the APA provisions in 5 U.S.C. 706 have disjunctive protections against actions that are arbitrary, capricious or an abuse of discretion. Perhaps an individual ruling could run afoul of those restrictions and thus be invalid in some special case, but we see no showing of such a violation here. As we have noted:

> The arbitrary and capricious standard of review ... applies to informal rule-making proceedings such as those provided in the SDWA. [Citation.] The United States Supreme Court has explained the arbitrary and capricious standard as follows:

> To make this finding the court must consider whether the decision was based on a consideration of the relevant factors and whether there has been a clear error of judgment. Although this inquiry into the facts is to be searching and careful, the ultimate standard is a narrow one. The court is not empowered to substitute its judgment for that of the agency.

* * *

The complaints made by ARCO do not warrant a holding that the EPA's decision to regulate the Garcia #1 as a Class I well was arrived at without a "consideration of the relevant facts," nor does the agency's decision reveal a "clear error of judgment" on the part of the EPA.

Accordingly, because we are "not empowered to substitute [our] judgment for that of the agency" (*Id.*), we decline to second-guess the EPA's decision to regulate the disposal of carbon dioxide waste fluids—including underground injection by the Garcia #1—more stringently than the disposal of hydrocarbon waste fluids. Insofar as ARCO's challenge to the merits of the EPA's administrative decision "really centers on the wisdom of the agency's policy," the challenge "must fail." *Chevron*, 467 U.S. at 866.

For the foregoing reasons, ARCO's petition for review is DENIED.

HARRIS v. UNITED STATES

19 F.3d 1090 (5th Cir.1994).

EMILIO M. GARZA, CIRCUIT JUDGE:

Plaintiff W.L. Harris brought suit in federal district court seeking a declaratory judgment that the Farmers Home Administration ("FmHA") had unlawfully placed wetland easements on his land and that the property declared by the FmHA to encompass wetlands actually did not. The district court denied relief, 820 F.Supp. 1018. Harris now appeals, and we affirm.

I

In 1987, the Grenada Bank of Mississippi foreclosed on 1,893 acres of farmland owned by Harris. The FmHA, which held a junior lien on the property, successfully bid for the property at the subsequent sale held by the bank. The following year, the United States Fish and Wildlife Service ("FWS"), pursuant to a request from the FmHA, inspected the property, found that it contained large areas of wetlands, and recommended that the FmHA impose wetland conservation easements on approximately 1,005 acres. In June 1988, the FmHA offered to let Harris lease-back or buy-back the farmland, subject to conservation easements imposed on the 1,005 acres. Harris opted to repurchase the land for $371,700, which was the land's fair market value with the conservation easements in place.... The wetland easements prevent Harris from farming the land and allow the FWS to manage water flow and other conditions on the land.

Harris subsequently sued the FmHA, contending that it had no authority to impose the wetland conservation easements. Harris alternatively contended that the FmHA's decision to impose the easements was arbitrary and capricious because much of the property designated as wetlands did not possess scientifically-accepted indicators of wetland status. The district court granted summary judgment for the United States as to Harris' first contention, holding that the FmHA had the authority to place wetland easements on the property that he repurchased. After a bench trial regarding the second claim, the district court found that the FmHA did not act in an arbitrary or capricious manner when imposing the easements because the land at issue constituted wetlands. Harris now appeals, contending that the district court erred with respect to both claims.

II

Executive Order 11990 requires that all federal agencies "take action to minimize the destruction, loss or degradation of wetlands, and to preserve and enhance the natural and beneficial values of wetlands in carrying out the agency's responsibilities for (1) acquiring, managing, and disposing of Federal lands and facilities...." Exec. Order No. 11990, § 1(a), 42 Fed.Reg. 26,961 (1977), reprinted as amended in 42 U.S.C. § 4321 note (1988). Moreover,

> when Federally-owned wetlands or portions of wetlands are proposed for lease, easement, right-of-way or disposal to non-Federal public or private parties, the Federal agency shall (a) reference in the conveyance those uses that are restricted under identified Federal, State or local wetlands regulations; and (b) attach other appropriate restrictions to the uses of properties by the grantee or

purchaser and any successor, except where prohibited by law; or (c) withhold such properties from disposal.

Id. § 4.... Both parties agree that this order, which was issued by President Carter pursuant to statutory authority, ... has the force and effect of a statute enacted by Congress. *See Eatmon v. Bristol Steel & Iron Works, Inc.*, 769 F.2d 1503 (11th Cir.1985). The FmHA contends that the order authorized it to impose the wetland conservation easements at issue. Harris, on the other hand, argues that the FmHA was "prohibited by law"—i.e., prohibited by the Food Security Act of 1985, Pub.L. No. 99–198, 99 Stat. 1526 (1985), and the Agricultural Credit Act of 1987, Pub.L. No. 100–233, 101 Stat. 1669 (1988)—from imposing the challenged easements.

A

Harris initially contends that 7 U.S.C. § 1985(e), ... which was added by the Agricultural Credit Act, prohibits the FmHA from imposing wetland easements on the property at issue because "no where in the language of [§ 1985] is the Secretary given the right to condition the exercise of leaseback/buyback rights on the acceptance of a wetlands easement." In essence, Harris' argument is that Congress prohibited the FmHA from imposing wetland conservation easements by not specifically codifying the FmHA's authority to do so. Nonetheless, there is no question that, in the absence of statutory authority to the contrary, Executive Order 11990 binds the FmHA. Thus, the issue presented is whether Congress sub-silentio rendered Executive Order 11990 void as it pertains to the buyback program by not specifically codifying the FmHA's authority to impose wetland easements. Harris relies upon four statutory provisions to support his contention that Congress barred the FmHA from imposing wetland conservation easements on property subject to the borrower's redemption rights.

1

Harris first asserts that language found in § 1985(e)(7) supports his interpretation of § 1985(e)(1)(A). Subsection (7) states:

> In the case of farmland administered under this chapter that is highly erodible land (as defined in section 3801 of Title 16), the Secretary may require the use of specified conservation practices on such land as a condition of the sale or lease of such land.

7 U.S.C. § 1985(e)(7). Because Congress did not similarly codify the FmHA's authority to impose such conditions of sale with regard to wetlands, Harris concludes that subsection (7) provides "strong evidence of Congress' intent not to subordinate the leaseback/buyback rights to any affirmative duty that the FmHA might have had under Executive Order 11990 to place wetlands easements on inventory land." However, an alternative—and more plausible—reading of Congress' inaction is that Congress felt no need to codify the FmHA's power to impose wetland easements because Executive Order 11990 already obliged the FmHA to do so. Consequently, we find Harris' contention unavailing.

2

Harris next argues that the language of 7 U.S.C. § 1997, which authorizes the FmHA to acquire conservation easements from delinquent borrowers, supports his reading of § 1985(e)(1)(A). Section 1997 allow the FmHA to "purchase" such easements

> by canceling that part of the aggregate amount of such outstanding loans of the borrower held by the Secretary . . . that bears the same ratio to the aggregate amount of the outstanding loans of such borrower held by the Secretary . . . as the number of acres of the real property of such borrower that are subject to such easement bears to the aggregate number of acres securing such loans.

7 U.S.C. § 1997(e). Harris concludes that because "Congress intended for the FmHA to 'purchase' conservation easements from distressed borrowers, Congress did not intend to empower the Secretary of Agriculture to extract a conservation easement by coercion from a farmer exercising his leaseback/buyback rights." Harris, however, overlooks the fact that the § 1997 program could not be used in this case because Grenada Bank, not the FmHA, foreclosed upon Harris' farm. Thus, the FmHA could not have purchased the easements from Harris as Harris did not own the property when the FmHA acquired it. Accordingly, Harris' reliance upon § 1997 is misplaced.

3

Harris next points to § 616 of the Agricultural Credit Act, which allows the FmHA, for conservation purposes, to transfer to a Federal or State agency any real property administered by the FmHA "with respect to which the rights of all prior owners and operators have expired." 7 U.S.C. § 2002. Harris argues that because "Congress expressly made leaseback/buyback rights superior to the right of the FmHA to transfer land under the 616 program . . ., it would seem logical that Congress also intended to make leaseback/buyback rights superior to the right of FmHA to exercise its authority under Executive Order 11990 to enhance wetlands." Harris fails to demonstrate, however, that the imposition of wetland conservation easements pursuant to Executive Order 11990 is inconsistent with the § 616 program. Indeed, Congress now has statutorily authorized the FmHA to impose easements on inventory land subject to the redemption provision of § 1985(e)(1)(A), . . . while at the same time retaining the § 616 program. Consequently, we find Harris' contention without merit.

4

Harris finally contends that 7 U.S.C. § 1985(g), which Harris concedes is not applicable here, . . . supports his interpretation of § 1985(e)(1)(A). Subsection (g) allows the FmHA to "establish perpetual wetland conservation easements to protect and restore wetlands or converted wetlands that exist on inventoried property, as determined by the Secretary in accordance with title XII of the Food Security Act of 1985 (16 U.S.C. § 3801 et seq.)." 7 U.S.C. § 1985(g)(1)(Supp. IV 1993).

Harris submits that Congress charged the FmHA with the duty to impose such easements because the FmHA did not have such a duty previously. Harris, however, fails to recognize that Congress, in adopting subsection (g), recognized the prior existing authority of the FmHA to impose wetland conservation easements. For example, the relevant Senate report noted that the enactment of subsection (g) would alleviate[ ]a problem with the current use of U.S. Fish and Wildlife Service easements on inventory property.... Easements can reduce the productive value of the property in some cases. For the FmHA borrower/owner who conveyed his or her property to the agency, and who exercises his or her redemption rights, the land could be worth less than when it was conveyed.

* * *

B

Harris has produced no evidence suggesting that Congress intended to repeal Executive Order 11990 as it applies to FmHA inventory land. *See Sedima, S.P.R.L. v. Imrex Co.*, 473 U.S. 479, 490, 105 S.Ct. 3275, 3281, 87 L.Ed.2d 346 (1985)(noting that if Congress wishes to change the law in a "novel" way, some mention of that intent should be present in the statute or its legislative history); *Farmer v. Employment Sec. Comm'n of N.C.*, 4 F.3d 1274, 1283–84 (4th Cir.1993)("It is settled law that repeal of a statute by implication is not favored."). Moreover, Executive Order 11990 and 7 U.S.C. § 1985(e)(1)(A) do not conflict such that the two cannot operate concurrently. *See* 1A Norman J. Singer, Sutherland Statutory Construction § 23.09, at 338 (5th ed. 1993)(noting that "in the absence of some affirmative showing of an intention to repeal, the only permissible justification for a repeal by implication is when the earlier and later statutes are irreconcilable or if the later act covers the whole subject of the earlier one and is clearly intended as a substitute"). Furthermore, subsection (e)(1)(B) states that "any purchase or lease under [§ 1985(e)(1)(A)] shall be on such terms and conditions as are established in regulations promulgated by the Secretary." 7 U.S.C. § 1985(e)(1)(B).... The regulations promulgated by the FmHA explicitly require that wetland conservation easements be placed on land sold pursuant to the buyback program authorized by § 1985. ... Accordingly, we cannot conclude that Congress, when authorizing the redemption program, intended to bar the FmHA from imposing wetland conservation easements under Executive Order 11990....

III

A

Harris' second claim is that the FmHA's designation of certain areas of his property as wetlands constitutes arbitrary and capricious action under the Administrative Procedure Act ("APA"), 5 U.S.C. § 706. "Under the APA, the administrative record is reviewed to determine whether the challenged action was arbitrary and capricious, an abuse of discretion, or otherwise not in accordance with law...." *State of Louisiana v.*

Verity, 853 F.2d 322, 326 (5th Cir.1988); see 5 U.S.C. § 706(2)(A). Under this "very narrow" standard of review, we may not "weigh the evidence in the record pro and con." Verity, 853 F.2d at 327. Instead, "our role is to review the agency action to determine whether the decision 'was based on a consideration of the relevant factors and whether there was a clear error of judgment.' " ... *Id.* (quoting *Motor Vehicle Mfrs. Ass'n of the United States v. State Farm Mut. Auto. Ins. Co.*, 463 U.S. 29, 43, 103 S.Ct. 2856, 2966–67, 77 L.Ed.2d 443 (1983)). "Thus, if the agency considers the factors and articulates a rational relationship between the facts found and the choice made, its decision is not arbitrary or capricious." *Id.* "Indeed, the agency's decision need not be ideal, so long as it is not arbitrary or capricious, and so long as the agency gave at least minimal consideration to relevant facts contained in the record." *Id.* (footnote omitted).

The Executive Order defines "wetlands" as

> those areas that are inundated by surface or ground water with a frequency sufficient to support and under normal circumstances does or would support a prevalence of vegetative or aquatic life that requires saturated or seasonally saturated soil conditions for growth and reproduction. Wetlands generally include swamps, marshes, bogs, and similar areas such as sloughs, potholes, wet meadows, river overflows, mud flats, and natural ponds.

Exec. Order No. 11990, § 7(c). While the Order does not provide a methodology for determining whether a specific parcel of land constitutes wetland, the parties nevertheless agree that property constitutes a wetland area only when both a wetland hydrology and hydric soils are present and the area's vegetation is predominately hydrophytic. ... Pursuant to those criteria, Charles McCabe, a FWS biologist, made the initial recommendation regarding Harris' property.... Harris contends that the process by which McCabe produced his proposed delineation was so flawed as to render McCabe's conclusions, the FWS's wetland delineation, and the FmHA's decision to implement the FWS's delineation arbitrary and capricious agency action.

B

Before conducting an on-site inspection of the property at issue, which consisted of four separate tracts of land, McCabe examined the topographical maps and aerial photographs for the applicable area to determine the boundaries of Harris' land. McCabe also examined the relevant soil surveys prepared by the United States Soil Conservation Service ("SCS") to ascertain whether the soils in the region surrounding Harris' property were hydric or non-hydric. McCabe further examined flood data accumulated by the Corps of Engineers to discern whether Harris' property fell within a flood plain. McCabe and two other biologists—one from the Mississippi Department of Wildlife Conservation and one from FWS Division of Wildlife Refuges—subsequently inspected Harris' land, spending a total of approximately seven hours on the four tracts. McCabe then formulated proposed wetland delineations, which he discussed with FWS Acting Field Supervisor Robert Barkley. McCabe, accompanied by Barkley, later inspected Harris' property a second time. After the latter inspection, Barkley, and the review committee of the FWS regional office, approved McCabe's report and recommendations that wetland easements be imposed on all four tracts of land.... The FmHA accepted the recommendations without change. Harris, relying primarily on the testimony of his expert, contends that McCabe's delineation is deficient for a multitude of reasons....

Harris initially contends that McCabe failed to employ a scientifically acceptable methodology when formulating his wetland easements recommendations because he was not aware of and did not refer to FWS publications dealing with wetland delineation. McCabe, however, testified that he followed the FWS-approved three parameter approach—which requires an examination of the land's vegetation, hydrology, and soils—when determining whether Harris' property included wetlands, although he admittedly did not specifically refer to the publications when formulating his recommendations. Although Harris attempted at trial to discredit McCabe, the district court chose to credit McCabe's testimony. On the cold record before us, we cannot say the district court erred in doing so. *See Anderson v. Bessemer City*, 470 U.S. 564, 573, 105 S.Ct. 1504, 1511, 84 L.Ed.2d 518 (1985)(noting that we must give "due regard to the trial court to judge the credibility of the witnesses"). Moreover, while McCabe may not have been as experienced in delineating wetlands as Dr. Heineke, McCabe did have sufficient expertise in wetland classification in that, at the time he inspected Harris' property, he had eighteen years experience dealing with wetlands and wetland issues and had delineated forty-four other properties.

Harris next argues that the FWS wetland delineation was fatally flawed because McCabe failed both to procure soil samples from the four tracts and to accurately measure whether the vegetation present on all four tracts was predominately hydrophytic.... However, the SCS soil surveys consulted by McCabe prior to his on-site inspection evidenced the presence of hydric soils on tracts I, II, and III. Moreover, based on prior experience, the SCS and the FWS previously had determined that, with very few exceptions, hydrophytic vegetation predominated on all land situated within the Mississippi delta area.... Additionally, maps prepared by the United States Department of Agriculture demonstrated that wetlands surrounded tracts I and III, and flood data gathered by the Army Corps of Engineers demonstrated that tracts I, II, and III were under water for extended periods of time at least one year out of every three. ... Finally, data obtained from the Corps of Engineers demonstrated that tract IV also was subject to frequent flooding.... Consequently, sufficient evidence supports the FmHA's decision to impose wetland easements on Harris' land.

Harris next points out that the easements imposed by the FmHA include not only wetlands, but also what the FWS termed "wetland buffer areas." ... Harris contends that Executive Order 11990 does not allow the FmHA to impose easements on land that does not satisfy the definition of wetlands. McCabe testified that buffer zones contained highly erodible land that, if protected by an easement, would help to both protect and allow proper management of the wetlands. Furthermore, Steve Gard, a FWS employee and an expert in the area of wetland science, explained that the FWS sometimes recommended that the FmHA impose an easement somewhat larger than the actual wetland area because the FWS needed to "block off" an area of land for management purposes. For example, Gard explained that if the FWS designated only "each and every" acre of wetland, an accurate description for surveying and title recording purposes would be impossible. Moreover, if the FWS attempted to manage water movement on such small areas, non-easement lands most likely would be flooded. Based upon such evidence, we conclude that the FmHA did not act arbitrarily or capriciously in imposing wetland easements on property considered to be part of a wetland buffer zone. *See* S.Rep. No. 357 at 217, reprinted in 1990 U.S.C.C.A.N. at 4871 (noting that buffer areas sometimes are needed "to produce a high quality wetland").

Finally, Harris argues that McCabe's delineation was deficient because McCabe failed to make or keep field notes recording the observations he made while inspecting the four tracts of land.... McCabe, however, testified as to both the observations he made while inspecting the property and the conclusions that he reached based on those observations. Moreover, as the district court concluded, evidence presented at trial "clearly indicates a wealth of institutional knowledge available to the agency participants, and upon which they drew[ ]in making the delineations in issue." ... Thus, while it certainly should not be standard agency procedure to discard such material, the facts presented here demonstrate that the FmHA's decision to implement the wetland delineations recommended by the FWS was not arbitrary and capricious.

IV

For the foregoing reasons, we AFFIRM the judgment of the district court.

NATURAL RESOURCES DEFENSE COUNCIL v. REILLY

983 F.2d 259 (D.C.Cir.1993).

EDWARDS, CIRCUIT JUDGE:

* * *

B. Legislative and Regulatory Responses to the "Refueling Vapor Recovery" Problem

Under the 1977 amendments to the CAA, EPA was required to promulgate ORVR regulations if it found ORVR to be a feasible and desirable means of controlling vapor emissions during refueling. Pub. L. No. 95–95, § 216, 91 Stat. 760–61 (1977).... Upon review of the information available to it in the late 1970's, EPA initially concluded that ORVR was "technically feasible." *See* 52 Fed. Reg. at 31,163 (describing conclusions reached in 1980). However, in order to avoid placing additional regulatory burdens on the ailing American automotive industry, EPA decided not to require ORVR systems at that time. *See* 46 FR 21,628, 21,629 (1981).

In 1984, EPA again took up the ORVR issue in a draft study entitled "Evaluation of Air Pollution Strategies for Gasoline Marketing Industry," EPA–45%–84–012A (July 1984). *See* 49 FR 31,706, 31,707 (1984)(announcing the public availability of the study). After thorough reconsideration, EPA concluded that ORVR was the preferred control technology and proceeded to detail proposed regulations for the implementation of mandatory ORVR. 52 Fed. Reg. at 31,162. In that same Federal Register Notice, EPA addressed the technical difficulties associated with a practical ORVR system. EPA concluded that ORVR was generally safe and that approximately two years of lead time would be sufficient for manufacturers to install ORVR in new models since most of the technology was already available. 52 Fed. Reg. at 31,202–03.

Researchers at NHTSA had a somewhat different view of the situation, for they had continuing concerns that ORVR would lead to an increase in crash and non-crash vehicle fires.... *See* 57 FR 13,220 (1992). Thus, before promulgating a final rule, EPA initiated further dialogue with NHTSA in order to address these issues.

NHTSA's concerns stemmed primarily from its view that ORVR would increase the complexity of fuel systems and concomitantly the risk of fire. EPA specifically responded to this concern in its 1988 draft report on the safety of ORVR. First, EPA challenged NHTSA's underlying assumption that there is a positive correlation between increased complexity and increased risk. EPA noted that the increasing design complexity of automobiles without significant safety degradation "strongly suggests that onboard systems of various design complexities could also be implemented safely." EPA Draft "Summary & Analysis of Comments Regarding Potential Safety Implications of Onboard Vapor Recovery Systems" at 3–35 (Aug. 1988) [hereinafter "EPA Draft"], reprinted in J.A. at 78. Second, even assuming that added complexity means added safety risk, EPA determined that ORVR systems need not be overly complex. According to the draft report, ORVR canister systems could be devised that would be simple extensions of present evaporative systems. *See id.* at 3–40. Thus, EPA found that "straightforward, reliable, and relatively inexpensive engineering solutions exist for each of the potential problems identified." *Id.*

In order to test this conclusion, EPA constructed a simple ORVR canister system and installed it in a test vehicle. *Id.* at 5–6. This vehicle adequately performed under limited testing conditions, leading EPA to summarize the experiment as follows:

> Onboard systems can be simple extensions or modifications of present evaporative systems. Further, modifications that are necessary can even simplify certain aspects of the current design. With the

proper design, no risk need be added, and in fact, refueling controls can offer several safety benefits.

Id. at 5–7. To further assess the safety of proposed ORVR systems, EPA contracted with an outside firm to complete an independent study. In September, 1988, after reviewing the risk of vehicle fire for ten different fuel system designs, the Battelle Institute's Transportation Safety Group concluded that the risk of fire was remote in all cases and that it would not be significantly impacted by the installation of ORVR. *See* EPA, Refueling Emission Controls: A Briefing for the National Highway Transportation Safety Administration at 25 (Apr. 21, 1989) (hereinafter "EPA Briefing"), reprinted in J.A. at 132.

During this period, EPA was also receiving further input from NHTSA. In October, 1988, NHTSA submitted its analysis of EPA's draft report as well as an analysis of the public comments EPA had received as a result of its proposed ORVR regulations. First, NHTSA reiterated that increased design complexity in fuel systems tends to result in greater fire risk. *See* DOT, Comments on the August 1988 EPA Draft at 9 (Oct. 1988), reprinted in J.A. at 505. In addition, NHTSA discounted the value of the tests done with the EPA prototype ORVR canister system since EPA neglected to account for certain problems that would arise under actual operating conditions, such as fuel leakage and lack of "drivability" (e.g., engine stalls and hesitation during acceleration). *See Id.* at 10. Thus, NHTSA contended that ORVR would add complexity to the system and increase, by an unquantified amount, safety hazards. *Id.* at 9. After reviewing NHTSA's assessment, and in view of imminent amendments to the CAA, EPA declined to issue final rules requiring ORVR systems. *See* 57 FR at 13,220.

In 1990, Congress again amended the CAA, this time establishing a comprehensive framework for controlling refueling emissions. Under sections 182(b)(3), (c), (d), and (e), Stage II controls are required in moderate, serious, severe, and extreme nonattainment areas. 42 U.S.C. § 7511a (Supp. 1990). Amended section 202(a)(6) of the CAA now mandates that EPA, after consultation with DOT regarding safety, shall promulgate standards for ORVR by November 15, 1991. . . . Pursuant to this statutory mandate, EPA reinitiated consultation with DOT, through NHTSA. NHTSA then embarked upon a further review of ORVR canister safety. Since actual ORVR systems were proprietary and not available for independent testing, NHTSA used components of, and data pertaining to, current evaporative systems to reach its conclusions. DOT Assessment at 11. NHTSA acknowledged that, because of availability problems, it did not consider or evaluate ORVR systems other than canisters. *See* DOT Review at 4.

NHTSA's final report was submitted to EPA in July, 1991. The report identified potential failure points of an ORVR canister system during operation. DOT Assessment at 7–8. However, this analysis was premised on four critical and unproven assumptions about ORVR canister systems. First, since ORVR systems will store more vapors than existing evaporative canisters, NHTSA hypothesized that the fire hazard posed by larger ORVR canisters would be greater than that of existing canisters. *Id.* at 3. Second, NHTSA speculated that the quantity of vapors being moved through the system during refueling will be large compared to that which passes through current evaporative systems. *Id.* at 9. Third, NHTSA assumed that the complexity of the ORVR canister system will be greater than present systems, thus increasing the possibility of component failure. *Id.* Finally, NHTSA contended that the increased quantity of fuel vapor being carried in the vehicle at any given time will lead to a greater chance of fire in the event of a crash in which canister integrity is lost and the contents of the canister are exposed to an ignition source. *Id.* Based on these assumptions, NHTSA concluded that:

> Under certain conditions representative of the motor vehicle crash and operating environment, ORVR refueling vapor recovery systems would result in a substantial increase in fire potential. These occurrences result in an increased safety risk and hence would have a negative impact on safety.

Id. at 10. Although NHTSA maintained that the testing conditions it used simulated real world environments, it recognized that the occurrence of these conditions would be unlikely. *Id.* at 11.

After publication of the study, EPA requested public comment on NHTSA's findings and conclusions. *See* 56 FR 43,682–83 (1991). In late September, a public hearing on the matter was held in which both EPA and NHTSA officials participated. *See* 57 Fed. Reg. at 13,221. EPA then asked NHTSA to review the presentations made at the hearing and to respond to public comments. NHTSA's technical evaluation, which followed on November 27, concluded:

> On this issue, the record is clear and unambiguous. Implementation of ORVR, regardless of prototype development and technological evolution, will increase safety risks. ORVR systems will require additional components and must manage, store, and transport larger quantities of flammable fuel vapor.... Thus, further technology development and operational successes or failures of prototype vehicles will not eliminate the fundamental safety issues associated with ORVR systems.

>   * * *

> NHTSA considers these risks to be inherent. We [NHTSA] believe that no amount of product development or engineering and quality control measures would fully alleviate these risks, regardless of lead time.

DOT Review at 4–5.

While this evaluation process was being completed, the November 15, 1991 deadline for the promulgation of ORVR standards passed without EPA action. Alleging that EPA had failed to abide by the statutory mandate in section 202(a)(6), NRDC filed suit in the Eastern

District of Virginia under section 304(a) of the CAA. *See* Natural Resources Defense Council v. Reilly, 788 F.Supp. 268 (E.D.Va.1992). Before the case could be concluded, however, EPA issued a Notice of Final Agency Action in which it determined that the safety risks of onboard systems outweighed the environmental benefits of such devices and that it would not, therefore, promulgate standards pursuant to section 202(a)(6). *See* 57 Fed. Reg. at 13,220–31. Noting that section 307(b)(1) of the CAA confers exclusive jurisdiction on the United States Court of Appeals for the District of Columbia Circuit to review Final Agency Action, the district court dismissed the case without prejudice. *NRDC v. Reilly*, 788 F.Supp. at 273–74. That decision has been appealed to the Fourth Circuit, which is holding the case in abeyance pending the outcome in this case. *NRDC v. Reilly*, No. 92–1534 (4th Cir.1992).

II. Discussion

The principal dispute in this case involves EPA's interpretation of section 202(a)(6) of the CAA. NRDC contends that the section contains an unambiguous requirement that EPA promulgate standards for ORVR systems. EPA, on the other hand, sees the "consultation" requirement contained in section 202(a)(6) as the last vestige of discretion permitted the Agency. In particular, the Agency argues that Congress did not intend that EPA promulgate ORVR standards if it found the systems to be inherently and unreasonably unsafe.

Since EPA is charged with administering the CAA, NRDC's challenge to its construction of this provision must be reviewed using the analysis provided by the Supreme Court in *Chevron USA, Inc. v. Natural Resources Defense Council Inc.*, 467 U.S. 837, 81 L.Ed.2d 694, 104 S.Ct. 2778 (1984).

If, under the first prong of [the] *Chevron* analysis, we can determine congressional intent by using "traditional tools of statutory construction," then that interpretation must be given effect. *United Food & Commercial Workers*, 484 U.S. at 123 (1987). If, on the other hand, "the statute is silent or ambiguous with respect to the specific issue," then we will defer to a "permissible" agency construction of the statute. *Chevron*, 467 U.S. at 848, 104 S.Ct. at 8781.

* * *

It is only legislative intent to delegate such authority that entitles an agency to advance its own statutory construction for review under the deferential second prong of *Chevron. See Chevron*, 467 U.S. at 843–44, 104 S.Ct. at 2781–82. "If Congress has explicitly left a gap for the agency to fill, there is an express delegation of authority. . . . Sometimes the legislative delegation to an agency on a particular question is implicit rather than explicit. In such a case, a court may not substitute its own construction of a statutory provision for a reasonable interpretation made by the administrator of an agency." *Id.*

Kansas City v. Department of Housing & Urban Dev., 287 U.S.App.D.C. 365, 923 F.2d 188, 191–92 (D.C.Cir.1991).

Given the plain and unmistakable language of section 202(a)(6), we need not proceed beyond the first step of the *Chevron* analysis. Section 202(a)(6) mandates that "within one year after November 15, 1990, the Administrator shall ... promulgate standards under this section requiring that new light duty vehicles ... shall be equipped with [ORVR] systems." 42 U.S.C. § 7521(a)(6)(Supp. 1990).... In this case, the language of the relevant section most manifestly obligates EPA to promulgate standards for ORVR systems. *See Hewitt v. Helms*, 459 U.S. 460, 471, 74 L.Ed.2d 675, 103 S.Ct. 864 (1983)("shall" is "language of an unmistakably mandatory character"); *Her Majesty the Queen v. USEPA*, 286 U.S.App.D.C. 171, 912 F.2d 1525, 1533 (D.C.Cir.1990) ("shall" signals mandatory action).

Where the authors of the CAA intended to create a conditional duty, they used the familiar words of condition. *See*, e.g., CAA § 112(d)(9) ... ("No standard for radionuclide emissions ... is required ... under this section if the Administrator determines, by rule, and after consultation with the Nuclear Regulatory Commission, that the regulatory program established by the Nuclear Regulatory Commission ... provides an ample margin of safety to protect the public health.") ...; CAA § 110(c)(1) ... ("The Administrator shall promulgate a Federal implementation plan at any time within the 2 years after the Administrator ... disapproves a State implementation plan submission in whole or in part, unless the State corrects the deficiency, and the Administrator approves the plan or revision, before the Administrator promulgates such Federal implementation plan.").... No such words of condition are found in the consultation requirement of section 202(a)(6) that derogate from EPA's duty to promulgate ORVR standards. Therefore, EPA exceeded its statutory authority by declining to issue the standards.

Recognizing that its only hope of prevailing in this case is to reach the deferential second step of *Chevron*, EPA posits two facets of the legislation as evidence of ambiguity. However, neither argument undermines the congressional intention plainly evinced by the "shall promulgate" mandate of section 202(a)(6).

A.   *The Consultation Requirement*

First, EPA argues that although section 202(a)(6) imposes a mandatory duty, the scope of that duty is circumscribed by the requirement that EPA consult with DOT regarding ORVR safety. EPA argues that the section does not specify how the consultation requirement "meshes" with the duty to promulgate standards, thus making the section at least ambiguous. We reject this argument because it is premised on a reading of "consultation" that would effectively result in DOT having a "veto" over any EPA action in compliance with the statutory duty to promulgate ORVR standards. This is a specious construction of the statute.

To begin with, the statute expressly provides that EPA "shall" promulgate standards "after" consultation with DOT, not "subject to" or "conditioned upon" that consultation.... Thus, no substantive result of the consultation is comprehended within the text that might vitiate EPA's mandatory duty to promulgate standards: no determination is required, no minimal standard for safety is articulated, and no particular measure or purpose of the consultation is specified. This does not mean that ORVR safety concerns will never be addressed. Sections 206(a)(3)(A) and 202(a)(4) of the Act provide for a later certification process to ensure that no system will be installed in an automobile for sale to the public unless it is safe. 42 U.S.C. §§ 7525(a)(3)(A), 7521(a)(4)(Supp. 1990); see also 40 C.F.R. Part 86 (regulatory certification process and standards). However, this safety evaluation comes at a later stage in the implementation of emission control systems. It does not affect the duty to promulgate standards in the first instance.

Read in context, the central purpose of section 202(a)(6) is to impose regulatory standards for ORVR systems over a given and detailed time frame. Inserted parenthetically in this structure is a requirement that EPA consult with DOT regarding safety issues. Contrary to EPA's contention, the fact that the DOT consultation is merely advisory does not make it meaningless. At least two reasons for the requirement are apparent: first, the process might have been meant to provide EPA with a better awareness of various systems so that ORVR standards might accurately conform to imminently available technology; conversely, the process might allow EPA to structure standards that will promote the design and development of safer systems. In any event, as a matter of statutory construction, such a general consultation clause will not normally render nugatory other substantive requirements in a statute. *See, e.g., Natural Resources Defense Council v. Train*, 166 U.S.App.D.C. 312, 510 F.2d 692, 704 (D.C.Cir.1974)(consultation requirement in Federal Water Pollution Control Act did not undermine a mandatory duty). So here, too, we find that it does not call into question the express command of the section.

Further, the structure of current section 202(a)(6) stands in stark contrast with that of its predecessor, which required EPA to determine the feasibility and desirability of ORVR prior to promulgating ORVR standards. In the former section, it was necessary for EPA to determine that such systems were safe as a condition precedent to the promulgation of ORVR standards. Thus, it was implicit in that statutory scheme that EPA exercise discretion in deciding whether or not to implement regulations for ORVR systems. By deleting the determination requirement in the new section, Congress sent an unmistakable message that the consultation requirement is not to be used by EPA to avoid its obligation to promulgate standards for ORVR systems.

It is important to note that this is not a case in which EPA has made an irrefutable finding that no ORVR system could be developed in the foreseeable future that would be safe. Both EPA and NHTSA restricted their analysis of ORVR to charcoal canister systems similar to those used in present evaporative systems. 57 Fed. Reg. at 13,230. Both agencies rationalized this limitation by pointing out the embryonic nature of other ORVR technologies. *See* DOT Review at 4 (other technologies not available for evaluation); 57 Fed. Reg. at 13,230 (EPA did not consider "undeveloped technologies"). Yet, this narrow review is not defensible on the facts of this case.

First, the statute clearly calls for EPA to evaluate ORVR "systems." The use of the plural defeats any implication that Congress intended EPA to consider only ORVR canister technology. *Cf. Association of American Railroads v. Costle*, 183 U.S.App.D.C. 362, 562 F.2d 1310, 1315 (D.C.Cir.1977)(reference to "equipment and facilities" in Noise Control Act of 1972 encompasses "all such equipment and facilities")(emphasis in original); *Natural Resources Defense Council v. USEPA*, 915 F.2d 1314, 1320 (9th Cir.1990)(use of plural in Clean Water Act foreclosed EPA from restricting the scope of its duties).

We have previously noted a distinction between provisions in the CAA that are "technology-based" and those that are "absolute." *See Natural Resources Defense Council v. USEPA*, 210 U.S.App.D.C. 205, 655 F.2d 318, 322 & 332 n. 25 (D.C.Cir.1981). Technology-based provisions require EPA to promulgate standards only after finding that the requisite technology exists or may be feasibly developed. *Id.* at 322. Absolute standards, on the other hand, require compliance with statutorily prescribed standards and time tables, irrespective of present technologies. *Id.* Absolute standards presume that industry can be driven to develop the requisite technologies.... In this case, the use of the word "systems" in section 202(a)(6), in combination with the statutorily fixed time table, indicates that this provision falls into the "absolute" category and, hence, is technology-forcing. There is nothing in the section warranting EPA's decision to limit its consideration of ORVR to a single existing technology. Moreover, this statutory command was not, EPA's protestations to the contrary notwithstanding, unrealistic. While it is true that alternative control methods are not production-ready, several are beyond the conceptualization stage and should have been amenable to engineering evaluation.

For instance, vapor condensers and vapor combusters have been considered as alternatives to canister containment systems, and both were sufficiently developed to be the subject of investigation by auto manufacturers in 1988. EPA Draft at 3–3. Perhaps the most promising alternative to canisters are the previously mentioned flexible fuel bladders. The record indicates that this option has been extensively researched and that EPA had information in its possession four years ago tending to show that bladder systems could be production-ready within one or two years.... There is simply no basis for us to believe that Congress was not aware that flexible bladders represented a plausible alternative to charcoal canisters or that Congress did not intend for EPA to consider them in promulgating ORVR standards. *See* S. REP. No. 228, 101st Cong., 2d Sess. 94 (1990)(specifically noting flexible fuel bladder alternative); see also 52 Fed. Reg. at 31,175 (bladders recognized as an alternative in 1987); *Id.* at 31,202 (bladders may improve fuel system safety). In addition, at least two other systems have been hypothesized which might eliminate or reduce many of the safety hazards that EPA perceived as attendant to ORVR canister systems. *See* U.S. Patent No. 4,880,135 (Nov. 14, 1989)(bellow tank); Memorandum from Karen Lostoski, Mechanical Engineer, EPA, to Public Docket No. A–87–11 (Sept. 9, 1988) (carbon cloth as a substitute for granulated activated carbon in ORVR canisters), reprinted in J.A. at 527 n. 14 Thus, in restricting its safety analysis to a single type of ORVR system, EPA disregarded its responsibility under the Act.

Moreover, with respect to ORVR canisters, it is not clear that either EPA or NHTSA concluded that these systems are incapable of being made reasonably safe. . . . Rather, it appears from the record that both EPA and NHTSA balanced the risks and benefits of ORVR against the risks and benefits of Stage II controls. *See* DOT Assessment at 3 (NHTSA weighed availability of Stage II controls in its ORVR safety assessment); 57 Fed. Reg. at 13,223 (EPA considers the availability of Stage II controls integral to decision); see also *Id.* at 13,221 (NHTSA concluded that "some risk" was inherent in ORVR canisters that was not present in Stage II controls); Letter from Jerry Ralph Curry, NHTSA, to William G. Rosenberg, Assistant Administrator for Air and Radiation, EPA (Oct. 31, 1991)("after weighing the alternatives," NHTSA would find ORVR an unreasonable safety risk), reprinted in J.A. at 464; EPA Briefing at 9a (relative effectiveness of ORVR and Stage II controls); cf. 57 Fed. Reg. at 13,223 (canister systems "potentially subject to additional failure modes"). . . . This reading is borne out by EPA's explanation of its final action that the decision not to promulgate ORVR standards was heavily dependent upon the ready availability of Stage II controls. *See id.* at 13,230.

Although EPA finally concluded that canister based systems present safety problems which are not "entirely capable of resolution," *Id.*, much of the data in the record directly contravenes this assertion. For instance, NHTSA assumed that ORVR canisters would add complexity to current fuel systems. . . . Yet, the EPA simple prototype proved that it was at least possible to build a simple ORVR canister system. . . . Moreover, the analytical approach used by NHTSA contains a logical flaw. NHTSA's tests seem to show that ORVR may increase risk under certain conditions. However, NHTSA presented no data on the likelihood of those conditions existing in the real world. Therefore, it is impossible to move directly from NHTSA's data to EPA's conclusion that ORVR canisters pose an unreasonable risk.

In addition, many of the benefits of ORVR that were recognized by EPA in its 1988 draft report were largely ignored in its final determination that ORVR is unreasonably unsafe. For instance, the number of service station fires . . . will almost certainly be reduced by ORVR. EPA Draft at 4–1. Second, repeated or prolonged dermal contact with liquid gasoline due to spillage can be reduced by ORVR, thus relieving the resultant skin irritation and dermatitis. *See id.* at 4–12. Perhaps most significantly, ORVR may help lower fuel tank pressures. . . . Greater fuel tank pressure leads to, among other things, fuel dispersion in tank rupture accidents. ORVR canister systems would require an increase in the size of the fuel tank venting orifices and thus decrease fuel tank pressures. *Id.* at 4–14. Finally, under operating conditions, vehicles sometimes create vapors that exceed the capacity of current evaporative canisters leading to so called "breakthrough" and the seepage of vapors into the engine compartment. Larger canisters in ORVR systems would capture and contain these vapors.

In short, the record as a whole does not substantiate a finding that ORVR systems present inherent and unreasonable safety risks. What is clear is that EPA has decided that ORVR canister systems are not worth the risk given that

> Stage II controls are a viable alternative. However, even were we to accept that Congress left some small amount of discretion in the statute for EPA to decline to require ORVR if it found such systems unreasonably hazardous, that discretion would be constrained to a measurement of the safety considerations of ORVR alone, weighed against the incremental environmental protection that ORVR systems would provide.... Thus, EPA's balancing of ORVR canisters against Stage II controls would still be an inappropriate basis upon which to decline to promulgate ORVR standards. ...

B. *The Lapse of Stage II Requirements*

EPA also argues that section 202(a)(6)'s provision for the lapse of Stage II requirements when EPA promulgates ORVR standards creates an ambiguity that warrants deference to the Agency's interpretation of the statute under the second step of *Chevron.* Specifically, section 202(a)(6) reads in pertinent part:

> The requirements of section 7511a(b)(3) of this title (relating to stage II gasoline vapor recovery) for areas classified under section 7511 of this title as moderate for ozone shall not apply after promulgation of such standards and the administrator may, by rule, revise or waive the application of the requirements of section 7511a(b)(3) of this title for areas classified under section 7511 of this title as Serious, Severe, or Extreme for ozone, as appropriate, after such time as the Administrator determines that onboard emissions control systems required under this paragraph are in widespread use throughout the motor vehicle fleet.

42 U.S.C. § 7521(a)(6)(Supp. 1990). The effective date of the Stage II requirements under section 182(b)(3) of the Act, 42 U.S.C. § 7511a(b)(3) (Supp. 1990), is November 15, 1992, one year after the date by which EPA was obligated to promulgate ORVR standards. EPA concludes from this that Congress provided for an alternative pollution control system in the event that EPA determined that ORVR is unsafe.

However, this reasoning relies on a specious reading of the statutory language. Section 202(a)(6) expressly provides for the termination of Stage II requirements after ORVR standards are promulgated; not if they are promulgated—the implication clearly being that ORVR standards will, at some future time, be promulgated and that Stage II will become unnecessary in certain nonattainment areas at that time. The Stage II requirements, then, are not so much an alternative to ORVR as they are an interim measure to provide environmental protection in the event that ORVR standards are inexplicably delayed.

This "fall-back" approach does not run afoul of any of our standard canons of interpretation. To begin with, there is no direct conflict between the two related sections of the CAA. If ORVR standards had been promulgated on time, the Stage II requirements in moderate nonattainment areas would merely have been superfluous. On the other hand, if EPA missed the statutory deadline—as it in fact has—some vapor emission control would be provided. Although perhaps not the most elegant framework, it was not unreasonable for Congress to provide for contingent environmental protection in the event that EPA missed the statutory deadline, given EPA's record with regard to implementing the CAA. *See NRDC v. Thomas*, 805 F.2d at 416 (EPA "behind the statutory timetable" of the CAA); *Sierra Club v. California*, 658 F.Supp. 165, 175 (N.D.Cal.1987)(EPA had "long-standing unwillingness to comply with" the CAA); see also 136 CONG. REC. S2,436 (daily ed. Mar. 8, 1990)("The history of the Clean Air Act demonstrates that we cannot rely on EPA to follow through on even its mandatory obligations.")(statement of Senator Lieberman). Thus, the overlap between sections 182(b)(3) and 202(a)(6) demonstrates not an ambiguity in the statute, but congressional prudence in providing for foreseeable administrative delays. . . .

It was suggested at oral argument that requiring EPA to promulgate ORVR standards at this point in time, now that the deadline has passed and Stage II controls have become mandatory in moderate and worse non-attainment areas, would impose inefficient double-controls in many areas. Yet, this is not precisely correct, since overlapping Stage II and ORVR controls will not result in complete duplication. As EPA explained in its Final Action, the benefits provided by ORVR are small . . . at fast and increase as fleet turnover occurs. 57 Fed. Reg. at 13,225. Even by the most optimistic view, it will be well into the twenty-first century before a substantial portion of the automobile fleet will be equipped with ORVR fuel systems. *See id.* (at least ten years until ORVR becomes an effective control). Stage II controls will provide important environmental protection in the areas with the worst ozone accumulation while this turnover takes place. In addition, by the terms of the statute, ORVR standards will only apply to light-duty vehicles. Whatever investment has already been made in Stage II controls for moderate nonattainment areas that would have been unnecessary had EPA promulgated ORVR standards on time will benefit the environment by capturing vapor emissions from heavy trucks, motorcycles, and other vehicles not encompassed within the ORVR standards. Thus, a literal reading of the statute does not lead to patently incoherent results. In any event, to the extent that double-control will occur now that the statutory deadline has passed, that contingency was so obvious that it must have been contemplated and accepted by Congress. It is not within the province of this court to second guess such clear legislative policy choices.

The converse problem was also raised at oral argument by EPA, which noted that a period of no control could occur in some moderate nonattainment areas if the requirements for Stage II controls cease to apply after the promulgation of ORVR standards and actual ORVR systems prove to be unreasonably unsafe so that they are denied certification under section 206(a)(3)(A). Although this is a legitimate concern for the Agency, it is not one that we can resolve.... The CAA provides that the requirements for Stage II controls shall not apply in moderate nonattainment areas once ORVR standards are promulgated. The possibility that ORVR systems will not reach the production fleet because of a failure to satisfy certification requirements must have been known to Congress when it passed the 1990 amendments. Thus, the scheme reflects an implicit policy decision by Congress. Whatever the wisdom of that decision, it is committed to Congress alone to make.

III.   Conclusion

The text of section 202(a)(6) clearly manifests a congressional intent that EPA promulgate ORVR standards. The requirement that EPA consult with DOT prior to promulgating the standards does not derogate from that mandatory duty. In addition, the provisions in the CAA for Stage II controls provide for an interim solution to the problem of ozone accumulation until ORVR systems become commonplace. ORVR and Stage II controls are not two alternative approaches between which EPA has discretion to choose. Moreover, even if we were to allow that Congress did not intend for EPA to require ORVR systems if EPA found that ORVR presented inherent and unreasonable safety risks, the record would not support such a finding. At most, it appears that EPA performed a net weighing of the risks and benefits of ORVR canisters relative to Stage II controls. In the end, EPA concluded that it preferred Stage II controls. However, that is not the equivalent of a finding that all ORVR systems present inherent and unreasonable safety risks. Thus, EPA's final decision must be set aside and ORVR standards promulgated in compliance with the CAA.

So Ordered.

WILLIAMS, CIRCUIT JUDGE, concurring: I reluctantly agree with the court that the "shall" of § 202(a)(6) is mandatory, as most "shalls" are, subject only to a very narrow escape hatch—one that would open only if EPA's consultation with the Department of Transportation yielded a finding that all plausible "onboard" (ORVR) systems "present inherent and unreasonable safety risks". Maj. Op. at 273. The EPA finding does not rise to that extreme level. Maj. Op. 268–71. I write separately for two reasons. First, I wish to identify yet another snag that this congressional choice may lead to—a snag that is, however, inherent in the sort of command-and-control, technology-forcing solution that Congress adopted. Second, I wish to emphasize that the exact character of the

EPA's decision under § 202(a)(4) is not before this court, so that our judgment necessarily leaves that issue open.

I

The majority opinion addresses two risks that the statute runs under our interpretation. First, it may leave these ozone-generating vapors substantially uncontrolled either by "onboard" systems installed by motor vehicle manufacturers or by "Stage II" controls installed by gas station operators. Maj. Op. at 273. Second, it may lead to overlapping controls by both. Maj. Op. at 272–73. There is yet a third risk-that auto and gasoline buyers will bear the expense of both systems (or much of that expense) yet secure the benefits of neither. Auto makers will incur at least the R & D costs of onboard controls (and auto buyers will bear them) because of the regulation required by our decision, yet, if none ever passes the ultimate safety test of § 202(a)(4), they will not be installed. Gasoline station operators may incur many of the costs of Stage II controls because they will apply in "moderate" (and worse) areas until such time as the EPA actually issues the required onboard regulation, but they will cease to apply in moderate areas once the onboard regulation issues, because thereafter (regardless of whether the onboard system ever can be installed), the last sentence of § 202(a)(6) specifies that the Stage II controls "shall not apply" in moderate areas after promulgation of the onboard standards. *See* Maj. Op. 264–65 n. 8.

As the majority observes of the no-control and the overlapping control scenarios, however, all this is implicit in the scheme. *See* Maj. Op. 272, 273. Congress evidently believed that a reasonably safe system of onboard controls was likely enough, and the value of securing them great enough, to justify running the various risks outlined in these opinions. The risks are, as the majority observes, perfectly obvious. Ours not to count the cost.

Is all this an inevitable cost in the quest for a clean environment? Under a system of either emissions fees or marketable permits, firms whose production or products pollute can be induced to invest in R & D for pollution-reducing devices under conditions substantially similar to those under which they invest in R & D for products whose demand is generated by consumers—investing up to the point where the marginal cost equals the marginal expected . . . revenues. The difference is simply that the marginal expected revenues take the form of emissions taxes averted, emission permit expenses averted, or revenues from the sale of emissions permits. Such systems offer comparatively efficient methods for addressing pollution, similar to the ways a market economy produces other goods. With rare exceptions, however, Congress has declined to use such methods. Accordingly, consumers must bear the burdens implicit in the statute that we interpret today.

II

The majority opinion suggests at 269–70 and 271 that the safety determination made by the EPA, prefiguring the one ultimately to be made before installment under § 202(a)(4), may not take into account the comparative effectiveness of Stage II controls. Perhaps so, but I should be most reluctant to reach any such conclusion. If system A posed a safety risk of 100 lives a year, one might conclude that that was an acceptable price for a 50% reduction in ozone if it were the only way of achieving the reduction. But if the same reduction could be achieved by system B, at a safety risk of only 10 lives a year and no material alternative drawbacks, it would be odd to find system A reasonable. The interaction that Congress specified between onboard and Stage II controls (in the last sentence of § 202(a)(6)) makes clear that Congress saw them as at least partial substitutes, as they plainly are as a matter of physics and technology. Under these circumstances, a court should not leap to the view that the "reasonableness" balancing called for by § 202(a)(4), see Maj. Op. 269 n. 15, precludes any consideration of the effect of the Stage II applications that legally depend on the absence of onboard controls.

Indeed, no party here argues that the § 202(a)(4) balancing must be so narrow. EPA, as the majority notes, regarded the two alternative methods as relevant to the § 202(a)(4) assessment on onboard devices. Maj. Op. at 269–70; see also 57 FR 13,220, 13,230/3 (April 15, 1992). Petitioners do not object to this element of EPA's reasoning. Rather, they make the much more limited argument that EPA was internally inconsistent in that it considered the safety benefits of Stage II controls at the gas stations where they would be installed without addressing the absence of control at the gas stations that would be uncontrolled even if Stage II controls were as broadly applicable as possible under the statute. See Reply Brief at 16–19 & n. 10. As the permissible scope of the § 202(a)(4) balance is not before us, there is no need to take any position on the subject. To the extent that the text, Maj. Op. 269–70, 271 is in tension with *Id.* 271 n. 21, plainly the footnote should be deemed controlling.

§ 3.4 PERMIT REVIEW PROCESS

EPA regulations provide that the Administrator may review permit decisions by Regional Administrators. See 40 C.F.R. § 124.19. Prior to February 13, 1992, this authority was exercised by the Administrator directly in concert with the Agency Judicial Officer. On February 13, 1992, the position of Agency Judicial Officer was abolished, and the Environmental Appeals Board was created to exercise the Administrator's review authority. See 40 C.F.R. § 22.04(a). The Board consists of three environmental judges.

CHANGES TO REGULATIONS TO REFLECT THE ROLE OF THE NEW ENVIRONMENTAL APPEALS BOARD IN AGENCY ADJUDICATIONS
57 Fed. Reg. 5320 (February 13, 1992).

SUMMARY: Under the environmental statutes administered by the Environmental Protection Agency, the Administrator has authority to decide appeals of permit decisions made by the Agency's Regional Administrators and administrative penalty decisions made by the Agency's Administrative Law Judges. Because it is unnecessary and impractical for the Administrator to make all such decisions, the Administrator has in the past either delegated authority to decide appeals in such cases to the Agency's Judicial Officers or decided such appeals himself primarily on the basis of recommendations from the Judicial Officers. As part of the response to an increasing level of administrative adjudications, the Administrator is creating a new entity called the Environmental Appeals Board to hear and decide the kinds of appeals that the Administrator formerly delegated to the Agency's Judicial Officers or decided on the basis of the Judicial Officers' recommendations. The rule promulgated herein makes technical changes to the rules of practice governing Agency permit and penalty decisions to bring such rules into conformity with the Administrator's action. The final rule delegates to the new Environmental Appeals Board the Administrator's authority to hear appeals of permit and penalty decisions. The rule also replaces references to the Judicial Officers and those references to the Administrator relating to appellate functions with references to the Environmental Appeals Board.

EFFECTIVE DATE: March 1, 1992.

* * *

THE ENVIRONMENTAL APPEALS BOARD

The Administrator has authority to decide appeals of permitting decisions made by Regional Administrators and appeals of administrative penalty decisions made by Administrative Law Judges. In implementing this authority, the Administrator has delegated authority to decide most kinds of appeals to the Agency's Judicial Officers (two EPA attorneys, one denominated the Chief Judicial Officer and the other denominated the Judicial Officer). The Administrator has retained authority to decide a few types of appeals, but has decided such appeals primarily on the basis of recommendations from the Agency's Judicial Officers.

The Agency is now creating a new entity called the Environmental Appeals Board, the purpose of which is to hear and decide appeals in cases that were formerly either delegated to the Judicial Officers or decided on the basis of the Judicial Officers' recommendations. The Judicial Officer positions at EPA Headquarters are being abolished. The establishment of the Board is being accomplished by the Administrator through internal Agency action. The purpose of the rule promulgated herein is only to make technical changes to the rules of practice governing Agency permit and penalty decisions to bring such rules into conformity with the Administrator's action.

The Board will be a permanent body with continuing functions. It will be composed of three Environmental Appeals Judges designated by the Administrator. The Board will decide each matter before it by majority vote in accordance with applicable statutes and regulations. Two Board members constitute a quorum, and if the absence or recusal of a Board member so requires, the Board may sit as a Board of two members. In the case of a tie vote, the matter shall be referred to the Administrator to break the tie.

The rule promulgated herein defines the Board and sets qualifications for Board members. It also includes express delegations of authority from the Administrator to the Board to hear and decide appeals of various types of cases. Under the old scheme, the rules of practice governing Agency adjudications did not actually delegate authority to the Judicial Officers (with the exception of the Equal Access to Justice Act regulations in part 17). Instead, the rules merely recognized the possibility of such a delegation, while the actual delegations were accomplished through an internal Agency document called the delegations manual. By contrast, under the rule promulgated herein, the rules of practice actually effect the delegation of the Administrator's authority. In addition, the rule replaces references to the Judicial Officer and those references to the Administrator related to appellate functions with references to the Environmental Appeals Board.

The approach adopted in this rule, while having the same practical effect as the previous approach, is designed to provide greater clarity. Under the old approach, in which delegations of authority were effected in a separate internal delegations manual, there was considerable confusion in the regulated community over the role of the Judicial Officers in Agency adjudications. The approach adopted in this rule reflects more clearly and directly the role of the Board as the final decisionmaker in Agency adjudications. Also, effecting the delegation directly in the regulation confers on the Board the dignity and stature that is appropriate for the Agency's highest adjudicative body. The old approach, in which the rules of practice merely recognized the possibility of a delegation, was rejected because it might have fostered the perception that the Board is an ad hoc, provisional body.

As a result of the rule promulgated today, the Board now holds delegated authority from the Administrator to hear and decide the following types of cases:

—Appeals of cases arising under the Equal Access to Justice Act (EAJA)(5 U.S.C. 504), which are governed by the procedures set out in part 17;

—Appeals of civil penalty cases arising under sections 3005(e), 3008, 9006, 11005 of the Solid Waste Disposal Act (RCRA), as amended (42 U.S.C. 6925, 6928, 6991(e), and 6992(d)), which are governed by the procedures set out in part 22;

—Appeals of civil penalty cases arising under section 211 of the Clean Air Act (CAA), as amended (42 U.S.C. 7545), which are governed by the procedures set out in part 22;

—Appeals of Class II penalty cases arising under section 309(g) of the Clean Water Act (CWA)(33 U.S.C. 1319(g)), which are governed by the procedures set out in part 22;

—Appeals of civil penalty cases arising under section 16(a) of the Toxic Substances Control Act (TSCA)(15 U.S.C. 2615(a)), which are governed by the procedures set out in part 22;

—Appeals of civil penalty cases arising under section 14(a) of the Federal Insecticide, Fungicide, and Rodenticide Act (FIFRA)(7 U.S.C. 1361(a)), which are governed by the procedures set out in part 22;

—Appeals of administrative penalty cases arising under section 325 of the Emergency Planning and Community Right to Know Act (EPCRA)(42 U.S.C. 11045), which are governed by the procedures set out in part 22;

—Appeals of civil penalties cases arising under sections 105 (a) and (f) of the Marine Protection, Research, Sanctuaries Act of 1972 (MPRSA)(33 U.S.C. 1415(a)), which are governed by the procedures set out in part 22;

—Appeals of administrative penalty cases arising under section 109 of the Comprehensive Environmental Response, Compensation, and Liability Act of 1980, as amended (CERCLA)(42 U.S.C. 9609), which are governed by the procedures set out in part 22;

—Appeals of civil penalty cases arising under section 1414(g)(3)(B) of the Safe Drinking Water Act as amended (42 U.S.C. 300g–3(g)(3)(B)), which are governed by the procedures set out in part 22;

—Appeals of cases arising under the Program Fraud Civil Remedies Act (31 U.S.C. 3801), which are governed by the procedures set out in part 27;

—Appeals of determinations under § 60.539, which deals with standards of performance for new residential wood heaters promulgated under the Clean Air Act;

—Appeals of Clean Air Act section 120 noncompliance penalty cases, which are governed by the procedures set out in part 66;

—Appeals of cases arising under the Clean Air Act involving control of air pollution from motor vehicles and motor vehicle engines, which are governed by the procedures set out in part 85;

—Appeals of cases arising under the Clean Air Act involving control of air pollution from new motor vehicles and new motor vehicle engines and certification and test procedures, which are governed by the procedures set out in part 86;

—Appeals of Spill Prevention, Containment and Control (SPCC) penalty cases arising under the Clean Water Act, which are governed by the oil pollution prevention regulations set out in part 114;

—Appeals from permit decisions made by Regional Administrators and Administrative Law Judges under the Clean Water Act (NPDES), which are governed by the procedures set out in part 124;

—Appeals from permit decisions made by Regional Administrators under RCRA, which are governed by the procedures set out in part 124;

—Appeals from permit decisions made by Regional Administrators and delegated States under the Clean Air Act (PSD permits), which are governed by the procedures set out in part 124;

—Appeals from permit decisions made by Regional Administrators under the Safe Drinking Water Act (UIC permits), which are governed by the procedures set out in part 124;

—Appeals of FIFRA cancellation, suspension and compensation cases, which are governed by the procedures set out in part 164;

—Appeals of cases under the Noise Control Act, which are governed by the procedures set out in part 209;

—Appeals from permit decisions made by Regional Administrators under the Marine Protection, Research, and Sanctuaries Act (MPRSA), which are governed by the procedures set out in part 222.

—Appeals of determinations under § 403.13, which deals with "fundamentally different factors" variances from Clean Water Act categorical pretreatment standards for publicly owned treatment works.

The Board will also have authority to decide appeals in cases arising under section 113(d) of the Clean Air Act, as soon as final action is taken on a proposed rule to make such cases subject to part 22. In addition, it is expected that the Administrator will, on occasion, ask the Board for advice and consultation on decisions that the Administrator has not delegated to the Board through these rule changes. In such cases, the Administrator may ask the Board to make findings of fact or conclusions of law, to prepare a recommended decision for the Administrator's consideration, or to serve as the final decisionmaker for the Agency, as is appropriate to a particular case.

The provisions promulgated herein to effect the delegation of the Administrator's authority to the Board provide that the delegation of authority does not preclude the Board from referring a particular case or motion to the Administrator for decision when the Board deems it appropriate to do so. The language of the provisions makes clear, however, that an appeal or motion for reconsideration of a Board decision must be directed to the Board. An appeal or motion for reconsideration directed to the Administrator will not be considered. One of the goals of the Board is to relieve the Administrator of the responsibility for responding to appeals. Allowing parties to petition the Administrator directly to hear an appeal or to overturn a Board decision would defeat this goal. It is expected that the Board will exercise its discretion to refer cases or motions to the Administrator directly to hear an appeal or to overturn a Board decision would defeat this goal. It is expected that the Board will exercise its discretion to refer cases or motions to the Administrator only in exceptional circumstances.

The rule promulgated herein also amends parts of Title 40 under which the Board will not have authority to hear appeals, but which contain incidental references to the Judicial Officer that need to be removed to reflect the abolition of that position. The following provisions have been amended for that purpose:

(1) Sections 57.103, 57.806, 57.809, relating to primary nonferrous smelter orders;

(2) Section 123.64, governing withdrawal of State NPDES programs;

(3) Section 223.4, relating to the revision, revocation, or limitation of ocean dumping permits under the Marine Protection, Research, and Sanctuaries Act;

(4) Section 233.53, relating to withdrawal of section 404 State program approval.

The Environmental Appeals Board will decide any appeals or related matters covered in this rule that are pending before a Judicial Officer or the Administrator at the time this rule becomes effective.

REASONS FOR THE CHANGE

The Environmental Appeals Board is being established to adapt the Agency's administrative appeals process to new realities facing the Agency. In recent years, the Agency has stepped up enforcement of the environmental statutes it is charged with administering. In addition, statutory amendments (most recently the Clean Air Act Amendments of 1990) have greatly increased the Agency's administrative penalty authority. This increase in administrative enforcement activity will continue to generate an increasing number of appeals to the Administrator. The Agency has also received a greater number of permit applications, resulting in more appeals from the permit decisions of Regional Administrators. As a result, the Agency needs to direct more resources to its administrative appeals process, so that it may keep pace with the growing case docket. The establishment of the Environmental Appeals Board will allow the Agency to do this. Another advantage of the Board is that it will allow for a broader range of input and perspective in administrative decisionmaking. It will do this in two ways. First, three individuals, rather than just one, will review each case, lending greater authority to the Agency's decisions. Second, the Board anticipates that, in appropriate cases, it will exercise its discretionary authority to grant or require oral argument, an authority that the Judicial Officers held under the rules but did not exercise. Another virtue of the Board is that it will make clear that the Administrator's enforcement authority (delegated to various Regional and Headquarters enforcement officers) and the Administrator's adjudicative authority are delegated to, and exercised by, separate and distinct components of the Agency, thus inspiring confidence in the fairness of Agency adjudications. Finally, the creation of the Board confers on Agency appellate proceedings the stature and dignity that are commensurate with the growing importance of such proceedings.

* * *

CIBA–GEIGY CORP. v. SIDAMON–ERISTOFF
3 F.3d 40 (2d Cir.1993).

JON O. NEWMAN, CHIEF JUDGE:

This case is before the Court upon the petition of Ciba–Geigy Corporation and Hercules Incorporated (collectively "Ciba"), the current and past operators of a hazardous waste site in Glen Falls, New York, for review of a Memorandum of Agreement between the Environmental Protection Agency and New York State, a decision of the Environmental Appeals Board, and two decisions of the EPA Regional Administrator. In each challenge, Ciba seeks to vindicate a narrow legal point: its contention that EPA cannot administer federal permits for hazardous waste sites in states that have their own federally approved hazardous waste programs under the Hazardous and Solid Waste Amendments ("HSWA") to the Resource Conservation and Recovery Act ("RCRA"). Because we conclude that Ciba has partially failed to exhaust administrative remedies, we dismiss the petition in part. As to the remaining aspects of the petition, we conclude that EPA's construction of RCRA is permissible, and deny the petition.

BACKGROUND

A brief review of the underlying statutory scheme will be helpful in understanding our disposition of this petition.

A. RCRA Permits

RCRA established "a comprehensive 'cradle-to-grave' system for regulating the management of hazardous wastes." 1 Susan M. Cooke, et al., The Law of Hazardous Waste § 1.01 at 1–4 (1993). The statute regulates generators of waste, transporters of waste, and operators of waste treatment, storage, and disposal facilities. *See* 42 U.S.C.A. §§ 6922–24 (West 1983 & Supp. 1993). Facility operators are required to obtain an operating permit. *See* 42 U.S.C. § 6925(a)(1988).

The statutory scheme contemplates an eventual delegation of permit-issuing authority from EPA to the states. States may submit to the EPA Administrator details of a proposed state hazardous waste program. 42 U.S.C. § 6926(b)(1988). The program must be "equivalent" to the federal RCRA program. *Id.* § 6926(b)(1). If the Administrator approves the program, the state carries out its program "in lieu" of the federal program. Id. § 6926(b). In particular, the state is responsible for the issuance and administration of permits. *Id.* However, even after approval of a state program, EPA retains significant involvement. EPA may bring enforcement actions, *see* 42 U.S.C. §§ 6928, 6973 (1988), and may inspect and monitor sites, *see* 42 U.S.C.A. §§ 6927, 6934 (West 1983 & Supp. 1993). *See generally Wyckoff Co. v. E.P.A.*, 796 F.2d 1197, 1200–01

(9th Cir.1986) (EPA may issue order under 42 U.S.C. § 6934 requiring operator to perform monitoring and report results to EPA even after state authorization).

The original version of RCRA primarily concentrated on ongoing management of hazardous wastes, and did not provide authority for mandating corrective action to cure past mismanagement of waste. Congress acted to close this gap in 1984 with enactment of HSWA. Among other requirements, HSWA requires that permits for facilities with an existing hazardous waste problem include a schedule for cleaning up the wastes. *See* 42 U.S.C. § 6924(u)-(v). HSWA also significantly complicated the division of authority between the federal government and the states. Concerned that regulations promulgated under HSWA be implemented as quickly as possible, Congress provided that new federal HSWA regulations would take effect in all states simultaneously, whether or not the state had an approved program under section 6926(b). *See* 42 U.S.C. § 6926(g)(1)(1988); Cooke § 1.03[3], at 1–20 to 1–21. If states wish to take over administration of these new regulations, they must amend their hazardous waste programs so as to be "substantially equivalent" to the federal HSWA regulations. Once this amendment is accomplished, the state may apply to the Administrator for "interim authorization . . . to carry out [the state] requirement in lieu of direct administration in the State by the Administrator of [the federal] requirement." Id. § 6926(g)(2). Eventually, states wishing to administer these regulations must adopt regulations fully equivalent to federal HSWA regulations, and obtain final authorization for the state HSWA program under section 6926(b).

In states that have obtained RCRA authorization under section 6926(b) but have not obtained authorization for HSWA regulations, whether under section 6926(g)(2) or section 6926(b), operators of most hazardous waste sites are required to obtain permits from both the state and EPA. *See American Iron and Steel Institute v. U.S. E.P.A.*, 280 U.S.App.D.C. 373, 886 F.2d 390, 403 (D.C.Cir.1989), cert. denied, 497 U.S. 1003 (1990); Cooke § 5.03[1], at 5–53 to 5–54. In practice, these dual permits apparently tend to overlap considerably and may even impose conflicting requirements since "it is not uncommon for the state and EPA to have different views on the same substantive issue. When this occurs, the applicant may get whipsawed between the two agencies." *See* John C. Chambers, Jr. & Peter L. Gray, Intergovernmental Relations: EPA and State Roles in RCRA and CERCLA, Nat. Resources & Env't, July 1989, at 7.

The statute does not contain specific provisions concerning the status of existing federal permits after a state obtains HSWA authorization under section 6926(g)(2) or section 6926(b). Under regulations adopted by EPA, the state is required to reissue permits to existing permittees. 40 C.F.R. § 271.13(d). . . . These state RCRA permits contain the requirements of both the previously issued state and federal permits. Id. At some point after issuance of the state RCRA permit, EPA will terminate the previous federal permit. *See* 40 C.F.R. § 271.8(b)(6).

B.   The New York Program

By 1986, the New York Department of Environmental Conservation ("DEC") had obtained authorization under section 6926(b), and thus ran the RCRA permitting process in New York. Following enactment of HSWA and the issuance of federal HSWA regulations, DEC adopted new regulations, and applied in September 1991 for authorization to administer these regulations. After a public comment period, the Administrator granted DEC "final authorization" on May 22, 1992. . . .

This authorization is reflected in a Memorandum of Agreement ("MOA") between EPA and DEC. The MOA includes provisions that concern the transfer and administration of existing federal permits. It appears to provide that while all pending permit applications will be transferred to DEC, existing federal permits will continue to be administered by EPA. Once DEC issues new permits containing all applicable requirements, EPA will consider termination of the federal permits on a case-by-case basis.

C.   The Pending Dispute

Ciba owns a paint pigment production facility in Glen Falls, New York. Various waste products were impounded at the site, largely in an open lagoon. In 1989, Ciba decided to close the site, and applied to DEC for an appropriate permit. Because the site contained hazardous wastes and DEC was not yet authorized to administer HSWA regulations, both DEC and EPA issued draft permits. The permits are in large measure identical, because DEC included clean-up requirements, as it had the right to do. Ciba submitted comments requesting that EPA not issue a permit. EPA responded that it could not accede to the request since the DEC permit might not cover all necessary requirements; EPA issued a federal permit in October 1991. Ciba sought review of the federal permit from the EPA Administrator. n3 During the pendency of the review process, the federal permit was automatically stayed. Ciba made two arguments in its review petition. It contended that the federal permit was improper because it substantially duplicated the state permit. It also contended that even if the federal permit could be issued prior to authorization of the New York HSWA program, the federal permit was required to contain an automatic termination provision triggered by state authorization. The Environmental Appeals Board ("EAB") denied the petition in a written opinion. Matter of CIBA–GEIGY Corp., RCRA Appeal No. 91–28 (Apr. 7, 1992). The EAB found (a) that EPA was required to administer the HSWA program prior to state authorization, even if the state had adopted substantially similar requirements and had included those requirements in its permit, and (b) that there was no requirement that the federal permit have an automatic termination provision. The EAB suggested that the termination of the federal permit would be resolved by the MOA between the state and EPA, or otherwise would be resolved by EPA after state authorization. The federal permit accordingly became effective (after some minor delays) on May 8, 1992—some two weeks before New York received authorization to administer its HSWA program. On July 2, 1992, Ciba requested that the Regional Administrator terminate the federal permit in light of the intervening authorization of the New York program. The Regional Administrator did not formally respond. However, counsel to the Regional Administrator stated in a phone call to counsel for Ciba that the Regional Administrator's lack of a response should be treated as a denial of the request.

DEC has not yet issued a new post-authorization permit to Ciba. Although EPA has suggested that it would voluntarily terminate the federal permit upon issuance of a new state permit to Ciba, EPA has also indicated that because New York is not authorized to administer 100 percent of HSWA requirements, some type of federal permit might remain necessary to cover those areas in which New York lacks authorization. However, EPA has never identified any specific HSWA requirements relevant to Ciba that only it can enforce.

On August 5, 1992, Ciba petitioned this Court pursuant to 42 U.S.C. § 6976(b)(1988) for review of (1) the EAB decision rejecting the petition for review of the October 1991 decision to issue the federal permit, (2) the May 1992 decision of the Regional Administrator to terminate the stay of the permit, (3) the July 1992 refusal of the Regional Administrator to terminate the permit upon request, and (4) the portions of the MOA failing to provide for automatic termination of a federal permit. For relief, Ciba requests that the permit be set aside or that the MOA be modified to provide for termination.

DISCUSSION

A. Exhaustion

At oral argument, the Court inquired of Ciba whether it had exhausted administrative remedies as to each of the three permitting decisions. We felt obligated to raise the issue sua sponte, since it directly related to the suitability of these matters for judicial review. *See Dettmann v. United States Department of Justice*, 802 F.2d 1472, 1476 n. 8, 256 U.S.App.D.C. 78 (D.C.Cir.1986). After reviewing Ciba's post-argument submission, we have concluded that of the permitting decisions, only the original decision to issue the permit is properly before us.

As an initial matter, we believe that there are really only two permitting decisions that Ciba seeks to challenge. This is because the second of the decisions—the Regional Administrator's May 1992 termination of the stay—is not meaningfully distinct from the two other permitting decisions. To the extent Ciba is complaining that the permit should not have been issued initially, that issue is brought before us by the petition for review of the October 1991 decision approved by the EAB. To the extent Ciba is complaining that new evidence—the authorization of New York's HSWA program in late May 1992—required that the permit not be made effective, that issue is presented by the July 1992 request to the Regional Administrator to terminate. The only sense in which the May 1992 decision is distinct from the July 1992 decision is that the Regional Administrator then chose to follow EPA regulations for lifting a stay after a challenged permit was affirmed by the EAB. *See*

40 C.F.R. § 124.16. We do not understand that Ciba wishes to challenge those regulations.

As to the two permitting challenges at issue, we conclude that administrative remedies have been exhausted as to the October 1991 decision but have not been exhausted as to the July 1992 decision. These conclusions stem from two sources. First, the relevant statute authorizes us to review only the "Administrator's action . . . in issuing, denying, modifying, or revoking any permit." 42 U.S.C. § 6976(b)(1) (emphasis added). The EAB's decision rejecting Ciba's petition for review of the original issuance of the permit constitutes action of the Administrator. *See* 40 C.F.R. § 22.04(a). However, the remaining two actions are actions by the Regional Administrator, Constantine Sidamon–Eristoff.

Second, EPA has adopted regulations creating express exhaustion requirements. For issuance of a permit, appeal to the EAB is a "prerequisite to the seeking of judicial review of the final agency action." 40 C.F.R. § 124.19(e). Ciba has complied with this requirement. However, Ciba has failed to comply with the parallel requirement for review of the Regional Administrator's refusal to terminate the permit. Such review is provided under 40 C.F.R. § 124.5(b), which allows an "informal appeal" to the Administrator of a Regional Administrator's refusal to terminate a permit. The regulation further provides that "this informal appeal is, under 5 U.S.C. § 704, a prerequisite to seeking judicial review." Id. n. 4 In its post-argument submission, Ciba argues that 40 C.F.R. § 124.5(b) is inapplicable because it applies only to requests to terminate under 40 C.F.R. § 124.5(a), and the request to terminate the federal permit because of approval of the state program could not have been made under section 124.5(a). We disagree. Section 124.5(a) provides that RCRA permits may be modified or terminated for the reasons specified in 40 C.F.R. §§ 270.41, 270.43. Section 270.41, in turn, provides that modification requests by the permittee are governed by 40 C.F.R. § 270.42, which allows for modification requests of any type, see id. § 270.42(d). While Ciba appears to be correct that the regulations contemplate termination per se only at the request of EPA, and only for egregious wrongdoing by the permittee, see 40 C.F.R. § 270.43, Ciba's goal of terminating the permit can be achieved by modifying the expiration date of the permit (which is currently November 12, 1996). Accordingly, the proper course for obtaining review of the refusal to terminate is to make a formal request under section 124.5(a) for a modification of the expiration date in compliance with the procedures outlined in section 270.42. If the Regional Administrator rejects the request, an informal appeal to the Administrator should be taken under section 124.5(b). Review would then be available in this Court under 42 U.S.C. § 6976(b)(1).

In its post-argument submission, Ciba also argues that EPA, by failing to mention exhaustion in its brief, has waived any defense based on exhaustion. Ciba is correct that under limited circumstances, an agency can waive an exhaustion defense. *See Weinberger v. Salfi,* 422 U.S. 749, 764–67, 45 L.Ed.2d 522, 95 S.Ct. 2457 (1975); 4 Kenneth C.

Davis, Administrative Law Treatise § 26:8, at 445 (1983). In *Salfi,* the Supreme Court reviewed the constitutionality of a Social Security Administration decision denying survivor's benefits to a widow on the ground she had been married to the deceased for less than nine months before his death. Although the petitioner had clearly not exhausted her claim within the agency, the Court found review appropriate because the Secretary had not raised an exhaustion defense, the applicant had presented "her claim at a sufficiently high level of review to satisfy the Secretary's administrative needs," and the Secretary had determined that "the only issue is the constitutionality of a statutory requirement, a matter which is beyond his jurisdiction to determine," and that the claim was otherwise valid. *Salfi,* 422 at 765. We believe that *Salfi* is distinguishable and that additional agency review would be quite helpful. The regulatory scheme is complex, the agency must construe both the statute and its own regulations, and no severable constitutional issue is presented.

B. Ripeness

EPA contends that the two remaining challenges—to the original permitting decision and to the MOA—are not ripe for adjudication by this Court. EPA points out that Ciba has identified no inconsistency between the state and federal permits and does not object to any specific decision requiring it to take any particular action in operating or cleaning up the site. Because Ciba seeks only to avoid the possibility of some future dispute, EPA asks that we dismiss the remaining portions of the petition as non-justiciable.

EPA relies on decisions under the Administrative Procedure Act that provide that agency action is not ripe unless the issue presented (i) is fit for judicial determination, in the sense that further factual development would not be helpful, and (ii) the withholding of court consideration would cause a hardship. *See Abbott Laboratories v. Gardner,* 387 U.S. 136, 149, 18 L.Ed.2d 681, 87 S.Ct. 1507 (1967). Arguably, decisions like Abbott Laboratories have limited relevance to Ciba's challenges, since RCRA specifically authorizes review in the Court of Appeals of the "Administrator's action (1) in issuing, denying, modifying, or revoking any permit under section 6925 ..., or (2) in granting, denying, or withdrawing authorization or interim authorization under section 6926." 42 U.S.C. § 6976(b). Thus, this may be a situation in which "Congress explicitly provides for our correction of the administrative process at a higher level of generality," see *Lujan v. National Wildlife Federation,* 497 U.S. 871, 894, 111 L.Ed.2d 695, 110 S.Ct. 3177 (1990), than the usual ripeness test demands. But see *W. R. Grace & Co.—Conn. v. U.S. E.P.A.,* 959 F.2d 360, 364–67 (1st Cir.1992) (applying general test of ripeness to permit dispute reviewable under 42 U.S.C. § 6976(b)(1)).

Even under the general test, however, we believe that the original permitting decision reviewed by the EAB is ripe for review. As to fitness, the issue is fairly well developed. We are well past the point where the agency has merely taken the position that it has the power to issue duplicative federal permits. Rather, the agency has issued the duplicative permit. In contrast to *W. R. Grace & Co.—Conn. v. U.S. E.P.A.,* 959 F.2d 360 (1st Cir.1992), in which the First Circuit declined to review a dispute over the mode of review of EPA modifications to a permit prior to the proposal of any actual modifications, it is difficult to see in this case how further factual development would make the legal question more fit for judicial review. *See* Duke Power Co. v. Carolina Environmental Study Group, Inc., 438 U.S. 59, 81–82, 57 L.Ed.2d 595, 98 S.Ct. 2620 (1978); American Petroleum Institute v. U.S. E.P.A., 285 U.S.App.D.C. 35, 906 F.2d 729, 739 (D.C.Cir.1990)("a 'purely legal question' ... is 'presumptively reviewable' "). As to hardship, Ciba points out that even if the federal permit does not impose different substantive requirements, it imposes burdensome procedural requirements. Ciba will be required to submit additional copies of all its plans, and await the approval of EPA before it can perform remediation activity. Whether duplicate filing obligations alone would suffice to warrant judicial review is debatable, but the need to await agency approval before taking action entitles Ciba to secure review of the agency's assertion of jurisdiction. That this dispute can grow worse does not mean that hardship does not exist now. *See Central Hudson Gas & Electric Corp. v. U.S. E.P.A.,* 587 F.2d 549, 558–60 (2d Cir.1978)(finding ripe EPA's assertion of jurisdiction to issue Clean Water Act permit, despite authorization of state program, prior to issuance of federal permit); *Sayles Hydro Associates v. Maughan,* 985 F.2d 451, 453–454 (9th Cir.1993)(federally licensed dam operator could challenge state permitting requirement on preemption grounds without awaiting state's imposition of inconsistent requirements under its permit); see generally *Natural Resources Defense Council, Inc. v. U.S. E.P.A.,* 859 F.2d 156 (D.C.Cir.1988)(in some cases, regulations requiring certain conditions in permits are ripe for review even before issuance of permits).

EPA also contends that Ciba's challenge to the MOA is not ripe. However, EPA's actual argument appears to be a standing argument: that Ciba may not challenge the MOA because it "has no impact on Ciba's conduct." EPA Brief at 23. EPA does not appear to contemplate that Ciba would be able to challenge the MOA itself at a later date. Instead, EPA insists that Ciba must await specific action by some agency under the MOA, and then may challenge that action. While we agree with EPA that any injury suffered by Ciba as a result of the MOA is slight, RCRA authorizes "any interested person" to challenge EPA's action in "granting, denying, or withdrawing authorization or interim authorization under section 6926." 42 U.S.C. § 6976(b). The MOA is the means by which EPA grants authorization under section 6926. *See* 40 C.F.R. §§ 271.8, 271.126. We do not believe that standing is lacking in a constitutional sense, since Ciba has suffered at least the minimal injury of being subjected to dual approval requirements and duplicative submission requirements, and because a change in the MOA would remedy Ciba's slight injury.

C. Merits

Ciba's surviving challenges on the merits present extremely narrow questions: whether EPA must include an automatic termination provision, triggered by state authorization, in pre-authorization federal permits, and whether an MOA must provide for the immediate termination of pre-existing federal permits. It is important to recognize what is not before us: the permissibility of EPA's general policy of continued administration, and perhaps issuance, of federal permits in authorized states. Most of Ciba's arguments are devoted to that question, a particularly difficult question since the lack of exhaustion has failed to make completely clear what EPA's position is on this question.

However, we will consider in turn each of Ciba's arguments as they apply to the narrow questions before us.

1. Judicial estoppel. Ciba's first argument is judicial estoppel. This argument rests on the contention that EPA took a position inconsistent with its current position in two District Court cases, *Chemical Waste Management, Inc. v. Templet,* 770 F.Supp. 1142 (M.D.La.1991), aff'd, 967 F.2d 1058 (5th Cir.1992), cert. denied, 122 L.Ed.2d 357, 113 S.Ct. 1048 (1993), and *Thompson v. Thomas,* 680 F.Supp. 1 (D.D.C.1987). This argument is unavailing. EPA was not even a party to the Chemical Waste Management case. In the *Thompson* case, which involved an attempt to force EPA to take discretionary enforcement actions against a dump, EPA argued that such a suit was not authorized by RCRA. The Court agreed, and suggested that the plaintiffs could bring a state court action against the dump in Wisconsin, since Wisconsin was an authorized state. Whatever consequence EPA's action in this litigation might have for EPA's broad policy on post-authorization administration, it is not at all relevant to either the question of whether a federal permit must include an automatic termination provision or the question of whether an MOA must provide for immediate termination of a federal permit upon issuance of a state permit.

2. Inconsistency with regulations. Ciba next argues that EPA's position is inconsistent with 40 C.F.R. § 271.8(b)(6), which provides:

> When existing permits are transferred from EPA to the State for administration, the Memorandum of Agreement shall contain provisions specifying a procedure for transferring the administration of these permits. If a State lacks the authority to directly administer permits issued by the Federal government, a procedure may be established to transfer responsibility for these permits.

NOTE: For example, EPA and the State and the permittee could agree that the State would issue a permit(s) identical to the outstanding Federal permit which would simultaneously be terminated.

Ciba contends that by adoption of this regulation, EPA committed itself to including termination provisions in federal permits and to immediately terminating federal permits upon state authorization. The simple answer is that this is not what the regulation says. The regulation says nothing about the content of permits. As to MOAs, the regulation requires only that they contain provision for transfer of existing permits; the content of those provisions is left open. The Note appended to the end of the section only suggests one method. There can be no doubt that the MOA has provisions governing the transfer of existing permits. Ciba just does not like those provisions. Moreover, other regulations adopted by EPA clearly contemplate the continued administration of federal permits after state authorization, at least to the point where the state issues a new state permit. *See,* e.g., 40 C.F.R. § 270.51(d).

    3. Impermissible construction of RCRA. Finally, Ciba contends that EPA's position is impermissible under the statute. The parties agree that resolution of this question is governed by *Chevron U.S.A., Inc. v. Natural Resources Defense Council, Inc.,* 467 U.S. 837, 81 L.Ed.2d 694, 104 S.Ct. 2778 (1984). Thus, Ciba may prevail only by showing that EPA's resolution of the issues is directly contrary to congressional intent, or that the statute is silent on the issues and the agency's resolution is unreasonable. Ciba devotes most of its brief to arguing under the first prong of *Chevron.* Section 6926(g)(2), which governs interim HSWA authorization, provides that

> The Administrator shall, if the evidence submitted shows the State requirement to be substantially equivalent to the [federal requirement], grant an interim authorization to the State to carry out such requirement in lieu of *direct administration* in the State by the Administrator of such requirement. [Emphasis added.]

Virtually identical language appears in section 6926(b), which governs final authorization. Ciba contends that the emphasized language means that after state authorization, the federal program is entirely displaced and EPA must immediately terminate or transfer any existing permits.

    Whatever this statutory language might signify for EPA's general policies on permit administration, it does not speak to the questions before the Court. The "direct administration" language cannot be read to specify any particular procedure for termination of federal permits, whether by an automatic termination provision in the permit or an immediate termination provision in the MOA, and does not specify any time limit by which federal involvement must cease.

    We thus reach the second prong of *Chevron.* Ciba must show that EPA's interpretation fails a highly deferential reasonableness test, applied with due regard to the statutory purpose. Congress' primary purpose in adopting RCRA and HSWA was protection of the environment and public health. While delegation to states was also an important purpose, EPA's refusal to include a termination provision in the original permit and its refusal to provide for immediate termination of federal permits cannot be said to be unreasonable. Continued administration of federal permits past the immediate moment of state authorization avoids the gap in regulation that might occur if the state failed to immediately issue a new permit containing all applicable requirements, and allows the state and federal regulators the opportunity to coordinate in an effective manner a gradual transfer of jurisdiction. *See Central Hudson Gas & Electric Corp. v. U.S. E.P.A.,* 587 F.2d 549, 561–62 (2d Cir.1978)(reasonable for EPA to issue federal permits under Clean Water Act, notwithstanding authorization of state permitting program, so as to "allow[] for the smooth transition from federal to state permit program")....

CONCLUSION

Ciba's petition for review of the July 1992 refusal to terminate the federal permit and of the May 1992 decision to terminate a stay of the federal permit is dismissed for failure to exhaust administrative remedies. The petition for review of the October 1991 issuance of the permit approved by the EAB in April 1992 and of the May 1992 MOA between EPA and New York is denied.

DEL ACKELS v. UNITED STATES EPA

7 F.3d 862 (9th Cir.1993).

SCHROEDER, CIRCUIT JUDGE:

INTRODUCTION

Petitioners Del Ackels, Stanley C. Rybachek, Rosalie A. Rybachek, Glenn Bouton, Donald Stein, Lela Bouton, and Richard Geraghty, are individual miners who have engaged in gold placer mining in Alaska. They filed this petition pro se asking us to review permits issued to them by the Environmental Protection Agency. The permits are National Pollutant Discharge Elimination System (NPDES) permits issued under the authority of the Clean Water Act, 33 U.S.C. §§ 1251–1387, pursuant to the regulatory framework established by the EPA. The permits impose effluent limitations, including numerical limits for specific pollutants in the discharge, and require specific technological practices miners must follow.

This court first considered NPDES permits for placer miners in *Trustees for Alaska v. EPA,* 749 F.2d 549 (9th Cir.1984). The opinion in that case described the sluicing process used to remove gold from "placers," which are alluvial or glacial deposits containing gold particles. This sluicing process results in the discharge of waste water which, if untreated, can create a serious environmental hazard to wildlife, particularly in the case of larger placer mining operations.

The permits we reviewed in Trustees were permits issued in 1976 and 1977. The permits we review here were issued in 1984, 1985 and 1987. The petitioners have demonstrated persistence, patience and perspicacity in pursuing their available remedies through a maze of regulatory procedures which brought them to this court after eight years of administrative appeals.... They argue effectively that the administrative framework is unduly burdensome and attenuated. Their challenges in this proceeding, however, are not to the regulatory system the EPA has established under the Clean Water Act, but to the substantive requirements that the EPA has imposed upon them in the NPDES permits. It is those substantive provisions which we must address.

The principal challenges are to the permit limitations on arsenic and turbidity. A third challenge is to the requirement that the miners monitor for settleable solids once each day of discharge, not once each day of sluicing.

Plaintiffs also challenge certain aspects of the State of Alaska's certification procedures. The Clean Water Act requires EPA to submit proposed permits to the appropriate state agency so that the state may certify that the permits are sufficiently strict to ensure compliance with state law water quality standards. There are in addition a number of challenges to the procedures the EPA followed in issuing permits. There are, finally, a number of issues raised that are moot or outside the jurisdiction of this court to consider.

We deal with each category in turn.

EFFLUENT LIMITATIONS: TURBIDITY AND ARSENIC

Turbidity

The original turbidity standard adopted by the EPA in the 1970s used the state water quality standard, measured 500 feet downstream. We held in Trustees that that standard was not sufficient to comply with the Act, and that the EPA was required to establish end-of-pipe effluent limitations for turbidity necessary to achieve state water quality standards. *See* 749 F.2d at 556–57.

In response to the Trustees decision, the EPA modified the 1985 permits to include end-of-pipe effluent limitations for turbidity of 5 NTUs ... above background, which is the Alaska water quality criteria. Accordingly, these permits provide that the state water quality criteria must be satisfied at the point of discharge.

Petitioners administratively challenged this limitation contending that the EPA should not have used the state water quality standard, but instead should have translated the turbidity standard into an effluent limitation for settleable solids by volume. They contended that the end-of-pipe effluent limitation for turbidity is not appropriate because turbidity is unstable and the permit limitation is not economically obtainable.

The Regional Administrator granted a hearing on this issue, and the ALJ found that the limitation was reasonable. The Administrator then denied review of this issue and the petitioners now challenge that decision.

The issue is whether the decision is supported by substantial evidence, and the record reflects that it is. *See Marathon Oil Co. v. EPA*, 564 F.2d 1253, 1266 (9th Cir.1977). Testimony introduced by both parties showed that turbidity, a measure of the water's cloudiness or the ability of water to scatter light, has little relationship to either the settleable solids or suspended solids at the NTU level in question. Organic matter as well as silt, minerals and metals affect turbidity.

Therefore it is not feasible to control turbidity by limiting suspended or settleable solids. The EPA correctly established a direct effluent limitation for turbidity. Further, there was evidence that there were technologies capable of meeting the turbidity limitation. Regardless of that fact, the limitation is necessary to comply with state water quality standards, and the Clean Water Act requires the permits to meet the state water quality standards. *See* 33 U.S.C. §§ 1311(b)(1)(C), 1313(c)(2). Accordingly, the economic and technological restraints are not a valid consideration.

Arsenic

Arsenic often occurs naturally in the soil in conjunction with gold in glacial placer deposits. When the miners complete their sluicing process, this arsenic is released in the wastewater. As with turbidity, the Act requires that the permit limitations meet state water quality criteria for arsenic. Petitioners' principal argument is that the EPA misinterpreted the state standard to require that the streams used in mining must be clean enough to provide a source of drinking water. The petitioners contend that the Alaska drinking water standard applies only to water that has already been treated for public distribution as drinking water.

The petitioners' reading of the Alaska water quality criteria is too strained for us to accept. The Alaska Water Quality Standards provide that "toxic and other deleterious organic and inorganic substances" in Alaska's water supply "shall not exceed Drinking Water Standards (18 AAC 80) or EPA Quality Criteria for Water ... as applicable to substance." Alaska Admin. Code tit. 18, § 70.020. The Alaska Drinking Water Standards in turn provide that the maximum contaminant concentration for arsenic in public water systems is 0.05 mg/l, *Id.* § 80.050(a)(1), and this is the limit EPA included in the permits.

Petitioners contend that the language in the Water Quality Standards mandates a choice between two different Drinking Water Standards sections, section 80.020 and section 80.050. According to petitioners, section 80.050 is applicable only to water that has already been treated for public distribution as drinking water and does not apply to their discharge. Petitioners contend that section 80.020 applies to their discharge and does not contain any specific numerical limit for arsenic.... The ALJ and the Administrator correctly rejected the petitioners' proposed reading of the water quality statutes. The statutes provide that when establishing a water quality standard for a particular toxic substance, one must find the numerical standard applicable to that substance in section 80.050. This is exactly what EPA did in establishing the effluent limitations and this interpretation of state law is reasonable and entitled to deference. *See Arkansas v. Oklahoma*, 117 L.Ed.2d 239, 112 S.Ct. 1046, 1058–59 (1992).

Petitioners also challenge the permit conditions regarding arsenic on the grounds that: (1) EPA failed to hold a hearing as mandated by this court in Trustees, and (2) the permits required improper procedures for testing for arsenic. These contentions lack merit.

In Trustees, we held that EPA was at a minimum required to hold a hearing on whether the permits should include limitations for arsenic, because evidence showed that arsenic posed an environmental problem. 749 F.2d at 556–57. By modifying the permits regarding arsenic, EPA went beyond this court's minimum requirement and took action to address the problem with which we were concerned. The miners then had a full evidentiary hearing before the ALJ on the issue of arsenic.

With respect to the testing procedures for arsenic required in the permits, the procedure is established by 40 C.F.R. pt. 136. The EPA correctly imposed this procedure in the permits.

FREQUENCY OF MONITORING

Section 308 of the Act grants EPA broad authority to require NPDES permitees to monitor, at such intervals as the Administrator shall prescribe, whenever it is required to carry out the objectives of the Act. 33 U.S.C. § 1318; 40 C.F.R. § 122.48. Petitioners contend that the Administrator erred by upholding the permits' requirement that discharge be monitored for settleable solids once per day of discharge instead of once per day of sluicing. The Administrator's decision that monitoring should take place once per day of discharge, however, is supported by substantial evidence. Petitioners contend that the provision will require them to remain at their sites to monitor discharge even during periods of inactivity and the off-season. The Administrator's decision did not so interpret the permits. Rather, monitoring is required only when there is discharge attributable to the existence of the mining operation. As explained in the Regional Administrator's Comments, this requirement is intended to encourage the operators to design their operations so that during periods of inactivity, there will be no discharge. The petitioners have not demonstrated that this requirement is unreasonable. Although they point to evidence in the record that monitoring once per day of sluicing was sufficient, the complete testimony was that such monitoring would be adequate only if the "mining operation had reached equilibrium," so that discharge occurred only when sluicing operations were taking place. Under these permits, the miners are permitted to monitor only when sluicing operations are taking place, provided that they have taken adequate safeguards to ensure that no discharges occur on any other days.

STATE CERTIFICATION ISSUES

Petitioners raise several challenges to the State's certification of the permits. Under the Act, EPA is required to submit proposed new or modified permits to the state for certification, and the state has authority to impose any more stringent terms or conditions necessary to ensure that the permits will meet state law water quality standards. Petitioners first contend that the state did not complete its certification within 60 days as required by 40 C.F.R. § 124.53(c)(3) and therefore the state's certification is invalid. Section 124.53(c)(3) provides that the state will be deemed to have waived its right to certify unless it exercises that right within 60 days. The Regional Administrator, however, may authorize a longer period upon finding that unusual circumstances require a longer time. 40 C.F.R. § 124.53(c)(3). We conclude that under this provision, and given Congress' intent to encourage state certification in order to protect the nation's waterways through a dual federal and state permitting process, EPA had discretion to accept state certification beyond the 60-day period.

Petitioners claim the state failed to provide state law authority for its imposition of a more stringent settleable solids limit. We conclude that the state properly indicated that this limit was based on Alaska Admin. Code tit. 18, § 70.020, which is the provision of Alaska law governing water quality for sediment. We must also reject petitioners' contention that the state certification is invalid because the state did not indicate which permit conditions could be made less stringent. This does not invalidate the certification but merely waives the State's right to object to any conditions subsequently made less stringent. 40 C.F.R. § 124.53(e)(3).

Petitioners also contend that when the state added the settleable solids limitation to the modified 1985 permits, EPA was then required to issue new draft permits because EPA had only noticed the permits for modification for turbidity and arsenic. Although the petitioners are correct that "when a permit is modified, only the conditions subject to modification are reopened," in this case the new conditions were added by the state, not EPA. EPA was required to forward the entire permit to the state, not merely the modified conditions, and once the state added the additional conditions, EPA was required to incorporate those conditions into the final permit and lacked authority to reject them. 33 U.S.C. § 1341(a); 40 C.F.R. § 124.53(a). Petitioners' only recourse is to challenge the state certification in state judicial proceedings. Miners Advocacy Council, amicus herein, has already litigated the validity of the State's certification of the modified 1985 permits, and lost. *See Miners Advocacy Council, Inc. v. Alaska Dep't of Envtl. Conservation*, 778 P.2d 1126, 1135 (Alaska 1989).

CHALLENGES TO ISSUANCE PROCEDURES

Petitioners challenge certain procedures EPA followed in issuing these permits. First, petitioners challenge the issuance of identical permits and contend that EPA must issue permits on a case-by-case basis and provide site-specific review. Petitioners' primary complaint here is that EPA should not have included the 0.2 ml/l limitation for settleable solids in all the 1985 and 1987 permits but should have calculated this limit on an individual basis. In 1988, however, the EPA promulgated national effluent guidelines establishing a 0.2 ml/l settleable solids limitation for the placer mining industry. 40 C.F.R. § 440.140–48. Thus, this issue is moot. Further, because EPA is not subject to the requirements of the Alaska Administrative Procedure Act, we must reject petitioners' claim that the issuance of identical permits constituted promulgation of a regulation in violation of the Alaska APA. *See Miners Advocacy Council*, 778 P.2d at 1135. Finally, the record shows that at least with respect to turbidity, individual applicants were allowed to present site-specific evidence and were issued modified permits on that basis.

Petitioners also claim that EPA erred by requiring them to comply with contested permit conditions while they challenged the permits through administrative and judicial appeals. This challenge is not to the permits, which we review, but to enforcement. To the extent petitioners challenge EPA's enforcement of contested conditions, they should do so as a defense to any enforcement proceedings in district court under section 309 of the Act, 33 U.S.C. § 1319(a), (b).

Petitioners also claim inadequate notice of enforceable conditions. Applicable administrative procedures provide for staying contested permit conditions during administrative appeals. *See* 40 C.F.R. § 124.60(c)(1). The record shows that EPA gave petitioners notice of uncontested conditions and contested, stayed conditions. EPA lacks authority to stay conditions imposed by state certification. Thus, petitioners' claims regarding notice of enforceable conditions lack merit.

Petitioners also contend that they were prejudiced because, when they requested a hearing on issuance procedures for the 1985 permits, the Regional Administrator denied a hearing yet the published notice erroneously included issuance procedures as one of the issues granted for hearing. Assuming arguendo the issue is not moot, we agree with the ALJ that because the miners had correct, individual notice of those issues denied for hearing and effectively appealed those issues, the error in the published notice was not prejudicial.

* * *

For the foregoing reasons, this court is not in a position to modify these permits or order further administrative proceedings on the basis of these challenges, which petitioners have ably pursued and presented. The petitions for review must be DENIED.

HECLA MINING CO. v. UNITED STATES EPA
12 F.3d 164 (9th Cir.1993).

Ferguson, Circuit Judge:

This case is a challenge brought pursuant to the Administrative Procedures Act (APA) 5 U.S.C. §§ 701–706, by Hecla Mining Company (Hecla) to decisions of the Environmental Protection Agency (EPA) made pursuant to §§ 304(l)(1)(B) and (C) of the Clean Water Act. 33 U.S.C. §§ 1314(l)(1)(B) and (C). The district court dismissed the action. We affirm for the reason that the challenged decisions of the EPA do not constitute the final agency action which is necessary to state a cause of action under the Act.

Hecla operates the Lucky Friday Mine located along the Coeur d'Alene River in Idaho. In its mining process, toxic pollutants are discharged into the river.

The Clean Water Act prohibits the discharge of any pollutants from a point source unless the discharge complies with the terms of a National Pollutant Discharge Elimination Systems ("NPDES") permit. The EPA has granted authority to 39 states to issue these permits. Idaho is not one of them. The Clean Water Act was amended by the Water Quality Act of 1987 (33 U.S.C. § 1311 et seq.) which placed greater emphasis on attaining state water quality standards. In order to attain water quality standards for toxic pollutants, § 304(1) requires states to submit to the EPA lists of, *inter alia*, (1) the state's navigable waters that, after the application of technology based controls, are not expected to meet prescribed water quality standards (the B list), and (2) those point sources discharging toxic pollutants that are responsible for impairing the achievement of water quality standards for the waters on List B (the C list).

The State of Idaho submitted its B and C lists to the EPA. Upon receipt of the lists, the EPA issued a proposed decision approving in part and disapproving in part the Idaho lists because they were underinclusive. The EPA then initiated a 120–day public comment period regarding the possible addition of waters and point sources to the Idaho lists. The EPA, after the public comment period, issued a proposal to amend Idaho's B list to include the South Fork of the Coeur d'Alene River and include the Lucky Friday Mine on the C list. Following a public comment period on its proposal, the EPA issued a decision adding the river and the mine to the appropriate lists.

Hecla in this action contends that the EPA exceeded its authority when, after it approved Idaho's B and C lists, it unilaterally amended them. It contends that the decision of the EPA to include the South Fork of the Coeur d'Alene River and the Lucky Friday Mine on Idaho's lists is final agency action because the decisions are final. It asserts that the river and mine are on the lists and that is a final decision.

We hold that the decision to include the river and mine on the lists is not the final agency action necessary to state a cause of action under § 704 of the APA. Finality of an agency action turns on whether the action was a definitive statement of the agency's position, had a direct and immediate effect on the day to day business of the complaining party, had the status of law and whether immediate compliance with the decision is expected. *F.T.C. v. Standard Oil Co.*, 449 U.S. 232, 239–40, 66 L.Ed.2d 416, 101 S.Ct. 488 (1980).

We concur with the Third and Fourth Circuits in concluding that EPA listing decisions do not constitute final agency action. Both circuits have held that listing decisions are merely preliminary steps in the § 304(*l*) process. *Munic. Auth. of Bor. of St. Marys v. E.P.A.*, 945 F.2d 67, 69 (3d Cir.1991); *P. H. Glatfelter Co. v. EPA*, 921 F.2d 516, 518 (4th Cir.1990).

In this case, the final agency decision that will require action on the part of Hecla is the issuance of a final NPDES permit. Until such a permit is issued there is no definitive statement on the EPA's position and no rules are established with which immediate compliance is required. Administrative agency action that serves only to initiate proceedings does not have the status of law or a direct and immediate effect on the day to day business of the complaining party.

The judgment of the district court dismissing the action is AFFIRMED.

§ 3.5   ADMINISTRATIVE PENALTIES

One of the most powerful enforcement incentives EPA has is its discretion to pursue a case as a civil, criminal or administrative manner. Under most federal environmental statutes, the conduct could be interpreted as either criminal or civil in nature. The following cases discuss the application of administrative penalties.

UNITED STATES v. MIDWEST SUSPENSION AND BRAKE

824 F.Supp. 713 (E.D.Mich.1993).

Opinion By: Lawrence P. Zatkoff

This matter is before the Court on the United States of America's ("the government's") civil action against defendant Midwest Suspension and Brake ("defendant" or "Midwest") under § 113 of the Clean Air Act, 42 U.S.C. § 7413, ... for alleged violations of § 112 of the Clean Air Act, 42 U.S.C. § 7412, the National Emission Standards for Hazardous Air Pollutants for Asbestos, 40 C.F.R. Part 61, Subpart M ("Asbestos NESHAP"), as well as alleged violations of an Administrative Order on Consent ("AO"), which Midwest and the government entered into pursuant to § 113(a)(3) of the Clean Air Act, 42 U.S.C. § 7413(a)(3). In this action, the government seeks civil penalties and injunctive relief against defendant. The Court presided over the bench trial in this matter from April 1, 1993—April 6, 1993 ("the trial"). Upon the Court's request at the close of the trial, both parties filed post-trial proposed findings of fact and conclusions of law.

During the bench trial, the Court had an opportunity to consider, and did consider, each witness's ability and opportunity to observe the facts and the events to which he and she testified; each witness's memory and manner while testifying; each witness's interest, bias, or prejudice; and the reasonableness of each witness's testimony considered in light of all the evidence admitted. Based upon the testimony produced during the trial, the exhibits admitted into evidence at trial, and the post-trial briefs that the parties have submitted to the Court, pursuant to Rule 52(a) of the Federal Rules of Civil Procedure, the Court sets forth below its findings of fact and conclusions of law.

* * *

C.   THE ADMINISTRATIVE ORDER

1.   *The Legal Import of the Administrative Order*

As noted above, on February 6, 1987, the AO between the government and Midwest became effective. The parties stipulated that the AO operates as a contract between Midwest and the government and that the AO is still in effect. In addition, the parties stipulated that each violation of the AO renders Midwest subject to injunctive relief and civil penalties of up to $25,000 per day for each violation pursuant to § 113(b) of the Clean Air Act, 42 U.S.C. § 7413(b). In *United States v. ITT Continental Baking Co.*, 420 U.S. 223, 95 S.Ct. 926, 43 L.Ed.2d 148 (1975), the Supreme Court, after reviewing its earlier cases, . . . stated that:

> since consent decrees and orders have many of the attributes of ordinary contracts,[] they should be construed basically as contracts, without reference to the legislation the Government originally sought to enforce but never proved applicable through litigation
>
> . . . .
>
> Since a consent decree or order is to be construed for enforcement purposes basically as a contract, reliance upon certain aids to construction is proper, as with any other contract. Such aids include the circumstances surrounding the formation of the consent order, any technical meaning words used may have had to the parties, and any other documents expressly incorporated in the decree. . . .

420 U.S. at 236–37, 238, 95 S.Ct at 934–35 . . . (footnote omitted). Accordingly, the AO in the case before this Court must be treated as a contract between the government and Midwest.

2.   *Midwest's Violations of the Administrative Order*

The government alleges that Midwest violated the AO on twenty-two (22) separate occasions. Each of these violations will be separately discussed below. The first violation of the AO is alleged to have occurred on June 12, 1987, when pieces of delining waste were found on the floor by the delining machine in the Midwest facility. These pieces were loose and not in a box. The government produced testimony supporting this allegation, as well as a photograph of the pieces of delining waste on the floor. This Court finds that this above-noted evidence supports a finding that Midwest violated P A(1)(a) of the AO (delining waste must fall into sturdy cardboard box).

The government also alleges that on June 12, 1987, Midwest violated the AO by allowing loose, exposed pieces of delining waste to be present in the dedicated dumpster. The government introduced sufficient evidence, in the form of Mr. Lins' testimony and a photograph, to support this allegation. As previously noted in this Opinion, this delining waste tested positive for asbestos. Based on the above evidence, this Court finds that Midwest violated P A(1)(a) of the AO (delining waste must fall into sturdy cardboard box, box must be securely closed, and sealed in shrink-wrapped plastic)(hereinafter "failure to containerize").

In addition, the government alleges that on June 12, 1987, an employee of Midwest dumped a can of dust from the delining operation into a compactor chute, and this amounts to two (2) separate violations of the AO. As noted above, Midwest, in the AO, stipulated that the delining waste is asbestos-containing waste. By allowing its employee to dump this asbestos-containing waste into the compactor chute of the non-dedicated dumpster, Midwest violated P A(2) of the AO (Midwest must segregate asbestos-containing waste material from all other non-asbestos containing trash)(hereinafter "failure to segregate") and P A(1)(a) of the AO (failure to containerize).

Finally, for the date of June 12, 1987, the government alleges that three (3) separate violations of the AO occurred when the dedicated dumpster was unload at the landfill resulting in at least three (3) boxes being broken open and, in addition, several boxes were not wrapped in shrink-wrapped plastic. As to the boxes braking open during the deposition, the parties stipulated that this was a violation of the AO. Stip. No. 50. In addition, this Court finds that the testimony of Mr. Lins and the photographs taken at the landfill on June 12, 1987, support a finding that some of the boxes were not sealed in shrink-wrapped plastic. Failure to seal the boxes in shrink-wrapped plastic constitutes a violation of the AO.

Accordingly, based on the above evidence, this Court finds that two (2) violations of the AO occurred on June 12, 1987, when the dedicated dumpster was unloaded at the landfill. That is, Midwest violated the AO by using boxes that broke upon when they were unloaded at the landfill and Midwest violated the AO by not sealing the boxes in shrink-wrapped plastic. This Court is not persuaded, however, by the government's argument that because three (3) boxes broke open that this amounts to three separate violations of the AO. To accept the government's position would mean that for every piece of delining waste that fell to the floor, as opposed to falling into a sturdy cardboard box, there would be a separate violation of the AO. For example, if the government discovered five (5) pieces of delining waste on the floor of the Midwest facility, the government, according to its own argument, could seek a $25,000 penalty for each piece of delining waste that was on the floor.... Such a position is untenable in light of the significant civil penalty imposed for each violation. Therefore, as noted above, this Court concludes that two (2) violations occurred on June 12, 1987, when the dedicated dumpster was unloaded at the landfill.

On June 29, 1988, the government contends that six (6) separate violations of the AO occurred. First, the government argues that an employee, by manually removing rivets from old brake shoes and allowing the linings and waste to fall to the floor, violated the AO's requirement that all delining waste fall directly into a sturdy cardboard box. The parties stipulated that this amounts to a violation of the AO. Stip. No. 53. In addition, this Court finds that the testimony presented at trial supports the government's allegation, and thus this Court finds that the above-described action by a Midwest employee violates P A(1)(a) of the

AO. The second violation which the government alleges occurred on June 29, 1988, was that an employee used a broom to sweep delining waste which was present on the floor of the delining area. The government presented sufficient testimony to support this allegation, and thus this Court finds that the employee's action of using a broom to sweep the delining waste is a violation of the AO's provision requiring that Midwest "vacuum the brake relining area (instead of sweeping) to pick up asbestos-containing material from the floor." P A(1)(c) of the AO. Furthermore, the parties stipulated that this is a violation of the AO. Stip. No. 55.

The parties also stipulated that Midwest used cardboard boxes which were not lined with plastic bags to dispose of waste from the delining process, including the delining table and the shot/sandblaster areas and that such action violated the AO's requirement that such waste be placed into plastic bags. Stip. Nos. 58 & 59. Based on the above stipulations, this Court finds that such action, as it relates to the sandblasting operation, violates P A(1)(b) of the AO.

Finally, for the date of June 29, 1988, the government contends that three (3) separate violations of the AO occurred when Mr. Murchison observed three (3) boxes of delining waste that were not closed tightly as required and the three (3) boxes were neither sealed in shrink-wrapped plastic nor labeled with asbestos warning labels. Mr. Murchison observed these boxes outside of the Midwest facility. The Court finds that the government introduced sufficient testimony at trial to support these allegation. In addition, the parties stipulated that on June 29, 1988, "three unwrapped, unlabeled boxes containing delining waste were on the ground outside of Midwest's facility," that these boxes were not securely closed, and thus the AO was violated. Stip. Nos. 56 & 57. This Court finds, however, that these actions constitute two (2) violations of the AO. One (1) violation of the AO's requirement that the boxes be securely closed and sealed in shrink-wrapped plastic ... and one (1) violation of the AO's requirement that the boxes have asbestos warning labels placed on them.

Next, the government contends that an additional six (6) violations of the AO occurred on August 3, 1989. These alleged violations can be summarized as follows: (1) loose pieces of delining waste on the floor of the dedicated dumpster; (2) loose pieces of delining waste on the ground outside of the dedicated dumpster; (3) several boxes containing delining waste did not have the proper asbestos warning labels on them (2 violations); and (4) at least 2 boxes in the dedicated dumpster were not properly wrapped in shrink-wrapped plastic (2 violations). This Court finds that the testimony of Mr. Murchison supports the government's allegations that these violations occurred. In addition, the parties also stipulated that all of these alleged violations did occur on August 3, 1989. Stip. Nos. 66 & 67. This Court finds, however, that these events amount to three (3) violations of the AO, instead of the six (6) violations which the government seeks to have this Court find. The first violation occurring when Midwest did not properly containerize the waste as was evidenced by the loose pieces of delining waste located both inside and dedicated dumpster and outside the dedicated dumpster on the ground. The second violation occurring when Midwest failed to properly label two (2) boxes and the third violation occurring when Midwest failed to properly seal the boxes in shrink-wrapped plastic.

In addition, the government alleges that on October 13, 1989, two (2) separate violations of the AO occurred when several boxes of delining waste broke open during the unloading of the dedicated dumpster at the landfill. The parties entered into a stipulation that on October 13, 1989, "several boxes of stripped brake block from the load broke open during the dumping." Stip. No. 72. The testimony of Lins also bears this out to be true. The boxes breaking open violates P A(1)(a) of AO (failure to properly containerize). For the reasons stated previously in this opinion, this Court holds that while two (2) boxes broke open, that this constitutes only one (1) violation of the AO.

Finally, the government alleges that on February 27, 1990, one (1) violation of the AO occurred when boxes or bags of delining or sand blast waste broke open during the unloading of the dedicated dumpster at the landfill. The testimony of Mr. Mauzy sufficiently supports this allegation. Accordingly, this Court finds that on February 27, 1990, Midwest violated P A(1)(a) of the AO.

Accordingly, the government has produced sufficient evidence for this Court to find that Midwest violated the AO sixteen (16) times.

D. CIVIL PENALTIES

1. *The Applicable Law*

As noted above, Midwest violated the AO sixteen (16) times, and Midwest caused four (4) visible emissions to occur in the case at bar. Accordingly, there are twenty (20) violations which are subject to the civil penalty provision of the Clean Air Act, Section 113(b) of the Clean Air Act, as amended by the 1990 Clean Air Act Amendments.... Section 113 provides, in part, that:

(b) Civil judicial enforcement

The Administrator shall, as appropriate, in the case of any person which is the owner or operator of an affected source, a major emitting facility, or a major stationary source, and may in the case of any other person, commence a civil action ... to assess and recover civil penalty of not more than $25,000 per day for each violation ... in any of the following instances:

* * *

(2) Whenever such person has violated ... any other requirement or prohibition of this subchapter ... including, but not limited to, a requirement or prohibition of any rule, order ... promulgated, issued, or approved under this chapter....

(e) Penalty assessment criteria

(1) In determining the amount of any penalty to be assessed under this section ... the court ... shall take into consideration (in addition to such other factors as justice may require) the size of the business, the economic impact of the penalty on the business, the violator's full compliance history and good faith efforts to comply, the duration of the violation as established by any credible evidence (including evidence other than the applicable test method), payment by the violator of penalties previously assessed for the same violation, the economic benefit of noncompliance, and the seriousness of the violation.

42 U.S.C. §§ 7413(b)(2) & (e)(1)(West Supp. 1993)....

Finally, this Court holds that, in calculating the amount of civil penalties to be imposed on defendant, this Court must start with the statutory maximum and make any downward adjustments based on the evidence adduced at trial. While this Court has not been directed to any cases decided under § 7413(e) of the Clean Air Act, the Sixth Circuit has held that "the Clean Air and Clean Waters Acts are in *pari materia* with one another." *United States v. Stauffer Chemical Co.*, 684 F.2d 1174, 1187 (6th Cir.1982), aff'd on other grounds, 464 U.S. 165, 104 S.Ct. 575, 78 L.Ed.2d 388 (1984)(citations omitted). The United States Court of Appeals for the Eleventh Circuit has held that, under the penalty provision of the Clean Water Act, "the point of departure for the district court should be the maximum fines for such violations permitted by the Clean Water Act." *Atlantic States Legal Foundation, Inc. v. Tyson Foods, Inc.*, 897 F.2d 1128, 1137 (11th Cir.1990). *See also A.A. Metal Constr. Co.*, 22 Envtl. L. Rep. at 21201. Based on the fact that the Clean Air Act and the Clean Water Act are in pari materia with one another, this Court finds the reasoning of *Tyson Foods* persuasive, and thus this Court will calculate the civil penalties to be imposed on defendant by starting with the statutory maximum of $25,000.00 per day for each violation, which equals $500,000.00 (twenty (20) violations multiplied by $25,000.00), and examining the requisite penalty assessment criteria to determine if any downward departure is required....

2. *Section 7413(E) Penalty Assessment Criteria*

With respect to the size of defendant's business, the evidence adduced at trial showed that Midwest delines between 30,000 and 32,000 brake shoes per year. In addition, Midwest stipulated that some of the brake shoes which Midwest rehabilitates contained asbestos. Based on this evidence, the government argues that this Court should find that the size of Midwest's business, with respect to brake shoe rehabilitation, is significant. No evidence was introduced, however, which would allow this Court to compare the size of Midwest's brake shoe rehabilitation business with other businesses involved in brake shoe rehabilitation. Therefore, this Court is unable to determine whether Midwest's business is significant. On the other hand, there was no evidence adduced at trial which indicated that Midwest's brake shoe rehabilitation business was small when compared to others in the business. Accordingly, this factor does not warrant a reduction in the maximum statutory penalty.

As to the economic impact of the penalty on defendant's business, this Court, for the reasons which follow, concludes that this factor warrants a significant reduction in the maximum statutory penalty. The government's witness at trial could not render an opinion with respect to what type of impact a $650,000.00 civil penalty would have on defendant's business. ... The government's witness did testify, however, that, in her opinion, defendant could withstand a penalty in excess of $600,-000.00, although the precise amount over $600,000.00 was not clarified. The government's witness also testified that defendant: (1) had accessed only 1.85 million dollars of the 2.5 million dollar line of credit with Michigan National Bank; (2) had allowed its accounts receivable to increase approximately $334,000.00 from the previous year and that out of the 1.6 million dollars in accounts receivable defendant only deemed $36,000.00 as uncollectible; (3) had a gross income of 10.819 million dollars for 1992; (4) had a net income of approximately $214,000.00 for 1992; and (5) had come through reasonably tough periods financially and that now Midwest is profitable and is generating positive case flow.

Based on the above, this Court finds that a reduction in the amount of $450,000.00 is warranted under this factor. First, while the government's witness testified that in 1992 Midwest had allowed its account receivable to increase by over $300,000.00, because defendant had not spent as much on turning its accounts receivable into cash as it had in 1991, this Court finds this testimony not persuasive. In light of the fact that in 1991 defendant spent $20,162.00 on credit and collection and that in 1992 defendant spent $19,130.00 on credit and collection, a difference of $1,032.00, this Court concludes that, in 1992, defendant attempted to turn its accounts receivable into cash with the same effort it used in the past, and thus the existence of a large of amount of accounts receivable does not warrant this Court finding that the civil penalty in this case should not be decreased.

Second, the fact that defendant can access a line of credit to pay the civil penalty is entitled to little weight, because defendant has secured this line of credit for reasons other than paying a civil penalty in this case. This Court finds that the most relevant information regarding defendant's ability to pay a civil penalty is found in the uncontested evidence that in 1992 defendant had gross sales above 10 million dollars and a net income of more than $200,000.00. This net income occurring after Midwest, according to the government's witness, had come through tough financial periods. Therefore, based on the above evidence, it is the opinion of this Court that the civil penalty against defendant should be reduced by $450,000.00 based on this statutory factor. This leaves the civil penalty in the amount of $50,000.00. An amount which represents 25% of defendant's net income for 1992. And thus an amount that is sufficient to deter Midwest from allowing future violations to occur and is sufficient to punish Midwest for its past violations.

Regarding the next factor, namely, defendant's full compliance history and good faith efforts to comply, the Court finds that this factor mitigates in favor of not allowing a reduction in the maximum penalty. The government presented sufficient evidence that defendant had regularly violated the Asbestos NESHAP and the AO over a number of years. In addition, defendant did not introduce any evidence with respect to its good faith efforts to comply with the Clean Air Act, the Asbestos NESHAP, or the AO. Accordingly, this factors weighs in favor of not reducing the statutory maximum penalty.

With respect to the duration of the violations as established by any credible evidence, this Court concludes that this factor does not warrant a reduction in the penalty to be imposed on defendant. As noted above, the government introduced ample evidence that the violations lasted from 1985 through 1991. Therefore, this factor does not weigh in favor of reducing the statutory maximum penalty.

The next factor, payment by defendant of penalties previously assessed for the same violations, is not implicated by the facts in this case, because there was no evidence adduced at trial that defendant previously paid a penalty for any of these violations. This brings the Court to the sixth factor, namely, the economic benefit of noncompliance. In *Tyson Foods, supra,* the Eleventh Circuit stated that "insuring that violators do not reap economic benefit by failing to comply with the statutory mandate is of key importance if the penalties are successfully to deter violations." 897 F.2d at 1141. In addition, in *A.A. METAL Constr. Co., supra,* the court noted "that the recovery of economic benefit is essential and that economic benefit should serve as the floor below which the maximum civil penalty should not be mitigated." 22 Envtl. L. Rep. at 21,201. Here, there was no evidence introduced at trial as to the exact amount of economic benefit defendant received through its noncompliance with the Clean Air Act.... This Court recognizes, however, that based on the evidence presented at trial, defendant received very little economic benefit from the violations. This case did not involve a defendant that intentionally buried asbestos-containing waste material in the ground or intentionally released asbestos-containing waste into the air in an effort to dispose of the waste. Here, defendant attempted to comply with all of the requirements. There is, however, no doubt in this Court's opinion that defendant did not handle the asbestos-containing waste material in a professional manner and that defendant failed to pay close enough attention to the details of the Asbestos NESHAP and the AO. Therefore, the Court finds that this factor neither establishes a floor below which the maximum civil penalty should not be reduced nor mitigates in favor of reducing the maximum civil penalty.

As to the last factor which this Court must address, that is, the seriousness of the violation, this Court finds that this factor does not require any downward adjustment in the amount of the penalty to be imposed on defendant. First, defendant does not dispute the fact that medical science has not established any minimum level of exposure to asbestos fibers which is considered to be safe to individuals exposed to the fibers. Therefore, as a matter of law, due to the fact the this case involves asbestos, this Court finds as a matter of law that the violations are very serious.

In addition, this case involves numerous violations of the AO. The AO was consented to by Midwest and was not unilaterally imposed on Midwest by the EPA. Midwest received a number of substantial benefits by entering into the AO, including but not limited to, the government not instituting an action in federal court seeking a substantial civil penalty and being able to negotiate with the EPA on the precise waste handling methods which Midwest would use at the facility. Notwithstanding these substantial benefits, Midwest failed to live up to its end of the bargain with respect to the AO. Consequently, the violations of the AO also are very serious violations.

Finally, this Court has one final comment before imposing the civil penalty on defendant. This Court is compelled to point out that defendant entered into numerous stipulations with the government in this case. Some stipulations involved facts and circumstances which there could have been a dispute over. Defendant decided, however, to stipulate to these facts, and thus allowed the government to present its case over the course of a few days, instead of over a course of a few weeks. While this, in and of itself, may not warrant a reduction in the amount of the civil penalty imposed in the case at bar, this Court wishes to acknowledge these actions.

Accordingly, after a thorough review of the relevant penalty assessment criteria set forth in 42 U.S.C. § 7413(e), the Court concludes that a civil penalty in the amount of $50,000.00 against defendant is proper. This amounts to $2,500.00 for each violation, which is a sufficient sum to deter defendant from future violations, as well as to penalize defendant for its past actions.

E. INJUNCTIVE RELIEF

The government seeks to have this Court affirmatively enjoin Midwest so that Midwest performs its rehabilitation of brake shoes at its Detroit facility in compliance with the key terms of the AO. In addition, the government proposes that the injunction could be terminated under the following conditions:

With at least thirty days prior, written notice to the United States, Midwest may petition the Court to lift this injunction upon certification to the Court either of the following:

(1) Midwest has complied continuously with this Court's injunction for at least twelve consecutive months subsequent to the date on which the Court's injunction was issued; or

(2) Midwest can certify specifically and affirmatively that it has not had on its facility—for any consecutive, eighteen-month period following entry of the injunction—any brake lining, new or used, that contained any asbestos, and further that Midwest warrants it will not allow on its premises any asbestos-containing brake lining,

new or used, at any time in the future. The United States shall have no less than 30 days after Midwest files any such petition to evaluate its merit and, if appropriate, oppose it.

It is axiomatic under federal law "that the basis for injunctive relief in the federal courts has always been irreparable injury and the inadequacy of legal remedies." *Weinberger v. Romero–Barcelo*, 456 U.S. 305, 312, 102 S.Ct. 1798, 1803, 72 L.Ed.2d 91 (1982)(injunctive relief under the Federal Water Pollution Control Act). Moreover, whether injunctive relief should be issued in within the equitable discretion of the court. *Id.* at 320, 102 S.Ct. at 1807.

Here, while this Court agrees with the government that its proposed injunction is reasonable, this Court declines to grant such injunctive relief. First, as the government emphasized in its post-trial brief, the primary goal of the civil penalty assessed against defendant under the Clean Air Act is deterrence. This Court has ordered defendant to pay a $50,000.00 civil penalty in this case. This is a significant penalty and it should be sufficient to deter defendant from future violations. Second, at this point in time, it cannot be said that the government is without adequate legal remedies; a requisite finding before an injunction can be issued. If defendant violates the AO in the future the government may bring a civil suit against defendant seeking an addition civil penalty. Indeed, if the government were forced to bring a civil suit in the future against defendant, then this Court may be more inclined to grant the government's request for injunctive relief based on the fact that the civil penalty assessed in the instant case had failed to deter defendant from violating the AO and the Asbestos NESHAP. Accordingly, the government's request for injunctive relief is DENIED.

§ 3.6   FREEDOM OF INFORMATION ACT

The Freedom of Information Act (FOIA) is an important tool available to the public to ensure that the government meets its administrative and enforcement obligations. A great deal of environmental data is reported to the agency under the various federal environmental statutes. it is not uncommon for plaintiff's attorneys to use FOIA to access this information and bolster the facts of their case.

ETHYL CORP. v. U.S.E.P.A.
25 F.3d 1241 (4th Cir.1994).

Niemeyer, Circuit Judge:

After the Environmental Protection Agency ("EPA") denied the application of Ethyl Corporation for a waiver of approval for a gasoline additive, Ethyl filed this action under the Freedom of Information Act to compel the production of records from the EPA relevant to the EPA's denial of the waiver application. In its complaint, Ethyl contended that the EPA did not conduct an adequate search for the documents requested and that other documents were discovered and improperly withheld.

Ethyl also requested discovery on these issues. The district court granted the EPA's motion for summary judgment, finding that Ethyl "failed to make a sufficient showing on an essential element of the case on which that party has the burden of proof." The court concluded: (1) the EPA's efforts in searching for information were adequate and no factual dispute was shown to exist; (2) the EPA's decision to withhold certain documents on the ground that they fell within the "deliberative process" privilege and the decision not to produce or describe other documents on the ground that they constituted personal, not agency, documents were proper as a matter of law; and (3) no discovery or in camera inspection was necessary to dispose of the case properly.

Because we conclude that factual questions remained on issues on which the EPA had the burden of proof, we vacate the judgment and remand the case for further proceedings.

I

In May 1990, Ethyl initiated an administrative proceeding before the EPA pursuant to § 211(f)(4) of the Clean Air Act, 42 U.S.C. § 7545(f)(4), seeking the EPA's approval of high-performance gasoline additive known as HiTEC 3000 (methylcyclopentadienyl manganese tricarbonyl). Section 211 prohibits use of a fuel additive until the manufacturer demonstrates that the additive will not interfere with the proper operation of any emission device or system. Pending completion of that proceeding, which Ethyl expects will be protracted, Ethyl requested a "fuel additive waiver" based on its own extensive and successful testing of HiTEC 3000. The EPA denied the application for a waiver on January 8, 1992, and on appeal, the issue was remanded to the EPA for further proceedings. *Ethyl Corp. v. Browner*, 989 F.2d 522 (D.C.Cir.1993).

On January 10, 1992 Ethyl submitted a request under the Freedom of Information Act ("FOIA"), 5 U.S.C. § 552, for EPA documents relating to the denial of Ethyl's waiver application, including "communications between the EPA and representatives of the automobile manufacturing industry" and portions of telephone logs and calendars reflecting such communications. In response to Ethyl's request, the EPA provided approximately 450 documents and identified 243 more which it declined to disclose on the grounds that the documents were used internally in the agency's deliberative process and were protected by the attorney-client and attorney work-product privileges. The EPA therefore took the position that these documents were exempt from disclosure under Exemption 5 of the FOIA, 5 U.S.C. § 552(b)(5). The EPA further noted that it was withholding an undisclosed number of documents that its employees had characterized as "personal." It did not identify those documents except to note that they consisted of calendars, telephone logs, and personal notes from telephone conversations and meetings.

When Ethyl moved to supplement the administrative record of its waiver application to include documents produced by the EPA, the EPA conducted a further review of the documents it had withheld and, concluding that 12 of them had been improperly withheld, provided them to Ethyl. With respect to the remaining withheld documents, Ethyl then filed an administrative appeal of its FOIA request. When the EPA failed to respond, Ethyl filed this action in August 1992, seeking a court order compelling the EPA to disclose the remaining documents it had identified as responsive but exempt from mandatory disclosure along with documents identified as personal.

Along with its complaint, Ethyl filed a motion to compel the production of a Vaughn index ... and served a set of interrogatories and requests for the production of documents. The EPA opposed Ethyl's discovery requests and took the position that it was not obliged to produce the Vaughn index until it filed a motion for summary judgment.

Although the district court stayed discovery until it could consider the EPA's motion for summary judgment, it entered an order directing the EPA to produce a Vaughn index. The order required the EPA to provide with respect to each withheld document: (1) its date; (2) its author and each recipient; (3) a description of its contents; (4) the reason for withholding its production, stated with sufficient specificity "to allow the court to determine whether the document has been properly withheld"; (5) any public interest determination made by the EPA concerning such withholding; and (6) "an identification of any reasonably segregable portions of a withheld document that may be disclosed to Ethyl, with a statement of all reasons for withholding the remainder of the document." Although the EPA filed a Vaughn index with the district court, it failed to provide most of the information required by the district court's order. Nevertheless, two days after producing the Vaughn index, the EPA determined that 79 more withheld documents could be released, and it provided them to Ethyl.

In February 1993, the EPA filed a motion for summary judgment relying on affidavits of David Kortum, the EPA official assigned the task of collecting the documents, and Mary Smith, the Director of the Field Operations and Support Division of the EPA's Office of Mobile Sources. The Smith affidavit revealed that five previously unidentified documents had been added to the Vaughn list and that another, which had been identified and withheld, was being produced. Ethyl states that on another occasion the EPA released three more documents. It contends that as of this time the number of documents being withheld totals 146....

The district court granted the EPA's motion for summary judgment on April 19, 1993, ruling that "the non-moving party [Ethyl] has failed to make a sufficient showing on an essential element of the case on which the party has the burden of proof." The court concluded that, based on the affidavits presented, the EPA had conducted "an adequate and thorough search" for responsive documents, and that Ethyl had failed to contradict the EPA's assertions in that regard. The court concluded that the only undisclosed documents were those listed on the EPA's Vaughn index, and based on information in the index, it concluded that the disputed documents were protected by the agency's "deliberative process privilege for pre-decisional and deliberative documents and that further disclosure would harm the public interest." The court also concluded that any purely factual materials in the withheld documents were not "reasonably segregable from the deliberative context of the documents." The court's findings were made on the basis of the Vaughn index and without the benefit of any in camera review.

Following the district court's ruling, Ethyl made a second FOIA request in July 1993, seeking further documents relating to the EPA's denial of its application for a gasoline additive waiver. In its second request, Ethyl asked the EPA to omit from its response any documents which had previously been produced in response to the first FOIA request. The EPA provided further documents in response to the second request, some previously produced, explaining that the agency had kept no record of which documents it had produced in response to the first FOIA request. Ethyl asserts that 17 documents produced in response to the second request were also responsive to the first request, and cites this fact as relevant to its contention that the EPA improperly withheld documents on the first request. It is unclear whether any of the 17 documents in question were listed on the Vaughn index of withheld documents that are the subject of this action.

II

The Freedom of Information Act was enacted to maintain an open government and to ensure the existence of an informed citizenry "to check against corruption and to hold the governors accountable to the governed." *NLRB v. Robbins Tire & Rubber Co.*, 437 U.S. 214, 242 (1978). While an efficient and effective democratic government is one that is open to the people and accountable to them, the people's access must be orderly and not so unconstrained as to disrupt the government's daily business. Although the Act recognizes these principles, it nevertheless is to be construed broadly to provide information to the public in accordance with its purposes; for the same reason, the exemptions from production are to be construed narrowly. *See United States Dep't of Justice v. Julian*, 486 U.S. 1, 8 (1988). Moreover, Congress explicitly provided that the agency called upon to provide documents bears the burden of demonstrating that any document withheld falls within a stated exemption. *See* 5 U.S.C. § 552(a)(4)(B)("the burden is on the Agency to sustain its action [of withholding a record under a stated exemption]").

The FOIA requires each governmental agency to provide information to the public on request if the request "reasonably describes" the record sought and is made in accordance with published agency rules for making requests. 5 U.S.C. § 552(a)(3). The agency is required to provide a response within 10 days of the receipt of the request on whether it will provide the information. 5 U.S.C. § 552(a)(6). Subsection 552(b) enumerates nine exemptions from the production requirement, but these exemptions apply to categories of information, and are not defined so as to protect entire documents, per se. *See Virginia Beach v. U.S. Dep't of Commerce*, 995 F.2d 1247, 1253 (4th Cir.1993). Thus, the Act provides:

Any reasonably segregable portion of a record shall be provided to any person requesting such record after deletion of the portions which are exempt from this subsection[(b)].

5 U.S.C. § 552(b). The United States District Courts are given jurisdiction to enjoin the Agencies from "withholding Agency records and to order the production of Agency records improperly withheld." 5 U.S.C. § 552(a)(4)(B).

On review of a district court's granting of summary judgment to the government in a FOIA action, we "must determine de novo whether, after taking all the evidence in the light most favorable to the non-movant, there remains no genuine issue of material fact and the government is entitled to judgment as a matter of law." *Virginia Beach*, 995 F.2d at 1252 (citing *Pulliam Invest. Co. v. Cameo Properties*, 810 F.2d, 1282, 1286 (4th Cir.1987)). Although any factual conclusions that place a document within a stated exemption of FOIA are reviewed under a clearly erroneous standard, "the question of whether a document fits within one of FOIA's prescribed exemptions is one of law, upon which the district court is entitled to no deference." *Id.* at 1252 n.12.

III

Ethyl Corporation first contends that the EPA's search for the requested documents failed to meet articulated standards of thoroughness. To buttress this allegation, Ethyl points to the fact that on each occasion the EPA was forced, either by court order or by the necessity of responding to a development in the litigation, to review withheld documents, it found that it had erroneously withheld documents subject to disclosure and consequently released such documents. It states that the EPA once had to amend the Vaughn list, and on another occasion, in response to the second FOIA request, it produced documents that were earlier requested but neither produced nor identified on the Vaughn list.

Ethyl also notes that in the EPA's first affidavit, David Kortum, who executed the affidavit on behalf of the EPA, stated that he contacted 25 individuals from eight separate EPA offices to obtain documents. When Ethyl provided a counter-affidavit that showed that more than 100 persons appeared to have participated in the review of Ethyl's waiver application, Kortum submitted a follow-up affidavit in which he indicated that he had communicated with 59 persons. Ethyl points out that the EPA did not, however, dispute the fact that more than 100 persons were involved, and it did not provide an explanation for why the remainder of the persons involved were not contacted for documents.

Finally, Ethyl contends that inadequate criteria were provided to EPA employees on how to differentiate between documents which are personal and those which belong to the agency and are theoretically subject to the FOIA. Ethyl observes that even though David Kortum was aware of the 10 factors contained in the EPA's FOIA Manual for distinguishing personal records from agency records, when he instructed EPA employees about Ethyl's request, he mentioned only 4 of the 10 factors, thus permitting employees to characterize as personal some documents which actually might be covered by the FOIA. As a consequence, Ethyl argues, when the EPA stated, "Certain documents requested by you are personal records, not agency documents, and thus, are not covered by FOIA," it may have excluded agency documents which should have been produced. The EPA described these personal documents generally as calendars, telephone logs, and notes of telephone conversations and meetings.

In response to Ethyl's arguments, the EPA asserts that its several affidavits show that its search for documents was thorough and adequate and that an effort of that quality is all that is required by law.

In judging the adequacy of an agency search for documents the relevant question is not whether every single potentially responsive document has been unearthed, *see, e.g., Perry v. Block*, 684 F.2d 121, 128 (D.C.Cir.1982), but whether the agency has "demonstrated that it has conducted a 'search reasonably calculated to uncover all relevant documents.'" *Weisberg v. United States Dep't of Justice*, 745 F.2d 1476, 1485 (D.C.Cir.1984)(quoting *Weisberg v. United States Dep't of Justice*, 705 F.2d 1344, 1350–51 (D.C.Cir.1983)). In demonstrating the adequacy of its search, however, an agency may not rest on an affidavit that simply avers that the search was conducted in a manner "consistent with customary practice and established procedure." Rather, the affidavit must be reasonably detailed, "setting forth the search terms and the type of search performed, and averring that all files likely to contain responsive materials (if such records exist) were searched" so as to give the requesting party an opportunity to challenge the adequacy of the search. *Oglesby v. United States Dep't of Army*, 920 F.2d 57, 68 (D.C.Cir. 1990).

In this case, a sufficient question has been raised about the EPA's methodology that we conclude that it was error to have ruled, as a matter of law, that the EPA met its burden of proof. First, on the question of whether a proper search was conducted of employees, we note that the employees were not properly instructed on how to distinguish personal records from agency records. An agency presented with a request for records under FOIA is required to produce only agency records, which are those that are either created or obtained by the agency and are subject to the control of the agency at the time the FOIA request is made. *See United States Dep't of Justice v. Tax Analysts*, 492 U.S. 136, 144–45 (1989). And personal records of an agency employee are not agency records and are not subject to the FOIA. The distinction, however, is more easily stated than applied. Not only is there difficulty in making the distinction between a personal record and an agency record, particularly when the record may not be required by agency procedure but is generated by the employee in the course of his work, but there is yet a more difficult problem in requiring employees in the first place to identify the existence of personal records. An agency cannot require an employee to produce and submit for review a purely personal document when responding to a FOIA request. On the other hand, it does control the employee to the extent that the employee works for the agency on agency matters. To clarify the distinction, the EPA published, in its FOIA Manual, 10 factors to be considered in determining whether a document is a personal or agency record, instructing that "employees should review each document in the context of all these criteria" ... Even though the EPA Manual directs that all 10 factors should be considered in determining whether a record is an agency or personal record, Kortum's affidavit indicates that he advised the employees to whom he spoke of only 4 of the factors.

An unresolved question is also created by Ethyl's statement, under oath, that over 100 employees were involved in considering and deciding the waiver application and by Kortum's affidavit which indicates that only 59 were actually contacted. Leaving unaddressed so large a group creates at least a question of fact as to whether the EPA met its burden of conducting a "search reasonably calculated to uncover all relevant documents."

Finally, the fact that 17 documents, responsive to the first request although not identified in response to that request, were supplied in response to a second FOIA request puts the adequacy of the search in connection with the first FOIA request in doubt.

For all of these reasons, we are not satisfied that the EPA met its burden of showing that it conducted an adequate search. "The burden is on the agency to demonstrate, not the requestor to disprove, that the materials sought, are not 'agency records.' " *Tax Analysts*, 492 U.S. at 142 n.3. At the least, a question of fact on the issue remains, precluding summary judgment for the EPA on this issue.

IV

The EPA claims that all of the 146 documents identified on the Vaughn list are subject to withholding on the basis of Exemption 5 of the FOIA, exempting from production records that are "interagency or intra-agency memorandums or letters which would not be available by law to a party other than an agency in litigation with the agency." 5 U.S.C. § 552(b)(5). Although some of these records were withheld on the basis of attorney-client and attorney work-product privileges, all of them were withheld on the basis of a privilege asserted to protect the EPA's deliberative processes, known as the "deliberative process" privilege. Ethyl does not contest the application of Exemption 5 to the attorney-client and attorney work-product documents. It does, however, challenge the EPA's assertion of the deliberative process privilege.

Defining the contours of the deliberative process privilege, the Supreme Court stated in *NLRB v. Sears, Roebuck & Co.*, 421 U.S. 132 (1975), "The cases uniformly rest the privilege on the policy of protecting the 'decisionmaking processes of government agencies,'; and focus on documents 'reflecting advisory opinions, recommendations and deliberations comprising part of a process by which governmental decisions and policies are formulated.' " *Id.* at 150 (citations omitted). Relying on the legislative history of the FOIA, the Court explained, "the point ... is that the 'frank discussion of legal or policy matters' in writing might be inhibited if the discussion were made public; and that the 'decisions' and 'policies formulated' would be the poorer as a result." *Id.* (citations omitted).

In addition to being deliberative, a record protected by the deliberative process privilege must also be predecisional, i.e. "prepared in order to assist an agency decisionmaker in arriving at his decision." *Renegotiation Board v. Grumman Aircraft Engineering Corp.*, 421 U.S. 168, 184 (1975). Stated differently, the privilege protects "recommendations, draft documents, proposals, suggestions, and other subjective documents which reflect the personal opinions of the writer rather than the policy of the agency." *Coastal States Gas Corp. v. Department of Energy*, 617 F.2d 854, 866 (D.C.Cir.1980). The deliberative process privilege, as with all of the exemptions contained in § 522(b), is to be construed narrowly, and the burden rests upon the government to be precise and conservative in its privilege claims. Thus, the privilege does not protect a document which is merely peripheral to actual policy formation; the record must bear on the formulation or exercise of policy-oriented judgment.

> To fall within the deliberative process privilege, materials must bear on the formulation or exercise of agency policy-oriented judgment. The deliberative process privilege, we underscore, is essentially concerned with protecting the process by which policy is formulated.... When material could not reasonably be said to reveal an agency's or official's mode of formulating or exercising policy-implicating judgment, the deliberative process privilege is inapplicable. *See Playboy Enterprises v. Dep't of Justice*, 677 F.2d 931, 935 (D.C.Cir.1982)(holding that fact report was not within privilege because compilers' mission was simply "to investigate the facts," and because report was not "intertwined with the policy-making process.")(quoting district court).

Petroleum Info. Corp. v. United States Dep't of Interior, 976 F.2d 1429, 1435 (D.C.Cir.1992)(internal citations omitted)(emphasis in the original).

One relevant factor to be considered in determining whether the deliberative process privilege applies to a record is the identity and position of the author and any recipients of the document, along with the place of those persons within the decisional hierarchy. *See Access Reports v. United States Dep't of Justice*, 926 F.2d 1192, 1195 (D.C.Cir.1991).

In the case before us, the Vaughn index articulates the Exemption 5 privilege in general terms, using FOIA language, and couples the statement of privilege for each document with a general description of the document. With respect to most of the documents listed on the index, neither the author nor the recipient of the document is identified. From this level of identification, it appears that many documents are no more than summaries or graphical representations of purely statistical data. Some are notes discussing contacts that EPA officials have had with other government agencies regarding Ethyl's waiver application. While most of the descriptions provided in the index are inadequate to determine whether the identified document is properly excluded by the deliberative process privilege, some that are adequate do not meet the applicable criteria for properly asserting the privilege.

The Vaughn index is a surrogate for the production of documents for in camera review, designed to enable the district court to rule on a privilege without having to review the document itself. It was developed in response to the Supreme Court's decision in *EPA v. Mink*, 410 U.S. 73 (1973), where the Court reversed a circuit ruling that would have mandated an in camera review by the district court of all documents withheld by the government in response to a FOIA request. Rather than impose such a rigid requirement, the Supreme Court introduced flexibility into the process. Appreciating the potential damage that disclosure, even to the district court, might have on the deliberative process of an agency, the Court observed that a review of the agency's decision to withhold a document does not automatically require an in camera inspection. The Court explained:

> Plainly, in some situations, in camera inspection will be necessary and appropriate. But it need not be automatic. An agency should be given the opportunity, by means of detailed affidavits or oral testimony, to establish to the satisfaction of the District Court that the documents sought fall clearly beyond the range of material that would be available to a private party in litigation with the agency. The burden is, of course, on the agency resisting disclosure, 5 U.S.C. § 552(a)(3), and if it fails to meet its burden without in camera inspection, the District Court may order such inspection.

Id. at 93. . . .

Defining a mechanism to take advantage of the flexibility allowed by Mink, the court in *Vaughn v. Rosen*, 484 F.2d 820 (D.C.Cir.1973), *cert. denied*, 415 U.S. 977 (1974), also recognized the pragmatic problem created by the unique dilemma inherent in, and one-sided nature of, a FOIA production. The producing party is saddled with the burden of demonstrating confidentiality without breaching the confidence, and it must carry this burden against the requesting party who lacks knowledge and therefore is helpless as an adversary.

> This lack of knowledge of the party seeking disclosure seriously distorts the traditional adversary nature of our legal system's form of dispute resolution. . . . In a case arising under the FOIA . . . the typical process of dispute resolution is impossible.

484 F.2d. at 824–25. While an in camera review was recognized to be available as a possible method of reviewing an agency decision, the court also recognized that such a process can be cumbersome and overburdening for the judiciary. The court in Vaughn thus directed that the government provide a detailed justification for its exemption and index the documents against the justification, fragmenting the documents into segregable parts. The court emphasized a need for specificity and itemization to permit the adversary process to function. If the index is so vague as to leave the district court with an inability to rule, then some other means of review must be undertaken, such as in camera review.

A review of EPA's Vaughn index in this case leaves the court without the ability to determine whether many of the documents fall within the claimed privilege, and absent sufficient information, the EPA fails to carry its burden of satisfying the requirements of demonstrating an exemption. Summaries and charts depicting the results of testing conducted by the agency would appear, without a more detailed explanation, not to have any deliberative character. But, most importantly, where the list fails to identify either the author or its recipient, those persons' relationships to the decisionmaking process cannot be identified and it becomes difficult, if not impossible, to perceive how the disclosure of such documents would result in a chilling effect upon the open and frank exchange of opinions within the agency. In short, little information is provided by much of the Vaughn index for testing the EPA's deliberative process privilege claims, leaving the district court and us entirely dependent upon the EPA's own assertions that the release of the documents in question would "significantly curtail ... the expression of such opinions, analyses, and recommendations in future deliberations."

The FOIA also provides that any agency may rely on an exemption only as to segregable portions of records, so that the agency must produce any "reasonably segregable portion of a record" that does not fall within an exemption. *See* 5 U.S.C. § 552(b). Thus, the statute requires partial disclosure of records "reflecting deliberative or policy making processes on the one hand, and purely factual, investigative matters on the other." Mink, 410 U.S. at 89. And the EPA, in this case, has the burden of showing that no segregable information exists. *See Army Times Publishing Co. v. Dep't of Air Force*, 998 F.2d 1067, 1071 (D.C.Cir.1993). We cannot determine from looking at the index whether it has attempted to meet this additional burden.

V

With respect to both the question of whether the EPA conducted an adequate search for records and the question of whether it justifiably has withheld 146 documents, the district court seems to have placed the burden of proof on Ethyl, contrary to the terms of the FOIA. Ethyl has raised significant factual questions, particularly in light of the fact that it does not have the benefit of any knowledge about the documents in question. The district court should have placed the burden on the EPA, conscious of the knowledge that "the plaintiff is at a distinct disadvantage in attempting to test the claims alleged by [the withholding agency]." *Exxon Corp. v. FTC*, 663 F.2d 120, 126 (D.C.Cir.1980). Because we conclude that open questions remain that cannot be disposed of on the present record by summary judgment, we vacate the summary judgment entered for the EPA and remand this case for further proceedings. The EPA has argued that if it is required to describe in more detail the documents it has withheld, then the confidentiality of the documents will be breached. If the district court is satisfied that the EPA cannot describe documents in more detail without breaching a properly asserted confidentiality, then the court is still left with the mechanism provided by the statute to conduct an in camera review of the documents. *See* 5 U.S.C. § 522(a)(4)(B).

VACATED AND REMANDED FOR FURTHER PROCEEDINGS.

Chapter 4

REGULATION OF TOXIC SUBSTANCES

Table of Sections

§ 4.1 THE TOXIC SUBSTANCES CONTROL ACT

Under the Toxic Substances Control Act (TSCA), 15 U.S.C.A. § 2601 *et seq*. EPA is authorized to prohibit, limit, or otherwise regulate the manufacture, processing, distribution, use, or disposal of a chemical that presents an unreasonable risk to health or the environment. All but small manufacturers who manufacture or process chemical substances must keep certain records and submit reports to EPA. Unless exempted under § 2604(h), all producers of a new chemical, or of an existing chemical for a significant new use, must notify EPA 90 days before producing a new chemical and may be required to submit test data before production begins. In addition, if anyone producing or distributing a chemical obtains information reasonably supporting the conclusion that the chemical presents a substantial risk of injury to health or the environment, they must notify the EPA Administrator immediately, unless they have actual knowledge that the Administrator has already been adequately informed.

ENVIRONMENTAL DEFENSE FUND v. REILLY
909 F.2d 1497 (D.C.Cir.1990).

ROBINSON, SENIOR CIRCUIT JUDGE.

Appellants, the Environmental Defense Fund and the National Wildlife Federation, jointly petitioned the Environmental Protection Agency (EPA) ... to issue, pursuant to the Toxic Substances Control Act, ... rules designed to protect human health and the environment from allegedly harmful dioxins and furans. EPA denied the petition in major part, whereupon appellants brought this suit in the District Court. Appellants contended that EPA's disposition of their request for rule-making contravened the Administrative Procedure Act (APA).... Appellants also invoked Section 21 of the Toxic Substances Control Act, which authorizes citizen petitions seeking promulgation of rules and orders under designated provisions thereof, and affords an opportunity for de novo district-court review of denials of such petitions.... The District Court awarded summary judgment to EPA on appellants' APA challenge, and that ruling is the subject of these appeals. The court later entered a consent decree settling all of appellants' Section 21 claims. We hold that appellants, having elected to pursue the Section 21 remedy to the results achieved by the settlement, cannot now resort to the APA.

I. BACKGROUND

A. The Toxic Substances Control Act

Enactment of this legislation in 1976 launched a "comprehensive program" ... to anticipate and forestall injury to health and the environment from activities involving toxic chemical substances.... Congress structured the Act to fill "conspicuous gaps" in the protection afforded by preexisting "fragmented and inadequate" statutes, ... and committed administration of the Act to EPA.... A brief resume of the Act's highlights serves the purposes of these appeals.

The Act provides in Section 4 for substance testing, ... and in Section 5 for notice of intent to manufacture new substances or existing substances for significant new uses.... Section 6 requires imposition of restrictions when the substance is hazardous, ... and Section 7 authorizes judicial proceedings for injunctive and other relief when danger is imminent.... Section 8 calls for retention and reporting of information, ... and Section 10 for research, monitoring and dissemination of data....

Section 6 is one of the most important features of the Act. It specifies that if EPA

> finds that there is a reasonable basis to conclude that the manufacture, processing, distribution in commerce, use, or disposal of a chemical substance or mixture ... presents or will present an unreasonable risk of injury to health or the environment, [the agency must] by rule apply one or more of [prescribed] requirements to such substance or mixture to the extent necessary to protect

adequately against such risk using the least burdensome require-ments. . . .

These requirements include limitations on manufacture, processing, distribution or use of such substances; . . . regulated methods of disposal of substances; . . . warnings and instructions; . . . notification of unrea-sonable risks of injury; . . and preparation and retention of records pertaining to manufacture, processing, monitoring and testing. . . . EPA is also empowered to issue orders exacting individual compliance with the Act.

Among a variety of mechanisms supplied for enforcement of the Act . . . are two entailing citizen activity. . . . Citizen participation is broadly permitted to "ensure that bureaucratic lethargy does not prevent the appropriate administration of this vital authority." . . . One form of citizen participation is authorized by Section 21, . . . and is central to the parties' dispute. By virtue of that section, "[a]ny person may petition [EPA] to initiate a proceeding for the issuance, amendment, or repeal of a rule . . . or an order" under designated provisions of the Act. . . . If EPA grants the petition, it must "promptly commence an appropriate proceeding." . . . If, however, a petition requesting issuance of a new rule is denied, or the agency fails to grant or deny the request within a designated period, the petitioner may obtain de novo review in a federal district court. . . . If the petitioner, once in court, meets a preponderance-of-the evidence standard, the court must order EPA to take suitable action. . . . A saving clause in Section 21 specifies that "the[se] remedies . . . shall be in addition to, and not in lieu of, other remedies provided by law." . . .

* * *

3M COMPANY (MINNESOTA MINING AND MANUFACTURING) v. BROWNER

17 F.3d 1453 (D.C.Cir.1994).

RANDOLPH, CIRCUIT JUDGE:

This petition for review of the Environmental Protection Agency's assessment of civil penalties turns on the meaning of 28 U.S.C. § 2462, the direct descendant of a statute of limitations enacted more than a century and a half ago. There are three questions. Does § 2462 apply to administrative proceedings? If so, is a proceeding to assess a civil penalty an action for the enforcement of a penalty within § 2462's meaning? If it is, does § 2462's five-year period of limitations begin running only when EPA reasonably could have been expected to detect the violations giving rise to the civil penalties?

I

Between August 1980 and July 1986, 3M unwittingly committed several violations of the Toxic Substances Control Act (TSCA), 15 U.S.C. §§ 2601–2629. On July 28, 1986, after the company became aware of its transgressions, it notified EPA's compliance office. The company had learned that one of its chemicals, Chemical A, ... was not on an EPA inventory of existing chemicals. Although 3M had believed that Chemical A came from a manufacturer in this country, the company's investigation revealed that 3M received the chemical from the manufacturer's Canadian affiliate.

At least ninety days before a new chemical may be imported, TSCA requires the importer to provide EPA with a Premanufacture Notice. 15 U.S.C. § 2604(a)(1). Because Chemical A was both new and imported, 3M's importation of Chemical A without the requisite notice violated this provision. In addition, 3M's brokers wrongly certified to Customs officials that TSCA's requirements had been met.

The mishap with Chemical A spurred 3M to review its other imported chemicals. Thus, it discovered a problem with Chemical B. This chemical has the same code and the same use as another chemical listed on the inventory of existing chemicals. When 3M imported Chemical B on various occasions between July 15, 1983, and August 4, 1986, it assumed Chemical B was not new and did not require a Premanufacture Notice. Closer inspection revealed that Chemical B was not identical to the chemical on the inventory. As with Chemical A, a Premanufacture Notice had been required but not submitted, and the Customs certifications regarding compliance with TSCA were incorrect. On September 16, 1986, 3M notified EPA of the violations concerning Chemical B.

Two years later, on September 2, 1988, EPA filed an administrative complaint against 3M seeking $1.3 million in civil penalties under § 16(a)(2)(A) of TSCA for 3M's failure to file Premanufacture Notices and for 3M's submitting inaccurate Customs certifications with respect to Chemicals A and B. Section 16(a)(2)(A), 15 U.S.C. § 2615(a)(2)(A), provides that the EPA Administrator shall assess civil penalties for violations of the Act "by an order made on the record after opportunity ... for a hearing...."

In its answer to the complaint, 3M interposed a statute of limitations—28 U.S.C. § 2462—claiming that the statute barred proceedings to impose penalties for 3M's importation of the chemicals without the requisite notices five years prior to EPA's complaint, that is, before September 1983. An EPA Administrative Law Judge ruled that no statute of limitations applied to § 16(a)(2)(A) proceedings. The ALJ found 28 U.S.C. § 2462 inapplicable on the grounds that it applied only to judicial proceedings; and that, in any event, civil penalty cases under § 16 of TSCA were not the sort of enforcement proceedings covered by § 2462. After the ALJ assessed a civil penalty of $104,720, 3M filed an administrative appeal with the EPA Chief Judicial Officer, who acts as the Administrator's delegate in these cases. The Chief Judicial Officer, "adopting and incorporating" the "applicable portions" of the ALJ's opinion, also ruled that § 2462 did not apply.... He then assessed a penalty against 3M of $130,650. This petition followed.

II

Any person who violates § 15 of TSCA, 15 U.S.C. § 2614, "shall be liable to the United States for a civil penalty in an amount not to exceed $25,000 for each such violation." 15 U.S.C. § 2615(a)(1). Before the EPA Administrator assesses a penalty pursuant to § 16(a)(2)(A), the alleged violator has the right to a hearing. 15 U.S.C. § 2615(a)(2)(A). If the hearing results in the Administrator's issuing an order fixing liability and setting the amount of the penalty, any person "aggrieved" has thirty days to file a petition for review in a federal court of appeals. 15 U.S.C. § 2615(a)(3).

While TSCA thus sets a deadline on the alleged violator's petition for judicial review, TSCA contains no provision limiting the time within which the EPA Administrator must initiate the administrative action. If there is such a time limit, it must be derived from the five-year statute of limitations, 28 U.S.C. § 2462, generally applicable to civil fines and penalties, which reads:

> Except as otherwise provided by Act of Congress, an action, suit or proceeding for the enforcement of any civil fine, penalty, or forfeiture, pecuniary or otherwise, shall not be entertained unless commenced within five years from the date when the claim first accrued if, within the same period, the offender or the property is found within the United States in order that proper service may be made thereon.

A

The most fundamental question raised by 3M's invocation of § 2462 is whether the statute applies to civil penalty cases brought before agencies. The question has received little attention in judicial opinions. In one case, the government and the defendant agreed that § 2462 "at least requires that any administrative action aimed at imposing a civil penalty must be brought within five years of the alleged violation." *United States v. Meyer*, 808 F.2d 912, 914 (1st Cir.1987). In three other cases, the courts have assumed, without discussion, that § 2462 covers administrative penalty proceedings. *See Williams v. United States Dep't of Transp.*, 781 F.2d 1573, 1578 n. 8 (11th Cir.1986); *H.P. Lambert Co. v. Secretary of the Treasury*, 354 F.2d 819, 822 (1st Cir.1965); *The A/S Glittre v. Dill*, 152 F.Supp. 934, 940 (S.D.N.Y.1957).... Reports of two congressional committees on unrelated legislation, cited in *Meyer*, also assumed that § 2462 "is applicable to administrative as well as judicial proceedings." S. REP. NO. 363, 89th Cong., 1st Sess. 7 (1965); *see* H.R. REP. NO. 434, 89th Cong., 1st Sess. 5 (1965).

It is easy to see why § 2462's application to administrative cases would be taken for granted. What cannot be "entertained" after § 2462's limitation period has expired is "an action, suit or proceeding." An agency's adjudication of a civil penalty case readily fits this description. In this case, EPA's regulations describe the agency's process for assessing civil penalties as a "proceeding." ...The Administrative Procedure Act, 5 U.S.C. § 554(b), which generally governs agency adjudications of civil penalties and which § 16(b) of TSCA expressly incorporates, calls agency adjudications "proceedings." So does the Judicial Code, see, e.g., 28 U.S.C. §§ 2344(1), 2347. See also 31 U.S.C. § 3730(e)(3), referring to an "administrative civil money penalty proceeding."

The ALJ nevertheless ruled that § 2462 related only to judicial "actions, suits or proceedings." He acknowledged that other administrative law judges had reached the opposite conclusion in TSCA penalty assessment cases.... Much of the ALJ's reasoning rested on the fact that § 2462's predecessor spoke of "suit or prosecution," and that the 1948 revision of the Judicial Code (of which more hereafter) replacing these words with "action, suit or proceeding" intended no change in substance. The ALJ therefore believed that regardless of whether EPA's assessment of a civil penalty was a "proceeding," it could not be considered a "suit or prosecution."

We wonder why not. According to the Administrative Procedure Act, agency attorneys who bring administrative complaints, including complaints for civil penalties, are performing "prosecuting functions." 5 U.S.C. § 554(d). *NLRB v. United Food & Commercial Workers,* 484 U.S. 112, 125–26, 98 L.Ed.2d 429, 108 S.Ct. 413 (1987), for example, holds that the NLRB General Counsel's decision to file an unfair labor practice complaint is "prosecutorial." The ATTORNEY GENERAL'S MANUAL ON THE ADMINISTRATIVE PROCEDURE ACT (at pp. 14, 55), prepared in 1947, points out that agency adjudications typically have "an accusatory flavor," and stresses the need for an agency's hearing officers to be independent of those engaged in the agency's "prosecution." The Supreme Court perceives no substantial distinction between the function performed by agency attorneys "presenting evidence in an agency hearing and the function of a prosecutor who brings evidence before a court." *Butz v. Economou,* 438 U.S. 478, 516, 57 L.Ed.2d 895, 98 S.Ct. 2894 (1978). Civil penalty proceedings under TSCA emulate judicial proceedings: a complaint is brought, the defendant answers, motions and affidavits are filed, depositions are taken, other discovery pursued, a hearing is held, evidence is introduced, findings are rendered and an order assessing a civil penalty is issued. 40 C.F.R. §§ 22.13–26. When that sequence of events takes place in a court, we have no trouble calling it a "prosecution," although the modern trend is to reserve the description for criminal cases. When the same sequence of events plays out before an administrative agency, it too may be—and has been—designated a "prosecution."

Given the reasons why we have statutes of limitations, there is no discernible rationale for applying § 2462 when the penalty action or proceeding is brought in a court, but not when it is brought in an administrative agency. The concern that after the passage of time "evidence has been lost, memories have faded, and witnesses have disappeared" pertains equally to fact-finding by a court and fact-finding by an agency. *Order of R.R. Telegraphers v. Railway Express Agency,* 321 U.S. 342, 349, 88 L.Ed. 788, 64 S.Ct. 582 (1944). Statutes of limitations also reflect the judgment that there comes a time when the potential defendant "ought to be secure in his reasonable expectation that the slate has been wiped clean of ancient obligations," Note, *Developments in the Law—Statutes of Limitations*, 63 HARV. L. REV. 1177, 1185 (1950). Here again it is of no moment whether the proceeding leading to the imposition of a penalty is a proceeding started in a court or in an agency. From the potential defendant's point of view, lengthy delays upset "settled expectations" to the same extent in either case. *See Board of Regents v. Tomanio*, 446 U.S. 478, 487, 64 L.Ed.2d 440, 100 S.Ct. 1790 (1980).

The ALJ also supported his ruling that no limitations period applied by invoking a maxim: statutes of limitations ought to be strictly construed in favor of the government. While this accurately recites the Supreme Court's general pronouncements, *see Badaracco v. Commissioner*, 464 U.S. 386, 391, 78 L.Ed.2d 549, 104 S.Ct. 756 (1984), there is another Supreme Court maxim, older still, a maxim specifically relating to actions for penalties and one pointing in quite the opposite direction: "In a country where not even treason can be prosecuted, after a lapse of three years, it could scarcely be supposed, that an individual would remain for ever liable to a pecuniary forfeiture." *Adams v. Woods*, 6 U.S. (2 Cranch) 336, 341, 2 L.Ed. 297 (1805)(Marshall, C.J.). Justice Story, sitting as a circuit justice in a civil penalty case, made the same point as Chief Justice Marshall: "it would be utterly repugnant to the genius of our laws, to allow such prosecutions a perpetuity of existence." *United States v. Mayo*, 26 F.Cas. 1230, 1231 (C.C.D. Mass.1813)(No. 15,754). *See also H.P. Lambert Co. v. Secretary of the Treasury*, 354 F.2d at 822; *United States v. Maillard*, 4 Ben. 459, 26 F.Cas. 1140, 1142 (S.D.N.Y. 1871)(No. 15,709).

We therefore reject this aspect of the ALJ's construction of § 2462. It is not entirely certain that the EPA's Chief Judicial Officer, whose order is the subject of our review, relied on any court-agency dichotomy in sustaining the ALJ's decision holding § 2462 inapplicable. Before us, EPA has chosen not to mount an argument in favor of this portion of the ALJ's reasoning. And so we move on.

B

If, as we have held, an administrative proceeding under § 16(a)(2) of TSCA is an "action, suit or proceeding," the question remains whether it is—in the language of § 2462—one "for the enforcement of" a civil penalty. EPA thinks not, because "enforcement" connotes an action to collect a penalty already imposed, whereas a proceeding under § 16(a)(2) merely assesses or imposes the penalty. EPA's distinction relies on § 16(a)(4), which authorizes the Attorney General to bring an action against the violator in federal district court to recover the amount, plus interest, of any civil penalty remaining unpaid after final judgment. That, EPA, says is the action for "enforcement," to which § 2462's five-year limitation applies.

As against this, 3M points out that if EPA is right, then there would be no limitations period and liability might be imposed no matter how distant the violation.... Yet *Adams v. Woods* tells us that with respect to penalty actions such a situation "could scarcely be supposed." "Enforce," 3M says, merely signifies "impose," which is what EPA seeks to do when it brings a civil penalty assessment case.

Both sides cite contemporary dictionaries in support of their readings. How to choose between these competing definitions of "enforcement"? History holds the key. For more than a century, § 2462's predecessors simply provided that "no suit or prosecution for any penalty or forfeiture, pecuniary or otherwise, accruing under the laws of the United States, shall be maintained" unless it is brought within five years "from the time when the penalty accrued." ... The word "enforcement" did not appear in the statute until the comprehensive revision of the Judicial Code, completed in 1948. The Reviser's Notes on the rewriting of § 2462's predecessor report: "Changes were made in phraseology." H.R. REP. NO. 308, 80th Cong., 1st Sess. A191 (1947).

A long line of Supreme Court decisions compels the conclusion that the rewording did not render the new statute different in substance from the old. When the Reviser's Notes describe the alterations as changes in phraseology, the well-established canon of construction is that the revised statute means only what it meant before 1948. *See, e.g., Keene Corp. v. United States*, 124 L.Ed.2d 118, 113 S.Ct. 2035, 2041 (1993); *Finley v. United States*, 490 U.S. 545, 554, 104 L.Ed.2d 593, 109 S.Ct. 2003 (1989); *Tidewater Oil Co. v. United States*, 409 U.S. 151, 162, 34 L.Ed.2d 375, 93 S.Ct. 408 (1972); *Fourco Glass Co. v. Transmirra Products Corp.*, 353 U.S. 222, 228, 1 L.Ed.2d 786, 77 S.Ct. 787 (1957).

EPA's reading of § 2462 therefore must be rejected. To adopt it would be to treat the Reviser's rewriting of § 2462 as a modification of the statute's substance. No one could have construed § 2462's immediate predecessor to mean what EPA urges. The pre–1948 version applied to any suit or prosecution "for" a penalty. Nothing restricted its operation to actions seeking to collect penalties already imposed in other proceedings, and we can discern no reason why Congress would have thought such a restriction desirable.... On the other hand, 3M's reading of "enforcement" to mean "imposition" is faithful to the canon recited above; it is consistent with one of the accepted definitions of "enforcement"; and it forecloses stale claims, one of the functions of a statute of limitations, since it is in the administrative proceeding that evidence is taken, findings are made and liability determined. Because assessment proceedings under TSCA seek to impose civil penalties, ... they are proceedings for the "enforcement" of penalties and § 2462 thus applies.

The same result may be reached on the basis, proposed by Judge Boggs, that "assessment is a prerequisite to, and thus a part of, the measures for the enforcement of a civil penalty." *Mullikin v. United States*, 952 F.2d 920, 933 n. 1 (6th Cir.1991)(concurring in part and dissenting in part). "It would seem quite odd to say that the very act that initiates the actions leading to the collection of the penalty, a stream of events that must at some point be a proceeding, is not itself part of the proceeding." *Id. See Yaffe Iron & Metal Co. v. EPA,* 774 F.2d 1008, 1012 (10th Cir.1985), characterizing a civil penalty administrative assessment proceeding under § 16(a)(2) of TSCA as an "enforcement action," a description also adopted by EPA attorneys in the administrative proceedings in this case.

Three courts of appeals, including the Sixth Circuit in the Mullikin case just cited, hold § 2462 inapplicable to the assessment of penalties by the Internal Revenue Service pursuant to 26 U.S.C. § 6700 or § 6701. ... In one of these cases, *Capozzi v. United States,* 980 F.2d 872 (2d Cir.1992), the court stated as an alternative holding ... that it "is the collection of amounts owed, not the assessment of them, that may be properly termed 'enforcement.' " 980 F.2d at 874–75 (footnote omitted). In adopting this definition, the *Capozzi* court neglected to consider how the word "enforcement" came to be inserted in the statute. The court therefore never analyzed whether, in light of the Reviser's Notes, it should have given such significance to § 2462's rewriting. Furthermore, the explanation the court did offer for its definition of "enforcement" does not survive close attention. The *Capozzi* court thought that "prior to the assessment" there can be "no fine, penalty or forfeiture"; "therefore, there is nothing to enforce until after the assessment is made." But if this is correct, if "enforcement" means only the collection of a previously assessed penalty and not the adjudication of liability for a civil penalty, then § 2462's five-year limitations period would not apply even to federal court actions to determine penalties. In view of the history of § 2462 and reasons why we have statutes of limitations, such a result is inconceivable.

Indeed, § 2462's application to cases in which the court first adjudicates liability and then sets the penalty or fine is unquestioned. . . .

III

The remaining issue concerns the meaning of § 2462's phrase "unless commenced within five years from the date when the claim first accrued." On the assumption that § 2462 applies, EPA contends, and the ALJ held, that its claim for penalties "first accrued" when it discovered 3M's violations, not beforehand when the company committed those violations.

A claim normally accrues when the factual and legal prerequisites for filing suit are in place. *United States v. Lindsay,* 346 U.S. 568, 569, 98 L.Ed. 300, 74 S.Ct. 287 (1954); *Oppenheim v. Campbell,* 187 U.S.App. D.C. 226, 571 F.2d 660, 662 (D.C.Cir.1978). While this appears to be a straightforward formulation, there may be complications: "The statutory period may begin either when the defendant commits his wrong or when substantial harm matures. This choice, unnecessary where the two events are simultaneous, becomes complex where considerable time intervenes; here the courts have generally looked to the substantive elements of the cause of action on which the suit is based." Note, *Developments in the Law—Statutes of Limitations,* 63 HARV. L. REV. at

1200. If the period always ran from the date of the wrong, actions by workers previously exposed to dangerous chemicals, for example, might be time-barred when brought years later after the workers' injuries manifested themselves. For cases involving such latent injuries or injuries difficult to detect, courts have developed the "discovery rule." We adopted the rule in *Connors v. Hallmark & Son Coal Co.*, 290 U.S.App. D.C. 170, 935 F.2d 336, 342 (D.C.Cir.1991), following the lead of the other courts of appeals.... The "discovery rule" rests on the idea that plaintiffs cannot have a tenable claim for the recovery of damages unless and until they have been harmed. Damage claims in cases involving hidden injuries or illnesses therefore are viewed as not accruing until the harm becomes apparent. The rule approved in *Connors*, in which we "borrowed" a local statute of limitations for a federal claim, is of this type—a "discovery of injury" rule. *Connors*, 935 F.2d at 341–42. Although use of the rule has not been restricted to personal injury actions, the rule has only been applied to remedial, civil claims. See supra note 13.

The rule EPA sponsors is of an entirely different sort. It is a "discovery of violation" rule having nothing whatever to do with the problem of latent injuries. The rationale underlying the discovery of injury rule—that a claim cannot realistically be said to accrue until the claimant has suffered harm—is completely inapposite. The statute of limitations on which EPA would engraft its rule is aimed exclusively at restricting the time within which actions may be brought to recover fines, penalties and forfeitures. Fines, penalties and forfeitures, whether civil or criminal, may be considered a form of punishment. *See Austin v. United States*, 125 L.Ed.2d 488, 113 S.Ct. 2801 (1993). In an action for a civil penalty, the government's burden is to prove the violation; injuries or damages resulting from the violation are not part of the cause of action; the suit may be maintained regardless of damage. Immediately upon the violation, EPA may institute the proceeding to have the penalty imposed. The penalty provision of TSCA, § 16(a)(1), says just that: "Any person who violates a provision of section 2614 of this title shall be liable to the United States for a civil penalty in an amount not to exceed $25,000 for each such violation." Because liability for the penalty attaches at the moment of the violation, one would expect this to be the time when the claim for the penalty "first accrued." ...

EPA's contrary arguments tend to disregard the limited role of the court in this case. We are interpreting a statute, not creating some federal common law. The provision before us, § 2462, is a general statute of limitations, applicable not just to EPA in TSCA cases, but to the entire federal government in all civil penalty cases, unless Congress specifically provides otherwise. We therefore cannot agree with EPA that our interpretation of § 2462 ought to be influenced by EPA's particular difficulties in enforcing TSCA.... And we cannot understand why Congress would have wanted the running of § 2462's limitations period to depend on such considerations. An agency may experience problems in detecting statutory violations because its enforcement effort is not sufficiently funded; or because the agency has not devoted an adequate number of trained personnel to the task; or because the agency's enforcement program is ill-designed or inefficient; or because the nature of the statute makes it difficult to uncover violations; or because of some combination of these factors and others. In this case, EPA suggests a remand for an evidentiary hearing on such matters and proposes a test: whether, "in the exercise of due diligence," EPA should have discovered 3M's violations earlier than it did. Brief of Respondents at 38 n.33. The subject matter seems more appropriate for a congressional oversight hearing. We seriously doubt that conducting administrative or judicial hearings to determine whether an agency's enforcement branch adequately lived up to its responsibilities would be a workable or sensible method of administering any statute of limitations. Nor do we understand how any of this relates to the reasons why we have a statute of limitations in penalty cases. An agency's failure to detect violations, for whatever reasons, does not avoid the problems of faded memories, lost witnesses and discarded documents in penalty actions brought decades after alleged violations are finally discovered. Most important, nothing in the language of § 2462 even arguably makes the running of the limitations period turn on the degree of difficulty an agency experiences in detecting violations.

When we return to the statutory language and ask what Congress meant when it required actions to be brought within five years from the date when a claim for a penalty "accrued," the answer readily presents itself. The meaning of this portion of § 2462 has been settled for more than a century. The word "accrued" first appeared in the 1839 version of the statute: the suit for a penalty had to be "commenced within five years from the time when the penalty or forfeiture accrued," Act of Feb. 28, 1839, ch. 36, § 4, 5 Stat. 321, 322. This language was carried over in the 1874 version (Rev. Stat. § 1047, 18 Stat. 193, 193 (1874), later codified at 28 U.S.C. § 791 (1911)), and modified slightly (without any substantive change) in the 1948 revision to read, as it does today, "unless commenced within five years from the date when the claim first accrued." See supra note 7.

In 1839, when Congress used the word "accrued," it could not possibly have intended the word to incorporate any discovery of violation rule. Only nine years earlier, the Supreme Court had rejected a discovery rule and held that a claim accrues at the moment a violation occurs. *Wilcox v. Plummer*, 29 U.S. (4 Pet.) 172, 181, 7 L.Ed. 821 (1830). Other Supreme Court opinions of the era consistently used the phrase "claim accrued" to mean the time at which a cause of action first existed, not the time when the violation was first discovered. *See, e.g., Meredith v. United States*, 38 U.S. (13 Pet.) 486, 493–94, 10 L.Ed. 258 (1839); *Bank of the United States v. Daniel*, 37 U.S. (12 Pet.) 32, 56, 9 L.Ed. 989 (1838); *Evans v. Gee*, 36 U.S. (11 Pet.) 80, 84, 9 L.Ed. 639 (1837); *New York v. Miln*, 36 U.S. (11 Pet.) 102, 144, 9 L.Ed. 648 (1837) (Thompson, J., dissenting on other grounds); *Montgomery v. Hernandez*, 25 U.S. (12 Wheat.) 129, 133–34, 6 L.Ed. 575 (1827). In a case decided under the

1839 version of § 2462, the government urged the court to hold—as EPA does here—that its claim for a forfeiture did not accrue until it discovered the violation. *Maillard*, 26 F.Cas. at 1143. The court rebuffed the government, ruling that the claim "did so accrue, as against the defendant in this case, when the offenses alleged were committed.... Ignorance does not prevent the running of the statute or the accruing of the forfeiture." *Id. See also In re Landsberg*, 14 F.Cas. 1065, 1067 (E.D.Mich.1870)(No. 8,041); *United States v. Hatch*, 26 F.Cas. 220, 224 (C.C.S.D.N.Y. 1824)(No. 15,325). Since then, the term "accrued" in § 2462 has been taken to mean that the running of the limitations period in penalty actions is measured from the date of the violation. *United States v. Core Lab.*, 759 F.2d 480, 482 (5th Cir.1985); *see also Smith v. United States*, 143 F.2d 228, 229 (9th Cir.1944); *United States v. Appling*, 239 F.Supp. 185, 194–95 (S.D.Tex.1965).... As the Fifth Circuit put it in *Core*, a "review of [cases under § 2462] clearly demonstrates that the date of the underlying violation has been accepted without question as the date when the claim first accrued, and, therefore, as the date on which the statute began to run." 759 F.2d at 482.

In light of the legal meaning of the word "accrued" in 1839, the retention of the word in the 1874 version of § 2462, and its appearance in the current statute, we hold that an action, suit or proceeding to assess or impose a civil penalty must be commenced within five years of the date of the violation giving rise to the penalty. We reject the discovery of violation rule EPA advocates as unworkable; outside the language of the statute; inconsistent with judicial interpretations of § 2462; unsupported by the discovery of injury rule adopted in non-enforcement, remedial cases; and incompatible with the functions served by a statute of limitations in penalty cases.

IV

EPA may not assess civil penalties against 3M for any violations of § 15 of TSCA allegedly committed by the company more than five years before EPA commenced its proceeding under 15 U.S.C. § 2615. The petition for review is granted, and the case is remanded for further proceedings consistent with this opinion.

Note

Until recently, polychlorinated biphenols (PCBs) were commonly used in transformer and dielectric fluids because of their fire resistant characteristics. PCB use currently is heavily restricted, because PCBs have been thought to be highly toxic, and their release into the environment is typically difficult and expensive to clean up. PCBs are specifically regulated under TSCA, 15 U.S.C.A. §§ 2601 *et seq*. Under TSCA, Congress directed EPA to phase out PCB manufacture and use in accord with a statutorily mandated timetable. The manufacture, processing, or distribution in commerce of PCBs is considered unlawful unless it is conducted in a "totally enclosed manner."

It is important to note, however, that electric utilities and others who currently use PCB-filled transformers and capacitors may maintain their existing equipment for its working life, provided it neither leaks nor requires major servicing, subject to specific requirements concerning equipment inspection, enclosure, labeling, and location. Consequently, PCB-filled electrical equipment still is commonly found inside and outside of many buildings. In some cases, that equipment is owned by the building owner and, in other cases, it is owned by the local electric utility. Building owners should determine whether such equipment exists on their premises and, if it does, who is responsible. TSCA imposes sizeable penalties on "any person" failing to adhere to its requirements. *See* 15 U.S.C.A. § 2615. Aside from potential TSCA penalties, building owners need to be aware of the substantial risk associated with a PCB fire. Such fires reportedly can result in the release of dioxins and furans that can quickly contaminate a building and result in massive cleanup costs, not to mention toxic tort suits by tenants and other building occupants.

§ 4.2 THE FEDERAL INSECTICIDE, FUNGICIDE, AND RODENTICIDE ACT

Under the Federal Insecticide, Fungicide, and Rodenticide Act (FIFRA), 7 U.S.C.A. § 135 *et seq.*, any distributor or seller of an insecticide, fungicide, or rodenticide must register and submit certain data to EPA. EPA then determines whether use of the pesticide will be allowed and, if so, under what conditions. Distributors or sellers must comply with certain labelling requirements. EPA also has broad authority to prohibit or limit the sale or use of a registered pesticide and may seize products posing imminent hazards to the public.

PITTS v. DOW CHEM. CO.
859 F.Supp. 543 (N.D.Ala.1994).

Opinion by: Myron H. Thompson

In this lawsuit, plaintiff Annie Mae Pitts—representing the estate of her deceased son, Willie Pitts—charges that the defendants are liable in tort for her son's death. Her son died while applying "Dursban TC," a pesticide manufactured, distributed, and sold by defendants. Defendants are Dow Chemical Company, Eli Lilly & Company, Van Waters & Rogers, Inc., DowElanco, Terra International, Inc., and Riverside Chemical Company, Inc.

* * *

1. The FIFRA Scheme of Pesticide Regulation and Labeling

FIFRA is a comprehensive regulatory statute governing the use, sale, and labeling of all pesticides sold in the United States. 7 U.S.C.A. § 136a. All pesticides sold or distributed in the United States must be registered with the EPA. 7 U.S.C.A. § 136a(a). A pesticide manufacturer seeking registration must submit proposed labeling and instructions for a pesticide, 7 U.S.C.A. § 136a(c)(1)(C), along with certain toxicological and other data generated from studies prescribed by the EPA. 40 C.F.R. §§ 158.240, 158.340, 158.390.

Upon receiving this information, the EPA cannot register a pesticide unless it finds that all of the following criteria have been met:

"(A) its composition is such as to warrant the proposed claims for it;

(B) its labeling and other material require [sic] to be submitted comply with the requirements of this subchapter;

(C) it will perform its intended function without unreasonable adverse effects on the environment; and

(D) when used in accordance with widespread and commonly recognized practice it will not generally cause unreasonable adverse effects on the environment."

7 U.S.C.A. § 136a(c)(5). "Unreasonable adverse effects on the environment" is defined as "any unreasonable risk to man or the environment, taking into account the economic, social, and environmental costs and benefits of the use of any pesticide." 7 U.S.C.A. § 136(bb).

When Congress amended FIFRA in 1972, it recognized that pesticides—many of which can be poisonous to humans as well as the target pests—have "both beneficial and deleterious" effects, and it designated the Administrator of the EPA as the party to conduct the necessary balancing analysis. Papas I, 926 F.2d at 1022 (quoting S. Rep. No. 92–838, 92nd Cong., 2d Sess., reprinted in 1972 U.S.C.C.A.N. 3993, 3996).... "The question [the Administrator] must decide," according to Congress, "is 'Is it better for man and the environment to register this pesticide, or is it better that this pesticide be banned?' " *Id.* at 1023 (quoting S. Rep. No. 92–838, at 4032–33). Congress explained that:

"He must consider hazards to farmworkers, hazards to birds and animals and children yet unborn. He must consider the need for food and clothing and forest products, forest and grassland cover to keep the rain when it falls, prevent floods, provide clear water. He must consider aesthetic values, the beauty and inspiration of nature, the comfort and health of man. All these factors he must consider, giving each its due."

Id.

Prior to registering a pesticide, the EPA must determine if the pesticide's "labeling and other material" meet FIFRA's detailed requirements. 7 U.S.C.A. § 136a(c)(5)(B). Labeling is defined to include "all labels and other written, printed, or graphic matter—(A) accompanying the pesticide ... at any time; or (B) to which reference is made on the label or literature accompanying the pesticide...." 7 U.S.C.A. § 136(p). Regulations promulgated pursuant to FIFRA specifically control the form and content of labels, including precautionary statements about risks to humans and directions for safe use. 40 C.F.R. §§ 156.10(h)(2)(1)(A), 156.10(i). Final labeling is approved by the EPA only if it is "adequate to protect the public from fraud and from personal

injury and to prevent unreasonable adverse effects on the environment."
40 C.F.R. § 156.10(i)(1)(i).

* * *

RUCKELSHAUS v. MONSANTO

467 U.S. 986, 104 S.Ct. 2862, 81 L.Ed.2d 815 (1984).

JUSTICE BLACKMUN delivered the opinion of the Court.

* * *

Appellee Monsanto Company (Monsanto) is an inventor, developer, and producer of various kinds of chemical products, including pesticides. Monsanto, headquartered in St. Louis County, Mo., sells in both domestic and foreign markets. It is one of a relatively small group of companies that invent and develop new active ingredients for pesticides and conduct most of the research and testing with respect to those ingredients . . .

These active ingredients are sometimes referred to as "manufacturing-use products" because they are not generally sold directly to users of pesticides. Rather, they must first be combined with "inert ingredients"—chemicals that dissolve, dilute, or stabilize the active components. The results of this process are sometimes called "end-use products," and the firms that produce end-use products are called "formulators." *See* the opinion of the District Court in this case, *Monsanto Co. v. Acting Administrator, United States Environmental Protection Agency*, 564 F.Supp. 552, 554 (E.D.Mo.1983). A firm that produces an active ingredient may use it for incorporation into its own end-use products, may sell it to formulators, or may do both. Monsanto produces both active ingredients and end-use products. *Ibid.*

The District Court found that development of a potential commercial pesticide candidate typically requires the expenditure of $5 million to $15 million annually for several years. The development process may take between 14 and 22 years, and it is usually that long before a company can expect any return on its investment. *Id.*, at 555. For every manufacturing-use pesticide the average company finally markets, it will have screened and tested 20,000 others. Monsanto has a significantly better-than-average success rate; it successfully markets 1 out of every 10,000 chemicals tested. *Ibid.*

Monsanto, like any other applicant for registration of a pesticide, must present research and test data supporting its application. The District Court found that Monsanto had incurred costs in excess of $23.6 million in developing the health, safety, and environmental data submitted by it under FIFRA. *Id.*, at 560. The information submitted with an application usually has value to Monsanto beyond its instrumentality in gaining that particular application. Monsanto uses this information to develop additional end-use products and to expand the uses of its registered products. The information would also be valuable to Monsanto's competitors. For that reason, Monsanto has instituted stringent security measures to ensure the secrecy of the data. *Ibid.*

It is this health, safety, and environmental data that Monsanto sought to protect by bringing this suit. The District Court found that much of these data "[contain] or [relate] to trade secrets as defined by the Restatement of Torts and confidential commercial information." *Id.,* at 562.

Monsanto brought suit in District Court, seeking injunctive and declaratory relief from the operation of the data-consideration provisions of FIFRA's § 3(c)(1)(D), and the data-disclosure provisions of FIFRA's § 10 and the related § 3(c)(2)(A). Monsanto alleged that all of the challenged provisions effected a "taking" of property without just compensation, in violation of the Fifth Amendment. In addition, Monsanto alleged that the data-consideration provisions violated the Amendment because they effected a taking of property for a private, rather than a public, purpose. Finally, Monsanto alleged that the arbitration scheme provided by § 3(c)(1)(D)(ii) violates the original submitter's due process rights and constitutes an unconstitutional delegation of judicial power.

After a bench trial, the District Court concluded that Monsanto possessed property rights in its submitted data, specifically including the right to exclude others from the enjoyment of such data by preventing their unauthorized use and by prohibiting their disclosure. 564 F.Supp., at 566. The court found that the challenged data-consideration provisions "give Monsanto's competitors a free ride at Monsanto's expense." *Ibid.* The District Court reasoned that § 3(c)(1)(D) appropriated Monsanto's fundamental right to exclude, and that the effect of that appropriation is substantial. The court further found that Monsanto's property was being appropriated for a private purpose and that this interference was much more significant than the public good that the appropriation might serve. 564 F.Supp., at 566–567.

The District Court also found that operation of the disclosure provisions of FIFRA constituted a taking of Monsanto's property. The cost incurred by Monsanto when its property is "permanently committed to the public domain and thus effectively destroyed" was viewed by the District Court as significantly outweighing any benefit to the general public from having the ability to scrutinize the data, for the court seemed to believe that the general public could derive all the assurance it needed about the safety and effectiveness of a pesticide from EPA's decision to register the product and to approve the label. *Id.,* at 567, and n. 4.

After finding that the data-consideration provisions operated to effect a taking of property, the District Court found that the compulsory binding-arbitration scheme set forth in § 3(c)(1)(D)(ii) did not adequately provide compensation for the property taken. The court found the arbitration provision to be arbitrary and vague, reasoning that the statute does not give arbitrators guidance as to the factors that enter into the concept of just compensation, and that judicial review is foreclosed except in cases of fraud. 564 F.Supp., at 567. The District Court also found that the arbitration scheme was infirm because it did not meet the requirements of Art. III of the Constitution. *Ibid.* Finally, the court found that a remedy under the Tucker Act was not available for the deprivations of property effected by §§ 3 and 10. 564 F.Supp., at 567–568.

The District Court therefore declared §§ 3(c)(1)(D), 3(c)(2)(A), 10(b), and 10(d) of FIFRA, as amended by the Federal Pesticide Act of 1978, to be unconstitutional, and permanently enjoined EPA from implementing or enforcing those sections. *See* Amended Judgment, App. to Juris. Statement 41a . . .

We noted probable jurisdiction. 464 U.S. 890 (1983).

III

In deciding this case, we are faced with four questions: (1) Does Monsanto have a property interest protected by the Fifth Amendment's Taking Clause in the health, safety, and environmental data it has submitted to EPA? (2) If so, does EPA's use of the data to evaluate the applications of others or EPA's disclosure of the data to qualified members of the public effect a taking of that property interest? (3) If there is a taking, is it a taking for a public use? (4) If there is a taking for a public use, does the statute adequately provide for just compensation?

For purposes of this case, EPA has stipulated that "Monsanto has certain property rights in its information, research and test data that it has submitted under FIFRA to EPA and its predecessor agencies which may be protected by the Fifth Amendment to the Constitution of the United States." App. 36. Since the exact import of that stipulation is not clear, we address the question whether the data at issue here can be considered property for the purposes of the Taking Clause of the Fifth Amendment.

This Court never has squarely addressed the applicability of the protections of the Taking Clause of the Fifth Amendment to commercial data of the kind involved in this case. In answering the question now, we are mindful of the basic axiom that " '[property] interests . . . are not created by the Constitution. Rather, they are created and their dimensions are defined by existing rules or understandings that stem from an independent source such as state law.' " *Webb's Fabulous Pharmacies, Inc. v. Beckwith,* 449 U.S. 155, 161 (1980), quoting *Board of Regents v. Roth,* 408 U.S. 564, 577 (1972). Monsanto asserts that the health, safety, and environmental data it has submitted to EPA are property under Missouri law, which recognizes trade secrets, as defined in § 757, Comment b, of the Restatement of Torts, as property. *See Reddi–Wip, Inc. v. Lemay Valve Co.,* 354 S.W.2d 913, 917 (Mo.App.1962); *Harrington v. National Outdoor Advertising Co.,* 355 Mo. 524, 532, 196 S.W.2d 786, 791 (1946); *Luckett v. Orange Julep Co.,* 271 Mo. 289, 302–304, 196 S.W. 740, 743 (1917). The Restatement defines a trade secret as "any formula, pattern, device or compilation of information which is used in one's business, and which gives him an opportunity to obtain an advantage over competitors who do not know or use it." § 757, Comment b. And the parties have stipulated that much of the information, research, and test data that Monsanto has submitted under FIFRA to EPA "contains or relates to trade secrets as defined by the Restatement of Torts." App. 36.

Because of the intangible nature of a trade secret, the extent of the property right therein is defined by the extent to which the owner of the secret protects his interest from disclosure to others. *See Harrington*, *supra*; *Reddi-Wip*, *supra*; Restatement of Torts, *supra*; *see also Kewanee Oil Co. v. Bicron Corp.*, 416 U.S. 470, 474–476 (1974). Information that is public knowledge or that is generally known in an industry cannot be a trade secret. Restatement of Torts, *supra*. If an individual discloses his trade secret to others who are under no obligation to protect the confidentiality of the information, or otherwise publicly discloses the secret, his property right is extinguished. *See Harrington*, *supra*; 1 R. Milgrim, Trade Secrets § 1.01[2] (1983).

Trade secrets have many of the characteristics of more tangible forms of property. A trade secret is assignable. *See, e.g., Dr. Miles Medical Co. v. John D. Park & Sons Co.*, 220 U.S. 373, 401–402 (1911); *Painton & Co. v. Bourns, Inc.*, 442 F.2d 216, 225 (C.A.2 1971). A trade secret can form the res of a trust, Restatement (Second) of Trusts § 82, Comment e (1959); 1 A. Scott, Law of Trusts § 82.5, p. 703 (3d ed. 1967), and it passes to a trustee in bankruptcy. *See In re Uniservices, Inc.*, 517 F.2d 492, 496–497 (C.A.7 1975).

Even the manner in which Congress referred to trade secrets in the legislative history of FIFRA supports the general perception of their property-like nature. In discussing the 1978 amendments to FIFRA, Congress recognized that data developers like Monsanto have a "proprietary interest" in their data. S. Rep. No. 95–334, at 31. Further, Congress reasoned that submitters of data are "entitled" to "compensation" because they "have legal ownership of the data." H. R. Conf. Rep. No. 95–1560, p. 29 (1978).... This general perception of trade secrets as property is consonant with a notion of "property" that extends beyond land and tangible goods and includes the products of an individual's "labour and invention." 2 W. Blackstone, *Commentaries* * 405; *see generally* J. Locke, *The Second Treatise of Civil Government*, ch. 5 (J. Gough ed. 1947).

Although this Court never has squarely addressed the question whether a person can have a property interest in a trade secret, which is admittedly intangible, the Court has found other kinds of intangible interests to be property for purposes of the Fifth Amendment's Taking Clause. *See, e.g., Armstrong v. United States*, 364 U.S. 40, 44, 46 (1960) (materialman's lien provided for under Maine law protected by Taking Clause); *Louisville Joint Stock Land Bank v. Radford*, 295 U.S. 555, 596–602 (1935)(real estate lien protected); *Lynch v. United States*, 292 U.S. 571, 579 (1934)(valid contracts are property within meaning of the

Taking Clause). That intangible property rights protected by state law are deserving of the protection of the Taking Clause has long been implicit in the thinking of this Court:

> "It is conceivable that [the term 'property' in the Taking Clause] was used in its vulgar and untechnical sense of the physical thing with respect to which the citizen exercises rights recognized by law. On the other hand, it may have been employed in a more accurate sense to denote the group of rights inhering in the citizen's relation to the physical thing, as the right to possess, use and dispose of it. In point of fact, the construction given the phrase has been the latter." *United States v. General Motors Corp.*, 323 U.S. 373, 377–378 (1945).

We therefore hold that to the extent that Monsanto has an interest in its health, safety, and environmental data cognizable as a trade-secret property right under Missouri law, that property right is protected by the Taking Clause of the Fifth Amendment.

* * *

IV

Having determined that Monsanto has a property interest in the data it has submitted to EPA, we confront the difficult question whether a "taking" will occur when EPA discloses those data or considers the data in evaluating another application for registration. The question of what constitutes a "taking" is one with which this Court has wrestled on many occasions. It has never been the rule that only governmental acquisition or destruction of the property of an individual constitutes a taking, for "courts have held that the deprivation of the former owner rather than the accretion of a right or interest to the sovereign constitutes the taking. Governmental action short of acquisition of title or occupancy has been held, if its effects are so complete as to deprive the owner of all or most of his interest in the subject matter, to amount to a taking." *United States v. General Motors Corp.*, 323 U.S., at 378. *See also PruneYard Shopping Center v. Robins*, 447 U.S. 74 (1980); *Pennsylvania Coal Co. v. Mahon*, 260 U.S. 393, 415 (1922).

As has been admitted on numerous occasions, "this Court has generally 'been unable to develop any "set formula" for determining when "justice and fairness" require that economic injuries caused by public action' " must be deemed a compensable taking. *Kaiser Aetna v. United States*, 444 U.S. 164, 175 (1979), quoting *Penn Central Transportation Co. v. New York City*, 438 U.S. 104, 124 (1978); *accord, Hodel v. Virginia Surface Mining & Reclamation Assn., Inc.*, 452 U.S. 264, 295 (1981). The inquiry into whether a taking has occurred is essentially an "ad hoc, factual" inquiry. *Kaiser Aetna*, 444 U.S., at 175. The Court, however, has identified several factors that should be taken into account when determining whether a governmental action has gone beyond "regulation" and effects a "taking." Among those factors are: "the character of the governmental action, its economic impact, and its interference with reasonable investment-backed expectations." *Prune-Yard Shopping Center v. Robins*, 447 U.S., at 83; *see Kaiser Aetna*, 444 U.S., at 175; *Penn Central*, 438 U.S., at 124. It is to the last of these three factors that we now direct our attention, for we find that the force of this factor is so overwhelming, at least with respect to certain of the data submitted by Monsanto to EPA, that it disposes of the taking question regarding those data.

A

A "reasonable investment-backed expectation" must be more than a "unilateral expectation or an abstract need." *Webb's Fabulous Pharmacies*, 449 U.S., at 161. We find that with respect to any health, safety, and environmental data that Monsanto submitted to EPA after the effective date of the 1978 FIFRA amendments—that is, on or after October 1, 1978 ... Monsanto could not have had a reasonable, investment-backed expectation that EPA would keep the data confidential beyond the limits prescribed in the amended statute itself. Monsanto was on notice of the manner in which EPA was authorized to use and disclose any data turned over to it by an applicant for registration.

Thus, with respect to any data submitted to EPA on or after October 1, 1978, Monsanto knew that, for a period of 10 years from the date of submission, EPA would not consider those data in evaluating the application of another without Monsanto's permission. § 3(c)(1)(D)(i). It was also aware, however, that once the 10–year period had expired, EPA could use the data without Monsanto's permission. §§ 3(c)(1)(D)(ii) and (iii). Monsanto was further aware that it was entitled to an offer of compensation from the subsequent applicant only until the end of the 15th year from the date of submission. § 3(c)(1)(D)(iii). In addition, Monsanto was aware that information relating to formulae of products could be revealed by EPA to "any Federal agency consulted and [could] be revealed at a public hearing or in findings of fact" issued by EPA "when necessary to carry out" EPA's duties under FIFRA. § 10(b). The statute also gave Monsanto notice that much of the health, safety, and efficacy data provided by it could be disclosed to the general public at any time. § 10(d). If, despite the data-consideration and data-disclosure provisions in the statute, Monsanto chose to submit the requisite data in order to receive a registration, it can hardly argue that its reasonable investment-backed expectations are disturbed when EPA acts to use or disclose the data in a manner that was authorized by law at the time of the submission.

Monsanto argues that the statute's requirement that a submitter give up its property interest in the data constitutes placing an unconstitutional condition on the right to a valuable Government benefit. *See* Brief for Appellee 29. But Monsanto has not challenged the ability of the Federal Government to regulate the marketing and use of pesticides. Nor could Monsanto successfully make such a challenge, for such restrictions are the burdens we all must bear in exchange for " 'the advantage of living and doing business in a civilized community.' " *Andrus v.*

Allard, 444 U.S. 51, 67 (1979), quoting *Pennsylvania Coal Co. v. Mahon*, 260 U.S., at 422 (Brandeis, J., dissenting); *see Day–Brite Lighting, Inc. v. Missouri*, 342 U.S. 421, 424 (1952). This is particularly true in an area, such as pesticide sale and use, that has long been the source of public concern and the subject of government regulation. That Monsanto is willing to bear this burden in exchange for the ability to market pesticides in this country is evidenced by the fact that it has continued to expand its research and development and to submit data to EPA despite the enactment of the 1978 amendments to FIFRA.... 564 F.Supp., at 561.

Thus, as long as Monsanto is aware of the conditions under which the data are submitted, and the conditions are rationally related to a legitimate Government interest, a voluntary submission of data by an applicant in exchange for the economic advantages of a registration can hardly be called a taking. *See Corn Products Refining Co. v. Eddy*, 249 U.S. 427, 431–432 (1919)("The right of a manufacturer to maintain secrecy as to his compounds and processes must be held subject to the right of the State, in the exercise of its police power and in promotion of fair dealing, to require that the nature of the product be fairly set forth"); *see also Westinghouse Electric Corp. v. United States Nuclear Regulatory Comm'n*, 555 F.2d 82, 95 (C.A.3 1977).

* * *

A fortiori, the Trade Secrets Act cannot be construed as any sort of assurance against internal agency use of submitted data during consideration of the application of a subsequent applicant for registration.... Indeed, there is some evidence that the practice of using data submitted by one company during consideration of the application of a subsequent applicant was widespread and well known.... Thus, with respect to any data that Monsanto submitted to EPA prior to the effective date of the 1972 amendments to FIFRA, we hold that Monsanto could not have had a "reasonable investment-backed expectation" that EPA would maintain those data in strictest confidence and would use them exclusively for the purpose of considering the Monsanto application in connection with which the data were submitted.

* * *

In summary, we hold that EPA's consideration or disclosure of data submitted by Monsanto to the agency prior to October 22, 1972, or after September 30, 1978, does not effect a taking. We further hold that EPA consideration or disclosure of health, safety, and environmental data will constitute a taking if Monsanto submitted the data to EPA between October 22, 1972, and September 30, 1978; ... the data constituted trade secrets under Missouri law; Monsanto had designated the data as trade secrets at the time of its submission; the use or disclosure conflicts with the explicit assurance of confidentiality or exclusive use contained in the statute during that period; and the operation of the arbitration provision does not adequately compensate for the loss in market value of the data that Monsanto suffers because of EPA's use or disclosure of the trade secrets.

V

We must next consider whether any taking of private property that may occur by operation of the data-disclosure and data-consideration provisions of FIFRA is a taking for a "public use." We have recently stated that the scope of the "public use" requirement of the Taking Clause is "coterminous with the scope of a sovereign's police powers." *Hawaii Housing Authority v. Midkiff, ante*, at 240; *see Berman v. Parker*, 348 U.S. 26, 33 (1954). The role of the courts in second-guessing the legislature's judgment of what constitutes a public use is extremely narrow. *Midkiff, supra*; *Berman, supra*, at 32.

* * *

Because the data-disclosure provisions of FIFRA provide for disclosure to the general public, the District Court did not find that those provisions constituted a taking for a private use. Instead, the court found that the data-disclosure provisions served no use. It reasoned that because EPA, before registration, must determine that a product is safe and effective, and because the label on a pesticide, by statute, must set forth the nature, contents, and purpose of the pesticide, the label provided the public with all the assurance it needed that the product is safe and effective. 564 F.Supp., at 567, and n. 4. It is enough for us to state that the optimum amount of disclosure to the public is for Congress, not the courts, to decide, and that the statute embodies Congress' judgment on that question. *See* 123 Cong. Rec., at 25706 (remarks of Sen. Leahy). We further observe, however, that public disclosure can provide an effective check on the decisionmaking processes of EPA and allows members of the public to determine the likelihood of individualized risks peculiar to their use of the product. *See* H. R. Rep. No. 95–343, p. 8 (1977) (remarks of Douglas M. Costle); S. Rep. No. 95–334, at 13.

We therefore hold that any taking of private property that may occur in connection with EPA's use or disclosure of data submitted to it by Monsanto between October 22, 1972, and September 30, 1978, is a taking for a public use.

VI

Equitable relief is not available to enjoin an alleged taking of private property for a public use, duly authorized by law, ... when a suit for compensation can be brought against the sovereign subsequent to the taking. *Larson v. Domestic & Foreign Commerce Corp.*, 337 U.S. 682, 697, ... (1949). The Fifth Amendment does not require that compensation precede the taking. *Hurley v. Kincaid*, 285 U.S. 95, 104 (1932). Generally, an individual claiming that the United States has taken his property can seek just compensation under the Tucker Act, 28 U.S. C. § 1491.... *United States v. Causby*, 328 U.S. 256, 267 (1946)("If there is a taking, the claim is 'founded upon the Constitution' and within the jurisdiction of the Court of Claims to hear and determine''); *Yearsley v. Ross Construction Co.*, 309 U.S. 18, 21 (1940).

* * *

Congress in FIFRA did not address the liability of the Government to pay just compensation should a taking occur. Congress' failure specifically to mention or provide for recourse against the Government may reflect a congressional belief that use of data by EPA in the ways authorized by FIFRA effects no Fifth Amendment taking or it may reflect Congress' assumption that the general grant of jurisdiction under the Tucker Act would provide the necessary remedy for any taking that may occur. In any event, the failure cannot be construed to reflect an unambiguous intention to withdraw the Tucker Act remedy. ''[Whether] or not the United States so intended,'' any taking claim under FIFRA is one ''founded . . . upon the Constitution,'' and is thus remediable under the Tucker Act. *Regional Rail Reorganization Act Cases*, 419 U.S., at 126. Therefore, where the operation of the data-consideration and data-disclosure provisions of FIFRA effect a taking of property belonging to Monsanto, an adequate remedy for the taking exists under the Tucker Act. The District Court erred in enjoining the taking.

* * *

JUSTICE WHITE took no part in the consideration or decision of this case.

JUSTICE O'CONNOR, concurring in part and dissenting in part.

I join all of the Court's opinion except for Part IV–B and the Court's conclusion, *ante*, at 1013, that ''EPA's consideration or disclosure of data submitted by Monsanto to the agency prior to October 22, 1972 . . . does not effect a taking.'' In my view public disclosure of pre–1972 data would effect a taking. As to consideration of this information within EPA in connection with other license applications not submitted by Monsanto, I believe we should remand to the District Court for further factual findings concerning Monsanto's expectations regarding interagency uses of trade secret information prior to 1972.

It is important to distinguish at the outset public disclosure of trade secrets from use of those secrets entirely within EPA. Internal use may undermine Monsanto's competitive position within the United States, but it leaves Monsanto's position in foreign markets undisturbed. As the Court notes, *ante*, at 1007, n. 11, the likely impact on foreign market position is one that Monsanto would weigh when deciding whether to submit trade secrets to EPA. Thus a submission of trade secrets to EPA that implicitly consented to further use of the information within the agency is not necessarily the same as one that implicitly consented to public disclosure.

It seems quite clear—indeed the Court scarcely disputes—that public disclosure of trade secrets submitted to the Federal Government before 1972 was neither permitted by law, nor customary agency practice before 1972, nor expected by applicants for pesticide registrations. The

Court correctly notes that the Trade Secrets Act, 18 U.S. C. § 1905, flatly proscribed such disclosures. The District Court expressly found that until 1970 it was Government "policy that the data developed and submitted by companies such as [Monsanto] be maintained confidentially by the [administrative agency] and was not to be disclosed without the permission of the data submitter." *Monsanto Co. v. Acting Administrator, EPA*, 564 F.Supp. 552, 564 (1983). Finally, the Court, *ante*, at 1009, n. 14, quotes from a 1972 statement by the National Agricultural Chemicals Association that "registration information submitted to the Administrator has not routinely been made available for public inspection." It is hard to imagine how a pre–1972 applicant for a pesticide license would not, under these circumstances, have formed a very firm expectation that its trade secrets submitted in connection with a pesticide registration would not be disclosed to the public.

The Court's analysis of this question appears in a single sentence: an "industry that long has been the focus of great public concern and significant government regulation" can have no reasonable expectation that the Government will not later find public disclosure of trade secrets to be in the public interest. *Ante*, at 1008. I am frankly puzzled to read this statement in the broader context of the Court's otherwise convincing opinion. If the degree of Government regulation determines the reasonableness of an expectation of confidentiality, Monsanto had as little reason to expect confidentiality after 1972 as before, since the 1972 amendments were not deregulatory in intent or effect. And the Court entirely fails to explain why the nondisclosure provision of the 1972 Act, § 10, 86 Stat. 989, created any greater expectation of confidentiality than the Trade Secrets Act. Section 10 prohibited EPA from disclosing "trade secrets or commercial or financial information." No penalty for disclosure was prescribed, unless disclosure was with the intent to defraud. The Trade Secrets Act, 18 U.S. C. § 1905, prohibited and still prohibits Government disclosure of trade secrets and other commercial or financial information revealed during the course of official duties, on pain of substantial criminal sanctions. The Court acknowledges that this prohibition has always extended to formal and official agency action. *Chrysler Corp. v. Brown*, 441 U.S. 281, 298–301 (1979). It seems to me that the criminal sanctions in the Trade Secrets Act therefore created at least as strong an expectation of privacy before 1972 as the precatory language of § 10 created after 1972.

The Court's tacit analysis seems to be this: an expectation of confidentiality can be grounded only on a statutory nondisclosure provision situated in close physical proximity, in the pages of the United States Code, to the provisions pursuant to which information is submitted to the Government. For my part, I see no reason why Congress should not be able to give effective protection to all trade secrets submitted to the Federal Government by means of a single, overarching, trade secrets provision. We routinely assume that wrongdoers are put on notice of the entire contents of the Code, though in all likelihood most of them have never owned a copy or opened a single page of it. It seems strange to assume, on the other hand, that a company like Monsanto, well served by lawyers who undoubtedly do read the Code, could build an expectation of privacy in pesticide trade secrets only if the assurance of confidentiality appeared in Title 7 itself.

The question of interagency use of trade secrets before 1972 is more difficult because the Trade Secrets Act most likely does not extend to such uses. The District Court found that prior to October 1972 only two competitors' registrations were granted on the basis of data submitted by Monsanto, and that Monsanto had no knowledge of either of these registrations prior to their being granted. 564 F.Supp., at 564. The District Court also found that before 1970 it was agency policy "that the data developed and submitted by companies such as [Monsanto] could not be used to support the registration of another's product without the permission of the data submitter." *Ibid*. This Court, however, concludes on the basis of two cited fragments of evidence that "the evidence against the District Court's finding seems overwhelming." *Ante*, at 1010, n. 14. The Court nevertheless wisely declines to label the District Court's findings of fact on this matter clearly erroneous. Instead, the Court notes that the "District Court did not find that the policy of the Department [of Agriculture] was publicly known at the time [before 1970] or that there was any explicit guarantee of exclusive use." *Ibid*. This begs exactly the right question, but the Court firmly declines to answer it. The Court simply states that "there is some evidence that the practice of using data submitted by one company during consideration of the application of a subsequent applicant was widespread and well known." *Ante*, at 1009 (footnote omitted). And then, without more ado, the Court declares that with respect to pre–1972 data Monsanto "could not have had a 'reasonable investment-backed expectation' that EPA would ... use [the data] exclusively for the purpose of considering the Monsanto application in connection with which the data were submitted." *Ante*, at 1010.

If one thing is quite clear it is that the extent of Monsanto's pre–1972 expectations, whether reasonable and investment-backed or otherwise, is a heavily factual question. It is fairly clear that the District Court found that those expectations existed as a matter of fact and were reasonable as a matter of law. But if the factual findings of the District Court on this precise question were not as explicit as they might have been, the appropriate disposition is to remand to the District Court for further factfinding. That is the course I would follow with respect to interagency use of trade secrets submitted by Monsanto before 1972.

MACDONALD v. MONSANTO CO.

27 F.3d 1021 (5th Cir. 1994).

E. GRADY JOLLY, CIRCUIT JUDGE:

This appeal raises the question of whether the labeling requirements of the Federal Insecticide, Fungicide and Rodenticide Act ("FIFRA"), 7

U.S.C. §§ 136–136y (1980 & Supp. 1993), preempt parallel state law labeling requirements. Because we find that FIFRA does indeed preempt state laws that are "different from or in addition" to FIFRA requirements, we reverse the district court's denial of summary judgment, and render judgment on this issue in favor of the defendants.

I

Plaintiff-appellee Charles MacDonald, a chemical sprayer for the Louisiana Department of Transportation and Development, suffered serious personal injuries allegedly caused by the phenoxy herbicide 2,4–D, which is produced by several different chemical companies. This herbicide was packaged in containers bearing labels approved by the Environmental Protection Agency ("EPA") pursuant to FIFRA requirements. MacDonald and his wife sued the chemical companies in Texas state court, claiming, *inter alia*, that the chemical companies failed, under state law, to label properly the herbicide and thereby failed, under state law, to warn him adequately of the dangers associated with 2,4–D. The defendants timely removed the suit to federal district court on diversity of citizenship grounds, and then moved for summary judgment, arguing that FIFRA preempts all state laws affecting labeling requirements. According to the defendants, because they complied with FIFRA labeling requirements (a fact uncontested in this appeal), and because FIFRA preempts state labeling requirements, they were entitled to summary judgment in their favor on the labeling issue. The district court disagreed, however, and denied their motion for summary judgment. The court held that the word "requirements" in § 136v(b) addressed only statutory or regulatory requirements—not common law requirements. *See Ferebee v. Chevron Chemical Co.*, 237 U.S.App.D.C. 164, 736 F.2d 1529 (D.C.Cir.1984), *cert. denied*, 469 U.S. 1062, 105 S.Ct. 545, 83 L.Ed.2d 432 (1984). Thus, the district court concluded that the MacDonald's state common law causes of action based on improper labeling and failure to warn were not preempted by FIFRA. Recognizing, however, that "there were substantial grounds for difference of opinion on the issue of preemption," the district court certified the issue for interlocutory appeal. Defendants-appellants Chevron Chemical Company and Ortho Products Division of Chevron Chemical Company (referred to collectively as "Chevron"), and Dow Chemical Company ("Dow") appeal the district court's denial of summary judgment. We granted this interlocutory appeal pursuant to 28 U.S.C. § 1292(b)(1993).

* * *

Dow and Chevron contend that FIFRA labeling requirements preempt state law requirements that relate to labeling. The Supremacy Clause of the Constitution invalidates any state laws that "interfere with, or are contrary to" federal laws. U.S. CONST. art. VI, cl. 2. Because of the Supremacy Clause, a state law that conflicts with federal law is "without effect." *Wisconsin Public Intervenor v. Mortier*, 501 U.S. 597, 111 S.Ct. 2476, 2482, 115 L.Ed.2d 532 (1991); *Maryland v. Louisiana*, 451 U.S. 725, 746, 101 S.Ct. 2114, 2128–29, 68 L.Ed.2d 576 (1981).

We begin our consideration of preemption questions with the presumption that historic police powers of the states are not superseded by federal law. *Rice v. Santa Fe Elevator Corp.*, 331 U.S. 218, 230, 67 S.Ct. 1146, 1152, 91 L.Ed. 1447 (1947). The police powers at issue here— health and safety matters—are matters that historically have been areas of state regulation. *See Hillsborough County v. Automated Medical Labs., Inc.*, 471 U.S. 707, 715–16, 105 S.Ct. 2371, 2376, 85 L.Ed.2d 714 (1985). This presumption against federal preemption of such state law may be overcome if Congress intended that the federal law preempt state law. *Rice v. Santa Fe Elevator Corp.*, 331 U.S. at 230, 67 S.Ct. at 1152. As the Supreme Court recently noted in *Cipollone v. Liggett Group, Inc.*,

> Congress' intent may be explicitly stated in the statute's language or implicitly contained in its structure and purpose. In the absence of an express congressional command, state law is pre-empted if that law actually conflicts with federal law, or if federal law so thoroughly occupies a legislative field as to make reasonable the inference that Congress left no room for the States to supplement it.

112 S.Ct. at 2617 (internal quotations and citations omitted).

In *Cipollone v. Liggett Group, Inc.*, the plaintiff, a woman who ultimately died of lung cancer after years of smoking, sued cigarette manufacturers under the state common law tort law for failure to warn consumers of the hazards of smoking. 112 S.Ct. at 2613. The cigarette manufacturer, however, argued that the Public Health Cigarette Smoking Act of 1969, 15 U.S.C. §§ 1331–1340 (1982 & Supp. 1994), preempted the state law claims. The cigarette manufacturers based their preemption argument on § 1334(b) of the Smoking Act, which provided that "no requirement or prohibition based on smoking and health shall be imposed under State law with respect to the advertising or promotion of any cigarettes the packages of which are labeled in conformity with the provisions of this Act." 15 U.S.C. § 1334(b)(1982). The Supreme Court held that "the phrase no 'requirement or prohibition' sweeps broadly and suggests no distinction between positive enactments and common law; to the contrary, those words easily encompass obligations that take the form of common law rules." *Cipollone v. Liggett Group, Inc.*, 112 S.Ct. at 2620. The Court cautioned, however, that § 1334(b) did not preempt all common law. For example, the Court noted that the statute preempting state labeling requirements did not preempt state law obligations to avoid marketing a product with a manufacturing defect or with a design defect. Id. at 2621. Thus, according to *Cipollone*, courts must compare the particular language of a statute's preemption provision with each common law claim asserted to determine whether the common law claim is in fact preempted. . . . *Id.*

Applying the reasoning articulated in *Cipollone* to FIFRA and the case at hand, the conclusion is manifest: FIFRA preempts conflicting state common law concerning the improper labeling of herbicides, which is the only common law claim raised in this appeal. As opinions from other courts have described, FIFRA provides a detailed scheme for regulating the content and format of labels for herbicides, ... and it requires all herbicides sold in the United States to be registered with the EPA. *See Worm v. American Cyanamid Co.*, 5 F.3d 744, 747 (4th Cir.1993)(discussing the details of FIFRA labeling requirements); *King v. E.I. Dupont De Nemours & Co.*, 996 F.2d at 1347 (discussing the details of FIFRA labeling requirements). In an effort to preserve uniformity of laws concerning labeling, FIFRA specifically mandates that "[a] State shall not impose or continue in effect any requirements for labeling or packaging in addition to or different from those required under this subchapter." 7 U.S.C. § 136v(b)(Supp. 1993).... If the encompassing words of the statute standing alone do not convince the skeptics, surely Cipollone leaves no doubt but that the FIFRA term "any requirements" makes no distinction between positive enactments and the common law. This is not to say, however, that not all common law is preempted by FIFRA—§ 136v(b) does not preempt common law that is unconcerned with herbicide labeling, nor does it preempt those state laws concerned with herbicide labeling that do not impose any requirement "in addition to or different from" the FIFRA requirements. *See Worm v. American Cyanamid Co.*, 970 F.2d 1301, 1307–08 (4th Cir.1992). Thus, we conclude, in accord with the clear language of the statute, that § 136v(b) preempts only those state laws that impose or effect different or additional labeling requirements....

The MacDonalds argue, however, that state common law tort judgments are not "requirements": the liable party is not "required" to change his label by a damage award, the argument goes, but may simply pay the judgment and leave the label as it is. We think this argument is sophistry. If plaintiffs could recover large damage awards because the herbicide was improperly labeled under state law, the undeniable practical effect would be that state law requires additional labeling standards not mandated by FIFRA; it cannot be presumed that businesses wish to bring about their own economic suicide. Consequently, such state labeling requirements would violate FIFRA's express prohibition against additional or different labeling requirements. We thus find that the express language of FIFRA clearly indicates that Congress intended that the federal act preempt conflicting state law, including state common law tort claims. We are far from alone in reaching this conclusion. *See King v. E.I. Dupont De Nemours & Co.*, 996 F.2d 1346 (1st Cir.1993), *cert. dismissed*, ___ U.S. ___, 114 S.Ct. 490, 126 L.Ed.2d 440 (1993)(holding that FIFRA preempts state common law causes of action); *Shaw v. Dow Brands, Inc.*, 994 F.2d 364 (7th Cir.1993)(holding that FIFRA preempts state common law causes of action); *Papas v. Upjohn Co.*, 985 F.2d 516 (11th Cir.1993), cert. denied, ___ U.S. ___, 114 S.Ct. 300, 126 L.Ed.2d 248 (1993) (holding that FIFRA preempts state common law causes of action); *Arkansas-Platte & Gulf Partnership v. Van Waters & Rogers, Inc.*, 981 F.2d 1177 (10th Cir.1993), cert. denied, ___ U.S. ___, 114 S.Ct. 60, 126 L.Ed.2d 30 (1993)(holding that FIFRA preempts state common law causes of action); *but see Ferebee v. Chevron Chem. Co.*, 237 U.S.App.D.C. 164, 736 F.2d 1529 (D.C.Cir.), *cert. denied,*

469 U.S. 1062, 105 S.Ct. 545, 83 L.Ed.2d 432 (1984)(holding that lack of direct conflict between the state and federal regulations compels a finding that FIFRA does not preempt state common law); *see also Stamps v. Collagen Corp.*, 984 F.2d 1416, 1424–25 (5th Cir.), *cert. denied*, ___ U.S. ___, 114 S.Ct. 86, 126 L.Ed.2d 54 (1993)(holding that the analysis used in *Ferebee* did not survive the *Cipollone* decision)....

IV

For the foregoing reasons, the decision of the district court to deny summary judgment is REVERSED, and we REMAND for entry of judgment accordingly.

REMANDED for entry of judgment.

JOHNSON, J., concurring in part, dissenting in the judgment.

The majority correctly decides that the Federal Insecticide, Fungicide and Rodenticide Act ("FIFRA") preempts both positive enactments and common law claims which differ from or add to FIFRA's labeling or packaging requirements. However, the majority fails to determine whether the specific common law claims raised in the case sub judice actually differ from or add to FIFRA's requirements. In this writer's view, the failure to warn and failure to adequately label claims at issue here are entirely consistent with FIFRA. They are not preempted.

The Supreme Court in *Cipollone v. Liggett Group, Inc.* made clear that a finding that a federal statute preempts common law actions in general is not tantamount to a finding that the statute preempts all common law actions. 112 S.Ct. 2608, 2621 (1992). Under the clear guidance of *Cipollone*, Courts must determine the scope of a statute's preemption provision. *Id.* at 2618. Any state law within the scope of the provision is preempted. However, "matters beyond that reach are not preempted." *Id.* To properly review a preemption claim, therefore, Courts must "fairly but—in light of the strong presumption against preemption—narrowly construe the precise language of [the preemption provision] and ... look to each of [the] common law claims [raised] to determine whether [they are] in fact preempted." *Id.* at 2621.

* * *

Consistent with FIFRA, the MacDonalds have claimed that the labels of the pesticides in question did not contain warnings or cautions which were adequate to protect Charles MacDonald's health. Hence, their state law claims do not add to or differ from FIFRA's requirements. ...Concededly, the MacDonalds must overcome the presumption that registered pesticides comply with FIFRA's registration provisions. However, under the plain language of the statute, registration of a pesticide does not conclusively prove that the pesticide was properly labeled ... 7 U.S.C. § 136a(f)(2).

By declining to determine whether the claims raised by the Mac-Donalds are consistent with FIFRA's broad labeling requirements, the majority fails to complete the preemption analysis mandated by Cipollone. In so doing, the majority has improperly allowed FIFRA to trample upon state law which is entirely consistent with the requirements set forth within the Act. Our federalism dictates that we refrain from extending federal power into state territory unless Congress intended such an extension. The majority pays short shrift to the ideals of federalism and comity so salient in this case. With such, this writer cannot agree and is therefore constrained to dissent.

BAILEY FARMS, INC. v. NOR–AM CHEMICAL COMPANY
27 F.3d 188 (6th Cir.1994).

SUHRHEINRICH, CIRCUIT JUDGE.

In this diversity action, plaintiff Bailey Farms, Inc., appeals the district court's dismissal of its negligence and breach of warranty claims against defendant NOR–AM Chemical Company. Defendant NOR–AM cross-appeals the district court's rulings that plaintiff's negligence claim was not preempted by the Federal Insecticide Fungicide and Rodenticide Act, 7 U.S.C.A. §§ 136–136y (1980 & Supp. 1993)("FIFRA"); and that plaintiff presented adequate proof to withstand summary judgment on the issue of causation.

For the reasons that follow, we AFFIRM.

I.

Plaintiff is a Michigan commercial farming corporation. Its sole shareholder and president is Howard Bailey. Defendant is a Delaware corporation. In 1989, plaintiff attempted for the first time to grow seedless watermelons in Michigan. Plaintiff purchased from defendant a soil fumigant, Vorlex, used for weed control. Plaintiff alleges that defendant, through its sales representative, misinformed him as to the proper use of the chemical, and that this improper use destroyed the 1989 crop.

Plaintiff brought suit in state court in May 1990, alleging negligence in advising about the proper use of Vorlex, and breach of warranty, and seeking incidental and consequential damages. Defendants removed the action, and later filed a motion for judgment on the pleadings or in the alternative, for summary judgment, raising three issues: (1) plaintiff's claims are preempted by FIFRA; (2) defendant had a valid disclaimer of all commercial warranties; and (3) plaintiff's complaint failed to state a valid claim for breach of warranty of fitness for a particular purpose. On October 1, 1991, the district court (Judge Enslen), ruled that plaintiff's claims were not preempted by FIFRA, that plaintiff had failed to create a genuine issue of fact as to defendant's assertion of a valid, enforceable disclaimer of warranties, and that plaintiff's negligence claim stated a question for a jury.

On August 13, 1992, defendant filed another motion to dismiss and/or for summary judgment, based upon the Michigan Supreme Court's recently issued decision in *Neibarger v. Universal Coops., Inc.,* 439 Mich. 512, 486 N.W.2d 612 (Mich.1992). *Neibarger* holds that a plaintiff may not recover in tort for economic loss caused by a defective product purchased for commercial purposes. In response, plaintiff argued that its claim was based on the tort of negligent misrepresentation, not on liability for a defective product; and that the transaction between the parties was for services and not goods, and therefore was not controlled by the Uniform Commercial Code as adopted by Michigan. On September 30, 1992, the lower court (Magistrate Judge Rowland) ... ruled that: (1) the "overall thrust" of the dealings between the parties was to purchase goods; and (2) although *Neibarger* was not precisely on point, plaintiff's negligent misrepresentation claim implicated the policies underlying the economic loss doctrine, thereby warranting the conclusion that the *Neibarger* doctrine barred plaintiff's claim. These timely appeals followed.

* * *

Plaintiff presents six subarguments in connection with its primary argument that its tort claim of negligent misrepresentation is not barred by the economic loss doctrine. We deal with each in turn.

1.

First, plaintiff argues that *Neibarger* does not apply because the economic loss doctrine, as defined by the *Neibarger* court, extends only to damages caused by defective products; and that plaintiff is not complaining that the product, Vorlex, worked improperly, but rather that he was negligently misinformed as to its proper use, resulting in the destruction of his crops. Plaintiff forgets that such a distinction was rejected in *Neibarger:*

> Plaintiffs' attempts to avoid the application of the UCC by arguing that there was no defect in the product, but that it was poorly designed or installed, are to no avail. At the heart of the complaints in these cases is the fact that the plaintiffs purchased products which proved inadequate for their purposes, causing them lost profits, and perhaps, consequential losses or property damages compensable in a timely suit under the provisions of the UCC.

486 N.W.2d at 622–23.

Although the watermelon crops at issue in this case also are technically "other property" than the purchased product, a successful crop was part of the commercial expectations for the fumigant, and the loss of that crop allegedly the result of a defect of the use of the purchased product. Similarly, at the heart of plaintiff's complaint is that the weed suppressant, through improper applications, proved inadequate and caused plaintiff consequential losses. We therefore reject this claim for the reasons stated in *Neibarger*.

2.

Next, plaintiff claims that *Neibarger* does not preclude a tort cause of action for misrepresentation. Defendant maintains that Michigan does not recognize the tort of negligent misrepresentation between commercial parties, and that decisions from other jurisdictions mandate that a negligent misrepresentation claim may only be asserted against a defendant in the business of supplying information.

Assuming, as did the district court, that the Michigan Supreme Court would not limit the tort of negligent misrepresentation to those defendants who are in the business of supplying information, we likewise agree with the lower court's prediction that the court would hold that the principles and rationale set forth in *Neibarger* bar any recovery for economic losses based upon the tort of negligent misrepresentation. We further agree with defendant that the claim nonetheless fails under Michigan law, which holds that an action in tort requires a breach of duty separate and distinct from a breach of contract. *Brock v. Consolidated Biomedical Lab.*, 817 F.2d 24, 25 (6th Cir.1987)(applying Michigan law to hold that Michigan law does not recognize a cause of action for negligent performance of a contract). We think equally true here that the "operative allegations in the claims would not arise without the existence of the putative contracts between the parties[,] [and that] such allegations therefore cannot be maintained as tort-based claims." *Merchants Publishing Co. v. Maruka Mach. Corp. of America*, 800 F.Supp. 1490, 1493 (W.D.Mich.1992)(actions for fraud, negligent misrepresentation and rescission of contract action with sale of faulty printing press cannot be maintained in tort under Michigan law because claims derive existence out of contracts between the parties). Finally, we note that the UCC contains a specific remedy for misrepresentation or fraud. See Mich. Comp. Laws Ann. § 440.2721 (West 1967).

3.

Third, plaintiff asserts that because NOR–AM's misrepresentations were not made until after the sale of goods was completed, the UCC does not apply. This contention is without merit. Pursuant to plaintiff's own admissions, advice and instruction were an expected aspect of the purchase of Vorlex, a basis of the commercial expectations of the parties, and clearly incidental to the sale. Furthermore, the UCC itself makes available remedies for defective products even after acceptance. *See, e.g.,* Mich. Comp. Laws Ann. § 440.2607 (West 1967).

4.

Fourth, plaintiff argues that its claims fall within tort policies, not contract principles, such that the economic loss doctrine should not apply. We disagree. Just as in *Neibarger,* the damages in this case were purely economic and consequential, and there was no accident or physical injury. Furthermore, plaintiff has a remedy for allegedly negligent representations by the seller pursuant to the warranty provisions of the UCC. See Mich. Comp. Laws Ann. § 440.2313 (West 1967 & Supp. 1993) (express warranties); and Mich. Comp. Laws Ann. §§ 440.2314, 440.2315 (West 1967)(implied warranties of merchantability and/or fitness for a particular purpose).

5.

Fifth, plaintiff claims that services, rather than goods, were the predominant reason that plaintiff purchased Vorlex and that the UCC and the economic loss doctrine therefore do not apply. We agree with the district court's assessment that the overall thrust of the dealings between the parties was to purchase goods. As pointed out by the district court, the cost of Vorlex, $8,251.65, made up most of the total invoice amount of $8,591.65. Bailey, in his deposition testimony, stated that he was looking primarily for an effective weed control when he purchased the Vorlex. Thus, under the test set forth in *Neibarger,* we conclude that the predominant factor of the parties agreement was a transaction of sale, with labor incidentally involved. *Neibarger,* 486 N.W.2d at 621 (adopting and applying *Bonebrake v. Cox,* 499 F.2d 951, 960 (8th Cir. 1974)).

6.

Plaintiff also contends that the destruction of its seedless watermelon crop amounts to a "disaster" and not a mere "disappointment." In *Citizens Ins. Co. of America v. Proctor & Schwartz, Inc.,* 802 F.Supp. 133 (W.D.Mich.1992), the court carved out a distinction it perceived was also recognized in *Neibarger,* that where economic loss is a "natural foreseeable result of product's defects," the "disappointed" commercial buyer is limited to contract remedies. However, where the defect results in a "sudden calamitous event" causing damage to other property, a "disaster," remediable in tort has occurred. *Citizens,* 802 F.Supp. at 140.

Assuming the validity of this distinction, we agree with the lower court that the loss was foreseeable and therefore more accurately characterized as a commercial disappointment than as an unforeseeable disaster for the simple reason that Bailey admittedly knew that Vorlex could kill the plants if the soil did not properly aerate. We therefore reject this argument.

B.

Plaintiff also appeals the district court's ruling that NOR–AM's disclaimer of warranties precluded plaintiff's breach of warranty claim. . . . Plaintiff presents three specific points of error.

1.

First, plaintiff claims that the disclaimer is not effective with respect to an implied warranty in tort claim. Plaintiff's argument fails for the reasons discussed above with respect to *Neibarger.* The cases relied on by plaintiff, *Citizens,* 802 F.Supp. at 133, and *Blanchard v. Monical Mach. Co.,* 84 Mich. App. 279, 269 N.W.2d 564 (Mich.App.1978) are distinguishable in that the claims in those cases were viable in tort. In *Citizens* the court disallowed recovery with respect to tort claims for losses resultant from damage to a peanut roaster and conveyer cleaner, but also held that the economic loss doctrine did not bar Citizens' tort claims for losses resultant from unanticipated, "disastrous" fire damage to other property. In *Blanchard,* recovery in tort was permitted where an employee was injured by a machine sold in an "as is" condition. In any event, the disclaimer here stated expressly that no agent of NOR–AM was authorized to make any warranties beyond those contained on the label. This argument is rejected.

2.

Second, referring to the above-quoted paragraph, plaintiff argues that because the Vorlex label contained no warranties to be disclaimed, the label is deceptive and confusing in that it "promises a warranty and then offers none." As pointed out by defendant, this argument is incorrect in that plaintiff received the Vorlex label and product information bulletin prior to purchase of Vorlex and could have relied on information therein which could serve as a basis for an express warranty. Secondly, both the UCC and common law allow defendant to disclaim implied warranties.

3.

Lastly, plaintiff contends that the disclaimer is unconscionable and should not be enforced. See Mich. Comp. Laws Ann. § 440.2302. Specifically, plaintiff claims that the disclaimer is one-sided and oppressive. However, plaintiff's admitted failure to read the Vorlex labeling, when he knew that he was required to do so by law, undercuts his claim that he had no bargaining power with respect to the disclaimer provision. In addition, the record reflects that plaintiff is not as inexperienced as he might suggest. He had been farming for over seventeen years, had over 1000 acres under cultivation at the time of the transaction, had performed custom farming for others in Florida, and most importantly, had prior experience with pesticides. We are not persuaded.

IV.

Because we are affirming the lower court as to both assignments of error raised by plaintiff, we need not address NOR–AM's cross-appeal.

For all the foregoing reasons, then, the judgment of the district court is AFFIRMED.

Discussion Problems

ChemUser, a chemical sprayer for the State A Department of Transportation and Development, suffered serious personal injuries allegedly caused by the phenoxy herbicide 2,4–D, which is produced by several different chemical companies. This herbicide was packaged in containers bearing labels approved by the Environmental Protection Agency ("EPA") pursuant to FIFRA requirements. ChemUser and his wife sued the chemical companies in state B court, claiming, *inter alia*, that the chemical companies failed, under state law, to label properly the herbicide and thereby failed, under state law, to warn him adequately of the dangers associated with 2,4–D.

The defendants timely removed the suit to federal district court on diversity of citizenship grounds and then moved for summary judgment, arguing that FIFRA preempts all state laws affecting labeling requirements. The Supremacy Clause of the United States Constitution provides that the laws of the United States "shall be the supreme Law of the Land ... any Thing in the Constitution or Laws of any state to the Contrary notwithstanding." U.S. Const., Art. VI, cl. 2. The preemption clause in FIFRA is found in section 136v, which provides:

(a) In general

A State may regulate the sale or use of any federally registered pesticide or device in the State, but only if and to the extent the regulation does not permit any sale or use prohibited by this subchapter.

(b) Uniformity

Such State shall not impose or continue in effect any requirements for labeling or packaging in addition to or different from those required under this subchapter.

Defendants argued that because they complied with FIFRA labeling requirements and because FIFRA preempts state labeling requirements, they were entitled to summary judgment in their favor on the labeling issue as well as on the questions of negligence, breach of implied warranties, strict liability and fraud.

You are the judge hearing the case. How do you rule? What elements will you look to in determining if the defendants did in fact comply with FIFRA? How do these elements compare with the elements of the various common law claims?

§ 4.3   THE OCCUPATIONAL SAFETY AND HEALTH ACT

The Occupational Safety and Health Act, 29 U.S.C.A. § 651 *et seq.*, which provides that "no employees will suffer material impairment of health or functional capacity from a lifetime of occupational exposure," sets forth *health standards* involving environmental contaminants in the work place. The Act regulates such issues as employee exposure to toxic chemicals, noise, and asbestos. In addition, the Act establishes a broad range of *safety standards* to minimize accidental injuries such as burns, cuts, broken bones, loss of limbs or eyesight, electrical shock, and death.

§ 4.4   THE CONSUMER PRODUCT SAFETY ACT

The Consumer Product Safety Act, 15 U.S.C.A. § 2051 *et seq.*, and related statutes such as the Hazardous Substances Act, 15 U.S.C.A. § 1261 *et seq.*, regulate chemicals and hazardous substances in consumer products. The Consumer Product Safety Commission, which administers these acts, is authorized to address only human safety questions derived from the use of consumer products and, as such, does not have authority over environmental problems.

§ 4.5   THE HAZARDOUS SUBSTANCES ACT

The Hazardous Substances Act, 15 U.S.C.A. § 1261 *et seq.*, regulates hazardous substances in interstate commerce. The statute is administered by the Consumer Product Safety Commission.

§ 4.6   THE FEDERAL FOOD, DRUG, AND COSMETIC ACT

The Federal Food, Drug, and Cosmetic Act, 21 U.S.C.A. § 301 *et seq.* (1988), is one of a number of federal statutes that regulate commercial products on the basis of health impact. Although such statutes do not regulate on the basis of environmental impact, they have much in common with environment-based product control statutes like TSCA and FIFRA in that they are primarily concerned with protection of human health and most often focus on cancer as the predominant health threat presented by toxic chemicals.

§ 4.7 ASBESTOS

Asbestos was used in constructing more than half of all buildings in the United States between 1940 and 1970. Asbestos or asbestos-containing material (ACM) may be found in cement products, acoustical plaster, fireproofing textiles, wallboard, ceiling tiles, vinyl floor tiles, thermal insulation and other materials. Exposure to airborne asbestos has been linked with asbestosis and mesothelioma, as well as with cancers of the lung, esophagus, stomach, colon and other organs. But the mere presence of asbestos might not pose a danger—ACM in good repair is not likely to release fibers into the air. It is when ACM becomes friable or when it is likely to be disturbed that it presents a potential health hazard.

EPA estimates that 733,000 public and commercial buildings in the United States contain friable ACM. To date, asbestos abatement has been conducted on only approximately 25,000 of these buildings. Proper asbestos abatement is costly. A prominent investment banking firm projected that asbestos abatement projects will cost $100 billion over the next 25 years. In some cases, the cost of asbestos abatement may exceed a building's original cost of construction.

At present, the primary asbestos concerns in the business context deal with regulatory compliance, asbestos abatement, and common law liability. EPA currently is phasing in an asbestos ban which will by 1997 prohibit the manufacture, importation, processing, and distribution in commerce of almost all asbestos or asbestos-containing products. 54 Fed. Reg. 29,460 (July 12, 1989)(codified at 40 C.F.R. §§ 763.160–763.179).

1. *General Regulatory Framework*

At the federal level, EPA, the Occupational Safety and Health Administration (OSHA) and the Department of Transportation (DOT) have asbestos regulations. EPA regulations cover the application and removal of ACM in buildings, and identification and abatement of asbestos in schools. EPA regulations also cover the industrial emission of asbestos fibers and the disposal of asbestos waste. OSHA regulations focus on worker protection. The DOT regulates the transportation of asbestos under the Hazardous Materials Transportation Act, as amended. 49 U.S.C.A. §§ 1801 *et seq*. The shipment of asbestos is subject to requirements for shipping papers, packing, marking, labelling and vehicle placarding. In addition to federal regulation, there are a variety of state provisions establishing requirements that reflect the federal programs and are in some cases more stringent.

2. Manufacturing and Using Asbestos

Some products containing asbestos may be manufactured so long as (1) there is no discharge of visible emissions to the outside air, or (2) methods prescribed by EPA are used to clean the emissions. 40 C.F.R. § 61.144. However, commercial and industrial uses of asbestos must be reported by persons who manufacture, import, or process ACM. TSCA, 15 U.S.C.A. §§ 2601–2654; 40 C.F.R. § 763.78. As noted previously, EPA has announced a ban of most asbestos products which is currently being phased in. By 1997, importation, manufacture, and distribution in commerce of almost all asbestos products will be banned. 40 C.F.R. §§ 763.160–763.179.

3. Occupational Safety

OSHA has promulgated regulations and standards applicable to all occupational exposures to ACM. *See* 29 C.F.R. §§ 1910.1001, 1926.58 (general industry and construction industry requirements, respectively). In particular, OSHA has established permissible exposure levels (PELs), monitoring and recordkeeping procedures, medical surveillance protocols, and warning requirements. Twenty-three states and territories have set up their own OSHA plans, which are either as rigorous as or more so than the federal standards.

4. Asbestos Inspection, Demolition, and Abatement Requirements

EPA promulgated a National Emission Standard for Hazardous Air Pollutants (NESHAP) for Asbestos, 40 C.F.R. §§ 61.140–156, pursuant to Clean Air Act §§ 112 and 301(a), 42 U.S.C.A. §§ 7412 and 7601(a). The NESHAP applies to manufacturing, demolition, renovation, asbestos mills, roadways, spraying, fabricating, insulating materials, and waste disposal. For demolition and renovation operations, the NESHAP imposes notification requirements, prescribes work procedures for asbestos emission control, and regulates disposal of ACM. As discussed above, . . . the 1990 Amendments to the Clean Air Act completely revised the system for controlling hazardous air pollutants. The 1990 Amendments designate 189 substances as hazardous air pollutants, including asbestos. The NESHAP for asbestos will remain in effect under amended § 112 until EPA reviews and revises it, if appropriate, to comply with the requirements of amended § 112(d). 42 U.S.C.A. § 7412(q)(1).

In addition, some states require inspection for and abatement of asbestos in buildings used for particular purposes (in addition to the federal and state programs regarding schools). In New York, for example, the prospectus for a proposed conversion of rental property to a condominium or cooperative must disclose the presence of any ACM in the building and recommend a protocol for asbestos abatement. The New York City Administrative Code also requires some form of asbestos abatement as a condition precedent to obtaining a building permit in certain situations. New York City is currently attempting to pass regulations imposing inspection and abatement requirements on virtually all building owners.

In addition, the requirement for asbestos abatement may be triggered by the renovation or demolition of buildings. Many states require inspection for asbestos and, if necessary, the formulation of an abatement plan as a condition to obtaining a building permit to renovate or demolish a building built before a certain date (usually around 1978).

In addition, many states operate licensing programs requiring training and licensing for members of asbestos-related occupations such as asbestos contractors or workers, asbestos inspectors, and asbestos management planners. Some states are beginning to require a permit for each specific asbestos abatement project

Discussion Problems

(1) Assume that a consumer interest group releases a study that determined that Chemical A is a probable carcinogen. The study is based on both empirical evidence from animal bioassays as well as elevated levels of cancer in humans living or working close to where the chemical is used. The U.S. Department of Health and Human Services (HHS) lists Chemical A as a substance reasonably anticipated to be a carcinogen in its Annual Report on Carcinogens.

(A) Under what statutory authority could chemical A be regulated when it is used as:

(1) an industrial solvent;

(2) a pesticide;

(3) a food or color additive;

(4) a contaminant in drinking water; and

(5) an air pollutant?

(B) What additional information, if any, could EPA, OSHA or the FDA request in order to be able to regulate Chemical A under each of the statutes identified above? Why?

(C) How stringently could Chemical A be regulated under each of these statutes?

(D) What common law causes of action might be invoked, if any?

(2) Suppose a neighborhood improvement association brings suit against a small company that owns and operate a local chemical manufacturing plant. Evidence revealed in anticipation of trial tends to indicate the following findings of fact will be found by the court:

Normal background risk of throat cancer in the neighborhood would be between 1 and 3 cases. The chemical plant discharged substantial quantities of a toxic substance known to cause throat cancer into both the air and the water for a period of ten years, but ceased these practices six years ago. The discharges were the result of sloppy management on the part of the chemical plant. Best estimates are that the plant's discharges increased the risk of throat cancer between 33 ⅓ and 66 ⅔ percent above the normal background risk. Four neighbors (all of whom are plaintiffs in the suit) have been diagnosed with throat cancer.

(A) What standards of causation might a court apply in evaluating this case? How would the prognosis of success differ under each of these causation standards?

(B) What factors would need to be considered in assessing whether or not the statue of limitations had run?

(C) Under what theories, if any, could other neighbors who were exposed to the toxic discharges but who have not yet contracted throat cancer bring suit? What would be the damages?

(3) Mrs. X is a nurse at the City General Hospital. Company A, Company B and Company C each manufacture a disinfectant solution that contain glutaraldehyde, a chemical compound designed to kill infectious viruses in hospital environments. During her employment at City General, Mrs. X regularly was exposed to each of these three products, which were used interchangeably and purchased intermittently depending on the various price and availability of the product. Mrs. X now suffers from respiratory disease and other chronic illnesses that she believe this exposure caused. What claims could Mrs. X raise? What obstacles might she face in bringing suit?

(4) In 1982, Ms. A purchased a log home. The sellers of the home had purchased it from Vermont Log Builders, Inc. ("Vermont Log"), in 1979. The component logs of this home had been treated with a product called "Woodlife," which contained the chemical pentachlorophenol ("PCP"). DAP, Inc. ("DAP") is the manufacturer of Woodlife. Three years later, Ms. A developed a rash on her face, which her doctor determined was caused by Woodlife. She vacated the house and comes to you for advice. What do you do, advise or want to know? What causes of action might she have? What are the limitations to the case?

Chapter 5

REGULATION OF SOLID AND HAZARDOUS WASTES—THE RESOURCE CONSERVATION AND RECOVERY ACT OF 1976

Table of Sections

---

§ 5.1 OVERVIEW

The primary federal statute under which solid and hazardous wastes are regulated is the Resource Conservation and Recovery Act of 1976 (RCRA), 42 U.S.C.A. § 6901 *et seq.* RCRA regulates "solid waste" in general, but contains especially detailed "cradle-to-grave" requirements for solid wastes that are classified as "hazardous waste."

EPA sets the technology based requirements under RCRA, but thereafter EPA may delegate to the states the implementation of the regulatory scheme. This is quite similar to the technique used in regulation of air and water pollution, where EPA sets the basic technical requirements and can then delegate the implementation and permitting to the states, on condition that the states have the necessary authority to act under state law and can demonstrate this fact to EPA. The state must implement the substantive regulatory requirements that EPA has prescribed, although states have discretion in interpreting them and in certain other areas in which EPA may have left the requirements open. Otherwise, state implementation is judged against quite concrete and specific EPA requirements established uniformly across the country at the national level. Almost every state in the United States currently has a hazardous waste program that has received final approval, although not all state programs address all aspects of hazardous waste permitting and enforcement covered by EPA's regulations. EPA thus retains authority over those aspects of regulation (such as corrective action for releases of hazardous wastes) not covered by an approved state program.

RCRA regulates *solid wastes* in general, but contains special detailed requirements relating to *solid wastes that are classified as hazardous waste.* Solid waste is defined as garbage, refuse, sludge, and other discarded material, including solid, liquid, semi-solid, and contained gaseous waste. 42 U.S.C.A. § 6903(27). Expressly excluded from the definition of solid waste are discharges regulated as point sources under the United States Clean Water Act, and nuclear waste as defined in the Atomic Energy Act.

Hazardous waste is defined as a solid waste which, because of its quantity, concentration, or other characteristics, may cause an increase in mortality or serious illness or may pose a hazard to health or the environment. 42 U.S.C.A. § 6903(5). Wastes can be classified as hazardous (1) if EPA lists the waste, or (2) if the waste tests hazardous due to its toxicity, *reactivity*, ignitability, or corrosiveness under tests that EPA prescribes. EPA has established four hazardous waste lists:

(1) hazardous wastes from non-specific sources, such as spent non-halogenated solvents or toluene, for example;

(2) hazardous wastes from specific sources, that is, wastes from a particular type of waste stream in a particular industry (*e.g.*, bottom sediment sludge from the treatment of waste waters from the wood-preserving industry); and

(3) two categories—toxic and acute—of discarded commercial chemical products and off-specification products and containers and spill residues of those products.

Once a solid waste is listed under RCRA or is classified as a hazardous waste, the *generation, transportation*, and the *treatment, storage, and disposal* of that waste are then pervasively regulated. Every person who generates or transports hazardous wastes or who owns or operates a treatment, storage, or disposal facility ("TSD" facility), must notify EPA (and the state agency if the state has implemented a state program) of his hazardous waste activities and obtain an identification number.

RCRA at a Glance

Section	Description
General	
§ 1002	Outline of statutory goals.
Subtitle C §§ 3001–3020	Hazardous Waste Management
§ 3001	Identification & Listing of Hazardous Wastes
§ 3002	Regulation of Hazardous Waste Generators
§ 3003	Regulation of Hazardous Waste Transporters
§ 3004	Regulation of Facilities that Treat, Store or Dispose (TSD) of Hazardous Wastes
§ 3005	TSD Permit Requirements
Subtitle D	State or Regional Solid Waste Plans
§§ 4001–4010	Requires EPA to establish guidelines for state solid waste management plans, including minimum criteria for municipal landfills.
	Enforcement Provisions
§ 3008	Provides for criminal, civil and administrative penalties
§ 7002	Authorizes citizens suits
§ 7003	Authorizes EPA injunctive action
§ 7006	Specifies judicial review of EPA decisions will occur in the DC Circuit
Subtitle I	Regulation of USTs
§ 9002	Requires UST owners to notify state authorities

§ 9003	Requires EPA to promulgate regulations concerning detection, prevention, correction of UST related problems, including financial assurance provisions
Subtitle J	Medical Waste Tracking Program
§ 11003	Required EPA to set up a demonstration program for tracking medical wastes in certain enumerated states or in states that opt into the program

AMERICAN MINING CONGRESS
v. UNITED STATES EPA
824 F.2d 1177 (D.C.Cir.1987).

Starr, Circuit Judge:

These consolidated cases arise out of EPA's regulation of hazardous wastes under the Resource Conservation and Recovery Act of 1976 ("RCRA"), as amended, 42 U.S.C. §§ 6901–6933 (1982 & Supp. III 1985). Petitioners, trade associations representing mining and oil refining interests, challenge regulations promulgated by EPA that amend the definition of "solid waste" to establish and define the agency's authority to regulate secondary materials reused within an industry's ongoing production process. In plain English, petitioners maintain that EPA has exceeded its regulatory authority in seeking to bring materials that are not discarded or otherwise disposed or within the compass of "waste."

I

RCRA is a comprehensive environmental statute under which EPA is granted authority to regulate solid and hazardous wastes. RCRA was enacted in 1976, and amended in 1978, 1980, and 1984. *See* The Quiet Communities Act of 1978, Pub. L. No. 95–609, 92 Stat. 3081; The Solid Waste Disposal Act Amendment of 1980, Pub. L. No. 96–482, 94 Stat. 2334; Hazardous and Solid Waste Amendments of 1984, Pub. L. No. 98–616, 98 Stat. 3221.

Congress' "overriding concern" in enacting RCRA was to establish the framework for a national system to insure the safe management of hazardous waste. H.R. Rep. No. 1491, 94th Cong., 2d Sess. 3 (1976). In passing RCRA, Congress expressed concern over the "rising tide" in scrap, discarded, and waste materials. 42 U.S.C. § 6901 (a)(2). As the statute itself puts it, Congress was concerned with the need "to reduce the amount of waste and unsalvageable materials and to provide for proper and economical solid waste disposal practices." *Id.* § 6901 (a)(4). Congress thus crafted RCRA "to promote the protection of health and the environment and to conserve valuable material and energy resources." *Id.* § 6902.

RCRA includes two major parts: one deals with non-hazardous solid waste management and the other with hazardous waste management. Under the latter, EPA is directed to promulgate regulations establishing a comprehensive management system. *Id.* § 6921. EPA's authority, however, extends only to the regulation of "hazardous waste." Because "hazardous waste" is defined as a subset of "solid waste," id. § 6903(5), the scope of EPA's jurisdiction is limited to those materials that constitute "solid waste." That pivotal term is defined by RCRA as

> any garbage, refuse, sludge from a waste treatment plant, water supply treatment plant, or air pollution control facility and other discarded material, including solid, liquid, semisolid or contained gaseous material, resulting from industrial, commercial, mining, and agricultural operations, and from community activities ...

42 U.S.C. § 6903(27).... As will become evident, this case turns on the the meaning of the phrase, "and other discarded material," contained in the statute's definitional provisions.

EPA's interpretation of "solid waste" has evolved over time. On May 19, 1980, EPA issued interim regulations defining "solid waste" to include a material that is "a manufacturing or mining by-product and sometimes is discarded." 45 Fed. Reg. 33,119 (1980). This definition contained two terms needing elucidation: "by-product" and "sometimes discarded." In its definition of "a manufacturing or mining by-product," EPA expressly excluded "an intermediate manufacturing or mining product which results from one of the steps in a manufacturing or mining process and is typically processed through the next step of the process within a short time." *Id.*

In 1983, the agency proposed narrowing amendments to the 1980 interim rule. 48 Fed. Reg. 14,472 (1983). The agency showed especial concern over recycling activities. In the preamble to the amendments, the agency observed that, in light of the interlocking statutory provisions and RCRA's legislative history, it was clear that "Congress indeed intended that materials being recycled or held for recycling can be wastes, and if hazardous, hazardous wastes." *Id.* at 14,473. The agency also asserted that "not only can materials destined for recycling or being recycled be solid and hazardous wastes, but the Agency clearly has the authority to regulate recycling activities as hazardous management." *Id.*

While asserting its interest in recycling activities (and materials being held for recycling), EPA's discussion left unclear whether the agency in fact believed its jurisdiction extended to materials recycled in an industry's on-going production processes, or only to materials disposed of and recycled as part of a waste management program. In its preamble, EPA stated that "the revised definition of solid waste sets out the Agency's view of its jurisdiction over the recycling of hazardous waste ... Proposed section 261.6 then contains exemptions from regulations for those hazardous waste recycling activities that we do not think require regulation." *id.* at 14,476. The amended regulatory description of "solid waste" itself, then, did not include materials "used or reused as effective substitutes for raw materials in processes using raw materials as principal feedstocks." *id.* at 14,508. EPA explained the exclusion as follows:

> [These] materials are being used essentially as raw materials and so ordinarily are not appropriate candidates for regulatory control. Moreover, when these materials are used to manufacture new products, the processes generally are normal manufacturing operations ... The Agency is reluctant to read the statute as regulating actual manufacturing processes.

Id. at 14,488. This, then, seemed clear: EPA was drawing a line between discarding and ultimate recycling, on the one hand, and a continuous or ongoing manufacturing process with one-site "recycling," on the other. If the activity fell within the latter category, then the materials were not deemed to be "discarded."

After receiving extensive comments, EPA issued its final rule on January 4, 1985. 50 Fed. Reg. 614 (1985). Under the final rule, materials are considered "solid waste" if they are abandoned by being disposed of, burned, or incinerated; or stored, treated, or accumulated before or in lieu of those activities. In addition, certain recycling activities fall within EPA's definition. EPA determines whether a material is a RCRA solid waste when it is recycled by examining both the material or substance itself and the recycling of "secondary materials" (spent materials, sludges, by-products, commercial chemical products, and scrap metal). These "secondary materials" constitute "solid waste" when they are disposed of; burned for energy recovery or used to produce a fuel; reclaimed; or accumulated speculatively. *Id.* at 618–19, 664.... Under the final rule, if a material constitutes "solid waste," it is subject to RCRA regulation unless it is directly reused as an ingredient or as an effective substitute for a commercial product, or is returned as a raw material substitute to its original manufacturing process.... *Id.* In the jargon of the trade, the latter category is known as the "closed-loop" exception. In either case, the material must not first be "reclaimed" (processed to recover a usable product or regenerated). *id.* EPA exempts these activities "because they are like ordinary usage of commercial products." *Id.* at 619.

* * *

II

Petitioners, American Mining Congress ("AMC") and American Petroleum Institute ("API"), challenge the scope of EPA's final rule. Relying upon the statutory definition of "solid waste," petitioners contend that EPA's authority under RCRA is limited to controlling materials that are discarded or intended for discard. They argue that EPA's reuse and recycle rules, as applied to in-process secondary materials, regulate materials that have not been discarded, and therefore exceed EPA's jurisdiction....

* * *

III

B

... we turn to the statutory provision at issue here. Congress, it will be recalled, granted EPA power to regulate "solid waste." Congress specifically defined "solid waste" as "discarded material." EPA then defined "discarded material" to include materials destined for reuse in an industry's ongoing production processes. The challenge to EPA's jurisdictional reach is founded, again, on the proposition that in-process secondary materials are outside the bounds of EPA's lawful authority. Nothing has been discarded, the argument goes, and thus RCRA jurisdiction remains untriggered.

* * *

1

... a complete analysis of the statutory term "discarded" calls for more than resort to the ordinary, everyday meaning of the specific language at hand. For, "the sense in which [a term] is used in a statute must be determined by reference to the purpose of the particular legislation." *Burnet v. Chicago Portrait Co.*, 285 U.S. 1, 6, 76 L.Ed. 587, 52 S.Ct. 275 (1932).... The statutory provision cannot properly be torn from the law of which it is a part; context and structure are, as in examining any legal instrument, of substantial import in the interpretive exercise. *See, e.g., Stafford v. Briggs*, 444 U.S. 527, 535, 63 L.Ed.2d 1, 100 S.Ct. 774 (1980); *Offshore Logistics, Inc. v. Tallentire*, 477 U.S. 207, 106 S.Ct. 2485, 2494, 91 L.Ed.2d 174 (1986); *Pennhurst State School v. Halderman*, 451 U.S. 1, 18–19, 67 L.Ed.2d 694, 101 S.Ct. 1531 (1981).

Application of "broad purposes" of legislation at the expense of specific provisions ignores the complexity of the problems Congress is called upon to address and the dynamics of legislative action. Congress may be unanimous in its intent to stamp out some vague social or economic evil; however, because its Members may differ sharply on the means for effectuating that intent, the final language of the legislation may reflect hard fought compromises. Invocation of the "plain purpose" of legislation at the expense of the terms of the statute itself takes no account of the processes of compromise and, in the end, prevents the effectuation of congressional intent.

106 S.Ct. at 689. That passage applies, we believe, with particular force here.

As we previously recounted, the broad objectives of RCRA are "to promote the protection of health and the environment and to conserve valuable material and energy resources ... " 42 U.S.C. § 6902. But that goal is of majestic breadth, and it is difficult, as Dimension Financial taught us, to pour meaning into a highly specific term by resort to grand purposes. Somewhat more specifically, we have seen that RCRA was enacted in response to Congressional findings that the "rising tide of scrap, discarded, and waste materials" generated by consumers and increased industrial production has presented heavily populated urban communities with "serious financial, management, intergovernmental, and technical problems in the disposal of solid wastes." *Id.* § 6901(a). In light of this problem, Congress determined that "federal action through financial and technical assistance and leadership in the development, demonstration, and application of new and improved methods and processes to reduce the amount of waste and unsalvageable materials and to provide for proper and economical solid waste disposal practices was necessary." *Id.* Also animating Congress were its findings that "disposal of solid and hazardous waste" without careful planning and management presents a danger to human health and the environment; that methods to "separate usable materials from solid waste" should be employed; and that usable energy can be produced from solid waste. *Id.* § 6901(b), (c), (d).

The question we face, then, is whether, in light of the National Legislature's expressly stated objectives and the underlying problems that motivated it to enact RCRA in the first instance, Congress was using the term "discarded" in its ordinary sense—"disposed of" of "abandoned"—or whether Congress was using it in a much more open-ended way, so as to encompass materials no longer useful in their original capacity though destined for immediate reuse in another phase of the industry's ongoing production process.

For the following reasons, we believe the former to be the case. RCRA was enacted, as the Congressional objectives and findings make clear, in an effort to help States deal with the ever-increasing problem of solid waste disposal by encouraging the search for and use of alternatives to existing methods of disposal (including recycling) and protecting health and the environment by regulating hazardous wastes. To fulfill these purposes, it seems clear that EPA need not regulate "spent" materials that are recycled and reused in an ongoing manufacturing or industrial process.... These materials have not yet become part of the waste disposal problem; rather, they are destined for beneficial reuse or recycling in a continuous process by the generating industry itself.

* * *

2

Our task in analyzing the statute also requires us to determine whether other provisions of RCRA shed light on the breadth with which Congress intended to define "discarded." As the Supreme Court reiterated a few years ago, in interpreting a statute, "we do not ... construe statutory phrases in isolation; we read statutes as a whole." *United States v. Morton*, 467 U.S. 822, 828, 81 L.Ed.2d 680, 104 S.Ct. 2769 (1984). The structure of a statute, in short, is important in the sensitive task of divining Congress' meaning.

In its brief, EPA directed us to a number of statutory provisions, arguing that they support its expansive definition of "discarded." This turned out, however, to be a wild goose chase through the labyrinthine maze of 42 U.S.C., for as counsel for EPA commendably recognized at oral argument, those statutory provisions speak in terms of "hazardous" (or "solid") waste.... In consequence, EPA's various arguments based on the statute itself are, upon analysis, circular, relying upon the term "solid waste" or "hazardous waste" to extend the reach of those very terms. This, all would surely agree, will not do.

Section 6935 addresses "used oil" collected by and utilized in the "oil recycling industry." Oil recyclers typically collect discarded used oils, distill them, and sell the resulting material for use as fuel in boilers. Regulation of those activities is likewise consistent with an every day reading of the term "discarded." It is only when EPA attempts to extend the scope of that provision to include the recycling of undiscarded oil at petroleum refineries that conflict occurs.

EPA has, however, advanced two arguments of potential merit based on specific RCRA provisions, and these therefore deserve our careful attention. First, EPA argues that § 6924(r)(2) of RCRA implicitly authorizes the agency to regulate recycled secondary materials. That subsection, we note at the outset, is highly specific; it exempts from a general labelling requirement fuels produced from petroleum refining waste containing oil if such materials (1) are "generated and reinserted on-site into the refining process" and (2) meet two other requirements, not relevant for our purposes.... It cannot go unnoticed that this subsection can be interpreted to come into play only where the material has become "hazardous waste" by being disposed of, and then is generated and reinserted on-site into the refining process. This interpretation, needless to say, would be singularly unhelpful to the agency's case, involving once more the now familiar problem of circularity of argument. EPA asserts, however, that the more natural reading of this provision is that materials generated and reinserted on-site into the refining process can be "hazardous waste," and are exempted from the otherwise applicable labelling requirement. The House Report explained in this regard:

> This provision provides a limited and conditional exemption from the labelling requirement for certain petroleum fuel refiners. Refineries often take oily refining wastes and reintroduce these wastes into the refining process where the oil component is incorporated into product [sic] and contaminants are removed. The committee does not believe that the refinery should automatically have to place a warning label on these fuels should EPA fail to exempt refineries from the labelling requirements within twelve months.

H.R. No. 198, 98th Cong., 2d Sess. at 43 (1984). Although we frankly agree that EPA's reading of this specific provision provides some support for its construction of RCRA's reach, it is, dispassionately viewed, of marginal force. For one thing, the provision has "no application to conventional fuels made by normal refining processes from recaptured hydrocarbon materials never intended to be discarded and never discarded." API's Reply Brief at 18–19. And, even more significantly, § 6924 itself is a provision defining "standards applicable to owners and operators of hazardous waste treatment, storage, and disposal facilities." This strongly suggests that the labelling subsection is directed at material which has indeed become hazardous waste, has reached a hazardous waste treatment facility, and is being recycled at that point.... Such a construction would, of course, render EPA's argument in this respect as circular as its other contentions.

Second, EPA argues that § 6924(q)(1) evinces Congressional intent to include recycled in-process materials within the definition of "solid waste." We note at the outset that this provision is likewise a subsection of § 6924 and is therefore directed towards hazardous waste treatment facilities. The ever-present circularity problem thus looms here as well. But that is not all. EPA's argument is deficient in other respects too. Section 6924(q)(1) commands the agency to promulgate standards applicable to persons who produce, market, distribute, or burn fuels produced from or otherwise containing hazardous waste.

The final sentence of that subparagraph states:

> For purposes of this subsection, the term "hazardous waste listed under section 6921 of this title" includes any commercial chemical product which is listed under section 6921 of this title and which, in lieu of its original intended use, is (i) produced for use as (or as a component of) a fuel, (ii) distributed for use as a fuel, or (iii) burned as a fuel.

Congress apparently added this language to override a then-existing EPA regulation which provided that unused commercial chemical products were solid wastes only when "discarded." 40 C.F.R. § 261.33 (1983). "Discarded" was at that time defined as abandoned (and not recycled) by being disposed, burned, or incinerated (but not burned for energy recovery). 40 C.F.R. § 261.2(c)(1983). As the House Report described the provision's scope:

> Hazardous waste, as used in this provision [6924(q)], includes not only wastes identified or listed as hazardous under EPA's regulations, but also includes any commercial chemical product (and related materials) listed pursuant to 40 C.F.R. § 261.33, which is not used for its original intended purpose but instead is burned or processed as fuel. (Under current EPA regulations, burning is not deemed to be a form of discard; hence listed commercial chemical products, unlike spent materials, by-products or sludges, are not deemed to be 'waste' when burned as fuel. They are only 'waste' when actually discarded or intended for discard.)

H.R. Rep. No. 198, 98th Cong., 1st Sess. 40.

We think it likely that in this provision Congress meant only to speak to the specific problem it identified—the burning of commercial chemicals as fuels, contrary to their original intended use. Congress addressed this problem by deeming the offending materials to be "discarded" and therefore within the statutory definition of "solid waste." This specific measure did not, however, revamp the basic definitional section of the statute. . . .

* * *

3

After this mind-numbing journey through RCRA, we return to the provision that is, after all, the one before us for examination. And that definitional section, we believe, indicates clear Congressional intent to limit EPA's authority. First, the definition of "solid waste" is situated in a section containing thirty-nine separate, defined terms. This is definitional specificity of the first order. The very care evidenced by Congress in defining RCRA's scope certainly suggests that Congress was concerned about delineating and thus cabining EPA's jurisdictional reach.

Second, the statutory definition of "solid waste" is quite specific. Although Congress well knows how to use broad terms and broad definitions, as for example, "waters of the United States" in Riverside Bayview, or in an altogether different setting, the term "intelligence source" in *CIA v. Sims*, 471 U.S. 159, 105 S.Ct. 1881, 85 L.Ed.2d 173 (1985), the definition here is carefully crafted with specificity. It contains three specific terms and then sets forth the broader term, "other discarded material." That definitional structure brings to mind a longstanding canon of statutory construction, ejusdem generis. Under that familiar canon, where general words follow the enumeration of particular classes of things, the general words are most naturally construed as applying only to things of the same general class as those enumerated. Lest the reader jump to unwarranted conclusions about an unwelcome renaissance of mechanical jurisprudence, we hasten to express our wariness of formalism and woodenness in the sensitive exercise of statutory construction. But, the precept of ejusdem generis contains more than a modicum of common sense and reason in the ascertainment of meaning. *See Department of State v. Washington Post Co.*, 456 U.S. 595, 600, 72 L.Ed.2d 358, 102 S.Ct. 1957 (1982)(specific terms are "benchmarks for measuring" the general term). Here, the three particular classes—garbage, refuse, and sludge from a water treatment plant, water supply treatment, or air pollution control facility—contain materials that clearly fit within the ordinary, everyday sense of "discarded." It is most sensible to conclude that Congress, in adding the concluding phrase "other discarded material," meant to grant EPA authority over similar types of waste, but not to open up the federal regulatory reach of an entirely new category of materials, i.e., materials neither disposed of nor abandoned, but passing in a continuous stream or flow from one production process to another. . . .

The term "disposal" means the discharge, deposit, injection, dumping, spilling, leaking, or placing of any solid waste or hazardous waste into or on any land or water so that such solid waste or hazardous waste or any constituent thereof may enter the environment or be emitted into the air or discharged into any waters, including ground waters.

42 U.S.C. § 6903(3). Far from indicating that Congress intended that the language used in its definitions be "functionally" interpreted, Congress' care and precision suggests that it intended to give the potentially vague terms that it was defining, such as "solid waste" and "disposal," specific content.

In sum, our analysis of the statute reveals clear Congressional intent to extend EPA's authority only to materials that are truly discarded, disposed of, thrown away, or abandoned. EPA nevertheless submits that the legislative history evinces a contrary intent. . . . Although we find RCRA's statutory language unambiguous, and can discern no exceptional circumstances warranting resort to its legislative history, we will nonetheless in an abundance of caution afford EPA the benefit of consideration of those secondary materials.

4

EPA points first to damage incidents cited by Congress in 1976 as justification for establishing a hazardous waste management system. *See* H.R. Rep. No. 1491, 94th Cong., 2d Sess. at 18, 22 (1976).... Neither of the incidents noted by EPA, however, involved commercial, in-process reuse or recycling activities. Instead, both incidents provide clear examples of waste disposal, which, of course, indisputably falls within EPA's jurisdiction conferred by RCRA.

EPA next asserts that the "most significant" aspect of the 1976 legislative history is the sense that Congress enacted broad grants of regulatory authority in order to " 'eliminate[] the last remaining loophole in environmental law.' " EPA Brief at 25–26 (quoting H.R. Rep. No. 1491, 94th Cong., 2d Sess. at 4). EPA, however, neglects to favor us with the entire sentence, and thereby misses the thrust of this passage. In pertinent part, the Report states as follows: "[The Committee] believes that the approach taken by this legislation eliminates the last remaining loophole in environmental law, that of unregulated land disposal of discarded materials and hazardous wastes." *Id.* ...

Wanting support for its position in the 1976 legislative history, EPA argues that the 1984 legislative history of RCRA amendments ratifies the agency's interpretation. The agency relies heavily on the following passage from the Report of the House Committee on Energy and Commerce, which states:

> This proposed section of the bill amends Section 6921 of RCRA to require the Administrator to issue regulations regarding use, reuse, recycling, and reclamation of hazardous wastes. This provision is intended to reaffirm the Agency's existing authority to regulate as [sic] hazardous waste to the extent it may be necessary to protect human health and the environment. The Committee affirms that RCRA already provides regulatory authority over these activities (which authority the Agency has exercised to a limited degree) and in this provision is amending to clarify that materials being used, reused, recycled, or reclaimed can indeed be solid and hazardous wastes and that these various recycling activities may constitute hazardous waste treatment, storage, or disposal.

H.R. Rep. No. 198, 98th Cong., 2d Sess. at 46 (1984).... This language is ambiguous at best. The Report refers to the agency's existing authority to regulate hazardous waste, ... which, as we saw before, renders EPA's argument circular. It is only in the context of "these activities"—regulation of "hazardous waste"—that the Report states that materials being used, reused, recycled, or reclaimed can be solid and hazardous wastes. Moreover, the Conference Report accompanying the bill enacted into law states: "The Conference substitute does not include the House provision on the use, reuse, recycling, and reclamation of hazardous waste. EPA has the authority to regulate such activities and an explicit mandate is not necessary." H.R. Conf. Rep. No. 1133, 98th Cong., 2d Sess. at 82 (1984).... Thus, with the exception of one passing phrase, which seems to us of limited probative value, ...EPA is unable to point to any portion of the legislative history which supports its expansive and counterintuitive interpretation of the pivotal term, "discarded." ...

We hasten to observe that even if the 1984 House or Conference Reports could reasonably be construed to support EPA's interpretation of its authority, they would be of limited value. "An assumption is not a law ... When uttered five years later it is mere commentary. Moreover, a committee is not the Congress. It cannot create a Congressional intent that did not exist, or amend a statute by a report." *Rogers v. Frito–Lay, Inc.*, 611 F.2d 1074, 1082 (5th Cir.1980), *cert. denied*, 449 U.S. 889, 101 S.Ct. 246, 66 L.Ed.2d 115 (1980). *Cf. Haig v. Agee*, 453 U.S. 280, 69 L.Ed.2d 640, 101 S.Ct. 2766 (1981)(Congressional acquiescence in long-standing executive interpretation indicates interpretation's validity); *Bob Jones Univ. v. United States*, 461 U.S. 574, 76 L.Ed.2d 157, 103 S.Ct. 2017 (1983).

To the contrary, a fair reading of the legislative history reveals intimations of an intent to regulate under RCRA only materials that have truly been discarded. Not only is the language of the legislative history fully consistent with the use of "discarded" in the sense of "disposed of," but it strains the language to read it otherwise. Most significantly in discussing its choice of the words "discarded materials" to define "solid waste," the House Committee stated:

> Not only solid wastes, but also liquid and contained gaseous wastes, semi-solid wastes and sludges are the subjects of this legislation. Waste itself is a misleading word in the context of the committee's activity. Much industrial and agricultural waste is reclaimed or put to new use and is therefore not a part of the discarded materials disposal problem the committee addresses.

H.R. Rep. No. 1491, 94th Cong., 2d Sess. at 2.... The Committee then went on to explain that "the term discarded materials is used to identify collectively those substances often referred to as industrial, municipal or post-consumer waste; refuse, trash, garbage, and sludge." *Id*..... Later in the Report, the Committee stated: "The overwhelming concern of the Committee, however, is the effect on the population and environment of the disposal of discarded hazardous wastes ... Unless neutralized or otherwise properly managed in their disposal, hazardous wastes present a clear danger ... " *Id.* at 3.... Throughout the Report, the Committee refers time and again to the problem motivating the enactment of RCRA as the disposal of waste.

In the Senate, a brief discussion took place as to the scope of the definition of "solid waste." In response to Senator Domenici's expression of concern that RCRA be aimed only at "the disposal of municipal and industrial wastes and not at the regulation of mining," Senator Randolph, the chairman of the Committee, unequivocally stated: "The bill definitely is directed at the disposal of municipal and industrial wastes."

122 Cong. Rec. 21,424 (1976).... To the extent this colloquy has probative value,.... it cuts squarely against expansive agency notions of the breadth of its jurisdictional reach.

After all is said and done, we are satisfied that the legislative history, rather than evincing Congress' intent to define "discarded" to include in-process secondary materials employed in an ongoing manufacturing process, confirms that the term was employed by the Article I branch in its ordinary, every day sense....

Here, in contrast, a literalistic reading of the statutory language would not lead to nonsensical results; indeed, the traditional meaning of "discarded"—disposed of—comports with Congress' statutorily defined purpose. *See supra* text at 16–20. In addition, the legislative history, as we have just detailed, contains clear indications of Congressional intent to cabin EPA's regulatory jurisdiction to materials that have been disposed of or abandoned. And, in light of the inconsistency of EPA's regulatory approach, this is not a case in which we can infer Congressional acquiescence in the agency's interpretation. Cf. also Riverside Bayview, 106 S.Ct. at 464–65 (administrative construction brought to Congress' attention through legislation specifically designed to supplant it); *Haig v. Agee*, 453 U.S. at 300 (Congress acquiesced in long-standing agency interpretation).

IV

We are constrained to conclude that, in light of the language and structure of RCRA, the problems animating Congress to enact it, and the relevant portions of the legislative history, Congress clearly and unambiguously expressed its intent that "solid waste" (and therefore EPA's regulatory authority) be limited to materials that are "discarded" by virtue of being disposed of, abandoned, or thrown away.... While we do not lightly overturn an agency's reading of its own statute, we are persuaded that by regulating in-process secondary materials, EPA has acted in contravention of Congress' intent.... Accordingly, the petition for review is

Granted.

* * *

MIKVA, CIRCUIT JUDGE, dissenting: The court today strains to overturn the Environmental Protection Agency's interpretation of the Resource Conservation and Recovery Act to authorize the regulation of certain recycled industrial materials. Under today's decision, the EPA is prohibited from regulating in-process secondary materials that contribute to the ominous problem that Congress sought to eradicate by passing the RCRA. In my opinion, the EPA has adequately demonstrated that its interpretation is a reasonable construction of an ambiguous term in a statute committed to the agency's administration. We therefore are obliged to defer to the agency's interpretation under the principles of *Chevron U.S.A., Inc., v. NRDC*, 467 U.S. 837, 81 L.Ed.2d 694, 104 S.Ct.

2778 (1984), and *INS v. Cardoza–Fonseca*, 480 U.S. 421, 107 S.Ct. 1207, 94 L.Ed.2d 434 (1987). I dissent.

Notes

1. Activities/Persons Subject to RCRA Regulation. Once a solid waste is listed under RCRA or is classified as a hazardous waste, the *generation, transportation*, and the *treatment, storage, and disposal* of that waste are then pervasively regulated. *See* 40 C.F.R. Parts 262–270 (1990). Every person who generates or transports hazardous wastes or who owns or operates a treatment, storage, or disposal facility (TSD facility), must notify EPA (and the state agency if the state has implemented a state program) of his hazardous waste activities and obtain an identification number.

2. Generators. A generator's first duty is to determine whether the waste he handles is classified as a hazardous waste. If the waste is hazardous, generators must obtain an EPA identification number and maintain records on the waste generated. There are also labelling and storage requirements, and generators must report each offsite shipment of hazardous waste to the government via a nationwide manifest system involving a series of documents in which they must specify the generator, the transporter, and the permitted treatment, storage, or disposal facility for which the waste is bound. Moreover, generators must use only transporters and TSD facilities that have an EPA identification number and are regulated under RCRA. *See* 40 C.F.R. § 262 (1990).

3. Transporters. Under RCRA, those who transport hazardous waste must obtain an EPA identification number before transporting any hazardous waste, and must document the amount, type, and delivery of the wastes to the permitted disposal facility. A transporter may only accept hazardous waste that is accompanied by a manifest signed by the generator, and must (1) sign the manifest himself and return a copy to the generator before leaving the generator's property, (2) keep the manifest with the hazardous waste at all times, (3) deliver the waste according to the instructions on the manifest, (4) date the manifest and obtain the signature of the TSD facility owner or operator (or next transporter), (5) retain a copy of the manifest for three years, and (6) give the remaining copies to the person receiving the waste. *See* 42 U.S.C.A. § 6923(a); 40 C.F.R. § 263.10 *et seq.* (1990). In addition, transporters must comply with all Department of Transportation (DOT) regulations under the Hazardous Materials Transportation Act, 49 C.F.R. Parts 171–179.

4. Treatment, Storage, and Disposal (TSD) Facilities. Those engaged in the treatment, storage, or disposal of the waste also are subject to regulatory standards. *See* 40 C.F.R. §§ 264–267 (1990). Permits are required for TSD facilities. *See* 42 U.S.C.A. § 6925. The standards that must be met by new and existing facilities to obtain permits are rigorous. Although the regulatory requirements chiefly include performance standards and statutory minimum technology standards for various types of facilities, there are also standards relating to such things as design, location, construction, operation, maintenance, insurance, and financial requirements for TSD facilities. *See* 42 U.S.C.A. § 6924.

This system was backfitted on to existing, as well as new, TSD storage facilities, and the regulatory technique used to do that was to bring all existing facilities under a temporary regulatory scheme (giving them what is called "interim status") pending application for and ultimate issuance of final licenses for existing sources. *See* 42 U.S.C.A. § 6925(e). This technique recognizes the difficulties involved in instantaneously imposing a new legal system on existing sources where permits are to be required, since it takes time to issue those permits.

In addition to the permit and regulatory requirements for TSD facilities, persons who treat, store, or dispose of hazardous wastes also are subject to the manifest system as they receive wastes and must send copies of the manifests to the generator to verify receipt of the waste.

5. Solid Waste Permit Requirements. Although RCRA imposes no requirements for permits upon those who transport or dispose of solid waste that is not hazardous, many states require a permit to operate a solid waste management facility.

6. Hazardous Waste Permits. Permits are required for facilities that treat, store, or dispose of hazardous waste. 42 U.S.C.A. § 6925. Facilities that were in existence on November 19, 1980, filed for a permit in accordance with an established schedule, *see* 40 C.F.R. § 270.73 (1990), and satisfy other conditions, are deemed to have permits and can continue to operate until the state authority issues or denies a permit. All other existing facilities must close until a permit is obtained. New facilities must obtain permits prior to commencement of construction. *See* 40 C.F.R. Part 270 (1990). The standards that existing and new facilities must meet to obtain permits are rigorous, and include requirements relating to training, security, design, testing, emergency planning, closure and post-closure care, financial responsibility, and compliance with the manifest system. 40 C.F.R. Parts 264, 265 (1990).

Generators who store hazardous waste on the site 90 days or more must have a permit to store hazardous waste. 40 C.F.R. § 262.34 (1990). Transporters of hazardous waste often must obtain permits under state, but not federal law.

CONNECTICUT COASTAL FISHERMEN'S ASSN. v. REMINGTON ARMS CO.
989 F.2d 1305 (2d Cir.1993).

CARDAMONE, CIRCUIT JUDGE:

Critical on this appeal is the meaning of the terms "solid waste" and "hazardous waste," as these terms are defined in the Solid Waste Disposal Act, 42 U.S.C. §§ 6901–6992 (1988), as amended by the Resource Conservation and Recovery Act of 1976 (RCRA), Pub. L. No. 94–580, 90 Stat. 2795 (1976), and the Hazardous and Solid Waste Amendments of 1984, Pub. L. No. 98–616, 98 Stat. 3221 (1984). Defining what Congress intended by these words is not child's play, even though RCRA has an "Alice in Wonderland" air about it. We say that because a careful perusal of RCRA and its regulations reveals that "solid waste" plainly means one thing in one part of RCRA and something entirely different in another part of the same statute.

"When I use a word," Humpty Dumpty said in a rather scornful tone, "it means just what I choose it to mean—neither more nor less."

"The question is," said Alice, "whether you can make words mean so many different things."

"The question is," said Humpty Dumpty, "which is to be master— that's all."

Lewis Carroll, *Through the Looking–Glass* ch. 6 at 106–09 (Schocken Books 1987)(1872). Congress, of course, is the master and in the discussion that follows, we undertake to discover what meaning Congress intended in its use of the words solid and hazardous waste.

Remington Arms Co., Inc. (Remington or appellant) has owned and operated a trap and skeet shooting club—originally organized in the 1920s—on Lordship Point in Stratford, Connecticut since 1945. Trap and skeet targets are made of clay, and the shotguns used to knock these targets down are loaded with lead shot. The Lordship Point Gun Club (the Gun Club) was open to the public and it annually served 40,000 patrons. After nearly 70 years of use, close to 2,400 tons of lead shot (5 million pounds) and 11 million pounds of clay target fragments were deposited on land around the club and in the adjacent waters of Long Island Sound. Directly to the north of Lordship Point lies a Connecticut state wildlife refuge at Nells Island Marsh, a critical habitat for one of the state's largest populations of Black Duck. The waters and shore near the Gun Club feed numerous species of waterfowl and shorebirds.

Plaintiff, Connecticut Coastal Fishermen's Association (Coastal Fishermen or plaintiff) brought suit against defendant Remington alleging that the lead shot and clay targets are hazardous wastes under RCRA and pollutants under the Clean Water Act (Act), 33 U.S.C. §§ 1251–1387 (1988 & Supp. II 1990). Remington has never obtained a permit under § 3005 of RCRA for the storage and disposal of hazardous wastes, 42 U.S.C. § 6925, or a National Pollutant Discharge Elimination System (pollution discharge) permit pursuant to § 402 of the Clean Water Act, 33 U.S.C. § 1342. Plaintiff insists that Remington must now clean up the lead shot and clay fragments it permitted to be scattered on the land and in the sea at Lordship Point. Because the debris constitutes an imminent and substantial endangerment to health and the environment under RCRA, we agree.

* * *

Turning now to Remington's appeal from the district court's RCRA ruling, plaintiff asserts that Remington has been operating an unpermitted facility for the treatment, storage or disposal of hazardous wastes in violation of 42 U.S.C. § 6925 (a citizens suit claim under § 6972(a)(1)(A)) and has created an "imminent and substantial endangerment" to human health and the environment under § 6972(a)(1)(B).

The district court did not distinguish between these causes of action in granting plaintiff summary judgment. Remington, as noted, never obtained a RCRA permit for the operation of its Gun Club facility, but contends that because lead shot and clay target debris are not "solid wastes"—and hence cannot be "hazardous wastes" regulated by RCRA—it is not subject to a permit requirement. In essence, Remington contends that RCRA does not apply to the Gun Club because any disposal of waste that occurred there was merely incidental to the normal use of a product.

RCRA establishes a "cradle-to-grave" regulatory structure for the treatment, storage and disposal of solid and hazardous wastes. Solid wastes are regulated under Subchapter IV §§ 6941–49a; hazardous wastes are subject to the more stringent standards of Subchapter III §§ 6921–39b. *See B.F. Goodrich Co. v. Murtha*, 958 F.2d 1192, 1201 (2d Cir.1992). Under RCRA "hazardous wastes" are a subset of "solid wastes." *See* 42 U.S.C. § 6903 (5). Accordingly, for a waste to be classified as hazardous, it must first qualify as a solid waste under RCRA. *See United Technologies Corp. v. EPA*, 261 U.S.App.D.C. 226, 821 F.2d 714, 716 n. 1 (D.C.Cir.1987). We direct our attention initially therefore to whether the lead shot and clay targets are solid waste.

* * *

The RCRA regulations create a dichotomy in the definition of solid waste. The EPA distinguishes between RCRA's regulatory and remedial purposes and offers a different definition of solid waste depending upon the statutory context in which the term appears. In its amicus brief, the EPA tells us that the regulatory definition of solid waste—found at 40 C.F.R. § 261.2(a)—is narrower than its statutory counterpart. The regulations define solid waste as "any discarded material" and further define discarded material as that which is "abandoned." 40 C.F.R. § 261.2(a). Materials that are abandoned have been "disposed of." 40 C.F.R. § 261.2(b). According to RCRA regulations, this definition of solid waste "applies only to wastes that also are hazardous for purposes of the regulations implementing Subtitle C of RCRA." 40 C.F.R. § 261.1(b)(1). As previously noted, Subtitle C [Subchapter III] contains more stringent handling standards for hazardous waste, and hazardous waste is a subset of solid waste.

The regulations further state that the statutory definition of solid waste, found at 42 U.S.C. § 6903(27), applies to "imminent hazard" lawsuits brought by the United States under § 7003, 42 U.S.C. § 6973. *See* 40 C.F.R. § 261.1(b)(2)(ii). This statement recognizes the special nature of the imminent hazard lawsuit under RCRA. Currently, RCRA authorizes two kinds of citizen suits. The first, under § 7002(a)(1)(A), 42 U.S.C. § 6972(a)(1)(A), enables private citizens to enforce the EPA's hazardous waste regulations and—according to 40 C.F.R. § 261.1(b)(1)—invokes the narrow regulatory definition of solid waste. The second type of citizen suit, under § 7002(a)(1)(B), 42 U.S.C. § 6972(a)(1)(B), authorizes citizens to sue to abate an "imminent and substantial endangerment to health or the environment." While the regulations do not specifically mention this second category of citizen suit, regulatory language referring to § 7003 must also apply to § 7002(a)(1)(B) because the two provisions are nearly identical. *Comite Pro Rescate de la Salud v. Puerto Rico Aqueduct and Sewer Auth.*, 888 F.2d 180, 187 (1st Cir.1989), *cert. denied*, 494 U.S. 1029, 108 L.Ed.2d 613, 110 S.Ct. 1476 (1990). Consequently, the broader statutory definition of solid waste applies to citizen suits brought to abate imminent hazard to health or the environment.

We recognize the anomaly of using different definitions for the term "solid waste" and that such view further complicates an already complex statute. Yet, we believe on balance that the EPA regulations reasonably interpret the statutory language. Hence, we defer to them. Dual definitions of solid waste are suggested by the structure and language of RCRA. Congress in Subchapter III isolated hazardous wastes for more stringent regulatory treatment. Recognizing the serious responsibility that such regulations impose, Congress required that hazardous waste—a subset of solid waste as defined in the RCRA regulations—be clearly identified. The statute directs the EPA to develop specific "criteria" for the identification of hazardous wastes as well as to publish a list of particular hazardous wastes. 42 U.S.C. § 6921 (a) & (b). By way of contrast, Subchapter IV that empowers the EPA to publish "guidelines" for the identification of problem solid waste pollution areas, does not require explanation beyond RCRA's statutory definition of what constitutes solid waste. *id.* § 6942(a). Hence, the words of the statute contemplate that the EPA would refine and narrow the definition of solid waste for the sole purpose of Subchapter III regulation and enforcement.

C. Regulatory Definition of Solid Waste

The EPA, as amicus, concludes that the lead shot and clay targets discharged by patrons of Remington's Gun Club do not fall within the narrow regulatory definition of solid waste. Again, this issue is one we need not resolve because plaintiff has failed to allege a valid claim, brought under the § 7002(a)(1)(A) citizen suit provision, that Remington violated § 6925 of RCRA.

Plaintiff first alleges that Remington is operating a hazardous waste disposal facility without a permit, in violation of § 6925. This claim alleges a "wholly past" RCRA violation and is dismissed under Gwaltney. The Supreme Court acknowledged that the language in the citizen suit provisions of the Clean Water Act and § 7002(a)(1)(A) of RCRA is identical, yielding the same requirement that plaintiff allege an ongoing or intermittent violation of the relevant statute. *Gwaltney*, 484 U.S. at 57 & n.2; *see also Ascon Properties, Inc. v. Mobil Oil Co.*, 866 F.2d 1149, 1159 (9th Cir.1989)(applying requirement of ongoing or intermittent violation to citizen suit brought under § 7002(a)(1)(A)). Because we find no valid allegation of a present violation with respect to Coastal Fishermen's Clean Water Act suit, we must reach the same result with respect to its first claim under § 7002(a)(1)(A) of RCRA.

Second, plaintiff alleges that Remington owns or is operating a hazardous waste storage facility without a permit in violation of § 6925. Because plaintiff's alleged "violation" would continue as long as the lead shot and clay targets are "stored" in the waters of Long Island Sound, Gwaltney does not bar this claim. But RCRA and its regulations do. RCRA defines "storage" as "the containment of hazardous waste, either on a temporary basis or for a period of years, in such a manner as not to constitute disposal of such hazardous waste." § 6903(33). Neither the statute nor its accompanying regulations define "containment," but "storage" is further defined in the regulations as "the holding of hazardous waste for a temporary period, at the end of which the hazardous waste is treated, disposed of, or stored elsewhere." 40 C.F.R. § 260.10 (1992). The lead shot and clay targets now scattered in the waters of Long Island Sound at no time have been contained or held.

Moreover, the very essence of Coastal Fishermen's complaint is that Remington left the debris in the sound with no intention of taking additional action. Hence, the alleged storage of the waste logically may not be an interim measure as the regulations require. Coastal Fishermen therefore failed to state a valid claim that Remington owns or operates a hazardous waste storage facility or that it violated § 7002(a)(1)(A). Because only such a violation would trigger application of the regulatory definition of solid waste, it is unnecessary to decide whether the lead shot and clay targets fall within RCRA's regulatory scope.

D. STATUTORY DEFINITION OF SOLID WASTE

Coastal Fishermen's allegation that the lead shot and clay target debris in Long Island Sound creates an "imminent and substantial endangerment" under § 7002(a)(1)(B) of RCRA need not meet the present violation hurdle. *See Gwaltney*, 484 U.S. at 57 n.2; *Ascon*, 866 F.2d at 1159. An imminent hazard citizen suit will lie against any "past or present" RCRA offender "who has contributed or who is contributing" to "past or present" solid waste handling practices that "may present an imminent and substantial endangerment to health or the environment." 42 U.S.C. § 6972(a)(1)(B). Therefore, under an imminent hazard citizen suit, the endangerment must be ongoing, but the conduct that created the endangerment need not be.

As already noted, RCRA regulations apply the broader statutory definition of solid waste to imminent hazard suits. The statutory definition contains the concept of "discarded material," 42 U.S.C. § 6903(27), but it does not contain the terms "abandoned" or "disposed of" as required by the regulatory definition. 40 C.F.R. §§ 261.2(a)(2), (b)(1). Amicus interprets the statutory definition of solid waste as encompassing the lead shot and clay targets at Lordship Point because they are "discarded." Specifically, the EPA states that the materials are discarded because they have been "left to accumulate long after they have served their intended purpose." Without deciding how long materials must accumulate before they become discarded—that is, when the shot is fired or at some later time—we agree that the lead shot and clay targets in

Long Island Sound have accumulated long enough to be considered solid waste. Compare AMC I, 824 F.2d at 1185–86 (in-process secondary materials destined for immediate reuse as part of ongoing production process are not subject to RCRA because not discarded) with *American Petroleum Inst. v. EPA*, 285 U.S.App.D.C. 35, 906 F.2d 729, 741 (D.C.Cir. 1990)(per curiam) (distinguishing AMC I on grounds that once product is "indisputably 'discarded'," it has become part of waste disposal problem and may be regulated under RCRA) and *American Mining Congress v. EPA*, 285 U.S.App.D.C. 173, 907 F.2d 1179, 1186–87 (D.C.Cir.1990)(AMC II)(same; deferring to the EPA's focus on potential environmental harm in determining whether material is discarded).

E. HAZARDOUS WASTE

Having resolved that the lead shot and clay targets are discarded solid waste, we next analyze whether they are hazardous waste. RCRA defines "hazardous waste" as

> a solid waste, or combination of solid wastes, which because of its quantity, concentration, or physical, chemical, or infectious characteristics may—

> * * *

> (B) pose a substantial present or potential hazard to human health or the environment when improperly treated, stored, transported, or disposed of, or otherwise managed.

42 U.S.C. § 6903 (5)(B).

Certain wastes have been listed by the EPA as hazardous pursuant to 40 C.F.R. § 261.30. Alternatively, a waste is considered hazardous if it exhibits any of the characteristics identified in 40 C.F.R. §§ 261.20 through 261.24: ignitability, *corrosivity*, *reactivity*, or toxicity. The district court granted summary judgment in favor of plaintiff on the issue of whether the lead shot qualified as a hazardous waste, but at the same time stated there were genuine issues of material fact as to whether the clay targets were hazardous waste. 777 F.Supp. at 194–95. Remington objects to both rulings.

1. Lead Shot

The district court concluded that the lead shot was hazardous waste as a matter of law because it satisfied the requirements of 40 C.F.R. § 261.24 for toxicity. *See* 777 F.Supp. at 194. That regulation provides that a solid waste is toxic, and therefore hazardous if, using appropriate testing methods, an "extract from a representative sample of the waste contains any of the contaminants listed ... at the concentration equal to or greater than" that specified. 40 C.F.R. § 261.24(a). For lead, the concentration threshold is 5.0 mg/L. *id.* table 1.

* * *

2. Clay Targets

Remington declares the clay targets cannot be hazardous waste merely because they contain hazardous wastes listed in 40 C.F.R. § 261.33(f). Regardless of whether this assertion properly interprets 40 C.F.R. § 261.33(d)(comment), it is irrelevant. The district court did not decide that there was a genuine issue as to whether the clay targets were hazardous because it was not yet determined whether they contain hazardous wastes listed in 40 C.F.R. § 261.33(f). Rather, it ruled this issue remained undecided because the appropriate tests to determine toxicity under 40 C.F.R. § 261.24 had not yet been completed. 777 F.Supp. at 195.

* * *

.... the judgment of the district court is affirmed, in part, and reversed, in part.

Note

Almost every state in America currently has a state program that has received final approval. Authorized states are required to go through the approval process again before they can administer any of the 1984 amendments. Until approval is obtained by a state, EPA is authorized to administer the 1984 amendments and issue permits containing new provisions required by the amendments in that state.

§ 5.2 LIABILITY FOR "IMMINENT HAZARDS"

One of the most powerful means for redressing past dumping of hazardous waste is the "imminent hazard" provision of RCRA, which authorizes EPA to bring suit for injunctive relief against any person who has contributed, or is contributing, to the past or present handling, storage, treatment, transportation, or disposal of solid or hazardous waste that may present an "imminent and substantial endangerment to health or the environment." Such persons may either be restrained from the activities causing the imminent and substantial endangerment or be ordered to take other action that may be necessary to deal with the problems, including, among other things, reimbursement of funds expended by EPA in connection with the site, site cleanup, and restoration of groundwater and other contaminated resources. This can result in millions of dollars of liability, since the cost of cleaning up a hazardous waste site is considerable. Liability of subsequent landowners is limited, however, to situations where they "could not reasonably be expected to have actual knowledge of the presence of hazardous waste at such facility or site and of its potential for release." RCRA § 3013(b), 42 U.S.C. § 6934(b).

In *United States v. Price*, 523 F.Supp. 1055, 1069–1074 (D.N.J.1981), *aff'd*, 688 F.2d 204 (3d Cir.1982), both the present owners of a dormant landfill and the sellers who owned and managed the landfill when it was in operation were held liable under RCRA to remedy the hazards posed by chemical dumping that occurred while the landfill was in operation.

The sellers were held liable because they had allowed the waste to be dumped on the site. The buyers were held liable, even though the seller had not informed the buyers of the hazardous waste disposal, because they "contribut[ed] to the disposal (i.e. leaking) of wastes merely by virtue of their studied indifference to the hazardous condition" that existed. *id.* at 1073. The court noted, however, that (1) the purchaser was a sophisticated real estate developer who "had a duty to investigate the actual conditions that existed on the property or take it as it was," (2) the purchase price reflected the fact that the property had been used as a landfill, and (3) the owners failed to abate the hazardous conditions on the land even after learning of them.

In addition to enforcement by EPA, RCRA authorizes citizens to bring suits against persons who violate any RCRA permit, regulation, or provision, or whose past or present handling, storage, treatment, transportation, or disposal of hazardous waste may present an "imminent and substantial endangerment to health or the environment." Citizens are required, however, to provide notice (60 days for suits alleging violations and 90 days for suits alleging imminent and substantial endangerment) to EPA, the state involved, and the offender before filing suit. Citizen suits are also authorized against EPA for failure to perform its duties.

§ 5.3   THE FEDERAL HAZARDOUS WASTE PROGRAM

This section reviews the principal elements of the federal hazardous waste program (often referred to as the *RCRA Subtitle C* program) which establishes minimum national standards for the generation, transportation, treatment, storage and disposal of hazardous waste. The program generally is implemented through individual state programs under federal EPA oversight, although not all states are authorized to enforce the Subtitle C program. Thus, as applied to individual states, many references in this chapter to the federal EPA would apply to a state enforcement agency.

Most states (whether authorized to enforce RCRA or not) supplement the federal program with additional, often more stringent, requirements for hazardous waste management. Accordingly, individual waste generators and handlers must consult applicable state statutes and regulations to identify the particular requirements to which they are subject.

One component of the hazardous waste program has a nearly universal application to American business: the hazardous waste identification rules (subsections A–B). Each business operator must consult these rules to determine if any of the waste streams generated or otherwise managed by his/her business constitute *hazardous waste*. If they do, the operator must identify and comply with the particular management standards applicable to those waste streams (subsection C).

1.   *Overview of Hazardous Waste Identification*

In essence, the hazardous waste identification rules separate the universe of waste into three discrete categories: (1) *hazardous waste,* which is regulated under Subtitle C of RCRA, (2) *non-hazardous solid waste*, which is regulated under Subtitle D of RCRA and a variety of state and local laws, and (3) material which is regulated (if at all) under non-RCRA programs, such as the Clean Water Act. The application of these rules to a particular waste stream is called a *hazardous waste determination*. Virtually *all* generators of waste in any form (even businesses as seemingly innocuous as retail stores and professional offices) must apply the hazardous waste identification rules to determine which of the three above-referenced categories their discrete waste streams fall within.

As a prelude to the discussion of hazardous waste identification, we note the special (and often confusing) significance of the term *solid waste*. In practice, many persons use *solid waste* to refer to *non-hazardous solid waste*, which normally is managed in municipal landfills and incinerators. In actuality, the term *solid waste* includes both *hazardous waste* and *non-hazardous solid waste*. As a result, wherever the hazardous waste identification rules exclude a substance from the definition of *solid waste*, that substance also is excluded from regulation as a *hazardous waste* and instead is regulated (if at all) under other environmental programs.

2. *The Step–by–Step Process of Identifying Hazardous Waste*

Hazardous Waste is any material that (1) satisfies the definition of a *solid waste*, (2) is *listed* as a hazardous waste by EPA, or exhibits one of four *characteristics* of hazardous waste, and (3) is not otherwise excluded from regulation under the RCRA Subtitle C program by the RCRA rules or by a site-specific determination. The hazardous waste identification process, which is required of all waste generators, includes an assessment of each discrete waste stream in light of these three elements.

Definition of Solid Waste. A generator first must determine if his/her waste stream constitutes a *solid waste*. Under RCRA, a *solid waste* is any *discarded* material that is not excluded from regulation by rule or variance.

Discarded Materials. A material is *discarded* if it is *abandoned, recycled,* or *inherently waste-like*. A material is *abandoned* if it is disposed of, burned or incinerated, or if it is accumulated, stored or treated before or in lieu of being disposed of, burned or incinerated. Virtually any discharge, deposit, injection, dumping, spilling, leaking, or placing of any material onto the land or into any groundwater or surface water body (whether intended or not) constitutes *disposal* and thereby generates a solid waste by virtue of *abandonment*.

The act of leaving a raw industrial material at an inactive manufacturing facility for more than 90 days also constitutes *abandonment*.

A material is *recycled* if it is used in a manner constituting disposal, burned for energy recovery, reclaimed or *accumulated speculatively* (*i.e.,* with the hope of selling it as a product or co-product, rather than managing it as a waste).

A material is *inherently waste-like* if it is designated as such by EPA. Generally, EPA will designate a material as inherently waste-like if it is normally disposed of, burned or incinerated, or contains certain toxic constituents, and EPA determines that the material poses a threat to human health or the environment when recycled.

Substances Which are Excluded from the Definition of Solid Waste. The RCRA statute and rule allow for certain substances to be excluded from the definition of *solid waste*, either categorically or on a case- and site-specific basis. Because the term *solid waste* includes both *hazardous waste* and *non-hazardous solid waste*, any substance excluded from the definition of *solid waste* also is excluded from regulation as a *hazardous waste* and instead is regulated (if at all) under other environmental programs. The most significant solid waste exclusions are summarized below.

Categorical Exclusions. The RCRA statute and rules exclude certain categories of materials from the definition of *solid waste* (and thereby exempt these substances from regulation as *hazardous wastes*). Examples of such exempted materials include (1) domestic sewage and other wastes handled by publicly owned treatment works (*POTWs*); (2) effluent discharges which are subject to NPDES discharge permits under the Clean Water Act; and (3) secondary materials which are reclaimed and returned to the original process in which they were generated (with certain restrictions).

Further, the RCRA program generally does not regulate as *solid waste* stored or transported raw (*i.e.*, unused) materials or chemicals, unless they are left unused or otherwise treated in a manner that causes them to be deemed *abandoned*.

Case-Specific Exemptions for Recyclable Materials. The RCRA rules provide a mechanism (called a *variance*) for removing *recyclable materials* from the RCRA program following the initial reclamation process. To obtain the variance, the generator or processor must be able to demonstrate that the initial reclamation process is so substantial that the resulting materials are more commodity-like than waste-like even though they are not yet commercial end products and have to be reclaimed further. Once the variance is obtained, the generator and processor could handle the material free from RCRA requirements, although any wastes generated from the further processing of the material would be subject to new hazardous waste determination.

Solid Wastes Which are Hazardous Wastes. A *solid waste* is also a *hazardous waste* if (1) it satisfies any of the following three conditions: (i) it is *listed* as a hazardous waste by EPA, (ii) it exhibits any one of four *characteristics* of hazardous waste (ignitability, *corrosivity*, *reactivity* and toxicity), or (iii) it is *mixed with*, *derived-from* or *contains* certain hazardous wastes; and (2) is not otherwise excluded from the regulation as a *solid waste* or *hazardous waste*. Further, certain materials that are mixed with, contained in or derived from the treatment of certain hazardous wastes also are regulated as hazardous wastes. The following table illustrates the types of solid wastes which are considered hazardous wastes:

Waste that Exhibits a Hazardous Characteristic	Wastes Specifically Listed as Hazardous	Wastes Mixed with a Listed Waste	Wastes "Derived From" a Listed Waste
Ignitability (I) 40 C.F.R. § 261.23	Hazardous from Nonspecific Sources (F) 40 C.F.R. § 261.31	EPA's Mixture Rule See 57 Fed. Reg. 7628 (1992).	EPA's "Derived-From" Rule See 57 Fed. Reg. 7628 (1992).
Corrosivity (C) 40 C.F.R. § 261.21	Hazardous from Specific Sources (K) 40 C.F.R. § 261.32		
Reactivity (R) 40 C.F.R. § 261.22	Acutely Hazardous Chemical Products (P) 40 C.F.R. § 261.33		
Toxicity (T) 40 C.F.R. § 261.24	Non-acutely Hazardous Chemical Products (U) 40 C.F.R. § 261.33(f)		

Listed Hazardous Wastes. EPA lists specific waste streams and waste constituents as *hazardous wastes* at sections 261.30–33 of the RCRA rules, wherein each substance is assigned a Hazardous Waste Number based on its source. Hazardous wastes from *specific sources*, such as bottom sediment sludge from the treatment of wood preserving wastewaters, are given a waste number starting with a "K", *e.g., K114.* Hazardous wastes from *non-specific sources*, such as spent degreasing solvents, are given identification numbers starting with an "F", *e.g., F001.*

AMERICAN PETROLEUM INST. v. UNITED STATES EPA

906 F.2d 729 (D.C.Cir.1990).

PER CURIAM.

These consolidated petitions for review challenge various aspects of a final Environmental Protection Agency ("EPA" or "agency") rule promulgated under the authority of the Resource Conservation and Recovery Act of 1976 ("RCRA") § 3004, 42 U.S.C. § 6924. The rule sets out land disposal prohibitions and treatment standards for "First–Third" scheduled wastes ("First–Third Rule"), 53 Fed.Reg. 31,138 (Aug. 17, 1988). . . .

The American Petroleum Institute, the American Iron and Steel Institute, the Chemical Manufacturers Association and the National Association of Metal Finishers (collectively "Industry Petitioners") challenge EPA's conclusion that the RCRA precludes the agency from considering land treatment, in conjunction with pretreatment, as an authorized method of treating hazardous wastes. Industry Petitioners also challenge EPA's abandonment of comparative risk analysis as a means of determining authorized treatment standards for hazardous wastes, claiming that the agency did not provide adequate reasons for abandoning this type of risk assessment.

The Natural Resources Defense Council, Chemical Waste Management, Inc. and the Hazardous Waste Treatment Council (collectively "NRDC") challenge the part of the First–Third Rule that establishes treatment standards for K061 hazardous waste. NRDC claims that EPA has unlawfully exempted the slag residues that result from the "treatment" of K061 in zinc smelters from the RCRA's restrictions on land disposal of hazardous wastes.

We agree with EPA that the RCRA does preclude land treatment in conjunction with pretreatment as a method of treating hazardous wastes. Additionally, we find that EPA provided adequate reasons for abandoning comparative risk analysis. However, because we find that EPA unlawfully exempted the residue produced from smelting K061 waste from the RCRA's restrictions on land disposal of hazardous wastes, we vacate that portion of the rule and remand to the agency for further rulemaking consistent with this opinion.

I. BACKGROUND

A. *Overview*

Subtitle C of the RCRA establishes "a 'cradle to grave' regulatory structure overseeing the safe treatment, storage and disposal of hazardous waste." *United Technologies Corp. v. EPA*, 261 U.S.App.D.C. 226, 821 F.2d 714, 716 (D.C.Cir.1987). Section 3001 of the RCRA, 42 U.S.C. § 6921, directs EPA to promulgate criteria for identifying the characteristics of hazardous waste, and for listing hazardous waste. In accordance with this directive, EPA has adopted a two-part definition of hazardous waste.

First, EPA has published several lists of specific hazardous wastes ("listed wastes") in which EPA has described the wastes and assigned a "waste code" to each one. 40 C.F.R. § 261, Subpart D. Second, EPA has identified four characteristics of hazardous wastes: ignitability, *corrosivity, reactivity* and extraction procedure toxicity. *See* 40 C.F.R. § 261.20–.24. Any solid waste exhibiting one or more of these characteristics is automatically deemed a "hazardous waste" subject to regulation under Subtitle C of the RCRA even if it is not a "listed" waste. *See Hazardous Waste Treatment Council v. EPA*, 274 U.S.App.D.C. 37, 861 F.2d 270, 271 (D.C.Cir.1988).

Once a waste is listed or identified as hazardous, its subsequent management is regulated. Treatment, storage and disposal of a hazardous waste normally can be undertaken only pursuant to a permit that specifies the conditions under which the waste will be managed. 42 U.S.C. §§ 6922–6925.

In the 1984 amendments to the RCRA, Congress shifted the focus of hazardous waste management away from land disposal to treatment alternatives, determining that:

> [Certain] classes of land disposal facilities are not capable of assuring long-term containment of certain hazardous wastes, and to avoid substantial risk to human health and the environment, reliance on land disposal should be minimized or eliminated.... [Land] disposal ... should be the least favored method for managing hazardous wastes.

42 U.S.C. § 6901(b)(7). Consistent with this finding, Subtitle C of the RCRA now prohibits hazardous wastes from being disposed of on the land unless one of two conditions is satisfied: (1) the Administrator of EPA determines, "to a reasonable degree of certainty, that there will be no migration of hazardous constituents from the disposal unit or injection zone for as long as the wastes remain hazardous." 42 U.S.C. § 6924(d), (e), (g), (m); or (2) the waste is treated to meet standards established by EPA pursuant to 42 U.S.C. § 6924(m). Section 6924(m)(1), which sets forth treatment requirements, provides:

> the Administrator shall, after notice and opportunity for hearings ..., promulgate regulations specifying those levels or methods of treatment, if any, which substantially diminish the toxicity of the waste or substantially reduce the likelihood of migration of hazardous constituents from the waste so that short-term and long-term threats to human health and the environment are minimized.

42 U.S.C. § 6924(m)(1).

To satisfy this directive, EPA required that the hazardous wastes subject to the standards be treated to levels that are achievable by performance of the "best demonstrated available technology" ("BDAT") or be treated by methods that constitute BDAT. *See* 51 Fed. Reg. 40,572, 40,578 (Nov. 7, 1986). EPA also explained that in setting BDATs it would compare the risk of various treatments for a particular waste with the risk of land disposal of that waste ("comparative risk" assessment).

* * *

III. CONCLUSION

EPA was correct in concluding that the RCRA's land disposal and hazardous waste treatment provisions preclude consideration of land treatment of hazardous wastes. Consequently, we deny the petition to review EPA's interpretation of the RCRA's land disposal and hazardous waste treatment provisions. Additionally, because EPA provided adequate reasons for abandoning comparative risk assessment, we deny the petition to review its decision in this regard. However, because EPA unlawfully exempted the K061 residues from the RCRA's land disposal restrictions, we grant the petition to review EPA's rulemaking on K061 wastes, vacate that part of the rule, and remand for further rulemaking consistent with this opinion.

So Ordered.

Notes

1. EPA also lists as hazardous wastes certain commercial chemical products, off-specification commercial chemical products, and certain chemical residues from spills and emptied containers if they are discarded, or if, in lieu of their original intended use, they are applied to the land or used as a fuel. These chemicals are classified as either *acute hazardous wastes*, which are given identification numbers starting with a "P" and listed at 40 C.F.R. § 261.33(e); or *toxic wastes*, which are given identification numbers starting with a "U" and listed at 40 C.F.R. § 261.33(f).

2. Hazard Codes. EPA assigns to each listed hazardous waste one or more Hazard Codes that identify the basis for listing. The Hazard Codes include "I" (ignitable), "C" (corrosive), "R" (reactive), "E" (toxicity characteristic), "H" (acute), and "T" (toxic). For wastes listed as toxicity characteristic ("E") or toxic ("T"), EPA identifies in Appendix VII to section 261 the particular constituents that cause the wastes to be listed.

3. Bases for Waste Listings. EPA lists as a hazardous wastes those substances which (1) exhibit a characteristic of hazardous waste (ignitability, *corrosivity*, *reactivity*, or toxicity); (2) are found to be acute hazardous wastes by being fatal to humans in low doses, or if toxicity data establish that the substances cause or contribute to serious illness; or (3) contain toxic constituents specifically listed by EPA in Appendix VIII to Part 261 of the RCRA rules and EPA determines, based on eleven specified criteria, that the substances pose a substantial present or potential hazard to human health or the environment when improperly treated, stored, transported or disposed. Because EPA's listing criteria overlap completely the four characteristics of hazardous waste, most *listed* hazardous wastes otherwise would qualify as *characteristic* hazardous wastes.

4. Delisting. RCRA allows individual generators of listed hazardous wastes to petition EPA to *delist* the waste generated at a particular facility. Petitioners may seek the delisting of listed wastes from specific sources, such as wastewater treatment sludges from the manufacturing and processing of explosives (K044), or non-specific sources, such as spent non-halogenated solvents (F003). To prevail, the delisting petitioner first must demonstrate to EPA that the particular waste stream generated at its facility does not exhibit the characteristic for which the waste stream was listed. For instance, a generator of coal (coking) tar decanter sludge (K087) would have to establish that the sludge generated at its facility does not contain harmful concentrations of phenols and naphthalene.

Second, the petitioner must satisfy EPA that the waste at issue could not properly be listed as a hazardous waste owing to other constituents or hazardous waste characteristics. At all events, a delisted waste remains subject to hazardous waste regulation if it exhibits any of the four characteristics of hazardous waste. Whether successful or not, a delisting proceeding invariably is costly and time-consuming.

EPA identifies all delisted facility-specific waste streams at Appendix IX to section 261 of the RCRA rules. Whether a decision to delist a particular substance applies to the waste streams previously generated at that facility, or applies only to future waste streams, is unresolved. The retroactive application of a delisting determination could obviate the need for corrective action at facilities where the delisted waste previously had been disposed.

5. Characteristic Hazardous Wastes. Waste streams that are not listed as hazardous wastes may nonetheless be regulated under the Subtitle C program if they exhibit one or more of four specified *characteristics* of hazardous waste, namely *ignitability, corrosivity, reactivity* and toxicity. Wastes exhibiting these characteristics are deemed to present a current or potential hazard to human health or the environment. The standards used to identify whether a particular waste stream exhibits a characteristic of hazardous waste are set forth in the table below:

Characteristic	Description
Ignitability	A solid waste generally exhibits the characteristic of *ignitability* if: (1) for most liquids, it has a flash point below 60°C (140°F); (2) it is a non-liquid capable under standard temperature and pressure of causing fire through friction, absorption of moisture or spontaneous chemical changes and, when ignited, burns so vigorously and persistently that it creates a hazard; or (3) it is an ignitable compressed gas or an oxidizer, as defined under the Hazardous Material Transportation Rules. All ignitable hazardous wastes are assigned the Hazardous Waste Number *D001*.
Corrosivity	A solid waste exhibits the characteristic of *corrosivity* if: (1) it is aqueous and has a pH less than or equal to 2 or greater than or equal to 12.5, or (2) it is a liquid and corrodes steel (SAE 1020) at a rate greater than 6.35 mm (0.250 inch) per year at 55°C (130°F). Corrosivity characteristic hazardous wastes are assigned the Hazardous Waste Number *D002*.
Reactivity	A solid waste generally exhibits the characteristic of *reactivity* if: (1) it normally is unstable and readily undergoes violent change without detonating; (2) when mixed with water, it reacts violently, forms potentially explosive mixtures or generates toxic gases, vapors or fumes; (3) it is a cyanide- or sulfide-bearing waste which, when exposed to normal pH conditions, can generate toxic gases,

	vapors or fumes; or (4) it readily is capable of detonation, explosive decomposition or reaction at standard temperature and pressure, or otherwise is capable of such reaction if subjected to heat or a strong initiating force. All reactive hazardous wastes are assigned the Hazardous Waste Number *D003*.
Toxicity	A solid waste generally exhibits the characteristic of *toxicity* if, using the Toxicity Characteristic Leaching Procedure (*TCLP*), the extract from a representative sample of the waste contains any of the forty constituents listed by EPA at 40 C.F.R. § 261.24 (Table 1) at concentrations at or above the applicable levels set forth in that table. A toxicity characteristic waste is assigned the Hazardous Waste Number corresponding to the contaminant listed on the above-referenced table, *e.g.*, *D043* (vinyl chloride).

6. Solid Wastes Which are Hazardous Wastes Owing to the Mixture, Derived–From and Contained–In Rules. Although a particular solid waste may not fall within the description of any listed hazardous waste, or exhibit a characteristic of hazardous waste, it may nonetheless be regulated as a hazardous waste under Subtitle C if it is (1) mixed with a hazardous waste, (2) derived from a hazardous waste, or (3) contains a hazardous waste. The rules which extend the scope of the Subtitle C program to cover these waste are known as the *mixture, derived-from,* and *contained-in* rules. These rules have been central to the scope and application of EPA's hazardous waste program since its adoption in 1980. EPA was forced to repromulgate the *mixture* and *derived-from* rules following a 1991 court decision finding procedural defects in the original issuance of these rules.

The *mixture rule* generally provides that if a non-hazardous solid waste is mixed with a listed hazardous waste, the resulting mixture is a hazardous waste. Certain mixtures of non-hazardous solid waste and listed hazardous waste may exit the hazardous waste program if the resulting substance no longer exhibits the particular characteristic of hazardous waste for which the listed hazardous waste originally was listed. The *mixture rule* does not specifically include mixtures of non-hazardous solid waste and *characteristic* hazardous waste; however, with some exceptions, any mixture that, by itself, exhibits any of the four characteristics of hazardous waste is a characteristic hazardous waste.

The *derived-from rule* provides that any solid waste which is generated from the treatment, storage or disposal of a *listed* hazardous waste, including any sludge, spill residue, ash, emission control dust, or leachate, remains subject to regulation as a hazardous waste unless the resulting waste is delisted. Wastes derived from *characteristic* hazardous wastes may exit the Subtitle C program if they no longer exhibit a characteristic of hazardous waste, although they may remain subject to certain restrictions against land disposal.

The *contained-in rule* provides that any wastes (*e.g.*, textiles and other absorbent materials) which contain a listed hazardous waste must be managed as if they were hazardous. The *contained-in rule* also applies to contaminated environmental media, such as soil and groundwater.

EPA designed the *mixture* and *derived-from* rules to close potential loopholes in the RCRA program, whereby solid waste generators might have avoided hazardous waste restrictions by diluting, mixing or treating substances which otherwise would be deemed hazardous. The agency confronted these loopholes during the public comment period following the 1978 issuance of the proposed RCRA rule and published the *mixture* and *derived-from rules* for the first time in its 1980 final RCRA regulation.

Numerous parties brought suit to challenge EPA's final RCRA rules claiming, among other things, that EPA's 1980 promulgation of the *mixture* and *derived-from* rules denied them an opportunity to review and comment on the rules. EPA contended that the two rules *flow[ed] from* the comments provided during the 1978–1980 rulemaking proceeding and were necessary to close the potential loopholes.

In 1991, a United States Court of Appeals panel agreed with the challengers and remanded the *mixture* and *derived-from* rules to EPA for republication in accordance with the Administrative Procedure Act. EPA thereafter reinstated the rules by republishing them for a new comment period.

7. Solid Wastes Which are Excluded from the Definition of Hazardous Waste. The hazardous waste identification rules exclude a number of *solid wastes* from the definition of *hazardous waste*. These substances are regulated as *non-hazardous solid wastes* under the RCRA Subtitle D program and under state and local solid waste rules (note, however, that each state is free to subject to hazardous waste regulation any substance which the federal program exempts from the definition of hazardous waste).

The most significant of the federal hazardous waste exclusions is household waste, which routinely is disposed of in municipal landfills or solid waste incinerators—disposal options which are not available for hazardous wastes. Other notable exclusions include solid waste generated by agricultural activity; mining overburden returned to the mine site; fly ash, bottom ash, and slag waste; flue gas emission control waste from the burning of coal or other fossil fuels; drilling fluids; certain wood or wood product wastes; certain wastes which exhibit the characteristic of toxicity (using the TCLP) because of chromium content alone; certain wastes from mining ores and minerals; and cement kiln dust waste.

8. The Special Status of Used Oil. Currently, used oil which is recycled or burned for energy recovery is not regulated as a *hazardous waste*, but instead it is subject to an array of specific management standards comparable to those applicable to hazardous waste. The regulation of used oil under RCRA has been the subject of considerable debate within and among Congress, EPA and state enforcement agencies, environmentalists and the regulated community. All parties agree that the RCRA program should promote used oil recycling under environmentally sound conditions. The principal point of contention is whether used oil management should be regulated as a *hazardous waste* under Subtitle C.

The hazardous waste treatment industry and many environmentalists have argued that the hazards posed by used oil constituents warrant the classification of used oil as a hazardous waste. Others have argued that the listing of used oil as a hazardous waste would inhibit used oil recycling efforts since many service stations and other entities would seek to avoid costly Subtitle C regulations by refusing to collect used oil from *do-it-yourselfers*.

The 1984 HSWA imposed set specific timetables for EPA to implement performance standards for oil recyclers and to determine whether to list used oil as a hazardous waste. EPA proposed management standards for oil recyclers in 1985, but never finalized these rules. In 1985 EPA proposed to list all used oils as hazardous based on the presence of toxic constituents in many samples. The agency withdrew the proposal in 1986, however, claiming that the stigma associated with a hazardous waste listing might discourage recycling. In 1988, a Federal Court of Appeals found that RCRA required the listing determination to be based on technical criteria rather than the stigmatic effects cited by EPA as the basis for its 1986 determination.

When the agency missed the statutory deadline for the listing decision, several parties brought suit against the agency to compel the determination. In 1991, EPA settled the suit by agreeing to make a final listing decision by May 1, 1992. On May 4, 1992, EPA announced that used oil destined for disposal would not be listed as a hazardous waste since it did not satisfy the technical requirements for listing provided by the RCRA statute. On September 10, 1992, EPA issued a final rule covering used oil that is recycled or burned for energy recovery. The rule sets forth management standards for used oil handlers and specifies that used oil managed in accordance with these standards is *not* a hazardous waste. The rule does not cover the disposal of waste oil mixtures and waste oil-contaminated media. For instance, if a property owner extracts petroleum-contaminated groundwater and transports it to a waste water treatment works for treatment and disposal under a Clean Water Act permit, the property would be subject to Subtitle C as a hazardous waste generator if the contaminated water, as extracted, exhibits a hazardous waste characteristic (*i.e.*, toxicity).

Owing to the long-standing uncertainties of federal used oil regulation, many states already have taken steps to regulate used oil, including mandatory recycling programs and licensing of used oil management facilities.

9. Sewage Sludge. Domestic sewage (and the sludges generated from the treatment thereof) is exempt from RCRA regulation and instead is regulated under the Clean Water Act. In February 1993, EPA issued a final rule governing the management of sewage sludge. The Sludge Rule imposes management standards on sewage sludge which is (1) applied to the land for a beneficial purpose (*e.g.*, distributed for use in home gardens), (2) land disposed and (3) incinerated.

§ 5.4 RCRA'S HAZARDOUS WASTE MANAGEMENT RULES

RCRA governs the management of hazardous wastes through a complicated system of statutes, rules, guidance documents, manifests, permits and, where necessary, compliance orders directed at individual waste facilities and other regulated parties. These mechanisms, including hazardous waste manifests, rules applicable to generators and transporters of hazardous waste, permitting requirements for facilities that treat, store or dispose of hazardous waste (so-called TSDs), and rules requiring the cleanup of contaminated hazardous waste facilities (the so-called *corrective action* rules), are discussed below.

1. *Hazardous Waste Manifests*

RCRA's manifest system manages and tracks each discrete quantity of hazardous waste from the *cradle* (the point of generation) to the *grave* (the point of disposal). The manifest, initially prepared by the generator, accompanies the waste shipment with the transporter and all subsequent handlers until the shipment reaches its final destination at a TSD facility. Each person or entity taking delivery of a hazardous waste shipment must possess a current permit and EPA identification number, and must, upon receipt, place these data on the manifest along with a dated, handwritten signature. TSDs also must check for any discrepancies in the manifest, *i.e.*, differences between the quantity or type of hazardous waste designated on the manifest and the quantity or type of hazardous waste actually received. Each party along the chain retains a copy of the manifest. Ultimately the TSD returns to the transporter and the generator a copy of the completed manifest with all signatures, certifications, identification numbers and other required information.

2. *Regulation of Hazardous Waste Generators*

A RCRA *generator* is any person, by site, whose act or process produces hazardous waste or whose act first causes a hazardous waste to become subject to regulation. While businesses and individuals do not require advance permission (in the form of a RCRA permit) to generate hazardous waste, generators are subject to management standards, reporting requirements and other restrictions. These requirements vary with respect to four principal categories of generators subject to RCRA: ordinary generators, conditionally exempt small quantity generators, intermediate quantity generators and farmers.

Ordinary Generators are those who generate in any calendar month more than 1,000 kilograms (kg) of hazardous waste or more than 1 kg of acute hazardous waste. Ordinary generators are required to

- obtain a generator identification number from EPA;
- comply with packaging, labeling and marking requirements applicable to hazardous waste containers;
- prepare and maintain for each discrete shipment of hazardous waste a manifest which identifies the permitted transporter(s) and destination TSD(s) for that shipment;

- confirm the delivery of each shipment to the permitted TSD (through the receipt from the TSD of the signed, completed manifest) and prepare an Exception Report in each instance where the manifest is not returned;

- submit biennial reports to EPA detailing the quantity and type(s) of hazardous waste generated at its facility and documenting its efforts to reduce the quantity and toxicity of waste produced;

- adhere to certain recordkeeping requirements regarding manifests, biennial and exception reports, and analytical testing results; and

- comply with export controls designed to ensure that the countries receiving hazardous waste shipments from the United States have consented to the importation of the wastes and have been given sufficient information regarding the nature of the waste to permit sound management practices.

Generators that also treat, store and accumulate hazardous waste for more than ninety days, or dispose of their own waste onsite also are regulated as TSD facilities. Generators that accumulate hazardous waste for less than ninety days need not apply for TSD permits but nonetheless are subject to certain rules governing the onsite containment of such waste. In August 1992, EPA amended the RCRA rules to allow generators to store certain non-liquid waste for up to ninety days in special *containment buildings* without being subject to land disposal treatment standards.

Conditionally exempt small quantity generators are those producing no more than 100 kg of hazardous waste per month. Such entities are exempted from many requirements otherwise applicable to ordinary generators provided they accumulate no more than 1,000 kgs of hazardous waste onsite at any given time. These generators *are* required to analyze the waste they produce to determine whether it is regulated, and must treat or dispose of the waste at a permitted TSD facility (either onsite or offsite) or at a state-licensed industrial solid waste facility. Small quantity generators otherwise are exempt from requirements applicable to generators, such as compliance with the manifest system; however, an offsite TSD facility may, if it chooses, require a small quantity generator to comply with such rules as a condition of accepting the wastes for treatment or disposal.

Intermediate quantity generators, *i.e.*, those who generate between 100 and 1,000 kgs of hazardous waste per month, are subject to somewhat greater restrictions than conditionally exempt small quantity generators. Intermediate quantity generators must obtain an EPA identification number; comply with all waste determination, containment and manifest requirements; transfer their hazardous waste only to transporters and TSD facilities with EPA identification numbers; and, if they treat or dispose of the waste onsite, comply with contingency plan and personnel training requirements. These generators may, subject to certain conditions, accumulate and store hazardous waste on site without a TSD permit for up to 180 days if the total quantity of waste does not exceed 6,000 kgs. These generators also are subject to all record-keeping and reporting requirements, except those for Biennial Reports.

Farmers generating pesticide wastes who otherwise would be *generators* under RCRA are exempt from hazardous waste disposal restrictions provided he/she triple rinses each emptied pesticide container and disposes of the pesticide residues in a manner consistent with the disposal instructions on the pesticide label, which in turn must conform to the requirements of the Federal Insecticide, Fungicide and Rodenticide Act (*FIFRA*).

3.   *Regulation of Hazardous Waste Transporters*

Like generators, hazardous waste transporters need not obtain operating permits but instead are subject to the RCRA transporters rules, which adopt by reference much of the Department of Transportation's (*DOT's*) hazardous materials transportation (*Hazmat*) rules.

The RCRA transporter rules require transporters of hazardous waste to obtain EPA identification numbers and to comply with the waste manifest and recordkeeping system. Transporters may store manifested shipments of hazardous waste at transfer facilities for up to ten days without becoming subject to TSD requirements. The rules also require transporters to contain or cleanup any release that occurs during transportation and to notify immediately the National Response Center in the event of a release.

The Hazardous Materials Transportation Act (*HMTA*), and DOT's Hazmat rules apply to *hazardous materials*, which are different from hazardous wastes. *Hazardous materials* are designated as such by DOT. The *HMTA* sets forth certain classes of materials that can be designated as hazardous materials, but otherwise relies on DOT's discretion to determine which materials, when transported in a particular quantity and form, may pose *an unreasonable risk to health and safety or property*.

The Hazmat rules apply to persons who transport in commerce packages that are used for the transportation of hazardous materials, and to those associated with packages that are held out for use in such transportation. *HMTA* uniformly regulates the transportation of hazardous materials between and among the states. The 1990 amendments to *HMTA* preempt local requirements that make impossible or impede compliance with the federal Hazmat rules, and also provide explicitly for the preemption of five classes of state/local regulation:

— the designation, description and classification of hazardous material;

— the packing, repacking, handling, labeling, marking and placarding of hazardous materials;

— the preparation, execution and use of shipping documents for such materials and the requirements respecting the number, content and placement of such documents;

— the written notification, recording and reporting of the unintentional release in transportation of hazardous materials; and

— the design, manufacturing, fabrication, marking, maintenance, reconditioning, repairing and testing of a package represented, marked certified, or sold as qualified to transport hazardous waste.

In these areas states and localities may only adopt and enforce laws, regulations, rules, standards and orders that are substantially the same as the provisions of the *HMTA* and the Hazmat rules.

States and localities are permitted some flexibility in restricting the transportation of hazardous materials to certain highways. Here, the *HMTA* directs DOT to issue federal procedural and substantive standards for (1) state and local adoption and enforcement of requirements with respect to highway routing, and (2) specific highway routes to be used. The statute sets out twelve factors that are to be used in establishing those routes, such as population density, type of highway and type of hazardous material. Any state highway routing restrictions which are inconsistent with these criteria are preempted. Further, states cannot impose restrictions that burden other states or localities, unless such restrictions are accepted by the affected parties and do not unreasonably burden interstate commerce.

The Hazmat rules cover areas such as shipping papers; marking; labeling; placarding; emergency response information; preparation of materials for transportation; carriage by rail, aircraft, vessel and public highway. EPA and DOT generally consult one another to avoid duplicative or conflicting transport requirements.

4. *Regulation of Treatment, Storage and Disposal Facilities*

RCRA's primary hazardous waste management regulations are directed at treatment, storage and disposal facilities (*TSD*). All TSD operators must obtain operating permits, which incorporate the waste management standards contained in section 264 of the RCRA rules.

A TSD permit application consists of two parts, called *Part A* and *Part B*. The Part A application supplies general information about the facility, such as its name, location and owner; a description of the activities which require the facility to obtain a RCRA permit; and a listing of all other permits received or applied for under RCRA or other regulatory programs. The Part B application, which is much more comprehensive, incorporates the substantive elements of the hazardous waste management rules and presents to EPA the operator's detailed proposal to manage hazardous waste in compliance with these rules.

Facilities already in existence when applicable RCRA rules were issued, and for which Part B permit applications are pending, are termed *interim status facilities* and are subject to the waste management standards of 40 C.F.R. § 265, which generally mirror those applicable to fully permitted facilities. Often the permit applicant does not seek to *operate* a

TSD at all, but is compelled by the RCRA rules to submit the application in order to *close* a waste disposal area within the facility.

RCRA operating permits are issued by EPA, or by state hazardous waste agencies that are approved to administer the RCRA hazardous waste program. Permitting requirements for TSDs vary with the type of waste management in which the operator seeks to engage. All TSDs, however, are subject to the minimum facility standards.

General Facility Standards. TSD operators must apply to EPA and obtain a TSD identification number and site-specific permit to treat, store or dispose hazardous waste. TSD operators further must comply with applicable location, design and construction standards and permit limitations; perform chemical analysis and waste identification; return completed manifests to generators from whom hazardous waste is received; comply with security and inspection standards; conduct personnel training programs; comply with specific requirements for managing highly volatile waste; check for discrepancies between waste manifests and waste actually received; maintain contingency plans for releases of hazardous waste; and comply with reporting and recordkeeping requirements.

Release Monitoring and Response. TSD operators must monitor their groundwater, soils and other areas of their facilities periodically for evidence of releases. When releases are discovered, TSD operators must undertake corrective action to cleanup the releases. Often the TSD's site-specific permit will establish groundwater protection standards to ensure that hazardous constituents do not exceed specified concentration levels. The permit will specify points of compliance within the facility where monitoring must be conducted and groundwater protection standards will apply.

Closure and Post–Closure Care. All TSDs ultimately must be *closed*, whereby the facility ceases to treat, store or dispose of hazardous waste and ceases to be subject to TSD operating and performance standards. In order to close a TSD, the facility must be placed in such a condition that minimizes the need for further maintenance, and controls or eliminates the escape of hazardous constituents from the facility. A *clean closure*, which must be completed within 180 days after the TSD receives its last shipment of hazardous waste, generally involves the treatment, removal from the facility, or disposal onsite of all remaining hazardous wastes in accordance with the closure plan, and a prohibition of further receipts of hazardous waste.

Certain types of TSDs also are subject to *post-closure* care, which generally involves at least 30 years of groundwater monitoring and reporting, and additional corrective action when necessary. The RCRA rules specify closure and post-closure standards for containers, tank systems, surface impoundments, waste piles, land treatment areas, landfills, incinerators, drip pads and other waste management units.

Closure and post-closure care is conducted pursuant to written closure and post-closure plans, which are submitted along with the TSD operator's permit application and are updated from time to time as relevant data become available. Closure plans must contain detailed descriptions of how each waste management unit will be closed; the steps needed to remove or decontaminate all hazardous waste residues and soils; groundwater monitoring, leachate collection and run-on and run-off controls; and the proposed timetable for closure of each unit. Further, TSD operators must maintain detailed written closure cost estimates and must demonstrate continuously their financial ability to implement their closure plans.

Within sixty days of completion of closure, a TSD operator must document and certify to EPA the completion of closure. The certification must be signed by a registered professional engineer. Similar requirements apply to post-closure plans, cost estimates and certifications.

IN RE CONSOLIDATED LAND DISPOSAL REGULATION LITIGATION
938 F.2d 1386 (D.C.Cir.1991).

GINSBURG, CIRCUIT JUDGE

In late 1982, a score of petitioners and intervenors sought review of the interim final hazardous waste land disposal regulations that the Environmental Protection Agency had issued in July of that year. Briefing was deferred while the parties pursued first legislative changes and then settlement talks. Now, after many parties have withdrawn, many issues have been settled or overtaken by events, and several of the original counsel have been succeeded by others -indeed by a new generation at the bar—three petitioners set before us two of the original 84 issues.

Petitioners American Iron and Steel Institute and Edison Electric Institute challenge the regulations insofar as they require a closed land disposal facility to obtain and abide by the terms of an EPA permit. 40 C.F.R. § 270.1(c); see 47 Fed. Reg. 32,336 (July 26, 1982)(scope of permit requirement, then codified in 40 C.F.R. Part 122). These petitioners contend that the regulations are arbitrary and capricious and exceed the agency's statutory authority, and that the agency improperly issued a portion of the post-closure permit regulation without prior notice and an opportunity for the public to comment.

Petitioner American Petroleum Institute challenges the regulations insofar as they establish groundwater monitoring and cleanup standards applicable to any disposal site located above an aquifer, without making specific provision for the exemption of sites above aquifers that are both contaminated to the point of being useless and isolated from other waters. API contends that because the further contamination of such an aquifer poses no threat to human health or the environment, the regulation is arbitrary and capricious and in excess of the EPA's authority. For the reasons set out below, we deny both petitions for review.

I. POST-CLOSURE PERMITS

The Resource Conservation and Recovery Act gave the EPA very broad authority to regulate the disposal of hazardous waste. Sections 3004 and 3005 respectively direct the agency to establish "performance standards, applicable to owners and operators of facilities for the treatment, storage, or disposal [TSD] of hazardous waste," 42 U.S.C. § 6924(a), and to issue regulations

> requiring each person owning or operating an existing [TSD] facility ... to have a permit issued pursuant to this section. [After the effective date of these regulations] the treatment, storage, or disposal of any such hazardous waste ... is prohibited except in accordance with such a permit.

42 U.S.C. § 6925(a). Pursuant to § 3005, the EPA requires that all hazardous waste disposal facilities "that received wastes after July 26, 1982, or that certified closure (according to § 265.115) after January 26, 1983" obtain a post-closure permit. 42 C.F.R. § 270.1(c). The petitioners contend that this regulation is inconsistent with the "common sense meaning of [§ 3005] ... that a permit is required and authorized only for facilities that currently are or will be treating, storing, or disposing of (i.e., 'managing') hazardous waste."

We approach this issue within the framework established in *Chevron U.S.A., Inc. v. NRDC*, 467 U.S. 837, 81 L.Ed.2d 694, 104 S.Ct. 2778 (1984). Because neither the petitioners nor the EPA claims that the Congress specifically addressed the question of requiring a post-closure permit for a disposal facility, we proceed under *Chevron* step two. Accordingly, we defer to the agency's interpretation of the statute so long as it is reasonable.

The EPA defines a "disposal" facility, for purposes of both § 3004 and § 3005, as any facility that received hazardous waste after the effective date of the permit requirement (November 19, 1980), regardless of whether the facility is currently open or closed. The petitioners concede that "a disposal facility that receives hazardous waste ... remains a 'disposal facility' subject to regulation [under § 3004] after it closes." They argue, however, that § 3005 is narrower in scope than § 3004; as they read § 3005, a permit is required only for on-going activities—the treatment, storage, or disposal of waste at such facilities—not for the facility itself post-closure.

The EPA maintains that it is reasonable to interpret broadly the term "disposal" in § 3005 in light of § 1004 of RCRA, which defines "disposal" very capaciously:

> the discharge, deposit, injection, dumping, spilling, leaking, or placing of any solid waste or hazardous waste into or on any land or water so that such solid waste or hazardous waste or any constituent thereof may enter the environment or be emitted into the air or be discharged into any waters, including ground waters.

42 U.S.C. § 6903(3). A TSD facility "at which hazardous wastes have been disposed by placement in or on the land" remains subject to both permitting (per § 3005) and regulation (per § 3004), the agency contends, because "such hazardous wastes or constituents may continue 'leaking' or 'may enter the environment or be emitted ... or discharged ...'" into the environment.

The petitioners, on the other hand, make the linguistic point that "disposal ... is not a continuing activity but occurs anew each time waste is placed into or on land." That may be one way in which the word is used in ordinary language, but is not necessarily how it is used in the statute; the equation of "disposal" with "leaking," which is a continuous phenomenon rather than a discrete event, is enough to blunt the sting of the petitioners' point. Theirs is at most an alternative reading of the statute, not an argument as to why the EPA's reading of the statute is unreasonable.

As to reasonableness, we note that the EPA also interpreted "disposal" to encompass the continuing presence of waste when it read § 3004(a) to authorize post-closure performance standards, see 45 Fed. Reg. 33,198 (May 19, 1980). The petitioners concede that authority to the agency, yet insist that the word "disposal" must be read differently when it appears in § 3005. We are constrained to disagree: the two sections were intended to work together (as evidenced by the cross references in §§ 3004(a)(7) and 3005(c)(1)), and divergent interpretations would create a gap in an otherwise complete scheme. We therefore hold that the agency is within its authority in requiring a post-closure permit as the means to implement its substantive regulatory authority under § 3004.

We need not reach the merits of the petitioners' argument that the EPA provided inadequate notice of the portion of its proposal that requires post-closure permits for disposal facilities that had operated under interim status while their permit applications were pending, but that had closed prior to EPA approval of those applications. At oral argument the petitioners forthrightly acknowledged that a remand solely in order to reopen the record for further comment would provide them no meaningful relief: the EPA fully understands their objections. Thus, having failed to obtain an order requiring the agency to reconsider its legal position, the petitioners would gain nothing from an order requiring the EPA to reopen the rulemaking record.

II. MONITORING UNUSABLE AQUIFERS

Section 3004 authorizes the EPA to enact only such performance standards "as may be necessary to protect human health and the environment." 42 U.S.C. § 6924(a). Pursuant to this authority, the EPA requires that the operator of a disposal site (1) monitor the ground water in the uppermost aquifer below the site in order to detect leaks (detection monitoring); (2) in the event of a leak, conduct further monitoring in order to determine whether the leaked substance exceeds the permissible concentration level (compliance monitoring); and if it does, (3) take remedial action to clean up the contaminated ground water. *See* 40 C.F.R. §§ 264.98 to .100. The regulation requires detection monitoring without exception, but provides for flexibility in the compliance monitoring and remedial stages. For example, the agency will exclude from the program a hazardous constituent "not capable of posing a substantial present or potential hazard to human health or the environment," taking into account a list of considerations bearing upon the quality, isolation, and likely use of the aquifer; and it will establish an alternate concentration level for a constituent that does not pose such a hazard below that concentration. 40 C.F.R. §§ 264.93, 264.94(a) & (b).

The petitioner contends that the EPA acted arbitrarily and capriciously by failing categorically to exempt from detection monitoring any site above an aquifer that is both "completely cut off from other bodies of groundwater or surface water" and "so contaminated that [it] cannot be put to any meaningful use." The agency also exceeded its statutory authority, according to the petitioner, because further contamination of such an isolated and unusable aquifer poses no conceivable threat to "human health [or] the environment."

The EPA responded skeptically to this claim in its rulemaking decision: "EPA believes that this would be an extremely rare situation, if indeed such a location exists, and has therefore, chosen not to establish an exemption at this time." 47 Fed. Reg. at 32,293. The agency also points out that the interim final regulation allows for adjustment in the response to a leak consistent with the quality of the aquifer, and that looking toward a final rule, it requested comments on the existence of such unusable aquifers as the petitioner posits. Absent evidence in the record before it, the agency declined the petitioner's invitation to fashion a special rule for a speculative circumstance.

The EPA cannot reasonably be required to create a blanket exemption for a hypothetical case unsupported by any evidence in the record, and the reality of which it doubts. Even in our leading case on the desirability of providing for the possibility of exemption from "general rules," *WAIT Radio v. FCC*, 135 U.S.App.D.C. 317, 418 F.2d 1153 (D.C.Cir.1969), upon which the petitioner principally relies, we spoke only of requests for waivers "accompanied by supporting data." *id.* at 1157. The agency has stated that it is open to just such a showing. It is now up to the petitioner to make a record that will support its claim that it is unreasonable for the agency not to provide for the exemption of unusable aquifers.

III. Conclusion

We hold that the challenged portions of the 1982 interim final regulations are within the substantive authority of the EPA, and that the agency's exercise of that authority was not arbitrary and capricious. Inasmuch as the petitioners no longer seek relief for any procedural error that may have attended the promulgation of the regulations, the petitions for review are

Denied.

Notes

1. Financial Assurance Requirements. Each permitted and interim status TSD operator must demonstrate continuously to EPA its financial ability to (1) satisfy third party liability claims arising from accidental releases of hazardous waste, and (2) complete closure and any applicable post-closure care in accordance with the TSD's written closure and post-closure plans. The minimum third party liability coverage amounts are set forth in the RCRA rules. The financial assurance requirements for closure and post-closure care are determined on a facility-specific basis as set forth below.

First, the TSD operator presents to EPA along with its permit application a detailed estimate of closure (and, if applicable, post-closure) costs. The closure cost estimate must equal the cost of final closure at the point in the facility's active life when the extent and manner of its operation would make closure the most expensive, as indicated by the closure plan. The estimate must be based on the costs to the TSD operator of hiring a third party to close the facility and may not incorporate any salvage value that may be realized upon the sale of hazardous waste. During the active life of the TSD, the operator periodically must adjust the closure cost estimate to account for inflation and to take into consideration any amendments to the written closure plan. Similar requirements apply to post-closure cost-estimates.

The RCRA rules allow TSD operators to choose from a number of financial mechanisms by which to demonstrate their current ability to pay for closure and post-closure costs. These include closure trust funds, surety bonds guaranteeing payment into a closure trust fund, surety bonds guaranteeing performance of closure, irrevocable letters of credit, closure insurance and the *financial test* and corporate guarantee for closure. The financial test mechanism, which generally does not entail the expenditure of assurance funds prior to closure, is available only to larger businesses that are able to demonstrate favorable debt/equity ratios, bond ratings, tangible working capital and net worth values in relation to the sum of the current closure, post-closure and *plugging and abandonment* cost estimates.

2. Air Emission Standards. Section 3004(n) of HSWA directed EPA to promulgate rules controlling air emissions from TSDs. In 1990, the agency issued rules covering emission from process vents and equipment leaks and in 1991 proposed rules for remaining emission sources. These rules seek primarily to prevent the volatization of organic compounds as they move through storage and treatment. The agency currently is contemplating a third phase of the program to address any residual emission risks posed by TSDs.

3. Facility–Specific Standards. In addition to the general TSD standards, the RCRA rules impose separate requirements on treaters, storers and disposers of hazardous waste.

Facility	Description
Treatment Facilities.	The *treatment* of hazardous waste includes any method, technique or

	process designed to change the physical, chemical or biological character or composition of any hazardous waste so as to neutralize such waste or so as to render such waste nonhazardous, safer for transport, amenable for recovery, amenable for storage or reduced in volume.
Storage Facilities.	A *storage* facility is one that contains hazardous waste, whether temporarily or for a period of years, in such a manner which does not constitute *disposal*. At some point in time, *storage* of hazardous waste ceases to be *temporary* and becomes instead permanent disposal. Since RCRA imposes a much more complicated regulation on disposers than on storers of hazardous waste, it is important to understand where *storage* ends and *disposal* begins. Unfortunately, the RCRA rules offer little guidance on this point and the issue generally remains unsettled.
Disposal Facilities.	One of RCRA's principal functions is to control the ultimate disposal of hazardous wastes at a *disposal facility*. A *disposal facility* is a facility at which hazardous waste is intentionally placed into or on any land or water and at which waste will remain after closure. The RCRA rules identify specific performance and operational standards for containers, tank systems, surface impoundments, waste piles, land treatment areas, landfills, incinerators, drip pads and other waste management units. The specific regulations governing the prohibition or limitation of the disposal of hazardous wastes on land (often referred to as the *land ban* rules).

Depending on the type of treatment employed, most treatment facilities are subject to the same regulatory standards applicable to storage and disposal facilities. For example, those land treatment facilities where treated hazardous waste remains after closure are considered disposal facilities and regulated accordingly. Similarly, most facilities which treat hazardous waste also are storage facilities and may be disposal facilities if the waste which is treated remains hazardous and is not transferred to a separate disposal facility.

Some facilities that *treat* wastes are regulated by other federal statutes and therefore are exempted from RCRA. The most significant exemptions from RCRA are those for totally enclosed treatment facilities, wastewater treatment units that discharge pursuant to a National Pollutant Discharge Elimination System (*NPDES*) permit, and elementary neutralization units. Recycling facilities are subject to limited RCRA standards.

The RCRA rules require land treatment facilities to monitor their leachate. The *Shell Oil* decision vacated these provisions along with the *mixture* and *derived-from* rule, owing to EPA's failure to provide the public with adequate notice of, and an opportunity on, these rules. EPA then republished these requirements in January 1992.

EPA and some state agencies explicitly differentiate between exempt facilities that handle regulated wastes and regulated facilities that handle exempt wastes. For example, as noted above, wastewater discharges pursuant to NPDES permits are exempt from the definition of hazardous waste. However, EPA asserts that the wastewaters located *upstream* from the discharge point are not exempt from hazardous waste regulation, even if the wastes are not spilled or otherwise released. EPA therefore requires such facilities to report the wastewaters as hazardous waste on annual generator forms and, if fees are to be paid based on the amount generated, fees must be paid on those wastewaters.

4. Boilers and Industrial Furnaces (BIFs). Prior to 1991, many generators burned their combustible hazardous wastes in boilers and industrial furnaces (**BIFs**), such as brick kilns. At that time, BIF operators who burned hazardous waste for energy recovery were subject to specific management standards but were otherwise exempt from TSD permitting requirements. All other burning of hazardous waste was regulated as *incineration*, which requires a RCRA permit. Owing to the rather fine distinction between incineration and burning for energy recovery, it appears that many prohibited often were—and still may be—burned in BIFs.

In February 1991, EPA issued a final rule subjecting all BIFs to permitting requirements and more stringent management standards particularly with respect to air emissions. The BIF rule accords interim status to BIF operators *in existence* on August 21, 1991 and exempts certain small quantity onsite burners.

Owing to the broad application of the BIF rule, EPA occasionally conducts public roundtable discussions on the implementation of this rule.

5. Hazardous Waste Recycling. The RCRA rules generally exempt from TSD permitting requirements the *reclamation* and *bona fide* recycling of hazardous waste, although the transportation and offsite storage of such waste prior to recycling is subject to permitting requirements. Further, the processing of such material which does not completely prepare the material for beneficial use is regulated as the *treatment* of hazardous waste, for which a RCRA treatment permit is required.

5. *Treatment Standards and Other Restrictions on Land Disposal*

In 1986, EPA began the staged elimination of land disposal as a management option for untreated hazardous waste. The Land Disposal Restrictions (or LDR program) bans some wastes, such as liquids, from land disposal altogether and conditions land disposal of other wastes on prior treatment.

EPA identified and divided into segments (called *Thirds*) hundreds of specific wastes which are subject to the LDR program. Each Third became subject to the LDR program on a separate date. Among those wastes which already have been banned from land disposal are liquid wastes containing solvents and dioxins, wastes bearing certain metals, particularly acidic wastes (2.0 pH or less) and wastes containing designated concentrations of PCBs and cyanides. The LDR program is implemented in conjunction with the TCLP, which must be used to determine if listed hazardous wastes are restricted from land disposal.

For all wastes subject to the LDR program, EPA has assigned one or more technology-based treatment standards which, if applied to the subject waste, permit subsequent land disposal of the treated product. Typical treatment standards include incineration, biodegradation, carbon adsorption and wet air oxidation.

EPA's June 1990 *Third Third* rule included treatment standards for characteristic wastes. This rule required the treatment of some toxicity characteristic wastes to concentrations below those designated under the TC rule. As a result, generators must reduce toxic concentrations to levels below those at which a waste exhibits the toxicity characteristic at the point of generation. This aspect of the *Third Third rule* was upheld by the D.C. Circuit Court of Appeals in 1992.

In August 1992, EPA issued treatment standards for *newly listed wastes* (wastes listed after November 8, 1984) and *hazardous debris* (debris that are contaminated with a listed hazardous waste or exhibit a characteristic of hazardous waste). The treatment options for hazardous debris include extraction, destruction and immobilization.

The LDR program *excludes* wastes generated by conditionally exempt small quantity generators (less than 100 kg/month), wastes identified or listed as hazardous after November 8, 1984 for which EPA has not promulgated land disposal prohibitions or treatment standards, pesticide wastes from farming activity and contaminated soil or debris from CERCLA/Superfund sites.

CHEMICAL WASTE MANAGEMENT, INC. v. UNITED STATES EPA

976 F.2d 2 (D.C.Cir.1992).

Opinion Per Curiam.

The Hazardous and Solid Waste Amendments of 1984 instituted a ban on the land disposal of classes of hazardous wastes unless certain conditions are met. Those amendments require the Environmental Protection Agency to follow a phased schedule for implementing the ban. In this case we consider various challenges to regulations implementing the final portion of this program, the so-called "third-third" rule, which largely covers the land disposal of wastes deemed hazardous because they possess certain defined characteristics.

Various petitioners raise multi-faceted challenges. A group of industry trade associations and companies ... (collectively, "industry petitioners") seek review of regulations mandating levels of treatment before land disposal that go beyond the removal of the attribute that led to the waste's classification as hazardous. These petitioners claim that the EPA lacked authority under the statute to require treatment to such levels. The Fertilizer Institute raises procedural and substantive objections to provisions that bar dilution of certain wastes as a form of treatment prior to discharge into the waters of the United States from treatment facilities licensed under the Clean Water Act. Finally, three companies attack the imposition of new testing requirements at disposal facilities as arbitrary and insufficiently clear.

We deny each of these petitions for review. Sections 3004(g)(5) and (m) of the Resource Conservation and Recovery Act ("RCRA") ... (which are reprinted in Appendix A hereto) give the EPA the statutory authority to mandate the treatment of wastes to levels beyond those at which the wastes present the characteristics that caused them to be deemed hazardous. The EPA provided adequate notice of its intent to bar dilution of certain hazardous wastes at water treatment facilities that meet the standards of the Clean Water Act facilities. The regulations provide sufficient guidance as to how this part of the rule will work, and the distinction drawn between types of hazardous wastes appears reasonable. The challenge by the individual companies to testing protocols established in this rule is rejected. The procedures are both clear and reasonable.

Several environmental organizations, as well as the Hazardous Waste Treatment Council, an association representing companies that treat hazardous waste (collectively, "NRDC petitioners"), present different objections. They assert that (1) the new rule's "deactivation" treatment standard impermissibly allows the dilution, rather than treatment with specified technologies, of many characteristic wastes prior to land disposal; (2) the rule authorizes placement of untreated formerly characteristic wastes in surface impoundments within Clean Water Act treatment systems, or into underground injection wells, in violation of RCRA; (3) it arbitrarily created treatment standards for chromium and lead wastes; and (4) the rule provides an exception to treatment standards for wastes burned in industrial furnaces along with wastes exempted by the Bevill Amendment that violates that provision. In addition, the Council and Chemical Waste Management, Inc., a large waste disposal company, challenge certain testing procedures imposed by the regulations as impermissibly vague.

The petitions brought by NRDC petitioners are granted in part and denied in part. Under the statute, dilution of characteristic hazardous wastes may constitute treatment, but only if no hazardous constituents are present following dilution that would endanger human health or the environment. The EPA concedes that dilution will not attain this result for certain characteristic wastes. For others, it has not made clear that dilution will meet the requirements for treatment. The standard is therefore vacated as to those wastes. The dilution of wastes in Clean Water Act facilities is acceptable so long as the toxicity of the waste discharged from the facility is minimized or eliminated consistent with RCRA. Similarly, disposal of wastes in underground injection wells may occur as long as the hazardous characteristics have been eliminated and any health and environmental dangers posed by hazardous constituents of the wastes are minimized.

We remand the lead and chromium standards because the EPA appears to have relied on data that does not support its conclusions. We also remand the exemption from regulation under Subtitle C of RCRA of wastes burned with wastes exempted under the Bevill Amendment for consideration in an ongoing rulemaking addressing that question. Finally, Chemical Waste Management's petition for review of test compliance procedures is denied. Testing procedures will be embodied in permits. Uncertainties over the standards can be resolved in the permit-writing process.

* * *

Subtitle C of the Resource Conservation and Recovery Act, 42 U.S.C. §§ 6921–6939b (1988), sets out a comprehensive regulatory system governing the treatment, storage, and disposal of hazardous wastes. Wastes are deemed hazardous in one of two ways: They possess one of the four hazardous characteristics identified by the EPA in 40 C.F.R. Part 261, Subpart C ("characteristic wastes"), *see id.* § 261.3(a)(2)(i) (1991), or have been found to be hazardous as a result of an EPA rulemaking. *See id.* Part 261, Subpart D ("listed wastes").

The four characteristics identified as hazardous are ignitability, *corrosivity*, *reactivity*, and extraction procedure ("EP") toxicity. The hazards presented by ignitable, corrosive, and reactive ("ICR") wastes are primarily, though not exclusively, the results of their physical properties. *See* 45 Fed. Reg. 33,066, 33,107–10 (1980). EP characteristic wastes contain toxic constituents. *Id.* at 33,107–12. These wastes remain hazardous until they cease to exhibit any of the characteristics identified in Subpart C. *See* 40 C.F.R. § 261.3(d)(1). Characteristic wastes comprise over fifty percent of all the hazardous wastes generated in the United States each year.

Although the EPA may list a waste if it possesses one of the four characteristics described above, in practice it will only list specific wastes that are either acutely hazardous or possess high levels of toxic constituents. *See id.*; 45 Fed. Reg. at 33,105–07. A listed waste loses its hazardous status only after a petition for its "delisting" is approved by the EPA in a notice-and-comment rulemaking. *See* 40 C.F.R. §§ 260.20, 260.22; *Shell Oil Co. v. EPA*, 950 F.2d 741, 749 (D.C.Cir.1991).

"Once a waste is listed or identified as hazardous, its subsequent management is regulated" under subtitle C of RCRA. *American Petroleum Inst. v. EPA*, 906 F.2d 729, 733 (D.C.Cir.1990)("API"). The waste enters RCRA's "cradle-to-grave" regulatory system; and "the waste's treatment, storage, and disposal is usually regulated by permit." *American Mining Congress v. EPA*, 907 F.2d 1179, 1182 (D.C.Cir.1990) ("AMC II"); see also RCRA §§ 3001–3004, 42 U.S.C. §§ 6921–6924. The management of a hazardous waste continues "until such time as it ceases to pose a hazard to the public." *Shell Oil*, 950 F.2d at 754.

Because "certain classes of land disposal facilities are not capable of assuring long-term containment of certain hazardous wastes," RCRA § 1002(b)(7), 42 U.S.C. § 6901(b)(7), Congress amended subtitle C in 1984 to prohibit land disposal of many hazardous wastes. The Hazardous and Solid Waste Amendments of 1984, Pub. L. No. 98–616, 98 Stat. 3221 (1984) ("1984 Amendments"), gave the EPA significant authority to regulate land disposal. The statute expressed a general policy preference that "reliance on land disposal should be minimized or eliminated." RCRA § 1002(b)(7), 42 U.S.C. § 6901(b)(7). A prohibition on disposal would apply unless the waste is treated so as to minimize the short-term and long-term threats to human health and the environment posed by toxic and hazardous constituents, RCRA § 3004(m), 42 U.S.C. § 6924(m), or unless the EPA finds that no migration of hazardous constituents from the facility will occur after disposal. *id.* § 3004(g)(5), 42 U.S.C. § 6924(g)(5); *see also Hazardous Waste Treatment Council v. EPA*, 886 F.2d 355, 357 (D.C.Cir.1989), *cert. denied*, 111 S.Ct. 139, 112 L.Ed.2d 106 (1990) ("HWTC III").

The 1984 Amendments specifically required the EPA to follow a phased schedule to implement the land disposal ban. They forbade the land disposal of hazardous wastes containing solvents and dioxins after November 8, 1986. RCRA § 3004(e), 42 U.S.C. § 6924(e). A select list of other wastes were barred from land disposal after July 8, 1987 ("California list" wastes). *Id.* § 3004(d), 42 U.S.C. § 6924(d). Finally, the amendments ordered the Agency to rank all remaining hazardous wastes on the basis of their intrinsic hazard and the volume generated annually and to divide the list into three parts. *Id.* § 3004(g)(4), 42 U.S.C. § 6924(g)(4). The Administrator was then charged with the task of promulgating final regulations for each third of the list. *See id.* § 3004(g)(5), 42 U.S.C. § 6924(g)(5). Unless the Administrator promulgated regulations for wastes in the last third of the list by May 8, 1990, they could not be land disposed. *Id.* § 3004(g)(6)(C), 42 U.S.C. § 6924(g)(6)(C).

Under the 1984 Amendments, the final regulations must

prohibit[ ] one or more methods of land disposal of the hazardous wastes listed on such schedule except for methods of land disposal which the Administrator determines will be protective of human health and the environment for as long as the waste remains hazardous.... For the purposes of this paragraph, a method of land disposal may not be determined to be protective of human health and the environment (except with respect to a hazardous waste which has complied with the pretreatment regulations promulgated under subsection (m) of this section) unless, upon application by an interested person, it has been demonstrated to the Administrator, to a reasonable degree of certainty, that there will be no migration of hazardous constituents from the disposal unit or injection zone for as long as the wastes remain hazardous.

RCRA § 3004(g)(5), 42 U.S.C. § 6924(g)(5). The Administrator must also promulgate treatment standards, compliance with which will authorize land disposal, at the same time he publishes the land ban. The treatment regulations shall

specify[ ] those levels or methods of treatment, if any, which substantially diminish the toxicity of the waste or substantially reduce the likelihood of migration of hazardous constituents from the waste so that short-term and long-term threats to human health and the environment are minimized.

Id. § 3004(m)(1), 42 U.S.C. § 6924(m)(1).

The regulations under review implement the land-ban program for the last third of the ranked list of wastes, the "third-third." They largely consist of treatment standards for characteristic wastes. *See* 55 Fed. Reg. 22,520–720 (1990). The final rule also modifies regulations governing characteristic wastes that are managed in treatment systems regulated through National Pollutant Discharge Elimination System permits issued under the Clean Water Act as well as regulations affecting those disposed of in underground injection wells regulated under the Safe Drinking Water Act. The rule establishes a variety of compliance requirements as well.

Fourteen petitions for review were filed and consolidated into this proceeding. Petitioners divided the case into three groups of issues for purposes of briefing and argument. The first focuses on industry petitioners' challenge to standards mandating treatment of characteristic wastes beyond the point at which they cease to display hazardous characteristics and on NRDC petitioners' challenge to dilution as a method of treatment. The second centers on the Clean Water Act and underground injection well questions. The third consists of the remaining issues. This opinion adopts the same approach.

II. TREATMENT STANDARDS FOR CHARACTERISTIC WASTES

* * *

In the final rule, the EPA revised many of its proposed treatment standards for ICR and toxic characteristic wastes. The EPA, however, did not back away from its basic position that it could require treatment below characteristic levels. Because "Congress has given apparently conflicting guidance on how the Agency should address land disposal prohibitions for characteristic wastes," the EPA "believes it has authority to reconcile these potential conflicts and to harmonize statutory provisions to forge a coherent regulatory system." 55 Fed. Reg. at

22,651. The EPA agreed with many participants in the comment period that "one permissible construction of the language in section 3004(g)" (which requires the promulgation of regulations "prohibiting ... methods of land disposal of the [listed] hazardous wastes") is that subtitle C rules applied only to hazardous wastes, and therefore the applicability of the land disposal regulations must be judged at the moment of disposal. 55 Fed. Reg. at 22,652. Ultimately, the EPA concluded that Congress did not state when the status of the waste should be evaluated for purposes of the ban on land disposal; therefore, the EPA could choose to regulate the waste "at the point of generation or at the point of disposal (and possibly at some other point or combination of the two)." *Id.*

While viewing its authority broadly, the EPA decided to exercise it sparingly:

> Today's rule reflects a decision to take limited, but nonetheless significant, steps within the point of generation framework. As a general matter, the Agency believes that the goals of [the program] may require application of standards which go beyond the characteristic level ... in some future cases.

Id. at 22,654. The final regulations call for treatment below characteristic levels for only a handful of wastes. Among ICR wastes, ignitable liquids with high total organic carbons (a subset of the subcategory of ignitable liquids for which the proposed rule required treatment to below characteristic levels by technology), *see id.* at 22,543–44, and reactive cyanides, *see id.* at 22,550c–51, would be subject to enhanced treatment. The Agency backed away from its original plan to mandate enhanced treatment for corrosive characteristic wastes.

The EPA determined that for most ICR wastes, treatment to characteristic levels would be sufficient. The Agency found upon review that

> the environmental concerns from the properties of ignitability, *corrosivity*, and *reactivity* are different from the environmental concern from EP toxic wastes. Toxic constituents can pose a cumulative impact on land disposal even where waste is below the characteristic level. Where wastes pose an ascertainable toxicity concern ... the Agency has developed treatment standards that address the toxicity concern and (in effect) require treatment below the characteristic level.... Otherwise, treatment that removes the properties of ignitability, *corrosivity*, and *reactivity*, fully addresses the environmental concern from the properties themselves.

Id. at 22,655.

The EPA also retreated from its emphasis on technology-based treatment in the final regulations, altering its position on the use of dilution as a method of treatment:

In all cases, the Agency has determined that for non-toxic hazardous characteristic wastes, it should not matter how the characteristic property is removed so long as it is removed. Thus, dilution is an acceptable treatment method for such wastes.

Id. at 22,532. The Agency included dilution within the ambit of the "deactivation" treatment standard. The final rule defined the standard as "deactivation to remove the hazardous characteristics of a waste due to its ignitability, *corrosivity*, and/or *reactivity.*" *Id.* at 22,693. As long as these characteristics are removed, any method can be employed under the final regulations. The EPA allowed full discretion among specified technological methods of treatment (such as neutralization or incineration) as well as dilution with water or other wastes. For toxic wastes, the prohibition on dilution remained. *See id.* at 22,656.

The Agency admitted that it

> believes the mixing of waste streams to eliminate certain characteristics is appropriate treatment for most wastes which are purely corrosive, or in some cases, reactive or ignitable. As a general matter, these are properties which can effectively be removed by mixing.

Id.. . . . It further conceded that

> this approach does not fully address the potential problem of toxic constituents that may be present in such wastes, nor encourages minimization or recovery of non-toxic characteristic hazardous wastes. EPA has determined that these potential problems should be addressed, if at all, in other rulemakings . . . and are too difficult to resolve in this proceeding, given the extraordinary pressures and limited review time imposed by the May 8 [1990] statutory deadline.

Id. at 22,665–66. Only in three subcategories of ICR wastes did the EPA mandate the use of technological treatment: reactive sulfides, 57 Fed. Reg. 8,086, 8,089 (1992)(technical correction to third-third rule); reactive cyanides, 55 Fed. Reg. at 22,551; and ignitable liquid nonwastewater wastes containing more than ten percent total organic compounds, *Id.* at 22,544. For all corrosive wastes, other ignitable liquid wastes (nonwastewaters with low total organic compounds and ignitable wastewaters), ignitable compressed gases, ignitable reactive wastes, explosive wastes, water reactives, and other reactives dilution would be acceptable. *Id.* at 22,543–53.

* * *

Industry petitioners contend that RCRA does not provide authority for the EPA to mandate treatment of characteristic wastes after their ignitability, corrosiveness, *reactivity*, or EP toxicity has been addressed. They make a straightforward argument: Subtitle C regulations attach to a waste only when it is hazardous. The moment a waste ceases to meet the regulatory definition of a hazardous waste, the EPA loses its authority to regulate further. Thus, in industry petitioners' view, RCRA's cradle-to-grave system covers waste only if it remains hazardous throughout its life and at the moment of its burial.

Industry petitioners point to a welter of provisions in RCRA where the words "hazardous waste" are used as proof that the statute applies only to waste defined as hazardous. Subtitle C, they explain, is entitled "Hazardous Waste Management," and the entire subtitle addresses that problem—the management of hazardous waste. They add that some statements by the EPA have suggested the same reading of the statute. *See*, e.g., 54 Fed. Reg. 1,056, 1,093 (1989)(a waste that no longer exhibits a hazardous characteristic "is no longer subject to the requirements of Subtitle C of RCRA").

In their view, the 1984 Amendments did not change this boundary. They point out that land disposal is defined in part as "any placement of such hazardous waste in a landfill, [or] surface impoundment," RCRA § 3004(k), 42 U.S.C. § 6924(k); that section 3004(g) similarly "prohibits one or more methods of land disposal of [ ]hazardous wastes," *Id.* § 6924(g)(5); and, finally, that section 3004(m) authorizes land disposal of hazardous waste that has been treated, suggesting to industry petitioners that the provision specifically authorizes only the disposal of wastes that remain hazardous after treatment. Thus, they conclude, the disposal restrictions can apply only to wastes that are hazardous at the moment of disposal.

In its brief, the EPA reiterates the rationales stated in its final rule: The key provisions of the land-ban program, sections 3004(g)(5) and (m), can be read as allowing the Agency to apply land disposal restrictions at any time it wishes; those provisions at a minimum contemplate activity that occurs before land disposal; section 3004(m)(1) requires treatment to avoid the prohibition on land disposal; and treatment must take place, by definition, before disposal occurs. This reading, the EPA adds, dovetails with the concern expressed in the report accompanying the Senate version of the 1984 Amendments, that hazardous waste not be diluted and then disposed of in landfills. *See* S. Rep. No. 284, 98th Cong., 1st Sess. 17 (1983)("Senate Report"). The Agency reasons that the subtitle C program can attach at the point of generation, and the broad language of section 3004(m)(1) allows additional treatment to remove risks posed by wastes beyond those inherent in the characteristic.

To succeed in their *Chevron* step one argument, industry petitioners must show that Congress "has directly spoken to the precise question at issue" and has "unambiguously expressed [its] intent." 467 U.S. at 842–43.... We find little support in the statute or our prior decisions for the notion that Congress mandated the line industry petitioners draw. These petitioners believe that the definition of a hazardous waste acts as a revolving regulatory door, allowing continual entrance and egress from RCRA's requirements. The key provisions of the statute support a contrary view—that hazardous waste becomes subject to the land disposal program as soon as it is generated.

RCRA directs the Administrator to "promulgate regulations identifying the characteristics of hazardous waste ... which shall be subject to the provisions of this subchapter." RCRA § 3001(b)(1), 42 U.S.C. § 6921(b)(1). This appears to bring a waste within the statutory scheme once it is identified as hazardous. Under the dictates of the 1984

Amendments, the Administrator "shall promulgate regulations . . . [banning land disposal for] any hazardous waste identified or listed under section 6921 of this title." RCRA § 3004(g)(4), 42 U.S.C. § 6924(g)(4). Again, the focus is on the identification of a waste as hazardous.

This reading of the statute is consistent with our prior interpretations. In *API*, we explained that "once a waste is listed or identified as hazardous, its subsequent management is regulated." *API*, 906 F.2d at 733. After the 1984 Amendments, we added, regulation of the waste included the prohibitions of section 3004. *Id.* In *Shell Oil*, we noted that the power to manage waste is created "at [the] point" a waste is defined as hazardous and discarded. *Shell Oil*, 950 F.2d at 754. Once in the system, we found that the power to manage hazardous waste provided by RCRA gave the EPA the authority to regulate waste until "it ceases to pose a hazard to the public." *Id.*; see also RCRA § 1004(7), 42 U.S.C. § 6903(7) (defining "hazardous waste management"). We therefore deferred to the EPA's determination that resource recovery from hazardous waste came within the Agency's subtitle C authority.

Industry petitioners nevertheless contend that we adopted the exact position they now advocate in *American Mining Congress v. EPA*, 824 F.2d 1177 (D.C.Cir.1987)("AMC I"). To be sure, in *AMC I*, we stated that the EPA's authority, in the first instance, extends only to waste that is identified as hazardous, *id.* at 1179, and that Congress took care in drafting the definition of solid waste to reflect its concern over the reach of the EPA's authority, ... But, as we emphasized in *Shell Oil*, the definitions of solid and hazardous wastes provide the keys to entrance into the RCRA system; "only materials that meet both definitions will come within the [RCRA] 'cradle-to-grave' regulatory scheme," *Shell Oil*, 950 F.2d at 754 . . .; and we also stated that once within the system, the waste will remain there so long as it poses a threat to the public health and safety. *Id. AMC I* turned on the question of whether secondary materials immediately reused within an industrial process had been "discarded" under the terms of RCRA. We concluded that they had not. *AMC I*, 824 F.2d at 1185–87. Our decision in that case stands for no more. *See Shell Oil*, 954 F.2d at 755–56.

The 1984 Amendments also provide the EPA with the authority to mandate treatment past the point at which a characteristic is removed. Section 3004(g)(5) requires the Administrator to promulgate regulations prohibiting land disposal of hazardous wastes "except with respect to a hazardous waste which has complied with the pretreatment regulations promulgated under subsection (m) of this section." 42 U.S.C. § 6924(g)(5). Subsection (m)(1), in turn, calls on the Administrator to

> specify[ ]those levels or methods of treatment, if any, which substantially diminish the toxicity of the waste or substantially reduce the likelihood of migration of hazardous constituents from the waste so that short-term and long-term threats to human health and the environment are minimized.

RCRA § 3004(m)(1), 42 U.S.C. § 6924(m)(1). The requirement that treatment "substantially diminish the toxicity" or substantially reduce the likelihood of migration of hazardous constituents suggests concerns that go beyond the characteristics identified in 40 C.F.R. Part 261, subpart C. Similarly, in concluding that the EPA had the authority to require technologies that go beyond the elimination of hazardous characteristics, we have noted that "minimize" offers a broad mandate: "To 'minimize' something is, to quote the Oxford English Dictionary, to 'reduce [it] to the smallest possible amount, extent, or degree.' " *HWTC III*, 886 F.2d at 361.

In *HWTC III*, the Chemical Manufacturer's Association ("CMA") attacked treatment standards for solvents under the land disposal program because the EPA required treatment of all solvents, not simply those deemed unsafe. *See id.* at 361. The CMA argued that this regime could result in treatment "below established levels of hazard," and therefore was an unreasonable interpretation of the Act. *Id.* at 362. We disagreed, noting that section 3004(m) demands that treatment minimize risks to health and the environment. Treatment might be unreasonable, we added, if the EPA required treatment of wastes that "posed no threat to human health or the environment." *Id.* at 363. That was not the case in *HWTC III*, nor is it true here.

We conclude that, in combination, sections 3004(g)(5) and (m) provide the EPA with authority to bar land disposal of certain wastes unless they have been treated to reduce risks beyond those presented by the characteristics themselves. We also find the Agency's assertion of regulatory authority over the wastes from the moment they are generated to be "based on a permissible construction of the statute." *Chevron*, 467 U.S. at 843.

E. NRDC Petitioners' Challenge to Deactivation Treatment Standard

NRDC petitioners ask this court to vacate the deactivation treatment standard as applied to ICR wastes because it authorizes the dilution of these wastes to eliminate their ignitability, corrosiveness, or *reactivity* rather than mandating use of technological treatment. NRDC petitioners rely on the language of section 3004(m)(1), statements in the legislative history of the 1984 Amendments, and the overall structure of the RCRA program as support for their position that treatment does not include dilution. They claim that some form of technology must be used to treat wastes in all instances.

They also contend that dilution fails to satisfy the statutory requirement that treatment minimize short-term and long-term threats to human health and the environment, or to substantially diminish the toxicity of the waste. In their view, the removal of these characteristics through dilution only affects the short-term risk that the waste will manifest that property; it does not address the threats posed by the hazardous organic and inorganic constituents of those wastes. NRDC petitioners also assert that the Agency's interpretation of RCRA fails *Chevron*'s second step because the statute does not permit a plea of time pressures as a reason for failing to require treatment at the levels mandated by section 3004(m). *See* 55 Fed. Reg. at 22,665–66.

We believe that dilution can, in principle, constitute an acceptable form of treatment for ICR wastes. We do not read the 1984 Amendments as mandating the use of the best demonstrated available technologies ("BDAT") in all situations. To reiterate, section 3004(m)(1) directs the Administrator to

> specify[ ]those levels or methods of treatment, if any, which substantially diminish the toxicity of the waste or substantially reduce the likelihood of migration of hazardous constituents from the waste so that short-term and long-term threats to human health and the environment are minimized.

42 U.S.C. § 6924(m)(1). NRDC petitioners insist that under the plain terms of this provision, the deactivation standard fails because dilution is not a "method of treatment." Although they acknowledge that the statutory definition of "treatment" is broad enough to encompass dilution, see RCRA § 1004(34), 42 U.S.C. § 6903(34), they maintain that Congress had a more exacting criterion in mind when it enacted section 3004(m).

We agree that the section imposes an exacting standard: It requires that treatment prior to land disposal "substantially diminish the toxicity of the waste or substantially reduce the likelihood of migration of hazardous constituents from the waste so that short-term and long-term threats to human health and the environment are minimized." RCRA 3004(m)(1), 42 U.S.C. § 6924(m)(1). But this provision does not bar dilution as a means of treating ICR wastes; instead, it defines the purposes that a method of treatment must achieve. Any treatment that meets those objectives is permissible. When read against RCRA's broad definition of treatment, we cannot say Congress clearly barred dilution as an acceptable methodology. *See Chevron*, 467 U.S. at 842–43.

NRDC petitioners advert to a number of statements in the legislative history that they believe make clear Congress's unexpressed intent to prohibit dilution as a form of treatment in all cases. They cite, for example, the committee report accompanying the Senate version of the 1984 Amendments, which notes that hazardous waste should be "transformed to a less hazardous chemical form through treatment." Senate Report at 17. More directly, the report states:

> The dilution of wastes by the addition of other hazardous wastes or any other materials during waste handling, transportation, treatment, or storage is not an acceptable method of treatment to reduce the concentration of hazardous constituents. Only dilution which occurs as a normal part of the process that results in the waste can be taken into account in establishing concentration levels.

Id. These petitioners also quote from Senator Moynihan's statement explaining the floor amendment that became section 3004(m): "The requisite levels or methods of treatment established by the Agency should be the best that has been demonstrated to be achievable." 130 Cong. Rec. 20,803 (1984)(statement of Sen. Moynihan). They infer from this that only treatment with technology will meet the standard of section 3004(m).

We are unpersuaded. The Senate committee version of the 1984 Amendments, which the committee report addresses, mandated the treatment of EP toxic wastes among the many others specified in the legislation. It did not require the treatment of ICR wastes. *See* Senate Report at 17–18. The strong statements cautioning against dilution as a means of treatment must be read in that context. Similarly, Senator Moynihan's statement referred to the particular problem of highly mobile, highly toxic wastes. *See* 130 Cong. Rec. S9,178. These citations to legislative history do not show that Congress spoke directly to the dilution of ICR wastes. *See Chevron*, 467 U.S. at 842–43.

We are more troubled by the question whether the dilution of certain ICR wastes will satisfy section 3004(m). Treatment must meet the standards established by that section, and its requirements are clear: It must remove the characteristic and reduce the presence of hazardous constituents when those constituents are present in sufficient concentrations to pose a threat to human health or the environment. The EPA's regulations "must be fully consistent with" those requirements. *NLRB v. United Food & Commercial Workers Union, Local 23*, AFL-CIO, 484 U.S. 112, 123, 108 S.Ct. 413, 98 L.Ed.2d 429 (1987). We find it unclear whether dilution is fully consistent with section 3004(m)'s treatment standards for all of the subcategories of ICR wastes for which the EPA has proscribed deactivation.

As we have explained, the proposed rule pointed to significant problems that could arise if dilution was accepted as a means of treating ICR wastes. In the final regulations, the Agency found that deactivation "addresses the environmental concern from the properties themselves." 55 Fed. Reg. at 22,655. The EPA admitted, however, that "the characteristic level is only one indicator of hazard and, thus, removal of the specific characteristic is not the same as assuring that the waste is safe." *Id.* at 22,651. It then acknowledged "that this approach does not fully address the potential problem of toxic constituents that may be present in [ICR] wastes, nor encourage[ ] minimization ... of non-toxic characteristic hazardous wastes." *Id.* at 22,665. The Agency's brief contains a similar admission. Brief for Respondent at 96–97.

Unfortunately, these confessions are not a substitute for a rule conforming to the statute's command. We conclude that the deactivation standard, in its present form, is permissible only in the case of corrosive wastes; and then only so long as they do not contain hazardous constituents that, following dilution, would themselves present a continuing danger to human health or the environment.

1. Ignitable Wastes

At oral argument, counsel for the EPA conceded that some ignitable wastes subject to the deactivation standard include hazardous or toxic constituents that will remain after dilution, perhaps at sufficient levels to pose a risk to human health and the environment. *See* also Reply Brief for NRDC petitioners at 12–14 (ignitable wastes have significant hazardous constituents); EPA, Final BDAT Background Document (May 1990), at 2–2 and 2–3, reprinted in Joint Appendix ("J.A.") at 456–57 (same). Further, in the proposed rule, the EPA barred dilution of all ignitable wastes because of the risk of emissions of volatile organic compounds during dilution and the possibility that the waste would regain its ignitability after dilution. *See also* BDAT Background Document at 2–10, reprinted in J.A. at 464 ("If the ignitable wastes are diluted, [volatile organic compounds] will ordinarily be emitted in concentrations far exceeding those emitted by treatment processes in which these volatiles are destroyed.").

The final regulations suggested a number of technology-based treatment methods that might be used for ignitable wastes, but in the end authorized dilution if it would remove the characteristic alone, except for ignitable wastes including more than ten percent total organic compounds. In its brief, the Agency stated that the problem of emissions and the possibility that the waste would regain its ignitability were not significant, that some dilution prior to treatment would be beneficial, and that the problem of VOC emissions, if any occur, would be "best addressed by establishing air emission limitations in the future." Brief for Respondent at 93.

In view of the EPA's position that treatment pursuant to section 3004(m) requires the removal of a waste's hazardous characteristic and the reduction of other hazardous constituents, and the Agency's concessions that constituents are present in some ignitable wastes subject to the deactivation standard, we vacate this part of the rule. To conform with its own reading of section 3004(m), the Agency must identify the ignitable wastes that include, after dilution, sufficiently high levels of hazardous constituents to pose a risk to human health or the environment, and propose a method of treatment that will deal with these threats. In addition, the Agency must address the problem of VOC emissions from ignitable wastes during dilution. The EPA's statement that it believes that VOC emissions can be controlled by changes in operating parameters is inadequate. It must state, with evidentiary support, that the risk of VOC emissions during dilution is minimal for ignitable wastes now subject to the deactivation standard, or it must require actions to minimize that risk.

2. *Corrosive Wastes*

The EPA asserts in its brief that the sole problem posed by corrosive wastes is their corrosiveness: "There are no hazardous constituents in the waste." Brief for Respondent at 94. Counsel for the EPA made essentially the same representation at oral argument. But NRDC petitioners come to a different conclusion. They point to the proposed rule, see 54 Fed. Reg. at 48,423 ("The Agency prefers neutralization of corrosive wastes over simple dilution because dilution simply creates a larger volume of wastes but does not treat or remove hazardous constituents in the wastes."), and a statement from the EPA's BDAT Background Document stating that some corrosive wastes do in fact possess hazardous constituents beyond their potential for corrosion. *See* BDAT Background Document at 3–2, reprinted in J.A at 485 ("Typically, corrosive wastes that are disposed of by deep well injection are likely to contain toxic organics, whereas landfilled wastes are likely (38 percent) to contain heavy metals."); *see also id.* at 3–7, reprinted in J.A. at 490 (residue from neutralized corrosive wastes can exhibit the characteristic of EP toxicity). NRDC petitioners acknowledge that corrosive wastes can be treated effectively by mixing acid and alkaline wastes; but they object to dilution with water because it will not treat the toxic constituents they claim are present in corrosive wastes. Reply Brief for NRDC petitioners at 15.

The final regulations themselves are somewhat ambiguous on the question of the presence of hazardous constituents. In discussing the deactivation standard applied to acids and alkalines, the EPA states that "many [corrosive] wastes also are hazardous for other reasons, and may require that additional treatment processes be employed besides neutralization, incineration or recovery." 55 Fed. Reg. at 22,549. The Agency also explains that

> *corrosivity* is not defined in the same way EP Toxic wastes are defined. *Corrosivity* is not based on a toxic constituent, where the environmental concern is mass-loading in the environment. With respect to the issue of toxics present in these corrosive wastes, EPA notes that if a corrosive waste also exhibits the toxicity characteristic, it must be treated to meet the treatment standard for the toxic constituent as well. . . .

Id. This explanation begs the question of what is required if the toxic constituent is present in insufficient quantities to cause the waste to be classified as EP toxic as well as corrosive, but in sufficient quantities to engage section 3004(m)'s concerns over residual effects.

We agree with the EPA that dilution can be an acceptable form of treatment of corrosive wastes. But in the face of this record, we cannot rely on the assertions made in the EPA's brief and oral argument that corrosive wastes pose no hazards other than those presented by this characteristic. If, however, the facts will support these assurances, the EPA may cure this defect and meet the requirements of section 3004(m) with a statement, backed by evidence, that the corrosive wastes subject to the deactivation standard do not contain hazardous constituents that pose a threat to human health and the environment. If such a statement may be made, the Agency should be able to revise its rulemaking prior to the issuance of the mandate in this case.

3. Reactive Wastes

With regard to reactive wastes, we have a problem of a different kind. Although, in the final regulations and in its brief, the EPA spoke of ICR wastes generally when it confessed that hazardous constituents might remain in some wastes following deactivation, see 55 Fed.Reg. at 22,655–56; Brief for Respondent at 96–97, we find nothing in the proposed or final regulations to suggest that reactive wastes contain such constituents, other than reactive cyanides and sulfides for which the EPA ordered technological treatment. Nor have NRDC petitioners identified any. Therefore, we have no basis for vacating the use of the deactivation standard for the remaining subcategories of reactive wastes because of the threat of migration of hazardous constituents.

The EPA, however, has only partially addressed the problem, raised in the proposed rule, of the effect of dilution on reactive wastes—that those wastes could display their reactive characteristic in the process of dilution. *See* 54 Fed. Reg. at 48,426. *See also* BDAT Background Document at 4–3, reprinted in J.A. at 503 (water reactives "(1) react violently with water; (2) form potentially explosive mixtures with water; or (3) when mixed with water, generate toxic gases, vapors, or fumes in a quantity sufficient to present a danger to human health or the environment."). In the final regulations, based on comments received, the EPA suggested that dilution with "certain organic liquids" prior to dilution with water would remove the risk of a violent reaction in the three subcategories of reactive wastes for which the deactivation treatment standard is permitted, allowing subsequent incineration or chemical treatment. 55 Fed. Reg. at 22,553. The Agency noted that it was "not restricting the use of this practice" for any reactive waste. *Id.*

The final regulations thus offer no assurance that dilution of explosive, water reactive, or other reactive wastes will not create a risk of violent reaction. The final regulations state that the Agency will not prohibit the practice of diluting wastes with other materials to reduce the risk of reaction, and suggest that this might be a useful step to take prior to technological treatment. This ignores the reality of the EPA's deactivation standard: Dilution of these wastes by any method is permissible if it removes the characteristic.

We grant, on narrow grounds, the petition for review as to reactive wastes. The Agency must limit dilution to methods that will curb the risk of violent reactions, mandate preliminary steps to prevent such reactions, require a technological treatment, or find, with the backing of evidence, that there is no significant risk of reaction present for any of the three subcategories of reactive wastes for which deactivation is a permissible form of treatment.

* * *

Finally, contrary to what the EPA suggests, it will not suffice that the Agency promises to fully address certain unresolved problems of hazardous constituents in future rulemakings. In enacting the 1984 Amendments, Congress imposed very strict deadlines. Moreover, it has chosen to enforce them by decreeing that any hazardous waste that is not covered by a valid regulation within the date specified will be denied land disposal. We understand the enormous difficulties that the Agency has undoubtedly faced, given competing obligations and the complexity of the task. Nevertheless, we cannot treat the final rule as other than that—the EPA's final response to the task entrusted to it by Congress. *Cf. State of Colorado v. Dep't of Interior*, 880 F.2d 481, 485 (D.C.Cir. 1989) (regulations promulgated by the deadline "constitute the [Agency's] complete response in compliance with the statutory requirements.").

III. THE EPA'S DILUTION RULES

The issues that we next face focus on challenges to the EPA's new dilution permissions, formulated to integrate RCRA requirements with Clean Water Act ("CWA") treatment systems and deep injection wells regulated pursuant to the Safe Drinking Water Act ("SDWA"). Contemporaneously with the promulgation of the third-third rule, the EPA amended a rule that had prohibited dilution of wastes in lieu of treatment. Pursuant to the amended rule, centralized CWA treatment systems may aggregate certain characteristic waste streams; the aggregation results in dilution that purportedly removes the hazardous characteristic without treatment. Under this new rule, dilution is allowed where the EPA has not specified a particular treatment method and where the CWA system includes a treatment protocol addressed to the types of characteristic wastes being aggregated. As a consequence of this rule, CWA treatment facilities may continue to use unlined surface impoundments as part of their treatment trains. The EPA also promulgated a new rule that permits the operators of deep injection wells to dilute all characteristic wastes, in lieu of treatment, prior to underground injection.

* * *

Petitioner's argument ... fails because listed wastes are, in any event, fundamentally different from characteristic wastes. As discussed in Part I of this opinion, listed wastes generally contain a certain substance that is per se harmful (such as arsenic). Dilution does nothing to remove that element from the waste stream and prevent it from entering the environment where it may reaccumulate. By contrast, some characteristic wastes may be altered permanently by dilution and, hence, it is reasonable to permit aggregation. In these cases, dilution and treatment are one and the same.

The fact that a rule may be justified on alternate grounds, however, will not normally save it from remand. *See SEC v. Chenery Corp.*, 318 U.S. 80, 95, 87 L.Ed. 626, 63 S.Ct. 454 (1943). Although the EPA does not offer this argument in its brief, it is well made in the final rule. The EPA explicitly linked its approach to the dilution prohibition to its view that dilution constituted acceptable treatment for some characteristic wastes.

Dilution rules are intended to prohibit dilution in lieu of treatment and to ensure that wastes are treated in appropriate ways. As discussed in the preamble sections on treatment of characteristic wastes, EPA believes the mixing of waste streams to eliminate certain characteristics is appropriate for most wastes which are purely corrosive, or in some cases, reactive or ignitable. As a general matter, these are properties which can effectively be removed by mixing. On the other hand, simple dilution is not effective treatment for toxic constituents. Dilution does not itself remove or treat any toxic constituent from the waste.

55 Fed. Reg. at 22,656. Thus, the EPA has adequately justified excluding listed wastes from the scope of Rule 268.3(b). *Cf. Syracuse Peace Council v. FCC*, 867 F.2d 654, 657 (D.C.Cir.1989)("if an agency relies on two grounds for a decision, a court may sustain it if one is valid and if the agency would clearly have acted on that ground even if the other were unavailable"), *cert. denied*, 493 U.S. 1019, 107 L.Ed.2d 737, 110 S.Ct. 717 (1990).

IV.   MISCELLANEA

Finally, various petitioners challenge four additional aspects of the third-third rule: (1) its requirement of periodic corroborative waste testing by disposers (industry petitioners); (2) its adoption of the characteristic level as the waste treatment standard for chromium (NRDC petitioners); (3) its exemption of "Bevill" unit residue from RCRA § 3004(m) standards (NRDC petitioners); and (4) its requirement that waste treatment standards be enforced by grab sampling rather than representative sampling (petitioner Chemical Waste Management, Inc.). . . . . we uphold as reasonable the EPA's corroborative testing and grab sampling requirements but remand for reconsideration the chromium treatment standard and the Bevill unit exemption.

* * *

D.   *"Grab" Sampling*

Finally, petitioner Chemical Waste Management ("CWM") asserts the final rule impermissibly requires compliance and enforcement based on "grab" samples rather than "representative" samples. Preliminarily, we note that a grab sample is a single test sample drawn from a single location, while a "representative" or "composite" sample consists of various samples drawn from different locations so as to yield a representative level for the waste. *See* RCRA Sampling Procedures Handbook 75 (1989), reprinted in J.A. at 1057. The final rule provides: "Where performance data exist based on both the analysis of composite samples and the analysis of grab samples, the Agency establishes the treatment standards based on the analysis of grab samples." 55 Fed. Reg. at 22,539. Implementing this preference, the rule amends 40 C.F.R. § 268.41(a) as follows: "Compliance with [the allowable waste concentrations established herein] is required based upon grab samples." 55 Fed. Reg. at 22,689. . . . The rule also provides that "enforcement of the disposal restrictions [be] based on grab samples." *Id.* at 22,539. n21 CWM challenges the new grab sample provisions on the grounds that they (1) are inconsistent with other regulations requiring that disposers use "representative" sampling to test waste levels and (2) are impermissibly vague. We find neither objection meritorious.

First, CWM argues that requiring grab samples, both for compliance and enforcement testing, is arbitrary because inconsistent with other regulations requiring disposal facilities to use representative sampling in developing waste analysis plans. *See* 40 C.F.R. §§ 264.13(a)(1) and 265.13(a)(1)(each stating: "Before an owner or operator treats, stores, or disposes of any hazardous wastes, or non-hazardous wastes if applicable under § 264.113(d), he must obtain a detailed chemical and physical analysis of a representative sample of the wastes."). We disagree.

As the EPA points out, it is facially reasonable to test compliance with a given standard under the same sampling method used to develop that standard, as the rule requires. Further, variation between results under the different methods will in large part be resolved through the EPA's adjustment of sampling results to account for the inevitable variability of content. *See* 55 Fed. Reg. at 22,539. To the extent that substantial variation may nevertheless result, an individual disposer can raise as a defense to enforcement the EPA's prior approval of its disposal plan, including the sampling method specified therein.

Finally, we summarily reject CWM's vagueness challenge to the grab sampling requirement. The EPA's published definition aside, *see* RCRA Sampling Procedures Handbook 75, reprinted in J.A. at 1057, the expression "grab sample" seems graphically self-defining. In fact, CWM's own discussion of the requirement's alleged arbitrariness demonstrates that it has experienced no difficulty in determining the phrase's meaning. Nevertheless, any vagueness that may inhere in the term can be resolved through explicit drafting of individual disposal permits.

V. CONCLUSION

For the reasons described above, the petitions for review are granted in part and denied in part.

* * *

Appendix A

42 U.S.C. § 6924(g)(5):

> not later than the date specified in the schedule published under this subsection, the Administrator shall promulgate final regulations prohibiting one or more methods of land disposal of the hazardous wastes listed on such schedule except for methods of land disposal which the Administrator determines will be protective of human health and the environment for as long as the waste remains hazardous, taking into account the factors referred to in subparagraph (A) through (C) of subsection (d)(1) of this section. For the purposes of this paragraph, a method of land disposal may not be determined to be protective of human health and the environment (except with respect to a hazardous waste which has complied with the pretreatment regulations promulgated under subsection (m) of

this section) unless, upon application by an interested person, it has been demonstrated to the Administrator, to a reasonable degree of certainty, that there will be no migration of hazardous constituents from the disposal unit or injection zone for as long as the wastes remain hazardous.

42 U.S.C. § 6924(m):

Treatment standards for waste subject to land disposal prohibition

(1) Simultaneously with the promulgation of regulations under subsection (d), (e), (f), or (g) of this section prohibiting one or more methods of land disposal of a particular hazardous waste, and as appropriate thereafter, the Administrator shall, after notice and an opportunity for hearings and after consultation with appropriate Federal and State agencies, promulgate regulations specifying those levels or methods of treatment, if any, which substantially diminish the toxicity of the waste or substantially reduce the likelihood of migration of hazardous constituents from the waste so that short-term and long-term threats to human health and the environment are minimized.

(2) If such hazardous waste has been treated to the level or by a method specified in regulations promulgated under this subsection, such waste or residue thereof shall not be subject to any prohibition promulgated under subsection (d), (e), (f), or (g) of this section and may be disposed of in a land disposal facility which meets the requirements of this subchapter. Any regulation promulgated under this subsection for a particular hazardous waste shall become effective on the same date as any applicable prohibition promulgated under subsection (d), (e), (f), or (g) of this section.

* * *

Notes

1. Variances. EPA may extend the effective date of a treatment standard upon a finding that inadequate treatment capacity is available to handle the particular waste. Such extensions are termed *national capacity variances*. EPA also may grant variances to specific waste streams where the generators or TSD operators can demonstrate that the designated treatment standards cannot be achieved or are otherwise inappropriate to the specific wastes. Persons seeking these variances, called *no-migration variances*, must be able to demonstrate to EPA that the land disposal of untreated waste will not result in the migration of hazardous constituents from the disposal unit for as long as the wastes remain hazardous. EPA issued procedural and substantive standards for no-migration variance petitions in August 1992.

Among the wastes for which EPA has granted LDR variances are mixed (radioactive and hazardous) waste and *hazardous soils* (soils which contain a listed hazardous waste or exhibit a characteristic of hazardous waste).

§ 5.5 CORRECTIVE ACTION

All RCRA TSD facilities that are permitted or are operating under interim status are required to cleanup current and former waste treatment, storage and disposal areas. This cleanup obligation, known as *corrective action*, is a permit condition of TSDs and an operating condition for interim status facilities.

The cleanup standards applicable to RCRA corrective action are comparable to those applied at CERCLA/Superfund facilities. Indeed, virtually any facility subject to RCRA corrective action requirements also could be compelled to remediate onsite conditions under CERCLA. Many TSD operators prefer to remediate their facilities under RCRA rather than CERCLA since RCRA corrective action generally provides greater flexibility, imposes fewer public participation requirements and, as a result, usually is less costly than CERCLA cleanups.

The 1984 amendments expanded EPA's authority to require cleanup of environmental problems caused by hazardous waste facilities. Corrective action is required for *releases* of hazardous waste or constituents, including those that have migrated "beyond the facility boundary," from any *solid waste management unit* at a TSD *facility* that is seeking or otherwise subject to a RCRA permit. The amendments also authorize EPA to require corrective action at *interim status facilities* whenever there is, or has been, a release of hazardous waste or constituents. RCRA permits issued after enactment of the HSWA amendments must require an operator to take corrective action for all releases of hazardous constituents at the TSD facility regardless of when the waste was placed in a unit or whether the unit is currently active.

VINELAND CHEM. CO. v. UNITED STATES EPA

810 F.2d 402 (3d Cir.1987).

STAPLETON, CIRCUIT JUDGE:

Vineland Chemical Company (ViChem) petitions this court to review the determination made by the U.S. Environmental Protection Agency (EPA or Agency) that ViChem had not satisfied the relevant certification requirements under the Resource Conservation and Recovery Act (RCRA) 42 U.S.C. § 6925(e)(2)(Supp. II 1984), and thus could no longer operate its hazardous waste disposal facility under "interim status."

We hold first that the Court of Appeals has jurisdiction to review this termination of interim status. The RCRA provision creating court of appeals jurisdiction authorizes review of permit decisions but is silent with respect to interim status terminations. 42 U.S.C. § 6976(b)(Supp. II 1984). While we find that interim status is not a permit in RCRA's statutory scheme, we hold that § 6976(b), when read in conjunction with the statutory history and the case law favoring court of appeals jurisdiction over petitions for review of agency action, establishes the requisite statutory basis for this court's jurisdiction.

On the merits of the petition for review, we hold that the EPA's interpretation of the statute to require certification by November 8, 1985 is reasonable and is compatible with both the statutory language and the intent of Congress, and therefore we defer to the EPA's construction. Given the EPA's interpretation of the statute, the factual determination that ViChem had failed to satisfy the certification requirements was supported by the record and was neither arbitrary nor capricious.

I.

Vineland Chemical Company operates two surface impoundments which are classified as land disposal facilities for hazardous wastes. RCRA forbids operation of a hazardous waste disposal facility without a permit. 42 U.S.C. § 6925(a)(Supp. II 1984). Prior to final administrative action on a permit application, however, qualified facilities are allowed to operate without a permit under a grandfather clause. Such permission to operate without a RCRA permit is termed "interim status." 42 U.S.C. § 6925(e) (Supp. II 1984).

Since 1980, ViChem has operated its surface impoundments under interim status, having satisfied the statutory requirements of 42 U.S.C. § 6925(e)(1). Interim status facilities must comply with operating requirements established by regulation. 40 C.F.R. § 265 (1985). Among the interim status operating requirements are the financial responsibility requirements at issue in this case. These regulations require operators to acquire liability insurance and provide financial assurances that there will be sufficient resources available for closure and post-closure costs.

. . .

In 1984, Congress amended RCRA to provide for termination of interim status for land disposal facilities, a classification which includes surface impoundments such as ViChem's, 50 Fed. Reg. 38,946, 38,947 (Sept. 25, 1985), if certain conditions were not satisfied. The 1984 amendment stated:

> In the case of each land disposal facility which has been granted interim status under this subsection before November 8, 1984, interim status shall terminate on the date twelve months after November 8, 1984, unless the owner or operator of such facility—
>
> (A) applies for a determination regarding the issuance of a permit under subsection (c) of this section for such facility before the date twelve months after November 8, 1984; and
>
> (B) certifies that such facility is in compliance with all applicable groundwater monitoring and financial responsibility requirements.

Pub. L. No. 98–616, § 213(a)(3), 98 Stat. 3221, 3241 (1984)(codified at 42 U.S.C. § 6925(e)(2)(Supp. II 1984)).

In accordance with § 6925(e)(2)(A), ViChem has submitted a Part B permit application to the New Jersey Department of Environmental Protection (DEP). The EPA has delegated responsibility for administering the RCRA permit program to the DEP as authorized by 42 U.S.C.

§ 6926. No final action has yet been taken on the ViChem permit application.

On November 8, 1985, ViChem submitted to the EPA a document certifying compliance with groundwater monitoring and liability insurance requirements.... The certification did not make any reference to financial assurances to cover closure and post-closure costs. On December 2nd, the EPA notified ViChem by letter that its interim status was terminated as of November 8, 1985 for failure to comply with the certification requirement of § 6925(e)(2)(B). The letter notified ViChem that it could not continue to operate, that it was required to submit a closure plan, and that continued operation could subject ViChem to both civil and criminal penalties. In a letter to the EPA dated December 27, 1985, ViChem attempted to correct the omission by certifying that it had been in compliance with all of the financial responsibility requirements as of November 8. The EPA's reply, dated January 30, 1986, reaffirmed its position that interim status had terminated as of November 8, 1985.

On February 28, 1986, ViChem filed the instant petition in this court, seeking review of the EPA's decision that ViChem's interim status had terminated. Subsequently, the EPA brought an enforcement action in the U.S. District Court of New Jersey.

* * *

ViChem asks this court to invalidate the EPA's termination of interim status for its two surface impoundments on the grounds that: 1) the EPA adopted an impermissible interpretation of § 6925(e)(2), and 2) the Agency's refusal to consider ViChem's submissions made after November 8 was arbitrary and capricious.

A.

ViChem argues that the EPA erred in interpreting § 6925(e)(2) to require submission of certification of compliance with the financial responsibility requirements by November 8, 1985. ViChem contends that the law should be construed to require facility operators to certify that they were in compliance by November 8, 1985, with no submission deadline specified.

The statute itself is most reasonably read to require that certification must be submitted by November 8. The statutory provision at issue states that "interim status shall terminate on the date twelve months after November 8, 1984, unless the owner or operator of such facility— (A) applies for ... a permit ... before the date twelve months after November 8, 1984; and (B) certifies that such facility is in compliance with all applicable groundwater monitoring and financial responsibility requirements." 42 U.S.C. § 6925(e)(2)(Supp. II 1984). Interim status thus terminates on November 8 unless the certification is made, strongly suggesting that Congress intended that certification be due by that date.

In addition to requiring a strained reading of the provision's language, ViChem's construction would leave the EPA in the woeful position of being unable to distinguish those facilities that no longer qualified for interim status from those which simply had not yet certified that they were in compliance as of November 8. Such a construction runs contrary to the clear Congressional intent to accelerate the EPA's enforcement activities. *See* H.R. Rep. No. 198, 98th Cong., 2nd Sess., Pt. I, at 44, reprinted in 1984 U.S. Code Cong. & Admin. News 5576, 5603 (one purpose of 1984 amendments was "to expedite the final permit review of major land disposal . . . facilities and close those facilities that cannot or will not meet the final standards at the earliest possible date").

Admitting some ambiguity in the statute itself, marked by the inclusion of a submission deadline in subsection (e)(2)(A) and the absence of such a date in subsection (e)(2)(B), we must consider the EPA's interpretation of the statute. "It is by now commonplace that 'when faced with a problem of statutory construction, this Court shows great deference to the interpretation given the statute by the officers or agency charged with its administration.'" *EPA v. National Crushed Stone Association*, 449 U.S. 64, 83, 66 L.Ed.2d 268, 101 S.Ct. 295 (1980)(quoting *Udall v. Tallman*, 380 U.S. 1, 16, 13 L.Ed.2d 616, 85 S.Ct. 792 (1965)). "An agency's construction of a statute it is charged with enforcing is entitled to deference if it is reasonable and not in conflict with the expressed intent of Congress." *United States v. Riverside Bayview Homes, Inc.*, 474 U.S. 121, 106 S.Ct. 455, 461, 88 L.Ed.2d 419 (1985), *Accord Chevron, U.S.A., Inc. v. Natural Resources Defense Council, Inc.*, 467 U.S. 837, 842–45, 81 L.Ed.2d 694, 104 S.Ct. 2778 (1984). The statute has consistently been interpreted by the Agency to require certification prior to November 8. . . . 50 Fed. Reg. 38,946 (Sept. 25, 1985); 50 Fed. Reg. 28,702, 28,723–24 (July 15, 1985). As we find this interpretation to be both reasonable and consonant with the intent of Congress, we are obliged to defer to the EPA's interpretation. Thus, we hold that the EPA did not err in requiring § 6925(e)(2)(B) certifications to be submitted by November 8, 1985.

* * *

Notes

1. The concept of corrective action dates back to the original enactment of RCRA in 1976, although the corrective action program lay mostly dormant until the passage of the HSWA in 1984. On July 27, 1990, EPA proposed a comprehensive rule to govern RCRA corrective action (the *proposed corrective action rule*). EPA hopes to issue a final version of the comprehensive rule sometime in 1993.

2. To expedite the cleanup process, EPA issued a final version of the component of this rule governing *corrective action management units* (CAMUs) and *temporary units*. This rule is referred to as the *CAMU rule*. The CAMU rule is designed to facilitate greater use of innovative, onsite treatment as compared with extraction for costly offsite treatment (such as incineration) and disposal. Among other things, the corrective action rule allows facilities to create onsite CAMUs to manage hazardous waste which is generated from the cleanup. The CAMUs are subject to specific management standards but are not subject to LDR restrictions and minimum technology requirements (*MTRs*) for land disposal facilities. Facilities also may create *temporary units* to manage hazardous waste for up to 180 days under less stringent management standards.

The CAMUs and temporary units may only be used for onsite remediation waste. They may not be used to manage ongoing process wastes (often termed *as-generated* wastes), wastes generated from offsite cleanups, or wastes that are generated onsite but treated offsite prior to disposal. Wastes that are not eligible for management in CAMUs must be managed in permitted TSDs in accordance with all applicable LDR treatment standards and MTRs. Notwithstanding these limitations, the availability of onsite CAMUs and temporary units can provide considerable cost savings as compared with conventional cleanups involving offsite treatment and disposal.

3. Sludge is the solid by-product of sewage treatment plants. Such plants, also known as publicly owned treatment works, typically treat both domestic wastestreams (from individual households) and industrial wastestreams (from industrial sources). The treatment produces an effluent-treated wastewater which is usually discharged in surface water. The solids removed in the treatment process compose the sludge.

4. Historical Overview of Corrective Action. The original 1976 RCRA statute included somewhat restrictive provisions for corrective action. Prior to the 1984 RCRA amendments (called HSWA), EPA could use the corrective action provision only to:

- require cleanups at facilities where past or present management of solid or hazardous waste may have presented an imminent and substantial endangerment of health or the environment;

- require operators to investigate and test for suspected releases that presented a substantial hazard to human health or the environment; and

- require corrective action for releases from active hazardous waste management units (called *regulated units*) at RCRA permitted facilities.

EPA's pre-HSWA corrective action authority did not extend to inactive units or units in which non-hazardous solid wastes were managed. Additionally, EPA could require corrective action at *interim status* facilities only by accelerating the permit process and then requiring corrective action as a condition of the permit.

The 1984 HSWA expanded EPA's corrective action authority to include both permitted and *interim status* RCRA facilities. Today, any newly issued or renewed TSD permit must require the TSD operator to remediate hazardous waste releases from all active *and inactive* Solid Waste Management Units (*SWMUs*) at the facility, regardless of the time at which waste was placed therein. Facilities permitted before November 8, 1984 (the effective date of HSWA) will have to comply with corrective action requirements when their permits expire or are reopened.

HSWA also extended corrective action requirements *beyond the boundaries* of permitted facilities. Thus, the operator of a TSD from which released hazardous constituents have migrated to neighboring lands must cleanup the neighboring properties unless the operator is unable to secure permission from local authorities and the affected property owners. This requirement applies to RCRA-permitted facilities and all landfills, surface impoundments and waste pile units that received hazardous waste after July 26, 1982.

For *interim status* facilities, *i.e.*, facilities that have not yet been permitted as TSDs, corrective action normally is imposed in the form of an administrative order, as opposed to a permit condition. EPA may enforce the corrective action order through judicial proceedings, if necessary. EPA's corrective action jurisdiction over interim status facilities is potentially more extensive than that applicable to permitted facilities because interim status corrective action orders may address releases other than those from SWMUs.

5. **Trigger for Corrective Action.** EPA asserts corrective action jurisdiction when it obtains information that there has been a *release* to the environment of a hazardous waste or constituent from (1) a SWMU at a permitted TSD facility or (2) at an interim status facility. Each of these terms, as they relate to corrective action jurisdiction.

6. **Releases Triggering Corrective Action.** For purposes of corrective action, a *release* is any spilling, leaking, pouring, emitting, emptying, discharging, injecting, pumping, escaping, leaching, dumping or disposing of hazardous wastes (including hazardous constituents) into the environment. This definition extends the reach of corrective action to include abandoned or discarded barrels, containers and other closed receptacles containing hazardous wastes or hazardous constituents. Moreover, the definition encompasses releases to all environmental media, including air, surface water, groundwater or land.

Two aspects concerning the meaning of release are noteworthy. First, releases triggering corrective action by permitted TSDs are limited to releases from SWMUs. Releases from non-SWMUs do not require corrective action. Second, under HSWA, a release of *any size* is sufficient to invoke corrective action. EPA no longer need establish as a prerequisite to corrective action jurisdiction that the release poses an imminent and substantial endangerment to public health or the environment.

UNITED STATES v. WASTE INDUS.

734 F.2d 159 (4th Cir.1984).

SPROUSE, CIRCUIT JUDGE:

After the Environmental Protection Agency (EPA) investigated the Flemington landfill waste disposal site in New Hanover County, North Carolina (the Flemington landfill) for possible water pollution in the surrounding area, the United States of America for the Administrator of the EPA initiated this action against Waste Industries, Inc.; Waste Industries of New Hanover County, Inc.; the New Hanover County Board of Commissioners; and the individual owner-lessors ... of land used for the Flemington landfill (all defendants will be referred to collectively as the landfill group). The EPA demanded affirmative action by the landfill group under section 7003 of the Resource Conservation and Recovery Act of 1976 (Act), 42 U.S.C. § 6973, to abate alleged threats to public health and the environment posed by hazardous chemicals leaking from the Flemington landfill, to monitor the area for further contamination, to reimburse the EPA for money spent on the area, and to provide residents with a permanent potable water supply.... The district court granted the landfill group's motion to dismiss under Federal Rule of Civil Procedure 12(b)(6) for failure to state a cause of action and the EPA brought this appeal. We reverse.

I

The district court, before ruling on the motion to dismiss, referred the case to a United States magistrate for factual development by order filed April 10, 1980. The magistrate issued lengthy factual findings which were taken as true by the district court for purposes of the motion. Essentially, the findings of fact showed that before 1968, New Hanover County, North Carolina (County) had no trash or solid waste disposal programs or facilities. Private trash and garbage dumps existed throughout the County, but most were simply the result of the public's disposal of garbage and waste on private property without the permission of the property owners. The County first began to address the problem in 1968 when it contracted with the city of Wilmington to use its landfill facilities. The County negotiated leases for two other landfill sites after finding that use of the Wilmington facility did not alleviate the problem. The County's experience with landfill operations was unsatisfactory, however, and in the fall of 1971, the County began looking for other solutions to its disposal problems. After some investigation, the County Board granted Waste Industries, Inc. and Waste Industries of New Hanover County, Inc. (referred to collectively as Waste Industries) an exclusive license to dispose of solid waste generated in the County.

Under the terms of the license, Waste Industries was to establish and operate landfills for the sanitary disposal of solid waste generated within the County on sites Waste Industries owned. Waste Industries was to obtain all licenses and permits for operation of the landfills. The license agreement contained several provisions common to County contracts at that time: it required (a) that Waste Industries hold the County harmless for claims arising out of Waste Industries' actions; (b) that Waste Industries provide a performance bond; and (c) that Waste Industries observe state and local regulations. It also, among other things, required Waste Industries to provide the County with a review of the volume of the material disposed. In return, Waste Industries gained an exclusive franchise to operate sanitary landfills within the County to provide sanitary disposal of solid waste, such as inflammable or toxic materials and industrial, commercial, and agricultural by-products. The Waste Industries—County agreement was renewed, rewritten, or amended in 1975, 1977, and 1978.

After signing the initial agreement in 1972, Waste Industries obtained several landfill sites, including the seventy-acre Flemington site leased from private owners. The Flemington leases granted Waste Industries sole use and control of the premises. The landfill Waste Industries then established on the site is situated in a hole from which sand has been removed, known as a "sand barrow pit"; the surrounding soil is composed of highly permeable sand. The Flemington landfill is within a mile of both the Cape New Fear and Northeast Cape New Fear Rivers. During the operation of the landfill, unknown quantities of solid and hazardous waste were buried at the site. These wastes began leaching through the sandy soil beneath them and into the groundwater aquifer below.

Before Waste Industries began operating the landfill, the residents of the Flemington community had high quality groundwater. Flemington area residents first noticed a decline in water quality in autumn 1977, when their water became foul in color, taste, and smell. Some residents suffered illnesses or side effects such as blisters, boils, and stomach distress they attribute to their use of well water. Residents complained to the County Board and demanded help.

In response to residents' demands, the County in 1978 placed surplus water tanks that it still operates in the Flemington area. Many residents, however, had found it difficult to use these tanks because of infirmity or disability. Many families wash their clothes at laundromats and drive to the homes of friends or relatives elsewhere to bathe. Others have abandoned their homes because of the contaminated water.

In addition to constructing the water tanks, the County in August 1978 referred the question of groundwater quality in and near the Flemington community to the North Carolina Department of Natural Resources and Community Development. The Department directed Waste Industries to cease disposing of waste at the Flemington landfill, which it did on June 30, 1979.

Meanwhile, the water contamination problem was brought to the attention of the EPA's regional office, which conducted hydrologic investigations of Flemington groundwater and well water in April, July, and September 1979. The September investigation was the broadest undertaken by the EPA and was designed to determine what landfill wastes were contaminating area groundwater and in what direction the contaminated aquifer groundwater was moving beneath the Flemington area. Analysis of Flemington area groundwater samples taken by the EPA revealed a large number of toxic, organic, and inorganic contaminants, including known carcinogens, resulting from improper disposal of waste at the Flemington landfill. The contaminants found beneath the landfill and in residential wells include tetrachloroethylene, benzene, trichloroethylene; 1, 2–dichloroethane; vinyl chloride, methylene chloride, and lead. These chemicals, migrating from the Flemington landfill, have been detected in residential wells at levels sufficient to affect adversely human health and the environment. The presence of chlorides, dichlorophenol, chlorobenzene, iron, manganese, phenol, and zinc has rendered the water in the wells unfit for human consumption because some of these chemicals are suspected carcinogens and all of them are a source of extremely bad taste or odor in water. Concentrations of lead, benzene, tetrachloroethylene, trichlorethylene, 1, 2–dichloroethane, and vinyl chloride found in three residential wells pose an unacceptably high risk of neurological damage in children and cancer in humans of any age.

After conducting its July 1979 tests, the EPA warned many local residents that continued use of their wells for any purpose would endanger their health, and informed the County that additional water tanks were needed to meet local residents' needs. The EPA helped the County obtain commitments for three-quarters of the funds needed to install a permanent water system in the Flemington community—half from the federal government and one-quarter from the state of North Carolina. The County initially approved the plan but later abandoned it. Finally, after the September 1979 testing established the landfill as a source of groundwater contamination, the EPA demanded that the County provide an adequate water supply to Flemington residents. A water system funded with federal, state, and local money is now in operation.

The new water system, however, has not solved the problem of escaping waste. As precipitation infiltrates the landfill waste and transports contaminants through permeable soil, the contaminants reach the local aquifer and move laterally through the aquifer in the direction of groundwater flow to the south and east. Tests indicate that the process of leaching and migration of contaminants will continue indefinitely unless remedial action is taken.

II

The EPA, in its initial complaint, requested preliminary and permanent injunctive relief requiring the appropriate parties: (1) to supply affected residents with a permanent and potable source of water; (2) to develop and implement a plan to prevent further contamination; (3) to restore the groundwater; (4) to monitor the area for further contamination; and (5) to reimburse the EPA for money spent in connection with the Flemington landfill. The EPA later withdrew its request for preliminary relief when the federal, state, and local governments, as described above, jointly funded the installation of a permanent safe water supply, but it continued to demand in its complaint a plan to prevent further contamination, the restoration of groundwater, site monitoring, and reimbursement.

The district court, in a thorough opinion, *United States v. Waste Industries*, 556 F.Supp. 1301 (E.D.N.C.1982), found that the EPA's claim for permanent injunctive relief failed to state a cause of action. It concluded that Waste Industries' failure to abate the leaching of contaminants was not actionable under section 7003 of the Act, because the provision was not intended to apply to past conduct that terminated before enforcement was sought. The district court arrived at this conclusion after considering the language of section 7003, its context, the section's use of the present tense, the location of the section within the complete statute, the section's possible emergency nature, its asserted solely jurisdictional nature, its legislative history, and the presumption against retroactive application of statutes.

On appeal, the EPA contends that the district court relied on erroneous premises to support its conclusion and argues that the broad remedial purposes of section 7003 can only be served by permitting actions such as this requiring malfeasant polluters to correct their past abuses of the environment. The landfill group, relying on the district court's reasoning, reads the statute restrictively. We disagree with this limited interpretation of section 7003 as restraining only active human conduct, and reverse. The stated rules of statutory construction simply do not apply and comparison to other statutes cited by the district court sheds no light on congressional purpose in enacting section 7003.

III

Section 7003 of the Act provides that [n]otwithstanding any other provision of this chapter, upon receipt of evidence that the handling, storage, treatment, transportation or disposal of any solid waste or hazardous waste may present an imminent and substantial endangerment to health or the environment, the Administrator may bring suit on behalf of the United States in the appropriate District Court to immediately restrain any person contributing to such handling, storage, treatment, transportation or disposal to stop such handling, storage, treatment, transportation, or disposal or to take such other action as may be necessary.

The landfill group contends, and the district court held, that this section does not authorize an action to correct hazardous conditions because it only regulates the wastes themselves before or as they are produced, not the conditions they later create. The fallacy of that contention is demonstrated by the indication of Congress that section 7003 remedies exist apart from the other provisions in the Act's structure. In addition, section 7003 stands apart from the other sections of the Act defining the EPA's regulatory authority. The regulatory scheme for hazardous wastes appears in subtitle C of the Act; the scheme for solid wastes, in subtitle D. In contrast, section 7003 appears in subtitle G, and it is designed to deal with situations in which the regulatory schemes break down or have been circumvented.

We do not attach the same significance to the location of section 7003 in the miscellaneous subtitle of the statute as did the lower court. This section is logically placed in the statutory structure to provide a remedy for environmental endangerment by hazardous or solid waste, whether or not those engaging in the endangering acts are subject to any other provision of the Act. Its application "notwithstanding any other provision of this chapter" indicates a congressional intent to include a broadly applicable section dealing with the concerns addressed by the statute as a whole.

The operative language of section 7003 authorizes the administrator to bring an action against any person contributing to the alleged disposal to stop such disposal "or to take such other action as may be necessary." 42 U.S.C. § 6973(a).... "Disposal" is defined in 42 U.S.C. § 6903(3) as follows:

> The term "disposal" means the discharge, deposit, injection, dumping, spilling, leaking, or placing of any solid waste or hazardous waste into or on any land or water so that such solid waste or hazardous waste or any constituent thereof may enter the environment or be emitted into the air or discharged into any waters, including ground waters.

The district court held, after a contextual analysis, that this language means only disposal by "active human conduct." We cannot agree. The term "disposal," it is true, is used throughout subtitle C in the sense that the Administrator can regulate current disposal of hazardous waste. In this way, the Act regulates current conduct of would-be polluters. But a strained reading of that term limiting its section 7003 meaning to active conduct would so frustrate the remedial purpose of the Act as to make it meaningless. Section 7003, unlike the provisions of the Act's subtitle C, does not regulate conduct but regulates and mitigates endangerments. The Administrator's intervention authorized by section 7003 is triggered by evidence that the "disposal of . . . hazardous waste may present an imminent and substantial endangerment." . . .

The inclusion of "leaking" as one of the diverse definitional components of "disposal" demonstrates that Congress intended "disposal" to have a range of meanings, including conduct, a physical state, and an occurrence. Discharging, dumping, and injection (conduct), hazardous waste reposing (a physical state) and movement of the waste after it has been placed in a state of repose (an occurrence) are all encompassed in the broad definition of disposal. "Leaking" ordinarily occurs when landfills are not constructed soundly or when drums and tank trucks filled with waste materials corrode, rust, or rot. Thus "leaking" is an occurrence included in the meaning of "disposal."

The district court's statutory analysis relied heavily upon the present-tense definition of "disposal" as indicative of an intent to restrain only ongoing human conduct. The Act, however, permits a court to order a responsible party to "stop" activities "or to take such other action as may be necessary" . . . to abate the endangerment. Such grammatical niceties as tense may be useful in arriving at a narrowly-sculpted meaning, but they are of little help in interpreting remedial statutes in which actions such as "may be necessary" are contemplated in order to abate gross dangers to a community. Since the term "disposal" is used throughout the Act, its definition in section 6903(3) must necessarily be broad and general to encompass both routine regulatory and the less common emergency situations. Thus it includes such diverse characteristics as "deposit, injection, dumping, spilling, leaking, or placing" wastes. We must assume that Congress included "leaking" as a definitional component of "disposal" for a purpose. We conclude that Congress made "leaking" a part of the definition of "disposal" to meet the need to respond to the possibility of endangerment, among other reasons.

Congress expressly intended that this and other language of the Act close loopholes in environmental protection. *Accord United States v. Price*, 523 F.Supp. 1055, 1071 (D.N.J.1981), *aff'd*, 688 F.2d 204 (3d Cir.1982); *United States v. Solvents Recovery Service*, 496 F.Supp. 1127, 1136 (D.Conn.1980). Limiting the government's enforcement prerogatives to cases involving active human conduct would open a gaping hole in the overall protection of the environment envisioned by Congress, a protection designed to be responsive to unpredictable occurrences. Without a means to respond to disasters precipitated by earlier poor planning, our nation's resources could be "conserved" from further harm, as the title of the Resource Conservation and Recovery Act suggests, but never "recovered" to their former wholesome condition.

IV

The landfill group argues that section 7003 was designed to control pollution only in emergency situations. The district court agreed, concluding that it was similar to other statutes designed by Congress solely to eliminate emergency problems. We find this position unsupportable, for the section's language stands in contrast to "emergency" type statutes. The language of section 7003 demonstrates that Congress contemplated circumstances in which the disposal of hazardous waste "may present an imminent and substantial endangerment" ...; therefore, the section's application is not specifically limited to an "emergency."

The Third Circuit, in its recent interpretation of the Act's section 7003, reached the same conclusion. It described section 7003 as having "enhanced the courts' traditional equitable powers by authorizing the issuance of injunctions when there is but a risk of harm, a more lenient standard than the traditional requirement of threatened irreparable harm." *United States v. Price*, 688 F.2d 204, 211 (3d Cir.1982). ... Thus the Third Circuit's interpretation of section 7003, far from limiting its application to emergency situations, gave full effect to this expansion of the courts' traditional powers.

V

Although strictly speaking there is little legislative history to assist us in our quest for exact congressional intent, the history of the Act's amendments is enlightening. The legislative history of the Act as originally enacted contains no specific discussion of the reach of section 7003 and no mention of the reasons for its insertion. The hastiness of the Act's passage in the final days of a congressional session has been well-documented. *See* Covens & Klucsik, The New Federal Role in Solid Waste Management: The Resource Conservation and Recovery Act of 1976, 3 Colum. J. Envtl. L. 205, 216–20 (1976). That the Act was intended to eliminate any remaining loopholes in statutory protection from toxic pollution, however, is plain from a consideration of the legislative history of the statute as a whole. H.R.Rep.No. 94–1491, 94th Cong., 2d Sess. at 4 (1976).

The focus of our attention, then, is not on the Act's legislative history, but on the legislative history of its 1980 amendments, in which various congressional committees addressed the issues of EPA authority under section 7003 and the purposes of this section. Later congressional ratification of the availability of section 7003 as a tool for abating hazards created by inactive solid and hazardous waste disposal sites such as the Flemington landfill has been consistent and authoritative. Although this is not legislative history as such, the views of subsequent Congresses on the same or similar statutes are entitled to some weight in the construction of previous legislation. *NLRB v. Bell Aerospace Co.*, 416 U.S. 267,275 (1974); *Red Lion Broadcasting Co. v. FCC*, 395 U.S. 367, 380–81, 23 L.Ed.2d 371, 89 S.Ct. 1794 (1969). Although the views of subsequent Congresses cannot override the unmistakable intent of the enacting one, *Teamsters v. United States*, 431 U.S. 324, 354 n. 39, 52 L.Ed.2d 396, 97 S.Ct. 1843 (1977), this is not a problem in this case because there was no absolutely "unmistakable intent" of Congress concerning section 7003. To the extent that the precise intent of the enacting Congress may be obscure, the views of subsequent Congresses should be given greater deference than they would be otherwise entitled to receive. *Seatrain Shipbuilding Corp. v. Shell Oil Co.*, 444 U.S. 572, 596, 63 L.Ed.2d 36, 100 S.Ct. 800 (1980).

Later reports issued by the House and Senate committees which developed the Act as originally passed have consistently confirmed the availability of section 7003 as a tool for abating hazards like the Flemington landfill. For example, a congressional report on hazardous waste disposal issued when the 1980 amendments were being drafted observed:

> Imminence in this section [7003] applies to the nature of the threat rather than identification of the time when the endangerment initially arose. The section, therefore, may be used for events which took place at some time in the past but which continues to present a threat to the public health or the environment.

Subcommittee on Oversight and Investigation of the Committee on Interstate and Foreign Commerce, Report on Hazardous Waste Disposal, H.R.Comm. Print No. 96–IFC 31, 96th Cong., 1st Sess. 32 (1979)(Eckhardt Report). After noting that "RCRA is basically a prospective act designed to prevent improper disposal of hazardous wastes in the future," the Eckhardt Report points out: "The only tool that [the Act] has to remedy the effects of past disposal practices which are not sound is its imminent hazard authority (section 7003)." *Id.* at 31. Accordingly, the authority to abate waste hazards is expansive:

> Section 7003 is designed to provide the Administrator with overriding authority to respond to situations involving a substantial endangerment to health or the environment, regardless of other remedies available through the provisions of the Act.

Id. at 32. *Accord United States v. Solvents Recovery Service*, 496 F.Supp. at 1137–38 .

It is true that some confusion has been created in the interpretation of section 7003 by the EPA's own earlier interpretation—since abandoned—of its authority under this section. The EPA at first took the position that because of its present tense language the statute was not intended to apply to inactive disposal facilities. 43 Fed. Reg. 58,984 (December 18, 1978). This narrow reading by the agency led the House Committee on Interstate and Foreign Commerce, one of the committees which had developed the original Act, to rebuke the EPA for its lack of vigor in using section 7003 and admonish the agency that section 7003 "should be used for abandoned sites as well as active ones." H.R.Rep. No. 96–191, 96th Cong., 1st Sess. 5 (1979). Not only did Congress reject the EPA's narrow view of its own authority, but the EPA later reversed its own early interpretation of section 7003. *See* 45 Fed. Reg. 33,170 (May 19, 1980). The agency's current view is, of course, entitled to substantial deference. *See Andrus v. Sierra Club*, 442 U.S. 347, 356–61, 60 L.Ed.2d 943, 99 S.Ct. 2335 (1979)(Supreme Court defers to Council on Environmental Quality's later reversal of earlier interpretation of regulations).

* * *

The landfill group accurately states that although the Act was passed in 1976, regulations promulgated under it were, in fact, not finally adopted until May 1980, some four months after this action was filed and eleven months after the Flemington landfill closed. It argues, therefore, that to grant the requested relief would be a retroactive application of the Act. Section 7003 does not, however, depend on regulations for its application. It became operative upon enactment without need for the promulgation of regulations. In fact, the regulations issued under the Act pertain to subtitle C and establish rules for safe management practices for persons handling hazardous wastes, not for situations covered by section 7003. The Flemington landfill was in operation for three years after the effective date of section 7003, so applying it to the landfill group has no retroactive effect.

VIII

Contrary to the district court holding, we conclude on the peculiar facts of this case that permanent mandatory injunctive relief is an appropriate remedy. The landfill group argues that no emergency exists and that CERCLA provides an adequate remedy at law. The EPA need not prove that an emergency exists to prevail under section 7003, only that the circumstances may present an imminent and substantial endangerment. It has been alleged that an imminent and substantial endangerment exists. We make no finding on whether the EPA will be able to meet its burden at trial. Since this case came to us in the posture of an appeal from the grant of a Rule 12(b)(6) motion to dismiss, we have viewed all the evidence in the light most favorable to the party opposing the motion, the EPA.

Finally, the landfill group contends that an injunction cannot issue because CERCLA provides an adequate remedy at law. This lawsuit was not brought in common-law equity, however, but pursuant to an express statutory command giving the EPA an injunctive remedy. Congress chose to enhance the courts' traditional equitable powers in order to protect the public and the environment. *United States v. Price*, 688 F.2d at 211. Any other decision would, in effect, interpret CERCLA as repealing the Act—a result obviously not intended by Congress.

For the reasons stated we reverse the district court's grant of the landfill group's motion to dismiss and remand for further proceeding consistent with this opinion.

Notes

1. **The court noted that:**

Section 7003 is a congressional mandate that the former common law of nuisance, as applied to situations in which a risk of harm from solid or hazardous wastes exists, shall include new terms and concepts which shall be developed in a liberal, not a restrictive, manner. This ensures that problems that Congress could not have anticipated when passing the Act will be dealt with in a way minimizing the risk of harm to the environment and the public. *Cf., e.g., United States v. Price*, 523 F.Supp. 1055, 1069, 1070 (D.N.J.1981); *United States v. Diamond Shamrock Corp.*, 12 Envtl.L.Rep. 20819 (N.D.Ohio 1981).

2. **Hazardous Wastes and Constituents.** EPA has taken the position that *hazardous wastes*, the releases of which are sufficient to invoke corrective action jurisdiction, include substances *in addition to* those merely subject to waste management restrictions as *listed* and *characteristic* hazardous wastes. Specifically, for purposes of corrective action, *hazardous wastes* are any substances falling within the *statutory* definition, *i.e.*, those capable of causing or contributing to any increases in mortality or illness or of posing a hazard to human health or the environment.

The proposed corrective action rule defines the term *hazardous constituent* to include any constituent identified in Appendix VIII to 40 C.F.R. § 261 (toxicity characteristic constituents) or in Appendix IX to 40 C.F.R. § 264 (groundwater monitoring list). For the most part, EPA intends to direct its corrective action rule to releases of the aforementioned Appendix VIII and Appendix IX pollutants.

EPA's interim status corrective action authority nominally applies only to releases of hazardous wastes and not hazardous constituents. EPA, however, has interpreted this authority to extend to hazardous constituents.

3. **SWMUs.** A SWMU (solid waste management unit) is any discernable unit at which solid wastes have been placed at any time, irrespective of whether the unit was intended for the management of solid or hazardous waste. Under this definition, the following units would be SWMUs:

- Regulated hazardous waste management units (defined in 40 C.F.R. § 264.90(a)(2) as any landfill, surface impoundment, waste pile or land treatment unit that received hazardous waste after July 26, 1982);

- Units that manage hazardous waste, but are exempt from permitting requirements (*e.g.*, wastewater treatment units and recycling units);

- Units where only non-hazardous solid wastes are managed;

- Units where hazardous or non-hazardous solid wastes previously were managed;

- Process units where solid wastes are or have been routinely and systematically released (*e.g.*, wood preservative *kickback drippage* area, loading and unloading areas for raw materials and products and solvent washing areas); and

- Industrial process collection sewers.

Passive leakage (*e.g.*, leakage from a chemical storage tank, emissions from production processes or a one-time spill of hazardous wastes) in a particular area would not create a SWMU since the release is not routine and systematic. EPA intends to address hazardous conditions at non-SWMU areas, however, using its broad permitting authority.

Further, the restriction of corrective action to releases from SWMUs applies only to permitted TSDs. EPA already may direct operators of *interim status facilities* to cleanup releases from non-SWMU areas.

1. *Facilities Subject to Corrective Action*

Corrective action requirements apply to all TSD operators seeking new or renewed operating permits to engage in active hazardous waste management. Operators of inactive TSDs (*i.e.*, those that have ceased hazardous waste management operations) also are subject to corrective action as a condition of the post-closure permits for such facilities. Interim status corrective action applies to several classes of TSD facilities including those that meet requirements for obtaining and maintaining interim status; those that have ceased active operations and have lost interim status; and those that should have obtained interim status, but did not. Facilities that operate Underground Storage Tanks (*USTs*) are subject to corrective action requirements under a separate section of the RCRA rules dealing solely with USTs.

Corrective action requirements do *not* apply to facilities that manage only non-hazardous solid wastes; facilities that generate hazardous waste and then transport the waste off-site for treatment, storage or disposal; and facilities that treat, store or dispose of hazardous wastes in ways that do not require a permit or interim status (*e.g.*, exempt wastewater treatment facilities).

The proposed corrective action rule defines *facility* to include all contiguous property under the control of the owner or operator of the TSD. This definition of facility was upheld in a decision of the U.S. District Court of Appeals. Property that is separated only by a public right-of-way is likely to be considered contiguous property. Thus, for permitted TSDs, corrective action is limited to releases from SWMUs but extends to the entire facility and to offsite properties that are contaminated as a result of a release from a SWMU.

2. *Corrective Action Procedure*

Corrective action begins at the time EPA permits a TSD facility or when the agency issues an administrative order to an interim status facility. The corrective action process consists of four stages: facility assessment, facility investigation, corrective measures study and, finally, implementation. Often these stages are planned and consolidated within a corrective action consent agreement between EPA and the facility owner/operator.

A *RCRA facility assessment* (*RFA*) serves to determine the likelihood that the facility has experienced a hazardous waste release and to eliminate from further investigation those facilities for which no evidence of a release exists. The *RFA*, which is conducted by EPA, involves the review of available information on the facility, the identification of SWMUs, a site visit to note visual evidence of releases and, in some cases, media sampling to confirm the absence or presence of releases. *RFAs* are targeted only at releases and do not examine the facility's entire process.

If the *RFA* indicates a release, EPA will direct the facility owner/operator to conduct a *RCRA facility investigation* (RFI). The RFI involves comprehensive media sampling and analysis to identify the vertical and areal extent of contamination of released constituents. The RFI also involves the designation of constituent *action levels* and a determination of whether such action levels have been exceeded. The facility owner/operator conducts the investigation pursuant to a written RFI workplan, which is submitted to EPA in advance for approval.

Generally, if the RFI indicates that a release from the facility has caused hazardous constituents to contaminate environmental media in excess of the designated action levels, EPA will direct the owner/operator to conduct a *corrective measure study* (*CMS*) to identify and evaluate corrective action alternatives and to recommend to EPA the most appropriate and cost-effective corrective action to be undertaken. Generally, contaminants are remedied through a combination of containment, stabilization, treatment and removal for offsite disposal. The selection of a particular corrective action plan among competing alternatives (often with widely varying costs) usually occurs through intensive negotiations between EPA and the facility owner/operator.

Upon agreement with EPA, the facility owner/operator *implements* the corrective action plan by designing, constructing and operating the selected waste management vehicles. At many corrective action sites, the mechanisms needed to contain, treat or remove soil and groundwater contaminants can be employed and retired within one to three years of initial implementation. Unfortunately, extended soil and groundwater monitoring, which routinely is included in any corrective action plan involving significant media contamination, can prolong indefinitely the completion of corrective action.

3. *Action Levels*

Action levels are defined concentrations of specific constituents which, if exceeded within a particular medium (*e.g.*, groundwater), may create a present or potential hazard to human health or the environment. The presence of hazardous constituent concentrations above designated action levels in any medium generally triggers a CMS, which leads to corrective action itself. Action levels, which are determined during the RFI, should be distinguished from *cleanup standards*—the designated constituent concentrations which corrective action (if determined to be necessary) ultimately seeks to *achieve*. The designation of action levels is a critical juncture in the cleanup process, however, since the action levels often will determine the scope and cost of the cleanup process.

EPA's proposed corrective action rule would permit, but not require, the agency to order a CMS if contamination from the release exceeds action levels. In some cases, the owner/operator of the facility may contest the presumption that a CMS is required when action levels are exceeded. Conversely, the fact that action levels have not been exceeded does not preclude EPA from requiring a CMS.

4. *Criteria for Determining Action Levels*

Action levels generally incorporate health-based standards (*e.g.*, maximum contaminant levels established under the Safe Drinking Water Act) if such standards have been established for the constituents found to have been released at the facility. If such standards are not available, action levels may be based on non-promulgated health-based levels provided the alternate standards satisfy four requirements:

- The concentrations must be derived in a manner consistent with EPA guidelines for assessing the health risks of environmental pollutants.
- Toxicological studies used to establish the alternate standards must have been conducted in accordance with EPA's TSCA Good Laboratory Practice Standard.
- The *non-threshold* concept must be used for assessing the risks associated with carcinogenicity. For *known* or *probable* (Class A or Class B) human carcinogens, concentrations used as action levels must correspond with a 1×10^{-6} upperbound excess cancer risk. For *possible* (Class C) human carcinogens a 1×10^{-5} upperbound excess cancer risk must be used.
- The *threshold* concept must be used in deriving the action levels associated with systemic toxicants (*i.e.*, toxic chemicals that cause effects other than cancer or mutations). Here, action levels must be concentrations to which human populations (including sensitive subgroups) could be exposed on a daily basis without appreciable risks of adverse effects during single lifetimes.

5. *Action Levels for Groundwater*

Action levels for groundwater constituents are based on applicable Maximum Contaminant Levels (*MCLs*) which EPA promulgates pursuant to the Safe Drinking Water Act. *MCLs* are applied as action levels even when the facility's groundwater currently is not used for drinking water and could not prospectively be so used. For these facilities, EPA will apply *MCL*-based action levels to trigger a CMS but may refrain from requiring the facility owner/operator to remediate groundwater to such values.

Where no *MCLs* exist for particular constituents found at a facility, action levels are based on non-promulgated health-based standards using the four criteria. Here, however, EPA will derive action levels based on the risks to a 70 kilogram adult consuming two liters of water per day over a 70–year lifetime.

6. *Action Levels for Ambient Air*

Action levels for ambient air constituents are based on EPA-verified health-based intake levels for inhalation when such standards are available for the constituents of concern. If these values are not available, action levels are based on valid inhalation studies that have not yet cleared the intra-agency verification process. The model for these levels is a 70 kg adult inhaling twenty cubic meters of air per day during a 70–year lifetime.

When inhalation studies are not available, action levels for air are based on oral studies with a conversion factor of one for route-to-route extrapolation. Oral studies are not used if the extrapolation from oral route to inhalation route is determined to be inappropriate, *e.g.*, where significant differences in absorption may apply.

Air action levels normally are measured at the facility boundary, although intra-facility points also may be used if individuals actually reside within the facility boundary, *e.g.*, a military base, or where other factors indicate that intra-facility air quality levels will have a significant impact on human health or the environment.

7. *Action Levels for Surface Water*

Action levels for surface water constituents are based on applicable numerical surface water quality standards, which EPA and state authorities promulgate pursuant to section 303 of the Clean Water Act (*CWA*). If EPA and the relevant state have issued only narrative water quality standards for constituents of concern, action levels may be based on the numeric interpretations of these narrative standards.

Where no applicable numeric or narrative standards have been established and the applicable surface water body at the facility is designated by the state as a drinking water source, action levels are based on MCLs (maximum contaminant levels) promulgated under the Safe Drinking Water Act. If neither water quality standards nor MCLs are available for particular hazardous constituents in a surface drinking water source, action levels are based on non-promulgated health-based standards using those four criteria. If the surface water body of concern is a non-drinking water source and no numerical or narrative standards for hazardous constituents of concern are available, EPA may consider the designated uses of the surface water in establishing action levels.

Sampling to determine whether action levels have been exceeded is undertaken at the point in the surface water where the highest concentrations of hazardous constituents released from onsite SWMUs are expected to occur. Even if action levels are not exceeded, EPA nonetheless may order a CMS if, for instance, human health or the environment may be threatened by contaminated sediments or the consumption of contaminated aquatic organisms.

8. Action Levels for Soil

Action levels for soil constituents are based on available health standards. Such values assume that human exposure occurs through consumption of contaminated soil. Action levels for PCBs (polychlorinated biphenyls) are based on cleanup standards established pursuant to TSCA (the Toxic Substances Control Act).

The analytical model for carcinogens is a 70 kg. adult ingesting 0.1 grams per day over seventy years. The analytical model for non-carcinogens is a 16 kg. child ingesting 0.2 grams per day over five years. Action levels for soil constituents would typically be measured at the surface, *i.e.*, the upper two feet of earth.

9. Selection of a Corrective Action Remedy

EPA will select a remedial alternative (which may include a combination of technologies) that satisfies the essential requirements of corrective action. These include (1) the attainment cleanup standards for each affected medium, (2) reducing or eliminating the source of the release and (3) compliance with all applicable waste management standards. Beyond these specific objectives, the remedy also must satisfy an overarching requirement to protect human health and the environment. This latter standard may require the owner/operator to undertake additional measures that are unrelated to media cleanup, source control or waste management (*e.g.* providing alternative drinking water supplies or constructing protective barriers around the facility).

The proposed corrective action rule identifies a number of factors to be considered in selecting among alternative remedial technologies. These include *long-term reliability and effectiveness* (source control technologies, such as stream stripping and chemical precipitation, that actually treat waste constituents are strongly preferred to those that are temporary and rely on containment structures); *the permanent reduction of* toxicity, *mobility or volume of waste*; *short-term effectiveness* (including risks to facility workers and the surrounding community during remediation); *implementability* (including start-up time, which can be lengthy for innovative or complicated technologies); and *cost*.

10. *Media Cleanup Standards*

Media cleanup standards are targeted concentrations of hazardous constituents that corrective action seeks to achieve through the application of remedial technologies. EPA will designate concentration standards for each environmental medium (groundwater, surface water, soil and ambient air) on a facility-specific basis.

For known or suspected carcinogens, concentrations are set at levels which represent an excess upperbound lifetime risk to an individual between 1×10^{-4} and 1×10^{-6}. A lifetime cancer risk of 1×10^{-6} is used as a point of departure, while allowing site- or remedy-specific factors to enter the evaluation as justification for risks higher than 1×10^{-6}. The risk to individuals posed by the media clean-up standard should not exceed 10^{-4}. For systemic toxicants, cleanup standards shall represent concentration levels to which the public (including sensitive subgroups) could be exposed on a daily basis without risk of adverse impacts during a lifetime.

In designating cleanup standards that satisfy the above-listed criteria EPA will consider the multiplicity of contaminants in the affected medium, exposure threats to sensitive environmental receptors, other sources of potential exposures to affected media and the reliability and practicality of the remedial technology to be employed.

The location at which compliance with cleanup standards is measured varies with the medium involved. For groundwater, the cleanup standard should be achieved throughout the area of contaminated groundwater. For ambient air, the point of compliance will typically be outside the facility boundary at the location of the most exposed individual. For surface water, compliance with the standard is required at the point where the released hazardous constituent enters the surface water. For soils, the point of compliance is near the surface of the soils since this is where the greatest likelihood exists of direct human contact.

11. *Conditional Remedies*

In cases where the cleanup process is lengthy and complex, EPA will allow the owner/operator to effect a *conditional remedy, i.e.,* a phased approach to cleanup. Conditional remedies must, at minimum, achieve media cleanup standards beyond the facility boundary as soon as practicable; prevent further environmental degradation by containing the source of the release and preventing further constituent migration; prevent significant exposures to the released constituents; continue constituent monitoring; provide financial assurance for the ultimate completion of the remedy; and comply with applicable waste management rules.

§ 5.6 WASTE MANAGEMENT DURING CORRECTIVE ACTION—CAMUS AND TEMPORARY UNITS

The February 1993 CAMU rule allows TSD operators to manage remediation waste in onsite CAMUs (corrective action management units) and temporary units which are not subject to formal TSD permitting requirements, LDR treatment standards or MTRs (minimum technology requirements) for land disposal units. CAMUs and temporary units may be utilized in cleanups of both permitted TSDs and *interim status* TSDs.

The final CAMU rule reflects an expanded role for CAMUs than that contemplated under the 1990 proposed corrective action rule. Specifically, the final CAMU rule provides that CAMUs need not consist exclusively of previously-contaminated areas of the facility, and that waste generated from the remediation of other parts of the facility may be excavated and transferred to CAMUs. The final rule also clarifies that facilities undergoing corrective action may designate and utilize more than one CAMU.

Temporary units consist of tanks and container storage areas located within the facility and used for treatment or storage of hazardous remediation waste. These units may be operated for up to one year, or longer if conditions warrant.

As noted above, CAMUs and temporary units may only be used for onsite *remediation wastes*; they may not be used to manage ongoing process wastes (often termed *as-generated* wastes), wastes generate from offsite cleanups or onsite wastes that are generated onsite but removed for offsite treatment. These wastes must be managed in permitted TSDs in accordance with all applicable LDR treatment standards and MTRs. Notwithstanding these limitations, the availability of onsite CAMUs and temporary units will provide considerable cost savings as compared with conventional cleanups involving offsite treatment and disposal.

§ 5.7 THE RELATIONSHIP BETWEEN RCRA CORRECTIVE ACTION AND CERCLA (SUPERFUND)

At the ground level, a RCRA corrective action and a government-ordered CERCLA cleanup virtually are indistinguishable. Both generally adhere to the same substantive media cleanup standards. Distinctions between the two forms of cleanup, which are outlined below, arise primarily in the areas of liability, cost-recovery and public participation.

- RCRA extends liability for corrective action only to owners/operators of a TSD facility. CERCLA extends cleanup liability to all parties associated with a site including generators, owners/operators and transporters.

- CERCLA imposes liability for damages to natural resources while RCRA does not.

- CERCLA allows the federal government to recover litigation expenses plus costs incurred in evaluating the site, performing the actual cleanup and overseeing the work done by potentially responsible parties (*PRPs*). The government does not perform corrective action and RCRA makes no provision for the government to recover oversight costs in corrective action proceedings.

- CERCLA authorizes any person who has expended money in cleanup activity to seek contribution from other PRPs (such as offsite sources of disposed waste) while RCRA provides no such right to contribution.

- CERCLA guarantees the public's right to participate (through public hearings and written comments to EPA) throughout various stages of the remediation process. A RCRA corrective action consent order generally is a matter of public record, but the public is not otherwise allowed to monitor or to participate in the decision-making process.

These differences generally make CERCLA remediation lengthier and more costly than RCRA corrective action. Accordingly, many facility owners/operators prefer RCRA corrective action to CERCLA remediation.

Whether a contaminated site ultimately is remedied through a RCRA corrective action or through CERCLA depends largely on the regulatory status of the facility. RCRA corrective action normally applies to *active* RCRA facilities or to former RCRA facilities undergoing *closure*. CERCLA generally applies to abandoned or inactive facilities where potentially responsible parties are unknown or are unable or unwilling to finance the cleanup. These delineations are not absolute. Indeed, they have been the subject of considerable debate between EPA and the regulated community.

In order to conserve Superfund funds and promote private cleanups, EPA promulgated a policy whereby facilities which potentially could be subject to both CERCLA and RCRA will be managed under RCRA and not listed on the National Priorities list, except where the owner or operator is unable or unwilling to take corrective action. *See* EPA, RCRA/NPL Listing Policy, 51 Fed. Reg. 21054, 21057–59 (1986). *See also United States v. Rohm & Haas Co.*, 2 F.3d 1265 (3d. Cir.1993), rehearing denied (Oct. 22, 1993)(asserting that the federal government's CERCLA response and oversight costs was inappropriate, because under published EPA policy the site should be managed under RCRA since R & H–DVI was willing to take corrective action and clean up the site at its own expense).

ALLIED–SIGNAL INC. v. UNITED STATES EPA

976 F.2d 1444 (D.C.Cir.1992).

Per Curiam

This case came to be heard on a petition for review off a final rule of the Environmental Protection Agency, and it was briefed and argued by counsel. The arguments have been accorded full consideration by the court and occasion no need for a published opinion. *See* D.C. Cir. Rule 14 (c). For the reasons stated in the accompanying memorandum, it is

ORDERED AND ADJUDGED by this Court that the petition for review be denied.

* * *

Allied–Signal opposes the decision of the Environmental Protection Agency ("EPA" or "Agency") to place the Prestolite Battery site on the National Priorities List ("NPL"). The EPA creates this list pursuant to powers granted by the Comprehensive Environmental Response, Compensation and Liability Act, 42 U.S.C. §§ 9601–9675 (1988)("CERCLA"), and uses it to identify the sites, nationwide, that deserve the highest priority for clean-up of hazardous substances or other pollutants.

Allied–Signal's argument is based on the overlapping clean-up authority of another statute, Subtitle C of the Resource Conservation and Recovery Act, 42 U.S.C. §§ 6921–6939 (1988)("RCRA"). The EPA has a longstanding policy to "defer listing [on the NPL] sites that could be addressed by the RCRA Subtitle C corrective action authorities." 54 Fed. Reg. 41,000, 41,004. The petitioner claims that RCRA Subtitle C applies to the Prestolite site, and that the EPA therefore should have deferred listing the site.

The EPA responds that it has declined to defer listing "sites where RCRA corrective action may not apply to all the contamination at the site." 53 Fed. Reg. 23,978, 23,982. A large proportion of the contamination at the Prestolite site is atmospherically-deposited lead. The Agency asserts that it included the site on the NPL because "it remains unclear if the atmospheric deposition of lead at the site can be considered a Solid Waste Management Unit (SWMU) subject to the RCRA corrective action authorities." Support Document for the Revised National Priorities List Final Rule, 6–38 (October 1989).

Since the briefs were filed in this case, this court has issued a decision in a similar case, *Apache Powder Co. v. United States* (D.C.Cir. 1992). The court there held that the uncertainty as to the applicability of RCRA clean-up authorities to the contamination of ground water by nitrates justified the Agency's decision not to defer listing the Apache site on the NPL. Apache is closely analogous to the present case. We therefore hold that Apache controls this case, and we accordingly deny Allied–Signal's petition for review.

We express concern, however, as to the EPA's recent tendency in such cases to fail to determine whether matters can be fully resolved under RCRA before invoking the tougher CERCLA statute, in spite of the Agency's claim that it tries to do just that.

We note that the parties are continuing to negotiate as to whether they can proceed under RCRA. If such an agreement is reached, it will serve the public interest by facilitating an early and thorough clean-up of the site.

Note

EPA has developed a set of criteria, now known collectively as the *NPL/RCRA Deferral Policy*, to determine whether to apply CERCLA or RCRA to facilities falling within the regulatory jurisdiction of both statutes. The NPL/RCRA Deferral Policy establishes a general preference for RCRA corrective action absent evidence that the facility owner/operator is unable or unwilling to pay for corrective action. This Policy acknowledges the advantages of RCRA corrective action over CERCLA remediation (faster response time, simplicity of negotiations, preservation of public resources and obviation of judicial cost-recovery actions) allow EPA to focus limited Superfund monies on orphaned sites for which potentially responsible parties are unwilling or unable to finance remediation and for which no other remedial authority is available. The following facilities generally are *not* eligible for RCRA corrective action under EPA's policy:

- *Pre-codification facilities*. These are facilities that ceased treating, storing or disposing hazardous waste prior to November 19, 1980 (the effective date of the RCRA rules) and by virtue of which are not subject to corrective action.

- *Facilities managing only RCRA-exempt materials*.

- *Non-TSD facilities*, *e.g.*, facilities of hazardous waste generators and transporters.

- Facilities whose owners/operators are *bankrupt* or otherwise insolvent or who have demonstrated a clear history of unwillingness to undertake corrective action.

- Facilities for which no Part A RCRA application was filed timely.

- *Converters*, *i.e.*, facilities that at one time treated or stored hazardous waste but since have converted to an activity for which a RCRA permit is not required (*e.g.*, generators who store hazardous waste for 90 days or less), and which have withdrawn their Part A applications and have EPA's acknowledgement of that withdrawal.

- *Protective filers*, *i.e.*, facilities that have not managed hazardous waste (and therefore are not subject to RCRA corrective action) but whose owners/operators filed Part A applications as a precautionary measure against future enforcement activity.

- *TSDs permitted prior to 1984 (HSWA)*.

EPA has acknowledged on several occasions that the RCRA Deferral Policy is not exhaustive or absolute and that the agency will exercise its discretion as to whether to apply the policy to specific facilities.

EPA's Office of Solid Waste and Emergency Response (*OSWER*) has published hundreds of directives and guidance documents which interpret RCRA statutory and regulatory requirements and identify the agency's enforcement procedures and priorities. OSWER periodically updates a catalog of these materials.

UNITED STATES v. COLORADO

990 F.2d 1565 (10th Cir.1993).

BALDOCK, CIRCUIT JUDGE.

This case examines the relationship between the Resource Conservation and Recovery Act of 1976 ("RCRA"), Pub. L. No. 94–580, 90 Stat. 2795, as amended by the Hazardous and Solid Waste Amendments of 1984 ("HSWA"), Pub. L. No. 98–616, 98 Stat. 3221 (codified as amended at 42 U.S.C. §§ 6901–6981 (West 1983 & Supp. 1992)), and the Comprehensive Environmental Response, Compensation, and Liability Act of 1980 ("CERCLA"), Pub. L. No. 96–510, 94 Stat. 2767, as amended by the Superfund Amendments and Reauthorization Act of 1986 ("SARA"), Pub. L. No. 99–499, 100 Stat. 1613 (codified as amended at 42 U.S.C. §§ 9601–9675 (West 1983 & Supp. 1992) and 26 U.S.C. § 9507 (West Supp. 1992)). At issue is whether a state which has been authorized by the Environmental Protection Agency ("EPA") to "carry out" the state's hazardous waste program "in lieu of" RCRA, see 42 U.S.C. § 6926(b)(West Supp. 1992), is precluded from doing so at a hazardous waste treatment, storage and disposal facility owned and operated by the federal government which the EPA has placed on the national priority list, see id. § 9605(a)(8)(B), and where a CERCLA response action is underway. *See* 42 U.S.C. § 9604 (West 1983 & Supp. 1992).

I.

The Rocky Mountain Arsenal ("Arsenal") is a hazardous waste treatment, storage and disposal facility subject to RCRA regulation, see 42 U.S.C. § 6924(a)(West Supp. 1992), which is located near Commerce City, Colorado in the Denver metropolitan area. The United States government has owned the Arsenal since 1942, and the Army operated it from that time until the mid–1980's. Without reiterating its environmental history, suffice it to say that the Arsenal is "one of the worst hazardous waste pollution sites in the country." *Daigle v. Shell Oil Co.,* 972 F.2d 1527, 1531 (10th Cir.1992)(footnote omitted). The present litigation focuses on Basin F which is a 92.7 acre basin located within the Arsenal where millions of gallons of liquid hazardous waste have been disposed of over the years.

A.

Congress enacted RCRA in 1976 "to assist the cities, counties and states in the solution of the discarded materials problem and to provide nationwide protection against the dangers of improper hazardous waste disposal." H.R. Rep. No. 1491, 94th Cong., 2d Sess. 11 (1976), reprinted in 1976 U.S.C.C.A.N. 6238, 6249. RCRA requires the EPA to establish performance standards, applicable to owners and operators of hazardous waste treatment, storage and disposal facilities "as may be necessary to protect human health and the environment." ... 42 U.S.C. § 6924(a) (West Supp. 1992). The EPA enforces RCRA standards by requiring owners and operators of facilities to obtain permits, ... see 42 U.S.C.

§ 6925 (West 1983 & Supp. 1992), and by issuing administrative compliance orders and seeking civil and criminal penalties for violations. *Id.* § 6928. The EPA may authorize states to "carry out" their own hazardous waste programs "in lieu of" RCRA and to "issue and enforce permits for the storage, treatment, or disposal of hazardous waste" so long as the state program meets the minimum federal standards.... 42 U.S.C. § 6926(b) (West Supp. 1992). *See* also H.R. Rep. No. 1491(I) at 32, reprinted in 1976 U.S.C.C.A.N. at 6270 (under RCRA, states retain "primary authority" to implement hazardous waste programs). However, RCRA does not preclude a state from adopting more stringent requirements for the treatment, storage and disposal of hazardous waste. 42 U.S.C. § 6929 (West Supp. 1992). *See* also *Old Bridge Chems., Inc. v. New Jersey Dep't of Envtl. Protection*, 965 F.2d 1287, 1296 (3d Cir.)("RCRA sets a floor not a ceiling for state regulation of hazardous wastes"), cert. denied, 121 L.Ed.2d 538, 113 S.Ct. 602 (1992). Once the EPA authorizes a state to carry out the state hazardous waste program in lieu of RCRA, "any action taken by [the] State [has] the same force and effect as action taken by the [EPA]...." 42 U.S.C. § 6926(d)(West 1983). The federal government must comply with RCRA or an EPA-authorized state program "to the same extent as any person...." ... 42 U.S.C. § 6961 (West 1983). In short, RCRA provides "a prospective cradle-to-grave regulatory regime governing the movement of hazardous waste in our society." ... H.R. Rep. No. 1016(I), 96th Cong., 2d Sess. 17 (1980), reprinted in 1980 U.S.C.C.A.N. 6119, 6120. *See* also Old Bridge, 965 F.2d at 1292 (RCRA is "principal federal statute regulating the generation, transportation, and disposal of hazardous wastes").

B.

Because RCRA only applied prospectively, it was "clearly inadequate" to deal with " 'the inactive hazardous waste site problem.' " H.R. Rep. No. 1016(I), at 17–18, reprinted in 1980 U.S.C.C.A.N. at 6120. Consequently, Congress enacted CERCLA in 1980 "to initiate and establish a comprehensive response and financing mechanism to abate and control the vast problems associated with abandoned and inactive hazardous waste disposal sites." *Id.* at 22, reprinted in 1980 U.S.C.C.A.N. at 6125. Among its provisions, CERCLA required the President to revise the "national contingency plan for the removal of ... hazardous substances" which would "establish procedures and standards for responding to releases of hazardous substances...." 42 U.S.C. § 9605(a)(West Supp. 1992). *See* also 40 C.F.R. pt. 300 (1992). When "any hazardous substance is released or there is a substantial threat of such a release into the environment," CERCLA authorizes the President to

> act, consistent with the national contingency plan, to remove or arrange for the removal of, and provide for remedial action relating to such hazardous substance ... at any time ... or take any other response measure consistent with the national contingency plan which the President deems necessary to protect the public health or welfare or the environment.

42 U.S.C. § 9604(a)(1)(West Supp. 1992). CERCLA finances these government response actions through the Hazardous Substance Superfund, see id. § 9611(a)(1); 26 U.S.C. 9507 (West Supp. 1992), and permits the government to seek reimbursement from responsible parties by holding them strictly liable. *Id.* § 9607(a). *See* also H.R. Rep. No. 1016, at 17, 1980 U.S.C.C.A.N. at 6120 (CERCLA establishes "a Federal cause of action in strict liability to enable [the EPA] to pursue rapid recovery of the costs ... of [response] actions"). *See, e.g., United States v. Hardage,* 982 F.2d 1436, 1443 (10th Cir.1992). CERCLA also requires the President to develop a national priority list, as part of the national contingency plan, which identifies "priorities among releases or threatened releases throughout the United States" for government response actions, id. § 9605(a)(8). *See* 40 C.F.R. pt. 300 app. B (1992), and the listing of a particular site on the national priority list is a prerequisite to a Superfund-financed remedial action at the site. 40 C.F.R. § 300.425(b)(1)(1992). We note that Superfund monies cannot be used for remedial actions at federal facilities, 42 U.S.C. § 9611(e)(3) (West Supp. 1992), but CERCLA otherwise applies to the federal government "to the same extent, both procedurally and substantively, as any nongovernmental entity." *Id.* § 9620(a)(1). In short, CERCLA is a remedial statute "designed to facilitate cleanup of environmental contamination caused by releases of hazardous substances." ... *Colorado v. Idarado Mining Co.,* 916 F.2d 1486, 1488, 1492 (10th Cir.1990), cert. denied, 113 L.Ed.2d 648, 111 S.Ct. 1584 (1991). *See also Daigle,* 972 F.2d at 1533.

II.

In November 1980, the Army, as the operator of the Arsenal, submitted to the EPA part A of its RCRA permit application ... which listed Basin F as a hazardous waste surface impoundment.... Appellants' App. at 413. By submitting the part A RCRA application, the Army achieved RCRA interim status. *See* supra note 2. In May 1983, the Army submitted part B of its RCRA permit application to the EPA which included a required closure plan for Basin F, Appellants' App. at 505, and the following month, the Army submitted a revised closure plan for Basin F. Appellants' App. at 471. *See* also supra notes 1 and 7. In May 1984, the EPA issued a notice of deficiency to the Army regarding part B of its RCRA permit application and requested a revised part B application within sixty days under threat of termination of the Army's interim status. Appellants' Br. Attach. 12. The Army never submitted a revised part B RCRA permit application to the EPA; rather, in October 1984, the Army commenced a CERCLA remedial investigation/feasibility study ("RI/FS"). ... Appellee's App. at 9, 30.

Effective November 2, 1984, the EPA, acting pursuant to 42 U.S.C. § 6926(b)(West Supp. 1992), authorized Colorado to "carry out" the Colorado Hazardous Waste Management Act ("CHWMA"), Colo. Rev. Stat. §§ 25–15–301 to 25–15–316 (1989 & Supp. 1992), "in lieu of" RCRA. *See* 49 Fed. Reg. 41,036 (1984). That same month, the Army submitted its part B RCRA/CHWMA permit application to the Colorado Department of Health ("CDH") which is charged with the administration and enforcement of CHWMA. Appellants' App. at 473. Notably, the part B application was the same deficient application that the Army submitted to the EPA in June 1983. *Id.* Not surprisingly, CDH found the application, specifically the closure plan for Basin F, to be unsatisfactory. *Id.*

Consequently, in May 1986, CDH issued its own draft partial closure plan for Basin F to the Army, *id.* at 481, and in October 1986, CDH issued a final RCRA/CHWMA modified closure plan for Basin F and requested the Army's cooperation in immediately implementing the plan. *Id.* at 393. The Army responded by questioning CDH's jurisdiction over the Basin F cleanup. *Id.* at 395–96.

In response to the Army's indication that it would not implement CDH's closure plan for Basin F, Colorado filed suit in state court in November 1986. Colorado sought injunctive relief to halt the Army's alleged present and future violations of CHWMA and to enforce CDH's closure plan for Basin F. The Army removed the action to federal district court, and moved to dismiss Colorado's CHWMA enforcement action claiming that "CERCLA's enforcement and response provisions pre-empt and preclude a state RCRA enforcement action with respect to the cleanup of hazardous wastes at the Arsenal." *Colorado v. United States Dept. of the Army*, 707 F.Supp. 1562, 1565 (D.Colo.1989).

In June 1986, the Army announced that it was taking a CERCLA interim response action with respect to Basin F. Appellee's App. at 20. In September 1986, the Army agreed with Shell Chemical Company . . . on an interim response action in which Shell would construct storage tanks with a total capacity of four million gallons to hold Basin F liquids. *Id.* In June 1987, the Army, the EPA, Shell and Colorado agreed on a Basin F interim response action which required the Army to remove contaminated liquids to the temporary storage tanks and contaminated sludges and soils to a temporary holding area until determination of a final Arsenal-wide remedy. *Id.* at 47–50. In August 1987, the Army requested that Colorado identify potential applicable or relevant and appropriate requirements ("ARAR's"), see 42 U.S.C. § 9621(d)(West Supp. 1992); infra note 20, for the Basin F interim response action, and, in October 1987, the Army requested comment on its plan, see 42 U.S.C. § 9621(f)(1)(E)(West Supp. 1992); however, Colorado did not respond to either of these requests. Appellee's App. at 21–22.

In October 1987, the Army advised Colorado that it was withdrawing its still pending part B RCRA/CHWMA permit application claiming that it was ceasing operations of all structures addressed in the application and that it intended to remediate Basin F pursuant to CERCLA. Appellants' App. at 398–400. The Army indicated that it would, however, comply with RCRA and CHWMA in accordance with CERCLA's provisions at 42 U.S.C. § 9620(i) and § 9621(d)(2)(A)(i). *Id.* at 399.

In December 1987, the Army transmitted a draft decision document for the Basin F interim response action to the EPA, Shell and Colorado and initiated a thirty day public comment period, see 42 U.S.C. § 9617

(West Supp. 1992). Appellee's App. at 22. In January 1988, the Army issued its decision document for the Basin F interim response action. Appellants' App. at 5. Thereafter, the Army began the Basin F interim response action, and, in December 1988, completed the removal of eight million gallons of hazardous liquid wastes from Basin F, relocating four million gallons to three lined storage tanks and four million gallons to a double-lined holding pond. Appellee's App. at 12. In addition, the Army removed 500,000 cubic yards of contaminated solid material from Basin F, dried it, and placed it in a sixteen acre, double lined, capped wastepile. *Id.* The Army also capped the Basin F floor.... *Id.*

In February 1989, the federal district court denied the Army's motion to dismiss Colorado's CHWMA enforcement action. The district court relied on several provisions of both RCRA and CERCLA, including CERCLA's provision for the application of state laws concerning removal and remedial action at federal facilities not listed on the national priority list. ... *Colorado v. United States Dep't of the Army*, 707 F.Supp. at 1569–70 (citing 42 U.S.C. § 9620(a)(4)). The district court found this provision to be particularly noteworthy in light of the fact that Basin F was not listed on the national priority list. *Id.* Furthermore, the district court expressed particular concern about the relationship between the Army and the EPA, noting that the EPA's "potential monitoring of the Army's Basin F cleanup operation under CERCLA does not serve as an appropriate or effective check on the Army's efforts," ... and that Colorado's involvement "would guarantee the salutary effect of a truly adversary proceeding that would be more likely, in the long run, to achieve a thorough cleanup." *Id.* at 1570. Thus, the district court held that Colorado was not precluded from enforcing CHWMA, pursuant to its EPA-delegated RCRA authority, despite the Army's cleanup efforts under CERCLA. *Id.*

In March 1989, the month following the district court's order, the EPA added Basin F to the national priority list.... 54 Fed. Reg. 10,512 (1989). The Army immediately moved for reconsideration of the district court's order in light of the EPA's listing of Basin F on the national priority list.

In September 1989, CDH, acting in accordance with the district court's February 1989 order, issued a final amended compliance order to the Army, pursuant to CDH's authority under CHWMA. The final amended compliance order requires the Army to submit an amended Basin F closure plan, as well as plans and schedules addressing soil contamination, monitoring and mitigation, groundwater contamination, and other identified tasks for each unit containing Basin F hazardous waste as required under CHWMA. Appellants' App. at 96–103. The final amended compliance order also requires that CDH shall approve all plans and that the Army shall not implement any closure plan or work plan prior to approval in accordance with CHWMA. *Id.* at 98.

As a result of the final amended compliance order, the United States filed the present declaratory action, invoking the district court's jurisdiction under 28 U.S.C. § 2201. The United States' complaint sought an order from the federal district court declaring that the final amended compliance order is "null and void" and enjoining Colorado and CDH from taking any action to enforce it. . . .

Id. at 13. Colorado counterclaimed requesting an injunction to enforce the final amended compliance order. . . . *Id.* at 35–41. On cross motions for summary judgment, the district court relied on CERCLA's provision which limits federal court jurisdiction to review challenges to CERCLA response actions, see 42 U.S.C. § 9613(h)(West Supp. 1992), and held that "any attempt by Colorado to enforce [] CHWMA would require [the] court to review the [Army's CERCLA] remedial action . . . prior to [its] completion" and that "such a review is expressly prohibited by [CERCLA] § 9613(h)." *United States v. Colorado,* 1991 WL 193519 (D.Colo. 1991)(Mem. Order & Op.). It is important to note that the district court distinguished its earlier order, which held that Colorado could enforce CHWMA despite the Army's CERCLA response action, Colorado v. United States Dep't of the Army, 707 F.Supp. at 1570, based on the EPA's intervening listing of Basin F on the national priority list. *United States v. Colorado,* 1991 WL 193519. In doing so, the district court appears to have implicitly relied on 9620(a)(4), which provides for the application of state laws concerning removal and remedial action at federal facilities not listed on the national priority list, in addition to § 9613(h). Based on this reasoning, the district court granted summary judgment to the United States on its claims for declaratory and injunctive relief, denied Colorado's cross-motion for summary judgment, and enjoined Colorado and CDH from taking "any action to enforce the[] final amended compliance order." *Id.* at 10–11.

III.

Colorado filed a timely notice of appeal from the district court's order giving us jurisdiction over this matter. 28 U.S.C. § 1291. Colorado contends that § 9613(h) is not applicable to a state's efforts to enforce its EPA-delegated RCRA authority, that listing on the national priority list is immaterial, and that the district court's order amounts to a determination that CERCLA preempts a state's EPA-delegated RCRA authority contrary to well-settled principles. . . . In addition to arguing that 9613(h) bars Colorado from enforcing its EPA-delegated RCRA authority, the United States alternatively contends that CERCLA's provision, which grants the President authority to select the remedy and allow for state input through the ARAR's process, see 42 U.S.C. § 9621 (West Supp. 1992), bars Colorado from enforcing state law independent of CERCLA. *See Hill v. Ibarra,* 954 F.2d 1516, 1525 n. 4 (10th Cir. 1992)("grant of summary judgment . . . may be upheld on any grounds supported by the record").

We review a district court order granting or denying summary judgment de novo, applying the same standard as the district court. *United States v. Hardage,* 985 F.2d 1427, 1432 (10th Cir.1993). Summary judgment is appropriate if "there is no genuine issue as to any material fact and ... the moving party is entitled to a judgment as a matter of law." Fed. R. Civ. P. 56(c). In applying this standard, we construe the factual record and reasonable inferences therefrom in the light most favorable to the party opposing summary judgment. *Hardage,* 985 F.2d at 1433.

As this is a case of statutory construction, our job is to effectuate the intent of Congress. *Colorado v. Idarado Mining Co.,* 916 F.2d 1486, 1494 (10th Cir.1990), cert. denied, 113 L.Ed.2d 648, 111 S.Ct. 1584 (1991). While our starting point is the statutory language, *Hallstrom v. Tillamook County,* 493 U.S. 20, 25, 28–29, 107 L.Ed.2d 237, 110 S.Ct. 304 (1989), we must also look to the design of the statute as a whole and to its object and policy. *Crandon v. United States,* 494 U.S. 152, 158, 108 L.Ed.2d 132, 110 S.Ct. 997 (1990). *See also King v. St. Vincent's Hosp.,* 116 L.Ed.2d 578, 112 S.Ct. 570, 574 (1991)(statute must be read as a whole because "meaning, plain or not, depends on context"). When Congress has enacted two statutes which appear to conflict, we must attempt to construe their provisions harmoniously. *Negonsott v. Samuels,* 933 F.2d 818, 819 (10th Cir.1991), aff'd, 507 U.S. 99, 113 S.Ct. 1119, 122 L.Ed.2d 457 (1993). *See also County of Yakima v. Confederated Tribes & Bands of Yakima Indian Nation,* 116 L.Ed.2d 687, 112 S.Ct. 683, 692 (1992)("Courts are not at liberty to pick and choose among congressional enactments, and when two statutes are capable of coexistence, it is [our] duty ... absent clearly expressed congressional intention to the contrary, to regard each as effective."). Even when a later enacted statute is not entirely harmonious with an earlier one, we are reluctant to find repeal by implication unless the text or legislative history of the later statute shows that Congress intended to repeal the earlier statute and simply failed to do so expressly. *United States v. Barrett,* 837 F.2d 933, 934 (10th Cir.1988). *See also Kremer v. Chemical Constr. Corp.,* 456 U.S. 461, 470, 72 L.Ed.2d 262, 102 S.Ct. 1883 (1982)("an implied repeal must ordinarily be evident from the language or operation of the statute"). We turn now to the application of these well-settled rules of statutory construction to this particular case.

IV.

The district court focused on CERCLA's provision governing civil proceedings which grants federal courts exclusive jurisdiction over all actions arising under CERCLA. 42 U.S.C. § 9613(b)(West Supp. 1992). As the district court recognized, § 9613(h) expressly limits this grant of jurisdiction by providing, with exceptions not relevant here, that "no Federal court shall have jurisdiction under Federal law ... to review any challenges to removal or remedial action selected under section 9604 of this title...." *Id.* § 9613(h). However, contrary to the district court's reasoning, § 9613(h) does not bar federal courts from reviewing a CERCLA response action prior to its completion; rather, it bars federal courts from reviewing any "challenges" to a CERCLA response actions. This is a critical distinction because an action by Colorado to enforce the final amended compliance order, issued pursuant to its EPA-delegated RCRA authority, is not a "challenge" to the Army's CERCLA response action. To hold otherwise would require us to ignore the plain language and structure of both CERCLA and RCRA, and to find that CERCLA implicitly repealed RCRA's enforcement provisions contrary to Congress' expressed intention.

A.

Congress clearly expressed its intent that CERCLA should work in conjunction with other federal and state hazardous waste laws in order to solve this country's hazardous waste cleanup problem. CERCLA's "savings provision" provides that "nothing in [CERCLA] shall affect or modify in any way the obligations or liabilities of any person ... under other Federal or State law, including common law, with respect to releases of hazardous substances or other pollutants or contaminants." 42 U.S.C. § 9652(d)(West 1983). Similarly, CERCLA's provision entitled "relationship to other laws" provides that "nothing in [CERCLA] shall be construed or interpreted as preempting any State from imposing any additional liability or requirements with respect to the release of hazardous substances within such State." 42 U.S.C. § 9614(a)(West 1983). By holding that § 9613(h) bars Colorado from enforcing CHWMA, the district court effectively modified the Army's obligations and liabilities under CHWMA contrary to § 9652(d), and preempted Colorado from imposing additional requirements with respect to the release of hazardous substances contrary to 9614(a).

As a federal facility, the Arsenal is subject to regulation under RCRA. *See* 42 U.S.C. § 6961 (West 1983). More importantly, because the EPA has delegated RCRA authority to Colorado, the Arsenal is subject to regulation under CHWMA. *Id. See also Parola v. Weinberger,* 848 F.2d 956, 960 (9th Cir.1988)(§ 6961 "unambiguously subjects federal instrumentalities to state and local regulation"). While the President has authority to exempt federal facilities from complying with RCRA or respective state laws "if he determines it to be in the paramount interest of the United States," 42 U.S.C. § (West 1983), nothing in this record indicates that the Army has been granted such an exemption with respect to its activities at the Arsenal. Thus, Colorado has authority to enforce CHWMA at the Arsenal, and "any action taken by [Colorado] ... [has] the same force and effect as action taken by the [EPA]...." *Id.* 6926(d)(West 1983).

Notwithstanding Colorado's RCRA authority over the Basin F cleanup, and CERCLA's express preservation of this authority, § 9613(h), which was enacted as part of SARA, limits federal court jurisdiction to review challenges to CERCLA response actions. Congress' expressed purpose in enacting § 9613(h) was "to prevent private responsible parties from filing dilatory, interim lawsuits which have the effect of slowing down or preventing the EPA's cleanup activities." H.R. Rep. No. 253(I), 99th Cong., 2d Sess. 266 (1985), reprinted in 1986 U.S.C.C.A.N. 2835, 2941 (emphasis added). Nonetheless, the language of § 9613(h) does not differentiate between challenges by private responsible parties and challenges by a state. Thus, to the extent a state seeks to challenge a

CERCLA response action, the plain language of § 9613(h) would limit a federal court's jurisdiction to review such a challenge. *See, e.g., Alabama v. EPA,* 871 F.2d 1548, 1557 (11th Cir.), cert. denied, 493 U.S. 991, 107 L.Ed.2d 535, 110 S.Ct. 538 (1989).

Be that as it may, an action by a state to enforce its hazardous waste laws at a site undergoing a CERCLA response action is not necessarily a challenge to the CERCLA action. For example, CDH's final amended compliance order does not seek to halt the Army's Basin F interim response action; rather it merely seeks the Army's compliance with CHWMA during the course of the action, which includes CDH approval of the Basin F closure plan prior to implementation. Thus, Colorado is not seeking to delay the cleanup, but merely seeking to ensure that the cleanup is in accordance with state laws which the EPA has authorized Colorado to enforce under RCRA. In light of §§ 9652(d) and 9614(a), which expressly preserve a state's authority to undertake such action, we cannot say that Colorado's efforts to enforce its EPA-delegated RCRA authority is a challenge to the Army's undergoing CERCLA response action.

The United States relies principally on two cases to support its claim that § 9613(h) bars any action by Colorado to enforce the final amended compliance order. In *Schalk v. Reilly,* 900 F.2d 1091 (7th Cir.), cert. denied, 498 U.S. 981, 112 L.Ed.2d 521, 111 S.Ct. 509 (1990), the Seventh Circuit held that § 9613(h) barred private citizens from bringing a CERCLA citizen suit which challenged a consent decree between the EPA and a responsible party on the grounds that failure to prepare an environmental impact statement violated the National Environmental Policy Act, 42 U.S.C. § 4321 et seq. 900 F.2d at 1095. Responding to the citizens' argument that they were not challenging the remedial action but rather merely asking that certain procedural requirements be met, the court held that "challenges to the procedure employed in selecting a remedy nevertheless impact the implementation of the remedy and result in the same delays Congress sought to avoid by passage of the statute; the statute necessarily bars these challenges." *Id.* at 1097.

While we do not doubt that Colorado's enforcement of the final amended compliance order will "impact the implementation" of the Army's CERCLA response action, we do not believe that this alone is enough to constitute a challenge to the action as contemplated under § 9613(h). The plaintiffs in *Schalk* were attempting to invoke the federal court's jurisdiction under CERCLA's citizen suit provision. *See* 42 U.S.C. § 9659 (West Supp. 1992). While one of the exceptions to § 9613(h)'s jurisdictional bar is for CERCLA citizen suits, such suits "may not be brought with regard to a removal where a remedial action is to be undertaken at the site." *Id.* § 9613(h)(4). Thus, the CERCLA citizen suit in *Schalk* was jurisdictionally barred by the plain language of the statute. *See* 900 F.2d at 1095. Accord Alabama v. EPA, 871 F.2d at 1557. Unlike the plaintiffs in *Schalk,* Colorado has not asserted and need not assert jurisdiction under CERCLA's citizen suit provision to enforce the final amended compliance order; therefore, *Schalk*'s reasoning does not apply.

Nonetheless, the plain language of § 9613(h) bars federal courts from exercising jurisdiction, not only under CERCLA, but under any federal law to review a challenge to a CERCLA remedial action. *See* 42 U.S.C. § 9613(h)(West Supp. 1992). In *Boarhead Corp. v. Erickson,* 923 F.2d 1011 (3d Cir.1991), the Third Circuit held that § 9613(h) barred the federal court from exercising federal question jurisdiction, 28 U.S.C. § 1331, under the National Historic Preservation Act, 16 U.S.C. § 470 et seq., in an action which sought to stay the EPA's CERCLA response action pending determination of whether property qualified for historic site status. 923 F.2d at 1021.

Like *Schalk*, *Boarhead* is also distinguishable from the present case. First, the plaintiff in *Boarhead* was a responsible party under CERCLA; therefore, permitting the plaintiff's action to proceed would have been contrary to Congress' expressed intent in enacting § 9613(h). Moreover, the plaintiff's complaint in *Boarhead* sought to stay the CERCLA remedial action; thus, the plaintiff's action under the Preservation Act clearly constituted a challenge to the CERCLA remedial action. *Boarhead*, 923 F.2d at 1015. *See also Alabama v. EPA*, 871 F.2d at 1559 (plaintiff's prayer for relief seeking to enjoin the EPA from participating in CERCLA remedial action "belied" plaintiff's assertion that it was not challenging the remedial action plan). Most importantly, the *Boarhead* court's application of § 9613(h) to the facts of that case did not "affect or modify in any way the obligations or liabilities" of a responsible party "under other Federal or State law ... with respect to releases of hazardous substances," see 42 U.S.C. § 9652(d)(West 1983), and did not "preempt[] [the] state from imposing any additional liability or requirements with respect to the release of hazardous substances." *See id.* § 9614(a). In light of the plain language of §§ 9652(d) and 9614(a), and our responsibility to give effect to all of CERCLA's provisions, *Boarhead* cannot control this case.

B.

Not only is the district court's construction of § 9613(h) inconsistent with §§ 9652(d) and 9614(a) of CERCLA, it is also inconsistent with RCRA's citizen suit provision. *See* 42 U.S.C. § 6972 (West 1983 & Supp. 1992). While CERCLA citizen suits cannot be brought prior to the completion of a CERCLA remedial action, *Schalk*, 900 F.2d at 1095, RCRA citizen suits to enforce its provisions at a site in which a CERCLA response action is underway can be brought prior to the completion of the CERCLA response action.

RCRA's citizen suit provision permits any person to commence a civil action against any other person, including the United States government or its agencies, to enforce "any permit, standard, regulation, condition, requirement, prohibition, or order which has become effective pursuant to" RCRA. 42 U.S.C. 6972(a)(1)(A)(West Supp. 1992). Such suits are prohibited if the EPA or the state has already "commenced and is diligently prosecuting" a RCRA enforcement action. *Id.* 6972(b)(1)(B). *See, e.g., Supporters to Oppose Pollution, Inc. v. Heritage Group,* 973 F.2d 1320, 1323–24 (7th Cir.1992). Federal courts have jurisdiction over such suits and are authorized "to enforce the permit, standard, regulation, condition, requirement, prohibition, or order...." 42 U.S.C. 6972(a)(West Supp. 1992).

RCRA's citizen suit provision also permits any person to commence a civil action against any other person, including the United States government or its agencies, to abate an "imminent and substantial endangerment to health or the environment...." *Id.* § 6972(a)(1)(B). These types of RCRA citizen suits are prohibited, not only when the EPA is prosecuting a similar RCRA imminent hazard action pursuant to 42 U.S.C. § 6973, but also when the EPA is prosecuting a CERCLA abatement action pursuant to 42 U.S.C. § 9606; the EPA is engaged in a CERCLA removal action or has incurred costs to initiate a RI/FS and is "diligently proceeding" with a CERCLA remedial action pursuant to 42 U.S.C. § 9604; or the EPA has obtained a court order or issued an administrative order under CERCLA or RCRA pursuant to which a responsible party is conducting a removal action, RI/FS, or remedial action. *Id.* § 6972(b)(2)(B). Federal courts have jurisdiction over RCRA citizen imminent hazard suits and are authorized "to restrain any person who has contributed or who is contributing to the past or present handling, storage, treatment, transportation, or disposal of any solid or hazardous waste ...." *Id.* § 6972(a).

By prohibiting RCRA citizen imminent hazard suits with respect to hazardous waste sites where a CERCLA response action is underway, while not prohibiting RCRA citizen enforcement suits with respect to such sites, Congress clearly intended that a CERCLA response action would not prohibit a RCRA citizen enforcement suit. Because the definition of "person" under RCRA includes a state, 42 U.S.C. § 6903(15)(West 1983), Colorado could enforce RCRA in federal court by relying on RCRA's citizen enforcement suit provision, 42 U.S.C. § 6972(a)(1)(West Supp. 1992), provided that it complied with the requisite notice provisions. *See id.* § 6972(b)(1)(A). *See also Hallstrom v. Tillamook County,* 493 U.S. 20, 26, 107 L.Ed.2d 237, 110 S.Ct. 304 (1989)("compliance with ... notice provision is a mandatory ... condition precedent for suit"). Because CHWMA became "effective" pursuant the EPA's delegation of RCRA authority to Colorado, and the final amended compliance order was issued pursuant to CHWMA, Colorado could arguably seek enforcement of the final amended compliance order in federal court pursuant to § 6972(a)(1). However, we need not decide this issue. While Colorado's counterclaim sought enforcement of the final amended compliance order in the district court, Colorado asserted the counterclaim solely under CHWMA, claiming that it was compulsory pursuant to Fed. R. Civ. P. 13(a), and seeking to invoke the district court's ancillary jurisdiction. *See* Appellants' App. at 30. Thus, we do not express any opinion on whether federal court jurisdiction over Colorado's counterclaim is proper under § 6972(a)(1)(A). Nonetheless, our discussion of this provision is relevant to our determination that Congress did not intend a CERCLA response action to bar a RCRA enforcement action, or an equivalent action by a state which has been authorized by EPA to enforce its state hazardous waste laws in lieu of RCRA.

C.

Rather than challenging the Army's CERCLA remedial action, Colorado is attempting to enforce the requirements of its federally authorized hazardous waste laws and regulations, consistent with its ongoing duty to protect the health and environment of its citizens. CERCLA itself recognizes that these requirements are applicable to a facility during the pendency of a CERCLA response action. *See Moskal v. United States,* 498 U.S. 103, 109–10, 112 L.Ed.2d 449, 111 S.Ct. 461 (1990)(statutes must be construed to give effect to "every clause and word"). Further, RCRA contemplates that enforcement actions may be maintained despite an ongoing CERCLA response action, and we cannot say that CERCLA implicitly repealed RCRA's enforcement provision given CERCLA's clear statement to the contrary. *See Manor Care, Inc. v. Yaskin,* 950 F.2d 122, 127 (3d Cir.1991)("Congress did not intend for CERCLA remedies to preempt complementary state remedies."). While the decision to use CERCLA or RCRA to cleanup a site is normally a "policy question[] appropriate for agency resolution," *Apache Powder Co. v. United States,* 296 U.S.App.D.C. 330, 968 F.2d 66, 69 (D.C.Cir.1992), the plain language of both statutes provides for state enforcement of its RCRA responsibilities despite an ongoing CERCLA response action. Thus, enforcement actions under state hazardous waste laws which have been authorized by the EPA to be enforced by the state in lieu of RCRA do not constitute "challenges" to CERCLA response actions; therefore, § 9613(h) does not jurisdictionally bar Colorado from enforcing the final amended compliance order.

* * *

... the United States candidly concedes, the district court's application of § 9620(a)(4) is incorrect. *See* Appellee's Br. at 36. At most, § 9620(a)(4) determines the controlling law, not federal court jurisdiction over actions by a state. Moreover, the district court's reasoning regards CHWMA as a state law "concerning removal and remedial action." While we recognize that CERCLA's definition of "removal and remedial action" is conceivably broad enough to encompass certain RCRA corrective actions, see 42 U.S.C. §§ 9601(23), 9601(24)(West Supp. 1992), we believe that had Congress intended § 9620(a)(4) to exclude states from enforcing their EPA-delegated RCRA responsibilities, it would have expressly said so. The district court's reasoning is contrary to § 9620(i) which expressly preserves the obligations of federal agencies "to comply with any requirement of [RCRA] (including corrective action requirements)." 42 U.S.C. § 9620(i)(West Supp. 1992). This provision indicates that Congress did not intend that RCRA, or state laws authorized by the EPA to be enforced in lieu of RCRA, to be equivalent to laws concerning removal and remedial actions.

Despite the United States' concession concerning the incorrect application of § 9620(a)(4), it argues that the listing of Basin F on the national priority list removes any doubt that Colorado's enforcement of CHWMA at the Arsenal is precluded by § 9613(h). However, the national priority list is nothing more than "the list of priority releases for long-term remedial evaluation and response." 40 C.F.R. § 300.425(b)(1992). It "serves primarily informational purposes, identifying for the States and the public those facilities and sites or other releases which appear to warrant remedial action." ... 9 S. Rep. No. 848, 96th Cong., 2d Sess. 60 (1980). Placement on the national priority list simply has no bearing on a federal facility's obligation to comply with state hazardous waste laws which have been authorized by an EPA delegation of RCRA authority or a state's ability to enforce such laws.

VII.

The United States alternatively contends that CERCLA's provision, which grants the President authority to select the remedy and allow for state input through the ARAR's process, see 42 U.S.C. § 9621 (West Supp. 1992), bars Colorado from enforcing state law independent of CERCLA. This is a curious argument in light of §§ 9614(a) and 9652(d) which expressly preserve state RCRA authority, and we find it to be without merit.

A.

While the United States does not dispute that Congress intended states to play a role in hazardous waste cleanup, the United States argues that the states' role when a CERCLA response action is underway is confined to CERCLA's ARAR's process.... Undoubtedly, CERCLA's ARAR's provision was intended to provide "a mechanism for state involvement in the selection and adoption of remedial actions which are federal in character." *Colorado v. Idarado Mining Co.,* 916 F.2d 1486, 1495 (10th Cir.1990), cert. denied, 113 L.Ed.2d 648, 111 S.Ct. 1584 (1991). *See also United States v. Akzo Coatings of Am., Inc.,* 949 F.2d 1409, 1455 (6th Cir.1991)(ARAR's provisions "reflect Congress' special concern that state interests in the health and welfare of their citizens be preserved, even in the face of a comprehensive federal environmental statute"). Nonetheless, nothing in CERCLA supports the contention that Congress intended the ARAR's provision to be the exclusive means of state involvement in hazardous waste cleanup.

Contrary to the United States' claim, Colorado is not invading the President's authority to select a CERCLA remedial action. Rather, Colorado is merely insuring that the Army comply with CHWMA which §§ 9614(a) and 9652(d) of CERCLA expressly recognize is applicable. Sections 9614(a) and 9652(d) were included within CERCLA when it was originally enacted in 1980. *See* Pub. L. No. 96–510, § 114(a), 302(d), 94 Stat. 2795, 2808 (1980). However, the ARAR's provision was not enacted until the 1986 amendments to CERCLA. *See* Pub. L. No. 99–499, § 121, 100 Stat. 1672 (1986). Certainly, Congress could not have intended the ARAR's provision to be the exclusive means of state involvement in hazardous waste cleanup as provided under §§ 9614(a) and 9652(d) when the ARAR's concept did not even come into being until six years after CERCLA was enacted.

Moreover, while the ARAR's provision requires the President to allow a state to participate in remedial planning and to review and comment on remedial plans, 42 U.S.C. § 9621(f)(1)(West Supp. 1992), it only allows states to ensure compliance with state law at the completion of the remedial action. *See* id. §§ 9621(d)(2)(A), 9621(f)(2), 9621(f)(3). However, §§ 9614(a) and 9652(d) expressly contemplate the applicability of other federal and state hazardous waste laws regardless of whether a CERCLA response action is underway. Given that RCRA clearly applies during the closure period of a regulated facility, see 40 C.F.R. § 264.228 (1992); id. § 265.228, the ARAR's provision cannot be the exclusive means of state involvement in the cleanup of a site subject to both RCRA and CERCLA authority.

Contrary to the United States' claim, permitting state involvement in hazardous waste cleanup outside of CERCLA's ARAR's process, based on independent state authority, does not render the ARAR's process irrelevant. When a state does not have independent authority over the cleanup of a particular hazardous waste site, the ARAR's provision insures that states have a meaningful voice in cleanup. However, when, as here, a state has RCRA authority over a hazardous waste site, §§ 9614(a) and 9652(d) expressly preserve the state's exercise of such authority regardless of whether a CERCLA response action is underway. . . .

B.

The United States also argues that to allow Colorado to enforce the final amended compliance order would violate CERCLA's provision that "no Federal, State, or local permit shall be required for the portion of any removal or remedial action conducted entirely onsite, where such remedial action is selected and carried out in compliance with [§ 9621]." 42 U.S.C. § 9621(e)(1)(West Supp. 1992). While this provision arguably conflicts with §§ 9652(d) and 9614(a) when a state has been authorized to issue and enforce RCRA permits, the facts of this case do not require us to reconcile the potential conflict. The final amended compliance order does not require the Army to obtain a permit. Rather, it merely requires the Army to update its existing RCRA/CHWMA permit application to include all units currently containing Basin F hazardous waste, see Appellants' App. at 101, as required by both RCRA and CHWMA regulations applicable to interim status facilities. . . . *See* 40 C.F.R. § 270.72(a)(3); 6 Colo. Code Regs. 1007–3 § 100.11(d)(1)(1993). Thus, enforcement of the final amended compliance order would not violate § 9621(e)(1).

C.

The United States also directs us to CERCLA's section governing "settlements," 42 U.S.C. § 9622 (West Supp. 1992), and specifically its provision, within the "special notice procedures" subsection, entitled "inconsistent response action." *Id.* § 9622(e)(6). This provision states that

> when either the President, or a potentially responsible party pursuant to an administrative order or consent decree under [CERCLA], has initiated a remedial investigation and feasibility study for a particular facility under this chapter, no potentially responsible party may undertake any remedial action at the facility unless such remedial action has been authorized by the President.

Id. While the relevance of § 9622(e)(6) to the present case is unclear, the United States relies on the EPA's interpretation of this provision in a policy statement concerning the listing of federal facilities on the national priority list. *See* 54 Fed. Reg. 10,520 (1989). In the course of discussing why it would not apply its policy of deferring placement of RCRA-subjected sites on the national priority list to federal facilities, the EPA recognized that when it undertakes a CERCLA response action at a site subject to state-delegated RCRA authority, a conflict may arise "from the overlap of the corrective action authorities of the two statutes." *Id.* at 10,522. The EPA takes the position that § 9622(e)(6) gives the EPA final authority over the remedy when the conflicting views of the EPA and a RCRA-authorized state cannot be resolved in regard to a site where a RI/FS has been initiated. *Id.* at 10,523. In the EPA's view, § 9622(e)(6)'s authorization requirement applies, not only to a potentially responsible party's independent remedial action, but also to any action by a party which has been ordered by the state under its RCRA authority "as both types of action could be said to present a potential conflict with a CERCLA authorized action." *Id.* Thus, in the case of a conflict between the EPA and the state, § 9622(e)(6) authorizes the EPA to withhold authorization to a potentially responsible party from going forward with a RCRA corrective action ordered by the state. *Id.* Not surprisingly, the United States argues for deference to the EPA's interpretation of § 9622(e)(6). *See Hill v. National Transp. Safety Bd.,* 886 F.2d 1275, 1278 (10th Cir.1989).

The EPA's interpretation of § 9622(e)(6) has several problems, not the least of which is that it permits the EPA to preempt state law contrary to § 9614(a) and to modify a responsible party's obligations and liabilities under state RCRA programs contrary to 9652(d). Section § 9622(e)(6) makes absolutely no mention of RCRA-authorized state actions, and it seems highly suspect that Congress intended this provision which is buried within a subsection entitled "notice provisions" in a section addressing settlements with private responsible parties to resolve conflicts between state-RCRA laws and CERCLA response actions. *See* H.R. Rep. No. 253(I), 99th Cong., 2d Sess. 100 (1985), reprinted in 1986 U.S.C.C.A.N. 2835, 2882 (§ 9622 was "designed to encourage and facilitate negotiated private party cleanup").

Moreover, applying the EPA's interpretation of § 9622(e)(6) to federal facilities is contrary to the plain language of CERLCA's section specifically addressing federal facilities. 42 U.S.C. § 9620 (West Supp.

1992). Congress expressly provided within the federal facilities section that "nothing in this section shall affect or impair the obligation of any department, agency or instrumentality of the United States to comply with any requirement of [RCRA] (including corrective action requirements)." *Id.* § 9620(i). While the EPA takes the position that its interpretation of § 9622(e)(6) is not inconsistent with § 9620(i) because RCRA requirements can be achieved through the ARAR's process pursuant to § 9621(d)(2), 54 Fed. Reg. at 10,526, the ARAR's process cannot be the exclusive means of a RCRA-authorized state's involvement in the cleanup of a RCRA-regulated site because otherwise a party's obligations under other federal and state hazardous waste laws would be modified during the closure period contrary to § 9652(d), and state law would be preempted contrary to § 9614(a). *See* supra. By the same reasoning, if the ARAR's process constituted a state's sole means of enforcing its RCRA program at a federal facility, the federal agency's RCRA obligations prior to completion of the CERCLA remedial action would be "affected or impaired" contrary to the plain language of § 9620(i). *See* H.R. Rep. No. 253(I), at 95, reprinted in 1986 U.S.C.C.A.N. at 2877 (federal facilities section "provides the public, states, and [the EPA] increased authority and a greater role in assuring the problems of hazardous substance releases are dealt with by expeditious and appropriate response actions").

Finally, § 9622(e)(6) is triggered by the initiation of a RI/FS. The federal facilities provision requires federal agencies to commence a RI/FS within six months after the facility is included on the national priority list, 42 U.S.C. § 9620(e)(1)(West Supp. 1992), and commence a remedial action within fifteen months of the study's completion, *Id.* § 9620(e)(2), while at the same time providing that this section does not affect or impair the agency's RCRA corrective action requirements. *Id.* § 9620(i). Certainly, Congress could not have intended to require a RI/FS and RCRA compliance in one section while at the same time barring RCRA compliance when a RI/FS is initiated in another section. As summed up by one commentator, "if placement on the [national priority list], completion of a RI/FS, and initiation of remedial action pursuant to [§ 9620] does not impair RCRA obligations, mere initiation of the required investigation cannot have this effect." Joseph M. Willging, Why the EPA's Current Policies on Potential CERCLA–RCRA Authority Conflicts May be Wrong, 1 Fed.Facilities Envtl.J 69, 82–83 (Spring 1990).

Because the EPA's interpretation of § 9622(e)(6) is "contrary to the plain and sensible meaning" of §§ 9622, 9614(a) and 9652(d), and, when applied to federal facilities, § 9620, we do not afford it any deference. Hill, 886 F.2d at 1278 (quotations omitted). In our view, § 9622(e)(6) does not bar a state from exercising its EPA-delegated RCRA authority at a federal facility where a RI/FS has been initiated.

VIII.

We REVERSE the district court's grant of summary judgement for Plaintiff–Appellee, the United States. We REMAND to the district court with instructions to VACATE the order prohibiting Defendants–Appellants, Colorado and CDH, from taking any action to enforce the final amended compliance order and for further.

§ 5.8   STATE REGULATION OF HAZARDOUS WASTE

RCRA is designed to allow states to assume principal enforcement jurisdiction over hazardous waste regulation. State environmental protection agencies prepare and submit to EPA for approval a state hazardous waste management plan, which must be no less protective of human health and the environment than the RCRA statute and rules. Once approved, the state agencies perform virtually all aspects of RCRA enforcement including permitting, investigations, oversight and the imposition of civil and administrative penalties for noncompliance. EPA oversees and provides technical and financial assistance to the delegated state enforcement agencies.

§ 5.9   INTERSTATE HAZARDOUS WASTE ISSUES

Interstate traffic in hazardous waste is a contentious issue between states such as South Carolina that operate commercial TSDs and those, like North Carolina, that lack sufficient merchant capacity to handle their own waste streams. States attempting to restrict inbound shipments of hazardous waste often run afoul of the Interstate Commerce Clause, a federal constitutional provision that generally prohibits states from protecting in-state interests against out-of-state competitors.

In two recent opinions, the U.S. Supreme Court reaffirmed that solid waste is an article of commerce protected by the Interstate Commerce Clause. Taken together, these opinions establish several important limitations on states' ability to restrict entries of out-of-state waste.

- States may not arbitrarily bar the entry of, or impose discriminatory taxes on, out-of-state waste, even when the restrictions apply equally to in-state, out-of-jurisdiction waste.

- Private landfills probably are not public resources that may be reserved by a state for the use of in-state generators.

- Planning requirements may not provide a legitimate basis for restricting out-of-state waste.

- The quarantine case analogy, which allows states to exclude noxious articles, probably does not apply to solid waste.

Prior to the Supreme Court's decisions, a U.S. Court of Appeals panel had affirmed a federal District Court's invalidation of a South Carolina law making it unlawful for any in-state TSD operator to accept hazardous waste originating in any other state which itself prohibited the delivery, treatment or storage of hazardous waste from South Carolina or which had not entered into a regional agreement on hazardous waste management.

The RCRA rules impose similar restraints on states seeking EPA approval of their hazardous waste management plans. EPA will not approve any plan which unreasonably restricts, impedes or operates as a ban on the free movement across the State border of hazardous waste from or to other States for treatment, storage or disposal at facilities authorized to operate under [RCRA] or an approved state program.

Congress, however, currently is considering legislation to allow states to regulate or restrict entries of out-of-state waste.

§ 5.10 WASTE MINIMIZATION: RCRA HAZARDOUS WASTE MINIMIZATION REQUIREMENTS

RCRA requires generators of hazardous waste to implement programs to minimize hazardous waste and to report periodically to EPA on the results of these efforts. Specifically, each generator currently must certify on all hazardous waste manifests that (1) it has a *program in place* to reduce the volume or quantity and toxicity of such waste to the degree determined by the generator to be economically practicable; and (2) the proposed method of treatment, storage or disposal is that *practicable* method currently available to the generator which minimizes the present and future threat to the human health and the environment.

Further, generators must submit Biennial Reports to EPA that identify (1) the efforts undertaken during the year to reduce the volume and toxicity of waste generated; and (2) the changes in volume and toxicity of waste actually achieved during the year in question in comparison with previous years, to the extent such information is available for years prior to November 8, 1984.

EPA defines *hazardous waste minimization* as the reduction, to the extent feasible, of hazardous waste that is generated prior to treatment, storage or disposal of the waste. Such minimization may be achieved by any source reduction or recycling activity that results in the reduction of the toxicity or total volume (or both) of hazardous waste generated. Minimization does *not* include transfers of hazardous constituents from one environmental medium to another, concentration conducted solely for volume reduction (unless, for example, concentration of the waste allowed for recovery of useful constituents prior to treatment and disposal), or dilution as a means of toxicity reduction.

EPA has published a draft non-binding guidance document to clarify to generators what constitutes a *program in place* for purposes of the certification requirement. EPA purposely has avoided interpreting what constitutes an economically *practicable* method of treatment, storage and disposal. Here, each generator takes into account its own particular circumstances in determining what measures are practicable.

§ 5.11 ENFORCEMENT OF HAZARDOUS WASTE REQUIRE-MENTS

Hazardous waste management standards are enforced primarily by administrative agencies such as EPA through permits, investigations, consent agreements, administrative orders and penalties, injunctions and civil and criminal proceedings. Private parties also may enforce these laws through citizens' suits, which are authorized by most federal environmental statutes and common law actions in nuisance, trespass and strict liability for ultrahazardous activity. RCRA's principal enforcement provisions are summarized below.

1. *Civil and Administrative Actions*

EPA may issue an administrative order requiring compliance whenever "any person" has violated or is violating any RCRA requirement and may assess a civil penalty up to $25,000 per violation per day for any past or current violation. The Administrator also may revoke a permit for failing to comply with the permit requirements under RCRA § 3005, 42 U.S.C. § 6925, or the performance standards applicable to owners and operators under RCRA §§ 3004, 3005(d), 42 U.S.C. §§ 6924, 6925(d). A permit also may be terminated for failing to comply with permit conditions. In addition to administrative proceedings, EPA may seek injunctive relief and civil penalties up to $25,000 per day in a federal district court for any violation of the hazardous waste management requirements.

EPA and state enforcement agencies may also, at their discretion, elect to enforce RCRA requirements through direct civil actions against suspected violators. Courts can issue injunctions against offending activities and impose civil penalties of up to $25,000 per day of violation. Where RCRA violations create imminent hazards, EPA and state agencies may seek court injunctions requiring defendants to abate the hazard created. In some instances, courts have required defendants to fund studies of the sites or consider remedial options, provide temporary or permanent alternative water supplies and conduct groundwater monitoring.

EPA and state authorities also may impose penalties, issue administrative orders requiring immediate or scheduled compliance, suspend or revoke operating permits (thereby imposing a virtual shutdown of affected facilities).

2. *Citizens' Suits*

Private citizens may bring direct actions against RCRA violators (including government agencies) where enforcement agencies decline to proceed diligently against the offending conduct. A prospective citizen-plaintiff must provide sixty or ninety days advance notice (depending on the nature of the suit) to both EPA and the alleged offender before bringing such actions. The citizens' suit is barred if EPA and the target of the suit take diligent steps to correct the alleged violation within the notification period.

If EPA fails to take enforcement action and the citizens' suit proceeds, the prevailing citizen-plaintiff may recover attorney and expert witness fees from the defendant, in addition to any civil or equitable relief otherwise available to EPA under the statute. EPA is afforded an opportunity to intervene in citizens' suits.

SUPPORTERS TO OPPOSE POLLUTION, INC. v. HERITAGE GROUP

973 F.2d 1320 (7th Cir.1992).

EASTERBROOK, CIRCUIT JUDGE.

Environmental Waste Control, Inc., operated the Four County Landfill in Indiana—poorly. The Environmental Protection Agency sued EWC under the Resource Conservation and Recovery Act of 1976 (RCRA), 42 U.S.C. §§ 6901–87, and obtained an order requiring EWC to close the dump, take some corrective action, and pay a fine of $2.8 million. *EPA v. Environmental Waste Control, Inc.,* 710 F.Supp. 1172 (N.D.Ind.1989), affirmed, 917 F.2d 327 (7th Cir.1990).

EWC has not paid the fine; it never could have paid such a sum. It is a thinly capitalized firm, almost a one-man band. (That man is Stephen W. Shambaugh, its CEO and half owner; James A. Wilkins owns the other half.) Even thinly capitalized firms have some working funds. Beginning in 1986 EWC borrowed money from firms affiliated with The Heritage Group, which to protect its investment did some supervision, but not enough to keep Shambaugh within the bounds of the law. Needless to say, Heritage has lost its investment. An entity calling itself Supporters to Oppose Pollution (StOP) believes that Heritage, having propped up EWC, should dig deeper into its pockets to pay for the cleanup. StOP apparently is willing to litigate perpetually in support of this position; the number of its lawsuits and the district judge's enthusiasm for them have been inversely related.

I

As a co-plaintiff in the EPA's action against EWC, StOP tried at the last minute to add Heritage as a defendant, contending that Heritage is EWC's alter ego under Indiana law. The EPA opposed the addition of Heritage, fearing that more parties would delay the suit. Heritage added that it is distinct from EWC, which ran the landfill without Heritage's aid between 1978 and 1986; neither Shambaugh nor Wilkins is employed by or an investor in Heritage. The district court rebuffed StOP's effort, in large measure because StOP, having neglected discovery, could not prove its claims of linkage. StOP did not appeal from the district court's order keeping Heritage out of the original suit. StOP has nonetheless tried four more times to involve Heritage, and we have appeals from three of these four additional efforts.

Congress authorized private citizens to enforce RCRA through litigation, 42 U.S.C. § 6972, and StOP filed such a suit, which we call SOP I. (StOP represents persons living close to the garbage, which has at least the potential to injure them, so the Constitution permits it to litigate. Compare *Lujan v. Defenders of Wildlife,* 119 L.Ed.2d 351, 112 S.Ct. 2130 (1992), with *Duke Power Co. v. Carolina Environmental Study Group, Inc.,* 438 U.S. 59, 57 L.Ed.2d 595, 98 S.Ct. 2620 (1978).) Section 6972 requires a would-be champion to try negotiation before litigation. To be precise, "no action may be commenced under subsection (a)(1)(B) of this section prior to ninety days after the plaintiff has given notice of the endangerment to ... any person alleged to have contributed" to the handling or storage of the waste. 42 U.S.C. § 6972(b)(2)(A)(iii). StOP ignored this rule, mailing Heritage a notice on July 14, 1989, and filing the complaint on July 24. StOP dismissed SOP I under Fed. R. Civ. P. 41(a) on November 17, 1989, shortly after *Hallstrom v. Tillamook County,* 493 U.S. 20, 107 L.Ed.2d 237, 110 S.Ct. 304 (1989), reiterated that § 6972 requires pre-suit notice, and not just a stay of the litigation.

The same day it dismissed SOP I, StOP filed SOP II, asserting that 90 days had passed since the notice mailed on July 14. The district judge dismissed SOP II because Heritage still had not received the 90 days of non-adversarial time that the statute contemplates. 1990 WL 258383. StOP argued that because it appended a claim that the landfill violates a permit or regulation under RCRA advance notice is not necessary. (StOP originally claimed that it was proceeding under § 6973, but only the EPA may enforce that statute. The district judge corrected the mis-citations when denying StOP's post-judgment motion. Although some confusion lingers in the parties' briefs, we treat SOP II as pursuing a claim under §§ 6924 and 6925.) The district judge replied that private parties are not authorized to invoke this branch of RCRA if the EPA has commenced and is diligently pursuing an action. 42 U.S.C. § 6972(b)(1)(B). Judge Miller held that the EPA had prosecuted the original action against EWC diligently and obtained substantial relief. If as StOP contends Heritage really is the alter ego of EWC, then relief already runs against Heritage and the EPA may claim the fruits of victory; if Heritage is not EWC's alter ago, then StOP has no claim on the merits. So it loses either way. StOP's appeal of this order is No. 91–1247.

The judgment dismissing SOP II was entered on August 1, 1990. On August 10 StOP served another notice on Heritage, and it filed suit (SOP III) on November 20. This suit met the fate of SOP II, as the judge reiterated his holding that RCRA gives the adversary 90 non-adversarial days before suit on the claim StOP raised. Because StOP's motion to reconsider the dismissal of SOP II was pending, Heritage had yet to receive any non-litigious time. 760 F.Supp. 1338 (1991). Judge Miller gave an alternative ground: claim preclusion (res judicata), for StOP was presenting a new legal theory in support of the same relief sought or obtained in the original suit. The appeal from this judgment is No. 91–1728.

Meanwhile EWC fled for bankruptcy, having insufficient assets to clean up the waste. StOP is among its creditors, having been awarded attorneys' fees in *EPA v. EWC,* 737 F.Supp. 1485 (1990). In SOP IV the group asked the judge to remove the bankruptcy case to district court (he declined) and attempted to commence supplemental "enforcement" proceedings against Heritage. Judge Miller found these barred by 11 U.S.C. § 362, the automatic stay in bankruptcy, because StOP, as a creditor, was trying to reach assets of the estate. 131 B.R. 410 (1991). To the extent StOP was trying to enforce a claim by the EWC estate against Heritage for contribution or indemnity, it is the wrong party. The claim belongs to EWC's trustee, not to creditors. And to the extent StOP was trying to add Heritage as a party, it was renewing a request the district judge had rejected in the same case. Once again the district judge invoked res judicata to clean up any residue. StOP's appeal from the judgment in SOP IV is No. 91–2884.

II

On the appeal of SOP II, plaintiff contests only the district court's conclusion that the EPA's action against EWC blocks a private action, under §§ 6924, 6925, and 6972(a)(1)(A), to enforce permits and regulations issued under RCRA. This is a subject on which notice is necessary, see § 6972(b)(1)(A), but the suit may follow immediately on the giving of notice. Private litigation under these sections is forbidden, however, if the EPA "has commenced and is diligently prosecuting a civil or criminal action in a court of the United States ... to require compliance with such permit, standard, regulation, condition, requirement, prohibition, or order." 42 U.S.C. § 6972(b)(1)(B). Notice that this statute refers to an action to "require compliance with such permit [or] regulation"—not an action against the private party's chosen adversary, but an action to require compliance. Judge Miller concluded that the EPA had filed, diligently pursued, and won, an action to require compliance with EWC's permit and federal regulations.

StOP does not challenge this conclusion so much as it contends that even though the EPA prevailed, the risk continues. EWC closed the dump, so no new hazardous materials are being deposited. But because EWC ran out of money to clean up the wastes, the risk to groundwaters continues. It is to curtail this risk that it must be allowed to bring in new, deep-pocket defendants, StOP insists. This approach supposes, however, that § 6972(b)(1)(B) applies only when the EPA has succeeded by the private party's definition of success. The statute does not require that the EPA succeed; it requires only that the EPA try, diligently.

Section 6972(b)(1)(B) belongs to a genre common to environmental laws under which citizen suits serve as goads to both the EPA and polluters without displacing the federal agency as the principal enforcer. When describing a similar provision in the Clean Water Act, the Supreme Court observed that citizen suits may supplement but not supplant public litigation. *Gwaltney of Smithfield, Ltd. v. Chesapeake Bay Foundation, Inc.*, 484 U.S. 49, 60, 98 L.Ed.2d 306, 108 S.Ct. 376 (1987). It gave a telling example. "Suppose that the Administrator identified a violator of the Act and issued a compliance order.... Suppose further that the Administrator agreed not to assess or otherwise seek civil penalties on the condition that the violator take some extreme corrective action, such as to install particularly effective but expensive machinery, that it otherwise would not be obliged to take. If citizens could file suit ... in order to seek the civil penalties that the Administrator chose to forgo, then the Administrator's discretion to enforce the Act in the public interest would be curtailed considerably." Id. at 60–61. An Administrator unable to make concessions is unable to obtain them. A private plaintiff waiting in the wings then is the captain of the litigation. And it makes no difference that this person chooses to sue another party. If as StOP insists EWC and Heritage really are the same entity, then the ability to sue Heritage is the ability to sue EWC for more than the EPA obtained, and fear of this liability will lead Heritage (that is, EWC) to fight to the death in the initial case.

To say, as StOP would, that the EPA is not "diligently prosecuting" the action if it does not sue the persons, or use the theories, the private plaintiff prefers would strip EPA of the control the statute provides. *North & South Rivers Watershed Ass'n v. Scituate*, 949 F.2d 552, 555–56 (1st Cir.1991), holds that an enforcement action under a part of the Clean Water Act containing a limitation materially identical to § 6972(b)(1)(B) bars private litigation even though the public plaintiff settled for declaratory and injunctive relief, while the private one demands damages. The first circuit concluded that under such statutes public agencies' litigation decisions may not be second-guessed by the device of filing an independent suit. Primary responsibility lies with public enforcers. "Merely because the State may not be taking the precise action [the private plaintiff] wants it to or moving with the alacrity [that plaintiff] desires does not entitle [the private plaintiff] to injunctive relief." *Id.* at 558.

"Diligent" prosecution is all the statute requires. Although StOP wants a trial on the question whether the EPA's prosecution was "diligent," such follow-up inquiries are appropriate only when the agency loses its suit and the private litigant insists that the agency had not tried hard enough. RCRA permits a follow-on private suit if the public suit was not prosecuted diligently. But if the agency prevails in all respects, that is the end; § 6972(b)(1)(B) does not authorize a collateral attack on the agency's strategy or tactics. At all events, there can be no serious question about the EPA's conduct of its suit. Judge Miller, who presided over that case as well as all four of StOP's later actions, found that the EPA prosecuted vigorously. It would be asinine to require Judge Miller to hold a new trial at which the only question would be whether he accurately assessed the conduct of the first trial.

Behind all of this fighting is StOP's belief that the EPA underestimates the seriousness of the risk posed by this landfill. Although RCRA provides some remedies, the heavy artillery lies in the Comprehensive Environmental Response, Compensation, and Liability Act of 1980 (CERCLA), 42 U.S.C. §§ 9601–26. Sections 106 and 107 of CERCLA, 42 U.S.C. §§ 9606–07, permit the EPA to direct almost anyone connected with hazardous waste to bear the costs of cleanup, and if they cannot or will not do so, to tap the "Superfund" for the necessary money. Several courts have held that the EPA may collect from parent corporations, corporate affiliates, and even major lenders that took a supervisory role. *E.g., United States v. Kayser–Roth Corp.*, 910 F.2d 24 (1st Cir.1990)(parent corporation); *United States v. Fleet Factors Corp.*, 901 F.2d 1550

(11th Cir.1990) (secured lender with a "capacity to influence" the borrower's waste disposal). *See also* David W. Leebron, Limited Liability, Tort Victims, and Creditors, 91 Colum. L. Rev. 1565, 1641–46 & n.227 (1991); Note, Cleaning up the Debris After Fleet Factors: Lender Liability and CERCLA's Security Interest Exemption, 104 Harv. L. Rev. 1249 (1991). Broad though it is, CERCLA has limits. *Edward Hines Lumber Co. v. Vulcan Materials Co.,* 861 F.2d 155 (7th Cir.1988); *Covalt v. Carey Canada Inc.,* 860 F.2d 1434, 1439 (7th Cir.1988). We need not decide whether to embrace decisions such as *Fleet Factors* or how they would apply to Heritage. If the hazards at the Four County Landfill are as serious as StOP thinks, then CERCLA holds the key to further relief. Doubtless StOP believes that it should be able to initiate a cleanup under CERCLA and send Heritage the bill, but that is not the way Congress wrote these statutes, and courts have no business bending one statute out of shape because litigants (or even the judges) believe that Congress should have written another statute differently.

* * *

StOP is playing games. It contends that it is unconstrained by the limitations on the use of supplemental and enforcement proceedings because it is "really" vindicating rights created by RCRA. And it contends that it is unconstrained by the limitations on citizen suits under RCRA because it is "really" enforcing the judgment in the EPA's suit. It can't have things both ways. For reasons we have explained its failure to appeal in EPA and *StOP v. EWC* means that it now can't have things either of these ways.

Fourth and finally, StOP appears to believe that Heritage removed assets from EWC, preventing that firm from fulfilling its obligations under the judgment. This is either a fraudulent conveyance action or a preference action, which in either event belongs to EWC's trustee in bankruptcy, not to one of EWC's creditors.

We recognize plaintiff's frustration over the effect that application of preclusion yields. Yet all litigants must accept the outcome of their cases, even if they wish in retrospect that they had acted differently. Plaintiff has had its day in court, has been heard out. Now it must STOP.

AFFIRMED.

PALUMBO v. WASTE TECHNOLOGIES INDUSTRIES

989 F.2d 156 (4th Cir.1993).

WILKINSON, CIRCUIT JUDGE:

After years of gathering state and federal permits for their hazardous waste incinerator, defendants here face a collateral challenge to the validity of those permits by certain citizens of West Virginia. The issue on this certified interlocutory appeal is whether the district court has subject matter jurisdiction over such a challenge, under the citizens' suit provision of the Resource Conservation and Recovery Act, 42 U.S.C.

§ 6972. We hold that it does not. Accordingly, we reverse the judgment of the district court, and remand with instructions to dismiss the complaint.

I.

The Resource Conservation and Recovery Act ("RCRA"), 42 U.S.C. §§ 6901 et seq., is a comprehensive regulatory system designed to promote the safe handling of solid and hazardous wastes. Toward this end, RCRA provides for the formal identification of certain solid wastes as hazardous; a system of written manifests for tracking shipments of hazardous wastes; and a permitting scheme to insure that handlers meet certain standards in treating, storing, and disposing of hazardous wastes. States may enact their own regulatory schemes to take care of hazardous wastes, as long as they comply with the minimum requirements of federal law.

Defendant Waste Technologies Industries ("WTI") is the Ohio partnership that owns the hazardous waste incinerator located in East Liverpool, Ohio, on the banks of the Ohio River. The remaining corporate defendants are the partners in WTI. The plaintiffs in this case are the Attorney General for West Virginia, acting as parens patriae for the citizens of West Virginia who oppose the operation of the incinerator; and the City of Chester, West Virginia, which sits directly across the Ohio River from the incinerator.

For more than ten years, defendants have been working to obtain and maintain the state and federal permits necessary to begin operating the East Liverpool incinerator. Defendants received their first permit on February 2, 1983, when the Ohio Environmental Protection Agency issued them an air pollution permit to install the incinerator at the East Liverpool site. Because the Ohio EPA had authority at that time to administer the federal Clean Air Act as well, the issuance of this permit brought the proposed incinerator into compliance with both the Ohio air pollution laws, Ohio Rev. Code § 3704, and the federal Clean Air Act, 42 U.S.C. §§ 7401 et seq.

On June 24 of the same year, the federal EPA issued the defendants a hazardous waste permit for the incinerator, as required by RCRA. Because the Ohio EPA did not have an EPA-authorized hazardous waste program at that time, the defendants had to obtain a separate state hazardous waste permit under Ohio Rev. Code § 3734. The Ohio EPA granted the state hazardous waste permit on April 27, 1984. The State of West Virginia challenged the issuance of the state permit in the Ohio appellate courts, but the Ohio Supreme Court ultimately affirmed the decision of the Ohio EPA. *West Virginia v. Ohio Hazardous Waste Facility Approval Bd.*, 28 Ohio St. 3d 83, 502 N.E.2d 625 (1986). In July 1990, and again in April 1991, the defendants applied separately to the Ohio EPA and the federal EPA for a number of changes to their hazardous waste permits, including the addition of a spray dryer. On December 18, 1991, the Ohio EPA approved these changes and issued the defendants a revised hazardous waste permit. An appeal of that decision, brought by the Attorney General for West Virginia and others, is pending before the Ohio Environmental Board of Review.

On February 3, 1992, the federal EPA likewise approved the modifications requested by the defendants. The Attorney General for West Virginia and others then sought review of that modification decision before the United States Environmental Appeals Board. On July 24, 1992, the Environmental Appeals Board rejected the petitioners' challenge. Under 42 U.S.C. § 6976(b), petitioners had ninety days to appeal the Board's ruling to an appropriate circuit court. They did not.

Instead, plaintiffs have pursued this action. On April 21, 1992, plaintiffs filed a nine-count complaint in the Northern District of West Virginia, challenging the validity of the defendants' state and federal hazardous waste permits, and seeking to enjoin the eventual operation of the East Liverpool incinerator. On May 22, WTI moved to dismiss the complaint on several grounds, including lack of subject matter jurisdiction. The plaintiffs then moved to amend their complaint to allege that the incinerator would pose an "imminent and substantial endangerment to health or the environment" under the RCRA citizens' suit provision, 42 U.S.C. § 6972(a)(1)(B). On October 9, the district court granted the plaintiffs' motions to amend, as well as the defendants' motion to dismiss Count VIII of the complaint for failure to state a claim upon which relief could be granted. The court denied, however, defendants' motion to dismiss Counts I–VII and IX, ruling that it did have subject matter jurisdiction over these counts under the "imminent and substantial endangerment" clause of § 6972(a)(1)(B). The district court then certified WTI's motion to file an interlocutory appeal on the issue of subject matter jurisdiction, which we granted. *See* 28 U.S.C. § 1292(b).

II.

The RCRA citizens' suit statute provides in relevant part as follows:

Any person may commence a civil action on his own behalf—

> (1)(A) against any person ... who is alleged to be in violation of any permit, standard, regulation, condition, requirement, prohibition, or order which has become effective pursuant to this chapter; or

> (B) against any person ... who has contributed or who is contributing to the past or present handling, storage, treatment, transportation, or disposal of any solid or hazardous waste which may present an imminent and substantial endangerment to health or the environment. . . .

42 U.S.C. § 6972(a). . . . Plaintiffs argue that the district court was correct to accept for jurisdictional purposes their allegations that the operation of the incinerator would pose an "imminent and substantial endangerment" under § 6972(a)(1)(B), and maintain that we are obliged to do the same. Defendants maintain that the facts, even as plaintiffs state them, do not give rise to the kind of "imminent and substantial endangerment" that § 6972(a)(1)(B) requires.

We agree with defendants that § 6972(a)(1)(B) does not cover this case. At bottom, plaintiffs' complaint is nothing more than a collateral attack on the prior permitting decisions of the federal EPA. The RCRA judicial review provision plainly forbids such an attack, in place of a direct appeal:

> Review of the Administrator's action ... in issuing, denying, modifying, or revoking any permit under section 6925 of this title ... may be had by any interested person in the Circuit Court of Appeals of the United States for the Federal judicial district in which such person resides.... Any such application shall be made within ninety days from the date of such issuance, denial, modification, revocation, ... or after such date only if such application is based solely on grounds which arose after such ninetieth day. Action of the Administrator with respect to which review could have been obtained under this subsection shall not be subject to judicial review in civil or criminal proceedings for enforcement.

42 U.S.C. § 6976(b).... Plaintiffs chose not to appeal the February 1992 modification decision to an appropriate circuit court; they are bound by that choice now. To the extent that plaintiffs challenge separately the permitting decisions of the Ohio EPA, they are denied jurisdiction on *Burford* abstention grounds. *Burford v. Sun Oil Co.*, 319 U.S. 315 (1943)(abstaining from review of complex state regulatory scheme, where state has established specialized tribunal to review that scheme); *see also Ada–Cascade Watch Co. v. Cascade Resource Recovery, Inc.*, 720 F.2d 897 (6th Cir.1983)(abstaining under *Burford* from review of Michigan's Hazardous Waste Management Act and Solid Waste Management Act). Ohio has taken great care to provide for specialized adjudication of its complicated environmental law scheme. Initial applications for hazardous waste permits are screened by the Ohio EPA and then reviewed by the Ohio Hazardous Waste Facility Approval Board. Ohio Rev. Code § 3734.05(D)(2)-(3). The members of this Board are the director of the Ohio EPA, the Ohio director of natural resources, the chairman of the Ohio water development authority, a university-employed chemical engineer, and a university employed geologist. *Id.* at § 3734.05(D)(1). Decisions of the Board may be appealed to the Franklin County Court of Appeals, and then to the Ohio Supreme Court. *Id.* at § 3734.05(D)(7). Subsequent permit revisions that the Ohio EPA approves may be appealed to the Ohio Environmental Board of Review, whose three members are each required to have "extensive experience in pollution control and abatement technology, ecology, public health, environmental law, economics of natural resource development, or related fields." *Id.* at § 3745.02. Decisions of the Environmental Board of Review may also be appealed to an intermediate court of appeals, and ultimately to the Ohio Supreme Court. *Id.* at § 3745.06. Plaintiffs are currently using this latter channel of review: an appeal of the Ohio EPA's December 1991 decision is pending before the Environmental Board of Review. Burford forbids us to interfere.

III.

A count-by-count examination of the substance of plaintiffs' complaint confirms that it is at root a collateral attack on the permitting decisions of the federal and Ohio EPAs. Count I alleges that WTI failed to notify either EPA that the members of the partnership had changed since the issuance of their hazardous waste permits, in violation of 42 U.S.C. § 6925 and 40 C.F.R. § 270.30(a). Count II builds on Count I, alleging that because the partners of WTI have changed, WTI has effectively transferred its permits to a new entity without modification or revocation-reissuance, in violation of 42 U.S.C. § 6925(c) and 40 C.F.R. §§ 270.40(a) and 270.30(*l*)(3). Count III parallels Count II, alleging that the permit modification allowing WTI to install spray dryers listed a new partner as the operator of the incinerator, again in violation of 42 U.S.C. § 6925 and 40 C.F.R. §§ 270.40 and 270.30. Count IV alleges that the owner of the land on which the incinerator is located did not sign WTI's hazardous waste permit applications, in violation of 40 C.F.R. §§ 270.10(b) and 270.40(a). All of these counts allege what are essentially technical violations in the EPA permitting process. On their face, they do not give rise to any "imminent and substantial endangerment to health or the environment," and the plaintiffs should have raised them on direct appeal, or with the relevant regulatory bodies.

Count V alleges that on January 30, 1991, the Ohio EPA notified the defendants that the incinerator was not in compliance with certain conditions of its state hazardous waste permit. Plaintiffs claim that the federal and Ohio EPAs should then have revoked the defendants' permit; plaintiffs do not allege, however, that the incinerator is currently in noncompliance. In essence, then, plaintiffs challenge the EPAs' decisions to give the defendants time to bring their incinerator into compliance with the terms of their permits. Once again, plaintiffs should have raised this issue on direct appeal, either from the federal EPA's permit modification decision in February 1992, or from the Ohio EPA's parallel decision in December 1991.

Count VI alleges that the federal and Ohio EPAs have failed to review whether the location of the incinerator is still suitable in light of new environmental standards. These standards are (1) the requirement that no hazardous waste facility be located within 2000 feet of a residence or school, imposed under Ohio Rev. Code § 3734.05(D)(6) in 1984; (2) the requirement that a hazardous waste facility be designed to avoid washout from a one-hundred year flood, also imposed under Ohio Rev. Code § 3734.05(D)(6) in 1984; (3) the Reference Air Concentration ("RAC") for lead, which the federal EPA promulgated under RCRA in 56 Fed. Reg. 7134 (Feb. 22, 1991); and (4) the "Guideline on Air Quality Models" prescribing a new model for determining whether a plant is in compliance with the secondary ambient air quality standard ("AAQS") for sulfur dioxide, which model the federal EPA revised in July 1986. Count VII overlaps with Count VI, and alleges that the federal and Ohio EPAs have failed to require the defendants, as conditions of their hazardous waste permits, to comply with the RAC for lead and secondary

AAQS for sulfur dioxide. Even if § 6972(a)(1)(B) is read to extend to non-RCRA violations as well, we emphasize again that plaintiffs' claims are simply expressions of displeasure with the alleged inadequacies of EPA review. Plaintiffs should have taken up these challenges with the appropriate agencies, or raised them on direct appeal from EPA permitting decisions, whether in state or federal court. "Generally, when jurisdiction to review administrative determinations is vested in the courts of appeals these specific, exclusive jurisdiction provisions preempt district court jurisdiction over related issues under other statutes." *Connors v. Amax Coal Co.*, 858 F.2d 1226, 1231 (7th Cir.1988); *accord Media Access Project v. FCC*, 280 U.S.App.D.C. 119, 883 F.2d 1063, 1067–69 (D.C.Cir.1989).

Finally, Count IX alleges that the operation of the incinerator will pose a public nuisance, under either federal or state common law. This count functions as little more than an "omnibus" count, reiterating under the guise of a common law claim plaintiffs' now-familiar dissatisfaction with the EPA permitting decisions. The count expressly incorporates the allegations of the preceding counts, alleges once again that the EPA permitting process was deficient, and then enumerates the ensuing risks in an attempt to give substance to the claim of nuisance. These risks are (1) the possibility of washout from a one-hundred year flood; (2) the production of mustard gas by the new spray dryer; and (3) the discharge of lead and other contaminants from the incinerator. All of these risks arise from the violations alleged in the first seven counts; all relate to EPA permitting decisions that plaintiffs should have challenged on direct appeal. Plaintiffs cannot evade the exclusive jurisdiction rule of § 6976 simply by slapping a nuisance label on the violations alleged in the first seven counts. Since the first seven counts fail to allege sufficient jurisdictional facts, the nuisance count fails as well. . . .

IV.

We conclude by re-emphasizing that when Congress has chosen to provide the circuit courts with exclusive jurisdiction over appeals from agency decisions, the district courts are without jurisdiction over the legal issues pertaining to those decisions—whether or not those issues arise from the statute that authorized the agency action in the first place. *Media Access*, 883 F.2d at 1067; *Connors*, 858 F.2d at 1231. *See also General Electric Uranium Management Corp. v. Department of Energy*, 246 U.S.App.D.C. 263, 764 F.2d 896, 903 (D.C.Cir.1985)("where it is unclear whether review jurisdiction is in the district court or the court of appeals the ambiguity is resolved in favor of the latter")(quoting *Denberg v. United States R.R. Retirement Bd.*, 696 F.2d 1193, 1197 (7th Cir.1983)). Plaintiffs cannot launch a grapeshot collateral attack on the permitting decisions of the EPA—invoking RCRA, the Clean Air Act, Ohio hazardous waste laws, and the common law of nuisance—and hope that one of these shots will land them in a federal district court. "The choice of forum is . . . for Congress and we cannot imagine that Congress intended the exclusivity vel non of statutory review to depend on the substantive infirmity alleged. The policy behind having a special review procedure in the first place similarly disfavors bifurcating jurisdiction over various substantive grounds between district court and the court of appeals." *City of Rochester v. Bond*, 195 U.S.App.D.C. 345, 603 F.2d 927, 936 (D.C.Cir.1979).

Adding another layer of collateral review for agency decisions threatens to put at naught the administrative process established by Congress. Plaintiffs who sue collaterally in a federal district court would be able to avoid the deferential standard of review that circuit courts must apply under the Administrative Procedure Act when hearing a direct appeal from an agency decision. 5 U.S.C. § 706. Plaintiffs would also be able to circumvent the limitations period during which they were required to post a direct appeal—ninety days in the case of RCRA. And the district court, as plenary fact-finder, would not be limited to the evidentiary record that the agency has accumulated during the months of permit proceedings and public hearings held prior to the issuance of the permit. In short, for an uncertain length of time after the agency issues the permit, the permit-holder would face the very real threat that the inquiry into the validity of its permit might be reopened in an altogether different forum. This threat will have one long-term effect: otherwise worthy permit applicants will weigh the formidable costs in delay and litigation, and simply will not apply. *See General Electric*, 764 F.2d at 903 ("exclusive jurisdiction in the court of appeals avoids duplicative review and the attendant delay and expense involved"). We see no evidence that Congress intended to eviscerate the very permitting process that Congress itself set up, and we will not do so by entertaining this suit.

For the foregoing reasons, the district court is without jurisdiction over this complaint. We remand this case with directions that it be dismissed.

MEGHRIG v. KFC WESTERN, INC.

___ U.S. ___, 116 S.Ct. 1251, 134 L.Ed.2d 121 (1996).

JUSTICE O'CONNOR delivered the opinion of the Court.

We consider whether § 7002 of the Resource Conservation and Recovery Act of 1976 (RCRA), 42 U.S.C. § 6972 (1988 ed.), authorizes a private cause of action to recover the prior cost of cleaning up toxic waste that does not, at the time of suit, continue to pose an endangerment to health or the environment. We conclude that it does not.

I

Respondent KFC Western, Inc. (KFC), owns and operates a "Kentucky Fried Chicken" restaurant on a parcel of property in Los Angeles. In 1988, KFC discovered during the course of a construction project that the property was contaminated with petroleum. The County of Los Angeles Department of Health Services ordered KFC to attend to the problem, and KFC spent $211,000 removing and disposing of the oil-tainted soil.

Three years later, KFC brought this suit under the citizen suit provision of RCRA, 90 Stat. 2825, as amended, 42 U.S.C. § 6972(a)(1988 ed.), seeking to recover these cleanup costs from petitioners Alan and Margaret Meghrig.

KFC claimed that the contaminated soil was a "solid waste" covered by RCRA, see 42 U.S.C. § 6903(27)(1988 ed.), that it had previously posed an "imminent and substantial endangerment to health or the environment," see § 6972(a)(1)(B), and that the Meghrigs were responsible for "equitable restitution" of KFC's cleanup costs under § 6972(a) because, as prior owners of the property, they had contributed to the waste's "past or present handling, storage, treatment, transportation, or disposal." See App. 12–19 (first amended complaint).

The District Court held that § 6972(a) does not permit recovery of past cleanup costs and that § 6972(a)(1)(B) does not authorize a cause of action for the remediation of toxic waste that does not pose an "imminent and substantial endangerment to health or the environment" at the time suit is filed, and dismissed KFC's complaint. App. to Pet. for Cert. A21–A23. The Court of Appeals for the Ninth Circuit reversed, over a dissent, 49 F.3d 518, 524–528 (1995)(Brunetti, J.), finding that a district court had authority under § 6972(a) to award restitution of past cleanup costs, id., at 521–523, and that a private party can proceed with a suit under § 6972(a)(1)(B) upon an allegation that the waste at issue presented an "imminent and substantial endangerment" at the time it was cleaned up, id., at 520–521.

The Ninth Circuit's conclusion regarding the remedies available under RCRA conflicts with the decision of the Court of Appeals for the Eighth Circuit in *Furrer v. Brown*, 62 F.3d 1092, 1100–1101 (1995), and its interpretation of the "imminent endangerment" requirement represents a novel application of federal statutory law. We granted certiorari to address the conflict between the Circuits and to consider the correctness of the Ninth Circuit's interpretation of RCRA, 515 U.S. ___, 116 S.Ct. 41, 132 L.Ed.2d 922 (1995), and now reverse.

II

RCRA is a comprehensive environmental statute that governs the treatment, storage, and disposal of solid and hazardous waste. *See Chicago v. Environmental Defense Fund*, 511 U.S. ___ (1994)(slip op., at 3–4). Unlike the Comprehensive Environmental Response, Compensation and Liability Act of 1980 (CERCLA), 94 Stat. 2767, as amended, 42 U.S.C. § 9601 et seq. (1988 ed. and Supp. V), RCRA is not principally designed to effectuate the cleanup of toxic waste sites or to compensate those who have attended to the remediation of environmental hazards. Cf. *General Electric Co. v. Litton Industrial Automation Systems, Inc.*, 920 F.2d 1415, 1422 (C.A.8 1990) (the "two ... main purposes of CERCLA" are "prompt cleanup of hazardous waste sites and imposition of all cleanup costs on the responsible party"). RCRA's primary purpose, rather, is to reduce the generation of hazardous waste and to ensure the proper treatment, storage, and disposal of that waste which is nonetheless generated, "so as to minimize the present and future threat to human health and the environment." 42 U.S.C. § 6902(b)(1988 ed.).

Chief responsibility for the implementation and enforcement of RCRA rests with the Administrator of the Environmental Protection Agency (EPA), see §§ 6928, 6973, but like other environmental laws, RCRA contains a citizen suit provision, § 6972, which permits private citizens to enforce its provisions in some circumstances.

Two requirements of § 6972(a) defeat KFC's suit against the Meghrigs. The first concerns the necessary timing of a citizen suit brought under § 6972(a)(1)(B): That section permits a private party to bring suit against certain responsible persons, including former owners, "who have contributed or who [are] contributing to the past or present handling, storage, treatment, transportation, or disposal of any solid or hazardous waste which may present an imminent and substantial endangerment to health or the environment." (Emphasis added.) The second defines the remedies a district court can award in a suit brought under § 6972(a)(1)(B): Section 6972(a) authorizes district courts "to restrain any person who has contributed or who is contributing to the past or present handling, storage, treatment, transportation, or disposal of any solid or hazardous waste . . . , to order such person to take such other action as may be necessary, or both." (Emphasis added.)

It is apparent from the two remedies described in § 6972(a) that RCRA's citizen suit provision is not directed at providing compensation for past cleanup efforts. Under a plain reading of this remedial scheme, a private citizen suing under § 6972(a)(1)(B) could seek a mandatory injunction, i.e., one that orders a responsible party to "take action" by attending to the cleanup and proper disposal of toxic waste, or a prohibitory injunction, i.e., one that "restrains" a responsible party from further violating RCRA. Neither remedy, however, is susceptible of the interpretation adopted by the Ninth Circuit, as neither contemplates the award of past cleanup costs, whether these are denominated "damages" or "equitable restitution."

In this regard, a comparison between the relief available under RCRA's citizen suit provision and that which Congress has provided in the analogous, but not parallel, provisions of CERCLA is telling. CERCLA was passed several years after RCRA went into effect, and it is designed to address many of the same toxic waste problems that inspired the passage of RCRA. Compare 42 U.S.C. § 6903(5)(1988 ed.)(RCRA definition of "hazardous waste") and § 6903(27)(RCRA definition of "solid waste") with § 9601(14)(CERCLA provision incorporating certain "hazardous substances," but not the hazardous and solid wastes defined in RCRA, and specifically not petroleum). CERCLA differs markedly from RCRA, however, in the remedies it provides. CERCLA's citizen suit provision mimics § 6972(a) in providing district courts with the authority "to order such action as may be necessary to correct the violation" of any CERCLA standard or regulation. 42 U.S.C. § 9659(c)(1988 ed.). But CERCLA expressly permits the Government to recover "all costs of removal or remedial action," § 9607(a)(4)(A), and it expressly permits the recovery of any "necessary costs of response, incurred by any ... person consistent with the national contingency plan," § 9607(a)(4)(B). CERCLA also provides that "any person may seek contribution from any other person who is liable or potentially liable" for these response costs. See § 9613(f)(1). Congress thus demonstrated in CERCLA that it knew how to provide for the recovery of cleanup costs, and that the language used to define the remedies under RCRA does not provide that remedy.

That RCRA's citizen suit provision was not intended to provide a remedy for past cleanup costs is further apparent from the harm at which it is directed. Section 6972(a)(1)(B) permits a private party to bring suit only upon a showing that the solid or hazardous waste at issue "may present an imminent and substantial endangerment to health or the environment." The meaning of this timing restriction is plain: An endangerment can only be "imminent" if it "threatens to occur immediately," Webster's New International Dictionary of English Language 1245 (2d ed. 1934), and the reference to waste which "may present" imminent harm quite clearly excludes waste that no longer presents such a danger. As the Ninth Circuit itself intimated in *Price v. United States Navy*, 39 F.3d 1011, 1019 (1994), this language "implies that there must be a threat which is present now, although the impact of the threat may not be felt until later." It follows that § 6972(a) was designed to provide a remedy that ameliorates present or obviates the risk of future "imminent" harms, not a remedy that compensates for past cleanup efforts. Cf. § 6902(b) (national policy behind RCRA is "to minimize the present and future threat to human health and the environment").

Other aspects of RCRA's enforcement scheme strongly support this conclusion. Unlike CERCLA, RCRA contains no statute of limitations, compare § 9613(g)(2)(limitations period in suits under CERCLA § 9607), and it does not require a showing that the response costs being sought are reasonable, compare §§ 9607(a)(4)(A) and (B)(costs recovered under CERCLA must be "consistent with the national contingency plan"). If Congress had intended § 6972(a) to function as a cost-recovery mechanism, the absence of these provisions would be striking. Moreover, with one limited exception, *see Hallstrom v. Tillamook County,* 493 U.S. 20, 26–27, 107 L.Ed.2d 237, 110 S.Ct. 304 (1989)(noting exception to notice requirement "when there is a danger that hazardous waste will be discharged"), a private party may not bring suit under § 6972(a)(1)(B) without first giving 90 days' notice to the Administrator of the EPA, to "the State in which the alleged endangerment may occur," and to potential defendants, see §§ 6972(b)(2)(A)(i)-(iii). And no citizen suit can proceed if either the EPA or the State has commenced, and is diligently prosecuting, a separate enforcement action, see §§ 6972(b)(2)(B) and (C).

Therefore, if RCRA were designed to compensate private parties for their past cleanup efforts, it would be a wholly irrational mechanism for doing so. Those parties with insubstantial problems, problems that neither the State nor the Federal Government feel compelled to address, could recover their response costs, whereas those parties whose waste problems were sufficiently severe as to attract the attention of Government officials would be left without a recovery.

Though it agrees that KFC's complaint is defective for failing properly to allege an "imminent and substantial endangerment," the Government (as amicus) nonetheless joins KFC in arguing that § 6972(a) does not in all circumstances preclude an award of past cleanup costs. See Brief for United States as Amicus Curiae 22–28. The Government posits a situation in which suit is properly brought while the waste at issue continues to pose an imminent endangerment, and suggests that the plaintiff in such a case could seek equitable restitution of money previously spent on cleanup efforts. Echoing a similar argument made by KFC, see Brief for Respondent 11–19, the Government does not rely on the remedies expressly provided in § 6972(a), but rather cites a line of cases holding that district courts retain inherent authority to award any equitable remedy that is not expressly taken away from them by Congress. *See, e.g., Porter v. Warner Holding Co.,* 328 U.S. 395, 90 L.Ed. 1332, 66 S.Ct. 1086 (1946); *Wyandotte Transp. Co. v. United States,* 389 U.S. 191, 19 L.Ed.2d 407, 88 S.Ct. 379 (1967); *Hecht Co. v. Bowles,* 321 U.S. 321, 88 L.Ed. 754, 64 S.Ct. 587 (1944).

RCRA does not prevent a private party from recovering its cleanup costs under other federal or state laws, see § 6972(f)(preserving remedies under statutory and common law), but the limited remedies described in § 6972(a), along with the stark differences between the language of that section and the cost recovery provisions of CERCLA, amply demonstrate that Congress did not intend for a private citizen to be able to undertake a clean up and then proceed to recover its costs under RCRA. As we explained in *Middlesex County Sewerage Authority v. National Sea Clammers Assn.,* 453 U.S. 1, 14, 69 L.Ed.2d 435, 101 S.Ct. 2615 (1981), where Congress has provided "elaborate enforcement provisions" for remedying the violation of a federal statute, as Congress has done with RCRA and CERCLA, "it cannot be assumed that Congress intended to authorize by implication additional judicial remedies for private citizens suing under" the statute. " 'It is an elemental canon of statutory construction that where a statute expressly provides a particular remedy or remedies, a court must be chary of reading others into it.' " *Id.,* at 14–15 (quoting *Transamerica Mortgage Advisors, Inc. v. Lewis,* 444 U.S. 11, 19, 62 L.Ed.2d 146, 100 S.Ct. 242 (1979)).

Without considering whether a private party could seek to obtain an injunction requiring another party to pay cleanup costs which arise after a RCRA citizen suit has been properly commenced, cf. *United States v. Price,* 688 F.2d 204, 211–213 (C.A.3 1982)(requiring funding of a diagnostic study is an appropriate form of relief in a suit brought by the Administrator under § 6973), or otherwise recover cleanup costs paid out after the invocation of RCRA's statutory process, we agree with the Meghrigs that a private party cannot recover the cost of a past cleanup effort under RCRA, and that KFC's complaint is defective for the reasons stated by the District Court. Section 6972(a) does not contemplate the award of past cleanup costs, and § 6972(a)(1)(B) permits a private party to bring suit only upon an allegation that the contaminated site presently poses an "imminent and substantial endangerment to health or the environment," and not upon an allegation that it posed such an endangerment at some time in the past. The judgment of the Ninth Circuit is reversed.

It is so ordered.

3.   *Common Law Actions*

Private citizens injured by releases of hazardous substances may seek civil and injunctive relief under common law theories of negligence, trespass, nuisance and strict liability for ultrahazardous activities. Generally such claims involve damage to lands arising from the migration of released hazardous constituents through surface runoff, groundwater and air pathways.

4.   *Criminal Penalties*

Persons committing *knowing violations* of RCRA face criminal fines of up to $50,000, and prison terms up to five years, per violation. Higher penalties may be imposed if the violation results in the *knowing endangerment* of any person.

The past few years have witnessed a steady increase in criminal prosecutions on RCRA and other environmental laws. The Justice Department's Land and Natural Resources Division announced a record number of criminal environmental prosecutions in 1990. The agency increased indictments 33% over 1989 levels and secured a conviction rate of ninety-five percent.

Many prosecutors prefer bringing charges arising from *reporting requirements* since such violations generally are easier to establish than other, more substantive environmental crimes and, therefore, offer better prospects for conviction. *False reports* may draw penalties under the Federal False Claims Act, in addition to applicable environmental statutes. Owing to federal sentencing guidelines, many first-time violators actually serve jail time. Clearly, the criminal risks of environmental violations as well as the willingness of the government to prosecute has shifted.

Many constitutional protections applicable to criminal proceedings, such as the privilege against self-incrimination, are unavailable to corporation-defendants, although individual corporate officials may invoke such shields for their personal defense.

UNITED STATES v. DEAN

969 F.2d 187 (6th Cir.1992).

CHARLES W. JOINER, SENIOR DISTRICT JUDGE.

Defendant Gale E. Dean appeals his convictions on one count of conspiracy to violate the Resource Conservation and Recovery Act (RCRA), 42 U.S.C. §§ 6901 et seq., in violation of 18 U.S.C. § 371; one count of failure to file documentation of hazardous waste generation, storage, and disposal as required by 42 U.S.C. § 6928(d)(4); and one count of storage of spent chromic acid without a Permit, one count of storage and disposal of chromic acid rinse water and wastewater sludges in a lagoon without a permit, and one count of disposal of paint sludge and solvent wastes in a pit without a permit, all in violation of 42 U.S.C. § 6928(d)(2)(A).

I.

Defendant's convictions arose out of the operation of the General Metal Fabricators, Inc. (GMF) facility in Erwin, Tennessee, which engaged in metal stamping, plating, and painting. The facility utilized hazardous chemicals and generated hazardous waste. The owners of GMF, Joseph and Jean Sanchez; as well as Dean, the production manager; and Clyde Griffith, the plant manager; were indicted for conspiracy to violate RCRA, and, individually, for violations of various sections of the statute. The district court granted defendant's motion to sever his trial from that of the other defendants.

RCRA provides a comprehensive system of oversight of hazardous materials, a system centered upon requirements that facilities utilizing such materials obtain permits, and maintain proper records of the treatment, storage, and disposal of hazardous substances. No permit was sought for the GMF facility. The hazardous waste disposal practices at GMF were discovered by chance by state waste-management authorities whose attention was caught, while driving to an appointment at another facility, by two 55–gallon drums abandoned among weeds on GMF's property.

As production manager, Dean had day-to-day supervision of GMF's production process and employees. Among his duties was the instruction of employees on hazardous waste handling and disposal. Numerous practices at GMF violated RCRA. GMF's plating operations utilized rinse baths, contaminated with hazardous chemicals, which were drained through a Pipe into an earthen lagoon outside the facility. In addition, Dean instructed employees to shovel various kinds of solid wastes from the tanks into 55–gallon drums. Dean ordered the construction of a pit, concealed behind the facility, into which 38 drums of such hazardous waste were tossed. The contents spilled onto the soil from open or corroded drums. Chemical analyses of soil and solid wastes, entered by stipulation at trial, revealed that the lagoon and the pit were contaminated with chromium. In addition, the pit was contaminated with toluene and xylene solvents. All of these substances are hazardous. Drums of spent chromic acid solution were also illegally stored on the premises.

Defendant was familiar with the chemicals used in each of the tanks on the production lines, and described to authorities the manner in which the contents of the rinse tanks were deposited in the lagoon. Material Safety Data Sheets (MSDS) provided to GMF by the chemical manufacturer clearly stated that various chemicals in use at GMF were hazardous and were subject to state and federal pollution control laws. The MSDS were given to investigators by Dean, who demonstrated his knowledge of their contents. The MSDS delivered with the chromic acid made specific reference to RCRA and to related EPA regulations. Dean informed investigators that he "had read this RCRA waste code but thought it was a bunch of bullshit."

II.

A.

Dean assigns as error numerous aspects of the proceedings in the trial court. We shall address first a number of contentions going to the scope and elements of RCRA's criminal provisions, which we think of primary importance among the issues raised by defendant. The first of these issues arises in connection with defendant's contention that the trial court erred in denying his motion for an acquittal on Count 4, because there was no evidence that defendant knew of RCRA's permit requirement. Defendant's characterization of the evidence is inaccurate; but moreover, we see no basis on the face of the statute for concluding that knowledge of the permit requirement is an element of the crime. The statute penalizes:

Any person who—

* * *

(2) knowingly treats, stores, or disposes of any hazardous waste identified or listed under this subchapter—

(A) without a permit under this subchapter or pursuant to title I of the Marine Protection, Research, and Sanctuaries Act (86 Stat. 1052); or

(B) in knowing violation of any material condition or requirement of such permit; or

(C) in knowing violation of any material condition or requirement of any applicable interim status regulations or standards. . . .

42 U.S.C. § 6928(d)(2). Defendant was convicted of violating subsection 6928(d)(2)(A).

The question of interpretation presented by this provision is the familiar one of how far the initial "knowingly" travels. Other courts of appeals have divided on this question. In *United States v. Johnson &*

Towers, Inc., 741 F.2d 662 (3d Cir.1984), *cert. denied*, sub nom., the Court of Appeals for the Third Circuit concluded that knowledge of the permit requirement was an element of the crime, observing:

> Treatment, storage or disposal of hazardous waste in violation of any material condition or requirement of a permit must be "knowing," since the statute explicitly so states in subsection (B). It is unlikely that Congress could have intended to subject to criminal prosecution those persons who acted when no permit had been obtained irrespective of their knowledge (under subsection (A)), but not those persons who acted in violation of the terms of a permit unless that action was knowing (subsection (B)). Thus we are led to conclude either that the omission of the word "knowing" in (A) was inadvertent or that "knowingly" which introduces subsection (2) applies to subsection (A).

Id. at 668 (footnote omitted).

The Court of Appeals for the Ninth Circuit disagreed with the Third Circuit in *United States v. Hoflin*, 880 F.2d 1033 (9th Cir.1989), *cert. denied*, 493 U.S. 1083, 107 L.Ed.2d 1047, 110 S.Ct. 1143 (1990). The Ninth Circuit noted first the well-established principle of statutory construction that courts will "give effect, if possible, to every clause and word of a statute," *United States v. Menasche*, 348 U.S. 528, 538–9, 99 L.Ed. 615, 75 S.Ct. 513 (1955)(citing *Inhabitants v. Ramsdell*, 107 U.S. 147, 152, 2 S.Ct. 391, 27 L.Ed. 431 (1883)), pointing out that the Third Circuit's reading of subsection 6928(d)(2)(A) would render mere surplusage the word "knowing" in subsections 6928(d)(2)(B) and (C). *Hoflin*, 880 F.2d at 1038. The Ninth Circuit also disagreed with the Third Circuit that there was anything illogical about reading subsections 6928(d)(2)(B) and (C) to have a knowledge requirement but subsection 6928(d)(2)(A) to have none. The Ninth Circuit observed that the permit requirement is intended to give the EPA notice that oversight of a facility is necessary (and, by implication, the force of the statutory scheme would be greatly diminished by exempting all who claimed ignorance of the statute's requirements). The difference in mens rea between the subsections signifies the relative importance, in the estimation of Congress, of the twin requirements of obtaining a permit and complying with the permit. This ranking is consistent with the greater likelihood that compliance with the permit will be monitored. The Court of Appeals for the Fourth Circuit agreed with the Ninth Circuit in *United States v. Dee*, 912 F.2d 741 (4th Cir.1990), *cert. denied*, 499 U.S. 919, 111 S.Ct. 1307, 113 L.Ed.2d 242 (1991).

All of the courts to address this question have reasoned by analogy from the holding of the Supreme Court in *United States v. International Minerals & Chemical Corp.*, 402 U.S. 558, 29 L.Ed.2d 178, 91 S.Ct. 1697 (1971). In that case, the indictment was brought under 18 U.S.C. § 834(f), which penalizes knowing violation of any regulation. The regulation at issue, enacted by the Interstate Commerce Commission, required shipping papers to reflect certain information concerning corrosive liquids being shipped. The question before the Supreme Court was whether knowledge of existence of the regulation was an element of the crime. The Court held that it was not, turning its decision upon the maxim that ignorance of the law is no excuse. The Court concluded its opinion by stating, with equal force here, that when "dangerous or deleterious devices or products or obnoxious waste materials are involved, the probability of regulation is so great that anyone who is aware that he is in possession of them or dealing with them must be presumed to he aware of the regulation." *Id.* at 565. The Court of Appeals for the Third Circuit mitigated its holding in *Johnson & Towers* somewhat in light of International Minerals, holding that knowledge of RCRA would be imputed to employees above a certain level of responsibility (no guidance was given concerning the level of responsibility required, on grounds that there was insufficient evidence in the record on the responsibilities of the employees at issue).

We agree with the reasoning of the Court of Appeals for the Ninth Circuit in *Hoflin*. The "knowingly" which begins § 6928(d)(2) cannot be read as extending to the subsections without rendering nugatory the word "knowing" contained in subsections 6928(d)(2)(B) and (C). Subsection 6928(d)(2)(A) requires knowing treatment (or knowing storage, or knowing disposal) of hazardous waste. It also requires proof that the treatment, or storage, or disposal, was done without a permit. It does not require that the person charged have known that a permit was required, and that knowledge is not relevant.

As to subsections 6928(d)(2)(B) and (C), the requirements are different. Here, the statute clearly requires in addition that if one is to be charged under 6928(d)(2)(B) with violating the terms of a permit or under 6928(d)(2)(C) with violating regulations then one must be aware of the additional requirements of the permit or regulation. To us the statute is clear, makes sense and does not contain the ambiguities or inconsistencies found by others.

The Court of Appeals for the Third Circuit hypothesized in the alternative that Congress inadvertently omitted the word "knowing" from subsection 6928(d)(2)(A), because, the court opined, the plain language reading of section 6928(d)(2) to which we adhere resulted in an "unlikely" statutory scheme. A general review of the reasonableness of legislative choices, however, is not among our statutory construction tools. The inquiry ends with a cogent means of reading the plain language of the statute. *United States Dep't of Energy v. Ohio*, U.S. , 112 S.Ct. 1627, 1635, 118 L.Ed.2d 255 (1992). The *Hoflin* court, moreover, adequately addressed the reasons Congress might have had for crafting the statute in this manner. Finally, we note that statutes which are designed to protect the public health and safety (as is RCRA, *Johnson & Towers*, 741 F.2d at 668) have consistently been distinguished in Supreme Court precedent as more likely candidates for diminished mens rea requirements. *Liparota v. United States*, 471 U.S. 419, 433, 85 L.Ed.2d 434, 105 S.Ct. 2084 (1985).

We do not agree with the suggestion in *Johnson & Towers* that section 6928(d)(2)(A) is in fact a strict liability crime if knowledge of the permit requirement need not be shown. The provision applies by its terms to any person who "knowingly treats, stores or disposes of hazardous waste." 42 U.S.C. § 6928(d)(2)(emphasis ours). The Supreme Court's pronouncement in *International Minerals*, quoted above, stands for the proposition that persons involved in hazardous waste handling have every reason to be aware that their activities are regulated by law, aside from the rule that ignorance of the law is no excuse. In this case, the documentation provided by the chemical manufacturer abundantly illustrates one means by which knowledge of hazardous waste laws is communicated. Accordingly, even absent the requirement of proof that the defendant knew of RCRA's permit provisions, the statute does not impose strict liability. The district court did not err in declining to grant defendant's motion for acquittal based on his alleged ignorance of RCRA's permit requirement.

B.

Defendant also contends that the district court should have granted his motion for acquittal because subsection 6928(d)(2)(A) was not intended to reach employees who are not "owners" or "operators" of facilities. By its terms, the provision applies to "any person." "Person" is a defined term meaning "an individual, trust, firm, joint stock company, corporation (including a government corporation), partnership, association, State, municipality, commission, political subdivision of a State, or any interstate body." 42 U.S.C. § 6903(15).

Defendant would be hard pressed to convince the court that he is not an "individual." He argues, however, that because only owners and operators of facilities are required to obtain permits, 42 U.S.C. § 6925, the penalty imposed for hazardous waste handling without a permit by subsection 6928(d)(2)(A) must apply only to owners and operators.

This contention is unpersuasive for numerous reasons. Of primary importance is the fact that it is contrary to the unambiguous language of the statute. *Cf. United States v. Northeastern Pharmaceutical & Chem. Co.*, 810 F.2d 726, 745 (8th Cir.1986), *cert. denied*, 484 U.S. 848, 98 L.Ed.2d 102, 108 S.Ct. 146 (1987). We agree with the Third Circuit that "had Congress meant in § 6928(d)(2)(A) to take aim more narrowly, it could have used more narrow language." *United States v. Johnson & Towers, Inc.*, 741 F.2d 662 (3d Cir.1984), *cert. denied*, sub nom. Second, while defendant's argument at first glance has logical appeal in relation to subsection 6928(d)(2)(A), the relevant language "any person" prefaces § 6928(d) generally. A number of separate crimes are set out in § 6928(d), several of them having nothing to do with the permit requirement (e.g., failure to maintain requisite documentation or to comply with regulations). Defendant's argument would accordingly impose a limitation on all of the crimes set out in § 6928(d) on a ground relevant to few of them. Third, even the logical appeal of the assertion does not withstand scrutiny. The fact that Congress chose to impose the permit requirement upon owners and operators does not undercut the value of further assuring permit compliance by enacting criminal penalties which would lead others to make inquiry into the permit status of facilities. Given that "such wastes typically have no value, yet can only be safely disposed of at considerable cost," *United States v. Hoflin*, 880 F.2d 1033, 1038 (9th Cir.1989), *cert. denied*, 493 U.S. 1083, 107 L.Ed.2d 1047, 110 S.Ct. 1143 (1990), facilities generating hazardous waste have a strong incentive to evade the law. Moreover, clean-up of the resulting environmental damage almost always involves far greater cost than proper disposal would have, and may be limited to containing the spread of the harm. Defendant argues that employees are the least likely persons to know facilities' permit status. However, employees of a facility are more able to ascertain the relevant facts than the general public, which the statute is intended to protect. In light of these factors, it was entirely reasonable for Congress to have created broad criminal liability. Fourth, it is far from clear that defendant is in fact not an "operator" of GMF, a term defined in the regulations to mean "the person responsible for the overall operation of a facility." 40 C.F.R. § 260.10 (1991). Finally, we agree with the Court of Appeals for the Third Circuit that this result is also supported by the decision of the Supreme Court in *United States v. Dotterweich*, 320 U.S. 277, 88 L.Ed. 48, 64 S.Ct. 134 (1943), and by the legislative history. *See Johnson & Towers, Inc.*, 741 F.2d at 665–7. We conclude that employees may be criminally liable under § 6928(d).

C.

Defendant contends that he should have been acquitted on Count 3 because the chromic acid at issue was not "hazardous waste" as required by 42 U.S.C. § 6928(d)(2)(A), set out above. The term "hazardous waste" is defined as:

> [A] solid waste, or combination of solid wastes, which because of its quantity, concentration, or physical, chemical, or infectious characteristics may—
>
> > (A) cause, or significantly contribute to an increase in mortality or an increase in serious irreversible, or incapacitating irreversible, illness; or
> >
> > (B) pose a substantial present or potential hazard to human health or the environment when improperly treated, stored, transported, or disposed of, or otherwise managed.

42 U.S.C. § 6903(5). Count 3 involved spent chromic acid solution which was being stored in drums at the facility. Dean contends that the chromic acid was not "hazardous" within the meaning of § 6903(5), apparently on the ground that the chromic acid did not pose a danger to human health in the conditions under which it was being stored at GMF. *American Mining Congress v. EPA*, 907 F.2d 1179, 1191 (D.C.Cir.1990), upon which defendant relies, contains nothing supporting this proposition, and is directed at an inapposite question of law.

Defendant does not deny that the "chemical . . . characteristics" of chromic acid involve a threat to human health, as was prominently stated in the MSDS provided by its vendor. It is not apparent from the plain language of the statute that it requires, as defendant would read it, that a hazardous waste present a threat to human health as a result of the manner in which it is being stored. We note that the definitions of "disposal" and "storage" under the statute are distinguished by the fact that the former is defined to mean placing the waste in a location where environmental contamination may result, while the latter is defined as "containment" of waste in a manner not constituting disposal, i.e., such that environmental contamination will not result. *See*, 42 U.S.C. §§ 9603(3), 9603(33). A substance contained in a manner which does not threaten environmental contamination presumably would not present a threat to human health. Substances being "stored" would accordingly not be "hazardous," therefore storage could never be a predicate for a RCRA violation. This result is clearly contrary to the terms of the statute, and highlights the fallacy in defendant's argument.

Moreover, construing the statute to Penalize storage of hazardous substances without a permit, without regard to whether the means of storage is itself unsafe, is in keeping with the statute's purposes. The requirement of a Permit is intended to remedy the danger to the public health (underscored by the events in this case) presented by facilities whose generation of hazardous waste is unknown to authorities charged with monitoring the handling of wastes, for the protection of the environment. *Cf. United States v. Hoflin*, 880 F.2d 1033, 1038–9 (9th Cir.1989), *cert. denied*, 493 U.S. 1083, 110 S.Ct. 1143, 107 L.Ed.2d 1047 (1990).

D.

Defendant asserts that he should have been acquitted on Count 4 because the discharges into the lagoon also were not "hazardous waste." This contention is based on defendant's assertion that the lagoon is a "point Source" governed by the Clean Water Act. 33 U.S.C. §§ 1251, 1254 et seq. To reach the issue presented by this assignment of error, it is necessary to delve into interlocking defined terms. As the definition of "hazardous waste" set out above makes clear, a hazardous waste must be a "solid waste." *See* 42 U.S.C. § 6903(27). A "solid waste" is defined as:

> Any garbage, refuse, sludge from a waste treatment plant, water supply treatment plant, or air pollution control facility and other discarded material, including solid, liquid, semi solid, or contained gaseous material resulting from industrial, commercial, mining, and agricultural operations, and from community activities, but does not include solid or dissolved material in domestic sewage, or solid or dissolved materials in irrigation return flows or industrial discharges which are point sources subject to permits under section 1342 of Title 33, or source, special nuclear, or by-product material as defined by the Atomic Energy Act. . . .

42 U.S.C. § 6903(27). A "point source" is defined in the clean Water Act as:

> Any discernible, confined and discrete conveyance, including but not limited to any pipe, ditch, channel, tunnel, conduit, well, discrete fissure, container, rolling stock, concentrated animal feeding operation, or vessel or other floating craft, from which pollutants are or may be discharged. This term does not include agricultural stormwater discharges and return flows from irrigated agriculture.

33 U.S.C. § 1362(14). Dean argues that the lagoon was a point source, because discharges into a nearby watercourse occurred, and therefore he was not properly indicted under RCRA for discharges into the lagoon.

The government points out that EPA regulations further define the distinction between the jurisdiction of RCRA and the Clean Water Act:

> This exclusion [from RCRA's "solid waste" definition] applies only to the actual point source discharge. It does not exclude industrial wastewaters while they are being collected, stored or treated before discharge, nor does it exclude sludges that are generated by industrial wastewater treatment.

40 C.F.R. § 261.4(a)(2) cmt. The meaning of the regulation is that it is only the actual discharges from a holding pond or similar feature into surface waters which are governed by the Clean Water Act, not the contents of the pond or discharges into it. Count 4 charged that Dean "did knowingly store and dispose of and cause the storage and disposal of hazardous waste, to wit: chromic acid rinse water and wastewater sludges from the coating of aluminum in an open lagoon." This accords with the distinction drawn by the regulation.

United States v. Earth Sciences, Inc., 599 F.2d 368, 373–74 (10th Cir.1979), upon which defendant relies, supports this reading of the regulation. In that case, the indictment was brought under the Clean Water Act on the basis of discharges from Earth Sciences' sump into a nearby stream. Earth Sciences' discharges into the sump, and the actual contents of the sump, are not addressed in the decision. The case is therefore consistent with our construction of the relationship between the statutes.

* * *

Notes

1. A person is subject to criminal liability if he knowingly:

(1) treats, stores, or disposes of hazardous waste without a permit, or transports a hazardous waste to a facility that does not have a permit;

(2) generates, handles, stores, treats, transports, or disposes of hazardous waste and knowingly destroys, alters, or conceals required records;

(3) makes a false statement, misrepresentation, or material omission in any permit application, permit, manifest, record, report, label, or manifest;

(4) transports hazardous waste without a manifest; or

(5) exports hazardous waste without the consent of the receiving country or in violation of an international agreement.

2. The offenses listed in (1) above are subject to a fine up to $50,000 per day of violation and/or up to *five years* in prison. The remaining offenses carry a fine up to $50,000 per day of violation and/or up to *two years* in prison. A second conviction doubles the potential fine and prison sentence. If the violator knows that the violation places another person in imminent danger of death or serious bodily injury, he is subject to a fine up to $250,000 and/or imprisonment up to *fifteen years*. "Organizations" that knowingly endanger persons as a result of a violation are subject to fines up to $1,000,000.

5. *Permit Shield*

SHELL OIL COMPANY v. ENVIRONMENTAL PROTECTION AGENCY
950 F.2d 741 (D.C.Cir.1991).

OPINION: PER CURIAM.

In these consolidated cases, petitioners challenge both the substance of several rules promulgated by the Environmental Protection Agency pursuant to the Resource Conservation and Recovery Act of 1976 and its compliance with the Administrative Procedure Act's rulemaking requirements.

Consolidated petitioners challenge two rules that categorize substances as hazardous wastes until a contrary showing has been made: the "mixture" rule, which classifies as a hazardous waste any mixture of a "listed" hazardous waste with any other solid waste, and the "derived-from" rule, which so classifies any residue derived from the treatment of hazardous waste. They argue that the EPA failed to provide adequate notice and opportunity for comment when it promulgated the mixture and derived-from rules, and that the rules exceed the EPA's statutory authority.

Three petitioners present separate challenges to other rules included in the same rulemaking. In the first, the American Mining Congress asserts that the EPA exceeded its statutory authority and failed to provide notice and opportunity to comment in defining "treatment" to include processes designed to recover valuable materials from the recycling of solid wastes. Second, the American Petroleum Institute attacks the EPA's requirement of "leachate monitoring" at land treatment facilities for failure to provide notice and opportunity to comment. (In land treatment, waste is placed upon land or incorporated into the surface soil. Leachate monitoring tests water that has passed through the soil to assure that hazardous wastes or their constituents are not migrating through it.) Finally, the Environmental Defense Fund challenges the EPA's "permit-shield" provision, a regulation that, with some exceptions, exempts a facility from enforcement proceedings for statutory violations if it is in compliance with its permit conditions.

We agree with petitioners that the EPA failed to give sufficient notice and opportunity for comment in promulgating the "mixture" and "derived-from" rules and the leachate monitoring requirement. We therefore remand the rules to the Secretary. We conclude that the regulatory definition of "treatment" does not comport with the statutory definition. The regulation of resource recovery, however, falls within the EPA's broad authority under Subtitle C to regulate hazardous waste management. Therefore, we deny the American Mining Congress's petition. We also reject its contention that the EPA failed to provide adequate notice of the regulation of resource recovery. As for the permit-shield provision, all parties agree that it cannot trump the citizen's statutory right to sue. As applied to the Agency, however, the regulation lies well within the limits of the EPA's enforcement discretion.

* * *

E. PERMIT–SHIELD PROVISION

The Environmental Defense Fund ("EDF") challenges the EPA's "permit as shield" provision that, with some exceptions, protects holders of RCRA permits from enforcement actions for violations of the underlying statute. . . . The provision currently reads:

> Compliance with an RCRA permit during its term constitutes compliance for purpose of enforcement, with Subtitle C of RCRA except for those requirements not included in the permit which become effective by statute, or which are promulgated under Part 268 of this chapter restricting the placement of hazardous wastes in or on the land. However, a permit may be modified, revoked and reissued, or terminated during its term for cause as set forth in §§ 270.41 and 270.43, or the permit may be modified upon the request of the permittee as set forth in § 270.42.

40 C.F.R. § 270.4(a)(1990). . . . The EDF argues that by insulating permittees from most enforcement actions, the permit-shield provision expressly contravenes the broad enforcement authority that RCRA grants to members of the general public in its citizen-suit provision, see 42 U.S.C. § 6972(a)(1988), and to the EPA in various other provisions, see id. §§ 6928(a); 6928(d). In the alternative, the EDF argues that the provision unreasonably curtails the EPA's enforcement powers. . . . We conclude that the EDF's citizen-suit challenge does not present a case or controversy requiring resolution, and its remaining challenges lack merit.

1. Statutory and Regulatory Background

RCRA requires owners and operators of hazardous waste treatment, storage, or disposal facilities to obtain a permit before commencing operations. 42 U.S.C. § 6925(a)(1988). Permits are valid for ten years, although permits for land disposal facilities are reviewed every five years. *Id.* § 6925(c)(3). Before granting a permit, the EPA must determine that the facility meets the requirements of 42 U.S.C. § 6924 and its implementing regulations. *Id.* § 6925(c)(1). These include any performance standards the EPA deems necessary to "protect human health and the environment." *Id.* § 6924(a).

The EPA promulgated the original version of the permit-shield provision in its 1980 base regulations. 45 Fed. Reg. 33,428 (40 C.F.R. § 122.13(a)). The EPA described the permit-shield rule as a binding principle under which it "will not take enforcement action against any person who has received a final RCRA permit except for noncompliance with the conditions of that permit." *Id.* 33,312. According to the Agency, the shield applies not only to the EPA enforcement actions, but also to enforcement actions brought by States and by citizens through RCRA's citizen-suit provision. *Id.* Although the permit-shield rule lacks explicit statutory authorization, the Agency asserts that the rule furthers the objectives of the RCRA permit program by protecting owners and operators of waste facilities against otherwise "unavoidable uncertainty as to the standing of their operations under the law," *id.*, and by conserving agency resources, which would be "barely sufficient to issue and renew RCRA permits, and review State permits." *Id.*

2. Conflict With Citizen–Suit Provision

The EDF first challenges the permit-shield provision on the ground that it conflicts with RCRA's citizen-suit provision, which states:

Except as provided in subsection (b) or (c) of this section, any person may commence a civil action on his own behalf—

(1)(A) against any person ... who is alleged to be in violation of any permit, standard, regulation, condition, requirement, prohibition, or order which has become effective pursuant to this chapter....

42 U.S.C. § 6972(a)(1)(A)(1988). The EDF contends that by restricting citizens to enforcement actions based on permit violations, the permit-shield provision expressly contravenes the statute's broad grant of authority to citizens to enforce violations of any "standard, regulation, condition, requirement, prohibition, or order." *Id.* Because "Congress has directly spoken to the precise question at issue," *Chevron,* 467 U.S. at 842, the EDF concludes that this court must strike down the inconsistent permit-shield provision insofar as it limits citizens' enforcement authority.

We do not decide the merits of the EDF's challenge. The EPA represents that although it believes its permit system will narrow the opportunities for citizen suits, "the Agency does not maintain that the shield precludes [such] suits." Brief for Respondent at 109. Although the EPA appears to have taken a different position when it first promulgated the rule, see 45 Fed. Reg. 33,312, it has evidently changed its mind. Therefore, as we do not have an actual controversy before us, we do not decide whether the permit provision could lawfully bar "citizen suits." *See Deakins v. Monaghan*, 484 U.S. 193, 199, 98 L.Ed.2d 529, 108 S.Ct. 523 (1988)("Article III of the Constitution limits federal courts to the adjudication of actual, ongoing controversies....").

3.   *Conflict with EPA's Enforcement Authority*

The parties dispute whether Congress has directly spoken to the question whether the EPA can limit its own enforcement actions to violations of permits, and, if not, whether the EPA nonetheless acted unreasonably by issuing the permit-shield rule.

The EDF argues that RCRA requires the EPA to do more than simply enforce permit provisions:

> Whenever ... the Administrator determines that any person has violated or is in violation of any requirement of [RCRA Subtitle C], the Administrator may issue an order assessing a civil penalty for any past or current violation, requiring compliance ... or the Administrator may commence a civil action

* * *

42 U.S.C. § 6928(a)(1)(1988).... According to the EDF, Congress's use of the broad phrase "any requirement" demonstrates that it intended the EPA to bring enforcement actions for all violations of RCRA's standards, even when those standards are not incorporated into a permit. The EDF points out that Congress used narrower language in RCRA's criminal enforcement provisions, which authorize criminal sanctions against any person who "knowingly treats, stores, or disposes of any hazardous waste ... in knowing violation of any material condition or requirement of [a] permit." *Id.* § 6928(d)(2)(B). As courts should "give effect, if possible, to every word that Congress has used in a statute," *Connecticut Dep't of Income Maintenance v. Heckler*, 471 U.S. 524, 530 n. 15, 85 L.Ed.2d 577, 105 S.Ct. 2210 (1985), the EDF concludes, the shield provision must fall.

The EDF's *Chevron* I argument is unavailing. Although the provision authorizes the EPA to enforce violations of "any requirement," it does not require that the EPA do so. On the contrary, the provision's use of the permissive word "may" guarantees the EPA's discretion in the civil enforcement arena. *See LO Shippers Action Committee v. ICC*, 273 U.S.App. D.C. 11, 857 F.2d 802, 806 (D.C.Cir.1988)("may" indicates the presence of regulatory discretion), *cert. denied*, 490 U.S. 1089, 104 L.Ed.2d 986, 109 S.Ct. 2429 (1989). Thus, as no other provision in RCRA even arguably addresses the question whether permit compliance can shield a permit-holder from EPA enforcement actions, we will strike down the permit-shield provision only if it is an unreasonable construction of the statute. *See Chevron*, 467 U.S. at 845.

The Supreme Court pointed out in *Heckler v. Chaney*, 470 U.S. 821, 84 L.Ed.2d 714, 105 S.Ct. 1649 (1985), that agencies are generally free to set their own enforcement agendas. In the Court's words, "an agency's decision not to prosecute or enforce, whether through civil or criminal process, is a decision generally committed to an agency's absolute discretion." *Id.* at 831. The Court noted that agency discretion with respect to enforcement decisions is generally desirable because

> an agency decision not to enforce often involves a complicated balancing of a number of factors which are peculiarly within its expertise. Thus, the agency must not only assess whether a violation has occurred, but whether agency resources are best spent on this violation or another, whether the agency is likely to succeed if it acts, whether the particular enforcement action requested best fits the agency's overall policies, and, indeed, whether the agency has enough resources to undertake the action at all.

Id. In short, in its view, "the agency is far better equipped than the courts to deal with the many variables involved in the proper ordering of its priorities." *Id.* at 831–32.

The Court adds, however, that

> Congress may limit an agency's exercise of enforcement power if it wishes, either by setting substantive priorities, or by otherwise circumscribing an agency's power to discriminate among issues or cases it will pursue.

Id. at 833. Here, as we indicated in rejecting EDF's argument that the plain language of the statute required us to set the shield provision aside, we see no congressional constraints on the EPA's exercise of enforcement discretion.

Chaney is not directly on point because there the agency had refused to take enforcement action in a single case. Here, by contrast, the EPA has announced, through rulemaking, that it will not take enforcement actions in a whole class of cases. For purposes of determining the reviewability of agency action, this distinction might make a difference, ... but for purposes of determining the reasonableness of the permit-shield rule, the policies underlying *Chaney* retain persuasive force.

We note in particular that the decisionmaking process that led to promulgation of the permit-shield provision involves the same "ordering of priorities" that the Supreme Court described in *Chaney*. The EPA has decided that the most efficient and effective way to pursue an enforcement strategy is to place all of the relevant RCRA requirements in a single permit for each permittee and then to focus its enforcement efforts solely on compliance with those permits. In arriving at its decision, the EPA balanced factors such as achieving compliance with all statutory and regulatory requirements, providing permittees with certainty about their legal obligations, and conserving the agency's own overtaxed resources. *See* 45 Fed. Reg. 33,311–12. At a minimum, then, *Chaney* suggests that rules like the permit-shield provision are presumptively reasonable under the second prong of *Chevron*. *See* 467 U.S. at 845.

Chaney distinguishes the case where "it could justifiably be found that the agency has 'consciously and expressly adopted a general policy' that is so extreme as to amount to an abdication of its statutory responsibilities." 470 U.S. at 833 n.4 (citing as an example *Adams v. Richardson*, 156 U.S.App. D.C. 267, 480 F.2d 1159 (D.C.Cir.1973)(en banc)). The EDF argues that we have such a situation here: If under the shield provision, a permit writer erroneously omits a regulatory or statutory provision from the permit, the holder of the permit will be free to violate RCRA for up to ten years. For its part, the EPA acknowledges that some of the errors in drafting permits will not be corrected during the life of the permit, see 45 Fed. Reg. 33,312, but the Agency also argues that the permit-shield provision does not constitute an abdication of statutory responsibilities. We find this argument persuasive.

First, the EPA explains that it plans to include all of the applicable statutory requirements in each permit and to enforce each permit fully. RCRA permits are subject to full public notice and comment. 40 C.F.R. §§ 124.10–124.19 (1990). Therefore, members of the public can ensure that proposed permits include all the requisite terms by submitting comments and participating in public hearings, *see id.* §§ 124.10–124.14, and by seeking administrative, *see id.* at § 124.19, and judicial, see 42 U.S.C. § 6976(b)(1988), review of each final permit. Next, the EPA points out that it can cure mistakes occurring in final permits by modifying ... or revoking and reissuing ... them, or by terminating them if it finds that the permittee misrepresented or failed to disclose material facts in the permit issuance process, see 40 C.F.R. § 270.43(a)(2)(1990), or that "the permitted activity endangers human health or the environment and can only be regulated to acceptable levels by permit modification or termination." *Id.* § 270.43(a)(3). Finally, the EPA stresses that the shield provision in no way limits its enforcement authority to respond to instances where the "handling, storage, treatment, transportation or disposal of any solid waste or hazardous waste may present an imminent and substantial endangerment to health or the environment." 42 U.S.C. § 6973(a)(1988).

Notwithstanding the permit-shield provision, then, the EPA retains sufficient flexibility to properly carry out its statutory responsibilities. Moreover, the insulating effect of the provision is limited both in scope and duration. The shield rule does not apply to self-implementing statutory provisions or to the regulatory restrictions on land disposal, and it can only preclude enforcement of standards omitted by mistake for up to ten years, the maximum permit term. We therefore uphold the permit-shield rule as a reasonable, self-imposed constraint on the Agency's enforcement discretion.

III. *Conclusion*

Because the EPA failed to provide adequate notice and opportunity for comment with regard to the mixture and derived-from rules and with regard to the leachate monitoring requirement, we vacate these rules and remand them to the Agency. We uphold the EPA's definition of "treatment" as consistent with clear congressional intent. Finally, we find the permit-shield regulation, as applied to the enforcement activities of the EPA, to fall within the Agency's discretion under RCRA.

The petitions for review are therefore granted in part and denied in part.

* * *

§ 5.12   CONSTITUTIONAL ISSUES

CHEMICAL WASTE MANAGEMENT, INC. v. HUNT

504 U.S. 334, 112 S.Ct. 2009, 119 L.Ed.2d 121 (1992).

JUSTICE WHITE delivered the opinion of the Court.

Alabama imposes a hazardous waste disposal fee on hazardous wastes generated outside the State and disposed of at a commercial facility in Alabama. The fee does not apply to such waste having a source in Alabama. The Alabama Supreme Court held that this differential treatment does not violate the Commerce Clause. We reverse.

I

Petitioner, Chemical Waste Management, Inc., a Delaware corporation with its principal place of business in Oak Brook, Illinois, owns and operates one of the Nation's oldest commercial hazardous waste land disposal facilities, located in Emelle, Alabama. Opened in 1977 and acquired by petitioner in 1978, the Emelle facility is a hazardous waste treatment, storage, and disposal facility operating pursuant to permits issued by the Environmental Protection Agency (EPA) under the Resource Conservation and Recovery Act of 1976 (RCRA), 90 Stat. 2795, as amended, 42 U.S.C. § 6901 et seq., and the Toxic Substances Control Act, 90 Stat. 2003, as amended, 15 U.S.C. § 2601 et seq. (1988 ed. and Supp. II), and by the State of Alabama under Ala. Code § 22–30–12(i)(1990). Alabama is 1 of only 16 States that have commercial hazardous waste landfills, and the Emelle facility is the largest of the 21 landfills of this kind located in these 16 States. . . .

The parties do not dispute that the wastes and substances being landfilled at the Emelle facility "include substances that are inherently dangerous to human health and safety and to the environment. Such waste consists of ignitable, corrosive, toxic and reactive wastes which contain poisonous and cancer causing chemicals and which can cause birth defects, genetic damage, blindness, crippling and death." . . . 584 So.2d 1367, 1373 (1991). Increasing amounts of out-of-state hazardous wastes are shipped to the Emelle facility for permanent storage each year. From 1985 through 1989, the tonnage of hazardous waste received per year has more than doubled, increasing from 341,000 tons in 1985 to 788,000 tons by 1989. Of this, up to 90% of the tonnage permanently buried each year is shipped in from other States.

Against this backdrop Alabama enacted Act No. 90–326 (the Act). Ala. Code §§ 22–30B–1 to 22–30B–18 (1990 and Supp. 1991). Among other provisions, the Act includes a "cap" that generally limits the amount of hazardous wastes or substances ... that may be disposed of in any 1–year period, and the amount of hazardous waste disposed of during the first year under the Act's new fees becomes the permanent ceiling in subsequent years. Ala. Code § 22–30B–2.3 (1990). The cap applies to commercial facilities that dispose of over 100,000 tons of hazardous wastes or substances per year, but only the Emelle facility, as the only commercial facility operating within Alabama, meets this description. The Act also imposes a "base fee" of $25.60 per ton on all hazardous wastes and substances disposed of at commercial facilities, to be paid by the operator of the facility. Ala. Code § 22–30B–2(a)(Supp. 1991). Finally, the Act imposes the "additional fee" at issue here, which states in full:

"For waste and substances which are generated outside of Alabama and disposed of at a commercial site for the disposal of hazardous waste or hazardous substances in Alabama, an additional fee shall be levied at the rate of $72.00 per ton." § 22–30B–2(b).

Petitioner filed suit in state court requesting declaratory relief against the respondents and seeking to enjoin enforcement of the Act. In addition to state law claims, petitioner contended that the Act violated the Commerce, Due Process, and Equal Protection Clauses of the United States Constitution, and was preempted by various federal statutes. The Trial Court declared the base fee and the cap provisions of the Act to be valid and constitutional; but, finding the only basis for the additional fee to be the origin of the waste, the Trial Court declared it to be in violation of the Commerce Clause. App. to Pet. for Cert. 83a–88a. Both sides appealed. The Alabama Supreme Court affirmed the rulings concerning the base fee and cap provisions but reversed the decision regarding the additional fee. The court held that the fee at issue advanced legitimate local purposes that could not be adequately served by reasonable nondiscriminatory alternatives and was therefore valid under the Commerce Clause. 584 So.2d, at 1390.

Chemical Waste Management, Inc., petitioned for writ of certiorari, challenging all aspects of the Act. Because of the importance of the federal question and the likelihood that it had been decided in a way conflicting with applicable decisions of this Court, Supreme Court Rule 10.1(c), we granted certiorari limited to petitioner's Commerce Clause challenge to the additional fee. 502 U.S. 1070 (1992). We now reverse.

II

No State may attempt to isolate itself from a problem common to the several States by raising barriers to the free flow of interstate trade. Today, in *Fort Gratiot Sanitary Landfill, Inc. v. Michigan Dept. of Natural Resources*, post, p. 353, we have also considered a Commerce Clause challenge to a Michigan law prohibiting private landfill operators from accepting solid waste originating outside the county in which their facilities operate. In striking down that law, we adhered to our decision in *Philadelphia v. New Jersey*, 437 U.S. 617 (1978), where we found New

Jersey's prohibition of solid waste from outside that State to amount to economic protectionism barred by the Commerce Clause:

> The evil of protectionism can reside in legislative means as well as legislative ends. Thus, it does not matter whether the ultimate aim of ch. 363 is to reduce the waste disposal costs of New Jersey residents or to save remaining open lands from pollution, for we assume New Jersey has every right to protect its residents' pocketbooks as well as their environment. And it may be assumed as well that New Jersey may pursue those ends by slowing the flow of all waste into the State's remaining landfills, even though interstate commerce may incidentally be affected. But whatever New Jersey's ultimate purpose, it may not be accompanied by discriminating against articles of commerce coming from outside the State unless there is some reason, apart from their origin, to treat them differently. Both on its face and in its plain effect, ch. 363 violates this principle of nondiscrimination.

> " 'The Court has consistently found parochial legislation of this kind to be constitutionally invalid, whether the ultimate aim of the legislation was to assure a steady supply of milk by erecting barriers to allegedly ruinous outside competition, *Baldwin v. G.A.F. Seelig, Inc.*, 294 U.S. [511,] 522–524 (1935); or to create jobs by keeping industry within the State, *Foster-Fountain Packing Co. v. Haydel*, 278 U.S. 1, 10 (1928); *Johnson v. Haydel*, 278 U.S. 16 (1928); *Toomer v. Witsell*, 334 U.S. [385,] 403–404 (1948); or to preserve the State's financial resources from depletion by fencing out indigent immigrants, *Edwards v. California*, 314 U.S. 160, 173–174 (1941).' " *Fort Gratiot Sanitary Landfill*, post, at (quoting *Philadelphia v. New Jersey, supra*, at 626–627).

> To this list may be added cases striking down a tax discriminating against interstate commerce, even where such tax was designed to encourage the use of ethanol and thereby reduce harmful exhaust emissions, *New Energy Co. of Ind. v. Limbach*, 486 U.S. 269, 279 (1988), or to support inspection of foreign cement to ensure structural integrity, *Hale v. Bimco Trading, Inc.*, 306 U.S. 375, 379–380 (1939). For in all of these cases, "a presumably legitimate goal was sought to be achieved by the illegitimate means of isolating the State from the national economy." *Philadelphia v. New Jersey, supra*, at 627.

> The Act's additional fee facially discriminates against hazardous waste generated in States other than Alabama, and the Act overall has plainly discouraged the full operation of petitioner's Emelle facility.... Such burdensome taxes imposed on interstate commerce alone are generally forbidden: "[A] State may not tax a transaction or incident more heavily when it crosses state lines than when it occurs entirely within the State." *Armco Inc. v. Hardesty*, 467 U.S. 638, 642 (1984); see also *Walling v. Michigan*, 116 U.S. 446, 455 (1886); *Guy v. Baltimore*, 100 U.S. 434, 439 (1880). Once a state tax is found to discriminate against out-of-state commerce, it is typically struck down without further inquiry. *See, e.g., Westinghouse Electric Corp. v. Tully*, 466 U.S. 388,

406–407 (1984); *Maryland v. Louisiana*, 451 U.S. 725, 759–760 (1981); *Boston Stock Exchange v. State Tax Comm'n*, 429 U.S. 318, 336–337 (1977).

The State, however, argues that the additional fee imposed on out-of-state hazardous waste serves legitimate local purposes related to its citizens' health and safety. Because the additional fee discriminates both on its face and in practical effect, the burden falls on the State "to justify it both in terms of the local benefits flowing from the statute and the unavailability of nondiscriminatory alternatives adequate to preserve the local interests at stake." *Hunt v. Washington Apple Advertising Comm'n*, 432 U.S. 333, 353 (1977); *see also Fort Gratiot Sanitary Landfill*, post, at 359; *New Energy Co., supra*, at 278–279. "At a minimum such facial discrimination invokes the strictest scrutiny of any purported legitimate local purpose and of the absence of nondiscriminatory alternatives." *Hughes v. Oklahoma*, 441 U.S. 322, 337 (1979).

The State's argument here does not significantly differ from the Alabama Supreme Court's conclusions on the legitimate local purposes of the additional fee imposed, which were:

> "The Additional Fee serves these legitimate local purposes that cannot be adequately served by reasonable nondiscriminatory alternatives: (1) protection of the health and safety of the citizens of Alabama from toxic substances; (2) conservation of the environment and the state's natural resources; (3) provision for compensatory revenue for the costs and burdens that out-of-state waste generators impose by dumping their hazardous waste in Alabama; (4) reduction of the overall flow of wastes traveling on the state's highways, which flow creates a great risk to the health and safety of the state's citizens." 584 So.2d, at 1389.

These may all be legitimate local interests, and petitioner has not attacked them. But only rhetoric, and not explanation, emerges as to why Alabama targets only interstate hazardous waste to meet these goals. As found by the Trial Court, "although the Legislature imposed an additional fee of $72.00 per ton on waste generated outside Alabama, there is absolutely no evidence before this Court that waste generated outside Alabama is more dangerous than waste generated in Alabama. The Court finds under the facts of this case that the only basis for the additional fee is the origin of the waste." App. to Pet. for Cert. 83a–84a. In the face of such findings, invalidity under the Commerce Clause necessarily follows, for "whatever [Alabama's] ultimate purpose, it may not be accomplished by discriminating against articles of commerce coming from outside the State unless there is some reason, apart from their origin, to treat them differently." *Philadelphia v. New Jersey*, 437 U.S., at 626–627; *see New Energy Co., supra*, at 279–280. The burden is on the State to show that "the discrimination is demonstrably justified by a valid factor unrelated to economic protectionism," ... *Wyoming v. Oklahoma*, 502 U.S. 437, (slip op., at 16)(1992) ..., and it has not carried this burden. *Cf. Fort Gratiot Sanitary Landfill*, post, at 361.

Ultimately, the State's concern focuses on the volume of the waste entering the Emelle facility.... Less discriminatory alternatives, however, are available to alleviate this concern, not the least of which are a generally applicable per-ton additional fee on all hazardous waste disposed of within Alabama, *cf. Commonwealth Edison Co. v. Montana*, 453 U.S. 609, 619 (1981), or a per-mile tax on all vehicles transporting hazardous waste across Alabama roads, *cf. American Trucking Assns., Inc. v. Scheiner*, 483 U.S. 266, 286 (1987), or an evenhanded cap on the total tonnage landfilled at Emelle, *see Philadelphia v. New Jersey*, 437 U.S., at 626, which would curtail volume from all sources.... To the extent Alabama's concern touches environmental conservation and the health and safety of its citizens, such concern does not vary with the point of origin of the waste, and it remains within the State's power to monitor and regulate more closely the transportation and disposal of all hazardous waste within its borders. Even with the possible future financial and environmental risks to be borne by Alabama, such risks likewise do not vary with the waste's State of origin in a way allowing foreign, but not local, waste to be burdened.... In sum, we find the additional fee to be "an obvious effort to saddle those outside the State" with most of the burden of slowing the flow of waste into the Emelle facility. *Philadelphia v. New Jersey*, 437 U.S., at 629. "That legislative effort is clearly impermissible under the Commerce Clause of the Constitution." *Ibid.*

Our decisions regarding quarantine laws do not counsel a different conclusion.... The Act's additional fee may not legitimately be deemed a quarantine law because Alabama permits both the generation and landfilling of hazardous waste within its borders and the importation of still more hazardous waste subject to payment of the additional fee. In any event, while it is true that certain quarantine laws have not been considered forbidden protectionist measures, even though directed against out-of-state commerce, those laws "did not discriminate against interstate commerce as such, but simply prevented traffic in noxious articles, whatever their origin." *Philadelphia v. New Jersey, supra*, at 629. As the Court has stated in Guy v. Baltimore, 100 U.S., at 443:

> "In the exercise of its police powers, a State may exclude from its territory, or prohibit the sale therein of any articles which, in its judgment, fairly exercised, are prejudicial to the health or which would endanger the lives or property of its people. But if the State, under the guise of exerting its police powers, should make such exclusion or prohibition applicable solely to articles, of that kind, that may be produced or manufactured in other States, the courts would find no difficulty in holding such legislation to be in conflict with the Constitution of the United States." *See also Reid v. Colorado*, 187 U.S. 137, 151 (1902); *Railroad Co. v. Husen*, 95 U.S. 465, 472 (1878).

The law struck down in *Philadelphia v. New Jersey* left local waste untouched, although no basis existed by which to distinguish interstate waste. But "if one is inherently harmful, so is the other. Yet New Jersey has banned the former while leaving its landfill sites open to the latter." 437 U.S., at 629. Here, the additional fee applies only to interstate hazardous waste, but at all points from its entrance into Alabama until it is landfilled at the Emelle facility, every concern related to quarantine applies perforce to local hazardous waste, which pays no additional fee. For this reason, the additional fee does not survive the appropriate scrutiny applicable to discriminations against interstate commerce.

Maine v. Taylor, 477 U.S. 131 (1986), provides no additional justification. Maine there demonstrated that the out-of-state baitfish were subject to parasites foreign to in-state baitfish. This difference posed a threat to the State's natural resources, and absent a less discriminatory means of protecting the environment—and none was available—the importation of baitfish could properly be banned. *Id.*, at 140. To the contrary, the record establishes that the hazardous waste at issue in this case is the same regardless of its point of origin. As noted in *Fort Gratiot Sanitary Landfill*, "our conclusion would be different if the imported waste raised health or other concerns not presented by [Alabama] waste." Post, at 367. Because no unique threat is posed, and because adequate means other than overt discrimination meet Alabama's concerns, *Maine v. Taylor* provides the State no respite.

III

The decision of the Alabama Supreme Court is reversed, and the cause remanded for proceedings not inconsistent with this opinion, including consideration of the appropriate relief to petitioner. *See McKesson Corp. v. Florida Division of Alcoholic Beverages & Tobacco*, 496 U.S. 18, 31 (1990); *Tyler Pipe Industries, Inc. v. Washington State Dept. of Rev.*, 483 U.S. 232, 251–253 (1987).

So ordered.

CHIEF JUSTICE REHNQUIST, dissenting.

I have already had occasion to set out my view that States need not ban all waste disposal as a precondition to protecting themselves from hazardous or noxious materials brought across the State's borders. *See Philadelphia v. New Jersey*, 437 U.S. 617, 629 (1978)(REHNQUIST, J., dissenting). In a case also decided today, I express my further view that States may take actions legitimately directed at the preservation of the State's natural resources, even if those actions incidentally work to disadvantage some out-of-state waste generators. *See Fort Gratiot Sanitary Landfill, Inc. v. Michigan Dept. of Natural Resources*, post, 504 U.S. 353, 368 (1992)(REHNQUIST, C.J., dissenting). I dissent today, largely for the reasons I have set out in those two cases. Several additional comments that pertain specifically to this case, though, are in order.

Taxes are a recognized and effective means for discouraging the consumption of scarce commodities—in this case the safe environment that attends appropriate disposal of hazardous wastes. Cf. 26 U.S.C. A. §§ 4681, 4682 (Supp. 1992)(tax on ozone-depleting chemicals); 26 U.S.C. § 4064 (gas guzzler excise tax). I therefore see nothing unconstitutional in Alabama's use of a tax to discourage the export of this commodity to other States, when the commodity is a public good that Alabama has helped to produce. *Cf. Fort Gratiot,* post, at 372 (REHNQUIST, C.J., dissenting)(slip op., at 5). Nor do I see any significance in the fact that Alabama has chosen to adopt a differential tax rather than an outright ban. Nothing in the Commerce Clause requires Alabama to adopt an "all or nothing" regulatory approach to noxious materials coming from without the State. *See Mintz v. Baldwin,* 289 U.S. 346 (1933) (upholding State's partial ban on cattle importation).

In short, the Court continues to err by its failure to recognize that waste—in this case admittedly hazardous waste—presents risks to the public health and environment that a State may legitimately wish to avoid, and that the State may pursue such an objective by means less Draconian than an outright ban. Under force of this Court's precedent, though, it increasingly appears that the only avenue by which a State may avoid the importation of hazardous wastes is to ban such waste disposal altogether, regardless of the waste's source of origin. I see little logic in creating, and nothing in the Commerce Clause that requires us to create, such perverse regulatory incentives. The Court errs in substantial measure because it refuses to acknowledge that a safe and attractive environment is the commodity really at issue in cases such as this, *see Fort Gratiot,* post, at 369, n. (REHNQUIST, C.J., dissenting). The result is that the Court today gets it exactly backward when it suggests that Alabama is attempting to "isolate itself from a problem common to the several States," ante, at 2012. To the contrary, it is the 34 States that have no hazardous waste facility whatsoever, not to mention the remaining 15 States with facilities all smaller than Emelle, that have isolated themselves.

There is some solace to be taken in the Court's conclusion, ante, at 9, that Alabama may impose a substantial fee on the disposal of all hazardous waste, or a per-mile fee on all vehicles transporting such waste, or a cap on total disposals at the Emelle facility. None of these approaches provide Alabama the ability to tailor its regulations in a way that the State will be solving only that portion of the problem that it has created, *see Fort Gratiot,* post, at 369, n. (REHNQUIST, C.J., dissenting). But they do at least give Alabama some mechanisms for requiring waste-generating States to compensate Alabama for the risks the Court declares Alabama must run.

Of course, the costs of any of the proposals that the Court today approves will be less than fairly apportioned. For example, should Alabama adopt a flat transportation or disposal tax, Alabama citizens will be forced to pay a disposal tax equal to that faced by dumpers from outside the State. As the Court acknowledges, such taxes are a permissible effort to recoup compensation for the risks imposed on the State. Yet Alabama's general tax revenues presumably already support the State's various inspection and regulatory efforts designed to ensure the Emelle facility's safe operation. Thus, Alabamians will be made to pay twice, once through general taxation and a second time through a specific disposal fee. Permitting differential taxation would, in part, do no more than recognize that, having been made to bear all the risks from such hazardous waste sites, Alabama should not in addition be made to pay more than others in supporting activities that will help to minimize the risk.

Other mechanisms also appear open to Alabama to achieve results similar to those that are seemingly foreclosed today. There seems to be nothing, for example, that would prevent Alabama from providing subsidies or other tax breaks to domestic industries that generate hazardous wastes. Or Alabama may, under the market participant doctrine, open its own facility catering only to Alabama customers. *See, e.g., White v. Massachusetts Council of Construction Employers, Inc.*, 460 U.S. 204, 206–208 (1983); *Reeves, Inc. v. Stake*, 447 U.S. 429, 436–437 (1980); *Hughes v. Alexandria Scrap Corp.*, 426 U.S. 794, 810 (1976). But certainly we have lost our way when we require States to perform such gymnastics, when such performances will in turn produce little difference in ultimate effects. In sum, the only sure byproduct of today's decision is additional litigation. Assuming that those States that are currently the targets for large volumes of hazardous waste do not simply ban hazardous waste sites altogether, they will undoubtedly continue to search for a way to limit their risk from sites in operation. And each new arrangement will generate a new legal challenge, one that will work to the principal advantage only of those States that refuse to contribute to a solution.

For the foregoing reasons, I respectfully dissent.

Note

The Supreme Court noted in a footnote that:

To some extent the State attempts to avail itself of the more flexible approach outlined in, *e.g., Brown–Forman Distillers Corp. v. New York State Liquor Auth.*, 476 U.S. 573, 579, 106 S.Ct. 2080, 2084, 90 L.Ed.2d 552 (1986), and *Pike v. Bruce Church, Inc.*, 397 U.S. 137, 142, 90 S.Ct. 844, 847, 25 L.Ed.2d 174 (1970), but this lesser scrutiny is only available "where other legislative objectives are credibly advanced and there is no patent discrimination against interstate trade." *Philadelphia v. New Jersey*, 437 U.S. 617, 624, 98 S.Ct. 2531, 2535, 57 L.Ed.2d 475 (1978). . . . We find no room here to say that the Act presents "effects upon interstate commerce that are only incidental," *ibid.*, for the Act's additional fee on its face targets only out-of-state hazardous waste. While no "clear line" separates close cases on which scrutiny should apply, "this is not a close case." *Wyoming v. Oklahoma*, 502 U.S. 437, 455, n. 12, 112 S.Ct. 789, 800, n. 12, 117 L.Ed.2d 1 (1992).

Do you agree? Why or why not? When should the lesser scrutiny be applied? Under what fact pattern could you find the lesser scrutiny should be applied in the environmental context, if ever?

Discussion Problems

Problem #1

In 1983, ABC Inc. ("ABC") purchased a railroad tie treating business located in New York from the XYZ Corporation ("XYZ"). ABC was owned by Owner and his business partner, Partner.

The tie treatment process consisted of first placing untreated green ties into a large cylinder and then adding creosote. The creosote then was heated to boiling. As water and natural wood alcohols were drawn out by a vacuum process, the creosote penetrated the ties. The water, wood alcohols and some creosote, collectively referred to in the industry as "bolton water," would vaporize in the cylinder, where it was then drawn off and run through condensation coils. This mixture, consisting of twenty-five percent creosote, thereafter was placed in a heated evaporation tank. Once in this tank, the creosote quickly settled to the bottom due to its heavier weight, forming sludge. The water then was boiled off so that the remaining creosote sludge could be suctioned out and placed into storage for re-use in the treatment process.

Subsequent to 1983, ABC began having problems with its treatment process. As a result, excess creosote often became contaminated or spilled from the system. ABC supervisors regularly directed employees to dispose of the contaminated creosote by soaking it up with sawdust and dumping it in remote areas of the ABC property. ABC never had applied for a RCRA "TSD" (treatment, storage or disposal) permit and, therefore, neither the New York State Department of Environmental Conservation ("DEC") nor the United States Environmental Protection Agency ("EPA") was aware that ABC regularly handled, and disposed of, creosote.

On October 30, 1986, a large, accidental creosote spill occurred at ABC. Contrary to Owner's instructions, this spill was reported to the DEC, which then began making periodic, pre-announced visits. With the exception of the October 30 spill, however, no regulatory agency had any knowledge or information of any other spill or disposal of creosote by ABC.

ABC began experiencing financial difficulties in 1987. Its problems were exacerbated when, early in June, ABC's boiler ceased to function properly. Without a properly functioning boiler, ABC could not recover the creosote sludge left over from the treatment process. ABC quickly began to run out of storage space for the bolton water, and ABC employees were directed to put the excess bolton water into a railroad tanker car that had recently delivered a shipment of new creosote. This tanker car remained on the ABC railroad spur and was used to store the bolton water generated by the treatment process.

During the time that the bolton water was being stored in the tanker car, Owner became concerned over ABC's daily accrual of "demurrage" or rental charges for keeping the tanker car beyond its normal return date. After two weeks had passed with no resolution of the boiler problems, Owner met with ABC Vice President of Operations and Plant Manager ("VP") and a company consultant. The three discussed several methods of disposing of the bolton water, including: (1) returning the tanker car full of bolton water (approximately 22,000 gallons) to the creosote manufacturer, which would have proper disposal facilities available to it; (2) hiring a hazardous waste remover to cart away and properly dispose of the bolton water; and (3) pumping the bolton water into a truck and disposing of it by spraying it out of the back of the truck while it drove along dirt roads in Sidney. Owner rejected the first two proposals as being too costly. He then proposed the spray truck scheme to VP and Thomas, who both objected and informed Owner that such a scheme would be illegal.

Shortly thereafter, Owner began to demand repeatedly that VP release the contents of the tanker car onto the ground. After VP refused, Owner informed him that he was going to release the creosote sludge himself. After one unsuccessful nocturnal attempt to release the creosote sludge, Owner returned a second time, at approximately three o'clock in the morning, and successfully released the entire contents of the tanker car directly onto the ground.

The next morning, in the presence of ABC employees, Owner admitted to VP that he had dumped the creosote sludge, but told those present that they would be fired if the release was reported to the Government. Owner then instructed VP to hire an outside contractor to cover the contaminated soil with rock and gravel. This was done, no report was made to either the DEC or the EPA, and the spill was never mentioned during subsequent inspections.

Financial conditions at ABC continued to deteriorate, and on August 6, 1987, XYZ exercised its rights under a note it held from the 1983 sale and removed Owner from operational control of ABC. Although Owner remained an equity owner, he and the entire ABC board were removed as directors in August of 1987. ABC then filed for chapter 11 bankruptcy sometime in the autumn of 1987.

In order to finance the purchase in 1983, ABC gave XYZ a promissory note for part of the purchase price. In the event of default on the note, XYZ had the right to remove the ABC board of directors and elect a new board.

In December of 1987, XYZ President, informed by VP of the June dumping, directed VP to arrange for the contaminated soil to be excavated and removed. Approximately five hundred and twenty cubic yards of soil were recovered from the site where Owner had released the creosote sludge. This soil was added to the pile of soil that was excavated after the spill in October of 1986.

ABC continued its financial slide and, by May of 1988, the entire facility was abandoned. Nothing was done to dispose of or safeguard either the tens of thousands of gallons of creosote left behind or the fifty-five gallon drums of hydrochloric acid and other hazardous chemicals that were abandoned. By the summer of 1988, the DEC learned that the site had been deserted and began piecing together details of its true condition.

You are the attorney for the DEC. You are asked to investigate this case and recommend whether civil or criminal prosecution should be commenced.

Problem #2

The Company & Co. ("the Company"), received from the Environmental Protection Agency ("EPA" or "the agency"), a corrective action permit under the Resource Conservation and Recovery Act ("RCRA"), 42 U.S.C.A. §§ 6901–92k.

Company, a major manufacturer of chemicals for industrial use, received a TSD permit in 1985. Between 1988 and 1989, EPA detected releases of potentially hazardous waste or constituents at Company's New Hampshire facility. In September 1989, the agency issued Company a corrective action permit, requiring the Company to investigate and, if necessary, remedy the releases.

The permit instructs Company, pursuant to a schedule of compliance, to submit to EPA a series of proposals and studies characterizing the nature and extent of any suspect release. For example, Company must supply EPA with a "RCRA Facility Investigation (RFI) Proposal" within three months of the permit's issuance. Over the next twenty-four or so months, Company is to provide EPA with approximately four more major submissions, the due dates of which are staggered to allow the results of earlier studies to inform subsequent work.

If a hazardous release is detected, Company will be required to provide EPA with a range of cleanup proposals, in the form of a "Corrective Measures Study (CMS) proposal." Within three months of EPA's approval of the proposal, Company will have to submit a CMS Report, which will include the Company's own recommendations for corrective measures. EPA then will select a remedial plan to be implemented by Company and revise Company's corrective action permit to include the cleanup measures.

The schedule of compliance allows twenty-eight months for completion of both the investigative and remedial phases of the corrective action program, excluding time for EPA review of Company's submissions.

The administrator of the EPA regional office charged with oversight of Company's facility ("the Regional Administrator") issued a "draft permit" to Company, for public comment, before issuing the final permit. The draft permit set forth the procedure by which EPA intends to review the proposals, reports, and studies submitted by Company during the investigative phase of its corrective action program. When EPA approves a submission—a proposal regarding the number and placement of sampling wells necessary for a particular study, for example—the approved specifications will become an enforceable part of the permit and binding upon Company. EPA may, however, reject a Company submission as deficient, and, over Company's objection, revise the particular proposal to conform to EPA's assessment of what corrective action requires. In such a case, EPA's recommendations, rather than those submitted by Company, become enforceable permit conditions.

Before EPA revises a submission, it will ask Company to submit a modified version addressing the deficiencies noted by the agency. If EPA remains dissatisfied with Company's recommendations, it will then amend the document itself, over the Company's objections, if necessary. Company's permit states that "if . . . [the Company's RFI] Proposal is not approved, the . . . [Regional Administrator] may . . . either require further modification or make such modifications as he deems necessary. . . . In the event that the [Regional Administrator] makes such modifications, the modified Proposal becomes the approved RFI Proposal." The same procedure governs the other submissions required under the permit.

In a set of written comments upon the draft, Company strenuously objected to this modification procedure, arguing that under RCRA and applicable regulations, as well as the Due Process Clause of the Fifth Amendment, it was entitled to impartial review of such unilateral agency action. Company argued to the Regional Administrator, as it does before us, that investigative phase tasks can be extremely costly and that, where Company and EPA disagree as to how a particular study ought to be conducted—whether five or fifty sampling wells ought to be drilled to determine a particular constituent level, for example—Company is entitled to judicial and/or administrative review.

The Regional Administrator rejected Company's claims in a published statement and issued the final version of the corrective action permit with the modification provisions intact. Company then petitioned the EPA Administrator for review of the Regional Administrator's action. In an opinion and order dated March 25, 1991, the EPA Administrator denied Company's petition, upholding the Regional Administrator's construction of RCRA, the regulations, and the Due Process Clause.

Company petitioned the Administrator of EPA for review of the permit, claiming that certain of its provisions violated RCRA, EPA regulations, and the Due Process Clause of the Fifth Amendment of the United States Constitution. The Administrator denied the petition.

You are a District Court Judge. Company seeks review of that decision in this court, reiterating its statutory and constitutional arguments. What result?

Problem #3

Company is a Delaware corporation that manufactures wire products at two facilities located in Michigan. Company's manufacturing process generates, and the company stores, materials such as hydrochloric acid, sulfuric acid, and alkaline wastes. These by-products are within the RCRA definition of "hazardous waste." As required by section 6925(a), Company applied to EPA for a permit for the treatment, storage, and disposal of the hazardous wastes it generated. *See* 40 C.F.R. § 270 [hereinafter TSD permit]. At present, its application remains pending, so that Company's facilities currently are operating under "interim status." 42 U.S.C.A. § 6925(e)(1). As part of the process of obtaining a permit, corrective action must be taken with regard to any releases of hazardous wastes. Interim status facilities that experience hazardous waste releases are also subject to corrective action. *Id.* at §§ 6924(u), 6928(h).

On March 24 and 25, 1987, EPA officials visited the facilities and performed visual site inspections. During that tour, the officials determined that there were several "solid waste management units" (SWMUs) at each facility and that corrective action would be necessary. On April 3, EPA formally notified Company that it was planning a sampling visit at Company's facilities as the next stage of the corrective action program required under sections 6924(u) and 6927. In the Notification Letters, EPA stated that it wanted to conduct a hazardous waste inspection and collect samples to determine the nature of any corrective action required at Company's facilities before granting the company a permit to store hazardous wastes. The Notification Letters also stated that EPA contractors were to assist with the sampling, and that representatives of the Michigan Department of Natural Resources would observe the inspection. Finally, the Letters identified thirty SWMUs at the facilities that would be targeted by the inspection team.

Company refused to consent to the inspection. It protested the breadth of EPA's intended sampling, and stated that section 6924(u) did not authorize the "fishing expedition" proposed by EPA. It also alleged that many of the proposed sampling sites were not SWMUs. Soon afterwards, Company filed a declaratory judgment action in the district court for the Northern District of Illinois. The complaint sought declaratory relief on the ground that EPA lacked authority under section 6924(u) to inspect the Company facilities and that any inspections allowed under sections 6924(u) and 6927(a) were limited to hazardous wastes specifically listed in the Code of Federal Regulations. Venue was grounded on the location in Chicago of the EPA Regional Administrator charged with overseeing RCRA enforcement at the facilities.

Three days after the filing of the complaint, EPA applied for and obtained ex parte an administrative search warrant to inspect the Company facilities from the United States magistrate in the district court for the Western District of Michigan. Attached to the warrant application was the affidavit of an EPA geologist. Geologist had been part of the EPA visual site inspection team that visited the Company facilities on March 24th and 25th; as a result of this inspection, she had determined that there were several SWMUs at each facility. She further stated that, based on her observations of discolored soil, surface water body sediments, discontinuities in vegetation, and odors, there had been releases of what may be hazardous wastes or constituents from some of the SWMUs. She believed the releases may have been hazardous wastes because they were near known SWMUs containing ignitable solid wastes, copper cyanide, lead, or waste water treatment sludges from electroplating operations. Geologist proposed taking no more than sixty solid waste, water, and air samples, including background samples, at the facilities. On July 15, 1987, three days after obtaining the warrant, EPA commenced execution.

On June 16, 1987, Company responded, filing in the district court for the Western District of Michigan: (1) a complaint seeking preliminary and permanent injunctive relief barring EPA from continuing the inspection and from using the inspection results; and (2) an emergency motion to quash the administrative search warrant and to transfer venue of all Michigan proceedings to the district court for the Northern District of Illinois. After conferring with the district judge presiding over the pending declaratory judgment action in the Northern District of Illinois, the chief judge of the Western District of Michigan ordered all proceedings transferred to Illinois.

You are the judge in the Northern District of Illinois. How do you find?

§ 5.13 UNDERGROUND STORAGE TANKS

In 1984, Congress amended RCRA to establish new requirements for dealing with environmental problems associated with underground storage tanks (USTs) containing petroleum or hazardous substances. 42 U.S.C.A. § 6991–6991i. These provisions require EPA to develop regulations implementing statutory requirements for corrosion protection; spill and overflow prevention; leak detection, correction and cleanup;

closure; and financial responsibility. These provisions were further amended in 1986 by the Superfund Amendment Reauthorization Act, Pub. L. No. 99–499, 100 Stat. 1613 (1986), to establish an Underground Storage Tank Trust Fund and to provide for a cleanup liability scheme similar to that imposed under CERCLA.

A UST is a tank, including underground piping connected to the tank, that has at least ten percent of its volume underground. 42 U.S.C. § 6991(1). Several types of tanks, however, are excluded by law or regulation from UST requirements. These include tanks used to store heating oil consumed on the premises where stored; emergency spill and overflow tanks; and tanks holding 110 gallons or less. *Id.*; 40 C.F.R. Part 280.10 (1990).

EPA has promulgated extensive regulations and financial responsibility requirements for USTs. Under EPA's rules, USTs installed after December 1988, must meet strict technical requirements governing installation, spill and overflow prevention, corrosion protection and leak detection. USTs installed before December 1988 (existing USTs), were required by December 1998 to meet requirements for (1) corrosion protection, and (2) spill and overflow prevention. Existing USTs also must meet leak detection requirements by one of several different methods. The deadline for meeting leak detection requirements depends on the tank's age. Leak detection methods also are specified for piping.

In addition, owners and operators of all tanks, whether new or existing, must (1) report and keep records of all known leaks, (2) take corrective actions in response to leaks, (3) follow closure requirements for tanks closed either temporarily or permanently, and (4) meet financial responsibility requirements for the cost of cleaning up a leak and compensating other people for bodily injury and property damage caused by any leaking UST. The amount of financial responsibility required depends on the type of business operated, the amount of throughput of the tank, and the number of tanks owned or operated by the entity.

NURAD, INC. v. HOOPER & SONS CO.
966 F.2d 837 (4th Cir.1992).

WILKINSON, CIRCUIT JUDGE:

This is a suit brought by the current owner of a piece of property for reimbursement of costs it incurred in removing from the property some underground storage tanks and their hazardous contents. The current owner sought reimbursement from previous owners and tenants at the site, claiming that they were liable under the Comprehensive Environmental Response, Compensation, and Liability Act (CERCLA) as "owners" or "operators" of the facility at the time of "disposal" of the hazardous substances. 42 U.S.C. § 9607(a)(2). The district court entered summary judgment against the original owner of the tanks and in favor of the other defendants.

We think the district court was correct both in holding that the original owner was liable under CERCLA and in holding that the tenant defendants were not liable as "operators" of the facility in question. We think it erred, however, in absolving certain of the previous owner defendants on the ground that they were not owners"at the time of disposal." By requiring proof of affirmative participation in hazardous waste disposal as a prerequisite to liability under § 9607(a)(2), the district court misconstrued both the statutory definition of "disposal" and a decision of this court interpreting that definition. We think the statute plainly imposes liability on a party who owns a facility at the time hazardous waste leaks from an underground storage tank on the premises. Any other result would substantially undermine CERCLA's goal of encouraging voluntary cleanup on the part of those in a position to do so.

I.

Plaintiff Nurad, Inc., brought this lawsuit to recover the costs it incurred in removing several underground storage tanks (USTs) from a piece of property it owns in Baltimore, Maryland. From 1905 to 1963, Wm. E. Hooper & Sons. Co. (the Hooper Co. or the Company) owned the site and adjacent properties, collectively known as Hooperwood Mills. At some point before 1935, the Hooper Co. began to install tanks for the storage of mineral spirits which it used to coat fabrics in its textile finishing plant. The Company continued to use the tanks for that purpose until 1962, when it shut down its finishing operations. At that time, the Hooper Co. abandoned the USTs and did not remove the mineral spirits.

In 1963, the Hooper Co. sold Hooperwood Mills to Property Investors, Inc. Frank Nicoll, as president and principal shareholder of Property Investors and its successor, Monumental Enterprises, Inc., leased several of the buildings on Hooperwood Mills to various tenants, none of which ever used the USTs. Then in 1976, Monumental Enterprises sold Hooperwood Mills to Kenneth Mumaw, who subdivided the property and sold a portion of it to Nurad.

Nurad's operations at the site involve the manufacture of antennae. In all its years at the site, Nurad apparently never used the USTs. In 1987, however, the Maryland Department of the Environment informed Nurad that the tanks had not been properly abandoned and required that they be removed from the ground or filled with sand or concrete within 180 days. Nurad sought assistance with the cleanup from several of the previous owners and tenants of the site, but they all refused. Nurad then hired an environmental consultant and a tank removal contractor to analyze the contents of the tanks and dispose of several of the tanks and the surrounding soil.

In 1990, Nurad filed this CERCLA suit, seeking reimbursement for approximately $226,000 in cleanup costs from former owners of the site (the Hooper Co., Nicoll, Mumaw, and Monumental Enterprises); from former tenants at the site (Allstates Moving & Storage, Raymond B. McMillan, Universal Laboratory Installations, Inc., and Monumental Millwork); and from James Hooper, Jr., and Lawrence Hooper (the

Hooper brothers), who were shareholders and directors of the Hooper Co. The district court decided the issues of liability on summary judgment. In its view, only the Hooper Co. was liable under CERCLA for costs incurred by Nurad in removing the tanks. The court found that the tenant defendants did not qualify as "operators" because they did not possess sufficient authority to control the hazardous waste at the facility. Further, the court ruled that certain of the previous owners were not liable because they were not owners "at the time of disposal." According to the district court, "disposal" necessarily contemplated some element of affirmative participation on the part of the defendant, and only the original owner actively dealt with hazardous substances at the site. Accordingly, the court granted summary judgment against the Hooper Co. and in favor of the other defendants. The court also granted Nurad's motion to bifurcate the issues of liability and damages, and entered final judgment pursuant to Rule 54(b) of the Federal Rules of Civil Procedure.

Both Nurad and the Hooper Co. appeal.

* * *

. . . we address Nurad's claims against the previous owners of the site, the Hooper Co. and Kenneth Mumaw. Neither the Hooper Co. nor Mumaw appeals from the district court's conclusion that they are prior owners of the facility. At oral argument, Mumaw did direct our attention to the fact that he held legal title to the property for only a short period of time. We do not think, however, that the word "owned" is a word that admits of varying degrees. Such equitable considerations as the duration of ownership may well be relevant at a later stage of the proceedings when the district court allocates response costs among liable parties, see 42 U.S.C. § 9613(f)(1), but we reject any suggestion that a short-term owner is somehow not an owner for purposes of § 9607(a)(2).

Because both the Hooper Co. and Mumaw are prior owners of the facility, we must ask whether recovery against them is nonetheless barred because no "disposal" of hazardous wastes took place on their watch. The district court took a narrow view of the word "disposal," limiting it to disposal by affirmative human conduct. Thus, the court concluded that the Hooper Co. was liable because it actively disposed of hazardous substances and then abandoned them in the USTs. The court held, however, that Mumaw was not liable—even though passive migration of hazardous substances may have occurred during his ownership—since he did not take an active role in managing the tanks or their contents.

We think the district court's restrictive construction of "disposal" ignores the language of the statute, contradicts clear circuit precedent, and frustrates the fundamental purposes of CERCLA. The statute defines "disposal" in 42 U.S.C. § 9601(29) by incorporating by reference the definition found in the Resource Conservation and Recovery Act (RCRA). That definition states:

The term "disposal" means the discharge, deposit, injection, dumping, spilling, leaking, or placing of any solid waste or hazardous waste into or on any land or water so that such solid waste or hazardous waste or any constituent thereof may enter the environment or be emitted into the air or discharged into any waters, including ground waters.

42 U.S.C. § 6903(3). Some of the words in this definition appear to be primarily of an active voice. *See Ecodyne Corp. v. Shah*, 718 F.Supp. 1454, 1457 (N.D.Cal.1989). This is true of "deposit," "injection," "dumping," and "placing." Others of the words, however, readily admit to a passive component: hazardous waste may leak or spill without any active human participation. The district court arbitrarily deprived these words of their passive element by imposing a requirement of active participation as a prerequisite to liability.

Indeed, this circuit has already rejected the "strained reading" of disposal which would limits meaning to "active human conduct." *United States v. Waste Ind., Inc.*, 734 F.2d 159, 164–65 (4th Cir.1984). In *Waste Industries*, the court held that Congress intended the 42 U.S.C. § 6903(3) definition of disposal "to have a range of meanings," including not only active conduct, but also the reposing of hazardous waste and its subsequent movement through the environment. *Id.* at 164. Here the district court attempted to distinguish *Waste Industries* on the ground that it involved the authority of the Environmental Protection Agency to demand cleanup by former owners and operators under RCRA. The district court thought that the *Waste Industries* definition was necessary to close a loophole in RCRA's environmental protection scheme, *see id.* at 165, and believed "that the only way for the *Waste Industries* court to preserve the EPA's ability to demand cleanup by the actual former owners and operators was to define 'disposal' in RCRA to cover completely passive repose or movement through the environment." In this CERCLA action, by contrast, the district court noted that the current owner and all prior owners were already defendants and in some cases were liable for cleanup costs.

We think the district court was bound to follow *Waste Industries* in interpreting the term "disposal." It is true that *Waste Industries* interpreted the definition in the context of RCRA, but Congress expressly provided that under CERCLA the term "shall have the meaning provided in section 1004" of RCRA (42 U.S.C. § 6903(3)). 42 U.S.C. § 9601(29). Moreover, the aim of both RCRA and CERCLA is to encourage the cleanup of hazardous waste conditions. Whether the context is one of prospective enforcement of hazardous waste removal under RCRA or an action for reimbursement of response costs under CERCLA, a requirement conditioning liability upon affirmative human participation in contamination equally frustrates the statutory purpose.

* * *

60 FED. REG. 46692

(September 7, 1995)

* * *

DESCRIPTION OF THE UST REGULATORY PROGRAM

Under the Hazardous and Solid Waste Amendments of 1984, Congress responded to the increasing threat to groundwater posed by leaking underground storage tanks by adding Subtitle I to the Resource Conservation and Recovery Act. Subtitle I required EPA to develop a comprehensive regulatory program for USTs storing petroleum or hazardous substances. Congress directed the Agency to publish regulations that would require owners and operators of new tanks and tanks already in the ground to prevent and detect leaks, cleanup leaks, and demonstrate that they are financially capable of cleaning up leaks and compensating third parties for resulting damages.

EPA's UST regulations, 40 CFR Parts 280 and 281, apply to any person who owns or operates an UST or UST system. The term "owner" is defined in the statute generally to mean any person who owns an UST used for the storage, use, or dispensing of substances regulated under Subtitle I of RCRA (which includes both petroleum and hazardous substances)(§ 9001(3), 42 USC 6991(3)). Owners are responsible for complying with the "technical requirements," "financial responsibility requirements," and "corrective action requirements" specified in the statute and regulations. These requirements are intended to ensure that USTs are managed and maintained safely, so that they will not leak or otherwise cause harm to human health and the environment. In addition, should a leak occur, the requirements provide that the owner is responsible for addressing the problem. These same requirements apply to any person who "operates" an UST system. The term "operator" is very broad and means "any person in control of, or having responsibility for, the daily operation of the underground storage tank" (§ 9001(4), 42 USC 6991(4)). As with owners, there may be more than one operator of a tank at a given time. Each owner and operator has obligations under the statute and regulations. In this respect, it is important to understand that a person may have obligations under Subtitle I either as an owner or as an operator, or both.

The following subsections describe briefly each of the major components of the UST regulatory program applicable to persons who own or operate USTs and UST systems.

A. UST Technical Standards

The technical standards of 40 CFR Part 280 referred to here include: Subpart B–UST systems: Design, Construction, Installation, and Notification (including performance standards for new UST systems, upgrading of existing UST systems, and notification requirements); Subpart C–General Operating Requirements (including spill and overfill control, corrosion protection, reporting and recordkeeping); Subpart D–Release Detection; § 280.50 (reporting of suspected releases) of Subpart E–Release Reporting, Investigation, and Confirmation; and Subpart G–Out of Service UST Systems (including temporary and permanent closure). These regulations impose obligations upon UST owners and operators, separate from the Subtitle I corrective action requirements discussed in Section II. B of this preamble.

1. Leak Prevention

Before EPA regulations were issued, most tanks were constructed of bare steel and were not equipped with release prevention or detection features. 40 CFR § 280.21 requires UST owners and operators to ensure that their tanks are protected against corrosion and equipped with devices that prevent spills and overfills no later than December 22, 1998. Tanks installed before December 22, 1988 must be replaced or upgraded by fitting them with corrosion protection and spill and overfill prevention devices to bring them up to new-tank standards. USTs installed after December 22, 1988 must be fiberglass-reinforced plastic, corrosion-protected steel, a composite of these materials, or determined by the implementing agency to be no less protective of human health and the environment, and must be designed, constructed, and installed in accordance with a code of practice developed by a nationally recognized association or independent testing laboratory. Piping installed after December 22, 1988 generally must be protected against corrosion in accordance with a national code of practice. All owners and operators must also ensure that releases due to spilling or overfilling do not occur during product transfer and that all steel systems with corrosion protection are maintained, inspected, and tested in accordance with § 280.31.

2. Leak Detection

In addition to meeting the leak prevention requirements, owners and operators of USTs must use a method listed in §§ 280.43 through 280.44 for detecting leaks from portions of both tanks and piping that routinely contain product. Deadlines for compliance with the leak detection requirements have been phased in based on the tank's age: The oldest tanks, which are most likely to leak, had the earliest compliance deadlines. Phase-in of the leak detection requirements was completed in 1993, and all UST systems should now be in compliance with these requirements.

3. Release Reporting

UST owners and operators must, in accordance with § 280.50, report to the implementing agency within 24 hours, or another reasonable time period specified by the implementing agency, the discovery of any released regulated UST substances, or any suspected release. Unusual operating conditions or monitoring results indicating a release must also be reported to the implementing agency.

4. Closure

Owners or operators who would like to take tanks out of operation must either temporarily or permanently close them in accordance with

40 CFR part 280 subpart G–Out-of-Service UST Systems and Closure. When UST systems are temporarily closed, owners and operators must continue operation and maintenance of corrosion protection and, unless all USTs have been emptied, release detection. If temporarily closed for three months or more, the UST system's vent lines must be left open and functioning, and all other lines, pumps, manways, and ancillary equipment must be capped and secured. After 12 months, tanks that do not meet either the performance standards for new UST systems or the upgrading requirements (excluding spill and overfill device requirements) must be permanently closed, unless a site assessment is performed by the owner or operator and an extension is obtained from the implementing agency. To close a tank permanently, an owner or operator generally must: Notify the regulatory authority 30 days before closing (or another reasonable time period determined by the implementing agency); determine if the tank has leaked and, if so, take appropriate notification and corrective action; empty and clean the UST; and either remove the UST from the ground or leave it in the ground filled with an inert, solid material.

5. *Notification, Reporting, and Recordkeeping*

UST owners who bring an UST system into use after May 8, 1986 must notify state or local authorities of the existence of the UST and certify compliance with certain technical and other requirements, as specified in § 280.22. Owners and operators must also notify the implementing agency at least 30 days (or another reasonable time period determined by the implementing agency) prior to the permanent closure of an UST. In addition, owners and operators must keep records of testing results for the cathodic protection system, if one is used; leak detection performance and upkeep; repairs; and site assessment results at permanent closure (which must be kept for at least three years).

B. *Corrective Action Requirements*

Owners and operators of UST systems containing petroleum or hazardous substances must investigate, confirm, and respond to confirmed releases, as specified in §§ 280.51 through 280.67. These requirements include, where appropriate: Performing a release investigation when a release is suspected or to determine if the UST system is the source of an off-site impact (investigation and confirmation steps include conducting tests to determine if a leak exists in the UST or UST system and conducting a site check if tests indicate that a leak does not exist but contamination is present); notifying the appropriate agencies of the release within a specified period of time; taking immediate action to prevent any further release (such as removing product from the UST system); containing and immediately cleaning up spills or overfills; monitoring and preventing the spread of contamination into the soil and/or groundwater; assembling detailed information about the site and the nature of the release; removing free product to the maximum extent practicable; investigating soil and groundwater contamination; and, in some cases, outlining and implementing a detailed corrective action plan for remediation.

C. Financial Responsibility Requirements

The financial responsibility regulations (40 CFR part 280 subpart H) require that UST owners or operators demonstrate the ability to pay the costs of corrective action and to compensate third parties for injuries or damages resulting from the release of petroleum from USTs. The regulations require all owners or operators of petroleum USTs to maintain an annual aggregate of financial assurance of $1 million or $2 million, depending on the number of USTs owned. Financial assurance options available to owners and operators include: Purchasing commercial environmental impairment liability insurance; demonstrating self-insurance; obtaining guarantees, surety bonds, or letters of credit; placing the required amount into a trust fund administered by a third party; or relying on coverage provided by a state assurance fund.

D. State Program Approval Regulations

Subtitle I of RCRA allows state UST programs approved by EPA to operate in lieu of the federal program. EPA's state program approval regulations under 40 CFR Part 281 set standards for state programs to meet.

E. Scope of the UST Program

This rule applies only to petroleum underground storage tanks that are subject to Subtitle I of RCRA. There are certain types or classes of tanks that are excluded from Subtitle I of RCRA. Therefore, the provisions of this rule do not apply to holders of security interests in excluded tanks. Among those tanks specifically excluded by statute are: Farm and residential tanks of 1,100 gallons or less capacity used for storing motor fuel for noncommercial purposes; tanks used for storing heating oil for consumptive use on the premises where stored; tanks stored on or above the floor of underground areas (such as basements or tunnels); septic tanks; systems for collecting stormwater or wastewater; and flow-through process tanks (42 U.S.C. § 6991(1)).

60 FED. REG. 52343
(October 6, 1995)

The Resource Conservation and Recovery Act of 1976, as amended (RCRA), authorizes the U.S. Environmental Protection Agency (EPA) to grant approval to states to operate their underground storage tank programs in lieu of the federal program. 40 CFR part 282 codifies EPA's decision to approve state programs and incorporates by reference those provisions of the state statutes and regulations that will be subject to EPA's inspection and enforcement authorities under sections 9005 and 9006 of RCRA subtitle I and other applicable statutory and regulatory provisions.

* * *

Section 9004 of the Resource Conservation and Recovery Act of 1976, as amended, (RCRA), 42 U.S.C. 6991c, allows the U.S. Environmental Protection Agency (EPA) to approve state underground storage tank programs to operate in the state in lieu of the federal underground storage tank program. EPA published a Federal Register document announcing its decision to grant approval to [State] (60 FR 12709, March 8, 1995). Approval was effective on April 7, 1995.

EPA codifies its approval of State programs in 40 CFR part 282 and incorporates by reference therein the state statutes and regulations that will be subject to EPA's inspection and enforcement authorities under sections 9005 and 9006 of subtitle I of RCRA, 42 U.S.C. 6991d and 6991e, and other applicable statutory and regulatory provisions.... This codification reflects the state program in effect at the time EPA granted [state] approval under section 9004(a), 42 U.S.C. 6991c(a) for its underground storage tank program. Notice and opportunity for comment were provided earlier on the Agency's decision to approve the [state] program, and EPA is not now reopening that decision nor requesting comment on it.

This effort provides clear notice to the public of the scope of the approved program in each state. By codifying the approved [State] program and by amending the Code of Federal Regulations whenever a new or different set of requirements is approved in [State], the status of federally approved requirements of the [State] program will be readily discernible. Only those provisions of the [State] underground storage tank program for which approval has been granted by EPA will be incorporated by reference for enforcement purposes.

To codify EPA's approval of [state]'s underground storage tank program, EPA has added section 282.94 to title 40 of the CFR. Section 282.94 incorporates by reference for enforcement purposes the State's statutes and regulations. Section 282.94 also references the Attorney General's Statement, Demonstration of Adequate Enforcement Procedures, the Program Description, and the Memorandum of Agreement, which are approved as part of the underground storage tank program under subtitle I of RCRA.

The Agency retains the authority under sections 9005 and 9006 of subtitle I of RCRA, 42 U.S.C. 6991d and 6991e, and other applicable statutory and regulatory provisions to undertake inspections and enforcement actions in approved states. With respect to such an enforcement action, the Agency will rely on federal sanctions, federal inspection authorities, and federal procedures, rather than the state authorized analogs to these provisions. Therefore, the approved [state] enforcement authorities will not be incorporated by reference. Section 282.94 lists those approved state authorities that would fall into this category.

The public also needs to be aware that some provisions of the State's underground storage tank program are not part of the federally approved state program. These non-approved provisions are not part of the RCRA subtitle I program because they are "broader in scope" than subtitle I of RCRA. See 40 CFR 281.12(a)(3)(ii). As a result, state provisions which are "broader in scope" than the federal program are not incorporated by reference for purposes of enforcement in part 282. Section 282.94 of the codification simply lists for reference and clarity the [state] statutory and regulatory provisions which are "broader in scope" than the federal program and which are not, therefore, part of the approved program being codified today. "Broader in scope" provisions cannot be enforced by EPA; the State, however, will continue to enforce such provisions.

§ 5.14   RCRA SUBTITLE J: MEDICAL WASTE TRACKING ACT

Numerous incidents of public exposure to improperly disposed medical waste resulted in Congress' passage of the Medical Waste Tracking Act of 1988. This act amended RCRA by adding subtitle J. The Act required EPA to develop a two-year demonstration tracking program for medical waste. The demonstration program set forth segregation, packaging, labeling, tracking, transportation, and recordkeeping requirements of medical waste generated in the covered States, and lists the wastes to be covered by the program. The emphasis of the tracking program was to assure the generator that the waste is delivered to a proper disposal facility.

Regulations promulgated to implement the Act applied only to medical waste generators in States that participated in the program. In addition, they applied to other handlers (transporters, transfer facilities, and treatment or disposal facilities) who manage regulated medical wastes that originated in a State that participates in the demonstration tracking program.

The Act also required EPA to submit a final report and two interim reports to Congress discussing the program's overall success and the information obtained from the program. The results of the demonstration program were designed to assist Congress in determining whether or not the provisions of the medical waste tracking program should be extended nationwide.

Certain states, including New Jersey, New York and Connecticut were obligated to participate in the program. Other states, such as the states contiguous to the Great Lakes and any other state that petitioned the EPA, had the option of participating in the program if they chose to do so. The requirements promulgated in the Federal Register on March 24, 1989, were effective on June 24, 1989 for certain medical wastes generated in these States.

In Indiana, Governor Bayh decided that Indiana would not participate in the program. Indiana had developed its own regulatory scheme for tracking medical waste and the federal scheme would preempt the Indiana program. According to the letter sent by Governor Bayh to the Administrator of the Environmental Protection Agency, the Indiana program needed to be in operation so that its effectiveness could be analyzed. The Governor's letter indicated that he felt that it would be premature to alter the present regulatory scheme as of April 1989. The Governor also wrote that the cost of the federal program to Indiana would be difficult to justify in light of the fiscal situation faced by Indiana at that time. This decision resulted in litigation.

Indiana was not alone. Each of the Great Lakes States (Illinois, Indiana, Michigan, Minnesota, Ohio, Pennsylvania, and Wisconsin) elected to opt out of the medical waste demonstration tracking program. As required under the MWTA, the Governors of these States notified the EPA Administrator of their intent to opt out.

Pursuant to section 11001 of the MWTA, on March 24, 1989 EPA released a Federal Register notice providing the States not identified in the Act an opportunity to participate in the demonstration program. The Governor of any State electing to participate was required to submit a letter petitioning the EPA Administrator to allow the State to participate. The Governors of the States of Louisiana and Rhode Island, the Mayor of the District of Columbia, and the Governor of the Commonwealth of Puerto Rico petitioned the Administrator to be included in the demonstration program. These petitions were accepted, and the June 6 Notice identified Louisiana, Rhode Island, the District of Columbia, and Puerto Rico as Covered States in addition to the States of Connecticut, New Jersey, and New York. The requirements of the demonstration program contained in the March 24 Federal Register notice were effective on July 24, 1989 for certain medical wastes generated in Louisiana, Rhode Island, the District of Columbia, and Puerto Rico.

States participating in the program included New York, New Jersey, Connecticut (effective 6/22/89), Rhode Island, and Puerto Rico (effective 7/24/89). In addition, two States originally elected to participate in the demonstration program, but later asked EPA to reconsider their participation. The Governor of Louisiana and the Mayor of the District of Columbia each requested removal from the program after initial requests to opt-into the program. Both requests were based on concerns that the respective jurisdictions would be unable to fully implement the program until well into the second year of the demonstration project. EPA granted the request for removing Louisiana and the District of Columbia from the list of Covered States, explaining as follows:

> EPA does not believe an effective program can be established in DC and Louisiana without strong support from those States. Therefore, it is in the interest of the demonstration program to remove those States. Effective August 24, 1989, medical waste generated in the District of Columbia and Louisiana is no longer subject to the requirements of the tracking program promulgated March 24, 1989.

The Act, thus, authorized a two-year pilot tracking program in only five states to ensure that medical waste was sent to proper disposal facilities.

Critics of the Act were concerned that the federal Medical Waste Tracking Act was not effective. They were concerned that the federal act would be difficult to comply with and would be frequently circumvented.

An innovative feature of the Medical Waste Tracking Act was that it contained a "knowing endangerment" section that imposed enhanced penalties on violators who knowingly place another person in imminent danger of death or serious bodily injury. The knowing endangerment section of the Medical Waste Tracking Act, however, expressly returns to the knowledge standard of the RCRA, requiring proof that the defendant "is aware or believes that his conduct is substantially certain to cause danger or serious bodily injury."

At the end of its term, Congress did not reauthorize the 2–year demonstration program that EPA had established under the Medical Waste Tracking Act of 1988. When it expired on June 22, 1991, EPA's regulations on medical waste in 40 C.F.R. Part 259 had applied in only five States.

Chapter 6

SUPERFUND

Table of Sections

§ 6.1 OVERVIEW

Congress enacted the Comprehensive Environmental Response, Compensation and Liability Act of 1980 ("CERCLA" or "Superfund"), 42 U.S.C.A. §§ 9601–9675, in the wake of "Love Canal" and the growing public concern about the dangers posed by hazardous waste sites. In Love Canal, a residential neighborhood was built over an abandoned hazardous substance site. Existing law precluded the homeowners from suing Hooker Chemical Company (the company factually responsible for the site contamination) due to lack of privity relationship between the homeowners and the polluter. Similarly, RCRA was unavailable as a remedy for the homeowners because the site was an abandoned, *inactive hazardous* waste site and RCRA regulates only *active* hazardous waste sites. CERCLA was enacted to remedy this gap in law.

CERCLA serves two "essential" yet independent purposes. First, the law gives the federal government the tools necessary for prompt and effective response to the problems created by abandoned hazardous wastes. Second, CERCLA holds those "responsible parties" accountable for the costs and responsibility of cleanup. The stated purpose of CERCLA was "to force polluters to pay for costs associated with remedying their pollution." The law was drafted so broadly, however, that many people who never participated in pollution (such as current owners) could be held liable for cleanup costs.

The following table illustrates the key provisions of CERCLA:

CERCLA at a Glance

Section	Description
§ 101	Definitions, including (1) owner & operator and (2) scope of innocent purchaser defense
§ 103	Release Notification Requirements for Hazardous Substances
§ 104	Authorizes EPA to conduct removal or remedial action consistent with NCP
§ 105	NCP requires establishing NPL through the hazard ranking system (HRS) and requires periodic revision of the NCP
§ 106	Authorizes issuance of unilateral administrative orders (UAO) requiring the abatement of releases or threat of release creating an imminent and substantial endangerment to health, welfare or the environment
§ 107(a)	Establishes liability for four classes of PRPs.

§ 107(b)	Establishes limited statutory defenses, including the third party defense, innocent purchaser defense and the inheritance defense
§ 111	Creates the Superfund
§ 113	Bars pre-enforcement review
§ 116	Establishes timetable for reviewing the NPL sites, commencement of RI/FSs and remedial action
§ 121	Establishes guidelines for setting cleanup standards
§ 122	Establishes standards for settlements with PRPs, including de minimis contributors

The Comprehensive Environmental Response, Compensation, and Liability Act of 1980 ("CERCLA" or "Superfund") authorizes the President of the United States:

√ to clean up "facilities"

√ at which "hazardous substances"

√ have been "released."

Congress, in 1980, gave EPA a $1.6 billion revolving fund, the "Superfund," to finance the enforcement and cleanup effort at the front end, pending reimbursement by responsible parties. In 1986, Congress enacted far-reaching amendments to Superfund (Superfund Amendments and Reauthorization Act or "SARA"), and gave EPA $8.5 billion more to finance Superfund. The reimbursement provisions of Superfund create huge civil liabilities for business because they allow EPA (and others) to sue businesses to recover:

√ "response costs" (the costs incurred in cleaning up, which amount to millions of dollars at a typical waste dump site), and

√ "natural resource damages" (which may ultimately prove to be even more expensive than cleanup costs).

These costs and damages can be recovered from a wide range of persons and businesses associated with the sites, known as "potentially responsible parties" or PRPs. The possibility of cost recovery has spawned three tiers of massive litigation. EPA (or the state or private party cleanup plaintiff) can recover cleanup costs from the PRP or PRPs they choose to sue (in the first tier of litigation) and those PRPs are left to bring separate legal actions (in the second tier of litigation) against other PRPs (or to join the other PRPs in the original action) to sort out, under evolving principles of "contribution" law, who ultimately bears how much of the responsibility for the cleanup costs. Finally, a third tier of litigation arises when PRPs bring lawsuits against their insurance carriers in an attempt to establish coverage under standard Comprehensive General Liability (CGL) or Environmental Impairment Liability (EIL) policies.

In a nutshell, Superfund imposes millions of dollars of joint and several, strict liability on hazardous waste generators and transporters and on an extremely broad range of persons who can be characterized under Superfund as past or present "owners" or "operators" of hazardous waste sites (including such persons as past and present landowners, real estate brokers, lessors and lessees, lenders, parties to project finance transactions, insurance companies, parent corporations, successor corporations, and officers, or other responsible corporate personnel of any of the above). The magnitude of Superfund liability, the Superfund standard of liability, and the broad range of persons subject to Superfund liability are discussed below in greater depth.

§ 6.2 ELEMENTS OF A CAUSE OF ACTION

To trigger liability, CERCLA section 107 requires a plaintiff must allege the following four elements:

(1) the waste disposal site is a "facility;"

(2) a "release" or "threatened release" of any "hazardous substance" from the facility has occurred;

(3) such "release" or "threatened release" has caused the plaintiff to incur response costs that are "consistent with the national contingency plan (NCP),"; and

(4) the defendant must qualify as one of four categories of "covered persons" subject to CERCLA liability.

CERCLA defines facility as "any building, structure, installation, equipment, pipe, ... well, pit, pond, lagoon, impoundment, ditch, landfill, storage container ... or any site where a hazardous substance has been deposited, stored, disposed of, or placed, or otherwise come to be located." With only limited exceptions, courts have interpreted this definition very broadly to include "every place where hazardous substances come to be located." "In order to show that an area is a 'facility' a plaintiff need only show that a hazardous substance has 'otherwise come to be located' there."

A release is defined as "any spilling, leaking, pumping, pouring, emitting, emptying, discharging, injecting, escaping, leaching, dumping, or disposing into the environment." Courts have repeatedly rejected any attempt to limit the broad coverage of this definition. The definition was meant to "encompass the entire universe of ways in which hazardous substances may come to exist in the environment." Most courts have interpreted the term as including both active and passive releases of hazardous substances. A release of hazardous substances is not limited to just one instance, but can occur each time a hazardous substance is disposed.

A split of authority exists concerning the issue of liability for so-called passive releases of hazardous substances. Some courts have held that such passive releases constitute a disposal for CERCLA purposes. *See, e.g., Nurad, Inc. v. William E. Hooper & Sons Co.*, 966 F.2d 837,

844–46 (4th Cir.1992). Others have rejected the notion that passive releases constitute disposals under CERCLA. *See, e.g., United States v. Petersen Sand and Gravel*, Inc., 806 F.Supp. 1346 (N.D.Ill.1992).

When federal courts have held that a passive release of hazardous substances did not constitute a disposal for CERCLA purposes, the cases involved scenarios where no disposal activity occurred during the period of alleged liability. Rather, during the period in question, waste, previously disposed of at the facility, migrated or leached into the soil or water thereby creating a contamination problem. *See, e.g., United States v. Petersen Sand & Gravel*, 806 F.Supp. 1346 (N.D.Ill.1992) (leaking and leaching of hazardous substances from barrels disposed at the facility prior to company's operation constitutes passive disposal for which no CERCLA liability attaches); *Ecodyne Corp. v. Shah*, 718 F.Supp. 1454, 1457 (N.D.Cal.1989)(CERCLA only provides "an action against prior owners or operators who owned the site at the time the hazardous substances were introduced into the environment."); *Snediker Developers Ltd. Partnership v. Evans*, 773 F.Supp. 984, 989 (E.D.Mich. 1991)("The mere migration of hazardous waste, without more, does not constitute disposal." Therefore, owners of property where hazardous waste had been dumped by others sixteen years earlier were not responsible for the spread of the waste matter during their period of ownership.); *In re Diamond Reo Trucks, Inc.*, 115 B.R. 559, 565 (Bkrtcy.Mich. 1990)("The mere ownership of the site during a period of time in which migration or leaching may have taken place, without any active disposal activities, does not bring [the defendant] within the liability provision of § 9607(a)(2).").

"Response Costs" are defined as those costs incurred in the removal of hazardous substances or any remedial action to clean up hazardous substances as well as any related enforcement activities. "Removal" is defined as "the cleanup or removal of released hazardous substances from the environment, such actions may be necessary taken in the event of the threat of release of hazardous substances into the environment." "Remedial action" is defined as "those actions consistent with permanent remedy taken instead of or in addition to removal actions in the event of a release or threatened release of a hazardous substance into the environment, to prevent or minimize the release of hazardous substances so that they do not migrate to cause substantial danger to present or future public health or welfare or the environment." In other words, removal actions are the short term activities necessary to stop contained contamination or adverse health effects from the site. Remedial activities are the long term cleanup strategies. Whether "response costs" have been incurred or not is a case by case determination. Response costs have been held to include:

√ medical monitoring;

√ security fencing or other measures to secure the site;

√ investigating, monitoring, testing and evaluation costs;

√ alternative water supplies;

√ prejudgment interest;

√ enforcement costs;

√ remedial actions, including storage, confinement, clay cover, neutralization, recycling or reuse, destruction, dredging or excavation, collection of leachate or runoff and on-site treatment or incineration; and

√ sometimes EPA oversight costs.

CERCLA does not distinguish between private and NPL sites in its liability section. Thus, one of the critical issues in CERCLA liability is whether or not the cleanup must be "consistent with the NCP" in order to be actionable. Some courts have held that cleanup costs must be consistent with the NCP in a private cause of action. Other courts, however, have held that consistency with NCP is only relevant as to apportionment of liability and not to the question of liability itself. To evaluate consistency with the NCP, a court must evaluate the following factors:

√ the nature of the action taken;

√ the imminence or the release or threatened release;

√ whether a state or federal agency found a threat to public health or safety;

√ whether an agency has recommended action to eliminate the threat; and

√ the costs, complexity and duration of the activity.

Absence of public notice and comment will not necessarily preclude cost recovery when the PRP cleaning up has notified the relevant regulatory agencies. There is a rebuttable presumption that costs incurred pursuant to a consent decree will be deemed consistent with the NCP.

Beyond cleanup costs, potentially responsible parties (PRPs) are also liable for "natural resource damages." While the price tag for these damages is not yet clear, this form of Superfund liability at NPL listed sites could ultimately prove to be even more expensive than cleanup costs. For example, at the Rocky Mountain arsenal site the initial claim for natural resource damages was $1.8 billion. Natural resource damages have not yet begun to be considered an issue in private CERCLA sites, but the statute does not differentiate between private and NPL listed sites with regards to natural resource damages. Moreover, natural resource damage settlements are subject to a Superfund requirement for a "reopener," a provision allowing the government to later sue a PRP if unknown natural resource damages is later discovered.

Unlike RCRA and other environmental statutes, for the purposes of CERCLA liability there is no threshold quantity or concentration of hazardous substance. A PRP may be liable regardless of how low the percentage of hazardous substance may be.

§ 6.3   LIABLE PARTIES

Causation is not an element of a CERCLA cause of action. The plaintiff is not required to link the defendant's conduct or the defendant's waste firmly to the release or threat of release. Nor must the defendant's conduct be considered unlawful in order to incur liability. The release or threat of release only need have emanated from a facility which the defendant owned, or to which defendant transported.

Under CERCLA, four classes of persons may be held liable:

> (1) current owner and operators;

> (2) past owners or operators at the time of disposal;

> (3) generators; and

> (4) transporters of hazardous waste that selected the disposal site.

Once it has been found that there is a responsible party and that a hazardous substance has been released at a CERCLA facility the court may, "allocate response costs among liable parties using such equitable factors as the court determines are appropriate." 42 U.S.C.A. § 9613(f)(1).

1.   Owners and Operators

UNITED STATES v. NORTHEASTERN PHARMACEUTICAL & CHEMICAL CO.

810 F.2d 726 (8th Cir.1986), *cert. denied*, 484 U.S. 848, 108 S.Ct. 146, 98 L.Ed.2d 102 (1987).

McMILLIAN, CIRCUIT JUDGE.

Northeastern Pharmaceutical & Chemical Co. (NEPACCO), Edwin Michaels and John W. Lee appeal from a final judgment entered in the District Court ... for the Western District of Missouri finding them and Ronald Mills jointly and severally liable for response costs incurred by the government after December 11, 1980, and all future response costs relative to the cleanup of the Denney farm site that are not inconsistent with the national contingency plan (NCP) pursuant to §§ 104, 107 of the Comprehensive Environmental Response, Compensation, and Liability Act of 1980 (CERCLA), 42 U.S.C. §§ 9604, 9607 (appeal No. 84–1837). For reversal, appellants argue the district court erred in (1) applying CERCLA retroactively, (2) finding Michaels and Lee individually liable, (3) failing to dismiss NEPACCO as a party defendant, (4) awarding response costs absent affirmative proof that the response costs were consistent with the NCP, (5) refusing to reduce the award of response costs by the amount of a prior settlement, and (6) denying appellants a jury trial.

* * *

The following statement of facts is taken in large part from the district court's excellent memorandum opinion, *United States v. Northeastern Pharmaceutical & Chemical Co.*, 579 F.Supp. 823 (W.D.Mo.1984)(NEPACCO). NEPACCO was incorporated in 1966 under the laws of Delaware; its principal office was located in Stamford, Connecticut. Although NEPACCO's corporate charter was forfeited in 1976 for failure to maintain an agent for service of process, NEPACCO did not file a certificate of voluntary dissolution with the secretary of state of Delaware. In 1974 its corporate assets were liquidated, and the proceeds were used to pay corporate debts and then distributed to the shareholders. Michaels formed NEPACCO, was a major shareholder, and was its president. Lee was NEPACCO's vice-president, the supervisor of its manufacturing plant located in Verona, Missouri, and also a shareholder. Mills was employed as shift supervisor at NEPACCO's Verona plant.

From April 1970 to January 1972 NEPACCO manufactured the disinfectant hexachlorophene at its Verona plant. NEPACCO leased the plant from Hoffman–Taff, Inc.; Syntex Agribusiness, Inc. (Syntex), is the successor to Hoffman–Taff. Michaels and Lee knew that NEPACCO's manufacturing process produced various hazardous and toxic by-products, including 2,4,5–trichlorophenol (TCP), 2,3,7,8–tetrachlorodibenzo-p-dioxin (TCDD or dioxin), and toluene. The waste by-products were pumped into a holding tank which was periodically emptied by waste haulers. Occasionally, however, excess waste by-products were sealed in 55–gallon drums and then stored at the plant.

In July 1971 Mills approached NEPACCO plant manager Bill Ray with a proposal to dispose of the waste-filled 55–gallon drums on a farm owned by James Denney located about seven miles south of Verona. Ray visited the Denney farm and discussed the proposal with Lee; Lee approved the use of Mills' services and the Denney farm as a disposal site. In mid-July 1971 Mills and Gerald Lechner dumped approximately 85 of the 55–gallon drums into a large trench on the Denney farm (Denney farm site) that had been excavated by Leon Vaughn. Vaughn then filled in the trench. Only NEPACCO drums were disposed of at the Denney farm site.

In October 1979 the Environmental Protection Agency (EPA) received an anonymous tip that hazardous wastes had been disposed of at the Denney farm. Subsequent EPA investigation confirmed that hazardous wastes had in fact been disposed of at the Denney farm and that the site was not geologically suitable for the disposal of hazardous wastes. Between January and April 1980 the EPA prepared a plan for the cleanup of the Denney farm site and constructed an access road and a security fence. During April 1980 the EPA conducted an on-site investigation, exposed and sampled 13 of the 55–gallon drums, which were found to be badly deteriorated, and took water and soil samples. The samples were found to contain "alarmingly" high concentrations of dioxin, TCP and toluene.

In July 1980 the EPA installed a temporary cap over the trench to prevent the entry and run-off of surface water and to minimize contamination of the surrounding soil and groundwater. The EPA also contracted with Ecology & Environment, Inc., for the preparation of a feasibility study for the cleanup of the Denney farm site. Additional on-site testing was conducted. In August 1980 the government filed its initial complaint against NEPACCO, the generator of the hazardous substances; Michaels and Lee, the corporate officers responsible for arranging for the disposal of the hazardous substances; Mills, the transporter of the hazardous substances; and Syntex, the owner and lessor of the Verona plant, seeking injunctive relief and reimbursement of response costs pursuant to RCRA § 7003, 42 U.S.C. § 6973 (count I). In September 1983 the feasibility study was completed.

In the meantime the EPA had been negotiating with Syntex about Syntex's liability for cleanup of the Denney farm site. In September 1980 the government and Syntex entered into a settlement and consent decree. Pursuant to the terms of the settlement, Syntex would pay $100,000 of the government's response costs and handle the removal, storage and permanent disposal of the hazardous substances from the Denney farm site. The EPA approved Syntex's proposed cleanup plan, and in June 1981 Syntex began excavation of the trench. In November 1981 the site was closed. The 55-gallon drums are now stored in a specially constructed concrete bunker on the Denney farm. The drums as stored do not present an imminent and substantial endangerment to health or the environment; however, no plan for permanent disposal has been developed, and the site will continue to require testing and monitoring in the future.

In August 1982 the government filed an amended complaint adding counts for relief pursuant to CERCLA §§ 104, 106, 107, 42 U.S.C. §§ 9604, 9606, 9607 (counts II and III). CERCLA was enacted after the filing of the initial complaint.

* * *

The district court found that dioxin, hexachlorophene, TCP, TCB (1,2,3,5-tetrachlorobenzene, also found at the Denney farm site), and toluene have high levels of toxicity at low-dose levels and are thus "hazardous substances" within the meaning of RCRA § 1004(5), 42 U.S.C. § 6903(5), and CERCLA § 101(14), 42 U.S.C. § 9601(14). 579 F.Supp. at 832, 845; *see also United States v. Vertac Chemical Corp.*, 489 F.Supp. 870, 874–79 (E.D.Ark.1980)(dioxin). The district court also found there was a substantial likelihood that the environment and human beings would be exposed to the hazardous substances that had been disposed of at the Denney farm site. 579 F.Supp. at 846 & n.28 (discussing meaning of "imminent and substantial endangerment" standard). A state geologist testified the Denney farm site is located in an area in which substances rapidly move through the soil and into the groundwater and, although no dioxin had been found in the water in nearby wells, dioxin had been found as far as 30 inches beneath the soil in the trench. *Id.* at 832–33.

* * *

CERCLA § 104, 42 U.S.C. § 9604, authorizes the EPA to take direct "response" actions, which can include either short-term "removal" actions or long-term "remedial" actions or both, pursuant to the NCP, with funds from the "Superfund," . . . and to seek recovery of response costs from responsible parties pursuant to CERCLA § 107, 42 U.S.C. § 9607, in order to replenish the Superfund. The EPA can also use CERCLA § 106, 42 U.S.C. § 9606, to seek injunctions to compel responsible parties to clean up hazardous waste sites that constitute an "imminent and substantial endangerment" to health and the environment. In the present case, count II sought injunctive relief pursuant to CERCLA § 106, 42 U.S.C. § 9606, and count III sought recovery of the government's past and future response costs pursuant to CERCLA §§ 104, 107, 42 U.S.C. §§ 9604, 9607.

* * *

The district court found NEPACCO liable as the "owner or operator" of a "facility" (the NEPACCO plant) under CERCLA § 107(a)(1), 42 U.S.C. § 9607(a)(1), and as a "person" who arranged for the transportation and disposal of hazardous substances under CERCLA § 107(a)(3), 42 U.S.C. § 9607(a)(3). 579 F.Supp. at 847. The district court found Lee liable as a "person" who arranged for the disposal of hazardous substances under CERCLA § 107(a)(3), 42 U.S.C. § 9607(a)(3), *id.* at 847–48, and as an "owner or operator" of the NEPACCO plant under CERCLA § 107(a)(1), 42 U.S.C. § 9607(a)(1), by "piercing the corporate veil." *Id.* at 848–49. The district court also found Michaels liable as an "owner or operator" of the NEPACCO plant under CERCLA § 107(a)(1), 42 U.S.C. § 9607(a)(1). *Id.* at 849.

Appellants concede NEPACCO is liable under CERCLA § 107(a)(3), 42 U.S.C. § 9607(a)(3), for arranging for the transportation and disposal of hazardous substances at the Denney farm site. Brief for Appellants at 25–26. Because NEPACCO's assets have already been liquidated and distributed to its shareholders, however, it is unlikely that the government will be able to recover anything from NEPACCO.

Appellants argue (1) they cannot be held liable as "owners or operators" of a "facility" because "facility" refers to the place where hazardous substances are located and they did not own or operate the Denney farm site, (2) Lee cannot be held individually liable for arranging for the transportation and disposal of hazardous substances because he did not "own or possess" the hazardous substances and because he made those arrangements as a corporate officer or employee acting on behalf of NEPACCO, and (3) the district court erred in finding Lee and Michaels individually liable by "piercing the corporate veil." Appellants have not claimed that any of CERCLA's limited affirmative defenses apply to them. *See* CERCLA § 107(b)(1), (2), (3), 42 U.S.C. § 9607(b)(1), (2),

(3)(no liability if defendant establishes by preponderance of evidence that release was caused solely by act of God, act of war, act or omission of third party other than employee or agent or by contract only if defendant establishes due care and precautions against foreseeable consequences taken); *see, e.g., United States v. Ward*, 618 F.Supp. at 897–98; *United States v. Conservation Chemical Co.*, 619 F.Supp. at 203–04; *see generally* Developments, 99 Harv. L. Rev. at 1543–48.

The government argues Lee can be held individually liable without "piercing the corporate veil," under CERCLA § 107(a)(3), 42 U.S.C. § 9607(a)(3), and that Lee and Michaels can be held individually liable as "contributors" under RCRA § 7003(a), 42 U.S.C.A. § 6973(a)(West Supp. 1986). For the reasons discussed below, we agree with the government's liability arguments. . . .

. . . Despite the findings by the district court, the government did not seek to impose liability upon NEPACCO, Lee and Michaels under CERCLA § 107(a)(1), 42 U.S.C. § 9607(a)(1), as the owners or operators of a facility where hazardous substances are located, and in these appeals the government has expressed no opinion with respect to "owner and operator" liability under the circumstances in the present case . . . The government further argues that it is unnecessary to decide whether Michaels would also be liable under CERCLA § 107(a)(3), 42 U.S.C. § 9607(a)(3), because RCRA § 7003(a), 42 U.S.C.A. § 6973(a)(West Supp. 1986), "so clearly fits the circumstances of this case." . . . The district court did not reach the question of Michaels' liability under CERCLA § 107(a), 42 U.S.C. § 9607(a). 579 F.Supp. at 849 n.31.

A. *Liability under CERCLA § 107(a)(1), 42 U.S.C. § 9607(a)(1)*

First, appellants argue the district court erred in finding them liable under CERCLA § 107(a)(1), 42 U.S.C. § 9607(a)(1), as the "owners and operators" of a "facility" where hazardous substances are located. Appellants argue that, regardless of their relationship to the NEPACCO plant, they neither owned nor operated the Denney farm site, and that it is the Denney farm site, not the NEPACCO plant, that is a "facility" for purposes of "owner and operator" liability under CERCLA § 107(a)(1), 42 U.S.C. § 9607(a)(1). We agree.

CERCLA defines the term "facility" in part as "any site or area where a hazardous substance has been deposited, stored, disposed of, or placed, or otherwise come to be located." CERCLA § 101(9)(B), 42 U.S.C. § 9601(9)(B); *see New York v. Shore Realty Corp.*, 759 F.2d 1032, 1043 n. 15 (2d Cir.1985). The term "facility" should be construed very broadly to include "virtually any place at which hazardous wastes have been dumped, or otherwise disposed of." *United States v. Ward*, 618 F.Supp. at 895 (definition of "facility" includes roadsides where hazardous waste was dumped); *see also United States v. Conservation Chemical Co.*, 619 F.Supp. at 185 (stereotypical waste disposal facility); *New York v. General Electric Co.*, 592 F.Supp. 291, 296 (N.D.N.Y.1984) (dragstrip); *United States v. Metate Asbestos Corp.*, 584 F.Supp. 1143, 1148 (D.Ariz. 1984)(real estate subdivision). In the present case, however, the place where the hazardous substances were disposed of and where the government has concentrated its cleanup efforts is the Denney farm site, not the NEPACCO plant. The Denney farm site is the "facility." Because NEPACCO, Lee and Michaels did not own or operate the Denney farm site, they cannot be held liable as the "owners or operators" of a "facility" where hazardous substances are located under CERCLA § 107(a)(1), 42 U.S.C. § 9607(a)(1).

* * *

VII. BURDEN OF PROOF OF RESPONSE COSTS

The district court found appellants had the burden of proving the government's response costs were inconsistent with the NCP, 579 F.Supp. at 580, and that response costs that are not inconsistent with the NCP are conclusively presumed to be reasonable and therefore recoverable, *id.* at 851. Appellants argue the district court erred in requiring them to prove the response costs were inconsistent with the NCP, not cost-effective or unnecessary. Appellants further argue the district court erred in assuming all costs that are consistent with the NCP are conclusively presumed to be reasonable. Appellants note that the information and facts necessary to establish consistency with the NCP are matters within the possession of the government.

We believe the district court's analysis is correct. CERCLA § 107(a)(4)(A), 42 U.S.C. § 9607(a)(4)(A), states that the government may recover from responsible parties "all costs of removal or remedial action ... not inconsistent with the [NCP]." The statutory language itself establishes an exception for costs that are inconsistent with the NCP, but appellants, as the parties claiming the benefit of the exception, have the burden of proving that certain costs are inconsistent with the NCP and, therefore, not recoverable. *See United States v. First City National Bank*, 386 U.S. 361, 366, 18 L.Ed.2d 151, 87 S.Ct. 1088 (1967). Contrary to appellants' argument, "not inconsistent" is not, at least for purposes of statutory construction and not syntax, the same as "consistent." *See, e.g., United States v. Ward*, 618 F.Supp. at 899; *United States v. Conservation Chemical Co.*, 619 F.Supp. at 186; *Lone Pine Steering Comm. v. EPA*, 600 F.Supp. 1487, 1499 (D.N.J.), *aff'd*, 777 F.2d 882 (3d Cir.1985), *cert. denied*, 476 U.S. 1115, 106 S.Ct. 1970, 90 L.Ed.2d 654 (1986); *New York v. General Electric Co.*, 592 F.Supp. at 303–04 (state action for recovery of response costs); *J.V. Peters & Co. v. Ruckelshaus*, 584 F.Supp. 1005, 1010 (N.D.Ohio 1984), *aff'd*, 767 F.2d 263 (6th Cir.1985).

The statutory scheme also supports allocation of the burden of proof of inconsistency with the NCP upon the defendants when the government seeks recovery of its response costs. As noted above, CERCLA § 107(a)(4)(A), 42 U.S.C. § 9607(a)(4)(A), provides that the federal government or a state can recover "all costs of removal or remedial action ... not inconsistent with the [NCP]." In comparison, CERCLA § 107(a)(4)(B), 42 U.S.C. § 9607(a)(4)(B), provides that "any other person," referring to any "person" other than the federal government or a state, can recover "any other necessary costs of response ... consistent with the [NCP]." That statutory language indicates that nongovernmental entities must prove that their response costs are consistent with the NCP in order to recover then. The statutory scheme thus differentiates between government and nongovernmental entities in allocating the burden of proof of whether response costs are consistent with the NCP. *See, e.g., United States v. Ward*, 618 F.Supp. at 899; *New York v. General Electric Co.*, 592 F.Supp. at 303–04 (state action for recovery of response costs).

The statutory language also supports the district court's reasoning that under CERCLA § 107(a)(4)(A), 42 U.S.C. § 9607(a)(4)(A), "all costs" incurred by the government that are not inconsistent with the NCP are conclusively presumed to be reasonable. CERCLA does not refer to "all reasonable costs" but simply to "all costs." Cf. Federal Water Pollution Control Act § 311(f)(FWPCA), 33 U.S.C. § 1321(f)(responsible parties are liable for "actual costs incurred" by the government for cleanup); *see, e.g., Union Petroleum Corp. v. United States*, 228 Ct. Cl. 54, 651 F.2d 734, 744 (1981)(construing "actual costs incurred" in 33 U.S.C. § 1321(f) to apply conclusive presumption of reasonableness). Case law interpreting the FWPCA is relevant because CERCLA defines the NCP by referring to the NCP mandated by the FWPCA. CERCLA §§ 101(31), 105, 42 U.S.C. §§ 9601(31), 9605; *see United States v. Conservation Chemical Co.*, 619 F.Supp. at 204 (noting cross-references in CERCLA to FWPCA); *United States v. Shell Oil Co.*, 605 F.Supp. at 1073–74 & n.4 (the NCP as revised to incorporate CERCLA was issued in 1982). . . .

Appellants also argue the district court erred in requiring them to establish that the government's cleanup actions were cost-effective and necessary. This argument challenges the government's choice of a particular cleanup method. We note, however, that CERCLA § 105(3), (7), 42 U.S.C. § 9605(3), (7), requires the EPA, as the agency designated by the President, to revise the NCP required by § 311 of the FWPCA, 33 U.S.C. § 1321, to include the "national hazardous substance response plan," which is specifically required by CERCLA to include "methods and criteria for determining the appropriate extent of removal, remedy, and other measures," and "means of assuring that remedial action measures are cost-effective." Consideration of whether particular action is "necessary" is thus factored into the "cost-effective" equation. The term "cost-effective" is defined by regulation as "the lowest cost alternative that is technologically feasible and reliable and which effectively mitigates and minimizes damage to and provides adequate protection of public health, welfare, or the environment." 40 C.F.R. § 300.68(j)(1986).

Because determining the appropriate removal and remedial action involves specialized knowledge and expertise, the choice of a particular cleanup method is a matter within the discretion of the EPA. The applicable standard of review is whether the agency's choice is arbitrary and capricious. As explained in *United States v. Ward*,

[i]f [appellants] wish the court to review the consistency of [the government's] actions with the NCP, then they are essentially alleging that the EPA did not carry out its statutory duties. The statute provides liability except for costs "not inconsistent" with the NCP. This language requires deference by this court to the judgment of agency professionals. [Appellants], therefore, may not seek to have the court substitute its own judgment for that of the EPA. [Appellants], may only show that the EPA's decision about the method of cleanup was "inconsistent" with the NCP in that the EPA was arbitrary and capricious in the discharge of their duties under the NCP.

618 F.Supp. at 900.

Here, appellants failed to show that the government's response costs were inconsistent with the NCP. Appellants also failed to show that the EPA acted arbitrarily and capriciously in choosing the particular method it used to clean up the Denney farm site.

* * *

X. CONCLUSION

In conclusion, we hold (1) CERCLA applies retroactively, (2) the government can recover its pre-enactment response costs under CERCLA, (3) RCRA imposes strict liability upon past off-site generators and transporters of hazardous substances, (4) Lee and Michaels can be held individually liable, (5) NEPACCO had the capacity to be sued, (6) appellants had the burden of proving the government's response costs were inconsistent with the NCP, (7) the government's award should not be reduced by the Syntex settlement, and (8) appellants did not have the right to a jury trial.

Accordingly, the judgment of the district court is affirmed in part, reversed in part and remanded for further proceedings consistent with this opinion. The district court's refusal to dismiss NEPACCO as a party defendant, retroactive application of CERCLA to pre-enactment conduct, imposition of individual liability upon corporate officers who actually control the handling and disposal of hazardous substances, placement upon the responsible parties of the burden of proof that the government's response costs are inconsistent with the NCP, refusal to reduce the award by the amount of the prior settlement, and denial of a jury trial are affirmed. The district court's refusal to allow the government to recover its response costs incurred before the enactment of CERCLA in 1980, refusal to impose strict liability upon past off-site generators and transporters of hazardous substances under RCRA § 7003(a), 42 U.S.C.A. § 6973(a)(West Supp. 1986), and imposition of liability upon appellants as owners or operators of a facility pursuant to CERCLA § 107(a)(1), 42 U.S.C. § 9607(a)(1), are reversed.

On remand, before awarding a specific amount of pre-enactment response costs to the government under CERCLA, the district court should afford appellants an opportunity to show that the government's pre-enactment response costs were inconsistent with the NCP. Alternatively, because the government also sought to recover the response costs it incurred before the enactment of CERCLA in the form of equitable relief as abatement costs under RCRA, on remand the district court could grant the government recovery of such costs as a matter of equitable discretion.

Notes

1. Ownership liability may be based on mere title ownership of the site. For example, a PRP could be held liable as an owner if a release or threat of release occurs during the PRP's ownership of the property even if that person did not cause or contribute to the release.

2. Operator liability is determined by virtue of control over the facility. Courts have developed concerning shareholder liability for environmental problems. They are as follows:

(1) the personal participation theory allows a court to hold a shareholder liable for CERCLA response costs if that individual personally and actively participated in disposal of the hazardous substance concerned;

(2) under the authority-to-control test, operator liability is imposed as long as one corporation had the capability to control, even if it was never utilized;

(3) under the actual control standard, operator liability will be incurred for the environmental violations when there is evidence of substantial control that is actually exercised over the activities;

(4) under the prevention test, the court reviews evidence of an individual's authority to control waste handling practices, including distribution of power in the corporation, percentage of shares owned, responsibility for waste disposal practices and neglect in that regard; and

(5) under the piercing the corporate veil theory, there can be no direct operator liability of shareholders, officers or directors under CERCLA unless the elements necessary to pierce the corporate veil are met.

Most courts subscribe to one of the first four theories and allow direct operator liability under CERCLA without the necessity of piercing the corporate veil.

2. Transporters

Only transporters who accept hazardous substances for shipment and participate in disposal site selection are held liable under CERCLA. The liability attaches when the transporters advice is a substantial contributing factor in the decision to dispose of hazardous waste at a particular facility. By contrast, generators need not have participated (or even known about) the site of disposal in order to be held liable.

STATES v. BFG ELECTROPLATING & MFG. CO., INC.

1990 WL 67983, 31 Env't. Rep. Cas. (BNA) 1183 (W.D.Pa.1990).

MEMORANDUM AND ORDER

BARRON P. McCUNE, SENIOR DISTRICT JUDGE.

* * *

BFG's motion for reconsideration of count II is two-pronged: (1) the sale of the used cinder blocks did not constitute "arranging for disposal" since the sale was for a useful purpose, i.e., home improvement and modification; and (2) even if the cinder block sale were considered an "arrangement for disposal", a "sale" does not constitute a "disposal" as defined under CERCLA and thus the sale was not a release or threatened release of hazardous substances.

While there is an absence of authority under § 107(a)(1) interpreting whether a "sale" is an "arrangement for disposal," the issue is discussed when considering liability as a generator under § 107(a)(3).

It is true that there is authority that when one sells a contaminated product there is no release. However, these are cases where a new product was sold in the ordinary course of defendants' business. The product contained some hazardous substance perhaps, but the defendant had merely sold it. A sale is not therefore always a release.

A sale may sometimes be a release. Where the sale was merely a means to get rid of the hazardous substance or where ownership was retained, the courts found liability. . . .

In *United States v. A & F Materials Co.*, Inc., 582 F.Supp. 842, (S.D.Ill.1984), McDonnell Douglas Corporation in the manufacture of jet aircraft generated a caustic solution which it sold to A & F. McDonnell Douglas argued that it was not liable because it had merely *sold* the caustic solution. The court rejected the argument and held that the relevant inquiry was *who decided* to place the material into the hands of a particular facility. *A & F Materials* has been followed in *United States v. Conservation Chemical Co.*, 619 F.Supp. 162 (W.D.Mo.1985) and *New York v. General Electric*, 592 F.Supp. 291 (E.D.N.Y.1984).

The instant action is more like *A & F Materials*. While the blocks were sold, they were not new and they were not sold in the normal course of BFG business. By way of a sale it was BFG's decision to place the cinder blocks on the property of plaintiffs.

We recognize that intent to dispose is not a requirement under CERCLA. *United States v. Conservation Chemical Co.*, 619 F.Supp. at 241. Nevertheless, courts do not hesitate "to look beyond defendants' characterizations to determine whether a transaction in fact involves an arrangement for disposal of a hazardous substance." *United States v. Aceto Agricultural Chemicals Corp.*, 872 F.2d 1373, 1381 (8th Cir.1989).

Turning to the character of the transaction, we resolved in plaintiffs' favor that the cinder blocks were part of the Consent Order and Agreement ("CA & O") and contaminated with hazardous substances. October Opinion at 8. As part of the CA & O, the cinder blocks were to be disposed of at an approved disposal facility. We find that since the cinder blocks were to be disposed of at a facility, the sale was clearly an "arrangement for disposal" as defined under § 107(a)(3) of CERCLA notwithstanding that the blocks were a useful substance for construction.

BFG argues that retained ownership of the disposed waste or exercise of some control over the manner or place of disposal is pivotal in determining whether or not a sale is an arrangement for disposal. However, there is no such requirement under CERCLA § 107(a)(3). *See New York v. General Electric*, 592 F.Supp. 291 (E.D.N.Y.1984).

It is clear from CERCLA's legislative history that "persons cannot escape liability by 'contracting away' their responsibility or by alleging that the incident was caused by the act or omission of a third party." *Id.* at 297 (citation omitted). Thus BFG's argument that it did not decide to dispose of the cinder blocks, but rather sold them with the expectation that they would be used for a useful purpose must fall. It was BFG's duty to dispose of the cinder blocks at an approved facility. They cannot so facilely circumvent liability by characterizing the disposal as a sale resulting in a release of hazardous substances into the environment by means of plaintiffs' actions.

The second prong of BFG's argument is that "arranged for disposal" under CERCLA § 107(3) is not dispositive of whether a sale constitutes a release under CERCLA § 107(a)(1).

As outlined in the October Opinion, " '[r]elease' is defined as 'any spilling, leaking, ... dumping or *disposing* into the environment ...' " October Opinion at 9 *quoting* CERCLA § 101(22), 42 U.S.C. § 9601(22). We found that since a disposal constitutes a release, when a sale constitutes an arrangement for a disposal that sale is also a release. *Id.*

BFG stresses that "disposal" refers to the physical discharge or placing of a solid or hazardous waste on land or water such that the solid or hazardous waste may enter the environment. 42 U.S.C. § 9601(29); 42 U.S.C. § 6903(3). BFG interprets an "arrangement for disposal" to refer to the situation wherein the person who created the hazardous substance arranged for its transport to a waste facility.

We concur with defendant's definitions. However, because arranging for disposal results in placing the solid waste or hazardous waste in a position such that it may enter the environment, we find "arrangement for disposal" is a subset of "disposal." Since BFG's sale of the cinder blocks was an arrangement for disposal, we conclude that the sale was also a disposal and therefore a "release" as defined in § 101(22) of CERCLA.

Accordingly, the motion for reconsideration of BFG is denied.

* * *

3. *Generators*

Generator liability attaches even where the generator intended the wastes to be disposed elsewhere. All that is needed to prove generator liability is that the generator possessed the hazardous substance and it ultimately was disposed at the facility.

KELLEY EX REL. MICHIGAN NATURAL RESOURCES COMMISSION v. ARCO INDUSTRIES CORP.

739 F.Supp. 354 (W.D.Mich.1990).

ENSLEN, DISTRICT JUDGE.

This case is now before the Court on third-party defendant E. I. DuPont de Nemours and Company's September 7, 1989 Motion to Dismiss. Also before me is a Motion to dismiss filed on September 21, 1989 by third-party defendant Northwest Coating Corporation. In the principal action, the State of Michigan and Arco Industries Corporation ("Arco") under the Comprehensive Environmental Response, Compensation and Liability Act ("CERCLA"), 42 U.S.C., § 9601 *et seq*. The principal action—a multi-party CERCLA case—was settled by a consent decree on October 11, 1989. The essence of the State's claim was that Arco had damaged the Schoolcraft, Michigan aquifer by contaminating the groundwater downgradient of its facility in that area with volatile organic compounds ("VOC").

Arco seeks to hold a dozen or so third-party defendants liable for contribution and indemnity. Three of those third-party defendants, E. I. DuPont de Nemours and Company ("DuPont"), Northwest Coatings Corporation ("Northwest"), and General Latex and Chemical Corporation ("General Latex") were suppliers to Arco. The other third-party defendants are persons that owned land near the site of the Arco facility, including the Village of Schoolcraft.

Third-party defendants DuPont, Northwest, and General Latex supplied Arco with various neoprene compounds for use in its manufacture of rubbergoods and products. As part of its manufacturing process, Arco would leach the rubber products manufactured from the neoprene and dispose of the resulting wastewater, along with other waste streams, by discharging it to a lagoon behind its plant facility. The process of "leaching" involved immersion of the rubber products into water. The process removed salt and other waste-soluble materials. Thus, some of the materials used in the manufacturing process—neoprene and neoprene latex (collectively "neoprene")—contained hazardous substances, including toluene, which were also leached out of the rubber products. These hazardous substances were discharged at the conclusion of the manufacturing process into Arco's seepage pond, and subsequently entered the aquifer. In its third-party complaint against DuPont, Arco claims that one of the contaminants identified in the State's complaint, toluene, was a by-product of the leaching process and seeks contribution and indemnity under the Comprehensive Environmental Response, Compensation and Liability Act, 42 U.S.C. § 9601 *et seq.* ("CERCLA"), as well as under common law theories of products liability and negligence.

In Arco's view, the suppliers of the neoprene, unlike Arco, each knew that the hazardous substances would leach out if Arco followed the treatment that each supplier recommended. Moreover, according to Arco, the hazardous substances were not, in any way, necessary to the proper functioning of the neoprene. In fact, Arco contends that hazardous substances could have been extracted prior to sale, without compromising the quality of the product.

Supplier Liability under CERCLA

Under a 1986 amendment to CERCLA, "[a]ny person may seek contribution from any other person who is liable or potentially liable under CERCLA." 42 U.S.C. § 9613(f)(1) ... This provision codifies the principle developed under federal common law that contribution should only be obtained from parties liable under the governing law. *Edward Hines Lumber Co. v. Vulcan Materials*, 685 F.Supp. 651, 654 (N.D.Ill. 1988). *See also Colorado v. ASARCO, Inc.*, 608 F.Supp. 1484, 1492 (D.Colo.1985); *United States v. Ward*, 22 Env't Rep. Cas. (BNA) 1235, 1238 (E.D.N.C.1984). I must therefore look to the Act to see if third party defendants here are responsible parties as defined in CERCLA and thus potentially liable for contribution.

Section 107 of CERCLA provides for liability against several types of responsible parties, including individual who arranged for disposal or treatment under § 107(a)(3), as follows:

> (3) any person who by contract, agreement, or otherwise arranged for disposal or treatment, or arranged with a transporter for transport for disposal or treatment, of hazardous substances owned or possessed by such person, by any other party or entity, at any facility or incineration vessel owned or operated by another party or entity and containing such hazardous substances....

42 U.S.C. § 9607(a)(3).

Arco's third party complaint alleges that DuPont and NorthWest "each arranged for the disposal of ... hazardous substances within the meaning of Section 107(a) of CERCLA, 42 U.S.C. Section 9607." Complaint at ¶10. Third party plaintiff argues to this Court that the provisions of § 107(a)(3) should be read broadly to include sellers of a hazardous substance where the hazardous substance is not a necessary component of a useful product. According to Arco, the traditionally liberal approach to CERCLA liability should be followed here, triggering liability for those who sell products containing hazardous substances.

CERCLA does not define the term "arrange" in § 107(a)(3); however, both disposal and treatment are defined by the Act.

The term "disposal" and "treatment" are defined by reference to the Solid Waste Disposal Act, 42 U.S.C., § 9601(29). That is, CERCLA provides that "disposal" and "treatment" shall have the same meaning as those terms do in the Solid Waste Disposal Act. *See id.* Thus, "treatment" is defined as:

> [a]ny method, technique, or process, including neutralization, designed to change the physical, chemical or biological character or composition of any hazardous waste so as to neutralize such waste or so as to render such waste nonhazardous, safer for transport, amenable for recovery, amenable for storage, or reduced in volume. Such term includes any activity or processing designed to change the physical form or chemical composition of hazardous waste so as to render it nonhazardous.

42 U.S.C § 4902(34).

The term "disposal" is defined as:

> [t]he discharge, deposit, injection, dumping, spilling, leaking, or placing of any solid waste or hazardous waste into or on any land or water so that such solid waste or hazardous waste or any constituent thereof may enter the environment or be emitted into the air or discharged into any waters, involving ground.

42 U.S.C § 6903(3).

Courts interpreting § 107(a)(3) have consistently held that the mere sale of a product is not "arranging for disposal" within the meaning of the statute. *See e.g., Prudential Insurance Co. v. United States Gypsum Co.*, 711 F.Supp. 1244 (D.C.N.J.1989); *Edward Hines Lumber Co. v. Vulcan Materials Co.*, 685 F.Supp. 651 (*aff'd*, 861 F.2d 155 (7th Cir. 1988)); *Florida Power & Light Co. v. Allis–Chalmers Corp.*, 15 Chem. Waste Lit. Rep. 1209, 18 ELR 20998 (S.D.Fla.1988); *United States v. Westinghouse Electric Corp.*, 22 Env't. Rep. Case ___ (S.D.Ind.1983). In *Prudential*, plaintiffs sought relief under CERCLA from defendants who had "manufactured, processed, marketed, distributed, supplied and/or sold" asbestos-containing products. The plaintiffs claimed that the conduct of the defendant suppliers constituted "disposal" of asbestos within the meaning of CERCLA. After reviewing relevant case law, the court stated:

> [A]s there was no affirmative act to get rid of the asbestos beyond the sale of it as part of a complete, useful product, for use in a building structure, the plaintiffs' allegations fail to reveal that there has been an arrangement for the disposal of hazardous materials....

Id.

The *Prudential* court looked at the plain meaning of "disposal," but stressed the language of the statute itself to reach its conclusion, writing "looking at the term disposal in the context of the statute, . . . it is clear that liability attaches to a party who has taken an affirmative act to dispose of a hazardous substance, that is, 'in some manner the defendant must have *dumped* his waste on the site at issue,' as opposed to convey a useful substance for a useful purpose." 711 F.Supp. at 1253 (quoting *Jersey City Redevelopment Authority v. PPG Industries*, 655 F.Supp. 1257, 1260 (D.N.J.1987), *aff'd*, 866 F.2d 1411 (3d Cir.1988)(emphasis in original)). The court in *Prudential* summarized the case law on this issue, recognizing that the sale of a product is not a *per se* disposal arrangement resulting in liability under CERCLA. *Id*. The facts in *Prudential* suggested only that "there had been a conveyance of a useful, albeit dangerous product, to serve a particular, intended purpose." *Id*. at 1254. To conclude that such a transaction "constituted a CERCLA-type disposal" would strain the interpretation of the relevant terms, the court decided. In light of that decision, defendants' motion to dismiss for failure to state a claim was granted. *Id*.

In *Edward Hines Lumber Co. v. Vulcan Materials Co.*, 685 F.Supp. 651, the district court held against the owner of a wood treatment plant who brought an action against several of its suppliers to determine who should be responsible for the costs of removing contaminants from the owner's facility. The facts in *Hines* closely parallel the facts here. The defendant in *Hines* had supplied wood treatment chemicals as a primary product, and the plaintiff's disposal of runoff from the product caused the contamination at issue. The *Hines* court rejected the plaintiff's attempt to impose liability on the suppliers of the wood treatment chemicals, holding instead that "liability for environmental damage under § 9607(a)(3) attaches only to parties who transact in a hazardous substance *in order to dispose or treat the substance*." *Id*. at 654. In so holding the court stated:

> [T]he mere sale of ... [hazardous] substances for use in the wood treatment process does not constitute arranging for the disposal or treatment of a hazardous substance, even when process runoff containing the substances is placed at the same site. The defendants have presented evidence indicating that they sold the substances solely for use in wood treatment and not for the disposal of their own wastes or by-products. [Plaintiff] Hines has presented no evidence to the contrary. Defendants did not decide how the hazardous substance would be disposed of after its use in the wood treatment process. That they knew or may have known that Hines stored the process runoff in a holding pond at the Mena site does not create a material issue as to their liability. Based on these undisputed facts, neither [of the defendants] are responsible parties under § 9607(a)(3), and we grant their motions for summary judgment as to such liability.

Citing a related case, the district court in *Hines* set limits that are *relevant* to this case. It wrote:

> [L]iability for releases under § 9607(a)(3) is not endless; it ends with that party who both owned the hazardous waste and made the crucial decision how it would be disposed of or treated, and by whom.

Hines, 685 F.Supp. at 655 (quoting *United States v. A & F Materials*, 582 F.Supp. 842, 845 (S.D.Ill.1984)).

Other cases have so held, including the district court in *Florida Power & Light Co. v. Allis Chalmers Corp.*, 15 Chem. Waste Lit. Rep. 1209, 18 E.D.R. 20998 (S.D.Fla.1988). In that case, the defendant manufacturers' motion for summary judgment was granted as to the plaintiffs' claim for contribution under CERCLA. Defendant manufactured electrical transformers which contained polychlorinated biphenyls, commonly known as PCBs. Florida Power & Light Company had purchased the transformers for use in its utility business. When the transformers neared the end of their useful life, Florida Power & Light contracted with another company for their sale as scrap. After salvaging what it could, the salvager, Pepper Steel & Alloys, Inc., disposed of the transformers at its disposal site. Under plaintiff Florida Power & Light's theory, the manufacturer of the transformers was liable for contribution under CERCLA for environmental damage resulting from the eventual disposal of PCBs. *Id.*

The *Florida Power & Light* court summarized the case law to hold that the sale of a useful product which contains a contaminant does not subject a seller to liability under CERCLA. *Id.* at 1560. According to that court:

> Liability under CERCLA is narrowly construed [here]; only the party who owns the *hazardous waste product* (as opposed to the useful product containing it) can be liable, and then only if that party is the one that decided how and by whom it would be treated and disposed. As noted in [the case of] *Conservation Chemical*, CERCLA imposes strict liability on that party.

Id.

Also, in *United States v. Westinghouse Electric Corp.*, the government sued Westinghouse under CERCLA for sending PCB contaminated waste to a landfill in Indiana. 22 Env't. Rep. Cas. 1230 (S.D.Ind.1983). Westinghouse then brought a third party complaint against Monsanto which had originally supplied the PCBs to Westinghouse for use as a dielectric fluid in electrical equipment manufactured by Westinghouse. The court in that case dismissed the CERCLA claims against Monsanto, holding that it is not alleged that Monsanto disposed of any hazardous waste and did not contract for removal or disposal of such waste. According to the *Westinghouse* court, Monsanto is thus not liable under the third party complaint to Westinghouse. *Id.* at 1233.

Third party plaintiff in the matter before us argues that the statutory language of CERCLA and federal common law confirms liability for third party defendants in this case who have sold a useful product with a hazardous substance not necessary to the functioning of the product, and thus of no use to the purchaser. ARCO further argues that the cases on this issue, including the ones this Court has just discussed, stand only for the proposition that a seller could be held liable for arranging the disposal of a hazardous waste product in the limited circumstances where the product could be shown *not to function at all* absent the hazardous substance. The policy behind such a rule, according to ARCO, is that useful products would undoubtedly be kept out of the market entirely if liability were imposed under these circumstances. In contrast, ARCO points to how the product sold to it by third party defendants could have been manufactured and sold without the neoprene, a hazardous waste with no vital purpose.

I believe that ARCO makes a clever distinction here, one that leads me to anticipate the possible positive results which would spring from such a rule. I cannot, however, substitute my own policy preferences for those quite evidently held by Congress when it enacted § 107(a)(3). Neither can I blind myself to the straightforward law set forth in the recent judicial opinions interpreting this section on this very issue. There is simply no language supporting ARCO's reading in these cases, in fact, if anything, the cases are careful to limit broad readings of the language "or otherwise arranged for" the disposal of hazardous substances. 42 U.S.C. § 9607(a)(3). *See, e.g., Prudential Insurance Co. v. United States Gypsum Co.,* 711 F.Supp. 1244 (D.C.N.J.1989); *Edward Hines Lumber Co. v. Vulcan Materials Co.,* 685 F.Supp. 651 N.D. Ill., *aff'd* 861 F.2d 155 (7th Cir.1988); *Florida Power & Light Co. v. Allis–Chalmers Corp.,* 15 Chem. Waste Lit. Rep. 1209, 18 ELR 20998 (S.D.Fla. 1988), *United States v. Westinghouse Electric Corp.,* 22 Env't. Rep. Cas. 1230 (S.D.Ind.1983).

Further, I choose not to rely on the few cases third party plaintiff cites directly. In one of these cases, *United States v. Aceto Agricultural Chemicals Corp.,* 872 F.2d 1373, 1381 (8th Cir.1989), the court in dicta recognized as correct, cases holding that the sale of a useful product incorporated into a product and then disposed of is not "arranging for a disposal." The court then went on to find this line of reasoning inapplicable to the case before it where the parties manufacturing and providing the substances retained ownership—there was no transfer of ownership of the hazardous substances. Instead, the owner of the contaminated site, a pesticide formulator, performed a process on products owned by defendants—who were manufacturer/providers—to mix and formulate the pesticide substances, eventually sending them back to the manufacturer or the manufacturer's customers. I find the *Aceto Agricultural Chemicals* base, as did the Eighth Circuit, inapplicable to a case similar to the one before me. *See id.*

Two other cases on which third party plaintiff ARCO relies are distinguishable. In *New York v. General Electric Co.,* the allegation that defendant sold used transformer oil—in order to dispose of it—was sufficient to state a claim of CERCLA liability. 592 F.Supp. 291 (N.D.N.Y.1984). To interpret § 107(a)(3), the court in *General Electric* focused on the defendant's argument that the sale of a hazardous substance to dispose of that substance was distinguishable from the actual disposal of the substance. The court rejected the distinction, finding that CERCLA liability attaches to the party who makes the decision to dispose of the substance. *Id.* I must agree with the court in

Edward Hines when it concluded that the *General Electric* case "in no way stated or implied that liability attaches to all transactions in a hazardous substance." 685 F.Supp. at 655.

The court in *Edward Hines* also found unpersuasive the argument that the case *United States v. Conservation Chemical*, 619 F.Supp. 162 (W.D.Mo.1985) should be read to support a markedly broad reading of § 107(a)(3). The *Conservation Chemical* case, "at most" wrote the court in *Edward Hines*, "stands for the proposition that summary judgment for a defendant on CERCLA liability is inappropriate when there is some evidence that the motivation behind a transaction was to dispose of a waste or by-product." 685 F.Supp. at 656.

Given all the foregoing, I conclude that the motions to dismiss which are before me should be granted. The law is straight forward; CERCLA liability is not available under the circumstances in this case. I will enter an appropriate order.

* * *

UNITED STATES v. CONSOLIDATED RAIL CORP.
729 F.Supp. 1461 (D.Del.1990)

MURRAY M. SCHWARTZ, SENIOR DISTRICT JUDGE.

* * *

ii. GENERATOR LIABILITY UNDER § 9607(A)(3)

The language of section 9607(a)(3) extends liability to persons who "by contract, agreement, or otherwise arranged for" the disposal of hazardous substances. While the legislative history of CERCLA sheds little light on the intended meaning of this phrase, courts have concluded that a liberal judicial interpretation is consistent with CERCLA's "over-whelmingly remedial" statutory scheme. *See United States v. Aceto Agricultural Chemicals Corp.*, 872 F.2d 1373, 1379–82 (8th Cir.1989). In order for there to be liability under section 9607(a)(3), a person need not have generated the hazardous substances, *United States v. Bliss*, 667 F.Supp. 1298, 1306 (E.D.Mo.1987), and a person need not have actual ownership or possession of the waste. *United States v. Ward*, 618 F.Supp 884, 890 (E.D.N.C.1985); *United States v. Northeastern Pharmaceutical and Chemical Co., Inc.*, 579 F.Supp. 823 (W.D.Mo.1984), *aff'd in part, rev'd in part*, 810 F.2d 726 (8th Cir.1986), *cert. denied*, 484 U.S. 848, 108 S.Ct. 146, 98 L.Ed.2d 102 (1987)(NEPACCO). The inquiry under section 9607(a)(3) turns on the determination of who made the crucial decision to dispose of hazardous substances under the Act, and thus falls within the class of responsible persons described in section 9607(a)(3). *Jersey City Redevelopment Authority v. PPG Industries*, 655 F.Supp. 1257, 1260 (D.N.J.1987), *citing United States v. A & F Materials*, 582 F.Supp. 842, 845 (S.D.Ill.1984). "It is the authority to control the handling and disposal of hazardous substances that is critical under the statutory scheme." *NEPACCO*, 810 F.2d at 743.

The decision to dispose is not merely limited to the determination of where the hazardous substances would be disposed or treated. *See United States v. Ward*, 618 F.Supp. 884 (E.D.N.C.1985). In that case, the court found generator liability in part because the defendant "clearly intended to have Burns, [an individual hired by the defendant], 'get rid of' the PCB-laden oil which had become a problem for him to maintain on . . . [the] premises." *Id.* at 895. Thus, liability may also be extended to generators "who did not make the crucial decision of how [the substances] would be disposed or treated, and by whom," *United States v. Aceto Agricultural Chemicals Corp.*, 699 F.Supp. 1384, 1389 (S.D.Iowa 1988), *aff'd in part, rev'd in part*, 872 F.2d 1373 (8th Cir.1989), where "[a]ny other decision . . . would allow defendants to simply 'close their eyes' to the method of disposal of their hazardous substances, a result contrary to the policies underlying CERCLA." *Id.* at 1382.

Third-party plaintiffs seek to impose liability on both BPB and Eklof as generators of hazardous wastes. Third-party plaintiffs allege that BPB had control over the decision to accept wastes for disposal or treatment at the Sealand site. Similarly, third-party plaintiffs assert that Eklof made the decision to dispose of the coal tar at the Sealand facility evidenced by the alleged negotiation of that sale.

a. Generator Liability as to BPB

Third-party plaintiffs argue that BPB's agreement with Sea–Port embodied an arrangement for the disposal or treatment of hazardous substances at the Sealand site. BPB contends that this analysis fails because they did not control the decision to place the waste in the Sealand facility. Third-party plaintiffs have only established that Hildreth provided Hawkins with the names of potential raw coal suppliers. (Hildreth Aff. at ¶ 14). There is no evidence that Hildreth made the decision to dispose of hazardous substances or performed any role in deciding which suppliers formed any role in deciding which suppliers would sell to Sea–Port or providing coal tar directly to Sea–Port.

Third-party plaintiffs also assert that BPB should be held to generator liability as a formulator of hazardous wastes. In *U.S. v. Aceto Agr. Chemicals Corp.*, 699 F.Supp. 1384 (S.D.Iowa 1988), *aff'd in part, rev'd in part*, 872 F.2d 1373 (8th Cir.1989), the Court denied defendants' motions to dismiss where defendants processed pesticides at the Aidex facility and received the end product. The Court found that the "formulator [Aidex] is more of an independent contractor than a purchaser, because the manufacturer normally maintains ownership of the technical grade pesticide, the work in progress and the commercial grade pesticide even after possession passes to the formulator." *Aceto* at 1387. *See also United States v. Velsicol Chemical Corporation*, 701 F.Supp. 140, 142 (W.D.Tenn.1987)(finding generator liability where defendants arranged for Arlington Blending to formulate and package products and defendant knew or should have known that there would be losses through spills or leaks and that wastes would be generated in the formulating process).

Third-party plaintiffs argue that BPB should be held liable as a generator under the *Aceto* standard. The record establishes that BPB assisted in locating the raw material inputs for the Sealand operation and received the output at rates substantially lower than market prices. In addition, BPB was the only one who received the coal tar from the operation of the Sealand site. Third-party plaintiffs combine these facts to infer that the Sealand facility was operated by BPB for the benefit of BPB indicating an implied relationship between Sea–Port and BPB akin to that in *Aceto*.

BPB contends that this analogy fails because in *Aceto* the raw materials were owned by the defendants and then shipped to Aidex for formulation. There is no such evidence in this case. In fact, although BPB did purchase all of the output from the Sealand facility, there is no evidence of a contractual obligation on the part of BPB to accept all of the output from the Sealand facility. The letter of agreement states:

> This is to confirm that The Burke–Parsons–Bowlby Corporation will purchase the hydrocarbon products supplied by Sealand, Ltd. . . . on a month to month basis for one year.

(Dkt. 436, Exhibit 1).

Although CERCLA was meant to be interpreted broadly, on this record there is no support for the inference that BPB controlled or had the authority to control the hazardous substances disposed or treated at the Sealand site. Therefore, BPB's motion for summary judgment that BPB was not a generator of the hazardous substances at the Sealand facility under 42 U.S.C. § 9607(a)(3) will be granted.

b. *Generator Liability as to Eklof*

Third-party plaintiffs contend that Eklof negotiated the deal to sell the coal tar to Sea–Port. The sole evidence relied upon by third-party plaintiffs to support this allegation is that Eklof's signature appears on the purchase order as a seller of the oil. Eklof by affidavit disputes whether an adverse inference may be drawn based on that signature. Eklof maintains that Eklof's signature only appears on the purchase order to acknowledge that Eklof considered the debt owed by M.R. Trading to be satisfied by the agreement of Sea–Port to pay directly to Eklof $.04 per gallon out of the purchase price. (Eklof Aff., Dkt. 458, Appendix A, Exhibit 1 at ¶ 15. . . .)

* * *

The most expansive reading of generator liability still requires that Eklof take some affirmative action to dispose of the waste that resulted in deposit or treatment at the Sealand site. In opposing the motion for summary judgment, third-party plaintiffs bear the burden of countering the sworn statement of Eklof with some affirmative evidence to support their contention that Eklof did participate in the decision to dispose of the oil. The fact that Eklof Marine wanted the oil off its barge is not enough.

The summary judgment record boils down to the following. An inference may be drawn from Eklof's signature on the bill of sale that Eklof Marine owned the oil and participated in negotiations to sell it. However, Eklof by affidavit has stated he was not the owner of the oil, did not participate in any fashion in the sale of the oil to Sealand and was powerless to effect the sale to Sealand.... Thus, unless testimony of Zeigler and Meyer may be used to rebut the Eklof affidavit, Eklof's position set forth in his affidavit is uncontroverted. Third-party plaintiffs assert that an inference may be drawn from the failure of Meyer to recollect the event, indicating that Meyer was not involved. The problem with third-party plaintiff's position is an inference that Meyer was not involved is a far cry from saying Eklof participated in or negotiated the sale. Moreover, as set forth *supra*, pp. 1471–1472, Meyer and Zeigler do not know how the sale was arranged. The statements of Meyer and Zeigler are not based upon personal knowledge as required by Fed. R. Civ. P. 56(e). Therefore, they cannot be employed to contradict or in any way weaken the Eklof affidavit. As a result, on this summary judgment record Eklof's affidavit is uncontradicted. The only inference that may be drawn from Eklof's signature on the bill of sale is that set forth in the Eklof affidavit. Therefore, Eklof's motion for summary judgment that it was not a generator of the hazardous substances at the Sealand facility under 42 U.S.C. § 9607(a)(3) will be granted.

* * *

§ 6.4   DEFENSES TO LIABILITY

CERCLA allows only a few statutory affirmative defenses. These defenses include: an act of G-d; an act of war and an act of an unrelated third party. This later third party affirmative defense includes what has been termed the "innocent purchaser" defense. Courts have interpreted these three statutory defenses very narrowly. For example, court found that heavy rains and high floodwaters were not acts of God for purposes of escaping CERCLA liability.

1. *Third Party Defense*

Past "owners or operators" and current "owners and operators" may assert certain defenses. One of these is a "third-party" defense, which provides that an owner may escape liability if the release of the hazardous substances was caused by a third-party and the owner can show that it took due care with regard to the risk of environmental contamination. To shield the defendant form liability, the defendant must show that:

    1) the hazardous contamination at the site was caused *solely* by other parties;

    2) no *direct or indirect contractual relationship existed* between it and the parties responsible for contaminating the site (for purpose of this element, contractual relationship is defined by statute to

include "land contracts, deeds or other instruments transferring title or possession");

3) it *did not know or have reason to know* of the contamination at the site at the time of purchase; and

4) it *exercised due care* with respect to the hazardous waste at the site.

Failure to prove any of these elements by a "preponderance of the evidence" precludes use of the defense.

The requirement that there be no contractual relationship has led to a great deal of litigation. For example, in *United States v. Monsanto Co.*, 858 F.2d 160, 167 (4th Cir.1988), 682 F.Supp. 706, 728 (D.R.I.1988), the Fourth Circuit held that two site-owners had not established the absence of a direct or indirect contractual relationship with the sublessee ("SCRDI"), the party causing the release, in part because they had accepted rent payments from SCRDI. In *O'Neil v. Picillo*, generators of hazardous wastes ultimately disposed of at the contaminated site argued that the release had to have been caused solely by third parties for whom they had no responsibility, claiming that the licensed waste transporters to whom they had consigned their wastes had no contact with the contaminated site. The court rejected the defendants' argument, however, finding that:

> The simple fact is that during the time the defendants consigned their waste to licensed disposers, some of that waste, in identifiable containers, came to rest at the Picillo site.... The defendants must demonstrate by a preponderance of the evidence that "a totally unrelated third party is the sole cause of the release.".... Absent any evidence along these lines, I must concluded that it is equally likely that either the licensed disposers or a subcontractor of the disposers deposited the waste at the site.

In *Washington v. Time Oil Co.*, 687 F.Supp. 529, 532 (W.D.Wash.1988), the court denied a motion for summary judgment by the defendant landowner, Time Oil, based on the innocent landowner defense. The court found that because Time Oil's subsidiary was also responsible for the contamination of the property, Time Oil had failed to establish that the release was caused solely by a third party for whom it was not responsible.

2. *Innocent Purchaser Defense*

An "innocent purchaser" may nonetheless escape liability if he purchased after the disposal of the hazardous substance and he did not know, or have reason to know, that the hazardous substance was disposed of on, in, or at the facility. "To establish that the defendant had no reason to know [of the hazardous substance] the defendant must have undertaken, at the time of acquisition, all appropriate inquiry into the previous ownership and uses of the property consistent with good commercial or customary practice in an effort to minimize liability." 42 U.S.C.A. § 9601. In interpreting that standard, the court "shall take into account any specialized knowledge or experience on the part of the defendant, the relationship of the purchase price to the value of the property if uncontaminated, commonly known or reasonably ascertainable information about the property, the obviousness of the presence or likely presence of contamination at the property, and the ability to detect such contamination by appropriate inspection." *Id.*

To qualify as an "innocent purchaser," one must have undertaken "all appropriate inquiry" into the previous ownership and uses of the property, consistent with "good commercial or customary practice" at the time of transfer. "Good commercial practice" is not defined in the statute. The innocent landowner defense has been repeatedly criticized for being vague regarding the extent of investigation necessary to show "due diligence." *United States v. Pacific Hide & Fur Depot, Inc.*, 716 F.Supp. 1341 (D.Idaho 1989). Numerous Congressional efforts to define this term and the term "all appropriate inquiry" have failed.

The legislative history of this section is also vague on the definition of "good commercial practice," indicating only that it requires that "a reasonable inquiry must have been made in all circumstances, in light of best business and land transfer principles." In deciding whether a defendant has complied with this standard, courts consider any specialized knowledge or expertise the defendant has, whether the purchase price indicated awareness of the presence of a risk of contamination, commonly known or reasonable information about the property, the obviousness of the presence of contamination at the property, and the ability to detect such contamination by appropriate inspection.

The statutory definition of "contractual relationship" includes land contracts, deeds, and other instruments transferring title unless the real property was acquired "after the disposal or placement of the hazardous substance" on it, and defendant establishes by a preponderance of the evidence:

(i) At the time the defendant acquired the facility, the defendant did not know and had no reason to know that any hazardous substance which is the subject of the release or threatened release was disposed of on, in, or at the facility;

(ii) the defendant is a government entity which acquired the facility by escheat, or through any other involuntary transfer or acquisition, or through the exercise of eminent domain authority by purchase or condemnation (the municipal defense); and

(iii) the defendant acquired the facility by inheritance or bequest (the "inheritance defense").

The legislative history shows that Congress meant to establish "a three-tier system" in these innocent landowner provisions: "Commercial transactions are held to the strictest standard; private transactions are given a little more leniency; and inheritances and bequests are treated the most leniently" of all. *United States v. Pacific Hide & Fur Depot, Inc.*, 716 F.Supp. 1341, 1348 (D.Idaho 1989)(the three defendant inheritees all obtained their initial interest by familial gift and their ultimate interest by a corporate event beyond their control). Although a large industry has developed providing services to ensure compliance with the dictates of the "innocent purchaser" defense, the courts have construed both the third party and the innocent purchaser defense extremely narrowly.

WICKLAND OIL TERMINALS v. ASARCO INC.

1988 WL 167247, 19 Envtl. L. Rep. 20855 (N.D.Cal.1988).

CONTI, DISTRICT JUDGE.

Plaintiff Wickland Oil Terminals ("Wickland") brings this action under the Comprehensive Environmental Response, Compensation and Liability Act of 1980 ("CERCLA"), 42 U.S.C. §§ 9601–9657, and state law seeking damages, declaratory relief, and indemnity against defendants Asarco, Inc. ("Asarco") and State Lands Commission of California ("State Lands") with respect to the disposal of allegedly hazardous wastes located on property owned and leased by plaintiff.

Specifically, plaintiff, in its federal claims, seeks: (1) a declaration that Asarco and State Lands are "wholly liable" to plaintiff for all of the necessary costs of response to the hazard posed by the slag; and (2) a declaration that Asarco and State Lands, between themselves, are "wholly liable" for all past and future necessary costs of response expended by any party, governmental or private.

* * *

Wickland has already spent in excess of $400,000 as part of a program to test the site and surrounding waters and to devise a remediation and containment program for the slag acceptable to the state agencies. The current remediation plan awaiting final agency approval entails first phase costs of $5–6 million.

* * *

The court will begin with Wickland's claim that it is an "innocent purchaser" since this contention is a necessary basis for Wickland's summary judgment motion and central to the counterclaims of defendants Asarco and State Lands. Subsection 107(b)(3) of CERCLA provides a defense where an otherwise liable party can show the release of a hazardous substance is attributable solely to a third party and there is not a contractual relationship between itself and the third party. Since Wickland, as vendee/lessee of the site, has a contractual relationship with the named third parties, Wickland must show by a preponderance of the evidence that at the time of acquisition of the property it "did not know and had no reason to know that any hazardous substance which is the subject of the release or threatened release was disposed of on, in, or at the facility." CERCLA § 101(35)(A)(i).

* * *

The undisputed facts show that the following information was known to Wickland at the time it acquired the Selby site. Wickland was aware of the presence of up to one million metric tons of metal slag and Roy Wickland had physically observed the large slag piles during his inspections of the Selby site. Roy Wickland and his environmental consultant Frank Boerger were aware that the slag contained lead and other heavy metals. Wickland was also aware that the slag was leaching into the bay and after a meeting with Fred H. Dierker, the Executive Director of the Regional Water Quality Control Board ("RWQCB"), Roy Wickland noted that "acid caused the lead deposits in the slag to break down and, consequently, water was carrying the lead into the Bay ... [o]ver the years, Asarco had a significant number of discharges in the Bay and, as a result, has had many discussions with the [RWQCB]." Defendant's Second Amended Statement of Material Facts Not in Dispute, Plaintiff's Response, P 47.

Wickland states that it understood from its consultations with RWQCB and others that the slag posed no present environmental risk and was inert. Yet, Wickland did perceive that there was a definite risk of future problems resulting from the slag. After his April 1977 meeting with RWQCB, Roy Wickland noted that : "as expected, Dierker could not assure me that there would not be any future water quality problems with this particular site." *Id.* In October 1977 Frank Boerger received a letter from RWQCB which stated: "Our current information indicates that leachate from the site will not produce toxic effects in the receiving waters, but this information is sketchy at best." *Id.* at p 63. In this letter Wickland was also advised to obtain legal advice about potential liability for "water quality and/or health problems" that could arise on the site. *Id.*

In addition to this information which Wickland possessed at the time of purchase, there was still more information readily available to Wickland. Wickland was allowed to perform test borings at the property and conduct other tests as it saw fit, but apparently did not avail itself of this opportunity. Wickland also did not examine the RWQCB files on the Selby site and was thus unaware of a tentative 1970 resolution which proposed setting discharge requirements for metals leaching from the site. Both Harding–Lawson Associates, a consulting firm hired by Wickland, and Landeis, Ripley and Diamond, Wickland's legal counsel, were familiar with the environmental problems posed by the slag and the need for a detailed study to determine the scope of the problems. In particular, the Landeis firm had represented the Dillingham Corporation which rescinded an earlier agreement to buy the site based in part on the environmental problems posed by the slag. Edgar Washburn of this firm who advised Wickland on the Selby site testified that the environmental problems with the slag were well-known. Nevertheless, Wickland states that it did not acquire this information.

Wickland claims that defendants Asarco and State Lands withheld material information concerning environmental problems at the site and that it was misled into believing that the slag posed no environmental problem. The statutory language of CERCLA, however, requires the purchaser to establish that it undertook an appropriate inquiry. This is particularly so since Congress intended that "those engaged in commercial transactions should ... be held to a higher standard of inquiry than those who are engaged in private residential transactions." H.R.Rep. No. 962, 99th Cong., 2d Sess. 187 (1986).

Moreover, Wickland's emphasis on what it knew about the environmental problems posed by the slag at the time of purchase is misplaced. The question for the purposes of Wickland's "innocent purchaser" defense is whether it knew or had reason to know that hazardous substances were "disposed of on, in, or at the facility." CERCLA § 101(35)(A)(i). The undisputed facts show that Wickland was aware of the obvious presence of the large slag piles on the site and knew that the slag contained lead and other heavy metals which are classified as hazardous substances. The court finds that Wickland is not entitled to the "innocent purchaser" defense under CERCLA sections 101(35)(A)(i) and 107(b). Therefore, Wickland is strictly liable under CERCLA § 107(a) regardless of whether it is at fault. *New York v. Shore Realty Corp.*, 759 F.2d 1032, 1043 (2d Cir.1985).

Accordingly, the court grants defendants' motions for partial summary judgment on their counterclaims and finds that the plaintiff is a party responsible under CERCLA for response costs at the Selby site. Because Wickland is a party responsible, the court denies Wickland's motion for partial summary judgment declaring that defendants Asarco and State Lands are wholly responsible for response costs at the Selby site ... The court also denies defendants' motions for summary judgment against Wickland because it finds that genuine issues of material fact remain with regard to the contractual and legal defenses raised by defendants and the apportionment of liability between the parties.

LASALLE NAT'L TRUST, N.A. v. SCHAFFNER
818 F.Supp. 1161 (N.D.Ill.1993).

* * *

CERCLA imposes liability, regardless of fault, on owner/operators of facilities and others where there is a release of hazardous substances. *See* § 9607(a)(1). For this reason, CERCLA liability is a form of strict liability. *See United States v. Monsanto Co.*, 858 F.2d 160, 167 (4th Cir.1988). Absent some exception, Levy, as a current owner/operator of the Chicagoland site, would be liable for cleanup under CERCLA. The statute includes certain enumerated defenses, however, including one commonly referred to as the "innocent landowner defense." 42 U.S.C. § 9607(b)(3); *United States v. Petersen Sand and Gravel, Inc.*, 806 F.Supp. 1346, 1351 (N.D.Ill.1992). Section 9607(b)(3) provides in relevant part:

There shall be no liability ... for a person ... who can establish ... that the release or threat of release of a hazardous substance and the damages resulting therefrom were caused solely by ... an act or omission of a third party other than ... one whose act or omission occurs in connection with a contractual relationship ... with the defendant ... if the defendant establishes ... that he exercised due care with respect to the hazardous substance concerned ... and he took precautions against foreseeable acts or omissions of any such third party and the consequences that could foreseeable result from such acts or omissions.

42 U.S.C. § 9607(b)(3).

The term "contractual relationship" in subsection (b) specifically includes land contracts. 42 U.S.C. § 9601(35). However, an innocent purchaser may nonetheless escape liability if he purchased after the disposal of the hazardous substance and he did not know, or have reason to know, that the hazardous substance was disposed of on, in, or at the facility. § 9701(35)(A)(i). "To establish that the defendant had no reason to know [of the hazardous substance] the defendant must have undertaken, at the time of acquisition, all appropriate inquiry into the previous ownership and uses of the property consistent with good commercial or customary practice in an effort to minimize liability." § 9701(35)(B). In interpreting that standard, the court "shall take into account any specialized knowledge or experience on the part of the defendant, the relationship of the purchase price to the value of the property if uncontaminated, commonly known or reasonably ascertainable information about the property, the obviousness of the presence or likely presence of contamination at the property, and the ability to detect such contamination by appropriate inspection." *Id.*

Chicagoland argues that Levy has failed to show, as is his burden, that he made "all appropriate inquiry" prior to purchasing the property. Although it is alleged that Levy hired a consultant for an environmental audit prior to the purchase, there is no evidence that this audit was "consistent with good commercial and customary practices." In fact, Chicagoland notes, Levy has brought a separate action against that consultant, Versar, Inc., alleging that the audit did not satisfy this standard. More importantly, Chicagoland argues that the report prepared by Versar should have alerted Levy to the potentiality of PCE contamination because it revealed that Chicagoland used PCE and noted staining on the concrete floor where the dry cleaning machines had been.

Versar's pre-purchase Phase I study for Levy indicated that the inspection of the facility "focused on identification of hazardous materials usage and storage practices." Versar Phase I Report attached to Versar Compl., Defs' Ex. F at 11. According to the report, "the building contains one 1,500 gallon perchloroethylene tank." *Id.* "The perchloroethylene tank is not diked for spell (sic) containment and a floor drain is located with (sic) 10 feet of the tank. This drain is connected to city sewers. If an uncontrolled release should occur, the drain would be a direct path to the environment." *Id.* Additionally, "[prior] to using Safety–Kleen [to pick-up PCE sludge and spent PCE filters], the [PCE] waste was disposed of [in] a common refuse dumpster and landfill. The disposal method for perchloroethylene used previous to the Safety–Kleen system raises a concern as to the possibility of the Chicagoland Laundry service becoming a potentially responsible party in environmental litigation." *Id.* at 12. Versar also performed a Phase II study for Levy to study known underground gas and oil storage tanks. The Versar Phase II report indicates "while completing the Phase II work, Versar noted that floors beneath removed dry cleaning machines were stained. These stains probably result from dry cleaning fluid leakage." *Id.* Phase II Report at 3. Genuine issues of material fact exist with respect to whether or not Levy made "all appropriate inquiry" sufficient to escape liability and whether he should be charged with knowledge of the contamination, precluding the innocent owner exception. Therefore summary judgment will be denied as to Chicagoland's CERCLA claims.

In opposition to the motion, Chicagoland also argued that even if Levy were found to be an innocent purchaser, he lost this defense to liability because of his actions at the property since the time of the purchase. Specifically, Chicagoland argues that the manner in which Levy's monitoring wells were installed and the nature of the hydrogeology of the sites suggests that contaminants may have spread as a result of Levy's testing activities. Therefore, Chicagoland argues, Levy cannot allege he took all "due care with respect to the hazardous substances concerned." Chicagoland's argument is based upon speculation contained in the affidavit of Joseph Adams, an environmental engineer. Adams speculates that exploratory borings by Levy's hired consultants "may have moved the contaminants to a lower sub-surface strata than where some of the original contamination was located." Adams Aff. at P 6. Levy has filed a motion to strike portions of the Adams affidavit, including the portion relied upon by Chicagoland. Because Levy's motion for summary judgment will be denied based upon the factual issues involving "all appropriate inquiry", Chicagoland's speculative exacerbation argument need not be addressed and Levy's motion to strike will be denied as moot.

* * *

Notes

1. Defining "all appropriate inquiry." An audit designed to satisfy the innocent purchaser defense is the minimum audit which a prospective purchaser should conduct in order to determine the potential environmental problems of a property or business to be purchased. Similarly, an audit designed to (1) allow a prospective Seller to establish an environmental baseline prior to sale or (2) ensure that the Seller's representations and warranties to the Buyer are in fact truthful will probably go well beyond the scope of the innocent purchaser defense. The scope of these additional audit procedures will vary depending upon the present and past usages of the property and the practices of the business to be sold. Thus, additional state and federal environmental statutes and common law should be considered when designing an environmental audit. Although these laws would not effect the availability of the "innocent purchaser defense," depending on the circumstances one or more of these statutes may be important in establishing baseline or determining market value.

2. The Duty To Disclose Under CERCLA. It should be noted that CERCLA imposes liability on past owners who acquired actual knowledge of a release or a threatened release during ownership and subsequently transferred ownership to another person without disclosing such knowledge. CERCLA § 101(35)(C). Thus, past owners (or current owners about to sell their property) who did not own during disposal, and would not otherwise be liable under § 107(a), may be held liable as current owners or operators under § 107(a)(1) if they failed to disclose to the purchaser any knowledge of contamination.

§ 6.5　STATUTORY EXCLUSIONS

In addition to the express statutory exemptions in CERCLA, there are certain statutory exemptions from CERCLA liability. These include:

- the secured creditor exemption;
- the petroleum exclusion;
- the consumer product exemption; and
- the pesticide exclusion.

1.　*The Secured Creditor Exemption*

The secured creditor exemption protects lenders who, without participating in the management of their debtor, hold indicia of ownership primarily to protect a security interest. This exemption was carved out to protect banks that held legal title to land in title theory states. Since lenders in such states are actual owners of the property, Congress wanted to clarify that this type of ownership alone would not give rise to CERCLA liability. Recent cases, upholding the secured creditor exemption include *Northeast Doran, Inc. v. Key Bank of Maine*, 15 F.3d 1 (1st Cir.1994), which held that mortgagee that promptly divests itself of title property is deemed to have held it only as security interest for a mortgage was protected by the exemption. Similarly, in *Kemp Industries v. Safety Light Corp.*, 857 F.Supp. 373 (D.N.J.1994), the prior titleholder who financed a construction project through a sale leaseback was held to be protected by the exemption. In *North Carolina v. W.R. Peele, Sr. Trust,* the court held that the secured creditor exemption does not pertain to property held in trust and that a CERCLA action could be maintained against a trust. This exemption will discussed in greater detail under the sub-part discussing lender liability under CERCLA.

2.　*The Consumer Product Exemption*

The statutory definition of facility under CERCLA excludes a "consumer product in consumer use." This exclusion has been termed the "consumer products exclusion." For example, applying this exclusion courts have held that CERCLA does not apply to asbestos that is incorporated into walls and ceilings of buildings. Certain courts have found the exclusion limited. "The exception is for facilities that are consumer products in consumer use, not for consumer products contained in facilities."

The legislative history reinforces ... that Congress intended to provide recovery only for releases or threatened releases from inactive and abandoned waste sites, not releases from useful consumer products in the structure of buildings. The sale of asbestos-containing products for useful consumption is not the "arranging for disposal" of a hazardous substance at a "facility", Section 107(a) of CERCLA, that the statute is designed to combat.

AMCAST INDUSTRIAL CORP. v. DETREX CORP.

2 F.3d 746 (7th Cir.1993).

POSNER, CIRCUIT JUDGE.

This appeal requires us to explore the outer limits of the "Superfund" statute—the Comprehensive Environmental Response, Compensation and Liability Act (CERCLA), 42 U.S.C. §§ 9601 et seq. We must decide whether, as the district court concluded, the Act extends to any chemical spill that creates an environmental hazard. This is an important question that has not until now been the subject of an appellate case. Our conclusion is that the spiller, but not the shipper of the chemical that spilled, is within the Act's long reach.

The facts are simple enough, and we shall make them even simpler where we can do so without affecting the analysis. The principal plaintiff, Elkhart (Amcast is its parent, and can be ignored), manufactures copper fittings at a plant in Indiana. One of the chemicals that it uses in the manufacturing process is the solvent trichloroethylene (TCE). Elkhart used to buy TCE in liquid form from a number of chemical manufacturers, including the defendant, Detrex. Detrex sometimes delivered the solvent in its own tanker trucks and sometimes hired a common carrier, Transport Services, to deliver it. In 1984, TCE was discovered in the groundwater beneath a pharmaceutical plant adjacent to Elkhart's plant. There is evidence that both Detrex's and Transport Services' drivers sometimes spilled TCE accidentally on Elkhart's premises while trying to fill Elkhart's storage tanks and that some of this spillage found its way into the groundwater beneath the pharmaceutical plant, although an expert hired by Detrex has estimated that out of almost 800 gallons of TCE that have been found in the soil and groundwater beneath the pharmaceutical plant, no more than 49 came from these delivery spills, the rest having leaked from the storage tanks or a waste-disposal pit or the plant itself or been spilled by other suppliers' drivers.

The Superfund statute, so far as bears on this case, imposes liability for "response costs" (the costs of eliminating an environmental hazard) on the "owner and operator of a ... facility" from which a hazardous substance has been released, § 9607(a)(1), and on "any person who by contract ... arranged for disposal or treatment, or arranged with a transporter for transport for disposal or treatment, of hazardous substances owned or possessed by such person." § 9607(a)(3). "Facility" is broadly defined as "(A) any building, structure, installation, equipment, pipe or pipeline . . ., well, pit, pond, lagoon, impoundment, ditch, landfill, storage container, motor vehicle, rolling stock, or aircraft, or (B) any site or area where a hazardous substance has been deposited, stored, disposed of, or placed, or otherwise come to be located." § 9601(9). Elkhart is admittedly a "responsible person," as an entity liable for response costs is called; but the statute permits one responsible person to recover all or part of its response costs from another. § 9607(a)(4)(B). Having spent more than $1 million on cleaning up the contamination caused by the spillage of TCE from its facility, Elkhart brought this suit to establish that Detrex was a responsible person, too, and to shift Elkhart's response costs (that is, the $1 million it had incurred in cleaning up the contamination) from itself to Detrex.

A potentially responsible person who, like Detrex, has been sued is entitled to seek, by way of counterclaim, contribution from the plaintiff for the amount of response costs fairly attributable to the conduct of the plaintiff as distinct from that of the defendant. § 9613(f). Rather than file a counterclaim against Elkhart, Detrex argued to the district judge that in the course of adjudicating Elkhart's claim he had to apportion responsibility for the costs between the parties. The judge rejected this argument, together with Detrex's more fundamental argument that it is not a responsible person within the meaning of the statute, and entered judgment in favor of Elkhart for the entire response costs that Elkhart had incurred. Eventually Detrex filed a separate action for contribution from Elkhart; that suit is pending in the district court. § 9613(f)(1); *United States v. R.W. Meyer, Inc.*, 932 F.2d 568, 571 n. 2 (6th Cir.1991). Detrex was entitled to proceed in that fashion. The statute is explicit that a counterclaim for response costs is not compulsory, §§ 9613(f)(1), (g)(3)(A), a result consistent with general law. Detrex's claim against Elkhart, dependent as it was on Elkhart's establishing Detrex's liability to it, had not matured when Elkhart's suit was filed. Fed. R. Civ. P. 13(a); *Harbor Ins. Co. v. Continental Bank Corp.*, 922 F.2d 357, 360 (7th Cir.1990); 6 Charles Alan Wright, Arthur R. Miller & Mary Kay Kane, *Federal Practice and Procedure* § 1411 at p. 83 (2d ed. 1990).

The argument that the judge had to apportion liability between Detrex and Elkhart in Elkhart's suit makes no sense, so we dispatch it at the outset. The statute is clear that whoever (like Elkhart) incurs costs in cleaning up a contaminated site can seek to recover them from any responsible person, and if the responsible person believes as Detrex does that his contribution to the mess was trivial and wants the point established promptly he can counterclaim for as large a percentage of the costs as he thinks he can prove was due to the plaintiff's own conduct. *United States v. R.W. Meyer, Inc.*, *supra*, 932 F.2d at 571 n. 2; *United States v. Mexico Feed & Seed Co.*, 764 F.Supp. 565, 573 (E.D.Mo.1991), rev'd in part on other grounds, 980 F.2d 478 (8th Cir.1992). The counterclaim if promptly filed will doubtless be tried at the same time as the main claim, so the defendant will at no time be out of pocket by more than the share of the response costs attributable to his own conduct. Obviously Detrex could have counterclaimed without giving up its main argument—that it is not a responsible person and therefore is not liable for any part of the response costs. We do not know why it waited and filed a separate suit.

The difficult question is whether Detrex is within the grasp of the Superfund law at all; if not, Elkhart's suit must fail irrespective of any division of responsibilities between Elkhart and Detrex. Elkhart argues that Detrex has forfeited this ground of appeal by failing to present it to the district court. Detrex had argued to the district court on a variety of grounds that it was not liable to the plaintiff under that law, and one of these grounds was that it was not an arranger for disposal or treatment. The fact that it did not marshal in support of this ground all the relevant legislative provisions and history did not work a forfeiture. *Dawson v. General Motors Corp.*, 977 F.2d 369, 372 n. ___ (7th Cir.1992); *Locke v. Bonello*, 965 F.2d 534, 536 n. 1 (7th Cir.1992); *cf. Bellotti v. Baird*, 428 U.S. 132, 143 n. 10, 49 L.Ed.2d 844, 96 S.Ct. 2857 (1976); *but see Elder v. Holloway*, 975 F.2d 1388, 1392–93 (1991), *rehearing en banc denied*, 984 F.2d 991 (9th Cir.1993) (per curiam), *cert. granted*, 113 S.Ct. 3033, 125 L.Ed.2d 721 (1993). But Detrex tacitly conceded in the district court that it was, though not an arranger for disposal, an owner of a facility, within the meaning of the statute. Detrex thus conceded a ground that it now seeks to raise with us, that it was not an owner of a facility; and failure to have presented to the district court a ground on which reversal is being urged is a more serious matter than failing to support a ground with the arguments or authorities that the appellate court finds persuasive. The rule in civil cases is that except with regard to jurisdictional issues and issues involving comity—the mutual respect owed by sovereigns and quasi-sovereigns, such as the states—a ground not raised in the district court cannot be used to reverse that court, *Old Republic Ins. Co. v. Federal Crop Ins. Corp.*, 947 F.2d 269, 276–77 (7th Cir.1991); *Zbaraz v. Hartigan*, 763 F.2d 1532, 1544 (7th Cir.1985), *aff'd by an equally divided Court under the name Hartigan v. Zbaraz*, 484 U.S. 171, 98 L.Ed.2d 478, 108 S.Ct. 479 (1987). The Supreme Court has told us, however, that the rule is not absolute, *Singleton v. Wulff*, 428 U.S. 106, 121, 49 L.Ed.2d 826, 96 S.Ct. 2868 (1976); *see also Arcadia v. Ohio Power Co.*, 498 U.S. 73, 77, 112 L.Ed.2d 374, 111 S.Ct. 415 (1990); id. at 86 (concurring opinion); *U.S. National Bank v. Independent Insurance Agents of America, Inc.*, 124 L.Ed.2d 402, 113 S.Ct. 2173, 2178–79 (1993), a point upon which we have built in carving an exception for plain errors in civil cases. (The civil rules contain no counterpart to Rule 52(a) of the criminal rules, which allows reversal on the basis of plain errors even if they had not been drawn to the attention of the trial court.) *Deppe v. Tripp*, 863 F.2d 1356, 1362 (7th Cir.1988). Occasional flat statements in our cases that there is no plain error doctrine in civil cases, *e.g., United States v. Caputo*, 978 F.2d 972, 974 (7th Cir.1992), which puzzled the court in *Hudak v. Jepsen of Illinois*, 982 F.2d 249, 251

n. 1 (7th Cir.1992), implicitly refer to error in jury instructions, a setting to which Rule 51 of the civil rules has been interpreted to make the doctrine of plain error inapplicable. *Deppe v. Tripp, supra*, 863 F.2d at 1361–62.

Forfeiture is a sanction, and sanctions should be related to harm done or threatened. In the rare case in which failure to present a ground to the district court has caused no one—not the district judge, not us, not the appellee—any harm of which the law ought to take note, we have the power and the right to permit it to be raised for the first time to us. *Rosser v. Chrysler Corp.*, 864 F.2d 1299, 1306 n. 7 (7th Cir.1988); *Charlton v. United States*, 743 F.2d 557, 561 n. 5 (7th Cir.1984)(per curiam). This is a suitable case in which to exercise our power of lenity. The new ground is fully argued in the brief of the appellant, so that Elkhart had—and it took—a full opportunity to respond. The ground rests entirely on a pure issue of statutory interpretation, as to which the district judge's view, while it would no doubt be interesting, could have no effect on our review, which is plenary on matters of law. It is unrealistic to think that if Detrex had made the argument to the district court and prevailed, there would have been no appeal. The appeal just would have been filed by Elkhart rather than by Detrex. The issue having been fully briefed and argued, there is no reason to defer its resolution to another case. There will be no better time to resolve the issue than now.

Each of the tanker trucks owned by Detrex in which it delivered TCE to Elkhart constituted prima facie a "facility" within the meaning of the Superfund law, § 9601(9)(A), contained a hazardous substance, namely TCE, and "disposed of" it when the truck spilled it, because the statute defines disposal to include spilling. §§ 6903(3), 9601(29). The statutory definition of facility excludes, however, a "consumer product in consumer use." § 9601(9). Neither party suggests that the term "consumer product" is limited to products used by consumers as distinct from ones consumed by business firms and other institutions. *Dayton Independent School District v. U.S. Mineral Products Co.*, 906 F.2d 1059, 1065–66 (5th Cir.1990), holds, correctly in our view, that asbestos products incorporated into walls and ceilings of school buildings are consumer products within the meaning of the Superfund law. The difficult question is whether the reference to consumer product in section 9601(9), the definition of "facility," is to be read literally.

If it is read literally, the only consumer product exempted by the statute is the consumer product that is a facility. The alternative is to read the exemption as referring to facilities that contain consumer products. Under this alternative reading, as long as Elkhart was using TCE in its plant in the ordinary course, with no spills or leaks, it was not the owner of a "facility" within the meaning of the statute. The *Dayton* decision even suggests that the school buildings themselves might have been consumer products within the meaning of the statute, 906 F.2d at 1065 n. 4, and likewise Elkhart's plant, so long as it was merely manufacturing useful products and not creating hazardous wastes. That, however, would be an extraordinarily strained reading of "consumer product."

Once Elkhart finished using the TCE in its manufacturing process—once consumer use passed over into waste disposal, as happened when Elkhart dumped the used TCE into a waste-disposal pit on its premises—Elkhart became, if the statutory reference to a facility that is a consumer product is interpreted to mean a facility that contains a consumer product, a responsible person, as a facility owner no longer sheltered by the exception for consumer products in consumer use. Continuing with this interpretation of the consumer-product exception, and assuming reasonably enough that the transportation of a consumer product to the customer is as much a consumer use as the consumption of the product in the customer's manufacturing process (the trucks themselves might be thought consumer products, within the extended meaning attached to this term in the *Dayton* footnote, but we reject so strained an interpretation of the term), we would conclude that until the TCE transported in Detrex's trucks spilled, it was a consumer product in consumer use. It ceased to be in consumer use when it spilled; but the spilled TCE was no longer in the trucks or any other property owned by Detrex, and when it hit the ground it was in premises owned by Elkhart, and Elkhart thus became the facility owner and a responsible person.

This approach does excessive violence to the statutory language. The exception is for facilities that are consumer products in consumer use, not for consumer products contained in facilities. Although read as it is written the exception is narrow, it is not meaningless, for the statute defines "facility" so broadly that it could be thought to include a can of lye. Since Detrex, not Elkhart, was responsible for the environmental damage resulting from the spillage of TCE from Detrex's trucks, there is no anomaly, so far as the purpose of the Superfund statute is concerned, in deeming Detrex a responsible person along with Elkhart. A literal interpretation that furthers the statute's purpose is hard to beat.

Irrespective of the issue of consumer product and consumer use, however, Detrex was a responsible person with respect to the TCE that was spilled by trucks owned by Transport Services only if by hiring Transport Services to carry the stuff to the Elkhart plant Detrex "arranged with a transporter for transport for disposal or treatment" of TCE. § 9607(a)(3). Detrex hired a transporter, all right, but it did not hire it to spill TCE on Elkhart's premises. Although the statute defines disposal to include spilling, the critical words for present purposes are "arranged for." The words imply intentional action. The only thing that Detrex arranged for Transport Services to do was to deliver TCE to Elkhart's storage tanks. It did not arrange for spilling the stuff on the ground. No one arranges for an accident, except in the sinister sense, not involved here, of "staging" an accident—that is, causing deliberate harm but making it seem accidental.

Statutes sometimes use words in nonstandard senses, and do so without benefit of a definitional section. (The Superfund statute does not define "arrange for.") Elkhart argues that we can tell that Congress was doing that here because the provision in question speaks of "disposal" and we know that "disposal" includes accidentally spilling. But since context determines meaning, the same word can mean different things in different sentences—to monopolize a conversation doesn't mean the same thing as to monopolize the steel industry—even in the same statute, especially when the statute does not attempt to impose a single meaning by defining the word. In the context of the operator of a hazardous-waste dump, "disposal" includes accidental spillage; in the context of the shipper who is arranging for the transportation of a product, "disposal" excludes accidental spillage because you do not arrange for an accident except in the Aesopian sense illustrated by the staged accident.

The words "arranged with a transporter for transport for disposal or treatment" appear to contemplate a case in which a person or institution that wants to get rid of its hazardous wastes hires a transportation company to carry them to a disposal site. If the wastes spill en route, then since spillage is disposal and the shipper had arranged for disposal—though not in that form—the shipper is a responsible person and is therefore liable for clean-up costs. But when the shipper is not trying to arrange for the disposal of hazardous wastes, but is arranging for the delivery of a useful product, he is not a responsible person within the meaning of the statute and if a mishap occurs en route his liability is governed by other legal doctrines. It would be an extraordinary thing to make shippers strictly liable under the Superfund statute for the consequences of accidents to common carriers or other reputable transportation companies that the shippers had hired in good faith to ship their products. *Indiana Harbor Belt R.R. v. American Cyanamid Co.*, 916 F.2d 1174, 1180–81 (7th Cir.1990). The language of the statute permits but does not compel such a result, and we can find no evidence that it was intended.

This conclusion does not create a regulatory void. Apart from common law liability of transportation companies for chemical spills, noted in our *Indiana Harbor Belt R.R.* decision, there are a variety of direct regulatory controls over the transportation of hazardous substances, illustrated by the Hazardous Materials Transportation Act, 49 U.S.C. App. §§ 1801 et seq. And Elkhart was responsible for the cost of cleaning up the contamination resulting from the spillage from Transport Service's trucks if it couldn't find any other responsible persons to whom to shift that cost in whole or in part.

We conclude that Detrex was liable under the Superfund statute for the spillage from its own trucks (though it may be able to shift some of that liability back to Elkhart by means of the counterclaim) but not the spillage from the trucks of the common carrier that it hired. The judgment for Elkhart is therefore affirmed in part and reversed in part and the case remanded to the district court for further proceedings consistent with this opinion.

* * *

3. *The Pesticide Exclusion*

The pesticide exemption, provides a very limited exception to CERC-LA liability under Sec. 107 by indicating "no person ... may recover ... for any response costs or damages resulting from the application of a pesticide product registered under the Federal Insecticide, Fungicide, and Rodenticide Act." *See Jordan v. Southern Wood Piedmont Co.,* 805 F.Supp. 1575, 1581–82 (S.D.Ga.1992)(rejecting in dicta wood treatment pesticide seller's arguments that pesticides are generally excluded from CERCLA); *United States v. Hardage,* 733 F.Supp. 1424 (W.D.Okl.1989). The exclusion covers only liability for "field application" of a pesticide. This exclusion is limited to pesticide application of pesticides registered under FIFRA. This is intended to mean the use of a pesticide in accordance with its purpose. Pesticide releases, including spilling of pesticides, are covered under CERCLA. Claimants who are injured by spilling, dumping, disposal, or leaking of pesticides, whether intentional or accidental, have recourse under CERCLA and are not protected by the pesticide exemption.

4. *The Petroleum Exclusion*

CERCLA defines "hazardous substance" by reference to substances listed under various other federal statutes. CERCLA expressly excludes from its "hazardous substance" definition "petroleum, including crude oil or any fraction thereof which is not otherwise specifically listed or designated as a hazardous substance...." Both the EPA and the courts interpret the petroleum exclusion to apply to petroleum products, even if a specifically listed hazardous substance, such as Chrysene, is indigenous to such products. The petroleum exclusion in CERCLA "does apply to unrefined and refined gasoline even though certain of its indigenous components and certain additives during the refining process have themselves been designated as hazardous substances within the meaning of CERCLA." EPA interprets the petroleum exclusion to apply to materials such as crude oil, petroleum feedstocks, and refined petroleum products, even if a specifically listed or designated hazardous substance is present in such products. EPA does not, however, consider materials such as waste oil to which listed CERCLA substances have been added to be within the petroleum exclusion.

COSE v. GETTY OIL CO.

4 F.3d 700 (9th Cir.1993).

PREGERSON, CIRCUIT JUDGE:

Don A. Cose and Darlene A. Cose ("the Coses") appeal the district court's grant of summary judgment dismissing their Comprehensive Environmental Response, Compensation and Liability Act ("CERCLA"), 42 U.S.C. § 9601, action against the Getty Oil Company ("Getty Oil"), et al. The CERCLA action sought recovery for response costs needed to clean subsurface crude oil tank bottom waste discovered on property purchased from Getty Oil. The tank bottom waste contains substances deemed hazardous under CERCLA. The district court based its dismissal on its conclusion that crude oil tank bottoms fall within CERCLA's petroleum exclusion. We disagree and therefore reverse.

BACKGROUND

Getty Oil produced crude oil from wells in the Tafts–Fellow area of Kern County, California. The oil was transported by Getty to its Avon refinery in Martinez, California via a pipeline route and pumping stations located at twelve-mile intervals. The crude oil was stored at the pumping stations in tanks and heated to reduce its viscosity. The oil was then pumped farther along the pipeline.

When crude oil is stored in tanks, suspended sedimentary solids in the crude oil settle to the bottom. Because water is heavier than oil, it separates from the oil and also collects at the bottom of the tank. The bottom layer of the tank is known as basic sediment and water, or "crude oil tank bottoms." Crude oil tank bottoms are typically drained from crude oil storage facilities and disposed of in nearby sumps.

One pumping station used by Getty Oil was located in Tracy, California. The sump facility for the Tracy pumping station was situated on nearby property called the "Gravel Pit." About once a week, the crude oil tank bottoms from the Tracy pumping station storage tanks were drained and dumped in the Gravel Pit. Getty Oil closed the Tracy pumping station by 1968, when a new pipeline system on a different route rendered the Tracy station obsolete.

In May 1974, Don A. Cose purchased the Gravel Pit, a 40–acre parcel of undeveloped land, from Getty Oil ... for $50,000. The complaint alleges that when Cose purchased the property, a layer of topsoil concealed the crude oil tank bottom materials dumped on the property and hence, a reasonable inspection of the premises did not disclose the dumped materials. The Coses contend that they discovered the presence of a "subsurface asphalt or tar-like material" on the property in November 1987 when they undertook to develop the property for housing. They then commissioned Kleinfelder, Inc., a soils and environmental engineering firm, to investigate the property further. The investigation included a preliminary assessment of the chemical composition of the oily waste found on the property. Of particular concern, the investigation revealed a "high concentration" (10.5 ppm) of Chrysene, a known carcinogen. Kleinfelder Report, at 4. The concentration level of Chrysene in crude oil in the region was determined to be 28.0 ppm. The Kleinfelder report recommended that "the waste, which contains concentrations of [petroleum hydrocarbons] that are considered hazardous by many regulatory agencies, be removed or stabilized prior to development of the site." Kleinfelder Report, at 1.

Based on the results of the Kleinfelder investigation, the Coses filed suit in federal district court under CERCLA to recover "response costs" needed to clean up the Gravel Pit property.... 42 U.S.C. § 9607(a)(3).

In response, Getty Oil moved for summary judgment. In its summary judgment motion, Getty Oil contended that the Coses could not prove that Getty Oil had disposed of a "hazardous substance" on the Gravel Pit property because CERCLA excludes from its "hazardous substances" definition crude oil tank bottoms.

The district court agreed and granted summary judgment in favor of Getty Oil. This appeal followed.

* * *

Congress enacted CERCLA in 1980 "to facilitate the cleanup of leaking hazardous waste disposal sites." *Ascon Properties, Inc. v. Mobil Oil Co.*, 866 F.2d 1149, 1152 (9th Cir.1989)(citing *Exxon Corp. v. Hunt*, 475 U.S. 355, 358–60, 89 L.Ed.2d 364, 106 S.Ct. 1103 (1986)). To further this purpose, Congress created a private cause of action for certain "response costs" against various types of persons who contributed to hazardous waste dumping at a specific site. *Ascon Properties,* 866 F.2d at 1152 (citing 42 U.S.C. § 9607(a)).

To state a prima facie case under CERCLA, 42 U.S.C. § 9607(a), a plaintiff must allege that: (1) the waste disposal site is a "facility" within the meaning of 42 U.S.C. § 9601(9); (2) a "release" or "threatened release" of a "hazardous substance" from the facility has occurred, id. § 9607(a)(4); (3) such release or "threatened release" will require the expenditure of response costs that are "consistent with the national contingency plan," id. §§ 9607(a)(4) and (a)(4)(B); and, (4) the defendant falls within one of four classes of persons subject to CERCLA's liability provisions. *Id.* at §§ 9607(a)(1)-(4); *Ascon Properties,* 866 F.2d at 1152.

Here, the district court granted summary judgment in favor of the defendants because it concluded as a matter of law that crude oil tank bottoms are not "hazardous substances" under CERCLA. Hence, the court held that the Coses could not establish a prima facie case under CERCLA because they could not show that Getty Oil had released a "hazardous substance."

CERCLA defines "hazardous substance" by reference to substances listed under various other federal statutes.... *See* 40 C.F.R. § 302.4 (comprehensive listing of CERCLA hazardous substances). But § 9601(14) of CERCLA expressly excludes from its "hazardous substance" definition "petroleum, including crude oil or any fraction thereof which is not otherwise specifically listed or designated as a hazardous substance under subparagraphs (A) through (F) of [§ 9601(14)].... "

Both the EPA and our court interpret the petroleum exclusion to apply to petroleum products, even if a specifically listed hazardous substance, such as Chrysene, is indigenous to such products. *See* EPA Memorandum, July 31, 1987; *Wilshire Westwood Assoc.,* 881 F.2d 801 (leaded gasoline falls within the petroleum exclusion despite hazardous indigenous components and additives). In *Wilshire,* we analyzed the plain meaning of CERCLA, its post-enactment legislative history, and the EPA's interpretation of the statute to reach the following conclusion:

> The petroleum exclusion in CERCLA does apply to unrefined and refined gasoline even though certain of its indigenous components and certain additives during the refining process have themselves been designated as hazardous substances within the meaning of CERCLA.

881 F.2d at 810 . . .

The EPA has followed this interpretation through its rules and memoranda. As the EPA explained in a Final Rule published April 4, 1985,

> EPA interprets the petroleum exclusion to apply to materials such as crude oil, petroleum feedstocks, and refined petroleum products, even if a specifically listed or designated hazardous substance is present in such products. However, EPA does not consider materials such as waste oil to which listed CERCLA substances have been added to be within the petroleum exclusion.

50 Fed. Reg. 13,460 (April 4, 1985). . . . *See also Mid Valley Bank v. North Valley Bank*, 764 F.Supp. 1377, 1384 (E.D.Cal.1991)(waste oil containing CERCLA hazardous substances does not fall under CERCLA's petroleum exclusion); *United States v. Western Processing Co.*, 761 F.Supp. 713, 722 (W.D.Wash.1991)(tank bottom sludge does not fall within the petroleum exclusion in part because the sludge at issue contained contaminants that were not indigenous to the crude oil itself).

If a specifically listed hazardous substance is indigenous to petroleum and is present as a result of the release of petroleum, such substance will fall within the petroleum exclusion unless it is present at a concentration level that exceeds the concentration level that naturally occurs in the petroleum product. *See, e.g., State of Washington v. Time Oil Co.*, 687 F.Supp. 529, 532 (W.D.Wash.1988)(contaminants in excess of amounts that would have occurred during the oil refining process and substances that would not have occurred due to the refining process do not fall under the petroleum exclusion).

Our court has not yet addressed the question whether the separated sediment and water that constitute crude oil tank bottoms fall within CERCLA's petroleum exclusion. This is the issue that we must decide.

The Coses contend that crude oil tank bottoms are discarded waste products and not fractions of the crude oil. Hence, the Chrysene, which is part of the tank bottom material dumped at the Gravel Pit, does not fall within the petroleum exclusion. In contrast, Getty Oil contends that crude oil tank bottoms are components of the crude oil. Hence, because the concentration level of the Chrysene found in the Gravel Pit does not exceed the concentration level found in regional crude oil, the tank bottoms fall within the petroleum exclusion. We address each argument in turn.

A. *Argument that Crude Oil Tank Bottoms Are Not "Petroleum, Including Crude Oil or a Fraction Thereof" Under CERCLA, 42 U.S.C. § 9601(14)*

1. *Definition of "Fraction" and "Petroleum"*

As a starting point, we will examine the definitions of the words "fraction" and "petroleum." Our court took judicial notice of these definitions in *Wilshire Westwood Assoc. v. Atlantic Richfield*, 881 F.2d at 803. In *Wilshire*, we defined "fraction" to mean "one of several portions (as of a distillate or precipitate) separable by fractionation and consisting either of mixtures or pure chemical compounds." *Id.* (citing Webster's Third New International Dictionary Unabridged (1981)).

Likewise, in *Wilshire* we defined "petroleum" as:

> An oily flammable bituminous liquid ... that is essentially a compound mixture of hydrocarbons of different types with small amounts of other substances (as oxygen compounds, sulfur compounds, nitrogen compounds, resinous and asphaltic components, and metallic compounds) ... and that is subjected to various refining processes (a fractional distillation, cracking, catalytic reforming, hydroforming, alkylation, polymerization) for producing useful products (as gasoline, naphtha, kerosene, fuel oils, lubricants, waxes, asphalt, coke, and chemicals....)

Id. .... Crude oil tank bottoms do not fall within the plain meaning of the definition of "fraction" or "petroleum."

Crude oil tank bottoms are comprised of water and sedimentary solids that settle out of the crude oil and create a layer of waste at the bottom of the crude oil storage tanks. Such tank bottoms accumulate naturally before the crude oil even reaches the refinery. Crude oil tank bottoms are not "one of several portions separable by fractionation" of crude oil, as required by our definition of "fraction."

Likewise, crude oil tank bottoms are never "subjected to various refining processes" as required by our "petroleum" definition.... Moreover, such tank bottoms are not used "for producing useful products." Rather, as evidenced at the Gravel Pit property, the substance is simply discarded waste.

Accordingly, the definitions of "fraction" and "petroleum" as adopted by our court urge a conclusion that crude oil tank bottoms do not fall within CERCLA's exclusion of "petroleum, including crude oil or a fraction thereof."

* * *

Because we conclude that the crude oil tank bottoms here at issue are not "petroleum" and therefore not subject to CERCLA's exclusion, the Chrysene found within the Gravel Pit's environmental samples is properly viewed as an independent "hazardous substance," rather than as a component of petroleum. Liability is imposed under CERCLA regardless of the concentration of the hazardous substances present in a defendant's waste, as long as the contaminants are listed "hazardous substances" pursuant to 40 C.F.R. § 302.4(a). *See Louisiana–Pacific Corp. v. ASARCO, Inc.*, 735 F.Supp. 358, 361 (W.D.Wa.1990), aff'd 909 F.2d 1260 (9th Cir.1990). Hence, the Coses need only show the presence of Chrysene to recover cleanup costs from Getty Oil under Sections 107(a)(3) of CERCLA, 42 U.S.C. § 9607(a)(3). Because the presence of Chrysene in the Gravel Pit is undisputed, we reverse the district court's grant of summary judgment and find Getty Oil liable for cleanup costs as a matter of law.

REVERSED.

§ 6.6 THE STANDARD OF LIABILITY UNDER CERCLA

CERCLA holds any or all of the PRPs liable:

- *strictly* (that is, without regard to fault or negligence),

- in the normal case of "indivisible" injury, *jointly and severally* (that is, any one contributing PRP can be held liable for the *entire* cleanup by EPA, the state, or the private plaintiff, and is left to his own devices to subsequently collect a "fair share" from other contributing PRPs), and

- for *pre-enactment conduct* and cleanup costs as well as post-enactment conduct and cleanup costs.

Thus, an owner or operator may be liable whether or not his conduct was legal under state and federal law at the time undertaken, unless the release meets the narrow definition of a "federally permitted release." Furthermore, a PRP may be liable even if a PRP contributed only a small amount of hazardous substances to a facility, whether or not the hazardous substances contributed to the site by the PRP are the ones the release of which required cleanup, and whether or not the PRP *caused* the release of the hazardous substances actually requiring the cleanup. In short, EPA (or the state or private party cleanup plaintiff) can extract cleanup costs from any PRP or group of PRPs that they choose to sue, and those PRPs are left to use the original action or separate legal actions among themselves (or among themselves and other PRPs that they find and join or sue) to sort out, under evolving principles of "contribution" law, who ultimately bears how much of the responsibility for the cleanup costs.

§ 6.7 MECHANISMS OF SUIT

There are numerous methods by which CERCLA allows cleanup of hazardous sites. First, CERCLA grants the President of the United States broad authority to provide for the cleanup of sites contaminated by hazardous substances. Most of this authority has been delegated to EPA via the regional EPA administrators.

Second, CERCLA also authorizes the United States to use "Superfund" monies to clean up a site. The government may then recover those response costs from the parties defined under the statute as responsible for the pollution.

Third, private parties may also maintain a cause of action for recovery of cleanup "response" costs and interest from other potentially responsible parties. Section 113 of CERCLA makes clear that one held liable under Section 107 may seek contribution from others also responsible for contaminating the site. Generally, § 113(f)(1) provides a right of contribution for any party against any other party who is or may be liable for the release or threatened release of hazardous substances. This private cause of action was designed to encourage the cleanup of environmental hazards by private individuals, who then may recover the costs of the cleanup from the parties responsible for the hazard. Even if a state has an effective voluntary remediation program in place and a party has received a covenant not to sue or No Further Action Letter, that party still cannot be shielded from a federal private cause of action even if the regional EPA administrator joined into an agreement with the state through a Memorandum of Understanding (MOU)(which binds the federal government).

§ 6.8 CONTRIBUTION

Contribution is the method by which a joint tortfeasor can compel a sharing of the liability burden with other parties responsible for the hurt. In the 1986 amendments, Congress codified the right of contribution for response costs among PRPs. CERCLA § 113(f)(1) allows a party who has incurred response costs to seek contribution from any person who is liable or potentially liable under section 107. A party may bring a contribution claim during or after a CERCLA § 106 proceeding or CERCLA § 107 cost recovery action, or at any time after they have incurred response costs.

The legislative history of SARA shows that Congress did try to soften the harshness of joint and several liability by expressly allowing a cause of action for contribution. Contribution may become an issue for the current or past owner of a brownfield site where that party wants to sue others for their past relationship to the site.

The majority rule is that where the harm is indivisible (as is usually the case with cleanup of CERCLA sites) liability under CERCLA is joint and several. The burden of demonstrating divisibility is placed on the defendant, the potentially responsible party (PRP). Congress allows EPA to enter into de minimis and de micromis settlements, but this is within EPA's discretion and is beyond the defendant's control.

Certain equitable factors, especially the relative culpability of the PRPs, can be considered by a court when allocating response costs among liable parties. These factors are not legal defenses, but are equitable criteria which the court may consider in apportioning CERCLA response costs. In allocating liability, many courts the factors set forth in *United States v. A & F Materials Co.* (the so-called "Gore factors"). These are:

(i) The ability of the parties to demonstrate that their contribution to a discharge, release or disposal of a hazardous waste can be distinguished;

(ii) The amount of the hazardous waste involved;

(iii) The degree of toxicity of the hazardous waste involved;

(iv) The degree of involvement by the parties in the generation, transportation, treatment, storage, or disposal of the hazardous waste;

(v) The degree of care exercised by the parties with respect to the hazardous waste concerned, taking into account the characteristics of such waste; and

(vi) The degree of cooperation by the parties with Federal, State or local officials to prevent any harm to the public health or the environment.

Once a court determines a party is liable under CERCLA § 107(a), that party must contribute its equitable share of response costs under CERCLA § 113(f)(1). In allocating CERCLA liability, a liable party's share may range from 0% to 100% of the CERCLA liability for the Site. The first, fourth and fifth "Gore factors" require a comparison of fault and causation among the liable parties. Thus, although CERCLA is a strict liability statute, culpability is considered in equitable apportionment of multiparty Superfund sites under CERCLA § 113.

CERCLA allocation cases suggest that the remaining Gore factors are primarily utilized when there is not a glaring distinction between the fault of numerous liable parties. Certain Gore factors appear primarily relevant to allocation of liability among generators, rather than between generators and owners/operators.

CERCLA expressly reserves the rights of private parties to contractually indemnify or release one another from liability. The right to shift liability is good as between the parties to the contract. A private indemnity agreement will not effect the right of the government to sue and hold any party liable under CERCLA. The private indemnity agreement will, however, allow a party sued to join the indemnitor in any action brought by the federal government for cleanup costs.

Whether a party agreed to release the other private party from CERCLA liability is, therefore, a matter of contract interpretation. Factors which have been considered include:

(1) whether the contract language addressed CERCLA-type liabilities,

(2) whether the scope of the contractual language is so broad that it permits an

CERCLA expressly reserves the rights of private parties to contractually indemnify or release one another from liability. Whether a party agreed to release the other private party from CERCLA liability is, therefore, a matter of contract interpretation. Factors which have been considered include:

> (1) whether the contract language addressed CERCLA-type liabilities,

> (2) whether the scope of the contractual language is so broad that it permits an inference regarding assumption of future-arising liabilities,

> (3) whether the agreement pre-dated or post-dated CERCLA's enactment,

> (4) whether the parties knew of the presence of hazardous wastes on the site,

> (5) whether the clean-up issues were addressed in the parties' negotiations, and

> (6) whether separate consideration was paid for the release of liability.

Courts have not been consistent in interpreting private indemnity agreements shifting environmental liabilities. Thus, even where private parties contractually allocate liability, they can not be certain that the liability shifting provisions will be enforced by courts between the parties (or in a contribution action brought by a private third party plaintiff). Moreover, since such contractual liability shifting will have no bearing on CERCLA liability to any federal governmental action, there is no way to contractually shift the risk of litigation (even if the indemnitor ultimately pays all costs as per the contract).

UNITED STATES v. R. W. MEYER, INC.
932 F.2d 568 (6th Cir.1991).

BERTELSMAN, DISTRICT JUDGE

This appeal involved the construction of the provisions of the Comprehensive Environmental Response, Compensation, and Liability Act (CERCLA) governing contribution actions among responsible parties following a cleanup of a hazardous waste site and an Immediate Removal Action by the Environmental Protection Agency (EPA). 42 U.S.C. §§ 9607, 9613(f)(1).

* * *

"This matter stems from a suit brought by the United States against Northernaire Plating Company ("Northernaire") for recovery of its costs in conducting an 'Immediate Removal Action' pursuant to the Comprehensive Environmental Response, Compensation & Liability Act (hereinafter, "CERCLA"), 42 U.S.C. § 9601, et seq. Northernaire owned and operated a metal electroplating business in Cadillac, Michigan. Beginning in 1972, it operated under a 10–year lease on property owned by R.W. Meyer, Inc. ("Meyer"). Northernaire continued operations until mid–1981 when its assets were sold to Toplocker Enterprises, Inc.

("Toplocker"). From July of 1975 until this sale, Willard S. Garwood was the president and sole shareholder of Northernaire. He personally oversaw and managed the day-to-day operations of the company.

"Acting upon inspection reports from the Michigan Department of Natural Resources ("MDNR"), the United States Environmental Protection Agency ("EPA") conducted an Immediate Removal Action at the Northernaire site from July 5 until August 3, 1983. Cleanup of the site required neutralization of caustic acids, bulking and shipment of liquid acids, neutralization of caustic and acid sludges, excavation and removal of a contaminated sewer line, and decontamination of the inside of the building. All of the hazardous substances found at the site were chemicals and by-products of metal electroplating operations.

"In an earlier opinion and order dated May 6, 1988, this court found the defendants Garwood, Northernaire, and Meyer jointly and severally liable to plaintiff for the costs of the Immediate Removal Action under Section 107(a) of CERCLA. 42 U.S.C. § 9607(a). *United States v. Northernaire Plating Co.*, 670 F.Supp. 742 (W.D.Mich.1987). The court awarded plaintiff $268,818.25 plus prejudgment interest. The court later determined the prejudgment interest due to be $74,004.97, making the total award to plaintiff $342,823.22.

"Each defendant, (Northernaire and Garwood moving together) has brought cross-claims for contribution against the other. Currently before the court are the summary judgment motions on these cross-claims.

"CERCLA specifically allows actions for contribution among parties who have been held jointly and severally liable:

"(1) Contribution

"Any person may seek contribution from any other person who is liable or potentially liable under section 9607(a) of this title, during or following any civil action under section 9606 of this title or under section 9607(a) of this title. Such claims shall be brought in accordance with this section and the Federal Rules of Civil Procedure, and shall be governed by Federal law. In resolving contribution claims, the court may allocate response costs among liable parties using such equitable factors as the court determines are appropriate. Nothing in this sub-section shall diminish the right of any person to bring an action for contribution in the absence of a civil action under section 9606 or section 9607 of this title.

"42 U.S.C. 9613(f)(1)."

Joint App., at 414–16.

* * *

Apparently, the parties allowed the building to degenerate into a true environmental disaster area. As this court observed in the former appeal:

"In March 1983, officials from the EPA and the Michigan Department of Natural Resources (MDNR) examined the property. Their examination was prompted by earlier reports of MDNR officials indicating that the building had been locked and abandoned and that a child had received chemical burns from playing around discarded drums of electroplating waste that were left outside the building. State tests on samples of the soil, sludge, and drum contents disclosed the presence of significant amounts of caustic and corrosive materials. During their examination of the site, EPA and MDNR officials observed drums and tanks housing cyanide littered among disarray outside the facility. Based on their observations outside the building, the officials determined that Northernaire had discharged its electroplating waste into a "catch" basin and that the waste had seeped into the ground from the bottom of the basin. The waste then entered a pipe that drained into a sewer line that discharged into the sewage treatment plant for the city of Cadillac."

Meyer, 889 F.2d at 1498–99 (footnote omitted).

In the former appeal, this court affirmed the decision of the trial court finding that the damage to the site had been "indivisible" and imposing joint and several liability on the present parties to reimburse the EPA for the removal costs for the cleanup of the building. . . .

The total cost of the cleanup plus prejudgment interest was $342,-823.22. In this subsequent contribution action, the trial court held that two-thirds of the liability should be borne by Northernaire and its principal shareholder, each contributing one-third each. But the court held that the remaining one-third ($114,274.41) should be borne by the appellant property owner.

The appellant attacks this apportionment, arguing strenuously that its responsibility should be limited to an amount apportioned according to the degree that the sewer line mentioned in the above quote contributed to the cleanup costs. Applying this approach, the appellant generously offers to pay $1,709.03. Appellees accept the trial court's apportionment.

The appellant also quibbles about certain statements made by the trial court in its opinion, stating that some facts recited were not supported by the record.

ANALYSIS

The trial court held that it was within its discretion to apply certain factors found in the legislative history of CERCLA in making its contribution apportionment. Although these factors were originally intended as criteria for deciding whether a party could establish a right to an apportionment of several liability in the EPA's initial removal action, the trial court found "these criteria useful in determining the proportionate share each party is entitled to in contribution from the other." Joint App., at 417.

The criteria mentioned are:

"(1) the ability of the parties to demonstrate that their contribution to a discharge release or disposal of a hazardous waste can be distinguished;

"(2) the amount of the hazardous waste involved;

"(3) the degree of toxicity of the hazardous waste involved;

"(4) the degree of involvement by the parties in the generation, transportation, treatment, storage, or disposal of the hazardous waste;

"(5) the degree of care exercised by the parties with respect to the hazardous waste concerned, taking into account the characteristics of such hazardous waste; and

"(6) the degree of cooperation by the parties with Federal, State, or local officials to prevent any harm to the public health or the environment."

Id. (citing *Amoco Oil Co. v. Dingwell*, 690 F.Supp. 78, 86 (D.Me.1988), aff'd sub nom. *Travelers Indemnity Co. v. Dingwell*, 884 F.2d 629 (1st Cir.1989); *United States v. A & F Materials Co.*, Inc., 578 F.Supp. 1249 (S.D.Ill.1984); H.R. No. 253 (III), 99th Cong., 2d Sess. 19, (1985), reprinted in 1986 U.S. Code Cong. & Admin. News 3038, 3042).

The trial court recognized that the lessee was the primary actor in allowing this site to become contaminated. (Appellant argues that the lessee was the only actor.) The trial court found, however, that in addition to constructing the defective sewer line which contributed to the contamination, appellant bore significant responsibility "simply by virtue of being the landowner." *Id.* at 418. The trial court observed further that appellant "neither assisted nor cooperated with the EPA officials during their investigation and eventual cleanup of the ... site." *Id.*

Chief Judge Hillman concluded, "As it is well within the province of this court, I have balanced each of the defendants' behavior with respect to the equitable guidelines discussed." *Id.* at 421. As a result of the balancing, he made the apportionment described above.

The trial judge was well within the broad discretion afforded by the statute in making the apportionment he did.

Congress intended to invest the district courts with this discretion in making CERCLA contribution allocations when it provided, "the court may allocate response costs among the liable parties using such equitable factors as the court determines are appropriate." 42 U.S.C. § 9613(f)(1)....

Essentially, appellant argues here that a narrow, technical construction must be given to the term "contribution," so that, as in common law contribution, contribution under the statute is limited to the percentage a party's improper conduct causally contributed to the toxicity of the site in a physical sense. This argument is without merit. On the contrary, by using the term "equitable factors" Congress intended to invoke the tradition of equity under which the court must construct a flexible decree balancing all the equities in the light of the totality of the circumstances. . . .

"It is well established that flexibility is proper in the successful shaping . . . of an equitable decree. *Swann v. Charlotte–Mecklenburg Board of Education*, 402 U.S. 1, 15, 91 S.Ct. 1267, 1275, 28 L.Ed.2d 554 reh'g denied 403 U.S. 1912 [912], 91 S.Ct. 2200, 29 L.Ed.2d 689 (1971); *United States v. City of Parma*, 661 F.2d 562, 563, 576 (6th Cir.1981)." . . .

In a highly persuasive decision, *Charles v. Charles*, 788 F.2d 960, 965 (3d Cir.1986), the court held that a Virgin Islands statute directing courts to consider the "equity of the case" in allocating marital property required the trial court to consider marital fault. The court observed that the statute authorized the trial court to "use a variety of means to obtain an equitable result." *Id.* at 966.

Noting the accepted definition of "equitable," the court observed:

"In this regard, Black's Law Dictionary, 482 (5th ed. 1979) defines 'equitable' as 'just'; conformable to principles of justice and right. Existing in equity; available or sustainable in equity, or upon the rules and principles of equity. 'Equity' is defined as 'justice administered according to fairness as contrasted with the strictly formulated rules of common law.' *Id.* at 484."

Id. at 965, n.13.

"The hallmark of a court of equity is its ability to frame its decree to effect a balancing of all the equities and to protect the interest of all affected by it, including the public." . . . Congress reemphasized that the trial court should invoke its moral as well as its legal sense by providing that the court use not just "equitable factors," which phrase already implies a large degree of discretion, but "such equitable factors as the court determines are appropriate." This language broadens the trial court's scope of discretion even further.

Thus, under § 9613(f)(1) the court may consider any factor it deems in the interest of justice in allocating contribution recovery. Certainly, the several factors listed by the trial court are appropriate, but as it recognized, it was not limited to them. No exhaustive list of criteria need or should be formulated. However, in addition to the criteria listed above, the court may consider the state of mind of the parties, their economic status, any contracts between them bearing on the subject, any traditional equitable defenses as mitigating factors . . . and any other factors deemed appropriate to balance the equities in the totality of the circumstances.

Therefore, the trial court quite properly considered here not only the appellant's contribution to the toxic slough described above in a technical causative sense, but also its moral contribution as the owner of the site. Review of the trial court's equitable balancing process is limited to a review for "abuse of discretion." . . . This is in accord with the principle of equity that the chancellor has broad discretion to frame a decree. . . .

This case, even though it involves over $300,000, is but a pimple on the elephantine carcass of the CERCLA litigation now making its way through the court system. Some of these cases involve millions or even billions of dollars in cleanup costs and hundreds or even thousands of potentially responsible parties.

I do not believe Congress intended to require meticulous findings of the precise causative contribution each of several hundred parties made to a hazardous site. In many cases, this would be literally impossible. . . . Rather, by the expansive language used in § 9613(f)(1) Congress intended the court to deal with these situations by creative means, considering all the equities and balancing them in the interests of justice. As recognized by a recent comprehensive scholarly article, this multi-factor approach takes into account more varying circumstances than common law contribution. . . .

"Courts are also following CERCLA Section 113(f) and taking 'equitable factors' into account in apportioning liability for response costs. The equitable factors which courts are examining in order to decide what kind of apportionment to make depend on the actual facts of each case. Nevertheless, many federal courts do consider common law equitable defenses such as unclean hands and caveat emptor as mitigating factors in deciding liability for response costs. This approach is in line with Congressional intent as long as courts do not consider these equitable defenses to be a total bar to a liability action, but merely mitigating factors in awarding damages. Courts are also using a modified comparative fault analysis that takes numerous factors such as culpability and cooperation into account in apportioning damages." . . .

Although such an approach "cannot be applied with mathematical precision, it is the fairest and most workable approach for apportioning CERCLA liability. . . . Such an approach furthers the legislative intent of encouraging the prompt cleanup of hazardous sites by those equitably responsible. . . . The parties actually performing the cleanup can look for reimbursement from other potentially responsible parties without fear that their contribution actions will be bogged down by the impossibility of making meticulous factual determinations as to the causal contribution of each party." Chief Judge Hillman was well within the equitable discretion afforded him by Congress in the way he handled this CERCLA contribution action.

AFFIRMED.

RALPH B. GUY, JR., CIRCUIT JUDGE, concurring.

Although I concur in the result reached by Judge Bertelsman, I write separately because this area of the law is both new and complex. In many, if not most, of these cases arising under CERCLA, multi-party liability will be involved. Unfortunately, for the parties as well as the courts, the sorting out of responsibility is not an easy task. I view this particular case as a close one, and want to set forth in more detail my reasons for concurrence.

* * *

UNITED STATES v. ALCAN ALUMINUM CORP.
990 F.2d 711 (2d Cir.1993).

CARDAMONE, Circuit Judge:

Alcan Aluminum Corporation (Alcan) and Cornell University appeal from an order of the United States District Court for the Northern District of New York, (McAvoy, J.), granting summary judgment in favor of appellees, United States and New York State, holding Alcan jointly and severally liable for cleanup of a hazardous waste site, and allowing Alcan to obtain contribution from Cornell. *United States v. Alcan Aluminum Corp.*, 755 F.Supp. 531 (N.D.N.Y.1991).

Alcan and a host of amicus briefs have presented us with a parade of horribles predicated on their view that under the district court opinion, hazardous substances include breakfast cereal, the soil, and nearly everything else upon which life depends, and that such an approach will make liable for response costs the butcher, the baker and the candlestick maker. They posit that to avoid such an absurd result, liability under the Comprehensive Environmental Response, Compensation and Liability Act of 1980 (CERCLA), 42 U.S.C. §§ 9601 et seq. (1988, Supp. I 1989 & Supp. II 1990), should not be imposed unless a responsible party has contributed some minimum concentration of a hazardous element or compound.

Admittedly, there is some force to this argument; yet, the government's response is also compelling. It notes that were we to limit liability in the manner Alcan and amici suggest, each potential defendant in a multi-defendant CERCLA case would be able to escape liability simply by relying on the low concentration of hazardous substances in its wastes, and the government would be left to absorb the clean-up costs. Several courts have already held such was not the aim of Congress.

In passing CERCLA Congress faced the unenviable choice of enacting a legislative scheme that would be somewhat unfair to generators of hazardous substances or one that would unfairly burden the taxpaying public. The financial burdens of toxic clean-up had been vastly underestimated—in 1980 when CERCLA was enacted $1.8 billion was thought to be enough. In 1986 when the Superfund Amendments and Reauthorization Act of 1986 (SARA), Pub. L. No. 99–499, 100 Stat. 1613 (1986), was passed, $100 billion was held to be needed. It may well be more today. It is of course the public-at-large that is already bearing the economic brunt of this enormous national problem. There may be unfairness in the legislative plan, but we think Congress imposed responsibility on generators of hazardous substances advisedly. And, even were it not advisedly, we still must take this statute as it is.

Having assessed CERCLA's plain meaning, its legislative history, and the case law construing it, we think the tension may be resolved by allowing a responsible party, like Alcan, to pay nothing if it can demonstrate that its pollutants, when mixed with other hazardous wastes, did not contribute to the release or the resulting response costs. In this respect we essentially adopt the Third Circuit's reasoning in *United States v. Alcan Aluminum Corp.*, 964 F.2d 252, 267–71 (3d Cir.1992)(Alcan–Butler). This approach is not intended to provide an escape hatch for CERCLA defendants; rather, it will permit such a defendant to avoid liability only when its pollutants contribute no more than background contamination.

BACKGROUND

A. Facts

From 1970 to 1977 Pollution Abatement Services (PAS) operated a waste disposal and treatment center on 15 acres of land in Oswego County, New York. The PAS facility there stored, processed, and disposed of chemical wastes from a number of sources; as a result the site became contaminated with hazardous substances. In 1977 the Environmental Protection Agency (EPA) and New York State undertook response and clean-up measures and spent over $12 million in the ensuing ten years on remedial actions.

Alcan used PAS during the 1970s and arranged for disposal or treatment there of 4.6 million gallons of oil emulsion. This emulsion— used in Alcan's manufacturing process—consisted mostly of water and mineral oil, along with small aluminum ingot shavings containing lead, copper, chromium, zinc, and cadmium compounds.

In 1974, a stock-pile of coal caught fire at Cornell University's Ithaca, New York campus. The local fire department extinguished it with water, and some of the run-off from the coal pile flowed into area streams. After consultation with New York environmental officials, Cornell collected this coal run-off water and neutralized it. For two years following the fire, Cornell sent 551,000 gallons of the neutralized run-off water to the Oswego PAS site. When in 1983 Cornell was notified of hazardous waste problems at the PAS site, it explained to the EPA what waste it had sent there for disposal. In March 1986 Cornell purportedly resolved any question of its liability with the EPA, which thereupon removed the University from its list of those parties potentially responsible for response costs at PAS.

* * *

II. LIABILITY UNDER CERCLA

A. Chronology

Before entering upon an analysis of the merits of this appeal it will be helpful to set forth an overview of CERCLA. In bringing an action under this Act, the government must establish that: (1) defendant is one of the four categories of covered persons listed under § 9607(a) as liable for the costs of remedial action, (2) the site of the clean-up is a facility under § 9601(9), (3) there is a release or threatened release of hazardous substances at the facility, (4) as a result of which plaintiff has incurred response costs, and (5) the costs incurred conform to the national contingency plan under § 9607(a)(4)(A) as administered by the EPA. *See B.F. Goodrich Co. v. Murtha*, 958 F.2d 1192, 1198 (2d Cir.1992). If the government establishes each of these elements on undisputed facts, and the defendant is unable to demonstrate by a preponderance of the evidence the existence of one of the three affirmative defenses set forth in § 9607(b), then plaintiff is entitled to summary judgment on the issue of liability, even when genuine issues of material fact remain as to appropriate damages. *See Amoco Oil Co. v. Borden, Inc.*, 889 F.2d 664, 668 (5th Cir.1989).

Liability may be decided first before the more complicated questions implicated in clean-up measures, which includes fixing the proportionate fault of liable parties. *Id.* at 667. Bifurcation and summary judgment provide powerful legal tools which, by effectively isolating the issues to be resolved, avoid lengthy and perhaps needless litigation. The existence of those procedural tools aids Congress' purpose by encouraging settlement discussions and speeding up remedial action. *See* id. at 668.

B.   Liability Issues

Alcan attempts to interpose a number of additional defenses to prevent the imposition of liability. It argues that a polluter should not be held liable unless: a) the concentration of hazardous substances in its wastes exceeds some minimum threshold; b) its wastes fall within certain EPA reporting requirements; and c) its wastes caused the government to incur response costs. Under the present reading of CERCLA none of these issues may be considered in imposing liability.

1.   Quantitative Thresholds for Hazardous Substances

CERCLA § 9601(14) defines "hazardous substance" by cross-referencing several other environmental statutes. The term includes: "(A) any substance" designated under the Clean Water Act, "(B) any element, compound, mixture, solution, or substance" under CERCLA § 9602, "(C) any hazardous waste" listed in § 3001 of the Solid Waste Disposal Act, "(D) any toxic pollutant" listed in § 307(A) of the Clean Water Act, "(E) any hazardous air pollutant listed under" § 112 of the Clean Air Act, and "(F) any imminently hazardous chemical substance or mixture" with respect to which the EPA has taken action. 42 U.S.C. § 9601 (14).... The statute on its face applies to "any" hazardous substance, and it does not impose quantitative requirements.

The breadth of § 9601(14) cannot be easily escaped, and we have expressly held that "quantity or concentration is not a factor." *Murtha*, 958 F.2d at 1200; *accord Alcan–Butler*, 964 F.2d at 259–61. We have also reasoned that "when Congress wanted to draw distinctions based on concentration or quantity, it expressly provided as much." *Murtha*, 958 F.2d at 1200; *accord Alcan–Butler*, 964 F.2d at 261 (same). The absence of such quantity requirements in CERCLA leads inevitably to the conclusion that Congress planned for the "hazardous substance" definition to include even minimal amounts of pollution. *See Eagle–Picher Indus., Inc. v. United States E.P.A.*, 245 U.S.App.D.C. 196, 759 F.2d 922, 927–28 (D.C.Cir.1985).

2. *EPA Definition of Hazardous Substances Under CERCLA*

Pursuant to § 9602(a), the EPA has designated certain substances as hazardous in 40 C.F.R. § 302.4 (1992) and the accompanying table. This regulation sets out broad headings of elements, within which are established specific reportable quantities ("RQs") of substances and chemical abstracts service registry numbers ("CASRNs"). Alcan admits that the elements in its oil emulsion fall within the broad categories listed by the EPA, but it notes that these elements are not given RQs and CASRNs. Thus, it argues that these elements should not be classified as hazardous under CERCLA, as all hazardous elements must have RQs and CASRNs. According to Alcan, a contrary interpretation renders the EPA regulation meaningless.

We need not dwell long on this argument. Besides the district court in this case, see *Alcan*, 755 F.Supp. at 538, two other courts have assessed and rejected this proposition. *See Alcan–Butler*, 964 F.2d at 262–63; *City of New York v. Exxon Corp.*, 766 F.Supp. 177, 181–83 (S.D.N.Y.1991)(also involving Alcan). Each of these courts has essentially determined that the RQs and CASRNs are irrelevant for CERCLA liability purposes. The EPA draws a vital distinction that makes this plain: RQs and CASRNs only go to reporting requirements, they do not address the issue of CERCLA liability. *See Exxon*, 766 F.Supp. at 182–83 (citing and quoting EPA interpretation in 50 Fed.Reg. 13,456, 13,461, 13,472–73 (April 5, 1985)). We believe this reasoning correct and therefore adopt it.

3. *Causation Under Cercla*

CERCLA § 9607(a) imposes strict liability on "any person who by contract, agreement, or otherwise arranged for disposal or treatment" of hazardous substances "from which there is a release, or a threatened release which causes the incurrence of response costs." § 9607(a)(3) and (4). The plain meaning of this language dictates that the government need only prove: (1) there was a release or threatened release, which (2) caused incurrence of response costs, and (3) that the defendant generated hazardous waste at the clean-up site. What is not required is that the government show that a specific defendant's waste caused incurrence of clean-up costs.

As earlier noted, there are "only" three defenses to imposition of liability on a generator: an act of God, an act of war, and an act or omission of a third party. 42 U.S.C. § 9607(b). In *State of New York v. Shore Realty Corp.*, 759 F.2d 1032, 1044 (2d Cir.1985), we held that the owner of a facility was liable under CERCLA without a finding of causation of the release because "including a causation requirement makes superfluous the affirmative defenses provided in section 9607(b)." *Id.* Our reading drew additional support from CERCLA's legislative history, from which we concluded that "Congress specifically rejected including a causation requirement" in this section. *Id.* Other circuits have reached the same conclusion. *See Alcan–Butler,* 964 F.2d at 265; *Dedham Water Co. v. Cumberland Farms Dairy, Inc.,* 889 F.2d 1146, 1152–54 (1st Cir.1989); *United States v. Monsanto Co.,* 858 F.2d 160, 170 (4th Cir.1988), cert. denied, 490 U.S. 1106, 104 L.Ed.2d 1019, 109 S.Ct. 3156 (1989). Hence, it seems plain that in addition to imposing a strict liability scheme, CERCLA does away with a causation requirement.

Alcan argues to the contrary, primarily relying upon the Fifth Circuit's decision in *Amoco Oil Co.,* 889 F.2d at 670, which it interprets as establishing a causal nexus requirement. Alcan further presses that in order for a causal connection to exist, there must be levels of hazardous substance above ambient or background. The Third Circuit assessed and rejected this assertion, noting that the Fifth Circuit did not hold that the factual inquiry concerning whether a release has caused response costs would implicate whether an alleged polluter's waste caused response costs. *Alcan–Butler,* 964 F.2d at 266. We agree with the Third Circuit that Amoco Oil is distinguishable.

III.   DIVISIBILITY

A.   *General Principles*

Having rejected Alcan's proffered defenses to liability, one would suppose there is no limit to the scope of CERCLA liability. To avoid such a harsh result courts have added a common law gloss onto the statutory framework. They have at once adopted a scheme of joint and several liability but at the same time have limited somewhat the availability of such liability against multiple defendants charged with adding hazardous substances to a Superfund site. *See, e.g., O'Neil v. Picillo,* 883 F.2d 176, 178–79 (1st Cir.1989), cert. denied, 493 U.S. 1071 (1990); *United States v. Chem–Dyne Corp.,* 572 F.Supp. 802, 808 (S.D.Ohio 1983). The Restatement (Second) of Torts § 433A (1965) has been relied upon in determining whether a party should be held jointly and severally liable, for the entire cost of remediating environmental harm at the site. *See,* e.g., *Alcan–Butler,* 964 F.2d at 268–69; *O'Neil,* 883 F.2d at 178; *Monsanto,* 858 F.2d at 171–73; see also R.W. Meyer, 889 F.2d at 1506–08. Under § 433A of the Restatement where two or more joint tortfeasors act independently and cause a distinct or single harm, for which there is a reasonable basis for division according to the contribution of each, then each is liable for damages only for its own portion of the harm. In other words, the damages are apportioned. But where each tortfeasor causes a single indivisible harm, then damages are not apportioned and each is liable in damages for the entire harm.

Based on these common law principles, Alcan may escape any liability for response costs if it either succeeds in proving that its oil emulsion, when mixed with other hazardous wastes, did not contribute to the release and the clean-up costs that followed, or contributed at most to only a divisible portion of the harm. *See Alcan–Butler,* 964 F.2d at 270. Alcan as the polluter bears the ultimate burden of establishing a reasonable basis for apportioning liability. *See Monsanto,* 858 F.2d at 172; *Chem–Dyne,* 572 F.Supp. at 810. The government has no burden of proof with respect to what caused the release of hazardous waste and triggered response costs. It is the defendant that bears that burden. To defeat the government's motion for summary judgment on the issue of divisibility, Alcan need only show that there are genuine issues of material fact regarding a reasonable basis for apportionment of liability. As other courts have noted, apportionment itself is an intensely factual determination. *See, e.g., Chem–Dyne,* 572 F.Supp. at 811.

In so ruling we candidly admit that causation is being brought back into the case—through the backdoor, after being denied entry at the frontdoor—at the apportionment stage. We hasten to add nonetheless that causation—with the burden on defendant—is reintroduced only to permit a defendant to escape payment where its pollutants did not contribute more than background contamination and also cannot concentrate. To state this standard in other words, we adopt a special exception to the usual absence of a causation requirement, but the exception is applicable only to claims, like Alcan's, where background levels are not exceeded. And, we recognize this limited exception only in the absence of any EPA thresholds.

Contrary to the government's position, commingling is not synonymous with indivisible harm, and Alcan should have the opportunity to show that the harm caused at PAS was capable of reasonable apportionment. It may present evidence relevant to establishing divisibility of harm, such as, proof disclosing the relative toxicity, migratory potential, degree of migration, and synergistic capacities of the hazardous substances at the site. *See Alcan–Butler,* 964 F.2d at 270 n.29, 271; *Monsanto,* 858 F.2d at 172 n.26.

Alcan declares that the response actions at PAS were attributable to substances such as PCB's, nitro benzene, phenol, dichlonoethone, toluene, and benzene. It contends that no soil contamination due to heavy metals was found there, and insists that the metallic constituents of its oil emulsion are insoluble compounds, submitting an affidavit supporting this theory of divisibility. The government submitted a declaration stating that metal contaminants like those found in Alcan's waste emulsion were present in environmental media at PAS, that the commingling of metallic and organic hazardous substances resulted in indivisible harm, and that though some forms of lead, cadmium and chromium are insoluble, they may chemically react with other substances and become water-soluble. These differing contentions supported by expert affidavits raise sufficient questions of fact to preclude the granting of summary judgment on the divisibility issue.

B. Timing of the Divisibility Issue

The Third Circuit concluded that a divisibility inquiry is one "best resolved at the initial liability phase" because it involves "relative degrees of liability." *See Alcan–Butler,* 964 F.2d at 270, n.29 (emphasis in original). Although we prefer this common sense approach, it may be contrary to the statutory dictates of CERCLA. In *Shore Realty Corp.,* 759 F.2d at 1032, we reviewed CERCLA's language and legislative history and concluded that the federal government through the EPA responds to releases or threatened releases of hazardous substances immediately and later attempts to collect the remediation costs from others. *See* id. at 1041. We also determined, as previously stated, that importing a causation requirement into the strict liability of § 9607(a) would render the affirmative defenses in § 9607(b) superfluous. *Id.* at 1044–45. Legislative support for that view is found in House Report No. 96–1016's statement of the purpose of the original bill. It envisioned that the EPA would "pursue rapid recovery of the costs" incurred in clean-up. H.R. Rep. No. 96–1016, 96th Cong., 2d Sess. 17, reprinted in 1980 U.S.C.C.A.N. 6119, 6120.

A similar review of the legislative history of CERCLA and the SARA amendments of 1986 was undertaken in *Murtha,* which construes the Act and its amendments to enable the EPA to respond "efficiently and expeditiously" to environmental threats and to hold the parties responsible liable for the cleanup costs in an action by the EPA to recoup them. *See Murtha,* 958 F.2d at 1198. In those cases where this burden of recoupment costs is unfair or disproportionate, such may be alleviated under § 9613(f)(1) after the response costs are fixed. *Id.* at 1206. Again, we are told in the Judicial Review portion of House Report No. 99–253(I) that "to avoid delay of cleanups and to minimize litigation, responsible parties would be allowed to challenge the cleanup remedy after acknowledging liability for the hazardous waste site." H.R. Rep. No. 99–253(I), 99th Cong., 2d Sess. 59, reprinted in 1986 U.S.C.C.A.N. 2835, 2841.... The administrator of the EPA, who was primarily responsible for drafting the SARA amendments, at the time of their enactment declared they would "expedite civil actions by requiring that separate suits be brought against other potentially liable parties for contribution after judgment or settlement in enforcement actions." *Id.* at 124, 1986 U.S.C.C.A.N. at 2906....

Consequently, the language of CERCLA and SARA and their legislative histories appear to demonstrate the following chronology: liability is fixed first and immediately for enforcement purposes; litigation later to sort out what contribution is owed and by whom as a result of the remediation effort. But we do not rule that this chronology be followed or that the *Alcan–Butler* approach of deciding divisibility at the initial liability phase of the case is the best way for the district court to proceed. Instead, the choice as to when to address divisibility and apportionment are questions best left to the sound discretion of the trial court in the handling of an individual case.

IV. CORNELL

A. Potentially Liable Party Under Cercla

Cornell believes it should be shielded from liability for contribution by virtue of having resolved its liability to the United States and the

State of New York. We discuss first whether Cornell is a potentially liable party under CERCLA § 9607.

CERCLA § 9613(f)(1) provides that "any person may seek contribution from any other person who is liable or potentially liable under section [9607(a)]." § 9613(f)(1). Of the four classes of individuals subject to liability under § 9607(a), Cornell submits that only the third—any person who by contract, agreement or otherwise arranged for disposal or treatment of hazardous substances—is relevant because it contracted to have its coal run-off sent to PAS. But, it continues, because the EPA removed the University from the list of those potentially responsible parties, a fortiori, it may not be a potentially liable party under § 9607(a). Alcan responds that Cornell's coal waste water was essentially the same as Alcan's oil emulsion, and that there is no principled basis under the statute for treating Cornell differently.

The statutory language imposes liability and contribution upon "any person" who arranges for disposal of waste at a facility. Under the plain meaning of this language it is difficult to see how Cornell could avoid being included. Cornell points to no cases that in fact have drawn the distinction it urges us to adopt. Hence, Cornell is a potentially liable party under § 9607(a)(3).

B. Retroactive Application of Sara

Cornell was removed by the EPA in March 1986 from the list of potentially responsible parties before the SARA amendments' proceedings for contribution under § 9613 became effective on October 17, 1986. Compelled contribution, in its view, could therefore only occur as a result of retroactive application of SARA.

If that statement reflected the whole matter, we would agree. There is a strong presumption against the retrospective application of a statute. It is familiar law, the Supreme Court instructs, that while judicial decisions operate retrospectively, statutes look only to the future. *See United States v. Security Indus. Bank*, 459 U.S. 70, 79, 103 S.Ct. 407, 74 L.Ed.2d 235 (1982). No law, including SARA, should be construed retrospectively unless Congress' purpose can be satisfied in no other way or unless the statutory language admits of no other meaning. *See United States Fidelity & Guar. Co. v. Struthers Wells Co.*, 209 U.S. 306, 314, 28 S.Ct. 537, 52 L.Ed. 804 (1908). Yet, in apparent conflict with this rule there is another principle: that a court should apply law existing at the time of its decision unless to do so is contrary to the plain meaning of a statute or would cause manifest injustice. *See Bradley v. Richmond Sch. Bd.*, 416 U.S. 696, 711, 94 S.Ct. 2006, 40 L.Ed.2d 476 (1974).

Fortunately, we need not choose between these conflicting precedents, *see Kaiser Aluminum & Chem. Corp. v. Bonjorno*, 494 U.S. 827, 836–37, 108 L.Ed.2d 842, 110 S.Ct. 1570 (1990), because in the case at hand the outcome is the same under either rule. *Cf. Litton Sys., Inc. v. American Tel. & Tel. Co.*, 746 F.2d 168, 170–71 (2d Cir.1984)(Bradley rule applies only to cases pending on direct appeal at time change in law occurs).

Prior to the 1986 SARA amendments to CERCLA, federal common law principles applied, and these rules did not shield Cornell from having contribution sought from it. *See United States v. Conservation Chem. Co.*, 628 F.Supp. 391, 402 (W.D.Mo.1985)(invoking 1977 Uniform Comparative Fault Act as to pre-SARA settlement). SARA's 1986 provision in § 9613(f) for a statutory cause of action for contribution codifies what had been generally held implicit under the 1980 Act. *See* H.R. Rep. No. 99–253 (I), 99th Cong., 2d Sess. 79, reprinted in 1986 U.S.C.C.A.N. 2835, 2861 (SARA "confirms" federal right of contribution under CERCLA). In that Act courts are granted implicit authority, using appropriate equitable factors, to "allocate response costs among liable parties." *O'Neil,* 883 F.2d at 179. Hence, we are not applying SARA retroactively in order to hold Cornell liable for contribution as the University asserts; rather, we are relying on common law principles that predated SARA.

C. *Required to Contribute*

The last point Cornell raises is that since it resolved its liability in an administratively approved settlement, it should be insulated from any requirement to contribute. CERCLA § 9613(f)(2) provides that a "person who has resolved its liability to the United States or a State in an administrative or judicially approved settlement shall not be liable for claims for contribution." § 9613(f)(2).

The district court thought § 9613 was inapplicable and that the EPA and Cornell did not settle any question of liability. Rather, it believed the government—employing prosecutorial discretion—simply chose not to sue Cornell. The University naturally views the situation quite differently. It asserts this is not a case of prosecutorial discretion. We are told instead that the government entered into negotiations with the University, requested and received technical studies from it, and ultimately decided not to hold it liable. This interaction, according to Cornell, constitutes an "administrative settlement."

Although this argument appears at first blush to be compelling, upon closer examination it does not carry the day. First, if the SARA amendments were to be applied retrospectively, the negotiations between Cornell and the EPA did not amount to an "administrative settlement" because those procedural steps necessary to effectuate a settlement under CERCLA § 9622 were not followed. Section 9622, which deals in part with de minimis settlements, states that a settlement "shall be entered as a consent decree or embodied in an administrative order setting forth the terms of the settlement," and where the total response costs exceed $500,000, as they do here, such an order may only be issued "with the prior written approval of the Attorney General." 42 U.S.C. § 9622(g)(4). Further settlement procedures set forth in § 9622(i)(1) include notice of such being published in the Federal Register, which concededly did not take place in the instant case. Only when these procedures are followed is a party shielded from a contribution claim.

Second, applying the SARA amendments prospectively, Cornell has not met the requirements for protection from contribution under federal common law. Under § 6 of the Uniform Comparative Fault Act, "[a] release, covenant not to sue, or similar agreement entered into by a claimant and a person liable discharges that person from all liability for contribution." *See Conservation Chem. Co.*, 628 F.Supp. at 402 (principles of 1977 Uniform Comparative Fault Act are "the most consistent with, and do the most to implement" congressional intent underlying CERCLA). The EPA merely advised Cornell that it was removing Cornell from the list of potentially responsible parties. The EPA and Cornell did not enter into a release, covenant not to sue, or any other similar, legally binding agreement.

We are satisfied therefore that the district court properly found Cornell liable or potentially liable under § 9607(a) of the Act and that federal common law rules under § 9613(f)(1) made Cornell liable to a suit for contribution. Having said this, we note that if at the directed hearing Alcan succeeds on any issue and has its contribution reduced, Cornell's share should also be reduced since it has been determined that its contribution is fixed at six percent of Alcan's. As an equitable consideration, the University should also be given an opportunity to have its waste water claim evaluated in the same light as Alcan's similar claim. If indeed, as Cornell claims, it can show that the University's wastes did not, when mixed with other wastes, contribute to the release or resultant response costs, then Cornell should succeed on this § 9604(a)(3) issue, and it would of course avoid any liability or contribution.

CONCLUSION

After careful consideration of all the other arguments raised by the parties, we find they do not need to be addressed as our opinion fully disposes of them. Accordingly, for the reasons stated the district court's amended final judgment of May 29, 1992 is affirmed, in part, and reversed, in part, and remanded for further proceedings, and the order of January 15, 1991 is also remanded for further proceedings, both consistent with this opinion.

Note

Evaluate the two *Alcan* decisions and the *Bell Petroleum* case on the CERCLA liability and allocation system. Is the judicial reliance on *The Restatement (Second) of Torts* § 443A appropriate?

§ 6.9   STAKEHOLDER LIABILITY

1. *Current Owners and Operators*

CERCLA Section 107(a)(1) provides that liability for the current "owner and operator" of a facility may be liable. Unless the landowner can successfully invoke the Section 107(b)(3) third party defense (which includes the "innocent" landowner defense, the inheritance defense and the municipal foreclosure defense), the present owner of a site may be liable under CERCLA *even if the release of the hazardous substance involved was caused entirely by a prior owner, lessee or former lessee.*

2.   Past Owners or Operators

Persons or businesses that owned land years ago are liable under Superfund for the cleanup of that land if:

- hazardous substances were disposed on the land while they owned it, or

- they learned of contamination during ownership and failed to disclose this information when the property was transferred (even if disposal did not occur their during ownership of the property).

Prior to enactment of the Superfund Amendments and Reauthorization Act ("SARA") in 1986, past owners of a site were liable under CERCLA only if waste disposal occurred while they owned the site. CERCLA Section 101(35)(C), as amended by SARA Section 101(f), however, provides that a prior owner also may be liable under Section 107(a)(1) where he acquired actual knowledge of a release or threatened release while he owned the property and subsequently "transferred ownership" to another person "without disclosure." Thus, a past owner not otherwise liable under Section 107(a) who discovers contamination during ownership must disclose the contamination to a purchaser or he will be held liable as a current owner or operator under Section 107(a)(1). Thus, a current "innocent landowner" who discovers contamination and wishes to sell finds himself faced with two undesirable alternatives: if he fails to disclose, he may be liable for cleanup costs; if he discloses, however, a prospective purchaser might insist on a lower price or may decide not to buy the property at all.

3.   The Scope of "Owner" or "Operator"

Past and present "owners" or "operators" of a contaminated site may be liable for cleanup costs and natural resource damages under CERCLA Section 107(a). The scope of the terms "owner" and/or "operator" is very broad and continues to broaden under evolving Superfund case law. Persons not obviously connected to the risk, such as passive lessors and lessees, real estate brokers, lenders, parties to project finance transactions, insurance companies, parent corporations, successor corporations, officers, shareholders, employees or other responsible corporate personnel of any of the above, may be liable as current or past "owners" and/or "operators" under Superfund.

Certain types of "owners," however, are exempt from Superfund liability, including secured creditors, innocent landowners who have no knowledge of present contamination, persons inheriting property and municipalities foreclosing on property. A great deal of litigation has arisen concerning the scope of these exclusion from liability.

4.   Successor Corporations

Superfund expressly includes corporations in the definition of "persons" subject to Superfund liability. A corporation that merges with or purchases the assets of a *present* owner or operator becomes a present owner or operator and will be strictly liable under CERCLA § 107(a)(1).

Where a corporation merges with or purchases the assets of a *past* owner or operator, the successor corporation is not automatically liable under CERCLA. Liability must be analyzed under traditional common law rules of corporate liability under which liability of a successor corporation depends on the structure of the corporate acquisition.

The traditional American corporate rule regarding successor liability is that the successor corporation is liable for all of the obligations and liabilities of its predecessor if the new corporation acquires ownership by merger, consolidation, or purchase of all the outstanding stock. Thus, a corporation that acquires another through merger or consolidation generally will acquire all of the predecessor's CERCLA liabilities, including those that arise from any assets ever owned or activities ever conducted by the predecessor (including Superfund liability for "off-site" disposal of hazardous substances) even if the assets were sold or the activities ended long before the acquisition. If the acquisition is through the sale or transfer of assets, however, the successor corporation generally does not acquire the predecessor's liabilities unless (1) the acquiring corporation expressly or impliedly agrees to assume such obligations, (2) the transaction amounts to a "de facto" consolidation or merger, (3) the purchasing corporation is merely a continuation of the selling corporation, or (4) the transaction was fraudulently entered into to escape liability. A fifth exception to the general rule is sometimes made where the transfer was without adequate consideration and provisions were not made for creditors of the transferor.

Courts rely heavily on the *de facto* merger exception to impose liability on successor corporations and are inclined to find that a particular transaction amounts to a de facto merger if (1) there is a continuation of the enterprise of the seller corporation, so that there is continuity of management, personnel, physical location, assets, and general business operations, (2) there is a continuity of shareholders that results from the purchasing corporation paying for the acquired assets with shares of its own stock, this stock ultimately coming to be held by the shareholders of the seller corporation so that they become a constituent part of the purchasing corporation, (3) the seller corporation ceases its ordinary business operations, liquidates, and dissolves as soon as practically possible, and (4) the purchasing corporation assumes those obligations (*e.g.*, contracts) of the seller ordinarily necessary for the uninterrupted continuation of normal business operations of the seller corporation.

Although courts generally have taken a cautious approach to judicial evolution of successor liability under the environmental statutes, there appears to be a trend toward expanding the liability of successor corporations. One federal appellate court stated that "national uniformity" must be considered in resolving successor liability issues to avoid circumvention of CERCLA goals by some state laws that unduly restrict successor liability and that "when choosing between the taxpayers or a successor corporation, the successor should bear the cost [of cleanup]." Several other federal courts have simply assumed the existence of successor liability in CERCLA cases without establishing successor liability standards.

In adopting a federal common law rule for piercing the corporate veil and holding a parent liable under Superfund for the activities of its subsidiary, the court in *United States v. Nicolet Inc.*, stated that:

> Where a subsidiary is or was at the relevant time a member of one of the classes of persons potentially liable under [Superfund]; and the parent had a substantial financial or ownership interest in the subsidiary; and the parent corporation controls or at the relevant time controlled the management and operations of the subsidiary, the parent's separate corporate existence may be disregarded.

The government has interpreted this language to mean that parent corporations may be held directly liable under Superfund whenever a parent actively participates in the management of a subsidiary that owns or operates a hazardous waste facility. Private industry, however, has taken the position that such a broad interpretation of the court's language is implausible—every parent would be liable if the test merely required a showing of control of a subsidiary's management and operations. Industry argues that the court's language must be read with traditional state law regarding corporate liability.

Although the majority of courts have held a parent corporation directly liable as an "owner or operator" under CERCLA § 107(a) for cleanup costs at a site operated by the corporation's subsidiary, in *Joslyn Corp. v. T.L. James & Co.*, 696 F.Supp. 222 (W.D.La.1988), *aff'd*, 893 F.2d 80 (5th Cir.1990). the Fifth Circuit expressly rejected the notion that parent corporations and corporate officers may be held liable as owners or operators under CERCLA without first piercing the corporate veil under traditional corporate law.

5. Lessors and Lessees

Although CERCLA does not expressly address landlord-tenant liability, courts have found that lessors and lessees may be held jointly and severally liable, as current and past "owners" and/or "operators," for cleanup costs under the Act. Lessors who lease their property to a lessee who creates an environmentally hazardous condition may be liable under CERCLA even if the owner did not create or contribute to the site. In addition, lessees, as tenants who are entitled to the exclusive use and enjoyment of the leased premises, may be liable as an "owner" or "operator" under CERCLA. Courts have held that a lessee is an "owner" for purposes of liability under CERCLA.

6. Corporate Officers and Shareholders

The general principle of corporate law is that absent special circumstances, a shareholder's liability is limited to the value of the shareholder's investment. Even with today's increased pressure to hold shareholders liable for environmental problems, courts continue to hold that shielding shareholders' from environmental liability remains a legitimate reason for incorporation.

In imposing personal liability for CERCLA response costs, the federal courts have been neither consistent nor predictable. As long as a shareholder retains the "capacity to control" of (1) the hazardous waste disposal practices or (2) the corporation itself, then the shareholder will remain at risk for litigation asserting the shareholder's liability under CERCLA or other environmental theories.

NEW YORK v. SHORE REALTY CORP.

759 F.2d 1032 (2d Cir.1985).

Oakes, Circuit Judge:

* * *

On February 29, 1984, the State of New York brought suit against Shore Realty Corp. ("Shore") and Donald LeoGrande, its officer and stockholder, to clean up a hazardous waste disposal site at One Shore Road, Glenwood Landing, New York, which Shore had acquired for land development purposes. At the time of the acquisition, LeoGrande knew that hazardous waste was stored on the site and that cleanup would be expensive, though neither Shore nor LeoGrande had participated in the generation or transportation of the nearly 700,000 gallons of hazardous waste now on the premises. The State's suit under CERCLA for an injunction and damages was brought in the United States District Court for the Eastern District of New York, Henry Bramwell, Judge. The complaint also contained pendent state law nuisance claims, based on both common law and N.Y.Real.Prop.Acts.Law § 841 (McKinney 1979). On October 15, 1984, the district court granted the State's motion for partial summary judgment. Apparently relying at least in part on CERCLA, it directed by permanent injunction that Shore and LeoGrande remove the hazardous waste stored on the property, subject to monitoring by the State, and held them liable for the State's "response costs," *see* 42 U.S.C. § 9607(a)(4)(A). In the alternative the court based the injunction on a finding that the Shore Road site was a public nuisance. Following a remand by this court on December 14, 1984, the district court on January 11, 1985, stated with more particularity the undisputed material facts underlying its decision finding defendants liable for the State's response costs and clarifying its earlier decision by basing the injunction solely on state public nuisance law. The court also modified its earlier decision by suggesting that CERCLA does not authorize injunctive relief in this case. . . .

We affirm, concluding that Shore is liable under CERCLA for the State's response costs. We hold that Shore properly was found to be a covered person under 42 U.S.C. § 9607(a); that the nonlisting by the Environmental Protection Agency ("EPA") . . . of the site on the National Priorities List ("NPL"), 42 U.S.C. § 9605(8)(B), is irrelevant to Shore's liability; that Shore cannot rely on any of CERCLA's affirmative defenses; but that, as suggested in the amicus brief filed for the United States and the district court's supplemental memorandum, injunctive relief under CERCLA is not available to the State. We nevertheless hold that the district court, exercising its pendent jurisdiction, properly granted the permanent jurisdiction, properly granted the permanent injunction based on New York public nuisance law. Moreover, we hold LeoGrande jointly and severally liable under both CERCLA and New York law.

* * *

LeoGrande incorporated Shore solely for the purpose of purchasing the Shore Road property. All corporate decisions and actions were made, directed, and controlled by him. By contract dated July 14, 1983, Shore agreed to purchase the 3.2 acre site, a small peninsula surrounded on three sides by the waters of Hempstead Harbor and Mott Cove, for condominium development. Five large tanks in a field in the center of the site hold most of some 700,000 gallons of hazardous chemicals located there, though there are six smaller tanks both above and below ground containing hazardous waste, as well as some empty tanks, on the property. The tanks are connected by a pipe to a tank truck loading rack and dockage facilities for loading by barge. Four roll-on/roll-off containers and one tank truce trailer hold additional waste. And before June 15, 1984, one of the two dilapidated masonry warehouses on the site contained over 400 drums of chemicals and contaminated solids, many of which were corroded and leaking. . . .

* * *

The purchase agreement provided that it could be voided by Shore without penalty if after conducting an environmental study Shore had decided not to proceed. LeoGrande was fully aware that the tenants, Applied Environmental Services, Inc., and Hazardous Waste Disposal, Inc., were then operating-illegally, it may be noted—a hazardous waste storage facility on the site. Shore's environmental consultant, WTM Management Corporation ("WTM"), prepared a detailed report in July 1983, incorporated in the record and relied on by the district court for its findings. The report concluded that over the past several decades "the facility ha[d] received little if any preventive maintenance, the tanks (above ground and below ground), pipeline, loading rack, fire extinguishing system, and warehouse have deteriorated." WTM found that there had been several spills of hazardous waste at the site, including at least one large spill in 1978. Though there had been some attempts at cleanup, the WTM testing revealed that hazardous substances, such as benzene, were still leaching into the groundwater and the waters of the bay immediately adjacent to the bulkhead abutting Hempstead Harbor. . . . After a site visit on July 18, 1983, WTM reported firsthand on the sorry state of the facility, observing, among other things, "seepage from the bulkhead," "corrosion" on all the tanks, signs of possible leakage from some of the tanks, deterioration of the pipeline and loading rack, and fifty to one hundred fifty-five gallon drums containing contaminated earth in one of the warehouses. The report concluded that if the current tenants "close up the operation and leave the material at the site," the owners would be left with a "potential time bomb." WTM estimated that the cost of environmental cleanup and monitoring would range from $650,000 to over $1 million before development could begin. After receiving this report Shore sought a waiver from the State Department of Environmental Conservation ("DEC") of liability as landowners for the disposal of the hazardous waste stored at the site. Although the DEC denied the waiver, Shore took title on October 13, 1983, and obtained certain rights over against the tenants, whom it subsequently evicted on January 5, 1984.

* * *

... Shore argues that it had nothing to do with the transportation of the hazardous substances and that it has exercised due care since taking control of the site. Who the "third part(ies)" Shore claims were responsible is difficult to fathom. It is doubtful that a prior owner here, since the acts or omissions referred to in the statute are doubtless those occurring during the ownership or operation of the defendant. Similarly, many of the acts and omissions of the prior tenants/operators fall outside the scope of section 9607(b)(3), because they occurred before Shore owned the property. In addition, we find that Shore cannot rely on the affirmative defense even with respect to the tenants' conduct during the period after Shore closed on the property and when Shore evicted the tenants. Shore was aware of the nature of the tenants' activities before the closing and could readily have foreseen that they would continue to dump hazardous waste at the site. In light of this knowledge, we cannot say that the releases and threats of release resulting of these activities were "caused solely" by the tenants or that Shore "took precautions against" these "foreseeable acts or omissions."

* * *

D. LEOGRANDE'S PERSONAL LIABILITY

We hold LeoGrande liable as an "operator" under CERCLA, 42 U.S.C. § 9607, for the State's response costs. Under CERCLA "owner or operator" is defined to mean "any person owning or operating" an onshore facility, *id.* § 9601(20)(A), and "person" includes individuals as well as corporations, *id.* § 9601(21). More important, the definition of "owner or operator" excludes "a person, who, without participating in the management of a ... facility, holds indicia of ownership primarily to protect his security interest in the facility." *Id.* § 9601(20)(A). The use of this exception implies that an owning stockholder who manages the corporation, such as LeoGrande, is liable under CERCLA as an "owner or operator." That conclusion is consistent with that of other courts that have addressed the issue. *See*, e.g., *United States v. Carolawn Co.*, 14 Envtl. L. Rep. (Envtl. L. Inst.) 20,699, 20–700 (D.S.C. June 15, 1984); *NEPACCO*, 579 F.Supp. at 847–48. In any event, LeoGrande is in charge of the operation of the facility in question, and as such is an "operator" within the meaning of CERCLA.

Turning to liability for abatement, it is debatable whether a New York court would hold LeoGrande personally liable by piercing the corporate veil. New York courts disregard the corporate form "reluctantly," *see Gartner v. Snyder*, 607 F.2d 582, 586 (2d Cir.1979), and while the State claims that LeoGrande dominated Shore and that Shore was undercapitalized, these allegations are probably insufficiently particularized. *See Walkovszky v. Carlton*, 18 N.Y.2d 414, 420, 223 N.E.2d 6, 10, 276 N.Y.S.2d 585, 590 (1966). Both the New York Court of Appeals and this court have been quite insistent that the corporate form will not be disregarded unless the opposing party shows that the corporate form is being used fraudulently or as a means of carrying on business for personal rather than corporate ends. *See Marine Midland Bank, N.A. v. Miller*, 664 F.2d 899, 903 (2d Cir.1981); *Walkovszky*, 18 N.Y.2d at 418, 420, 223 N.E.2d at 8, 10, 276 N.Y.S.2d at 588–90. The State's claim has not at this stage risen to that level.

Nevertheless, we hold LeoGrande liable for the abatement of the nuisance without piercing the corporate veil. New York courts have held that a corporate officer who controls corporate conduct and thus is an active individual participant in that conduct is liable for the torts of the corporation. *See State v. Ole Olsen, Ltd.*, 35 N.Y.2d 979, 324 N.E.2d 886, 365 N.Y.S.2d 528 (1975); *LaLumia v. Schwartz*, 23 A.D.2d 668, 669, 257 N.Y.S.2d 348, 350 (1965). We need not address whether he is liable merely as an officer of Shore, for it is beyond dispute that LeoGrande specifically directs, sanctions, and actively participates in Shore's maintenance of the nuisance. *See also Escude Cruz v. Ortho Pharmaceutical Corp.*, 619 F.2d 902, 907 (1st Cir.1980)(citing federal cases pronouncing this rule of liability for corporate officers). This general rule is particularly appropriate in the public nuisance context where " 'everyone who ... participates in the ... maintenance ... of a nuisance are liable jointly and severally.' " *Schenectady Chemicals*, 117 Misc.2d at 966, 459 N.Y.S.2d at 976 (quoting 17 Carmody–Wait 2d Actions for Waste, Nuisance and Trespass § 107:59, at 334 (1979)); *accord Caso v. District Council 37, American Federation of State, County & Municipal Employees*, 43 A.D.2d 159, 163, 350 N.Y.S.2d 173, 178 (1973).

As a final note however, the district court should take into account one additional factor in supervising its injunction, a principle limiting perhaps to some extent, LeoGrande's liability for the future costs of abatement. The injunctive remedy is an equitable one; that abatement expenses may become prohibitive and disproportionate therefore may be taken into consideration. *See* Restatement, *supra*, § 839 comment f [sic]; *id.* § 936.

* * *

Note

1. Recommendations to Avoid Environmental Liability. In order to avoid environmental liability under CERCLA or other environmental statutes, an investing shareholder should:

- remain at arms length from the actual operational control of the corporation;

- avoid contract language which would allow the shareholder to influence corporate conduct if the shareholder so chose;

- ensure that corporate formalities (such as issuance of stock, holding regular shareholder meetings, and assurance that all officers and directors are functional) are respected;

- ensure that adequate capitalization ratios are maintained by the corporation;

- regardless of corporate title, avoid the appearance of dominating or influencing corporate decisionmaking.

These recommendations are, of course, predicated on the notion that avoidance of environmental liabilities is the shareholder's paramount concern. Often shareholders will chose to remain involved in corporate affairs and risk potential environmental liability in the hopes that sound corporate management coupled with (and perhaps due to) their early involvement will prevent the liability from ever arising.

2. Summary of the Law of Shareholder Liability. These rules are predicated on the four general theories of liability courts have developed concerning shareholder liability for environmental problems. These theories have not always been consistent with established principles of corporate law. The four theories of liability are as follows:

(1) personal participation;

(2) control of corporate conduct;

(3) the prevention test; and

(4) piercing the veil.

The personal participation theory allows a court to hold a shareholder liable for CERCLA response costs if that individual personally and actively participated in disposal of the hazardous substance concerned. The control of corporate conduct theory allows a corporate shareholder to be held liable for CERCLA response costs due to their corporate capacity to control actions of the corporation.

The prevention test was adopted by the Sixth Circuit. The prevention test encompasses two elements. First, the court will examine the actual authority the individual in question has within the organization. This analysis demands that the court examine not only the official title the individual holds within the corporation, but it also involves a realistic assessment of the actual authority held by the individual taking into account the actual distribution of power within the corporation based on corporate hierarchy and the percentage of the corporation's shares which the individual might own.

The second prong of the prevention test analyzes what the individual did with the authority he or she had. The court will look not only at misfeasance and nonfeasance, but will also consider as a mitigating factor whether the individual undertook "clear measures to avoid or abate the hazardous waste damage." Thus, "active, direct, knowing efforts to prevent or abate the contamination may work for—not against—a corporate defendant where the acts suggest the individual tried but was unable to prevent or abate the unlawful waste disposal."

Under the traditional corporate law theory of piercing the corporate veil, a court may not hold a corporate shareholder individually liable for CERCLA response costs unless circumstances are such that the court to disregard to the corporate veil. Such factors include:

- whether the corporation is adequately capitalized;
- whether the daily operations of the corporation are separate and distinct from those of its shareholder;
- whether formal barriers between the management of the corporation and its shareholder are erected and maintained, with each functioning in its respective own best interest;
- whether persons coming in contact with the corporation are appraised of the separate nature of the corporation's identity;
- whether the corporation files consolidated income tax returns with its shareholder;
- whether the operating capital of the corporation is financed by its shareholder; and, if so, to what extent;
- the extent to which separate books and accounts are kept for the corporation;
- the extent of common departments and business;
- whether separate meetings of shareholders and directors are held;
- whether the shareholder is permitted to determine policies of the corporation;
- the extent to which contracts favor the shareholder over the corporation;
- whether the shareholder pays the salaries, expenses or losses of the corporation;
- the extent to which the corporation does business only with or on behalf of the shareholder or related companies;
- the extent to which corporate formalities are generally observed by both the shareholder and the corporation;
- the extent to which not piercing the corporate veil would work an injustice on the claimant; and
- the connection of the shareholder to the corporation's tort or contract giving rise to the suit.

Courts look at the totality of the facts and circumstances to determine whether it is appropriate to pierce the corporate veil. The majority of courts apply a different standard to personal injury cases than they do to contract disputes in determining whether it is appropriate to pierce the corporate veil. In tort cases, most courts do not require a finding of fraud as an element of proving that one corporation acted as the alter ego of another, especially where the corporation is under capitalized. In contract cases, however, fraud is an essential element of an alter ego finding. The courts different treatment of tort and contract cases, requiring a more difficult showing in contract cases, is predicated on the fact that in contract cases the claimant voluntarily dealt with the defendant, whereas in tort cases the claimant is considered the unwilling victim of the act or omission of the defendant corporation. Accordingly, courts balance different factors to determine whether the shareholder dominated the finances, policies and practices of the corporation.

Discussion Problem

In 1950, Active Past Owner buried a drum of PCBs on his agricultural lot. In 1970, Passive Past Owner duly conducted an all appropriate inquiry with an environmental audit of the lot, but never discovered the single drum of PCBs. Passive Past Owner bought the lot the next day. In 1980, Congress passed CERCLA which retroactively holds PRPs strictly and joint and severally liable for response costs incurred in cleaning up a contaminated facility. Among the list of PRPs are current owners and any person who owned the facility *at the time of disposal*. The only three defenses available to a PRP were (1) an act of God, (2) an act of war, or (3) an act or omission of a third party other than one whose act or omission occurred in connection with a contractual relationship with the defendant so long as the PRP (a) exercised due care with respect to the hazardous substance and (b) took precautions against foreseeable acts or omissions of any such third party. In the 1986 Superfund Amendment and Reauthorization Act ("SARA"), Congress amended CERCLA to, in essence, add a fourth defense known as the "innocent purchaser" defense. Basically, it releases a PRP from liability if at the time the PRP purchased the property, the PRP, upon all appropriate inquiry, did not know or have reason to know that any hazardous substance was disposed of on, in, or at the facility. The defense is only available, if the PRP acquired the property **after the disposal** or placement of the hazardous substance on, in, or at the facility. Furthermore, **past** owners or operators are **not** eligible for the defense. Finally, a PRP who initially qualifies for the defense can lose it and become liable like a current owner, if during his ownership the PRP obtains actual knowledge of a release of hazardous substance and subsequently sells it to another person without disclosing such knowledge.

In December 1987, the undetected PCB drum corroded and began leaking into the groundwater. In January, 1988, Passive Current Owner duly conducted an all appropriate inquiry with an environmental audit of the lot, but never discovered the buried single drum of PCBs because they had just begun leaking a month before. In 1993, the landowner neighboring the lot got sick. The local health department traced the problem to his drinking well. EPA traced the contaminated groundwater back to the corroded drum of PCBs on the lot. The lot was listed on the National Priority List ("NPL"), EPA spent $32 million in response costs cleaning up the site, and every person who owned or operated the site is insolvent, except for Passive Past Owner. Given that CERCLA defines "disposal" to include the "spilling" or "leaking" of any hazardous waste into or on any land or water so that such hazardous waste may enter the environment, is Passive Past Owner a PRP without a defense?

7. *Prospective Purchasers*

Prospective purchasers shy away from contaminated properties, despite their often desirable location, for one simple reason: the environmental liability associated with them is uncertain and seemingly unending. As a result of the environmental liabilities, contaminated real estate may now have a large negative value, as may businesses that own such property. Insurance policies covering past conduct may not cover these liabilities and current insurance generally cannot be obtained. Many prospective purchaser contemplating transactions involving brownfield properties believe that they are playing a new American form of "Russian Roulette."

Federal environmental laws create two main categories of risk for investments in brownfield properties—regulatory risks and liability risks. The regulatory risks arise from a myriad of complicated environmental laws that regulate such matters as impact assessment, standard-setting, licensing. Compliance with these laws can be quite expensive, can constrain management's decision-making capacity, and can, in some cases, altogether preclude operation of a business. Failure to comply with these regulatory laws can result in exposure to fines and penalties that can reach more than $25,000 per day and can result in imprisonment in extreme cases.

Despite the great cost, regulatory risks are generally quantifiable. Thus, *even more significant than the regulatory risks, are the civil liability risks associated with past or present ownership or operation of sites containing hazardous substances or of a company that created such wastes and shipped them offsite.* Association with property contaminated by hazardous substance, or with a company that owns or operates such property, can result in millions of dollars of liability for cleanup costs, personal injury, or property damage under CERCLA, state Superfund-like laws and the state common law, respectively. The Superfund law imposes a harsh, retroactive civil liability scheme under which all past and present owners and operators associated with a hazardous waste site. Even those that did not create or contribute to the hazardous condition, may be held liable for cleanup costs unless they qualify for certain extremely limited defenses. Persons associated with contaminated property must also contend with potential toxic tort liability under the common law. As one commentator explained:

> . . . . industrial practices in both rural and urban areas of the United States have left a legacy of contamination that affects all sectors of the real estate industry. Owners, lenders, borrowers and users throughout the country encounter serious impediments in financing and developing real property as a consequence of cleanup costs and unknown liability. Indeed, the mere presence of a contaminant, even in small concentrations, has a chilling and often fatal effect on real estate investment and development.

Mark A. Chertok and Mark A. Levine, *States Address Development Of "Slightly" Contaminated Land*, New York Law Journal (Nov. 17, 1993).

The extent of the civil liabilities created by Superfund is often staggering, even at relatively small sites. The high cleanup costs often reflect the inherent physical difficulty of coping with subsurface ground-water pollution and the aggregated cost of cleanup after years of neglect. Their magnitude also reflects large elements of public fear about the effects of toxic and carcinogenic substances and extravagant, unrealistic public expectations as to the diminution in risk levels that can be achieved on an economically practicable basis.

The following table describes market evidence of impairments of brownfields that often deter prospective purchasers from investing in these otherwise desirable properties:

Market	Costs
For Lease	Lower effective rents More concessions Higher vacancies Greater turnover Slower lease-up Longer marketing time Fewer prospective tenants Expanding competitive supply
For Sale	Lower sale prices More concessions Slower sellout More days on the market Fewer prospective buyers Expanded competitive supply
Operating Expenses	Increased marketing costs Increased turnover costs Increased costs of monitoring, maintenance, emergency response & communications Increased insurance costs Reduced coverage Cost of indemnification or bonding
Financing and Settlement	Higher yield requirements More due diligence costs to seller Extended settlement terms Indemnification, bonding, personal guarantees Higher loan-to-value ratios Shorter terms Higher rates Higher coverage ratios More points Seller financing

Congress' intention in 1980 when it passed CERCLA to deal with the problem of contaminated property was for the expense of cleanup to be funded primarily by those who were responsible for the creation of the environmental harm and their successors. For many sites identification of a solvent responsible party with the resources necessary to remediate the environmental harm is impossible. Clean up of these so-called "orphan" sites usually requires the expenditure of Superfund dollars.

Furthermore, any person who knowingly purchases contaminated real property—orphaned or not—may be held strictly liable under CERCLA for the response costs in spite of the fact that such an owner may not have in any way contributed to the contamination. This has an obvious chilling effect on economic redevelopment and investment in contaminated property, encouraging developers to seek out other, possibly undeveloped, sites to avoid potential Superfund liability thereby eliminating any hope EPA might have of recovering response costs from the sale of such sites. Carol Browner described the problem as follows:

> Current law extends to both past and prospective owners of contaminated sites. As a result, the market value of older industrial sites can be depressed, because the specter of Superfund liability diminishes the attractiveness of investing in industrial areas. Many claim that prospective owners who want to develop property have an economic incentive to use undeveloped, or 'greenfield', sites to avoid potential Superfund liability, thereby contributing to suburban sprawl and exacerbating chronic unemployment often found in inner-city industrial areas.

Statement of Carol M. Browner, Administrator, U.S. Environmental Protection Agency before the Subcommittee on Transportation and Hazardous Materials of the Committee on Energy and Commerce, U.S. House of Representatives (February 3, 1994) at page 6.

Recognizing this deficiency, EPA has, in a limited number of cases, entered into prospective agreements with purchasers of contaminated property in which the EPA covenants to not sue the purchaser in exchange for some environmental benefit (e.g., reimbursement to the Superfund, a program of clean-up). EPA originally published the criteria governing these agreements in 1989, but has only very recently seriously begun to implement this option.

To date, EPA has negotiated *only fourteen* prospective purchaser agreements—much too few to have a significant economic impact beyond the immediate local communities in which the affected properties are located. Although EPA has received numerous requests for covenants not to sue from prospective purchasers of contaminated property. EPA's historical policy was "not to become involved in private real estate transactions." Six of the fourteen prospective purchaser agreements in place have been negotiated within the past 18 months.

The circumstances in which EPA has historically been willing to consider such an agreement have been very limited:

> . . . a covenant not to sue a prospective purchaser might appropriately be considered if an enforcement action is anticipated and if performance of or payment for cleanup would not otherwise be available except from the Superfund and if the prospective purchaser participates in a clean-up. A prospective purchaser may participate in cleanup either through the payment of a substantial sum of money . . . to be applied towards a clean-up of the site or through a commitment to perform substantial response actions.

OSWER Directive at 25–26.

EPA's historic reservations about prospective purchaser agreements. EPA has expressed three primary concerns that mitigate against entering such an agreement:

> (1) an inadequate or incomplete site investigation makes it difficult to assess the impact and compatibility of the activities proposed by the prospective purchaser;

> (2) the remedy ultimately selected may present a health risk incompatible with the activities proposed by the prospective purchaser. The sites with which the EPA is concerned are, by definition, sites at which there has been a release or threatened release of hazardous substances and which pose a genuine health risk;

> (3) until the potentially responsible parties are identified, the EPA cannot adequately assess whether there is anything to be gained by entering a prospective purchaser agreement.

As a precursor to cleanup of a site is listed on the NPL, EPA conducts (or directs a responsible party to conduct) a Remedial Investigation/Feasibility Study ("RI/FS"). The purpose of the remedial investigation is to collect and analyze data concerning the environmental condition of the site to be used to define the objectives of the response action, to develop remedial action alternatives, and to undertake an initial screening and detailed analysis of the alternatives; the "feasibility study" emphasizes data analysis and is generally performed concurrently and in an interactive fashion with the remedial investigation for the purpose of developing and evaluating options for remedial action. Until the RI/FS is conducted and extent of contamination determined, the necessary remedy will be unknown. Since the EPA is unable to say what the remedy is, "it may be impossible to determine whether the proposed activities of the prospective purchaser at the site (for example, operating a manufacturing facility or developing the property) will interfere with any remedy ultimately selected by the [EPA]."

Development and commercial use of such contaminated sites may be dangerous to those persons present at the site and the purchasers future activities may aggravate or contribute to the contamination. Furthermore, if the remedy selected calls for something less than the destruction of all contaminants below health based levels, there may be a risk that unknown future uses are inconsistent with the remedy or may interfere with an ongoing cleanup.

Even before EPA includes a property on the NPL it has an obligation to conduct a remedial preliminary assessment and site investigation to evaluate whether the site poses a threat to human health. This authority and responsibility to investigate contaminated sites also includes the obligation to identify, whenever possible, the potentially responsible parties who caused or contributed to the environmental harm. Until these potentially responsible parties are identified and their financial viability assessed, the EPA will be unable to determine whether it is "receiving a benefit which otherwise could not be obtained." Furthermore, the benefit gained from an agreement with a prospective purchaser may ultimately serve as a "set-off" against future cost recovery against any viable responsible parties—a result wholly unintended by the EPA.

The "appropriate case" for a prospective purchaser agreement under the 1989 Guidance. In spite of these concerns, as early as 1989 EPA recognized that "in an appropriate case, entering into a covenant not to sue with a prospective purchaser of contaminated property ... may result in an environmental benefit through a payment to be applied to clean-up of the site or a commitment to perform response action." In determining what is a appropriate case, EPA applied the following five criteria:

- ✓ the likelihood of an enforcement action.
- ✓ whether or not it will receive a substantial benefit for cleanup that would not otherwise be available.
- ✓ whether the "continued operation of the facility or new site development, with the exercise of due care, will not aggravate or contribute to the existing contamination or interfere with the remedy."
- ✓ whether "due consideration" has been given to the effect which continued operations at the facility or new development are likely to have on the health risks to those persons likely to be present at the site.
- ✓ whether the prospective purchaser is financially viable.

Since it was considered contrary to EPA policy to become involved in purely private commercial transactions, EPA would "not entertain requests or covenants not to sue from prospective purchasers unless an [EPA] enforcement action is contemplated with respect to the facility." **The practical effect of this restrictive criteria was to limit prospective purchaser agreements to sites either "listed or proposed for listing on the NPL, those facilities at which [Superfund] monies have been expended, or those facilities which are the subject of a pending enforcement action."**

The presumption was that EPA would not enter into a prospective purchaser agreement. If the EPA determined "that its anticipated response costs can be recouped through other means, such as the filing and enforcement of a federal lien, such covenants will not be entertained." Similarly, in determining whether site development would aggravate the site remedy, EPA tended to not enter into an agreement.

Traditional elements of a prospective purchaser agreement. If the prospective purchaser satisfies certain specified criteria, including demonstrating his financial viability, and EPA determines that it is in the public's interest to enter into a covenant not to sue, an agreement could be executed between the prospective purchaser, the current owner of the facility, and the Regional Administrator of EPA, with the concurrence of the Assistant Administrator of the Office of Solid Waste and Emergency Response, the Assistant Administrator of the Office of Enforcement and Compliance Assurance, and the Attorney General. Based on the 1989 guidance provide by EPA's Office of Solid Waste and Emergency Response (OSWER), prospective purchaser agreement must have contained the following elements:

Key Element	Description
Consideration.	The prospective purchaser must agree to certain preconditions in exchange for the EPA's covenant not to sue for civil liability under sections 106 and 107(a) of CERCLA and section 7003 of RCRA arising from contamination of the facility which exists as of the date of acquisition of the facility. Specifically, the prospective purchaser must agree: ♦ to make either a cash payment toward cleanup activities or, alternatively, perform removal or remedial activities; ♦ not to assert any claim against the United States or the Superfund arising from contamination of the facility which exists as of the date of acquisition of the facility, or to seek any other costs, damages, or attorney's fees from the United States arising out of response activities at the facility; ♦ to file in the local land records a notice acceptable to EPA, stating that hazardous substances were disposed of on the site and that EPA makes no representation as to the appropriate use of the property; ♦ and to grant an irrevocable right of entry to the EPA, its response action contractors, and other persons performing response actions under EPA oversight for the purpose of taking response actions at the facility and for monitoring compliance with the agreement.
Reservation of rights.	EPA expressly reserves the right to assert claims against all persons other than the purchaser as well as the right to assert claims against the prospective purchaser for any activity not set forth in the covenant not to sue. The latter includes things such as: ● a contamination after the date of acquisition by the purchaser resulting from the purchaser's operation of the facility or by any person, ● any exacerbation of contamination existing prior to the date of acquisition, ● any failure to cooperate and/or interference with response activities at the facility, ● any failure to exercise due care with respect to any contamination at the facility, and ● any and all criminal liability.

Key Element	Description
	Where the Federal natural resource trustee has not agreed in writing to the covenant not to sue, the agreement generally expressly reserves natural resource damage claims.
Scope of response actions.	The agreement does not limit or restrict "the nature or scope of response actions which may be undertaken by the EPA in exercising its authority under federal law" even to the extent that such response actions interfere with the purchaser's operation, "including closure of the facility or a part thereof."
Disclaimer.	EPA expressly disclaims any finding as to the risks to human health and the environment which may be posed by contamination at the facility or any representation that the property is fit for any particular use.
Compliance with applicable laws and duty to exercise due care.	The purchaser is subject to the requirements of all federal and state laws and regulations, including the duty to exercise due care with respect to hazardous substances at the facility.

The ultimate conclusion to be drawn by a purchasers seeking the protection afforded by historic prospective purchaser agreements was that the although EPA guidance gave the agency flexibility in entering into prospective purchaser agreements, the likelihood of using this device to reduce the liability of prospective purchasers was remote. First, **the transaction must involve a site listed on the NPL, which means most brownfield sites are not eligible even for consideration in EPA's current prospective purchaser program.** Second, the EPA must have incurred or is likely to incur response costs at the site. Thus, the program was ineligible to sites which were only marginally contaminated and subject to cleanup by a volunteer (perhaps under pressure from his lender). Third, what the purchaser must have proposed to pay or perform is proportionate to the risk he is seeking to avoid and is, therefore, "substantial." Thus, many prospective purchasers felt it was better to risk development without the added transaction costs of the negotiation process preceding the entering into a prospective purchaser agreement.

On May 25, 1989, EPA issued a new guidance document that replaced the 1989 policy. This new policy, which will be discussed in greater detail later in the report, is designed to make the prospective purchaser agreement a more viable option than it hitherto had been. The effectiveness of this brand new policy, of course, remains to be seen. It does, however, at least purport to state a fundamental shift in EPA's traditional policy of not using the prospective purchaser agreement as a tool in the brownfields context.

8. Developers

Developers have been held potentially liable for CERCLA cleanup costs in the redevelopment of polluted sites. For example, in *Tanglewood*

East Homeowners v. Charles–Thomas, Inc., 849 F.2d 1568 (5th Cir.1988), the Fifth Circuit upheld the district court's refusal to dismiss a CERCLA claim against a lender, residential developers, construction companies, and real estate agents and agencies, all of whom participated in the development of a subdivision built on contaminated property. It is not at all clear from the opinion on what basis the court concluded that certain of these parties (especially the lender and real estate brokers) could be held liable under CERCLA. The court did not specifically address the developers in its discussion of "present owners," "past owners" or "past arrangers and transporters." (Indeed, it is difficult to see how brokers or lenders can fall into any of the categories, even given the court's broad interpretation of the categories.) Nevertheless, the fact that the Fifth Circuit upheld the district court's refusal to dismiss the claims against the defendants, which included the developers, real estate brokers, and others has created great discomfort for developers of potentially contaminated sites. This fear of liability led one commentator to conclude that, "Unless Congress authorizes the EPA to grant developers releases from liability, new inner-city cleanup programs may be of limited value."

Another case illustrating the concerns of developers is *City of North Miami v. Berger*, 828 F.Supp. 401 (E.D.Va.1993). In that case, a CERCLA action arouse out of the ill-fated efforts of the City of North Miami, Florida and various entities and individuals to develop a municipal recreational complex on city-owned property in south Florida. Those efforts included the 1974 to 1980 operation of a state permitted landfill at the site, a landfill that was later alleged to be the source of hazardous substance releases. From its inception, the Munisport development project faced intense regulatory scrutiny as well as pressure from various private interest groups. The City sought recovery from the developer of the property, his attorney, the key shareholders in the development corporation, the demolition company working on the site and the construction company hired to undertake the development. Although not all parties were ultimately held liable, the case signalled the great litigation risk inherent in development of polluted sites.

9. *Parties to Project Finance Transactions*

Many large project financing involving real estate and industrial facilities are structured as sale/leasebacks, combining sale, lease and loan transactions, each of which must be analyzed from the standpoint of environmental risks. In each type of transaction, the legal risk to the various participants normally turns on their status as "owners" or "operators" of an industrial facility or a piece of real estate.

In the traditional sale/leaseback:

√ The owner of an industrial facility (who is usually also its operator) sells the project by transferring legal title to an entity, usually a bank or trust company serving as trustee under a grantor trust formed by an investor, who will provide the equity in the transaction and who will become the beneficial owner of the project through the trust.

√ The owner-trustee, as lessor, leases the facility back to the original owner, as lessee, who will continue to operate it under a long-term lease.

√ In a "leveraged" lease deal, the owner-trustee obtains a loan from one or more financial institutions (sometimes the debt is raised through a public offering) secured by an assignment of the lessor's rights under the lease and by a mortgage on the lessor's interest in the project, in order to finance that portion of the purchase price and transaction expenses not covered by the investor's equity contribution. The lender's recourse is restricted to its collateral, and neither the owner-trustee nor the equity investor will have any personal liability for repayment of the loan. The lease assignment and mortgage typically introduces another bank or trust company into the transaction, who will hold the collateral for the lenders' benefit as indenture trustee under the terms of an indenture.

Although it is fundamental in sale/leasebacks that the owner-trustee/lessor be treated as the owner of the project for federal income tax purposes so that the equity investor, through the grantor trust, will be entitled to depreciation, interest deductions and other significant tax benefits, from the standpoint of environmental law, this creates an immediate tension with the objective that the owner-trustee and the equity investor (not to mention the lenders) avoid, to the extent possible, the environmental responsibilities imposed on the "owner" or "operator" of the facility (or "persons" engaged in certain conduct).

When a project financing is structured to include a sale, a lease, a mortgage, or all three, the impact of "owner" and "operator" (and "person") liability on each party to the transaction in his capacity as seller, buyer, lessor, lessee, mortgagor and mortgagee must be considered. Borrowers in a project financing will normally fall into at least several of these categories and will have direct regulatory compliance and civil liability risks. Owner-trustees and equity investors run certain risks of also falling into one or more of these categories. Lenders, while not normally falling into any of them directly, will bear derivative risks related to the possibility of (1) borrower insolvency and (2) diminished collateral value due to the impact of environmental laws on the borrower. Further, under CERCLA, RCRA, the state equivalents and other environmental laws, lenders themselves have been considered "owners," "operators," and perhaps "persons" upon foreclosure or in difficult "workout" situations. Thus, these lenders can become directly liable for regulatory compliance costs or civil liabilities of unprecedented magnitude, well beyond the value of the loan or the collateral involved.

10. Lessors and Lessees

Although CERCLA does not expressly address landlord-tenant liability, courts have found that lessors and lessees may be held jointly and severally liable, as "owners" and/or "operators," for cleanup costs under the Act. Lessors who lease their property to a lessee who creates an environmentally hazardous condition may be liable under CERCLA even if the owner did not create or contribute to the site. In *United States v. Argent Corp.*, 21 Env't Rep. Cas. (BNA) 1354 (D.N.M. May 4, 1984), for example, the court held that an owner who leased a warehouse to a business generating hazardous waste was liable under CERCLA as an "owner" even though the lessor had no other connection to the lessee's operation. *Cf. United States v. Northernaire Plating Co.*, 670 F.Supp. 742, 748 (W.D.Mich.1987)(owner who leased facility to disposing party was precluded from asserting a third party defense because of the contractual relationship between the owner and the lessee).

In addition, lessees, as tenants who are entitled to the exclusive use and enjoyment of the leased premises, may be liable as an "owner" or "operator" under CERCLA. Courts have held that a lessee is an "owner" for purposes of liability under CERCLA. In *United States v. South Carolina Recycling and Disposal, Inc. (SCRDI)*, the district court held that the Columbia Organic Chemical Company ("COCC"), the lessee and sublessor of a Superfund site known as the Bluff Road site on which it also had operated a facility for reclaiming and recycling waste chemicals, was an "owner" under CERCLA, "apart and distinct" from its activities as an "operator." 653 F.Supp. 984, 1003 (D.S.C.1984), *aff'd sub. nom.*, *United States v. Monsanto*, 858 F.2d 160 (4th Cir.1988), *cert. denied*, 490 U.S. 1106, 109 S.Ct. 3156, 104 L.Ed.2d 1019 (1989). The district court reasoned that the lessee "maintained control and responsibility for the use of the property and, essentially, stood in the shoes of the property owners." *Id.* Looking to the definition of "owner or operator" in section 101(20)(A), the court also noted that "site control is an important consideration in determining who qualifies as an owner." *Id.*

Apart from liability as owners or operators under CERCLA, lessors and lessees also may be liable to third parties under common law theories for both the cleanup of hazardous waste and for any personal injury or property damage resulting from the hazardous waste.

CALIFORNIA v. BLECH

976 F.2d 525 (9th Cir.1992).

TASHIMA, DISTRICT JUDGE.

I

The issue in this case is whether the Comprehensive Environmental Response, Compensation, and Liability Act of 1980, 42 U.S.C. §§ 9601–9675 ("CERCLA"), as interpreted in *3550 Stevens Creek Associates v. Barclays Bank of California*, 915 F.2d 1355 (9th Cir.1990), creates a right of action by a tenant against a landlord to recover the costs of cleaning up asbestos dust accidentally released into leased space when walls containing asbestos were damaged by fire.

II

Appellant California Department of General Services (the "Department"), a state agency, leased commercial office space from appellee Blech. On March 2, 1989, a fire released asbestos from materials in the walls of the building into the leased space. Asbestos dust covered the floor, furniture, typewriters, and files, making use of the space unsafe. The Department requested Blech abate the hazard. Blech declined to do so. The Department decontaminated the area at its own expense and filed this cost recovery action against Blech under CERCLA section 107(a)(1)(A), which provides: "The owner and operator of a vessel or a facility ... from which there is a release, or threatened release which causes the incurrence of response costs, of a hazardous substance, shall be liable for ... all costs of removal or remedial action incurred by ... a State...." 42 U.S.C. § 9607(a)(1)(A).

Blech moved to dismiss for failure to state a claim upon which relief could be granted. The district court dismissed the action. *Anthony v. Blech*, 760 F.Supp. 832 (C.D.Cal.1991).

III

We held in *Stevens Creek* that CERCLA did not authorize the present owner of a building to recover from a prior owner the cost of removing asbestos installed in the building by the prior owner. The suit was brought under CERCLA section 107(a)(2), which provides for recovery from "any person who at the time of disposal of any hazardous substance owned or operated any facility at which such hazardous substances were disposed of." 42 U.S.C. § 9607(a)(2).

We rejected the claim principally on the ground that in installing the asbestos material, the prior owner had not "disposed of" it within the meaning of section 107(a)(2). 915 F.2d at 1359–62.

The present suit was brought against the present owner of a building under section 107(a)(1), 42 U.S.C. § 9607(a)(1), rather than against a past owner of a building under section 107(a)(2), 42 U.S.C. § 9607(a)(2). Section 107(a)(1) simply provides for recovery of removal costs from "the owner or operator of ... a facility ... from which there is a release, or threatened release which causes the incurrence of response costs, of a hazardous substance...." As the district court noted, section 107(a)(1) does not condition recovery from a present owner upon the owner's "disposal" of the hazardous substance as does section 107(a)(2). 760 F.Supp. at 835.... Thus, the dispute between the parties as to whether failure to abate the asbestos dust constituted a "disposal" is irrelevant to this case.

However, *Stevens Creek* also cited an alternative ground for rejecting the claim for the cost of removing asbestos building material used in a structure. We concluded that, aside from the question of "disposal" under section 107(a)(2), there is no basis for inferring an intention by Congress to create a private cause of action under CERCLA for recovery of the cost of removing asbestos building materials from a structure when no release of hazardous substances outside the structure is alleged. 915 F.2d at 1362–65.

As we noted in *Stevens Creek*, the only discussion of Congress's intent with respect to asbestos removal occurred during the discussion of the so-called "building materials exception" to CERCLA adopted in 1986. *Id.* at 1363–64. That exception reads: "The President shall not provide for a removal or remedial action under this section in response to a release or threat of release ... from products which are part of the structure of, and result in exposure within, residential buildings or business or community structures." CERCLA section 104(a)(3)(B), 42 U.S.C. § 9604(a)(3)(B).

We recognized in *Stevens Creek* that the plain language of this exception appears to limit its direct impact to remedial actions by the federal government. We concluded, however, that section 104(a)(3)(B) and pertinent legislative history reflected an intention on the part of Congress to exclude from CERCLA recovery by any party of costs incurred under circumstances in which the President was not authorized by CERCLA to respond; specifically, when the release or threatened release is (1) from a product that is part of the structure of the building; and (2) the resulting exposure is wholly within the structure. 915 F.2d at 1363–65.

Both circumstances are present in this case: (1) although appellant argues the asbestos dust ceased to be part of the structure when released into the leased space by fire, the release was clearly "from products which are part of the structure," 42 U.S.C. § 9604(a)(3)(B) ...; and (2) there is no allegation in the complaint that the release resulted in exposure outside the structure itself. Accordingly, CERCLA created no private cause of action for removal costs.

* * *

11. *Public and Private Lenders*

Although CERCLA contains a "security interest" exemption that excludes from the definition of "owner or operator" any "person, who, without participating in the management of a vessel or facility, holds indicia of ownership primarily to protect his security interest in the vessel or facility," a lender may nevertheless become liable as a present or past an "owner" or "operator" under Superfund by:

  √ assuming too much control over his debtor,

  √ foreclosing on contaminated land, or

  √ causing a release of hazardous substances.

As an owner or operator, the lender could be liable for cleanup costs or natural resource damages well beyond the amounts it originally had at risk in the lending transaction.

Although the security interest exemption has in fact protected most lenders from Superfund liability, the lending community became greatly concerned about potential Superfund liability when one court held a foreclosing lender liable a present owner and operator under CERCLA and another court suggested in dicta that a "capacity to control" the operations at a facility might be sufficient to void the statutory protection. In addition, in 1989 the Federal Home Loan Bank Board highlighted the following concerns environmentally contaminated properties could pose for both public and private lender:

√ reduced value of collateral;

√ inability of borrowers to repay loans if they must also cover site cleanup costs;

√ preemption of a mortgage loan security by state environmental cleanup liens (so-called "superlien" laws) enforced in certain states;

√ potential for the lender to become directly liable for the cost of cleanup of the site if it engages in workout activities or forecloses on the property;

√ the concern that the lender may be forced to chose between foregoing collateral interest and not foreclose on property or incur significant cleanup costs under CERCLA;

√ the possibility that the borrower would not maintain the facility in an environmentally safe manner and corresponding fears of liability if the lender either monitors or fails to monitor the environmental affairs of the debtor.

These concerns and the decline of available capital for certain high risk industries led to increased lender surveillance of environmentally contaminated properties as well as difficulties for certain businesses to secure loans on properties at risk for environmental problems. As one commentator observed:

Private developers, even if determined to acquire an old property, often are stymied by lenders concerned about their inheritance of liability, devaluation of collateral, and the effect of cleanup costs on the project's vitality.

Reed D. Rubinstein, *Shortening the 10–Foot Pole*, The Connecticut Law Tribune (May 15, 1995).

EPA issued a "Lender Liability Rule" to calm lenders' fears and provide them guidance about what actions would and would not constitute "participation in management," causing them to lose their statutory protection. Although the rule addressed only Superfund liabilities (and did not address any other state or federal causes of action) was "welcomed by the banking community as a good solution to their problem."

EPA's rule was, however, struck down by the D.C. Court of Appeals on the grounds that EPA lacked statutory authority to issue the rule. Recent efforts to revise CERCLA to grant authority to promulgate a new lender liability rule have failed. The administration continues to support such efforts.

"New federal regulations should help get polluted urban properties off lenders' untouchable list." On May 4, 1995 regulations were amended to provide an incentive for bankers and developers to help rescue cities with polluted industrial properties. "For the first time, lenders subject to the federal Community Reinvestment Act (CRA)—aimed at directing capital into poor neighborhoods—can claim CRA credit for loans made to help clean up and redevelop urban, industrial property." The new rule, orchestrated by Environmental Protection Agency Administrator Carol Browner, was designed to complement the EPA's new "Brownfields Action Agenda." The effectiveness of these new regulations, of course, remains to be seen.

12. *Remediation Contractors*

In 1986, Congress enacted certain limited protections for government hired remediation contractors under SARA. 42 U.S.C.A. § 9619(c) allows EPA to relieve contractors from liability for their negligent acts under certain very restricted circumstances. The indemnity provided by EPA must be written and will only be for the contractor's negligence. There is no protection for gross negligence or intentional misconduct. In order to be eligible for this "indemnity and hold harmless agreement" the contractor must show that insurance is not available to the contractor at a fair and reasonable price despite the contractors diligent effort to obtain insurance coverage.

In addition, § 119 (a)(1) states:

> A person who is a response action contractor with respect to any release or threatened release of a hazardous substance or pollutant or contaminant from a vessel or facility shall not be liable under this title or under any other Federal law to any person for injuries, costs, damages, expenses, or other liability (including but not limited to claims for indemnification or contribution and claims by third parties for death, personal injury, illness or loss of or damage to property or economic loss) which results from such release or threatened release.

Id. § 9619(c)(5)(1994). The final regulations implementing Superfund Response Action Contractor (RAC) Indemnification were implemented on Jan. 25, (1993). See 58 Fed. Reg. 5972 (1993). **Indemnification applies only to response action contractor liability which results from a release of any hazardous substance or pollutant or contaminant if such release arises out of EPA contracted response action activities.** Where EPA exercises its discretionary authority to grant indemnity and hold harmless agreements with RACs, EPA generally requires the indemnification agreement to include deductibles and place limits on the amount of indemnification to be made available.

Although SARA exclusions for EPA hired RACS proved certain limited protections where EPA agrees to give an "indemnity and hold harmless agreement," these exclusions apply (in the CERCLA context) almost solely to NPL listed sites. Remediation contractors hired by private PRPs enjoy no such protection. For example, the 9th Circuit squarely addressed the question of independent contractor liability in *Kaiser Aluminum & Chemical Corp. v. Catellus Development. Corp.*, 976 F.2d 1338 (9th Cir.1992). The court reversed a ruling dismissing a third party complaint contribution costs under § 9613(f) of CERCLA against James L. Ferry & Sons ("Ferry"), a construction contractor. The dispute arose when Catellus Development Corp.'s (Catellus) predecessor sold land to the City of Richmond, California ("Richmond"), who then hired Ferry to "excavate and grade a portion of the land for a proposed housing development." Ferry spread some of the displaced soil containing hazardous substances over other parts of the property. Richmond sued Catellus to recover a portion of the clean-up costs. In response, Catellus "filed a third-party complaint against Ferry for contribution under 42 U.S.C. § 9613(f)(1), alleging that Ferry exacerbated the extent of contamination by extracting the contaminated soil from the excavation site and spreading it over uncontaminated areas of the property."

The Court reiterated the "well-settled rule that 'operator' liability under section § 9607(a)(2) only attaches if the defendant had authority to control the cause of the contamination at the time the hazardous substances were released into the environment." The court held that the allegations that Ferry "excavated the tainted soil, moved it away from the excavation site, and spread it over uncontaminated portions of the property," were sufficient to support a claim that a hazardous substance was disposed of. It based this holding on the finding in *Tanglewood* that "the dispersal of contaminated soil during the excavation and grading of a development site," constitutes a disposal, and that a disposal can occur during the subsequent movement or dispersal of hazardous substances.

The Court next examined if the contractor could be found liable under § 9607(a)(3). The court stated "[l]iability for releases under § 9607(a)(3) is not endless; it ends with that party who both owned the hazardous waste and made the crucial decision how it would be disposed of or treated, and by whom." Concluding that plaintiff had "not alleged that Abbott owned any hazardous waste or made any decision on how it would be disposed," the Court held that Plaintiff's claim under (a)(3) was untenable.

There is no due diligence defense to liability for contractors like there is for landowners. Thus, even a contractor that used its best efforts to discover any hazardous substances and used state of the art technology in an effort to discover such contamination can be held liable for remedial measures if they failed to discover the contamination and dispose of it in a proper manner. Moreover, since disposal technologies are still in their infancy and waste disposed of in an EPA approved landfill has an expected life of no more than 100 years, contractors have no way of cutting off liability under CERCLA for future cleanup even where cleanup was undertaken in a legal, permitted and state of the art manner.

13. *Insurance Carriers*

The advent of strict, retroactive, joint and several liability for the generation, transportation, or disposal of toxic or hazardous waste spawned litigation and debate nationwide over the precise meaning of the words in the nation's various Comprehensive General Liability's (CGL) policies:

> Since Congress passed the Comprehensive Environmental Response, Compensation and Liability Act in 1980, the legislation, commonly known as "Superfund", has led to a long and expensive battle over who is to pay for cleaning up past pollution at industrial sites.... Insurers claim that all this has led to a "deep-pocket syndrome", with the firm with the most insurance being singled out to pay the lion's share of a clean-up bill, even if it was not the most insurance being singled out to pay the lion's share of a clean-up bill, even if it was not the worst offender. If the insurance industry has to pick up much of the tab for pollution, the result could be even more devastating than a big natural catastrophe. To cope with this threat companies have boosted their reserves. A.M. Best estimates that the industry's "survival ratio", which measures the number of years it would take to exhaust reserves based on the present rate of claims, will have risen to 6.9 at the end of the year, up from 5.2 in 1990.

The Economist at 9 (December 3, 1994). Because it is derived from standard insurance industry forms, the basic language in virtually all CGL policies is identical. *See* George Pendygraft, et al., *Who Pays for Environmental Damage: Recent Developments in CERCLA Liability and Insurance Coverage Litigation*, 21 Ind. L. Rev. 117, 140 (1988).

The huge Superfund and toxic tort risks associated with the nations polluted industrial sites have become essentially uninsurable. The casualty insurance industry buffeted by the effects of declining interest rates on its investment income, has been stung by the willingness of many courts to impose liability for "gradual" pollution under CGL policies, and appalled by Congress' attempt to create huge new liabilities for conduct that was insured (and premium levels gauged) when no such liabilities existed. Thus, led by the London reinsurers, for quite a while insurers withdrew from the U.S. market, refusing to write insurance to cover any form of environmental risk.

In a study published in March 1994, A.M. Best, an insurance rating agency, estimated that if Superfund was not reformed, domestic and foreign insurers in America could end up paying as much as $1.5 trillion in environmental liability claims over the next 25 years. A study published in 1992 by the RAND Corporation, concluded that some 88% of the cash paid out by insurers on Superfund-related claims in 1986–91 had been spent on defending policy-holders and on litigation to decide who should be responsible for clean-ups. *Id.*

PRPs typically pursue their insurance carriers in an attempt to establish coverage under standard CGL or Environmental Impairment

Liability (EIL) policies. Carriers vigorously resisted such coverage, arguing that (1) CERCLA cleanup costs are not "damages" under the policies, (2) the "pollution exclusion clause" bars coverage in most cases, and (3) policies pre-dating the enactment of CERCLA do not cover an insured's payments to the government in a CERCLA cost recovery suit. Court are divided as to whether cleanup costs are compensable under the property damage provision of the standard CGL policies. Courts are also divided as to whether there is coverage even when the insured was ordered to undertake cleanup of the pollution itself.

Coverage under the CGL policy is triggered by an "occurrence"— "an accident, including continuous or repeated exposure to conditions, which results in *bodily injury* or *property damage* neither expected nor intended from the standpoint of the insured[.]" The standard form CGL policy issued between 1970 and 1985 includes the following pollution exclusion clause:

This insurance does not apply:

* * *

(f) to *bodily injury* or *property damage* arising out of the discharge, dispersal, release or escape of smoke, vapors, soot, fumes, acids, alkalis, toxic chemicals, liquids or gases, waste materials or other irritants, contaminants or pollutants into or upon land, the atmosphere or any water course or body of water; but this exclusion does not apply if such discharge, dispersal, release or escape is *sudden and accidental* . . . .

Policies issued prior to 1970 generally included no such exclusion and may serve as a basis for finding insurance coverage for pollution predating many of the federal environmental statutes.

The meaning of the pollution exclusion and other limiting phrases in insurance contracts is critical as insurance companies, private parties, the government, users of landfills and waste sites, and property owners ask whether the insurance company must defend relevant lawsuits or indemnify the insured against liability to third persons. Interpretation of insurance contracts is a matter of state law. The nation's courts are hopelessly split, and as one judge noted, "[t]he cases swim the reporters like fish in a lake." Indeed, there are different interpretations both between states and among state and federal courts within the same state. Some jurisdictions interpret the contract language as ambiguous, interpret it broadly, and generally rule in favor of the insured. Others deem the words unambiguous, interpret them narrowly under the "plain meaning" doctrine, and limit coverage to damages from instantaneous polluting events. This approach usually favors the insurance company. Indeed, although "insure" means "to make sure, certain, or secure," the only certainty in CGL policies is that of expensive, extended, and exasperating litigation.

Sometimes insurance coverage is found, sometimes it is not. Sometimes an insurance company will defend a CERCLA action and sometimes it will not. It is clear that there is no enough insurance capacity to cover all environmental problems that may potentially be covered by CGL and other insurance policies. It is this lack of capacity that has created such uncertainty in the insurance market. Allowing insurance coverage for CERCLA cleanups has will undoubtedly continue to put some insurance companies out of business; state courts interpreting insurance contracts undoubtedly feel this political pressure.

14. State, County and City Government

The 600–member U.S. Conference of Mayors announced "that abandoned industrial sites, dubbed 'brownfields,' are the top environmental problem facing America's cities." Municipalities have a "critical interest in industrial redevelopment." "Public managers are faced with the fiscal reality that their cities' older sections have increased or disproportionate risk of environmental contamination." As once commentator explained:

> Contaminated industrial sites constitute a serious problem for the nation's cities. Once flourishing factories and mills produced goods that improved lives and won wars. In the process, they supported generations of workers and kept towns growing. Their peak is past and their future are bleak. Many are vacant and deteriorating, leaving blanks on the tax rolls and symbolizing decline to nearby residents.
>
> In older cities, factories often lie on the river or harbor and in the old inner city core. Restoration of these sites to productive use is a high priority of public officials and community leaders. Abandoning the facilities, transportation links, and other infrastructure simply weakens the community.... the road to recovery is littered with obstacles.

Randy Lee Loftis, *EPA Targets Toxic Sites in Nation's Urban Areas Development Gets Boost From Cleanup Plan*, THE DALLAS MORNING NEWS (March 13, 1995). Another commentator focused the blame even more squarely on CERCLA:

> The Comprehensive Environmental Response, Compensation, and Liability Act (CERCLA) and other environmental regulations, however, cast doubt on the wisdom of municipal ownership of risks associated with fee simple ownership of land. The city is a "potentially responsible party" (i.e., "deep pocket") in the chain of title. Further, research suggests that the perceived risk of redevelopment of contaminated sites may lead to market failure, because investors overvalue the possibility of excessive expense beyond their actual cleanup costs. Hence, there may be a stigma attached to polluted properties beyond actual costs.

Simons, Robert, *How clean is clean? contaminated property development*, Appraisal J. (July 1994). *See also* Ellen JoAnne Gerber, *Industrial Property Transfer Liability: Reality versus Necessity*, 40 Cleveland State L. Rev. 177–208 (1992); Tex Ann Reid, Edward M. Clar, Anthony M. Diecidue, and Mark F. Johnson, *Assessing a Municipality's Ability to Pay*

Superfund Cleanup Costs, Federal Environmental Restoration Conference and Exhibitions (Washington, D.C.: Federal Environmental Restoration Conference and Exhibitions 1992); Bill Mundy, *The Impact of Hazardous and Toxic Material on Property Value: Revisited* , Appraisal J. 463–471 (October 1992); Peter J. Patchin, *Contaminated Properties— Stigma Revisited*, Appraisal J. 168–172 (April 1991). These concerns have led many "cities such as Buffalo do not even foreclose on abandoned industrial complexes in redevelopment zones because the potential for staggering cleanup costs and liability claims once they take ownership." Deborah Cooney, et al., Revival of Contaminated industrial Sites: Case Studies (Northeast- Midwest Inst. 1992). *See also* Mike Dries, *A Long Road to Urban Redevelopment*, 12 Milwaukee Bus. J. 1 (May 13, 1995).

"Municipalities and other local governments also can find the financial burden of Superfund liability difficult to carry, whether they incur liability as the 'owners or operators' of municipal landfills at which hazardous waste was disposed of, or as 'generators' or 'transporters' of trash ('municipal solid waste' or 'MSW') sent to a private landfill where it became mixed with hazardous wastes." Testimony of Lois Schiffer, Assistant Attorney General, Environment and Natural Resources Division Department of Justice before the Senate Environment Superfund, Waste Control and Risk Assessment Superfund, FDCH Congressional Testimony (April 27, 1995). The federal government does not generally pursue municipalities who sent only MSW to a landfill, but private PRPs very often do sue municipalities. Private PRPs often complain that the large volume of the trash contributed by the municipalities severely raises the cost of the remedies at these "co-disposal" sites. For example, in *New Jersey v. Gloucester Envtl. Mgmt. Servs.,* 821 F.Supp. 999 (D.N.J.1993), one of the Generator Groups involved in the litigation surrounding the Gloucester Environmental Management Services, Inc. ("GEMS") Landfill, a Superfund site ranked twelfth on EPA's NPL, filed a Third–Party Complaint against 52 municipalities, seeking contribution from these local municipalities arising from their alleged generation and disposal of hazardous substances at the landfill. Recognizing the complexity of the problem the court said:

> American households are said to dispose of about 1.6 million tons of hazardous waste annually (i.e., an estimated one percent of the 160 million tons of total municipal solid waste).... The municipal solid waste, with its hazardous component, is said to present a considerable hazardous potential ... at certain sites. While the potential for harm from release of hazardous components at a typical municipal landfill may not be great, this potential may be greatly aggravated at a Superfund site in which municipal wastes in high volumes contribute their hazardous components to the hazardous industrial wastes also on site to yield formidable problems of containment and remediation. It is the volume of hazardous substances in municipal waste, and not the isolated or occasional paint can or pesticide from the

individual household, that potentially threatens the environment in a material way as envisioned by CERCLA.

821 F.Supp. 999 (D.N.J.1993). Thus, most court have held that the municipalities could be held liable under CERCLA. As one court explained:

> It is clear from the definition of "person" in 42 U.S.C. § 9601(21) that municipalities are explicitly included as PRPs for purposes of the liability provisions of 42 U.S.C. § 9607(a).... Additional evidence of this Congressional intent to consider municipalities as PRPs comes from CERCLA's limited exceptions to potential municipal liability which are found in 42 U.S.C. §§ 9601 (20)(D) and 9607(d)(2).... If Congress had the ability to make explicit exemptions from liability in these sections, it had the ability to make exemptions in 42 U.S.C. § 9607(a). The fact that municipalities are "persons" under CERCLA and that no such exceptions were made for municipalities under 42 U.S.C. § 9607(a) is compelling evidence that Congress intended municipalities to be held liable as PRPs under § 9607(a)....

Communities should recognize that potential liability under CERCLA applies regardless of whether the HHW [household waste] was picked up as a part of a community's routine waste collection service and disposed of in a municipal waste landfill ... or if the HHW was gathered as part of a special collection program and taken to a hazardous waste landfill....

Id.

Hence, under CERCLA, if a municipality arranges for the disposal or treatment of hazardous substances, it may be held liable for contribution or response costs under the CERCLA if a subsequent release or threatened release requires cleanup efforts. "The concentration of hazardous substances in municipal solid waste—regardless of how low a percentage—is not relevant in deciding whether CERCLA liability is incurred." The fact that Municipal Solid Waste is not specifically mentioned as a hazardous substance does not exempt it from CERCLA's reach. Most courts reached this conclusion despite noting the magnitude of potential liability cities may suffer.

The courts noted that municipalities, like private parties, are not completely without recourse from CERCLA liability. They can bring third party contribution actions:

> Appellant municipalities are not without recourse to avoid inequitable and disproportionate burdens that may arise from their liability as third-party contributors. Courts have the authority to "allocate response costs among liable parties using such equitable factors as the court determines are appropriate." § 9613(f)(1). An array of equitable factors may be considered in this allocation process, including the relative volume and toxicity of the substances for disposal of which the municipalities arranged, the relative cleanup costs

incurred as a result of these wastes, the degree of care exercised by each party with respect to the hazardous substances, and the financial resources of the parties involved. Consequently, the amount of liability imposed will not necessarily be a function solely of the total volume of municipal waste disposed of in the landfills, but rather will be a function of the extent to which municipal dumping of hazardous substances both engendered the necessity, and contributed to the costs, of cleanup.

Id. This judicial recommendation for municipal protection is only partial. As one court recognized:

This court emphasizes the limited nature of its holding. **We are not holding that municipalities will be held equally culpable with other PRPs.** . . . That was not the issue presented to us, and even CERCLA suggests that municipalities should not be held equally culpable due to the relatively low toxicity level of MSW. . . . Section 113(f)(1) of CERCLA . . . gives courts the discretion to resolve contribution actions according to "such equitable factors as the court determines are appropriate." . . . In enacting CERCLA, members of Congress repeatedly emphasized the environmental degradation and harm caused by industrial hazardous substances, . . . and nothing in this opinion displaces to municipalities any part of the burden that must be predominantly shouldered by the industrial generators and haulers of such wastes. But nothing in the statute or legislative history excludes municipalities from bearing an appropriate share of liability at a Superfund site. **We are merely holding that a municipality that has generated or arranged for the disposal of municipal solid wastes at a facility may be liable under CERCLA § 107(a)(3) for an equitable share of responsibility** upon a third-party contribution claim under CERCLA § 113(f). . . .

Id. Under current law, there is no way for a municipality to protect itself from the risk of extensive litigation draining its already scarce resources only to ultimately found that the municipalities fair share in a site is zero dollars. Although no damages must be paid, the cost of litigation and the depletion of legal resources has caused many municipalities great consternation when addressing redevelopment issues in the context of brownfield sites.

Practice Problems

This case grows out of the ill-fated efforts of the City of North Miami, Florida ("City") and various entities and individuals to develop a municipal recreational complex on city-owned property in south Florida. Those efforts included the 1974 to 1980 operation of a landfill at the site, a landfill that is alleged to be the source of hazardous substance releases. The City seeks to recover from defendants the past and future costs associated with the cleanup and remediation of these hazardous substance releases pursuant to the cost recovery provisions of the Comprehensive Environmental Response Compensation and Liability Act ("CERCLA"), 42 U.S.C.A. § 9601 et seq.

In October 1972, the City entered into a lease agreement with Company, a Florida corporation formed by some of the defendants, under which the City leased to Company 281 acres of raw land. Pursuant to the lease agreement, Company agreed to develop the land and construct a municipal recreational complex featuring two 18–hole golf courses. In return, the City agreed to lease the property as improved to Company for thirty years, during which time Company would operate the complex and retain the lion's share of the revenues earned. Company was jointly controlled by Shareholder 1 and Shareholder 2, each holding 32.5% of the shares. Shareholder 2 served as President of the corporation and Shareholder 1 was its Treasurer. The remaining minority shares of Company were distributed among various consultants needed to develop the raw land into a recreational facility. Included among these consultants was Consultant, Company's of Company's shares.

Soon after the execution of the 1972 lease agreement, the parties agreed to permit Company to operate a landfill on the property in order to raise the level of the terrain and help defray the costs of constructing the golf courses. The City and Company amended the lease in 1974 to reflect this agreement. Shortly thereafter, the Company landfill began accepting household garbage, construction debris, vegetative materials, and industrial and commercial refuse. Company retained the services of defendant Engfirm, an engineering firm, to prepare the engineering plans and drawings for the project, assist in obtaining the necessary permits, and provide engineering and consulting services in connection with the operation of the landfill. In addition, Company contracted with ABC Demolition Co. to develop the property, operate the landfill, and construct the golf courses and other recreational facilities. Like Company, ABC was controlled by Shareholder 1 and Shareholder 2, with each owning 50% of the shares and Shareholder 1 serving as ABC's President. The Company landfill operated from 1974 to 1980. During this time, the landfill accepted over 6 million cubic yards of solid wastes, including some hospital wastes and some known toxic wastes, though the precise quantities of these wastes are disputed. Operation of the landfill, Company's sole business activity, generated approximately $8 million in revenue for Company.

From its inception, the Company development project faced intense regulatory scrutiny. In January 1975, in response to an enforcement action by the Florida Department of Pollution Control (which subsequently became the Department of Environmental Regulation or "DER"), Company applied for a temporary operating permit for the landfill. This permit issued on May 9, 1975, and reissued on September 21, 1976. It named Company as the operator and the City as the owner and imposed a variety of specific operating conditions. A full DER operating permit issued on June 8, 1979. In addition, because the eastern end of the site included approximately 103 acres of wetlands, Company obtained a dredge and fill permit from DER on January 5, 1976, which was modified on March 21, 1977. Both of the dredge and fill and the landfill operating permits were subject to the issuance of a comparable dredge and fill permit from the U.S. Army Corps of Engineers under the Federal Water Pollution Control Act; 33 U.S.C.A. § 1344. The federal permit issued on March 15, 1976 and expired on March 15, 1979. Permits for the landfill were also obtained from various other local entities, including the Dade County Fire Department. Additionally, the landfill was closely monitored by the Metropolitan Dade County Department of Environmental Resources and the U.S. Environmental Protection Agency ("EPA").

Not surprisingly, the landfill was subjected to private as well as public scrutiny. The project faced opposition from the Florida Audubon Society and from a small but vocal group or neighboring citizens. Given the rigorous regulatory climate and the vigorous local opposition, the City, Company, and ABC often found themselves enmeshed in administrative proceedings and civil litigation. In fact, during the operation of the landfill, Company was cited for numerous violations of permit conditions and regulatory requirements. Among these violations were the placement of waste in the groundwater, failure adequately to cover the garbage, disposal of hazardous wastes on site, illegal acceptance of hospital wastes, and improper placement of waste within thirty feet of lakes. Defendant Consultant handled all legal proceedings relating to the project, including matters relating to these violations.

In March 1980, the DER notified Company and the City of its intent to revoke the landfill operating permit and the state dredge and fill permit based on the various permit and regulatory violations. A year later, following the requisite administrative proceedings, DER revoked these permits. Meanwhile, EPA had been expressing increasing concern that ammonia leachate from the landfill would contaminate groundwater which, in turn, would migrate into the adjacent State Mangrove Preserve. As a result, apparently, of this concern, EPA vetoed Company's request for renewal and extension of the Corps of Engineers dredge and fill permit, which had expired on March 15, 1979. Without the permit, Company could not take steps to fill the 103 acres of wetlands that constituted the eastern portion of the tract. This, in turn, made it impossible to construct the planned 36–hole golf course on the site, thereby threatening the economic viability of the entire project. Thus it was that in July 1980, Company, faced with the state permit revocation proceedings and the EPA's announced intent to veto any Corps of Engineers dredge and fill permits, ceased its landfill operations. This ultimately doomed the entire project and Company as well. Company was dissolved a year later.

On September 8, 1983, EPA listed the Company landfill on its CERCLA "National Priorities List" of uncontrolled hazardous release sites. EPA sent letters of potential liability to Shareholder 2, Shareholder 1, Consultant, Company, ABC, the City, and others. In accordance with established CERCLA procedures, EPA conducted a series of extensive environmental investigations of the site, which included comprehensive sampling of surface water; groundwater, soils and sediments. The results of these investigations were set forth in a series of reports, which concluded that hazardous substances had leached out of the landfill into the groundwater, imperiling the adjacent state Mangrove Preserve and, potentially, the more distant Biscayne Bay. More specifically, the report of EPA's remedial investigation, found that groundwater, surface water, sediment and soils all contained organic and inorganic chemicals, many of them CERCLA hazardous substances, chiefly at the relatively low concentration levels typically associated with municipal solid waste landfills. But this report also found that "chronic toxicity was typically observed among the aquatic species exposed the groundwater samples collected from the landfill area." Indeed, another report, the Mangrove Study found that ammonia leachate had surfaced in the preserve and presented a "significant threat to aquatic life."

In March 1990, EPA published its "Proposed Plan" for remedial action. The public was invited to comment on this plan, and EPA thereafter held a public meeting in North Miami on the subject. After consideration of public comments, EPA on July 26, 1990, issued its Record of Decision ("ROD"), in which it set forth appropriate remedial action and documented in detail the agency's basis for requiring this action. EPA subsequently urged all potentially liable parties under CERCLA to undertake this remedial action voluntarily. Only the City heeded EPA's call. On March 20, 1992, the City entered into a Consent Decree with EPA in the United States District Court for the Southern District of Florida. Under this Consent Decree, the City assumed responsibility for remediation the landfill site. As a result, the City has incurred substantial costs, including, but not limited to, reimbursement of past EPA response costs; technical studies, investigation, and engineering costs; and "enforcement" costs related to the instant lawsuit. Nor is this the end of the matter; it is likely that the City will incur additional costs in the future.

Please evaluate the respective potential liabilities and defenses of each of the parties. Please also consider the potential insurance coverage and insurers' duty to defend each of the respective PRPs.

§ 6.10　FEDERAL LIEN AUTHORITY FOR RESPONSE COSTS

The 1986 Superfund Amendments authorize a federal lien for all cleanup costs and damages for which a person is liable to EPA under CERCLA. Under Superfund, all costs and expenses for which a site owner is considered liable will constitute a lien in favor of the United States on all of such party's real property that is subject to or affected by a removal or remedial action. The lien attaches immediately upon expenditure of the funds and without any judicial intervention and continues in effect until the liability for costs incurred has been satisfied or becomes unenforceable (*e.g.*, through operation of the statute of limitations). *The lien does not, however, take priority over previously perfected security interests and attaches only to the real property affected by a clean up action.*

REARDON v. UNITED STATES
947 F.2d 1509 (1st Cir.1991).

TORRUELLA, CIRCUIT JUDGE

After removing hazardous substances from property belonging to the Reardons, EPA filed a notice of lien on the property for the amount spent. *See* 42 U.S.C. § 9607(*l*). The Reardons sued to have the notice of lien removed, arguing that they were not liable for the cleanup costs, that the lien was overextensive in that it covered parcels not involved in the clean-up, and that the filing of the lien notice without a hearing deprived them of property without due process. The district court, in

Reardon v. United States, 731 F.Supp. 558 (D.Mass.1990), decided that it did not have jurisdiction to hear the Reardons' two statutory claims. It ruled that although jurisdiction existed to hear the constitutional claim, the filing of a lien did not amount to a taking of a significant property interest protected by the due process clause. It therefore denied the Reardons' motion for a preliminary injunction, and dismissed their complaint. The Reardons appealed and a panel of this court ruled in their favor on statutory grounds. *Reardon v. United States*, 922 F.2d 28 (1st Cir.1990)(withdrawn). We now consider the appeal en banc. After closely considering applicable law, including most notably the recent case of *Connecticut v. Doehr*, U.S. , 59 U.S.L.W. 4587, 111 S.Ct. 2105, 115 L.Ed.2d 1 (1991), we conclude that the district court correctly decided that it did not have jurisdiction to consider the Reardons' statutory claims, but we find that the CERCLA lien provisions do violate the fifth amendment due process clause.

I. BACKGROUND

A. Facts. In 1979, Paul and John Reardon purchased a 16–acre parcel in Norwood, Massachusetts, adjacent to an electric equipment manufacturing plant site known as the "Grant Gear" site, and named it "Kerry Place." In 1983, the Massachusetts Department of Environmental Quality Engineering, responding to a report of a nearby resident, tested soil samples from both properties and discovered extremely high levels of polychlorinated biphenyls ("PCBs") on the Grant Gear site and on Kerry Place where it bordered Grant Gear. EPA then investigated the site. Finding the same high levels of PCBs, it authorized an immediate clean-up of the contaminated areas. Between June 25 and August 1, 1983, EPA removed 518 tons of contaminated soil from the two properties. It then notified the Reardons that it had removed all soil with concentrations of PCBs known to be above the safe limit, but informed them that additional areas of contamination might exist, in which case EPA might undertake additional clean-up work.

In 1984, the Reardons subdivided Kerry Place into a number of parcels; they sold five of those parcels and retained ownership of the others. In October 1985, EPA notified the Reardons that, as current owners of Kerry Place, they might be liable under §§ 106 and 107 of the Comprehensive Environmental Response, Compensation, and Liability Act ("CERCLA"), 42 U.S.C. §§ 9606 & 9607, along with ten other present and prior owners of the properties, for the clean-up costs.

In August 1987, EPA again investigated the properties to assess the feasibility of a long-term remedy for any remaining contamination. New testing showed that soil in several areas on Kerry Place was still contaminated with PCBs. In April 1988, EPA informed the Reardons of these results. The Reardons told EPA that they intended to clean up their property themselves. EPA advised the Reardons to coordinate any offsite disposal plans with EPA and to obtain EPA's approval of a treatment or disposal facility. In January 1989, the Reardons informed

EPA that they had completed their own clean-up of Kerry Place, without having attempted coordination with or sought the approval of EPA.

On March 23, 1989, EPA filed a notice of lien with the Norfolk County Registry of Deeds pursuant to § 107(l) of CERCLA, 42 U.S.C. § 9607(l), on all of the Kerry Place parcels still owned by the Reardons. The lien was for an unspecified amount, as it secured payment of "all costs and damages covered by" 42 U.S.C. § 9607(l) for which the Reardons were liable under § 107(a) of CERCLA, 42 U.S.C. § 9607(a). Five days later, EPA notified the Reardons that it had filed the notice of lien. On July 12, 1989, EPA informed the Reardons that they could settle EPA's claims against them for $336,709, but noted that this amount did not limit the Reardons' potential liability. On September 29, 1989, EPA selected a long-term remedy for the Kerry Place and Grant Gear sites estimated to cost $16,100,000.

B. Procedural History. The Reardons filed a complaint and a motion for preliminary injunction in the United States District Court for the District of Massachusetts. They argued that they were entitled to have the notice of lien removed for three reasons. First, the Reardons maintained that they qualified as "innocent landowners" under § 107(b) of CERCLA, 42 U.S.C. § 9607(b), and therefore were not liable for any clean-up costs. Second, 42 U.S.C. § 9607(l) provides for a lien on only that property "subject to or affected by a removal or remedial action," 42 U.S.C. § 9607(l)(1)(B); the Reardons claim that since some of their Kerry Place parcels were not "subject to or affected by" the clean-up, EPA erred in filing a notice of lien covering all of those parcels. Third, they asserted that EPA's imposition of the lien without a hearing violated the due process clause of the fifth amendment to the United States Constitution.

The district court held that § 113(h) of CERCLA, 42 U.S.C. § 9613(h), divested it of jurisdiction to hear the Reardons' "innocent landowner" and "overbroad lien" claims. It found that the same section also purported to divest it of jurisdiction to hear the due process claim, but held that Congress was without power to place such a limitation on its jurisdiction. Turning to the merits of the due process claim, the district court held that the lien imposed by § 107(l) did not amount to a taking of a "significant property interest" protected by the due process clause. The court therefore denied the motion for a preliminary injunction and dismissed the complaint.

The Reardons appealed, and a panel of this court found in their favor. The panel opinion construed § 9613(h) so as to permit judicial review of the statutory challenges to the lien, and did not reach the due process issue. In response to EPA's petition for rehearing, however, a majority of the court voted to grant a rehearing en banc. Although the court en banc finds for the plaintiffs, as did the panel, we do so on constitutional rather than statutory grounds.

* * *

III.   THE DUE PROCESS CLAIM

The Supreme Court has established a two-part analysis of due process challenges to statutes which, like this one, involve property rather than liberty interests. One must first ask whether the statute authorizes the taking of a "significant property interest" protected by the fifth amendment. *E.g.*, *Fuentes v. Shevin*, 407 U.S. 67, 86, 32 L.Ed.2d 556, 92 S.Ct. 1983 (1972). If there is no significant property interest involved, the inquiry is at an end. If there is, one proceeds to examine what process is due in the particular circumstances. *E.g.*, *id.*; *Mathews v. Eldridge*, 424 U.S. 319, 335, 47 L.Ed.2d 18, 96 S.Ct. 893 (1976). We shall address each issue in turn.

A.   The Deprivation. The district court, relying primarily on *Spielman-Fond, Inc. v. Hanson's, Inc.*, 379 F.Supp. 997 (D.Ariz.1973) (three judge panel), *aff'd mem.*, 417 U.S. 901, 94 S.Ct. 2596, 41 L.Ed.2d 208 (1974), found that the filing of a federal lien under 42 U.S.C. § 9607(*l*) did not amount to a deprivation of a significant property interest; thus, the court did not reach the second step of the analysis. However, a Supreme Court case decided after the district court had issued its decision (indeed, after oral argument at the en banc rehearing of this appeal) has clarified the law in this area considerably, and has precluded continued reliance on the Court's summary affirmance in *Spielman-Fond*.

In *Connecticut v. Doehr*, 501 U.S. 1 (1991), a unanimous Court held that a Connecticut attachment statute violated the due process clause. The Court held that the attachment lien on plaintiff Doehr's real property deprived him of a significant property interest within the meaning of the due process clause. The Court stated:

> For a property owner like Doehr, attachment ordinarily clouds title; impairs the ability to sell or otherwise alienate the property; taints any credit rating; reduces the chance of obtaining a home equity loan or additional mortgage; and can even place an existing mortgage in technical default where there is an insecurity clause.

Doehr, ___ U.S. at ___. It concluded that "even the temporary or partial impairments to property rights that attachments, liens, and similar encumbrances entail are sufficient to merit due process protection." *Id.* . . . .And, in a footnote, it disposed of its summary affirmance in *Spielman-Fond* by noting that "[a] summary disposition does not enjoy the full precedential value of a case argued on the merits and disposed of by a written opinion." *Id.* at ___ n. 4 (citing *Edelman v. Jordan*, 415 U.S. 651, 671, 39 L.Ed.2d 662, 94 S.Ct. 1347 (1974)). *See also id.* at ___ (Rehnquist, C.J., concurring)(*Spielman-Fond* should not be read to mean that the imposition of a lien is not a deprivation of a significant interest in property).

In light of these comments, we cannot but conclude that the lien on real property created in 42 U.S.C. § 9607(*l*) amounts to deprivation of a "significant property interest" within the meaning of the due process clause. The EPA's lien has substantially the same effect on the Reardons as the attachment had on the plaintiff in *Doehr*—clouding title, limiting alienability, affecting current and potential mortgages. We thus turn to the second, more difficult, part of the analysis.

B. What Process is Due. The *Doehr* Court reaffirmed the "now familiar threefold inquiry," *id*. at ___, required to determine what process is due. That inquiry requires a court to balance

> "the private interest that will be affected by the official action;" "the risk of an erroneous deprivation of such interest through the procedures used, and the probable value, if any, of additional or substitute safeguards;" and lastly "the Government's interest, including the function involved and the fiscal and administrative burdens that the additional or substitute procedural requirement would entail."

Id. (quoting *Mathews v. Eldridge*, 424 U.S. 319, 335, 47 L.Ed.2d 18, 96 S.Ct. 893 (1976)). We apply the *Mathews* test to the facts of this case.

(1) The Affected Private Interest. The federal lien here, like the attachment lien in *Doehr*, does not deprive the landowner of possession and use of his property. As *Doehr* said, the effect of such a lien—clouding title, impairing the ability to alienate the property, tainting credit ratings, and reducing the chance of obtaining any further mortgage—"is less than the perhaps temporary total deprivation of household goods or wages." *Id*. However, the interests that the federal lien affects—the same as the interests affected in *Doehr*—are "significant." *Id*. We note in addition that the CERCLA statute contemplates the filing of a notice of lien well before clean-up procedures are completed, with the result that the lien is not for any sum certain, but for an indefinite amount. This would seem to increase the lien's effect on the landowner's property interests, since a potential buyer or mortgage lender could not identify any limit on the government's interest in the property short of its full value.

(2) The Risk of Current Procedures and the Value of Additional Safeguards. This part of the analysis encompasses several considerations. First, we must weigh the nature of the issues which would indicate whether the federal lien in this case has been correctly filed. Are these issues "uncomplicated matters that lend themselves to documentary proof," *Mitchell v. W.T. Grant Co.*, 416 U.S. 600, 609, 40 L.Ed.2d 406, 94 S.Ct. 1895 (1974), thereby minimizing the risk that the lien would be wrongfully filed? Or are the issues "highly factual?" *Doehr*, ___ U.S. at ___.

This case falls somewhere between the two extremes. The initial issue of liability under CERCLA is quite straightforward. Section 107(a) of CERCLA, 42 U.S.C. § 9607(a), makes owners of "facilities" strictly liable for, among other things, all response costs incurred by the United States "not inconsistent with the national contingency plan." Ownership of land, and the physical presence of hazardous substances on land, are matters that are subject to relatively simple resolution. Whether the response costs were incurred consistently with the national contingency plan is an issue which may be highly factual, but it is usually a matter of the amount, and not the existence, of liability. More likely to be "highly factual" is the determination whether certain of the owner's parcels of land are "subject to or affected by" EPA's response action. Similarly, on the issue of the landowner's liability, EPA admits in its brief that the "concepts of due care, foreseeability, objective and subjective knowledge, some of which are unique in CERCLA to the innocent landowner defense, are extremely fact-intensive." EPA Supplementary Brief at 16–17.

Second, we must consider what procedural safeguards, if any, CERCLA provides against erroneous filing of a lien.

a. The right to a judicial hearing. CERCLA provides no such safeguards. It provides for no pre-deprivation proceedings at all—not even the ex parte "probable cause" hearing judged insufficient in *Doehr*. *See Doehr* at ___ (describing Connecticut attachment procedure).

Nor does CERCLA provide for an immediate post-deprivation hearing. . . . The first hearing the property owner is likely to get is at the enforcement proceeding, or cost recovery action, brought by EPA. This action may be brought several years after the notice of lien is filed; it is limited only by a rather complicated statute of limitations, see 42 U.S.C. § 9613(g)(2), which gives EPA three years after a removal action is completed or six years after a remedial action is commenced to bring such a suit. The running of the statute of limitations is entirely within EPA's control. Since the government may take its own sweet time before suing, and since the removal or remedial action may itself take years to complete, the lien may be in place for a considerable time without an opportunity for a hearing.

"Mere postponement of judicial enquiry is not a denial of due process if the opportunity given for ultimate judicial determination of liability is adequate." *Phillips v. Commissioner*, 283 U.S. 589, 596, 75 L.Ed. 1289, 51 S.Ct. 608 (1931). But the CERCLA statute of limitations on liens throws the "ultimate judicial determination" so far into the future as to render it inadequate. Indeed, in this respect the CERCLA scheme resembles the replevin statutes in *Fuentes v. Shevin*, where the Court held that the debtor may not be "left in limbo to await a hearing that might or might not 'eventually' occur." *Mitchell v. W.T. Grant Co.*, 416 U.S. at 618 (discussing *Fuentes v. Shevin*).

b. Posting of a Bond. The Court has recognized that requiring the filing party to post a bond may provide the property owner important protection against wrongful filing; in *Doehr*, four members of the Court suggested that due process always requires a plaintiff's bond in the context of an attachment. *See Doehr*, ___ U.S. at ___ (plurality). CERCLA does not require EPA to post a bond when filing the notice of federal lien.

c. Action for damages. In *Doehr*, the State of Connecticut argued that the availability of a double damages remedy for suits that are commenced without probable cause was an important protection against misuse of the attachment provisions; however, four members of the Court did not find the availability of such a suit to be an adequate procedural safeguard. Four members of the court explained in detail why an action for damages would never prove adequate:

> The necessity for at least a prompt postattachment hearing is self-evident because the right to be compensated at the end of the case, if the plaintiff loses, for all provable injuries caused by the attachment is inadequate to redress the harm inflicted, harm that could have been avoided had an early hearing been held. An individual with an immediate need or opportunity to sell a property can neither do so, nor otherwise satisfy that need or recreate the opportunity. The same applies to a parent in need of a home equity loan for a child's education, an entrepreneur seeking to start a business on the strength of an otherwise strong credit rating, or simply a homeowner who might face the disruption of having a mortgage placed in technical default.

Doehr, ___ U.S. at ___ (plurality).

In this case, EPA asserts that the Reardons might recover damages for the wrongful filing of a lien by filing a suit under the Tucker Act, 28 U.S.C. § 1491(a)(1) claiming that the lien was a taking without compensation in violation of the fifth amendment. The Reardons counter that a Tucker Act suit would not be possible in this case. It appears to us that recovery under the Tucker Act would be, at best, questionable, and any potential relief or recovery would be inadequate in the same way described by the *Doehr* Court. *See Bowen v. Massachusetts*, 487 U.S. 879, 914, 101 L.Ed.2d 749, 108 S.Ct. 2722 (1988); *United States v. Testan*, 424 U.S. 392, 398, 47 L.Ed.2d 114, 96 S.Ct. 948 (1976).

(3) The Government's Interest. The third consideration is "'the Government's interest, including the function involved and the fiscal and administrative burdens that the additional or substitute procedural requirement would entail.'" *Doehr*, ___ U.S. at ___ (quoting *Mathews v. Eldridge*, 424 U.S. 319, 335, 47 L.Ed.2d 18, 96 S.Ct. 893 (1976)). This factor encompasses a number of points.

    a.   Recognized Interest in the Property. First, the Court has considered whether the party seeking to impose a lien on property has a recognized interest in the particular property which it is seeking to protect. *See Doehr*, ___ U.S. at ___ n. 4, ___ ; *Mitchell v. W.T. Grant Co.*, 416 U.S. at 603. For example, in *Mitchell* the parties stipulated that defendant W.T. Grant Co., which had sold goods on installment to plaintiff Mitchell, had a vendor's lien on the goods. The Court found that an ex parte order to sequester those goods did not violate due process. *See Mitchell*, 416 U.S. at 604 ("The reality [in this case] is that both seller and buyer had current, real interests in the property.... Resolution of the due process question must take account not only of the interests of the buyer of the property but those of the seller as well."). In contrast, in *Doehr* the attached property served only to ensure the availability of assets to satisfy a possible judgment in a tort action unrelated to the property. *See Doehr,* ___ U.S. at ___.

In this case, the government does not have any prior recognized interest in the Reardons' property. Under 42 U.S.C. § 9607(1), of course, a federal lien is created by operation of law before the government files a notice of lien. But that lien attaches to particular real property only if (1) the property is owned by a person who is liable to the United States for CERCLA clean-up costs, and (2) the property is "subject to or affected by a removal or remedial action." 42 U.S.C. § 9607(*l*)(1). The Reardons assert that they are not liable, and that some of the property on which a federal lien has been noticed has not been subject to or affected by a removal or remedial action. Nor has any court ever found that either of these conditions has been satisfied. Thus we cannot say that the government has a present, recognized interest in the property.

We believe this conclusion is consistent with the Court's remarks in *Doehr* about the *Spielman-Fond* case. The Court, explaining why its summary affirmance in *Spielman-Fond, Inc. v. Hanson's Inc.,* 417 U.S. 901, 41 L.Ed.2d 208, 94 S.Ct. 2596 (1974), did not control in *Doehr,* stated:

The facts of *Spielman-Fond* presented an alternative basis for affirmance in any event. Unlike the case before us, the mechanic's lien statute in *Spielman-Fond* required the creditor to have a pre-existing interest in the property at issue. 379 F.Supp. 997. As we explain below, a heightened plaintiff interest in certain circumstances can provide a ground for upholding procedures that are otherwise suspect.

Doehr, ___ U.S. at ___ n. 4. In his concurrence, Chief Justice Rehnquist reiterates this distinction:

But in *Spielman-Fond, Inc., supra,* there was, as the Court points out in fn. 4 [sic], ante, an alternate basis available to this Court for affirmance of that decision. Arizona recognized a pre-existing lien in favor of unpaid mechanics and materialmen who had contributed labor or supplies which were incorporated as improvements to real property. The existence of such a lien upon the very property ultimately posted or noticed distinguishes those cases from the present one, where the plaintiff had no pre-existing interest in the real property which he sought to attach.

Id. at ___ (Rehnquist, C.J., concurring). Although these comments are brief, we think the Court's reasoning is as follows. At the time *Spielman-Fond* was decided, the relevant Arizona statute provided:

Every person who labors or furnishes materials, machinery, fixtures or tools in the construction, alteration, or repair of any building, or other structure or improvement whatever, shall have a lien thereon for the work or labor done of materials, machinery, fixtures or tools furnished.

Ariz. Rev. Stat. § 33–981 (1973). The landowners in *Spielman-Fond* apparently did not deny that "defendants Yanke and Hanson's furnished labor and materials to plaintiffs in connection with the development of plaintiffs' mobile home park." *Spielman-Fond*, 379 F.Supp. 997. Thus, they could not deny that, under the terms of the Arizona statute, Yanke and Hanson's had a lien on the property. In the instant case, by contrast, the Reardons do not admit that the conditions under which the government would have a lien on their property are fulfilled.

Of course, the Reardons cannot claim that the underlying action is entirely unrelated to the attached property, as was the case in *Doehr*. But, taking the Reardons' contentions as true, a cleanup undertaken by EPA on portions of the Reardons' property is too minimal a connection to justify bootstrapping a lien on all the parcels.

Relying on the apparent constitutionality of a mechanic's lien as a basis for upholding the CERCLA lien fails for three further reasons. First, a *Spielman-Fond* type of mechanic's lien rests on a voluntary agreement between the contracting parties. Proof of an agreement establishes a connection between the parties, and, where the service has indisputably been rendered, creates a rebuttable presumption of at least some liability on the part of the landowner. There is no such voluntary agreement here. Moreover, mechanic's lien statutes typically provide for dissolution of the lien unless the mechanic takes further action. For example, the Arizona statute in *Spielman-Fond* gave the property owner an opportunity to challenge the lien and provided a six month period after which the lien was dissolved if an action was not brought to enforce it. Ariz. Rev. Stat. Ann. § 33–998. *See also, e.g.,* Maine Rev. Stat. Ann. tit. 10, §§ 3253, 3255; Mass. Gen. L. ch. 254, §§ 8, 11; N.H. Rev. Stat. Ann. § 447:9. Finally, mechanic's liens, unlike CERCLA liens, are validated by their established place in the law of the land—pre-dating the Constitution itself.

b. Exigent Circumstances. The absence of notice and a hearing may be justified by exigent circumstances. As the Court said in *Doehr*, finding a lack of such circumstances:

> There was no allegation that Doehr was about to transfer or encumber his real estate or take any other action during the pendency of the action that would render his real estate unavailable to satisfy a judgment. Our cases have recognized such a properly supported claim would be an exigent circumstance permitting post-poning any notice or hearing until after the attachment is effected. *See Mitchell, supra,* at 609; *Fuentes,* supra, at 90–92; *Sniadach,* 395 U.S. 337, 339, 23 L.Ed.2d 349, 89 S.Ct. 1820. Absent such allegations, however, the plaintiff's interest in attaching the property does not justify the burdening of Doehr's ownership rights without a hearing to determine the likelihood of recovery.

Doehr, ___ U.S. at ___.

As in *Doehr*, there is nothing in this case suggesting that a transfer or encumbrance of the parcels retained by the Reardons was imminent. And a special feature of CERCLA makes a claim of exigent circum-stances even less likely than in the usual lien case. Under the CERCLA liability provisions, any subsequent owner of property who knew at the time of purchase that hazardous wastes were located on the premises would become liable for clean-up costs, and the property could be sold to satisfy a judgment against that subsequent owner. *See* 42 U.S.C. § 9607. Hence, the transfer of property would likely affect the government's interest in recovering cleanup costs less than the average transfer would affect the interest of the average potential judgment creditor.

c. The Added Burden of Additional Procedural Requirements. The due process calculus also involves consideration of "the fiscal and administrative burdens that the additional or substitute procedural requirement would entail." *Doehr*, ___ U.S. at ___ (quoting *Mathews v. Eldridge*, 424 U.S. 319, 335, 47 L.Ed.2d 18, 96 S.Ct. 893 (1976)). In this case, the minimum additional procedural requirements would be notice of an intention to file a notice of lien and provision for a hearing if the property owner claimed that the lien was wrongfully imposed. This would seem to be a relatively simple matter. Moreover, the Constitution certainly allows the process due to be tailored to fit the realities of the situation. *Mitchell v. W.T. Grant Co.*, 416 U.S. at 610. For example, EPA may only need to demonstrate probable cause or reason to believe that the land would be "subject to or affected by" a cleanup, or that the landowner was not entitled to an "innocent landowner" defense.

Of course, EPA might seek to place a lien on property during the very early stages of a response action, when it did not have sufficient proof that a particular parcel of property was going to be "subject to or affected by" that action. However, we do not believe that EPA has a legitimate interest in exceeding the limits of its authority under CERCLA, and we see nothing wrong with requiring EPA to delay filing a notice of lien until it can show that the statutory prerequisites for filing the notice have been satisfied.

EPA argues that the present case can be distinguished from *Doehr* in five respects: (1) the EPA's interest in the Reardons' property before attachment of the lien; (2) the availability of a Tucker Act damages action; (3) the presence of exigent circumstances; (4) the interest of the United States in protecting the federal fisc; and (5) the purportedly minimal risk of erroneous attachment in this case. Our discussion above has already addressed the first three of these arguments. We will now consider the last two.

It does not seem that the fact that the United States, rather than a private party, is seeking the lien, should weigh in favor of the statute's constitutionality. Indeed, since the due process clause protects against government deprivation, just the opposite would seem to be the case. There is one situation, the federal tax lien, where the government's financial well-being may justify the draconian deprivation of its citizens' property. But an EPA lien is not on the level of a federal tax lien. The tax lien is a law unto itself, and arises from administrative necessity (as well as direct constitutional authority, see U.S. Const. art. I, § 8) not present here. . . .

As for EPA's final point, we simply do not see how the risk of erroneous deprivation in this case can be characterized as minimal. Rather, the risk seems greater than it was in *Doehr*. In that case, a judge considered the merits ex parte before authorizing the attachment, the plaintiff could attain an immediate post-attachment hearing, and a double damage remedy was available to compensate for, and to deter, error. Here, there is no prior neutral proceeding, no double damage remedy, and no post-attachment review for what may be many years. Unless EPA is immune from error—which we doubt—the risk of mistake is not minimal.

IV. Conclusion

In sum, we find that CERCLA 9613(h) does not bar federal jurisdiction over the due process claim in this case; that the deprivation caused by the CERCLA lien is significant; that, at least when the landowner has raised a colorable defense, the issues may be quite factual; that the lien statute completely lacks procedural safeguards; that the government has no recognized pre-existing interest in the property; that the statute has no "exigent circumstances" requirement (nor have any such circumstances been shown in this case); and that additional procedural requirements are likely to place significant, but not overwhelming, administrative burdens on the government. As applied in this case, the statute thus deprives persons of property with far less process than the State of Connecticut provided in the attachment law found unconstitutional in *Doehr*. Thus, we are constrained to find that the CERCLA lien provisions, by not providing, at the very least, notice and a pre-deprivation hearing to a property owner who claims that the property to be encumbered is not "subject to or affected by a removal or remedial action," violate the fifth amendment due process clause. . . .

Cyr, Circuit Judge (dissenting).

Although the majority makes a respectable case that 42 U.S.C. § 9613(h), as interpreted, violates the due process clause, I cannot accede to its failure to observe governing rules of statutory construction which warrant an interpretation more consonant with the CERCLA statute and the Constitution.

* * *

Due process analysis requires that we consider the effects of the CERCLA lien on the Reardons' property rights, as applied in this case. In my opinion, considering the important governmental interests involved and the relatively insignificant risk of any unwarranted, uncompensable, short-term deprivation of the Reardons' property rights, a prompt postdeprivation hearing at the instance of the Reardons would satisfy the due process analysis required by *Doehr* and *Mathews*. As I believe the statute is reasonably interpreted as permitting a prompt postdeprivation challenge at the instance of innocent landowners and is therefore constitutional, I respectfully dissent.

Notes

1. The states with environmental lien statutes are Alaska, Arkansas, Connecticut, Illinois, Indiana, Iowa, Kentucky, Louisiana, Maine, Maryland, Massachusetts, Michigan, Minnesota, Montana, New Hampshire, New Jersey, Ohio, Oregon, Pennsylvania, Tennessee, and Texas. The states with superlien statutes are Connecticut, Louisiana, Maine, Massachusetts, New Hampshire, and New Jersey.

2. The *Reardon* decision relied heavily on the rationale of *Connecticut v. Doehr*, 501 U.S. 1 , 111 S.Ct. 2105, 115 L.Ed.2d 1 (1991), which did not involve an environmental lien statute. Was *Reardon* correct in applying the same standard of review to determine the constitutionality of an environmental lien statute as that of other attachment liens? In consideration of CERCLA's important public health and environmental protection purposes, should the courts relax strict due process requirements for the environmental lien statute?

3. Under the *Doehr* and *Reardon* analyses, an environmental lien statute, in order to pass constitutional muster, must provide at the minimum notice and a pre-attachment hearing, unless an immediate post-attachment hearing is provided in the face of exigent circumstances. Do you agree with *Reardon* that such due process safeguards Bill not frustrate congressional intent to authorize prompt response to environmental emergencies without the need to await judicial determination of liability?

4. As noted, environmental liens can cause many practical problems for the property owner, lender, developer, or creditor. How will the due process protections required by *Reardon* alleviate these problems?

5. Are environmental superliens really necessary to protect a government's interest in securing repayment of pollution cleanup expenditures? Interestingly, the trend toward superliens has faltered. Since 1988, Arkansas and Tennessee deleted superlien provisions from their cleanup statutes, and efforts to create environmental superliens in Kansas, New York, and Pennsylvania were defeated.

6. A title search will not reveal the potential existence of the superlien, even though the property may be subject for many years to an ongoing governmental investigation and hazardous substance cleanup, during which a lien could be imposed at any time. The presence of hazardous material on land, and the concomitant possibility of governmental liens, does not constitute a title defect covered by a title insurance policy. *See Lick Mill Creek Apartments v. Chicago Title Ins. Co.*, 231 Cal.App.3d 1654, 283 Cal.Rptr. 231 (1991); *Chicago Title Ins. Co. v. Kumar*, 24 Mass.App.Ct. 53, 506 N.E.2d 154, 156 (1987). This problem is alleviated in states which require the government to record notice as soon as it designates the property as a contaminated site or begins to expend funds to investigate or clean up the property. *See, e.g.*, Tenn. Code Ann. § 68–46–209 (1987 & Supp. 1991).

§ 6.11 NATIONAL CONTINGENCY PLAN/NATIONAL PRIORITY LIST

Before Congress created the EPA and long before Congress enacted the CERCLA, 42 U.S.C.A. §§ 9601–9675, there was a National Contingency Plan ("NCP"). It was then called the National Oil and Hazardous Substances Pollution Contingency Plan. In 1968, a group of federal agencies developed the first NCP, which was a multi-agency strategy for dealing with environmental disasters. In 1970, Congress incorporated the NCP into the Federal Water Pollution Control Act, 33 U.S.C.A. §§ 1251–1376, and pursuant to its directive, the President issued the first published NCP. Water and Environmental Quality Improvement Act of 1970, Pub. L. No. 91–224, 84 Stat. 91, § 102 (1970); 35 Fed. Reg. 8508 (1970). The NCP, which acquired its current name—the National Oil and Hazardous Substances Pollution Contingency Plan, 36 Fed. Reg. 16,215 (1971)—in 1971, was revised a number of times throughout the 1970s. *See* 37 Fed. Reg. 2808 (1972); 38 Fed. Reg. 21,888 (1973); 45 Fed. Reg. 17,832 (1980). By 1980, a comprehensive NCP was in place, although it applied only to discharges into waters regulated by the Clean Water Act. *Id.* "It did not apply to releases to groundwater or soil, and it did not provide authority or funding for long-term federal response to chronic hazards."

CERCLA came next. Enacted in 1980, CERCLA provided "for liability, compensation, cleanup, and emergency response for hazardous substances released into the environment and the cleanup of inactive waste disposal sites." Pub. L. No.96–510, 94 Stat. 2767, 2767. The NCP plays a prominent role under CERCLA. Section 104(a)(1) of CERCLA authorizes the President "to act, consistent with the national contingency plan, to remove or arrange for the removal of, and provide for remedial action relating to such hazardous substance, pollutant, or contaminant at any time …, or take any other response measure consistent with the national contingency plan which the President deems necessary to protect the public health or welfare or the environment." 42 U.S.C.A. § 9604(a)(1). The NCP thus "provides the organizational structure and procedures" for responding to hazardous waste threats. 40 C.F.R. § 300.1. It is the means by which EPA implements CERCLA.

When Congress enacted CERCLA in 1980, it directed the President to revise and republish the NCP in light of the new law. 42 U.S.C. § 9605(a). Pursuant to section 115 of CERCLA, the President assigned EPA the responsibility of amending the NCP. *See* 42 U.S.C. § 9615; Exec. Order No. 12,316, 46 Fed. Reg. 42,237 (1981); Exec. Order No. 12,580, 52 Fed. Reg. 2923 (1987). In 1982, EPA issued a new version of the NCP. 47 Fed. Reg. 31,180 (1982). EPA revised the NCP again in 1985. 50 Fed. Reg. 47,912 (1985). When Congress passed the Superfund Amendments and Reauthorization Act of 1986 ("SARA"), Pub. L. No. 99–499, 100 Stat. 1613, which significantly revised the statute, Congress directed the President to revise the NCP again to reflect the changes in CERCLA. 42 U.S.C. § 9605(b). EPA issued these revisions to the NCP in 1990. 55 Fed. Reg. 8666 (1990). Thus, CERCLA, as amended, requires that the NCP include and periodically update a list of national priorities among the known releases or threatened releases of hazardous substances, pollutants, or contaminants throughout the United States. The

National Priorities List ("NPL") which is Appendix B to 40 CFR part 300 constitutes this list.

Section 105 of CERCLA amends the NCP to include criteria prioritizing releases throughout the U.S. before undertaking remedial action at uncontrolled hazardous waste before undertaking remedial action at uncontrolled hazardous waste sites. The Hazard Ranking System (HRS) is a model that is used to evaluate the relative threats to human health and the environment posed by actual or potential releases of hazardous substances, pollutants, and contaminants. The HRS criteria take into account the population at risk, the hazard potential of the substances, as well as the potential for contamination of drinking water supplies, direct human contact, destruction of sensitive ecosystems, damage to natural resources affecting the human food chain, contamination of surface water used for recreation or potable water consumption, and contamination of ambient air.

The HRS score is crucial since it is the primary mechanism used to determine whether a site is eligible to be included on the National Priorities List (NPL). Only sites on the NPL are eligible for Superfund-financed remedial actions. HRS scores are derived from the sources described in this information collection, including field reconnaissance, taking samples at the site, and reviewing available reports and documents. States record the collected information on HRS documentation worksheets and include this in the supporting reference package. States then send the package to the EPA region for a completeness and accuracy review, and the Region then sends it to EPA Headquarters for a final quality assurance review. If the site scores above the NPL designated cutoff value, and if it meets the other criteria for listing, it is then eligible to be proposed on the NPL.

The NPL is intended primarily to guide the EPA in determining which sites warrant further investigation to assess the nature and extent of public health and environmental risks associated with the site and to determine what CERCLA-financed remedial action(s), if any, may be appropriate. The NPL is not intended to define the boundaries of a site or to determine the extent of contamination.

EPA identifies sites which appear to present a significant risk to public health, welfare, or the environment and it maintains the NPL as the list of those sites. Sites on the NPL may be the subject of Fund-financed remedial actions. Any site deleted from the NPL remains eligible for Fund-financed remedial actions in the unlikely event that conditions at the site warrant such action. Sites may be deleted from the list after notice and comment by the public. Section 300.66(c)(8) of the NCP states that Fund-financed actions may be taken at sites deleted from the NPL. Deletion of a site from the NPL does not affect responsible party liability or impede EPA efforts to recover costs associated with response efforts.

NATIONAL PRIORITIES LIST FOR UNCONTROLLED HAZARDOUS WASTE SITES

60 Fed. Reg. 20330 (April 25, 1995).

* * *

In 1980, Congress enacted the Comprehensive Environmental Response, Compensation, and Liability Act, 42 U.S.C. 9601–9675 ("CERCLA" or "the Act"), in response to the dangers of uncontrolled hazardous waste sites. CERCLA was amended on October 17, 1986, by the Superfund Amendments and Reauthorization Act ("SARA"), Public Law No. 99–499, stat. 1613 et seq. To implement CERCLA, EPA promulgated the revised National Oil and Hazardous Substances Pollution Contingency Plan ("NCP"), 40 CFR Part 300, on July 16, 1982 (47 FR 31180), pursuant to CERCLA section 105 and Executive Order 12316 (46 FR 42237, August 20, 1981). The NCP sets forth the guidelines and procedures needed to respond under CERCLA to releases and threatened releases of hazardous substances, pollutants, or contaminants. EPA has revised the NCP on several occasions. The most recent comprehensive revision was on March 8, 1990 (55 FR 8666).

Section 105(a)(8)(A) of CERCLA requires that the NCP include "criteria for determining priorities among releases or threatened releases throughout the United States for the purpose of taking remedial action * * * and, to the extent practicable taking into account the potential urgency of such action, for the purpose of taking removal action." "Removal" actions are defined broadly and include a wide range of actions taken to study, clean up, prevent or otherwise address releases and threatened releases. 42 USC 9601(23). " 'Remedial' actions" are those "consistent with permanent remedy, taken instead of or in addition to removal actions * * *." 42 USC 9601(24).

Pursuant to section 105(a)(8)(B) of CERCLA, as amended by SARA, EPA has promulgated a list of national priorities among the known or threatened releases of hazardous substances, pollutants, or contaminants throughout the United States. That list, which is Appendix B of 40 CFR Part 300, is the National Priorities List ("NPL").

CERCLA section 105(a)(8)(B) defines the NPL as a list of "releases" and as a list of the highest priority "facilities." The discussion below may refer to the "releases or threatened releases" that are included on the NPL interchangeably as "releases," "facilities," or "sites."

CERCLA section 105(a)(8)(B) also requires that the NPL be revised at least annually. A site may undergo remedial action financed by the Trust Fund established under CERCLA (commonly referred to as the "Superfund") only after it is placed on the NPL, as provided in the NCP at 40 CFR 300.425(b)(1). However, under 40 CFR 300.425(b)(2) placing a site on the NPL "does not imply that monies will be expended." EPA may pursue other appropriate authorities to remedy the releases, including enforcement action under CERCLA and other laws.

CERCLA section 305 provides for a legislative veto of regulations promulgated under CERCLA. Although *INS v. Chadha*, 462 U.S. 919, 103 S.Ct. 2764, 77 L.Ed.2d 317 (1983) cast the validity of the legislative veto into question, EPA has transmitted a copy of this regulation to the Secretary of the Senate and the Clerk of the House of Representatives. Three mechanisms for placing sites on the NPL for possible remedial action are included in the NCP at 40 CFR 300.425(c)(55 FR 8845, March 8, 1990). Under 40 CFR 300.425(c)(1), a site may be included on the NPL if it scores sufficiently high on the Hazard Ranking System ("HRS"), which EPA promulgated as Appendix A of 40 CFR Part 300. On December 14, 1990 (55 FR 51532), EPA promulgated revisions to the HRS partly in response to CERCLA section 105(c), added by SARA. The revised HRS evaluates four pathways: ground water, surface water, soil exposure, and air. The HRS serves as a screening device to evaluate the relative potential of uncontrolled hazardous substances to pose a threat to human health or the environment. As a matter of Agency policy, those sites that score 28.50 or greater on the HRS are eligible for the NPL.

Under a second mechanism for adding sites to the NPL, each State may designate a single site as its top priority, regardless of the HRS score. This mechanism, provided by the NCP at 40 CFR 300.425(c)(2), requires that, to the extent practicable, the NPL include within the 100 highest priorities, one facility designated by each State representing the greatest danger to public health, welfare, or the environment among known facilities in the State.

The third mechanism for listing, included in the NCP at 40 CFR 300.425(c)(3), allows certain sites to be listed regardless of their HRS score, if all of the following conditions are met:

√ The Agency for Toxic Substances and Disease Registry (ATSDR) of the U.S. Public Health Service has issued a health advisory that recommends dissociation of individuals from the release.

√ EPA determines that the release poses a significant threat to public health.

√ EPA anticipates that it will be more cost-effective to use its remedial authority (available only at NPL sites) than to use its removal authority to respond to the release.

EPA promulgated an original NPL of 406 sites on September 8, 1983 (48 FR 40658). The NPL has been expanded since then, most recently on December 16, 1994 (59 FR 65206).

The NPL includes two sections, one of sites that are evaluated and cleaned up by EPA (the "General Superfund Section"), and one of sites being addressed by other Federal agencies (the "Federal Facilities Section"). Under Executive Order 12580 (52 FR 2923, January 29, 1987) and CERCLA section 120, each Federal agency is responsible for carrying out most response actions at facilities under its own jurisdiction, custody, or control, although EPA is responsible for preparing an HRS score and determining whether the facility is placed on the NPL. EPA is not the lead agency at these sites, and its role at such sites is accordingly less extensive than at other sites. The Federal Facilities Section includes those facilities at which EPA is not the lead agency.

DELETIONS/CLEANUPS

EPA may delete sites from the NPL where no further response is appropriate under Superfund, as explained in the NCP at 40 CFR 300.425(e)(55 FR 8845, March 8, 1990). To date, the Agency has deleted 75 sites from the General Superfund Section of the NPL, most recently Olmsted County Sanitary Landfill, Oronoco, Minnesota (60 FR 8570, February 15, 1995); Boise Cascade/Onan Corp./Medtronics, Inc., Fridley, Minnesota (60 FR 8570, February 15, 1995); Kent City Mobile Home Park, Kent City, Michigan (60 FR 14645, March 20, 1995); Crystal City Airport, Crystal City, Texas (60 FR 15247, March 23, 1995); Radium Chemical Co., Inc., New York City, New York (60 FR 15489, March 24, 1995); Independent Nail Co., Beaufort, South Carolina (60 FR 16808, April 3, 1995); and Wilson Concepts of Florida, Inc., Pompano Beach, Florida (60 FR 17004, April 4, 1995).

EPA also has developed an NPL construction completion list ("CCL") to simplify its system of categorizing sites and to better communicate the successful completion of cleanup activities (58 FR 12142, March 2, 1993). Sites qualify for the CCL when:

(1) any necessary physical construction is complete, whether or not final cleanup levels or other requirements have been achieved;

(2) EPA has determined that the response action should be limited to measures that do not involve construction (e.g., institutional controls); or

(3) the site qualifies for deletion from the NPL. Inclusion of a site on the CCL has no legal significance.

In addition to the 74 sites that have been deleted from the NPL because they have been cleaned up (the Waste Research and Reclamation site was deleted based on deferral to another program and is not considered cleaned up), an additional 217 sites are also in the NPL CCL, all but three from the General Superfund Section. Thus, as of March 1995, the CCL consists of 291 sites.

Cleanups at sites on the NPL do not reflect the total picture of Superfund accomplishments. As of February 28, 1995, EPA had conducted 660 removal actions at NPL sites, and 2,382 removal actions at non-NPL sites. Information on removals is available from the Superfund hotline.

* * *

II.   Purpose and Implementation of the NPL

PURPOSE

The legislative history of CERCLA (Report of the Committee on Environment and Public Works, Senate Report No. 96–848, 96th Cong., 2d Sess. 60 (1980)) states the primary purpose of the NPL:

The priority lists serve primarily informational purposes, identifying for the States and the public those facilities and sites or other releases which appear to warrant remedial actions. Inclusion of a facility or site on the list does not in itself reflect a judgment of the activities of its owner or operator, it does not require those persons to undertake any action, nor does it assign liability to any person. Subsequent government action in the form of remedial actions or enforcement actions will be necessary in order to do so, and these actions will be attended by all appropriate procedural safeguards.

The purpose of the NPL, therefore, is primarily to serve as an informational and management tool. The identification of a site for the NPL is intended to guide EPA in determining which sites warrant further investigation to assess the nature and extent of the public health and environmental risks associated with the site and to determine what CERCLA-financed remedial action(s), if any, may be appropriate. The NPL also serves to notify the public of sites that EPA believes warrant further investigation. Finally, listing a site serves as notice to potentially responsible parties that the Agency may initiate CERCLA-financed remedial action.

IMPLEMENTATION

After initial discovery of a site at which a release or threatened release may exist, EPA may begin a series of increasingly complex evaluations. The first step, the Preliminary Assessment (PA), is a low-cost review of existing information to determine if the site poses a threat to the public health or the environment. If the site presents a serious imminent threat, EPA may take immediate removal action. If the PA shows that the site presents a threat but not an imminent threat, EPA generally will perform a more extensive study called the Site Inspection (SI). The SI involves collecting additional information to better understand the extent of the problem at the site, screen out sites that will not qualify for the NPL, and obtain data necessary to calculate an HRS score for sites that warrant placement on the NPL and further study. To date EPA has completed approximately 37,000 PAs and approximately 18,000 SIs.

The NCP at 40 CFR 300.425(b)(1) limits expenditure of the Trust Fund for remedial actions to sites on the NPL. However, EPA may take enforcement actions under CERCLA or other applicable statutes against responsible parties regardless of whether the site is on the NPL. Although, as a practical matter, the focus of EPA's CERCLA enforcement actions has been and will continue to be on NPL sites. Similarly, in the case of CERCLA removal actions, EPA has the authority to act at any site, whether listed or not, that meets the criteria of the NCP at 40 CFR 300.415(b)(2)(55 FR 8842, March 8, 1990).

EPA's policy is to pursue cleanup of NPL sites using all the appropriate response and/or enforcement actions available to the Agency, including authorities other than CERCLA. The Agency will decide on a site-by-site basis whether to take enforcement or other action under

CERCLA or other authorities prior to undertaking response action, to proceed directly with Trust Fund-financed response actions and seek to recover response costs after cleanup, or do both. To the extent feasible, once sites are on the NPL, EPA will determine high-priority candidates for CERCLA-financed response action and/or enforcement action through both State and Federal initiatives. EPA will take into account which approach is more likely to accomplish cleanup of the site most expeditiously while using CERCLA's limited resources as efficiently as possible.

Although it is a factor that is considered, the ranking of sites by HRS scores does not by itself determine the sequence in which EPA funds remedial response actions, since the information collected to develop HRS scores is not sufficient to determine either the extent of contamination or the appropriate response for a particular site (40 CFR 300.425(a)(2), 55 FR 8845). Additionally, resource constraints may preclude EPA from evaluating all HRS pathways. Only those that present significant environmental risk or are sufficient to make a site eligible for the NPL may be evaluated. Moreover, the sites with the highest scores do not necessarily come to the Agency's attention first, so that addressing sites strictly on the basis of ranking would in some cases require stopping work at sites where it already was underway. In addition, site listings based on the ATSDR Health Advisory Criteria or designated by states as highest priorities would not have HRS scores.

More detailed studies of a site are undertaken in the Remedial Investigation/Feasibility Study ("RI/FS") that typically follows listing. The purpose of the RI/FS is to assess site conditions and evaluate alternatives to the extent necessary to select a remedy (40 CFR 300.430(a)(2)). The RI/FS takes into account the amount of contaminants released into the environment, the risk to affected populations and environment, the cost to remediate contamination at the site, and the response actions that have been taken by potentially responsible parties or others. Decisions on the type and extent of response action to be taken at these sites are made in accordance with 40 CFR 300.415 and 40 CFR 300.430.

After conducting these additional studies, EPA may conclude that initiating a CERCLA remedial action using the Trust Fund at some sites on the NPL is not appropriate because of more pressing needs at other sites, or because a private party cleanup already is underway pursuant to an enforcement action. Given the limited resources available in the Trust Fund, the Agency must carefully balance the relative needs for response at the numerous sites it has studied. It is also possible that EPA will conclude after further analysis that the site does not warrant remedial action.

RI/FS at Proposed Sites

An RI/FS may be performed at sites proposed in the Federal Register for placement on the NPL (or even sites that have not been proposed for placement on the NPL) pursuant to the Agency's removal authority under CERCLA, as outlined in the NCP at 40 CFR 300.415. Although an RI/FS generally is conducted at a site after it has been placed on the NPL, in a number of circumstances the Agency elects to conduct an RI/FS at a site proposed for placement on the NPL in preparation for a possible Superfund-financed response action, such as when the Agency believes that a delay may create unnecessary risks to public health or the environment. In addition, the Agency may conduct an RI/FS to assist in determining whether to conduct a removal or enforcement action at a site.

Facility (Site) Boundaries

The Agency's position is that the NPL does not describe releases in precise geographical terms, and that it would be neither feasible nor consistent with the limited purpose of the NPL (as the mere identification of releases), for it to do so.

CERCLA section 105(a)(8)(B) directs EPA to list national priorities among the known "releases or threatened releases." Thus, the purpose of the NPL is merely to identify releases that are priorities for further evaluation. Although a CERCLA "facility" is broadly defined to include any area where a hazardous substance release has "come to be located" (CERCLA section 101(9)), the listing process itself is not intended to define or reflect the boundaries of such facilities or releases. Of course, HRS data upon which the NPL placement was based will, to some extent, describe which release is at issue. That is, the NPL site would include all releases evaluated as part of that HRS analysis (including noncontiguous releases evaluated under the NPL aggregation policy, described at 48 FR 40663 (September 8, 1983)).

EPA regulations provide that the "nature and extent of the threat presented by a release" will be determined by an RI/FS as more information is developed on site contamination (40 CFR 300.68(d)). During the RI/FS process, the release may be found to be larger or smaller than was originally thought, as more is learned about the source and the migration of the contamination. However, this inquiry focuses on an evaluation of the threat posed. The boundaries of the release need not be defined. Moreover, it generally is impossible to discover the full extent of where the contamination "has come to be located" before all necessary studies and remedial work are completed at a site. Indeed, the boundaries of the contamination can be expected to change over time. Thus, in most cases, it will be impossible to describe the boundaries of a release with certainty.

For these reasons, the NPL need not be amended if further research into the extent of the contamination expands the apparent boundaries of the release. Further, the NPL is only of limited significance, as it does not assign liability to any party or to the owner of any specific property. *See* Report of the Senate Committee on Environment and Public Works, Senate Rep. No. 96–848, 96th Cong., 2d Sess. 60 (1980), quoted above and at 48 FR 40659 (September 8, 1983). If a party contests liability for releases on discrete parcels of property, it may do so if and when the

Agency brings an action against that party to recover costs or to compel a response action at that property.

At the same time, however, the RI/FS or the Record of Decision (which defines the remedy selected, 40 CFR 300.430(f)) may offer a useful indication to the public of the areas of contamination at which the Agency is considering taking a response action, based on information known at that time. For example, EPA may evaluate (and list) a release over a 400–acre area, but the Record of Decision may select a remedy over 100 acres only. This information may be useful to a landowner seeking to sell the other 300 acres, but it would result in no formal change in the fact that a release is included on the NPL. The landowner (and the public) also should note in such a case that if further study (or the remedial construction itself) reveals that the contamination is located on or has spread to other areas, the Agency may address those areas as well.

This view of the NPL as an initial identification of a release that is not subject to constant re-evaluation is consistent with the Agency's policy of not rescoring NPL sites:

> EPA recognizes that the NPL process cannot be perfect, and it is possible that errors exist or that new data will alter previous assumptions. Once the initial scoring effort is complete, however, the focus of EPA activity must be on investigating sites in detail and determining the appropriate response. New data or errors can be considered in that process.... [T]he NPL serves as a guide to EPA and does not determine liability or the need for response. (49 FR 37081)(September 21, 1984).

See also City of Stoughton, Wisc. v. U.S. EPA, 858 F.2d 747, 751 (D.C.Cir.1988):

> Certainly EPA could have permitted further comment or conducted further testing [on proposed NPL sites]. Either course would have consumed further assets of the Agency and would have delayed a determination of the risk priority associated with the site. Yet * * * "the NPL is simply a rough list of priorities, assembled quickly and inexpensively to comply with Congress' mandate for the Agency to take action straightaway." *Eagle-Picher [Industries v. EPA] II*, 759 F.2d [922,] at 932 [(D.C.Cir.1985)].

It is the Agency's policy that, in the exercise of its enforcement discretion, EPA will not take enforcement actions against an owner of residential property to require such owner to undertake response actions or pay response costs, unless the residential homeowner's activities lead to a release or threat of release of hazardous substances, resulting in the taking of a response action at the site (OSWER Directive #9834.6, July 3, 1991). This policy includes residential property owners whose property is located above a ground water plume that is proposed to or on the NPL, where the residential property owner did not contribute to the contamination of the site. EPA may, however, require access to that property during the course of implementing a clean up.

* * *

ECONOMIC IMPACTS

The costs of cleanup actions that may be taken at any site are not directly attributable to placement on the NPL. EPA has conducted a preliminary analysis of economic implications of today's amendment to the NPL. EPA believes that the kinds of economic effects associated with this revision generally are similar to those effects identified in the regulatory impact analysis (RIA) prepared in 1982 for the revisions to the NCP pursuant to section 105 of CERCLA and the economic analysis prepared when amendments to the NCP were proposed (50 FR 5882, February 12, 1985). The Agency believes the anticipated economic effects related to adding sites to the NPL can be characterized in terms of the conclusions of the earlier RIA and the most recent economic analysis.

Inclusion of a site on the NPL does not itself impose any costs. It does not establish that EPA necessarily will undertake remedial action, nor does it require any action by a private party or determine its liability for site response costs. Costs that arise out of site responses result from site-by-site decisions about what actions to take, not directly from the act of listing itself. Nonetheless, it is useful to consider the costs associated with responding to the sites included in this rulemaking.

The major events that follow the proposed listing of a site on the NPL are a search for potentially responsible parties and a remedial investigation/feasibility study (RI/FS) to determine if remedial actions will be undertaken at a site. Design and construction of the selected remedial alternative follow completion of the RI/FS, and operation and maintenance (O & M) activities may continue after construction has been completed.

EPA initially bears costs associated with responsible party searches. Responsible parties may bear some or all the costs of the RI/FS, remedial design and construction, and O & M, or EPA and the States may share costs.

The State cost share for site cleanup activities is controlled by Section 104(c) of CERCLA and the NCP. For privately operated sites, EPA will pay for 100% of the costs of the RI/FS and remedial planning, and 90% of the costs associated with remedial action. The State will be responsible for 10% of the remedial action. For publicly-operated sites, the State cost share is at least 50% of all response costs at the site, including the RI/FS and remedial design and construction of the remedial action selected. After the remedy is built, costs fall into two categories:

— For restoration of ground water and surface water, EPA will share in startup costs according to the criteria in the previous paragraph for 10 years or until a sufficient level of protectiveness is achieved before the end of 10 years.

— For other cleanups, EPA will share for up to 1 year the cost of that portion of response needed to assure that a remedy is operational and functional. After that, the State assumes full responsibilities for O & M.

In previous NPL rulemakings, the Agency estimated the costs associated with these activities (RI/FS, remedial design, remedial action, and O & M) on an average per site and total cost basis. EPA will continue with this approach, using the most recent (1994) cost estimates available. The estimates are presented below. However, there is wide variation in costs for individual sites, depending on the amount, type, and extent of contamination. Additionally, EPA is unable to predict what portions of the total costs responsible parties will bear, since the distribution of costs depends on the extent of voluntary and negotiated response and the success of any cost-recovery actions.

* * *

Costs to the States associated with today's final rule arise from the required State cost-share of: (1) 10% of remedial actions and 10% of first-year O & M costs at privately-operated; and (2) at least 50% of the remedial planning (RI/FS and remedial design), remedial action, and first-year O & M costs at publicly-operated sites. States will assume the cost for O & M after EPA's period of participation. Using the budget projections presented above, the cost to the States of undertaking Federal remedial planning and actions, but excluding O & M costs, would be approximately $7 million. State O & M costs cannot be accurately determined because EPA, as noted above, will share O & M costs for up to 10 years for restoration of ground water and surface water, and it is not known if the site will require this treatment and for how long. Assuming EPA involvement for 10 years is needed, State O & M costs would be approximately $14.7 million.

Placing a hazardous waste site on the final NPL does not itself cause firms responsible for the site to bear costs. Nonetheless, a listing may induce firms to clean up the sites voluntarily, or it may act as a potential trigger for subsequent enforcement or cost-recovery actions. Such actions may impose costs on firms, but the decisions to take such actions are discretionary and made on a case-by-case basis. Consequently, precise estimates of these effects cannot be made. EPA does not believe that every site will be cleaned up by a responsible party. EPA cannot project at this time which firms or industry sectors will bear specific portions of the response costs, but the Agency considers: the volume and nature of the waste at the sites; the strength of the evidence linking the wastes at the site to the parties; the parties' ability to pay; and other factors when deciding whether and how to proceed against the parties.

Economy-wide effects of this amendment to the NPL are aggregations of efforts on firms and State and local governments. Although effects could be felt by some individual firms and States, the total impact of this amendment on output, prices, and employment is expected to be negligible at the national level, as was the case in the 1982 RIA.

BENEFITS

The real benefits associated with today's amendment are increased health and environmental protection as a result of increased public awareness of potential hazards. In addition to the potential for more Federally-financed remedial actions, expansion of the NPL could accelerate privately-financed, voluntary cleanup efforts. Listing sites as national priority targets also may give States increased support for funding responses at particular sites.

As a result of the additional CERCLA remedies, there will be lower human exposure to high-risk chemicals, and higher-quality surface water, ground water, soil, and air. These benefits are expected to be significant, although difficult to estimate in advance of completing the RI/FS at these sites.

* * *

V. Regulatory Flexibility Act Analysis

The Regulatory Flexibility Act of 1980 requires EPA to review the impacts of this action on small entities, or certify that the action will not have a significant impact on a substantial number of small entities. By small entities, the Act refers to small businesses, small government jurisdictions, and nonprofit organizations.

While this rule revises the NCP, it is not a typical regulatory change since it does not automatically impose costs. As stated above, adding sites to the NPL does not in itself require any action by any party, nor does it determine the liability of any party for the cost of cleanup at the site. Further, no identifiable groups are affected as a whole. As a consequence, impacts on any group are hard to predict. A site's inclusion on the NPL could increase the likelihood of adverse impacts on responsible parties (in the form of cleanup costs), but at this time EPA cannot identify the potentially affected businesses or estimate the number of small businesses that might also be affected.

The Agency does expect that the listing of the sites in this NPL rule could significantly affect certain industries, or firms within industries, that have caused a proportionately high percentage of waste site problems. However, EPA does not expect the listing of these sites to have a significant economic impact on a substantial number of small businesses.

In any case, economic impacts would occur only through enforcement and cost-recovery actions, which EPA takes at its discretion on a site-by-site basis. EPA considers many factors when determining enforcement actions, including not only the firm's contribution to the problem, but also its ability to pay. The impacts (from cost recovery) on small governments and nonprofit organizations would be determined on a similar case-by-case basis.

For the foregoing reasons, I hereby certify that this rule does not have a significant economic impact on a substantial number of small entities. Therefore, this regulation does not require a regulatory flexibility analysis.

UNFUNDED MANDATES REFORM ACT OF 1995

Under Section 202 of the Unfunded Mandates Reform Act of 1995, signed into law on March 22, 1995, EPA must prepare a statement to accompany any rule where the estimated costs to State, local, or tribal governments in the aggregate, or to the private sector, will be $100 million or more in any one year. Under Section 205, EPA must select the most cost-effective and least burdensome alternative that achieves the objective of the rule and is consistent with statutory requirements. Section 203 requires EPA to establish a plan for informing and advising any small governments that may be significantly impacted by the rule.

EPA has determined, since adding sites to the NPL does not in itself require any action by any party, and does not determine the liability of any party for the cost of cleanup at the site, that this rule does not include a Federal mandate that may result in estimated costs of $100 million or more to either State, local or tribal governments in the aggregate, or to the private sector.

TEX TIN CORP. v. U.S. ENVIRONMENTAL PROTECTION AGENCY
992 F.2d 353 (D.C.Cir.1993).

RANDOLPH, CIRCUIT JUDGE:

The Comprehensive Environmental Response, Compensation and Liability Act of 1980 directed the President to establish a list of "national priority" sites most in need of federal remedial attention. *See* 42 U.S.C. § 9605(a)(8)(B). The Environmental Protection Agency then promulgated regulations creating a mathematical model called the Hazard Ranking System (HRS), 40 C.F.R. pt. 300, app. A, to determine the sites deserving of inclusion on the National Priorities List (NPL), see 40 C.F.R. pt. 300, app. B. Using the HRS, the Agency evaluates the observed or potential release of hazardous substances into surface water, groundwater and air and quantifies the environmental risks a site poses. The risk and magnitude of hazardous release into each of these three pathways is separately rated and then combined into an aggregate score; all sites receiving an HRS score of 28.50 or greater are listed on the NPL. *See generally Bradley Mining Co. v. United States Environmental Protection Agency*, 297 U.S.App.D.C. 348, 972 F.2d 1356, 1357–58 (D.C.Cir.1992).

The Agency first declared its intention to include petitioner Tex Tin's Texas City, Texas, smelting facility on the NPL in August 1990. *See* 55 FR 35,502, 35,508 (1990). Tex Tin sought expedited review of that decision in a petition challenging "the criteria EPA used for the air route score" component of the HRS. *See Tex Tin Corp. v. United States*

Environmental Protection Agency, 290 U.S.App.D.C. 202, 935 F.2d 1321, 1323 (D.C.Cir.1991)(per curiam)("Tex Tin I"). According to Tex Tin, the Agency had not sufficiently supported its claim that arsenic, present in tin slag waste piles on the site, could "reasonably be expected to be transported away from the facility via the air route." *See* 40 C.F.R. pt. 300, app. A, § 5.2 (1990). If the "reasonably ... expected" standard had not been met, the Agency erred in considering arsenic's toxicity when it computed the air-route component of the HRS. This court viewed the basis for the Agency's treatment of the arsenic as obscure and remanded "for a reasoned explanation for the conclusion that the arsenic is reasonably likely to be transported via the air route." 935 F.2d at 1324. n. 1

On remand, the Agency issued a nine-page "Explanation" defending its initial treatment of the tin-based arsenic, see U.S. Environmental Protection Agency, Memorandum Re: Explanation of Tex Tin NPL Listing (Aug. 5, 1991)("Agency Explanation"), and invited the company to comment. After Tex Tin submitted a voluminous legal and scientific response, the Agency placed in the administrative record a further justification of its position. *See* U.S. Environmental Protection Agency, Memorandum Re: Response to Comments of Tex Tin Corp. (Dec. 6, 1991)("Agency Response"). Tex Tin then brought the current petition for review presenting the question whether the Agency adequately responded to our remand order....

Because the NPL represents only a "rough list" of priority sites, *Eagle-Picher Industries, Inc. v. United States Environmental Protection Agency*, 245 U.S.App.D.C. 196, 759 F.2d 922, 932 (D.C.Cir.1985), and because the listing of a facility itself produces no official consequences, *see generally Kent County, Delaware Levy Court v. United States Environmental Protection Agency*, 295 U.S.App.D.C. 288, 963 F.2d 391, 394 (D.C.Cir.1992), some Agency "imprecision" in HRS calculations is tolerable. Bradley Mining Co., 972 F.2d at 1359. Nevertheless, the imprecision may rise to such a level that agency action becomes arbitrary and capricious and not otherwise in accordance with law. *See* 5 U.S.C. § 706(2)(A); *National Gypsum Co.*, 968 F.2d at 45.

Conflicting assertions about the physical and chemical properties of tin slag are at the heart of this dispute. Both sides agree that arsenic is present in tin slag. Because of the physiochemical composition of tin slag (an unwanted by-product of tin smelting), pure arsenic does not separate from the rest of the slag except at extremely high temperatures. It is at least possible, however, that small, arsenic-laden slag particles might exist. While these particles would not be pure arsenic, the Agency nonetheless considers them toxic for the purposes of the HRS. ...Particles smaller than 75 microns in diameter—dust—are "entrainable," that is, capable of becoming airborne. There is disagreement about whether the tin slag at the Tex Tin facility is "reasonably likely" to emit dust, through erosion or other processes. The investigation of this subject has proceeded theoretically: to date, there has been no documented instance of the release of arsenic-laden dust from Tex Tin's tin slag. This fact alone would not necessarily doom the Agency's position. The regulation's "can-reasonably-be-expected" language assumes that the risk of release is enough for purposes of the HRS. *See Tex Tin I,* 935 F.2d at 1323.

The Agency's primary argument, both in support of its initial listing and on remand, is that uncovered tin slag waste piles are, by their nature, likely to produce entrainable dust particles. In its Explanation on remand, the Agency cited a number of studies finding that particulate releases from slag piles "commonly occur as a result of wind erosion, vehicular traffic, and site operations." Agency Explanation at 2. The studies were of piles of iron and steel slag and crushed rock. *See id.* Tex Tin responded with an affidavit from Peter A. Wright, an expert metallurgist familiar with the Tex Tin site. Wright claimed that whatever the Agency's experience with other types of waste piles, the tin slag at the Tex Tin facility was unlikely to generate any entrainable dust. In particular, Wright noted that the Tex Tin facility produced its slag by pouring out the molten materials, slowly cooling the materials, and then breaking the solid mass into large pieces with a back-end loader. Wright stated that this process itself "does not generate dust," and that slag created by this "air cooled" method would be "very unlikely" to generate dust through wind erosion or other processes. Faced with this detailed and specific evidence, the Agency's Response merely cited again the general waste pile studies. *See* Agency Response at 6, 15–17.

We are thus confronted with a state of affairs reminiscent of Tex Tin I. Then, as now, we had only the Agency's "conclusory statements" (935 F.2d at 1323) to weigh against specific scientific evidence Tex Tin provided. Despite the "cursory nature of the NPL listing process," the Agency may not "base a listing decision on unsupported assumptions." *National Gypsum Co.,* 968 F.2d at 44. With respect to the Agency's primary argument, we again conclude that the Agency has supplied nothing more than unsupported assumptions to back up its conclusion that arsenic-laden dust particles are likely to come from the tin slag.

On remand, the Agency supplemented the record with studies and observations of the Tex Tin plant. (Because Tex Tin was able fully to examine and comment upon these items during the remand, the Agency appropriately considered them in reaching its present decision. *See, e.g., National Grain & Feed Ass'n v. OSHA,* 903 F.2d 308, 310–11 (5th Cir.1990).) The Agency tells us these new studies lend further support to its conclusion that because the tin slag will produce dust, particles containing arsenic will become airborne. We remain unconvinced.

The Agency's 1991 site characterization study found arsenic present in a variety of materials other than the tin slag at the Tex Tin location. *See* Agency Explanation at 4–5. This information, however, is not responsive to our remand order in Tex Tin I, which required the Agency to justify its conclusion that the tin slag was a likely source of arsenic emissions. *See* 935 F.2d at 1324. It is too late for the Agency to base its listing on a new theory for the source of arsenic. *Cf. Anne Arundel County, Md. v. United States Environmental Protection Agency*, 295 U.S.App.D.C. 309, 963 F.2d 412, 418 (D.C.Cir.1992).

The Agency also reports the results of a sampling of the tin slag piles it took from the Tex Tin facility in July 1991, showing entrainable dust particles present in the piles in concentrations of 0.2 to 2.8 percent. *See* Agency Explanation at 6–7. The problem is that the Agency never conducted any chemical analysis to confirm that the particles came from the tin slag. It is as if dust accumulated on an automobile's windshield; one could not simply infer that the dust came from the window glass rather than the air. So here, Tex Tin claims—entirely plausibly, it seems to us—that the small particles blew onto the uncovered piles from elsewhere. The fact remains that the Agency has never documented a single speck of dust with a chemical composition associating it with Tex Tin's tin slag. Given this gaping evidentiary hole, the Agency was not entitled merely to assume that the untested dust particles on the tin slag pile were produced by the slag.

Finally, the Agency notes that the 1991 site characterization study found high concentrations of arsenic in soil adjacent to the Tex Tin facility. *See* Agency Explanation at 5. Tex Tin attributes these concentrations to the plant's smokestack, which for years had a federal permit to emit more than 8000 pounds of arsenic annually.... Given the volume, the smokestack qualifies as a much more likely source, at least in the absence of any chemical analysis linking the arsenic found in the soil to the tin slag. The Agency claims that the documented presence of the arsenic in the surrounding soil is at least "probabilistic" evidence that the tin slag is likely to release arsenic. *See* Agency Response at 20. This confuses correlation with causation. Without any evidence showing that the tin slag releases dust or is likely to do so, the presence of arsenic in the soil merely points to the one known source of arsenic, the smokestack.

The Agency has failed to comply with our remand order. Once again it has come up with insufficient support for its conclusion that the tin slag at Tex Tin's site is "reasonably likely" to emit arsenic into the air. Tex Tin's petition for review is granted and the company's Texas City, Texas, facility is ordered deleted from the NPL.

Petition for Review Granted.

THE CERCLA SITE LISTING PROCESS AT A GLANCE

Site Identified

I

Included on CERCLIS

I

Preliminary Assessment

I

Hazard Ranking

I

National Listing of Sites

I

Remedial Investigation/feasibility Study (RI/FS)

I

Record of Decision (ROD)

I

Remedial Design

I

Remedial Action

I

Site Clean

[Possible Recording of Deed or Land Use Restrictions Depending on Cleanup Standard Used]

I

Site Delisted From NPL

§ 6.12 CLEAN UP AND REMEDIATION

SUPERFUND ACCELERATED CLEANUP MODEL (SACM!)

THE NEW SUPERFUND PARADIGM

INTRODUCTION

The present Superfund program operates within a complex and, at times, circuitous pattern that was designed ten years ago to accommodate a new and complicated law, then tinkered with as the program lurched from its infancy. The result has been a somewhat "jerry built" structure, altered to fit everyone's perceived needs and a host of conflicting expectations, but basically satisfying few. Early implementation focused on numerous intricate administrative and legal requirements. However, recent budget emphasis has dramatically shifted towards construction, policy emphasis has moved from Fund to enforcement. Various committees and work groups continue to suggest ways to speed up the process. Congress will soon consider many ideas for restructuring under Reauthorization.

Amidst this evolution, however, a few facts are unlikely to change—the public does not understand our present process or grasp the full scope of our work. It wants faster cleanups, and believes that enough money has been given to Superfund to get the job done. The bottom line is that we can expect neither a lowering of expectations, nor a rise in resources. These factors have crystallized into a new focus on radically speeding up and streamlining the program.

BACKGROUND

The current system for Superfund cleanups is based on two discrete programs—remedial and removal. The remedial component is a series of steps to define and address long term cleanup sites on the National Priorities List (NPL). Separate and apart are the activities of the removal program. These sites enter our system through a different "door," usually the States (through the National Response Center) seeking our help at a specific release. Some are spontaneous "screaming emergencies," others are prioritized for short term action as money becomes available. While the removal program generally does not address groundwater, many of the other risks and response actions associated with the two programs are similar. Yet, there are enormous differences between remedial and removal actions regarding the depth of investigation, and cost and time expended to complete a cleanup.

In summary, the innate complexity of our process and our heretofore unsuccessful attempts to portray progress have left the Superfund program highly vulnerable to criticism. Therefore, we must focus attention on a few major outcomes that the *public will value.*—We must make sure we deliver these outcomes and do it in terms the public will understand. For this reason, the new Superfund paradigm must be:

- simple and flexible—to allow fastest possible, worst first, risk reduction;

- free of administrative contrivances that divide and diffuse the *totality of reduced risk* at remedial and removal sites;

- realistically achievable in that we make realistic cleanup commitments and deliver them on time; and

- focused on rapid protection of people and the environment and disconnected from the single and unattainable goal of returning all groundwater to pristine condition.

THE NEW SUPERFUND ACCELERATED CLEANUP MODEL

Under this paradigm *all* sites on which Superfund takes any kind of cleanup action are Superfund sites. The distinctions between "remedial" and "removal" are eliminated. Rather than viewing these two entities as separate *programs*, they are viewed as separate *legal authorities* with different, but complimentary, application at Superfund sites.

Rather than entering the program through one of two doors marked "remedial" or "removal," all sites through one marked "Superfund." All **site assessment** takes place in one program, combining, as appropriate, elements of present removal assessments, PA/SIs, RI/FSs, and risk assessments. During the assessment process, a Regional Decision Team institutes short term activities *that address all threats to the health and safety of the existing population*. These actions include cleanup activities generally taking no more than three or, at the most, five years—a reasonable time frame based on the program's demonstrated ability to identify and address immediate risks to people and the environment within three to five years.

These activities are published in the *Federal Register* (for public information purposes only, not as a rulemaking) on an **Early Action List**. It is crucial to note here, that though these actions are "short term" and quickly implemented, they could eliminate *the majority of human risk* from Superfund sites. Enforcement activities would commence with immediate PRP notification, expedited orders/negotiation, and opportunity for voluntary cleanup. Because the vast majority of risk reduction occurs in this part of the program, most of EPA's public participation/information activities are focused here. Community relations and opportunities for Technical Assistance Grants (TAGs) continue as they do today. The State role is confirmed in its present configuration; further, they can continue with their own State-funded programs, resulting in a net increase of cleaned-up sites nationwide.

The Regional Decision Team can also determine if and when long term remediation (e.g., groundwater restoration) is appropriate. Sites would then be placed on the **Long Term Remediation List** (formerly known as the NPL), and cleaned up over many years. Regional Decision Teams could also decide that no Federal action was appropriate or that the site should be deferred to RCRA or other response authority.

The major parameters of this concept are outlined below.

1. *Single Site Assessment Function*. There are a number of redundancies in the beginning of the program as it is structured today. Hazardous waste sites can receive numerous similar, but sequential, assessments before any kind of cleanup begins. Sites are evaluated by the removal program (removal assessments), the site assessment program (PAs, SIs, Expanded SIs, and Hazard Ranking System (HRS) scoring), the remedial program (RIs, baseline risk assessments, and FSs), and even the RCRA program. ATSDR, State, local, and private party assessments may also occur. Many, if not most of these assessments start from scratch,

> they do not necessarily take into consideration the information and data generated by the studies that preceded them. This happens not only because of the obvious financial incentives to the contractor community and the human inclination to distrust the work of others, but because each part of the program is gathering data to respond to its particular perceived need. The

site-assessment program wants to know if it will score on the HRS; the removal program wants to know if the site is going to blow up; the remedial program wants to know the extent of the groundwater plume, the size of the cap, etc.

Large amounts of time and money are expended on the process of executing separate contracts, mobilizing sampling teams, designing sampling strategies, modifying health and safety plans, etc., as each part of the program goes out to "feel a different part of the elephant." Assessment, in all of its forms, now absorbs far more time than any other part of the process. The public believes that the program has been cleaning up sites for ten years with little result. It does not know that much of this time has been spent in various parts of the assessment process. Whole steps in this redundant process must be combined if the goal of expediting cleanup is to be achieved. The FIT/TAT contract mechanism could support this combined assessment effort and thereby assist in blending the remedial/removal "cultures."

In some Regions, there will be no reason for a two-staged screening function (PA followed by SI) since there will be no backlog of sites to be screened. *Discovered sites could be screened once and, if serious, go directly to RI level data collection and risk assessment.* Appropriate short term cleanup activity, combined with public participation/outreach, and expedited enforcement action (i.e., PRP search, information gathering, and notification) could begin immediately. **These changes in the assessment process could save several years, since the level and type of risk posed by the site would be understood and often eliminated prior to listing**.

Placing all site assessment activities in one area would require the development of new protocols but they would serve many needs. Rigid QA/QC procedures would assure the integrity and multiple-usability of the data developed.

2. *Regional Decision/Management Teams.* Regions often know the most likely course of action to remediate a site well before the decision process allows them to act. In future years that capacity certainly will expand. The Region Decision Teams would "traffic cop" sites onto the Early Action List and/or score long term restoration actions such as groundwater sites for inclusion on the Long Term Remediation List. In addition, standards for both remediation levels and technologies are likely to have been developed and accepted. This move toward standardization will both speed up the decision making process and allow increased flexibility in the staging or timing of various activities. The chief benefits are the ability to:

- make early action decisions while studies continue;
- carry out relatively short term cleanup steps that may in many cases be all that is necessary without triggering the site listing process;

- stay flexible while various activities are going on, rather than keeping functions in rigid and sequential boxes;
- effectively utilize the decision making expertise in the Regions, delegating where appropriate (e.g., standard remedy selection), to the project manager level to speed cleanups; and
- realize time and cost economies.

Regional Decision/Management Teams would require the skills of the most experienced managers (Fund and Enforcement), site and risk assessors, on-scene coordinators (OSC), remedial project managers (RPM), Community Relations coordinators and State officials, as appropriate. The OSC and RPM individual site management function would eventually become combined, which would further increase the efficiency of the process. Enforcement orders and negotiations would be conducted within strict deadlines. Cleanup could be performed by PRPs and appropriately overseen by the Agency. Training and commitment on the part of Superfund Headquarters and Regional management can help overcome different cultures that now exist and use the combined expertise in the remedial, removal, and enforcement programs to achieve the common goal of risk reduction.

3. *Early Actions.* Risks at NPL sites fall into a number of categories, but most commonly are associated with the direct contact with wastes or contaminated soil, or drinking contaminated water from groundwater sources. Source control steps taken early in the remedial process, such as drum removal, soil cleanup and access restraints, as well as alternate drinking water provision, frequently provide substantial risk reduction to existing populations. Actions taken under removal authorities are designed to address just such risks.

Early Actions would be an expansion of current removal activities. In fact, we have already interpreted and expanded removal authority to allow continuing cleanup actions at NPL sites if consistent with remedial actions (e.g., Radium, Chemical, White Chemical, Avtex, Publicker). True emergency situations such as train derailments would continue to be handled as they are today. Surface cleanup associated with remedial actions, (i.e., actions other than long term groundwater pump and treat or extensive site restoration technologies such as large mining site cleanups, wetlands/estuaries remediation, or extended incineration projects), would be carried out through the Early Action phase of the program. This would include activities as:

- waste and soil removal,
- preventing access,
- capping landfills,
- moving people,
- providing alternate drinking water sources.

Most important, *all immediate threats to public health and safety would be addressed* in this part of the process. While standardized cleanups for similar sites would expedite many cleanups, innovative technology would be used whenever it is faster, more efficient, more acceptable to the public, less expensive, or less environmentally impactive. Both standardized and innovative treatment technologies offer opportunities for cost efficiencies.

The public could be notified of activities at these Superfund site through a quarterly *Federal Register* notice—the Early Action List. *Sites would be listed when the decision to cleanup was made, then documented and delisted when the work was completed.* Public input would be achieved through all the mechanisms (possible including TAGs) that are now used by the program's community relations professionals. Most important, Superfund progress would be measured against *all* of its risk reduction activities and most of those activities would be completed rapidly. Under the New Superfund Accelerated Cleanup Model, the Agency would commit itself first and foremost to substantially reducing or eliminating threats to public health and the environment within a specified time frame and that time frame would be short. **This commitment would be EPA's primary measure of success**.

4. *Long Term Remediation*. Sites requiring groundwater restoration or long term remediation (e.g., mining sites, extended incineration projects, wetlands/estuaries) would be published in the *Federal Register* on the Long Term Remediation List. They would not be placed there until the need for such remediation activities was clearly established by the site assessment function. Many sites would already have been addressed under the Early Action phase, eliminating the need to evaluate many of the issues that hold up RODs today. Enforcement opportunities would be vigorously pursued using the full arsenal of Enforcement tools to obtain PRP participation. Community Relations would be performed and public participation fostered. Innovative technologies and standardized cleanups would be used, as appropriate. **Of greatest benefit, the public would understand that the actions placed on this list would require many years, if not decades, to clean up, but would pose no immediate threat at all to existing populations**. Removing the groundwater restoration question to a separate part of the decision making process would also allow for a more reasonable evaluation of the benefits and costs of such restoration. Public policy makes could then more reasonably decide which groundwater resources warrant priority action given limited funding.

IMPLEMENTATION

This concept has been developed in Headquarters and discussed with several Regions. The next step is to hypothetically run some sites through the proposed process and see if there are any unforeseen "stoppers." After receiving Agency management approval, as well as DOJ endorsement, appropriate White House, OMB and Congressional contacts would be briefed. The next step would be tested on a pilot basis in one or two Regions. Various Regional pilots are being reviewed for utility in the execution of the process. The timing is very opportune considering the congruence of current recommendations for improving and streamlining Superfund.

CONCLUSION

A program guaranteeing prioritized public health protection at all sites, without programmatic distinction, within five years of site identification, and having, as a separate activity, the long and difficult job of environmental media restoration, has a better chance of being understood, appreciated, and, therefore, publicly supported.

Counting the totality of risk reduction rather than focusing on NPL site deletions, is a simple, uncontrived, and true expression of the work of the program. It fulfills several of our most basic needs in building public confidence. First and most important, it focuses the program on the very substantial risk reduction that is now achieved, and achievable. Second, it focuses on the distinction between sites with the risk reduced to safe levels because of completed surface cleanup and those sites presenting no immediate threat, but requiring decades to complete. And third, it supplies what the public expects, and has every reason to expect from a program called "Superfund" the achievement of appropriate cleanup at large numbers of sites.

* * *

§ 6.13 OTHER STATUTES REGULATING HAZARDOUS WASTES

CERCLA is not the only statute regulating hazardous wastes or similarly hazardous substances. The table below illustrates other major federal statutes that may be invoked in the regulation and cleanup of hazardous substances and other toxic materials:

Table of Other Statutes Regulating Hazardous Wastes

Statute	Citation	Purpose
Clean Water Act	33 U.S.C. § 1251	Regulate surface water quality
Marine Protection Research and Sanctuaries Act	16 U.S.C. § 1401	Limit ocean dumping
Safe Drinking Water Act	40 U.S.C. §§ 300f–300j–10	Protect drinking water
Clean Air Act	42 U.S.C. § 7401	Improve air quality
Resource Conservation and Recovery Act	42 U.S.C. § 6901	Regulate hazardous and solid wastes

Statute	Citation	Purpose
Comprehensive Environmental Response, Compensation, and Liability Act	42 U.S.C. § 9601	Cleanup abandoned hazardous waste sites
Surface Mining Regulate and Reclamation Act	30 U.S.C. § 1201	Regulate pollution from surface coal mines
Nuclear Waste Policy Act	42 U.S.C. § 10101	Regulate disposal of high-level radioactive wastes
Low Level Radioactive Waste Policy Act	42 U.S.C. § 2021b	Regulate disposal of low-level radioactive wastes
Uranium Mill Tailings Radiation Control Act	42 U.S.C. § 7901	Regulate uranium mill tailings
Toxic Substances Act	15 U.S.C. § 2601	Regulate chemical substances

CERCLA STUDY GUIDE QUESTIONS

1. What is the significance of the National Contingency Plan (NCP) in CERCLA?

2. Does the NCP specify a type of remedy to employ in a given circumstance?

3. What is the difference between a CERCLA removal action and a CERCLA remedial action?

4. How are CERCLA sites identified?

5. What is the significance of the Comprehensive Environmental Response and Liability Information System (CERCLIS)?

6. When will EPA conduct a Preliminary Assessment (PA)?

7. What is the NPL hazardous ranking system?

8. What criteria are used in the NPL hazardous ranking system?

9. What is the likely success of a challenge to a site listing on the NPL?

10. Explain how the Superfund Comprehensive Accomplishments Plan (SCAP) should affect the EPAs nationwide strategic plan for addressing hazardous waste sites.

11. Explain what is a Remedial Investigation/Feasibility Study (RI/FS) and when it should be conducted.

12. What cleanup standards are required by CERCLA § 121?

13. What is a Record of Decision (ROD) and why is it important to the CERCLA process?

14. What state input is allowed/required under CERCLA?

15. When can a PRP conduct a judicial pre-enforcement review of EPA response actions or administrative orders?

16. What is the scope of EPA's investigatory power under CERCLA Section 104(e)? What is the typical § 104(e) process?

17. What elements are necessary to state a prima facie case under CERCLA § 107?

18. Who are the four statutorily enumerated types of persons that can be named as a PRP?

19. List and describe the statutory defenses and statutory exemptions which might be available to certain classes of PRPs.

20. Explain the difference between a Removal and a Remedial action.

21. What methods are used for CERCLA Site Identification?

22. Describe the NPL hazardous ranking system.

23. What Cleanup Standards are set under CERCLA?

24. What are "Applicable or Relevant and Appropriate Requirements" (ARARs)?

25. What is the role of Remedy Selection Criteria and ARARs Under the NCP?

26. To what extent is Pre-enforcement Review of CERCLA actions allowed? barred?

27. What is a Section 104(e) letter and what is the significance of receiving one?

Chapter 7

COMMUNITY–RIGHT–TO–KNOW AND EMERGENCY PLANNING REQUIREMENTS

Table of Sections

---

§ 7.1 INTRODUCTION

The Emergency Planning and Community Right–To–Know Act of 1986 (EPCRA) was enacted as Title III of the 1986 Superfund Amendments. 42 U.S.C. §§ 11001–11050 (1988). EPCRA imposes detailed chemical release and inventory reporting requirements on businesses that handle "toxic chemicals," "hazardous chemicals," and "extremely hazardous chemicals."

EPCRA establishes four principal reporting or notification requirements for owners or operators of facilities at which certain substances are produced, processed, used, or stored. Under specified circumstances, facility owners or operators must provide:

(1) notification to the state emergency response commission of the presence of a substance or substances at the facility in excess of EPA-established threshold planning quantities (TPQs) for extremely hazardous substances and emergency notification of releases of extremely hazardous chemicals and hazardous substances;

(2) information from material safety data sheets (MSDs) for hazardous chemicals;

(3) emergency and hazardous chemical inventory forms; and

(4) toxic chemical release forms.

EPCRA at a Glance

Section	Discussion
§ 301	Establishes state emergency response commissions (SERCs) and local emergency planning committees (LEPC)
§ 302	Requires EPA to publish list of extremely hazardous substances. Requires facilities with more than the threshold amounts to notify the SERC & LEPC
§ 303	Requires LEPC to prepare a comprehensive emergency response plan. Specifies minimum content for such plans
§ 304	Requires owners and operators of facilities to notify community emergency response coordinators of release of extremely hazardous substances
§§ 311 & 312	Requires owners and operators of OSHA regulated facilities to submit Material Safety Data Sheets (MSDSs) and an emergency and hazardous chemical inventory form to SERC, LEPC and the local fire department
§ 313	Requires owners and operators of facilities with more than 10 full time employees and that are in SIC codes 20–39 to complete a toxic chemical release form reporting releases of each of more than 300 chemicals used in quantities that exceed the threshold amounts in a calendar year and file the report with the EPA and the state by July 1 of each year Requires EPA to establish a computer database, the national toxic release inventory (TRI)
§ 325	Provides for civil, administrative and criminal penalties
§ 326	Authorizes citizen suits against owners and operators of facilities that fail to comply with the law & against EPA for failure to enforce the law

Section 313 of EPCRA requires certain facilities manufacturing, processing, or otherwise using listed toxic chemicals to report their environmental releases of such chemicals annually. Beginning with the 1991 reporting year, such facilities must also report pollution prevention and recycling data for such chemicals, pursuant to section 6607 of the Pollution Prevention Act (42 U.S.C.A. 13106). When enacted, section 313 established an initial list of toxic chemicals that was comprised of more than 300 chemicals and 20 chemical categories. Section 313(d) authorizes

EPA to add chemicals to or delete chemicals from the list, and sets forth criteria for these actions. EPA has added chemicals to and deleted chemicals from the original statutory list. Under section 313(e)(1), any person may petition EPA to add chemicals to or delete chemicals from the list. Pursuant to EPCRA section 313(e)(1), EPA must respond to petitions within 180 days either by initiating a rulemaking or by publishing an explanation of why the petition is denied.

Section 313(d)(4) of EPCRA provides, "Any revision [to the section 313 list] made on or after January 1 and before December 1 of any calendar year shall take effect beginning with the next calendar year. Any revision made on or after December 1 of any calendar year and before January 1 of the next calendar year shall take effect beginning with the calendar year following such next calendar year." EPA interprets this delayed effective date provision to apply only to actions that add chemicals to the section 313 list; EPA may, at its discretion, make deletions from the list and amendments to listings immediately effective.

§ 7.2 FILING WITH STATE EMERGENCY RESPONSE COMMISSION (SERC)

EPA's regulations implementing the emergency planning and notification requirements are codified at 40 C.F.R. Part 355 (1990). They require the owner or operator of a facility at which extremely hazardous substances are present in amounts equal to or in excess of the TPQs to provide notice to the State Emergency Response Commission (SERC) by May 17, 1987, or within sixty days after the facility first becomes subject to the requirements of this section, whichever is later. The facility owner or operator also must designate a facility representative who will participate in the local emergency planning process as a facility emergency response coordinator. This notice must have been provided on or before September 17, 1987, or thirty days after establishment of a local emergency planning committee (LEPC), whichever is later.

§ 7.3 MSDS

EPA's regulations implementing material safety data sheets (MSDS) and chemical inventory forms are codified at 40 C.F.R. Part 370. The regulations apply to the owner or operator of any facility at which a hazardous chemical for which an MSDS is required is present in amounts equal to or greater than 10,000 lbs., or at which an extremely hazardous substance is present in amounts greater than 500 lbs. (or 55 gallons) or the TPQ, whichever is less. The owner or operator must submit either (1) an MSDS for each chemical or (2) a list of hazardous chemicals with other appropriate information. That information must have been submitted by October 17, 1987 (or three months after the facility first becomes subject to the rule). *See* 40 C.F.R. § 370.20, 370.21 (1990). The MSDSs or chemical list must be submitted to the SERC, the LEPC, and the fire department with jurisdiction over the facility.

§ 7.4   OTHER REPORTING REQUIREMENTS

Owners or operators of facilities at which hazardous chemicals are present in amounts over 10,000 lbs. during the preceding calendar year, or at which extremely hazardous substances are present in amounts greater than or equal to 500 lbs. (or 55 gallons) or the TPQ during the previous calendar year, must have filed an emergency and hazardous chemical inventory form by March 1, 1988 (or March 1 of the first year after the facility first becomes subject to the subpart.) Owners and operators of facilities at which hazardous chemicals or extremely hazardous substances are present in amounts *less* than these levels, but greater than 0, must also file these reports at a later date.

There are two types of inventory forms. Tier I reports require information on the maximum amount, daily average amount, number of days on site, and general location on site of all hazardous chemicals and extremely hazardous substances. Tier II reports are much more detailed.

By March 1990, or March 1 of the third year after the facility first becomes subject to the subpart as stated in the regulations, and annually thereafter, facilities must file inventory forms for all hazardous chemicals present at the facility during the preceding calendar year in amounts equal to or greater than 10,000 lbs., or for extremely hazardous substances present at the facility in an amount equal to or greater than 500 lbs. (or 55 gallons) or the TPQ, whichever is less.

Owners or operators of facilities at which hazardous chemicals or extremely hazardous substances are located also must be prepared to submit a Tier II form providing more detailed information to the SERC, LEPC, or the fire department, or any other person upon written request.

HULS AMERICA, INC. v. BROWNER

889 F.Supp. 1 (D.D.C.1995).

Thomas F. Hogan, District Judge.

Before the Court are cross-motions for summary judgment concerning a chemical listing under the Emergency Planning and Community Right-to-Know Act of 1986 (EPCRA), 42 U.S.C. § 11001 et seq. This action arises because the defendants, Carol M. Browner and the United States Environmental Protection Agency (EPA), denied the petition of the plaintiff, Huls America, Inc. (Huls), to remove isophorone diisocyanate (IPDI) from a list of "extremely hazardous substances" established by EPCRA. For the reasons discussed below, the Court will deny the plaintiff's motion for summary judgment and grant the defendants' motion for summary judgment.

I.   Background

EPCRA was signed into law in 1986 at Title III of the Superfund Amendments and Reauthorization Act of 1986. Pub L. No. 99–499, 100 Stat. 1613 (1986). Congress passed the law to encourage state and local planning for accidental releases of certain chemicals called "extremely hazardous substances" (EHSs). Pursuant to 42 U.S.C. § 11002, a facility must notify the relevant state agency of the presence of an EHS in excess of its "threshold planning quantity."

Congress mandated that the original EHS list be identical to the list EPA published for its Chemical Emergency Preparedness Program (CEPP). Isophorone diisocyanate (IPDI) was one of the chemicals originally designated through CEPP. As a result, IPDI was automatically designated as an EHS when EPCRA became law in 1986. The original EHS list was published in the Federal Register on November 17, 1986. 51 Fed. Reg. 41,570. Congress authorized EPA to revise the EHS list under the criteria set forth in EPCRA. These criteria are the subject of the action between Huls and EPA.

On November 25, 1992, Huls petitioned EPA to remove IPDI from the EHS list. Huls is one of the leading marketers of IPDI in the United States. Huls contended that leaving the chemical on the EHS list would create significant reporting burdens for its customers and would generate a public misconception that IPDI poses serious and immediate risks if released.

On October 12, 1994, EPA published a notice in the Federal Register denying Huls' petition to remove IPDI from the EHS list. 59 Fed. Reg. 51,816. Huls then sought judicial review by instituting this action. In Huls' motion for summary judgment, Huls argues that EPA acted contrary to the plain meaning of EPCRA by denying the petition. In addition, Huls claims that EPA's decision to keep IPDI on the EHS list was arbitrary and capricious.

II. ANALYSIS

* * *

The plaintiff's suit is governed by the Administrative Procedure Act (APA). The Court can only set aside EPA's decision to keep IPDI on the EHS list if the Court finds that EPA acted in a manner that was arbitrary, capricious, an abuse of discretion, or otherwise not in accordance with the law. 5 U.S.C. § 706(2)(A). The Court must consider whether the agency's decision was based on a consideration of the relevant factors and whether the agency made a clear error in judgment. The Court cannot substitute its own judgment for that of the agency. *Citizens to Preserve Overton Park, Inc. v. Volpe*, 401 U.S. 402, 416, 28 L.Ed.2d 136, 91 S.Ct. 814 (1971). This standard is highly deferential to the agency and rests on a presumption that the agency's action was valid. *International Fabricare Institute v. EPA*, 297 U.S.App.D.C. 331, 972 F.2d 384, 389 (D.C.Cir.1992).

* * *

1. *Plain Meaning of the EPCRA Statute*

Huls claims that EPA acted in a manner contrary to the plain meaning of the statute when the agency refused to remove IPDI from the EHS list. The statute reads in pertinent part as follows: "The

Administrator may revise the list ... from time to time. Any revisions to the list shall take into account the toxicity, *reactivity*, volatility, dispersability, combustability, or flammability of a substance." 42 U.S.C. § 11002(a)(4).... Huls complains that EPA did not consider all of the listed factors when it denied the petition.

EPA relied primarily upon one factor, toxicity, in deciding that IPDI should remain on the EHS list. EPA claims quite properly that it did not need to consider all six factors from the statute when amending the EHS list. The word "or" normally has a disjunctive connotation that here only requires EPA to examine one or some of the statutory factors. EPA, therefore, presented a reasonable interpretation of the statute which the Court cannot question. "When a court reviews an agency's construction of the statute which it administers, ... the question for the court is whether the agency's answer is based on a permissible construction of the statute." *Chevron v. Natural Resources Defense Council*, 467 U.S. 837, 842–43, 81 L.Ed.2d 694, 104 S.Ct. 2778 (1984). Even if the language of EPCRA could be considered ambiguous, the Court must give deference to a reasonable agency interpretation. "[The court] need not pass on whether there are valid alternative readings of [the statute].... The only question ... is whether [the Administrator's] interpretation of [the statute] is reasonable." *International Union, UMW v. Federal Mine Safety and Health Administration*, 287 U.S.App.D.C. 166, 920 F.2d 960, 963 (D.C.Cir.1990).

2. *Arbitrary and Capricious*

Huls claims that the Court should set aside EPA's denial of its petition in accordance with § 706(2)(A) of the APA. Huls contends that EPA did not give adequate reasons for denying the petition and that EPA was arbitrary and capricious in relying on only one type of toxicity data. Toxicity can be measured in a variety of ways, including oral toxicity, inhalation toxicity, and dermal toxicity. EPA relied upon the inhalation toxicity of IPDI to deny Huls' petition. Huls notes that IPDI does not meet the oral or dermal toxicity thresholds that EPA allegedly normally uses to determine whether a substance should be on the EHS list. Huls also challenges EPA's reliance on inhalation toxicity by emphasizing the low vapor pressure of IPDI. Vapor pressure is the measure of the volatility of a substance. According to Huls, IPDI's low vapor pressure means that at normal atmospheric conditions, the maximum amount of IPDI that could volatilize into the air is unlikely to exist in quantities high enough to cause serious injury by inhalation.

EPA, however, did present credible evidence that IPDI can be toxic when inhaled even at low concentrations. EPA cited commonly used toxicity data from the "Registry of Toxic Effects of Chemical Substances" database maintained by the National Institute of Occupational Health and Safety (NIOSH). The NIOSH data show that the inhalation toxicity for IPDI is over the threshold required for placing a chemical on the EHS list. Under the regulations promulgated pursuant to EPCRA, a substance with a median inhalation lethal concentration of less than 0.50

milligrams per liter would qualify for inclusion on the EHS list. 51 Fed. Reg. 41,574 (1986). The NIOSH database shows, and Huls does not dispute, that IPDI has a median lethal concentration of 0.26 milligrams per liter. Furthermore, EPA states that even though IPDI has a low vapor pressure under normal atmospheric conditions, facilities will often use the chemical under higher pressures and temperatures that will increase IPDI's volatility.

Huls also asserts that EPA incorrectly interpreted the NIOSH data. Huls notes that EPA extrapolated the NIOSH data from animal studies conducted under extreme conditions which were unlikely to occur in reality and bore no relationship to the accidental release scenarios which prompted Congress to pass EPCRA. In deciding if EPA has acted in an arbitrary and capricious manner, the Court must be "particularly deferential when reviewing agency actions involving policy decisions based on uncertain technical information." *New York v. Reilly,* 297 U.S.App.D.C. 147, 969 F.2d 1147, 1150–51 (D.C.Cir.1992). When the Court is faced with conflicting interpretations of evidence that could lead to two rational conclusions, it gives deference to the interpretation offered by the agency. "Even if the evidence supports both sides of an issue, [the court] will sustain the agency 'if a reasonable person could come to either conclusion on that evidence.' " Id. at 1150 (quoting *Public Citizen Health Research Group v. Tyson,* 254 U.S.App.D.C. 253, 796 F.2d 1479, 1485 (D.C.Cir.1986)). In addition, when EPA "is evaluating scientific data within its technical expertise ... 'in an area characterized by scientific and technological uncertainty[,] ... this court must proceed with particular caution, avoiding all temptation to direct the agency in a choice between rational alternatives.' " *International Fabricare Institute v. EPA,* 297 U.S.App.D.C. 331, 972 F.2d 384, 389 (D.C.Cir.1992)(quoting *Environmental Defense Fund, Inc. v. Costle,* 188 U.S.App.D.C. 95, 578 F.2d 337, 339 (D.C.Cir.1978)). EPA argues that it is customary to use animal data to determine toxicity for regulatory purposes and claims that it is capable of reasonably extrapolating the data to human conditions. 59 Fed. Reg. 51,819 (1994). Based on the information supplied by EPA, the Court cannot conclude that EPA has acted in an arbitrary and capricious manner by relying on only the inhalation toxicity data and by employing the NIOSH animal studies.

While the above analysis suffices to determine that EPA was not arbitrary and capricious, the Court also notes that EPA did consider the evidence that Huls presented and responded by proposing to increase the threshold planning quantity for IPDI. 59 Fed. Reg. 51,820 (1994). This would mean that facilities could keep more IPDI on site without becoming subject to EPCRA's reporting requirements. This action is a further sign that EPA did not act in an arbitrary or capricious fashion in denying Huls' petition.

III. CONCLUSION

Huls believes that EPA misinterpreted the EPCRA statute and was arbitrary and capricious in denying Huls' petition to remove IPDI from the EHS list. The Court, however, gives deference to agencies when they make reasonable analyses of scientific and technical information in their own area of expertise and when they make reasonable interpretations of statutes that they must administer. EPA proffered a reasonable interpretation of the word "or" in 42 U.S.C. § 11002(a)(4) that prevents the Court from finding that EPA acted contrary to the plain meaning of the statute in relying upon toxicity data. In addition, the Court finds that EPA presented credible data in an area of EPA expertise to show that EPA's denial of the petition was not arbitrary and capricious simply because it focused upon inhalation toxicity as reported in the NIOSH database. The Court will, therefore, deny Huls' motion for summary judgment and grant EPA's motion for summary judgment. An order will be issued to accompany this opinion.

§ 7.5 ENFORCEMENT

Persons who fail to comply with the emergency planning notification and release reporting requirements are subject to civil penalties of up to $25,000 for each violation or $25,000 for each day during which the violation continues. Subsequent violations are subject to civil penalties up to $75,000 for each day of violation. Knowing or willful failure to provide the required notices is punishable by fines of up to $25,000 or imprisonment for not more than two years, or both. Repeat offenses are subject to fines of up to $50,000 or imprisonment for not more than five years or both.

WILLIAMS v. LEYBOLD TECHNOLOGIES, INC.
784 F.Supp. 765 (N.D.Cal.1992).

Opinion by: EDWARD A. INFANTE

* * *

This is a citizen's enforcement action arising under the Emergency Planning and Community Right–To–Know Act ("EPCRA"), 42 U.S.C. Sec. 11001 *et seq*. The Complaint alleges that the defendant, Leybold Technologies Inc. ("Leybold"), failed to timely submit certain hazardous chemical information, in the form of a Material Safety Data Sheet ("MSDS"), to proper local authorities as required by one of the EPCRA reporting provisions, 42 U.S.C. Sec. 11021(a)(1), and the United States Environmental Protection Agency ("EPA") regulations promulgated thereunder. Plaintiff Christopher Williams ("Williams") admits that by the time this suit was filed, because EPA has modified the applicable regulations, Leybold was no longer, nor is it presently, in violation of Sec. 11021(a)(1). However, plaintiff contends that EPCRA authorizes citizen suits seeking civil penalties for wholly past violations.

Plaintiff seeks 1) civil penalties for violation of Sec. 11021(a)(1), pursuant to 42 U.S.C. Sec. 11045, and 2) attorney's fees and costs. The parties have cross-moved for summary judgment.

The material facts are not in dispute. From October 1984 through August 1990 Leybold employed Williams as a process technician at its facility located at 1876 Hartog Drive in San Jose. From 1986 to 1990 Leybold used nickel and nickel compounds in its manufacturing operations at the Hartog Drive facility. Pursuant to EPCRA, Leybold was required to submit a MSDS for nickel and nickel compounds to local agencies by August 25, 1988. Leybold has never submitted a MSDS for nickel or nickel compounds as required by EPCRA.

In July 1990, the United States EPA ("EPA") modified the EPCRA regulations, eliminating reporting requirements for hazardous substances present in amounts of less than 10,000 pounds. 40 C.F.R. Sec. 370.20. The amount of nickel and nickel compounds present at the Leybold facility never exceeded 40 pounds. The Complaint in this action was filed on May 30, 1991.

Williams has satisfied the essential elements necessary to prevail in a citizen suit under EPCRA. *See,* 42 U.S.C. Sec. 11046. Leybold is an operator of a facility within the meaning of EPCRA. 42 U.S.C. Sec. 11049(4). Nickel and nickel compounds are listed hazardous substances under 29 C.F.R. Sec. 1910(Z). Leybold's failure to file a MSDS for nickel and nickel compounds violated EPCRA. *See,* 42 U.S.C. Sec. 11021(a)(1). On September 10, 1990, Williams gave notice of this EPCRA violation to the Administrator of the EPA as required by 42 U.S.C. Sec. 11046(d), and the EPA is not prosecuting an action under this section. 42 U.S.C. Sec. 11046(e).

* * *

III.   DISCUSSION

A.   *Emergency Planning and Right to Know Act ... ("EPCRA") Structure—Past Violations*

EPCRA provides, in pertinent part, that:

> The owner or operator of any facility which is required to prepare or have available a MSDS for a hazardous chemical under the Occupational Safety and Health Act of 1970 and the regulations promulgated under that act (29 U.S.C. Sec. 651 *et seq.*) shall submit a MSDS for each such chemical or a list of such chemicals as described in paragraph (2) to each of the following:
>
> (A) the appropriate local emergency planning committee;
>
> (B) the State emergency response commission;
>
> (C) the fire department with jurisdiction over the facility.

42 U.S.C. Sec. 11021(a)(1). The first EPA regulations promulgated under EPCRA required MSDSs to be submitted to the above listed agencies by all facilities where any hazardous chemicals were present between 10,-000 and zero pounds. Under those regulations Leybold was required to submit an MSDS to the appropriate agencies by August 25, 1988.

Leybold did not submit a MSDS for nickel, a hazardous chemical pursuant to OSHA regulations. 29 C.F.R. Sec. 1910(Z).

In July 1990, the EPA promulgated new EPCRA regulations, which reduced the threshold level of hazardous chemical which triggers the reporting requirements under Section 11021(a)(1). The new regulations only require reporting for hazardous chemicals present at the facility at any one time in amounts equal to or greater than 10,000 pounds. Neither nickel nor nickel compounds, which are classified as hazardous chemicals, were ever present at the Leybold facility in amounts greater than 30—40 pounds.

It is undisputed that Leybold is no longer in violation of EPCRA, nor was it at the time Williams filed the Complaint in this action. Williams relies on *Atlantic States Legal Foundation, Inc. v. Whiting Roll-Up Door Manufacturing Corp.*, 772 F.Supp. 745 (W.D.N.Y.1991) to support his contention that EPCRA authorizes citizen suits for reporting violations which are not continuing at the time the suit was filed.

The *Atlantic States* court framed the issue before it as: Does EPCRA authorize citizen suits for reporting violations which are not continuing at the time the lawsuit was filed? *Id.* at 749. The court examined the language of the statute and held:

The plain language of EPCRA's reporting, enforcement and civil penalty provisions, when logically viewed together, compel a conclusion that EPCRA confers federal jurisdiction over citizen lawsuits for past violations.

Atlantic States involved a defendant who filed a MSDS only after it received notice that a suit was about to be filed against it. At the time the suit was filed the defendant was still required to submit an MSDS. Although *Atlantic States* did not involve a subsequent change in the federal regulations requiring reporting, nevertheless, its reasoning is sound and fully applicable here. In the absence of a "clearly expressed intention to the contrary" the court must rely on the plain language of the statute. *Consumer Product Safety Commission v. GTE Sylvania, Inc.*, 447 U.S. 102, 108, 100 S.Ct. 2051, 2056, 64 L.Ed.2d 766 (1980). EPCRA required Leybold to submit an MSDS by August 25, 1988. EPCRA authorizes citizen suits against any person (other than a government entity) who violates the reporting requirement of Section 11021(a)(1). The statute does not expressly require a continuing violation at the time of filing suit, but rather authorizes a suit against any person who failed to submit an MSDS by the applicable deadline. . . .

EPCRA's legislative history establishes that the dual purposes of EPCRA are to (1) provide the public with information regarding the presence of hazardous chemicals in their communities, and (2) to establish emergency planning and notification requirements which would protect the public in the event of a release of hazardous chemicals. *See*, H.CONF.REP. NO. 962 99th Cong., 2d. Sess. (1986), reprinted in 1986 U.S.Code Cong. & Admin. News 3276. As the *Atlantic States* court pointed out, the filing of the MSDS is necessary to achieving the underlying purpose of EPCRA.

[The filing of the MSDS] is obviously a critical first step to achieving the intent of EPCRA, for without the filing of this information, state and local officials would have no way of receiving the necessary information regarding hazardous chemicals to make available to the public and to formulate an effective emergency response plan. *Atlantic States*, 772 F.Supp. 745, 751. Together, the legislative history and the plain language of the statute compel the conclusion that past violations are not exempt from EPCRA's citizen suit provisions.

B.   The EPCRA Penalty Provision

Defendant relies on an analysis of the factors set out in *Kennedy v. Mendoza–Martinez*, 372 U.S. 144, 9 L.Ed.2d 644 , 83 S.Ct. 554 (1963) to support its contention that the civil penalty provision of Section 11045(c)(2) is actually a criminal penalty in order to rely on the principle that the repeal of a criminal statute prevents prosecution under the statute. The Supreme Court has repeatedly held that whether a statutorily defined penalty is civil or criminal is a matter of statutory construction. *United States v. Ward*, 448 U.S. 242, 248, 65 L.Ed.2d 742 , 100 S.Ct. 2636 (1980). *See, e.g., One Lot Emerald Cut Stones v. United States*, 409 U.S. 232, 237, 93 S.Ct. 489, 493 , 34 L.Ed.2d 438 (1972).

* * *

The statute establishes $10,000 per day of violation as an upper limit on the fine which may be imposed, but permits imposition of a lower fine. Therefore, the sanction is not so punitive as to transform what was clearly intended as a civil remedy into a criminal penalty. *See, Ward*, at 249.

Furthermore, application of the *Kennedy* factors to this case confirms that the penalty provided by Section 11045(c)(2) is civil. Defendant contends that because the statute exacts money from a violator, it imposes a large affirmative disability. Applying the *Kennedy* factors in *Ward*, the Supreme Court did not find that a maximum penalty of $5,000 was punitive.

* * *

Although there is apparently no criminal statute for the identical violation, EPCRA does provide criminal penalties for other reporting violations. Furthermore, the sole purpose of the penalties under Section 11045 is to ensure that the public receives information about the location of hazardous materials within the community, thus enabling the community to develop emergency response plans. EPCRA has no alternative purpose. These factors provide further support for finding that the penalty at issue is civil. Since Congress expressly intended the penalty provided by 42 U.S.C. Section 11045(c)(2) to be civil, and an application of the *Kennedy* factors to this case provides no basis for finding it to be criminal or quasi-criminal, the Court finds that the penalty is civil.

IV. Conclusion

The plaintiff may bring a citizen enforcement action pursuant to 42 U.S.C. Section 11046 seeking civil penalties for a past failure to comply with 42 U.S.C. Section 11021(a)(1) even though the defendant came into compliance prior to the filing of the complaint. Since plaintiff has established all statutory requirements for a citizen suit under EPCRA, and defendant has raised no other defenses, plaintiff is entitled to summary judgment on his claim that Leybold is liable for violation of the EPCRA reporting requirements. Accordingly, plaintiff's motion for summary judgment is hereby GRANTED, and defendant's counter motion for summary judgment is hereby DENIED.

* * *

ATLANTIC STATES LEGAL FOUNDATION, INC. v. BUFFALO ENVELOPE CO.
1991 WL 183772 (W.D.N.Y.1991).

Opinion by: SKRETNY

* * *

Now before this Court is the motion of the defendant Buffalo Envelope Company, a division of American Envelope Company ("defendant"), to dismiss the Complaint for this Court's lack of subject matter jurisdiction pursuant to Fed.R.Civ.P. 12(b)(1).

The plaintiff predicates this Court's jurisdiction on 42 U.S.C. § 11046.

This lawsuit is a citizen's enforcement action arising under the Emergency Planning and Community Right–To–Know Act ("EPCRA"), 42 U.S.C. § 11001 *et seq.* . . . In Count One of the Complaint, plaintiff Atlantic States Legal Foundation, Inc. ("plaintiff") alleges that the defendant has failed to submit timely hazardous chemical information to proper state and federal authorities pursuant to EPCRA § 313, 42 U.S.C. § 11023 ("§ 313"), for the 1987 and 1988 reporting years. Although the plaintiff concedes that as of the date of suit the defendant has filed all required information under § 313 for the 1987 and 1988 reporting years, the plaintiff maintains that EPCRA authorizes a citizen suit, such as this, to recover civil penalties for wholly past violations, that is, even where the defendant has "come into" compliance with EPCRA's reporting provisions before the plaintiff commenced suit. Plaintiff seeks the following relief: 1) a declaratory judgment regarding defendant's liability for failure to meet the reporting requirements contained in § 313; 2) pursuant to EPCRA § 325(c), 42 U.S.C. § 11045 ("§ 325"), civil penalties for violations of § 313; 3) an Order of this Court authorizing plaintiff to inspect the defendant's records for EPCRA compliance; 4) an Order of this Court requiring the defendant to provide plaintiff copies of materials which the defendant submits to the United States Environmental Protection Agency ("EPA") through 1991; and 5) attorneys' fees and costs.

Moving to dismiss this lawsuit, the defendant argues that EPCRA does not afford citizens, such as plaintiff, a right to sue for wholly past violations. Since, according to the defendant, the evidence demonstrates defendant's compliance with § 313 before plaintiff filed this lawsuit, the defendant argues that this Court lacks jurisdiction of plaintiff's lawsuit. . . .

* * *

EPCRA Generally

A consultation of the entirety of EPCRA's provisions reveals that the statute has two central objectives: public access to centralized information, at a reasonably localized level, concerning hazardous chemicals used, produced or stored in the community and the use of this information to formulate and administer local emergency response plans in case of a hazardous chemical release.

To achieve these objectives, EPCRA contains three reporting provisions, § 311—313, which require owners or operators of a facility, as that term is defined at § 329(4), 42 U.S.C. § 11049(4), to submit certain specified information with respect to hazardous chemicals maintained at threshold levels to responsible state, local and, in the case of § 313, federal authorities. Additionally, EPCRA §§ 301—305 provide for the formation of state and local emergency response commissions and planning committees designed to receive and collect this reported information, make the information available to the public, and develop emergency response plans should a chemical release occur.

In this lawsuit, the plaintiff alleges that the defendant has failed to meet the reporting requirement contained at § 313. This Court will now address § 313 in greater detail.

A. EPCRA § 313

Section 313 requires completion of a Toxic Chemical Release Inventory Form, commonly known as the EPA Form R ("Form R"), for those chemicals which are included on the "List of Section 313 Chemicals," contained at 40 C.F.R. § 372.65. Facilities which release certain toxic chemicals must report total emissions of these toxic chemicals to the EPA and to State officials. With respect to an initial compliance date, § 313(a) provides that the initial Form R " . . . shall be submitted to the Administrator and to an official or officials of the States designated by the Governor on or before July 1, 1988, and annually thereafter on July 1 and shall contain data reflecting releases during the preceding calendar year."

B. EPCRA Citizen Suit Enforcement & Civil Penalty Provisions

With respect to a citizen's right to sue an owner or operator for failure to meet any of EPCRA's reporting requirements, § 326, 42 U.S.C.

§ 11046 ("§ 326"), contains EPCRA's citizen enforcement provision. § 326 in relevant part provides:

(a) Authority to bring civil actions

(1) Citizen suits except as provided in subsection (e) of this section, any person may commence a civil action on his own behalf against the following:

(A) An owner or operator of a facility for failure to do any of the following:

* * *

(iv) Complete and submit a toxic chemical release form under section 11023(a) [§ 313] of this title. . . .

With respect to violations of EPCRA § 313, § 326 must be read in conjunction with § 325, EPCRA's civil penalty provision. § 325(c) provides in relevant part:

(1) Any person (other than a governmental entity) who violates any requirement of section 11022 or 11023 of this title, shall be liable to the United States for a civil penalty in an amount not to exceed $25,000 for each such violation . . .

(3) Each day a violation described in paragraph (1) or (2) continues shall, for purposes of this subsection, constitute a separate violation.

(4) The Administrator may assess any civil penalty for which a person is liable under this subsection by administrative order or may bring an action to assess and collect the penalty in the United States district court for the district in which the person from whom the penalty is sought resides or in which such person's principal place of business is located.

FACTS

Plaintiff is a not-for-profit citizens environmental organization. (Complaint, para. 6). Defendant is a manufacturing facility presently located at 100 Centre Drive in Orchard Park, New York. (Fitzgerald Supp., para. 4). In December 1988, defendant relocated its facility from 270 Michigan Avenue, Buffalo, New York to the Orchard Park address. (Fitzgerald Supp., para. 4).

By letter dated May 15, 1990 signed by Charles Tebbutt, Esq., plaintiff transmitted to defendant a Notice Of Intent To Sue ("Notice Letter"). The Notice Letter stated, in accordance with § 326(d), that upon expiration of sixty (60) days from the date of the Notice Letter, " . . . the Atlantic States Legal Foundation will file a civil action in federal district court . . ." pursuant to the citizen suit provision contained in § 326(a). The Notice Letter identified alleged violations of, *inter alia,* § 313 as the reason for plaintiff's imminent suit. Specifically, the Notice Letter alleged that the defendant had . . . failed to accurately complete and submit . . . C. Toxic Chemical Release Forms (EPA Form

Rs) by July 1, 1988, and annually thereafter, pursuant to Section 313 of EPCRA, 42 U.S.C. 11023. (Complaint, exh. A).

On June 28, 1990, Robert Fitzgerald, defendant's President, filed Form Rs for the 1987, 1988 and 1989 reporting years to the EPA EPCRA reporting Center and the New York State Emergency Response Commission. These submissions were filed under the name of American Envelope Co./Buffalo Division. (Fitzgerald, para. 4 and exhs. A & B thereto).

On October 30, 1990, the plaintiff filed this lawsuit.

DISCUSSION

A. *EPCRA's Authorization of Citizen Suits for Past Violations*

The plaintiff does not dispute that the defendant submitted complete Form Rs pursuant to § 313 for the 1987 and 1988 reporting years before plaintiff filed this lawsuit ... It is also undisputed that prior to receiving plaintiff's Notice Letter, the defendant failed to file the required information under § 313. (Fitzgerald, paras. 4–8 and exhs. A and B thereto).

Maintaining that EPCRA authorizes citizen suits for wholly past reporting violations, that is, for late filed reports which have been filed by the time of suit, plaintiff seeks, *inter alia,* civil penalties for the defendant's failure to report according to the initial compliance date contained in § 313.

Defendant moves for dismissal based on this Court's lack of subject matter jurisdiction arguing that EPCRA does not afford citizens the right to sue for failure to report under § 313 where the defendant has filed the required information before the lawsuit is filed.

Thus this Court must decide this narrow issue: Does EPCRA authorize citizen suits for reporting violations which are not continuing at the time the lawsuit is filed. This is an issue of first impression. Having considered all arguments, based on the statute's plain language and the legislation's underlying purpose, which is well documented by its legislative history, this Court must conclude in the affirmative.

Absent "... a clearly expressed legislative intention to the contrary," this Court must conclusively rely on the words of the statute. *Consumer Product Safety Commission v. GTE Sylvania, Inc.*, 447 U.S. 102, 108, 100 S.Ct. 2051, 2056, 64 L.Ed.2d 766 (1980). Accordingly, since this Court locates no legislative intention to the contrary, it initially examines the plain language of EPCRA.

The plain language of EPCRA's reporting, enforcement and civil penalty provisions, when logically viewed together, compel a conclusion that EPCRA confers federal jurisdiction over citizen lawsuits for past violations.

As noted above, § 326(a)(1) authorizes citizen suits against an owner or operator for "... failure ..." to, *inter alia*, complete and submit a Form R pursuant to § 313. Sections 325(c)(1) and (2) authorize citizen suit civil penalties against "any person (other than a government entity) who violates any requirement . . ." of, *inter alia,* 313.   As also noted above, § 313 establishes a mandatory date for initial compliance. . . .

It logically follows that these mandatory compliance dates must be considered to constitute § 313 "requirements" for purposes of the citizen suit civil penalty provision under § 325, as Congress' choice of the word "shall" in § 313 indicates.

In this case, it is undisputed that the defendant failed to report information pursuant to § 313 by the compliance date therein. The defendant argues that § 326 does not authorize a citizen suit " . . . for failure to complete and submit a form, on time, but rather to complete and submit a form, period." (d. memo., p. 6)(emphasis supplied).   Defendant's interpretation, however, ignores § 313's plain language, for the compliance date in § 313 constitutes a requirement; the unequivocal language of § 313 requires initial reporting on a date certain. Thus, this Court cannot reconcile the defendant's interpretation with EPCRA's civil penalty provision which authorizes civil penalties against "any person . . . who violates any requirement . . ." of EPCRA's reporting provisions. § 325(c)(1) & (2).

Moreover, this Court's acceptance of the defendant's interpretation would render gratuitous the compliance date for initial submissions which Congress placed in § 313.

EPCRA's underlying purpose, well documented by its legislative history, supports the conclusion that citizens may sue for violations which no longer continue at time of suit.

> Congress designed the concept of the emergency response plan, which necessarily depends on accurate and current information, as a public safety measure in case of a hazardous chemical release. The preamble to the Conference report describes the Senate and House versions of EPCRA as . . . programs to provide the public with important information on the hazardous chemicals in their communities, and to establish emergency planning and notification requirements which would protect the public in the event of a release of hazardous chemicals.

H. REP. NO. 962, 99th Cong., 2d Sess. (1986), *reprinted in* 1986 U.S.C.C.A.N. 3276. EPCRA's legislative history often refers to protection of the public health and environment. *See, e.g.,* H. REP. NO. 99–253 ("each Emergency Response Plan must be designed to protect public health and the environment in the event of a hazardous substance emergency. . . .")(Id., 1986 U.S.C.C.A.N. at 2896).

As noted above, and as evident from these general statements, EPCRA embodies two fundamental objectives: public access to information concerning hazardous chemicals in the community and use of this information to formulate and administer local emergency response plans in case of a hazardous chemical release. The relative achievement of these objectives, then, depends on accurate and current information. Via the reporting requirements contained in §§ 311–313, Congress has placed the burden on facility owners or operators to submit this information to appropriate officials who can then implement an emergency response plan. If owners or operators fail to comply with the reporting requirements, including their mandatory compliance dates, the development and success of emergency response plans would be seriously, if not critically, undercut, and the entire thrust of EPCRA could be defeated. To the extent owners and operators, such as the defendant, delay reporting beyond the compliance dates which Congress placed in §§ 311—313, the public has access to less information and emergency response plans are based on incomplete information. Moreover, the public has no mechanism to ensure the accuracy of information which is unreported. EPCRA provides that mechanism. Clearly, for all these reasons, to overlook EPCRA's reporting deadlines, such as defendant has done here with respect to § 313, would subvert the objectives of EPCRA.

In support of its motion, the defendant relies on *Gwaltney of Smithfield v. Chesapeake Bay Foundation, Inc.*, 484 U.S. 49, 108 S.Ct. 376, 98 L.Ed.2d 306 (1987), where the Supreme Court held the citizen suit provision of the Clean Water Act, § 505(a), 33 U.S.C. § 1365(a) ("505(a)"), did not confer federal jurisdiction over citizen suits for wholly past violations.

In *Gwaltney*, the citizen suit provision of the Clean Water Act provided in relevant part that

> ... any citizen may commence a civil action on his own behalf—(1) against any person ... who is alleged to be in violation of (A) an effluent standard or limitation under this chapter or (B) an order issued by the Administrator or a State with respect to such a standard or limitation....

Id. 484 U.S. at 55, 108 S.Ct. at 380.

Examining the plain statutory language, the statutory scheme, and the statute's legislative history the Supreme Court concluded that the "... alleged to be in violation ..." language did not confer federal jurisdiction of citizen lawsuits for wholly past violations.

Initially the Court found that, although ambiguous, the "... to be in violation ..." clause contemplated a "... continuous or intermittent violation—that is, a reasonable likelihood that a past polluter will continue to pollute in the future." Rejecting the argument that Congress committed a careless accident by incorporating this language and citing the Clean Air Act, 42 U.S.C. § 7604, as an example, the Court noted that Congress used "... identical language ..." in citizen suit provisions contained in other statutes which authorized only prospective relief. *Id*., 484 U.S. at 57, 108 S.Ct. at 381. The Court emphasized that "... the pervasive use of the present tense ..." throughout § 505 buttressed the conclusion that the provision contemplated only prospective application. *Id*., 484 U.S. at 59, 108 S.Ct. at 382.

Next, the Court found the Clean Water Act's notice provision irreconcilable with an interpretation that citizen suits may address wholly past violations. § 505(b)(1)(A) requires that citizens give 60 days notice of their intent to sue to the alleged violator, EPA Administrator and appropriate State officials. Since, pursuant to § 505(b)(1)(B), the commencement of an enforcement action by the Administrator or State within the 60 day notice period barred a citizen enforcement suit, the Court concluded, " . . . it follows logically that the purpose of notice to the alleged violator is to give it an opportunity to bring itself into complete compliance with the [Clean Water] Act and thus likewise render unnecessary a citizen suit." Therefore, the Court said, if citizen suits could target solely past violations, the notice requirement to past violators " . . . becomes gratuitous." *Id.*, 484 U.S. at 60, 108 S.Ct. at 382–83.

Lastly, the Court found that the legislative history of the Clean Water Act supported the conclusion that its citizen suit provision remained inapplicable to suits for past violations. *Id.*, 484 U.S. at 61—63, 108 S.Ct. at 383–84.

However, this Court finds Gwaltney distinguishable from this case. The factors cited by the Supreme Court to support its holding that the Clean Water Act did not authorize citizen suits for wholly past violations are substantially diminished with respect to EPCRA in this case.

First, the plain language of EPCRA's citizen suit provision is different than its Clean Water Act counterpart. Section 326 authorizes citizen suits for an owner's or operator's "failure to" comply with EPCRA's reporting requirements, while § 505 authorizes citizen suits against a person " . . . who is alleged to be in violation . . ." of certain provisions of the Clean Water Act. The natural reading of the EPCRA provision at least would seem to include past acts of noncompliance, while a natural reading of the Clean Water Act provision, as the Supreme Court has held, indicates that the statute contemplates only prospective relief. This reading of § 326, of course, is supported by viewing § 326 along with § 325 which authorizes civil penalties against "any person . . . who violates any requirement . . . " of EPCRA, including its reporting provisions which require initial submissions by dates certain.

Moreover, unlike § 505 of the Clean Water Act, EPCRA § 326 does not contain "pervasive use of the present tense . . ." which might indicate its restricted applicability to continuing or intermittent violations. In fact, the venue provision contained at § 326(b)(1) states that "any action under subsection (a) of this section against an owner or operator of a facility shall be brought in the district court for the district in which the alleged violation occurred." . . . Contrary to the defendant's interpretation, this clause arguably suggests that § 326 contemplates past violations.

Although § 326(d)(1)(2) contains a notice provision like that in the Clean Water Act before the Court in *Gwaltney*, since *Gwaltney*, Congress has demonstrated that, in its view, such a notice provision is not irreconcilable with an authorization of suit for wholly past violations. Recently Congress amended the Clean Air Act citizen suit provision, 42 U.S.C. § 7604(a), to afford citizens the right to sue for past violations although Congress left a similar 60 day notice provision intact.... Therefore, the fact that Congress amended the Clean Air Act citizen suit provision to allow suits for past violations while simultaneously leaving the Clean Air Act's notice provision unchanged undercuts the importance of the Supreme Court's discussion in *Gwaltney* that Congress would not have placed such a notice provision in a statute where it also intended authorize citizen suits for past violations.

In sum, this Court holds that the plaintiff may bring a citizen enforcement action pursuant to § 326(a) to seek civil penalties for failure to comply with § 313 even though the plaintiff alleges no continuing violations of § 313 at the time it commenced suit. Therefore, this Court must deny the defendant's motion to dismiss the Complaint for this Court's lack of subject matter jurisdiction.

* * *

§ 7.6   EPCRA AUDITS

IN THE MATTER OF SARA LEE CORP.

1993 WL 489798 (E.P.A.) (Nov. 4, 1993).

Environmental Appeals Judge, U.S. Environmental Protection Agency, Washington, D.C.

* * *

C.   EPCRA/CERCLA § 103(A) COMPLIANCE AUDIT

Sara Lee agrees that the internal audit conducted to review and report on the compliance of Sara Lee's continental U.S. manufacturing and food services distribution facilities with Sections 304, 311, 312 and 313 of EPCRA and Section 103(a) of CERCLA has been and will be conducted as follows:

1.   Scope of Audit: This audit, and the stipulated penalties identified in section V.C.7 below, shall apply only to Sara Lee's continental U.S. manufacturing and food services distribution facilities purchased and/or owned by Sara Lee during the three-year period preceding the execution of this Consent Agreement. The audit shall exclude Sara Lee's facilities sold or otherwise taken out of active operation prior to the date of execution of this Consent Agreement. However, for those facilities still owned or leased by Sara Lee and still in active operation at the time of the execution of this Consent Agreement, the audit shall cover the full three-year period, including the period prior to Sara Lee's ownership. "Active operation" means a facility which currently employs a paid staff and is engaged in some form of manufacturing or processing activities.

2.   Independent Auditor: Sara Lee's EPCRA and CERCLA § 103 audit activities have been and will continue to be conducted by indepen-

dent third parties, i.e., either trained outside consultants or trained in-house personnel who do not report to the management of the facility being audited. Oversight of auditing activities is provided by the Director of Environmental Affairs who is independent of any facility management personnel. The reports required under Paragraph V.C.4 of this Agreement shall be prepared and submitted by either the auditor or the Director of Environmental Affairs.

3.   Audit Initiation/Termination: Auditing activities related to this CACO began in December of 1991 and shall be completed within 250 days of the date of execution of the Consent Order by the Environmental Appeals Board.

4.   Reporting Requirements: Sara Lee agrees to submit the following reports during the course of the EPCRA/CERCLA § 103(a) audit:

a.   Initial Report. The initial report shall be submitted within 60 days of receipt of the executed Consent Order. The initial report shall list the Sara Lee facilities to be audited or already audited. The initial report shall also describe the records already audited and the procedures employed to audit such records ("the protocol"), and confirm that such audit procedures will encompass all the records necessary to comply with this Agreement.

b.   Final Report. The final report shall be submitted within 60 days following the completion of the audit. The final report shall provide in a cumulative fashion a list of the facilities and chemicals reviewed at each facility which meets Tier II and Form R threshold requirements for EPCRA and CERCLA § 103(a) reporting requirements, and a summary of the violations detected and the actions taken to remedy and mitigate the violations. The final report must also include: (1) a statement signed by a responsible corporate official certifying that the audit has been conducted and that the audit protocol was followed; and (2) to the extent practicable, an accounting for all costs incurred in conducting the audit, including all internal costs and all fees paid to consultants for audit-related work.

5.   Immediately Reportable Events/Duty to Mitigate: Discovery of any of the following acts or omissions during the period covered by the audit shall constitute an immediately reportable event:

a.   failure to notify immediately the National Response Center of a release of a reportable quantity of a hazardous substance, or failure to provide all of the required information, as required by CERCLA § 103(a) and the applicable regulations;

b.   failure to notify immediately the State Emergency Response Commission and/or the Local Emergency Planning Committee of a release of a hazardous substance or an Extremely Hazardous Substance (EHS), as required by EPCRA § 304 and the applicable regulations;

    c.   failure to provide written followup notification of an emergency release to the State Emergency Response Commission and/or the Local Emergency Planning Committee as soon as practicable, as required by EPCRA § 304(c) and the applicable regulations;

    d.   failure to submit an MSDS as required by EPCRA § 311 and the applicable regulations;

    e.   failure to submit emergency and hazardous chemical inventory forms as required by EPCRA § 312 and the applicable regulations; and

    f.   failure to submit toxic chemical release forms ("Form Rs") timely as required by EPCRA § 313 and the applicable regulations.

Sara Lee is required to submit to EPA a written notice of each immediately reportable event discovered during the audit within 10 working days of confirmation of the event. The notice shall describe the nature and extent of the reportable event and indicate the steps taken, or being taken by Sara Lee to cure or mitigate the violation.

Sara Lee agrees to cure potential CERCLA § 103(a) violations by providing the required notification as specified in CERCLA § 103(a) and the applicable regulations. Sara Lee agrees to cure potential EPCRA § 304(a) violations by providing the required notification to the applicable authorities as specified in EPCRA § 304(a). Sara Lee agrees to cure potential EPCRA § 304(c) violations by providing written followup emergency notice to the applicable authorities as specified in EPCRA § 304(c) and the applicable regulations. Sara Lee agrees to cure potential EPCRA § 311, § 312 and § 313 violations by submitting the required MSDS form, emergency and hazardous chemical inventory form, and/or toxic chemical release form to the applicable authorities as specified in the statute and accompanying regulations.

    6.   Reporting Period: The time periods to be covered by the audit shall be as follows:

    a.   CERCLA § 103(a): Three years prior to the date of execution of this Consent Agreement.

    b.   EPCRA § 304(c): Three years prior to the date of execution of this Consent Agreement.

    c.   EPCRA § 311: Three years prior to the date of execution of this Consent Agreement.

    d.   EPCRA § 312: Three years prior to the date of execution of this Consent Agreement.

    e.   EPCRA § 313: Three years prior to the date of execution of this Consent Agreement.

    7.   Stipulated Penalties: The stipulated penalties set forth below shall apply for only those violations that are reported under the EPCRA/CERCLA § 103(a) compliance audit and which are remedied. Once a violation is reported and remedied, the stipulated penalty establishes the limit of Sara Lee's CERCLA § 103(a) and EPCRA § 304, § 311, § 312

and § 313 liability for that violation. The amount assessed by EPA for a particular violation will depend upon the circumstances of the violation, however, per-day penalties will not be assessed. Otherwise, the applicable Enforcement Response Policy will serve as EPA's guide in calculating an appropriate penalty.

Sara Lee agrees to pay the following stipulated penalties:

a. Each violation of CERCLA § 103(a) shall be assessed on a per-violation basis. The penalty, under this section, shall not exceed $20,000 per violation.

b. Each violation of EPCRA § 304(a) shall be assessed on a per-violation basis. The penalty, under this section, shall not exceed $20,000 per violation; reporting to the LEPC, the SERC, or the local fire department constitute three separate points of compliance and therefore the failure to report to all three constitutes three separate violations.

c. Each violation of EPCRA § 304(c) shall be assessed on a per-violation basis. The penalty, under this section, shall not exceed $10,000 per violation; reporting to the LEPC, the SERC, or the local fire department constitutes three separate points of compliance and therefore the failure to report all three violations constitutes three separate violations.

d. Each violation of EPCRA § 311 shall be assessed on a per-violation basis. The penalty, under this section, shall not exceed $8,000 per violation; reporting to the LEPC, the SERC, or the local fire department constitutes three separate points of compliance and therefore the failure to report all three violations constitutes three separate violations. However, for purposes only of this Consent Agreement and Consent Order, where all three points of compliance have been violated with respect to a given chemical, the total penalty for the three violations shall not exceed $20,000.

e. Each violation of EPCRA § 312 shall be assessed on a per-violation basis. The penalty, under this section, shall not exceed $8,000 per violation; reporting to the LEPC, the SERC, or the local fire department constitutes three separate points of compliance and therefore the failure to report all three violations constitutes three separate violations. However, for purposes only of this Consent Agreement and Consent Order, where all three points of compliance have been violated with respect to a given chemical, the total penalty for the three violations shall not exceed $20,000.

f. Each late-reporting violation of EPCRA § 313 shall be assessed on a per-violation basis. The penalty, under this section, shall not exceed $15,000 per chemical, per facility.

g. Each data-quality violation of EPCRA § 313 shall be assessed on a per-violation basis. The penalty, under this section, shall not exceed $10,000 per violation.

8. Retention of Enforcement Authority: EPA reserves the right to take appropriate enforcement action, under the applicable enforcement response policy or penalty policy, for those CERCLA § 103(a) and EPCRA § 304, § 311 and § 313 violations not reported to EPA under this audit, or for those violations reported under this audit but which are not remedied under the terms of this Agreement.

D.   EPCRA AND CERCLA § 103 COMPLIANCE PROGRAM

The EPCRA and CERCLA § 103 compliance program already developed and implemented by Sara Lee includes the following elements:

1. Educational and training efforts directed to specific employees which emphasize the importance of, and corporate procedures for, complying with EPCRA and the emergency release reporting requirements of CERCLA § 103. Such efforts stress EPCRA fundamentals and the fact that failure to comply with EPCRA may result in the interruption of manufacture or use of the substance, adversely affecting business operations. These employees include division vice presidents of operations, plant managers, division environmental coordinators, plant environmental coordinators, and other selected people.

2. The conduct of training involving at least eight (8) hours initially for the targeted employees, and eighty (80) hours initially for auditors, with sixteen (16) hours per year thereafter for auditors.

3. The development and distribution of manuals including EPCRA and CERCLA § 103 compliance information as a guide to the basic requirements of EPCRA and CERCLA § 103, with an explanation of reporting requirements under those statutes and applicable regulations. The Manual directs employees to those persons within Sara Lee with responsibility for compliance and reporting under EPCRA and CERCLA § 103.

4. A report describing a corporate training program, which has been submitted to EPA prior to signature of this Consent Agreement and Consent Order.

VI.   *Other Matters*

A. This Agreement may be modified only upon written approval by EPA and Sara Lee.

B. Nothing in this Consent Agreement and Consent Order shall relieve Sara Lee of the duty to comply with all applicable EPCRA regulations or other applicable environmental statutes.

C. This Consent Agreement shall be binding upon the Parties to this action, as well as upon their successors and assigns. The undersigned representative of each Party to this Consent Agreement certifies that he or she is duly authorized by the Party whom he or she represents to enter into the terms and bind that Party to it.

D. This Consent Agreement shall take full effect upon the signing of the Consent Order by a member of EPA's Environmental Appeals Board or his or her designated representative.

E. Sara Lee's obligations under this Consent Agreement shall end when it has paid the civil penalty and any stipulated penalties in accordance with the Consent Agreement and Consent Order, and has completed the CERCLA § 103(a) and EPCRA § 304 and § 311, § 312 and § 313 compliance audit specified in Paragraphs V.C and V.D of this Agreement.

F. All of the terms and conditions of this Consent Agreement together comprise one Agreement, and each of the terms and conditions is in consideration for all of the other terms and conditions. In the event that this Consent Agreement (or one of more of its terms and conditions) is held invalid, or is not executed by all of the signatory parties in identical form, or is not approved in such identical form by a member of the EPA's Environmental Appeals Board or his or her designated representative, then the entire Consent Agreement shall be null and void.

G. This matter shall constitute a "history of prior violations" by Sara Lee Corporation's Forest, Mississippi facility, its Design Foods facility, Fort Worth, Texas, and its Hillshire Farm & Kahn's facility, New London, Wisconsin, as that phrase is used in the EPCRA § 313 ERP and the EPCRA § 304/CERCLA § 103 Penalty Policy.

H. Failure to remit the civil penalties provided herein will result in this matter being forwarded to the U.S. Department of Justice for collection of the amount due, plus stipulated penalties and interest at the statutory judgment rate provided for in 28 U.S.C. § 1961 as in effect on the date of execution of the Consent Order.

I. Unless otherwise provided in the Agreement, whenever the Agreement requires notice or submission of reports, information or documents, such information shall be submitted to the following persons:

* * *

Consent Order

The United States Environmental Protection Agency as Complainant, and Sara Lee Corp. ("Sara Lee"), as Respondent, the Parties herein, having signed and consented to the entry of the Consent Agreement hereto attached and incorporated by reference into this Consent Order,

NOW, THEREFORE, IT IS ORDERED THAT:

1. Respondent Sara Lee Corporation shall comply with all terms of the Consent Agreement;

2. Respondent is assessed a civil penalty of $118,830;

3. Respondent shall, within thirty (30) calendar days of the date of this Order, forward a cashier's or certified check in the amount of $12,750 and payable to the order of the "EPA Hazardous Substance Superfund," to the following address:

U.S. Environmental Protection Agency Headquarters,
ATTENTION: Superfund Accounting,

P.O. Box 360582M,
Pittsburgh, PA 15251

and

4. Respondent shall, within thirty (30) calendar days of the date of this Order, forward a certified or cashier's check in the amount of $106,080 and payable to the order of the "Treasurer of the United States of America," to the following address:

U.S. Environmental Protection Agency,
Hearing Clerk,
P.O. Box 360277M,
Pittsburgh, PA 15251

* * *

§ 7.7 SMALL BUSINESS RELIEF

ALTERNATE THRESHOLD FOR FACILITIES WITH LOW ANNUAL REPORTABLE AMOUNTS; TOXIC CHEMICAL RELEASE REPORTING; COMMUNITY RIGHT–TO–KNOW

59 Fed. Reg. 61488 (Nov. 30, 1994).

ACTION: Final rule.

EPA is establishing an alternate threshold for those facilities with low annual reportable amounts of a listed toxic chemical. These are facilities that would otherwise meet reporting requirements under section 313 of the Emergency Planning and Community Right-to-Know Act of 1986 (EPCRA). A facility that meets the current section 313 reporting thresholds, but estimates that the total annual reportable amount of the chemical does not exceed 500 pounds per year, can take advantage of an alternate manufacture, process, or otherwise use threshold of 1 million pounds per year, for that chemical, provided that certain conditions are adhered to. EPA is establishing this alternate threshold in response to petitions received from the Small Business Administration and the American Feed Industry Association, and in consideration of the future management of the Toxic Release Inventory (TRI).

* * *

This rule is issued under section 313(f)(2) and section 328 of the Emergency Planning and Community Right-to-Know Act of 1986 (EP-CRA), 42 U.S.C. 11023(f)(2) and 11048. EPCRA is also referred to as Title III of the Superfund Amendments and Reauthorization Act of 1986 (SARA).

Section 313 of EPCRA, 42 U.S.C. 11023, requires certain facilities which manufacture, process, or otherwise use listed toxic chemicals in excess of the applicable threshold quantities to report their environmental releases of such chemicals annually. The threshold quantities are established in section 313(f)(1). EPA has authority to revise these threshold amounts pursuant to section 313(f)(2); however, such revised threshold amounts must obtain reporting on a substantial majority of total releases of the chemical at all facilities subject to section 313. A revised threshold may be based on classes of chemicals or categories of facilities.

Beginning with the 1991 reporting year, such facilities also began reporting source reduction and recycling data for listed chemicals, pursuant to section 6607 of the Pollution Prevention Act, 42 U.S.C. 13106. This information is submitted on EPA Form 9350–1 (Form R) and compiled in an annual Toxic Release Inventory (TRI). Each covered facility must file a separate Form R for each listed chemical manufactured, processed, or otherwise used in excess of the reporting thresholds established in section 313(f)(1). Section 328, 42 U.S.C. 11048, provides EPA with general rulemaking authority to develop regulations necessary to carry out the purposes of the Act.

B. BACKGROUND

On August 8, 1991, the Small Business Administration (SBA) petitioned EPA to exempt from TRI reporting requirements, facilities reporting relatively low volumes of chemicals released and transferred off-site. The petition proposed that EPA establish a tiering system within the list of reportable chemicals under EPCRA section 313. The petition suggested a division of the list to be based on a combination of chemical toxicity and amounts reported to TRIB. Those chemicals deemed to have high toxicity concerns and/or are reported in relatively low volumes nationally, would have a lower "exemption" threshold (such as 10 pounds for the sum of releases and transfers) or would be reported on a much more simplified form. Those chemicals with lower toxicity concerns and are reported in relatively high volumes would be subject to a much higher "exemption" level, such as 5,000 pounds for the sum of releases and transfers.

* * *

EPA received a similar request in a petition from the American Feed Industry Association (AFIA) on February 14, 1992. AFIA requested an exemption of Standard Industrial Classification (SIC) code 2048 from TRI reporting. The general basis of this request is that facilities in SIC code 2048, "Prepared Feeds and Feed Ingredients for Animals and Fowls, Except Dogs and Cats," have such small releases of the listed chemicals (primarily feed additives) that the industry as a whole does not contribute information that furthers the purposes of EPCRA, therefore, the imposition of TRI reporting on the feed industry is unfair. The AFIA petition suggested, as an alternative to their request of an SIC code deletion, that EPA adopt the approach proposed in the SBA petition.

* * *

EPA decided to focus on a revision of current reporting requirements that would be applied to all industries subject to section 313, as opposed to a revision restricted to target industrial sectors or SIC codes.

EPA therefore considers this rule as a response to both the AFIA and SBA petitions.

* * *

EPA is establishing an alternate threshold for those facilities with a low amount of a listed toxic chemical in their "annual reportable amount" (in the proposal, this amount was referred to as "total waste"). Contingent upon OMB approval, the alternate threshold rule will be effective for activities beginning January 1, 1995. EPA will publish a technical amendment in the Federal Register when the reporting additions have been approved by OMB. This reporting modification will enable facilities otherwise meeting reporting requirements under section 313 of EPCRA to take advantage of a higher threshold than those set out in 40 CFR 372.25 for any listed toxic chemical, if the annual reportable amounts of that toxic chemical did not exceed 500 pounds for the combined total quantities released at the facility, disposed within the facility, treated at the facility (as represented by amounts destroyed or converted by [*61490] treatment processes), recovered at the facility as a result of recycle operations, combusted for the purpose of energy recovery at the facility, and amounts transferred from the facility to off-site locations for the purpose of recycle, energy recovery, treatment, and/or disposal. These volumes correspond to the sum of amounts reportable for data elements on EPA Form R (EPA Form 9350–1; Rev. 12/4/93) as Part II column B or sections 8.1 (quantity released), 8.2 (quantity used for energy recovery on-site), 8.3 (quantity used for energy recovery off-site), 8.4 (quantity recycled on-site), 8.5 (quantity recycled off-site), 8.6 (quantity treated on-site), and 8.7 (quantity treated off-site).

The alternate threshold applies to a defined category of facilities on a per chemical basis. The alternate manufacture, process, or otherwise use threshold for a specific chemical at a facility meeting the category definition would be an amount greater than 1 million pounds per year. Specifically, if a facility manufactures, processes, or otherwise uses 1 million pounds or less of a chemical annually, and if 500 pounds or less of that chemical is present in their annual reportable amount, then the alternate reporting option is available to that facility for that chemical. Other chemicals at the facility that do not meet the criteria for the alternate threshold would continue to be reported on Form R as currently required.

To take advantage of the alternate threshold, a facility is required to: (1) Submit an

annual certification statement indicating that the facility met the requirements for use of the alternate threshold for the specific chemical and (2) maintain and make available upon request accurate records substantiating the calculations supporting the facility's claim of eligibility for the alternate threshold for each chemical.

II. *Explanation of This Threshold Modification*

This final rule establishes an alternate threshold for purposes of submitting reports under section 313 of EPCRA. The key factors that govern the application of this alternate threshold are, the sum of amounts of the listed toxic chemical in their annual reportable amount, and the quantity of that chemical being manufactured, processed, or otherwise used within the facility.

Current reporting thresholds set forth in EPCRA section 313(f)(1) apply to the manufacture, process, or otherwise use of listed section 313 chemicals. In short, these are activity-based thresholds. EPCRA section 313(f)(2) also provides EPA with the flexibility to revise the established activity-based threshold amounts in section 313(f)(1) and apply such revised thresholds to individual chemicals, classes of chemicals, or categories of facilities. However, any modification of a threshold must continue to obtain reporting on a substantial majority of total releases of the chemical at all facilities subject to the requirements of section 313.

This final rule first establishes a category of facilities based on the annual sum of a listed toxic chemical in their annual reportable amount. By establishing this category of facilities, a threshold modification can then be applied selectively to that category. A facility becomes part of this category if at least one toxic chemical, otherwise reportable, does not exceed the 500 pound criterion for that chemical in their annual reportable amount. Annual reportable amount is defined as the combined total quantities released at the facility, disposed within the facility, treated at the facility (as represented by amounts destroyed or converted by treatment processes), recovered at the facility as a result of recycle operations, combusted for the purpose of energy recovery at the facility, and amounts transferred from the facility to off-site locations for the purpose of recycle, energy recovery, treatment, and/or disposal. These volumes correspond to the sum of amounts reportable for data elements on EPA Form R (EPA Form 9350–1; Rev. 12/4/93) as Part II column B or sections 8.1 (quantity released), 8.2 (quantity used for energy recovery on-site), 8.3 (quantity used for energy recovery off-site), 8.4 (quantity recycled on-site), 8.5 (quantity recycled off-site), 8.6 (quantity treated on-site), and 8.7 (quantity treated off-site).

A facility in this category is then eligible to take advantage of an alternate manufacture, process, or otherwise use threshold of 1 million pounds for that specific chemical. Hence, if the facility meets the criterion of having no more than 500 pounds in its annual reportable amount of a listed toxic chemical, and for that chemical, the facility does not exceed the manufacture, process, or otherwise use threshold of 1 million pounds, then that facility may submit a certification statement for that chemical in lieu of a full Form R. A facility eligible to apply the alternate threshold and choosing to submit a certification statement must keep records substantiating the facility's eligibility determination. If EPA subsequently determines that the facility was ineligible to apply the alternate threshold, then the Agency can bring an enforcement action with respect to non-reporting of Form R.

* * *

Chapter 8

WATER POLLUTION

Table of Sections

---

§ 8.1 INTRODUCTION

1. *History of Water Pollution Regulations*

Regulation of pollution in waters of the United States is perhaps the oldest of all *federal* environmental statutes. Under the Federal Rivers and Harbors Act of 1899, 33 U.S.C.A. §§ 401, 403 (West 1988 & Supp. 1993), it was and still is illegal to commence the construction of a bridge, dam, dike, or causeway in navigable waters without a "Section 9" permit from the Army Corps of Engineers (the Corps)(for dams and dikes) or the Secretary of Transportation (for bridges and causeways). The consent of Congress also is required if the navigable water is interstate, and consent of the appropriate state legislature is required if the navigable portion of the navigable water is solely within the boundaries of one state.

A "Section 10" permit is required for construction of other improvements that may obstruct navigability, *e.g.*, piers, weirs, jetties, pipelines, and power lines, or any other work in or affecting navigable waters, *e.g.*, dredging, filling, or excavating. Consent of Congress or a state legislature is not required for this type of construction. Structures in navigable water must also comply with applicable rules of the Coast Guard. *See* 33 C.F.R. Part 114 *et seq.* (1990).

It is the legacy of the Federal Rivers and Harbors Act of 1899 which created split jurisdiction with regard to regulation of wetlands—jurisdiction being split between the EPA and the Corps.

There is no one federal statute currently regulating the hydrological cycle. There is no comprehensive scheme regulating all United States waters (as opposed to the statutory "waters of the United States"). Instead, the water cycle in regulated on a federal level through a patchwork of complicated statutes that address pollution on a piecemeal basis. the problem with this patchwork approach, of course, is that many of the more important pollution protection issues are left completely unregulated on a federal level. The prime example of this lack of regulation is the increased problem of agricultural runoff from non-point sources. Excessive pesticides, fertilizers and top soil from farm lands contribute heavily to the pollution in our nations streams, rivers and bays.

Below is a table of the various federal environmental laws which contribute to the regulation of the hydrological cycle:

Body of Water/ Portion of the Hydrological Cycle	Name of Federal Statute
Rivers	Rivers & Harbors Act Oil Pollution Act of 1990
Oceans	Oil Pollution Act of 1990 Ocean Dumping Act Coastal Zone Management Act Coastal Barriers Resources System Act
Groundwaters	Safe Drinking Water Act RCRA CERCLA
Air	Clean Air Act—Title IV (Acid Rain)

Notice that groundwaters that are not drinking water sources or which are not subject to RCRA or CERCLA corrective action are not regulated under federal law; although some states have defined groundwaters as "waters of the state" for purposes of state law.

2. The Clean Water Act at a Glance

The Clean Water Act (CWA or the Act), as amended, 33 U.S.C.A. § 1251 *et seq.* (West 1988 & Supp. 1993), establishes a comprehensive scheme for regulating all sources of "pollution" and discharges of "pollutants" to "waters of the United States." A water is considered a water of the United States if it is:

√ A water affecting interstate commerce;

√ An interstate water;

√ An intrastate water affecting interstate commerce;

√ A tributary of the above;

√ A territorial sea; or

√ A wetland adjacent to the above.

Any addition of pollution to navigable waters from "any discernible, confined, and discrete conveyance, including but not limited to any pipe, ditch, channel, tunnel, conduit, well, discrete fissure, or container" (i.e. a "point source"), is prohibited, except as provided in the conditions of a National Pollutant Discharge Elimination System permit issued by EPA or an authorized state agency. The CWA also regulates storm water point source discharges, the discharge of dredged or fill material, and oil spills, among other things.

The goal of the Act is to "restore and maintain the chemical, physical and biological integrity of the nation's waters." Ironically, the CWA set the ambitious (and yet to be achieved) goal of having all waters of the United Stated fishable and swimmable by 1983. In addition, all discharges of pollutants into surface waters were to be eliminated by 1985.

The CWA is a federal program that can be delegated to the states. It is designed as a state/federal partnership, with the federal government providing the "floor"—the minimum regulation required across the country. States are free to impose regulations which exceed federal requirements. Laws are considered to exceed federal standards if they are *more* protective of health and the environment. EPA is responsible for implementing CWA requirements and has promulgated extensive regulations to that end.

The CWA consists of four primary permitting programs, which will be discussed in greater detail later in the chapter:

√ National Pollution Discharge Elimination System ("NPDES") Permits (the § 402 program);

√ Wetlands Permits (the § 404 program);

√ Stormwater permits; and

√ Publicly Owned Treatment Works (POTWs).

Section	Description
§ 101	Goals
§§ 201–219	Establishes Construction Grant Programs
§ 301	Establishes Effluent Limitations; Serves as statutory basis for § 402 NPDES permit program
§ 302	Establishes Water Quality Related Effluent Limitations
§ 303	Requires states to adopt Water Quality Standards that are subject to EPA approval
§ 304	Federal Water Quality Criteria and Guidelines
§ 306	Requires EPA to set New Source Performance Standards based on best demonstrated control technology
§ 307	Toxic and Pretreatment Effluent Standards
§ 309	Authorizes enforcement through issuance of compliance orders and administrative, civil and criminal penalties
§ 319	Nonpoint source management programs
§ 402	Establishes NPDES Permit Program
§ 404	Establishes Dredge & Fill Permit Program— Serves as Basis for Federal Regulation of Wetlands
§ 505	Citizen suit provisions
§ 509	Authorizes judicial review of certain EPA rulemaking in US Court of Appeals

§ 8.2 NATIONAL POLLUTANT DISCHARGE ELIMINATION SYSTEM

The CWA's primary regulatory program is the National Pollutant Discharge Elimination System (NPDES). Under the CWA, an NPDES permit is required for any discharges of pollutants from "point sources" to navigable waters of the United States. *See* 33 U.S.C.A. § 1342. The term "point source" is defined as "any discernible, confined and discrete conveyance, including, but not limited to, any pipe, ditch, channel, tunnel, conduit, well, discrete fissure, container, rolling stock, concentrated animal feeding operation, or vessel or other floating craft, from which pollutants are or may be discharged." 33 U.S.C.A. 1362. The terms "pollution" and "pollutant" are defined very broadly to include virtually any parameter, constituent, or water quality characteristic, subject only to certain, limited exceptions. Courts have construed "waters of the United States" broadly to encompass virtually all water bodies, including wetlands.

Note that "indirect discharges," such as discharges of sanitary wastes, are not subject to NPDES requirements. Rather, they are regulated by the local publicly owned treatment works (POTW) to which wastes are discharged. The POTW must comply with federal and state pretreatment program requirements. *See* 33 U.S.C.A. § 1317(c); 40 C.F.R. Part 403 (1990).

While the CWA initially gives EPA authority to issue such permits, the Agency may delegate that authority to the states, subject to oversight by EPA. State NPDES programs, and permits issued thereunder, must meet minimum federal standards, but the Act reserves to the states the right to set more stringent limitations, requirements, or conditions.

EPA promulgated regulations specifying the types of requirements that NPDES permits must contain. *See generally* 40 C.F.R. Parts 122–125 (1990). Under EPA's NPDES regulations, permits must require point source dischargers to comply with any applicable effluent limitations guidelines or New Source Performance Standards (NSPS). Permits also must assure compliance with applicable state water quality standards. In addition, the permit must contain a host of "boiler-plate" requirements for proper operation and maintenance of the facility, compliance monitoring, recordkeeping, monthly compliance reporting, and timely notification if permit limits are exceeded.

NPDES permits expire at the end of five years, unless the permittee files a complete application for renewal at least 180 days before the expiration of the permit. In that case, when EPA (or, in some cases, the state) is the permit issuer, the permit continues in effect even though the effective date of the permit has passed and a new permit has not been issued. Permits may not be transferred without proper notice to and approval from the permit issuer.

The CWA provides for development and application of several kinds of effluent limitations and standards. Most of these are incorporated in a source's NPDES permit as numerical restrictions on the concentration or mass of pollutants discharged.

1. *Technology–Based Standards for Existing Sources*

The CWA provides for three phases of progressively more stringent technology-based "effluent limitations guidelines" for categories and subcategories of existing industrial point sources. 33 U.S.C.A. § 1311. The first phase, to have been achieved in 1977, required discharges to be treated by "the best practicable control technology currently available" (BPT). The second phase, to have been achieved by various dates dependent on the date the guidelines were promulgated, but no later than March 31, 1989, required discharges of toxic pollutants (such as heavy metals) and non-toxic/non-conventional pollutants (such as chlorine and iron) to be treated by "the best available technology economically achievable" (BAT). The third phase, to have been achieved by various dates dependent on the date of promulgation of the guidelines, but no later than March 31, 1989, required discharges of "conventional" pollutants (such as biological oxygen demand, suspended solids, fecal coliform, acid, and oil and grease) to be treated with "the best conventional pollutant control technology" (BCT), depending on the pollutant involved. The EPA publishes generic "effluent limitation guidelines" specifying the pollutant effluent levels that BPT, BCT, and BAT are capable of achieving for various industries at 40 C.F.R. Parts 400–460. Unless a variance from the guidelines is obtained or more stringent water quality-based limits are imposed, the levels specified by the guidelines generally are incorporated in NPDES permits as effluent limitations.

Discharges from new or significantly modified sources directly into navigable waters must comply with "new source performance standards" (NSPS), which reflect the greatest degree of effluent reduction achievable through application of the "best available demonstrated control technology." A "new source" is one that commenced construction after publication of proposed NSPS that will apply to it, if the standards are in fact thereafter adopted in accordance with the Act.

ARKANSAS v. OKLAHOMA
503 U.S. 91, 112 S.Ct. 1046, 117 L.Ed.2d 239 (1992).

STEVENS, J.

Pursuant to the Clean Water Act, 86 Stat. 816, as amended, 33 U.S.C. § 1251, et seq., the Environmental Protection Agency (EPA) issued a discharge permit to a new point source in Arkansas, about 39 miles upstream from the Oklahoma state line. The question presented in this litigation is whether the EPA's finding that discharges from the new source would not cause a detectable violation of Oklahoma's water quality standards satisfied the EPA's duty to protect the interests of the downstream State. Disagreeing with the Court of Appeals, we hold that the Agency's action was authorized by the statute.

I

In 1985, the City of Fayetteville, Arkansas, applied to the EPA, seeking a permit for the City's new sewage treatment plant under the National Pollution Discharge Elimination System (NPDES). After the appropriate procedures, the EPA, pursuant to § 402(a)(1) of the Act, 33 U.S.C. § 1342(a)(1), issued a permit authorizing the plant to discharge up to half of its effluent (to a limit of 6.1 million gallons per day) into an unnamed stream in northwestern Arkansas.... That flow passes through a series of three creeks for about 17 miles, and then enters the Illinois River at a point 22 miles upstream from the Arkansas–Oklahoma border.

The permit imposed specific limitations on the quantity, content, and character of the discharge and also included a number of special conditions, including a provision that if a study then underway indicated that more stringent limitations were necessary to ensure compliance with Oklahoma's water quality standards, the permit would be modified to incorporate those limits. App. 84.

Respondents challenged this permit before the EPA, alleging, inter alia, that the discharge violated the Oklahoma water quality standards.

Those standards provide that "no degradation [of water quality] shall be allowed" in the upper Illinois River, including the portion of the River immediately downstream from the state line. . . .

Following a hearing, the Administrative Law Judge (ALJ) concluded that the Oklahoma standards would not be implicated unless the contested discharge had something more than a "mere de minimis impact" on the State's waters. He found that the discharge would not have an "undue impact" on Oklahoma's waters and, accordingly, affirmed the issuance of the permit. App. to Pet. for Cert. in No.90–1262, pp. 101a–103a (emphasis deleted).

On a petition for review, the EPA's Chief Judicial Officer first ruled that § 301(b)(1)(C) of the Clean Water Act requires an NPDES permit to "impose any effluent limitations necessary to comply with applicable state water quality standards." . . . *Id.*, at 116a–117a. He then held that the Act and EPA regulations offered greater protection for the downstream State than the ALJ's undue impact standard suggested. He explained the proper standard as follows:

> [A] mere theoretical impairment of Oklahoma's water quality standards—i.e., an infinitesimal impairment predicted through modeling but not expected to be actually detectable or measurable—should not by itself block the issuance of the permit. In this case, the permit should be upheld if the record shows by a preponderance of the evidence that the authorized discharges would not cause an *actual detectable violation* of Oklahoma's water quality standards. *Id.*, at 117a (emphasis in original).

On remand, the ALJ made detailed findings of fact and concluded that the City had satisfied the standard set forth by the Chief Judicial Officer. Specifically, the ALJ found that there would be no detectable violation of any of the components of Oklahoma's water quality standards. *Id.*, at 127a–143a. The Chief Judicial Officer sustained the issuance of the permit. *Id.*, at 145a–153a.

Both the petitioners in No. 90–1262 (collectively Arkansas) and the respondents in this litigation sought judicial review. . . . Arkansas argued that the Clean Water Act did not require an Arkansas point source to comply with Oklahoma's water quality standards. Oklahoma challenged the EPA's determination that the Fayetteville discharge would not produce a detectable violation of the Oklahoma standards.

The Court of Appeals did not accept either of these arguments. The court agreed with the EPA that the statute required compliance with Oklahoma's water quality standards, see 908 F.2d 595, 602–615 (C.A.10 1990), and did not disagree with the Agency's determination that the discharges from the Fayetteville plant would not produce a detectable violation of the those standards. *Id.*, at 631–633. Nevertheless, relying on a theory that neither party had advanced, the Court of Appeals reversed the Agency's issuance of the Fayetteville permit. The court first ruled that the statute requires that where a proposed source would discharge effluents that would contribute to conditions currently constituting a violation of applicable water quality standards, such [a] proposed source may not be permitted. *Id.*, at 620. Then the court found that the Illinois River in Oklahoma was already degraded, that the Fayetteville effluent would reach the Illinois River in Oklahoma, and that that effluent could be expected to contribute to the ongoing deterioration of the scenic [Illinois R]iver in Oklahoma even though it would not detectably affect the River's water quality. *Id.*, at 621–629.

The importance and the novelty of the Court of Appeals' decision persuaded us to grant certiorari. 499 U.S. (1991). We now reverse.

II

Interstate waters have been a font of controversy since the founding of the Nation. E. g., Gibbons v. Ogden, 9 Wheat. 1 (1824). This Court has frequently resolved disputes between States that are separated by a common river, *see, e.g., Ohio v. Kentucky,* 444 U.S. 335 (1980), that border the same body of water, *see, e. g., New York v. New Jersey,* 256 U.S. 296 (1921), or that are fed by the same river basin, *see, e.g., New Jersey v. New York,* 283 U.S. 336 (1931).

Among these cases are controversies between a State that introduces pollutants to a waterway and a downstream State that objects. *See, e.g., Missouri v. Illinois,* 200 U.S. 496 (1906). In such cases, this Court has applied principles of common law tempered by a respect for the sovereignty of the States. *Compare id.,* at 521, *with Georgia v. Tennessee Copper Co.,* 206 U.S. 230, 237 (1907). In forging what may not improperly be called interstate common law, *Illinois v. Milwaukee,* 406 U.S. 91, 105–106 (1972)(*Milwaukee I*), however, we remained aware that new federal laws and new federal regulations may in time pre-empt the field of federal common law of nuisance. *Id.,* at 107.

In *Milwaukee v. Illinois,* 451 U.S. 304 (1981)(*Milwaukee II*), we held that the 1972 Amendments to the Federal Water Pollution Control Act did just that. In addressing Illinois' claim that Milwaukee's discharges into Lake Michigan constituted a nuisance, we held that the comprehensive regulatory regime created by the 1972 Amendments pre-empted Illinois' federal common law remedy. We observed that Congress had addressed many of the problems we had identified in *Milwaukee I* by providing a downstream State with an opportunity for a hearing before the source State's permitting agency, by requiring the latter to explain its failure to accept any recommendations offered by the downstream State, and by authorizing the EPA, in its discretion, to veto a source State's issuance of any permit if the waters of another State may be affected. *Milwaukee II,* 451 U.S., 325–326.

In *Milwaukee II,* the Court did not address whether the 1972 Amendments had supplanted state common law remedies as well as the federal common law remedy. *See id.,* at 310, n. 4. On remand, Illinois argued that § 510 of the Clean Water Act, 33 U.S.C. § 1370, expressly preserved the State's right to adopt and enforce rules that are more stringent than federal standards. . . . . The Court of Appeals accepted Illinois' reading of § 510, but held that that section did no more than to save the right and jurisdiction of a state to regulate activity occurring within the confines of its boundary waters. *Illinois v. Milwaukee,* 731 F.2d 403, 413 (C.A.7 1984), cert. denied, 469 U.S. 1196 (1985).

This Court subsequently endorsed that analysis in *International Paper Co. v. Ouellette,* 479 U.S. 481 (1987), in which Vermont property owners claimed that the pollution discharged into Lake Champlain by a paper company located in New York constituted a nuisance under Vermont law. The Court held the Clean Water Act taken as a whole, its purposes and its history "pre-empted an action based on the law of the affected State and that the only state law applicable to an interstate discharge is the law of the State in which the point source is located." *Id.,* at 493, 487. Moreover, in reviewing § 402(b) of the Act, the Court pointed out that when a new permit is being issued by the source State's permit-granting agency, the downstream state

> does not have the authority to block the issuance of the permit if it is dissatisfied with the proposed standards. An affected State's only recourse is to apply to the EPA Administrator, who then has the discretion to disapprove the permit if he concludes that the discharges will have an undue impact on interstate waters. § 1342(d)(2). . . . Thus the Act makes it clear that affected States occupy a subordinate position to source States in the federal regulatory program. *Id.,* at 490–491. . . .

Unlike the foregoing cases, this litigation involves not a State-issued permit, but a federally issued permit. To explain the significance of this distinction, we comment further on the statutory scheme before addressing the specific issues raised by the parties.

III

The Clean Water Act anticipates a partnership between the States and the Federal Government, animated by a shared objective: to restore and maintain the chemical, physical, and biological integrity of the Nation's waters. 33 U.S.C. § 1251(a). Toward this end, the Act provides for two sets of water quality measures. Effluent limitations are promulgated by the EPA and restrict the quantities, rates, and concentrations of specified substances which are discharged from point sources. *See* 33 U.S.C. §§ 1311, 1314. Water quality standards are, in general, promulgated by the States and establish the desired condition of a waterway. *See* 33 U.S.C. § 1313. These standards supplement effluent limitations so that numerous point sources, despite individual compliance with effluent limitations, may be further regulated to prevent water quality from falling below acceptable levels. *EPA v. California ex rel. State Water Resources Control Board,* 426 U.S. 200, 205, n. 12 (1976).

The EPA provides States with substantial guidance in the drafting of water quality standards. *See* generally 40 CFR pt. 131 (1991)(setting forth model water quality standards). Moreover, § 303 of the Act requires, inter alia, that state authorities periodically review water quality standards and secure the EPA's approval of any revisions in the standards. If the EPA recommends changes to the standards and the State fails to comply with that recommendation, the Act authorizes the EPA to promulgate water quality standards for the State. 33 U.S.C. § 1313(c).

The primary means for enforcing these limitations and standards is the National Pollution Discharge Elimination System (NPDES), enacted in 1972 as a critical part of Congress' complete rewriting of federal water pollution law. *Milwaukee II*, 451 U.S., at 317. Section 301(a) of the Act, 33 U.S.C. § 1311(a), generally prohibits the discharge of any effluent into a navigable body of water unless the point source has obtained an NPDES permit. Section 402 establishes the NPDES permitting regime, and describes two types of permitting systems: state permit programs that must satisfy federal requirements and be approved by the EPA, and a federal program administered by the EPA.

Section 402(b) authorizes each State to establish its own permit program for discharges into navigable waters within its jurisdiction. 33 U.S.C. § 1342(b). Among the requirements the state program must satisfy are the procedural protections for downstream States discussed in *Ouellette* and *Milwaukee II. See* 33 U.S.C. §§ 1342(b)(3), (5). n7 Although these provisions do not authorize the downstream State to veto the issuance of a permit for a new point source in another State, the Administrator retains authority to block the issuance of any state-issued permit that is outside the guidelines and requirements of the Act. 33 U.S.C. § 1342(d)(2)....

In the absence of an approved state program, the EPA may issue an NPDES permit under § 402(a) of the Act. (In this case, for example, because Arkansas had not been authorized to issue NPDES permits when the Fayetteville plant was completed, the permit was issued by the EPA itself.) The EPA's permit program is subject to the same terms, conditions, and requirements "as a state permit program. 33 U.S.C. § 1342(a)(3). Notwithstanding this general symmetry, the EPA has construed the Act as requiring that EPA-issued NPDES permits also comply with § 401(a). That section, which predates § 402 and the NPDES, applies to a broad category of federal licenses, and sets forth requirements for any applicant for a Federal license or permit to conduct any activity including, but not limited to, the construction or operation of facilities, which may result in any discharge into the navigable waters." 33 U.S.C. § 1341(a). Section 401(a)(2) appears to prohibit the issuance of any federal license or permit over the objection of an affected State unless compliance with the affected State's water quality requirements can be insured....

IV

The parties have argued three analytically distinct questions concerning the interpretation of the Clean Water Act. First, does the Act require the EPA, in crafting and issuing a permit to a point source in one State, to apply the water quality standards of downstream States? Second, even if the Act does not require as much, does the Agency have the statutory authority to mandate such compliance? Third, does the Act provide, as the Court of Appeals held, that once a body of water fails to meet water quality standards no discharge that yields effluent that reach the degraded waters will be permitted?

In this case, it is neither necessary nor prudent for us to resolve the first of these questions. In issuing the Fayetteville permit, the EPA assumed it was obligated by both the Act and its own regulations to ensure that the Fayetteville discharge would not violate Oklahoma's standards. *See* App. to Pet. for Cert. in No. 90–1262, pp.116a–117a, and n.14. As we discuss below, this assumption was permissible and reasonable and therefore there is no need for us to address whether the Act requires as much. Moreover, much of the analysis and argument in the briefs of the parties relies on statutory provisions that govern not only federal permits issued pursuant to §§ 401(a) and 402(a), but also state permits issued under § 402(b). It seems unwise to evaluate those arguments in a case such as this one, which only involves a federal permit.

Our decision not to determine at this time the scope of the Agency's statutory obligations does not affect our resolution of the second question, which concerns the Agency's statutory authority. Even if the Clean Water Act itself does not require the Fayetteville discharge to comply with Oklahoma's water quality standards, the statute clearly does not limit the EPA's authority to mandate such compliance.

Since 1973, EPA regulations have provided that an NPDES permit shall not be issued when the imposition of conditions cannot ensure compliance with the applicable water quality requirements of all affected States. . . . 40 CFR § 122.4(d)(1991); see also 38 Fed. Reg. 13533 (1973); 40 CFR § 122.44(d)(1991). Those regulations—relied upon by the EPA in the issuance of the Fayetteville permit—constitute a reasonable exercise of the Agency's statutory authority.

Congress has vested in the Administrator broad discretion to establish conditions for NPDES permits. Section 402(a)(2) provides that for EPA-issued permits the Administrator shall prescribe conditions for such permits to assure compliance with the requirements of [§ 402(a)(1)] and such other requirements as he deems appropriate. 33 U.S.C. § 1342(a)(2) (emphasis supplied). Similarly, Congress preserved for the Administrator broad authority to oversee state permit programs:

> No permit shall issue . . . if the Administrator . . . objects in writing to the issuance of such permit as being outside the guidelines and requirements of this chapter. 33 U.S.C. § 1342(d)(2).

The regulations relied on by the EPA were a perfectly reasonable exercise of the Agency's statutory discretion. The application of state water quality standards in the interstate context is wholly consistent with the Act's broad purpose, to restore and maintain the chemical, physical, and biological integrity of the Nation's waters. 33 U.S.C. § 1251(a). Moreover, as noted above, § 301(b)(1)(C) expressly identifies the achievement of state water quality standards as one of the Act's central objectives. The Agency's regulations conditioning NPDES permits are a well-tailored means of achieving this goal.

Notwithstanding this apparent reasonableness, Arkansas argues that our description in *Ouellette* of the role of affected States in the permit process and our characterization of the affected States' position as subordinate, see 479 U.S., at 490–491, indicates that the EPA's application of the Oklahoma standards was error. We disagree. Our statement in *Ouellette* concerned only an affected State's input into the permit process; that input is clearly limited by the plain language of § 402(b). Limits on an affected State's direct participation in permitting decisions, however, do not in any way constrain the EPA's authority to require a point source to comply with downstream water quality standards.

Arkansas also argues that regulations requiring compliance with downstream standards are at odds with the legislative history of the Act and with the statutory scheme established by the Act. Although we agree with Arkansas that the Act's legislative history indicates that Congress intended to grant the Administrator discretion in his oversight of the issuance of NPDES permits, ... we find nothing in that history to indicate that Congress intended to preclude the EPA from establishing a general requirement that such permits be conditioned to ensure compliance with downstream water quality standards.

Similarly, we agree with Arkansas that in the Clean Water Act Congress struck a careful balance among competing policies and interests, but do not find the EPA regulations concerning the application of downstream water quality standards at all incompatible with that balance. Congress, in crafting the Act, protected certain sovereign interest of the States; for example, § 510 allows States to adopt more demanding pollution-control standards than those established under the Act. Arkansas emphasizes that § 510 preserves such state authority only as it is applied to the waters of the regulating State. Even assuming Arkansas's construction of § 510 is correct, cf. id., at 493, that section only concerns state authority and does not constrain the EPA's authority to promulgate reasonable regulations requiring point sources in one State to comply with water quality standards in downstream States.

For these reasons, we find the EPA's requirement that the Fayetteville discharge comply with Oklahoma's water quality standards to be a reasonable exercise of the Agency's substantial statutory discretion. *Cf. Chevron U.S.A. Inc. v. Natural Resources Defense Council, Inc.,* 467 U.S. 837, 842–845 (1984).

V

The Court of Appeals construed the Clean Water Act to prohibit any discharge of effluent that would reach waters already in violation of existing water quality standards.... We find nothing in the Act to support this reading.

The interpretation of the statute adopted by the court had not been advanced by any party during the agency or court proceedings. Moreover, the Court of Appeals candidly acknowledged that its theory has apparently never before been addressed by a federal court. 908 F.2d, at

620, n.39. The only statutory provision the court cited to support its legal analysis was § 402(h), *see id.,* at 633, which merely authorizes the EPA (or a state permit program) to prohibit a publicly owned treatment plant that is violating a condition of its NPDES permit from accepting any additional pollutants for treatment until the ongoing violation has been corrected. *See* 33 U.S.C. § 1342(h).

Although the Act contains several provisions directing compliance with state water quality standards, *see,* e. g., 33 U.S.C. § 1311(b)(1)(C), the parties have pointed to nothing that mandates a complete ban on discharges into a waterway that is in violation of those standards. The statute does, however, contain provisions designed to remedy existing water quality violations and to allocate the burden of reducing undesirable discharges between existing sources and new sources. *See,* e. g., 33 U.S.C. § 1313(d). Thus, rather than establishing the categorical ban announced by the Court of Appeals—which might frustrate the construction of new plants that would improve existing conditions—the Clean Water Act vests in the EPA and the States broad authority to develop long-range, area-wide programs to alleviate and eliminate existing pollution. *See,* e. g., 33 U.S.C. § 1288(b)(2).

To the extent that the Court of Appeals relied on its interpretation of the Act to reverse the EPA's permitting decision, that reliance was misplaced.

VI

The Court of Appeals also concluded that the EPA's issuance of the Fayetteville permit was arbitrary and capricious because the Agency misinterpreted Oklahoma's water quality standards. The primary difference.... between the court's and the Agency's interpretation of the standards derives from the court's construction of the Act. Contrary to the EPA's interpretation of the Oklahoma standards, the Court of Appeals read those standards as containing the same categorical ban on new discharges that the court had found in the Clean Water Act itself. Although we do not believe the text of the Oklahoma standards supports the court's reading (indeed, we note that Oklahoma itself had not advanced that interpretation in its briefs in the Court of Appeals), we reject it for a more fundamental reason—namely, that the Court of Appeals exceeded the legitimate scope of judicial review of an agency adjudication. To emphasize the importance of this point, we shall first briefly assess the soundness of the EPA's interpretation and application of the Oklahoma standards and then comment more specifically on the Court of Appeals' approach.

As discussed above, EPA regulations require an NPDES permit to comply with the applicable water quality requirements of all affected States. 40 CFR § 122.4(d)(1991). This regulation effectively incorporates into federal law those state law standards the Agency reasonably determines to be applicable. In such a situation, then, state water quality standards—promulgated by the States with substantial guidance from the EPA . . . and approved by the Agency—are part of the federal law of water pollution control.

Two features of the body of law governing water pollution support this conclusion. First, as discussed more thoroughly above, we have long recognized that interstate water pollution is controlled by federal law. *See* supra, at ___. Recognizing that the system of federally approved state standards as applied in the interstate context constitutes federal law is wholly consistent with this principle. Second, treating state standards in interstate controversies as federal law accords with the Act's purpose of authorizing the EPA to create and manage a uniform system of interstate water pollution regulation.

Because we recognize that, at least insofar as they affect the issuance of a permit in another State, the Oklahoma standards have a federal character, the EPA's reasonable, consistently held interpretation of those standards is entitled to substantial deference. *Cf. INS v. National Center for Immigrants' Rights,* 502 U.S. (1991)(slip op., at 6); *Chevron U.S.A., Inc. v. Natural Resources Defense Council, Inc.,* 467 U.S. 837 (1984). In this case, the Chief Judicial Officer ruled that the Oklahoma standards—which require that there be "no degradation" of the upper Illinois River—would only be violated if the discharge effected an "actually detectable or measurable" change in water quality. App. to Pet. for Cert. in No. 90–1262, p. 117a.

This interpretation of the Oklahoma standards is certainly reasonable and consistent with the purposes and principles of the Clean Water Act. As the Chief Judicial Officer noted, "unless there is some method for measuring compliance, there is no way to ensure compliance." *Id.,* at 118a, n.16 (internal quotation marks omitted; citation omitted). Moreover, this interpretation of the Oklahoma standards makes eminent sense in the interstate context: if every discharge that had some theoretical impact on a downstream State were interpreted as "degrading" the downstream waters, downstream States might wield an effective veto over upstream discharges.

The EPA's application of those standards in this case was also sound. On remand, the ALJ scrutinized the record and made explicit factual findings regarding four primary measures of water quality under the Oklahoma standards: eutrophication, . . . aesthetics, . . . dissolved oxygen, . . . and metals. . . . In each case, the ALJ found that the Fayetteville discharge would not lead to a detectable change in water quality. He therefore concluded that the Fayetteville discharge would not violate the Oklahoma water quality standards. Because we agree with the Agency's Chief Judicial Officer that these findings are supported by substantial evidence, we conclude that the Court of Appeals should have affirmed both the EPA's construction of the regulations and the issuance of the Fayetteville permit.

In its review of the EPA's interpretation and application of the Oklahoma standards, the Court of Appeals committed three mutually compounding errors.

First, the court failed to give due regard to the EPA's interpretation of its own regulations, as those regulations incorporate the Oklahoma standards. Instead the court voiced its own interpretation of the governing law and concluded that "where a proposed source would discharge effluents that would contribute to conditions currently constituting a violation of applicable water quality standards, such [a] proposed source may not be permitted." 908 F.2d, at 620. As we have already pointed out, that reading of the law is not supported by the statute or by any EPA regulation. The Court of Appeals sat in review of an agency action and should have afforded the EPA's interpretation of the governing law an appropriate level of deference. *See generally Chevron,* supra, at 842–844.

Second, the court disregarded well-established standards for reviewing the factual findings of agencies and instead made its own factual findings. The troubling nature of the court's analysis appears on the face of the opinion itself: at least four times, the court concluded that "there was substantial evidence before the ALJ to support" particular findings which the court thought appropriate, but which were contrary to those actually made by the ALJ. 908 F.2d, at 620, 625, 627, 629. Although we have long recognized the substantial evidence" standard in administrative law, the court below turned that analysis on its head. A court reviewing an agency's adjudicative action should accept the agency's factual findings if those findings are supported by substantial evidence on the record as a whole. *See* generally *Universal Camera Corp. v. NLRB,* 340 U.S. 474 (1951). The court should not supplant the agency's findings merely by identifying alternative findings that could be supported by substantial evidence.

Third, the court incorrectly concluded that the EPA's decision was arbitrary and capricious. This error is derivative of the court's first two errors. Having substituted its reading of the governing law for the Agency's, and having made its own factual findings, the Court of Appeals concluded that the EPA erred in not considering an important and relevant fact—namely, that the upper Illinois River was (by the court's assessment) already degraded.

As we have often recognized, an agency ruling is "arbitrary and capricious if the agency has ... entirely failed to consider an important aspect of the problem." *Motor Vehicle Mfrs. Assn. of United States, Inc. v. State Farm Mutual Automobile Insurance Co.,* 463 U.S. 29, 43 (1983). However, in this case, the degraded status of the River is only an "important aspect" because of the Court of Appeals' novel and erroneous interpretation of the controlling law. Under the EPA's interpretation of that law, what matters is not the River's current status, but rather whether the proposed discharge will have a "detectable effect" on that status. If the Court of Appeals had been properly respectful of the Agency's permissible reading of the Act and the Oklahoma standards, the court would not have adjudged the Agency's decision arbitrary and capricious for this reason.

In sum, the Court of Appeals made a policy choice that it was not authorized to make. Arguably, as that court suggested, it might be wise to prohibit any discharge into the Illinois River, even if that discharge would have no adverse impact on water quality. But it was surely not arbitrary for the EPA to conclude—given the benefits to the River from the increased flow of relatively clean water ... and the benefits achieved in Arkansas by allowing the new plant to operate as designed—that allowing the discharge would be even wiser. It is not our role, or that of the Court of Appeals, to decide which policy choice is the better one, for it is clear that Congress has entrusted such decisions to the Environmental Protection Agency.

Accordingly, the judgment of the Court of Appeals is

Reversed.

COMMITTEE TO SAVE MOKELUMNE RIVER v. EAST BAY MUN. UTIL. DIST.

13 F.3d 305 (9th Cir.1993).

PREGERSON, CIRCUIT JUDGE:

The East Bay Municipal Utility District and the members of the California Regional Water Quality Control Board, Central Valley Region, defendants below, appeal the district court's order granting partial summary judgment in favor of the Committee to Save the Mokelumne River. The district court, in a well-written, well-reasoned opinion, found that defendants owned and operated the Penn Mine facility, and that the facility discharged pollutants into the Camanche Reservoir and Mokelumne River without a permit, in violation of the Clean Water Act, 33 U.S.C. §§ 1251–1376. On appeal, defendants contend that (1) Mine Run Dam, part of the Penn Mine facility, is not subject to the discharge permit requirements of the Clean Water Act; (2) the Water Board is immune from liability under the Act; and (3) summary judgment was improper because a triable issue of material fact exists whether there has been an "addition of pollutants" within the meaning of the Clean Water Act.

We have jurisdiction under 28 U.S.C. § 1292(b). We affirm.

BACKGROUND

The Penn Mine property is the site of an abandoned copper and zinc mine that operated intermittently from the 1860s through the 1950s. The companies that mined the site left behind reactive mine tailings, waste rock, and excavated ores. When exposed to oxygen and water, these materials form "acid mine drainage," which contains high concentrations of aluminum, cadmium, copper, zinc, iron, and sulfuric acid. Unless impeded, rain water falling on the site carries this acid mine drainage downhill, in the form of surface runoff, into the Mokelumne River.

In the 1960s, the East Bay Municipal Utility District (the "District") acquired a portion of the Penn Mine property to build the Camanche Reservoir. The District owns water rights on the Mokelumne and supplies water to towns and cities east of San Francisco. In 1978, the District, joined by the California Regional Water Quality Control Board, Central Valley Region (the "Board"), constructed the Penn Mine Facility (the "facility") in an attempt to reduce the threat of continued toxic runoff from the site. The facility consists of Mine Run Dam and the Mine Run Dam Reservoir surface impoundment, along with a series of other impoundments, drainage ditches, pipes, valves, culverts, and channels. The Mine Run Dam and most of the Mine Run Dam Reservoir are located on property owned by the District. A small portion of the Mine Run Dam Reservoir extends onto property owned by a defunct mining company.

The facility was designed to capture contaminated surface water flowing through the site, and to contain and evaporate the water through a ponding and recirculation system, preventing the contamination from reaching the reservoir and river below. Each of the two drainages once occupied by Hinkley Run and Mine Run creeks, which formerly flowed through the site, now contains a cascade of three impoundments. Water contaminated with toxic pollutants runs off the mine site and collects in the upper impoundments and then flows to the lower impoundments, eventually collecting in the Mine Run Dam Reservoir. A pump and pipe owned by the Board recirculates polluted water from Mine Run Dam Reservoir back into the upper impoundments located in the former Mine Run Creek drainage basin. Defendants operate that pump.

The facility also consists of two principal diversion ditches that divert the surface flows of Hinkley Run and Mine Run creeks around the abandoned mine site. Those diversion ditches are intended to isolate the facility from the unpolluted flows of these two creeks by diverting the streams around the facility and directly into the Mokelumne River and Camanche Reservoir, below.

As part of the facility's ongoing operation, various pipes, channels, and gullies carry polluted runoff from the mine tailings and dikes into the Mine Run Dam Reservoir and other facility impoundments. In addition, from time to time, water and drainage collected in the Mine Run Dam Reservoir have passed over the spillway or through the dam's discharge valve into the Mokelumne River and Camanche Reservoir.

The Clean Water Act (the "Act"), 33 U.S.C. §§ 1251–1376, is intended to "restore and maintain the chemical, physical, and biological integrity of the Nation's waters." 33 U.S.C. § 1251(a). In pursuit of this goal, the Act prohibits the "discharge of any pollutant" into navigable waters from any "point source" without a permit. See 33 U.S.C. § 1311(a) (except as otherwise provided in the Act, the discharge of any pollutant ("NPDES")); § 1362(12)(defines "discharge of a pollutant" as "any addition of any pollutant to navigable waters from any point source").

The Committee to Save the Mokelumne River (the "Committee") initiated this suit against the District and members of the Board under the citizen suit provisions of the Act, 33 U.S.C. § 1365. The Committee seeks a judgment declaring that defendants have discharged pollutants from the Penn Mine facility without a permit, in violation of the Clean Water Act, and enjoining defendants from discharging pollutants from the facility until they have obtained an NPDES permit to do so. The Committee also seeks an order requiring defendants to devise a remedial plan to remove and dispose of contaminated sediment in the reservoir.

Defendants moved to dismiss this action on a number of procedural and substantive grounds. At the same time, the Committee moved for summary judgment on the issue of defendants' liability under the Act. The district court denied defendants' motion and granted judgment in favor of the Committee on the issue of liability.

On appeal from the district court's order of summary judgment in favor of the Committee, defendants raise four issues. They contend that the district court erred in granting partial summary judgment in favor of the Committee because (1) Mine Run Dam is not subject to the discharge permit requirements of the Clean Water Act; (2) a material issue of fact exists as to whether defendants have "discharged a pollutant" within the meaning of the Act; (3) defendants' activities in constructing and operating the facility are regulatory, and therefore cannot constitute "additions of pollutants" under the Act; (4) the Eleventh Amendment immunizes defendants from liability under the Clean Water Act. We address each of these arguments in turn.

Discussion

A. Is Mine Run Dam subject to the Clean Water Act's permit requirements? To establish a violation of the Act's NPDES requirements, a plaintiff must prove that defendants (1) discharged, i.e., added (2) a pollutant (3) to navigable waters (4) from (5) a point source. *National Wildlife Federation v. Gorsuch*, 224 U.S.App.D.C. 41, 693 F.2d 156, 165 (D.C.Cir.1982). Defendants concede that acid mine drainage is a "pollutant," that the Mokelumne River is among the covered "navigable waters," and that the spillway and valve of the Mine Run Dam and Reservoir are "point sources" ... from which polluted water has entered the Mokelumne River. They contest only the issue whether they have "added" pollutants to the Mokelumne.

Defendants argue that under well-established case law, the Mine Run Dam is not subject to the Clean Water Act's permit requirements because it is a dam that "does no more than impound navigable waters and impede their flow in the Mokelumne River." In support of this contention, defendants rely on two decisions that held that the specific dams at issue in those cases were not subject to the discharge permit requirements because they did not "discharge pollutants," i.e., " 'add' pollutants from the outside world to" navigable water. *See National*

Wildlife Federation v. Consumers Power Co., 862 F.2d 580, 584 (6th Cir.1988); *Gorsuch,* 693 F.2d at 174–75. These cases are inapposite here because the Penn Mine facility does "discharge pollutants" as that term is defined by the Act and relevant regulations.

In both *Consumer Power Co.* and *Gorsuch,* plaintiffs sought to compel dam operators to comply with the discharge permit requirements of the Clean Water Act. In Gorsuch, plaintiffs argued that dam-induced water quality changes caused by the impoundment and release of water were a "discharge of pollutants" within the meaning of Act. In both cases, the court held that the dams at issue did not "discharge a pollutant" because the dams did not add pollutants "from the outside world." *Consumers Power Co.,* 862 F.2d at 584; *Gorsuch,* 693 F.2d at 174–75. Neither case categorically exempts all dams from the discharge permit requirements of the Clean Water Act.

This case clearly is distinguishable from *Gorsuch* and *Consumer Power Co.* because the Penn Mine facility does not pass pollution from one body of navigable water into another. Rather, the source of pollution added to the Mokelumne River is "surface runoff that is collected or channelled by" defendants from the abandoned mine site. Such surface runoff is expressly listed under the definition of "discharge of a pollutant" contained in the regulations. *See* 40 C.F.R. § 122.2 ("Discharge of a pollutant means ... additions of pollutants into waters of the United States from: surface runoff which is collected or channelled by man").

In this case, defendants have admitted that acid mine drainage from the abandoned mine site is channelled into the Penn Mine facility and collects in the Mine Run Dam Reservoir. District Answer pp. 18, 24; Board Answer Par. Par. 18, 22. Defendants also admit that "water and drainage collected in Mine Run Dam Reservoir had, from time to time, passed over the spillway or through the valve into the Mokelumne River and Camanche Reservoir." District Answer Par. 21. *See* also Board Answer pp. 18, 21, 22. These admissions, in turn, conclusively establish that defendants "discharge a pollutant" from the Penn Mine facility within the meaning of the Clean Water Act, making them subject to the Act's permit requirements.

B. Have defendants raised a genuine issue of material fact so as to preclude summary judgment for the Committee? Defendants also argue that a material issue of fact exists as to whether there is an "addition of pollutants," making improper the district court's grant of summary judgment. Specifically, defendants rely on evidence that the acidity of water flowing into the Mokelumne River through the Penn Mine facility is not greater now than it was before the dam was constructed. In effect, defendants contend that they are liable under the Clean Water Act only if the facility produces a net increase in the acidity of the surface runoff compared to the acidity of the runoff before the facility was constructed.

This argument misapprehends the focus of the Clean Water Act. The Act does not impose liability only where a point source discharge creates a net increase in the level of pollution. Rather, the Act categorically prohibits any discharge of a pollutant from a point source without a permit. 33 U.S.C. §§ 1311(a), 1342(a); *Consumer Power Co.,* 862 F.2d at 582. Thus, the factual issue raised by defendants concerning the historical level of pollution compared to the current level of pollution is not material to the resolution of the Committee's claim, and therefore does not preclude summary judgment on the issue of liability.

Defendants have already admitted that acid mine drainage is channelled into and collects in the Penn Mine facility, and then is released over the Mine Run Dam's spillway or through its valve into the Camanche Reservoir and the Mokelumne River. Consequently, they have admitted to each of the elements needed to establish liability under the Clean Water Act. Defendants have (1) discharged a pollutant (i.e., collected and channeled surface runoff containing acid mine drainage into the reservoir and then added the polluted runoff); (2) into navigable waters (i.e., the Mokelumne); (3) from a point source (i.e., the dam's spillway and valve); (4) without a discharge permit. *See Gorsuch,* 693 F.2d at 165. Because the statute does not require the Committee to show that a greater level of pollution enters the Mokelumne now than was the case before the Penn Mine facility was constructed, the district court properly granted judgment in the Committee's favor on the issue of liability.

C. Are actions taken by regulatory authority to prevent or reduce discharges subject to the Clean Water Act's permit requirements?

Defendants also argue that "the State cannot be held liable [under the Clean Water Act] for the activities which it has performed pursuant to its regulatory responsibilities." Although they concede that no case has so held, they contend that analogous cases under the Comprehensive Environmental Response, Compensation and Liability Act ("CERCLA") do lend support to their argument.

As the district court pointed out, in the cases cited by defendants, the absence of governmental liability under CERCLA rests squarely on express statutory exemptions. *See* Order at 34–35 & n.32 (citing 42 U.S.C. §§ 9607(a)(1) & (2), and 42 U.S.C. § 9601). The Clean Water Act contains no such exemption. Given the absence of any statutory authority to exempt the Board or District from liability under the Clean Water Act, the district court did not err in finding that defendants are liable under the Act.

D. Does the Eleventh Amendment immunize the Water Board from liability under the Clean Water Act?

The Water Board argues that "the District Court could not consider the construction that took place prior to the filing of the lawsuit because of Eleventh Amendment considerations." However, the Committee seeks only prospective equitable relief, which is not barred by the Eleventh Amendment. *See Pennhurst State School & Hosp. v. Halderman,* 465 U.S. 89, 104–05, 79 L.Ed.2d 67, 104 S.Ct. 900 (1984)(citing *Ex Parte Young,* 209 U.S. 123), it relates to ongoing or future violations. Thus, defendants' Eleventh Amendment argument is without merit.

CONCLUSION

We conclude that the district court properly granted summary judgment in favor of the Committee on the issue of defendants' liability under the Clean Water Act.

AFFIRMED.

FERNANDEZ, CIRCUIT JUDGE, concurring:

I concur, but write separately because my position may be somewhat more narrowly based than the position of the majority.

As I understand it, the pollutants in question used to be carried into the Mokelumne River by Mine Run Creek and Hinkley Run Creek. The water from those creeks, and other water, ran across the tailings from the mines and became polluted. The creeks then carried that water to the river. The project has diverted those creeks so that they will stay clean and has captured polluted runoff so that it can be released in a more measured way. In other words, it seems that unregulated quantities of pollutants were flowing into the river and causing fish kills and the like long before EBMUD and the Board did anything at all. Those entities sought to eliminate the disasters caused by that unregulated flow and that is why the project was built. The result has been a significant improvement in the river's environment and a boon to aquatic life.

The majority appears to agree with appellee's position that the project is a point source in the sense that the Environmental Protection Agency could not determine that a NPDES permit was not required. I am not so sure. It seems to me that, given the history of this project, the EPA could properly have determined that this really is much more like the dams in *National Wildlife Fed'n v. Consumers Power Co.,* 862 F.2d 580 (6th Cir.1988), and *National Wildlife Fed'n v. Gorsuch,* 224 U.S.App. D.C. 41, 693 F.2d 156 (D.C.Cir.1982), than it is like the typical point source that truly does add pollution to navigable waters. *See* 33 U.S.C. § 1362(12). If it had, we would have shown that determination great deference.... *See Consumers Power,* 862 F.2d at 584–85. It did not. In fact, the information before the district court and before us indicates that the EPA considers the project to be a point source, which does require a permit containing numerous onerous conditions.

Appellants earnestly argue that the EPA's approach, and that of the appellee's, will not serve the long-term purpose of bettering the aquatic environment. They indicate that it takes no genius or epopt to see what the message will be. Do nothing! Let someone else take on the responsibility. Let the water degrade, let the fish die, but protect your pocketbook from vast and unnecessary expenditures. Do not try to bring some order out of environmental chaos. In short, appellants suggest that no Odysseus or Daedalus crafted the policy which we are now asked to follow. Perhaps they are correct; I suspect they are.

Nevertheless, we are not policymakers. We must simply apply the law. The majority opinion demonstrates that with great clarity.

Therefore, I concur.

Discussion Problem

In 1987, Congress amended the Federal Water Pollution Control Act (commonly referred to as the Clean Water Act or CWA), allowing the Environmental Protection Agency (EPA or Agency) to authorize Indian Tribes as "States" for purposes of assuming primary authority over various water quality regulatory programs in-lieu of the federal government. Thus, certain Tribes are now eligible under CWA section 518 to assume primacy over regulating the quality of their surface waters in much the same manner as States. Specifically, approved Tribes will now have the authority to establish water quality standards for those waters flowing through Indian lands.

Similar to other environmental statutes containing "treatment-as-States" (TAS) provisions, however, Congress has not clearly defined how tribes are to be treated nor the scope and role of tribal authority once approved under the CWA. Rather, it has placed enormous responsibility on the EPA to develop administrative mechanisms implementing this expansion of tribal authority. As the Agency establishes its rules and regulations in this regard, it sails further into the complex and murky waters where the principles of federalism, state sovereignty, and tribal sovereignty combine to impact environmental regulation within the reservations. As tribes step forward to "reclaim" regulatory authority over their waters, various jurisdictional disputes are certain to arise inside the reservations. For example, the extent of tribal authority to regulate the activities of non-Indians within the reservations affecting reservation surface water resources is unclear under current case law and the CWA.

"Tribes v. States" disputes are likely to arise when an approved Tribe establishes water quality standards more stringent than those applicable to a permitted upstream discharger releasing into the same body of water. EPA established a dispute resolution mechanism for resolving water quality-related disputes between Tribes and states, but this process did not prevent litigation in this area as is evidenced by the recent case of *Albuquerque v. Browner*.

How would you handle the questions raised when tribal rights conflict with those of neighboring states?

2. *New Source Performance Standards*

Section 306 of the CWA dictates that discharges of a pollutant from new or significantly modified sources directly into navigable waters must comply with New Source Performance Standards (NSPS), which reflect the degree of effluent reduction achievable through application of the "best available demonstrated control technology." New plants must install the best and most efficient production processes and wastewater treatment technologies. As a result, NSPS should represent the most stringent controls attainable through the application of the best available control technology for all pollutants (i.e., conventional, nonconventional, and toxic pollutants). In establishing NSPS, EPA is directed to take into consideration the cost of achieving the effluent reduction and any non-water quality environmental impacts and energy requirements. For purposes of NSPS, a "new source" is defined as a source in which construction was commenced *after publication of the proposed* NSPS that will apply to that source.

3. Water Quality Standards

The CWA also contains a separate water quality standards program. The states may designate appropriate uses for waters within their borders, and adopt criteria (in effect, ambient pollutant levels) that will allow such uses. These use designations and criteria constitute "water-quality standards" that are subject to EPA review. If a state fails to adopt these standards, EPA may adopt them for the state. 33 U.S.C.A. § 1313(c).

Once water quality standards have been established, states are responsible for establishing a total maximum daily load (TMDL) of particular pollutants necessary to implement water quality standards. 33 U.S.C.A. § 1313(d). The TMDLs are allocated among the various dischargers to a water body and eventually are used as a basis to establish water quality-based NPDES permit limits. In areas where technology-based effluent limitations (BPT, BCT, BAT, and NSPS) are inadequate to maintain water quality standards, more stringent permit limitations designed to do so may be imposed. 33 U.S.C.A. §§ 1311(b)(1)(C), 1314(*l*).

AMERICAN PAPER INST. v. UNITED STATES EPA
996 F.2d 346 (D.C.Cir.1993).

WALD, CIRCUIT JUDGE:

In these consolidated petitions for review, the American Paper Institute, Inc., the USX Corporation, Westvaco Corporation, the City of Akron, Ohio and a host of utilities contest several new Environmental Protection Agency ("EPA") regulations interpreting the Clean Water Act ("CWA" or the "Act") and its amendments. The petitioners primarily take issue with an EPA rule requiring writers of pollution discharge permits to use one of three methods to interpret state water quality standards containing so-called "narrative criteria" (e.g., "no toxics in toxic amounts") so as to create precise chemical-specific effluent limitations in those permits. For the reasons discussed below, we find the regulation in question as well as other, related regulations challenged by petitioners to constitute reasonable, authorized attempts at necessary gap-filling in the CWA statutory scheme. Accordingly, we deny the petitions for review.

I.

In enacting the CWA, Congress sought to "restore and maintain the chemical, physical, and biological integrity of the Nation's waters." 33 U.S.C. § 1251 (a). Toward that end, Congress constructed a system in which discharges of pollutants into the waters of the United States from "point sources"—"discernable, confined and discrete conveyances," 33 U.S.C. § 1362(14), such as factory pipes—are normally permissible only if made pursuant to the terms of a National Pollution Discharge Elimination System ("NPDES") permit. *See* 33 U.S.C. §§ 1311(a), 1342. Under the Act, those licenses must be obtained from the EPA or, in the approximately 40 states the EPA has authorized to administer their own NPDES program, from a designated state agency. *See* 33 U.S.C. § 1342(a)-(d); *see also* 57 Fed.Reg. 43,733, 43,734–35 (1992) (listing states with permitting authority). In either case, section 301 of the Act mandates that every permit contain (1) effluent limitations that reflect the pollution reduction achievable by using technologically practicable controls, see 33 U.S.C. § 1311(b)(1)(A), and (2) any more stringent pollutant release limitations necessary for the waterway receiving the pollutant to meet "water quality standards." 33 U.S.C. § 1311(b)(1)(C).

Of primary importance in this case is section 301's second requirement—i.e., that permits contain discharge limitations sufficient to assure that the receiving waterway satisfies water quality standards. Under the CWA, the water quality standards referred to in section 301 are primarily the states' handiwork. State water quality standards in effect at the time of the Act's passage in 1972 were deemed to be the initial water quality benchmarks for CWA purposes (so long as the standards passed an EPA review). *See* 33 U.S.C. § 1313(a). The states were to revisit and, if necessary, revise those initial standards at least once every three years—a process commonly known as triennial review. *See* 33 U.S.C. § 1313(c)(1). Triennial reviews consist of public hearings in which current water quality standards are examined to assure that they "protect the public health or welfare, enhance the quality of water and serve the purposes" of the Act. 33 U.S.C. § 1313 (c)(2)(A). Additionally, the CWA directs states to consider a variety of competing policy concerns during these reviews, including a waterway's "use and value for public water supplies, propagation of fish and wildlife, recreational purposes, and agricultural, industrial, and other purposes." *Id.*

In accord with Congress' intent to cast the states in the featured role in the promulgation of water quality standards, the EPA may step in and promulgate water quality standards itself only in limited circumstances. It may act only where (1) it determines that a state's proposed new or revised standard does not measure up to CWA requirements and the state refuses to accept EPA-proposed revisions to the standard or (2) a state does not act to promulgate or update a standard but, in the EPA's view, a new or revised standard is necessary to meet CWA muster. *See* 33 U.S.C. § 1313(c)(3)-(4).

The water quality standards that emerge from this state/federal pas de deux have two primary components: designated "uses" for a body of water (e.g., public water supply, recreation, agriculture) and a set of "criteria" specifying the maximum concentration of pollutants that may be present in the water without impairing its suitability for designated uses. *See* 33 U.S.C. § 1313(c)(2)(A). Criteria, in turn, come in two varieties: specific numeric limitations on the concentration of a specific pollutant in the water (e.g., no more than .05 milligrams of chromium per liter) or more general narrative statements applicable to a wide set of pollutants (e.g., no toxic pollutants in toxic amounts). ...*See* also *Environmental Defense Fund, Inc. v. Costle,* 211 U.S.App.D.C. 313, 657 F.2d 275, 288 (D.C.Cir.1981)(approving the use of narrative criteria). In deciding what criteria suit particular designated uses, the states are not left entirely to their own devices. As required by the CWA, see 33 U.S.C. § 1314(a)(1), the EPA has promulgated a set of recommended numeric criteria for certain listed pollutants that the states can, and quite often do, refer to in selecting appropriate criteria. *See* 57 Fed.Reg. 60,848, 60,874 (1992)(EPA notes that states generally rely on recommended criteria in establishing water quality standards).

Of course, the water quality standards by themselves have no effect on pollution; the rubber hits the road when the state-created standards are used as the basis for specific effluent limitations in NPDES permits. As noted above, once a water quality standard has been promulgated, section 301 of the CWA requires all NPDES permits for point sources to incorporate discharge limitations necessary to satisfy that standard. *See, e.g., Westvaco Corp. v. EPA,* 899 F.2d 1383, 1385 (4th Cir.1990). On its face, section 301 imposes this strict requirement as to all standards—i.e., permits must incorporate limitations necessary to meet standards that rely on narrative criteria to protect a designated use as well as standards that contain specific numeric criteria for particular chemicals. The distinctive nature of each kind of criteria, however, inevitably leads to significant distinctions in how the two types of criteria are applied to derive effluent limitations in individual permits. When the standard includes numeric criteria, the process is fairly straightforward: the permit merely adopts a limitation on a point source's effluent discharge necessary to keep the concentration of a pollutant in a waterway at or below the numeric benchmark. Narrative criteria, however, present more difficult problems: How is a state or federal NPDES permit writer to divine what limitations on effluent discharges are necessary to assure that the waterway contains, for example, "no toxics in toxic amounts"? Faced with this conundrum, some permit writers threw up their hands and, contrary to the Act, simply ignored water quality standards including narrative criteria altogether when deciding upon permit limitations. *See Natural Resources Defense Council v. EPA,* 915 F.2d 1314, 1317 (9th Cir.1990). Additionally, when standards containing narrative criteria were enforced—often through the device of whole effluent discharge limitations based on biological monitoring techniques, ... *see* 48 Fed. Reg. 51,400, 51,402 (1983)(noting that biological monitoring is one method of testing compliance with narrative criteria)—the lack of standardized procedures made it impossible to even approximate consistency in the translation of criteria into permit limitations. *Cf.* 57 Fed.Reg. 60,848, 60,851 (1992). Moreover, the biological monitoring techniques relied on to enforce narrative criteria were better suited to assuring protection of aquatic life than human health. *See* 131 Cong. Rec. 15,324 (1985)(Statement of Senator Stafford). Thus, in the EPA's view, the lack of a required procedure for developing water-quality-based permit limits from narrative criteria hamstrung attempts to fulfill the statutory requirement that NPDES permits contain limitations necessary to meet all water quality standards. *See* 54 Fed.Reg. 23,868, 23,877 (1989)(noting that the EPA's legal obligation to assure that NPDES permits meet all applicable water quality standards could not be set aside until states promulgate numeric water quality criteria for all their standards).

II.

A. Interpreting Narrative Criteria to Create Chemical-specific Limitations

To address these difficulties, the EPA promulgated the regulation under attack here, 40 C.F.R. § 122.44(d)(1)(vi). That rule requires NPDES permit writers to use one of three mechanisms to translate relevant narrative criteria into chemical-specific effluent limitations. Specifically, the regulation provides that a permit writer must establish effluent limits from narrative criteria by using (1) a calculated numeric water quality criterion derived from such tools as a proposed state numeric criterion or an "explicit state policy or regulation interpreting its narrative water quality criterion"; (2) the EPA recommended numeric water quality criteria, but only on a "case-by-case basis" and "supplemented where necessary by other relevant information"; and/or (3) assuming certain conditions are met, limitations on the discharge of an "indicator parameter," i.e., a different pollutant also found in the point source's effluent. . . .

We employ familiar principles in reviewing the disputed regulation. Unless we find that the EPA's rule contravenes the unambiguously conveyed intent of Congress as to this precise issue, we will reject the petitioners' challenge so long as the regulation appears designed to implement the statutory scheme by reasonable means. *See generally Chevron USA Inc. v. Natural Resources Defense Council, Inc.*, 467 U.S. 837, 843–44, 81 L.Ed.2d 694, 104 S.Ct. 2778 (1984).

In arguing that the EPA's rule flunks the first prong of this test, the petitioners highlight the alleged tension between the regulation's delegation of authority to a permit writer to interpret narrative criteria in each particular case and the CWA system, outlined above, in which generally applicable water quality standards are adopted by the states only after public input and the weighing of the competing policy considerations set out in the Act. In function if not in form, petitioners argue, the EPA regulation requires states to cede their standard-setting authority to an unaccountable bureaucrat: "Under the EPA regulations challenged here . . . water quality standards (or at least the required 'criteria' portion of water quality standards) are created on a case-by-case basis for individual discharges by an EPA or state permit writer. . . . " Petitioners' Brief at 24.

We are unpersuaded. As we understand it, the regulation does not supplant—either formally or functionally—the CWA's basic statutory framework for the creation of water quality standards; rather, it provides alternative mechanisms through which previously adopted water quality standards containing narrative criteria may be applied to create effective limitations on effluent emissions. As long as narrative criteria are permissible—and the petitioners do not contend that they are not—and must be enforced through limitations in particular permits, a permit writer will inevitably have some discretion in applying the criteria to a particular case. The general language of narrative criteria can only take the permit writer so far in her task. Of course, that does not mean that the language of a narrative criterion does not cabin the permit writer's authority at all; rather, it is an acknowledgement that the writer will have to engage in some kind of interpretation to determine what chemical-specific numeric criteria—and thus what effluent limitations—are most consistent with the state's intent as evinced in its generic standard. The EPA's new regulation merely requires that permit writers engage in this task to create chemical-specific limitations on discharges of pollutants and gives those writers three tools with which to do this work in a fairly regularized fashion. *See* 54 Fed.Reg. 23,868, 23,877 (1989); *see also id.* at 23,875 ("State narrative water quality criteria provide the legal basis for establishing effluent limits under paragraphs (d)(1)(v) and (d)(1)(vi) of today's regulations."). The regulation thus seems to provide an eminently reasonable means of effectuating the intent of the previously adopted narrative criteria as well as Congress' own intent, made explicit in section 301 of the CWA, that all state water quality standards be enforced through meaningful limitations in individual NPDES permits.

* * *

Petitioners' final argument of substance against the EPA's rule derives from section 303(c)(2)(B) of the CWA, 33 U.S.C. § 1313(c)(2)(B). . . . That subsection, enacted as part of the 1987 Water Quality Amendments, required states, in their next triennial reviews, to formulate numeric criteria for certain priority toxic pollutants listed in the EPA guidelines. If numeric criteria for those listed toxics were "not available," the provision mandated that states enact criteria based on biological monitoring techniques. The petitioners claim that this amendment would have been totally unnecessary if Congress thought that the EPA had the authority to interpret preexisting narrative criteria into numeric criteria. Not so. First, section 303's directives say nothing about chemicals other than the listed toxics. There are thus many pollutants of concern for which section 303 does not require numeric criteria. Additionally, even as to the listed chemicals for which states had to adopt numeric criteria, the regulation at issue complements section 303 quite nicely. The regulation allowed permit writers to put in place new chemical-specific limitations through interpretation of existing narrative criteria until states had an opportunity to adopt specific numeric criteria—which would of course avoid the inevitable marginal imprecision inherent in the interpretive task required under the EPA regulation—in the course of their next triennial review. *See* 54 Fed. Reg. at 23,877 (describing the EPA regulation as an "interim measure" until states formulate numeric criteria). Although, as the petitioners point out,

Congress did not expressly authorize use of such an interim measure, the agency's initiative seems a preeminent example of gap-filling in the interest of a continuous and cohesive regulatory regime; the EPA has plugged an obvious hole in the CWA scheme in a way that is both reasonable and consistent with (1) Congress' long-standing directive that permits contain limitations necessary to meet all water quality standards and (2) Congress' more recently expressed preference, evident in section 302(c)(2)(B), for numeric criteria. In sum, we see no problem with the agency's efforts. . . .

B. The EPA's Reading of the Term "Applicable Standard"

Besides requiring that states adopt numeric criteria for priority toxic pollutants, the 1987 Water Quality Amendments included a provision intended to focus regulatory attention on "toxic hotspots"—waters where, even with the implementation of best available technology controls, severe toxic contamination would still exist. Specifically, Congress required states to compile three lists of impaired waters. Section 304(*l*)(1)(A) of the CWA mandated submission to the EPA of an "A(i) List" of waters that cannot attain or maintain the "water quality standards for such waters reviewed, revised, or adopted in accordance with" section 303(c)(2)(B) of the CWA—which, as discussed above, required states to create numeric criteria for priority toxics during their next triennial review—as well as an "(A)(ii) List" of waters that were not anticipated to reach "that water quality which shall assure protection of public health, public water supplies, [and other uses]." 33 U.S.C. § 1314(*l*)(1)(A). The third list, included in section 304(*l*)(1)(B) and known as the "B List," consisted of waters for which the state did not expect "the applicable standard under section 1313 [requiring states to set water quality standards to] be achieved after [technology-based] requirements . . . are met, due entirely or substantially to discharges from point sources of any [listed] toxic pollutants." 33 U.S.C. § 1314(*l*)(1)(B). Each state was also required to file, in 1989, a list (the "C List") of point sources "preventing or impairing" the quality of waters on the first three lists. See 33 U.S.C. § 1314(*l*)(1)(C); see also Natural Resources Defense Council, 915 F.2d at 1320–22 (invalidating EPA regulation that required listing of only the point sources that impaired waters on the B List). For all C List point sources discharging into B List waters, states had to file an individual control strategy ("ICS")—a plan to reduce point source discharges to a degree sufficient to allow a waterway to attain water quality standards within three years. See 33 U.S.C. § 1314(*l*)(1)(D); 40 C.F.R. § 123.46(a). Through regulation, the EPA has defined an ICS as a final or draft NPDES permit accompanied by supporting documents showing how the permit's limitations would allow the water segment to attain relevant water quality standards within three years. See 40 C.F.R. § 123.46(c).

Since the EPA's current interpretation of the statute holds that only point sources discharging into B List waters are subject to the high-priority procedures of the ICS program, whether a waterway qualifies for the B List is an issue with critical practical consequences. Waters are to be placed on the B List if the state does not expect "the applicable standard under section 1313 [requiring states to set water quality standards to] be achieved after [technology-based] requirements ... are met, due entirely or substantially to discharges from point sources of any [listed] toxic pollutants." 33 U.S.C. § 1314(l)(1)(B). The statute does not go on to specify what constitutes an "applicable standard" under section 304(l)(1)(B), but the EPA has defined the term as follows:

Applicable standard means a numeric criterion for a priority pollutant promulgated as part of a state water quality standard. Where a state numeric criterion for a priority pollutant is not promulgated as part of a state water quality standard, for the purposes of listing waters "applicable standard" means the state narrative water quality criterion to control a priority pollutant ... interpreted on a chemical-by-chemical basis by applying a proposed state criterion, an explicit state policy or regulation, or an EPA national water quality criterion, supplemented with other relevant information.

40 C.F.R. § 130.10(d)(4).

Petitioners argue that this definition is both inconsistent with the CWA and arbitrary and capricious. n8 In their view, by referring to "applicable standards," Congress meant only already existing standards containing numeric criteria; the EPA's regulation is consequently invalid to the extent it considers standards based on narrative criteria to be "applicable." Petitioners contend that "applicable standards" cannot have been meant to include standards containing narrative criteria because, since all states have narrative "no toxics" standards, the EPA's reading would result in there always being an "applicable" standard. This reading is untenable, the argument goes on, because it effectively strikes the allegedly limiting adjective "applicable" from the statute. Elaborating on this theory, petitioners note that in contrast to subsection (A), where Congress referred simply to "water quality standards" in specifying the content of the A(i) list, in subsection (B) Congress used the term "applicable standard." By using these different terms, they contend, Congress indicated that the A(i) and B Lists were to refer to differing sets of water quality standards. Finally, petitioners seek support for their more limited interpretation of "applicable standards" from CWA section 303(c)(2)(B), the subsection that requires states to create numeric criteria for toxic pollutants during their next triennial review. Read together, they say, section 304(l)(1)—the section that requires the states to create these one-time-only lists and mandates that states formulate ICSs for at least some of the point sources discharging into those waters—and section 303(c)(2)(B) show that Congress intended to "require states to promulgate the numerical water quality criteria for toxic pollutants that Congress believed was necessary to regulate discharges of those pollutants, while at the same time requiring that those limited situations where applicable [numeric] water quality standards for toxic pollutants were already known to be violated be addressed promptly through the development of Individual Control Strategies, even prior to promulgation of additional [numeric] water quality criteria under CWA Section 303(c)(2)(B)." Reply Brief at 22–23.

These arguments (as well as others raised by petitioners n9) do not convince us that the EPA's broader construction of the term "applicable standard" is unreasonable. *See* generally *Chevron,* 467 U.S. at 843–44 (where statute is ambiguous on a particular question, we defer to any reasonable construction proffered by the implementing agency). The terms "standards" and "applicable standards" are used in the statute in totally different contexts to refer to totally different sets of water quality standards. The "standards" governing the (A)(i) List, which includes all waters that will not meet new numeric criteria to be enacted during each state's forthcoming triennial review due to pollution from point or nonpoint sources, are obviously future, statutorily prescribed standards. The "applicable standards" governing the B list, in contrast, focus on identifying waters that do not meet existing water quality standards because of point source pollution and thus mark a different set of troubled waters than those on the A(i) list; there is accordingly no reason why a major difference in meaning should be ascribed to a minor difference in phraseology. Moreover, in its own context, the EPA's definition of "applicable standard" seems quite reasonable, if indeed not required. Standards based on narrative criteria were among those "applicable" to state waters at the time of the 1987 amendments to the CWA, and, despite the petitioners' speculations to the contrary (based largely on the alleged interplay between this subsection and section 303(c)(2)(B), see supra page 18), there is no evidence in the text or history of the CWA or its amendments that Congress was concerned only with violations of numeric criteria. Thus, we conclude that the term "applicable standards" may plausibly be interpreted to include all standards that apply to state waters—including those standards that contain narrative criteria. *See Natural Resources Defense Council,* 915 F.2d at 1319 n. 5 ("Paragraph B refers to all water quality standards. . . . ")(emphasis added); see generally Chevron, 467 U.S. at 844 (where there has been an implicit delegation of a particular question to the expert agency, "a court may not substitute its own construction of a statutory provision for a reasonable interpretation made by the administrator" of that agency). . . .

* * *

For the foregoing reasons, we deny the petitions for review.

Note

The NPDES permit procedures are codified at 40 C.F.R. parts 122–36. EPA issues new or modified permits to individual applicants after public notice and opportunity for public comment. 40 C.F.R. §§ 122.21, 122.62, 124.3, 124.10. If a hearing is requested or if the Regional Administrator finds there is a significant degree of public interest, EPA may hold a hearing prior to issuing the permits. *Id.* § 124.12. Once EPA issues final permits, an interested party may request an evidentiary hearing. *Id.* § 124.74. If the request for a hearing is granted, the hearings are conducted by an Administrative Law Judge. *Id.* § 124.81. A party may appeal the ALJ's decision, or the denial of a hearing request, to the Administrator. *Id.* § 124.91. An appeal to the Administrator is a prerequisite for judicial review. *Id.* § 124.15. The Administrator's decision denying review or on the merits constitutes final agency action. *Id.* § 124.91(e).

4. *POTWs and Pretreatment Programs*

The Clean Water Act (CWA), as amended, and the regulations promulgated thereunder, proscribes generally the discharge of pollutants to waters of the United States unless those discharges comply with the standards specified in the Act. The CWA obligates the Administrator of the USEPA to promulgate regulations establishing limits on the types and amounts of pollutants discharged from various industrial, commercial, and public sources of wastewater. Armco, Inc. v. United States, 869 F.2d 975, 978 (6th Cir.1989).

CWA calls upon the administrator to establish effluent limitations for "direct dischargers," which are sources that discharge pollutants directly to waters of the United States. Under § 301, the administrator is obligated to establish effluent limitations requiring direct dischargers to employ "best practicable control technology" (BPT) by 1977 and "best available demonstrated control technology" (BAT) by 1989. 33 U.S.C.A. § 1311. Newly constructed facilities that directly discharge pollutants are obligated to comply with "new source performance standards" established pursuant to § 306. 33 U.S.C.A. § 1316.

Section 301(b)(1)(B), requires that publicly owned treatment works (POTWs) which directly discharge wastewater meet limitations requiring "secondary treatment" of all wastewater collected from residential, commercial, and industrial customers. 33 U.S.C.A. § 1311(b)(1)(B). Direct dischargers, including POTWs, are required to obtain a National Pollutant Discharge Elimination System (NPES) permit in order to directly discharge wastewater to any waters of the United States. Under § 402, wastewater dischargers must comply with the CWA standards. 33 U.S.C.A. § 1342.

In addition to requirements imposed upon "direct dischargers," the CWA also requires that an "indirect discharger," one whose wastes are collected and treated at a POTW rather than directly discharged into waters of the United States, "pretreat" its wastewater in order to remove any pollutant (including toxic pollutants) that " ... interferes with, passes through or otherwise is incompatible with such works." *See* § 307(b)(1), FWPCA, as amended, 33 U.S.C.A. § 1317(b)(1). An extensive description of the pretreatment program is set forth in NRDC v. EPA, 790 F.2d 289 (3d Cir.1986).

Section 307(b), provides for the administrator to establish "pretreatment standards for introduction of pollutants into treatment works ... which are publicly owned for those pollutants which are determined not to be susceptible to treatment by such treatment works or which would interfere with the operation of such treatment works." 33 U.S.C.A.

§ 1317(b). Pretreatment standards for iron and steelmaking facilities, such as those of Armco, were promulgated by USEPA in final form on May 27, 1982 and are set forth in 40 C.F.R. Part 420.

In order to avoid redundant treatment of wastewater passing from an industrial user through a POTW prior to discharge to surface waters, Congress in 1977 amended § 307(b)(1) of CWA to set up a procedure through which one who discharged indirectly could obtain a removal "credit" reflecting the amount of pollutants removed from its wastewater as a result of treatment by a POTW. Section 307(b)(1), 33 U.S.C.A. § 1317(b)(1), provides that:

> If, in the case of any toxic pollutant under subsection (a) of this section introduced by a source into publicly owned treatment works, the treatment by such works removes all or any part of such toxic pollutant and the discharge from such works does not violate the effluent limitation or standard which would be applicable to such toxic pollutant if it were discharged by such source other than through a publicly owned treatment works, and does not prevent sludge use or disposal by such works in accordance with section 1345 of this title, then the pretreatment requirements for the sources actually discharging such toxic pollutant into such publicly owned treatment works may be revised by the owner or operator or of such works to reflect the removal of such toxic pollutant by such works.

Sources discharging wastes to municipal sewers for treatment by publicly owned treatment works (POTWs) must comply with general and categorical "pretreatment standards," published by EPA at 40 C.F.R. Parts 400–471. Under EPA's regulations, POTWs are required to develop "pretreatment programs" designed to assure industrial users' compliance with pretreatment standards, and the terms of such programs are incorporated in the POTWs' NPDES permits. *See* 40 C.F.R. Part 403 (1990).

CHEMICAL MANUFACTURERS ASSOCIATION v. NRDC
470 U.S. 116, 105 S.Ct. 1102, 84 L.Ed.2d 90 (1985).

WHITE, J.

These cases present the question whether the Environmental Protection Agency (EPA) may issue certain variances from toxic pollutant effluent limitations promulgated under the Clean Water Act, 86 Stat. 816, as amended, 33 U.S.C. § 1251 *et seq*. . . .

I

As part of a consolidated lawsuit, respondent Natural Resources Defense Council (NRDC) sought a declaration that § 301(*l*) of the Clean Water Act, 33 U.S.C. § 1311(*l*), prohibited EPA from issuing "fundamentally different factor" (FDF) variances for pollutants listed as toxic under the Act. Petitioners EPA and Chemical Manufacturers Association

(CMA) argued otherwise. To understand the nature of this controversy, some background with respect to the statute and the case law is necessary.

The Clean Water Act, the basic federal legislation dealing with water pollution, assumed its present form as the result of extensive amendments in 1972 and 1977. For direct dischargers—those who expel waste directly into navigable waters—the Act calls for a two-phase program of technology-based effluent limitations, commanding that dischargers comply with the best practicable control technology currently available (BPT) by July 1, 1977, and subsequently meet the generally more stringent effluent standard consistent with the best available technology economically achievable (BAT)....

Indirect dischargers—those whose waste water passes through publicly owned treatment plants—are similarly required to comply with pretreatment standards promulgated by EPA under § 307 of the Act, 33 U. S. C. § 1317(b), for pollutants not susceptible to treatment by sewage systems or which would interfere with the operation of those systems. Relying upon legislative history suggesting that pretreatment standards are to be comparable to limitations for direct dischargers, see H. R. Rep. No. 95–830, p. 87 (1977), and pursuant to a consent decree, EPA has set effluent limitations for indirect dischargers under the same two-phase approach applied to those discharging waste directly into navigable waters.

Thus, for both direct and indirect dischargers, EPA considers specific statutory factors and promulgates regulations creating categories and classes of sources and setting uniform discharge limitations for those classes and categories. Since application of the statutory factors varies on the basis of the industrial process used and a variety of other factors, EPA has faced substantial burdens in collecting information adequate to create categories and classes suitable for uniform effluent limits, a burden complicated by the time deadlines it has been under to accomplish the task. Some plants may find themselves classified within a category of sources from which they are, or claim to be, fundamentally different in terms of the statutory factors. As a result, EPA has developed its FDF variance as a mechanism for ensuring that its necessarily rough-hewn categories do not unfairly burden atypical plants. Any interested party may seek an FDF variance to make effluent limitations either more or less stringent if the standards applied to a given source, because of factors fundamentally different from those considered by EPA in setting the limitation, are either too lenient or too strict....

The 1977 amendments to the Clean Water Act reflected Congress' increased concern with the dangers of toxic pollutants. The Act, as then amended, allows specific statutory modifications of effluent limitations for economic and water-quality reasons in §§ 301(c) and (g). Section 301(l), however, added by the 1977 amendments, provides:

"The Administrator may not modify any requirement of this section as it applies to any specific pollutant which is on the toxic pollutant list under section 307(a)(1) of this Act." 91 Stat. 1590.

In the aftermath of the 1977 amendments, EPA continued its practice of occasionally granting FDF variances for BPT requirements. The Agency also promulgated regulations explicitly allowing FDF variances for pretreatment standards and BAT requirements. Under these regulations, EPA granted FDF variances, but infrequently....

As part of its consolidated lawsuit, respondent NRDC here challenged pretreatment standards for indirect dischargers and sought a declaration that § 301(*l*) barred any FDF variance with respect to toxic pollutants. In an earlier case, the Fourth Circuit had rejected a similar argument, finding that § 301(*l*) was ambiguous on the issue of whether it applied to FDF variances and therefore deferring to the administrative agency's interpretation that such variances were permitted. *Appalachian Power Co. v. Train*, 620 F.2d 1040, 1047–1048 (1980). Contrariwise, the Third Circuit here ruled in favor of NRDC, and against petitioners EPA and CMA, holding that § 301(*l*) forbids the issuance of FDF variances for toxic pollutants. *National Assn. of Metal Finishers v. EPA*, 719 F.2d 624 (1983). We granted certiorari to resolve this conflict between the Courts of Appeals and to decide this important question of environmental law. 466 U.S. 957 (1984). We reverse.

* * *

JUSTICE MARSHALL, with whom JUSTICE BLACKMUN and JUSTICE STEVENS join, and with whom JUSTICE O'CONNOR joins as to parts I, II, and III, dissenting.

In these cases, the Environmental Protection Agency (EPA) maintains that it may issue, on a case-by-case basis, individualized variances from the national standards that limit the discharge of toxic water pollutants. EPA asserts this power in the face of a provision of the Clean Water Act that expressly withdraws from the agency the authority to "modify" the national standards for such pollutants. The Court today defers to EPA's interpretation of the Clean Water Act even though that interpretation is inconsistent with the clear intent of Congress, as evidenced by the statutory language, history, structure, and purpose. I had not read our cases to permit judicial deference to an agency's construction of a statute when that construction is inconsistent with the clear intent of Congress.

I

The Clean Water Act requires the EPA Administrator to regulate two types of industrial facilities: (1) "direct" dischargers, i.e., facilities that discharge waste water directly into navigable waters; and (2) "indirect" dischargers, i.e., facilities that discharge waste water into publicly owned treatment works prior to discharge into navigable waters. For both types of requirements, EPA conducts rulemaking proceedings and promulgates nationwide, categorical limitations, that is, limitations applicable to categories of dischargers (e.g., iron and steel plants).

The Act provides for the phased implementation of progressively more stringent requirements for direct dischargers. By July 1, 1977, existing direct dischargers were required to meet effluent limitations based on the "best practicable control technology currently available" (BPT). § 301(b)(1)(A), 86 Stat. 844, 33 U.S.C. § 1311(b)(1)(A). By July 1, 1984, such dischargers were obligated to meet limitations based on the "best available technology economically achievable" (BAT). § 301(b)(2)(A). . . .

Indirect dischargers are subject to "pretreatment" standards applicable to pollutants, including toxic pollutants, that are not susceptible to treatment by or would interfere with the operation of public treatment facilities. § 307(b). Pursuant to a consent decree, EPA has set limitations on existing indirect dischargers using the same two-phase scheme used for direct dischargers. See ante, at 119. Thus, pretreatment standards for existing indirect dischargers are set by reference to BPT and BAT levels.

In 1978, EPA issued pretreatment regulations that contained a variance provision for "fundamentally different factors" (FDF). *See* 43 Fed.Reg. 27,757 (1978). An FDF variance is a case-by-case adjustment of the relevant nationwide standard. *See* 40 CFR § 403.13(b)(1)(1984). A discharger may obtain such a variance if the factors relating to its discharges are fundamentally different from those taken into account by EPA in setting the nationwide standard. § 403.13(c)(ii).

In a petition for review filed in the Court of Appeals for the Third Circuit, respondent NRDC challenged the FDF variance provision on two grounds. First, it argued that EPA lacked the inherent authority to issue such variances. Second, it argued that even if, in general, EPA had the authority to grant such variances, it could not do so in the case of toxic pollutants, because § 301(*l*), which was enacted as part of the 1977 amendments to the Act, bans all "modifications" from the toxic standards. The Third Circuit agreed with the latter argument, holding that § 301(*l*) prohibits FDF variances in the case of toxic pollutants. *National Assn. of Metal Finishers v. EPA*, 719 F.2d 624, 644–646 (1983). The court remanded the variance provision back to EPA without considering the question of EPA's inherent authority to grant such variances. . . .

EPA advances—and the Court defers to—two independent statutory constructions in support of its position that § 301(*l*) does not ban FDF variances from the toxic standards. First, EPA argues that § 301(*l*) prohibits only modifications otherwise expressly allowed by two other statutory provisions—§§ 301(c) and (g)—and thus does not apply to FDF variances, which are nonstatutory. The plain meaning of § 301(*l*), the changes made prior to enactment to the bill containing this provision, and the clearly expressed congressional objectives in enacting § 301(*l*)— to deal vigorously and comprehensively with the extremely serious environmental problem caused by toxic pollutants—establish that this provision's scope was meant to be considerably broader than that attributed to it by EPA. As part of its effort to strengthen the control of toxic pollutants, Congress clearly intended to prohibit all exceptions to the nationwide, categorical standards.

Second, in a strained attempt to characterize the challenged variances in a way that would bring them outside the scope of the § 301(*l*) prohibition, EPA contends that the case-by-case FDF variance procedure provides a permissible alternative to the statutory mechanism for "revising" standards. The Court defers to this argument, and in so doing, it ignores the relevance of the central feature of the 1972 amendments to the Act—that Congress pointedly determined that water pollution control standards should take the form of general rules, to apply uniformly to categories of dischargers. As a result, the Court validates outcomes substantially less protective of the environment than those mandated by Congress. The only view of FDF variances consistent with the scheme of the Clean Water Act is that they are individual exceptions that soften the hardship of general rules. As such, they are undoubtedly disallowed by § 301(*l*).

These cases are not about whether exceptions are useful adjuncts to regulatory schemes of general applicability. That is a policy choice on which courts should defer to Congress in the first instance, and to the administrative agency in the absence of a clear congressional mandate. Here, Congress has made the policy choice. It has weighed competing goals and determined that, whatever the general merits of exceptions schemes, they are simply inappropriate in the context of the control of toxic water pollution. As a result, an exceptions scheme such as the one challenged here simply cannot stand.

* * *

For the foregoing reasons, it is apparent that § 301(*l*) prohibits FDF variances from the pretreatment standards for toxic pollutants. I therefore dissent.

JUSTICE O'CONNOR, dissenting.

I join Parts I, II, and III of JUSTICE MARSHALL's dissent. They accurately demonstrate that the Court's interpretation of § 301(*l*) of the Clean Water Act, 33 U.S.C. § 1311(*l*), is inconsistent with the language of the statute and its legislative history. In my opinion, this alone is sufficient grounds for affirming the judgment of the Court of Appeals. I express no view as to Part IV of the dissent because I think it is not necessary to the disposition of these cases.

* * *

5. *Storm Water Discharges*

EPA struggled for many years to develop a regulatory program for point source discharges of storm water runoff. Each attempt to issue

NPDES regulations for storm water discharges has, however, met with legal challenges from industry and environmental groups. Finally, in 1987, Congress amended the CWA to place a moratorium until October, 1992 on NPDES permit requirements for storm water, except for five classes of storm water point sources that EPA is specifically directed to regulate. *See* 33 U.S.C. § 1342(p). Included among the discharges subject to immediate regulation are discharges of storm water "associated with industrial activity" and discharges from large and medium-sized "municipal separate storm sewer systems." Although EPA was required to issue final permit application rules for these discharges by February 4, 1989, it failed to meet the deadline. On December 7, 1988, EPA finally published proposed permit application regulations. 53 Fed. Reg. 49,416. Under the statute, industrial storm water dischargers were supposed to have filed NPDES permit applications by February 4, 1990, but the proposed permit application rules implementing this requirement were ambiguous and the resulting confusion caused many businesses to miss the deadline.

EPA issued final storm water permit application regulations on November 16, 1990. 55 Fed. Reg. 47,990 (to be codified at 40 C.F.R. Parts 122, 123, and 124). The CWA provides that EPA must issue permits by February 4, 1991. EPA did not comply with that deadline. The final rules provide that facilities with unpermitted discharges of storm water must apply for an individual permit for these discharges. Alternatively, groups of similarly situated storm water dischargers may choose to participate in a "group application" which would consist of two parts—(1) a general narrative description of the discharges covered (due by September 18, 1991), and (2) a detailed set of analytical data collected by a representative subset of the applicants covered (due by May 18, 1992). *See* 56 Fed. Reg. 12,098 (March 21, 1991).

As a third alternative, EPA may issue a "general permit" applicable to a broad range of industrial storm water point sources. Industrial dischargers located in states for which EPA is the permit issuer, or which have and decide to exercise their general permit authority, may opt to be covered under such a permit. In lieu of filing a separate application, a covered facility need only submit a notice of intent to be covered by a general permit.

FACT SHEET FOR THE MULTI–SECTOR STORMWATER GENERAL PERMIT
PART II
58 Fed. Reg. 61146 (November 19, 1993).

In 1972, the Federal Water Pollution Control Act (also referred to as the Clean Water Act (CWA)) was amended to provide that the discharge of any pollutant to waters of the United States from any point source is unlawful, except if the discharge is in compliance with a National Pollutant Discharge Elimination System (NPDES) permit.

For a number of reasons, EPA and authorized NPDES States have failed to issue NPDES permits for the majority of point source discharges of storm water. Recognizing this, Congress added Section 402(p) to the CWA in 1987 to establish a comprehensive framework for addressing storm water discharges under the NPDES program. Section 402(p)(4) of the CWA clarifies the requirements for EPA to issue NPDES permits for storm water discharges associated with industrial activity. On November 16, 1990 (55 Fed.Reg. 47,990), EPA published final regulations which define the term "storm water discharge associated with industrial activity." These regulations also set forth NPDES permit application requirements for storm water discharges associated with industrial activity and storm water discharges from certain municipal separate storm sewer systems. The regulations presented three permit application options for storm water discharges associated with industrial activity. The first option was to submit an individual application consisting of Forms 1 and 2F. The second option was to become a participant in a group application. The third option was to file a Notice of Intent (NOI) to be covered under a general permit in accordance with the requirements of an issued general permit.

* * *

EPA estimates that about 100,000 facilities nationwide discharge storm water associated with industrial activity (not including oil and gas exploration and production operations). The large number of facilities addressed by the regulatory definition of "storm water discharge associated with industrial activity" has placed a tremendous administrative burdens on EPA and States with authorized NPDES programs to issue and administer permits for these discharges.

To provide a reasonable and rational approach to addressing this permitting task, the Agency has developed a strategy for issuing permits for storm water discharges associated with industrial activity. In developing this strategy, the Agency recognized that the CWA provides flexibility in the manner in which NPDES permits are issued,,.... and has used this flexibility to design a workable permitting system. In accordance with these considerations, the permitting strategy (described in more detail in 57 Fed.Reg. 11,394) describes a four-tier set of priorities for issuing permits for these discharges:

Tier I–Baseline Permitting–One or more general permits will be developed to initially cover the majority of storm water discharges associated with industrial activity.

Tier II–Watershed Permitting–Facilities within watersheds shown to be adversely impacted by storm water discharges associated with industrial activity will be targeted for individual or watershed-specific general permits.

Tier III–Industry–Specific Permitting–Specific industry categories will be targeted for individual or industry-specific general permits.

Tier IV–Facility–Specific Permitting–A variety of factors will be used to target specific facilities for individual permits.

* * *

II. Types of Discharges Covered

On November 16, 1990 (55 Fed.Reg. 47,990), EPA promulgated the regulatory definition of "storm water discharge associated with industrial activity" which addresses point source discharges of storm water from eleven major categories of industrial activities. Industrial activities from all of these categories with the exception of construction activities participated in the group application process. The information contained in the group applications indicates that type and amount of pollutants discharged in storm water varies from industrial activity to industrial activity because of the variety of potential pollutant sources present in different industrial activities, as well as the variety of pollution prevention measures commonly practiced by each of the regulated industries. To facilitate the process of developing permit conditions for each of the 1200 group applications submitted, EPA classified groups into 29 industrial sectors where the nature of industrial activity, type of materials handled and material management practices employed were sufficiently similar for the purposes of developing permit conditions. Each of the industrial sectors were represented by one or more groups which participated in the group application process.

* * *

AMERICAN MINING CONGRESS v. EPA
965 F.2d 759 (9th Cir.1992).

Ferguson, Circuit Judge:

The American Mining Congress ("AMC") challenges the Environmental Protection Agency's ("EPA's") recent Clean Water Act ("CWA") storm water discharge rule, National Pollutant Discharge Elimination System Permit Application Regulations for Storm Water Discharges, 55 Fed. Reg. 47,990, 48,065 (1990)(to be codified at 40 C.F.R. § 122.26(b)(14)(iii)), because it requires storm water discharge permits for "inactive mining operations." *Id.* at 48,065. AMC contends that the rule contravenes Congressional intent, is arbitrary and capricious, is improperly retroactive, and was promulgated in violation of certain procedural requirements. We uphold EPA's storm water rule.

I

Background

Congress enacted the CWA ..., 33 U.S.C.A. §§ 1251–1387 (West 1986 & Supp. 1991), "to restore and maintain the chemical, physical, and biological integrity of the Nation's waters." CWA § 101(a), 33 U.S.C.A. § 1251(a). See *Rybachek v. EPA,* 904 F.2d 1276, 1282 (9th Cir.1990). The Act seeks to accomplish this objective principally by controlling "point source" pollution....

The Act prohibits the "discharge of any pollutant" from a point source except as authorized by a National Pollutant Discharge Elimination System ("NPDES") permit. *See* CWA § 301(a), 33 U.S.C. § 1311(a);

CWA § 402, 33 U.S.C. § 1342. The CWA authorizes EPA to issue an NPDES permit containing conditions that implement various requirements of the Act. CWA § 402(a)(1), 33 U.S.C. § 1342(a)(1)....

Storm water discharges are a significant source of environmental pollution. 55 Fed. Reg. at 47,990–92; see 132 Cong. Rec. 32,381 (1986). Since 1973, EPA has issued several rules that have attempted to address the appropriate regulation of storm water runoff. Each rule has been the focus of substantial controversy.

Following the enactment of the CWA in 1972, EPA promulgated NPDES permit regulations exempting uncontaminated storm water discharges from regulation on the basis of administrative infeasibility. These regulations were challenged and set aside in *NRDC v. Costle*, 568 F.2d 1369, 1377 (D.C.Cir.1977), on the ground that EPA could not exempt categories of point sources from the statute's permitting requirements. Following this decision, EPA issued proposed and final rules covering storm water discharges in 1980, 1982, 1984, 1985 and 1988. These rules were challenged at the administrative level and in the courts.

In 1987, Congress passed the Water Quality Act ... ("WQA") amendments to the CWA, setting explicit and firm deadlines for EPA regulation of storm water discharges. Section 402(p) of the Act establishes a moratorium until October 1, 1992 on permits for storm water discharges, with five exceptions including an exception for "discharges associated with industrial activity." CWA § 402(p)(2)(B), 33 U.S.C. § 1342(p)(2)(B). Section 402(p) also outlines an incremental, or "phase-in" approach to issuance of storm water discharge permits. The purpose of this approach was "to allow EPA ... to focus [its] attention on the most serious problems." 133 Cong. Rec. 991 (1987) (statement of Rep. Stangeland). Section 402(p) required EPA to promulgate rules regulating permit application procedures in a staggered fashion.

In response to the 1987 amendments, EPA published its proposed storm water rule on December 7, 1988. National Pollutant Discharge Elimination System Permit Application Regulations for Storm Water Discharges, 53 Fed. Reg. 49,416 (1988). After extensive public comment, EPA issued the final rule on November 16, 1990. 55 Fed. Reg. 47,990.

EPA's final storm water rule defines "discharges associated with industrial activity" to include contaminated discharges from both active and inactive mines. EPA excluded from the category, however, discharges from inactive coal mines reclaimed under the Surface Mining Control and Reclamation Act ("SMCRA"), 30 U.S.C.A. §§ 1201–1328 (West 1986 & Supp. 1991), and from inactive non-coal mines reclaimed under applicable federal or state laws after the rule's effective date. 55 Fed. Reg. at 48,033, 48,065–66. As a result of this exclusion, such point source discharges are not required to obtain NPDES permits until after the expiration of the storm water permit moratorium.

II

DISCUSSION

* * *

Section 402(p)(2)(B) of the CWA, 33 U.S.C. § 1342(p)(2)(B), authorizes EPA to require a permit for any storm water discharge "associated with industrial activity." AMC contends that EPA's regulation of discharges from inactive mines under this section contravenes Congress' intent.

AMC argues that the plain language of the statute authorizes EPA to regulate only discharges from "industrial activity." Since no "activity" occurs at an inactive mine, AMC reasons, the statute prohibits EPA from requiring permits for discharges from such mines.

AMC's reading of the statute ignores a significant part of the language at issue. Section 402(p)(1)(B) allows EPA to require a permit for "[a] discharge associated with industrial activity." (Emphasis added.) Congress did not stipulate that the activity must occur concurrently with the discharge of storm water. EPA has determined that discharges from areas of past industrial activity at a variety of facilities, including mines, may be "associated with" that industrial activity. See 40 C.F.R. § 122.26(b)(14)(definition of "discharge associated with industrial activity" includes discharges from "areas where industrial activity has taken place in the past and significant materials remain and are exposed to storm water"). This conclusion is consistent with the language of the statute. . . .

AMC also looks to the terms of CWA § 402(*l*), which states that "the Administrator shall not require a permit . . . for discharges of stormwater runoff from mining operations . . . composed entirely of flows . . . which are not contaminated by contact with" polluting materials. (Emphasis added.) AMC argues that "operations" are by definition ongoing, and that the use of the term "operations" in this section demonstrates Congress' intent, throughout the WQA, to regulate only present activities. Section 402(*l*) does not support AMC's argument. The section does not make the term "discharge associated with industrial activity" in § 402(p) any less ambiguous. Even accepting AMC's argument that "operations" must be currently active, this exemption does not necessarily imply that only active operations were to be regulated under § 402(p) or any other provisions of the CWA.

In reviewing EPA's storm water rule, we must also examine the legislative history to determine whether Congress expressed a clear intent. See *NLRB v. United Food & Commercial Workers Union,* 484 U.S. 112, 123, 98 L.Ed.2d 429 , 108 S.Ct. 413 (1987). We find that Congress left it up to EPA to define a "discharge associated with industrial activity," specifying only that the term refers to discharges "directly related to manufacturing, processing or raw materials storage areas at an industrial plant" and not to "discharges associated with parking lots and administrative and employee buildings." 132 Cong. Rec. 31,968 (1986); 133 Cong. Rec. 985 (1987).

AMC argues that nothing in the legislative history reflects a Congressional intent to impose permitting requirements on inactive mines. Regardless of whether this is true, principles of statutory construction require AMC to demonstrate not simply that Congress failed to address the issue, but that Congress, if it had addressed the issue, would not have sanctioned EPA's interpretation. Chevron, 467 U.S. at 845. If Congress has failed to address the issue, or if the statute is silent or ambiguous, we must defer to EPA's reasonable interpretation of the statute. *Chevron,* 467 U.S. at 843; *Wyckoff,* 796 F.2d at 1200.

We find nothing in AMC's citations to the legislative history to suggest that Congress would not have allowed EPA to require permits for inactive mines. AMC directs us to references in which Congress discussed the regulation of storm water runoff in the context of active mines, without mentioning inactive mines. AMC first examines section 402(*l*)(2), 33 U.S.C. § 1342(*l*)(2), which states that uncontaminated storm water discharges from mining operations are exempt from permitting. Although Congress discussed this section in the context of active mines, the legislative history provides no indication that Congress intended to exempt contaminated discharges from inactive mines.

AMC also examines CWA section 301(p), 33 U.S.C. § 1311(p), which relaxes, under limited circumstances, the applicable effluent limitations with respect to pH, iron, and manganese for discharges from coal remaining at inactive sites. The section merely relaxes specific effluent limitations for certain permits when they are issued; it does not exempt any site from the requirement to obtain a permit. The Congressional discussions of this section say nothing about CWA section 402(p)(2)(B).

AMC cites statements made during the floor debate in the House to the effect that the new provisions would "reduce the universe of permits required for stormwater from millions to thousands." These statements, however, referred specifically to discharges from municipal storm sewers, not discharges associated with industrial activity. *See* 132 Cong.Rec. 31,964 (statement of Rep. Snyder); *Id.* at 31,968 (statement of Rep. Rowland). These statements do not support AMC's claim that Congress intended to regulate only a small number of sources under the industrial activity provision.

Since CWA section 402(p)(2)(B) and its legislative history are silent regarding whether storm water discharges from inactive mines fall within the definition of "[a] discharge associated with industrial activity," we must uphold EPA's interpretation so long as it is "reasonable." *Wyckoff,* 796 F.2d at 1200.

We conclude that EPA's regulation meets the reasonableness standard. EPA noted that some mine sites represent a significant source of contaminated storm water runoff. 55 Fed. Reg. at 48,033. This finding is well documented, *see, e.g.,* 46 Fed. Reg. 3,136, 3,144 (1981), and AMC has not challenged it. Moreover, EPA has exempted from the permitting requirement mine sites where storm water does not come into contact with any overburden, raw material, byproduct, or waste product. 40 C.F.R. § 122.26(b)(14)(iii). This exemption narrows EPA's regulation of inactive mines to only those sites at which storm water discharge is likely to have become contaminated through association with industrial activity.

EPA's interpretation is also consistent with the overall goals of the statute. Congress intended to allow EPA to adopt an orderly permitting process that would address the major contributors of pollutants, including industrial discharges, first. 133 Cong. Rec. 991 (1987)(statement of Rep. Stangeland). Since inactive as well as active mines may be significant sources of pollutants, their inclusion in the first phase is consistent with Congress' intent.

In sum, we hold that EPA's regulation of inactive mines under CWA section 402(p)(2)(B), 33 U.S.C. § 1342(p)(2)(B), is consistent with the plain language and legislative history of the statute and is reasonable.

* * *

2. Consistency With EPA's Past Practice

We also reject AMC's contention that the regulation of inactive mines contradicts EPA's past practice and is therefore arbitrary and capricious. AMC notes that in prior rulemakings to set effluent limitation guidelines for mining discharges, EPA has established guidelines only for active mining areas. See 40 C.F.R. §§ 434.10, 434.11(b), 440.132(g)(1991). However, this observation does not support AMC's contention. AMC confuses the operation of an effluent guideline with the more general requirement to obtain a permit.

Effluent limitation guidelines establish uniform national standards for the technology-based limits required in each NPDES permit. CWA § 304(b), 33 U.S.C. § 1314(b). EPA's decision not to promulgate effluent guidelines for a category of sources does not mean that those sources are exempt from permitting requirements. All point sources that discharge pollutants, including point sources that discharge pollutants from inactive mines, require a permit. EPA's decision not to establish a guideline for discharges from inactive mines means only that permits for such discharges are issued on an individual basis. See Coal Mining Point Source Category; Effluent Limitations Guidelines and New Source Performance Standards, 50 Fed. Reg. 41,296, 41,298 (1985)(sites reclaimed under SMCRA are subject to NPDES requirements, although not to the general effluent limitation guidelines). Thus, EPA's classification of discharges from inactive mines as "associated with industrial activity" is consistent with its earlier practice, in which such mines were also subject to NPDES permit requirements.

* * *

F. Retroactivity

AMC argues, next, that EPA's rule requiring permits for discharges from inactive mines unlawfully imposes retroactive liability on owners and operators of those mines.

Agencies generally do not have the authority to issue rules having retroactive effect in the absence of an express Congressional grant of such authority. *Bowen v. Georgetown Univ. Hosp.,* 488 U.S. 204, 208, 102 L.Ed.2d 493 , 109 S.Ct. 468 (1988). A rule has retroactive effect if "an act lawful at the time it was done" is "rendered unlawful and the actor called to account for a completed, now-condemned deed in the halls of justice." *Ralis v. RFE/RL, Inc.,* 770 F.2d 1121, 1127 (D.C.Cir.1985). In other words, a retroactive rule is one that alters the past legal consequences of past actions. *Bowen,* 488 U.S. at 219 (Scalia, J., concurring).

EPA's storm water rule requires only that owners or operators apply for permits for future discharges from inactive mines. Although the rule may reduce the financial attractiveness of mine ownership, it does not impose liability for past conduct.

AMC argues that EPA's storm water discharge rule is impermissible because it imposes liability on owners of mines where mining activities were conducted only in the past. We disagree. AMC ignores the distinction between merely "affecting rights" and "retroactively imparting an obligation cum liability." *Ralis,* 770 F.2d at 1127. A rule with exclusively future effect, such as a change in the tax laws taxing future income from existing trusts, is not made retroactive by the fact that it will "unquestionably affect past transactions (rendering [ ]previously established trusts less desirable in the future)." *Bowen,* 488 U.S. 219 at 219–20 (Scalia, J., concurring).

EPA's rule does not penalize inactive mine owners for mining activities or contaminated discharges that occurred in the past; it regulates discharges of contaminated storm water that occur in the future. ... The fact that the present contamination is the result of past mining activities does not make EPA's rule retroactive.

The rule may frustrate the economic expectations of some inactive mine owners, who may need to install treatment systems or implement storm water management practices in order to comply with the permit requirements. But regulations are not retroactive merely because they require a change in existing practices. Moreover, the rule effectuates Congress' intent to require dischargers to minimize or eliminate discharges of pollutants so as to achieve the water quality goals of the Act. CWA §§ 101(a), 301(a), 402(a), 33 U.S.C. § 1251(a), 1311(a), 1342(a). We hold, therefore, that EPA's storm water rule does not impose retroactive liability on owners of inactive mines.

* * *

CONCLUSION

EPA's rule including storm water discharges from inactive mines within the definition of discharges "associated with industrial activity" is consistent with Congressional intent, and is not arbitrary and capricious. The petition for review is DENIED.

IN RE: LIQUID AIR PUERTO RICO CORPORATION

NPDES Appeal No. 92–1
Permit No. PR 0001352
Order Remanding in Part and Denying Review in Part
United States Environmental Protection Agency
1994 WL 200538 (E.P.A.)
May 5, 1994

Opinion of the Board by JUDGE McCALLUM.

Liquid Air Puerto Rico Corporation ("Liquid Air") seeks review of the denial of its evidentiary hearing request by U.S. EPA Region II in connection with the renewal of the NPDES permit for Liquid Air's small industrial gas manufacturing facility in Catano, Puerto Rico. Because Liquid Air has eliminated its process wastewater and cooling water discharge from its operations, leaving it with stormwater as the only remaining point source of discharge, Liquid Air claims that EPA no longer has authority to require an NPDES permit for the facility. Pursuant to section 402(p) of the Clean Water Act, EPA may not impose a permit requirement for certain discharges composed entirely of stormwater. Liquid Air asserts that its stormwater discharge is exempt under this statutory provision. For the reasons set forth below, we remand one condition of the permit for further action consistent with this opinion, and deny review of all other issues.

I. BACKGROUND

Section 402(p) was enacted into law by the Water Quality Act of 1987, ... which established a phased approach to bringing stormwater discharges under regulatory coverage.... Section 402(p) provides, in pertinent part:

(p) Municipal and industrial stormwater discharges

    (1) General rule

Prior to October 1, 199[4], ... the Administrator * * * shall not require a permit under this section for discharges composed entirely of stormwater.

    (2) Exceptions

Paragraph (1) shall not apply with respect to the following stormwater discharges:

    (A) A discharge with respect to which a permit has been issued under this section before February 4, 1987.

    (B) A discharge associated with industrial activity.

(C) A discharge from a municipal separate storm sewer system serving a population of 250,000 or more.

(D) A discharge from a municipal separate storm sewer serving a population of 100,000 or more but less than 250,000.

(E) A discharge for which the Administrator * * * determines that the stormwater discharge contributes to a violation of a water quality standard or is a significant contributor of pollutants to waters of the United States.

33 U.S.C. § 1342(p). Under section 402(p)(1), EPA cannot require an NPDES permit for discharges consisting entirely of stormwater until October 1, 1994, except for those discharges identified under section 402(p)(2). After October 1, 1994, all stormwater discharges will presumably require an NPDES permit....

This proceeding evolved from Liquid Air's effort to renew the NPDES permit issued to its small industrial gas manufacturing facility n5 by Region II in 1983.... The 1983 permit authorized Liquid Air to discharge "process, cooling, and stormwater" from a single outfall, Outfall 001. On January 5, 1988, near the expiration of the 1983 permit's five-year term, Liquid Air informed Region II that it had successfully separated the stormwater and the process wastewater into two outfalls. On June 27, 1988, Liquid Air submitted an application to renew its NPDES permit. The application reflected Liquid Air's discharges from the two outfalls, but specifically added that Outfall 001 discharged both stormwater and "water table drainage."

On August 14, 1989, slightly more than a year after it had filed its permit application, but before the Region had prepared a draft permit, Liquid Air informed the Region that it wanted to withdraw the application. At this time, Liquid Air had eliminated its process wastewater discharge at Outfall 002, thus leaving the stormwater and water table drainage discharge at Outfall 001 as the only discharge at the facility. According to Liquid Air, this discharge was exempt from the NPDES permit requirements until October 1, 1994 under the "moratorium" for stormwater permits provided by section 402(p)(1) of the Clean Water Act, ... and thus no permit was required for the facility.

After the passage of another year, Region II responded to Liquid Air's request to withdraw its permit application. It explained to Liquid Air that its construction of section 402(p) of the Clean Water Act was different from Liquid Air's and that an NPDES permit was required for the discharge under that section of the Act.... Noting that the permitting moratorium set forth in section 402(p)(1) applies only to discharges "composed entirely of stormwater," Region II advised Liquid Air that the moratorium does not apply to its discharge because the discharge is not composed entirely of stormwater, but consists also of groundwater, as indicated by Liquid Air's reference to "water table drainage" in its permit application. As alternative bases for requiring a permit, the Region explained that even if the moratorium did apply, Liquid Air's discharge falls within three of the exceptions contained in section

GELTMAN MODERN ENV LAW—21

402(p)(2).... Aug. 1, 1990 Letter at 1. Region II further advised Liquid Air that if Liquid Air did not contact the Region within ten days to definitively withdraw its application for renewal, Region II would proceed to issue the NPDES permit based upon the application previously submitted by Liquid Air.

Liquid Air evidently did not contact the Region because on August 25, 1990, Region II issued a draft permit for Liquid Air's stormwater discharge. Liquid Air filed comments on the draft permit on September 20, 1990, again disputing the Region's conclusion that an NPDES permit can be required prior to October 1, 1994. In its comments, Liquid Air did not dispute the presence of groundwater in the stormwater discharge, but asserted that this fact should not be dispositive as Liquid Air has "undertaken to eliminate sources of groundwater infiltration into the facility stormwater system * * *." ...

Repeating its previous determination that Liquid Air's discharge is composed of stormwater and groundwater, and thus is not entitled to the moratorium because it is not entirely composed of stormwater, the Region issued the renewed permit in final form on September 28, 1990. On November 21, 1990, Liquid Air requested an evidentiary hearing on the permit to dispute the Region's authority to issue a permit for this stormwater discharge before the October 1, 1994 moratorium expired. The request specified three factual, and six legal, issues focussing on the section 402(p) issue. .... It did not provide any information on the status of Liquid Air's efforts to eliminate groundwater infiltration from its stormwater discharge, and instead merely challenged, as a matter of law, the Region's jurisdiction to exercise any authority over groundwater under the NPDES program.

One year later, Region II denied Liquid Air's evidentiary hearing request on November 27, 1991. The Region concluded that Liquid Air's request did not set forth material issues of fact relevant to the issuance of the permit as required by 40 C.F.R. § 124.75, and therefore an evidentiary hearing was not required. The Region also addressed each of the issues of law raised in Liquid Air's evidentiary hearing request. This appeal followed....

II. ANALYSIS

Under the rules governing NPDES permit proceedings, there is no review as a matter of right from the denial of an evidentiary hearing request. *See In re J & L Specialty Products Corp.*, NPDES Appeal No. 92–22, at 12 (EAB, Feb. 2, 1994). Ordinarily, a petition for review of a denial of an evidentiary hearing request is not granted unless the denial of the request is clearly erroneous or involves an exercise of discretion or policy that is important and therefore should be reviewed. *Id.*; 40 C.F.R. § 124.91(a). The Agency's longstanding policy is that NPDES permits should be finally adjudicated at the Regional level, and that the power to review NPDES permit decisions should be exercised only "sparingly." *See* 44 Fed. Reg. 32,887 (June 7, 1979); *see, e.g., In re City of Hollywood Florida*, NPDES Appeal No. 92–21 at 3 n.1 (EAB, Mar. 21, 1994). The petitioner has the burden of demonstrating that review should be granted. *See, e.g., In re American Cyanamid Company,* NPDES Appeal No. 92–18 at 5 (EAB, Sept. 27, 1993).

A. Legal Issues

Evidentiary hearings are granted pursuant to 40 C.F.R. § 124.75(a)(1) to resolve "material issues of fact relevant to the issuance of the permit." Liquid Air maintains that it has been erroneously or arbitrarily and capriciously denied "a right to a hearing on * * * disputed issues of * * * law." Notice of Appeal at 5. This argument is without merit. Although legal issues may be raised in an evidentiary hearing request, "they cannot themselves provide a basis for an evidentiary hearing, a procedure reserved for factual issues." *In re Town of Seabrook, N.H.,* NPDES Appeal Nos. 93–2, 93–3, at 13 (EAB, Sept. 28, 1993). Although legal questions related to factual issues for which an evidentiary hearing has been granted may be addressed in the course of an evidentiary hearing, *In re 446 Alaska Placer Miners,* NPDES Appeal No. 84–13 (CJO, Apr. 2, 1985), that situation does not apply here, since no evidentiary hearing on factual issues has been granted.

Where there is no evidentiary hearing, legal issues that were raised in the request for an evidentiary hearing can nevertheless be reviewed on appeal from the denial of the request, 40 C.F.R. § 124.74(b)(1)(note), provided the petitioner demonstrates that the legal issues merit review under the standards noted previously. On appeal, Liquid Air seeks review of the questions of law that are chiefly intended to determine the applicability of one or more of the statutory exceptions to the moratorium for stormwater discharges.... Because the Region determined that Liquid Air's discharge is not a qualifying stormwater discharge in the first instance, and because Liquid Air has not persuaded us that the Region erred in making that determination, there is no need to address the statutory exceptions to the moratorium. Accordingly, we conclude that none of the six legal issues identified by Liquid Air warrant review. Our more specific reasons follow.

The permitting moratorium in section 402(p)(1) provides that "[p]rior to October 1, 199[4], the Administrator * * * shall not require a permit under this section for discharges composed entirely of stormwater." 33 U.S.C. § 1342(p)(emphasis added). Thus, under the plain terms of the statute, the permitting moratorium applies only to discharges that are composed entirely of stormwater. As explained in the legislative history of section 402(p):

> Before October 1, 199[4], relief from the permit requirement is afforded only to discharges composed entirely of stormwater. Storm sewers that discharge any other type of effluent or into which pollutants are introduced by means other than incidental to stormwater runoff are required to obtain a permit.

H.R. Conf. Rep. No. 1004, 99th Cong., 2d Sess. 158 (Oct. 15, 1986) (emphasis added).

The Region concluded that Liquid Air's sole discharge is not subject to the permitting moratorium because it is not composed entirely of stormwater. Liquid Air's permit application indicates that the discharge consists of "facility stormwater and water table drainage," in other words, stormwater and groundwater. The Agency, in defining "stormwater" in 40 C.F.R § 122.26(b)(13), ... specifically decided not to include groundwater infiltration in the definition of stormwater. 55 Fed. Reg. 47,996 (Nov. 16, 1990).... The Agency recognized that stormwater, as surface water runoff, differs from groundwater, which has a longer exposure to pollutants in the soil. *Id.* Therefore, the Region correctly concluded that because Liquid Air's discharge contains stormwater and groundwater infiltration, the discharge is not composed entirely of stormwater, and thus the relief afforded by the moratorium is not available for the discharge.

Liquid Air asserts for the first time on appeal that during the pendency of its request for an evidentiary hearing it eliminated the discharge of the groundwater infiltration, so that the discharge is now entirely stormwater. Notice of Appeal at 7.... Liquid Air had not made any such assertion in its evidentiary hearing request or in any other submissions to the Region prior to the issuance of the permit. Although Liquid Air's earlier comments on the draft permit did mention that Liquid Air was in the process of eliminating groundwater from the stormwater outfall, there is nothing in the record indicating that Liquid Air ever notified or certified to the Region that groundwater had been eliminated. Accordingly, the Region had no basis for knowing when or whether Liquid Air's efforts would meet with success. Moreover, even after the Region subsequently denied the evidentiary hearing request (12 months after the request was made and 14 months after receiving Liquid Air's comments on the draft permit), Liquid Air's appeal gives no indication that it had ever provided the Region with any confirmation of its factual contentions. Thus, it appears from the record that Liquid Air's appeal represents the first formal notice to the Region of Liquid Air's factual contention that the discharges from the stormwater outfall consist solely of stormwater.

Quite obviously this information comes too late in the process, for it did not come to the Region's attention until after it had made its final permit determination and after it had denied the evidentiary hearing request. Under the rules governing NPDES permits, it is expected that information will be submitted with the response to comments on the draft permit or in the request for a evidentiary hearing. *See generally* 40 C.F.R. §§ 124.13 and 124.74(b)(1). In these circumstances, the Region cannot be charged with any reviewable error for having issued a permit that was predicated on the discharge at Outfall 001 being composed of stormwater and groundwater. This is the factual information that the Region had at the time, and it came from Liquid Air's permit application. We are evaluating the validity of the Region's action based upon the facts available to the Region at the time it made its determination. The Region was entitled to rely upon that information. Therefore, Liquid

Air is not entitled to benefit from the moratorium on permitting storm-water discharges. . . .

Our decision does not mean that Liquid Air can never ask the Region to revoke the permit because groundwater infiltration has been eliminated from the stormwater discharge. If Liquid Air wishes to press such a claim, the appropriate procedure to follow is for Liquid Air to seek a permit modification (revocation) under 40 C.F.R. § 122.62(a)(1) ("Alterations"). This procedure appears to be reasonably suited to the facts and circumstances of this case. . . . Other means of addressing the issue are either no longer available or are not as well suited to the circumstances. For example, the opportunity for Liquid Air to withdraw its application to renew its permit has passed, so that option is no longer available. Also, in our judgment, a remand of this issue to the Region for further fact finding would not be appropriate. The ultimate purpose of such a remand would be to determine whether Liquid Air is correct in contending that it is not required to have a permit; yet, such a contention is conceptually at odds with Liquid Air having applied for the permit in the first instance. The procedural regulations under which Liquid Air has made its application for a renewed NPDES permit are, as one would expect, intended to facilitate the issuance of permits to those who apply for them. The regulations tacitly assume that the person applying for the permit wants a permit, whereas in this instance Liquid Air is applying for a permit that it contends is not needed. . . . Under these circumstances, it is our position that the onus is on Liquid Air to establish its case in a manner that respects the fundamental permit-issuing goals of the procedures. Thus, we will not remand the permit to accomplish a purpose inconsistent with those goals. The permit modification (revocation) procedure referred to above is more suited to the situation now confronting Liquid Air.

B. Factual Issues

Under 40 C.F.R. § 124.75(a)(1), the Regional Administrator must grant an evidentiary hearing request that "sets forth material issues of fact relevant to the issuance of the permit." An issue of fact is material for the purposes of § 124.75(a)(1) if it might affect the outcome of the proceeding. *J & L Specialty Products,* supra, at 13 (citing *In re Mayaguez Regional Sewage Treatment Plant,* NPDES Appeal No. 92–23, at 12–13 (EAB, Aug. 23, 1993)). Liquid Air's evidentiary hearing request fails to meet this requirement, and therefore Liquid Air has failed to demonstrate that the Region clearly erred in denying its evidentiary hearing request.

In setting forth material issues of fact purportedly requiring an evidentiary hearing, Liquid Air's evidentiary hearing request reads:

III. QUESTIONS OF FACT

Requestor submits that the following facts are in dispute and were any decided in favor of Requestor, the proposed NPDES permit would have to be withdrawn by EPA Region 2:

a. Whether the stormwater presently discharged from Requestor's facility contains pollutants and contaminants associated with industrial activity.

b. Whether the stormwater presently discharged from Requestor's facility is directly related to manufacturing, processing or raw materials storage areas at an industrial plant.

c. Whether there is contained within the stormwater presently discharged from Requestor's facility significant amounts of pollutants.

Request for Evidentiary Hearing at 8. Each of the three factual questions pertains to whether Liquid Air's stormwater discharge falls within two of the exceptions to the permitting moratorium that the Region provided as alternative bases for issuing the permit.... We conclude that these alleged factual issues are not material to the issuance of the permit. For the reasons set forth above, the Region appropriately relied upon another basis for issuing the permit, namely, that based upon the facts known to the Region when it issued the permit as well as when it subsequently denied the evidentiary hearing request, Liquid Air's discharge is not encompassed by the permitting moratorium provided in Clean Water Act section 402(p)(1). Where, as here, the moratorium does not apply to the stormwater discharge, it is not necessary to examine whether the discharge is within any exceptions to the moratorium, and therefore, any factual questions relating to the applicability of the exceptions are not material to the issuance of the permit.

III. OTHER ISSUES

[*32]

A. *Special Condition 17*

Pursuant to section 401 of the Clean Water Act, 33 U.S.C. § 1341, ... the Puerto Rico Environmental Quality Board ("EQB") issued a water quality certification ("WQC") indicating that Liquid Air's proposed discharge, as represented in the permit renewal application, will not violate Puerto Rico's water quality standards if the effluent limitations contained in Table A–1 of the certification are met. In addition to effluent limitations, Table A–1 also contains monitoring requirements necessary to establish compliance with the effluent limitations. The WQC also contained a section entitled "Special Conditions." Although the certification contained twenty "Special Conditions," only one, Special Condition 17, is at issue here, as follows:

No monitoring by the permittee will be required for discharge 001 (Table A–1) if (1) within thirty (30) days after the effective date of the NPDES permit, the petitioner submits, for EQB approval, a Best Management Practices Plan (BMPP) for the control of pollutants in the storm water runoff and (2) within thirty (30) days after the date of approval of the BMPP, the petitioner should implement such plan. Failure to implement and comply with the BMPP shall submit the permittee to compliance with the requirements established in Table A–1 and in special conditions 18 and 19.

Special Condition 17 was not included in the draft permit, but was incorporated into the final permit pursuant to Liquid Air's request. *See* Comments at 4–5. . . .

The portion of the final permit reflecting Special Condition 17 is set forth below, highlighted with the Region's modifications thereto:

> The monitoring requirements for the water quality based limits included in Table A–1 of the WQC for discharges 001, may be deleted from the WQC, upon permittee's request if (1) within thirty (30) days after the effective date of the NPDES Permit, the petitioner submits, for EQB approval a Best Management Practices Plan (BMPP) for the control of pollutants in stormwater runoff and (2) within thirty (30) days after the date of the approval of the BMPP, the petitioner should implement such plan. Failure to implement and comply with the BMPP shall submit the permittee to compliance with the WQC requirements established in Table A–1 and in special conditions 12 and 13.

> Nevertheless, after EQB's modification of the WQC, in order to pursue any reduction in the requirements of the NPDES permit, the permittee must request modification from EPA. Since EPA could choose to impose discharge limitations based upon Best Professional Judgement, deletion of requirements by EQB would not necessarily result in a decision by EPA to delete all stormwater requirements.

Permit at 7.

. . .

On appeal, Liquid Air contends that the final permit arbitrarily and capriciously places additional administrative burdens upon Liquid Air in contravention of Puerto Rico's right to determine what measures are necessary to protect its water quality standards. Liquid Air asserts that as contained in the WQC, Special Condition 17 is self-executing, and that if Puerto Rico approves Liquid Air's BMPP and Liquid Air implements the BMPP, Special Condition 17 expressly provides that no monitoring will be required. . . . According to Liquid Air, Region II has added two more contingencies that must be met before monitoring will not be required: first, that Liquid Air obtain a modification of the WQC from Puerto Rico, and second, that Liquid Air then obtain a permit modification from Region II. In Liquid Air's view, these permit conditions are arbitrary and capricious because they are not contained in the WQC.

In response, the Region explains that it added clarifying language to Special Condition 17 when it incorporated that provision into the final permit "to inform the permittee that this Special Condition should not be interpreted to mean that EQB's approval of, and [Liquid Air's] implementation of, a BMPP would in and of itself constitute a permit modification." Response to Petition at 6. Further, the Region added, "because the NPDES program is not delegated to the Commonwealth of Puerto Rico, the proper procedure is for EPA, and not EQB, to grant or issue a permit modification relieving [Liquid Air] of a reporting requirement." *Id.*

The Region's analysis is faulty. The Region has turned a self-executing provision in the WQC to a non-self-executing condition in the permit. In attempting to justify this deviation from the WQC, the Region has framed the debate in terms of who has the authority to amend the NPDES permit—EPA or EQB. This argument, however, misses the mark. As Liquid Air points out, it is clear that the Region, in its discretion, could have made Special Condition 17 a separate and self-executing provision of the permit. Little or no modification to Special Condition 17 would be required to achieve that result. The Region's discussion of who has the authority to amend the permit fails to address why the self-executing component of Special Condition 17 was eliminated in the first instance, and why such a change from the terms of the WQC should be upheld here. Consequently, we have no basis for upholding the Region's decision to modify Special Condition 17. Therefore, we are remanding this portion of the permit to the Region for it to either incorporate Special Condition 17 into the permit as it appears in the WQC, or provide another basis for changing the self-executing nature of Special Condition 17. . . .

B. Standard Permit Conditions

On appeal, Liquid Air contends that the final permit erroneously and arbitrarily or capriciously contains "twenty-nine pages of standard terms and conditions set forth in the permit which have been historically prepared for and applied to high volume and pollutant loaded industrial wastewater discharges," and therefore are not applicable to stormwater discharges. Notice of Appeal at 14. The focus of Liquid Air's objection is not entirely clear from this language. The entire permit is twenty-nine pages in length, so perhaps Liquid Air is asserting that the entire permit is unwarranted because the discharge is of stormwater and not industrial wastewater. If this is the true nature of Liquid Air's objection, it is without merit. As explained above, Liquid Air has not shown that the Region was without a legal basis for issuing the permit for this stormwater discharge. An NPDES permit regulating stormwater may parallel, and in some ways duplicate, an NPDES permit regulating industrial wastewater, because the goal of both permits is the same—to assure that the discharge complies with the Clean Water Act. . . .

The Region interpreted Liquid Air's objection as a challenge to the inclusion of "standard" terms in the permit. . . . Assuming that Liquid Air intended to challenge the standard conditions that are set forth in the permit, we agree with the Region that this issue was not raised during the public comment period as required by 40 C.F.R. § 124.76, and good cause has not been demonstrated for the failure to raise it at that time. Accordingly, this issue cannot be raised for the first time in this petition for review. *Town of Seabrook, supra,* at 7.

Liquid Air argues that it did raise this issue during the public comment period, referring to that portion of its comments in which it proposed two alternatives to issuing the draft permit: undertaking a stormwater monitoring program for six months and then submitting a new stormwater discharge permit application under the newly promulgated regulations, or operating under the proposed permit provided the permit contains Special Condition 17. We agree with the Region that these proposed alternatives to issuing the permit do not in any way encompass an objection to the standard permit conditions contained in the draft permit.

IV. CONCLUSION

For the reasons set forth above, we conclude that the Regional Administrator did not clearly err in denying Liquid Air's request for an evidentiary hearing. The permit condition incorporating Special Condition 17 of the WQC is remanded to the Region for further action consistent with this opinion. Review of all other legal issues raised in the petition for review is hereby denied. Final Agency action for all issues concerning this permit shall occur upon completion of the administrative appeals process to the Board from the remanded proceeding. 40 C.F.R. § 124.91(f)(3).

So ordered.

6. *Enforcement*

The CWA's primary regulatory program is the National Pollutant Discharge Elimination System (NPDES). Under the CWA, an NPDES permit is required for any discharges of pollutants from "point sources" to navigable waters of the United States. *See* 33 U.S.C.A. § 1342. The term "point source" is defined as "any discernible, confined and discrete conveyance, including, but not limited to, any pipe, ditch, channel, tunnel, conduit, well, discrete fissure, container, rolling stock, concentrated animal feeding operation, or vessel or other floating craft, from which pollutants are or may be discharged." 33 U.S.C.A. 1362. The terms "pollution" and "pollutant" are defined very broadly to include virtually any parameter, constituent, or water quality characteristic, subject only to certain, limited exceptions. Courts have construed "waters of the United States" broadly to encompass virtually all water bodies, including wetlands.

While the Act initially gives EPA authority to issue such permits, the Agency may delegate that authority to the states, subject to oversight by EPA. State NPDES programs, and permits issued thereunder, must meet minimum federal standards, but the Act reserves to the states the right to set more stringent limitations, requirements, or conditions.

EPA has promulgated regulations specifying the types of requirements that NPDES permits must contain. *See generally* 40 C.F.R. Parts 122–125 (1990). Under EPA's NPDES regulations, permits must require point source dischargers to comply with any applicable effluent limitations guidelines or New Source Performance Standards (NSPS). Permits also must assure compliance with applicable state water quality standards. In addition, the permit must contain a host of "boiler-plate" requirements for proper operation and maintenance of the facility, compliance monitoring, recordkeeping, monthly compliance reporting, and timely notification if permit limits are exceeded.

NPDES permits expire at the end of five years, unless the permittee files a complete application for renewal at least 180 days before the expiration of the permit. In that case, when EPA (or, in some cases, the state) is the permit issuer, the permit continues in effect even though the effective date of the permit has passed and a new permit has not been issued. Permits may not be transferred without proper notice to and approval from the permit issuer.

Clean Water Act Enforcement Provisions at a Glance

Section	Description of Relevant Enforcement Provision
§ 308	Authorizes monitoring and reporting requirements by delegated enforcement authority
§ 309(a)	Authorizes issuance of administrative compliance orders
§ 309(b)	Authorizes civil enforcement actions for injunctive relief
§ 309(c)	Provides for criminal penalties
§ 309(d)	Provides for civil penalties
§ 309(e) & (f)	Requires EPA to join states as defendants in suits against municipalities; Authorizes suits against POTWs for violation of pretreatment regulations
§ 309(g)	Authorizes administrative penalties
§ 402(h)	Authorizes ban on new sewer hookups to POTWs violating discharge permits
§ 504	Authorizes EPA to sue to restrain any source from polluting waters, provided the pollution is an imminent or substantial endangerment to public health or welfare
§ 505	Authorizes citizens suits for civil and injunctive relief against persons violating effluent standard or order. Provides for attorney fees
§ 508	Gives EPA authority to blacklist Clean Water Act violators, barring them from all federal contracts and loans

7. *Citizens' Suits*

VILLAGE OF OCONOMOWOC LAKE
v. DAYTON HUDSON CORP.

24 F.3d 962 (7th Cir.1994).

EASTERBROOK, CIRCUIT JUDGE.

Target Stores, a division of Dayton Hudson Corporation, is building a warehouse (which it calls a "distribution center") in the City of Oconomowoc, Wisconsin. It holds all necessary state and local permits. Federal clearance is unnecessary, for the Environmental Protection Agency has authorized Wisconsin to perform the tasks required by the Clean Air and Clean Water Acts. The Village of Oconomowoc Lake, a nearby municipality, wishes the warehouse would disappear. We have for decision one among more than a dozen suits and administrative proceedings the Village has commenced in pursuit of that objective.

Warehouses do not spew pollutants, but they have indirect effects. Trucks that carry goods to and from the warehouse emit nitrogen oxides and other gasses. A well-sited warehouse cuts down on wasted movement of goods, and therefore on pollution in the United States as a whole, but increases the volume of emissions nearby. While parked near the warehouse trucks drip oil, which collects in the runoff from a storm. A few inches of rain falling on a large paved surface means many acre-feet of water. This warehouse has a retention pond, from which the water seeps into the ground—carrying hydrocarbons and other unwelcome substances, the Village fears.

State officials concluded that the warehouse would be such a trivial source of pollution that it should not be classified as a "major source" requiring full scrutiny. The Village wanted a federal judge to inquire further, but the judge declined to cooperate. The Clean Air Act requires permits only for "stationary sources" of pollution. A definitional provision provides not only that vehicles are not "stationary sources" but also that vehicular emissions are not attributed to the buildings served as points of origin or destination. 42 U.S.C. § 7602(z); see also 42 U.S.C. § 7410(a)(5)(C). Whatever requirements the state has added to federal law must be enforced in state court, the judge held. As for the rainwater runoff: the Clean Water Act regulates discharges into "navigable waters from a point source". 33 U.S.C. § 1362(12). Parking lots and retention ponds are not exactly "navigable," but another statute defines "navigable waters" as all "waters of the United States". 33 U.S.C. § 1362(7). Some water from the pond evaporates into the air, and the rest seeps into the ground. Even though ground water eventually reaches streams, lakes, and oceans, the court held, it is not part of the "waters of the United States". The district court accordingly dismissed the complaint under Fed. R. Civ. P. 12(b)(1).

As a rule, persons wishing to sue under the Clean Air Act must give 60 days' notice to the potential defendant. 42 U.S.C. § 7604(b). Notice provisions pervade environmental statutes, and would-be plaintiffs often appear to be desperate to evade them. *Hallstrom v. Tillamook County,* 493 U.S. 20, 107 L.Ed.2d 237, 110 S.Ct. 304 (1989); *Supporters to Oppose Pollution, Inc. v. Heritage Group,* 973 F.2d 1320 (7th Cir.1992). Why plaintiffs are unwilling to wait even 60 days—when an effort to jump the queue may lead to outright dismissal of the case under *Hallstrom*—eludes us. The Village filed suit only three days after giving notice. To justify this expedition, it invoked 42 U.S.C. § 7604(a)(3), which is not subject to the 60–day rule. Although this enabled it to sue 57 days sooner than it could have done had it used § 7604(a)(1) as the foundation for the suit, the strategy does little besides illustrate the adage that haste makes waste. (This saying predates the Clean Air Act and shows that not all waste is within federal jurisdiction.)

Section 7604(a)(3) permits a citizen to file a civil action:

> against any person who proposes to construct or constructs any new or modified major emitting facility without a permit required under ... part D of subchapter I of this chapter (relating to nonattainment) or who is alleged to be in violation of any condition of such permit.

The warehouse is in a "nonattainment" area, and the Village contends that it lacks the permit required for a "major emitting facility". Wisconsin treated the warehouse as a minor rather than a major source. But to use § 7604(a)(3) the Village had to show that "part D of subchapter I of this chapter" requires a major-facility permit, and it is impossible to see how this could be so. Recall that the warehouse itself does not emit pollutants and that the Clean Air Act does not require the attribution of motor-vehicle emissions to stationary sources. 42 U.S.C. § 7410(a)(5)(A), (C); *see also South Terminal Corp. v. EPA,* 504 F.2d 646, 668 n. 24 (1st Cir.1974). "Part D of subchapter I" does not require Dayton Hudson to obtain a permit; any such requirement must come from Wisconsin law and therefore cannot serve as the foundation for suit under § 7604(a)(3).

If the Village had waited for the prescribed 60 days, it would have been eligible to use § 7604(a)(1), which authorizes citizen suits against any person ... who is alleged to be in violation of (A) an emission standard or limitation under this chapter or (B) an order issued by the Administrator or a State with respect to such a standard or limitation. If this had been the foundation of the suit, and if we were to assume that the emissions from trucks going to and from the warehouse violate Wisconsin's implementation plan—for the state has elected to regulate such indirect emissions despite the lack of federal compulsion to do so— then it would have been necessary to decide whether a provision of a state plan going beyond the federal minima is "an emission standard or limitation under this chapter". States must clear their implementation plans with the EPA and enforce them faithfully; it is accordingly possible to characterize a state's rules as "an emission standard or limitation under this chapter" in the sense that it is adopted under the chapter and includes rules that satisfy the chapter. It may even be that rules going beyond federal requirements are essential to satisfy federal law. How could that be? Suppose the EPA approved a plan that was less stringent in some respects than the EPA would have demanded, only because in other respects it did more than federal law required and the rules, taken as a whole, would produce the desired cleanliness. Then failure to comply with the "extra" rules would reduce air quality below the federal minimum. The EPA believes that federal courts (and the Administrator) may enforce provisions in state plans. 40 C.F.R. § 51.165(a)(1)(xiv). We need not decide whether this means enforcement under § 7604(a)(1), as some courts have held. E.g., *Coalition Against Columbus Center v. New York City*, 967 F.2d 764, 771 (2d Cir.1992); *Delaware Valley Citizens Council v. Davis*, 932 F.2d 256, 265–67 (3d Cir.1991). *See also Sierra Club v. Larson*, 2 F.3d 462, 469 (1st Cir.1993)(remarking that indirect-source rules in a state implementation plan "may at least in some circumstances be within the purview of a citizens suit under 42 U.S.C. § 7604."). *But see Atlantic States Legal Foundation, Inc. v. Eastman Kodak Co.*, 12 F.3d 353, 358–60 (2d Cir.1993)(provisions of state plans exceeding federal requirements are not enforceable under provisions of the Clean Water Act parallel to § 7604). There will be ample opportunity for full consideration when the need arises.

The Village's claim under the Clean Water Act does not depend on any state rule or plan. This time the obstacle is the limitation of the Act's coverage to the "waters of the United States." Rainwater runoff from the 110–acre site (including 25 acres of paved parking) will collect in a 6–acre artificial pond. The pond is supposed to retain oil, grease, and other pollutants while "exfiltrating" the water to the ground below. The Clean Water Act is a broad statute, reaching waters and wetlands that are not navigable or even directly connected to navigable waters. *United States v. Riverside Bayview Homes, Inc.*, 474 U.S. 121, 88 L.Ed.2d 419, 106 S.Ct. 455 (1985). But not even the EPA shares Justice Story's view that the national government has regulatory power over every drop of water: "It was said of the late Justice Story, that if a bucket of water were brought into his court with a corn cob floating in it, he would at once extend the admiralty jurisdiction of the United States over it." Note, 37 Am. L. Rev. 911, 916 (1903). *See DeLovio v. Boit*, 7 Fed.Cas. 418 (No. 3,776)(CC Mass.1815). The Agency's regulatory definition of "waters of the United States" includes "intrastate lakes, rivers, streams (including intermittent streams), mudflats, sandflats, wetlands, sloughs, prairie potholes, wet meadows, playa lakes, or natural ponds, the use, degradation or destruction of which could affect interstate or foreign commerce". 40 C.F.R. § 230.3(s)(3). *Hoffman Homes, Inc. v. Administrator, EPA*, 999 F.2d 256, 260–61 (7th Cir.1993), concluded that the EPA did not exceed its power when promulgating this definition but that even a rule with such broad scope did not cover a one-acre wetland 750 feet from a small creek. A six-acre retention pond, farther from a body of surface water, is an easier case. The EPA's definition speaks of "natural ponds"; Dayton Hudson built an artificial pond.

What of the possibility that water from the pond will enter the local ground waters, and thence underground aquifers that feed lakes and streams that are part of the "waters of the United States"? Justice Story's bucket was part of the navigable waters in this sense. We know from *Wickard v. Filburn,* 317 U.S. 111, 87 L.Ed. 122, 63 S.Ct. 82 (1942), that wheat a farmer bakes into bread and eats at home is part of "interstate commerce" because these activities affect the volume of interstate shipments. On a similar rationale all ground waters could be thought within the power of the national government. *Inland Steel Co. v. EPA,* 901 F.2d 1419, 1422 (7th Cir.1990)(reserving the question). But the Clean Water Act does not attempt to assert national power to the fullest. "Waters of the United States" must be a subset of "water"; otherwise why insert the qualifying clause in the statute? (No one suggests that the function of this phrase is to distinguish domestic waters from those of Canada or Mexico.) Neither the Clean Water Act nor the EPA's definition asserts authority over ground waters, just because these may be hydrologically connected with surface waters.

The omission of ground waters from the regulations is not an oversight. Members of Congress have proposed adding ground waters to the scope of the Clean Water Act, but these proposals have been defeated, and the EPA evidently has decided not to wade in on its own. The most concerted effort in Congress occurred in 1972, and the Senate Committee on Public Works explained why it had not accepted these proposals:

> Several bills pending before the Committee provided authority to establish Federally approved standards for groundwaters which permeate rock, soil, and other subsurface formations. Because the jurisdiction regarding groundwaters is so complex and varied from State to State, the Committee did not adopt this recommendation.

S. Rep. No. 414, 92d Cong., 1st Sess. 73 (1972). *See also Exxon Corp. v. Train,* 554 F.2d 1310, 1325–29 (5th Cir.1977)(recounting this history). In other words, Congress elected to leave the subject to state law—and Wisconsin has elected to permit Target Stores to build a warehouse that will affect the local ground waters.

Decisions not to enact proposed legislation are not conclusive on the meaning of the text actually enacted. Laws sometimes surprise their authors. But we are confident that the statute Congress enacted excludes some waters, and ground waters are a logical candidate. Two courts have held that ground waters are not part of the (statutory) "waters of the United States." *Exxon; Kelley v. United States,* 618 F.Supp. 1103 (W.D.Mich.1985). The possibility of a hydrological connection cannot be denied, *see Sierra Club v. Colorado Refining Co.,* 838 F.Supp. 1428 (D.Colo.1993); *McClellan Ecological Seepage Situation v. Cheney,* 763 F.Supp. 431, 437 (E.D.Cal.1989), but neither the statute nor the regulations makes such a possibility a sufficient ground of regulation. On several occasions the EPA has noted the potential connection between ground waters and surface waters, but it has left the regulatory definition alone. *E.g.,* Preamble to NPDES Permit Application Regulations for Storm Water Discharges, 55 Fed. Reg. 47,990, 47,997 (Nov. 16, 1990)("This rulemaking only addresses discharges to waters of the United States, consequently discharges to ground waters are not covered by this rulemaking (unless there is a hydrological connection between the ground water and a nearby surface water body.")) Collateral reference to a problem is not a satisfactory substitute for focused attention in rulemaking or adjudication. By amending its regulations, the EPA could pose a harder question. As the statute and regulations stand, however, the federal government has not asserted a claim of authority over artificial ponds that drain into ground waters.

AFFIRMED

MANION, CIRCUIT JUDGE, concurring.

I agree with the court's holding that the plaintiff's claims invoking the Clean Air Act and the Clean Water Act should fail. For whatever reason the Village of Oconomowoc Lake wishes the warehouse would disappear (be it political, environmental, or simple resentment because it doesn't get a bite at the tax base), the regulations under the Clean Air and Clean Water Acts do not facilitate the attack. In addition, I would not speculate how to characterize a citizen's suit under § 7604(a)(1). Before federal courts begin deciding under the Clean Air Act whether or not such things as shopping malls are permissible because of their side effects, we should ensure that Congress has specifically authorized the EPA to regulate at that level. Nor would I suggest that the EPA can figuratively "wade in" to ground water as part of the waters of the United States without first having specific direction from Congress to do so. This would take more than a simple amendment of regulations by the administrators at the EPA. Regulations are promulgated at the direction of Congress, and at this juncture, Congress has not permitted collateral attacks against parking lots, septic tanks, and sprinkler systems—the natural consequence if we were to approve the interpretation espoused by the plaintiffs.

§ 8.3 WETLANDS DREDGE–AND–FILL PROGRAM

Section 404 of the CWA gives the Army Corps of Engineers (Corps) jurisdiction to issue permits for the discharge of any "dredged" or "fill material" into "waters of the United States," including wetlands. In addition, § 10 of the Rivers and Harbors Act of 1899 requires a Corps permit for any work in waters that are "navigable" in fact. The Corps has established regulations allowing issuance of consolidated permits under CWA § 404 and § 10 of the Rivers and Harbors Act. Those regulations establish criteria for determining whether or not a permit should be granted, appeal procedures, and minimum requirements that must be included in all permits. *See* 33 C.F.R. Parts 320–330 (1990).

Under § 404 of the CWA, before "dredged" or "fill" material may be discharged in any wetland, an individual permit must be obtained from the United States Army Corps of Engineers. 33 U.S.C.A. § 1344(a); 33 C.F.R. § 323.3 (1990). In layman's terms, "wetlands" constitute those areas that are "inundated or saturated" with water frequently enough so that they support "vegetation . . . adapted for life in saturated soil conditions." *See* 33 C.F.R. § 328.3(b)(1990). Wetlands usually are associated with swamps and marshes, but they often are located in areas where there is little visible surface water. Recent studies report as much as 87 percent of undeveloped land in some locales near waterbodies may be considered wetlands subject to federal regulation. Thus, one should not automatically assume that an apparently dry piece of land is not a wetland.

While the legal definitions of "dredged" and "fill" material are complex, as a practical matter, dredged or fill material includes virtually any solid material placed or redistributed in a wetland. There are, however, specified, limited exceptions to the 404 permit requirement. Also, the Corps has issued so-called "general permits" which authorize certain activities nationwide, as long as specific conditions are met. The EPA has broad authority to "veto" any individual permits issued by the Corps where the proposed projects will entail "unacceptable adverse effects." EPA has used this veto power on a number of occasions to disrupt large commercial development projects. It is, therefore, imperative that applications for § 404 permits address the likely concerns of both the Corps and EPA.

In deciding whether to grant a 404 permit, the Corps examines a host of complex technical factors under a myriad of federal laws and regulations, including the National Environmental Policy Act, the Fish and Wildlife Coordination Act, the Coastal Zone Management Act, the Endangered Species Act, and others. In general, however, no permits will be issued if there is a "practicable alternative" to the proposed project which would have a less adverse impact on the aquatic ecosystem. For projects that do not require access to the water, there is a presumption that "practicable alternatives" to the proposed wetlands site exist, and that these alternatives will entail a less adverse impact.

The states also have enacted regulatory programs to protect wetlands. These programs usually consist of permitting requirements similar to § 404.

As a result of the various federal and state regulatory regimes for wetlands, a business transaction can be impacted substantially and can involve negotiations and filings with a number of agencies. The penalties for ignoring or violating wetlands regulations can be harsh, including large civil penalties and restoration of damaged wetlands to their original appearance and condition. Consequently, it is important that any investigation of property to be acquired in the United States that could conceivably involve wetlands include an assessment by a qualified expert of whether the property qualifies as wetlands. If so, the permitting process should be initiated well in advance (6 to 10 months) of any closing.

UNITED STATES v. RIVERSIDE BAYVIEW HOMES
474 U.S. 121, 106 S.Ct. 455, 88 L.Ed.2d 419 (1985).

WHITE, J., delivered the opinion for a unanimous Court.

This case presents the question whether the Clean Water Act (CWA), 33 U.S.C. § 1251 et seq., together with certain regulations promulgated under its authority by the Army Corps of Engineers, authorizes the Corps to require landowners to obtain permits from the Corps before discharging fill material into wetlands adjacent to navigable bodies of water and their tributaries.

I

The relevant provisions of the Clean Water Act originated in the Federal Water Pollution Control Act Amendments of 1972, 86 Stat. 816, and have remained essentially unchanged since that time. Under §§ 301 and 502 of the Act, 33 U.S.C. §§ 1311 and 1362, any discharge of dredged or fill materials into "navigable waters"—defined as the "waters of the United States"—is forbidden unless authorized by a permit issued by the Corps of Engineers pursuant to § 404, 33 U.S.C. § 1344. n1. After initially construing the Act to cover only waters navigable in fact, in 1975 the Corps issued interim final regulations redefining "the waters of the United States" to include not only actually navigable waters but also tributaries of such waters, interstate waters and their tributaries, and nonnavigable intrastate waters whose use or misuse could affect interstate commerce. 40 Fed. Reg. 31,320 (1975). More importantly for present purposes, the Corps construed the Act to cover all "freshwater wetlands" that were adjacent to other covered waters. A "freshwater wetland" was defined as an area that is "periodically inundated" and is "normally characterized by the prevalence of vegetation that requires saturated soil conditions for growth and reproduction." 33 CFR § 209.120(d)(2)(h) (1976). In 1977, the Corps refined its definition of wetlands by eliminating the reference to periodic inundation and making other minor changes. The 1977 definition reads as follows:

> "The term 'wetlands' means those areas that are inundated or saturated by surface or ground water at a frequency and duration sufficient to support, and that under normal circumstances do support, a prevalence of vegetation typically adapted for life in saturated soil conditions. Wetlands generally include swamps, marshes, bogs and similar areas." 33 CFR§ 323.2(c)(1978).

In 1982, the 1977 regulations were replaced by substantively identical regulations that remain in force today. *See* 33 CFR § 323.2 (1985)....

Respondent Riverside Bayview Homes, Inc. (hereafter respondent), owns 80 acres of low-lying, marshy land near the shores of Lake St. Clair in Macomb County, Michigan. In 1976, respondent began to place fill materials on its property as part of its preparations for construction of a housing development. The Corps of Engineers, believing that the property was an "adjacent wetland" under the 1975 regulation defining "waters of the United States," filed suit in the United States District Court for the Eastern District of Michigan, seeking to enjoin respondent from filling the property without the permission of the Corps.

The District Court held that the portion of respondent's property lying below 575.5 feet above sea level was a covered wetland and enjoined respondent from filling it without a permit. Civ. No. 77–70041 (Feb. 24, 1977)(App. to Pet. for Cert. 22a); Civ. No. 77–70041 (June 21, 1979) (App. to Pet. for Cert. 32a). Respondent appealed, and the Court of Appeals remanded for consideration of the effect of the intervening 1977 amendments to the regulation. 615 F.2d 1363 (1980). On remand, the District Court again held the property to be a wetland subject to the Corps' permit authority. Civ. No. 77–70041 (May 10, 1981)(App. to Pet. for Cert. 42a).

Respondent again appealed, and the Sixth Circuit reversed. 729 F.2d 391 (1984). The court construed the Corps' regulation to exclude from the category of adjacent wetlands—and hence from that of "waters of the United States"—wetlands that were not subject to flooding by adjacent navigable waters at a frequency sufficient to support the growth of aquatic vegetation. The court adopted this construction of the regulation because, in its view, a broader definition of wetlands might result in the taking of private property without just compensation. The court also expressed its doubt that Congress, in granting the Corps jurisdiction to regulate the filling of "navigable waters," intended to allow regulation of wetlands that were not the result of flooding by navigable waters. ...Under the court's reading of the regulation, respondent's property was not within the Corps' jurisdiction, because its semiaquatic characteristics were not the result of frequent flooding by the nearby navigable waters. Respondent was therefore free to fill the property without obtaining a permit ...

We granted certiorari to consider the proper interpretation of the Corps' regulation defining "waters of the United States" and the scope of the Corps' jurisdiction under the Clean Water Act, both of which were called into question by the Sixth Circuit's ruling. 469 U.S. 1206 (1985). We now reverse.

II

The question whether the Corps of Engineers may demand that respondent obtain a permit before placing fill material on its property is primarily one of regulatory and statutory interpretation: we must determine whether respondent's property is an "adjacent wetland" within the meaning of the applicable regulation, and, if so, whether the Corps' jurisdiction over "navigable waters" gives it statutory authority to regulate discharges of fill material into such a wetland. In this connection, we first consider the Court of Appeals' position that the Corps' regulatory authority under the statute and its implementing regulations must be narrowly construed to avoid a taking without just compensation in violation of the Fifth Amendment.

We have frequently suggested that governmental land-use regulation may under extreme circumstances amount to a "taking" of the affected property. *See, e.g., Williamson County Regional Planning Comm'n v. Hamilton Bank*, 473 U.S. 172 (1985); *Penn Central Transportation Co. v. New York City*, 438 U.S. 104 (1978). We have never precisely defined those circumstances, *see id.*, at 123–128; but our general approach was summed up in *Agins v. Tiburon*, 447 U.S. 255, 260 (1980), where we stated that the application of land-use regulations to a particular piece of property is a taking only "if the ordinance does not substantially advance legitimate state interests . . . or denies an owner economically viable use of his land." Moreover, we have made it quite clear that the mere assertion of regulatory jurisdiction by a governmental body does not constitute a regulatory taking. *See Hodel v. Virginia Surface Mining & Reclamation Assn.*, 452 U.S. 264, 293–297 (1981). The reasons are obvious. A requirement that a person obtain a permit before engaging in a certain use of his or her property does not itself "take" the property in any sense: after all, the very existence of a permit system implies that permission may be granted, leaving the landowner free to use the property as desired. Moreover, even if the permit is denied, there may be other viable uses available to the owner. Only when a permit is denied and the effect of the denial is to prevent "economically viable" use of the land in question can it be said that a taking has occurred.

If neither the imposition of the permit requirement itself nor the denial of a permit necessarily constitutes a taking, it follows that the Court of Appeals erred in concluding that a narrow reading of the Corps' regulatory jurisdiction over wetlands was "necessary" to avoid "a serious taking problem." 729 F.2d, at 398. . . . We have held that, in general, "[equitable] relief is not available to enjoin an alleged taking of private property for a public use, duly authorized by law, when a suit for compensation can be brought against the sovereign subsequent to a taking." *Ruckelshaus v. Monsanto Co.*, 467 U.S. 986, 1016 (1984) (footnote omitted). This maxim rests on the principle that so long as compensation is available for those whose property is in fact taken, the governmental action is not unconstitutional. *Williamson County, supra*, at 194–195. For precisely the same reason, the possibility that the application of a regulatory program may in some instances result in the taking of individual pieces of property is no justification for the use of narrowing constructions to curtail the program if compensation will in any event be available in those cases where a taking has occurred. Under such circumstances, adoption of a narrowing construction does not constitute avoidance of a constitutional difficulty, *cf. Ashwander v. TVA*, 297 U.S. 288, 341–356 (1936)(Brandeis, J., concurring); it merely frustrates permissible applications of a statute or regulation. . . . Because the Tucker Act, 28 U.S. C. § 1491, which presumptively supplies a means of obtaining compensation for any taking that may occur through the operation of a federal statute, *see Ruckelshaus v. Monsanto Co., supra*, at 1017, is available to provide compensation for takings that may result from the Corps' exercise of jurisdiction over wetlands, the Court of

Appeals' fears that application of the Corps' permit program might result in a taking did not justify the court in adopting a more limited view of the Corps' authority than the terms of the relevant regulation might otherwise support.

* * *

III

Purged of its spurious constitutional overtones, the question whether the regulation at issue requires respondent to obtain a permit before filling its property is an easy one. The regulation extends the Corps' authority under § 404 to all wetlands adjacent to navigable or interstate waters and their tributaries. Wetlands, in turn, are defined as lands that are "inundated or saturated by surface or ground water at a frequency and duration sufficient to support, and that under normal circumstances do support, a prevalence of vegetation typically adapted for life in saturated soil conditions." 33 CFR § 323.2(c)(1985)(emphasis added). The plain language of the regulation refutes the Court of Appeals' conclusion that inundation or "frequent flooding" by the adjacent body of water is a sine qua non of a wetland under the regulation. Indeed, the regulation could hardly state more clearly that saturation by either surface or ground water is sufficient to bring an area within the category of wetlands, provided that the saturation is sufficient to and does support wetland vegetation.

The history of the regulation underscores the absence of any requirement of inundation. The interim final regulation that the current regulation replaced explicitly included a requirement of "[periodic] inundation." 33 CFR § 209.120(d)(2)(h)(1976). In deleting the reference to "periodic inundation" from the regulation as finally promulgated, the Corps explained that it was repudiating the interpretation of that language "as requiring inundation over a record period of years." 42 Fed. Reg. 37,128 (1977). In fashioning its own requirement of "frequent flooding" the Court of Appeals improperly reintroduced into the regulation precisely what the Corps had excised . . .

Without the nonexistent requirement of frequent flooding, the regulatory definition of adjacent wetlands covers the property here. The District Court found that respondent's property was "characterized by the presence of vegetation that requires saturated soil conditions for growth and reproduction," App. to Pet. for Cert. 24a, and that the source of the saturated soil conditions on the property was ground water. There is no plausible suggestion that these findings are clearly erroneous, and they plainly bring the property within the category of wetlands as defined by the current regulation. In addition, the court found that the wetland located on respondent's property was adjacent to a body of navigable water, since the area characterized by saturated soil conditions and wetland vegetation extended beyond the boundary of respondent's property to Black Creek, a navigable waterway. Again, the court's finding is not clearly erroneous. Together, these findings establish that respondent's property is a wetland adjacent to a navigable waterway. Hence, it is part of the "waters of the United States" as defined by 33 CFR § 323.2 (1985), and if the regulation itself is valid as a construction of the term "waters of the United States" as used in the Clean Water Act, a question which we now address, the property falls within the scope of the Corps' jurisdiction over "navigable waters" under § 404 of the Act.

IV

A

An agency's construction of a statute it is charged with enforcing is entitled to deference if it is reasonable and not in conflict with the expressed intent of Congress. *Chemical Manufacturers Assn. v. Natural Resources Defense Council, Inc.*, 470 U.S. 116, 125 (1985); *Chevron U.S. A. Inc. v. Natural Resources Defense Council, Inc.*, 467 U.S. 837, 842–845 (1984). Accordingly, our review is limited to the question whether it is reasonable, in light of the language, policies, and legislative history of the Act for the Corps to exercise jurisdiction over wetlands adjacent to but not regularly flooded by rivers, streams, and other hydrographic features more conventionally identifiable as "waters."

* * *

"For this reason, the landward limit of Federal jurisdiction under Section 404 must include any adjacent wetlands that form the border of or are in reasonable proximity to other waters of the United States, as these wetlands are part of this aquatic system." 42 Fed. Reg. 37,128 (1977).

We cannot say that the Corps' conclusion that adjacent wetlands are inseparably bound up with the "waters" of the United States—based as it is on the Corps' and EPA's technical expertise—is unreasonable. In view of the breadth of federal regulatory authority contemplated by the Act itself and the inherent difficulties of defining precise bounds to regulable waters, the Corps' ecological judgment about the relationship between waters and their adjacent wetlands provides an adequate basis for a legal judgment that adjacent wetlands may be defined as waters under the Act.

This holds true even for wetlands that are not the result of flooding or permeation by water having its source in adjacent bodies of open water. The Corps has concluded that wetlands may affect the water quality of adjacent lakes, rivers, and streams even when the waters of those bodies do not actually inundate the wetlands. For example, wetlands that are not flooded by adjacent waters may still tend to drain into those waters. In such circumstances, the Corps has concluded that wetlands may serve to filter and purify water draining into adjacent bodies of water, *see* 33 CFR § 320.4(b)(2)(vii)(1985), and to slow the flow of surface runoff into lakes, rivers, and streams and thus prevent flooding and erosion, *see* §§ 320.4(b)(2)(iv) and (v). In addition, adjacent wetlands may "serve significant natural biological functions, including food chain production, general habitat, and nesting, spawning, rearing and resting sites for aquatic ... species." § 320.4(b)(2)(i). In short, the Corps has concluded that wetlands adjacent to lakes, rivers, streams, and other bodies of water may function as integral parts of the aquatic environment even when the moisture creating the wetlands does not find its source in the adjacent bodies of water. Again, we cannot say that the Corps' judgment on these matters is unreasonable, and we therefore conclude that a definition of "waters of the United States" encompassing all wetlands adjacent to other bodies of water over which the Corps has jurisdiction is a permissible interpretation of the Act. Because respondent's property is part of a wetland that actually abuts on a navigable waterway, respondent was required to have a permit in this case....

* * *

C

We are thus persuaded that the language, policies, and history of the Clean Water Act compel a finding that the Corps has acted reasonably in interpreting the Act to require permits for the discharge of fill material into wetlands adjacent to the "waters of the United States." The regulation in which the Corps has embodied this interpretation by its terms includes the wetlands on respondent's property within the class of waters that may not be filled without a permit; and, as we have seen, there is no reason to interpret the regulation more narrowly than its terms would indicate. Accordingly, the judgment of the Court of Appeals is

Reversed.

* * *

Discussion Problems

Problem 1

Potential Plaintiffs, who refer to themselves collectively as Concerned Area Residents For the Environment ("CARE"), are a group of land owners who live near XYZ Farms, a dairy farm in the town of Castile, in upstate New York. XYZ Farm is one of the largest dairy farms in the State of New York. It employs twenty-eight full-time and nine part-time employees. As of 1992, it owned 1,100 crop acres and had an animal population of 1,290 head of mature cows with over 900 head of young cattle, heifers and calves, making a total of 2,200 animals.

Unlike old-fashioned dairy farms, XYZ's operations do not involve pasturing the cows. Instead, the cows remain in their barns except during the three times per day milking procedure. Also unlike old-fashioned dairy farms where the accumulated manure was spread by a manure spreader, XYZ's rather enormous manure operations are largely performed through the use of storage lagoons and liquid cow manure. The storage lagoons number five on the main farm property ("A Farm"). One four-acre manure storage lagoon has a capacity of approximately six-to-eight million gallons of liquid cow manure.

In connection with this particular manure storage lagoon, XYZ has installed a separator which pumps the cow manure over a mechanical device which drains off the liquid and passes the solids out through a compressing process. The solids that remain are dropped into bins for transport while the liquid runs by gravity through a pipe to the four-acre manure storage lagoon. This separated liquid was apparently used for the purpose of washing down the barns where the cows are housed.

Insofar as application of the manure as fertilizer to the land is concerned, there is a center pivot irrigation system for spreading liquid manure over the fields. The diameter of the circle of this irrigation system can be modified to conform to the field on which the application is being made. A series of pipes connects the pivot to the liquid manure storage lagoons. The pivot is self-propelled with the height of the arc from the manure spray being somewhere between 12 and 30 feet.

XYZ also spreads its manure with a hard hose traveler which is a long piece of plastic tubing on a large reel. The traveler can be unwound and has a nozzle on the end which can send liquid manure 150 feet in either direction making a 300–foot-wide swath for purposes of fertilizing farm fields. The height of the arc from the projected spray is "a couple of feet higher" than that of the center pivot irrigator. Since 1988, a piping system consisting of a six-inch aluminum pipe and running under both the state highway and a town road to a lagoon on at least one XYZ Farm other than the "A Farm," has transported liquid manure from the storage lagoon to various locations without the use of vehicles.

XYZ also uses conventional manure spreading equipment including spreaders pulled by tractors and self-propelled vehicles which, generally speaking, have a 5,000 gallon capacity for liquid manure. These vehicles were used to spread manure from the smaller lagoons on the "A Farm" which do not receive liquid manure processed through the separation system. XYZ's manure spreading record reflects the application of millions of gallons of manure to its fields.

You represent CARE. They want to know whether the farm is in violation of any environmental laws or regulations.

Problem 2

Company, a Tennessee corporation, owns and operates an industrial waste landfill in McMinn County, Tennessee. This landfill utilizes two ponds that receive wastewater from the landfill site. Client claims that the landfill site is contaminated with pollutants and discharges it into two streams through the two ponds. One pond, pond #2, on the back side of the landfill, discharges into a small tributary of Rogers Creek that runs across residential property. The other pond, pond #1, on the front side of the landfill, discharges into a tributary of Meadow Branch, which flows through farms and residential property and is used for watering livestock.

Company has not received a National Pollutant Discharge Elimination System ("NPDES") permit from the Tennessee Department of Conservation, Division of Water Pollution, for the discharges from either of the two ponds. Client claims that an NPDES permit is required for such discharges under the Clean Water Act, 33 U.S.C.A. § 1251 to 1376. Because Company has no NPDES permit, Client would like to seek injunctive relief from and civil penalties for the alleged discharges.

You represent Client. What do you do, advise or want to know in evaluating their prognosis for success on the merits?

Problem 3

Company X operates oil and gas wells at a site in Orange County, California, leased from ABC Corporation. These operations produce drilling wastes which are presently discharged into the surrounding environment. In July 1978, the Fish and Wildlife Service of the United States Department of the Interior requested that the Santa Ana Region of the State Board (Regional Board) adopt an order declaring Company X's disposal site a "wetlands" subject to the jurisdiction of the Act and its companion California statute, Cal. Water Code § 13370 et seq. Following a meeting at the site between Company X, the EPA and the Regional Board, and after a public hearing, the Regional Board concluded that the area "cannot be defined as national wetlands. Therefore, an NPDES permit is not necessary."

The Amigos, an interested environmental group, would like to petition the State Board for review of the Regional Board's decision pursuant to Cal.Water Code § 13320. Amigos also wants to approach EPA with its concerns about the discharges.

You are the attorney for Amigos. What is your legal recommendation? What additional information do you need, if any?

Problem 4

The K reactor at the XYZ River Site ("SRS") is a nuclear reactor that has been used by the Department of Energy ("DOE") since 1954 to produce tritium and plutonium for nuclear weapons. The K reactor and two other nuclear reactors at the SRS, the L and P reactors, are currently the nation's only source of tritium. Tritium, an essential component of nuclear fusion or "hydrogen" bombs, gradually decays over time, and thus must be periodically replenished in the weapons in which it is used.

The K, L, and P reactors have been closed since April 1991 for maintenance and safety upgrades. In February 1993, DOE issued a formal decision announcing its plan to restart the K reactor in the Third Quarter of 1995. The restart date has been postponed several times, and current plans are to restart the reactor within the Fourth Quarter of 1995.

The K reactor is cooled by drawing water from the XYZ River, circulating it once through the reactor cooling system, and then discharging the water into Indian Grave Branch, a tributary of the XYZ River that eventually rejoins the river through Steel Creek, approximately six miles from the point of discharge. Pursuant to the Clean Water Act, 33 U.S.C.A. § 1311, DOE has a National Pollutant Discharge Elimination System ("NPDES") permit for the K reactor's cooling water discharge. DOE does not deny that the K reactor consistently violated the thermal limits of its NPDES permit from January 1, 1984 until it was shut down in April 1988, causing substantial environmental damage to approximately 670 acres of wetlands on SRS property. Further, DOE concedes that, if the K reactor is allowed to reopen as scheduled, the resulting effluent will still not meet the standards of the NPDES permit.

DOE is presently constructing a cooling tower that will allow the K reactor to meet the requirements of the NPDES permit. DOE represents that the tower will be completed no later than December 1995, and possibly earlier. Once construction of the tower is completed, the operation of the reactor must be temporarily suspended to allow the cooling system of the reactor to be tied in to the cooling tower. DOE represented to the trial court that this also would be accomplished by December 1995. DOE has pledged not to run the K reactor at over 50% of full power until the cooling tower is completed, but admits that even under this proviso, the effluent will not fall within the NPDES permit's thermal limitations.

Plaintiffs, the National Resources Defense Council, Inc. and the Energy Research Foundation (collectively, hereinafter, "NRDC"), contend that operation of the K reactor without the cooling tower would cause irreparable damage to the ecological system of the XYZ River. Specifically, NRDC claims that restarting the reactor would destroy the modest recovery that has been made in the 670 acres of wetlands that were previously damaged by the operation of the reactor. Also, NRDC contends that damage will spread to adjoining areas of the wetlands at the rate of up to 10–12 acres per year. Finally, NRDC claims that operation of the reactor will render up to 3000 additional acres of wetlands inhospitable as a habitat for various species of wildlife indigenous to the wetlands. NRDC brought a citizen suit under the Clean Water Act, 33 U.S.C.A. § 1365(a), to block DOE's reopening of the K reactor before completion of the cooling tower.

You are the judge. How do you decide? Please include the legal basis for your decision.

Problem 5

Mr. & Mrs. Jones, jointly owned two parcels of property located in Florida, adjacent to the East Bay, an arm of the Gulf of Mexico. Earlier, in 1994, the United States Army Corps of Engineers (the "Corps") determined that a major portion of one of the lots was a wetland. At that time the land was owned by Lewis W. Seller, who planned to build a retirement home on the property, had placed some red clay fill on the site in preparation to build a driveway. Upon discovery of this activity, the Corps issued a cease and desist order to Seller, which informed him that it would be necessary to obtain authorization from the Corps prior to placing fill material on real estate designated as wetlands. The order instructed him to either restore the area to its former state or to obtain an after-the-fact permit from the Corps. The unrestored property was later acquired by the Jones, with full knowledge of the problems surrounding its partial designation as wetlands. They continued to deposit dirt and sand fill on the wetlands area without a permit despite receiving two additional cease and desist letters. They also enlarged an existing drainage ditch causing it to become subject to the ebb and flow of the tide.

You are the attorney for the Jones. Please advise them of the civil and criminal penalties which may be associated with their activities, if any.

§ 8.4 OIL SPILLS

Section 311 of the CWA prohibits the discharge of harmful amounts of oil or hazardous substances into waters of the United States. Persons in charge of a facility or vessel from which there is such a discharge must notify the appropriate state agency and EPA or the Coast Guard immediately. Determinations of which substances are "hazardous" and what constitutes a "harmful" amount are made by EPA and published at 40 C.F.R. Parts 110 and 116–117. EPA regulations also require sources that have discharged oil in harmful quantities, or reasonably could be expected to do so, to prepare a "Spill Prevention Control and Countermeasure Plan" (SPCC), which may require installation of equipment for spill prevention and containment. *See* 40 C.F.R. Parts 112 and 114 (1990).

In response to the EXXON VALDEZ oil spill in Alaska and other spills, Congress amended § 311 when it enacted the Oil Pollution Act of 1990 (OPA), Pub. L. No. 101–380, 104 Stat. 484 (1990); 33 U.S.C.A. §§ 2701–2761 (West Supp. 1991), to consolidate and rationalize oil and hazardous substance spill response mechanisms under various federal laws. To accomplish this, OPA's provisions, among other things:

(1) strengthen the authority of the federal government under § 311 to order oil removal action or to conduct the removal action itself;

(2) create a single fund, the Oil Spill Liability Trust Fund, to pay for oil spill response and other costs;

(3) revise SPCC requirements for onshore facilities, offshore facilities, and vessels;

(4) impose more stringent standards for equipment and operation of tank vessels, including a requirement for double hulls;

(5) increase civil and criminal penalties for spills of oil and hazardous substances; and

(6) create a comprehensive federal liability program for all spills of oil to navigable waters, the exclusive economic zone (EEZ) and shorelines.

The exclusive economic zone is the ocean area established by Presidential Proclamation Numbered 5030, dated March 10, 1983. It roughly includes coastal waters out to 200 nautical miles.

Many of OPA's non-liability requirements will have an impact on the economic wellbeing on businesses involved in maritime and oil-related activities and are discussed below.

Financial Responsibility Requirements

Several OPA provisions make clear that responsible parties (RPs) of vessels, offshore facilities, and deepwater ports are the primary insurers against claims for removal costs and oil discharge damages. For vessels, RPs are persons owning, operating or chartering the vessel by demise, excluding cargo owners. For onshore facilities, RPs are the owners and operators. For offshore facilities, RPs include the lessee, permittee, or holder of the area in which the facility is located, or the holder of a right of use and easement for the area, excluding a governmental entity. For deepwater ports, licensees are RPs, and for pipelines, owners or operators. OPA § 1002(a)

These RPs must provide evidence of financial responsibility. OPA § 1016. Methods of satisfying financial responsibility requirements include evidence of insurance, a surety bond, a guarantee, or a letter of credit.

RPs for vessels over 300 gross tons, using any place subject to U.S. jurisdiction, must establish and maintain evidence of financial responsibility up to the maximum liability limitation applicable to the vessel. RPs also must demonstrate financial responsibility for vessels using the EEZ to tranship or lighter oil destined for a place subject to U.S. jurisdiction. For those RPs that own or operate more than one vessel, financial responsibility requirements for all vessels may be satisfied by providing evidence of responsibility to meet "the amount of the maximum liability applicable to the vessel having the greatest maximum liability." Id. RPs for offshore facilities and deepwater ports also must show financial responsibility.

These requirements are similar to CWA § 311, but OPA increases the liability limits and, hence, the level of financial responsibility that must be shown. Similar to § 311, vessels whose RPs violate these requirements may be denied access to U.S. ports and waters, seized, detained, forfeited, and sold.

SPCC Requirements

OPA revises CWA § 311(j)(5) concerning vessel and facility response plans. OPA § 4202. By February 1993, covered entities must prepare and submit for approval an SPCC plan, or cease handling, storing, or transporting oil. These requirements apply to tank vessels, offshore facilities, and any onshore facility that "because of its location, could reasonably be expected to cause substantial harm to the environment by discharging into or on the navigable waters, adjoining shorelines, or the exclusive economic zone [EEZ]."

The legislative history of these provisions makes clear that the SPCC requirements do not supersede or supplant similar planning and reporting requirements under other federal statutes, but must be harmonized with existing requirements.

Standards for Vessel Equipment and Construction

OPA includes provisions concerning vessel equipment and construction that will impose compliance costs on vessel owners. All newly-constructed tank vessels must have double hulls, and existing single hull tankers must be phased out beginning in 1995. Also, by 2010, all single hulled vessels over 5,000 gross tons will be prohibited from operating until conversion. OPA § 4115. By 2015, all vessels under 5,000 gross tons must be equipped with a double hull or an equally effective double containment system.

Two other vessel equipment standards apply to U.S. flag vessels and foreign vessels calling at U.S. ports or sailing in the EEZ. Tank vessels over thirty years old will be subject to periodic gauging of plate thickness, to determine compliance with minimum plating thickness requirements to be established by the Coast Guard. OPA § 4109. Vessels also must comply with minimum standards for overfill warning, oil tank level, and oil pressure monitoring devices. OPA § 4110.

§ 8.5   SAFE DRINKING WATER ACT

The Safe Drinking Water Act, 42 U.S.C.A. § 300f *et seq.* (West 1982 & Supp. 1991), provides substantive and procedural requirements for "public water supply systems." A "public water supply system" is defined as "a system for the provision of piped water for human consumption, if such system has at least fifteen service connections or regularly serves at least twenty-five individuals." 42 U.S.C.A. § 300f(4). The definition includes a broad range of facilities and systems that are not traditionally considered to be "water systems," such as schools, hotels, restaurants, gas stations, factories, private housing developments, and other facilities that have their own wells or surface water supplies and have the requisite number of service connections or persons. The statute, which was amended most recently in 1986, requires EPA to set strict requirements for levels of contaminants in drinking water and to impose monitoring, reporting, public notification, and other requirements on such water supply systems.

EPA's regulations divide public water systems into two classes: "community water systems" and "non-community water systems." Community water systems cover all water systems of the requisite size that serve year-round residents. Non-community water systems are defined as "public water system[s] that [are] not ... community water system[s]." 40 C.F.R. § 141.2 (1990). Under the original regulatory scheme, virtually all corporate water suppliers were considered non-community water systems, and, as such, were subject only to limited regulatory requirements.

Prompted by the 1986 amendments, EPA has modified its regulatory approach towards corporate suppliers. On July 8, 1987, EPA established new regulations that impose substantially more stringent requirements on "non-transient, non-community water systems" (NTNCWSs). *See* 52 Fed. Reg. 25,690, 25,694 col. 3 (July 8, 1987). Such systems include any "public water system that is not a community water system and that regularly serves at least 25 of the same persons over six months per year." 40 C.F.R. § 141.2 (1990). These NTNCWSs will be required to comply with a host of new tap standards (known as maximum contaminant levels or "MCLs") and monitoring, reporting, public notice, record-keeping, and other requirements that EPA plans to promulgate. To date,

EPA has issued final MCLs for approximately fifty contaminants and has proposed MCLs for several others. Certain NTNCWSs serving less than 3,300 people were required to begin sampling to determine compliance with certain MCLs by January 1, 1991. 40 C.F.R. § 141.24(g)(1990). In its latest promulgation of new MCLs, EPA also adopted a new drinking water monitoring strategy. 56 Fed. Reg. 3,526 (Jan. 30, 1991). The Standard Monitoring Framework will require compliance monitoring on a standard nine-year cycle for all systems, including NTNCWSs, beginning January 1, 1993. Water systems must continue to comply with any existing monitoring requirements until they are superseded by the new requirements. The new MCLs also may necessitate the installation of treatment facilities that may be relatively costly to construct, operate, and maintain. Furthermore, under the 1986 amendments, EPA has issued treatment technique regulations that may eventually require most NTNCWSs to install filtration and disinfection systems. 40 C.F.R. Part 141, subpart H (1990).

In addition, each MCL or treatment technique that EPA promulgates carries with it certain compliance monitoring requirements that are likely to be more burdensome than those that formerly applied. Aside from compliance monitoring requirements, certain NTNCWSs also may be required to conduct and report the results of periodic monitoring for as many as 51 unregulated contaminants. *See* 40 C.F.R. §§ 141.35, 141.40 (1990).

Finally, NTNCWSs are subject to strict public notification requirements. On October 28, 1987 EPA promulgated a rule requiring NTNCWSs to provide expeditious notice to their consumers, in the same modes used by community water systems, following virtually any violation of the drinking water regulations. 52 Fed. Reg. 41,534, 41,538 col. 2 (Oct. 28, 1987); *see* 40 C.F.R. §§ 141.32, 141.34, 141.35 (1990).

1. *Drinking Water Regulation*

ARCO OIL & GAS CO. v. EPA

14 F.3d 1431 (10th Cir.1993).

HOLLOWAY, CIRCUIT JUDGE.

ARCO Oil and Gas Company ("ARCO") petitions for review of a June 14, 1990 finding by the Administrator of the Environmental Protection Agency ("EPA") that EPA Region VIII properly required ARCO to obtain a Class I EPA permit pursuant to the Safe Drinking Water Act ("SDWA"), 42 U.S.C. 300f to 300f–26 (1988), for operation of ARCO's Garcia #1 injection well in Colorado. Prior to the EPA's reclassification of the well, the Garcia #1 had been regulated as a Class II well by the Colorado Oil and Gas Conservation Commission ("COGCC"). We affirm the EPA Administrator's decision and deny ARCO's petition.

I

Since 1982, ARCO has been operating a gas extraction and processing project in Huerfano County, Colorado. The gas extracted by ARCO consists primarily of carbon dioxide (96%) and is used for enhanced oil recovery in Texas. In connection with ARCO's extraction activity, certain waste fluids are brought to the surface and subsequently disposed of in ARCO's Garcia #1 well, an underground injection well. . . .

On April 12, 1985, the EPA Region VIII directed Arco to apply for a Class I permit for the Garcia #1 well. I R., Doc. 4. In so doing, the agency relied on its characterization of the waste fluids disposed of in the Garcia #1 as "hazardous," "industrial" or "municipal" waste within the meaning of 40 C.F.R. 144.6(a)(1)-(2)(defining Class I wells). Designation of the Garcia #1 as a Class I well would result in direct—and more burdensome—regulation of the well by the EPA rather than continued regulation by the COGCC. . . .

ARCO objected, contending that the Garcia #1's waste fluids should instead be characterized as fluids "brought to the surface in connection with . . . conventional oil or natural gas production" within the meaning of 40 C.F.R. 144.6(b)(1), resulting in continued Class II designation of the Garcia #1 and regulation by the COGCC. I R., Doc. 6. ARCO's position was, and is, premised on its interpretation of the phrase "natural gas production" in 144.6(b)(1) as broadly encompassing carbon dioxide production of the kind undertaken by ARCO in connection with its Huerfano project.

Despite its objection to the EPA's reclassification, ARCO hedged its bets and applied for a Class I permit. Four years later, EPA Region VIII issued the requested Class I permit, indicating that the designation of Garcia #1 as a Class I well was appropriate because "the definition of 'natural gas' for the purpose of the underground injection control regulations was intended to include only 'energy-related' hydrocarbon series gases such as methane and butane," not carbon dioxide. I R., Doc. 2, Addendum at 2. This reading of the regulations was consistent with the EPA's advice to the COGCC in early 1984 that "the meaning of 'natural gas' in our regulations includes low molecular weight flammable gases and not just any naturally occurring gas." I R., Doc. 15 at 2.

In accordance with applicable administrative procedures (40 C.F.R. 124.19), ARCO petitioned for review to the EPA Administrator. I R., Doc. 1. The Administrator denied ARCO's petition, concluding ARCO did not demonstrate "that the Region's permit determination [was] either clearly erroneous (legally or factually) or that it involved an important question of policy or exercise of discretion warranting review." Petitioner's Opening Brief, Attach. A.

In its petition to this court, ARCO requests that we set aside the EPA's construction of the SDWA and its regulations. In the alternative, if the EPA's construction is upheld and the reclassification of the Garcia #1 as a Class I well is affirmed, ARCO urges us to invalidate the reclassification pursuant to the Administrative Procedures Act as "arbitrary, capricious, an abuse of discretion, or otherwise not in accordance with law.... " 5 U.S.C. 706. According to ARCO, "there is no rational basis for regulating the disposal of produced water from carbon dioxide operations more stringently than the disposal of produced water from hydrocarbon operations." Petitioner's Opening Brief at 20–21.

* * *

We first address whether the EPA properly characterized waste fluids disposed of in ARCO's Garcia #1 injection well as "hazardous," "industrial" or "municipal" waste within the meaning of 40 C.F.R. 144.6(a)(1)-(2), or whether the waste fluids should have been characterized as fluids "brought to the surface in connection with ... conventional oil or natural gas production" under 144.6(b)(1).

The initial step in our analysis is to determine "whether Congress has directly spoken to the precise question at issue," i.e., whether Congress itself has defined the term "natural gas" in the context of the SDWA and its regulations. *Chevron,* 467 U.S. at 842; accord *Good Samaritan Hospital v. Shalala,* 124 L.Ed.2d 368, 113 S.Ct. 2151, 2157 (1993)("the starting point in interpreting a statute is its language"). In so doing, we must consider the language of the relevant statutory scheme as illuminated by "the provisions of the whole law, and ... its object and policy." *Aulston,* 915 F.2d at 589. *See also Sullivan v. Everhart,* 494 U.S. 83, 89, 108 L.Ed.2d 72, 110 S.Ct. 960 (1990)(" 'in ascertaining the plain meaning of the statute, the court must look to the particular statutory language at issue, as well as the language and design of the statute as a whole' ")(quoting *K Mart Corp. v. Cartier, Inc.,* 486 U.S. 281, 291, 100 L.Ed.2d 313, 108 S.Ct. 1811 (1988)).

1

The SDWA makes reference to "natural gas" in two sections, neither of which provides any clear insight into the intended meaning of that term. First, concerning underground injection of fluids brought to the surface in connection with oil and natural gas production, 300h(b)(2) of the statute provides:

> Regulations of the Administrator under this section for State underground injection control programs may not prescribe requirements which interfere with or impede—
>
> (A) the underground injection of brine or other fluids which are brought to the surface in connection with oil or natural gas production or natural gas storage operations, or
>
> (B) any underground injection for the secondary or tertiary recovery of oil or natural gas, unless such requirements are essential to assure that underground sources of drinking water will not be endangered by such injection.

(Emphasis added.) Second, with respect to the kinds of underground injection covered by the SDWA, 300h(d)(1) of the statute (a 1980 amendment) excludes injection of "natural gas for purposes of storage." (Emphasis added.) . . .

Apart from simply employing the term "natural gas," the SDWA does not elaborate on the term's intended meaning or scope. As we recognized in *Exxon,* "in the absence of more specific linguistic evidence of Congress's intention than the [mere] use of the term 'natural gas,' we cannot say on the basis of the statute's plain language that Congress has spoken directly to the question at issue." 970 F.2d at 761. Accordingly, in order to discern the intended meaning of the term used, we consult relevant secondary authorities, a task we previously undertook in both *Exxon,* 970 F.2d at 760–61, and *Aulston,* 915 F.2d at 589–90. However, because our definitional inquiry in this case is the same as in *Exxon* and *Aulston,* we need not repeat the analysis here. Suffice it to say, we are not aware of any post-Exxon authorities that in any way alter or affect our previous conclusions. Accordingly, we conclude, once again, that "the term 'natural gas' is ambiguous" and " 'fairly and reasonably has more than one meaning.' " *Exxon,* 970 F.2d at 760–61 (citation omitted); *Aulston,* 915 F.2d at 589 ("the operative word 'gas' has numerous meanings in common speech, in the natural sciences, and in various legal and industrial contexts").

Under the first prong of *Chevron,* then, the only remaining question is whether the legislative history reveals Congress' intent concerning the meaning and scope of the term "natural gas." Only if the legislative history is "extremely clear" in this regard is it determinative on the issue. *Exxon,* 970 F.2d at 761.

The legislative history of the SDWA sheds precious little light on the intended meaning and scope of the term "natural gas" as used therein. ARCO attributes great significance to the fact that the House Report accompanying the statute reveals a congressional intent to limit "constraints on energy production activities." H.R. Rep. No. 1185, 93d Cong., 2d Sess. 29 (1974), U.S. Code Cong. & Admin. News at 6484. Inasmuch as the carbon dioxide extracted by ARCO in connection with its Huerfano operation is used for enhanced oil recovery in Texas, ARCO portrays the operation—including that of the Garcia #1—as a favored "energy production activity" encompassed by the House Report. However, the report simply does not reveal whether Congress considered production of carbon dioxide one of the "energy production activities" to be protected, much less whether Congress viewed carbon dioxide as falling within the definition of "natural gas." . . .

Moreover, to the extent the report reflects a concern about excessive regulation of the oil and gas industry in general, it expressly subjects this concern to the overriding goal of protecting the quality of drinking water. Specifically, the report states that constraints which "could stop or substantially delay production of oil or natural gas" should be "as limited in scope as possible while still assuring the safety of present and potential sources of drinking water." *Id.* (emphasis added). As we observed in *Phillips Petroleum Co.:*

If a requirement "is essential to assure that underground sources of drinking water will not be endangered," then it is of no import whether underground injections are impeded. [42 U.S.C. 300h–1(c).] Indeed, the clear overriding concern of Congress was that of "assuring the safety of present and potential sources of drinking water." H.R.Report No. 1185, 93d Cong., 2d Sess. at 31, U.S.Code Cong. & Admin. News 1974 p. 6484.... The phrase " 'underground injection which endangers drinking water sources' is to be liberally construed so as to effectuate the preventative and public health protective purposes of the [SDWA]." [*Id.*]

Id. at 560.

Because Congress' concern about undue interference with oil and gas production is secondary and expressly subject to the primary goal of ensuring clean water, the legislative history cited by ARCO in no way mandates that we override the EPA and adopt the broad construction or the term "natural gas" urged by ARCO.... Instead, we conclude that neither the language of the SDWA, nor the relevant legislative history reveals a clear congressional intent to treat carbon dioxide as "natural gas" within the meaning of the Act.

2

We next consider whether the EPA's narrow interpretation of the term "natural gas" is "a permissible construction of the [SDWA]" (*Chevron,* 467 U.S. at 842–43), i.e., whether the construction is " 'rational and consistent with the statute.' " *Sullivan,* 110 S.Ct. at 964 (quoting *NLRB v. United Food & Commercial Workers,* 484 U.S. 112, 123, 98 L.Ed.2d 429, 108 S.Ct. 413 (1987)). Accord *Salt Lake City v. Western Area Power Admin.,* 926 F.2d 974, 981 (10th Cir.1991)("when an administering agency's interpretation of a statute is challenged, and traditional tools of statutory construction yield no relevant congressional intent, the reviewing court must determine if the agency's construction is a permissible one"); *Aulston,* 915 F.2d at 597 ("we will defer to the [EPA's] interpretation unless it is inconsistent with the purpose and policy of the [statute]"). As recently reiterated by the Supreme Court:

> Confronted with an ambiguous statutory provision, we generally will defer to a permissible interpretation espoused by the agency entrusted with its implementation. ... Of particular relevance is the agency's contemporaneous construction which "we have allowed ... to carry the day against doubts that might exist from a reading of the bare words of a statute." *FHA v. The Darlington, Inc.,* 358 U.S. 84, 90, 79 S.Ct. 141, 145, 3 L.Ed.2d 132 (1958).

Good Samaritan Hospital, 113 S.Ct. at 2159.

This is not the first time we have been asked to consider the propriety of EPA interpretations of the SDWA. In *Phillips Petroleum Co.,* we considered whether the EPA properly invoked the SDWA to make regulations applicable to Indian lands. We defined the relevant standard of review as follows:

Because Congress has conferred ... sweeping authority on the [EPA] Administrator, courts afford considerable deference to the EPA's construction of the statutory scheme that it is entrusted to administer.... We need not find that the EPA's interpretation is the only permissible construction but only that the EPA's understanding of the statute is a sufficiently rational one to preclude a court from substituting its judgment for that of the EPA.... "The need for judicial restraint is further heightened by the realization that courts do not share the [Administrator's] expertise in this highly technical area." [*American Mining Congress v. Marshall*, 671 F.2d 1251, 1255 (10th Cir.1982).]

Phillips Petroleum Co., 803 F.2d at 558 (citations omitted).

Affording the appropriate measure of deference to the EPA and recognizing the Administrator's technical expertise in this area, we find the agency's interpretation of "natural gas" as excluding carbon dioxide to be permissible and consistent with the purpose and policy of the SDWA. The overriding purpose of the Act is "to insure the quality of publicly supplied water" by "regulating the endangerment of underground drinking water sources." *Id.* at 547. Here, the EPA's narrow interpretation of the term "natural gas" has the effect of subjecting carbon dioxide injection wells to stricter regulatory scrutiny and placing a greater number of wells under direct EPA oversight. This result is consistent with the statutory goal of treating water pollution as "a national concern," the causes and effects of which are "national in scope" and which therefore require "national standards for protection of public health." *Id.* at 555 (quoting H.R. Rep. No. 1185, 93d Cong., 2d Sess. 1 (1974), U.S. Code Cong. & Admin. News 1974, p.6454). Because "Congress emphasizes a national policy of clean water[] so, therefore, must we in interpreting the statute." *Id.* Accordingly, we are compelled to conclude that the EPA's interpretation of "natural gas" in the context of the SDWA "gives effect to the central purposes of [the] statute[] and is consequently permissible." *Exxon*, 970 F.2d at 763. "We should be especially reluctant to reject the agency's current view which, as we see it, so closely fits 'the design of the statute as a whole and ... its object and policy.'" *Good Samaritan Hospital*, 113 S.Ct. at 2161 (quoting *Crandon v. United States*, 494 U.S. 152, 158, 108 L.Ed.2d 132, 110 S.Ct. 997 (1990))....

B

Lastly, we address ARCO's alternative contention that regulation of the Garcia #1 as a Class I well is arbitrary and capricious and therefore in violation of the Administrative Procedures Act, 5 U.S.C. 706. ARCO says the produced waters from its Sheep Mountain wells are "virtually identical" to waters from wells producing mainly hydrocarbon gases; equipment and production methods for those Sheep Mountain wells are "virtually identical" to equipment and production methods for wells producing mainly hydrocarbon gases; ARCO injects the largely carbon dioxide gas stream from the field into old oil wells to enhance oil recovery; and Congress intended to limit as much as possible regulatory constraints on the oil and gas industry. Thus, ARCO concludes it is arbitrary and capricious to impose Class I regulation on the Garcia #1 well.

We are not persuaded. A very similar argument was discussed in *Exxon*, 970 F.2d at 763, where Exxon argued that the common carrier requirement emanating from the Secretary's ruling would "unduly burden the carbon dioxide industry and create perverse incentives to produce artificial carbon dioxide." We disagreed, holding that Exxon's argument struck us as a matter more appropriately addressed to the agency, and that the challenge really centered on the wisdom of the agency's policy, rather than on whether it was a reasonable choice within a gap left by Congress. *Id.* Here we have already upheld the administrative interpretation that carbon dioxide is not "natural gas" within the meaning of 40 C.F.R. 144.6(b)(1) as proper. This essentially disposes of ARCO's contention on arbitrariness.

It is true that the APA provisions in 5 U.S.C. 706 have disjunctive protections against actions that are arbitrary, capricious or an abuse of discretion. Perhaps an individual ruling could run afoul of those restrictions and thus be invalid in some special case, but we see no showing of such a violation here. As we have noted:

> The arbitrary and capricious standard of review ... applies to informal rule-making proceedings such as those provided in the SDWA. [Citation.] The United States Supreme Court has explained the arbitrary and capricious standard as follows:
>
> > To make this finding the court must consider whether the decision was based on a consideration of the relevant factors and whether there has been a clear error of judgment. Although this inquiry into the facts is to be searching and careful, the ultimate standard is a narrow one. The court is not empowered to substitute its judgment for that of the agency.

Citizens to Preserve Overton Park v. Volpe, 401 U.S. 402, 416, 91 S.Ct. 814, 823–24, 28 L.Ed.2d 136 (1971)(citations omitted).

Phillips Petroleum Co., 803 F.2d at 558 (emphasis added).

The complaints made by ARCO do not warrant a holding that the EPA's decision to regulate the Garcia #1 as a Class I well was arrived at without a "consideration of the relevant facts," nor does the agency's decision reveal a "clear error of judgment" on the part of the EPA.

Accordingly, because we are "not empowered to substitute [our] judgment for that of the agency" *(id.),* we decline to second-guess the EPA's decision to regulate the disposal of carbon dioxide waste fluids—including underground injection by the Garcia #1—more stringently than the disposal of hydrocarbon waste fluids. Insofar as ARCO's challenge to the merits of the EPA's administrative decision "really centers on the wisdom of the agency's policy," the challenge "must fail." *Chevron,* 467 U.S. at 866.

For the foregoing reasons, ARCO's petition for review is DENIED.

HICKEY'S CARTING INC. v. UNITED STATES EPA

978 F.2d 66 (2d Cir.1992).

PER CURIAM:

Plaintiff Hickey's Carting, Inc. ("Hickey"), appeals from a final judgment of the United States District Court for the Eastern District of New York, Leonard D. Wexler, Judge, denying its request for cancellation or modification of an administrative order of respondent United States Environmental Protection Agency ("EPA" or "Agency") that requires Hickey to comply with the Safe Drinking Water Act ("Act" or "SDWA"), 42 U.S.C. § 300f et seq. (1988), and to pay a $17,000 penalty for past violations of the Act. On appeal, Hickey contends principally that the court erroneously denied it judicial review and should have found mitigating circumstances justifying a reduction in penalty. Finding no merit in any of Hickey's arguments, we affirm.

The material facts do not appear to be in dispute. Hickey, at its facility in Suffolk County, New York, operated three wells, consisting of one storm drain located under a trash compactor and two bottomless drums inserted into a storage floor area. These wells were in violation of 40 C.F.R. §§ 144.11 and 144.12 (1991), regulations promulgated by EPA under the Act. Suffolk County authorities notified Hickey of the violation twice in 1989. Obtaining no results, the County contacted EPA.

On June 26, 1990, several weeks after inspecting Hickey's premises, EPA notified Hickey by certified mail that the wells were in violation of SDWA provisions, and it directed Hickey to apply for a permit or submit a plan for closure. The notice stated that failure to comply within 30 days would subject Hickey to a civil penalty. Hickey did not respond. On August 10, 1990, EPA notified Hickey that it would be subject to penalties for failure to respond to the June 26 notice, and gave Hickey 20 days in which to respond to the August letter. Hickey did not respond.

On September 27, 1990, EPA notified Hickey that it proposed to enter an order requiring Hickey to, inter alia, cease injecting fluids into the wells and pay a $17,000 penalty for its past violations. This notice also informed Hickey of its right to oppose the proposed order:

> You are hereby offered an opportunity to submit written comments on the proposed order and/or to request a hearing, within 30 days of receipt of this notice, under 1423(c)(3), 42 U.S.C. § 300h–2(c)(3). EPA will conduct any hearing pursuant to the procedures required by this section of the Act. A hearing will formally offer you an opportunity to show cause why the enclosed order should not be issued, why its terms should be modified, or why the penalty should be reduced or waived. A request for a hearing must be in writing and must specify the factual and legal issues that you believe are in

dispute and the specific factual and legal grounds on which you intend to base your defense. . . .

* * *

If you choose not to request a hearing as provided above, EPA will review any comments submitted on the proposed order and will thereafter determine whether to issue the order.

Whether or not you request a hearing, you may confer informally with EPA concerning the alleged violations or the amount of the proposed penalty. . . .

PLEASE NOTE THAT A REQUEST FOR AN INFORMAL CONFERENCE DOES NOT EXTEND THE 30–DAY TIME PERIOD DURING WHICH COMMENTS AND/OR A WRITTEN REQUEST FOR A HEARING MUST BE SUBMITTED.

Hickey did not respond to this September 27 notice within the 30–day period.

Hickey finally met with EPA in mid-November 1990 in an effort to avert the proposed penalty. Negotiations were unsuccessful, and in March 1991 EPA issued its order requiring Hickey to, inter alia, cease injecting fluids into the wells and to pay a $17,000 penalty.

In May 1991, Hickey commenced the present action, seeking to have the EPA's order set aside on the grounds that it was not supported by substantial evidence and was an abuse of discretion. Hickey argued that it had made efforts to cure its violations and had discussed those efforts with EPA beginning in mid-November 1990, and that it therefore deserved to have the penalty reduced.

The district court, after hearing argument, denied Hickey's application, stating in part as follows: "I find substantial evidence for the hearing officer's decision. You cannot sit back and do nothing and then say oh, I was thinking about it and working on it without their knowledge." Judgment was entered denying the relief requested by Hickey and ordering it to pay the $17,000 penalty.

Hickey appeals, contending principally (a) that the court erroneously denied it judicial review because of its failure to seek an evidentiary hearing on EPA's proposed order, and (b) that the court should have found that Hickey's mitigation efforts justified a reduction in penalty. We reject all of its arguments.

First, we disagree with the characterization of the district court's decision as a ruling that Hickey was not entitled to judicial review. The court noted that Hickey had been given 30 days in which to respond to the proposed order and had defaulted—while continuing to use the wells—and ruled that EPA was not required to base agency decisions on conduct of Hickey that occurred after its default. The court itself reviewed EPA's decision and found, inter alia, that there was substantial evidence to support it.

On the merits, Hickey contends that the court should have required EPA to reduce its penalty on account of Hickey's efforts to cure its violations. We see no error. The district court is not to disturb an EPA order unless there is not substantial evidence on the record to support the Agency's finding of a violation or unless the penalty constitutes an abuse of discretion. 42 U.S.C. § 300h–2(c)(6)(1988). Hickey concedes that it violated the Act. Further, the record reveals that EPA arrived at the $17,000 penalty by applying its standard "penalty policy" assessment formula. In light of the lengthy duration of Hickey's uncured violations, its repeated failures to respond to notices from EPA and Suffolk County, and its eventual default in responding to the final notice, the district court properly declined to find that the Agency's refusal to consider Hickey's postdefault conduct was an abuse of discretion.

We have considered all of Hickey's arguments on this appeal and have found them to be without merit. The judgment of the district court is affirmed.

2. *Underground Injection Control (UIC)*

The SDWA establishes a regulatory mechanism to insure the quality of publicly supplied drinking water. Part C of the SDWA establishes a regulatory program designed to prevent the endangerment of underground drinking water sources. In particular, Part C envisions a joint federal-state system to regulate the discharge of pollutants by injection wells into underground water systems.

Underground injection is defined by the SDWA to mean the "subsurface emplacement of fluids by well injection." Section 1421(d)(1), 42 U.S.C.A. § 300h(d)(1). Underground injection is a potentially widespread hazardous waste disposal practice that poses serious threats to groundwater sources of drinking water. Congress was particularly aware of the potential adverse effects of oil and gas related injection. The House Committee on Interstate and Foreign Commerce noted the "energy production companies are using injection techniques to increase production and dispose of unwanted brines brought to the surface during production.... Part C is intended to deal with all of the foregoing situations insofar as they may endanger underground drinking water sources." H.R.Rep. No. 1185, 93d Cong., 2d Sess. 29 (1974).

The EPA was directed to promulgate regulations establishing the minimum requirements for state underground injection control programs. 42 U.S.C.A. § 300h. Specifically, section 1421 of the SDWA, 42 U.S.C.A. § 300h, provides in part:

(a)(1) The Administrator shall publish proposed regulations for State underground injection control programs within 180 days after December 16, 1974. Within 180 days after publication of such proposed regulations, he shall promulgate such regulations with such modifications as he deems appropriate. Any regulation under this subsection may be amended from time to time.

In requiring the EPA to promulgate minimum requirements for effective state programs to prevent underground injection which endangers drinking water sources, Congress intended to ratify EPA's policy of deep well injection. (*See* 39 Fed.Reg. 12,922–3, April 19, 1974). This policy was first adopted by the Federal Water Quality Administrator of the Department of the Interior on October 15, 1970. The policy opposes storage or disposal of contaminants by subsurface injection without strict control and clear demonstration that such wastes will not interfere with present or potential subsurface water supplies, contaminate interconnected surface waters or otherwise damage the environment.

Comm. on Interstate and Foreign Commerce, Safe Drinking Water Act, H.R.Rep. No. 1185, 93d Cong., 2d Sess. 29 (1974).

No injection is to be allowed that may endanger "drinking water sources." Section 1421(b)(1), 42 U.S.C.A. § 300h(b)(1). An injection is presumed to endanger drinking water sources if it might result in a public water system's "not complying with any national primary drinking water regulation" or might otherwise adversely affect the public health. Section 1421(d)(2), 42 U.S.C.A. § 300h(d)(2).

Individual states may apply and receive approval ("primacy") to implement their own underground injection control programs if they meet the minimum requirements established by the EPA's regulations. Section 1422, 42 U.S.C.A. § 300h–1. In order to be approved, a State program:

(A) shall prohibit, effective on the date on which the applicable underground injection control program takes effect, any underground injection in such State which is not authorized by a permit issued by the State (except that the regulations may permit a State to authorize underground injection by rule);

(B) shall require (i) in the case of a program which provides for authorization of underground injection by permit, that the applicant for the permit to inject must satisfy the State that the underground injection will not endanger drinking water sources, and (ii) in the case of a program which provides for such an authorization by rule, that no rule may be promulgated which authorizes any underground injection which endangers drinking water sources;

(C) shall include inspection, monitoring, record-keeping, and reporting requirements; and

(D) shall apply (i) as prescribed by § 300j–6(b) of this title, to underground injections by Federal agencies, and (ii) to underground injections by any other person whether or not occurring on property owned or leased by the United States.

Section 1421(b)(1), 42 U.S.C.A. § 300h(b)(1).

If a state fails to adopt or adequately enforce an approved underground injection control program, the EPA must install its own federally administered program for the state or that part of the state not covered by an EPA approved program. Section 1422(c), 42 U.S.C.A. § 300h–1(c).

WESTERN NEBRASKA RESOURCES COUNCIL v. EPA
793 F.2d 194 (8th Cir.1986).

FAGG, CIRCUIT JUDGE.

Western Nebraska Resources Council (WNRC) has filed a petition for review before this court. That petition challenges two actions of the Environmental Protection Agency (EPA or agency) taken under authority of Part C of the Safe Drinking Water Act, 42 U.S.C. §§ 300h to 300h–4. The statutory source of this court's jurisdiction to consider WNRC's petition is found at 42 U.S.C. § 300j–7(a).

I. BACKGROUND

The Safe Drinking Water Act (SDWA or Act) identifies underground injection wells as a potential source of pollution to our nation's underground sources of drinking water (i.e. aquifers). To protect these sources of drinking water, Congress directed EPA to promulgate regulations governing the adoption of state-enforced underground injection control (UIC) programs. 42 U.S.C. §§ 300h(a), 300h–1. As a part of these regulations, EPA was directed to establish minimum requirements that must be adopted and implemented by all EPA approved UIC programs. *Id.* §§ 300h(b), 300h–1(b)(1)(A)(i).

EPA promulgated regulations governing state UIC programs and establishing minimum requirements for these programs in 1980. *See* 45 Fed.Reg. 33,418–513 and 45,500–12 (1980) (presently codified as amended at 40 C.F.R. Parts 124, 144, 145, and 146). These regulations generally prohibit all new underground injection wells unless authorized by permit. *See* 40 C.F.R. § 144.31. Further, a permit may not be granted where underground injection may cause a violation of any national primary drinking regulation or may otherwise adversely affect human health. *Id.* § 144.12; *see* 42 U.S.C. § 300h(d)(2).

To further assure the protection of our nation's drinking water, the agency's UIC regulations included a broad definition of an underground source of drinking water. 45 Fed.Reg. at 33,424. That definition, as last amended in 1982, provides:

> Underground source of drinking water (USDW) means an aquifer or its portion:
>
>> (a)(1) Which supplies any public water system; or
>>
>> (2) Which contains a sufficient quantity of ground water to supply a public water system; and
>>
>> (i) Currently supplies drinking water for human consumption; or
>>
>> (ii) Contains fewer than 10,000 mg/l total dissolved solids; and (b) Which is not an exempted aquifer.

40 C.F.R. § 144.3.

Because that definition was sufficiently broad to encompass some aquifers that will never be used as sources of drinking water, EPA, as a corollary, also adopted criteria for identifying exempted aquifers. 45 Fed.Reg. at 45,502. These criteria, last amended in 1982, provide that an aquifer (or a portion of an aquifer) may be exempted if

(a) It does not currently serve as a source of drinking water; and

(b) It cannot now and will not in the future serve as a source of drinking water because:

(1) It is mineral, hydrocarbon or geothermal energy producing, or can be demonstrated by a permit applicant as part of a permit application for a Class II or III operation to contain minerals or hydrocarbons that considering their quantity and location are expected to be commercially producible.

(2) It is situated at a depth or location which makes recovery of water for drinking water purposes economically or technologically impractical;

(3) It is so contaminated that it would be economically or technologically impractical to render that water fit for human consumption; or

(4) It is located over a Class III well mining area subject to subsidence or catastrophic collapse; or

(c) The total dissolved solids content of the ground water is more than 3,000 and less than 10,000 mg/l and it is not reasonably expected to supply a public water system.

40 C.F.R. § 146.4. The identification of an exempt aquifer may, in certain circumstances, allow the underground injection of contaminants to be permitted where it would otherwise be prohibited.

Before underground injection will be permitted, however, the state, after notice and an opportunity for a public hearing, must itself identify and approve the aquifer exemption. *Id.* § 144.7(b)(3). That exemption (with one exception inapplicable here) must then be authorized by EPA as a revision to the state's approved UIC program. *Id.* §§ 144.7(b)(3), 145.32. Further, even after an aquifer exemption is approved by EPA, the construction and operation of any underground injection well will be subject to strict controls, *see, e.g., id.* §§ 144.21—144.70, 146.1—146.52, which will include a continuing prohibition on the movement of any contaminated fluids into nonexempt underground sources of drinking water, *see id.* § 144.12.

Once EPA had promulgated regulations governing state UIC programs, states began to submit applications to EPA seeking approval of their UIC programs. *See* 42 U.S.C. § 300h–1(b). To gain EPA approval, a state's application must demonstrate (1) that the state has adopted and will implement a UIC program consistent with the minimum requirements established by the agency's regulations; and (2) that the state will keep such records and make such reports as may be required by the agency. *Id.* § 300h–1(b)(1)(A)(i)–(ii). After a state's UIC program application is approved by rule, *see id.* § 300h–1(b)(2), the state retains primary enforcement responsibility (primacy) until EPA by rule determines otherwise. *Id.* § 300h–1(b)(3).

In March of 1982, the State of Nebraska submitted a UIC program application to EPA. The Nebraska UIC program submitted (and as eventually approved) contained a definition of an underground source of drinking water and criteria for identifying an exempt aquifer consistent with the regulations promulgated by the agency. If anything, the state's definition of an underground source of drinking water was broader than that required by the agency, and its criteria for identifying an exempt aquifer were slightly more restrictive than the criteria adopted by the agency. *See* 40 C.F.R. § 145.11(a).

Approximately two years later, on June 12, 1984, the agency, by publication, gave notice of its approval of the Nebraska UIC program application. 49 Fed.Reg. 24,133 (1984). As required by 42 U.S.C. § 300h–1(b)(2), the agency's approval of that program was made by rule and is presently codified at 40 C.F.R. § 147.1401. For purposes of judicial review, the regulation approving Nebraska's UIC program (and the UIC program itself) became effective on June 26, 1984. *See* 49 Fed.Reg. at 24,133; 40 C.F.R. § 147.1401.

Prior to final approval of the Nebraska UIC program, the state, on March 28, 1984, submitted a proposed aquifer exemption to EPA for its approval. That proposed revision had not been submitted as part of Nebraska's original UIC program proposal.

At the time Nebraska sought approval of the exemption, EPA approval of the overall Nebraska UIC program was already imminent. Rather than further delay final approval of the overall Nebraska UIC program while considering the state's proposed aquifer exemption, the agency gave final approval to the Nebraska UIC program, allowing Nebraska to achieve primacy. *See* 42 U.S.C. § 300h–1(b)(3). The agency then proceeded to review the state's aquifer exemption request as a proposed revision to Nebraska's UIC program. *See* 40 C.F.R. §§ 144.7(b)(3), 145.32. Under the circumstances of this case, the agency's decision to approve the Nebraska UIC program and then consider the proposed exemption in a separate administrative action, even if reviewable, was clearly reasonable.

The aquifer exemption requested by Nebraska was for a 3,000 acre portion of an aquifer located near Crawford, Nebraska (Chadron aquifer). That exemption was intended to make possible the granting of an underground injection well permit to Wyoming Fuel Company. In turn, that permit would authorize Wyoming Fuel Company to develop underground injection wells for the subsurface mining of uranium.

After receiving Nebraska's request, EPA gave public notice of the request, accepted public comments, and on June 21, 1984, conducted a public hearing at Crawford, Nebraska. After considering all available data and taking into account all public comments, the agency approved a very small portion of the requested aquifer exemption.

Specifically, rather than approve the 3,000 acre exemption requested, the agency approved only a 6.7 acre exemption. That narrow exemption was further limited to the lower portion of the Chadron aquifer formation. The overlying formations within the 6.7 acre area were not exempted. In granting a limited aquifer exemption, essentially intended to allow the establishment of a research and development area by Wyoming Fuel Company, EPA sought to verify conclusively the validity of its determinations before approving any more extensive aquifer exemption.

EPA's approval of the limited 6.7 acre exemption was published on February 7, 1985. 50 Fed.Reg. 5,253 (1985). For purposes of judicial review, the agency's decision was promulgated on February 21, 1985. *Id.*

WNRC filed its petition on April 4, 1985. WNRC challenges EPA's approval of the entire Nebraska UIC program as well as the agency's separate approval of the 6.7 acre aquifer exemption. Although related, these administrative determinations constituted separate and independent administrative actions and for purposes of judicial review must be treated as such.

* * *

III. EPA Approval of a Limited 6.7 Acre Aquifer Exemption

Before reviewing the merits of EPA's 6.7 acre aquifer exemption, we address briefly two preliminary contentions raised by WNRC. First, WNRC argues the Safe Drinking Water Act does not authorize EPA to grant aquifer exemptions under any circumstances. In advancing that argument, WNRC attacks directly the agency's authority to promulgate regulations dealing with (1) the identification of exempt aquifers, 40 C.F.R. § 144.7(b), (2) the substantial and nonsubstantial revision of state UIC programs, *id.* § 145.32(b), and (3) the criteria to be applied in determining what may be considered an exempt aquifer, *id.* § 146.4.

* * *

The decision of whether a proposed UIC program revision is substantial or nonsubstantial lies with the agency. Even if reviewable, that decision, made internally and without a hearing, could be reversed only upon a showing that the decision was "arbitrary, capricious, an abuse of discretion, or otherwise not in accordance with law." *See* 5 U.S.C. § 706(2)(A). No such showing has been made by WNRC.

We turn finally to the substance of EPA's approval of the 6.7 acre aquifer exemption. WNRC's challenge to the agency's approval of that exemption was filed within the 45–day time limit of section 300j–7(a) and thus may be considered by this court.

As stated, the 6.7 acre aquifer exemption approved by the agency was a nonsubstantial program revision that could be approved without formal rulemaking. The parties agree that our review of that action is limited to determining whether the agency's action was "arbitrary, capricious, an abuse of discretion, or otherwise not in accordance with law." 5 U.S.C. § 706(2)(A); *see Citizens to Preserve Overton Park v. Volpe,* 401 U.S. 402, 416, 28 L.Ed.2d 136, 91 S.Ct. 814 (1971); *see also Montgomery County v. United States Environmental Protection Agency,* 662 F.2d 1040, 1042 (4th Cir.1981) (applying the arbitrary and capricious test under section 300j–7 in a nonrulemaking context).

Review under the arbitrary and capricious standard is quite limited, and this court may not substitute its views for those of the agency.

Nevertheless, the agency must examine the relevant data and articulate a satisfactory explanation for its action including a "rational connection between the facts found and the choice made." In reviewing that explanation, we must "consider whether the decision was based on a consideration of the relevant factors and whether there has been a clear error of judgment."

Motor Vehicle Manufacturers Association v. State Farm Mutual Automobile Insurance Co., 463 U.S. 29, 43, 77 L.Ed.2d 443, 103 S.Ct. 2856 (1983) (citations omitted).

We note that WNRC has made no contention that the substantial evidence test should apply in this case. *See* 5 U.S.C. § 706(2)(E). Arguably, in cases in which the program revision is made by rule after a hearing required by statute, *see* 42 U.S.C. § 300h–1(b)(4), that standard may be applicable, *see* 5 U.S.C. § 706(2)(E), and could in some cases lead to a different result. However, even if WNRC had asserted the applicability of the substantial evidence test, our thorough review of the well-developed agency record convinces us that under either standard of review no basis exists for overturning the agency's determination.

In reaching its decision, EPA properly considered a number of relevant factors. These factors included (1) whether the 6.7 acre area meets the agency's criteria for exempted aquifers, (2) the various comments received from interested groups and individuals, (3) the impact of the proposed mining project on the environment in general and on surrounding sources of drinking water in particular, (4) the impact of the proposed mining project on human health, (5) restoration of the mining site and removal of contaminants from the exempt aquifer area, and (6) reasonable alternatives to the exemption as well as alternatives to the type of mining proposed by Wyoming Fuel Company. *See generally* 50 Fed.Reg. 5,253–59 (1985).

In its decision, the agency initially presented its determination that the 6.7 acre area exempted met the agency's criteria for classification as an exempt aquifer. *See* 40 C.F.R. § 146.4 (quoted ante slip op. at p. 3). First, after examining the data available to it, EPA found no one currently uses the 6.7 acre portion of the aquifer as a source of drinking water. In fact, the agency found that no water wells were currently located within the entire 3,000 acre area proposed by the state in its exemption request. *See* 50 Fed.Reg. at 5,253–54; *see also* 40 C.F.R. § 146.4(a).

Second, the agency found the 6.7 acre area to contain uranium and found further that this uranium is expected to be producible commercially. *See* 50 Fed.Reg. at 5,254; *see also* 40 C.F.R. § 146.4(b)(1). Coupled with its initial finding, this second determination was sufficient to place the 6.7 acre area within the agency's definition of an exempt aquifer. EPA, in the alternative, however, also found the 6.7 acre area to be so contaminated by uranium that it would be economically or technologically impractical to render the water in that area fit for human consumption. *See* 50 Fed.Reg. at 5,254; *see also* 40 C.F.R. § 146.4(b)(3).

On the basis of these findings, the agency concluded that the 6.7 acre area met the agency's criteria for identifying an exempt aquifer. Our review of the record convinces us that the agency's factual findings are supported by substantial evidence. Further, these findings place the 6.7 acre area within the agency's criteria for identifying an exempt aquifer, and as a result the agency's determination that the area meets these criteria is clearly reasonable.

The agency's determination that the 6.7 acre area of the Chadron aquifer met its exemption requirement did not end the agency's inquiry. Rather, as was appropriate under the circumstances, a number of other factors were considered and a number of other findings were made by EPA. First, the agency found that no significant adverse impact on human health or on the environment as a whole (including surrounding sources of water) would result from the limited 6.7 acre exemption. 50 Fed.Reg. at 5,255–57. The agency also concluded that the type of mining to be made possible by the limited exemption would enhance the long-term productivity of the uranium field while not adversely affecting the long-term productivity of the area as a whole. *Id.* at 5,257–58. Our review of the record again convinces us these findings, which flow from a reasoned exercise of the agency's particular expertise in the area of environmental safety, are supported by substantial evidence.

Based on these further findings, which involved those factors relevant to the agency's decision under the circumstances of this case, the agency granted a limited exemption primarily intended to allow the establishment of a research and development project. Further, as a part of its approval, the agency emphasized the exacting protective and restorative measures required to be implemented under the terms of the Wyoming Fuel Company permit. Finally, the agency emphasized that once the project was fully developed and more complete data available, a decision on any further exemption could then be made. In taking this action, the agency acted with reasoned caution and well within the scope of its permissible discretion. Thus, finding no basis on which to overturn the agency's determination, we reject WNRC's challenge to the 6.7 acre aquifer exemption.

IV. Conclusion

WNRC's challenge to EPA's approval of the Nebraska UIC program is dismissed as untimely. Further, WNRC's challenge to certain regulations promulgated by the agency is dismissed as untimely and as brought in the wrong forum. Finally, because the agency's action was supported by substantial evidence and was neither arbitrary, capricious, an abuse of discretion, nor otherwise contrary to law, WNRC's procedural and substantive challenges to the agency's approval of the 6.7 acre aquifer exemption are rejected.

NATURAL RESOURCES DEFENSE COUNCIL, INC. v. U.S. EPA

824 F.2d 1258 (1st Cir.1987).

Campbell, Chief Judge.

This is a petition to review the standards promulgated by the Environmental Protection Agency ("EPA") for the long-term disposal of high level radioactive waste under the Nuclear Waste Policy Act of 1982, 42 U.S.C. §§ 10101–10226 (1982). The states of Maine and Vermont, and the Natural Resources Defense Council, Conservation Law Foundation of New England, and Environmental Policy Institute were the original petitioners. Later Minnesota and Texas also challenged the same standards in separate proceedings. All suits have been consolidated in this circuit. A coalition of nuclear power utilities has been permitted to intervene.

I. Statutory Background

The challenged standards were written by the EPA to regulate harmful releases into the environment from radioactive waste stored in repositories planned for its disposal. (The standards also regulate releases occurring while the waste is being managed prior to its disposal.)

The waste in question is derived from the fissioning of nuclear fuel in commercial nuclear power plants and in military reactors. Some of the material is first reprocessed so as to recover unfissioned uranium and plutonium. Reprocessing results in a transfer of most of the radioactivity into acidic liquids that are later converted into solid radioactive waste. Some spent nuclear fuel is not reprocessed and itself becomes a waste. Collectively this waste is called high level waste ("HLW"). It is extremely toxic and will maintain its toxicity for thousands of years.

Recognizing the need for repositories within which to dispose safely of the growing amounts of HLW, Congress in 1982 enacted the Nuclear Waste Policy Act ("NWPA"), 42 U.S.C. §§ 10101 et seq. The Act provides for a coordinated effort within the federal government to design, construct and operate nationally at least two HLW disposal facilities. 42 U.S.C. § 10134(2)(A). Without foreclosing other disposal methods, Congress focused in the NWPA on the creation of repositories located deep underground. These will depend on the surrounding underground rock formations together with engineered barriers, to contain safely the radioactivity from these wastes. *See* H.R.Rep. No. 491, 97th Cong., 2d Sess. 29–34, reprinted in 1982 U.S.Code Cong. & Admin.News 3,792, 3,795–3,800.

The underground repositories are expected to be constructed using conventional mining techniques in geologic media such as granite, basalt (solidified lava), volcanic tuff (compacted volcanic ash) or salt. The solidified high level waste will be housed in canisters placed in boreholes drilled into the mine floor. When the repository is full, it will be backfilled and sealed. *See* Background Information Document for Final Rule at 4–1, 4–2.

In the NWPA, Congress prescribed a complex process for selecting the sites of the high level waste repositories. We shall summarize the selection process since it is relevant to an overall understanding of the standards in question. The Department of Energy ("DOE") begins the process by naming states containing "potentially acceptable sites." 42 U.S.C. § 10136(a). Within 90 days of identification, DOE must tell the governors and legislatures of the identified states where these sites are. Simultaneously, DOE must adopt guidelines for the selection of sites in various geologic media. 42 U.S.C. § 10132(a). DOE is then to apply the guidelines to the potentially acceptable sites and nominate at least five sites as suitable for characterization as candidate sites for the first repository. 42 U.S.C. § 10132(a), (b)(1)(A). Under this format, DOE in February of 1983 identified nine potentially acceptable sites (a Nevada site in tuff; a Washington site in basalt; two Texas sites in bedded salt; two Utah sites in bedded salt; one Louisiana site in a salt dome; and two Mississippi sites in salt domes). *See* Background Information Document for Final Rule at 4–2.

The Act required DOE to recommend to the President three of the nominated sites for detailed characterization studies. 42 U.S.C. § 10132(b)(1)(B). The President may then approve or disapprove a nominated site. 42 U.S.C. § 10132(c). In December 1984 DOE tentatively identified five sites for possible detailed site characterization. Three of these sites were formally recommended for detailed site characterization studies (Yucca Mountain site in Nevada; Deaf Smith County site in Texas; and the Hanford site in Washington). *See* Background Information Document at 4–5.

Nominated sites recommended and approved by the President are then to be characterized by DOE. 42 U.S.C. § 10133. After conducting the detailed site characterization studies, DOE must make a recommendation to the President concerning the final site approval. Before DOE recommends a site it must hold public hearings, must notify any affected state or Indian tribe, and must prepare an environmental impact statement for each site to be recommended to the President. The President must then submit to Congress an endorsement of one site from the three sites characterized and recommended by DOE. 42 U.S.C. § 10134(a)(2)(A).

The site recommended by the President becomes the approved site for the first repository after 60 days, unless the affected state or Indian tribe submits to Congress a notice of disapproval. 42 U.S.C. § 10135(b). If such notice of disapproval is received, the site is disapproved unless, during the first 90 days after receipt of the notice, Congress passes a resolution of repository siting approval. 42 U.S.C. § 10135(c). The same site approval process is prescribed for the selection of a second federal repository site.

Several federal agencies share responsibility for building, licensing and laying down standards for the HLW repositories. The Department of Energy is to design, build and operate each federally owned repository. 42 U.S.C. § 10134. However, the Nuclear Regulatory Commission ("NRC") has responsibility to license the repositories. 42 U.S.C. § 10134(d). Under its licensure powers, the NRC regulates the construction of the repositories, licenses the receipt and possession of high level radioactive waste at the repositories, and authorizes the closure and decommissioning of repositories. See 42 U.S.C. § 10141(b).

The EPA also has a major regulatory role. The Act provides that EPA,

> pursuant to authority under other provisions of law, shall, by rule, promulgate generally applicable standards for protection of the general environment from offsite releases from radioactive material in repositories.

42 U.S.C. § 10141(a) ... The language, "pursuant to authority under other provisions of law," refers to the EPA's responsibility and authority under the Atomic Energy Act of 1954, 42 U.S.C. § 2201(b). The Reorganization Plan No. 3 of 1970 (which was the vehicle used by the executive branch to organize the newly formed Environmental Protection Agency), transferred to the EPA certain functions of the Atomic Energy Commission to the extent that such functions of the Commission consist of establishing generally applicable environmental standards for the protection of the general environment from radioactive material.

Reorganization Plan No. 3 of 1970, 3 C.F.R. § 1072 (1966–70 compilation).

It is these generally applicable HLW environmental standards, recently promulgated by the EPA pursuant to the directive of the NWPA, which we are now called upon to review. DOE must follow these standards when siting, designing, constructing and operating the repositories. See 10 C.F.R. Part 960 (1987). The NRC must likewise obey them when licensing the repositories. See 10 C.F.R. Part 60 (1987). EPA's standards will also apply to defense-related DOE facilities (not licensed by the NRC) which store and dispose of defense-related waste.

II. The High Level Waste Environmental Standards

The HLW environmental standards have two parts. Subpart A, 40 C.F.R. § 191.01–.05 (1986), entitled "Environmental Standards for Management and Storage," sets individual exposure limits from radiation releases during the management, interim storage, and preparation for disposal of the radioactive wastes. Subpart A requires that the management and storage of HLW during this phase be conducted in such a manner as to provide reasonable assurances that the total annual exposure to any individual member of the public shall not exceed a stated limit (25 millirems to the whole body, 75 millirems to the thyroid, and 25 millirems to any other critical organ), 40 C.F.R. § 191.03. Subpart A also allows the EPA to issue alternative standards for waste management and storage operations at DOE disposal facilities that are not regulated by the NRC (i.e., DOE defense-related facilities), 40 C.F.R. § 191.04.

Subpart B, 40 C.F.R. § 191.11–.18 (1986), entitled "Environmental Standards for Disposal," is intended to ensure long-term protection of public health and the environment from releases of radiation after the HLW has been stored in the chosen manner. Although this subpart was developed having in mind storage at underground repositories, the standards are said to apply also to any other disposal method that may be chosen. . . .

Subpart B comprises four different types of environmental standards. The first type is the general containment requirements, 40 C.F.R. § 191.13. These require that nuclear waste disposal systems be designed to provide a reasonable expectation, based on performance assessment, that the cumulative releases of radiation to anywhere in the "accessible environment," for 10,000 years after disposal, shall not exceed certain designated levels. . . .

The term "accessible environment" is defined as the atmosphere; land surfaces; surface waters; oceans; and all of the "lithosphere" that is beyond the "controlled area." 40 C.F.R. § 191.12(k). The "lithosphere," as defined, includes the entire solid part of the earth below the surface, including any ground water contained within it. 40 C.F.R. § 191.12(j). The "controlled area" is the surface and underground area (and any ground water found therein) immediately surrounding the repository "that encompasses no more than 100 square kilometers and extends horizontally no more than 5 kilometers in any direction" from the disposed waste. 40 C.F.R. § 191.12(g).

These definitions taken together show that the general containment requirements limit the total, cumulative releases of radiation, for 10,000 years, anywhere in the environment, outside the controlled area. Within the controlled area itself, the general containment requirements are inapplicable and, therefore, they place no limits on radiation releases.

An example of how the general release limits apply is found in the limits for uranium. The repositories must be designed to give reasonable assurance that for the radionuclide uranium (and all its isotopes) the total radiation release, over a 10,000–year period, to the entire accessible environment (including any ground water) must be less than 100 curies (per 1,000 metric tons of heavy metal waste disposed of).... Similar limits are established for other radionuclides, e.g., Americium–241, –243; Plutonium–238, –239, –240, –242. *See* Table of Release Limits for Containment Requirements, 40 C.F.R. Part 191, Appendix A (1986). According to the EPA, the above general containment requirements constitute the principal protection mechanism of the HLW environmental standards. If cumulative releases are within these levels, overall adverse health effects upon the general population will be low. The EPA estimates that the general containment requirements limit population risks from the disposal of these wastes to "no more than the midpoint of the range of estimated risks that future generations would have been exposed to if the uranium ore used to create the wastes had never been mined." 50 Fed.Reg. 38,072, col. 1 (Sept. 19, 1985).

The second type of environmental standard found in Subpart B is the assurance requirements, 40 C.F.R. § 191.14. These are a kind of practical backup to the cumulative release requirements just mentioned.

The assurance requirements provide, among other things, that "active institutional controls" over disposal sites be maintained for as long a period of time as is practicable after disposal. 40 C.F.R. § 191.14(a). (Active institutional controls include actions like controlling public access to a site, performing maintenance operations and cleaning up releases.) Other facets of the assurance requirements are as follows: that disposal arrangements be monitored in the future to detect deviations from expected performance, 40 C.F.R. § 191.14(b); that there be permanent markers, records and archives (so-called "passive institutional controls") to indicate to future generations the presence and location of the dangerous waste, 40 C.F.R. § 191.14(c); that disposal systems not rely on just one type of barrier to isolate waste, but rather employ both engineered and natural barriers, 40 C.F.R. § 191.14(d); that repository sites be selected that avoid areas where it is reasonable to expect future exploration for scarce or easily accessible resources, 40 C.F.R. § 191.14(e); that disposal systems be such that, for a reasonable time after disposal, most of the radioactive waste can be removed, 40 C.F.R. § 191.14(f).

The assurance requirements are applicable only to disposal facilities that are not regulated by the NRC (i.e., certain DOE national defense-related facilities) because in its comments on the originally proposed rule, the NRC objected to inclusion of the assurance requirements, arguing that they transcended the EPA's authority to set generally applicable environmental standards. The NRC felt that the assurance requirements were not environmental standards at all but rather were simply ways of ensuring compliance with environmental standards. Since it is the NRC's responsibility to make sure that the repositories comply with the different regulations, the NRC saw the EPA's assurance requirements as an intrusion upon the NRC's jurisdiction. The agencies ultimately resolved the dispute by (1) making the EPA's assurance requirements applicable only to facilities not licensed by the NRC, and (2) by having the NRC modify its regulations where necessary to incorporate the essence of the EPA's assurance requirements. *See* 50 Fed.Reg. 38,072, col. 3.

When the EPA published a first draft of its standards, Subpart B only included the two standards so far described (general containment requirements and assurance requirements). *See* Proposed Rule, 40 C.F.R. Part 191, 47 Fed.Reg. 58,196 (Dec. 29, 1982). The EPA at first believed that these two proposed standards—aimed to keep the total radiation release over a 10,000–year period below specified safe limits— would suffice. Later, however, it was persuaded to add so-called individual protection requirements, to deal with the possibility that radioactivity might be concentrated in specific areas. Release limits designed to protect individuals were thought necessary because, while overall releases to the environment as a whole would be within tolerable limits, particular individuals might end up being exposed to excessively large doses of radiation: for example, radiation from waste eventually released into, and concentrated in, ground water that is in the immediate vicinity of a repository. The EPA explained that

> Since ground water generally provides relatively little dilution, anyone using such contaminated ground water in the future may receive a substantial radiation exposure (e.g., several rems per year or more). This possibility is inherent in collecting a very large amount of radioactivity in a small area.

See 50 Fed.Reg. 38,077, col. 3. Therefore, after the notice and comment period, two additional provisions, the individual protection requirements, and the ground water protection requirements, were added to Subpart B of the final rule. These were mainly intended to protect individuals located near a repository who might be exposed to contamination emanating from the site.

The individual protection requirements, 40 C.F.R. § 191.15, require that disposal systems be designed to provide a reasonable expectation that, for 1,000 years after disposal, the annual radiation exposure to any member of the public in the accessible environment shall not exceed 25 millirems to the whole body or 75 millirems to any organ. The standard requires that in assessing the anticipated performance of a repository, all potential so-called "pathways" of radiation releases from the repository must be considered. The term "potential pathway" represents the expected scenario of how the released radioactivity will travel from the repository to the accessible environment and ultimately to individuals. There are various possible pathways which could result in exposures to individuals. These possible pathways include, for example, direct releases via seepage to the land surface and then to food crops ingested by man; or similar releases travelling to a river or to an ocean and then to fish which man would ingest; or releases to ground water that is used for drinking. *See* Background Information Document for Final Rule at Chapter 7.

As discussed above, the Agency was concerned about individual exposures especially because of the possibility that radiation might be released to and become concentrated in ground water, some of which might permeate even the rock surrounding a repository and might find its way, in time, to supplies of ground water beyond the site. Since ground water contaminated by seepage from the site might be used for drinking water, the individual protection requirements expressly require that in determining whether a repository will comply with the annual exposure limits, the assessments must assume that individuals consume all their drinking water (two liters per day) from any "significant source" of ground water . . . outside of the controlled area. This express requirement places an indirect limit on releases to ground water outside of the controlled area (the "controlled area" being, as already described, the area occupied by the repository and a specified surface and below-ground area surrounding the repository, *see* definition supra).

The fourth section of Subpart B is the special source ground water protection requirements, 40 C.F.R. § 191.16. The term "ground water protection requirements" is somewhat misleading. The provision does not protect ground water generally but only ground water of a very special type within or very near "controlled areas." Thus these requirements apply only to Class I ground waters, as defined by the EPA's Ground–Water Protection Strategy, . . . that also meet the following three conditions:

> (1) They are within the controlled area or near (less than five kilometers beyond) the controlled area; (2) they are supplying drinking water for thousands of persons as of the date that the Department [of Energy] selects the site for extensive exploration as a potential location of a disposal system; and (3) they are irreplaceable in that no reasonable alternative source of drinking water is available to that population.

See 40 C.F.R. § 191.12(n).

The radiation concentration limits set by this rule are similar to the maximum radiation concentration limits established under the Safe Drinking Water Act, 42 U.S.C. §§ 300f–j, for community water systems. *See* 40 C.F.R. Part 141. As with the individual protection requirements, the ground water protection requirements will apply only for the first 1,000 years after disposal.

Class I ground waters . . . are defined as ground waters that are highly vulnerable to contamination because of local hydrological characteristics and that are also either irreplaceable (i.e., there is no reasonable alternative source of drinking water) or vital to a particularly sensitive ecological system. Environmental Protection Agency, Ground–Water Protection Strategy at 5–6 (August 1984).

The ground water protection requirements thus apply to an extremely narrow category of ground water found within, or within five kilometers of, the repository site. The Agency explained that the ground water protection requirements provision is necessary and adequate to avoid any significant degradation of this important ground water resource. *See* 50 Fed.Reg. 38,074 (Sept. 19, 1985). The practical effect of these requirements seems less to provide ongoing regulation than simply to deter the choosing of a site containing ground water of this especially valuable kind upon which "thousands of persons" already depend. If this were the real purpose, however, the EPA did not say so in so many words.

* * *

IV. Do EPA's Regulations Violate the Safe Drinking Water Act?

Part C of the Safe Drinking Water Act, 42 U.S.C. § 300h (1982) ("SDWA"), indicates that the EPA has a duty to assure that underground sources of drinking water will not be endangered by any underground injection. Petitioners argue here that endangerment of such drinking water is bound to result if HLW is disposed of, underground, under standards no more stringent than the EPA's current HLW regulations. Since violations of the SDWA are inevitable, so petitioners argue, the present regulations are "not in accordance with law" and hence invalid.

To understand this argument we must first look at the SDWA, an Act which preceded the NWPA. The SDWA was enacted in 1974 to assure safe drinking water supplies, protect especially valuable aquifers, ... and protect drinking water from contamination by the underground injection of waste. The SDWA required the EPA to promulgate standards to protect public health, by setting either (1) maximum contaminant levels for pollutants in a public water supply, or (2) a treatment technique to reduce the pollutants to an acceptable level if the maximum contaminant level is not economically or technologically attainable. Maximum contaminant levels are to be established at a level having no known or adverse human health effect, with an adequate margin for safety. 42 U.S.C. § 300g–1(b)(1)(B). The EPA has established maximum contaminant levels for man-made radionuclides, *see* 40 C.F.R. § 141.16, as well as a maximum contaminant level for naturally occurring radium, *see* 40 C.F.R. § 141.15.

These standards apply to "public water systems" which regularly supply water to 15 or more connections or to 25 or more individuals at least 60 days per year. 42 U.S.C. § 300f(4); 40 C.F.R. § 141.1(e). The public water system has the responsibility to make sure the water it supplies meets these limits. In effect, the community water system must either clean up existing water if below standard, or find a new water supply which meets the maximum contaminant levels. The EPA is given certain powers to enforce its standards. 42 U.S.C. § 300g–3(b).

The SDWA also authorizes EPA to designate, on its own initiative or upon petition, an area as having an aquifer which is the sole source of the area's water supply and which would create a significant hazard to public health if contaminated. Once an area is so designated, no federal assistance may be provided for any project in the area which EPA determines may contaminate the aquifer. *See* 42 U.S.C. § 300h–3(e).

The SDWA's only provision for directly regulating pollution-causing activities is found in Part C, 42 U.S.C. § 300h. There Congress sought to protect underground sources of drinking water from what are termed "underground injections." Underground injection is the subsurface emplacement of contaminating fluids ... by well injection. 42 U.S.C. § 300h(d)(1). Part C requires the EPA to promulgate regulations governing underground injection control programs.

The EPA is directed to publish a list of each state for which an underground injection control program would be necessary to assure that underground injection would not endanger drinking water sources. 42 U.S.C. § 300h–1(a). The EPA has listed all states as needing underground injection control programs. 40 C.F.R. § 144.1(e).

The EPA is also required to promulgate regulations governing state underground injection control programs to ensure that the state programs prevent underground injection which could endanger drinking water sources. 42 U.S.C. § 300h(a)(1), (b)(1). If a state program does not comply with the EPA's regulations, the EPA itself is to promulgate a regulatory program for that state and enforce compliance. 42 U.S.C. § 300h–1(c). To be approved by EPA, a state control program has to meet certain standards. It must prevent underground injection unless authorized by permit or rule; it may authorize underground injection only where it is demonstrated that the injection will not endanger drinking water sources; and it shall include inspection, monitoring, recordkeeping and reporting requirements. 42 U.S.C. § 300h(b)(1)(A)–(C). State regulatory programs (as well as any EPA regulations for non-complying states) apply to underground injections by federal agencies as well as all others. 42 U.S.C. § 300h(b)(1)(D).

In requiring EPA to regulate state underground injection control programs, Congress restrained the EPA's authority in several ways in order to accommodate existing state programs and avoid disrupting oil and gas production. EPA's regulations may not interfere with or impede the production or recovery of oil or natural gas, unless such requirements are essential to assure that underground sources of drinking water will not be endangered by such injection. 42 U.S.C. § 300h(b)(2). EPA's regulations are to reflect the variations in geologic, hydrological or historical conditions between the states. 42 U.S.C. § 300h(b)(3)(A). To the extent feasible, EPA is not to promulgate rules which unnecessarily disrupt state underground injection control programs that were earlier in effect. 42 U.S.C. § 300h(b)(3)(B). Congress made it clear, however, that, despite the deference the EPA was to afford the states, the goal of protecting underground drinking water was to be preeminent. The SDWA states,

> Nothing in this section shall be construed to alter or affect the duty to assure that underground sources of drinking water will not be endangered by any underground injection.

42 U.S.C. § 300h(b)(3)(C). This language in particular, petitioners say, establishes that the EPA has an overriding statutory mandate, unaffected by the NWPA, to protect underground drinking water against endangerment.

The SDWA defines what is meant by the term "endanger":

Underground injection endangers drinking water sources if such injection may result in the presence in underground water which supplies or can reasonably be expected to supply any public water system of any contaminant, and if the presence of such contaminant may result in such system's not complying with any national primary drinking water regulation or may otherwise adversely affect the health of persons.

42 U.S.C. § 300h(d)(2).

Petitioners assert that the EPA, in promulgating the HLW standards, has violated this so-called "no endangerment mandate" because its rules will allow underground injections that result in radiation contamination of underground drinking water supplies.

Analysis of petitioners' argument requires us to address several questions: (1) whether storage of HLW in underground repositories will constitute an "underground injection" as that term is used in the SDWA; (2) whether the EPA's HLW standards sanction activities that will "endanger drinking water," as that phrase is used in the SDWA; and (3) whether, if the two previous questions are answered in the affirmative, EPA's HLW regulations are contrary to law or, if not, are nonetheless arbitrary and capricious. We shall deal with each of these questions in turn.

(1) Does Storage Of HLW In Underground Repositories Constitute Underground Injection?

What petitioners call the no endangerment provision of the SDWA, 42 U.S.C. § 300h(b)(3)(c), indicates that the EPA has a duty "to assure that underground sources of drinking water will not be endangered by any underground injection." For the Agency to have violated that duty by adopting the present HLW regulations, it is necessary that the proposed placing of HLW in underground repositories constitute an "underground injection." The SDWA defines underground injection as the "subsurface emplacement of fluids by well injection." 42 U.S.C. § 300h(d)(1) (emphasis added). The EPA, in its regulations enacted pursuant to the SDWA, has defined the terms "fluids" and "well injection."

Well injection is the "subsurface emplacement of fluids through a bored, drilled or driven well; or through a dug well, where the depth of the dug well is greater than the largest surface dimension." 40 C.F.R. § 146.3.

The Department of Energy, in its Mission Plan, has described how the HLW will be disposed of underground. The HLW will be removed from transportation casks, packaged and then transferred underground through the waste-handling shaft. "Once underground, the wastes will be emplaced in boreholes...." Mission Plan at 33. Thus it seems that waste will be "emplaced underground through a bored, drilled or driven shaft."

The EPA has defined the term "fluids" broadly as including a "material or substance which flows or moves whether in a semi-solid, liquid, sludge, gas or any other form or state." 40 C.F.R. § 146.3. This definition was taken directly from the legislative history which made it clear that "the definition of 'underground injection' is intended to be broad enough to cover any contaminant which may be put below ground level and which flows or moves, whether the contaminant is in semi-solid, liquid, sludge, or any other form or state." H.R.Rep. No. 1185, 93d Cong., 2d Sess., reprinted in 1974 U.S.Code Cong. & Admin.News 6454, 6483. The definition of high level waste in the NWPA shows that at least some of the waste material to be disposed of originates in a liquid form. The term "high-level radioactive waste" means—

> (A) the highly radioactive material resulting from the reprocessing of spent nuclear fuel, including liquid waste produced directly in reprocessing and any solid material derived from such liquid waste that contains fission products in sufficient concentrations....

42 U.S.C. § 10101(12). According to the EPA, the waste to be stored underground will be converted, before storage underground, into a solid. *See* Background Information Document at 3–4. This does not mean that the contemplated waste disposal system is not an underground injection, since the definition of fluids (following the directive in the legislative history, *see* supra) is very broad and includes waste "in any other form or state" if it flows or moves. 40 C.F.R. § 146.3. The dangerous component of this waste, i.e., the radiation, regardless of whatever "form or state" it is emitted from, will flow or move, thus having the capacity to do harm to drinking water sources far distant from the original site as more conventional injected fluids would do. The HLW waste rules "apply to radionuclides that are projected to move into the 'accessible environment' during the first 10,000 years." *See* Preamble, 50 Fed.Reg. 38,071, col. 2. The definition of "barrier" in the regulations includes a structure which prevents or substantially "delays movement" of water or radionuclides toward the accessible environment. 40 C.F.R. § 191.12(d).

The Arizona Nuclear Power Project, et al., intervenors in this case, argue that disposal of this radioactive waste underground is not the "type" of underground disposal that Congress was concerned with when it enacted Part C of the SDWA. Intervenors claim that the type of underground injection which disturbed Congress was a method whereby contaminants were injected into the subsurface and allowed to disperse freely into the general environment. Intervenors assert that the type of disposal contemplated by the HLW rules is different because the waste will be packaged in containers, and will be surrounded by barriers that are designed to isolate this waste from the environment. Thus, they conclude, Part C does not apply to this disposal system.

While Congress may have been especially concerned with a different type of underground disposal when it passed Part C of the SDWA, this does not negate its overall intent to protect future supplies of drinking water against contamination. Unusable ground water is unusable ground water no matter whether the original source of the pollution arrived in a loose, free form manner, or in containers injected into the ground. We find no language in the SDWA showing that Congress meant to regulate only certain forms of underground pollution, while overlooking other forms of contamination of ground water via underground injection. Indeed, the legislative history indicates that the phrase "underground injection which endangers drinking water sources" was to have the broadest applicability:

> It is the Committee's intent that the definition be liberally construed so as to effectuate the preventative and public health protective purposes of the bill. The Committee seeks to protect not only currently-used sources of drinking water, but also potential drinking water sources for the future.... The Committee was concerned that its definition of "endangering drinking water sources" also be construed liberally. Injection which causes or increases contamination of such sources may fall within this definition even if the amount of contaminant which may enter the water source would not by itself cause the maximum allowable levels to be exceeded. The definition would be met if injected material were not completely contained in the well, and if it may enter either a present or potential drinking water source, and if it (or some form into which it might be converted) may pose a threat to human health or render the water source unfit for human consumption.

H.R.Rep. No. 1185, 93d Cong., 2d Sess., reprinted in 1974 U.S.Code Cong. & Admin.News at 6484.

We believe that the narrow and constrained reading of Part C of the SDWA advocated by intervenors would do violence to the intent of Congress. We decline that reading.

We conclude that the primary disposal method being considered, underground repositories, would likely constitute an "underground injection" under the SDWA.

(2) Do The Regulations Under Review Sanction Activities That Will "Endanger Drinking Water"?

Part C of the SDWA, 42 U.S.C. § 300h(b)(3)(c), speaks of the EPA's duty "to assure that underground sources of drinking water will not be endangered by any underground injection." .... Assuming, as discussed above, that the planned disposal of HLW in underground repositories amounts to "underground injection," will such injection, if carried out under the EPA's current HLW standards, "endanger" underground sources of drinking water? We believe the answer is "yes."

As noted, the term "endanger" is defined in the SDWA to include any injection which may result in the presence "in underground water which supplies or can reasonably be expected to supply any public water system of any contaminant ... if the presence of such contaminant may result in such system's not complying with any national primary drinking water regulation." 42 U.S.C. § 300h(d)(2). Measured against this definition, the HLW standards permit contamination of most categories of underground water within the so-called controlled area without restriction of any type. More fundamentally, they permit water supplies outside the controlled area to be contaminated by radiation up to individual exposure levels that exceed the levels allowed in national primary drinking water regulations. It follows that the HLW regulations under review not only do not "assure" the non-endangerment of underground sources of drinking water, but sanction disposal facilities allowing certain levels of endangerment as that term is used in the SDWA....

* * *

(3) Does Noncompliance With SDWA Make The Regulations Contrary To Law Or Arbitrary And Capricious?

We have determined in sections (1) and (2) above that the challenged HLW regulations pertain to underground injection, and that the standards they provide will allow underground sources of drinking water to be "endangered" within the meaning of the SDWA. We must now ask whether the foregoing conclusions cause the current regulations to be contrary to law or arbitrary and capricious. The EPA asserts that the no endangerment provision of the SDWA applies to the EPA only in its role as administrator under the SDWA. In its different role as regulator of the disposal of high level waste under the NWPA, the Agency argues that it is free to adopt standards different from the ground water standards established under SDWA. EPA also makes other arguments supporting the proposition that the SDWA is irrelevant to our review of the HLW standards. *See* infra.

In analyzing the relation between the SDWA's no endangerment provision and the HLW standards, we divide our discussion into two parts: (A) Non-compliance with the SDWA in the controlled area, and (B) Non-compliance outside the controlled area.

Briefly summarized, our conclusion in respect to (A) is that when enacting the Nuclear Waste Policy Act of 1982, 42 U.S.C. §§ 10101–10226 (1982), Congress was aware that the area in immediate proximity to the buried HLW would likely be dedicated as a natural protective barrier, and hence could become contaminated. We read the NWPA as containing, by implication, authority for the EPA to depart from SDWA standards in any "controlled area." It follows that insofar as the regulations under review permit radiation contamination of ground water located within the controlled area itself, they are not contrary to law nor do we find them to be arbitrary and capricious.

In respect to (B) our conclusion is different. We find no evidence that Congress expected the HLW standards to permit underground sources of drinking water outside the controlled area to be degraded to levels beneath the standards EPA had established under the SDWA. At very least, such permitted degradation, without any accompanying explanation showing a clear need or justification for a different and lower standard than the SDWA prescribes, is arbitrary and capricious.

* * *

VII. CONCLUSION

Because the EPA did not consider the interrelationship of the high level waste rules and Part C of the Safe Drinking Water Act and thus failed either to reconcile the two regulatory standards or to adequately explain the divergence, we find that the Agency was arbitrary and capricious in its promulgation of the individual protection requirements. We must therefore remand to the Agency for further consideration. *See, e.g., Motor Vehicle Manufacturers Association v. State Farm Mutual Automobile Insurance Co.,* 463 U.S. 29, 57, 77 L.Ed.2d 443, 103 S.Ct. 2856 (1983) (where agency failed to supply reasoned analysis for its decision, remand to agency for further consideration necessary); *Federal Power Commission v. Transcontinental Gas Pipe Line Corp.,* 423 U.S. 326, 331, 46 L.Ed.2d 533, 96 S.Ct. 579 (1976) (where agency's decision not sustainable on administrative record, decision must be vacated and the matter remanded for further consideration). We are also remanding the individual protection requirements for further consideration because the Agency has not provided an adequate explanation for selecting the 1,000 year design criterion. Further, we find that the ground water protection requirements were promulgated without proper notice and comment as required by the Administrative Procedure Act, 5 U.S.C. § 553(c). We therefore remand for further notice and comment procedures. *See PPG Industries, Inc. v. Costle,* 212 U.S.App.D.C. 355, 659 F.2d 1239 (D.C.Cir.1981) (where EPA failed to fully meet notice requirements, remand was appropriate to allow agency to consider issues raised by parties in properly noticed rulemaking). We reject the petitioners' remaining challenges to the high level waste rules. Accordingly, the petition for review of the HLW rules is granted with respect to the issues of the individual and ground water protection requirements, and is denied with respect to the remaining challenges. The HLW rules, 40 C.F.R. Part 191 (1986), except for Subpart A of 40 C.F.R. Part 191 (1986), are vacated and remanded to the Agency for further proceedings not inconsistent with this opinion.

So ordered.

Notes

1. EPA published a "Ground–Water Protection Strategy" in August 1984. This policy was an in depth policy statement designed to help provide consistency and coordination among the many EPA programs that relate either directly or indirectly to ground water quality. Other EPA programs involving ground water cleanup include: RCRA, CERCLA and OPA. EPA's strategy document was not adopted through rulemaking, because it has no one statutory authority. Rather the strategy was intended to be implemented through the various EPA regulatory programs that involve ground water.

2. Under EPA's ground water strategy ground waters are defined in two classes:

> **Class I ground waters** are defined "as ground waters that are highly vulnerable to contamination because of local hydrological characteristics and that are also either irreplaceable (i.e., there is no reasonable alternative source of drinking water) or vital to a particularly sensitive ecological system.

> **Class II ground waters** are defined as all other ground water that is currently used or potentially available for drinking water or other beneficial use.

> **Class III ground waters** are ground water supplies that are not considered as potential sources of drinking water because of heavy salinity or other contamination.

See Environmental Protection Agency, Ground–Water Protection Strategy at 5–6 (August 1984).

The second class comprises most of the usable ground water in the United States.

3. An aquifer is an underground geologic formation, group of formations, or part of a formation that is capable of yielding a significant amount of water to a well or spring. *See* 40 C.F.R. § 146.3.

3. *Groundwater Regulation Generally*

Although contamination of groundwater has been a source of increasing concern in the United States in recent years, there currently is no comprehensive federal legislation addressing the issue. Although the CWA requires states, as a precondition to approval of their NPDES programs, to "control the discharge of pollutants into wells," EPA has no direct authority to regulate disposal of pollutants by subsurface injection. EPA instead relies upon authority under the Safe Drinking Water Act (SDWA), 42 U.S.C.A. § 300 *et seq.*, to regulate such discharges via an underground injunction control program. *See* 40 C.F.R. Parts 144–148 (1990).

There is no comprehensive system of federal groundwater regulation. Groundwaters that are drinking waters are regulated under the SDWA.

Contaminated groundwaters are regulated in cleanup through the Resource Conservation and Recovery Act, 42 U.S.C.A. § 6901 *et seq.* and CERCLA. The National Contingency Plan (NCP), a framework for implementation of Superfund, America's environmental cleanup program, sets forth cleanup standards for groundwater remediation at Superfund sites. EPA's approach to groundwater remediation has been to operate within the framework of its Groundwater Protection Strategy, which establishes different degrees of groundwater protection based on vulnerability, use, and value. The recently finalized NCP acknowledges this approach and addresses groundwater response actions separately. *See* 55 Fed. Reg. 8,666 (March 8, 1990).

BAMFORD v. UPPER REPUBLICAN NATURAL RESOURCES DISTRICT

245 Neb. 299, 512 N.W.2d 642 (1994).

BOSLAUGH, J.

In these two cases which were consolidated for briefing and argument in this court, the plaintiffs-appellants, Gregory L. Bamford, Bamford Partnership, Dan Adler, and Robin Roth, sought to prevent the enforcement of a cease and desist order issued by defendant-appellee, Upper Republican Natural Resources District (URNRD). URNRD issued its cease and desist order on March 12, 1992, to prevent the appellants from withdrawing ground water from nine wells until the issuance of an additional allocation permitting further withdrawals. In response, on March 26, 1992, the appellants filed a petition in case No. S-92-562, pursuant to Neb. Rev. Stat. § 84-917 (Cum. Supp. 1992), seeking a review of URNRD's issuance of the cease and desist order. On that date, the appellants also filed a separate petition in case No. S-92-563 seeking an injunction enjoining URNRD from enforcing its March 12 cease and desist order. In its answer to the appellants' petition for injunctive relief, URNRD filed a counterclaim seeking an injunction enjoining the appellants from withdrawing ground water until the appellants' wells were granted another allocation of ground water.

Following a trial on the action for injunctive relief, the district court denied the injunction sought by the appellants and granted the injunction sought by URNRD. In addition, after a review, in accordance with § 84-917(5), of URNRD's action in issuing the March 12 cease and desist order, the district court determined that the cease and desist order was properly issued and dismissed the petition which the appellants had filed pursuant to § 84-917. The appellants now appeal the decisions of the district court.

Before reviewing the appellants' assignments of error, it is helpful to provide some minimal background. We first note that center-pivot irrigation systems have been installed on each of the nine wells which are involved in this case. Appellant Gregory Bamford is the owner of land irrigated by five wells; those five tracts or "circles" are farmed by his tenant, appellant Roth. Land irrigated by the other four wells is owned by appellant Bamford Partnership; those four circles are farmed by appellant Adler.

The land irrigated by the appellants' nine wells falls within the jurisdiction of URNRD and is within an area which, in 1977, was designated a ground water "control area." *See* Neb. Rev. Stat. § 46-658 (Reissue 1988). Although § 46-658(5) provides procedures for modification of a control area designation, the control area encompassing the appellants' wells remains unchanged. Consequently, the withdrawal of ground water from the appellants' wells is subject to the limitations imposed by URNRD. *See* Neb. Rev. Stat. § 46–666 (Reissue 1988).

In 1978, URNRD adopted rules regarding the withdrawal of ground water from wells within the district, and such withdrawals have been subject to regulation by URNRD since that time. In 1988, URNRD adopted an order allocating 75 acre-inches of ground water per irrigated acre for the 5–year period commencing January 1, 1988, and ending December 31, 1992. (Neb. Rev. Stat. § 46–657 (Reissue 1988) defines an acre-inch as "the amount of water necessary to cover an acre of land one inch deep.") Thus, in 1988, URNRD issued an allocation of 15 acre-inches per year for 5 years, but irrigators would be allowed to withdraw in excess of 15 acre-inches per year for each irrigated acre, so long as total withdrawals during the 5–year period did not exceed 75 acre-inches per irrigated acre.

In determining the total allocation available to the appellants during the 5–year period, URNRD and the appellants agreed to a "pooling" of the appellants' nine wells. Under this pooling arrangement, allocations of water which were not withdrawn from any of the nine wells could be withdrawn from any of the other nine wells. Thus, withdrawals from any single well could exceed the 75–acre-inch allocation, but total withdrawals from all nine wells could not exceed the 5–year allocation of 75 acre-inches per irrigated acre. Nevertheless, at the end of 1991, i.e., the fourth year of the allocation period, the appellants' withdrawals of ground water from the nine pooled wells had exceeded the 75–acre-inch allocation by approximately 12 acre-inches per irrigated acre. While the four wells owned by Bamford Partnership had a remaining allocation of approximately 25 acre-inches per irrigated acre at the end of 1991, the five wells owned by Gregory Bamford had exceeded their allocations by approximately 41 acre-inches per irrigated acre, thus resulting in the 12–inch "deficit" for the nine pooled wells.

Because the appellants' nine pooled wells had, at the end of 1991, withdrawn all of the ground water allocated to those wells for the 5–year period ending December 31, 1992, URNRD conducted a hearing to determine whether a cease and desist order should be issued due to the appellants' withdrawals of ground water in excess of the amount allocated. Appellant Gregory Bamford testified at this February 11, 1992, hearing. Following the hearing, URNRD issued its March 12, 1992, cease and desist order to prevent further withdrawal of ground water until the issuance of another allocation. Appellants now contend that in upholding URNRD's cease and desist order, the district court erred in (1) finding that URNRD's issuance of the cease and desist order was not arbitrary and capricious, (2) finding that the appellants' nine wells were pooled, (3) denying appellants the right to use water underlying their land when evidence failed to show that the underground water supply was insufficient for all other water users, (4) finding that the Nebraska Ground Water Management and Protection Act was constitutional, and (5) finding that the appellants were not entitled to compensation for the taking of their property.

In reviewing the appellants' assignments of error in connection with their petitions, we first consider whether issues are presented which we may properly decide. The appellants' petitions primarily sought injunctive relief and a reversal of URNRD's issuance of the cease and desist order. However, it is apparent that the cease and desist order affected the appellants during 1992 only. The record shows that the appellants were entitled to and would have been issued an additional allocation of ground water in 1993, and statements by the appellants' counsel made during oral argument indicate that the cease and desist order was effective during 1992 only.

In *Koenig v. Southeast Community College,* 231 Neb. 923, 925–26, 438 N.W.2d 791, 794 (1989), this court stated:

> At the heart of this action is the request for an injunction. The purpose of an injunction is the restraint of actions which have not yet been taken. Remedy by injunction is generally preventative, prohibitory, or protective, and equity will not usually issue an injunction when the act complained of has been committed and the injury has been done. [Citations omitted.] In this case the matter is fait accompli, and the action has been taken. No court could now prohibit what has already taken place.... As to injunction, the case has become moot.

As in *Koenig,* issues relating only to the cease and desist order which affected the appellants during 1992 have become moot; the matter is a fait accompli. Thus, we do not address the appellants' contention that URNRD's issuance of the cease and desist order was arbitrary and capricious. Nevertheless, we note that the evidence is uncontroverted that at the end of 1991, the fourth year of the 5–year allocation period, the appellants' withdrawals of ground water from the nine pooled wells had exceeded the amount allocated. Similarly, while the record does support the district court's determination that the nine wells were pooled, the appellants' assignment of error regarding the pooling of the nine wells is relevant only with respect to the moot issue of the propriety of URNRD's cease and desist order.

Although the passage of time has rendered moot those issues relating only to issuance of URNRD's cease and desist order, we are cognizant of additional language contained in *Koenig* which states:

> There is an exception to the general rule regarding moot questions which should be examined. That exception applies to cases involving matters of public interest.... The public interest exception to the rule precluding consideration of issues on appeal due to mootness requires a consideration of the public or private nature of the question presented, desirability of an authoritative adjudication for future guidance of public officials, and the likelihood of future recurrence of the same or a similar problem.

Id. at 926–27, 438 N.W.2d at 795. We now address the appellants' remaining assignments of error, as those assignments of error involve matters of public interest likely to arise in future similar cases.

The appellants contend that the district court erred in denying them the right to use water underlying their land when evidence failed to show that the underground water supply was insufficient for all other water users. This contention is apparently based upon Nebraska's common law of ground water, i.e.: " 'The owner of land is entitled to appropriate subterranean waters found under his land, but ... if the natural underground supply is insufficient for all owners, each is entitled to a reasonable proportion of the whole.... ' " *Sorensen v. Lower Niobrara Nat. Resources Dist.,* 221 Neb. 180, 188, 376 N.W.2d 539, 546 (1985).

At the February 11, 1992, hearing conducted by URNRD, and also at the trial conducted by the district court with respect to the appellants' petition for injunctive relief, the appellants did present evidence relating to the available supply of water in the Ogallala aquifer, from which water was being withdrawn, and the effect of such withdrawals upon other water users. However, such evidence was not relevant in this case, because the question whether conditions existed requiring the regulation of the withdrawal of ground water from the appellants' wells (i.e., the question whether the underground water supply was sufficient for all users) was settled when the Director of Water Resources, pursuant to § 46–658, designated a control area encompassing appellants' nine wells. That designation effectively established that the underground water supply was insufficient for all owners using that supply. Furthermore, the record indicates that the order designating the control area was entered on August 1, 1977, and it is apparent no petition was filed seeking a review of that order within the 30 days specified by § 84–917. *See B. T. Energy Corp. v. Marcus,* 222 Neb. 207, 382 N.W.2d 616 (1986). Nor has the control area designation been modified pursuant to § 46–658(5). Thus, the question whether the underground water supply was insufficient for all water users was not an issue properly before either the district court or URNRD at its February 11, 1992, hearing.

The appellants also assert that they are entitled to a ground water allocation greater than the 75–acre-inch 5–year allocation granted to all wells regulated by URNRD. Again, however, the time has passed to challenge that order. The record shows that URNRD adopted the 75–acre-inch order in January or February 1988, and the appellants apparently did not timely seek a review of that URNRD decision. Furthermore, the appellants do not contend and the record does not suggest that URNRD failed to comply with the notice and public hearing requirements of Neb. Rev. Stat. § 46–663.01 (Reissue 1988) when it adopted the 75–acre-inch allocation for the 5–year period ending December 31, 1992. The 75–acre-inch allocation having been previously adopted and not challenged, at its February 11 hearing URNRD was left to consider only whether the appellants' withdrawals of water had exceeded the allocated amount and whether a cease and desist order should therefore be issued.

URNRD then determined that the appellants had exceeded their 75–acre-inch allocation, and in accordance with Neb. Rev. Stat. § 46–663(5)(Reissue 1988) and its own procedural rules, URNRD issued its cease and desist order.

The appellants next challenge the constitutionality of statutory provisions authorizing URNRD's issuance of a cease and desist order. In doing so, the appellants state that the Nebraska Ground Water Management and Protection Act is both vague and overbroad. *See, also, State v. Copple,* 224 Neb. 672, 401 N.W.2d 141 (1987). However, the argument which the appellants articulate presents only a vagueness question in the form of an assertion that the applicable statutory provisions are an unconstitutional delegation of legislative authority. As stated in *Kwik Shop v. City of Lincoln,* 243 Neb. 178, 182–83, 498 N.W.2d 102, 106 (1993):

> It is axiomatic that statutes are afforded a presumption of constitutionality, and the unconstitutionality of a statute must be clearly established before it will be declared void. *State v. Kipf,* 234 Neb. 227, 450 N.W.2d 397 (1990). Even when a law is constitutionally suspect, a court will attempt to interpret it in a manner consistent with the Constitution. *See id. See,* also, *State ex rel. Wright v. Pepperl,* 221 Neb. 664, 380 N.W.2d 259 (1986). The burden of establishing the unconstitutionality of a statute is on the one attacking its validity. *In re Guardianship and Conservatorship of Sim,* 225 Neb. 181, 403 N.W.2d 721 (1987).

When a legislative enactment is challenged on vagueness grounds, the issue is whether the two requirements of procedural due process are met: (1) adequate notice to citizens and (2) adequate standards to prevent arbitrary enforcement. *Kolender v. Lawson,* 461 U.S. 352, 103 S.Ct. 1855, 75 L.Ed.2d 903 (1983); *City of Lincoln v. ABC Books, Inc.,* 238 Neb. 378, 470 N.W.2d 760 (1991). *See, also, Grayned v. City of Rockford,* 408 U.S. 104, 92 S.Ct. 2294, 33 L.Ed.2d 222 (1972); *State v. Fellman,* 236 Neb. 850, 464 N.W.2d 181 (1991). "In other words, due process requires that an enactment supply (1) a 'person of ordinary intelligence a reasonable opportunity to know what is prohibited' and (2) 'explicit standards for those who apply [it].' " *ABC Books, Inc.,* 238 Neb. at 382, 470 N.W.2d at 764 (quoting *Grayned,* supra).

In re Application U–2, 226 Neb. 594, 413 N.W.2d 290 (1987), presented an issue similar to the issue raised by the appellants. The court stated:

> Appellants ... argue that § 46–226.01 is an unconstitutional delegation of legislative authority and that it does not contain adequate legal standards to govern the director's review of an application. We find no merit in this claim. We have held that where the Legislature has provided reasonable limitations and standards for carrying out the delegated duties, no unconstitutional delegation of legislative authority exists. *Mann v. Wayne County Board of Equalization,* 186 Neb. 752, 186 N.W.2d 729 (1971). Section § [sic]

46–226.02 sets out specific conditions which must be met before the director may approve an application. . . .

In addition, Neb. Rev. Stat. § 46–209 (Reissue 1984) gives DWR jurisdiction "over all matters pertaining to water rights for irrigation, power, or other useful purposes. . . . " The Legislature has recognized the expertise and experience needed to determine the difficult questions presented in the overall water situation in this state when it required, by Neb. Rev. Stat. § 46–701 (Reissue 1984), that the director of DWR be a professional engineer with at least 5 years' experience in a position of responsibility in irrigation work.

This court has recognized the difficulties inherent in requiring the Legislature to spell out each standard in complex fields in areas where expanding technology and complex theories daily change. In *State ex rel. Douglas v. Nebraska Mortgage Finance Fund,* 204 Neb. 445, 465, 283 N.W.2d 12, 24 (1979), we stated:

> "The question of how far the Legislature should go in filling in the details of the standards which an administrative agency is to apply raises large issues of policy in which the Legislature has a wide discretion, and the court should be reluctant to interfere with such discretion. Such standards in conferring discretionary power upon an administrative agency must be reasonably adequate, sufficient, and definite for the guidance of the agency in the exercise of the power conferred upon it and must also be sufficient to enable those affected to know their rights and obligations. . . . The modern tendency is to be more liberal in permitting grants of discretion to an administrative agency in order to facilitate the administration of laws as the complexity of economic and governmental conditions increases."

Similarly, in *Anderson v. Tiemann,* 182 Neb. 393, 401–02, 155 N.W.2d 322, 328 (1967), we stated: "Delegation of legislative power is most commonly indicated where the relations to be regulated are highly technical or where regulation requires a course of continuous decision."

In re Application U–2, 226 Neb. at 607–09, 413 N.W.2d at 299–300.

We now turn to the statutory provisions bearing upon the issuance of the March 12 cease and desist order, first noting that with respect to the following quoted sections, § 46–657 provides requisite definitions. That section states:

> As used in the Nebraska Ground Water Management and Protection Act . . .
>
> (6) District shall mean a natural resources district operating pursuant to Chapter 2, article 32;
>
> (7) Director shall mean the Director of Water Resources;
>
> * * *
>
> (14) Board shall mean the board of directors of a district. . . .

Section 46–658, further, provides:

An area may be designated a control area by the director following a hearing initiated in accordance with subsection (3) of this section if it shall be determined, following evaluation of relevant hydrologic and water quality data, history of developments, and projection of effects of current and new development, that development and utilization of the ground water supply has caused or is likely to cause within the reasonably foreseeable future the existence of either of the following conditions:

(a) An inadequate ground water supply to meet present or reasonably foreseeable needs for beneficial use of such water supply; or

(b) Dewatering of an aquifer, resulting in a deterioration of the quality of such ground water sufficient to make such ground water unsuitable for the present purposes for which it is being utilized.

(2) When determining whether to designate a control area because of the existence of any of the conditions listed in subsection (1) of this section, the director's considerations shall include, but not be limited to, whether conflicts between ground water users are occurring or may be reasonably anticipated or whether ground water users are experiencing or will experience within the foreseeable future substantial economic hardships as a direct result of current or anticipated ground water development or utilization.

(3) A hearing to designate a control area may be initiated by a district whenever it has information, sufficient in the opinion of the board of directors, to require that any portion of such district should be designated as a control area....

(4)(a) Within thirty days after a hearing has been initiated pursuant to subsection (3) of this section, the director shall consult with the district and fix a time and place for a public hearing to consider the information supplied and to hear any other evidence....

(b) At the hearing, all interested persons shall be allowed to appear and present testimony. The Conservation and Survey Division of the University of Nebraska, the Nebraska Natural Resources Commission, and the Department of Environmental Control shall offer as evidence any information in their possession which they deem relevant to the purposes of the hearing. After the hearing and after any studies or investigations conducted by or on behalf of the director as he or she deems necessary, the director shall determine whether a control area shall be designated. If the director determines that no control area shall be established, he or she shall issue an order declaring that no control area shall be designated.

(c) If the director determines that a control area shall be established, he or she shall consult with such relevant state agencies named in subdivision (b) of this subsection and with the district or districts affected and determine the boundaries of the control area, taking into account the considerations enumerated in subsection (1) of this section, the effect on political subdivisions, and the socioeconomic and administrative factors directly affecting the ability to implement and carry out local ground water management, control, and protection.

In addition, § 46–666 states:

(1) A district in which a control area has been designated pursuant to subsection (1) of section 46–658 shall by order adopt one or more of the following controls for the control area:

(a) It may determine the permissible total withdrawal of ground water for each day, month, or year and allocate such withdrawal among the ground water users;

* * *

(2) In adopting, amending, or repealing any control authorized by subsection (1) of this section ... the district's considerations shall include, but not be limited to, whether it reasonably appears that such action will mitigate or eliminate the condition which led to designation of the control or management area, will encourage a high degree of water use efficiency, or will improve the administration of the area.

(3) The adoption, amendment, or repeal of any authorized control in a control area shall be subject to the approval of the director. The director may hold a public hearing to consider testimony regarding the control prior to the issuance of an order approving or disapproving the adoption, amendment, or repeal of the control.... In approving the adoption, amendment, or repeal of an authorized control in a control area, the director's considerations shall include, but not be limited to, those enumerated in subsection (2) of this section.

* * *

(5) If the district determines, following a public hearing conducted pursuant to section 46–665, that depletion or contamination of the ground water supply in the control area or any portion of the control area is so excessive that the public interest cannot be protected solely through implementation of reasonable controls adopted pursuant to subsection (1) of this section, it may, with the approval of the director, close all or a portion of the control area to the issuance of any additional permits for a period of one calendar year. Such areas may be further closed thereafter by a similar procedure for additional one-year periods....

Finally, § 46–663 states:

Regardless of whether or not any portion of a district has been designated as a control, management, or special ground water quality protection area, in order to administer and enforce the Nebraska

Ground Water Management and Protection Act and to effectuate the policy of the state to conserve ground water resources, a district may:

* * *

(5) Issue cease and desist orders, following ten days' notice to the person affected stating the contemplated action and in general the grounds for the action and following reasonable opportunity to be heard, to enforce any of the provisions of the act or of orders or permits issued pursuant to it, to initiate suits to enforce the provisions of orders issued pursuant to the act, and to restrain the construction of illegal wells or the withdrawal or use of water from such wells.

We find that the above-cited statutes provide adequate notice to citizens and adequate enforcement standards regarding the establishment of control areas, the adoption of rules to control water usage, and the issuance of cease and desist orders to prevent violations of such rules. As in *In re Application U–2,* 226 Neb. 594, 610, 413 N.W.2d 290, 301 (1987), the applicable statutory provisions "clearly outlined the legal field of battle and [are] not unconstitutional."

We finally address the appellants' contention that the issuance of a cease and desist order in this case is tantamount to a regulatory "taking," and their claim that the district court therefore erred in failing to award them compensation as a result of the issuance of the cease and desist order. With respect to this issue, we point out that the issue of compensation was, in fact, not before the district court, since the appellants' petitions sought only a review of the action of URNRD in issuing the cease and desist order and an injunction which would have prevented the enforcement of that order. The appellants' petition did ask the district court to overturn URNRD's cease and desist order on the ground that the statute under which it was authorized and issued resulted in an unconstitutional taking of property without just compensation. In that regard, we note that there is no constitutional limitation on the right to take private property for public use under the power of eminent domain, except as to the right to just compensation. *See Hammer v. Department of Roads,* 175 Neb. 178, 120 N.W.2d [*313] 909 (1963). However, the appellants' petitions did not seek such compensation, and the appellants therefore failed to properly place that issue before the district court. In any event, however, the appellants' analysis fails to support their takings claim.

The appellants attempt to lay a foundation for their takings claim by citing language from *Sorensen v. Lower Niobrara Nat. Resources Dist.,* 221 Neb. 180, 376 N.W.2d 539 (1985). [***26] In *Sorensen,* 221 Neb. at 191–92, 376 N.W.2d at 548, this court stated that "the right of an owner of overlying land to use ground water is an appurtenance constituting property protected by Neb. Const. art. I, § 21: 'The property of no person shall be taken or damaged for public use without just compensation therefor.'" However, ground water, as defined in § 46–657, is owned by the public, and the only right held by an overlying landowner is in the use of the ground water. *In re Application U–2,* supra. Furthermore, placing limitations upon withdrawals of ground water in times of shortage is a proper exercise of the State's police power. *See Sporhase v. Nebraska ex rel. Douglas,* 458 U.S. 941, 102 S.Ct. 3456, 73 L.Ed.2d 1254 (1982).

Quoting *Olson v. City of Wahoo,* 124 Neb. 802, 248 N.W. 304 (1933), *State ex rel. Douglas v. Sporhase,* 208 Neb. 703, 705, 305 N.W.2d 614, 617 (1981), rev'd on other grounds 458 U.S. 941, 102 S.Ct. 3456, 73 L.Ed.2d 1254 (1982), recites Nebraska's common law of ground water:

> "The ... rule is that the owner of land is entitled to appropriate subterranean waters found under his land, but he cannot extract and appropriate them in excess of a reasonable and beneficial use upon the land which he owns, especially if such use is injurious to others who have substantial rights to the waters, and if the natural underground supply is insufficient for all owners, each is entitled to a reasonable proportion of the whole.... "

Under this rule, when the underground water supply is sufficient for all users, a landowner is entitled to reasonable and beneficial use of that supply. Apparently with that in mind, the appellants point to language in *Prather v. Eisenmann,* 200 Neb. 1, 7, 261 N.W.2d 766, 770 (1978), stating: "Under the reasonable use doctrine, two neighboring landowners ... can withdraw all the supply he [sic] can put to beneficial and reasonable use. What is reasonable is judged solely in relationship to the purpose of such use on the overlying land." The appellants then conclude that they were entitled to withdraw as much water as was required to use their land as they chose—in this case, to grow a corn crop.

The appellants' reliance on *Prather* is improvident, for the court specifically found that under the circumstances of that case, the water supply was sufficient for all users. Contrarily, as discussed previously, the designation of a control area which included the appellants' irrigated land established that in this instance the available supply of water was insufficient for all users.

In addition, while the common-law rule for ground water was adopted in *Olson,* supra, the Legislature has the power to determine public policy with regard to ground water and can alter the common law governing the use of ground water. *See Sorensen,* supra. *See,* also, *Sporhase,* supra.

Finally, the appellants state that they were deprived of all economic use of their land during 1992 and argue that under *Lucas v. South Carolina Coastal Council, U.S.,* 112 S.Ct. 2886, 120 L.Ed.2d 798 (1992), they were therefore entitled to compensation. In *Lucas,* the Court found that a landowner was entitled to compensation because South Carolina's Coastal Zone Management Act prohibited all economically beneficial use of his land. However, the appellants' assertions in this instance are little more than a claim that because they could not withdraw enough water to grow a corn crop, they were therefore deprived of all economic use of their land. The record here fails to show that the appellants were, in fact, deprived of all economic use of their land in 1992, and, if only for that reason, Lucas is inapplicable under the circumstances presented here.

For the reasons stated in the opinion, the appeal in case No. 92–563 is dismissed as moot; the judgment in case No. S–92–562 is affirmed.

Note

While there is not a comprehensive *federal* program regulating ground-water, many *states* already have such programs in place.

§ 8.6 COASTAL ZONE MANAGEMENT ACT OF 1972—PROTECTION OF COASTAL AREAS

The Coastal Zone Management Act of 1972 (CZMA), (West 1985 & Supp. 1991), includes provisions that affect commercial uses, activities, or projects conducted in or on coastal waters and adjacent shorelands. The term "coastal zone" means coastal waters and adjacent shorelands of the coastal states, including islands, salt marshes, wetlands, and beaches. In Great Lakes waters, the zone extends to the international boundary between the U.S. and Canada.

The principal purpose of CZMA, which is administered by the Department of Commerce (DOC), is to provide management grants to coastal states which develop programs for preservation of natural and cultural resources associated with coastal areas. Under these programs, which must be reviewed by DOC for consistency with statutory criteria, states may restrict land and water uses, including building and development, in coastal and estuarine areas to achieve CZMA's purposes. The states may carry out those coastal zone plans (CZPs) through state laws or local ordinances. CZPs can have a significant impact on siting of industrial facilities in specified coastal zone areas. Any company considering locating a plant or conducting industrial activity in a coastal zone area should consult any relevant CZP.

In the Coastal Zone Act Reauthorization Amendments of 1990 (CZARA), Congress reauthorized CZMA through 1995. Omnibus Reconciliation Act of 1990, Publ. L. No. 101–508, Subtitle C, 104 Stat. 764 (1990). Many of CZARA's provisions will increase the impact of CZMA on coastal zone activities. For instance, to take account of the effects of global warming, Congress expanded the scope of CZMA by defining coastal zones to include geographical areas likely to be affected by sea level rise. CZMA § 1453(1). By establishing eight new grant programs, CZARA also expanded the types of building and development activities a state's CZP may affect. CZPs now will affect, among other activities, management and protection of wetlands, and siting and impact management for energy facilities. Energy facilities can include electric generating plants, petroleum refineries and associated facilities, gasification plants, liquified natural gas facilities, uranium enrichment or nuclear fuel processing facilities, oil and gas facilities, deepwater ports, pipelines and transmissions, and terminals associated with any of those facilities. 16 U.S.C.A. § 1453.

By 1994, CZPs also must address urban run-off and control of non-point source pollution. Additional provisions require CZP measures for assessing and maintaining the levels of water quality required under state water quality standards. 16 U.S.C.A. § 1455(b).

Discussion Problem

The Coastal Zone Management Act of 1972 (CZMA) was enacted to "preserve, protect, develop, and where possible, to restore or enhance, the resources of the Nation's coastal zone for this and succeeding generations." In response to the mandates of the CZMA, states have passed coastal management plans (CMPs). These plans usually contain land use restrictions designed to limit the construction of erosion control devices and habitable structures within the coastal zone as a means of preventing the continued depletion of fragile, limited coastal resources.

The Fifth Amendment of the United States Constitution provides that private property may not be taken for public purposes without just compensation. This amendment has been used repeatedly since 1972 to raise challenges to the limits placed on development of private property within the coastal zone. While many of the challenges to state CMPs have been unsuccessful, the case-by-case approach taken by the Court and the uncertainties surrounding the takings clause have had a chilling effect on state legislatures trying to slow the destruction of their states' coastal zones.

Various alternative techniques or methods of protection have been used to protect coastal resources and avoid takings claims. Use of the public trust doctrine and mitigation requirements potentially offer the most hope for effective preservation.

Both private landowners and the public have rights that must legally and ethically be protected. How would you recommend resolving these tensions?

§ 8.7 MARINE PROTECTION, RESEARCH AND SANCTUARIES ACT OF 1972 ("MPRSA") AND THE OCEAN DUMPING BAN ACT OF 1988

Under the Marine Protection, Research and Sanctuaries Act of 1972, as amended by the Ocean Dumping Ban Act of 1988, Pub. L. No. 100–688, Title I, 102 Stat. 4139 (1988), codified at, 33 U.S.C.A. § 1401 *et seq.* (West 1988 & Supp. 1993), a federal permit is required to transport most materials from the United States into the ocean for dumping. In addition, the actual dumping of materials transported from outside the United States into the U.S. territorial sea or into the contiguous zone must be authorized by a permit. Ocean dumping permits are granted by EPA, except in the case of the dumping of dredged material, where the responsibility rests with the Corps of Engineers. *See* 40 C.F.R. Part 220 *et seq.* (1990).

UNITED STATES v. COUNTY OF NASSAU

733 F.Supp. 563 (E.D.N.Y.1990).

JACOB MISHLER, UNITED STATES DISTRICT JUDGE.

Defendants, County of Nassau and Nassau County Department of Public Works ("Nassau"), move to modify the Consent Decree and Enforcement Agreement ("Decree") "so ordered" on August 2, 1989 by deleting from Article V, Dewatering Measures For Land Based Management Of Sewage Sludge—the schedule requiring Nassau to construct and operate dewatering equipment capable of processing 100 percent of Nassau's sludge by December 31, 1991. The application does not affect Nassau's obligation to have dewatering equipment capable of processing 50 percent of its sludge by June 30, 1991. Article V, para. 7....

Nassau's request for modification of the Decree is based on its decision to use a private vendor to fulfill its obligations which, in turn, was a result of requests for proposals issued on March 1, 1989 and July 10, 1989. Article IV, "Solicitation of Proposals For Land–Based Management of Sewage Sludge." Paragraphs 4 and 5 of Article IV state in pertinent part:

> 4. Any party may propose modification of the schedules for implementation of land-based management of sewage sludge as a result of the process set forth in paragraph IV.B.1, 2 and 3 by January 15, 1990....

> 5. If the parties agree to seek a modification of paragraph V, VI or VII hereof, they shall seek one as appropriate in accordance with paragraph XII no later than February 28, 1990. If there is no agreement, any party may petition the court for a modification or may seek relief from the milestone events set forth in paragraphs VI and VII in accordance with paragraphs XII and XIV, as appropriate....

Nassau's motion seeks relief from the time schedule imposed and to substitute a schedule in keeping with Nassau's decision to contract with a private vendor. Nassau argues that "[under] this alternative system, optimally the sludge would not be disposed of in a landfill, but would be put into a form where the sludge could be reused. The full operation of this system is to commence by December 31, 1994." (Nassau brief, p. 4)

History and Background Leading to the Decree

Congress enacted the Marine Protection, Research and Sanctuaries Act of 1972 ("MPRSA"), 33 U.S.C. § 1401 et seq., declaring that it is the policy of the United States "to regulate the dumping of all types of materials into ocean waters and to prevent or strictly limit the dumping into ocean waters of any material which would adversely affect human health, welfare or amenities, or the marine environment, ecological systems, or economic potentialities." 33 U.S.C. § 1401. In 1974 and 1975, the United States Environmental Protection Agency ("EPA") required ocean dumpers to apply for permits. In 1976, only nine major municipalities including Nassau continued ocean dumping on EPA permits which provided a schedule with a view to end ocean dumping by December 31, 1981. Congress reinforced the goal to end ocean dumping by amending the MPRSA in 1977 by requiring an end to ocean dumping of sewage sludge by December 31, 1981, P.L. 95–153 and by requiring an end to ocean dumping of industrial waste by December 31, 1981, P.L. 96–572.

Between 1977 and 1981 the EPA and New York State gave financial assistance to Nassau and other municipalities for the purpose of developing alternatives to ocean dumping. Nassau constructed a dewatering facility at Cedar Creek in 1981. It did not become fully operational. The interpretation of the December 31, 1981 deadline for ending ocean dumping in the 1977 amendments to MPRSA in *City of New York v. United States Environmental Protection Agency,* 543 F.Supp. 1084, 1088 (S.D.N.Y.1981) placed the effectiveness of that date in doubt. Nassau entered into a consent decree with the EPA permitting the continued dumping of sewage sludge into the ocean.

The Ocean Dumping Ban Act of 1988 ("Act") amended the MPRSA, inter alia, by prohibiting the dumping of sewage sludge into the ocean after August 14, 1989 unless permitted by the EPA. The House amendment required all dumpers, within six months of enactment, to enter into one of two types of agreements—a compliance agreement for those who could end ocean dumping by the deadline and an enforcement agreement for those who could not meet the deadline. 33 U.S.C. § 1401. The enforcement decree was to phase out such ocean dumping. The Act makes it unlawful to dump sewage sludge in the ocean after December 31, 1991.

The Decree outlines a plan in which Nassau will cease ocean disposal of 50 percent of its sewage sludge by June 30, 1991 and all dumping of sewage sludge by December 31, 1991 through implementation of interim measures. Article V sets a time schedule for dewatering the sludge.... Article VI sets the schedule for disposal or reuse of the dewatered sludge. The long-term plan contemplates the incorporation of the equipment and procedures developed in the interim plan.

Present Facilities

In 1981 Nassau constructed the Cedar Creek Wastewater pollution Control plant. Its operation was suspended as a result of the decision in *City of New York v. United States Environmental Protection Agency,* supra. Cedar Creek will be fully operational by June 30, 1991. Sewage treatment plants exist at Bay Park and Inwood, but they are not functioning as dewatering facilities.

The sewage sludge from Inwood, Belgrave and West Long Beach is hauled to Bay Park. The sewage sludge from Cedar Creek is piped to Bay Park. All the sewage sludge from these communities together with the sewage sludge from Bay Park is placed on barges and dumped in the

ocean at a site off the continental shelf designated as "the 106 mile site."
. . .

MODIFICATION OF A CONSENT DECREE

Fed.R.Civ.P. 60(b) provides that a court may relieve a party from a final judgment, order, or proceeding when, inter alia, it is "no longer equitable that the judgment should have prospective application" or "any other reason justifying relief from the operation of the judgment." Fed.R.Civ.P. 60(b)(5) & (6). A court deciding a Rule 60(b) motion "must balance the policy in favor of hearing a litigant's claims on the merits against the policy in favor of finality." *Kozlowski v. Coughlin,* 871 F.2d 241, 246 (2d Cir.1989); *Kotlicky v. United States Fidelity & Guaranty Company,* 817 F.2d 6, 9 (2d Cir.1987)(citing 11 C. Wright & A. Miller, Federal Practice and Procedure, § 2857 (1973)).

The oft-quoted Swift standard for modifying a consent decree provides that "[the] inquiry for us is whether the changes are so important that dangers, once substantial, have become attenuated to a shadow. . . . Nothing less than a clear showing of grievous wrong evoked by new and unforeseen conditions should lead us to change what was decreed after years of litigation with the consent of all concerned." *United States v. Swift & Co.,* 286 U.S. 106, 119, 76 L.Ed. 999, 52 S.Ct. 460 (1932). *See also United States v. American Society of Composers,* 586 F.Supp. 727, 728–29 (S.D.N.Y.1984); *Air Transport Association of America v. Professional Air Traffic Controllers Organization,* 516 F.Supp. 1108, 1111 (E.D.N.Y.1981), aff'd, 667 F.2d 316 (2d Cir.1981). As explained in *United States v. United Shoe Machinery Corp.,* 391 U.S. 244, 20 L.Ed.2d 562, 88 S.Ct. 1496 (1968), a decree may be changed by an appropriate showing, but may not be changed in the "interests of the defendants if the purposes of the litigation as incorporated in the decree . . . have not been fully achieved." *Id.* at 248.

In determining whether modification is appropriate, the analysis must begin by identifying the "essential purpose or purposes of the decree in question, and weighing the impact of the proposed modification on that ultimate objective." *Kozlowski,* supra, at 247. The party seeking modification bears the burden of clearly showing that modification " 'is essential to attaining the goal of the decree.' " *Id.* at 247 (quoting *New York State Association for Retarded Children v. Carey,* 706 F.2d 956, 969 (2d Cir.1983)(Friendly, J.)). Once done, the movant must then show that "each change prunes the decree deftly, changing only as much as is required and leaving the ability to obtain the ultimate goal intact." *Id.* at 248.

Determining the goal of the decree turns on its construction. Although enforced as judicial acts, consent decrees are construed as contracts. *United States v. ITT Continental Baking Co.,* 420 U.S. 223, 236–37, 43 L.Ed.2d 148, 95 S.Ct. 926 (1975); *Canterbury Belts Ltd. v. Lane Walker Rudkin, Limited,* 869 F.2d 34, 38 (2d Cir.1989). Thus, the meaning and purpose of a consent decree should be discerned from the "four corners" of the decree. *United States v. Armour & Co.,* 402 U.S.

673, 681–82, 29 L.Ed.2d 256, 91 S.Ct. 1752 (1971); *Canterbury Belts,* supra, at 38. The explicit language of the decree is given its plain meaning and is afforded great weight. *Berger v. Heckler,* 771 F.2d 1556, 1568 (2d Cir.1985). *See also United States v. Atlantic Refining Co.,* 360 U.S. 19, 22–23, 3 L.Ed.2d 1054, 79 S.Ct. 944 (1959); *Vertex Distributing, Inc. v. Falcon Foam Plastics, Inc.,* 689 F.2d 885, 892–93 (9th Cir.1982); *Artvale, Inc. v. Rugby Fabrics Corp.,* 303 F.2d 283, 284 (2d Cir.1962). If terms in the decree are ambiguous, the court may consider evidence surrounding its negotiation. *ITT Continental Baking Co.,* supra, at 238 n. 11; *Canterbury,* supra, at 38.

Additional considerations inform the construction of a consent decree adopted to enforce a statute. Just as a court must consider whether the decree adequately protects the public interest in approving the consent decree, it must also consider the public interest in modifying that decree. *United States v. Wheeling–Pittsburgh Steel Corporation,* 866 F.2d 57, 59–60 (3d Cir.1988)(modification of decree entered under the Clean Air Act, as amended, 42 U.S.C. § 7502(a)(1)(1983)); *Citizens for a Better Environment v. Gorsuch,* 231 U.S.App.D.C. 79, 718 F.2d 1117, 1126 (D.C.Cir.1983)(approval of settlement agreement pursuant to Federal Water Pollution Control Act Amendments of 1972, §§ 101 et seq.); *State of New York v. Town of Oyster Bay,* 696 F.Supp. 841, 843 (E.D.N.Y.1988)(approval of consent decree pursuant to the Comprehensive Environmental Response, Compensation & Liability Act (CERCLA), 42 U.S.C. § 9601 et seq.); *United States v. Seymour Recycling Corp.,* 554 F.Supp. 1334, 1337 (S.D.Ind.1982)(approval of consent decree pursuant to the Resource Conservation and Recovery Act, 42 U.S.C. § 6901 et seq., the Clean Water Act, 33 U.S.C. § 1251 et seq., and CERCLA). Thus, in construing the decree, the congressional policy decision embodied in the statute it was adopted to enforce is given great weight. *Wheeling–Pittsburgh,* supra, at 60. *See System Federation No. 91 v. Wright,* 364 U.S. 642, 651, 5 L.Ed.2d 349, 81 S.Ct. 368 (1961)("[Just] as the adopting court is free to reject agreed upon terms as not in furtherance of statutory objectives, so must it be free to modify the terms of a consent decree when a change in law brings those terms in conflict with statutory objectives."). In addition, the language of the statute and the legislative history accompanying may limit the court's equitable discretion to modify the decree in contravention of the statute.

In support of its request to modify the schedule for construction and operation of the dewatering plant, Nassau argues that its primary intention is "to find an alternative solution to constructing dewatering facilities at either its Bay Park or Inwood Sewage Treatment Plant sites because proper time has not been allowed to evaluate long-term facilities at any of the County facilities or long-term proposals from private vendors." (Fangmann Aff., para. 3). Nassau also states that its intent in seeking modification is "to produce a reusable product at the earliest possible date to avoid the limited short term aspect of landfilling of dewatered sludge." (Fangmann Aff., para. 4). However, the county recognizes that "even the private vendors must utilize dewatering and landfilling on an interim basis," but argues that the private vendors are better able than the county to contract with available landfills and pursue other options. (Fangmann Aff., para. 30).

In addition, Nassau argues that the schedule set forth in Article V of the decree is too "tight" and does not allow enough time for "a thorough planning effort or public involvement program to consider the construction of a dewatering facility." (Fangmann Aff., para. 6). Finally, the county argues that there are substantial adverse environmental impacts from constructing dewatering facilities at either Inwood or Bay Park. (Fangmann Aff., para. 38–41). In particular, the increased truck traffic through the "narrow residential streets" of Bay Park "leaves the Bay Park site as unacceptable." (Fangmann Aff., para. 39). Construction of the dewatering plant at Inwood is unacceptable because of the "limitation on available property" at the site, due in part to the sewage plant's proximity to tidal wetlands. (Fangmann Aff., para. 40).

The county also argues that the decree contemplates "a two-stage plan that the county must follow to cease the ocean dumping of sewage sludge." (Def. Brief, p. 3). The first stage of the plan is the interim requirements: 50 percent of the county's sludge must be disposed of in a land-based management by June 30, 1991, and 100 percent of the county's sludge must be disposed of by December 31, 1991. n5 According to the county, this first stage also has two tracks. (Nassau brief, p. 4). The first track requires Nassau to submit requests for proposals (RFPs) from the private sector for land-based management. The purpose of these requests is to locate a private vendor that can meet the county's obligations. As Nassau notes, the decree itself specifies that the parties are to meet and discuss the proposals. Article IV, para. A. In addition, if the proposals are "sufficiently promising," then either party may request modification of the schedule for implementing the land-based sludge management. Article IV, para. B, sec. 4.

The second track of this first stage requires the county to build and implement the land-based sludge management. Articles V and VI. The purpose of these two tracks, according to Nassau, is to provide it with flexibility. They contend that the modification clause in the decree must have been intended to allow the county the option of pursuing either the private vendor or county track, depending on which was found to be superior.

This two track construction of the decree is incorrect. By the plain meaning of its terms, Nassau "shall implement dewatering measures for land-based management of sewage sludge in compliance with the following milestone events: ... [commence] on-site construction of all sludge dewatering facilities by June 30, 1990." Article V, para. 6. Nassau was to solicit proposals for "land-based sludge management options," Article IV, and to select a "land-based alternative," Article IV, para. 8, sec. 2, that is, proposals for the disposal of the dewatered sludge.

The November 1989 Nassau County's Draft Generic Environmental Impact Statement Interim Report No. 3, which supplements the December 1988 Evaluation of Long–Term Sludge Disposal Alternatives, shows that Nassau county clearly understood its obligations under the decree to implement dewatering measures. Nassau County environmentally analyzed four alternatives to incineration and beneficial-use alternatives. Each of the fourteen proposals required dewatering at Inwood or Bay Park and Cedar. More importantly, each of the proposals identified dewatering as the precedent to land-based management of the sludge. (Kiselica Aff., para. 20 & 21).

If dewatering was considered part of "land-based management," one would expect the RFPs deadlines to be tied to the dewatering schedule. But they are not. For example, the deadline for the "[complete] final design of all sludge dewatering facilities" is March 31, 1990. Article V, para. 2. However, all information gathered by Nassau as a result of the RFPs was not to be presented to the United States and the State until December 31, 1989.

Rather than follow the decree's mandate regarding land-based management, Nassau's Final Request for Proposals issued on July 10, 1989 did not provide for dewatered sludge from Bay Park and Inwood. (DeZolt Aff., para. 63 & 64). In addition, Nassau incorrectly limited the proposals to only address wet sludge from the Bay Park/Inwood plants and by using the process only to identify long-term options rather than to satisfy the interim goals of land-based management. (DeZolt Aff., para. 67.). Nassau is free to select a private vendor to build and construct its dewatering equipment. Several of the responses to the RFPs in fact offered an option for sludge management in Inwood or Bay Park. (Kiselica Aff., para. 36). However, all finalist vendors considered by Nassau involve remote-site processing of wet sludge. Rather than follow the purpose of the decree, Nassau appears to be pursuing its own agenda.

The essential purpose of the decree is clear: to end all ocean dumping by December 31, 1991. The Conference Report states: "It's clear that we cannot count on the EPA which has earned the name the Environmental Procrastination Agency. We need a firm deadline, in the law, to end the ocean dumping of sewage sludge and industrial waste. Only then, will alternatives be put in place. Only then, will the dumping stop." Senate Debate and Conference, Vol. 134 Cong.Rec. S16685 (daily ed. Oct. 18, 1988) (Statement of Senator Lautenberg). The Conference Report also states:

> In the event that the dumper cannot meet the deadline through the use of a long-term alternative, the dumper must try to utilize interim measures to meet the deadline. EPA and the State must assist the dumper in identifying such interim measures to meet the deadline. EPA and the State must assist the dumper in identifying such interim measures and EPA must not sign an enforcement agreement to allow dumping to continue past the 1991 date where reasonable interim measures exist to end the dumping prior to the deadline. EPA's focus in entering into agreements with the existing

dumpers must be to end he ocean dumping of sewage sludge and industrial waste at the earliest possible time.

Senate Debate and Conference, Vol. 134 Cong.Rec. S16685–16686 (daily ed. Oct. 18, 1988)(Statement of Senator Lautenberg).

The legislative history of the Ocean Dumping Ban Act shows not only that Congress wanted to close every legal loophole that the municipalities could find to delay that deadline, but expresses its anger and frustration that the nine municipalities had evaded the 1981 deadline for the cessation of ocean dumping. The Conference Report states:

This legislation should never have been added. Over a decade ago, congress thought it had banned ocean dumping. Unfortunately, New York City and other dumpers took the Environmental Protection Agency to court as the deadline approached and won. The case not only eliminated the 1981 deadline, it also effectively ended any chance that ocean dumping would come to a halt at any time without a new law.

Senate Debate and Conference, Vol. 134 Cong.Rec. S16689 (daily ed. Oct. 18, 1988)(Statement of Senator Biden).

The purpose of the decree, which was entered into pursuant to the Ocean Dumping Ban Act, was to end ocean dumping without delay. As apparent from the above quotes, Congress clearly intended to severely limit the equitable discretion of a court to extend the compliance dates of a dumper.

Not only has Nassau incorrectly interpreted the purpose of the decree, they have failed to demonstrate that the proposed modification would further the purpose of the decree. First, the dates suggested by the proposals, which state that the facilities will be in operation by December 31, 1991, cannot be relied upon. There is no guarantee that a contract will be negotiated and there is no guarantee that a remote site will receive the appropriate permits and have its environmental review process completed in time to meet the milestone in Section VI, para. 1, which requires that the county execute the contracts for interim land-based disposal of 50 percent of its sludge by March 31, 1991. (Kiselica Aff., para. 62 & 63).

For example, the state law requirements for siting a dewatering away from the location of the wastewater treatment plant where the sludge is generated involve both a public hearing and administrative review of contested issues. (DeZolt Aff., para. 27–29). Approval of the remote site will also involve a preliminary environmental review, application completeness, public notice requirements and opportunity for public comment, and record preparation. (DeZolt Aff., para. 29). Receiving approval alone for a remote site may entail a delay of over a year. (DeZolt Aff., para. 29). Nassau has essentially completed the environmental review process necessary to site a dewatering facility at Bay Park or Inwood. (DeZolt Aff., para. 34).

Second, any remote site chosen by the county will likely encounter substantial public opposition that will engender further delay. The only two remote sites mentioned in the proposals are Staten Island and Pennsylvania. The Ocean Dumping Ban Act contains a prohibition on the disposal of any sewage sludge in Staten Island, including sludge generated by Staten Island.... The governor of Pennsylvania recently imposed a moratorium on additional out-of-state dumping of sludge in Pennsylvania. (Fangmann Aff., Ex. G). The proposed modification by Nassau will only frustrate the purpose of the Decree by delaying the end of ocean dumping.

The Ocean Dumping Ban Act was intended to promote the interest of the general public in clean and safe ocean waters. The existence of diseased fish too toxic to eat, the existence of garbage and medical waste on the shores and beaches, the closure of one-third of all shellfish beds in the United States, and the death of marine animals has been traced to ocean dumping. Senate Debate and conference, Vol. 134 Cong.Rec. S16685 (daily ed. Oct. 18, 1988)(Statement of Senator Lautenberg). The Act expresses a national policy to safeguard the oceans and end ocean dumping. ...Thus, a consideration of the public interest also dictates that modification of the Decree be denied.

Not only has Nassau failed to demonstrate that the modification will advance the purpose of the decree, it has failed to demonstrate any new and unforeseen conditions that would require modification of the decree, much less "a clear showing of grievous wrong evoked by new and unforeseen conditions." *Swift,* supra, 286 U.S. at 119. First, Nassau anticipated substantial public opposition to siting the facility at Bay Park or Inwood before it signed the Decree. (Kiselica Aff., para. 4). Nassau was also aware that the space limitations at Inwood and the residential character of Bay Park would be an area of concern in siting the dewatering facility. (Kiselica Aff., para. 25). In addition, contrary to Nassau's assertions, these problems are not substantial and could be mitigated. (Kiselica Aff., para. 40–49).

Nassau's motion for modification of the Decree is denied.

Chapter 9

AIR POLLUTION

Table of Sections

§ 9.1 HISTORY OF AIR POLLUTION LAW

The Clean Air Act has been with us for nearly three decades. During that time, the Act has evolved from a set of principles to guide states in controlling sources of air pollution (the 1967 Air Quality Act), to a lengthy series of control requirements prescribed by the federal government and administered in coordination with the states.

The following table briefly describes the complex myriad of laws that has come to be known as the Clean Air Act:

The Clean Air Act at a Glance		
Title I	§ 108	Requires EPA to identify "air pollutants" and to publish air quality criteria
	§ 109	Requires EPA to adopt nationally uniform ambient air quality standards (NAAQS)
	§ 110	Requires states to develop and submit SIPs to EPA for approval to assure that air quality meets at least NAAQS
	§ 111	Establishes the New Source Performance Standards permit program (NSPS). Requires EPA to establish uniform technology based standards for major new stationary sources of air pollution
	§ 112	Mandates technology based standards to reduce listed hazardous air emissions from major new sources in designated industry categories
Part C	§§ 160–169A	Establishes Prevention of Significant Deterioration (PSD) program for areas that exceed NAAQSs
Part D	§§ 171–178	Establishes nonattainment program for areas that fail to meet NAAQS (so called non-attainment areas)
Title II	§§ 202–216	Provisions Relating To Mobile Sources
Title III	§ 304	Hazardous Air Pollutants— Authorizes citizen suits
	§ 307	Authorizes judicial review exclusively in the DC Circuit
Title IV	§§ 401–416	Acid Deposition Control

| Title V | §§ 501–507 | Establishes the Operating Permit Program |
| Title VI | §§ 601–617 | Stratospheric Ozone Protection |

This evolution in air quality regulation has tracked advances in our understanding of the environment. As our knowledge of the environment has improved, new concerns have emerged, and shortcomings have been identified in methods provided by the Act for regulating air pollution. A brief review of the experience with the Clean Air Act from the 1960s through the 1980s is helpful to an understanding of the multiple layers of regulatory requirements that now exist.

1. The Air Quality Act of 1967

In response to concerns with deteriorating urban air quality, Congress in 1967 enacted the Air Quality Act. *See* Air Quality Act of 1967, Public Law 90–148, 42 U.S.C.A. §§ 1857 *et seq.* (1967). The 1967 Act focused on regulation of ambient air quality to protect public health and welfare. The purposes of the 1967 Act were:

- To protect and to enhance the quality of the Nation's resources so as to promote the public health and welfare and the productive capacity of its population;

- To initiate and to accelerate a national research and development program to achieve the prevention and control of air pollution;

- To provide technical and financial assistance to state and local governments in connection with the development and execution of their air pollution prevention and control programs; and

- To encourage and to assist the development and operation of regional air pollution control programs. § 101(b).

The centerpiece of this regulatory program was the development of air quality "criteria" by the Department of Health, Education, and Welfare's ("HEW") Air Quality Advisory Board, for widespread and pervasive air pollutants. §§ 107(b)(1), 110. The "criteria" were to "accurately reflect the latest scientific knowledge" on the health and welfare effects of individual pollutants, such as sulfur dioxide (SO_2), nitrogen oxides (NO_X), and particulate matter (PM). § 107(b)(2). While Congress gave the federal government, through the HEW, the responsibility for developing air quality criteria, air quality problems were viewed principally as local concerns. Congress therefore gave the states the responsibility for developing, administering and enforcing specific standards based on the federal criteria. § 108.

With regard to mobile sources, the Act directed the Secretary of HEW to establish nationally-applicable emission standards and a fuel and fuel additive registration program. §§ 202, 210. The Act required that these standards take into account economic and technological feasibility. § 202.

These first efforts at air quality control were hampered by scientific uncertainties and technical difficulties that continue to challenge regulatory agencies today. For example, the criteria document development process proved long and cumbersome. States had difficulty translating the information made available by HEW into source-specific standards. Among other things, techniques for relating air quality to source-specific emissions (*e.g.*, atmospheric dispersion models) were not well-developed.

Moreover, the focus on improvement of ambient air quality through state and local action proved unduly narrow. Since air quality is influenced by regional as well as local factors, more broadly-based regulatory programs and control methods were needed.

2. *The 1970 Clean Air Act*

This early experience with air quality regulation provided a starting point for comprehensive amendments to the Clean Air Act in 1970. *See* Clean Air Act (as amended), Public Law 91–604, 42 U.S.C.A. §§ 1857 *et seq.* (1970). The 1970 Amendments remain the centerpiece of the present-day system of air quality regulation.

In order to overcome the inertia experienced in implementing the 1967 Act, Congress in 1970 gave the federal government a more prominent role in the regulation of air quality. Now, not only was the federal government required to develop air quality criteria describing levels of air quality associated with specific public health and welfare concerns (i.e., "criteria documents"), but the federal government, through the newly created Environmental Protection Agency ("EPA"), was to establish national ambient air quality standards ("NAAQS") that define specific levels of air quality that must be achieved in order to protect public health and welfare. §§ 108, 109. The NAAQS, in turn, would be used as the basis for individual source emission limitations to be established by the states in "state implementation plans" ("SIPs"). § 110.

Furthermore, Congress directed EPA to develop regulatory guidance to be used by states in implementing the NAAQS for individual sources through the SIPs, and provided criteria for EPA to use in reviewing the adequacy of these SIPs. Congress gave EPA a continuing oversight role to ensure that states continued to implement and to enforce the requirements of the Act pertaining to the NAAQS. § 110(a).

In an attempt to make this system of air quality regulation work in a timely fashion, Congress began to use regulatory deadlines to spur administrative decisionmaking. For example, in response to delays experienced in criteria document development and implementation of associated air pollution control measures, Congress set deadlines for development of air pollution criteria documents, for development of NAAQS based on those documents, and for state development and EPA review of SIPs. §§ 108(a), 109(a)(1), 110(a).

Under the 1970 Amendments, therefore, if a state did not develop an adequate SIP, or did not act in a timely fashion to adopt a SIP, or did not respond promptly to a notice from EPA that its SIP failed to meet the requirements of the Act, EPA would step in to implement the Act for the state. § 110(c). This basic federal-state partnership regarding air quality-based controls remains the centerpiece of Clean Air Act regulation today.

Besides creating a more detailed scheme for the protection of public health and welfare through ambient air quality regulation, Congress in 1970 expressed concern with the preservation of existing air quality where air quality was better than required by the NAAQS. Reflecting this concern, Congress adopted stringent control technology requirements for new sources (*i.e.*, the new source performance standards, or "NSPS" program of § 111 of the Act), and made clear in the general purposes clause that a key objective guiding implementation of the Act was the "prevention of significant deterioration" of air quality in clean air areas. *See Sierra Club v. Ruckelshaus*, 344 F.Supp. 253 (D.D.C.), *aff'd per curiam*, 4 Env't. Rep. Cas. (BNA) 1815 (D.C.Cir.1972), *aff'd by an equally divided Court sub nom. Fri v. Sierra Club*, 412 U.S. 541, 93 S.Ct. 2770, 37 L.Ed.2d 140 (1973).

Congress in 1970 also began to address pollution problems other than those associated with the "criteria" pollutants regulated under the NAAQS. For example, Congress in 1970 enacted the first program to regulate "hazardous air pollutants," or air toxics, as § 112 of the Act.

Finally, Congress grappled separately with the issue of mobile source pollution. §§ 202–234. Recognizing the political and technical difficulties associated with control of vehicle tailpipe emissions, Congress balanced environmental and economic concerns and set specific, technology-forcing emissions standards and deadlines for attainment. § 202(b)(1)(A)(B) and (2).

3. *The 1977 Clean Air Act Amendments*

In the early 1970s, EPA and the states began to implement the basic regulatory programs of the 1970 Amendments, including the NAAQS, the NSPS, and the hazardous air pollutant programs. These activities produced controversies that gave rise to the first wave of litigation under the Clean Air Act, and ultimately led to comprehensive amendments to the Act in 1977.

The 1977 Clean Air Act Amendments first of all refined the basic programs of the 1970 Act. For example, Congress adjusted the dates for attainment of the NAAQS (§ 171(a), (b)), 42 U.S.C.A. § 7502(a)(1)(2) and (b),[1] and provided additional guidance for development by the states of programs for areas that remained out of compliance with the NAAQS (*i.e.*, the "nonattainment" SIP requirements). § 109. With respect to the hazardous air pollutants program, Congress directed EPA to consider regulation of several specific pollutants (radionuclides, arsenic, and polycyclic organic matter), and required EPA to make regulatory decisions

---

1. The 1977 Amendments to the Clean Air Act are codified at 42 U.S.C.A. § 7401, *et seq.* Subsequent citations to the Clean Air Act in this section of this chapter are to this codification of the Act.

regarding these and other pollutants according to specific deadlines. §§ 120, 112.

Second, Congress in the 1977 Amendments further broadened the goals of the Act, and more specifically defined the scope of EPA's regulatory obligations. For example, Congress codified the prevention of significant deterioration ("PSD") program, *See Alabama Power Co. v. Costle*, 636 F.2d 323 (D.C.Cir.1979); CAA § 111(a)(1), 42 U.S.C.A. § 7411(a)(1), and adopted requirements aimed at improving visibility in national parks. § 169A. Congress also adopted limitations on dispersion credit to address concerns with the long range transport of air pollution. CAA § 123(a), *see Natural Resources Defense Council v. Thomas*, 838 F.2d 1224 (D.C.Cir.1988), *cert. denied*, 488 U.S. 888, 109 S.Ct. 219, 102 L.Ed.2d 210 (1988); *Sierra Club v. EPA*, 719 F.2d 436 (D.C.Cir.1983), *cert. denied*, 468 U.S. 1204, 104 S.Ct. 3571, 82 L.Ed.2d 870 (1984). These broad, welfare-based concerns foreshadowed a debate that would continue through the 1980s regarding the need for even more extensive legislation addressing acid rain and visibility.

Finally, as the scope of the Clean Air Act expanded, Congress began to use the Clean Air Act as a tool for addressing social policy. With respect to the NSPS program, for example, Congress acted to protect the nation's reserves of high sulfur coal and the jobs of high sulfur coal miners by adopting a requirement that large, new fossil fuel-fired boilers install "flue gas desulfurization" systems, or SO_2 scrubbers. *See* S. Ackerman & W. Hassler, *Clean Coal, Dirty Air*, Yale University Press (1981) at 32–33, 98–99.

4. *Efforts to Implement the Clean Act Through the 1980s*

The Clean Air Act after the 1977 Amendments can be summarized in terms of three categories of programs. The first category addresses air quality regulation. In this category fall the NAAQS and SIP programs (§§ 109, 110), which are designed to regulate wide-spread and pervasive pollution problems. The substances addressed by the NAAQS are referred to as "criteria pollutants." These include SO_2, NO_X, particulates (PM), carbon monoxide (CO), lead, ozone and non-methane hydrocarbons (including volatile organic compounds or "VOCs"). All sources of air pollution are subject to the NAAQS, and are regulated as necessary through emission limitations set by states in SIPs.

The SIPs are the principal Clean Air Act tool for control of emissions from existing stationary sources of air pollution. In areas with clean air, emission limitations in SIPs must be set at a level that ensures that compliance with the NAAQS is maintained. In areas that do *not* attain the NAAQS (*i.e.*, in "nonattainment areas") sources are subject to more stringent controls, designed to bring those areas into attainment with the NAAQS. For example, in order to bring nonattainment areas into compliance with the NAAQS, states must develop requirements that ensure "reasonable further progress" towards attainment, and large existing stationary sources of nonattainment pollutants must install "reasonably available control technology" ("RACT"). § 172(b)(2).

The second category of programs addressed by the 1977 Amendments involves regulation of new and modified sources of air pollution, which includes application of stringent control technology requirements to these sources. *See* §§ 111, 165, 173. Categories of sources that cause or contribute to significant air pollution are subject to the new source performance standard ("NSPS") program, pursuant to which emission limitations are set to reflect "best adequately demonstrated control technology." § 111(a)(1)(C). New sources in areas that attain the NAAQS are also subject to the prevention of significant deterioration ("PSD") preconstruction permitting program, which requires compliance with (1) "air quality increments" that represent levels of ambient air quality more stringent than the NAAQS, § 163, and (2) control technology requirements that must be at least as stringent as NSPS (*i.e.*, that must reflect "best available control technology," or "BACT," for that individual source). § 165(a). New and modified sources in areas that do not attain the NAAQS are subject to a different preconstruction permitting program, under which they must (1) offset projected emissions increases of nonattainment pollutants with emission reductions of those pollutants at existing facilities, and (2) install control technology to achieve the lowest achievable emission rate ("LAER") for that pollutant that is feasible for that source category or similar source categories. § 173.

The third category of programs under the 1977 Amendments addresses special pollution problems. The most important of these programs concern national emission standards for hazardous air pollutants ("NESHAP"), and protection of visibility in national parks. §§ 112, 169A.

Substantial administrative resources have been devoted to implementation of these Clean Air Act programs since 1977. Congress' most recent efforts to guide and to expedite regulation of air pollution through the 1990 Amendments to the Clean Air Act can be understood best in light of EPA's experience with implementation of the Act after 1977.

5. *The NAAQS/SIP Program*

The NAAQS for criteria pollutants were put in place in the early 1970s in response to the 1970 Amendments. The Act called upon EPA to review these standards at five year intervals, in order to determine whether more stringent standards were necessary to protect public health and welfare.

Pursuant to this mandate, EPA after 1977 periodically reviewed the "primary" (*i.e.*, health-based) NAAQS for SO_2, NO_X, PM, CO, ozone and lead. During the 1980s, this review produced a new primary ambient standard for small particles, minor adjustments to the CO standard, and a host of administrative proceedings and litigation regarding the need to revise the NAAQS for other criteria pollutants.

For example, EPA in 1987 completed a revision to the PM NAAQS, in which it changed the basis for the standard from total particulate matter to "PM–10," or particles with a median aerodynamic diameter of ten microns or less (*i.e.*, small particles). 52 Fed. Reg. 24,634 (1987). States thereafter grappled with how to implement this standard through the SIP process—an effort that took much longer than the nine months allotted by the 1977 Act. This delay resulted in district court litigation, in which citizen group plaintiffs undertook to force EPA to set SIP requirements for the states. *Sierra Club v. Reilly*, No. 89–3408 (D.D.C. filed Dec. 20, 1989).

With respect to the NAAQS for ozone, EPA again undertook a review proceeding after the 1977 Amendments. The failure to conclude this proceeding and to revise the standard led to litigation and, in response to that litigation, an Agency notice indicating that the data that existed as of the date of completion of the last review of the ozone criteria document (in 1988) did not establish that a revision to the NAAQS was appropriate. 57 Fed. Reg. 35,542 (1992). The Agency promptly began another review of the ozone standard after issuance of this notice, and plans to complete that review and issue a revised criteria document expeditiously.

Since many areas of the country have had difficulty attaining even the existing NAAQS for ozone, EPA in 1987 proposed a policy for bringing such areas into attainment with the NAAQS. 52 Fed. Reg. 45,044 (1987). Under EPA's proposed policy, sanctions for failure to meet the Act's attainment deadlines (*e.g.*, a moratorium on new construction) would not apply as long as the SIP for the area was revised to provide for reasonable further progress towards attainment, with a demonstration of attainment within a set period of time. *Id.* at 45,044–5. This policy statement prompted litigation that cast doubt on EPA's authority to allow states to structure a flexible approach to attainment, and raised the spectre of both greater federal involvement in nonattainment areas and of restrictions on industrial growth, unless Congress acted to extend the 1987 attainment deadline. 832 F.2d 1071 (9th Cir.1987).

EPA also considered during the 1980s the adoption of a stringent, short-term average (i.e., five-minute to one-hour) NAAQS for SO_2, in order to protect asthmatics. In 1989, EPA was ordered by the District Court for the Southern District of New York to complete its review of the primary SO_2 NAAQS, 870 F.2d 892 (2d Cir.1989), but that review has not yet been completed.

In addition to the primary NAAQS, EPA has reviewed the secondary NAAQS for particulate matter, SO_2, and other pollutants. (These are the NAAQS which address public welfare concerns.) Among other things, EPA has had under consideration for a number of years whether to set a fine particle standard (PM–2.5) to protect visibility, and whether to adopt a more stringent secondary NAAQS for SO_2 to address acid deposition. 52 Fed. Reg. 24670 (1987). Once again, citizen groups have sought to speed the pace of these administrative proceedings through litigation. *See, e.g., Environmental Defense Fund v. Thomas*, 870 F.2d 892 (2d Cir.1989), *cert. denied*, 493 U.S. 991, 110 S.Ct. 537, 107 L.Ed.2d 535 (1989); *Natural Resources Defense Council v. EPA*, 902 F.2d 962 (D.C.Cir.1990).

As can be seen, EPA's implementation of the NAAQS through the 1980s was characterized by litigation addressing both the substance and timing of regulatory action. The heated controversy over the substance and timing of NAAQS revisions led Congress to address the scope and nature of EPA's responsibilities with respect to the NAAQS in the 1990 Amendments to the Act, by providing new deadlines for Agency action and more specific directions as to how to implement the NAAQS.

6. *New Source Control Programs*

The control technology program for new and modified sources of air pollution (i.e., the NSPS program) proved to be among the more successful Clean Air Act programs during the 1980s. As of the end of the decade, EPA had developed NSPS for over sixty source categories. Moreover, given the difficulty EPA experienced with hazardous air pollution regulation during the 1980s, EPA had begun in the late 1980s to examine how the NSPS program might be used to regulate hazardous air pollutants. 51 Fed. Reg. 22,384 (1986).

Rulemaking to establish and to revise NSPS, however, proved increasingly costly and time-consuming. Perhaps the most important developments with respect to the new source control programs during the late 1980s, therefore, came through policy statements and guidance. Two issues exemplify EPA's efforts to find a means other than legislative rulemaking to implement the new source programs.

The first issue concerns when an existing source is "modified" so that it becomes subject to the more stringent new source control standards. Under the so-called *WEPCo* doctrine, EPA stated that if equipment has deteriorated so that a facility cannot operate up to its original design capacity, work undertaken to repair the facility to restore that original design capacity will result in application of more stringent new source standards, unless that work can be characterized as "routine repair, replacement, or maintenance." *See* Letter from Don R. Clay, EPA Acting Assistant Administrator for Air & Radiation, to John W. Boston, Vice President, Wisconsin Electric Power Company (February 15, 1989); Letter from Lee Thomas, EPA Administrator, to John W. Boston, *WEPCo* (October 14, 1988); Memorandum from Don R. Clay, EPA, to David A. Kee, EPA Region V, Director Air and Radiation Division (September 9, 1988). The Seventh Circuit set aside EPA's decision with respect to the PSD preconstruction permitting program, *Wisconsin Electric Power Co. ("WEPCo") v. Reilly*, 893 F.2d 901 (7th Cir.1990), and in response to that decision, EPA has issued an interpretive rule, as well as specific rule changes applicable to the electric utility industry, addressing when existing sources that undertake repair or replacement projects become subject to the NSPS, PSD and nonattainment programs. 57 Fed. Reg. 32,314 (1992).

The second issue concerns how best available control technology ("BACT") is to be established for individual new or modified sources during the PSD permitting process. Under the so-called "top-down" BACT policy announced in 1987, EPA has required new sources to apply the most stringent control technology available, unless use of that technology is shown to be infeasible at a given source. This policy has been applied to require control technology decisions more stringent than the traditional BACT standard, and which resemble the more restrictive control technology standards in nonattainment areas (known as the "lowest achievable emission rate," or "LAER" standard). Litigation regarding the guidance memoranda that embody the top-down BACT policy resulted in a settlement agreement, pursuant to which EPA agreed to undertake rulemaking clarifying the BACT standard. *American Paper Institute v. EPA*, No. 89–1428, *et al.* (D.C. Cir., filed July 1990). Lengthy debate between EPA and the Bush Administration, however, prevented issuance of a rule, with the result that the top-down BACT controversy will have to be addressed by the Clinton Administration. Both the *WEPCo* guidance and the top-down BACT policy reflect an effort on the part of EPA to find more simple means of implementing the Act, given the time consuming nature of legislative rulemaking.

7. *Specific Pollution Problems*

Besides the ambient air quality and new source control programs, the Act as amended in 1977 addressed several specific pollution problems. EPA's efforts to implement these programs have been no less controversial than its efforts to implement the NAAQS and new source programs.

a. *Hazardous Air Pollutants*

In 1970, Congress adopted a regulatory program (§ 112 of the Act) targeted at a limited number of especially hazardous substances. S. Rep. No. 1196, 91st Cong., 2d Sess. 418 (1970). In 1977, Congress required EPA to regulate several specific pollutants under this provision.

The statutory language implementing this program (§ 112 of the Act) was written broadly. That is, § 112 directed EPA to list as a hazardous air pollutant *any* substance that can cause serious health problems when emitted to the ambient air. Once listed, Congress required EPA to regulate the listed substance at a level that would protect public health with an ample margin of safety.

Virtually every aspect of this statutory directive resulted in litigation during the 1980s. For example, environmental interest groups argued that EPA had an obligation to list for regulation under this provision every known or probable carcinogen. Once a substance was listed, they argued that EPA was obligated to regulate every possible source category of that substance, regardless of the magnitude of risk associated with emissions from the source category. In setting emission standards, these groups argued that EPA was required to eliminate all risk of adverse health effects. Finally, they argued that EPA had no authority to consider costs and technological feasibility in setting emission standards under § 112.

Ironically, many of these questions were answered by courts in the Second Circuit and the D.C. Circuit, *Natural Resources Defense Council v. Thomas*, 885 F.2d 1067 (2d Cir.1989); *Natural Resources Defense Council v. EPA*, 824 F.2d 1146 (D.C.Cir.1987), and EPA was proceeding to finalize a number of § 112 decisions, as the Act was amended to revise in its entirety the hazardous air pollutant program to address the issues debated during the 1980s.

b. Visibility Protection

In 1980, under § 169A of the 1977 Amendments, EPA adopted the so-called "Phase I" visibility program addressing "plume blight" (*i.e.*, visible plumes) in national parks. 45 Fed. Reg. 34,763 (1980). EPA did not address the more widespread problem of "regional haze" that was not clearly attributable to a single, identifiable source of pollution. Rather, given the lack of techniques for attributing regional haze to specific sources, EPA left this concern for regulation in a future, Phase II program. *Id.* at 34,764. Since EPA never undertook a Phase II regulatory proceeding, the limited scope of the visibility program gave rise during the 1980s to a number of lawsuits, including an attempt to force EPA to set a secondary NAAQS for fine particles. *See, e.g., Natural Resources Defense Council v. EPA*, 902 F.2d 962 (D.C.Cir.1990), *vacated in part*, Order of January 2, 1991.

While resisting undertaking a rulemaking to develop a Phase II regulatory program in light of the significant scientific uncertainties, EPA did take a step in the direction of regional haze regulation in the case of an individual source, where the constituents of the plume of that source were claimed to be a significant contributor to regional haze. Based on the alleged contribution of the Salt River Project's Navajo Power Plant to regional haze in the Grand Canyon. 54 Fed. Reg. 36,948 (1989). EPA required imposition on this source of "best available retrofit technology" ("BART") under the Phase I visibility program, which resulted in control expenditures in excess of $1 billion for the facility. This decision, which was upheld by the U.S. Court of Appeals for the 9th Circuit, *Central Arizona Water Conservation District, et al. v. EPA*, 990 F.2d 1531 (9th Cir.1993), sets an important precedent for regulation of other sources that contribute to haze in national parks, and signals the Agency's continuing search for ways to set general policy through means other than the traditional rulemaking process.

c. International Air Pollution

During the 1980s, EPA was the target of persistent litigation attempting to force it to regulate acid deposition under § 115, the international air pollution provision of the Clean Air Act. After several years of litigation, the courts dismissed the lawsuits, and told the plaintiff environmental groups and states to seek relief by filing an administrative petition with the Agency under § 115 of the Act (which creates an administrative mechanism for addressing international air pollution problems). Administrative petitions were filed in mid–1988. At the same time, the Administration undertook an effort to conclude an international agreement with Canada addressing transboundary pollution problems. Most activity in this area was overtaken, however, by the 1990 Amendments to the Act.

8. *The Clean Air Act Amendments of 1990*

Implementation of the 1970 and 1977 Amendments was shaped by heated debate over the costs and benefits of air pollution control. The high costs of regulation and uncertainties as to the nature and magnitude of associated benefits created sharp differences among interest groups, states, and regions of the country. EPA's attempts to reconcile these differences led to delays in implementing key provisions of the Act, in spite of Congress' frequent use of statutory deadlines.

These political differences led Congress to begin to re-evaluate the balances it struck in the 1977 Amendments as early as 1980. At that time, industry sought legislative refinements to the 1977 Amendments—arguing, for example, for more flexibility and less Agency interference in the SIP process and in new source permitting. Environmental groups focused initially on expanding the Act to regulate more directly pollution that contributes to public welfare concerns such as "acid deposition," and later expanded their focus to include more detailed regulation of air toxics and nonattainment pollutants.

During the 1980s, the political controversies generated by clean air regulation proved no less difficult for Congress to resolve than for the Agency. After ten years of political stalemate, Congress in October 1990 enacted extensive amendments to the Clean Air Act, which were signed into law by President Bush on November 15, 1990. *See* Clean Air Act (as amended), Public Law No. 101–549, 104 Stat. 2399 (1990).

The 1990 Amendments are more lengthy and complex than any previous environmental legislation. They are also far different in form and content than the changes sought by industry and environmental groups in the early 1980s.

In amending the Clean Air Act in 1990, Congress decided not to change the direction of its earlier programs of air quality regulation. Rather, Congress accepted what it had created in 1970 and 1977, and added to that structure. Thus, for example, while Congress enacted a comprehensive operating permit program in 1990 to group together all source-specific requirements in one document, it did not abandon the SIP program. While Congress created a comprehensive regulatory program addressing acid rain, it did not abandon earlier attempts to regulate acid deposition, including the international air pollution and stack height provisions of the 1977 Amendments. And even though the

Agency had difficulty meeting statutory deadlines under the 1977 Amendments, Congress set many more deadlines for Agency action in the 1970 Amendments. As a result, the 1990 Amendments create substantial new regulatory responsibilities while leaving in place most of the pre-existing system of air pollution control. Whether this new combination of statutory directives and regulatory responsibilities will produce more effective clean air regulation remains to be seen. Below is a table outlining the provisions of the Clean Air Act Amendments of 1990:

Title	Description
Title I	Provisions For Attainment And Maintenance of National Ambient Air Quality Standards
Title II	Provisions Relating To Mobile Sources
Title III	Hazardous Air Pollutants
Title IV	Acid Deposition Control
Title V	Permits
Title VI	Stratospheric Ozone Protection
Title VII	Provisions Relating To Enforcement
Title VIII	Miscellaneous Provisions
Title IX	Clean Air Research
Title X	Disadvantaged Business Concerns
Title XI	Clean Air Employment Transition Assistance

The Clean Air Act reflects the culmination of over two decades of regulatory development and political debate. Over this period, more authority has gradually been given to EPA to implement regulatory requirements, and to control the states' application of those requirements. Under the 1967 Act, the federal government provided guidance and technical support to states. By contrast, under the 1990 Amendments, EPA has a much more central role. For example, it must define the minimum content of operating permits that apply to virtually all sources; it must approve state permit programs; and it has broad authority to veto state permit decisions and to revoke state permit programs. EPA must implement the air toxics and acid deposition programs. EPA enforcement authority is greatly enhanced. This expansion of authority at the federal level has the potential for making air quality regulation less responsive to state and local needs.

Congress in the 1990 Amendments to the Act has given increasingly specific guidance to EPA on how to exercise its regulatory authority. At the same time, Congress has greatly expanded the Agency's regulatory responsibilities. For example, under the 1990 Amendments, EPA does not have to determine what specific hazardous air pollutants to list for regulation, or what source categories to regulate, or whether to set control technology-based air toxics emission standards. Rather, it must regulate *every* major source category of each of 189 pollutants using sophisticated control technology standards. It is unclear whether Congress' more specific guidance will enable the Agency to deal any more efficiently with its extensive regulatory duties.

The Act's strict deadlines for EPA action will continue to place competing demands on limited Agency resources. For example, under the SIP program, the Agency has deadlines for classifying areas according to attainment status, for issuing control technology guidance, and for reviewing state plans. Under the NSPS program, the Agency has deadlines for revising NSPS and setting new NSPS. Under the hazardous air pollutant program, the Agency has deadlines for identifying source categories and for adopting emission standards. Under the new permit program, the Agency has deadlines for issuing regulations that establish requirements for state programs and for a substitute federal program. Under the acid deposition program, the Agency has deadlines for issuing regulations that establish a trading system, a federal permit program, and the specifics of the allowance system.

The Agency's resources will inevitably be less than adequate to deal with all of these deadlines and regulatory proceedings. Indeed, the Agency has already missed many regulatory deadlines under the 1990 Amendments, thereby creating difficulties for industries and states in determining how best to achieve their respective obligations under the Act. The result, as a practical matter, may be to give a greater role to district courts in setting the Agency's regulatory priorities, through the citizen suit provision of the Act.

Finally, given the difficult if not impossible implementation task given to EPA by Congress in the 1990 Amendments, the success of air quality regulation may ultimately depend upon the ability of EPA to move beyond the political controversy and delay associated with the command-and-control approach to regulation that has traditionally been at the heart of the Clean Air Act, to bring market forces to bear on regulatory issues. To date, Congress' principal attempt to introduce market forces into the regulatory process is the acid deposition program of the 1990 Amendments. The Agency and the states, however, have authority under the 1990 Amendments to apply such principles to other regulatory programs. The effectiveness of the Act over the next decade will depend in large measure on the ability of EPA and the states to use this authority to introduce more flexibility into Clean Air Act regulation and enforcement.

In sum, the Clean Air Act Amendments of 1990 contain substantial and complex new regulatory requirements. It is unclear whether Congress' effort to guide the Agency through this maze of requirements with a combination of specific statutory directives and regulatory deadlines will bear fruit. Implementation of the 1990 Amendments will call on the Agency to set realistic priorities, to be more open with respect to its regulatory plans, and to demonstrate a willingness to invite and to act on early public input.

§ 9.2 AIR QUALITY PLANNING

Before enactment of the 1990 Amendments, the Act was implemented primarily through state implementation plans ("SIP"), which spell out the emission limitations applicable to individual sources of air pollution. The following table describes the steps necessary for a state to develop a SIP under the CAA:

CAA Section	Description of the SIP Process
§ 107 Designate AQCRs	AQCRs are designated. They are the basic jurisdiction for air quality management. They are often metropolitan areas, but all areas of the nation, even clean, rural areas, are in an AQCR. Procedures are specified for dividing AQCRs into compliance and nonattainment areas for each criteria pollutant. Nonattainment areas for some criteria pollutants are further classified according to the severity of pollution.
§ 108 List Regulated Air Pollutants	EPA lists air pollutants to be regulated and twelve months later, EPA issues a "Criteria Document" and, simultaneously, a "Control Techniques Document" for each pollutant.
§ 109 Issue Air Quality Standards	EPA issues numerical standards, based on documents developed under section 108. These standards are the NAAQS. The "Primary Standard" is health based, and provides an adequate margin of safety; theoretically, there is no economic test in setting NAAQS. "Secondary Standards" are more stringent and are designed to protect the public welfare.
§ 110 Adopt SIP & Submit SIP to EPA	After EPA promulgates CAA section 109 standards, each State must adopt a SIP and submit it to EPA for approval for each AQCR in the state. Under CAA sections 309 and 109(d), EPA is required to review primary and secondary standards every five years. Each time these standards change, the SIP must also be changed. Legislative changes in statutory requirements also require SIP revisions. EPA must approve each SIP. After EPA approves the SIP, a State has to implement the SIP and bring its AQCRs into compliance. If EPA does not approve, the SIP must be returned to the State for changes. If the State does not prepare an adequate SIP, EPA must prepare a Federal Implementation Plan (FIP).
§§ 160–169 Attainment Area Requirements (PSDs)	This subpart C of subchapter I imposes additional requirements on areas that meet the NAAQS. These are known as prevention of significant deterioration (PSD) areas.

§§ 171–193 Nonattainment Area Requirements	This subpart D of subchapter I imposes additional requirements on areas that fail to meet the NAAQS.
§ 175A SIP Revisions	This section imposes SIP revision requirements to include maintenance plans for nonattainment areas that seek redesignation to attainment status.

The Clean Air Act provided only for a *preconstruction* permitting program for major new sources of air pollution, or major modifications of those sources. Preconstruction permitting is addressed under the prevention of significant deterioration (PSD) program of Title I, Part C, of the Act, and the nonattainment area provisions of Title I, Part D of the Act.

The following flow chart describes the framework of the CAA permitting scheme form the standpoint of the six criteria pollutants:

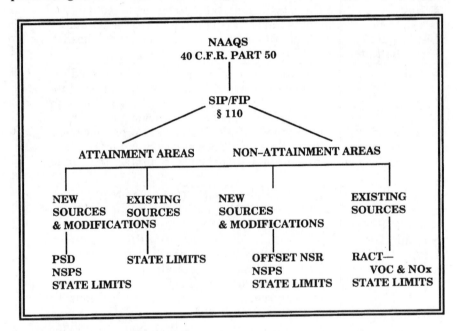

While many states established their own operating permit programs for air pollution sources during the 1970s and 1980s, EPA maintained that it had no authority to require or to enforce these state operating permits until the late 1980s. In 1989, the Agency issued guidance addressing when permits issued pursuant to a state operating permit program authorized by a federally-approved SIP could be considered to embody "federally enforceable" emission limits and operating restrictions. 54 Fed. Reg. 27,274 (1989).

The 1990 Amendments changed the basic approach to regulation of existing sources of air pollution by establishing a new *federal* operating permit program that applies to virtually all sources. The heart of the operating permit program is in Title V of the Act. Additional aspects of the new operating permit program are addressed in Title IV (the acid rain program) and Title III (the air toxics program). This federal operating permit program does not replace, but rather is in addition to, the preconstruction permitting requirements of the federal CAA and existing state permit programs.

The operating permit program of the 1990 Amendments is designed to be run by the states, but only after EPA gives the states guidance on the program, and only with close oversight by EPA. Under Title V, EPA must develop through rulemaking detailed guidelines that the states must follow in setting up their individual operating permit programs. EPA must also judge the adequacy of each state program, and may write and administer permit programs in states that do not develop such programs in a timely manner.

A state then must develop its Title V program based upon EPA's guidance, and the state program is subject to review and approval by EPA. Even after a state permit program is in effect, however, EPA continues to play a role in the review of individual permits issued by the states, and may veto any permit that it concludes does not properly implement applicable CAA requirements. After a permit is issued, EPA may terminate, modify, or revoke the permit upon determining that cause exists to do so.

The new operating permit program covers all major stationary sources, and many other sources as well. Once the program is in effect, each covered source will have to apply for and operate in compliance with the terms of an operating permit that contains (1) enforceable emission limitations (including the emission limitations of the applicable SIP); (2) a schedule for complying with any statutory requirements not yet being met; (3) inspection, monitoring, and reporting requirements; and (4) other conditions and measures as necessary to assure compliance with CAA requirements.

EPA's Title V rules make clear that the operating permit program is to be essentially procedural in nature. That is, Title V permits are to include the requirements that otherwise apply to a source under the Clean Air Act, and Title V does *not* authorize development of new substantive requirements.[1] It is unclear, however, whether this basic principle is being respected as states proceed to develop Title V operating permit programs.

§ 9.3   NONATTAINMENT

Title I of the 1990 Amendments contains new requirements for areas that do not attain ambient air quality standards, including areas in violation of the NAAQS for CO, PM–10, and the two precursors of

§ 9.2

1. *See* 40 C.F.R. § 70.1. (All citations in the text of this Chapter to 40 C.F.R. Part 70 will hereafter refer to the section number only.)

ozone—volatile organic compounds ("VOCs") and NO$_X$. The Amendments emphasize an incremental approach to attainment of these standards, ranking areas by the seriousness of the nonattainment problem, and providing more stringent controls and longer deadlines for areas with more serious nonattainment problems.

CHEVRON v. NRDC
467 U.S. 837, 104 S.Ct. 2778, 81 L.Ed.2d 694 (1984).

JUSTICE STEVENS delivered the opinion of the Court.

In the Clean Air Act Amendments of 1977, Pub. L. 95–95, 91 Stat. 685, Congress enacted certain requirements applicable to States that had not achieved the national air quality standards established by the Environmental Protection Agency (EPA) pursuant to earlier legislation. The amended Clean Air Act required these "nonattainment" States to establish a permit program regulating "new or modified major stationary sources" of air pollution. Generally, a permit may not be issued for a new or modified major stationary source unless several stringent conditions are met. . . . The EPA regulation promulgated to implement this permit requirement allows a State to adopt a plantwide definition of the term "stationary source." . . . Under this definition, an existing plant that contains several pollution-emitting devices may install or modify one piece of equipment without meeting the permit conditions if the alteration will not increase the total emissions from the plant. The question presented by these cases is whether EPA's decision to allow States to treat all of the pollution-emitting devices within the same industrial grouping as though they were encased within a single "bubble" is based on a reasonable construction of the statutory term "stationary source."

I

The EPA regulations containing the plantwide definition of the term stationary source were promulgated on October 14, 1981. 46 Fed. Reg. 50766. Respondents . . . filed a timely petition for review in the United States Court of Appeals for the District of Columbia Circuit pursuant to 42 U. S. C. § 7607(b)(1). . . . The Court of Appeals set aside the regulations. *Natural Resources Defense Council, Inc. v. Gorsuch*, 222 U.S. App. D. C. 268, 685 F.2d 718 (1982).

The court observed that the relevant part of the amended Clean Air Act "does not explicitly define what Congress envisioned as a 'stationary source,' to which the permit program . . . should apply," and further stated that the precise issue was not "squarely addressed in the legislative history." *Id.*, at 273, 685 F.2d, at 723. In light of its conclusion that the legislative history bearing on the question was "at best contradictory," it reasoned that "the purposes of the non-attainment program should guide our decision here." *Id.*, at 276, n. 39, 685 F.2d, at 726, n. 39. . . . Based on two of its precedents concerning the applicability of the bubble concept to certain Clean Air Act programs, . . . the court stated that the bubble concept was "mandatory" in programs designed merely to maintain existing air quality, but held that it was "inappropriate" in programs enacted to improve air quality. *Id.,* at 276, 685 F.2d, at 726. Since the purpose of the permit program—its "raison d'etre," in the court's view—was to improve air quality, the court held that the bubble concept was inapplicable in these cases under its prior precedents. Ibid. It therefore set aside the regulations embodying the bubble concept as contrary to law. We granted certiorari to review that judgment, 461 U.S. 956 (1983), and we now reverse.

The basic legal error of the Court of Appeals was to adopt a static judicial definition of the term "stationary source" when it had decided that Congress itself had not commanded that definition. Respondents do not defend the legal reasoning of the Court of Appeals. . . . Nevertheless, since this Court reviews judgments, not opinions, . . . we must determine whether the Court of Appeals' legal error resulted in an erroneous judgment on the validity of the regulations.

* * *

In the 1950's and the 1960's Congress enacted a series of statutes designed to encourage and to assist the States in curtailing air pollution. *See generally Train v. Natural Resources Defense Council, Inc.,* 421 U.S. 60, 63–64 (1975). The Clean Air Amendments of 1970, Pub. L. 91–604, 84 Stat. 1676, "sharply increased federal authority and responsibility in the continuing effort to combat air pollution," 421 U.S., at 64, but continued to assign "primary responsibility for assuring air quality" to the several States, 84 Stat. 1678. Section 109 of the 1970 Amendments directed the EPA to promulgate National Ambient Air Quality Standards (NAAQS's) . . . and § 110 directed the States to develop plans (SIP's) to implement the standards within specified deadlines. In addition, § 111 provided that major new sources of pollution would be required to conform to technology-based performance standards; the EPA was directed to publish a list of categories of sources of pollution and to establish new source performance standards (NSPS) for each. Section 111(e) prohibited the operation of any new source in violation of a performance standard.

Section 111(a) defined the terms that are to be used in setting and enforcing standards of performance for new stationary sources. It provided:

"For purposes of this section:

* * *

"(3) The term 'stationary source' means any building, structure, facility, or installation which emits or may emit any air pollutant." 84 Stat. 1683.

In the 1970 Amendments that definition was not only applicable to the NSPS program required by § 111, but also was made applicable to a requirement of § 110 that each state implementation plan contain a procedure for reviewing the location of any proposed new source and preventing its construction if it would preclude the attainment or maintenance of national air quality standards. . . .

In due course, the EPA promulgated NAAQS's, approved SIP's, and adopted detailed regulations governing NSPS's for various categories of equipment. In one of its programs, the EPA used a plantwide definition of the term "stationary source." In 1974, it issued NSPS's for the nonferrous smelting industry that provided that the standards would not apply to the modification of major smelting units if their increased emissions were offset by reductions in other portions of the same plant. . . .

NONATTAINMENT

The 1970 legislation provided for the attainment of primary NAAQS's by 1975. In many areas of the country, particularly the most industrialized States, the statutory goals were not attained. . . . . In 1976, the 94th Congress was confronted with this fundamental problem, as well as many others respecting pollution control. As always in this area, the legislative struggle was basically between interests seeking strict schemes to reduce pollution rapidly to eliminate its social costs and interests advancing the economic concern that strict schemes would retard industrial development with attendant social costs. The 94th Congress, confronting these competing interests, was unable to agree on what response was in the public interest: legislative proposals to deal with nonattainment failed to command the necessary consensus. . . .

In light of this situation, the EPA published an Emissions Offset Interpretative Ruling in December 1976, see 41 Fed. Reg. 55,524, to "fill the gap," as respondents put it, until Congress acted. The Ruling stated that it was intended to address "the issue of whether and to what extent national air quality standards established under the Clean Air Act may restrict or prohibit growth of major new or expanded stationary air pollution sources." *Id.*, at 55,524–55,525. In general, the Ruling provided that "a major new source may locate in an area with air quality worse than a national standard only if stringent conditions can be met." *Id.*, at 55,525. The Ruling gave primary emphasis to the rapid attainment of the statute's environmental goals. . . . Consistent with that emphasis, the construction of every new source in nonattainment areas had to meet the "lowest achievable emission rate" under the current state of the art for that type of facility. *See* Ibid. The 1976 Ruling did not, however, explicitly adopt or reject the "bubble concept." . . .

IV

The Clean Air Act Amendments of 1977 are a lengthy, detailed, technical, complex, and comprehensive response to a major social issue. A small portion of the statute—91 Stat. 745–751 (Part D of Title I of the amended Act, 42 U.S.C. §§ 7501–7508)—expressly deals with nonattainment areas. The focal point of this controversy is one phrase in that portion of the Amendments. . . . .

Basically, the statute required each State in a nonattainment area to prepare and obtain approval of a new SIP by July 1, 1979. In the interim those States were required to comply with the EPA's interpretative Ruling of December 21, 1976. 91 Stat. 745. The deadline for attainment of the primary NAAQS's was extended until December 31, 1982, and in some cases until December 31, 1987, but the SIP's were required to contain a number of provisions designed to achieve the goals as expeditiously as possible. . . . .

Most significantly for our purposes, the statute provided that each plan shall

"(6) require permits for the construction and operation of new or modified major stationary sources in accordance with section 173. . . . " Id., at 747.

Before issuing a permit, § 173 requires (1) the state agency to determine that there will be sufficient emissions reductions in the region to offset the emissions from the new source and also to allow for reasonable further progress toward attainment, or that the increased emissions will not exceed an allowance for growth established pursuant to § 172(b)(5); (2) the applicant to certify that his other sources in the State are in compliance with the SIP, (3) the agency to determine that the applicable SIP is otherwise being implemented, and (4) the proposed source to comply with the lowest achievable emission rate (LAER). . . .

The 1977 Amendments contain no specific reference to the "bubble concept." Nor do they contain a specific definition of the term "stationary source," though they did not disturb the definition of "stationary source" contained in § 111(a)(3), applicable by the terms of the Act to the NSPS program. Section 302(j), however, defines the term "major stationary source" as follows:

"(j) Except as otherwise expressly provided, the terms 'major stationary source' and 'major emitting facility' mean any stationary facility or source of air pollutants which directly emits, or has the potential to emit, one hundred tons per year or more of any air pollutant (including any major emitting facility or source of fugitive emissions of any such pollutant, as determined by rule by the Administrator)." 91 Stat. 770.

V

The legislative history of the portion of the 1977 Amendments dealing with nonattainment areas does not contain any specific comment on the "bubble concept" or the question whether a plantwide definition of a stationary source is permissible under the permit program. It does, however, plainly disclose that in the permit program Congress sought to accommodate the conflict between the economic interest in permitting capital improvements to continue and the environmental interest in improving air quality. Indeed, the House Committee Report identified the economic interest as one of the "two main purposes" of this section of the bill. It stated:

"Section 117 of the bill, adopted during full committee markup establishes a new section 127 of the Clean Air Act. The section has two main purposes: (1) to allow reasonable economic growth to continue in an area while making reasonable further progress to assure attainment of the standards by a fixed date; and (2) to allow States greater flexibility for the former purpose than EPA's present interpretative regulations afford.

"The new provision allows States with nonattainment areas to pursue one of two options. First, the State may proceed under EPA's present 'tradeoff' or 'offset' ruling. The Administrator is authorized, moreover, to modify or amend that ruling in accordance with the intent and purposes of this section.

"The State's second option would be to revise its implementation plan in accordance with this new provision." H. R. Rep. No. 95–294, p. 211 (1977)....

The portion of the Senate Committee Report dealing with nonattainment areas states generally that it was intended to "supersede the EPA administrative approach," and that expansion should be permitted if a State could "demonstrate that these facilities can be accommodated within its overall plan to provide for attainment of air quality standards." S. Rep. No. 95–127, p. 55 (1977). The Senate Report notes the value of "case-by-case review of each new or modified major source of pollution that seeks to locate in a region exceeding an ambient standard," explaining that such a review "requires matching reductions from existing sources against emissions expected from the new source in order to assure that introduction of the new source will not prevent attainment of the applicable standard by the statutory deadline." Ibid. This description of a case-by-case approach to plant additions, which emphasizes the net consequences of the construction or modification of a new source, as well as its impact on the overall achievement of the national standards, was not, however, addressed to the precise issue raised by these cases.

Senator Muskie made the following remarks:

"I should note that the test for determining whether a new or modified source is subject to the EPA interpretative regulation [the Offset Ruling]—and to the permit requirements of the revised implementation plans under the conference bill—is whether the source will emit a pollutant into an area which is exceeding a national ambient air quality standard for that pollutant—or precursor. Thus, a new source is still subject to such requirements as 'lowest achievable emission rate' even if it is constructed as a replacement for an older facility resulting in a net reduction from previous emission levels.

"A source—including an existing facility ordered to convert to coal—is subject to all the nonattainment requirements as a modified source if it makes any physical change which increases the amount of any air pollutant for which the standards in the area are exceeded."

123 Cong. Rec. 26847 (1977).

VI

As previously noted, prior to the 1977 Amendments, the EPA had adhered to a plantwide definition of the term "source" under a NSPS program. After adoption of the 1977 Amendments, proposals for a plantwide definition were considered in at least three formal proceedings.

In January 1979, the EPA considered the question whether the same restriction on new construction in nonattainment areas that had been included in its December 1976 Ruling should be required in the revised SIP's that were scheduled to go into effect in July 1979. After noting that the 1976 Ruling was ambiguous on the question "whether a plant with a number of different processes and emission points would be considered a single source," 44 Fed. Reg. 3,276 (1979), the EPA, in effect, provided a bifurcated answer to that question. In those areas that did not have a revised SIP in effect by July 1979, the EPA rejected the plantwide definition; on the other hand, it expressly concluded that the plantwide approach would be permissible in certain circumstances if authorized by an approved SIP. It stated:

"Where a state implementation plan is revised and implemented to satisfy the requirements of Part D, including the reasonable further progress requirement, the plan requirements for major modifications may exempt modifications of existing facilities that are accompanied by intrasource offsets so that there is no net increase in emissions. The agency endorses such exemptions, which would provide greater flexibility to sources to effectively manage their air emissions at least cost." Ibid. . . .

In April, and again in September 1979, the EPA published additional comments in which it indicated that revised SIP's could adopt the plantwide definition of source in nonattainment areas in certain circumstances. *See id.*, at 20,372, 20,379, 51,924, 51,951, 51,958. On the latter occasion, the EPA made a formal rulemaking proposal that would have permitted the use of the "bubble concept" for new installations within a plant as well as for modifications of existing units. It explained:

" 'Bubble' Exemption: The use of offsets inside the same source is called the 'bubble.' EPA proposes use of the definition of 'source' (see above) to limit the use of the bubble under nonattainment requirements in the following respects:

"i. Part D SIPs that include all requirements needed to assure reasonable further progress and attainment by the deadline under section 172 and that are being carried out need not restrict the use of a plantwide bubble, the same as under the PSD proposal.

"ii. Part D SIPs that do not meet the requirements specified must limit use of the bubble by including a definition of 'installation' as an identifiable piece of process equipment." ...

Significantly, the EPA expressly noted that the word "source" might be given a plantwide definition for some purposes and a narrower definition for other purposes. It wrote:

"Source means any building structure, facility, or installation which emits or may emit any regulated pollutant. 'Building, structure, facility or installation' means plant in PSD areas and in nonattainment areas except where the growth prohibitions would apply or where no adequate SIP exists or is being carried out." *Id.*, at 51,925....

The EPA's summary of its proposed Ruling discloses a flexible rather than rigid definition of the term "source" to implement various policies and programs:

"In summary, EPA is proposing two different ways to define source for different kinds of NSR programs:

"(1) For PSD and complete Part D SIPs, review would apply only to plants, with an unrestricted plant-wide bubble.

"(2) For the offset ruling, restrictions on construction, and incomplete Part D SIPs, review would apply to both plants and individual pieces of process equipment, causing the plant-wide bubble not to apply for new and modified major pieces of equipment.

"In addition, for the restrictions on construction, EPA is proposing to define 'major modification' so as to prohibit the bubble entirely. Finally, an alternative discussed but not favored is to have only pieces of process equipment reviewed, resulting in no plant-wide bubble and allowing minor pieces of equipment to escape NSR regardless of whether they are within a major plant."

Id., at 51,934.

In August 1980, however, the EPA adopted a regulation that, in essence, applied the basic reasoning of the Court of Appeals in these cases. The EPA took particular note of the two then-recent Court of Appeals decisions, which had created the bright-line rule that the "bubble concept" should be employed in a program designed to maintain air quality but not in one designed to enhance air quality. Relying heavily on those cases, ... EPA adopted a dual definition of "source" for nonattainment areas that required a permit whenever a change in either the entire plant, or one of its components, would result in a significant increase in emissions even if the increase was completely offset by reductions elsewhere in the plant. The EPA expressed the opinion that this interpretation was "more consistent with congressional intent" than the plantwide definition because it "would bring in more sources or modifications for review," 45 Fed. Reg. 52,697 (1980), but its primary legal analysis was predicated on the two Court of Appeals decisions.

In 1981 a new administration took office and initiated a "Government-wide reexamination of regulatory burdens and complexities." 46 Fed. Reg. 16,281. In the context of that review, the EPA reevaluated the various arguments that had been advanced in connection with the proper definition of the term "source" and concluded that the term should be given the same definition in both nonattainment areas and PSD areas.

In explaining its conclusion, the EPA first noted that the definitional issue was not squarely addressed in either the statute or its legislative history and therefore that the issue involved an agency "judgment as how to best carry out the Act." Ibid. It then set forth several reasons for concluding that the plantwide definition was more appropriate. It pointed out that the dual definition "can act as a disincentive to new investment and modernization by discouraging modifications to existing facilities" and "can actually retard progress in air pollution control by discouraging replacement of older, dirtier processes or pieces of equipment with new, cleaner ones." Ibid. Moreover, the new definition "would simplify EPA's rules by using the same definition of 'source' for PSD, nonattainment new source review and the construction moratorium. This reduces confusion and inconsistency." Ibid. Finally, the agency explained that additional requirements that remained in place would accomplish the fundamental purposes of achieving attainment with NAAQS's as expeditiously as possible.... These conclusions were expressed in a proposed rulemaking in August 1981 that was formally promulgated in October. See id., at 50,766.

VII

In this Court respondents expressly reject the basic rationale of the Court of Appeals' decision. That court viewed the statutory definition of the term "source" as sufficiently flexible to cover either a plantwide definition, a narrower definition covering each unit within a plant, or a dual definition that could apply to both the entire "bubble" and its components. It interpreted the policies of the statute, however, to mandate the plantwide definition in programs designed to maintain clean air and to forbid it in programs designed to improve air quality. Respondents place a fundamentally different construction on the statute. They contend that the text of the Act requires the EPA to use a dual definition—if either a component of a plant, or the plant as a whole, emits over 100 tons of pollutant, it is a major stationary source. They thus contend that the EPA rules adopted in 1980, insofar as they apply to the maintenance of the quality of clean air, as well as the 1981 rules which apply to nonattainment areas, violate the statute....

STATUTORY LANGUAGE

The definition of the term "stationary source" in § 111(a)(3) refers to "any building, structure, facility, or installation" which emits air pollution. See supra, at 846. This definition is applicable only to the NSPS program by the express terms of the statute; the text of the statute does not make this definition applicable to the permit program.

Petitioners therefore maintain that there is no statutory language even relevant to ascertaining the meaning of stationary source in the permit program aside from § 302(j), which defines the term "major stationary source." *See supra,* at 851. We disagree with petitioners on this point.

The definition in § 302(j) tells us what the word "major" means—a source must emit at least 100 tons of pollution to qualify—but it sheds virtually no light on the meaning of the term "stationary source." It does equate a source with a facility—a "major emitting facility" and a "major stationary source" are synonymous under § 302(j). The ordinary meaning of the term "facility" is some collection of integrated elements which has been designed and constructed to achieve some purpose. Moreover, it is certainly no affront to common English usage to take a reference to a major facility or a major source to connote an entire plant as opposed to its constituent parts. Basically, however, the language of § 302(j) simply does not compel any given interpretation of the term "source."

Respondents recognize that, and hence point to § 111(a)(3). Although the definition in that section is not literally applicable to the permit program, it sheds as much light on the meaning of the word "source" as anything in the statute. . . . As respondents point out, use of the words "building, structure, facility, or installation," as the definition of source, could be read to impose the permit conditions on an individual building that is a part of a plant. . . . A "word may have a character of its own not to be submerged by its association." *Russell Motor Car Co. v. United States,* 261 U.S. 514, 519 (1923). On the other hand, the meaning of a word must be ascertained in the context of achieving particular objectives, and the words associated with it may indicate that the true meaning of the series is to convey a common idea. The language may reasonably be interpreted to impose the requirement on any discrete, but integrated, operation which pollutes. This gives meaning to all of the terms—a single building, not part of a larger operation, would be covered if it emits more than 100 tons of pollution, as would any facility, structure, or installation. Indeed, the language itself implies a "bubble concept" of sorts: each enumerated item would seem to be treated as if it were encased in a bubble. While respondents insist that each of these terms must be given a discrete meaning, they also argue that § 111(a)(3) defines "source" as that term is used in § 302(j). The latter section, however, equates a source with a facility, whereas the former defines "source" as a facility, among other items.

We are not persuaded that parsing of general terms in the text of the statute will reveal an actual intent of Congress. . . . We know full well that this language is not dispositive; the terms are overlapping and the language is not precisely directed to the question of the applicability of a given term in the context of a larger operation. To the extent any congressional "intent" can be discerned from this language, it would appear that the listing of overlapping, illustrative terms was intended to enlarge, rather than to confine, the scope of the agency's power to regulate particular sources in order to effectuate the policies of the Act.

LEGISLATIVE HISTORY

In addition, respondents argue that the legislative history and policies of the Act foreclose the plantwide definition, and that the EPA's interpretation is not entitled to deference because it represents a sharp break with prior interpretations of the Act.

Based on our examination of the legislative history, we agree with the Court of Appeals that it is unilluminating. The general remarks pointed to by respondents "were obviously not made with this narrow issue in mind and they cannot be said to demonstrate a Congressional desire.... " *Jewell Ridge Coal Corp. v. Mine Workers,* 325 U.S. 161, 168–169 (1945). Respondents' argument based on the legislative history relies heavily on Senator Muskie's observation that a new source is subject to the LAER requirement.... But the full statement is ambiguous and like the text of § 173 itself, this comment does not tell us what a new source is, much less that it is to have an inflexible definition. We find that the legislative history as a whole is silent on the precise issue before us. It is, however, consistent with the view that the EPA should have broad discretion in implementing the policies of the 1977 Amendments.

More importantly, that history plainly identifies the policy concerns that motivated the enactment; the plantwide definition is fully consistent with one of those concerns—the allowance of reasonable economic growth—and, whether or not we believe it most effectively implements the other, we must recognize that the EPA has advanced a reasonable explanation for its conclusion that the regulations serve the environmental objectives as well. *See supra,* at 857–859, and n. 29; *see also supra,* at 855, n. 27. Indeed, its reasoning is supported by the public record developed in the rulemaking process, ... as well as by certain private studies....

Our review of the EPA's varying interpretations of the word "source"—both before and after the 1977 Amendments—convinces us that the agency primarily responsible for administering this important legislation has consistently interpreted it flexibly—not in a sterile textual vacuum, but in the context of implementing policy decisions in a technical and complex arena. The fact that the agency has from time to time changed its interpretation of the term "source" does not, as respondents argue, lead us to conclude that no deference should be accorded the agency's interpretation of the statute. An initial agency interpretation is not instantly carved in stone. On the contrary, the agency, to engage in informed rulemaking, must consider varying interpretations and the wisdom of its policy on a continuing basis. Moreover, the fact that the agency has adopted different definitions in different contexts adds force to the argument that the definition itself is flexible, particularly since Congress has never indicated any disapproval of a flexible reading of the statute.

Significantly, it was not the agency in 1980, but rather the Court of Appeals that read the statute inflexibly to command a plantwide definition for programs designed to maintain clean air and to forbid such a definition for programs designed to improve air quality. The distinction the court drew may well be a sensible one, but our labored review of the problem has surely disclosed that it is not a distinction that Congress ever articulated itself, or one that the EPA found in the statute before the courts began to review the legislative work product. We conclude that it was the Court of Appeals, rather than Congress or any of the decisionmakers who are authorized by Congress to administer this legislation, that was primarily responsible for the 1980 position taken by the agency.

POLICY

The arguments over policy that are advanced in the parties' briefs create the impression that respondents are now waging in a judicial forum a specific policy battle which they ultimately lost in the agency and in the 32 jurisdictions opting for the "bubble concept," but one which was never waged in the Congress. Such policy arguments are more properly addressed to legislators or administrators, not to judges. . . .

In these cases the Administrator's interpretation represents a reasonable accommodation of manifestly competing interests and is entitled to deference: the regulatory scheme is technical and complex, . . . the agency considered the matter in a detailed and reasoned fashion, . . . and the decision involves reconciling conflicting policies. . . . Congress intended to accommodate both interests, but did not do so itself on the level of specificity presented by these cases. Perhaps that body consciously desired the Administrator to strike the balance at this level, thinking that those with great expertise and charged with responsibility for administering the provision would be in a better position to do so; perhaps it simply did not consider the question at this level; and perhaps Congress was unable to forge a coalition on either side of the question, and those on each side decided to take their chances with the scheme devised by the agency. For judicial purposes, it matters not which of these things occurred.

Judges are not experts in the field, and are not part of either political branch of the Government. Courts must, in some cases, reconcile competing political interests, but not on the basis of the judges' personal policy preferences. In contrast, an agency to which Congress has delegated policymaking responsibilities may, within the limits of that delegation, properly rely upon the incumbent administration's views of wise policy to inform its judgments. While agencies are not directly accountable to the people, the Chief Executive is, and it is entirely appropriate for this political branch of the Government to make such policy choices—resolving the competing interests which Congress itself either inadvertently did not resolve, or intentionally left to be resolved by the agency charged with the administration of the statute in light of everyday realities.

When a challenge to an agency construction of a statutory provision, fairly conceptualized, really centers on the wisdom of the agency's policy, rather than whether it is a reasonable choice within a gap left open by Congress, the challenge must fail. In such a case, federal judges—who have no constituency—have a duty to respect legitimate policy choices made by those who do. The responsibilities for assessing the wisdom of such policy choices and resolving the struggle between competing views of the public interest are not judicial ones: "Our Constitution vests such responsibilities in the political branches." *TVA v. Hill,* 437 U.S. 153, 195 (1978).

We hold that the EPA's definition of the term "source" is a permissible construction of the statute which seeks to accommodate progress in reducing air pollution with economic growth. "The Regulations which the Administrator has adopted provide what the agency could allowably view as ... [an] effective reconciliation of these twofold ends.... " *United States v. Shimer,* 367 U.S., at 383.

The judgment of the Court of Appeals is reversed.

It is so ordered.

JUSTICE MARSHALL and JUSTICE REHNQUIST took no part in the consideration or decision of these cases.

JUSTICE O'CONNOR took no part in the decision of these cases.

Note

The definition of "major source" is not consistent throughout the Clean Air Act. The chart below describes the variations in definition for purposes of the different sections of the statute:

MAJOR SOURCE DEFINITIONS

Major Source	Definitions based on "emits or potential to emit"
PSD	100 tons per year of any pollutant from the stationary source list § 169 *or* 250 tons per year of any pollutant from any source
Nonattainment	major source varies depending on N/A classification for ozone, CO and PM_{10}. can be as low as 5 tons per year of VOC, for stationary source or group of sources under common control and located in contiguous area
§ 112 hazardous air pollutants	stationary source, or group of stationary sources under common control and located in contiguous area emitting 10 tons per year of *any* hazardous air pollutant *or* 25 tons of *any combination* of hazardous air pollutants
§ 302 general definition	stationary facility or source of air pollutants which directly emits or has potential to emit 100 tons per year or more of any air pollutant, including source of fugitive emissions as determined by Administrator.

1. *State Implementation Plans ("SIPs")*

After the 1990 Amendments, the Act continues to require the implementation of NAAQS in both attainment and nonattainment areas through the state implementation plan ("SIP") program of § 110. The 1990 Amendments, however, make certain procedural and substantive changes in the SIP process, to increase federal control and state accountability.

For example, as under the pre–1990 Act, states are to adopt and to revise SIPs after notice and a public hearing, and in accordance with criteria prescribed by the Act and by EPA. Moreover, once adopted by the state, the SIP must be reviewed by EPA to determine its adequacy in light of these criteria.

The 1990 Amendments allow EPA 12 months (rather than the current four months) to act once a SIP is submitted for federal review. § 110(k)(2). Moreover, the legislation makes clear that EPA will be allowed to approve or to disapprove individual aspects of a SIP submittal, without approving or rejecting the submittal as a whole. § 112(k)(3). As under the pre–1990 Act, EPA must promulgate a federal implementation plan ("FIP") if a state fails to submit a satisfactory SIP or SIP revision.

Section 110(a)(2) sets out the requirements for a SIP:

Elements of a SIP

√ enforceable emission limitations and other control measures including economic incentives;
√ an appropriate monitoring and data analyzing program that provides data to EPA;
√ an enforcement program;
√ adequate provisions to prevent interstate and international air pollution;
√ adequate personnel, funding, and authority under state law to carry out the implementation plan;
√ to the extent prescribed by EPA, requiring statutory sources to monitor, report and make emissions data available to the public;
√ to provide emergency response authority;
√ to provide procedures for revision of the SIP if it is necessary in order to meet NAAQS or additional requirements established under the CAA;
√ to meet the additional requirements of CAA Title I Part D in a plan for nonattainment areas;
√ to meet the requirements of: section 121 in relation to consultation, section 127 relating to public notification, and CAA Title I Part C relating to prevention of significant deterioration of air quality and visibility protection;
√ to provide for the performance of such air quality modeling as EPA may prescribe and for the submission of such data to EPA;
√ to require the owner of each major stationary source to pay a fee sufficient to cover the costs of running and enforcing a permit program;
√ to provide for the consultation and participation by local political subdivisions affected by the plan.

See Arnold W. Reitze, Jr., AIR POLLUTION LAW (1995).

For each pollutant covered by Title I, there are specific, new substantive requirements that must be incorporated into SIPs. These requirements have stimulated a great deal of regulatory activity, since existing SIPs must be revised to reflect these changes.

COALITION FOR CLEAN AIR v. UNITED STATES ENVIRONMENTAL PROTECTION AGENCY
971 F.2d 219 (9th Cir.1992).

NORRIS, CIRCUIT JUDGE:

California's South Coast Air Basin has the dirtiest air in the United States.... Twenty-two years have passed since Congress first enacted legislation requiring implementation plans to attain national air quality standards, and yet today the South Coast still lacks implementation plans for ozone and carbon monoxide. In 1989, EPA entered into a settlement agreement with appellants requiring it to perform its statutory duty and promulgate federal implementation plans for the South Coast on an expeditious schedule. EPA now argues that, when Congress passed the Clean Air Act Amendments of 1990, it relieved EPA of this obligation and returned the implementation plan process to square one. We disagree and reverse the district court's decision vacating the settlement agreement and dismissing the case. *Coalition for Clean Air v. EPA,* 762 F.Supp. 1399 (C.D.Cal.1991). We remand to the district court for reinstatement of the agreement and direct the court to establish an expeditious schedule for EPA to promulgate final implementation plans for the South Coast.

I

The Clean Air Act was passed in 1963, but it was the Clean Air Amendments of 1970, Pub. L. No. 91–604, 84 Stat. 1676 (1970), that gave the Clean Air Act the basic structure it retains today. See generally *Train v. NRDC,* 421 U.S. 60, 63–64, 95 S.Ct. 1470, 43 L.Ed.2d 731 (1975)(discussing pre–1970 statutes). The 1970 Amendments created "a federal-state partnership for the control of air pollution." *Abramowitz v. EPA,* 832 F.2d 1071, 1073 (9th Cir.1987). Section 109 of the Act, as amended, directed EPA to establish National Ambient Air Quality Standards ("NAAQS") for any air pollutants that might endanger public health or welfare. Clean Air Act ("CAA") § 109, 84 Stat. at 1679–80. EPA issued NAAQS for six pollutants in 1971, including carbon monoxide ("CO") and ozone.... Responsibility for meeting these standards fell, in the first instance, to the states, which were required to submit State Implementation Plans ("SIPs") by 1972 that would provide for attainment of the NAAQS by 1975. CAA § 110(a)(1), 84 Stat. at 1680. EPA was required to review the SIPs and to disapprove any that failed to meet the requirements of the Act, including the attainment of NAAQS by the statutory deadline. CAA § 110(a)(2), 84 Stat. at 1680–81. If EPA disapproved a SIP, the 1970 Amendments required that EPA adopt a Federal Implementation Plan ("FIP") that would meet the requirements of the Act and take the place of the disapproved SIP. CAA § 110(c), 84 Stat. at 1681–82.

In February 1972, California submitted a SIP for the South Coast to EPA. On May 31, 1972, EPA announced its disapproval of major portions of the SIP. 37 Fed. Reg. 10,842, 10,851–10,855 (1972). At that point, EPA was statutorily required to adopt a FIP for the South Coast but failed to act. As the result of a citizens' suit, EPA was placed under a court order to prepare a FIP by January 15, 1973 that would provide for attainment of NAAQS no later than 1977. *Riverside v. Ruckelshaus,* Civ. No. 72–2122–H, 4 Envt'l Rep. Cas. (BNA) 1728, 1731 (C.D. Cal. Nov. 16, 1972). During 1973, EPA issued several proposed FIPs that contained extreme provisions including gas rationing. *See, e.g.,* 38 Fed. Reg. 2,194, 2194–2200 (1973); 38 Fed. Reg. 31,232, 31,232–31,255 (1973). On October 15, 1976, EPA revoked its proposed gas rationing regulations, which were due to take effect in 1977, because of "the seriously disruptive social and economic consequences of such regulations," in spite of the fact that the revocation would "render the affected [implementation plans] defective as a legal matter, since such [plans] will no longer contain regulations which provide for NAAQS attainment." 41 Fed. Reg. 45,565 (1976).

Faced with widespread failure by the states to attain NAAQS, Congress amended the Clean Air Act again in 1977, to give "nonattainment" areas more time. Pub. L. No. 95–95, 91 Stat. 685 (1977). The deadline for NAAQS attainment was extended to 1982. CAA § 172, 91 Stat. at 746–48. On July 25, 1979, California submitted a SIP for the South Coast Air Basin requesting an extension of the ozone and CO attainment dates to 1987. EPA proposed to disapprove the SIP because California had failed to adopt a motor vehicle inspection and maintenance program, which was required as a condition for granting such an extension. 45 Fed. Reg. 21,271, 21,271–21,282 (1980). EPA took final action disapproving the SIPs for ozone and CO on January 21, 1981. 46 Fed. Reg. 5,965, 5,975 (1981).

In 1982, California submitted extensive revisions to its proposed South Coast SIPs for ozone and CO. These 1982 proposed SIPs acknowledged that even if the plans were fully implemented, the South Coast would fail to attain the ozone and CO NAAQS by 1987. 48 Fed. Reg. 5074, 5082–5083 (1983). On February 3, 1983, EPA proposed to disapprove the 1982 SIPs. *Id.* at 5074. California submitted further revisions, and EPA took final action on July 30, 1984, approving the CO and ozone control measures without requiring any demonstration that those measures would achieve attainment by the statutory deadline. EPA simply noted that it was deferring any final approval or disapproval of the SIP's attainment provisions. 49 Fed. Reg. 30,300, 30,305 (1984); *see Abramowitz,* 832 F.2d at 1074.

In September 1984, a citizen timely petitioned this court for review of the EPA's 1984 decision. We held that "EPA exceeded its authority under the Clean Air Act by approving the control measures without determining whether those measures would demonstrate attainment by the December 31, 1987 statutory deadline." *Abramowitz,* 832 F.2d at 1072–73. We remanded "with the specific instruction that EPA disapprove the relevant portions of the SIP and face up to implementing the measures which are to be triggered by failure to meet attainment requirements." Id. at 1073. In compliance with our order, EPA disapproved the South Coast SIPs for ozone and CO on January 22, 1988, triggering once again EPA's statutory obligation to adopt FIPs for the South Coast Air Basin. 53 Fed. Reg. 1,780 (1988).

On February 22, 1988, appellants Coalition for Clean Air and the Sierra Club filed this citizens' suit to enforce EPA's obligation to promulgate ozone and CO FIPs for the South Coast. In March 1989, EPA entered into a settlement agreement with plaintiffs, which obligated it to prepare, propose, and promulgate final FIPs for the South Coast. Because of the 1989 San Francisco earthquake, the district court extended EPA's deadline for publishing the proposed FIPs from April 30 to July 31, 1990. EPA finally published the proposed FIPs on September 5, 1990, and agreed to finalize them by February 28, 1991. 55 Fed. Reg. 36,458, 36,458–36,576 (1990).

In the meantime, EPA sought across-the-board relief from its statutory obligation to promulgate FIPs from Congress, which had begun to consider new amendments to the Clean Air Act. In September 1989, at EPA's urging, the Senate passed an amendment that would have left promulgation of FIPs to EPA's discretion. See S. 1630, 101st Cong., 1st Sess., § 105 (1989). In May 1990, a House Committee deleted this language, which prompted a letter from EPA Administrator Reilly complaining that the House action would require promulgation of a FIP imposing "across-the-board, draconian measures devastating the country's largest industrial area," an obvious reference to the South Coast Air Basin. 136 Cong. Rec. H2771, H2887 (daily ed. May 23, 1990). However, Administrator Reilly's complaint went unheeded by Congress. The House language retaining EPA's mandatory obligation to promulgate a FIP whenever it disapproves a SIP was ultimately enacted by Congress and signed into law by President Bush on November 15, 1991 as part of the Clean Air Act Amendments of 1990. Pub. L. No. 101–549, 104 Stat. 2399 (1990).

On November 30, 1991, EPA filed a motion asking the district court to vacate the settlement agreement and dismiss the case on the basis of the 1990 Amendments. EPA argued that Congress could not have intended to continue EPA's obligation to promulgate FIPs for the South Coast under the settlement agreement because the 1990 Amendments contained new criteria and new timetables for attainment, which EPA claimed the states must address in the first instance. Under EPA's interpretation of the 1990 Amendments, its mandatory obligation to promulgate FIPs would be triggered only if California failed to submit adequate SIPs under the new deadlines. The earliest date FIPs would be required for the South Coast under this interpretation of the 1990 Amendments is April 15, 1998. The district court granted EPA's motion to vacate the settlement agreement and dismissed the case. This appeal followed. . . .

Appellants make two arguments in support of their position that EPA is currently obligated to promulgate ozone and CO FIPs for the South Coast. First, they argue that § 110(c)(1)(B) of the Clean Air Act, as amended, did not relieve EPA of its obligation to promulgate these FIPs. Second, they argue that even if § 110(c)(1) had been amended to relieve EPA of its FIP obligation, the Amendments' Savings Clause— § 193 of the Clean Air Act—would have preserved EPA's obligation under the settlement agreement. Because we hold that § 110(c)(1)(B) imposes a current obligation on EPA to promulgate ozone and CO FIPs for the South Coast, we do not reach the Savings Clause question.

II

EPA's statutory obligation to promulgate FIPs is contained in § 110(c)(1) of the Clean Air Act, as amended in 1990:

The Administrator shall promulgate a Federal implementation plan at any time within 2 years after the Administrator–

(A) finds that a State has failed to make a required submission or finds that the plan or plan revision submitted by the State does not satisfy the minimum criteria established under section 7410(k)(1)(A) of this title, or

(B) disapproves a State implementation plan submission in whole or in part, unless the State corrects the deficiency, and the Administrator approves the plan or plan revision, before the Administrator promulgates such Federal implementation plan.

42 U.S.C. § 7410(c)(1). Appellants contend that under subsection (B), EPA is obligated to promulgate ozone and CO FIPs for South Coast based on its disapproval in January 1988 of California's proposed SIPs. EPA, on the other hand, contends that § 110(c)(1), as amended in 1990, was intended to operate prospectively only, so that EPA's obligation to promulgate a FIP for the South Coast will be triggered only if California fails to submit a SIP that meets the requirements of the Clean Air Act by the deadlines set forth in the 1990 Amendments.

A

We begin with the language of the provision: "The Administrator shall promulgate a Federal implementation plan at any time within 2 years after the Administrator ... disapproves a State implementation plan submission in whole or in part." This language is not, by its terms, limited to EPA's disapproval of "newly submitted" SIPs or SIPs "submitted under the 1990 Amendments." Instead it refers to disapproval of state implementations plans generally, either in whole or in part. EPA must promulgate a FIP within two years of such disapproval, unless the state submits and EPA approves revisions to the SIP that correct the deficiency. Since EPA disapproved the South Coast SIPs in January 1988, the statute on its face requires EPA to promulgate FIPs for the South Coast by January 1990. . . .

We recognize that EPA's obligation under § 110(c)(1) is put in the future tense. However, the time referred to by the word "shall" is two years from any of the triggering events listed in the provision, not two years from enactment of the 1990 Amendments. . . . Triggering event (A) actually includes two separate events: (1) EPA's finding that a state has failed to make a required submission, and (2) EPA's finding that a submission fails to meet the minimum criteria for completeness established under § 7410(k)(1)(A). Since § 7410(k)(1)(A) was added by the 1990 Amendments, it appears that the second of these findings could only occur after enactment of the 1990 Amendments. However, neither the first of these findings nor triggering event (B)—disapproval of "a State implementation plan submission in whole or in part"—contains any similar temporal limitation. Since these events could occur in the past or in the future, the use of the future tense "shall" to express EPA's obligation does not indicate Congress' intent that § 110(c)(1) operate prospectively only. In other words, if "disapproves" refers to past disapprovals as well as to future ones, "shall" is the appropriate word to describe obligations which may already have been triggered as well as those which may be triggered in the future.

However, EPA argues that the word "disapproves" cannot refer to past disapprovals because it is phrased in the present tense. EPA relies heavily on *Gwaltney v. Chesapeake Bay Found., Inc.*, 484 U.S. 49, 57–59, 98 L.Ed.2d 306, 108 S.Ct. 376 (1987), in which the Supreme Court interpreted a provision authorizing citizens' suits against persons "alleged to be in violation of" pollution permits as requiring continuous or intermittent violations. However, that case involved more than use of the present tense. It also involved the phrase "in violation," which, coupled with the present tense, suggests a focus on current violations that use of the present tense by itself would not. Moreover, EPA's argument proves too much. As appellants point out, the Clean Air Act, as amended, uses the present tense frequently. For example, Congress uses the present tense to establish criminal liability for "any person who knowingly—(A) makes any false material statement, . . . (B) fails to notify or report as required under this Act; . . ." 42 U.S.C. § 7413(c)(2)(emphasis added). Yet clearly the 1990 Amendments do not forgive criminal violations that occurred prior to the Amendments just because Congress speaks in the present tense. The present tense is commonly used to refer to past, present, and future all at the same time. We believe that Congress used the present tense word "disapproves" because it did not wish to limit § 110(c)(1)(B)'s reach to either past or future disapprovals.

Unlike Judge Noonan, we attach no weight to the fact that Congress chose to repeal an awkwardly drafted § 110(c)(1) and replace it with a clearer version. *See* Dissent at 7752–53. The new § 110(c)(1) contains the same triggering events as the old § 110(c)(1). Judge Noonan asserts that subsection (B) of the amended § 110(c)(1) is new, *see* Dissent at 7755, but it is not. The current subsection (B) merely incorporates the old subsection (B), which required promulgation of a FIP when a SIP was determined not to meet the requirements of the Act. See 84 Stat. at 1681–82. Judge Noonan also focuses on the fact that the 1990 Amendments added a new triggering event: EPA's finding that a submission fails to meet the minimum criteria for completeness established under § 7410(k)(1)(A). *See* Dissent at 7753. He says there is no reason to ignore subsection (A) in interpreting subsection (B). Id. at 7755. The problem with this analysis is that Congress put the word "or" between (A) and (B). Indeed, Congress put the word "or" between the two separate triggering events contained in subsection (A). Clearly Congress intended that EPA's obligation to promulgate a FIP would be triggered by any one of the three triggering events contained in § 110(c)(1) as amended.

In short, the plain language of § 110(c)(1)(B) supports appellants' contention that EPA is currently obligated to promulgate FIPs for the South Coast based on its January 1988 disapproval of California's proposed SIPs.

B

EPA also argues that requiring it to promulgate FIPs for the South Coast at this time would be inconsistent with the 1990 Amendments as a whole because those Amendments impose new deadlines and change certain requirements of the Clean Air Act. The district court found this argument persuasive. It reasoned that if the Act were interpreted to continue EPA's existing obligation to promulgate FIPs for the South Coast, "there would be the anomaly that the SIP prepared by the State under the former criteria and rejected is to be replaced by a FIP prepared under new criteria that the State has never had an opportunity to address." Coalition for Clean Air, 762 F.Supp. at 1401. Of course, the proper contents of FIPs for the South Coast are not before us, and we need not decide whether EPA would be required to meet any additional requirements imposed by the 1990 Amendments in promulgating FIPs for the South Coast. The sole question on appeal is whether EPA's obligation to promulgate such FIPs survived the 1990 Amendments. We therefore consider the 1990 changes in the Act's deadlines and requirements for the limited purpose of deciding whether an "anomaly" would result from enforcing the plain language of § 110(c)(1)(B).

On closer inspection, we find that no such anomaly exists. EPA points to the fact that the 1990 Amendments extend the deadlines for attainment of ozone and CO standards for the South Coast until 2010 and 2000 respectively. 42 U.S.C. § 7511(a)(1); id. § 7512(a)(1). Yet the FIP that EPA has proposed to adopt for the South Coast, ostensibly under the requirements of the old Clean Air Act, provided for attainment of these standards on precisely the same schedule. 55 Fed. Reg. 36,458, 36,500 (1990). Thus, EPA cannot claim that continuing its obligation to promulgate a FIP for the South Coast will deny the region any extra time to which they would be entitled under the 1990 Amendments....

EPA also argues that the 1990 Amendments require new measures to control oxides of nitrogen (NOx) and volatile organic compounds (VOCs), which are precursors of ozone, which the state must address in the first instance. 42 U.S.C. § 7511a(f). However, there is no reason the state may not propose these new measures as revisions to the FIP under the timetables provided in the 1990 Amendments just as the state would be required to do if a FIP had been in effect when those Amendments were adopted. See 42 U.S.C. § 7511a(e). Appellants have not argued that EPA's continuing obligation to promulgate FIPs relieves the state of any new obligations imposed by the 1990 Amendments.

Finally, EPA points out that the 1990 Amendments authorize it, under certain conditions, to approve SIP provisions for the attainment of ozone standards for the South Coast that anticipate new control techniques or the improvement of existing techniques and base attainment on the use of such technological advances. 42 U.S.C. § 7511a(e)(5). This new provision may allow EPA to approve some parts of the ozone SIP that it disapproved in 1988, and Judge Noonan points out that it would "make nonsense" of the 1990 Amendments not to give effect to this provision. *See* Dissent at 7756. However, under § 110(c)(1), EPA has authority to approve a SIP that meets the requirements of the Act at any time prior to the actual promulgation of a FIP. 42 U.S.C. § 7410(c)(1). Thus, there appears to be nothing to stop EPA from allowing California to rely on anticipated technology by approving SIP provisions that now meet the requirements of the Act.

Running throughout EPA's argument is the notion that federal involvement necessarily preempts state planning to control air pollution. However, this is a misconception. The Clean Air Act creates "a federal-state partnership for the control of air pollution," *Abramowitz v. EPA*, 832 F.2d at 1073, which continues after EPA's obligation to promulgate a FIP has been triggered. n9 As we have just observed, the state may propose and EPA may approve revisions to a proposed SIP that meet the requirements of the Act at any time prior to the actual promulgation of a FIP. 42 U.S.C. § 7410(c)(1).... Even after a FIP is promulgated, the states remain responsible for submitting revisions to the FIP if EPA changes the air quality standards, see 42 U.S.C. § 7410(a)(1), or if Congress changes the provisions of the Act, *see,* e.g., 42 U.S.C. § 7511a(e).... Thus, we fail to see how enforcing the plain terms of § 110(c)(1)(B) will create an unintended anomaly.

* * *

2. *Specific Nonattainment Pollutants*

a. *Ozone*

New provisions address the obligation of existing sources to install reasonably available control technology ("RACT") for the two pollutants that contribute to ozone formation—volatile organic compounds ("VOCs") and nitrogen oxides ("NO_x"). For example, EPA is required to issue a list of source categories for which control technique guidelines for RACT have not been published. EPA must then publish the guidelines pursuant to a rolling schedule contained in the legislation. Under the CAA, ozone nonattainment areas are designated as:

√ Marginal

√ Moderate

√ Serious

√ Severe 1

√ Severe 2

√ Extreme

Stationary sources that are not covered by a control technique guidelines document and that emit certain levels of VOCs will also be required to install RACT. Moreover, states with ozone nonattainment areas will have to revise their SIPs to address various new requirements, including annual, incremental reductions in emissions of VOCs. States are given authority to require NO_X emission reductions in ozone nonattainment areas that are ranked as having "moderate" or more serious nonattainment problems, and EPA is required to develop guidance with respect to control techniques for NO_X. Finally, failure of a state to meet statutorily prescribed "milestones" for reduction of VOC and NO_X emissions can expose the state to sanctions. Sanctions include a cutoff of federal highway funds and a higher offset ratio for construction or modification of major stationary sources. These VOC and NO_X nonattainment requirements are generally addressed in §§ 181–185B of the Act.

b. Carbon Monoxide

The Amendments require that states with CO nonattainment areas include in their plans specific substantive emission reduction requirements (e.g., RACT for major existing sources, stringent air quality and control technology permit requirements for major new and modified sources, and mobile source fleet requirements). Emission reduction targets must be met by specific deadlines in order that the overall deadline for attainment is met. If states fail to meet these interim "milestones," EPA must impose sanctions and require revisions to the SIP to ensure compliance. *See* §§ 186–87. CO nonattainment are designated as:

√ Moderate; or

√ Serious

c. PM–10

The Amendments contain substantive requirements for PM–10 similar to those for ozone and CO nonattainment areas. For example, states must implement all reasonably available control measures for major sources, and designate periodic emission reduction milestones until attainment is achieved. EPA is directed to promulgate control technique guidelines for reasonably available control measures and best available control measures for PM–10 emissions from both major stationary sources and area sources. *See* §§ 188–90. PM–10 nonattainment areas are designated as:

√ Moderate; or

√ Serious

Ozone, CO, and PM–10 SIP revisions are all to provide for automatic implementation of contingency measures if an area fails to attain the NAAQS by the mandated deadline. States are to adopt these contingency measures as regulations prior to the deadline for attainment, to ensure that these back-up measures can go into effect without delay if the target date is missed.

§ 9.4 NEW SOURCE PERFORMANCE STANDARDS

Under § 111 of the CAA, EPA has established special technology-based emission standards applicable to new or modified existing stationary sources that fall into certain categories. 40 C.F.R. Part 60 (1990). Among the approximately 50 industrial categories of stationary sources for which New Source Performance Standards (NSPS) have been developed are steel mills, fossil fuel-fired generating plants, oil refineries, incinerators, asphalt concrete plants, and kraft pulp mills. The NSPS, which are applicable to any stationary source that "commences construction" or "modification" after the date the NSPS are published in proposed form in the *Federal Register*, limit the amount of certain pollutants that may be emitted by new or modified facilities within each category. The 1990 Amendments require EPA by November 15, 1996 to propose NSPS for all categories of stationary sources previously listed under § 111 for which standards have not been proposed.

Owners or operators of new or modified sources are required to notify EPA of any new construction or modification beforehand and to conduct performance tests of the facility at maximum production to demonstrate compliance with applicable NSPS.

U.S. v. NARRAGANSETT IMPROVEMENT CO.
571 F.Supp. 688 (D.R.I.1983)

EPA claimed the defendant had not complied with the NSPS. The defendant who manufactured and sold asphalt concrete claimed its facility was not subject to the NSPS.

Between June 11, 1973 and July 15, 1974, Narragansett replaced equipment at a cost of $337,000. The cost of the integral part of the plant that was not replaced was about $300,000. The replacement activity did not materially increase productive capacity nor did the plant exceed the NSPS emission limitations, found at 40 C.F.R. § 60.92. The replacements, according to an EPA memorandum, probably decreased emissions. The plant was also in compliance with all emissions requirements of the State of Rhode Island. Thus, the principal effect on Narragansett if EPA prevailed was that they would have to perform emission testing at a cost ranging from $3000 to $10,000, but they would have been unlikely to be forced to reduce emissions.

Under the regulations in effect in 1973, at the time the work was completed, the NSPS only applied to newly constructed or modified plants. Under regulations first proposed October 15, 1974, three months after the work was completed, a third category called "reconstruction" also subjected a facility to the NSPS.

The court held that the plain meaning of "construction" keeps these replacements from being within the meaning of "construction." Construction is something new and original that did not exist before. Therefore, defendants' actions were not construction.

Narragansett also did not make a "modification" because a modification only occurs when a change results in an increase in the amount or type of air pollutants emitted by the source. As long as the level of emissions does not increase there is no modification....

Finally, EPA claimed the renovation constituted a "reconstruction" of a stationary source. Reconstruction does not require an increase in emissions, but under 40 C.F.R. § 60.15 reconstruction is defined to exist when "The fixed capital cost of the new components exceeds 50 percent of the fixed capital cost that would be required to construct a comparable entirely new facility." The court refused to apply this regulation retroactively to an activity completed before the regulation was proposed at 39 Fed. Reg. 36,946 (Oct. 15, 1974) and finalized at 40 Fed. Reg. 58,416 (Dec. 16, 1975). The court found the new regulation to be an abrupt departure from the established statutory scheme. To impose these post-reconstruction requirements would not be equitable. EPA's interest in applying the NSPS did not outweigh the prejudice to the defendants' interests. Judgment was for the defendant.

Note

1. The NSPS program examines maximum hourly emission rates, expressed in kilograms per hour. An hourly emissions rate may be determined by a stack test or calculated from the product of the instantaneous emissions rate, i.e., the amount of pollution emitted by a source, after control, per unit of fuel combusted or material processed (such as pounds of sulfur dioxide emitted per ton of coal burned) times the production rate (such as tons of coal burned per hour). See 40 CFR 60.14.

Emissions increases for NSPS purposes are determined by changes in the hourly emissions rates at maximum physical capacity. On the other hand, the NSR regulations examine total emissions to the atmosphere. For applicability determination purposes, emissions increases under NSR are determined by changes in annual emissions as expressed in tons per year (tpy).

2. The philosophy of control using NSPS of the CAA is that as old sources need to be replaced, they will become subject to NSPS. Thus, as sources age they would become subject to greater control of air pollution. The sources would be covered by NSPS if new or major modifications of existing sources. This philosophy differs from the approach taken under the CWA which imposed its standards on **both** existing and new sources. Under the CWA there was no real advantage not to modify sources whereas under the CAA an existing source was not regulated or was not regulated as stringently. By the addition of permits in Title V of the 1990 CAA Amendments, the CAA is moving away from the dichotomy between new and existing facilities.

3. Modification or reconstruction can subject a facility to NSPS when the modification or reconstruction causes and increase in the amount of any air pollutant emitted **or** causes emission of any air pollutant not previously emitted. Modification is defined as any physical change in, or change in the method of operation of, a stationary source which increases the amount of any air pollutant emitted by such source or which results in the emission of any air pollutant not previously emitted. § 111(a)(4). Reconstruction occurs when the fixed capital cost of the new components exceeds 50% of the fixed capital cost that would be required to construct a comparable entirely new facility.

1. *New Source Review*

Title I of the CAA has three programs specifically designed to ensure that no new air pollution—whether from new sources or from modifications to existing sources—can be emitted unless the source complies with new source requirements.

The 1970 CAA required EPA to promulgate technology-based NSPS applicable to the construction or modification of stationary sources that cause or contribute significantly to air pollution which may reasonably be anticipated to endanger public health or welfare [see CAA section 111(b)(1)(A), 42 U.S.C. 7411(b)(1)(A)]. The NSPS provisions were "designed to prevent new air pollution problems" by regulating newly-constructed sources and changes occurring at existing sources that result in emissions increases (see National Asphalt Pavement Assoc. v. Train, 539 F.2d 775, 783 (D.C.Cir.1976); see also H.R. Rep. No. 1146, 91st Cong., 2d Sess. 3, reprinted in 1970 U.S. Code Cong. & Admin. News 5356, 5358). Congress defined the term "modification" as "any physical change in, or change in the method of operation of, a stationary source which increases the amount of any air pollutant emitted by such source or which results in the emission of any air pollutant not previously emitted" [see CAA section 111(a)(4), 42 U.S.C. 7411(a)(4)].

In 1977, Congress adopted additional amendments to the CAA. These changes included preconstruction permitting requirements for major new and modified sources under two programs, prevention of significant deterioration (PSD) and nonattainment NSR (respectively, parts C and D of the CAA). Congress intended these programs to apply generally where industrial changes might increase pollution in an area. Alabama Power Co. v. Costle, 636 F.2d 323, 400 (D.C.Cir.1979). Congress incorporated in parts C and D the same definition of the term "modification" set forth in the NSPS provisions [see CAA section 111(a)(4), 169(2)(C), and 171(4)].

The NSR program for PSD (CAA sections 160–169) applies in attainment areas, i.e., those areas which have attained the national ambient air quality standards (NAAQS). To receive a PSD permit, a prospective major new source or major modification must (among other things) show that (1) it will not cause or contribute to a violation of the available air quality "increment" (designed to prevent ambient air quality from deteriorating by more than certain specified levels), (2) it will not cause or contribute to a violation of a NAAQS, and (3) it will use the "BACT," which must be at least as stringent as any applicable NSPS or hazardous pollutant standard under section 112 of the CAA.

Part D of the 1977 Amendments applies to nonattainment areas, i.e., those areas which have not met the NAAQS under section 109. To receive a permit in such areas, major new and modified sources must (among other things) (1) obtain emissions offsets, thereby assuring that reasonable progress toward attainment of the NAAQS will occur, and (2) comply with the "lowest achievable emission rate (LAER)" (see CAA sections 171–173).

2. *The Two–step Test for Modifications*

The modification provisions of the NSPS and NSR programs are based on the broad NSPS definition of "modification" in section 111(a)(4) of the CAA. That section contemplates a two-step test for determining whether activities at an existing facility constitute a modification subject to new source requirements. In the first step, which is largely the same for NSPS and NSR, the reviewing authority determines whether a physical or operational change will occur. If so, the reviewing authority proceeds in the second step to determine whether the physical or operational change will result in an emissions increase over baseline levels. In this second step, the applicable rules branch apart, reflecting the fundamental distinctions between the technology-based provisions of NSPS and the air quality-based provisions of NSR.

§ 9.5 PREVENTION OF SIGNIFICANT DETERIORATION (PSD)

The EPA's regulations implementing the PSD and nonattainment programs require preconstruction review for sources undertaking building a new facility or undertaking a "major modification," i.e., a physical change or change in the method of operations "that would result in a significant net emissions increase of any pollutant subject to regulation under the CAA." See 40 CFR 52.21(b)(2)(i), 52.24(f)(5). The current PSD program is set forth in two sets of regulations. One of the regulations cited (40 CFR 52.21) is part of the Federal PSD permit program which applies as part of a Federal implementation plan for States that have not submitted a PSD program meeting the regulatory requirements of 40 CFR 51.166 [standards for PSD provisions in State implementation plans (SIP)].

In most States where the Federal requirements apply, EPA has delegated the authority to implement the PSD program back to the State. Roughly two-thirds of the States are implementing their own PSD program pursuant to an EPA-approved SIP. Sections 52.21 and 51.166 have identical modification provisions. The EPA's regulations for nonattainment areas are set forth at 40 CFR § 51.165, 52.24 and in part 51, Appendix S. These sections contain applicability provisions regarding modification that are largely identical to those in the PSD provisions.

The table below describes how to approach a PSD permitting problem:

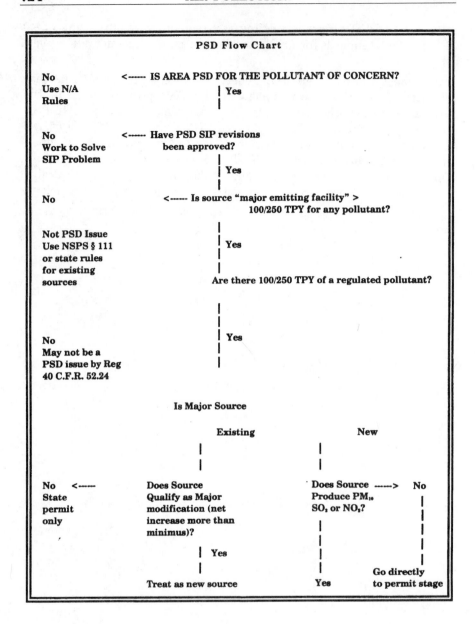

PSD Flow Chart

No
Use N/A
Rules
<----- IS AREA PSD FOR THE POLLUTANT OF CONCERN?
| Yes

No
Work to Solve
SIP Problem
<----- Have PSD SIP revisions
       been approved?
| Yes

No
<----- Is source "major emitting facility" >
       100/250 TPY for any pollutant?

Not PSD Issue
Use NSPS § 111
or state rules
for existing
sources
| Yes

Are there 100/250 TPY of a regulated pollutant?

No
May not be a
PSD issue by Reg
40 C.F.R. 52.24
| Yes

Is Major Source

Existing   New
| |
| |

No   <-----
State
permit
only
Does Source
Qualify as Major
modification (net
increase more than
minimus)?
| Yes

Does Source -----> No
Produce PM₁₀
SO₂ or NO₂?
| Go directly
| to permit stage

Treat as new source   Yes

See Arnold W. Reitze, Jr., Air Pollution Law (1995).

1. Existing Stationary Sources

Existing stationary sources include all stationary sources except those for which construction, modification or relocation began on or after the effective date of the applicable state air pollution regulations. Prior to the 1990 Amendments, which require operating permits for virtually all sources, a permit was not required and states were *not required* to impose any controls on an existing source if it was in an area of attainment for that pollutant. The requirements of the new operating permit program are discussed below. Of course, many states have implemented emission standards and other requirements for such sources as part of their SIPs, and also may require individual source operating permits.

2. *New or Modified Stationary Sources*

New or modified "major stationary sources" in attainment areas are subject to the PSD (prevention of significant deterioration) permit program under the CAA. A "major stationary source" is defined as one that (1) falls within one of certain enumerated industrial classifications and emits (or has the potential to emit) 100 or more tons/year of a regulated pollutant or (2) emits 250 or more tons/year of a regulated pollutant. *See* 40 C.F.R. § 51.18(i)(1990). A "major modification" is generally defined as any physical change or change in the method of operation of an affected facility that significantly *increases* the amount of any air pollutant emitted or causes the emission of a new air pollutant. The PSD program seeks to preserve existing areas of clean air by using a permit system to limit increases in the baseline concentrations of air pollutants regulated under the Clean Air Act. Thus far, EPA has only set PSD increments for sulfur dioxide, nitrogen dioxide, and particulates.

All new or modified facilities requiring PSD permits must install the "Best Available Control Technology" (BACT) for each pollutant, meet each applicable PSD increment and emission standards under the SIP and 40 C.F.R. Parts 60–61 (including NSPS), and conform to a number of other requirements. 42 U.S.C. § 7475(a)(4).

Operating permits also will be required for new or modified major stationary sources, in addition to PSD preconstruction permits. The following flow chart describes how to analyze the new source review process:

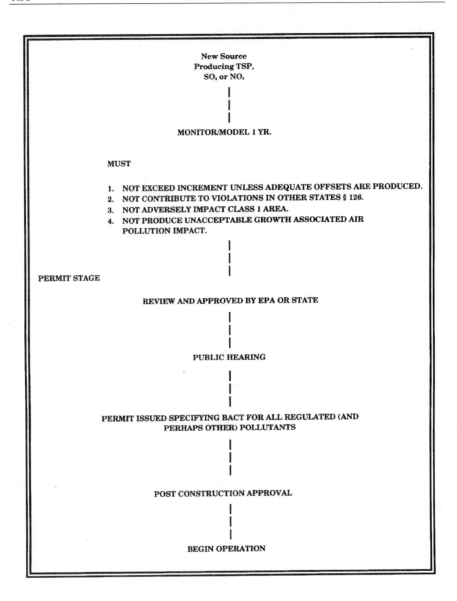

New Source
Producing TSP,
SO₂ or NO₂

MONITOR/MODEL 1 YR.

MUST

1. NOT EXCEED INCREMENT UNLESS ADEQUATE OFFSETS ARE PRODUCED.
2. NOT CONTRIBUTE TO VIOLATIONS IN OTHER STATES § 126.
3. NOT ADVERSELY IMPACT CLASS 1 AREA.
4. NOT PRODUCE UNACCEPTABLE GROWTH ASSOCIATED AIR POLLUTION IMPACT.

PERMIT STAGE

REVIEW AND APPROVED BY EPA OR STATE

PUBLIC HEARING

PERMIT ISSUED SPECIFYING BACT FOR ALL REGULATED (AND PERHAPS OTHER) POLLUTANTS

POST CONSTRUCTION APPROVAL

BEGIN OPERATION

See Arnold W. Reitze, Jr., Air Pollution Law (1995).

CITIZENS AGAINST THE REFINERY'S EFFECTS, INC., v. ENVIRONMENTAL PROTECTION AGENCY

643 F.2d 178 (4th Cir.1981).
Rehearing and Rehearing En Banc Denied April 8, 1981.

Citizens Against the Refinery's Effects (CARE) appeals from a final ruling of the Administrator of the Environmental Protection Agency (EPA) approving a permit for the prevention of significant deterioration

(PSD) of air quality issued to the Hampton Roads Energy Company (HREC). After reviewing the application, analyzing the modeling data submitted by the HREC, and digesting numerous public comments, EPA determined that the refinery would not cause significant deterioration of air quality in the Portsmouth area. We affirm the action of the Administrator in issuing the permit.

To obtain a PSD permit, the applicant must submit to EPA an "air quality dispersion" model which predicts whether the facility (1) violates the national standards, or (2) will contribute to air pollution in excess of that allowed by the PSD regulations for the attainment area involved. 42 U.S.C. § 7475. Guidelines for the modeling format have been developed and published by EPA in conjunction with private industry. After public comments were solicited, this modeling guideline was incorporated by reference into the regulations. 40 C.F.R. 52.21(m). Included in the guidelines are various modeling devices designed to limit application of the theoretical models. Mathematical threshold calculations known as "significance levels" were approved by EPA and included in the guideline after notice and public comments were received....

HREC has been attempting for seven years to build a 184,000 barrel refinery in Portsmouth, Virginia, the first refinery in over twenty years to be built on the east coast. For purposes of the PSD permit, Portsmouth is a Class II attainment area. HREC submitted an application for a PSD permit to EPA on June 28, 1978.... On August 4, 1978, HREC submitted the requisite air quality modeling analysis, thus fulfilling the PSD permit requirements.

On August 17, 1978, EPA notified HREC that its application was considered complete as of August 4, 1978. In analyzing the application, EPA (1) reviewed the refinery's impact upon national standards; (2) contracted with an independent consultant to assess the refinery pollution abatement devices to make sure these complied with applicable regulations; and (3) conducted an analysis of air quality impact which resulted in additional permit conditions designed to control SO_2 emissions. EPA issued a proposed permit on October 16, 1979, and public hearings were held in November of 1979. As a result of comments received at those hearings, EPA requested additional carbon monoxide information from HREC. EPA evaluated the additional information and issued the final permit on January 25, 1980.

CARE makes three major attacks on EPA's issuance of the permit to construct the refinery. First, they argue that the modeling analysis submitted by HREC was inaccurate and therefore underpredicted the effect of the refinery on air quality in Portsmouth. Second, CARE contends that EPA should have considered the HREC application complete when the carbon monoxide data was submitted in January, 1979, rather than in August of 1978. Such a change in the completion date would bring HREC under the new monitoring requirements of the 1977 Clean Air Amendments and require a full year of air quality monitoring data from the refinery. 42 U.S.C. section 7475(e)(2). Third, CARE argues that the significance levels approved by EPA in the modeling devices caused the agency to disregard data from the model which should have been considered. . . .

Analysis of modeling results required for PSD applications is a highly technical area particularly within the expertise of the EPA, and thus the agency interpretation should be given great weight by the court. FPC v. Florida Power & Light Co., 404 U.S. 453 (1972), reh. den. 405 U.S. 948, (1972). Yet CARE argues that this Court must examine in great detail the technical modeling data submitted to the agency and, in considering this data as well as materials outside the record, determine that EPA approval of the HREC permit was unlawful. This we cannot do.

In their first attack, CARE raises questions about four aspects of the air dispersion model submitted by HREC. First, CARE argues that the model should have incorporated five years of weather data instead of the one year of data actually used. The EPA modeling guidelines recommend that five years of data be used. See 40 CFR § 51.21(m) incorporating by reference Guideline on Air Quality Models, EPA–45%–78–027 (1978). EPA permitted the use of only one year of data because only one year was locally obtainable and compatible with the computer model used. . . . To hold EPA rigidly subject to the suggestions in the modeling guideline would elevate mere agency recommendations to the stature of a regulation, and thus tie the hands of any agency giving guidance to the public in following its regulations.

Second, CARE argues that EPA erred in deciding that HREC had filed its application before one of the other pollution sources, since both applications were filed on the same day. This decision is critical, the second applicant must include potential pollution from the first applicant in its modeling analysis. *See* 40 CFR § 52.21(*o*)(2)(ii). Absent a clear error of judgment, the agency will generally be upheld on a discretionary decision such as who filed first. . . . The primary concern is clean air; as long as EPA considers both applications and the polluting effect of both sources, the agency determination of who files first is a matter of judgment left within the province of the administrator. . . .

Third, CARE contends that the model was inaccurate because sulfur dioxide "removal rates" . . . were originally used and later were improperly removed from the model. EPA contends that a "worst case" analysis was used, and that the removal rates were taken out from the days where the effect was most intense. This is a disagreement of experts, and as such the discretion of the agency is to be given great weight, absent evidence of arbitrary and capricious actions. . . .

Finally, CARE argues that the nitrous oxide input into the model was inaccurate by a factor of ten, thereby creating inaccurate base readings. EPA argues that the error was not raised in public comments before the agency and therefore may not be considered by this Court. . . . The facts demonstrate here that the error which was raised during the public comment period was of a lesser degree than the error presented on appeal. EPA did consider the lesser error in the model and decided it wasn't significant. Given CARE's demonstrated ability to accurately assess information and given the need for specific, accurate objections during the technical administrative process, EPA was justified in considering only the lesser modeling error as presented by CARE and in ruling accordingly. . . .

Beyond the errors in the dispersion model, CARE contends that the agency also erred in concluding that the application was complete as of August 4, 1978. . . .

The regulations establish the date of a "complete" application as the date all materials necessary for approval have been filed. 40 CFR § 52.21(r)(1). Just because additional information is found necessary after the agency begins to analyze the submission during the public comment stage does not mean that the application is incomplete. . . .

Lastly, CARE argues that the significance levels used in the models to prevent the theoretical from becoming the absurd contravene the meaning and purpose of the statute. The significance levels, designed to key the modeler into only "significant" levels of incremental pollution, are included in the modeling guidelines and apply only to modeling. Thus these levels are not designed for the absolute NAAQS requirements of the Act. Appellant's reliance upon statutory limits on air pollution is misplaced because the levels adopted by EPA were to be used in measuring the application of the theoretical model instead of actual air pollution.

The deference normally given administrative agencies in interpreting their own regulations as well as the highly technical nature of the modeling techniques make the EPA particularly well suited to make determinations as to whether to issue a PSD permit or not. Where, as here, the agency did nothing which may be construed as arbitrary, capricious, an

> abuse of discretion, or outside the statute, the only course possible is to affirm the final action of the administrator.

In the final analysis, Petitioners had a different interpretation of the rather disparate and equivocal scientific data in the record. Notwithstanding Petitioners' challenge, the Final Rule was the result of a site-specific informal rulemaking process that included virtually unprecedented cooperation between the governmental agency and the directly affected parties. . . . Petitioners' arguments provided no reason for the court disruptively to interject itself into the picture. Because Congress delegated to EPA the power to "regulate on the borders of the unknown," this court will not interfere with the agency's "reasonable interpretations of equivocal evidence." . . . EPA's actions in promulgating the Final Rule were reasonable and within the bounds of its statutory authority, and not arbitrary and capricious.

The Districts' petition for review and motion to supplement the administrative record were accordingly DENIED.

3. *In Non–Attainment Areas*

a. *Existing Stationary Sources*

The 1990 Amendments add additional requirements to the non-attainment program, imposing an incremental approach to meeting attainment deadlines for CO, particulates (or PM–10), and the two precursors of ozone—VOC and NOx. EPA must classify each area designated non-attainment, according to the degree to which the existing air quality falls below the applicable standard. For example, the classifications for ozone non-attainment areas range from "Marginal" to "Extreme." 42 U.S.C.A. 7511(a). The date on which the NAAQS for ozone must be attained depends upon the area classification.

For existing stationary sources in non-attainment areas for a pollutant, the CAA requires that a state implementation plan impose all "reasonably available control measures" on sources of the pollutant. States are responsible for devising the plans, but they must follow EPA criteria and obtain approval from EPA. Under the 1990 Amendments, existing stationary sources could be required to reduce emissions of CO, PM–10, VOC, and NOx.

Under the 1990 Amendments, operating permits will be required for existing sources in non-attainment areas. Such permits could include any emissions reductions required by the SIP.

b. *New or Modified Stationary Sources*

The Clean Air Act requires that a new or modified major stationary source that emits, or has the potential to emit, at least 100 tons per year (TPY) of any criteria pollutant for which the area is non-attainment obtain a permit before commencing construction. 42 U.S.C.A. § 7502(c)(5). The 1990 Amendments tighten the definition of "major stationary source" and progressively lower the amount of emissions that will trigger the application of the non-attainment provisions to a new or modified source. The amount depends upon the specific pollutant and the designation of the area as Moderate or more serious. For example, in the provisions applicable to ozone, the definition of "major stationary source" is expanded to include any stationary source that emits or has the potential to emit VOC of (1) at least 50 TPY in a Serious area, (2) at least 25 TPY in a Severe area, (3) at least 10 TPY in an Extreme area, and (4) at least 5 TPY in a Moderate area when the SIP incorporates alternative incremental VOC emissions reductions specified in the statute. 42 U.S.C.A. 7511(b)-(e).

The permit review process is designed to ensure that "reasonable further progress" toward attainment of the NAAQS is not impeded by construction of the new or modified source.

In order to obtain a non-attainment preconstruction permit, the source must demonstrate that emissions will be controlled to a level reflecting the lowest achievable emission rate (LAER), which is defined in the CAA to mean the most stringent emission limitation (unless it is shown to be unachievable) in any SIP in the country, or the lowest emission limitation achieved in practice anywhere in the country, applicable to any source in the same category. 42 U.S.C.A. 7501. Moreover, the source must show that other sources owned or operated by the applicant in the state are in compliance, or on a schedule for compliance, with all applicable emission limits. Finally, the source must either provide enforceable emissions reductions from the same source or other sources in the same non-attainment region as "offsets" to its emissions or show that increases in emissions are within any growth allowance that has been built into the SIP control strategy. *See generally* 40 C.F.R. Part 51, Appendix S (1990). The 1990 Amendments provide varying offset ratios for VOC, CO, and PM–10, depending upon the area's non-attainment classification.

Operating permits will be required for new or modified stationary sources in non-attainment areas, in addition to non-attainment preconstruction permits.

c. *Operating Permits*

The 1990 Amendments create an important new permitting scheme. Previously, operating permits have not been required by federal law, though many state laws provide for such permits. Under the 1990 Amendments, EPA will be required to promulgate minimum requirements for state permit programs by November 15, 1991. During the next four years, the states must adopt and obtain EPA approval of permit programs, and applicants must file applications. This means that covered sources will be required to have operating permits in about five to seven years. 42 U.S.C.A. 7661 *et seq.*

The permit will consolidate into one document all of the requirements applicable to a particular source. Permits must include emissions limits, compliance schedules, and monitoring and reporting requirements. Sources subject to the acid deposition provisions will be required to install and operate continuous emissions monitors or some alternative method to provide information of the same type and accuracy. Permittees will have to submit quarterly reports and certify every six months that they are in compliance. Permits also must allow government representatives the right to enter and inspect the permitted facility to ensure compliance.

One goal of the new permit requirements purportedly is to simplify the procedures for establishing and modifying a facility's pollution control obligations. Currently, any source-specific modification must go through the SIP revision process, which can be a time-consuming process. Under the new system, the state would revise the permit. EPA would have 45 days to review the permit. If EPA fails to object to the issuance of a permit that does not comply with the requirements of the Act within this 45 day period, a citizen can petition EPA to act within 60 days (and seek judicial relief if EPA fails to act). If EPA does not act and no petition to act is filed, the revised permit goes into effect.

Permits also must include provisions for fees to cover the states' and EPA's costs in administering these programs. Under the new SIP provisions, major sources must pay permit fees sufficient to cover the costs of reviewing any permit application and the "reasonable cost" of implementing and enforcing the terms and conditions of the permit. The Amendments suggest that fees of $25 per ton for emissions of regulated pollutants (up to 4,000 tons per pollutant) would be appropriate.

d. Permit Transfer

Federal regulations presently do not contain any specific procedures for permit transfers. State regulations, however, may contain such requirements and should be examined. Although no specific permit transfer mechanism is provided, federal regulations provide that a change in ownership of a stationary source is *not* a major modification. 40 C.F.R. § 51.165(a)(V)(A)(1990)(non-attainment areas) and 40 C.F.R. § 51.166(b)(2)(iii)(g)(1990)(attainment areas).

In addition, EPA has prepared a draft policy on PSD permit modifications that provides guidance for revising any EPA-issued PSD permit. *See* EPA, PSD Permit Modifications: Policy Statement on Changes to a Source, Permit Applications, or an Issued Permit and on Extensions to Construction Schedules (EPA Policy Statement), dated July 5, 1985. In this policy statement, EPA proposes that changes in the "company name" or "operator" generally are to be treated as permit amendments requiring little or no review, with no public participation requirements. EPA emphasized, however, that there may be instances where a change in ownership may warrant review or public participation, such as the "change of ownership" of a proposed source to a company that has been involved in highly controversial projects or has received public attention as a result of the manner in which other air pollution sources owned by this company were operated.

§ 9.6 HAZARDOUS AIR POLLUTANTS

Before the 1990 Amendments, EPA was required to list as hazardous air pollutants substances likely to increase the risk of death or serious illness. Emission standards, known as NESHAPs, were then established for these pollutants at a level designed to protect public health with an ample margin of safety. Prior to 1990, EPA had addressed 33 substances under § 112, by deciding either to list or not to list the substance, and had additional substances under consideration for listing.

The 1990 Amendments significantly alter the scheme for air toxics regulation, based in part on congressional dissatisfaction with the pre–1990 § 112 program, and in part on the publicity generated by EPA's first Toxic Release Inventory (compiled from reports required by the Emergency Planning and Community Right to Know Act of 1986). Under the 1990 Amendments, § 112 of the Act would shift from a pollutant-by-pollutant, health-based regulatory approach, to regulation of categories of sources using technology-based standards. Examples of air toxics that must be regulated by EPA include VOCs such as benzene, and metals such as chromium, cadmium, and manganese.

§ 9.7   OPERATING PERMITS

The Clean Air Act Amendments of 1990 create an important new permitting program. Previously, operating permits were not required by federal law, though many state laws provided for such permits. Under Title V of the 1990 Amendments, however, EPA is required to promulgate minimum requirements for state permit programs within one year of enactment. § 502(b). EPA issued these Title V rules in July 1992.

One purpose of the new permit program is to consolidate into one document all of the requirements applicable to a particular source, including how the general rules contained in a SIP will be applied to specific sources. In addition to Title V, Title IV addresses permit requirements for acid rain sources. The intent of the 1990 Amendments, however, is eventually to consolidate all permitting requirements into one process.

Permits must include emission limits, compliance schedules, and monitoring and reporting requirements. § 504(a). Permittees will have to submit quarterly reports and certify every six months that they are in compliance. Permits must also allow for inspection and entry to ensure compliance. Sources subject to the acid rain provisions of Title IV will be required to install and operate continuous emission monitors or some alternative method to provide information of the same type and accuracy.

Another goal of the new operating permit program is to simplify the procedures for establishing and modifying a facility's pollution control obligations. Currently, any source-specific modification in emission reduction requirements must go through the SIP revision process. The state must first develop and propose the change. EPA then must either approve or disallow the revision through notice and comment rulemaking. This has proven to be a time-consuming process.

Under the new system, the state would issue the operating permit. EPA would have 45 days to review the permit. If EPA fails to object to the issuance of a permit that does not comply with the requirements of the Act within this 45 day period, a citizen can petition EPA to act within 60 days (and seek judicial relief if EPA fails to act). Significantly, if EPA does not object to the permit within the 45–day review period, and the permit is issued, the permit goes into effect whether or not a member of the public files an administrative petition. § 505.

State permit programs must include provisions for fees to cover the state's costs in administering the program. Under the new operating permit provisions, major sources must pay permit fees sufficient to cover the costs of developing and implementing the permit program. Upon receipt of a permit, the "reasonable costs" of implementing and enforcing the terms and conditions of the permit must be collected. The

Amendments suggest that fees of $25 per ton for emissions of regulated pollutants (up to 4,000 tons per regulated pollutant) would be appropriate to fund administration of state permit programs. § 502(b)(3).

Whether the operating permit program will in fact simplify a facility's pollution control obligations will depend in large measure on how EPA and the states implement this program. Among other things, since the SIP process is left in place, an individual facility may have to go through *both* the SIP and permitting procedures to revise its compliance obligations, unless the respective roles of the SIP and the permit program are clearly defined by the state. Moreover, while Title V operating permits are intended to include only those standards required by a federal regulation or by the SIP, integration of pre-existing state permits with Title V permits could result in the inclusion of non-federal requirements in Title V permits. Unless the Title V permit clearly delineates which requirements are based on federal law, and which are based on state law, state operating restrictions would become federally enforceable and require time consuming federal permit modification procedures to change—a result that would restrict the operational flexibility of industrial sources.

§ 9.8 ACID DEPOSITION CONTROL

One of the major new regulatory programs of the 1990 Amendments concerns the control of precursors of acid deposition—i.e., SO_2 and NO_X. The centerpiece of this program is the establishment of an emissions allowance and trading regime for SO_2. EPA has undertaken several rulemakings to implement these provisions, and issued the basic rules addressing the allowance trading and monitoring system in October 1992, and the allowance allocation rules in March 1993.

Under § 403 of the Act, sources subject to the Title IV SO_2 program (principally, large fossil-fuel fired electric utility boilers) will be assigned SO_2 "allowances". An allowance is an authorization to emit one ton of SO_2. A plant's emissions will not be allowed to exceed its allowances, or it will be subject to penalties that are designed to be more costly than compliance. EPA's regulations provide for a system to track and record the allowances.

The 1990 Amendments specify that allowances are not a property right and can be limited, revoked or modified. In the future, Congress intends to consider whether affected sources should be allowed to trade NO_X for SO_2 emissions, based upon a study to be conducted by EPA.

Under § 408, a unit's allowance allocation will be made as part of the permitting process. As part of that process, a compliance plan must be submitted providing an implementation schedule, and indicating whether the owner or operator of the facility intends to obtain additional allowances in order to comply with the Act.

EPA must also issue regulations setting up a system for allowance auctions to be held annually. § 416. Anyone eligible to hold allowances may purchase at the auction. Holders of allowances can also contribute to the auction and receive a pro rata share of the monies collected. The Amendments specify that the auction is to be conducted so as to ensure the orderly functioning of the national market for allowances, and to preserve competition in the electric power industry. EPA is given the option of discontinuing or altering the frequency of the auction by undergoing another rulemaking if it determines that an auction is not necessary. The first allowance auction took place on March 29, 1993.

EPA is also required to establish by regulation a reserve of allowances that owners and operators of new utility units can purchase from the Agency as a last resort if they cannot obtain them elsewhere. To be eligible to purchase from the reserve, owners and operators will have to show that they made good faith efforts to purchase from other allowance holders. Under § 416 of the Act, EPA is to require owners and operators of new units to make a "vigorous showing" that allowances are not otherwise available. In the regulations implementing the reserve system, EPA has set strict criteria for establishing the requisite showing for access to the reserve. 57 Fed. Reg. 65,606–07 (1991)(40 C.F.R. §§ 73.74–73.77).

The Agency must also issue regulations providing criteria and procedures for allowing owners and operators of sources not covered by Title IV (e.g., industrial facilities and small utility boilers) to voluntarily opt into the program by electing certain sources normally not eligible to receive allowances. § 410. The purpose of this provision is to increase the amount of allowances available. However, sources that opt into the program would then become subject to all of the other permitting and monitoring requirements of this program.

EPA is to establish allowable emission rates for NO_x emissions from coal-fired electric utility boilers. § 407. Additionally, EPA must revise the standards of performance for SO_2 and NO_x emissions from fossil-fuel fired steam generating units, including both utility and non-utility units.

61 FED. REG. 15,934

(April 10, 1996)
Notice of the 1996 EPA SO₂ Allowance Auctions Results.

Pursuant to Title IV of the Clean Air Act and 40 CFR Part 73, the EPA is responsible for implementing a program to reduce emissions of sulfur dioxide (SO_2), a precursor of acid rain. The centerpiece of the SO_2 control program is the allocation of transferable allowances, or authorizations to emit SO_2, which are distributed in limited quantities to existing utility units and which eventually must be held by virtually all utility units to cover their SO_2 emissions. These allowances may be transferred among polluting sources and others, so that market forces may govern their ultimate use and distribution, resulting in the most cost-effective sharing of the emissions control burden. EPA is directed under Section 416 of the Act to conduct annual sales and auctions of a small portion of allowances (2.8%) withheld from the total allowances allocated to utilities each year. Sales and auctions are expected to stimulate and support the allowance market and to provide a public source of allowances, particularly to new units for which no allowances are allocated. In the Fall of 1992, EPA delegated the administration of the EPA allowance auctions and sales to the Chicago Board of Trade (CBOT). Today, the Acid Rain Division is giving notice of the results of the fourth annual SO_2 allowance auctions that were conducted by the CBOT on March 25, 1996.

For rules governing the conduct of the auctions and sales *see* 40 CFR Part 73, Subpart E.

I. OFFERS

A. *Total Allowances Available for Auction*

In the spot auction (year 1996 allowances sold), a total of 158,000 allowances were offered for sale: 150,000 that were withheld from the utilities and an additional 8,000 that were voluntarily contributed from utilities. In the 6–year advance auction (year 2002 allowances sold), a total of 32,000 allowances were offered for sale: 25,000 that were unsold from the 1995 direct sale and an additional 7,000 that were contributed from utilities. In the 7–year advance auction (year 2003 allowances sold), a total of 107,000 allowances were offered for sale: 100,000 that were withheld from the utilities and an additional 7,000 that were contributed . . . .

* * *

§ 9.9 MOBILE SOURCES

The 1990 Amendments substantially tighten mobile source emission standards. The Amendments require automobile manufacturers to reduce tailpipe emissions of hydrocarbons (HC) and NO_X, for example, by 35 percent and 60 percent, respectively,

beginning with 40 percent of the vehicles sold in 1994 and increasing to 100 percent of vehicles sold in 1996. § 202. The Amendments also require a further 50 percent reduction in mobile source emissions of these pollutants beginning in 2003, unless EPA finds that these more stringent standards are not necessary, technologically feasible, or cost effective.

In addition to establishing new mobile source emission standards, the Amendments establish two new fuels-related programs designed to achieve emission reductions. §§ 211(k) and 241–50. The first of these programs—the reformulated fuels program—requires the use of reformulated gasoline in certain CO and severe ozone nonattainment areas beginning in 1992 and 1995, respectively. Among other things, reformulated gasoline must be blended to achieve reductions in VOCs and tailpipe emissions of toxic air pollutants.

The second fuels program is the clean fuel vehicle program. Under this program, automobiles operating on "clean alternative fuels" (*e.g.,* methanol, ethanol, natural gas, and reformulated gasoline) must meet even more stringent emission standards. The clean fuel vehicle program will be implemented in two ways: (1) by establishing a California pilot test program that requires the production and sale of 300,000 clean fuel vehicles annually by 1999; and (2) by requiring operators of centrally-fueled fleets of ten or more vehicles in certain CO and ozone nonattainment areas to purchase and use clean fuel vehicles beginning in 1998.

NATURAL RESOURCES DEFENSE COUNCIL v. REILLY
983 F.2d 259 (D.C.Cir.1993).

Edwards, Circuit Judge:

The 1990 amendments to the Clean Air Act ("CAA") altered section 202(a)(6) to require the Environmental Protection Agency ("EPA"), after "consultation" with the Department of Transportation ("DOT"), to promulgate standards by November 15, 1991, that would require new "light-duty" vehicles ... to be equipped with onboard refueling vapor recovery ("ORVR") systems over a specified phase-in period. After consulting with DOT, EPA concluded that the safety risks of ORVR systems were unreasonable given the availability of alternative mechanisms for controlling refueling vapor emissions and declined to promulgate ORVR standards by the statutory deadline. This decision was Noticed as a Final Agency Action in April, 1992. 57 Fed.Reg. 13,046 (1992). In explaining its decision, EPA contended that amended section 202(a)(6) contained residual authority for EPA to exercise discretion in deciding whether to promulgate ORVR standards if the Agency determined that ORVR was unreasonably unsafe. The Natural Resources Defense Council ("NRDC") initiated this suit, alleging that EPA lacked discretion under the statute and that its failure to promulgate ORVR standards was therefore unlawful.

Because the language of section 202(a)(6) plainly imposes a mandatory duty, we agree that EPA's decision not to promulgate ORVR standards was beyond the pale of its statutory authority. There is nothing in the statute to substantiate EPA's claim for residual discretionary authority, nor is there ambiguity that would warrant deference by this court to EPA's construction. Furthermore, EPA's findings regarding ORVR safety do not establish that all such systems present inherent and unreasonable safety risks. We are thus not faced with a situation in which a literal reading of the section produces nonsensical results. Whatever doubts EPA may have about the wisdom of choices implicit in the statute must be raised with Congress. This court is not the proper forum in which to argue the relative merits of those choices. Therefore, the Final Agency Action is set aside and EPA is ordered to promulgate ORVR standards in compliance with the CAA.

* * *

THE NEW YORK STATE AUTOMOBILE DEALERS ASSOCIATION v. THE NEW YORK STATE DEPARTMENT OF ENVIRONMENTAL CONSERVATION

827 F.Supp. 895 (N.D.N.Y.1993).

THOMAS J. MCAVOY

Plaintiffs challenge the new motor vehicle emission regulations for model year 1994 vehicles ("1994 standards") contained at 6 N.Y.C.R.R. Part 218 ("Part 218 Regulations"), which were adopted by the New York State Department of Environmental Conservation (DEC). Like the plaintiffs in *MVMA v. Jorling,* 92–CV–869 (McAvoy, C.J.), the instant plaintiffs allege that DEC's adoption of the Part 218 Regulations violates § 177 of the Clean Air Act, 42 U.S.C. § 7507....

The complaint contains two causes of action. In their first cause of action, plaintiffs allege that the 1994 standards adopted by DEC are not identical to the California standards for which a waiver has been granted by the Environmental Protection Agency (EPA). In their second cause of action, plaintiffs allege that in adopting the 1994 standards DEC failed to comply with the two year leadtime requirement of § 177. Presently before the court is plaintiffs' motion for summary judgment pursuant to Fed.R.Civ.P. 56.

* * *

DEC has adopted two sets of California's new motor vehicle emission standards pursuant to § 177 of the Clean Air Act. Under this regulatory scheme, only those new motor vehicles which comply with the applicable emission standards contained in the Part 218 Regulations may be registered in the State of New York. Therefore, new motor vehicles which are designed to comply with the less stringent emission standards established by the EPA ("the federal standards") may not be registered in New York.

The first set of standards adopted by DEC are the standards applicable to model year 1993 and 1994 vehicles. This first set of standards was originally adopted by DEC on October 22, 1990. The second set of standards, and the set at issue in the MVMA v. Jorling action, are the Low Emission Vehicle (LEO) standards applicable to model years 1995 and beyond. This second set of standards was adopted on April 28, 1992 following the California Air Resource Board's (CARB) adoption of the LEV/Clean Fuels (CF) Program, and made effective on May 28, 1992. In the second rulemaking, DEC repealed and simultaneously readopted the standards for model years 1993 and 1994, with one change from those prior standards. The change in the $^{1993}/_{1994}$ standards was the deletion of the medium duty truck standards. However, according to DEC, there were no other changes.

II

Plaintiff New York State Automobile Dealers Association (NYSADA) is a not-for-profit association which represents approximately 1400 auto dealers in the State. Plaintiffs Syracuse Automobile Dealers Associations (SADA), Rochester Automobile Dealers Association (RADA), Niagara Frontier Automobile Dealers Association (NFADA), and Capital Region Automobile Dealers Association (CRADA) are all corporations organized by regional auto dealers for the purpose of, inter alia, advancing the interests of their members in judicial proceedings. In their complaint, plaintiffs allege that when CARB adopted the LEV/CF Program it modified and supplemented the model year 1994 standards, providing for, inter alia, alternative certification between pre-LEV and LEV standards. They argue that the Part 218 Regulations concerning the 1994 model year are therefore not identical to the California standards for that model year. Furthermore, they allege that the re-adoption of the standards for the 1994 model year on April 28, 1992 violates the two year leadtime provision of § 177. Finally, it is alleged in the complaint that plaintiffs will suffer immediate and irreparable injury as a direct result of the enforcement of the model year 1994 emission standards.

As alleged in the complaint, and explained in the affidavit of Norma Sharpe, Executive Vice–President of NYSADA, automobile manufacturers are currently demanding that plaintiffs' members place their orders for the 1994 model year. (Complaint at p. 17; Sharpe Affidavit at p. 14). Accordingly, plaintiffs' members must know whether to purchase vehicles which conform to the federal emission standards or the "California" standards adopted by DEC. (*Id.*). Therefore, they argue that the threat of harm is immediate. Since defendants have challenged plaintiffs' standing, however, it is important to understand how plaintiffs will allegedly be harmed.

New York is the only state which has adopted the California standards for 1994; therefore, model year 1994 vehicles sold in states other than California and New York need only comply with the less stringent federal standards. If the 1994 standards are enforced in New York, plaintiffs' members will only be permitted to sell California certified vehicles for registration in New York. (Complaint at pp. 18–19). It is alleged in the complaint that because plaintiffs' members rely on their ability to trade with out-of-state dealers, the enforcement of the 1994 standards will preclude them from satisfying consumer demand for a particular vehicle by trading for such a vehicle with an out-of-state dealer. (*Id.*). Plaintiffs further allege that California certified vehicles are more expensive than federally certified vehicles, and therefore enforcement of the 1994 standards will place their members at a competitive disadvantage relative to out-of-state dealers. (*Id.* at p. 20). Finally, it is alleged in the complaint, upon information and belief, that manufacturers will not be producing all models of their vehicles to meet the California standards, and therefore enforcement of the 1994 standards will limit the vehicle models which plaintiffs' members will be able to offer. (*Id.* at p. 21). While plaintiffs' affidavits elaborate further on these three different injuries alleged in the complaint, for the purposes of the instant motion, the court will focus solely on the allegations in the complaint.

* * *

Plaintiffs allege that enforcement of the 1994 standards will effectively preclude them from trading with out-of-state dealers to satisfy consumer demand. (Complaint at pp. 18–19.) They argue that this is an economic injury sufficient to constitute an injury-in-fact. The court disagrees.

Absent enforcement of the 1994 standards, a dealers' quest for a particular vehicle sought by a customer would not be limited by that particular vehicle's emission certification; therefore, plaintiffs' members would have a larger collection of vehicles with which to trade in order to satisfy consumer demand. Through enforcement of the 1994 standards, DEC will limit these searches to a sub-category of the larger collection of vehicles—specifically, California certified vehicles. It does not, however, directly preclude plaintiffs' members from trading with dealers outside of New York State. Rather, enforcement of the 1994 standards only restricts plaintiffs' members to trading for California certified vehicles. In fact, whether a New York dealer will be able to trade with an out-of-state dealer is as much a function of the out-of-state dealer's decision to carry California certified vehicles as it is a function of DEC's enforcement of the 1994 standards.

Nevertheless, even assuming that the practical effect of DEC's enforcement of the 1994 standards will be to preclude plaintiffs' members from trading with out-of-state dealers, that does not translate into an economic injury.... Plaintiffs have not alleged in the complaint how such a restriction causes them economic harm through lost profits, impaired competitive position, or otherwise. At oral argument, plaintiffs' counsel argued that by limiting the collection of vehicles with which dealers may trade, enforcement of the 1994 standards might lead to lost sales for dealers because it may take longer to locate a particular vehicle which satisfies a customer's specific demands. However, the threat of losing a sale due to consumer impatience is both conjectural and hypothetical, and therefore insufficient to constitute an injury-in-fact....

Stripped down to its core, plaintiffs' central thesis is that enforcement of the 1994 standards will make it more difficult to satisfy consumer demand. While under the 1994 standards plaintiffs' members will be restricted to selling California certified vehicles for registration in New York, the market in which they sell these vehicles will be similarly restricted. As a result of DEC's enforcement of the 1994 standards, the New York registered new motor vehicle market will be defined as those vehicles which are certified to the California standards. Consequently, consumer demand within New York State will only be satisfied by California certified vehicles. Therefore, plaintiffs' members' ability to satisfy consumer demand will not be adversely affected by their inability to purchase federally certified vehicles from out-of-state dealers or auctions. Moreover, enforcement of the 1994 standards will not place plaintiffs' members at any competitive disadvantage with respect to out-of-state dealers insofar as the New York market is concerned. The effect of DEC's enforcement of the 1994 standards on plaintiffs' members is no different than its effect on out-of-state dealers.... As far as the 1994 standards are concerned, an out-of-state dealer's ability to satisfy consumer demand within the New York market is no greater than any of plaintiffs' members. Therefore, even assuming that enforcement of the 1994 standards will preclude plaintiffs' members from trading with out-of-state dealers to satisfy consumer demand, that does not constitute a concrete and particularized injury.

Next, plaintiffs allege that California certified vehicles are more expensive than comparable federally certified vehicles. They allege that this inequality of price will result in a loss of bargaining power for New York dealers, and will further handicap them in their ability to trade with out-of-state dealers. (Complaint at p. 20). The court finds that this alleged harm is likewise insufficient to satisfy the injury-in-fact requirement of Article III.

Beyond the conclusory allegation in the complaint, plaintiffs have failed to explain exactly how the price differential will result in a loss of bargaining power for New York dealers. As explained above, the effect of DEC's enforcement of the 1994 standards will be to restrict the New York market to California certified vehicles. With respect to that market, all dealers, both New York dealers and out-of-state dealers, are in an equal bargaining position. Likewise, all dealers are in an equal bargaining position with respect to the market for federally certified vehicles. Therefore, the alleged price differential will not disadvantage New York dealers in their ability to trade with out-of-state dealers, and consequently, does not constitute an injury-in-fact.

Finally, plaintiffs allege, upon information and belief, that manufacturers will not be producing all models of their vehicles to meet the California standards, and therefore enforcement of the 1994 standards will limit the selection of vehicles which they will be able to offer. Once again, plaintiffs are claiming that their ability to satisfy consumer demand will be impaired. However, even assuming that a manufacturer's decision to produce only a limited number of models to meet the California standards constitutes an injury to plaintiffs' members, such an injury is not fairly traceable to the allegedly unlawful conduct.

The allegedly illegal conduct challenged in the complaint is DEC's failure to comply with the requirements of § 177 in adopting the 1994 standards. The line of causation between this allegedly unlawful conduct and a manufacturer's decision to produce a particular model vehicle to meet the California standards is attenuated at best. The harm alleged here results from the independent decisions of the vehicle manufacturers and not from defendants' allegedly unlawful conduct. Plaintiffs have not alleged that DEC's adoption of the 1994 standards was in any way causally connected to any manufacturer's decision to limit the number of models produced to meet the California standards.

The court recognizes that in the absence of the 1994 standards, plaintiffs members would not be limited to selling California certified vehicles for registration in New York. However, the harm alleged in the complaint is not that enforcement of the 1994 standards will limit plaintiffs' members to selling California certified vehicles. Rather, plaintiffs allege that the manufacturers will not be producing all models to meet the California standards, and that by enforcing the 1994 standards DEC is restricting plaintiffs' members to selling only that class of vehicles which the manufacturers decide to produce according to the California standards. While a manufacturer may consider the enforcement of the 1994 standards in New York as a factor in determining which models to produce according to the California standards, such a decision is certainly not fairly traceable to defendants' allegedly unlawful conduct.

* * *

Having considered the papers submitted and the arguments of counsel, the court finds that plaintiffs' members have not satisfied the constitutional requirements of standing implicit in Article III. However, even assuming that plaintiffs' members could satisfy the requirements of Article III, neither § 209 nor § 177 of the clean Air Act can be read as granting plaintiffs' members a right to the judicial relief which they seek....

ETHYL CORPORATION v. BROWNER

989 F.2d 522 (D.C.Cir.1993).

WILLIAMS, CIRCUIT JUDGE:

Ethyl Corporation seeks review of the Environmental Protection Agency's denial of Ethyl's application for a waiver for a fuel additive, MMT, ... a manganese-based additive designed to prevent auto engine knocking. *See* § 211(f)(4) of the Clean Air Act, 42 U.S.C. § 7545(f)(4). The Administrator acknowledges that evidence developed since denial of the waiver has undermined the stated basis for denial, and asks that we remand the matter to the Agency for further consideration, including review of other possible bases for denial that the Agency alluded to but did not resolve in its explanation of the original denial. Ethyl resists the remand, arguing that we must decide whether the denial was erroneously issued, because (it says) the statutory scheme entitles it to receive the waiver if the denial was in error. Because we conclude that illegality at the time of denial would not entitle Ethyl to that remedy, we think it inappropriate to review the now stranded decision, and we remand the case to the Administrator.

Section 211(f)(1) of the Clean Air Act prohibits the sale of fuels and fuel additives that are not "substantially similar" to those in use in vehicles or engines certified since 1974. 42 U.S.C. § 7545(f)(1). Section 211(f)(4), however, provides that upon application by a manufacturer; the Administrator may waive the prohibition of § 211(f)(1) if he determines that the applicant has established that its additive will not "cause or contribute" to the failure of vehicles to comply with the emission standards to which they have been certified. In the interests of assuring timely action by the EPA, the same section provides a sanction for failure to act within 180 days: If the Administrator has not acted to rant or deny an application under this paragraph within [180] days of receipt of such application, the waiver authorized by this paragraph shall be treated as granted.

42 U.S.C. § 7515(f)(4).

Ethyl applied on July 12, 1991 for a § 211(f)(4) waiver to permit the addition of MMT to unleaded gasoline. . . . The Administrator denied the application on January 8, 1992, within the 180–day statutory period, solely because test data submitted by the Ford Motor Co. indicated that "factors other than those taken into account in Ethyl's test program"— particularly, the "driving cycle," or speed at which the vehicle is typically driven—"may significantly and adversely influence the magnitude of the emissions increase caused by the addition of [MMT] to unleaded gasoline." 57 Fed. Reg. 2,535, 2,541 (Jan. 22, 1992). Because the Administrator regarded the Ford data as sufficient rounds for denying the application, he declined to reach several other issues, such as the effect of MMT on public health, which might otherwise have affected his decision. Id.

Ethyl petitioned this court for review of the Administrator's decision, claiming that the Administrator's reliance on the Ford data was arbitrary, capricious, and inconsistent with the purposes underlying the Clean Air Act. Soon thereafter the EPA began settlement discussions with Ethyl. In the course of these discussions Ethyl provided EPA with the results of tests completed since the original decision. Because Ethyl's tests undermined the view that the driving cycle altered the effect of MMT on emissions, the Administrator moved this court for a remand of the administrative record to allow the agency to consider the new evidence and make a new decision. We commonly grant such motions, preferring to allow agencies to cure their own mistakes rather than wasting the courts' and the parties' resources reviewing a record that both sides acknowledge to be incorrect or incomplete. . . . Ethyl opposed the motion, arguing that erroneous denial of a waiver was a nullity, thus calling into play the provision for automatic issuance of a waiver where the EPA fails to act within 180 days. We deferred action on the EPA motion until oral argument so as to decide the matter with a better understanding of the context and of Ethyl's theory.

Ethyl derives its remedial argument from § 211(f)(4)'s provision that if the Administrator "has not acted to grant or deny an application" within 180 days of receipt, the waiver "shall be treated as granted." Thus it equates unlawful denial with inaction. In assessing this claim, we hasten to note that its acceptance would not leave the country unalterably exposed to harmful additives, for § 211(c) empowers the EPA to ban the use of any additive found to cause health problems or to impair the operation of an emissions control device....

The statute does not compel Ethyl's result. It says that the agency must act with speed to stave off an involuntary waiver grant, not that it must act with perfection. Ethyl, to support its proposed extension of the statutory language, points to *American Methyl Corp. v. EPA*, 242 U.S.App.D.C. 148, 749 F.2d 826 (D.C.Cir.1984). But there we held only that when the EPA has granted a waiver, and has then come to believe the grant mistaken, it may revoke the waiver only by means of the procedure set out in § 211(c). The case does not address the issue of mistaken denials, nor does its logic support Ethyl's interpretation of the 180–day time limit. Indeed, the only link between this case and American Methyl is that both deal with the question of remedying an agency mistake; but as American Methyl dealt with the effect of a remedy explicitly provided by Congress for erroneous grant of a waiver (§ 211(c)), it has no direct application here.

We do not see that the policy of § 211(f)(4)'s automatic issuance provision naturally extends to mistaken denials. Automatic issuance is itself a dramatic, even extreme, penalty for agency delay; given the tradition of allowing agencies to reconsider their actions where events pending appeal draw their decision in question, we see no basis to extend Congress's remedy for delay into a similarly radical remedy for error.

Accordingly, we remand the case to the EPA to redetermine within 180 days whether to grant or deny Ethyl's § 211(f)(4) application.

§ 9.10 STRATOSPHERIC OZONE PROTECTION

Title VI of the 1990 Amendments incorporates into the Clean Air Act the goals of the Montreal Protocol on Substances that Deplete the Ozone Layer. The Protocol, which was most recently amended in November 1992, requires its signatories (including the United States) to restrict the production and consumption (defined as production plus imports minus exports of bulk chemicals) of chlorofluorocarbons (CFCs), halons, methyl chloroform, carbon tetrachloride, and hydrochlorofluorocarbons (HCFCs). As amended in November 1992, the Protocol requires the complete phase out of all listed CFCs, methyl chloroform, and carbon tetrachloride by 1996, and of halons by 1994. The phaseout of HCFCs is to be accomplished over a longer time period stretching out to 2020–2040. Finally, the 1992 amendments require that production and consumption of hydrobromofluorocarbons (HBFCs) be phased out beginning in 1996 and add methyl bromide to the list of controlled substances.

In 1988, EPA issued final rules implementing the Protocol in the United States. 53 Fed. Reg. 30,598 (1988)(40 C.F.R. Part 82). These rules established a system for allocating production and consumption allowances for ozone-depleting substances based on 1986 levels of production and imports, and established a system for trading these allowances. 40 C.F.R. §§ 82.4–82.12 (1991). In 1989, this regulatory system was supplemented with an excise tax on most sales of CFCs and other ozone-depleting chemicals.

Although Title VI largely mirrors the requirements of the Montreal Protocol as they existed in 1990, it contains more stringent interim targets and an earlier phase-out of methyl chloroform. EPA has proposed a further acceleration of these targets in response to new scientific information, the 1992 amendments to the Montreal Protocol, and petitions to the Agency. Title VI also requires EPA to promulgate regulations to ensure the "lowest achievable levels" of emissions in all user sectors, to ban nonessential products, to limit the use of harmful substitutes, to establish standards and requirements regarding the use, recycling and disposal of CFCs and certain other substances in appliances and industrial process refrigeration, to establish standards and requirements regarding servicing of motor vehicle air conditioners, to mandate warning labels, and to establish a safe alternatives program. Some of these regulations have been promulgated, others have been proposed, and some have not yet reached the proposal stage.

The provisions of the Montreal Protocol and of Title VI are directed at the reduction and eventual discontinuance of the production and consumption of ozone-depleting substances. The statute lists the substances that are to be controlled and mandates that their production and consumption be phased out over a specified time period depending on the ozone-depletion potential of the substances. In addition, Title VI immediately bans specific uses of controlled substances that Congress deemed to be nonessential and authorizes the EPA Administrator to promulgate rules banning additional nonessential uses.

§ 9.11 ENFORCEMENT

The 1990 Amendments significantly expand the enforcement authorities of EPA and private citizen groups. For example, EPA now has authority to issue field citations and to assess administrative penalties. The amounts of civil penalties have been increased, liability for criminal penalties has been expanded, and potential criminal penalties have been made more severe. *See generally* § 113.

Private citizen groups can bring civil penalty actions, as well as actions seeking injunctive relief (as was provided for in the pre–1990 Act). The authority of citizen groups to bring district court actions to control the scope and pace of Agency action has been expanded. *See* § 304(a).

The following table describes the enforcement options currently available under the CAA:

Enforcement Option	CAA Section/Description
Informal	Telephone calls On-site visits Warning letters

Notice of Violation (NOV)	§ 113(a)(1) allows issuance of formal warning letter where a violation of a SIP or permit has occurred. Notice must be issued 30 days before further enforcement action is taken to both the source of the violation and the state in which it occurs. EPA may: issue an administrative compliance order; issue an administrative order assessing penalties under section 113(d); commence a civil action under section 113(b) to require compliance, collect any fees owed, and assess and collect penalties (including noncompliance penalties assessed and owed under section 120); or issue both a compliance order and an administrative penalty order. Correction of the violation within the thirty day period following notice does not affect EPA's authority to take the enforcement action authorized by section 113(a). EPA may also pursue criminal penalties under section 113(c) or seek noncompliance penalties under section 120 or seek an emergency order under section 303.
Administrative Order	EPA compliance orders, except orders to a state prohibiting construction or modification of major stationary sources under section 113(a)(5), must state a specified deadline for compliance, not more than one year from issuance, and are not renewable. The § 113 order, except an order for violation of section 112 (dealing with hazardous emissions), is not effective until the recipient has been given opportunity to confer with EPA about the alleged violation. A copy of the order must be sent by EPA to the appropriate state air pollution control agency, and if the order is issued to a corporation, to the appropriate corporate officers. Compliance orders may not be final actions and, hence, are not appealable under CAA section 307. The compliance order will not take effect until the person to whom it is issued has had the opportunity to confer with the Administrator unless the order involves a violation of the hazardous air pollution requirements of section 112.
Field Citations— § 113(d)(3)	A new provision in the 1990 CAA provides the Administrator with the authority to issue regulations creating a field citation program. This program allows EPA to deal with minor violations by assessing civil penalties not to exceed $5000 per day of violation. The term minor violation is not defined but the Senate viewed minor violations as those discovered during the course of an inspection or for routine violations of reporting or recordkeeping requirements. A person subject to a field citation may request a hearing. If a hearing is not requested, the penalty assessment becomes final. The hearing for a field citation is not subject to the Administrative Procedure Act. Review of an assessment is in a federal district court with venue based on a substantial evidence review.
Administrative civil penalties— § 113(d)(1)	The Administrator may issue an administrative order assessing civil penalties of up to $25,000 per day of violation. The total penalty may not exceed $200,000 and the first alleged date of violation can occur no more than twelve months prior to the initiation of the administrative action. Either or both of these limitations can be waived where the Administrator and the Attorney General jointly decide to do so. The statute provides no guidance as to how this authority is to be exercised, but the statute does say that these determinations are not subject to judicial review. The civil penalty provisions apply to virtually every violation of the CAA except subchapter II, dealing with mobile sources, which has its own civil penalty provision.

Court imposed civil penalties	§ 113(b) dictates that EPA may commence a civil action for a permanent or temporary injunction, or to assess and recover a civil penalty of not more than $25,000 per day for each violation, or both. Liability for civil penalties for violation of section 113 is based on strict liability principles and does not require a "knowing" violation. Civil actions for violation of a SIP or a permit may be commenced only during a period of federally assumed enforcement or more than thirty days following a section 113(a)(1) notice of violation (NOV). The 1990 CAA Amendments added section 113(e) to clarify the rules for penalty assessments by the Administrator or the courts. Factors to be considered are: "the size of the business, the economic impact of the penalty on the business, the violator's full compliance history and good faith efforts to comply, the duration of the violation as established by any credible evidence (including evidence other than the applicable test method), payment by the violator of penalties previously assessed for the same violation, the economic benefit of noncompliance, and the seriousness of the violation." CAA § 113(e), 42 U.S.C. § 7413(e).
Judicial equitable remedies	§ 113(b) gives EPA the power to seek injunctions, civil penalties or both under section 113(b). In addition, the court may award costs of litigation including reasonable attorney and expert witness fees. EPA has authority to seek injunctions under the CAA, but the process that is used is based on traditional common law equity practice. Injunctions are commonly used to enforce orders requiring emission sources to monitor and report under CAA section 114. An injunction usually is not granted to close down a business unless there is a serious and imminent threat to public health or other serious problem.　Normally an injunction includes: √ a compliance schedule with interim requirements; √ a schedule for installing the necessary pollution control equipment or measures; √ a final compliance date; √ stipulated penalties for failure to meet the requirements of the injunction.
Noncompliance penalties	The amount of the administrative penalty is to be based on the amount needed for deterrence which is the sum of the economic benefit of noncompliance plus an additional amount to account for the seriousness of the violation. EPA may adjust this gravity component downward based on the extent of the violator's cooperation.
Criminal actions	Knowing violation (§ 113(c)(1)) Knowing false statement (§ 113(c)(2)) Knowing failure to pay a fee (§ 113(c)(3)) Negligent endangerment (§ 113(c)(4)) Knowing endangerment (§ 113(c)(5))

See Arnold W. Reitze, Jr., AIR POLLUTION LAW (1995).

NATURAL RESOURCES DEFENSE COUNCIL v. REILLY

983 F.2d 259 (D.C.Cir.1993).

EDWARDS, CIRCUIT JUDGE:

D.　CIVIL PENALTIES

1.　*The Applicable Law*

As noted above, Midwest violated the AO sixteen (16) times, and Midwest caused four (4) visible emissions to occur in the case at bar.

Accordingly, there are twenty (20) violations which are subject to the civil penalty provision of the Clean Air Act, Section 113(b) of the Clean Air Act, as amended by the 1990 Clean Air Act Amendments.... Section 113 provides, in part, that:

(b) Civil judicial enforcement

The Administrator shall, as appropriate, in the case of any person which is the owner or operator of an affected source, a major emitting facility, or a major stationary source, and may in the case of any other person, commence a civil action ... to assess and recover civil penalty of not more than $25,000 per day for each violation ... in any of the following instances:

. . .

(2) Whenever such person has violated ... any other requirement or prohibition of this subchapter ... including, but not limited to, a requirement or prohibition of any rule, order ... promulgated, issued, or approved under this chapter....

(e) Penalty assessment criteria

(1) In determining the amount of any penalty to be assessed under this section ... the court ... shall take into consideration (in addition to such other factors as justice may require) the size of the business, the economic impact of the penalty on the business, the violator's full compliance history and good faith efforts to comply, the duration of the violation as established by any credible evidence (including evidence other than the applicable test method), payment by the violator of penalties previously assessed for the same violation, the economic benefit of noncompliance, and the seriousness of the violation.

42 U.S.C. §§ 7413(b)(2) & (e)(1)(West Supp. 1993)(emphasis added)....

Finally, this Court holds that, in calculating the amount of civil penalties to be imposed on defendant, this Court must start with the statutory maximum and make any downward adjustments based on the evidence adduced at trial. While this Court has not been directed to any cases decided under § 7413(e) of the Clean Air Act, the Sixth Circuit has held that "the Clean Air and Clean Waters Acts are in pari materia with one another." *United States v. Stauffer Chemical Co.*, 684 F.2d 1174, 1187 (6th Cir.1982), *aff'd on other grounds*, 464 U.S. 165, 104 S.Ct. 575, 78 L.Ed.2d 388 (1984)(citations omitted). The United States Court of Appeals for the Eleventh Circuit has held that, under the penalty provision of the Clean Water Act, "the point of departure for the district court should be the maximum fines for such violations permitted by the Clean Water Act." *Atlantic States Legal Foundation, Inc. v. Tyson Foods, Inc.*, 897 F.2d 1128, 1137 (11th Cir.1990). See also *A.A. Metal Constr. Co.*, 22 Envtl. L. Rep. at 21201. Based on the fact that the Clean Air Act and the Clean Water Act are in pari materia with one another, this Court finds the reasoning of Tyson Foods persuasive, and thus this Court will calculate the civil penalties to be imposed on defendant by starting with the statutory maximum of $25,000.00 per day for each violation, which equals $500,000.00 (twenty (20) violations multiplied by $25,000.00), and examining the requisite penalty assessment criteria to determine if any downward departure is required....

2. Section 7413(e) Penalty Assessment Criteria

With respect to the size of defendant's business, the evidence adduced at trial showed that Midwest delines between 30,000 and 32,000 brake shoes per year. In addition, Midwest stipulated that some of the brake shoes which Midwest rehabilitates contained asbestos. Based on this evidence, the government argues that this Court should find that the size of Midwest's business, with respect to brake shoe rehabilitation, is significant. No evidence was introduced, however, which would allow this Court to compare the size of Midwest's brake shoe rehabilitation business with other businesses involved in brake shoe rehabilitation. Therefore, this Court is unable to determine whether Midwest's business is significant. On the other hand, there was no evidence adduced at trial which indicated that Midwest's brake shoe rehabilitation business was small when compared to others in the business. Accordingly, this factor does not warrant a reduction in the maximum statutory penalty.

As to the economic impact of the penalty on defendant's business, this Court, for the reasons which follow, concludes that this factor warrants a significant reduction in the maximum statutory penalty. The government's witness at trial could not render an opinion with respect to what type of impact a $650,000.00 civil penalty would have on defendant's business.... The government's witness did testify, however, that, in her opinion, defendant could withstand a penalty in excess of $600,-000.00, although the precise amount over $600,000.00 was not clarified. The government's witness also testified that defendant: (1) had accessed only 1.85 million dollars of the 2.5 million dollar line of credit with Michigan National Bank; (2) had allowed its accounts receivable to increase approximately $334,000.00 from the previous year and that out of the 1.6 million dollars in accounts receivable defendant only deemed $36,000.00 as uncollectible; (3) had a gross income of 10.819 million dollars for 1992; (4) had a net income of approximately $214,000.00 for 1992; and (5) had come through reasonably tough periods financially and that now Midwest is profitable and is generating positive case flow.

Based on the above, this Court finds that a reduction in the amount of $450,000.00 is warranted under this factor. First, while the government's witness testified that in 1992 Midwest had allowed its account receivable to increase by over $300,000.00, because defendant had not spent as much on turning its accounts receivable into cash as it had in 1991, this Court finds this testimony not persuasive. In light of the fact that in 1991 defendant spent $20,162.00 on credit and collection and that in 1992 defendant spent $19,130.00 on credit and collection, a difference of $1,032.00, this Court concludes that, in 1992, defendant attempted to turn its accounts receivable into cash with the same effort it used in the past, and thus the existence of a large of amount of accounts receivable does not warrant this Court finding that the civil penalty in this case should not be decreased.

Second, the fact that defendant can access a line of credit to pay the civil penalty is entitled to little weight, because defendant has secured this line of credit for reasons other than paying a civil penalty in this case. This Court finds that the most relevant information regarding defendant's ability to pay a civil penalty is found in the uncontested evidence that in 1992 defendant had gross sales above 10 million dollars and a net income of more than $200,000.00. This net income occurring after Midwest, according to the government's witness, had come through tough financial periods. Therefore, based on the above evidence, it is the opinion of this Court that the civil penalty against defendant should be reduced by $450,000.00 based on this statutory factor. This leaves the civil penalty in the amount of $50,000.00. An amount which represents 25% of defendant's net income for 1992. And thus an amount that is sufficient to deter Midwest from allowing future violations to occur and is sufficient to punish Midwest for its past violations.

Regarding the next factor, namely, defendant's full compliance history and good faith efforts to comply, the Court finds that this factor mitigates in favor of not allowing a reduction in the maximum penalty. The government presented sufficient evidence that defendant had regularly violated the Asbestos NESHAP and the AO over a number of years. In addition, defendant did not introduce any evidence with respect to its good faith efforts to comply with the Clean Air Act, the Asbestos NESHAP, or the AO. Accordingly, this factors weighs in favor of not reducing the statutory maximum penalty.

With respect to the duration of the violations as established by any credible evidence, this Court concludes that this factor does not warrant a reduction in the penalty to be imposed on defendant. As noted above, the government introduced ample evidence that the violations lasted from 1985 through 1991. Therefore, this factor does not weigh in favor of reducing the statutory maximum penalty.

The next factor, payment by defendant of penalties previously assessed for the same violations, is not implicated by the facts in this case, because there was no evidence adduced at trial that defendant previously paid a penalty for any of these violations. This brings the Court to the sixth factor, namely, the economic benefit of noncompliance. In *Tyson Foods, supra,* the Eleventh Circuit stated that "insuring that violators do not reap economic benefit by failing to comply with the statutory mandate is of key importance if the penalties are successfully to deter violations." 897 F.2d at 1141. In addition, the in *A.A. Mactal Constr. Co., supra,* the court noted "that the recovery of economic benefit is essential and that economic benefit should serve as the floor below which the maximum civil penalty should not be mitigated." 22 Envtl. L. Rep. at 21,201. Here, there was no evidence introduced at trial as to the exact amount of economic benefit defendant received through its noncompliance with the Clean Air Act.... This Court recognizes, however, that based on the evidence presented at trial, defendant received very little economic benefit from the violations. This case did not involve a defendant that intentionally buried asbestos-containing waste material in the ground or intentionally released asbestos-containing waste into the air in an effort to dispose of the waste. Here, defendant attempted to comply with all of the requirements. There is, however, no doubt in this Court's opinion that defendant did not handle the asbestos-containing waste material in a professional manner and that defendant failed to pay close enough attention to the details of the Asbestos NESHAP and the AO. Therefore, the Court finds that this factor neither establishes a floor below which the maximum civil penalty should not be reduced nor mitigates in favor of reducing the maximum civil penalty.

As to the last factor which this Court must address, that is, the seriousness of the violation, this Court finds that this factor does not require any downward adjustment in the amount of the penalty to be imposed on defendant. First, defendant does not dispute the fact that medical science has not established any minimum level of exposure to asbestos fibers which is considered to be safe to individuals exposed to the fibers. Therefore, as a matter of law, due to the fact the this case involves asbestos, this Court finds as a matter of law that the violations are very serious.

In addition, this case involves numerous violations of the AO. The AO was consented to by Midwest and was not unilaterally imposed on Midwest by the EPA. Midwest received a number of substantial benefits by entering into the AO, including but not limited to, the government not instituting an action in federal court seeking a substantial civil penalty and being able to negotiate with the EPA on the precise waste handling methods which Midwest would use at the facility. Notwithstanding these substantial benefits, Midwest failed to live up to its end of the bargain with respect to the AO. Consequently, the violations of the AO also are very serious violations.

Finally, this Court has one final comment before imposing the civil penalty on defendant. This Court is compelled to point out that defendant entered into numerous stipulations with the government in this case. Some stipulations involved facts and circumstances which there could have been a dispute over. Defendant decided, however, to stipulate to these facts, and thus allowed the government to present its case over the course of a few days, instead of over a course of a few weeks. While this, in and of itself, may not warrant a reduction in the amount of the civil penalty imposed in the case at bar, this Court wishes to acknowledge these actions.

Accordingly, after a through review of the relevant penalty assessment criteria set forth in 42 U.S.C. § 7413(e), the Court concludes that a civil penalty in the amount of $50,000.00 against defendant is proper. This amounts to $2,500.00 for each violation, which is a sufficient sum to deter defendant from future violations, as well as to penalize defendant for its past actions.

E. INJUNCTIVE RELIEF

The government seeks to have this Court affirmatively enjoin Midwest so that Midwest performs its rehabilitation of brake shoes at its Detroit facility in compliance with the key terms of the AO. In addition, the government proposes that the injunction could be terminated under the following conditions:

With at least thirty days prior, written notice to the United States, Midwest may petition the Court to lift this injunction upon certification to the Court either of the following:

(1) Midwest has complied continuously with this Court's injunction for at least twelve consecutive months subsequent to the date on which the Court's injunction was issued; or

(2) Midwest can certify specifically and affirmatively that it has not had on its facility—for any consecutive, eighteen-month period following entry of the injunction—any brake lining, new or used, that contained any asbestos, and further that Midwest warrants it will not allow on its premises any asbestos-containing brake lining, new or used, at any time in the future. The United States shall have no less than 30 days after Midwest files any such petition to evaluate its merit and, if appropriate, oppose it.

It is axiomatic under federal law "that the basis for injunctive relief in the federal courts has always been irreparable injury and the inadequacy of legal remedies." *Weinberger v. Romero–Barcelo*, 456 U.S. 305, 312, 102 S.Ct. 1798, 1803, 72 L.Ed.2d 91 (1982)(injunctive relief under the Federal Water Pollution Control Act). Moreover, whether injunctive relief should be issued in within the equitable discretion of the court. Id. at 320, 102 S.Ct. at 1807.

Here, while this Court agrees with the government that its proposed injunction is reasonable, this Court declines to grant such injunctive relief. First, as the government emphasized in its post-trial brief, the primary goal of the civil penalty assessed against defendant under the Clean Air Act is deterrence. This Court has ordered defendant to pay a $50,000.00 civil penalty in this case. This is a significant penalty and it should be sufficient to deter defendant from future violations. Second, at this point in time, it cannot be said that the government is without adequate legal remedies; a requisite finding before an injunction can be issued. If defendant violates the AO in the future the government may bring a civil suit against defendant seeking an addition civil penalty. Indeed, if the government were forced to bring a civil suit in the future against defendant, then this Court may be more inclined to grant the government's request for injunctive relief based on the fact that the civil penalty assessed in the instant case had failed to deter defendant from violating the AO and the Asbestos NESHAP. Accordingly, the government's request for injunctive relief is DENIED.

IV Conclusion

For all of the aforementioned reasons this Court concludes that defendant, Midwest Suspension and Brake, has violated the Administrative Order sixteen (16) times and has violated the Asbestos NESHAP on four (4) occasions. The Court ORDERS defendant to pay a civil penalty in the amount of $50,000.00 to the United States Treasury. Finally, the government's request for injunctive relief enjoining defendant from future violation of the Administrative Order is DENIED....

IT IS SO ORDERED.

§ 9.12 THEMES FOR THE 1990S

Congress in the 1970 and 1977 Amendments to the Clean Air Act created an extensive program of air quality and control technology-based regulation for existing and new sources of air pollution. These requirements spawned numerous and complex administrative proceedings, as well as litigation addressing both the Agency's substantive obligations and its schedule for action. In many instances, these provisions are still being implemented by EPA.

EPA's rules and guidance under the pre–1990 Act will continue to impose important regulatory obligations during the coming decade. The experience with air pollution regulation through the 1980s, however, suggests several themes that will be important to implementation of the 1990 Amendments to the Act.

First, air pollution is not merely a local concern, but must be addressed in a broader geographical context. This necessity has led to efforts to redefine the federal-state relationship in ways that strengthen the federal partner. In this regard, experience has shown that a strong federal hand may be important to timely implementation of air quality requirements. The continuing challenge for EPA in implementing the Act will be to find the proper balance of federal compulsion and state discretion to reconcile national, regional, and local interests.

Second, to ensure that the federal government acts, Congress has increasingly relied on deadlines for regulatory action, as well as greater detail in enabling legislation in an attempt to resolve difficult policy decisions for the Agency. Merely telling the Agency to act by a date certain does not guarantee timely action, however, as the experience of the 1980s has shown. Indeed, of the numerous statutory deadlines in the 1977 Amendments, only one—regarding an air quality modeling conference—was met by the Agency. Similarly, the use of increasingly detailed statutory directives does not necessarily lead to quicker regulatory action. "Detail" often means increased complexity—a factor that can work against the goal of expediting Agency action. Timely implementation of the 1990 Amendments will require careful allocation of Agency resources and an honest effort to avoid ideological disputes.

Third, as deadlines proliferate and statutory language becomes more complex, the Agency will be forced to look for alternative means of meeting its statutory obligations. This trend was evident during the 1980s, as the Agency moved away from legislative rulemaking in several areas to explore alternative implementation strategies that require less public involvement, and therefore supposedly less controversy and delay. Policy guidance and adjudicatory determinations have begun to play and will continue to play a greater role in Clean Air Act implementation.

Finally, as public health-related standards have been implemented, Congress has turned its attention to welfare-related concerns, including preservation of existing levels of air quality in clean areas. This broadening of the goals of the Act has resulted in an escalation in the costs of regulation. The escalating costs of clean air regulation has, in turn, provided a strong incentive for market-oriented solutions to air quality problems. Congress specifically adopted a market-oriented approach to regulation of acid rain in the 1990 Amendments, and encouraged EPA and the states to employ market mechanisms in other areas of air quality regulation. The success of the Clean Air Act over the next decade will be influenced by how well EPA and the states exercise this authority.

Congress and EPA's struggles with the complexities of clean air regulation through the 1980s suggest several themes for the 1990s—more federal oversight, an emphasis on alternatives to traditional legislative rulemaking, and a search for innovative ways to control the escalating costs of clean air regulation. These themes are brought into focus by the Clean Air Act Amendments of 1990, the most lengthy and complex piece of environmental legislation ever enacted by Congress.

Chapter 10

CONSERVATION LAWS

Table of Sections

§ 10.1   ACTIVITIES ON FEDERAL LANDS

There are a number of statutes that restrict the use of federal lands. Environmental controls are especially stringent for those lands that have been designated as national parks, forests, wildlife refuges, game systems, or wilderness areas. Most commercial uses are prohibited within such lands. Activities not covered by a flat prohibition usually must be authorized by the federal department responsible for the administration of the particular lands. For example, the construction of power lines, pipelines, or roads through national wilderness areas may be carried out if authorized by a permit from the Secretary of the Interior.

SALMON RIVER CONCERNED CITIZENS v. ROBERTSON
32 F.3d 1346 (9th Cir.1994).

TANG, SENIOR CIRCUIT JUDGE:

Appellants (collectively, "SRCC") ... challenge the vegetation management policy for the Pacific Southwest Region adopted by the Chief Forester for the United States Forest Service ("Forest Service" or

"Service"). In particular, SRCC challenges the environmental impact statement underlying the policy and issued under the provisions of the National Environmental Policy Act ("NEPA"), 42 U.S.C. § 4332. The district court granted summary judgment in favor of the Forest Service. SRCC appeals, arguing that the impact statement is inadequate under NEPA. The Forest Service counters that SRCC lacks standing to press its action, and that its claims lack merit. We find that SRCC has standing, but affirm the district court's summary judgment in favor of the Forest Service.

* * *

The Forest Service is obliged under the National Forest Management Act of 1976 ("NFMA"), 16 U.S.C. § 1601 *et seq.*, to prepare and implement land and resource management plans for our National Forests, one objective being to produce a continuous supply of timber for logging.... The Service implements this objective through reforestation.... Because competition from other plants often prevents achieving timber yield objectives, the Forest Service intervenes to assist the growth of trees through vegetation management....

The FEIS at issue in this case evaluates the use of herbicides as part of the vegetation management plan for the Pacific Southwest Region (Region 5). The lands claimed to be most likely affected are located in Northern California and the Sierra Nevada, totaling approximately six million of the total twenty million acres of National Forest System land in the Region.

The Impact Statement is the culmination of public and private efforts over the last twenty years. The previous environmental impact statement was published in 1974. As a result of increased public concerns about human health and safety, the environment, changes in applicable federal law, and the development of new information and technology, the process of updating that impact statement began in 1981. The process led to a revised impact statement that was published and released for public comment in mid–1983.

In 1984, while the revised impact statement was still under consideration, the Forest Service initiated a moratorium on herbicide use in Region 5. The impetus for this decision was two judicial decisions in which this Circuit precluded government agencies from relying solely on herbicide registration by the U.S. Environmental Protection Agency ("EPA") to verify herbicide safety for normal use. As a result, this Circuit required agencies to undertake a worst case analysis concerning the safety of herbicides. *See Save Our Ecosystems v. Clark*, 747 F.2d 1240 (9th Cir.1984); *Southern Oregon Citizens Against Toxic Sprays v. Clark*, 720 F.2d 1475 (9th Cir.1983), *cert. denied*, 469 U.S. 1028, 83 L.Ed.2d 372, 105 S.Ct. 446 (1984).

In response to these two decisions and public comment, the Service supplemented the revised impact statement. With assistance from various consultants, the supplement was published and circulated for public comment in 1986. It included a worst case analysis of the risks from herbicide use to human health, soils, water quality, and wildlife.

The Forest Service published the FEIS now in issue in December 1988. The Impact Statement incorporates and responds to public comments to both the revised impact statement and the 1986 supplement. In doing so, the Impact Statement identifies and evaluates eight alternative vegetation management programs, each employing several methods of controlling vegetation, including mechanical, thermal, manual, chemical, and biological controls.... Each alternative emphasizes a specific objective, such as, cost-effectiveness, maximizing timber production, maximizing employment opportunities, preservation of nontimber resources, or minimizing or prohibiting the use of herbicides.

More pertinent to the issues before us, the FEIS evaluates the effect of each of the eight alternatives on, *inter alia*, soil and water quality, air quality, vegetation, wildlife, fisheries, human health and safety, cultural resources, and scenic quality. The Impact Statement also evaluates the socioeconomic effects of each alternative, including an analysis of economic efficiency and the cost of alternative approaches.

The evaluation of the effects on human health and safety considers risks to forest workers and to the public from the use of thirteen herbicides. The Forest Service accomplished its analysis by applying a "risk assessment" methodology. This methodology compares doses of an herbicide that people may get from applying the herbicide, or from being near an application site, with doses that produced no observable adverse effects in test animals and were considered safe in laboratory studies. Because various factors contributed to uncertainty in this process, ... however, the Service employed several other analytical approaches to conduct a more comprehensive assessment of the risks to human health: hazard analysis, exposure analysis, and risk analysis....

The resulting risk assessment addresses the potential for herbicides to cause general systemic effects, heritable mutations, synergistic effects, cumulative effects, and effects on sensitive individuals. Unfortunately, missing or unavailable information regarding exposures or certain ill effects produced gaps in the data. These gaps are "evaluated in terms of [their] importance in determining human health risks ... and in terms of the cost and delay required to supply the information." FEIS at 4–63. As a result, this aspect of the risk assessment includes an assessment of the effects of herbicide applications under three scenarios: a normal or realistic scenario, an abnormal or conservative scenario, and an accident or worst case scenario....

Based on these analyses, the FEIS recommends that the Forest Service adopt Alternative 1 as its vegetation management program, which seeks to "maximize flexibility for professional foresters to select the most appropriate treatments, based on site-specific conditions and other considerations, consistent with achieving land management objectives." *Id.* at 2–14. More specifically, this alternative "allows use of all methods to treat competing vegetation ... adequate ... to meet the timber yield objectives.... However, herbicides are to be used only when essential.... " *Id.* at 2–14–17.

The Regional Forester adopted the Impact Statement's recommendation, delegating to district foresters, for the most part, the discretion to apply herbicides at the project level.... On June 1, 1989, SRCC appealed the ROD in an administrative proceeding, securing a partial stay precluding the use of herbicides during the pendency of the appeal. On January 1, 1991, the Forest Service affirmed the Regional Forester's decision to select Alternative 1 as modified in the ROD, approved the FEIS, and denied SRCC's request for a new impact statement. Furthermore, the Service lifted the moratorium on its use of herbicides in Region 5, and quashed the stay. The Forest Service found the Regional Forester's decision to be neither arbitrary nor capricious. The Service also found that the FEIS adequately disclosed and discussed the potential risks to human health from the use of herbicides. It noted, in particular, that many of the issues and concerns raised by SRCC were site-specific concerns not within the scope of a programmatic document such as the FEIS.

SRCC then pursued its challenges of the FEIS and the ROD against the Forest Service in federal district court. Both parties moved for summary judgment, the Service contending that the complaint was insufficient in either establishing SRCC's standing, or merit requiring declaratory or injunctive relief. Although it rejected the defense that SRCC failed to establish its standing and that the case was not ripe, the district court granted the Forest Service's summary judgment, concluding that the Impact Statement, its risk assessment in particular, satisfied the requirements of NEPA. SRCC appeals that decision.

* * *

We find that SRCC has standing to challenge the FEIS and ROD. We are compelled, however, to reject SRCC's claims that the FEIS fails to adequately address cumulative effects, evaluate inert ingredients, and disclose and evaluate the risks to chemically sensitive individuals.

§ 10.2 ACTIVITIES IN MARINE SANCTUARIES

Under the Marine Protection, Research and Sanctuaries Act of 1972, as amended, 16 U.S.C.A. § 1431 *et seq.*, permits authorizing activities in marine sanctuaries are valid only if the Secretary of Commerce certifies that the proposed activities are consistent with the purposes of the Marine Protection, Research and Sanctuaries Act and can be carried out within the regulations for the sanctuary. The Secretary of Commerce is authorized to designate as marine sanctuaries any ocean waters, coastal waters, or Great Lakes and their connecting waters that he finds to have important conservation, recreational, ecological, or aesthetic values.

§ 10.3 PROTECTION OF WILD AND SCENIC RIVERS

Under the Wild and Scenic Rivers Act, 16 U.S.C.A. § 1271 *et seq.*, a federal agency may not issue a permit for the construction of any water resources project on a river designated as a wild and scenic river, if the project would have a direct and adverse effect on the environmental values of the river.

§ 10.4 PROTECTION OF ENDANGERED SPECIES

Under the Endangered Species Act, 16 U.S.C.A. § 1531 *et seq.*, it is illegal to capture, possess, or sell any species of fish or wildlife that has been designated as an endangered species, unless such action is authorized by a permit issued by the Secretary of the Interior or Secretary of Commerce. Such permits are usually issued only where the purpose of the activity is to enhance the survival of the species or to make scientific studies, although an exemption from the prohibition can sometimes be obtained by making a showing of economic hardship.

BABBITT v. SWEET HOME CHAPTER OF COMMUNITIES FOR A GREAT OREGON

___ U.S. ___, 115 S.Ct. 2407, 132 L.Ed.2d 597 (1995).

JUSTICE STEVENS delivered the opinion of the Court.

The Endangered Species Act of 1973, 87 Stat. 884, 16 U.S.C. § 1531 (1988 ed. and Supp. V)(ESA or Act), contains a variety of protections designed to save from extinction species that the Secretary of the Interior designates as endangered or threatened. Section 9 of the Act makes it unlawful for any person to "take" any endangered or threatened species. The Secretary has promulgated a regulation that defines the statute's prohibition on takings to include "significant habitat modification or degradation where it actually kills or injures wildlife." This case presents the question whether the Secretary exceeded his authority under the Act by promulgating that regulation.

I

Section 9(a)(1) of the Endangered Species Act provides the following protection for endangered species: ...

"Except as provided in sections 1535(g)(2) and 1539 of this title, with respect to any endangered species of fish or wildlife listed pursuant to section 1533 of this title it is unlawful for any person subject to the jurisdiction of the United States to— .....

(B) take any such species within the United States or the territorial sea of the United States[.]" 16 U.S.C. § 1538(a)(1).

Section 3(19) of the Act defines the statutory term "take":

"The term 'take' means to harass, harm, pursue, hunt, shoot, wound, kill, trap, capture, or collect, or to attempt to engage in any such conduct." 16 U.S.C. § 1532(19).

The Act does not further define the terms it uses to define "take." The Interior Department regulations that implement the statute, however, define the statutory term "harm":

"Harm in the definition of 'take' in the Act means an act which actually kills or injures wildlife. Such act may include significant habitat modification or degradation where it actually kills or injures wildlife by significantly impairing essential behavioral patterns, including breeding, feeding, or sheltering." 50 CFR § 17.3 (1994).

This regulation has been in place since 1975. . . .

A limitation on the § 9 "take" prohibition appears in § 10(a)(1)(B) of the Act, which Congress added by amendment in 1982. That section authorizes the Secretary to grant a permit for any taking otherwise prohibited by § 9(a)(1)(B) "if such taking is incidental to, and not the purpose of, the carrying out of an otherwise lawful activity." 16 U.S.C. § 1539(a)(1)(B).

In addition to the prohibition on takings, the Act provides several other protections for endangered species. Section 4, 16 U.S.C. § 1533, commands the Secretary to identify species of fish or wildlife that are in danger of extinction and to publish from time to time lists of all species he determines to be endangered or threatened. Section 5, 16 U.S.C. § 1534, authorizes the Secretary, in cooperation with the States, see 16 U.S.C. § 1535, to acquire land to aid in preserving such species. Section 7 requires federal agencies to ensure that none of their activities, including the granting of licenses and permits, will jeopardize the continued existence of endangered species "or result in the destruction or adverse modification of habitat of such species which is determined by the Secretary . . . to be critical." 16 U.S.C. § 1536(a)(2).

Respondents in this action are small landowners, logging companies, and families dependent on the forest products industries in the Pacific Northwest and in the Southeast, and organizations that represent their interests. They brought this declaratory judgment action against petitioners, the Secretary of the Interior and the Director of the Fish and Wildlife Service, in the United States District Court for the District of Columbia to challenge the statutory validity of the Secretary's regulation defining "harm," particularly the inclusion of habitat modification and degradation in the definition. . . . Respondents challenged the regulation on its face. Their complaint alleged that application of the "harm" regulation to the red-cockaded woodpecker, an endangered species, . . . and the northern spotted owl, a threatened species, . . . had injured them economically. App. 17–23.

Respondents advanced three arguments to support their submission that Congress did not intend the word "take" in § 9 to include habitat modification, as the Secretary's "harm" regulation provides. First, they correctly noted that language in the Senate's original version of the ESA would have defined "take" to include "destruction, modification, or curtailment of [the] habitat or range" of fish or wildlife, . . . but the Senate deleted that language from the bill before enacting it. Second, respondents argued that Congress intended the Act's express authorization for the Federal Government to buy private land in order to prevent habitat degradation in § 5 to be the exclusive check against habitat modification on private property. Third, because the Senate added the term "harm" to the definition of "take" in a floor amendment without debate, respondents argued that the court should not interpret the term so expansively as to include habitat modification.

The District Court considered and rejected each of respondents' arguments, finding "that Congress intended an expansive interpretation of the word 'take,' an interpretation that encompasses habitat modification." 806 F.Supp. 279, 285 (1992). The court noted that in 1982, when Congress was aware of a judicial decision that had applied the Secretary's regulation, *see Palila v. Hawaii Dept. of Land and Natural Resources*, 639 F.2d 495 (C.A.9 1981) (*Palila I*), it amended the Act without using the opportunity to change the definition of "take." 806 F.Supp. at 284. The court stated that, even had it found the ESA " 'silent or ambiguous' " as to the authority for the Secretary's definition of "harm," it would nevertheless have upheld the regulation as a reasonable interpretation of the statute. *Id.*, at 285 (quoting *Chevron U.S.A. Inc. v. Natural Resources Defense Council*, Inc., 467 U.S. 837, 843, 81 L.Ed.2d 694, 104 S.Ct. 2778 (1984)). The District Court therefore entered summary judgment for petitioners and dismissed respondents' complaint.

A divided panel of the Court of Appeals initially affirmed the judgment of the District Court. 303 U.S.App.D.C. 42, 1 F.3d 1 (C.A.D.C. 1993). After granting a petition for rehearing, however, the panel reversed. 305 U.S.App.D.C. 110, 17 F.3d 1463 (C.A.D.C.1994). Although acknowledging that "the potential breadth of the word 'harm' is indisputable," id., at 1464, the majority concluded that the immediate statutory context in which "harm" appeared counseled against a broad reading; like the other words in the definition of "take," the word "harm" should be read as applying only to "the perpetrator's direct application of force against the animal taken. . . . The forbidden acts fit, in ordinary language, the basic model 'A hit B.' " *Id.*, at 1465. The majority based its reasoning on a canon of statutory construction called noscitur a sociis, which holds that a word is known by the company it keeps. *See Neal v. Clark*, 95 U.S. 704, 708–709, 24 L.Ed. 586 (1878).

The majority claimed support for its construction from a decision of the Ninth Circuit that narrowly construed the word "harass" in the Marine Mammal Protection Act, 16 U.S.C. § 1372(a)(2)(A), *see United States v. Hayashi*, 5 F.3d 1278, 1282 (1993); from the legislative history of the ESA; . . . from its view that Congress must not have intended the purportedly broad curtailment of private property rights that the Secretary's interpretation permitted; and from the ESA's land acquisition provision in § 5 and restriction on federal agencies' activities regarding habitat in § 7, both of which the court saw as evidence that Congress had not intended the § 9 "take" prohibition to reach habitat modification. Most prominently, the court performed a lengthy analysis of the 1982 amendment to § 10 that provided for "incidental take permits" and concluded that the amendment did not change the meaning of the term "take" as defined in the 1973 statute. . . .

Chief Judge Mikva, who had announced the panel's original decision, dissented. *See* 17 F.3d at 1473. In his view, a proper application of Chevron indicated that the Secretary had reasonably defined "harm," because respondents had failed to show that Congress unambiguously manifested its intent to exclude habitat modification from the ambit of "take." Chief Judge Mikva found the majority's reliance on noscitur a sociis inappropriate in light of the statutory language and unnecessary in light of the strong support in the legislative history for the Secretary's interpretation. He did not find the 1982 "incidental take permit" amendment alone sufficient to vindicate the Secretary's definition of "harm," but he believed the amendment provided additional support for that definition because it reflected Congress' view in 1982 that the definition was reasonable.

The Court of Appeals' decision created a square conflict with a 1988 decision of the Ninth Circuit that had upheld the Secretary's definition of "harm." *See Palila v. Hawaii Dept. of Land and Natural Resources,* 852 F.2d 1106 (1988) (*Palila II*). The Court of Appeals neither cited nor distinguished *Palila II*, despite the stark contrast between the Ninth Circuit's holding and its own. We granted certiorari to resolve the conflict. 513 U.S. (1995). Our consideration of the text and structure of the Act, its legislative history, and the significance of the 1982 amendment persuades us that the Court of Appeals' judgment should be reversed.

II

Because this case was decided on motions for summary judgment, we may appropriately make certain factual assumptions in order to frame the legal issue. First, we assume respondents have no desire to harm either the red-cockaded woodpecker or the spotted owl; they merely wish to continue logging activities that would be entirely proper if not prohibited by the ESA. On the other hand, we must assume arguendo that those activities will have the effect, even though unintended, of detrimentally changing the natural habitat of both listed species and that, as a consequence, members of those species will be killed or injured. Under respondents' view of the law, the Secretary's only means of forestalling that grave result—even when the actor knows it is certain to occur ...—is to use his § 5 authority to purchase the lands on which the survival of the species depends. The Secretary, on the other hand, submits that the § 9 prohibition on takings, which Congress defined to include "harm," places on respondents a duty to avoid harm that habitat alteration will cause the birds unless respondents first obtain a permit pursuant to § 10.

The text of the Act provides three reasons for concluding that the Secretary's interpretation is reasonable. First, an ordinary understanding of the word "harm" supports it. The dictionary definition of the verb form of "harm" is "to cause hurt or damage to: injure." Webster's Third New International Dictionary 1034 (1966). In the context of the ESA, that definition naturally encompasses habitat modification that results in actual injury or death to members of an endangered or threatened species.

Respondents argue that the Secretary should have limited the purview of "harm" to direct applications of force against protected species, but the dictionary definition does not include the word "directly" or suggest in any way that only direct or willful action that leads to injury constitutes "harm." ... Moreover, unless the statutory term "harm" encompasses indirect as well as direct injuries, the word has no meaning that does not duplicate the meaning of other words that § 3 uses to define "take." A reluctance to treat statutory terms as surplusage supports the reasonableness of the Secretary's interpretation. *See, e.g., Mackey v. Lanier Collection Agency & Service, Inc.,* 486 U.S. 825, 837, 100 L.Ed.2d 836, 108 S.Ct. 2182, and n. 11 (1988)....

Second, the broad purpose of the ESA supports the Secretary's decision to extend protection against activities that cause the precise harms Congress enacted the statute to avoid. In *TVA v. Hill,* 437 U.S. 153, 98 S.Ct. 2279, 57 L.Ed.2d 117 (1978), we described the Act as "the most comprehensive legislation for the preservation of endangered species ever enacted by any nation." *Id.,* at 180. Whereas predecessor statutes enacted in 1966 and 1969 had not contained any sweeping prohibition against the taking of endangered species except on federal lands, see id., at 175, the 1973 Act applied to all land in the United States and to the Nation's territorial seas. As stated in § 2 of the Act, among its central purposes is "to provide a means whereby the ecosystems upon which endangered species and threatened species depend may be conserved.... " 16 U.S.C. § 1531(b).

In *Hill,* we construed § 7 as precluding the completion of the Tellico Dam because of its predicted impact on the survival of the snail darter. See 437 U.S. at 193. Both our holding and the language in our opinion stressed the importance of the statutory policy. "The plain intent of Congress in enacting this statute," we recognized, "was to halt and reverse the trend toward species extinction, whatever the cost. This is reflected not only in the stated policies of the Act, but in literally every section of the statute." *Id.,* at 184. Although the § 9 "take" prohibition was not at issue in *Hill,* we took note of that prohibition, placing particular emphasis on the Secretary's inclusion of habitat modification in his definition of "harm." ... In light of that provision for habitat protection, we could "not understand how TVA intends to operate Tellico Dam without 'harming' the snail darter." *Id.,* at 184, n. 30. Congress' intent to provide comprehensive protection for endangered and threatened species supports the permissibility of the Secretary's "harm" regulation.

Respondents advance strong arguments that activities that cause minimal or unforeseeable harm will not violate the Act as construed in the "harm" regulation. Respondents, however, present a facial challenge to the regulation. *Cf. Anderson v. Edwards,* 514 U.S. ___, ___, n. 6 (1995)(slip op., at 11); *INS v. National Center for Immigrants' Rights,*

Inc., 502 U.S. 183, 188, 116 L.Ed.2d 546, 112 S.Ct. 551 (1991). Thus, they ask us to invalidate the Secretary's understanding of "harm" in every circumstance, even when an actor knows that an activity, such as draining a pond, would actually result in the extinction of a listed species by destroying its habitat. Given Congress' clear expression of the ESA's broad purpose to protect endangered and threatened wildlife, the Secretary's definition of "harm" is reasonable. . . .

Third, the fact that Congress in 1982 authorized the Secretary to issue permits for takings that § 9(a)(1)(B) would otherwise prohibit, "if such taking is incidental to, and not the purpose of, the carrying out of an otherwise lawful activity," 16 U.S.C. § 1539(a)(1)(B), strongly suggests that Congress understood § 9(a)(1)(B) to prohibit indirect as well as deliberate takings. *Cf. NLRB v. Bell Aerospace Co. Division of Textron, Inc.,* 416 U.S. 267, 274–275, 40 L.Ed.2d 134, 94 S.Ct. 1757 (1974). The permit process requires the applicant to prepare a "conservation plan" that specifies how he intends to "minimize and mitigate" the "impact" of his activity on endangered and threatened species, 16 U.S.C. § 1539(a)(2)(A), making clear that Congress had in mind foreseeable rather than merely accidental effects on listed species. . . . No one could seriously request an "incidental" take permit to avert § 9 liability for direct, deliberate action against a member of an endangered or threatened species, but respondents would read "harm" so narrowly that the permit procedure would have little more than that absurd purpose. "When Congress acts to amend a statute, we presume it intends its amendment to have real and substantial effect." *Stone v. INS,* 514 U.S. __, (1995)(slip op., at 10). Congress' addition of the § 10 permit provision supports the Secretary's conclusion that activities not intended to harm an endangered species, such as habitat modification, may constitute unlawful takings under the ESA unless the Secretary permits them.

> The Court of Appeals made three errors in asserting that "harm" must refer to a direct application of force because the words around it do. . . . First, the court's premise was flawed. Several of the words that accompany "harm" in the § 3 definition of "take," especially "harass," "pursue," "wound," and "kill," refer to actions or effects that do not require direct applications of force. Second, to the extent the court read a requirement of intent or purpose into the words used to define "take," it ignored § 9's express provision that a "knowing" action is enough to violate the Act. Third, the court employed noscitur a sociis to give "harm" essentially the same function as other words in the definition, thereby denying it independent meaning. The canon, to the contrary, counsels that a word "gathers meaning from the words around it."

Jarecki v. G. D. Searle & Co., 367 U.S. 303, 307, 6 L.Ed.2d 859, 81 S.Ct. 1579 (1961). The statutory context of "harm" suggests that Congress meant that term to serve a particular function in the ESA, consistent with but distinct from the functions of the other verbs used to define "take." The Secretary's interpretation of "harm" to include indirectly injuring endangered animals through habitat modification permissibly interprets "harm" to have "a character of its own not to be submerged by its association." *Russell Motor Car Co. v. United States*, 261 U.S. 514, 519, 67 L.Ed. 778, 43 S.Ct. 428 (1923)....

Nor does the Act's inclusion of the § 5 land acquisition authority and the § 7 directive to federal agencies to avoid destruction or adverse modification of critical habitat alter our conclusion. Respondents' argument that the Government lacks any incentive to purchase land under § 5 when it can simply prohibit takings under § 9 ignores the practical considerations that attend enforcement of the ESA. Purchasing habitat lands may well cost the Government less in many circumstances than pursuing civil or criminal penalties. In addition, the § 5 procedure allows for protection of habitat before the seller's activity has harmed any endangered animal, whereas the Government cannot enforce the § 9 prohibition until an animal has actually been killed or injured. The Secretary may also find the § 5 authority useful for preventing modification of land that is not yet but may in the future become habitat for an endangered or threatened species. The § 7 directive applies only to the Federal Government, whereas the § 9 prohibition applies to "any person." Section 7 imposes a broad, affirmative duty to avoid adverse habitat modifications that § 9 does not replicate, and § 7 does not limit its admonition to habitat modification that "actually kills or injures wildlife." Conversely, § 7 contains limitations that § 9 does not, applying only to actions "likely to jeopardize the continued existence of any endangered species or threatened species," 16 U.S.C. § 1536(a)(2), and to modifications of habitat that has been designated "critical" pursuant to § 4, 16 U.S.C. § 1533(b)(2).... Any overlap that § 5 or § 7 may have with § 9 in particular cases is unexceptional, *see, e.g., Russello v. United States*, 464 U.S. 16, 24, 78 L.Ed.2d 17, 104 S.Ct. 296, and n. 2 (1983), and simply reflects the broad purpose of the Act set out in § 2 and acknowledged in *TVA v. Hill*.

We need not decide whether the statutory definition of "take" compels the Secretary's interpretation of "harm," because our conclusions that Congress did not unambiguously manifest its intent to adopt respondents' view and that the Secretary's interpretation is reasonable suffice to decide this case. *See generally Chevron U.S.A. Inc. v. Natural Resources Defense Council, Inc.*, 467 U.S. 837, 81 L.Ed.2d 694, 104 S.Ct. 2778 (1984). The latitude the ESA gives the Secretary in enforcing the statute, together with the degree of regulatory expertise necessary to its enforcement, establishes that we owe some degree of deference to the Secretary's reasonable interpretation. *See* Breyer, *Judicial Review of Questions of Law and Policy*, 38 Admin. L. Rev. 363, 373 (1986)....

III

Our conclusion that the Secretary's definition of "harm" rests on a permissible construction of the ESA gains further support from the legislative history of the statute. The Committee Reports accompanying the bills that became the ESA do not specifically discuss the meaning of "harm," but they make clear that Congress intended "take" to apply broadly to cover indirect as well as purposeful actions. The Senate Report stressed that "'take' is defined ... in the broadest possible manner to include every conceivable way in which a person can 'take' or attempt to 'take' any fish or wildlife." S. Rep. No. 93–307, p. 7 (1973). The House Report stated that "the broadest possible terms" were used to define restrictions on takings. H. R. Rep. No. 93–412, p. 15 (1973). The House Report underscored the breadth of the "take" definition by noting that it included "harassment, whether intentional or not." *Id.*, at 11.... The Report explained that the definition "would allow, for example, the Secretary to regulate or prohibit the activities of birdwatchers where the effect of those activities might disturb the birds and make it difficult for them to hatch or raise their young." Ibid. These comments, ignored in the dissent's welcome but selective foray into legislative history, see post, at 14–16, support the Secretary's interpretation that the term "take" in § 9 reached far more than the deliberate actions of hunters and trappers.

Two endangered species bills, S. 1592 and S. 1983, were introduced in the Senate and referred to the Commerce Committee. Neither bill included the word "harm" in its definition of "take," although the definitions otherwise closely resembled the one that appeared in the bill as ultimately enacted. See Hearings on S. 1592 and S. 1983 before the Subcommittee on Environment of the Senate Committee on Commerce, 93d Cong., 1st Sess., pp. 7, 27 (1973)(hereinafter Hearings). Senator Tunney, the floor manager of the bill in the Senate, subsequently introduced a floor amendment that added "harm" to the definition, noting that this and accompanying amendments would "help to achieve the purposes of the bill." 119 Cong. Rec. 25683 (July 24, 1973). Respondents argue that the lack of debate about the amendment that added "harm" counsels in favor of a narrow interpretation. We disagree. An obviously broad word that the Senate went out of its way to add to an important statutory definition is precisely the sort of provision that deserves a respectful reading.

The definition of "take" that originally appeared in S. 1983 differed from the definition as ultimately enacted in one other significant respect: It included "the destruction, modification, or curtailment of [the] habitat or range" of fish and wildlife. Hearings, at 27. Respondents make much of the fact that the Commerce Committee removed this phrase from the "take" definition before S. 1983 went to the floor. See 119 Cong. Rec. 25663 (1973). We do not find that fact especially significant. The legislative materials contain no indication why the habitat protection provision was deleted. That provision differed greatly from the regulation at issue today. Most notably, the habitat protection in S. 1983 would have applied far more broadly than the regulation does because it made adverse habitat modification a categorical violation of the "take" prohibition, unbounded by the regulation's limitation to habitat modifications that actually kill or injure wildlife. The S. 1983 language also failed to qualify "modification" with the regulation's limiting adjective "significant." We do not believe the Senate's unelaborated disavowal of the provision in S. 1983 undermines the reasonableness of the more moderate habitat protection in the Secretary's "harm" regulation. . . .

The history of the 1982 amendment that gave the Secretary authority to grant permits for "incidental" takings provides further support for his reading of the Act. The House Report expressly states that "by use of the word 'incidental' the Committee intends to cover situations in which it is known that a taking will occur if the other activity is engaged in but such taking is incidental to, and not the purpose of, the activity." H. R. Rep. No. 97–567, p. 31 (1982). This reference to the foreseeability of incidental takings undermines respondents' argument that the 1982 amendment covered only accidental killings of endangered and threatened animals that might occur in the course of hunting or trapping other animals. Indeed, Congress had habitat modification directly in mind: both the Senate Report and the House Conference Report identified as the model for the permit process a cooperative state-federal response to a case in California where a development project threatened incidental harm to a species of endangered butterfly by modification of its habitat. See S. Rep. No. 97–418, p. 10 (1982); H. R. Conf. Rep. No. 97–835, pp. 30–32 (1982). Thus, Congress in 1982 focused squarely on the aspect of the "harm" regulation at issue in this litigation. Congress' implementation of a permit program is consistent with the Secretary's interpretation of the term "harm."

IV

When it enacted the ESA, Congress delegated broad administrative and interpretive power to the Secretary. See 16 U.S.C. §§ 1533, 1540(f). The task of defining and listing endangered and threatened species requires an expertise and attention to detail that exceeds the normal province of Congress. Fashioning appropriate standards for issuing permits under § 10 for takings that would otherwise violate § 9 necessarily requires the exercise of broad discretion. The proper interpretation of a term such as "harm" involves a complex policy choice. When Congress has entrusted the Secretary with broad discretion, we are especially reluctant to substitute our views of wise policy for his. See Chevron, 467 U.S. at 865–866. In this case, that reluctance accords with our conclusion, based on the text, structure, and legislative history of the ESA, that the Secretary reasonably construed the intent of Congress when he defined "harm" to include "significant habitat modification or degradation that actually kills or injures wildlife."

In the elaboration and enforcement of the ESA, the Secretary and all persons who must comply with the law will confront difficult questions of proximity and degree; for, as all recognize, the Act encompasses a vast range of economic and social enterprises and endeavors. These questions must be addressed in the usual course of the law, through case-by-case resolution and adjudication.

The judgment of the Court of Appeals is reversed.

It is so ordered.

JUSTICE O'CONNOR, concurring.

My agreement with the Court is founded on two understandings. First, the challenged regulation is limited to significant habitat modification that causes actual, as opposed to hypothetical or speculative, death or injury to identifiable protected animals. Second, even setting aside difficult questions of scienter, the regulation's application is limited by ordinary principles of proximate causation, which introduce notions of foreseeability. These limitations, in my view, call into question *Palila v. Hawaii Dept. of Land and Natural Resources,* 852 F.2d 1106 (C.A.9 1988) (*Palila II*), and with it, many of the applications derided by the dissent. Because there is no need to strike a regulation on a facial challenge out of concern that it is susceptible of erroneous application, however, and because there are many habitat-related circumstances in which the regulation might validly apply, I join the opinion of the Court.

In my view, the regulation is limited by its terms to actions that actually kill or injure individual animals. JUSTICE SCALIA disagrees, arguing that the harm regulation "encompasses injury inflicted, not only upon individual animals, but upon populations of the protected species." Post, at 4–5. At one level, I could not reasonably quarrel with this observation; death to an individual animal always reduces the size of the population in which it lives, and in that sense, "injures" that population. But by its insight, the dissent means something else. Building upon the regulation's use of the word "breeding," JUSTICE SCALIA suggests that the regulation facially bars significant habitat modification that actually kills or injures hypothetical animals (or, perhaps more aptly, causes potential additions to the population not to come into being). Because "impairment of breeding does not 'injure' living creatures," JUSTICE SCALIA reasons, the regulation must contemplate application to "a population of animals which would otherwise have maintained or increased its numbers." Post, at 5, 22.

I disagree. As an initial matter, I do not find it as easy as JUSTICE SCALIA does to dismiss the notion that significant impairment of breeding injures living creatures. To raze the last remaining ground on which the piping plover currently breeds, thereby making it impossible for any piping plovers to reproduce, would obviously injure the population (causing the species' extinction in a generation). But by completely preventing breeding, it would also injure the individual living bird, in the same way that sterilizing the creature injures the individual living bird. To "injure" is, among other things, "to impair." Webster's Ninth New Collegiate Dictionary 623 (1983). One need not subscribe to theories of "psychic harm," cf. post, at 22, n. 5, to recognize that to make it impossible for an animal to reproduce is to impair its most essential physical functions and to render that animal, and its genetic material, biologically obsolete. This, in my view, is actual injury.

In any event, even if impairing an animal's ability to breed were not, in and of itself, an injury to that animal, interference with breeding can cause an animal to suffer other, perhaps more obvious, kinds of injury.

The regulation has clear application, for example, to significant habitat modification that kills or physically injures animals which, because they are in a vulnerable breeding state, do not or cannot flee or defend themselves, or to environmental pollutants that cause an animal to suffer physical complications during gestation. Breeding, feeding, and sheltering are what animals do. If significant habitat modification, by interfering with these essential behaviors, actually kills or injures an animal protected by the Act, it causes "harm" within the meaning of the regulation. In contrast to JUSTICE SCALIA, I do not read the regulation's "breeding" reference to vitiate or somehow to qualify the clear actual death or injury requirement, or to suggest that the regulation contemplates extension to nonexistent animals.

There is no inconsistency, I should add, between this interpretation and the commentary that accompanied the amendment of the regulation to include the actual death or injury requirement. *See* 46 Fed. Reg. 54,748 (1981). Quite the contrary. It is true, as JUSTICE SCALIA observes, post, at 5, that the Fish and Wildlife Service states at one point that "harm" is not limited to "direct physical injury to an individual member of the wildlife species," see 46 Fed. Reg. 54,748 (1981). But one could just as easily emphasize the word "direct" in this sentence as the word "individual." * Elsewhere in the commentary, the Service makes clear that "section 9's threshold does focus on individual members of a protected species." *Id.*, at 54,749. Moreover, the Service says that the regulation has no application to speculative harm, explaining that its insertion of the word "actually" was intended "to bulwark the need for proven injury to a species due to a party's actions." *Ibid.; see also ibid.* (approving language that "Harm covers actions ... which actually (as opposed to potentially), cause injury"). That a protected animal could have eaten the leaves of a fallen tree or could, perhaps, have fruitfully multiplied in its branches is not sufficient under the regulation. Instead, as the commentary reflects, the regulation requires demonstrable effect (i.e., actual injury or death) on actual, individual members of the protected species.

By the dissent's reckoning, the regulation at issue here, in conjunction with 16 U.S.C. § 1540(1), imposes liability for any habitat-modifying conduct that ultimately results in the death of a protected animal, "regardless of whether that result is intended or even foreseeable, and no matter how long the chain of causality between modification and injury." Post, at 3–4; see also post, at 10. Even if § 1540(1) does create a strict liability regime (a question we need not decide at this juncture), I see no indication that Congress, in enacting that section, intended to dispense with ordinary principles of proximate causation. Strict liability means liability without regard to fault; it does not normally mean liability for every consequence, however remote, of one's conduct. See generally W. Keeton, D. Dobbs, R. Keeton, & D. Owen, *Prosser and Keeton on Law of Torts* 559–560 (5th ed. 1984)(describing "practical necessity for the restriction of liability within some reasonable bounds" in the strict liability context). I would not lightly assume that Congress, in enacting a strict liability statute that is silent on the causation question, has dispensed with this well-entrenched principle. In the absence of congressional abrogation of traditional principles of causation, then, private parties should be held liable under § 1540(1) only if their habitat-modifying actions proximately cause death or injury to protected animals. *Cf. Benefiel v. Exxon Corp.,* 959 F.2d 805, 807–808 (C.A.9 1992)(in enacting the Trans–Alaska Pipeline Authorization Act, which provides for strict liability for damages that are the result of discharges, Congress did not intend to abrogate common-law principles of proximate cause to reach "remote and derivative" consequences); *New York v. Shore Realty Corp.,* 759 F.2d 1032, 1044, and n. 17 (C.A.2 1985)(noting that "traditional tort law has often imposed strict liability while recognizing a causation defense," but that, in enacting CERCLA, Congress "specifically rejected including a causation requirement"). The regulation, of course, does not contradict the presumption or notion that ordinary principles of causation apply here. Indeed, by use of the word "actually," the regulation clearly rejects speculative or conjectural effects, and thus itself invokes principles of proximate causation.

Proximate causation is not a concept susceptible of precise definition. *See* Keeton, *supra,* at 280–281. It is easy enough, of course, to identify the extremes. The farmer whose fertilizer is lifted by tornado from tilled fields and deposited miles away in a wildlife refuge cannot, by any stretch of the term, be considered the proximate cause of death or injury to protected species occasioned thereby. At the same time, the landowner who drains a pond on his property, killing endangered fish in the process, would likely satisfy any formulation of the principle. We have recently said that proximate causation "normally eliminates the bizarre," *Jerome B. Grubart, Inc. v. Great Lakes Dredge & Dock Co.,* 513 U.S. , (1995)(slip op., at 9), and have noted its "functionally equivalent" alternative characterizations in terms of foreseeability, *see Milwaukee & St. Paul R. Co. v. Kellogg,* 94 U.S. 469, 475, 24 L.Ed. 256 (1877)("natural and probable consequence"), and duty, *see Palsgraf v. Long Island R. Co.,* 248 N.Y. 339, 162 N.E. 99 (1928). *Consolidated Rail Corp. v. Gottshall,* 512 U.S. ___, (1994)(slip op., at 13). Proximate causation depends to a great extent on considerations of the fairness of imposing liability for remote consequences. The task of determining whether proximate causation exists in the limitless fact patterns sure to arise is best left to lower courts. But I note, at the least, that proximate cause principles inject a foreseeability element into the statute, and hence, the regulation, that would appear to alleviate some of the problems noted by the dissent. *See, e.g.,* post, at 8 (describing "a farmer who tills his field and causes erosion that makes silt run into a nearby river which depletes oxygen and thereby [injures] protected fish").

In my view, then, the "harm" regulation applies where significant habitat modification, by impairing essential behaviors, proximately (foreseeably) causes actual death or injury to identifiable animals that are protected under the Endangered Species Act. Pursuant to my interpretation, *Palila II*—under which the Court of Appeals held that a state agency committed a "taking" by permitting feral sheep to eat mamane-naio seedlings that, when full-grown, might have fed and sheltered endangered palila—was wrongly decided according to the regulation's own terms. Destruction of the seedlings did not proximately cause actual death or injury to identifiable birds; it merely prevented the regeneration of forest land not currently inhabited by actual birds.

This case, of course, comes to us as a facial challenge. We are charged with deciding whether the regulation on its face exceeds the agency's statutory mandate. I have identified at least one application of the regulation (*Palila II*) that is, in my view, inconsistent with the regulation's own limitations. That misapplication does not, however, call into question the validity of the regulation itself. One can doubtless imagine questionable applications of the regulation that test the limits of the agency's authority. However, it seems to me clear that the regulation does not on its terms exceed the agency's mandate, and that the regulation has innumerable valid habitat-related applications. Congress may, of course, see fit to revisit this issue. And nothing the Court says today prevents the agency itself from narrowing the scope of its regulation at a later date.

With this understanding, I join the Court's opinion.

JUSTICE SCALIA, with whom THE CHIEF JUSTICE and JUSTICE THOMAS join, dissenting.

* * *

As I understand the regulation that the Court has created and held consistent with the statute that it has also created, habitat modification can constitute a "taking," but only if it results in the killing or harming of individual animals, and only if that consequence is the direct result of the modification. This means that the destruction of privately owned habitat that is essential, not for the feeding or nesting, but for the breeding, of butterflies, would not violate the Act, since it would not harm or kill any living butterfly. I, too, think it would not violate the Act—not for the utterly unsupported reason that habitat modifications fall outside the regulation if they happen not to kill or injure a living animal, but for the textual reason that only action directed at living animals constitutes a "take."

* * *

The Endangered Species Act is a carefully considered piece of legislation that forbids all persons to hunt or harm endangered animals, but places upon the public at large, rather than upon fortuitously accountable individual landowners, the cost of preserving the habitat of endangered species. There is neither textual support for, nor even evidence of congressional consideration of, the radically different disposition contained in the regulation that the Court sustains. For these reasons, I respectfully dissent.

PALILA v. HAWAII DEPT. OF LAND
& NATURAL RESOURCES

852 F.2d 1106 (9th Cir.1988).

O'SCANNLAIN, CIRCUIT JUDGE:

This is the fourth round of judicial activity involving a six-inch long finch-billed bird called palila, found only on the slopes of Mauna Kea on the Island of Hawaii.

An endangered species under the Endangered Species Act ("Act"), 16 U.S.C. § 1531–43 (1982), the bird (Loxioides bailleui), a member of the Hawaiian honeycreeper family, also had legal status and wings its way into federal court as a plaintiff in its own right. The Palila (which has earned the right to be capitalized since it is a party to this proceeding) is represented by attorneys for the Sierra Club, Audubon Society, and other environmental parties who obtained an order directing the Hawaii Department of Land and Natural Resources ("Department") to remove mouflon sheep from its critical habitat. Sports hunters, represented by the Hawaii Rifle Association, among others, had intervened to dispute the contention that the Palila was "harmed" by the presence of mouflon sheep. Hence, these appeals.

* * *

I

The Department argues that the district court construed the definition of "harm" in 50 C.F.R. § 17.3 too broadly.... The scope of the definition of harm is important because it in part sets the limit on what acts or omission violate the Act's prohibition against "taking" an endangered species....

In making this argument, the Department suggests dichotomy between "actual" and "potential" harm. The Department believes that actual harm only includes those acts which result in the immediate destruction of the Palila's food sources; all other acts are "potential" harm no matter how clear the casual link and beyond the reach of the Act. Thus, the Department challenges the district court's finding that habitat destruction which could drive the Palila to extinction constitutes "harm."

We inquire whether the district court's interpretation is consistent with the Secretary's construction of the statute since he is charged with enforcing the Act, and entitled to deference if his regulation is reasonable and not in conflict with the intent of Congress. *See United States v. Riverside Bayview, Inc.*, 474 U.S. 121, 131 (1985).

While promulgating a revised definition of harm, the Secretary noted that harm includes not only direct physical injury, but also injury caused by impairment of essential behavior patterns via habitat modification that can have significant and permanent effects on a listed species. 46 Fed. Reg. 54,748, 54,750 (1981)(codified at 50 C.F.R. § 17.3). Moreover, in that same promulgation notice, the Secretary let stand the district court's construction of harm in *Palila I. Id.* at 54749–50. In *Palila I*, the district court construed harm to include habitat destruction that could result in the extinction of the Palila—exactly the same type of injury at issue here. *See generally Palila I*, 471 F.Supp. at 985. We conclude that the district court's inclusion within the definition of "harm" of habitat destruction that could drive the Palila to extinction falls within the Secretary's interpretation.

The Secretary's inclusion of habitat destruction that could result in extinction follows the plain language of the statute because it serves the overall purpose of the Act, which is "to provide a means whereby the ecosystems upon which endangered species and threatened species depend may be conserved.... " 16 U.S.C. § 1531(b). The definition serves the overall purpose of the Act since it conserves the Palila's threatened ecosystem (the mamane-naio woodland).

The Secretary's construction of harm also consistent with the policy of Congress evidenced by the legislative history. For example, in the Senate Report on the Act: " 'Take' is defined in ... the broadest possible manner to include every conceivable way in which a person can 'take' or attempt to 'take' any fish or wildlife." S. Rep. No. 307, 93d Cong., 1st Sess. (1973), *reprinted in* 1973 U.S. Code Cong. & Admin. News 2989, 2995. The House Report said that the "harassment" form of taking would "allow, for example, the Secretary to regulate or prohibit the activities of birdwatchers where the effect of those activities might disturb the birds and make it difficult for them to hatch or raise their young." H.R. Rep. No. 412, 93d Cong., 1st Sess. (1973), *reprinted in* 4 House Miscellaneous Reports on Public Bills, 93d Cong., 1st Sess. 11 (1973). If the "harassment" form of taking includes activities so remote from actual injury to the bird as birdwatching, then the "harm" form of taking should include more direct activities, such as the mouflon sheep preventing any mamane from growing to maturity....

II

The Department contends that the district court erred when it found an unlawful "taking" within the meaning of section 9 of the Act. (Section 9—codified as 16 U.S.C. § 1538—lists the conduct prohibited by the Act). The Department argues that no taking exists because the evidence shows that (1) a huntable number of sheep (a flock large enough to sustain sports hunting) could co-exist with the Palila; and (2) the Palila are doing poorly because of the recently removed feral sheep and goats, not the mouflon sheep. Our review is for clear error. *Oregon Envtl. Council v. Kunzman*, 817 F.2d 484, 493 (9th Cir.1987).

A. Co-existence

The Department's witnesses conceded that a large number of mouflon sheep in one area could significantly damage the mamane-naio woodlands and thereby drive the Palila to extinction. However, these witnesses maintained that a huntable number of mouflon sheep could co-exist with the Palila. In support of its co-existence thesis, the Department makes four arguments. First, since the removal of the feral sheep and goats, the mamane-naio woodland has regenerated. This regeneration will support both the mouflon sheep and the Palila. Second, the Department has begun a number of regeneration projects (replanting, fertilizing, etc.). Third, the mouflon sheep would not cause significant degradation if the Department controlled their density. Fourth, the population of the Palila has increased since January 1985.

The Sierra Club's witnesses controverted the Department's thesis of co-existence. First, although regeneration (new mamane seedlings and sprouts) has occurred in many areas, it takes twenty-five years for the mamane seedlings and sprouts to become mature trees capable of providing food and shelter for the Palila. However, for the first ten to fifteen years of this growth period, the mouflon sheep can kill the mamane trees and no significant regeneration would occur, at least not sufficient to sustain the Palila unless the trees survive to twenty-five years of age. Second, the Sierra Club's witnesses showed that the Department's additional programs as an alternative to removal of the mouflon sheep would not work. Third, they disagreed with the premise that the mouflon sheep population could co-exist with the Palila if the Department controlled their density. Fourth, the Sierra Club witnesses stated that the Palila's population, despite short-term fluctuations, has been static over the long term.

The Sierra Club witnesses put forth their own thesis: Because the grazing and the browsing habits of the mouflon sheep destroy the mamane woodland upon which the Palila depend entirely for their existence, the sheep must be removed. This thesis received the support of the one of the state's witnesses. This witness conceded that he believes that the mouflon sheep must be removed to ensure the survival of the Palila.

The Sierra Club's witnesses are not contradicted by the documentary evidence (i.e., studies of the Palila, mouflon sheep, etc.), and the Sierra Club witnesses advanced a coherent and plausible thesis. On the issue of co-existence, then, the district court's decision to accept the Sierra Club's witnesses' testimony as more credible cannot be clearly erroneous.

B. Feral Sheep and Goats Versus Mouflon Sheep

The Department's witnesses asserted that there had been significant regeneration wherever the feral animals had been removed. The Sierra Club's witnesses agreed, but they went on to argue that where mouflon sheep have appeared, no significant regeneration has occurred.

On the question of which animals—the feral sheep and goats or the mouflon—damage the mamane, the district court again gave more credibility to the Sierra Club's witnesses; this preference cannot be clearly erroneous where the Sierra Club's witnesses were not contradicted by documentary evidence. Indeed, the testimony given by the Sierra Club witnesses—noticeable regeneration has occurred only where the feral animals have been removed and no mouflon sheep have appeared—is both plausible and consistent.

We affirm the district court's finding that the Department's permitting mouflon sheep in the area constitutes a "taking" of the Palila's habitat. The district court made its findings based on the testimony of the Sierra Club witnesses, which was not contradicted by extrinsic evidence. Therefore, the district court's findings should not be held clearly erroneous. *See Anderson v. City of Bessemer City, N.C.*, 470 U.S. 564, 575 (1985)("When a trial judge's finding is based on his decision to credit the testimony of one of two or more witnesses, each of whom has told a coherent and facially plausible story that is not contradicted by extrinsic evidence, that finding, if not internally inconsistent, can virtually never be clear error").

III

Under this resolution of the appeal, we do not reach the issue of whether harm includes habitat degradation that merely retards recovery. The district court's (and the Secretary's) interpretation of harm as including habitat destruction that could result in extinction, and findings to that effect are enough to sustain an order for the removal of the mouflon sheep....

Conclusion

The district court's finding of habitat degradation that could result in extinction constitutes "harm." The district court's finding of a "taking" was not clearly erroneous. We do not reach the issue of whether the district court properly found that harm included habitat degradation that prevents recovery of an endangered species.

CHRISTY v. HODEL

857 F.2d 1324 (9th Cir.1988), *cert. denied.*, 490 U.S.
1114, 109 S.Ct. 3176, 104 L.Ed.2d 1038 (1989)

ALARCON, CIRCUIT JUDGE:

Plaintiffs–Appellants Richard P. Christy (Christy), Thomas B. Guthrie (Guthrie), and Ira Perkins (Perkins) appeal from the district court's grant of summary judgment in favor of Defendants–Appellees Donald P. Hodel, Secretary of the Interior (Secretary) and the United States Department of Interior (Department). The district court rejected plaintiffs' claim that the Endangered Species Act (ESA) and certain regulations promulgated thereunder are unconstitutional as applied because they prevent plaintiffs from defending their sheep by killing grizzly bears. The court also rejected plaintiffs' claims that the ESA unlawfully delegated legislative authority to the Secretary and that the Secretary exceeded his lawful authority in promulgating the regulations at issue. We affirm.

I. FACTS

Christy owned 1700 head of sheep. On or about June 1, 1982, he began grazing the sheep on land he had leased from the Blackfeet Indian Tribe. The land was located adjacent to Glacier National Park in Glacier County, Montana.

Beginning about July 1, 1982, bears attacked the herd on a nightly basis. The herder employed by Christy frightened the bears away with limited success by building fires and shooting a gun into the air. Christy sought assistance from Kenneth Wheeler, a trapper employed by the United States Fish and Wildlife Service. Wheeler set snares in an attempt to capture the bears.

By July 9, 1982, the bears had killed approximately twenty sheep, worth at least $1200. That evening, while Christy and Wheeler were on the leased land together, Christy observed two grizzly bears emerge from the forest. One of the bears quickly retreated to the trees. The other bear moved toward the herd. When the animal was 60–100 yards away, Christy picked up his rifle and fired one shot, which hit the bear. It ran a short distance, then fell to the ground. Christy approached the bear and fired a second shot into its carcass to ensure that it was dead.

Wheeler's subsequent efforts to capture any bears were unsuccessful. On July 22, 1982, the Tribe agreed to terminate the lease and to refund Christy's money. On July 24, 1982, Christy removed his sheep from the leased land, having lost a total of 84 sheep to the bears during the lease term.

Pursuant to authority conferred by the ESA, the Secretary has listed the grizzly bear (Ursus arctos horribilis) as a threatened species throughout the 48 contiguous states. 50 C.F.R. § 17.11(h)(1987). Regulations promulgated by the Department forbid the "taking" of grizzly bears, except in certain specified circumstances. *See id.* § 17.40(b). . . .

The Department assessed a civil penalty of $3,000 against Christy for killing a grizzly bear in violation of the ESA and the regulations. On August 13, 1984, at Christy's request, the Department held an administrative hearing. At the hearing, Christy admitted that he had killed the bear knowing it to be a grizzly, but contended that he did so in the exercise of his right to defend his sheep. The administrative law judge (ALJ) upheld the imposition of a penalty but lowered the amount to $2,500.

Christy filed an administrative appeal, arguing that the imposition of a penalty violated his alleged constitutional right to defend his sheep. The appeal was denied on the ground that the Department had no jurisdiction to determine the constitutionality of federal laws or regulations.

On January 30, 1986, Christy instituted the present action. Also named as plaintiffs are Guthrie and Perkins, who have pastured flocks of sheep in Teton County, Montana. Guthrie and Perkins allege that they, too, have lost sheep to grizzly bears. They allege that they were informed by the United States Fish and Wildlife Service that they would be fined if they harmed or killed a grizzly bear, even in defense of their sheep. Guthrie alleges that, "[a]s a result of his losses to the grizzly bears and the harassment of the flock by the bears in the years 1984 and 1985, Guthrie sold all the merchantable sheep from his flock in 1985."

Plaintiffs seek a permanent injunction restraining defendants from enforcing the ESA and the grizzly bear regulations against them. Christy seeks a declaration that the Department's application of the ESA and the regulations to him in the administrative proceeding deprived him of "his fundamental right to possess and protect his property," deprived him of his property and liberty without just compensation or due process, and deprived him of equal protection of the laws. Guthrie and Perkins seek a declaration that the promulgation of the regulations was unconstitutional on the same grounds asserted by Christy. All plaintiffs seek a declaration that application of the ESA and the regulations to them in circumstances where they are defending their property is unconstitutional. Plaintiffs also seek declarations that the ESA contained an unconstitutional delegation of legislative power to the Secretary and that the Secretary exceeded his delegated authority in promulgating the regulations.

The Department filed a counterclaim against Christy seeking judgment in the amount of $2,500, plus interest, representing the unpaid penalty assessed against him by the ALJ. The Department lodged the administrative record with the district court.

On July 23, 1986, the defendants filed a motion for summary judgment. The defendants relied on the facts alleged in the complaint and on the administrative record. In response, plaintiffs asserted that "genuine issues of material fact exist as to allegations of Plaintiffs' Complaint." Plaintiffs, however, submitted no affidavits or other evidence in opposition to the defendants' motion.

On May 4, 1987, the district court issued a Memorandum and Order granting the defendants' motion for summary judgment. The court found that "the material facts preceding and arising from this lawsuit are not in dispute." The court ruled that the defendants were entitled to judgment as a matter of law. The court rejected plaintiffs' argument that there is a fundamental right to possess and protect property. Accordingly, the court evaluated the ESA and the grizzly bear regulations under the "rational basis" test and found that they satisfied that test. The court next rejected plaintiffs' contention that the loss of their sheep constituted a taking of their property by the federal government without just compensation. The court held that damage to private property by protected wildlife does not constitute a taking.

The court further concluded that "the ESA is a valid delegation of legislative authority," and that "the regulations at issue are a rational reflection of Congressional will, properly promulgated under the authority vested in the Secretary of the Interior." Finally, the court affirmed the penalty assessed against Christy by the ALJ, finding that it was supported by substantial evidence contained in the administrative record. Plaintiffs now appeal from the judgment entered against them.

* * *

III. Discussion

A grant of summary judgment is reviewed de novo. *Coverdell v. Department of Social & Health Services*, 834 F.2d 758, 761 (9th Cir. 1987). We must determine, "viewing the evidence in the light most favorable to the nonmoving party, whether there are any genuine issues of material fact and whether the district court correctly applied the relevant substantive law." *Id.* at 761–62.

Plaintiffs contend that entry of summary judgment was improper because "many genuine issues of material fact are unresolved." In their motion for summary judgment, the defendants relied on facts set forth in plaintiffs' own complaint, together with the administrative record. Plaintiffs submitted no evidence, by affidavit or otherwise, in opposition to the defendants' motion.

When a defendant's motion shows that there are no genuine issues of material fact, a plaintiff's unsupported assertion to the contrary is insufficient to forestall summary judgment. "Once the moving party shows the absence of evidence [to support the nonmoving party's case], the burden shifts to the nonmoving party to designate ' "specific facts showing that there is a genuine issue for trial." ' " *Id.* at 769 (quoting *Celotex Corp. v. Catrett*, 477 U.S. 317, 324 (1986), quoting Fed. R. Civ. P. 56(e)). Because plaintiffs failed to demonstrate the existence of any genuine issues of material fact, ... we need only determine whether the district court correctly applied the relevant law to the facts of record.

A. Do the ESA and the Regulations, as Applied, Deprive Plaintiffs of Property Without Due Process?

Plaintiffs contend that application of the ESA and the regulations so as to prevent them from defending their sheep against destruction by grizzly bears deprives them of property without due process, in violation of the fifth amendment.... The first step in our analysis is to determine the standard to be applied in reviewing the challenged legislation.

Strict judicial scrutiny of legislation that allegedly violates the due process clause is reserved for those enactments that "impinge upon constitutionally protected rights." *San Antonio Indep. School Dist. v. Rodriguez*, 411 U.S. 1, 40 (1973). When legislation impairs the exercise of a "fundamental" right, the government "must prove to the Court that the law is necessary to promote a compelling or overriding interest." 2 Rotunda § 15.4, at 59; *accord Beller v. Middendorf*, 632 F.2d 788, 808 (9th Cir.1980), *cert. denied*, 452 U.S. 905, 454 U.S. 855 (1981).

On the other hand, when the legislative enactment infringes on no fundamental right, "the law need only rationally relate to any legitimate end of government." 2 Rotunda § 15.4, at 59; *accord Beller*, 632 F.2d at 808. The law will be upheld if the court can hypothesize any possible basis on which the legislature might have acted. *See supra* note 2.

The right claimed by the plaintiffs in this action is the right "to protect their property from immediate destruction from federally protected wildlife." In their opening brief, plaintiffs characterize this as a "natural and fundamental constitutional right." In their reply brief, plaintiffs backtrack somewhat, arguing that the right "should be deemed fundamental."

Certain state courts have construed their own constitutions to protect the sort of right claimed by the plaintiffs in this case. *See, e.g., Cross v. State*, 370 P.2d 371, 376, 377 (Wyo.1962)(due process clause in state constitution construed to guarantee "the inherent and inalienable right to protect property"); *State v. Rathbone*, 110 Mont. 225,___, 100 P.2d 86, 90 (1940)(state constitution expressly guaranteed the right "of acquiring, possessing, and protecting property"); *see generally* Annotation, *Right to Kill Game in Defense of Person or Property*, 93 A.L.R.2d 1366 (1964). No court, however, has construed the United States Constitution to protect such a right. *See Mountain States Legal Found. v. Hodel*, 799 F.2d 1423, 1428 n. 8 (10th Cir.1986)(en banc)(noting the absence of authority on the question), *cert. denied*, 107 S.Ct.

The ESA expressly provides that no civil penalty shall be imposed on a defendant who proves that, in killing a member of a threatened species, the defendant was acting in self-defense or in defense of others. 16 U.S.C. § 1540(a)(3)(1982); *see* 50 C.F.R. § 17.40(b)(1)(i)(B)(1987) ("Grizzly bears may be taken in self-defense, or in defense of others ..."). The defendant may raise the same defense in criminal prosecutions under the ESA. 16 U.S.C. § 1540(b)(3)(1982). The ESA makes no mention, however, of a right to kill a member of a threatened species in defense of property ... One circuit court has opined that this omission evinces a congressional view that no such right exists under the United States Constitution. *See Mountain States*, 799 F.2d at 1428 ...

The U.S. Constitution does not explicitly recognize a right to kill federally protected wildlife in defense of property. Plaintiffs, nevertheless, urge that we infer such a right, in much the same way that the Supreme Court has inferred a constitutional right to privacy despite the absence of language expressly recognizing such a right. *See Griswold v. Connecticut*, 381 U.S. 479, 484–85 (1965)(state law forbidding married couples from using contraceptives violated constitutional right to privacy).

The Supreme Court has recently expressed reluctance "to discover new fundamental rights imbedded in the Due Process Clause." *Bowers v. Hardwick*, 478 U.S. 186, 194 (1986). The Court explained:

> There should be ... great resistance to expand the substantive reach of [the due process clauses of the fifth and fourteenth amendments], particularly if it requires redefining the category of rights deemed to be fundamental. Otherwise, the Judiciary necessarily takes to itself further authority to govern the country without express constitutional authority.

Id. at 195. The Court in *Bowers* refused to recognize a fundamental constitutional right of homosexuals to engage in sodomy, rejecting the argument that the constitutional right to privacy extended to protect such conduct. *Id.* at 190–94. The Court's reticence to "redefin[e] the category of rights deemed to be fundamental" is further manifested by the Court's refusal to find a fundamental right to such necessities as education, *Rodriguez*, 411 U.S. at 37, and adequate housing, *Lindsey v. Normet*, 405 U.S. 56, 74 (1972).

The Supreme Court's teaching is clear and unmistakable—federal courts should refrain from divining new fundamental rights from the due process clauses of the fifth and fourteenth amendments, at least when the claimed right is neither "implicit in the concept of ordered liberty," *Palko v. Connecticut*, 302 U.S. 319, 325 (1937), overruled on other grounds, *Benton v. Maryland*, 395 U.S. 784 (1969), or "deeply rooted in this Nation's history and tradition," *Moore v. City of East Cleveland*, 431 U.S. 494, 503 (1977)(op. of Powell, J.). Thus, we recently "heed[ed] the Supreme Court's counsels of caution" and refused to extend the right to privacy to include the right of a prison inmate to be free from a state official's unauthorized disclosure of intimate photographs of the inmate's wife. *Davis v. Bucher*, No. 87–3694, slip op. 9397, 9401, 9403 (9th Cir. Aug. 2, 1988).

In light of the Supreme Court's admonition that we exercise restraint in creating new definitions of substantive due process, we decline plaintiffs' invitation to construe the fifth amendment as guaranteeing the right to kill federally protected wildlife in defense of property. In so doing, we do not minimize the seriousness of the problem faced by livestock owners such as plaintiffs nor do we suggest that defense of property is an unimportant value. We simply hold that the right to kill federally protected wildlife in defense of property is not "implicit in the concept of ordered liberty" nor so "deeply rooted in this Nation's history and tradition" that it can be recognized by us as a fundamental right guaranteed by the fifth amendment.

Because of our determination that the killing of grizzly bears to protect sheep is not a fundamental right enjoyed by the plaintiffs, we are not required to subject the ESA and the grizzly bear regulations to strict scrutiny. Instead, we must determine whether those enactments rationally further a legitimate governmental objective.

Plaintiffs do not argue that preservation of threatened species is an impermissible objective, or that Congress lacks authority to pursue that objective. Plaintiffs contend, rather, that the ESA and the grizzly bear regulations do not rationally further that objective. Plaintiffs' position appears to be that regulations preventing citizens from protecting their property against depredating bears will inevitably generate a backlash, including "unlawful killings resulting from the gross unfairness of the existing system."

We do not agree that the ESA and the regulations have no rational basis. Congress's intent in enacting the ESA was "to halt and reverse the trend towards species extinction, whatever the cost." *Tennessee Valley Authority v. Hill*, 437 U.S. 153, 184 (1978). The regulations at issue plainly advance this goal by forbidding the killing of grizzly bears, except in certain limited circumstances. *See* 50 C.F.R. § 17.40(b)(1)(i)(1981).

The regulations recognize the concerns and accommodate the needs of owners of livestock and other property by authorizing the killing of nuisance bears by government officials when efforts to live-capture such bears have been unsuccessful. *See id.* § 17.40(b)(1)(i)(C). The regulations are reasonable in requiring private citizens to seek the assistance of experienced government officials, who may be expected to protect the public interest, rather than leaving every individual free to kill a "nuisance bear" whenever he or she deems it necessary. *See State v. Webber*, 85 Or. App. 347, 350–51, 736 P.2d 220, 222 (state statute requiring owner to obtain permit before killing depredating wildlife was "a reasonable restraint on defendant's right to protect his property"), *review denied*, 304 Or. 56, 742 P.2d 1187 (1987).

Moreover, the regulations do not forbid plaintiffs from personally defending their property by means other than killing grizzly bears. *See supra* note 4; *see also Barrett v. State*, 220 N.Y. 423, , 116 N.E. 99, 101–02 (1917)(state statute forbidding molestation or disturbance of wild beavers held constitutional because it left property owners free to fence their land or to drive away destructive beavers).

For the foregoing reasons, the ESA and the grizzly bear regulations, as applied to prevent plaintiffs from killing such bears in defense of their property; do not deprive plaintiffs of their property without due process of law.

B. Do the ESA and the Regulations, as Applied, Deny Plaintiffs Equal Protection of the Laws?

Plaintiffs also argue that the ESA and the grizzly bear regulations, as applied to prevent them from killing grizzly bears to protect their sheep against imminent destruction, deny them equal protection of the laws.

The due process clause of the fifth amendment has been construed to require the federal government to accord every person within its jurisdiction equal protection of the laws. *See Jimenez v. Weinberger*, 417 U.S. 628, 637 (1974)(referring to "the equal protection of the laws guaranteed by the due process provision of the Fifth Amendment"); *Bolling v. Sharpe*, 347 U.S. 497, 499 (1954)(invalidating racial segregation of public schools under the fifth amendment); *Eskra v. Morton*, 524 F.2d 9, 13 (7th Cir.1975)("The United States, as well as each of the several States, must accord every person within its jurisdiction the equal protection of the laws.").

"In order to subject a law to any form of review under the equal protection guarantee, one must be able to demonstrate that the law classifies persons in some manner." 2 Rotunda § 18.4, at 343–44. A classification may be demonstrated in one of three ways: by showing that the law, on its face, employs a classification; by showing that the law is applied in a discriminatory fashion; or by showing that the law is "in reality . . . a device designed to impose different burdens on different classes of persons." *Id.* at 344.

Once a legislative classification has been demonstrated, it will be subjected to strict judicial scrutiny if it employs a "suspect" class or if it classifies in such a way as to impair the exercise of a fundamental right. 2 Rotunda § 15.4, at 60; id. § 18.3, at 323; *see Clark v. Jeter*, 108 S.Ct. 1910, 1914 (1988)("Classifications based on race or national origin, and classifications affecting fundamental rights, are given the most exacting scrutiny.")(citations omitted). On the other hand, "where the law classifies persons on a non-suspect basis for the exercise of liberties which are not fundamental constitutional rights," the law will be upheld if it rationally relates to a legitimate governmental objective. 2 Rotunda § 15.4, at 60; *see Dandridge v. Williams*, 397 U.S. 471, 485 (1970)(in the area of economics and social welfare, legislative classification satisfies requirements of equal protection if it has some "reasonable basis" and if any state of facts can be conceived to justify it). . . .

Plaintiffs argue that the ESA and the grizzly bear regulations classify persons along two lines. "The first classification," they contend, "is between a group of persons who, like Plaintiffs, are raising livestock near grizzly bear habitat and all remaining citizens and taxpayers of the U.S." Plaintiffs have made no showing, however, that the ESA or the grizzly bear regulations employ such a classification. This is certainly not a classification that appears on the face of the challenged enactments. Nor have the plaintiffs proffered any evidence to suggest that the prohibition on the killing of grizzly bears is applied with greater severity against persons raising livestock near grizzly bear habitat . . . Finally, plaintiffs do not contend that the enactments constitute a device for imposing excessive burdens on such persons. In short, the first so-called classification identified by plaintiff—persons raising livestock near grizzly bear habitat—is simply not a classification made by the ESA or by the grizzly bear regulations.

The second classification identified by plaintiffs "is that which allows a certain group of people to hunt and kill grizzly bears under certain conditions for sport while withholding this same authority to livestock owners like Plaintiffs, even in immediate defense of their stock." This classification appeared on the face of the regulations as they read at all times relevant to this case:

> Northwestern Montana. If it is not contrary to the laws and regulations of the State of Montana, a person may hunt grizzly bears in the Flathead National Forest, the Bob Marshall Wilderness Area, and the Mission Mountains Primitive Area of Montana: Provided, that if in any year in question 25 grizzly bears have already been killed for whatever reason in that part of Montana, including the Flathead National Forest, the Bob Marshall Wilderness Area and the Mission Mountains Primitive Area, which is bounded on the north by the United States–Canadian Border, on the east by U.S. Highway 91, on the south by U.S. Highway 12, and on the west by

Montana–Idaho State line, the Director shall post and publish a notice prohibiting such hunting, and any such hunting for the remainder of that year shall be unlawful. . . .

50 C.F.R. § 17.40(b)(1)(i)(E)(1981).

Plaintiffs do not contend that the foregoing classification is "suspect," and no case so holds. Nor does this classification impair the exercise of any fundamental constitutional right. *See* Part III(A) *supra.* Accordingly, the classification should be upheld if it satisfies the "rational basis" test, i.e., if any state of facts can be conceived to justify it.

Plaintiffs argue that no rational basis supports the provision for sport hunting of grizzly bears: "Not only is the hunting of a threatened species unrelated to the goals of the Act, it is in complete derogation of its purposes, i.e. the preservation of threatened species. Indeed, given the threatened nature of their existence, allowing hunters to take even one [grizzly bear] arguably would be in direct conflict with the Act. Since this classification is in complete contradiction of the purposes of the Act, it can in no way have even a rational relationship to the purposes of the Act, as a matter of law."

Plaintiffs' argument is premised on the unsupported assumption that a program of carefully controlled killings of bears in limited geographic regions cannot promote "conservation" and, therefore, necessarily conflicts with the purpose of the ESA. On the contrary, Congress expressly contemplated that "in the extraordinary case where population pressures within a given ecosystem cannot be otherwise relieved," conservation may require "regulated taking." 16 U.S.C. § 1532(3)(1982). Further, although it expressly prohibited the killing of endangered species, Congress delegated to the Secretary the task of determining whether the killing of threatened species should also be prohibited. *Compare id.* § 1538(a)(1)(B)(imposing general prohibition on killing of endangered species) with *id.* § 1533(d)(Secretary "shall issue such regulations as he deems necessary and advisable to provide for the conservation of" threatened species). Congress authorized, but did not require, the Secretary to forbid the killing of threatened species. *Id.* § 1533(d). This legislative scheme reflects Congress's conclusion that certain killings of a threatened species could be consistent with the goal of conserving that species.

The Secretary had a rational basis for authorizing "regulated taking" of grizzly bears, by means of sport hunting, in those regions specified in the regulations. The basis is set forth in Amendment Listing the Grizzly Bear of the 48 Coterminous States as a Threatened Species, 40 Fed. Reg. 31,734–35 (1975) [hereinafter Amendment]. Briefly, relying on investigations by Fish and Wildlife Service biologists, data submitted by the Governors of Colorado, Idaho, Montana, Washington, and Wyoming, and comments filed by interested members of the public, the Director of the Fish and Wildlife Service, on behalf of the Secretary, determined that "grizzly bear population pressures definitely exist in the Bob Marshall Ecosystem." *Id.* at 31,735. The Director considered easing such pressures through live-trapping and transplantation of the animals but rejected that approach as "too dangerous and too expensive to be used with sufficient frequency to relieve ... the population pressures." *Id.* The Director concluded that "[a] limited amount of regulated taking is necessary." *Id.*

The Director then considered whether such regulated "taking" should be accomplished through the isolated killing of nuisance bears or through seasonal sport hunting. The Director concluded that isolated killings, while necessary, were "not sufficient to prevent numerous depredations and threats to human safety. This is because the occasional killing of one bear does not create a fear of man among the grizzly bear population in general." *Id.* A carefully controlled seasonal hunt, on the other hand, would both relieve the population pressures and condition the bears "to avoid all areas where humans are encountered," thus minimizing human-bear contact and the resultant risks to both. *Id.* Accordingly, the Director ruled that the best system of relieving the population pressures in the Bob Marshall Ecosystem would be "to combine limited taking of specific nuisance bears with a closely regulated sport hunt." *Id.* The promulgated regulations strictly controlled the total number of bears killed each year by mandating the cessation of hunting in any year "where the total number of bears killed for whatever reason ... reaches 25 bears for that year." *Id.* . . . .

In light of the foregoing, the regulations authorizing a carefully controlled and limited sport hunt of grizzly bears in designated geographic regions had a rational basis. Plaintiffs have proffered no evidence to suggest otherwise. The classification employed by the regulations, therefore, does not deny plaintiffs equal protection of the laws.

C. Do the ESA and the Regulations Effect a "Taking" of Plaintiffs' Property Without Just Compensation, in Violation of the Fifth Amendment?

The fifth amendment provides that private property shall not "be taken for public use, without just compensation." U.S. Const. amend. V. This prohibition applies only to takings by the federal government. *See Twin Cities Chippewa Tribal Council v. Minnesota Chippewa Tribe*, 370 F.2d 529, 533 (8th Cir.1967)(citing *Koch v. Zuieback*, 316 F.2d 1, 2 (9th Cir.1963)) ... Plaintiffs contend that by protecting grizzly bears, the Department has transformed the bears into "governmental agents" who have physically taken plaintiffs' property.

The defendants analyze this case under the principles applicable to regulatory takings. Plaintiffs, on the other hand, insist that their property has been physically taken, because their sheep have been "destroyed, killed, and rendered absolutely useless by the bear's act."

The defendants properly focus on the regulations, promulgation of which constituted governmental action. The regulations themselves, however, do not purport to take, or even to regulate the use of, plaintiffs' property. The regulations leave the plaintiffs in full possession of the complete "bundle" of property rights to their sheep. Perhaps because plaintiffs recognize this fact, they choose to focus on the conduct of the bears. Undoubtedly, the bears have physically taken plaintiffs' property, but plaintiffs err in attributing such takings to the government.

Numerous cases have considered, and rejected, the argument that destruction of private property by protected wildlife constitutes a governmental taking. The pertinent cases were recently summarized by the Tenth Circuit:

> Of the courts that have considered whether damage to private property by protected wildlife constitutes a "taking," a clear majority have held that it does not and that the government thus does not owe compensation. The Court of Claims rejected such a claim for damage done to crops by geese protected under the Migratory Bird Treaty Act in *Bishop v. United States*, 126 F.Supp. 449, 452–53 (Ct.Cl.1954), *cert. denied*, 349 U.S. 955 (1955). The United States Court of Appeals for the Seventh Circuit rejected a similar claim under the Federal Tort Claims Act in *Sickman v. United States*, 184 F.2d 616 (7th Cir.1950), *cert. denied*, 341 U.S. 939 (1951). Several state courts have also rejected claims for damage to property by wildlife protected under state laws. *See, e.g., Jordan v. State*, 681 P.2d 346, 350 n. 3 (Alaska App.1984)(defendants were not deprived of their property interest in a moose carcass by regulation prohibiting the killing of a bear that attacked the carcass because "their loss was incidental to the state regulation which was enacted to protect game"); *Leger v. Louisiana Department of Wildlife & Fisheries*, 306 So.2d 391 (La.Ct.App.), *writ of review denied*, 310 So.2d 640 (La.1975)(because wildlife is regulated by the state in its sovereign, as distinct from its propriety [sic] capacity, the state has no duty to control its movements or prevent it from damaging private property); *Barrett v. State*, 220 N.Y. 423, 116 N.E. 99 (N.Y.Ct.App.1917)(damage to timber by beavers not compensable because the state has a general right to protect wild animals as a matter of public interest, and incidental injury by them cannot be complained of); *see also Collopy v. Wildlife Commission, Department of Natural Resources*, 625 P.2d 994 (Colo.1981); *Maitland v. People*, 93 Colo. 59, 63 23 P.2d 116, 117 (1933); *Cook v. State*, 192 Wash. 602, 74 P.2d 199, 203 (1937); *Platt v. Philbrick*, 8 Cal.App.2d 27, 30, 47 P.2d 302, 304 (1935). *But see State v. Herwig*, 17 Wis.2d 442, 117 N.W.2d 335 (1962); *Shellnut v. Arkansas State Game & Fish Commission*, 222 Ark. 25, 258 S.W.2d 570 (1953).

Mountain States, 799 F.2d at 1428–29. The Tenth Circuit held that damages to private property caused by federally protected wild burros did not constitute a taking under the fifth amendment. *Id.* at 1431.

Plaintiffs do not challenge the constitutional power of Congress to enact legislation to protect threatened species. Yet plaintiffs would, in effect, require that the government insure its citizens against property damage inflicted by such species. The federal government does not "own" the wild animals it protects, nor does the government control the conduct of such animals ... *See Douglas v. Seacoast Products, Inc.*, 431 U.S. 265, 284 (1977)("It is pure fantasy to talk of 'owning' wild fish, birds, or animals. Neither the State nor the Federal Government ... has title to these creatures until they are reduced to possession by skillful capture."). Plaintiffs assume that the conduct of the grizzly bears is attributable to the government but offer not explanation or authority to support their assumption.

Plaintiffs cite the following language from a recent Supreme Court opinion in support of their argument that the government should compensate them for the killing of their sheep by grizzly bears: "It is axiomatic that the Fifth Amendment's just compensation provision is 'designed to bar Government from forcing some people alone to bear public burdens which, in all fairness and justice, should be borne by the public as a whole.'" *First English Evangelical Lutheran Church v. County of Los Angeles*, 107 S.Ct. 2378, 2388 (1987)(quoting *Armstrong v. United States*, 364 U.S. 40, 49(1960)). The foregoing principle is inapplicable to the present case, because neither the ESA nor the grizzly bear regulations "force" plaintiffs to bear any burden. The losses sustained by the plaintiffs are the incidental, and by no means inevitable, result of reasonable regulation in the public interest. As one state court has aptly noted:

> Wherever protection is accorded [to wild animals] harm may be done to the individual. Deer or moose may browse on his crops; mink or skunks kill his chickens; robins eat his cherries. In certain cases the Legislature may be mistaken in its belief that more good than harm is occasioned. But this is clearly a matter which is confided to its discretion. It exercises a governmental function for the benefit of the public at large, and no one can complain of the incidental injuries that may result.

Barrett v. State, 220 N.Y. at 424, 116 N.E. at 100.

For the foregoing reasons, we hold that the ESA and the grizzly bear regulations do not effect a taking of plaintiffs' property by the government so as to trigger the just compensation clause of the fifth amendment, and that the government is not answerable for the conduct of the bears in taking plaintiffs' property.

* * *

CHRISTY v. LUJAN

490 U.S. 1114, 109 S.Ct. 3176, 104 L.Ed.2d 1038 (1989).

OPINION: The petition for a writ of certiorari is denied.

JUSTICE WHITE, dissenting.

Petitioner is a herder who grazed his sheep on leased land near Glacier National Park. Between July 1 and July 9, 1982, grizzly bears from the park killed 20 of petitioner's sheep. Requests for assistance from park rangers yielded no results, and efforts to frighten away the bears were unsuccessful. On July 9, when two grizzlies emerged from the forest and approached petitioner's sheep, he shot and killed a bear. Grizzlies, however, are "endangered species;" petitioner's killing of the bear thus violated the Endangered Species Act, which makes it unlawful to "harass, harm pursue, hunt, shoot, wound, kill, trap, capture, or collect" grizzlies and other animals protected by the statute. 16 U.S. C. § 1538(a)(1). Petitioner was consequently assessed a $2,500 penalty for shooting the bear.

Petitioner then filed this action in District Court, seeking to enjoin enforcement of the Act against herders like himself, and resisting payment of the $2,500 penalty. Petitioner claimed, *inter alia*, that his actions in defense of his livestock were protected by the Due Process Clause of the Fifth Amendment; alternatively, petitioner contended that the Act resulted in an uncompensated "taking" of his property. Both the District Court and the Ninth Circuit rejected these claims, and this petition ensued.

I would grant the petition for certiorari to consider petitioner's constitutional claims. Petitioner's claim of a constitutional right to defend his property is not insubstantial. A man's right to defend his property has long been recognized at common law, *see* W. Blackstone, *Commentaries* * 138–140, and is deeply-rooted in the legal traditions of this country, *see, e.g., Beard v. United States*, 158 U.S. 550, 555 (1895). Having the freedom to take actions necessary to protect one's property may well be a liberty "deeply rooted in this Nation's history and tradition," *Moore v. East Cleveland*, 431 U.S. 494, 503 (1977)(opinion of Powell, J.), and therefore, entitled to the substantive protection of the Due Process Clause. In any event, petitioner's claim to such protection presents an interesting and important question-the proper resolution of which is not altogether clear-that merits plenary review.

Even more substantial is petitioner's claim that the Endangered Species Act operates as a governmental authorization of a "taking" of his property; leaving him uncompensated for this taking violates the Fifth Amendment, petitioner contends. There can be little doubt that if a federal statute authorized park rangers to come around at night and take petitioner's livestock to feed the bears, such a governmental action would constituted a "taking." The Court of Appeals below, and the United States in its submission here, distinguish such a case from this one, by noting that the United States "does not 'own' the wild animals it protects, nor does the government control the conduct of such animals." 857 F.2d 1324, 1335 (C.A.9 1988); *see* Brief of the Respondents 7.

Perhaps not; but the government does make it unlawful for petitioner to "harass, harm, [or] pursue" such animals when they come to take his property-and perhaps a government edict barring one from resisting the loss of his property is the constitutional equivalent of an edict taking such property in the first place. Thus, if the government decided (in lieu of the food stamp program) to enact a law barring grocery store owners from "harassing, harming, or pursuing" people who wish to take food off grocery shelves without paying for it, such a law might well be suspect under the Fifth Amendment. For similar reasons, the Endangered Species Act may be suspect as applied in petitioner's case.

In sum, sustaining grizzly bears is a worthwhile and important governmental objective. But it "is axiomatic that the Fifth Amendment's just compensation provision is 'designed to bar Government from forcing some people alone to bear public burdens which, in all fairness and justice, should be borne by the public as a whole.'" *First English Evangelical Lutheran Church v. County of Los Angeles*, 482 U.S. 304, 318–319 (1987)(quoting *Armstrong v. United States*, 364 U.S. 40, 49 (1960)). Here, petitioner has been asked to bear the burden of feeding endangered grizzlies-or at the least, has been estopped from taking measures necessary to prevent the use of his property for this purpose. Thus, it seems quite possible that petitioner has been denied the Fifth Amendment's protection against uncompensated takings.

Because I think that petitioner's constitutional claims present interesting and important questions that merit our attention, I dissent from the Court's denial of review in this case.

MOUNTAIN STATES LEGAL FOUND. v. HODEL
799 F.2d 1423 (10th Cir.1986), *cert. denied*, 480 U.S. 951, 107 S.Ct. 1616, 94 L.Ed.2d 800 (1987).

McKay, Circuit Judge.

The Mountain States Legal Foundation and the Rock Springs Grazing Association (collectively referred to hereinafter as "the Association") brought this action on behalf of their members against the Secretary of the Interior and other government officials to compel them to manage the wild horse herds that roam public and private lands in an area of southwestern Wyoming known locally as the "checkerboard." ... The checkerboard comprises over one million acres of generally high desert land and has been used by the Association since 1909 for the grazing of cattle. The lands involved in this case are in the Rock Springs District of the checkerboard, an area approximately 40 miles wide and 115 miles long. Record, vol. 1 at 17; Appellant's Brief at 5–6. In this area of the checkerboard, the Association's cattle roam freely on property owned by the Association and on the alternate sections of land owned by the federal government. Thousands of wild horses also roam these lands.

* * *

The Association alleges that the Secretary has disregarded its repeated requests to remove wild horses from its lands, that it is prohibited by section 1338 of the Act from removing the wild horses itself, and that the wild horses grazing on its lands have eroded the topsoil and consumed vast quantities of forage and water. In support of its Fifth Amendment claim, the Association argues that "it is the panoply of management responsibilities set forth in the Act and its regulations, including [section 1334], which ... subject the United States to liability due to its pervasive control over the horses' existence." Appellant's Supp. Brief on Rehearing En Banc at 8.... In our prior opinion in this case, a panel of this court, with one judge dissenting, found that the government's "complete and exclusive control" over wild horses made the Wild Free–Roaming Horses and Burros Act "unique" in the field of wildlife protection legislation. 740 F.2d at 794. This degree of control, the court said, was potentially "significant" in determining the government's liability under the Fifth Amendment. *Id.* With the benefit of additional briefing and oral argument, it is now apparent to us that, in the area of wildlife protection legislation, there is nothing novel about the nature and degree of the government's control over wild horses and burros.

At the outset, it is important to note that wild horses and burros are no less "wild" animals than are the grizzly bears that roam our national parks and forests. Indeed, in the definitional section of the Act, Congress has explicitly declared "all unbranded and unclaimed horses and burros on public lands" to be "Wild horses and burros." 16 U.S.C. § 1332(b)(1982) ....

* * *

It is well settled that wild animals are not the private property of those whose land they occupy, but are instead a sort of common property whose control and regulation are to be exercised "as a trust for the benefit of the people." *Geer v. Connecticut*, 161 U.S. 519, 528–29, 40 L.Ed. 793, 16 S.Ct. 600 (1896), overruled on other grounds, *Hughes v. Oklahoma*, 441 U.S. 322, 60 L.Ed.2d 250, 99 S.Ct. 1727 (1979) ... The governmental trust responsibility for wildlife is lodged initially in the states, but only "in so far as its exercise may not be incompatible with, or restrained by, the rights conveyed to the Federal government by the Constitution." *Id.* at 528. *See* also *Martin v. Lessee of Waddell*, 41 U.S. (16 Pet.) 367, 410, 10 L.Ed. 997 (1842). Neither state nor federal authority over wildlife is premised upon any technical "ownership" of wildlife by the government. Although older decisions sometimes referred to government "ownership" of wildlife, that language has been deemed "a fiction expressive in legal shorthand of the Importance to its people that a State have power to preserve and regulate the exploitation of an important resource." *Toomer v. Witsell*, 334 U.S. 385, 402, 92 L.Ed. 146, 68 S.Ct. 1156 (1948). As the Supreme Court declared, "It is pure fantasy to talk of 'owning' wild fish, birds, or animals. Neither the States nor the Federal Government ... has title to these creatures until they are reduced to possession by skillful capture." *Douglas v. Seacoast Products, Inc.*, 431 U.S. 265, 284, 52 L.Ed.2d 304, 97 S.Ct. 1740 (1977)(citing *Missouri v. Holland*, 252 U.S. 416, 434, 64 L.Ed. 641, 40 S.Ct. 382 (1920); *Geer v. Connecticut*, 161 U.S. at 539–40 (Field, J., dissenting)).

In exercising their powers "to preserve and regulate the exploitation of an important resource," both the state and federal ... governments have often enacted sweeping and comprehensive measures to control activities that may adversely affect wildlife. For example, the Marine Mammal Protection Act, 16 U.S.C. §§ 1361–1407 (1982 & Supp. II 1984), establishes plenary federal authority for the conservation of marine mammals and preempts entirely state laws pertaining to their taking. 16 U.S.C. § 1379(a)(1982). While the Wild and Free–Roaming Horses and Burros Act makes it illegal to "maliciously" cause the death or harassment of a wild horse or burro, 16 U.S.C. § 1338(a)(3)(1982), the Marine Mammal Protection Act establishes a federal moratorium of indefinite duration against any "taking" of a marine mammal, a term defined to include harassing, hunting, capturing, or killing, whether done maliciously or not. 16 U.S.C. § 1362(12)(1982). Indeed, even unintentional, inadvertent takings that occur incidental to an otherwise lawful activity are strictly regulated and, for "depleted" marine mammal species, prohibited altogether. 16 U.S.C. § 1371(a)(4)(A), (5)(A)(1982). These prohibitions apply despite the fact that the hearty appetites of some marine mammal species for fish and shellfish often put them in conflict with human competitors for the same resource. Moreover, the mere presence of sea otters in an area may restrict the rights of oil companies or developers to exploit resources that would otherwise produce handsome returns. *See* H.R. Rep. No. 124, 99th Cong., 1st Sess. 16 (1985). Despite their losses, those individuals and corporations are prohibited from "taking" the otters, and they are unable to call upon the government to remove them—as a private landowner can do when bothered by wild horses. *See id.* at 19.

Another wildlife species, the bald eagle, is protected not by one federal law, but by three: the Migratory Bird Treaty Act, 16 U.S.C. §§ 703–712 (1982), the Bald and Golden Eagle Protection Act, 16 U.S.C. §§ 668–668d (1982) and (in 48 states at least) the Endangered Species Act, 16 U.S.C. §§ 1531–1543 (1982 & Supp. 1984). Together, these statutes authorize a degree of federal control at least as "complete and exclusive" as that provided by the Wild Free–Roaming Horses and Burros Act. Indeed, in many respects their commands are far more sweeping. For example, not only is it illegal under each of these laws to capture or kill bald eagles, but the Bald and Golden Eagle Protection Act prohibits removing or destroying their nests or collecting their feathers. 16 U.S.C. § 668(a) (1982). . . .

In addition, the Endangered Species Act makes it illegal to "harass, harm, pursue, hunt, shoot, wound, kill, trap, capture, or collect" any endangered species or attempt to do so, again without regard to whether such actions are done maliciously. 16 U.S.C. §§ 1532(19), 1538(a)(1982). The prohibition against "harming" an endangered species is especially broad, having been construed to mean that one who maintains on his own land grazing animals that so modify natural habitat as to cause indirect injury to endangered species can be required to remove those grazing animals from his land. *Palila v. Hawaii Department of Land and Natural Resources*, 471 F.Supp. 985, 995, 999 (D.Hawaii 1979), *aff'd*, 639 F.2d 495 (9th Cir.1981) . . . Thus, even though eagles and other endangered species often prey on privately-owned livestock and poultry, the Endangered Species Act prohibits self-help measures which have the effect of "harming" such predators.

. . . The Endangered Species Act authorizes as an affirmative defense to prosecutions for violations of that Act that the defendant acted to protect himself or another person from bodily harm. 16 U.S.C. § 1540(a)(3), (b)(3)(1982). No similar statutory defense exculpates actions to protect property. Several state courts have held that, as a matter of state constitutional law, a person may kill wildlife contrary to the state's conservation laws where such action is necessary to protect his property. *See, e.g., Cross v. State*, 370 P.2d 371 (Wyo.1962). No case has yet addressed whether a similar right exists under the United States Constitution, though the bodily injury defense contained in the Endangered Species Act suggests a congressional view that it does not.

Because the Wild Free–Roaming Horses and Burros Act only prohibits the harassment of wild horses when it is done "maliciously," 16 U.S.C. § 1338(a)(3)(1982), it is not clear that the appellants are completely prevented from taking measures to protect their forage from wild horses without running afoul of the proscriptions of the Act. For example, neither Wyoming nor federal law prohibits the Association from fencing out wild horses and burros. In *Anthony Wilkinson Live Stock Co. v. McIlquam*, 14 Wyo. 209, 83 P. 364 (1905), the court upheld a landowner's right to erect a lawful fence to keep out his neighbor's trespassing cattle. Although the fence cut off the neighbor's access to public grazing lands, the court concluded that so far as the mere right to build fences on his land is concerned, [a landowner] is not prohibited by any law or rule that we are aware of from building a fence along one, or two, or three sides of his premises, or through the center thereof, or upon any other part of his land, if he so chooses, unless by so doing he invades some right of another, or violates some public stature. *Id.* at ___, 83 P. at 369. In *Camfield v. United States*, 167 U.S. 518, 42 L.Ed. 260, 17 S.Ct. 864 (1897), the Supreme Court addressed the right of a landowner to enclose his property when it lies in a checkerboard arrangement with public land. In that case, the government maintained that a private landholder could not fence in his odd-numbered lots since to do so would also enclose the even-numbered federal lots. Rejecting the government's argument, the court observed that this was a contingency which the government was bound to contemplate in giving away the odd-numbered sections. So long as the individual proprietor confines his inclosure to his own land, the government has no right to complain, since he is entitled to the complete and exclusive enjoyment of it . . . . *Id.* at 528.

With respect to each of these federal wildlife protection statutes, the degree of governmental control over activities affecting the wildlife in question cannot be said to be different in character from that mandated by the Wild and Free–Roaming Horses and Burros Act. Indeed, in some of these examples, the governmental control over the wildlife is more pervasive, more sweeping, and more restrictive than that provided by the Wild Free–Roaming Horses and Burros Act.

Many state wildlife conservation laws provide similar, comprehensive control over activities affecting protected species. Most states, for example, have enacted endangered species laws containing prohibitions that parallel those contained in federal wildlife protection laws. *See, e.g.,* Cal. Fish & Game Code §§ 2050–2098 (West 1984 & Supp. 1986); Colo. Rev. Stat. §§ 33–2–101 to–108 (1984); Ga. Code Ann. §§ 27–3–130 to–132 (1986); Ill. Ann. Stat. ch. 8, §§ 331–341 (Smith-Hurd 1975 & Supp. 1986); Ind. Code Ann. §§ 14–2–8.5–1 to–15 (Burns 1981 & Supp. 1986); Iowa Code Ann. §§ 109A.1–10 (West 1984); Md. Nat. Res. Code Ann. §§ 10–2A–01 to–09 (1983 & Supp. 1985); Neb. Rev. Stat. §§ 37–430 to–438 (1984).

The foregoing discussion demonstrates the fallacy in the Association's argument that the wild horses are, in effect, instrumentalities of the federal government whose presence constitutes a permanent governmental occupation of the Association's property. In structure and purpose, the Wild Free–Roaming Horses and Burros Act is nothing more than a land-use regulation enacted by Congress to ensure the survival of a particular species of wildlife. It is not unique in its impact on private resource owners.

Of the courts that have considered whether damage to private property by protected wildlife constitutes a "taking," a clear majority have held that it does not and that the government thus does not owe compensation. The Court of Claims rejected such a claim for damage done to crops by geese protected under the Migratory Bird Treaty Act in *Bishop v. United States*, 130 Ct. Cl. 198, 126 F.Supp. 449, 452–53 (Ct.Cl.1954), *cert. denied*, 349 U.S. 955 75 S.Ct. 884, 99 L.Ed. 1279 (1955).The United States Court of Appeals for the Seventh Circuit rejected a similar claim under the Federal Tort Claims Act in *Sickman v. United States*, 184 F.2d 616 (7th Cir.1950), *cert. denied*, 341 U.S. 939, 71 S.Ct. 999, 95 L.Ed. 1366 (1951). Several state courts have also rejected claims for damage to property by wildlife protected under state laws. *See, e.g., Jordan v. State*, 681 P.2d 346, 350 n. 3 (Alaska App.1984) (defendants were not deprived of their property interest in a moose carcass by regulation prohibiting the killing of a bear that attacked the carcass because "their loss was incidental to the state regulation which was enacted to protect game"); *Leger v. Lousiana Dept. of Wildlife and Fisheries*, 306 So.2d 391 (La.Ct.App.), *writ of review denied*, 310 So.2d 640 (La.1975)(because wildlife is regulated by the state in its sovereign, as distinct from its proprietary capacity, the state has no duty to control its movements or prevent it from damaging private property); *Barrett v. State*, 220 N.Y. 423, 116 N.E. 99 (N.Y.Ct.App.1917)(damage to timber by beavers not compensable because the state has a general right to protect wild animals as a matter of public interest, and incidental injury by them cannot be complained of). *See also Collopy v. Wildlife Commission, Department of Natural Resources*, 625 P.2d 994 (Colo.1981); *Maitland v. People*, 93 Colo. 59, 63, 23 P.2d 116, 117 (1933); *Cook v. State*, 192 Wash. 602, 74 P.2d 199, 203 (1937); *Platt v. Philbrick*, 8 Cal.App.2d 27, 47 P.2d 302, 304 (1935). *But see State v. Herwig*, 17 Wis.2d 442, 117

N.W.2d 335 (1962); *Shellnut v. Arkansas State Game & Fish Commission*, 222 Ark. 25, 258 S.W.2d 570 (1953).

The majority view that rejects takings claims for damage caused by protected wildlife is consistent with the Supreme Court precedent that controls our decision. In *Andrus v. Allard*, 444 U.S. 51, 62 L.Ed.2d 210, 100 S.Ct. 318 (1979), the Court clarified its stance on the takings clause:

Penn Central Transportation Co. v. New York City, 438 U.S. 104, 123–128, 57 L.Ed.2d 631, 98 S.Ct. 2646 (1978), is our most recent exposition on the Takings Clause. That exposition need not be repeated at length here. Suffice it to say that government regulation—by definition—involves the adjustment of rights for the public good. Often this adjustment curtails some potential for the use or economic exploitation of private property. To require compensation in all such circumstances would effectively compel the government to regulate by purchase. "Government hardly could go on if to some extent values incident to property could not be diminished without paying for every such change in the general law." *Pennsylvania Coal Co. v. Mahon*, 260 U.S. 393, 413, 67 L.Ed. 322, 43 S.Ct. 158 (1922); *see Penn Central, supra*, at 124.

The Takings Clause, therefore, preserves governmental power to regulate, subject only to the dictates of " 'justice and fairness.' " *Ibid.*; *see Goldblatt v. Hempstead*, 369 U.S. 590, 594, 8 L.Ed.2d 130, 82 S.Ct. 987 (1962). There is no abstract or fixed point at which judicial intervention under the Takings Clause becomes appropriate. Formulas and factors have been developed in a variety of settings. *See Penn Central, supra*, at 123–128. Resolution of each case, however, ultimately calls as much for the exercise of judgment as for the application of logic. *Id.* at 65; *see Loretto v. Teleprompter Manhattan CATV Corp.*, 458 U.S. 419, 73 L.Ed.2d 868, 102 S.Ct. 3164 (1982). More recently, in *Hodel v. Virginia Surface Mining & Reclamation Ass'n*, 452 U.S. 264, 69 L.Ed.2d 1, 101 S.Ct. 2352 (1981), *overruled on other grounds*, *Garcia v. San Antonio Metropolitan Transit Authority*, 469 U.S. 528, 105 S.Ct. 1005, 83 L.Ed.2d 1016 (1985), the Court emphasized that, in cases involving alleged unconstitutional takings of private property, it "has generally 'been unable to develop any "set formula" for determining when "justice and fairness" require that economic injuries caused by public action be compensated by the government, rather than remain disproportionately concentrated on a few persons.' Rather, it has examined the 'taking' question by engaging in essentially ad hoc, factual inquiries that have identified several factors—such as the economic impact of the regulation, its interference with reasonable investment backed expectations, and the character of the government action—that have particular significance." *Kaiser Aetna v. United States*, 444 U.S. 164, 175, 62 L.Ed.2d 332, 100 S.Ct. 383 (1979) (citations omitted). *Id.* at 295.

In an unbroken line of cases, the Supreme Court has sustained land-use regulations that are reasonably related to the promotion of the public interest, consistently rejecting the notion that diminution in property value, standing alone, constitutes a taking under the Fifth

Amendment. *See, e.g., Goldblatt v. Town of Hempstead*, 369 U.S. 590, 8 L.Ed.2d 130, 82 S.Ct. 987 (1962)(ordinance prohibiting excavation below certain level did not constitute a taking of land used for sand and gravel mining); *Miller v. Schoene*, 276 U.S. 272, 72 L.Ed. 568, 48 S.Ct. 246 (1928)(statute which mandates the destruction of red cedar trees in order to protect apple orchards held not to constitute a taking); *Village of Euclid v. Ambler Realty Co.*, 272 U.S. 365, 71 L.Ed. 303, 47 S.Ct. 114 (1926)(enactment of zoning ordinance limiting uses of unimproved property reducing property's value by seventy-five percent did not constitute a taking); *Hadacheck v. Sebastian*, 239 U.S. 394, 405, 60 L.Ed. 348, 36 S.Ct. 143 (1915)(ordinance precluding the manufacture of brick did not constitute a taking even though it reduced value of petitioner's land to less than one-tenth its prior value). In the regulatory context, the Court has said, "the 'taking' issue ... is resolved by focusing on the uses the regulations permit." *Penn Central Transportation Co. v. New York City*, 438 U.S. 104, 131, 57 L.Ed.2d 631, 98 S.Ct. 2646 (1978).

It is well settled that a land-use regulation may effect a taking if it "does not substantially advance legitimate state interests ... or denies an owner economically viable use of his land...." *Agins v. City of Tiburon*, 447 U.S. 255, 260, 65 L.Ed.2d 106, 100 S.Ct. 2138 (1980)(citations omitted). *But* in *Kleppe v. New Mexico*, 426 U.S. 529, 49 L.Ed.2d 34, 96 S.Ct. 2285 (1976), the Supreme Court recognized the important governmental interest in preserving wild horses and burros in their natural habitat, citing congressional findings that their preservation would " 'contribute to the diversity of life within the Nation and enrich the lives of the American People.' " *Id.* at 535 (citing 16 U.S.C. § 1331 (1970 ed., Supp. IV)). The provisions of the Wild Free–Roaming Horses and Burros Act advance this important governmental interest.

The Association has not argued, or even suggested that the Act deprives it of the "economically viable use" of its property. Rather, it contends that the consumption of forage by the wild horses, standing alone, requires the government to pay just compensation. In determining whether a particular land-use regulation deprives a property owner of the "economically viable use" of his land, the court must examine the impact of the regulation on the property as a whole. *Penn Central*, 438 U.S. at 130–31. The Ninth Circuit has explained:

> It is well settled that taking jurisprudence does not divide a single parcel into discrete segments or attempt to determine whether rights in a particular segment of a larger parcel have been entirely abrogated. The Supreme Court has long since rejected any contention that denial of the use of a portion of a parcel of property is so bound up with the investment-backed expectations of a claimant that government deprivation of the right to use a portion of the property in issue invariably constitutes a taking, irrespective of the impact of the restriction on the value of the parcel as a whole. *Penn Central, supra*, 438 U.S. at 130, n.27, 98 S.Ct. at 2662, n.27. *MacLeod v. Santa Clara County*, 749 F.2d 541, 547 (9th Cir.1984), *cert. denied*, 472 U.S. 1009, 105 S.Ct. 2705, 86 L.Ed.2d 721 (1985).

Considering the economic impact on the Association's property as a whole, the Act does not interfere with the Association's "distinct investment-back expectations" of using its property for grazing cattle. Nor does it impair the Association's right to hold the property for investment purposes. *See id.* at 547 n.7. Moreover, the Association has not been deprived of its "right to exclude" the wild horses and burros. *See supra* note 8 (discussion of right to fence property); *Kaiser Aetna v. United States*, 444 U.S. 164, 179–80, 62 L.Ed.2d 332, 100 S.Ct. 383 (1979). Admittedly, the grazing habits of the wild horses have diminished the value of the Association's property. But "a reduction in the value of property is not necessarily equated with a taking." *Andrus v. Allard*, 444 U.S. at 66. In this case, the reduction in the value of the property pales in comparison to that sustained in *Village of Euclid v. Ambler Realty Co.*, 272 U.S. at 384 (75% of property value lost) and *Hadacheck v. Sebastian*, 239 U.S. at 405 (92.5% of property value lost).

Whether a particular land-use regulation gives rise to a taking under the Fifth Amendment is essentially an ad hoc inquiry. Although the economic burden imposed on the Association is significant, the Association has not even contended that it has been deprived of the "economically viable use" of its lands. In view of the important governmental interest involved here, we conclude that no taking has occurred and that the district court correctly granted summary judgment for the government. Because no taking occurred, we also affirm the trial court's dismissal of the Association's claim against the Director of the BLM.

* * *

Barrett, Circuit Judge, dissenting.

I must respectfully dissent. I continue to adhere to the reasoning of the prior opinion by a panel of this court reversing and remanding the grant of summary judgment on the basis that wild free-roaming horses and burros are not "wild animals." *Mountain States Legal Foundation v. Clark*, 740 F.2d 792 (10th Cir.1984), vacated sub nom. *Mountain States Legal Foundation v. Hodel*, 765 F.2d 1468 (10th Cir.1985). Assuming, however, that the animals protected under the Wild Free–Roaming Horses and Burros Act, 16 U.S.C. § 1331–1340 (the Act), are "wild animals," I would nonetheless dissent from the majority opinion. RSGA should not be precluded from litigating its "taking" claim as a matter of law given the Act's unique wildlife protection scheme. Summary judgment is inappropriate and this case should be remanded to the district court to determine whether the facts here, i.e., the amount of damage to RSGA's property and the cause of that damage, entitle RSGA to relief under the Taking Clause of the Fifth Amendment.

I disagree with the majority's characterization of the Act as "nothing more than a land-use regulation enacted by Congress to ensure the survival of a particular species of wildlife." *Mountain States Legal Foundation v. Hodel*, 799 F.2d 1423. The plain and unambiguous language of the Act makes clear that Congress intended that wild free-roaming horses and burros be maintained on public lands and not on private lands. Unlike the treatment of wildlife in other federal statutes wild free-roaming horses and burros under the Act are by definition specific to the public lands. As I read the Act, Congress did not intend to burden private landowners but rather intended to have the Government assume the complete responsibility for maintaining as well as protecting these animals.

In the section of the Act entitled "Congressional findings and declarations of policies," 16 U.S.C. § 1331, Congress expressly stated: "It is the policy of Congress that wild free-roaming horses and burros shall be protected from capture, branding, harassment, or death; and to accomplish this they are to be considered in the area where presently found, as an integral part of the natural system of the public lands.".... Wild free-roaming horses and burros are defined as "all unbranded and unclaimed horses and burros on public lands of the United States ..." 16 U.S.C. § 1332(b).... "Range" is defined as "the amount of land necessary to sustain an existing herd or herds of wild free-roaming horses and burros, which does not exceed their known territorial limits, and which is devoted principally but not necessarily exclusively to their welfare in keeping with the multiple-use management concept for the public lands ..." 16 U.S.C. § 1332(c).... "Public Lands" is defined as "any lands administered by the Secretary of the Interior through the Bureau of Land Management or by the Secretary of Agriculture through the Forest Service." 16 U.S.C. § 1332(e).

The Act directs the Secretary to manage wild free-roaming horses and burros on and as part of the public lands:

> The Secretary is authorized and directed to protect and manage wild free-roaming horses and burros as components of the public lands, and he may designate and maintain specific ranges on public lands as sanctuaries for their protection and preservation ... The Secretary shall manage wild free-roaming horses and burros in a manner that is designed to achieve and maintain a thriving natural ecological balance on the public lands.

16 U.S.C. § 1333(a).... Section 1334 of the Act also makes clear Congress' express intent that wild free-roaming horses or burros be maintained on the public lands and not on private lands: "If wild free-roaming horses or burros stray from public lands onto privately owned lands, the owners of such land may inform the nearest Federal marshall or agent of the Secretary, who shall arrange to have the animals removed." 16 U.S.C. § 1334.... While a private landowner may choose to maintain these animals on his property, *id.*, it is clear under the Act that the Secretaries have an affirmative and mandatory duty to remove wild horses from private lands at the request of landowners, consistent with congressional intent that these horses be maintained on public lands. Therefore, if the Wild Free–Roaming Horses and Burros Act is a land-use regulation, it is only with respect to public, not private lands.

The majority not only incorrectly characterizes the Wild Free–Roaming Horses and Burros Act as a land-use regulation, but also inappropriately compares the Act with other federal wildlife statutes. My research reveals that the Wild Free–Roaming Horses and Burros Act is the only federal wildlife act which imposes a duty upon an agency of the federal government to manage and to maintain wildlife specifically on the public lands. Again, assuming arguendo, that wild horses and burros are "wild animals," the Act is nonetheless unique in the duty Congress imposed on the Secretaries of the Interior and Agriculture to maintain and to manage these animals on the public lands. The specific and identifiable duty imposed upon the executive branch to maintain and to manage these animals on public lands is the feature which makes the Act unique among federal wildlife statutes. While other wildlife conservation laws may also authorize and require exclusive governmental control over wildlife, this Act is unique insofar as the complete and total control of the government over wild free-roaming horses and burros is tied to public lands.

The "taking" issue before us in this case is specific to the Wild Free–Roaming Horses and Burros Act. Properly stated, the issue is whether damage to private property by wild horses caused by the failure of the Government to remove the horses from private lands at the request of landowners constitutes a violation of the Fifth Amendment Taking Clause under the Act? Assuming that a private landowner's property is damaged by a failure of the Government to maintain and to manage wild horses and burros on public lands as required by the Act, I believe there can be a violation of the Fifth Amendment Taking Clause. Therefore, summary disposition of RSGA's "taking" claim is inappropriate.

The Fifth Amendment of the United States Constitution provides in relevant part: "nor shall private property be taken for public use without just compensation." While the Supreme Court has apparently never addressed the issue of whether property damage caused by wild animals can constitute a taking, *see generally*, Note, *"The Liability of the Federal Government for the Trespass of Wild Horses and Burros,"* 20 Land & Water L. Rev. 493, 506 (1985), the majority applies the "land-use regulation" taking cases to this case. As noted above, I do not believe this is a land-use regulation case nor do I believe this case can be decided as a matter of law based upon prior Supreme Court decisions.

The Supreme Court has often stated that there is no "set formula" for determining when justice and fairness require that economic injuries caused by public action (or inaction) must be deemed a compensable taking. *Ruckelshaus v. Monsanto Co.*, 467 U.S. 986, 1005, 81 L.Ed.2d 815, 104 S.Ct. 2862 (1984)(citations omitted).

We have eschewed the development of any set formula for identifying a "taking" forbidden by the Fifth Amendment, and have relied instead on ad hoc factual inquiries into the circumstances of each particular case. To aid in this determination, however, we have identified three factors which have "particular significance:" (1) "the economic impact of the regulation on the claimant;" (2) "the extent to which the regulation has interfered with distinct investment-backed expectations;" and (3) "the character of the governmental action." *Connolly v. Pension Benefit Guaranty Corp.*, 475 U.S. 211, 106 S.Ct. 1018, 1026, 89 L.Ed.2d 166 (1986)(citations omitted).

While the general rule is that a Fifth Amendment taking claim is to be determined on a case by case basis, the Supreme Court has held that a permanent physical invasion by the Government constitutes a taking per se without regard to other factors that a court might ordinarily examine. *Loretto v. Teleprompter Manhattan CATV Corp.*, 458 U.S. 419, 432, 73 L.Ed.2d 868, 102 S.Ct. 3164 (1982). All other taking claims not involving a permanent physical invasion must be resolved by an ad hoc inquiry considering the factors set forth above. *Id.* RSGA apparently does not contend that the presence of wild horses upon its property constitutes a permanent physical occupation. Therefore, the resolution of RSGA's taking claim in this case must be made upon a review of the facts in light of the factors articulated by the Supreme Court.

The Supreme Court has stated: "The purpose of forbidding uncompensated takings of private property for public use is 'to bar Government from forcing some people alone to bear public burdens which, in all fairness and justice, should be borne by the public as a whole.'" *Connolly*, 106 S.Ct. at 1027, quoting *Armstrong v. United States*, 364 U.S. 40, 49, 4 L.Ed.2d 1554, 80 S.Ct. 1563 (1960). In this case it is not only fair and just that the Government not impose a burden on a few individuals to sustain wild free-roaming horses and burros, but it is also the express intent of Congress that private landowners not be required to share the burden of sustaining these animals which compete with livestock for scarce and valuable high plains forage. RSGA should be given an opportunity to demonstrate how and to what extent it has been harmed by the failure of the Secretaries to remove the horses from its property. The majority concedes that "the economic burden imposed on the Association is significant ..." *Mountain States Legal Foundation v. Hodel*, 799 F.2d 1423. In light of the direct impact of the Secretaries' action under the Act on RSGA's land, I am not prepared to hold as matter of law that a compensable "taking" has not occurred in this case. I would therefore reverse the district court's holding that "the use of private lands by excess horses under the Act does not rise to the level of a Fifth Amendment violation" and remand the case to the district court for fact-finding consistent with the Supreme Court's previous holdings regarding "taking" claims.

I fully concur in the views expressed by Judge Seth in his separate dissenting opinion.

HOLLOWAY, CHIEF JUDGE, joins in the dissents of JUDGE SETH and JUDGE BARRETT.

§ 10.5   PROTECTION OF MARINE ANIMALS

Under the Marine Mammal Protection Act, 16 U.S.C.A. § 1361 *et seq.*, it is generally illegal to take or import any marine mammal that has been designated as a depleted or endangered species unless the activity is authorized by a permit for scientific research issued by the Secretary of the Interior or the Secretary of Commerce.

§ 10.6   PROTECTION OF MIGRATORY BIRDS

Under the Migratory Bird Treaty Act, 16 U.S.C.A. § 703 *et seq.*, it is illegal to hunt, possess, transport, sell, import, or export any migratory bird without a permit from the U.S. Fish and Wildlife Service (or from the Department of Agriculture for importing or exporting). Captive-reared migratory waterfowl (*e.g.*, mallard ducks) are exempt from this permit requirement if certain conditions are met.

§ 10.7   PROTECTION OF FISH AND WILDLIFE

Under the Fish and Wildlife Coordination Act, 16 U.S.C.A. § 661 *et seq.*, whenever a federal agency considers a permit application for work in a body of water, it must give the same consideration to wildlife conservation as it gives to other factors. Before issuing the permit, the agency must consult with the United States Fish and Wildlife Service, Department of the Interior, and with the head of the state agency exercising administration over the affected wildlife resources.

§ 10.8   PRESERVATION OF HISTORIC SITES

Under the National Historic Preservation Act, 16 U.S.C.A § 470 *et seq.*, whenever a federal agency undertakes or licenses a project that will alter any terrain in such a way that significant scientific, historical, or archeological data is threatened, the agency must notify the Secretary of the Interior. The Secretary lists significant districts, sites, buildings, and objects in the National Register. To preserve these sites, the Secretary is authorized to make grants from the National Trust for Historic Preservation.

§ 10.9   REGULATION OF SURFACE MINING—THE SURFACE MINING CONTROL AND RECLAMATION ACT OF 1977

The Surface Mining Control and Reclamation Act of 1977 (SMCRA), 30 U.S.C.A.§ 1201 *et seq.*, regulates the environmental impact of surface coal mining, the reclamation of abandoned mines, and research and instruction regarding mining and mineral resources. Under SMCRA, it is illegal to engage in surface coal mining operations unless such mining is authorized by a permit issued by a state pursuant to a federally approved state program or by the Secretary of the Interior. Among other things, permit applicants generally must submit geological and hydrological information on the site, detailed maps of the mining area, a reclamation plan, and an insurance certificate that covers surface mining liability.

An application fee is assessed, and the applicant must provide opportunities for public review.

After mining, the operator must restore the land to its prior use capacity and contour. Variances may be granted under certain circumstances.

NATIONAL COAL ASSOCIATION AND AMERICAN MINING CONGRESS v. LUJAN
979 F.2d 1548 (D.C.Cir.1992).

GINSBURG, RUTH B., CIRCUIT JUDGE:

This is an action for judicial review of regulations issued by the Secretary of the Interior on February 8, 1988 under the Surface Mining Control and Reclamation Act (SMCRA), 30 U.S.C. §§ 1201 et seq. (1988). Plaintiffs–Appellants are two associations of coal producers, the National Coal Association and the American Mining Congress (NCA/AMC); the challenged regulations, implementing SMCRA § 518(f), 30 U.S.C. § 1268(f), provide for the assessment of individual civil penalties against officers, directors, and agents of corporate mine operators. The district court, in an unelaborated one-sentence order responding to cross-motions for summary judgment, held for the Secretary. National Coal Association v. United States Department of the Interior, No. 88–951 (D.D.C. July 19, 1991).

In this appeal, NCA/AMC first seek an order remanding the case to the district court for an explanation of its decision. Alternately, in the event that we reach the merits, NCA/AMC urge us to set aside the regulations on individual civil penalties as arbitrary, capricious, and inconsistent with law. The Secretary initially contends that the plaintiff trade associations lack standing to sue; on the merits, the Secretary maintains that the regulations are sound and should be affirmed. We hold that the trade associations NCA/AMC have standing to sue. Because a remand would entail unwarranted protraction, we reach the merits and uphold the regulations.

I. BACKGROUND

Enacted "to protect society and the environment from the adverse effects of surface coal mining operations," 30 U.S.C. § 1202(a), SMCRA establishes an enforcement scheme that includes civil and criminal penalties. See 30 U.S.C. § 1268. This dispute involves the relationship between two of SMCRA's civil penalty provisions and the regulations issued under each. The first, which the Secretary calls "a primary enforcement mechanism," see Brief for the Federal Appellees at 4, provides for civil penalties against holders of strip-mining permits:

Any permittee who violates any permit condition or who violates any other provision of this subchapter, may be assessed a civil penalty by the Secretary.... Such penalty shall not exceed $5000 for each violation. Each day of continuing violation may be deemed a separate violation for purposes of penalty assessments. In determining the amount of the penalty, consideration shall be given to the permittee's history of previous violations at the particular surface coal mining operation; the seriousness of the violation, including any irreparable harm to the environment and any hazard to the health or safety of the public; whether the permittee was negligent; and the demonstrated good faith of the permittee charged in attempting to achieve rapid compliance after notification of the violation.

30 U.S.C. § 1268(a)(subsection (a)). The parties refer to subsection (a) as the "corporate civil penalties" provision.

Supplementing the provision on corporate civil penalties, and directly at issue in this litigation, SMCRA authorizes the imposition of civil penalties on individual representatives of corporate permittees:

> Whenever a corporate permittee violates a condition of a [Federal] permit[,] ... any director, officer, or agent of such corporation who willfully and knowingly authorized, ordered, or carried out such violation ... shall be subject to the same civil penalties, fines, and imprisonment that may be imposed upon a person under subsections (a) and (e) [criminal penalties] of this section.

30 U.S.C. § 1268(f)(subsection (f)). The Secretary refers to subsection (f), among with provisions for injunctive relief, criminal prosecution, and permit suspension or revocation, as "alternate enforcement mechanisms." *See* Brief for the Federal Appellees at 4–6.

In 1979, the Office of Surface Mining Reclamation and Enforcement (OSMRE, a constituent of the Department of the Interior) issued permanent program regulations to implement subsection (a)'s corporate civil penalty prescriptions. *See* 44 Fed. Reg. 15,461 (1979), codified at 30 C.F.R. § 845 (1991). n1 Under the subsection (a) regulations, OSMRE determines the gravity of the permit holder's violation and sets the amount of assessed penalties according to a "point system." Under the point system, a permittee is assigned a score in four categories derived from the factors listed in subsection (a): (1) history of previous violations; (2) "seriousness" of the violation (determined in part by "the extent of potential or actual damage, in terms of area and impact on the public or environment"); (3) degree of any negligence or greater fault involved in the violation; and (4) good faith in attempting to achieve compliance. *See* 30 C.F.R. § 845.13. The point total for the violation determines the amount of the permittee's penalty. *See* 30 C.F.R. § 845.14 (penalty table).

Upon finding that a penalty is in order, OSMRE sends the permittee a "proposed assessment"; within 30 days of receipt of OSMRE's proposal, the permittee may request an "assessment conference" to review the proposal, informally, with an OSMRE "conference officer." *See* 30 C.F.R. § 845.18. Within 30 days after the assessment conference is held, the conference officer "shall either ... settle the issues" or "affirm, raise, lower, or vacate the penalty." 30 C.F.R. § 845.18(b)(3). If dissatisfied with the conference outcome, the permittee may request a formal administrative hearing and, ultimately, petition for judicial review. *See*

30 C.F.R. § 845.19. Pending pursuit and completion of administrative and judicial review of a corporate penalty, the permittee must place in an escrow account the entire amount assessed by OSMRE. *See* 30 U.S.C. 1268(c); 30 C.F.R. § 845.19.

The agency did not propose regulations to implement subsection (f), the individual civil penalties provision, until several years after it developed and installed the subsection (a) corporate civil penalties regulations. In 1980 and 1983, however, OSMRE issued successive internal directives "providing guidance concerning implementation" of subsection (f). *See, e.g.,* OSMRE Directive, *Individual Civil Penalty Assessment* (issued October 11, 1983), reprinted in Joint Appendix (J.A.) at 47. The directives described circumstances in which agency personnel should consider seeking individual civil penalties under subsection (f). *See* id., J.A. at 47–49 (listing "site criteria" and "individual criteria"). Under the heading "Procedures," the directives stated: "Hearings and conference procedures for individual penalties will be the same as procedures developed for hearings and conferences for regular penalties." *Id.,* J.A. at 49.

In 1986, in response to a consent decree settling a "citizen suit" brought against the Secretary by environmental organizations, OSMRE proposed regulations implementing subsection (f). *See* 51 Fed. Reg. 46,838 (1986). These proposed regulations on individual civil penalties differed from the previously issued corporate regulations in two relevant respects. First, the individual penalty scheme did not provide for assessment conferences. Second, to set the amount of the penalty, the proposed subsection (f) regulations used, in lieu of a point system, a more open-ended balancing of the relevant statutes considerations, tailored to fit individuals. The proposed regulations delineated three factors: the individual's involvement in previous violations; the seriousness of the violation; and the individual's good faith in attempting to achieve rapid compliance. *See* 51 Fed. Reg. at 46,842. The "seriousness" criterion, as stated in the proposed individual regulations, contained a key parenthetical component, one that does not appear in the corporate regulations; the new component concerned the cost of reclamation:

> (2) The seriousness of the violation ... (as indicated by the extent of damage and/or the cost of reclamation), including any irreparable harm to the environment and any hazard to the health or safety of the public[.]

Id. .... On February 8, 1988, with no alternation of the 1986 text significant here, OSMRE issued final regulations governing individual civil penalties. *See* 53 Fed. Reg. 3,664 (1988), codified at 30 C.F.R. § 846 (1991).

Suing to set aside the final rule containing the individual penalty prescriptions, NCA/AMC trained their attack on the agency's failure to include in the subsection (f) individual penalty regulations two key features included in the subsection (a) corporate penalty regulations: the assessment conference and the point system. *See* 30 U.S.C.

§ 1276(a)(1)(rules promulgated under SMCRA may be set aside on judicial review if they are "arbitrary, capricious, or otherwise inconsistent with law"). On cross-motions for summary judgment, and after full briefing by the parties, the district court ruled for the Secretary without stating reasons for the court's decision.

II. Threshold Questions

A. *Standing*

The Secretary argues, for the first time in the case, that the two plaintiff trade associations lack standing to challenge the individual penalty regulations. In a nutshell, the Secretary points out that NCA/AMC's members are coal companies. The challenged regulations, however, apply only to individuals. According to the Secretary, NCA/AMC have not demonstrated that regulations on penalties for individuals threaten the trade associations or their corporate members with any injury. We find utterly unpersuasive the Secretary's endeavor in this context to divorce the corporation from those who act in its name.

We first recite settled law on the representational capacity of entities like NCA/AMC. An association has standing if its members would have standing to sue in their own right; if it seeks to protect interests germane to its organizational purpose; and if individual members' participation is not required for proper disposition of the litigation. *See Hunt v. Washington State Apple Advertising Comm'n,* 432 U.S. 333, 343, 53 L.Ed.2d 383, 97 S.Ct. 2434 (1977).

Insisting that NCA/AMC's coal company members lack the causally-connected and redressable injury essential to standing, see Allen v. Wright, 468 U.S. 737, 751, 82 L.Ed.2d 556, 104 S.Ct. 3315 (1984), the Secretary observes that penalties paid by individuals "do not increase the liability of [NCA/AMC member] coal companies." Brief for the Federal Appellees at 17. The obligation of plaintiffs' member companies to indemnify their officers and agents, the Secretary continues, "would not constitute sufficient injury because the extent of the member companies' responsibility would be determined by independent action, namely the knowing and willful conduct of the members' officers, directors, or agents." *Id.* (citing *Simon v. Eastern Ky. Welfare Rights Org.,* 426 U.S. 26, 41–42, 96 S.Ct. 1917, 48 L.Ed.2d 450 (1976)). Because a corporate entity ultimately can act only through a human agent, the Secretary's argument appears more formal than substantial.

Arguably, NCA/AMC's coal company members themselves could proceed on behalf of their officers, directors, and agents—the individuals who are subject to subsection (f) penalties—and the trade associations could stand in for those companies. *See New York State Club Ass'n v. New York City,* 487 U.S. 1, 9–10, 101 L.Ed.2d 1, 108 S.Ct. 2225 (1988)(an association composed of associations has standing to sue if the constituent associations would have standing to sue on behalf of their individual members); *United States v. Westinghouse Corp.,* 638 F.2d 570, 574 (3d Cir.1980)(corporation has standing to assert employees' privacy rights implicated by administrative subpoena for employees' medical records).

We do not consider that prospect, however, because we are satisfied that the companies' own economic interests are vitally affected by the subsection (f) regulations.

The very purpose of the individual penalties for which subsection (f) provides is to impel permittee compliance with SMCRA by giving those who act for the corporation strong cause to adhere to the law and to abate violations promptly. As the agency declared when it issued the regulations, the subsection (f) civil penalty rule is designed "to insure that the requirements of the Act are met"; OSMRE expected that a corporate official would opt to "order the corporate permittee to abate the violation" rather than face stiff individual penalties. 53 Fed. Reg. at 3672. Given the raison d'etre for individual penalties, moreover, it cannot be seriously doubted that coal companies fall within the zone of interests regulated by subsection (f). *See Clarke v. Securities Industry Ass'n,* 479 U.S. 388, 394–400, 93 L.Ed.2d 757, 107 S.Ct. 750 (1987); see also 30 U.S.C. § 1276(a)(1)(affording right to judicial review of SMCRA rulemakings to "any person who participated in the administrative proceedings and who is aggrieved by the action of the Secretary").

Unlike *Simon v. Eastern Ky. Welfare Rights Org.,* 426 U.S. at 42–44, the causal link between the allegedly unlawful action and the alleged injury here is not "speculative." Sure and swift individual penalty imposition, the agency itself reasoned, would propel corporate action, thereby advancing the objectives Congress set in MCRA. No one has suggested any cause to doubt the agency's reasoning on this point. In short, the agency's justification for rendering individual penalty enforcement more efficient and effective belies the standing objection it lately asserts.

In addition to the matter of member standing, the other requirements for associational standing are met. The interests the two plaintiff trade associations seek to protect are germane to their organizational goals of ensuring a favorable regulatory environment and economic health for coal companies. *See Humane Society of the United States v. Hodel,* 268 U.S.App.D.C. 165, 840 F.2d 45, 58 (D.C.Cir.1988)("undemanding" germaneness test requires "mere pertinence between litigation subject and organizational purpose"). Finally, there is no apparent reason why this suit requires the participation of individual companies. NCA/AMC have standing to sue.

B. Remand

NCA/AMC acknowledge that a remand for district court explanation of its summary judgment is not dictated by law. *See* Fed. R. Civ. P. 52(a) (stating that "findings of fact and conclusions of law are unnecessary on decisions of motions under Rule ... 56"). Nevertheless, the trade associations urge the large and practical importance to litigants and this court of explicitly reasoned decisionmaking in the court of first instance. A responsible accounting for its decision by the district court, we agree, informs both the litigants and this court; such an accounting serves the twin objectives of fairness to the parties and judicial economy. Our federal court system works best when the courts that form the foundation of the system give to the litigants and to the judges next in line the full benefit of their analysis. *See, e.g., National Wildlife Fed'n v. Hodel,* 268 U.S.App.D.C. 15, 839 F.2d 694 (D.C.Cir.1988)(affirming in large part several district court decisions that substantially reduced number of issues in controversy); *In re Korean Air Lines,* 265 U.S.App.D.C. 39, 829 F.2d 1171 (D.C.Cir.1987), affirming order and adopting opinion of district court in 664 F.Supp. 1488 (D.D.C.1987), *aff'd sub nom. Chan v. Korean Air Lines, Ltd.,* 490 U.S. 122, 109 S.Ct. 1676, 104 L.Ed.2d 113 (1989); *Universal Health Servs. of McAllen, Inc. v. Sullivan,* 770 F.Supp. 704 (D.D.C.1991), *aff'd mem.,* 978 F.2d 745 (D.C.Cir.1992).

In this case, however, several considerations lead us to resist a remand. The issues presented are few and clearly defined; the case has been well briefed and argued; it is our obligation in any event to review the administrative record de novo, and here that record is not dense. *Cf. Randolph–Sheppard Vendors of America, Inc. v. Harris,* 202 U.S.App. D.C. 341, 628 F.2d 1364, 1368 (D.C.Cir.1980)(refusing to remand for district court clarification where no facts were in dispute and record was adequate to enable this court to review agency rules de novo). Mindful of the years it has taken to complete the SMCRA penalty provision rulemakings, and unwilling further to delay final decision on the regulations, we proceed to the merits of NCA/AMC's case.

III. VALIDITY OF THE SUBSECTION (F) REGULATIONS

NCA/AMC portray the Secretary's decision not to include the assessment conference procedure or the point system in the subsection (f) regulations as a "reversal of the agency's former views"; under *Motor Vehicle Mfrs. Ass'n v. State Farm Mutual Life Ins. Co.,* 463 U.S. 29, 41– 42, 77 L.Ed.2d 443, 103 S.Ct. 2856 (1983) (*State Farm*), NCA/AMC assert, such a reversal must be supported by "reasoned analysis." The Secretary responds that because formal regulations had never before been issued under subsection (f), OSMRE was working on a clean slate; hence, OSMRE was not required to justify its choice not to copy exactly the procedures adopted years earlier in the subsection (a) regulations. *See State Farm,* 463 U.S. at 42 ("An agency changing its course by rescinding a rule is obligated to supply a reasoned analysis for the change beyond that which may be required when an agency does not act in the first instance."). . . . Neither side, we conclude, has it entirely right.

Subsections (a) and (f) are interrelated and cross-referenced; the statutory provision applicable to individuals incorporates, in part, those governing corporations. Moreover, the agency relied on the corporate procedures when it framed interim, internal directives on individual penalties. *See supra* p. 5. This statutory relationship and regulatory history made it incumbent on OSMRE to say why it chose to depart from the corporate scheme when it adopted the individual regulations.

But concise statement would do. The challenged individual penalty regulations were not a volte-face as was the change at issue in *State*

Farm. See 463 U.S. at 41–42. There, an agency abandoned without cogent explanation a policy option it had earlier studied extensively and strongly endorsed. *See id.* at 46–51. Here, by contrast, the agency has not abandoned or rescinded a policy; it has simply refused permanently to extend to individual penalty enforcement certain policy approaches developed in the context of corporate penalties. In promulgating the regulations on corporate penalties, the agency did not purport to address individual penalties as well. OSMRE's initial directives on individual penalties were notably provisional in character. In this setting, the burden of explanation derived from *State Farm* is relatively light.

A. Assessment Conferences

The assessment conference procedure was part of the initial corporate penalty scheme in 1977, and was incorporated into the permanent program regulations issued in 1979. *See* 30 C.F.R. § 723.18 (1991); 30 C.F.R. § 845.18 (1991). The preamble to the 1977 interim regulations described the assessment conference as an opportunity "to discuss informally the facts relevant to the proposed assessment and reach an agreement on the proper assessment without a formal hearing." 42 Fed. Reg. 62,639, 62,672 (1977). In its discussion of the 1979 corporate penalty regulations, the agency further explained:

> The conference procedure insures the Office of correct assessments by taking into account good faith and any other relevant information. This prevents the underpayment of overpayment of the penalty into escrow, and provided a much greater measure of due process to the operator, who is assured of an opportunity to be heard and to obtain a correction of the penalty before having to put his money into escrow.

44 Fed. Reg. 14,902, 15,309 (1979).

The subsection (f) individual penalty regulations proposed in 1986 included no assessment conference. OSMRE explained that the basic reason for the conference was inapplicable to subsection (f) penalties because individuals, unlike corporate violators, were not required to prepay penalties into escrow pending administrative and judicial review. *See* 51 Fed. Reg. at 46,841. In response to a commenter who had suggested that the subsection (f) regulations provide for assessment conferences, the agency comprehensively explained:

> The rules provide an adequate opportunity for administrative review through (the Department of the Interior's Office of Hearings and Appeals [OHA]). No need exists to create an additional level of administrative review in OSMRE. As was previously stated, the corporate official is not required to pre-pay the assessment as a prior condition to requesting a hearing with OHA; thus no due process violation exists. Moreover, the notice of proposed assessment against the corporate official will contain a detailed narrative explanation of the reasons for the assessment and the amount assessed, so that the corporate official will clearly understand why OSMRE believes that an individual civil penalty is justified. It has been OSMRE's experi-

ence with corporate violations that almost everyone requests both an assessment conference and a hearing with OHA, so that rather than eliminate administrative waste and inconvenience a conference simply would add another step in the process and increase the government's administrative costs. Finally, an individual civil penalty will be assessed only for knowing and willful conduct. Questions concerning such conduct may be better resolved by an administrative law judge, rather than an assessment conference officer.

53 Fed. Reg. at 3,671. There is no need for more words on this issue. This uncommonly concise, complete and convincing agency explanation fully satisfies *State Farm's* demand for "reasoned analysis." 463 U.S. at 42.

B. the "Same Penalties" Clause of Subsection (F)

Subsection (f) declares individual directors, officers, or agents subject to the "same civil penalties, lines, and imprisonment that may be imposed upon a person under subsections (a) and (e) of this section." 30 U.S.C. § 1268(f).... NCA/AMC argue that OSMRE ignored this requirement when it adopted procedures for setting the amounts of individual penalties that did not conform to the procedures previously established for corporate penalties. In particular, NCA/AMC attack the agency's failure to use the point system in the subsection (f) penalty scheme and its adoption of a novel measure of "seriousness" explicitly based on reclamation costs.

SMCRA is administered by an office of the Department of the Interior. We must defer to that agency's interpretation of the "same penalties" provision unless the agency's reading is contrary to the statute's instruction, or is unreasonable. *See Chevron U.S.A. Inc. v. Natural Resources Defense Council, Inc.,* 467 U.S. 837, 842–43, 81 L.Ed.2d 694, 104 S.Ct. 2778 (1984). In promulgating the individual penalty regulations, OSMRE explained that it construed the subsection (a) "same penalties" language "to mean that the relevant criteria of [subsection (a)] are to be applied, and that the daily ceiling in [subsection (a)] on the amount of the penalty must be observed when assessing an individual civil penalty." 53 Fed. Reg. at 3669. But, the agency added, the "same penalties" provision does not require "the amount of the penalty assessed against the individual to be the same as that assessed against the corporation." *Id.*

We find no explicit or implicit instruction in subsection (f) telling us whether the "same penalties" requirement means that the corporate and individual penalty assessments must be calculated using the identical methodologies, or whether, as the agency maintains, "same penalties" means only that the criteria of subsection (a) must also be used in subsection (f) analysis and that the penalty ceilings must be the same. The text of the statute does make it plain that the factors for assessing corporate and individual penalties are not identical; notably, the corporate provisions require consideration of "whether the permittee was negligent," while the subsection (f) provisions are inapplicable unless the individual director, officer, or agent acted "willfully and knowingly."

This difference heightens our skepticism regarding the trade associations' position that Congress intended the "same penalties" language to require precisely parallel assessment methodologies.

NCA/AMC have indicated what Congress might have said to convey the meaning the trade associations urge. Subsection (f) uses the words "same civil penalties." On brief, NCA/AMC translate these words to command the same "civil penalty scheme." Brief of Appellants at 16. . . . Nothing coming from Congress obliged the agency to agree. In sum, the statute is silent on the methods the agency should use in fixing the amount of the penalty, and OSMRE reasonably concluded that the "same penalties" phrase did not require adoption of the point system for individual penalties. We take up infra at pp. 16–17 NCA/AMC's further argument that, even if not ruled out by statute, the agency's abandonment of the point system in the individual penalties regulation was arbitrary and capricious.

We treat next NCA/AMC's statutory objection to OSMRE's use of reclamation costs in the individual penalty assessment calculus. The corporate penalty regulations assign gravity-of-violation points for seriousness based on "the extent of the potential or actual damage, in terms of area and impact on the public or environment[.]" 30 C.F.R. § 845.13(b)(2)(ii)(1991). The individual penalty regulations include as a measure of the seriousness of a violation "the cost of reclamation." 30 C.F.R. § 846.14(a)(2)(1991). We see no reason why the "cost of reclamation" does not fit within the statutory criterion of "seriousness" or why the agency should be locked into the subsection (a) regulations' formulation of that criterion. *See Chevron*, 467 U.S. at 863–64 ("An initial agency interpretation is not instantly carved in stone. On the contrary, the agency, to engage in informed rulemaking, must consider varying interpretations and the wisdom of its policy on a continuing basis."). Again, we agree with the agency that the "same civil penalties" language of subsection (f) does not mandate the degree of conformity NCA/AMC ask us to impose.

C. Rationality of Reclamation Costs

Having concluded that the statute did not bar OSMRE's departures from the corporate penalties regulation when it framed the individual penalties regulation, we consider, finally, NCA/AMC's charges that the agency's resort to reclamation costs and its omission of the point system were inadequately explained. When it issued the subsection (f) individual penalty regulations, OSMRE stated that, in its view, "the amount of money it will cost to abate the violation and/or reclaim the affected area" could serve as "one accurate indicator" of the extent of environmental damage. 53 Fed. Reg. at 3,669. OSMRE then explained that using reclamation costs in assessing penalties appropriately advanced a statutory scheme in which individual penalties are an alternative mechanism of enforcing permittee compliance:

> OSMRE intends in some instances to propose an individual civil penalty which equals or exceeds the cost of abating the violation

under the theory that it would be more economical for the corporate official to order the corporate permittee to abate the violation than to pay the penalty. . . .

53 Fed. Reg. at 3,672. The agency thus justified the reclamation costs standard as an incentive for corporate officials to ensure compliance with SMCRA. We see nothing unreasonable here. Again, we cannot fault the agency, in face of the rationality of its position, simply because the regulations on corporate penalties do not similarly refer to reclamation costs. . . .

D.   Rationality of Omitting Point System

Relying once more on State Farm, NCA/AMC contend that OSMRE failed adequately to explain why the point system, although used in the regulations governing corporate penalties, was not used in the individual penalty regulations. The trade associations feature statements made in 1979 by then Acting Secretary James A. Joseph when the subsection (a) regulations issued. The Acting Secretary praised the point system as "the only adequate way to achieve rational and consistent assessments" and said that "careful thought" had been given to the weights assigned the respective criteria. 44 Fed. Reg. at 15,305–06. NCA/AMC argue that the point system could have accounted for relevant differences between individuals and corporations, and underscore that the subsection (a) point system was based on MSHA regulations, which apply to corporate and individual penalties alike. *See id.*

> When it promulgated the individual penalty regulations in 1988, OSMRE explained that, based on an examination of "existing rules and policies related to the assessment of civil penalties," the point system does not appear practical for, nor strictly applicable to, the assessment of individual civil penalties [and] does not give the Secretary sufficient flexibility to assess a penalty which fairly considers the particular actions or inactions of an individual. For example, [the corporate penalty regulations] consider the history of the permittee's previous violations without respect to the individual's involvement with them.

53 Fed. Reg. at 3,664. The agency thus decided that the point system applicable to corporate violators was inappropriate for individual violations. The path the agency has taken on this point "may reasonably be discerned." *See State Farm,* 463 U.S. at 43 (quoting *Bowman Transportation, Inc. v. Arkansas–Best Freight System, Inc.,* 419 U.S. 281, 286, 42 L.Ed.2d 447, 95 S.Ct. 438 (1974)). Substantial modifications would have been required to create a point system applicable to subsection (f) cases. In addition to modifying the history-of-previous-violations criterion, a point system for individuals would have to adjust for the different mens rea standard (individual violations, but not corporate violations, require knowing and willful misconduct). The agency's new emphasis on reclamation costs would also require attention. *See* 53 Fed. Reg. at 3,670 ("The penalty assessed against the corporate permittee under the point

system for the seriousness of the violation in many instances may not cover the actual cost to repair the damage to the environment.'').

OSMRE evidently decided, in light of its experience administering the subsection (a) corporate penalty provisions, that the point system was not well suited to individual violations. We cannot gainsay that experience and judgment.... Nor can we impose on the agency a requirement of perfect consistency. OSMRE may eventually decide to alter the corporate regulations once the individual provisions have been tested. NCA/AMC surely do not urge that the agency embark on such a change now.

Conclusion

NCA/AMC have standing to challenge the individual penalty regulations because those regulations directly affect the interests of the associations' corporate members. While we and the litigants would have been aided by a reasoned district court decision, considerations specific to this case counsel against a remand. Because the individual civil penalty regulations under review are not "arbitrary, capricious, or otherwise inconsistent with law," the judgment of the district court in favor of the Secretary is

Affirmed.

Appendix

DEFINITION OF KEY ENVIRONMENTAL TERMS AND ACRONYMS

ACBM: Asbestos containing building materials

ACM: Asbestos Containing Materials

Administrator: The Administrator of the United States Environmental Protection Agency.

AgSTAR: a voluntary program which encourages the widespread use of technologies to increase livestock production profits.

AICP: American Institute of Certified Planners

ANPRM: Advanced Notice of Proposed Rulemaking

ARAR: Applicable or Relevant and Appropriate requirements for hazardous substance cleanups under CERCLA.

AOX: Adsorbable Organic Halides

APA: Administrative Procedures Act

APA: American Planning Association

AQCR: Air Quality Control Region

ASLA: American Society of Landscape Architechs

AST: Aboveground storage tank

BACM: Best Available Control Measures

BACT: Best Available Control Technology

BART: Best Available Retrofit Technology

BAT: Best available technology

BDAT: Best demonstrated available (treatment) technology

BNA: Bureau of National Affairs

BLM: Bureau of Land Management

BOD: Biochemical Oxygen Demand

BPT: Best practical technology

BMA: Beachfront Management Act

BSR: Business for Social Responsibility

BTU: British Thermal Unit

CAA: Clean Air Act

CAMU: Corrective Action Management Unit described under RCRA

CARB: California Air Resources Board

CAS: Chemical Abstract Number

CBD: Central Business District

CBEC: Concentration-based exemption criteria

CEQA: California Environmental Quality Act

CFCs: Chloroflourocarbons

CEM: Continuous Emission Monitoring

CERCLA: Comprehensive Environmental Response, Compensation, and Liability Act

CERCLIS: CERCLA Information System

CERES: The Coalition for Environmentally Responsible Economies

CFR: Code of Federal Regulations

CFCs: Chloroflurocarbons

CLF: Conservation Law Foundation

CMS: Corrective measure study

CMSA: Consolidated Metropolitan Statistical Area

CORE: Congress on Racial Equality

CRF: USEPA/NBS-approved Certified Reference Material

CO: Carbon Monoxide

Corps: United States Army Corps of Engineers

CPI: Consumer Price Index

CTGs: Control Technique Guidelines

CWA: Clean Water Act

DE: Deep Ecology

DEIS: Draft Environmental Impact Statement

Dfe: Design for the Environment

DP: Rawlsian Difference Principle

DOE: Department of Energy

DOI: Department of Interior

DOT: Department of Transportation

DSEIS: Draft Supplemental Environmental Impact Statement

EA: Environmental Assessment

EC: European Community

ECHO: Expanded Characteristics Option

ECRA: New Jersey Environmental Cleanup Responsibility Act

EEC: European Economic Community

EHS: Extremely Hazardous Substance defined in EPCRA Title III

EIL: Environmental impairment liability insurance

EIS: Environmental impact statement

EPA: Environmental Protection Agency

EPD: State Environmental Protection Division to which a release of an EHS in a RQ should be reported under SARA Title III.

EPCRA: Emergency Planning and Community Right to Know Act

ESA: Endangered Species Act

Existing Source: any stationary source other than a new source.

FAE: Federally Assumed Enforcement

FEIS: Final Environmental Impact Statement

FHWA: Federal highway administration

FIFRA: Federal Insecticide, Fungicide, and Rodenticide Act

FIP: Federal Implementation Plan

FIRREA: Federal Institutions Reform, Recovery, and Enforcement Act of 1989

FLM: Federal Land Manager

Form R: Toxic chemical release reporting form required under EPCRA Title III

FOIA: Freedom of Information Act

FONSI: Finding of No Significant Impact

FPC: Federal power commission

FSEIS: Final Supplemental Environmental Impact Statement

FWPCA: Federal water pollution control act of 1972

G1: msids used to begin test (also know as adults)

G2: generation 2 (produced by generation 1)

GACT: Generally Available Control Technology

GCWR: Gross combination weight rating

GEP: Good engineering practice

gpm: Grams Per Mile

Hazardous Air Pollutants: In CAA, an air pollutant to which no ambient air quality standard is applicable and which in the judgment of the Administrator causes, or contributes to, air pollution which may reasonably be anticipated to result in an increase in mortality or an increase in serious irreversible, or incapacitating reversible, illness.

Hazardous Chemical: OSHA term

Hazardous Material: A DOT term in the HMTA

Hazardous Substance: CERCLA term defined in 40 CFR 302

Hazardous Waste: RCRA term defined in 40 CFR 260 and 261

HC: Hydrocarbon

HCFCs: Hydrofloroflourocarbons

HCP: Habitual Conservation Plan

HEPA: High-efficiency particulate air filter

HEW: Department of Health, Education and Welfare

HMTA: Hazardous Materials Transportation Act

HOCs: Halogenated organic compounds

HRGC: High resolution gas chromotography

HRMS: High resolution mass spectrometry

HRS: Hazard Ranking System used under CERCLA to score and compare the relative risk of contaminated disposal sites.

HSWA: Hazardous and Solid Waste Amendments of 1984

HWIR: Hazardous Waste Identification Rule

H_{Sys}: the carbon adsorption system efficiency calculated when each absorber vessel has an individual exhaust stack.

HSWA: Hazardous and Solid Waste Amendments to RCRA

HVAF: High velocity air filter

HVAC: Heating/air conditioning unit in a building

H_v: the individual carbon absorber vessel (v) achieved for the duration of the emission test

HWM facility: Hazardous waste management facility

ICS: Intermitten control system

Interstate Air Pollution Control Agency: an air pollution control agency established by two or more states or two or more municipalities located in different states.

IPP: Independent Power Producer

ISO: industrial Standards Organization

ISRA: New Jersey Industrial Site Recovery Act. Revised the New Jersey Environmental Cleanup Responsibility Act (ECRA).

ISTEA: Intermodal Surface Transportation Efficiency Act

LA: Load allocation

LAER: Lowest Achievable Emission Rate. Clean air act term, defining the rate of emissions from a source which reflects:

- The most stringent emission limitation which is contained in an applicable SIP of any state for such class or category of source, unless the owner or operator of the proposed source demonstrates that such limitations are not achievable; or

- the most stringent emission limitation which is achieved in practice by such class or category of sources, whichever is more stringent. Lowest achievable emission rates shall never be less stringent than the applicable NSPS.

LC(50): A test that uses living organisms such as fish to measure the relative toxicity of an effluent.

LDR: Land disposal restrictions

LEPC: Local Emergency Planning Committee established under EPCRA as the local focal point for reporting chemical storage and emergency response planning activities.

LOQ: Level of quantitation

LOT: Light-off time

LPC: Limiting permissible concentration

LULU: Locally Unwanted Land Uses

LWK: Live weight killed

MACT: Maximum Achievable Control Technology

Major Stationary Source or Major Emitting Facility: Any stationary facility or source of air pollutants which directly emits, or has the potential to emit, 100 tons per year or more of any air pollutant (including any major emitting facility or source of fugitive emissions of any such pollutant, as determined by rule by the Administrator).

MATC: Maximum acceptable toxicant concentration

MB: Marginal Benefits

Mbbi: one thousand barrels (one barrel is equivalent to 42 gallons)

MBE: Minority business enterprise

MC: Marginal Costs

MCL: Maximum Contaminant Level in the SDWA

MCLG: Maximum Contaminant Level Goal in the SDWA

MCW unit capacity

MD & A: Management Discussion & Analysis (Item 303 of Regulation S–K; data included on Forms 10K & 10Q)

mg/l: milligram per liter

Mgal: one thousand gallons

ml/l: Milliliters per liter

Modification: any physical change in, or change in the method of operation of, a stationary source which increases the amount of any air pollutant emitted by such source or which results in the emission of any air pollutant not previously emitted.

MPO: Metropolitan Planning Organization

MSA: Metropolitan Statistical Area

MSDS: Material Safety Data Sheet

MSW: Municipal-type solid waste

MSWLF: Municipal solid waste landfill

MTP: Maximum total trihalmethance potential

MTRs: Minimum technology requirements (for land disposal facilities)

MW: Megawatts

MWC: Municipal waste combuster

Mwh: Megawatts per hour

MWTA: Medical Waste Tracking Act

NAAQS: National Ambient Air Quality Standards established under the Clean Air Act.

NAMS: National air monitoring station

NBS SRM: National Bureau of Standards Standard Reference Material

NCP: National Contingency Plan established under CERCLA

NEPA: National Environmental Policy Act

NESHAP: National Emission Standards for Hazardous Pollutants in the CAA.

New Source: any stationary source, the construction or modification of which is commenced after the publication of regulations (or, if earlier, proposed regulations) prescribing a standard of performance which will be applicable to such facility.

NIMBY: Not in My Backyard

NJDEP: New Jersey Dept. of the Environment

NICE3: An EPA voluntary program aimed a promoting energy efficiency.

NIOSH: National Institute for Occupational Safety and Health of the U.S. Department of Health and Human Services.

NMOG: Nonmethane Organic Gas

NMFS: National Marine Fisheries Service

NOAA: National Oceanic and Atmosphere Administration

NOEC: No observed effect concentration

Nonattainment Area: for any air pollutant, an area which is shown by monitored data or which is calculated by air quality modeling (or other methods determined by the Administrator to be reliable) to exceed any national ambient air quality standard for such pollutant.

NO_x: Nitrogen Oxides

NP–1: A mixture of two chemicals found in household and hospital disinfectants used to prevent the growth of microorganisms on freshly cut lumber.

NRC: Nuclear Regulatory Commission

NRC: National Response Center

NRR: Noise reduction rating

NRT: National Response Team

NSF: National Strike Force

NSPS: New Source Performance Standards (CWA)

NSR: New Source Review

NPDES: National Pollution Discharge Elimination System established under the Clean Water Act.

NPDWR: National Primary Drinking Water Regulations in the SWDA.

NPL: National Priorities List of hazardous sites ranked through the use of the Hazard Ranking System under CERCLA.

NRC: National Response Center operated by the Coast Guard, and the point of contact for reportable releases under CERCLA.

NSDWR: National Secondary Drinking Water Regulations in the SWDA.

NSPS: New Source Performance Standard in the CAA.

NSPS: New Source Performance Standard under the Clean Air Act.

NTNCWS: Non-transient non-community water system

NWPA: Nuclear Waste Policy Act of 1982

O_3: Ozone

O & G: Oil and grease

O & M: Oil and maintenance

OCR: Office of Civil Rights

OEC: Observed effect concentration

OECD: Organization for Economic Cooperation and Development

OEM: Original equipment manufacturer

OPPTS: EPA's Office of Prevention, Pesticides & Toxic Substances

ORD: Office of Research of Research & Development

OSC: On-scene coordination

OSHA: Occupational Safety and Health Administration

OSWER: Office of Solid Waste and Emergency Response (EPA)

Owner or Operator: any person who owns, leases, operates, controls, or supervises a stationary source in the CAA or a TSD facility in RCRA.

PA: Preliminary Assessment under the CERCLA remediation process.

PCA: Production Compliance Audit

PCB: Polychorinated biphenol

PCW: Post-consumer waste

PERI: Public Environmental Reporting Initiative

Plan: Ground Transportation Plan

PIAT: Public information assist team

POM: Polycyclic Organic Matter

PM: Particulate Matter

PM–10: Particulate Matter with a Median Aerodynamic Diameter of 10 microns or less

PMN: Pre-manufacturing Notice in the TSCA.

PPIC: Pollution Prevention Information Clearinghouse

POTW: Publicly owned treatment works

PRP: Potentially responsible party (under CERCLA)

PSD: Prevention of Significant Deterioration in the CAA

PSES: pretreatment standards for existing sources

PSNS: pretreatment standards for new sources

PUC: [State] Public Utility Commission

PURPA: Public Utilities Regulatory Policies Act

QF: Qualifying facility

RACM: Reasonably Available Control Measures

RACT: Reasonably Available Control Technology

RCRA: Resource Conservation and Recovery Act

RF: Response factor

RO: Rated output

RFA: RCRA facility assessment

RFG: reformulated gasoline

RFI: RCRA facility investigation

RI/FS: Remedial investigation/ feasibility study (under CERCLA)

ROD: Record of decision (CERCLA)

RQ: Reportable Quantity for a spilled material established under CERCLA.

RP: Responsible party (under CERCLA)

RWQCB: Regional Water Quality Control Board

SARA: Superfund Amendments and Reauthorization Act

SAROAD: Storage and retrieval Aeromitric Data system

SCF: Standard cubic feet

SCS: Supplemental control system

SDWA: Safe Drinking Water Act

SEA: Securities Exchange Act of 1934

SEC: Securities Exchange Commission

SERC: State Emergency Response Commission under EPCRA Title III

SI unit: a unit of measure in the International System of Units (Sievert).

SIC Code: Standard Industrial Classification Code

SIP: State Implementation Plan in the CAA

SLAMS: State or Local Air Monitoring Stations

Sm^3: Standard cubic meters

SN: Smoke number

SO_2: Sulfur Dioxides

SOW: statement of work

SOV: Single Occupant Vehicle

sq m: area plated expressed in square meters

SPCC Plan: Spill Prevention Control and Countermeasure Plan required for petroleum products under the Clean Water Act.

SPLP: Synthetic Precipitation Leaching Procedure

SRF: State water pollution control revolving fund.

SS: the pollutant parameter total suspended solids.

SSA: Sole source aquifer

SSC: Scientific Support Coordinator

Stationary Source: any building, structure, facility, or installation which emits or may emit any air pollutant.

STEP: Strategies for Today's Environmental Partnership

Subtitle C: RCRA's hazardous waste management program

Subtitle D: RCRA's non-hazardous solid waste management program

SWMU: Solid waste management unit

TC: Toxicity characteristic

TCLP: Toxic Characteristic Leaching Procedure test used to identify Hazardous Wastes.

TDR: Transferable development rights

TDS: Total dissolved solids

TFE: Two factor egalitarianism

TIP: Transportation Improvement Program

Title V permit: Permit issued under Title V of the Clean Air Act amendments of 1990.

TMDL: Total maximum daily load

TPQ: Threshold Planning Quantity defined in EPCRA Title III

TOC: Total organic compounds

TOVALOP: Tank owners voluntary agreement concerning liability for oil pollution

TPQ: threshold planning quantity for an extremely hazardous substance as defined in 40 CFR Part 355.

tpy: Tons Per Year

TRC: Total residual chlorine

TRS: Total Reduced Sulfur

TSCA: Toxic Substances Control Act

TSD permit: Treatment, storage and disposal permit issued under RCRA.

TSDF: Treatment, Storage, or Disposal Facility permitted under RCRA.

TSS: Total Suspended Solids

TTO: Total toxic organics

TVA: Tennessee Valley Authority

TWS: transient non-community water system (serves less than 25 of the same people over six months per year).

UIC: Underground injection control program, part C of SDWA

ULI: Urban Land Institute

UORA: Used Oil Recycling Act

UN: United Nations

UNEP: United Nations Environment Programme

UNCTAD: the United Nations Commission on Trade and Development

USCG: U.S. Coast Guard

USDA: U.S. Dept. of Agriculture

USDW: Underground source of drinking water

UST: Underground Storage Tank

VE: Value engineering

VHAP: Volatile hazardous air pollutant

VMT: Vehicle Miles Travelled

VOC: Volatile Organic Compounds

VOL: Volatile organic liquid

WAS: Water quality standards

WAVE: The Water Alliances for Voluntary Efficiency

WL: Working level

WLA: Wasteload allocation

W_{oi}: the weight fraction of VOC in each coating (i) applied at an affected coating operation during a nominal 1–month period as determined by Method 24.

WQM: Water quality management plan

WQS: Water quality standards

ZID: Zone of initial dilution

1933 Act: Securities Act of 1933

1934 Act: Securities Exchange Act of 1934

33/50 Program: EPA's voluntary emission reduction program initiated under EPA Administrator William Reilly.

*

Index

References are to pages

References are to pages

†